W9-BOD-799

To my daughters, Joanne and Stacey
—PDE

To my wife Ellie and children, Grace and Christian
—RFH

To my husband Brittan, my children Loic, Maclean, Quinn and Kay, and my understanding co-authors LK and CW.
—MLM

To my wife Aline.
—AH

Cambridge Business Publishers

FINANCIAL & MANAGERIAL ACCOUNTING FOR MBAs, First Edition, by Peter D. Easton, Robert F. Halsey, Mary Lea McAnally, and Al Hartgraves.

ISBN 0-9787279-1-6

Bookstores & Faculty: to order this book, contact the company via email **customerservice@cambridgepub.com** or call 800-619-6473.

Retail Customers & Students: to order this book, please visit the book's website and order directly online.

For permission to use material from this text, contact the company via email **permissions@cambridgepub.com**.

Printed in the United States of America.
10 9 8 7 6 5 4 3 2

Managerial Accounting	Feature Companies	Real Organizations Referenced in Assignments
MODULE 14 Managerial Accounting for MBAs	Hewlett-Packard, Dell Computer	Amazon.Com, Canon, Cook County Hospital, Cornell University, Dell Computer, Emory University, Exxon Mobil, Hilton Hotels, Honda, Kimberly-Clark, Kohl's Department Store, L.L.Bean, Procter & Gamble, Royal Dutch/Shell, Time Warner, Toyota, United Parcel Service, Xerox Corporation
MODULE 15 Cost Behavior, Activity Analysis, and Cost Estimation	Air Tran, American, Bombardier, ComAir, Delta, Embraer, Fairchild-Dornier, JetBlue, Mesa Air, Northwest, Southwest, SkyWest, United	DHL, LensCrafters, Papa John's
MODULE 16 Cost-Volume-Profit Analysis and Planning	Amazon.Com, Cisco Systems, Inktomi, Microsoft, Webvan, Yahoo	JetBlue, Papa John's, Paper Mate, Southwest Airlines
MODULE 17 Relevant Costs and Benefits for Decision Making	AT&T, Cunningham Motor Company, Microsoft, StarTek Inc., Time Warner	Apple, Hewlett-Packard, MicroAge, Inc., Sanmina-SCI
MODULE 18 Product Costing: Job and Process Operations	Ace Hardware, DaimlerChrysler, Freightliner, Home Depot, Lowe's, Navistar International, Paccar, Robert Bosch Tool Corporation, Rotozip Tool Corporation, Sears, USG Corporation	Callaway Golf Company, Milliken & Company, Herman Miller, Inc., JIF, J.M. Smucker Company
MODULE 19 Product Costing: Assigning Indirect Costs	Enviro-Recovery Corporation, Oshkosh Truck Corporation, Shimano, SRAM Corporation	Panasonic Company, Pennington Group, Sherwin-Williams, Timberland Company
MODULE 20 Operational Budgeting and Profit Planning	Georgia Pacific, Home Depot, International Paper, 7-Eleven, Smurfit-Stone, Target, Wal-Mart, Weyerhaeuser	Datek
MODULE 21 Performance Assessment: Standard Costs, Flexible Budgets, and Variance Analysis	Gateway Corporation	Casio, Forza, LensCrafters, Nortel, Phillips Petroleum, Regal Flags and Poles, Sony
MODULE 22 Segment Reporting, Transfer Pricing, and Balanced Scorecard	C. H. Robinson Worldwide, Procter & Gamble, Verizon	IBM Corporation, Six Flags Theme Parks, Watkins Associated Industries
MODULE 23 Pricing and Other Product Management Decisions	Ballard Power Systems, DaimlerChrysler, Ford, General Motors, Honda, Toyota	Earthlink, Inc., General Electric, Marriott International, Redback Networks, Sue Bee Honey

First

Financial & Manageria Accounting for MBAs

PETER D. EASTON

ROBERT F. HALSEY

MARY LEA McANALL

AL HARTGRAVE

Cambridge
BUSINESS PUBLISHERS

ABOUT THE AUTHORS

The combined skills and expertise of Easton, Halsey, McAnally, and Hartgraves create the ideal team to author the first new financial and managerial accounting textbook for MBAs in more than a generation. Their collective experience in award-winning teaching, consulting, and research in accounting and analysis provides a powerful foundation for this innovative textbook.

PETER D. EASTON is an expert in accounting and valuation and holds the Notre Dame Alumni Chair in Accountancy in the Mendoza College of Business. Professor Easton's expertise is widely recognized by the academic research community and by the legal community. Professor Easton is a Principal in Chicago Partners LLC, where he serves as a consultant on accounting and valuation issues.

Professor Easton holds undergraduate degrees from the University of Adelaide and the University of South Australia. He holds a graduate degree from the University of New England and a PhD in Business Administration (majoring in accounting and finance) from the University of California, Berkeley.

Professor Easton's research on corporate valuation has been published in the *Journal of Accounting and Economics, Journal of Accounting Research, The Accounting Review, Contemporary Accounting Research, Review of Accounting Studies,* and *Journal of Business Finance and Accounting.* Professor Easton has served as an associate editor for 11 leading accounting journals and he is currently an associate editor for the *Journal of Accounting Research, Contemporary Accounting Research, Journal of Business Finance and Accounting,* and *Journal of Accounting, Auditing, and Finance.* He is an editor of the *Review of Accounting Studies.*

Professor Easton has held appointments at the University of Chicago, the University of California at Berkeley, Ohio State University, Macquarie University, the Australian Graduate School of Management, the University of Melbourne, and Nyenrode University. He is the recipient of numerous awards for excellence in teaching and in research. Professor Easton regularly teaches accounting analysis and security valuation to MBAs. In addition, Professor Easton has taught managerial accounting at the graduate level.

ROBERT F. HALSEY is an associate professor at Babson College. He received his MBA and PhD from the University of Wisconsin. Prior to obtaining his PhD he worked as the chief financial officer (CFO) of a privately held retailing and manufacturing company and as the vice president and manager of the commercial lending division of a large bank.

Professor Halsey teaches courses in financial and managerial accounting at both the graduate and undergraduate levels, including a popular course in financial statement analysis for second year MBA students. He has also taught numerous executive education courses for large multinational companies through Babson's School of Executive Education as well as for a number of stock brokerage firms in the Boston area. He is regarded as an innovative teacher and has been recognized for outstanding teaching at both the University of Wisconsin and Babson College. He is the recipient of an Ernst & Young Fellowship and is a member of the Beta Gamma Sigma and Phi Eta Sigma honor societies.

Professor Halsey's research interests are in the area of financial reporting, including firm valuation, financial statement analysis, and disclosure issues. He is the coauthor of *Financial Statement Analysis,* published by McGraw-Hill/Irwin, and has publications in *Advances in Quantitative Analysis of Finance and Accounting, The Journal of the American Taxation Association, Issues in Accounting Education, The Portable MBA in Finance and Accounting* (3rd ed.), the *CPA Journal, AICPA Professor/Practitioner Case Development Program,* and in other accounting and analysis journals. He has also developed exam preparation materials for the CFA examination and administers numerous CFA review courses in the Northeast.

MARY LEA McANALLY is an associate professor and Mays Research Fellow at Texas A&M University. Professor McAnally teaches financial accounting and reporting in the MBA and Executive programs. Her casebook (co-authored with D. Eric Hirst), "Cases in Financial Reporting" is published by Prentice Hall. She has received several faculty-determined teaching awards including the Beazley Award and the Trammell/CBA Foundation Award. She has also received numerous student-initiated awards including the MBA Teaching Award at UT (1995, 2000, 2001, 2002), the MBA Association Distinguished Faculty Award at A&M (2003 and 2004) and the Class of 1997 Award for Outstanding and Memorable Faculty Member (2002). In 2006, the A&M Association of Former Students granted Professor McAnally the Distinguished Achievement Award.

Professor McAnally's research interests include accounting and disclosure of stock options, and accounting for risk. She has published articles in the leading academic journals including *Journal of Accounting and Economics, Journal of Accounting Research, The Accounting Review, Contemporary Accounting Research,* and *Journal of Accounting Auditing and Finance.* In 2005, Professor McAnally received the Mays Business School Research Achievement Award. She works closely with doctoral students and has served on numerous doctoral committees. She was the director of A&M's doctoral program until 2007.

Professor McAnally is active in the American Accounting Association and its FARS section and has been involved with the New Faculty Consortium, the FASB conference, several doctoral consortia and the KPMG PhD project.

Professor McAnally holds an undergraduate degree from the University of Alberta and a PhD from Stanford University. She is a Chartered Accountant (Canada) and Certified Internal Auditor. Prior to arriving at A&M in 2002, Professor McAnally held positions at University of Texas at Austin, University of Calgary, University of Alberta, Canadian National Railways, and Dunwoody and Company Chartered Accountants.

AL L. HARTGRAVES is Professor of Accounting at the Goizueta Business School at Emory University in Atlanta, Georgia. He is also a frequent Guest Professor at Johannes Kepler University in Linz, Austria and at the Helsinki School of Economics and Business Administration in Finland. His published scholarly and professional articles have appeared in The Accounting Review, Accounting Horizons, Management Accounting, Journal of Accountancy, Journal of Accounting and Public Policy and many other journals. Students at Goizueta Business School have selected him on six occasions to receive the Distinguished Educator Award. In 2002 he received Emory University's highest teaching award, The Scholar/Teacher Award, and in 2003 he was recognized as the Accounting Educator of the Year by the Georgia Society of CPAs. He has been recognized as an Outstanding Faculty Member in two editions of The Business Week Guide to the Best Business Schools. He is a Certified Public Accountant (inactive) and a Certified Management Accountant, having received the Certificate of Distinguished Performance on the CMA exam. He received his Ph.D. from Georgia State University.

Welcome to *Financial & Managerial Accounting for MBAs*. Our main goal in writing this book was to satisfy the needs of today's business manager by providing the most contemporary, engaging, and user-oriented textbook available. This book is the product of extensive market research including focus groups, market surveys, class tests, manuscript reviews, and interviews with faculty from across the country. We are grateful to the students and faculty who provided us with useful feedback during the preparation of this book.

TARGET AUDIENCE

Financial & Managerial Accounting for MBAs is intended for use in full-time, part-time, executive, and evening MBA programs that include a combined financial and managerial accounting course as part of the curriculum, and one in which managerial decision making and analysis are emphasized. This book easily accommodates mini-courses lasting several days as well as extended courses lasting a full semester.

INNOVATIVE APPROACH

Financial & Managerial Accounting for MBAs is managerially oriented and focuses on the most salient aspects of accounting. It teaches MBA students how to read, analyze, and interpret accounting data to make informed business decisions. This textbook makes accounting **engaging, relevant,** and **contemporary.** To that end, it consistently incorporates **real company data,** both in the body of each module and throughout assignment material.

FLEXIBLE STRUCTURE

The MBA curricula, instructor preferences, and course lengths vary across colleges. Accordingly and to the extent possible, the 23 modules that make up *Financial & Managerial Accounting for MBAs* were designed independently of one another. This modular presentation enables each college and instructor to "customize" the book to best fit the needs of their students. Our introduction and discussion of financial statements constitute Modules 1, 2, and 3. Module 4 presents the analysis of financial statements with an emphasis on profitability analysis. Modules 5 through 10 highlight major financial accounting topics including assets, liabilities, equity, and off-balance-sheet financing. Module 11 explains adjusting and forecasting financial statements. Module 12 introduces simple valuation models. Module 13 concludes with a comprehensive case on Kimberly-Clark and acts as a capstone for the financial accounting portion of the course. Module 14 introduces managerial accounting and is followed by a discussion of cost behavior and cost estimation in Module 15. Module 16 explains cost-volume-profit analysis while Module 17 focuses on using relevant costs to make business decisions. Job and process costing are covered in a single module, Module 18, followed by Module 19 on the assignment of indirect costs. The remaining modules, 20 through 23, highlight managerial accounting topics ranging from operational budgets and variance analysis to segment reporting and product pricing.

MANAGERIAL EMPHASIS

As MBA instructors, we recognize that the core MBA accounting course is not directed toward accounting majors. *Financial & Managerial Accounting for MBAs* embraces this reality. This book highlights **reporting, analysis, interpretation,** and **decision making.** In the financial accounting modules, we incorporate the following **financial statement effects template** when relevant to train MBA students in understanding the economic ramifications of transactions and their impacts on all key financial statements. This analytical tool is a great resource for MBA students in learning accounting and applying it to their future courses and careers. Each transaction is identified in the "Transaction" column. Then, the dollar amounts (positive or negative) of the financial statement effects are recorded in the appropriate balance sheet or income statement columns. The template also reflects the statement of cash flow effects (via the cash column) and the statement of stockholders' equity effects (via the contributed capital and earned capital columns). The earned capital account is immediately updated to reflect any income or loss arising from each transaction (denoted by the arrow line from net income to earned capital). This template is instructive as it reveals the financial impacts of transactions, and it provides insights into the effects of accounting choices.

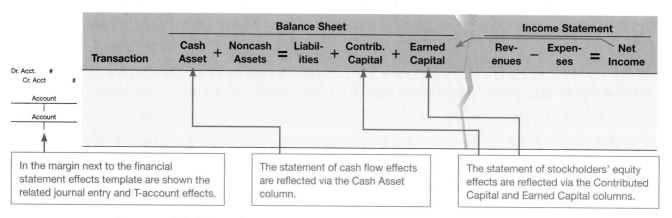

Tomorrow's MBA graduates must be skilled in using financial statements to make business decisions. These skills often require application of ratio analyses, benchmarking, forecasting, valuation, and other aspects of financial statement analysis to decision making. Furthermore, tomorrow's MBA graduates must have the skills to go beyond basic financial statements and to interpret and apply nonfinancial statement disclosures, such as footnotes and supplementary reports. This book, therefore, emphasizes real company data, including detailed footnote and other management disclosures, and shows how to use this information to make managerial inferences and decisions. This approach makes accounting interesting and relevant for all MBA students.

INNOVATIVE PEDAGOGY

Financial & Managerial Accounting for MBAs includes special features specifically designed for the MBA student.

Focus Companies for Each Module

In the financial accounting portion of the book, each module's content is explained through the accounting and reporting activities of real companies. To that end, each module incorporates a "focus company" for special emphasis and demonstration. The enhanced instructional value of focus companies comes from the way they engage MBA students in real analysis and interpretation. Focus companies were selected based on the industries that MBA students typically enter upon graduation. We apply a similar approach for the managerial accounting modules, but limited access to internal accounting information prevents us from illustrating all managerial accounting topics using real company data. We do, however, incorporate real world examples throughout each module. Each managerial accounting module is presented in context using real world scenarios from industries and companies ranging from technology and telecommunications to services, retail, and manufacturing.

Focus Company by Module

MODULE 1 Berkshire Hathaway	**MODULE 9** Accenture	**MODULE 17** AT&T, Microsoft, Time Warner
MODULE 2 Apple	**MODULE 10** Southwest Airlines	**MODULE 18** Ace, Home Depot, Lowes
MODULE 3 Apple	**MODULE 11** Procter & Gamble	**MODULE 19** Oshkosh Truck, Shimano, SRAM
MODULE 4 Home Depot	**MODULE 12** Johnson & Johnson	**MODULE 20** 7-Eleven, Target, Wal-Mart
MODULE 5 Pfizer	**MODULE 13** Kimberly-Clark	**MODULE 21** Gateway
MODULE 6 Cisco	**MODULE 14** HP, Dell, Compaq	**MODULE 22** Procter & Gamble, Verizon
MODULE 7 Google	**MODULE 15** American, United, JetBlue	**MODULE 23** Ford, GM, Honda, Toyota
MODULE 8 Verizon	**MODULE 16** Amazon, Webvan, Yahoo!	**APPENDIX B** Starbucks

Real Company Data Throughout

Market research and reviewer feedback tell us that one of instructors' greatest frustrations with other MBA textbooks is their lack of real company data. We have gone to great lengths to incorporate real company data throughout each module to reinforce important concepts and engage MBA students. We engage nonaccounting MBA students specializing in finance, marketing, management, real estate, operations, and so forth, with companies and scenarios that are relevant to them. For representative examples, **SEE PAGES 4-5; 5-5; 6-11.**

Managerial and Decision Making Orientation

One primary goal of a MBA accounting course is to teach students the skills needed to apply their accounting knowledge to solving real business problems and making informed business decisions. With that goal in mind, Managerial Decision boxes in each module encourage students to apply the material presented to solving actual business scenarios. For representative examples, **SEE PAGES 5-15; 6-12; 8-23; 16-19; 17-5.**

Research Insights for MBAs

Academic research plays an important role in the way business is conducted, accounting is performed, and students are taught. It is important for students to recognize how modern research and modern business practice interact. Therefore, we periodically incorporate relevant research to help students understand the important relation between research and modern business. For representative examples, **SEE PAGES 4-18; 5-26; 11-7.**

Mid-Module and Module-End Reviews

Accounting can be challenging—especially for MBA students lacking business experience or previous exposure to business courses. To reinforce concepts presented in each module and to ensure student comprehension, we include mid-module and module-end reviews that require students to recall and apply the accounting techniques and concepts described in each module. For representative examples, **SEE PAGES 4-14; 8-6; 11-9; 16-13; 17-7.**

Excellent, Class-Tested Assignment Materials

Excellent assignment material is a must-have component of any successful textbook (and class). We went to great lengths to create the best assignments possible from contemporary financial statements. In keeping with the rest of the book, we used real company data extensively. We also ensured that assignments reflect our belief that MBA students should be trained in analyzing accounting information to make business decisions, as opposed to working on mechanical bookkeeping tasks. Assignments encourage students to analyze accounting information, interpret it, and apply the knowledge gained to a business decision. There are five categories of assignments: **Discussion Questions**, **Mini Exercises**, **Exercises**, **Problems**, and **Cases**. For representative examples, **SEE PAGES 4-34; 6-45; 10-31; 16-29; 18-41.**

SUPPLEMENT PACKAGE

For Instructors

Electronic Solutions Manual: Created by the authors, the *Solutions Manual* contains complete solutions to all the assignment material in the text.

PowerPoint: The PowerPoint slides outline key elements of each module.

Electronic Test Bank: The test bank includes multiple-choice items, matching questions, short essay questions, and problems.

Website: All instructor materials are accessible via the book's Website (password protected) along with other useful links and information. www.cambridgepub.com

For Students

Website: Useful links are available to students free of charge on the book's website. www.cambridgepub.com

ACKNOWLEDGMENTS

This book benefited greatly from the valuable feedback of focus group attendees, reviewers, students, and colleagues. We are extremely grateful to them for their help in making this project a success.

Ashiq Ali, *University of Texas—Dallas*
Steve Baginski, *University of Georgia*
Eli Bartov, *New York University*
Dan Bens, *University of Arizona*
Denny Beresford, *University of Georgia*
Mark Bradshaw, *Harvard University*
John Briginshaw, *Pepperdine University*
Stephen Brown, *Emory University*
Mary Ellen Carter, *University of Pennsylvania*
Agnes Cheng, *University of Houston*
Doug Clinton, *Northern Illinois University*
Gary Colbert, *University of Colorado—Denver*
Carol Dee, *University of Colorado—Denver*
Elizabeth Demers, *INSEAD*
Vicki Dickinson, *University of Florida*
Jeffrey Doyle, *University of Utah*
Thomas Dyckman, *Cornell University*
James Edwards, *University of South Carolina*
John Eichenseher, *University of Wisconsin*
Gerard Engeholm, *Pace University*
Mark Finn, *Northwestern University*
Richard Frankel, *Washington University*
Julia Grant, *Case Western Reserve University*
Karl Hackenbrack, *Vanderbilt University*
Michelle Hanlon, *University of Michigan*
Al Hartgraves, *Emory University*
Carla Hayn, *University of California—Los Angeles*
Frank Heflin, *Florida State University*
Eleanor Henry, *Southeast Missouri State University*
Clayton Hock, *Miami University*
Judith Hora, *University of San Diego*
Court Huber, *University of Texas—Austin*
Richard Hurley, *University of Connecticut*
Ross Jennings, *University of Texas—Austin*
Paul Juras, *Wake Forest University*
Sanjay Kallapur, *Purdue University*
Saleha Khumawala, *University of Houston*
Ron King, *Washington University*
Krishna Kumar, *George Washington University*
Lisa Kutcher, *University of Oregon*
Brian Leventhal, *University of Illinois—Chicago*
Elliott Levy, *Bentley College*
Joshua Livnat, *New York University*
Barbara Lougee, *University of California—Irvine*

Luann Lynch, *University of Virginia—Darden*
Greg Miller, *Harvard University*
Melanie Mogg, *University of Minnesota*
Steve Monahan, *INSEAD*
Dale Morse, *University of Oregon*
Dennis Murray, *University of Colorado—Denver*
Sandeep Nabar, *Oklahoma State University*
Doron Nissim, *Columbia University*
Susan Parker, *Santa Clara University*
Stephen Penman, *Columbia University*
Mark Penno, *University of Iowa*
Kathy Petroni, *Michigan State University*
Christine Petrovits, *New York University*
Glenn Pfeiffer, *Chapman College*
Kirk Philipich, *University of Michigan—Dearborn*
Morton Pincus, *University of California—Irvine*
Grace Pownall, *Emory University*
Ram Ramanan, *University of Notre Dame*
Susan Riffe, *Southern Methodist University*
Jane Saly, *University of St. Thomas*
Andrew Schmidt, *Columbia University*
Chandra Seethamraju, *Washington University*
Stephen Sefcik, *University of Washington*
Kenneth Shaw, *University of Missouri*
Paul Simko, *University of Virginia—Darden*
Pam Smith, *Northern Illinois University*
Sri Sridharan, *Northwestern University*
Charles Stanley, *Baylor University*
Jens Stephan, *University of Cincinnati*
Phillip Stocken, *Dartmouth College*
K.R. Subramanyam, *University of Southern California*
Gary Taylor, *University of Alabama*
Sam Tiras, *University of Buffalo*
Mark Vargus, *University of Texas—Dallas*
James Wallace, *Claremont Graduate School*
Charles Wasley, *University of Rochester*
Greg Waymire, *Emory University*
Edward Werner, *Drexel University*
Jeffrey Williams, *University of Michigan*
David Wright, *University of Michigan*
Michelle Yetman, *University of California—Davis*
Tzachi Zack, *Washington University*
Xiao-Jun Zhang, *University of California—Berkeley*

In addition, we are extremely grateful to George Werthman and the entire team at Cambridge Business Publishers for their encouragement, enthusiasm, and guidance. We have had a very positive textbook authoring experience with this book thanks, in large part, to our publisher.

Peter   *Bob*   *Mary Lea*   *Al*

March 2007

BRIEF CONTENTS

	About the Authors		iii
	Preface		iv
MODULE	1	Financial Accounting for MBAs	1-1
MODULE	2	Introducing Financial Statements and Transaction Analysis	2-1
MODULE	3	Constructing Financial Statements and Analyzing Transactions	3-1
MODULE	4	Analyzing and Interpreting Financial Statements	4-1
MODULE	5	Reporting and Analyzing Operating Income	5-1
MODULE	6	Reporting and Analyzing Operating Assets	6-1
MODULE	7	Reporting and Analyzing Intercorporate Investments	7-1
MODULE	8	Reporting and Analyzing Nonowner Financing	8-1
MODULE	9	Reporting and Analyzing Owner Financing	9-1
MODULE	10	Reporting and Analyzing Off-Balance-Sheet Financing	10-1
MODULE	11	Adjusting and Forecasting Financial Statements	11-1
MODULE	12	Analyzing and Valuing Equity Securities	12-1
MODULE	13	Comprehensive Case	13-1
MODULE	14	Managerial Accounting for MBAs	14-1
MODULE	15	Cost Behavior, Activity Analysis, and Cost Estimation	15-1
MODULE	16	Cost-Volume-Profit Analysis and Planning	16-1
MODULE	17	Relevant Costs and Benefits for Decision Making	17-1
MODULE	18	Product Costing: Job and Process Operations	18-1
MODULE	19	Product Costing: Assigning Indirect Costs	19-1
MODULE	20	Operational Budgeting and Profit Planning	20-1
MODULE	21	Performance Assessment: Standard Costs, Flexible Budgets, and Variance Analysis	21-1
MODULE	22	Segment Reporting, Transfer Pricing, and Balanced Scorecard	22-1
MODULE	23	Pricing and Other Product Management Decisions	23-1
APPENDIX A		Compound Interest Tables	A-1
APPENDIX B		Constructing the Statement of Cash Flows	B-1
APPENDIX C		Chart of Accounts with Acronyms	C-1
APPENDIX D		Quick Review	D-1
		Glossary	G-1
		Index	I-1

CONTENTS

MODULE One

Financial Accounting for MBAs 1-1

Focus Company: Berkshire Hathaway 1-1
Reporting On Business Activities 1-3
Financial Accounting Information: Demand and Supply 1-5
  Demand for Information 1-5
  Supply of Information 1-7
Financial Statements 1-8
  Balance Sheet 1-8
  Income Statement 1-10
  Statement of Stockholders' Equity 1-12
  Statement of Cash Flows 1-13
  Financial Statement Linkages 1-14
  Information Beyond Financial Statements 1-15
Mid-Module Review 1-15
Profitability Analysis 1-16
  Return on Net Operating Assets 1-16
  Components of Return on Net Operating Assets 1-16
  Return on Equity 1-18
  Financial Accounting and Business Analysis 1-18
Module-End Review 1-20
Appendix 1A: Accessing SEC Filings Using EDGAR 1-21
Appendix 1B: Accounting Principles and Governance 1-23

MODULE Two

Introducing Financial Statements and Transaction Analysis 2-1

Focus Company: Apple 2-1
Introduction 2-3
Balance Sheet 2-5
  Assets—Reflecting Investing Activities 2-5

  Liabilities and Equity—Reflecting Financing Activities 2-7
Income Statement 2-12
  Revenue Recognition and Matching 2-13
  Reporting of Transitory Items 2-14
Statement of Stockholders' Equity 2-14
Statement of Cash Flows 2-15
  Statement Format and Data Sources 2-16
  Cash Flow Computations 2-17
Mid-Module Review 2-19
Articulation of Financial Statements 2-21
  Retained Earnings Reconciliation 2-21
  Financial Statement Linkages 2-22
Transaction Analysis and Accounting 2-23
  Recording Transactions 2-24
  Adjusting Accounts 2-24
  Preparing Financial Statements 2-25
Module-End Review 2-29
Appendix 2A: Additional Information Sources 2-30

MODULE Three

Constructing Financial Statements and Analyzing Transactions 3-1

Focus Company: Apple 3-1
Introduction 3-3
Accounting for Transactions 3-4
  Financial Statement Effects Template 3-4
  Introduction to Transaction Analysis 3-5
  Capital Investment 3-5
  Asset (Inventory) Acquisition 3-6
  Revenue and Expense Recognition 3-6
  Capital Distributions 3-7
Mid-Module Review 1 3-8
Accounting Adjustments (Accruals) 3-8
  Prepaid Expenses (Assets) 3-11
  Unearned Revenues (Liabilities) 3-11
  Accrued Expenses (Liabilities) 3-12
  Accrued Revenues (Assets) 3-12
  Trial Balance Preparation and Use 3-13
Mid-Module Review 2 3-15
Financial Statement Preparation 3-16
  Income Statement 3-16
  Balance Sheet 3-17

Statement of Stockholders' Equity 3-18
Statement of Cash Flows 3-18
Closing Process 3-21
Module-End Review 3-22
Appendix 3A: Closing Process Using Journal Entries 3-24

MODULE **Four**
Analyzing and Interpreting Financial Statements 4-1

Focus Company: Home Depot 4-1
Introduction 4-3
Return On Equity (ROE) 4-4
Operating Return (RNOA) 4-5
Mid-Module Review 1 4-8
RNOA Disaggregation into Margin and Turnover 4-12
Mid-Module Review 2 4-14
Nonoperating Return 4-16
Liquidity and Solvency 4-18
Liquidity Analysis 4-19
Solvency Analysis 4-20
Limitations of Ratio Analysis 4-21
Module-End Review 4-22
Appendix 4A: Vertical and Horizontal Analysis 4-23
Appendix 4B: Nonoperating Return Component of ROE 4-25

MODULE **Five**
Reporting and Analyzing Operating Income 5-1

Focus Company: Pfizer 5-1
Introduction 5-3
Operating Income Components 5-5
Revenues 5-5
Research and Development (R&D) Expenses 5-11
Restructuring Expenses 5-14
Mid-Module Review 1 5-16
Income Tax Expenses 5-17
Adequacy of the Deferred Tax Asset Valuation 5-22
Mid-Module Review 2 5-23
Operating Components 'Below-the-Line' 5-23

Extraordinary Items 5-24
Earnings Per Share 5-24
Foreign Currency Translation 5-26
Module-End Review 5-27

MODULE **Six**
Reporting and Analyzing Operating Assets 6-1

Focus Company: Cisco Systems 6-1
Introduction 6-3
Accounts Receivable 6-4
Allowance for Uncollectible Accounts 6-5
Footnote Disclosures 6-7
Analysis Implications 6-8
Mid-Module Review 1 6-12
Inventory 6-13
Capitalization of Inventory Cost 6-13
Inventory Costing Methods 6-14
Footnote Disclosures 6-16
Lower of Cost or Market 6-17
Financial Statement Effects of Inventory Costing 6-18
Tools of Inventory Analysis 6-20
LIFO Liquidations 6-24
Mid-Module Review 2 6-24
Property, Plant and, Equipment (PPE) 6-26
Capitalization of Asset Costs 6-26
Depreciation 6-27
Asset Sales and Impairments 6-31
Footnote Disclosures 6-33
Analysis Implications 6-34
Module-End Review 6-35

MODULE **Seven**
Reporting and Analyzing Intercorporate Investments 7-1

Focus Company: Google 7-1
Introduction 7-3
Passive Investments 7-5
Acquisition and Sale 7-5
Mark-to-Market versus Cost 7-6
Investments Marked to Market 7-7

Financial Statement Disclosures 7-8
Investments Reported at Cost 7-10
Mid-Module Review 1 7-11
Investments with Significant Influence 7-13
Accounting for Investments with Significant Influence 7-13
Equity Method Accounting and ROE Effects 7-15
Mid-Module Review 2 7-16
Investments with Control 7-18
Accounting for Investments with Control 7-18
Module-End Review 7-27
Appendix 7A: Equity Method Mechanics 7-28
Appendix 7B: Consolidation Accounting Mechanics 7-30
Appendix 7C: Accounting for Derivatives 7-31

MODULE **Eight**

Reporting and Analyzing Nonowner Financing 8-1

Focus Company: Verizon Communications 8-1
Introduction 8-3
Current Liabilities 8-4
Accounts Payable 8-4
Accounts Payable Turnover (APT) 8-5
Mid-Module Review 1 8-6
Accrued Liabilities 8-7
Mid-Module Review 2 8-9
Current Nonoperating Liabilities 8-10
Mid-Module Review 3 8-11
Long-Term Nonoperating Liabilities 8-12
Pricing of Debt 8-12
Effective Cost of Debt 8-15
Reporting of Debt Financing 8-16
Financial Statement Effects of Debt Issuance 8-16
Effects of Discount and Premium Amortization 8-17
Financial Statement Effects of Bond Repurchase 8-19
Financial Statement Footnotes 8-20
Credit Ratings and the Cost of Debt 8-21
Module-End Review 8-25
Appendix 8A: Compound Interest 8-25
Appendix 8B: Economics of Gains and Losses on Bond Repurchases 8-29

MODULE **Nine**

Reporting and Analyzing Owner Financing 9-1

Focus Company: Accenture 9-1
Introduction 9-3
Contributed Capital 9-4
Classes of Stock 9-5
Accounting for Stock Transactions 9-7
Stock Compensation Plans 9-9
Mid-Module Review 1 9-11
Earned Capital 9-12
Cash Dividends 9-12
Mid-Module Review 2 9-14
Stock Dividends and Splits 9-14
Mid-Module Review 3 9-16
Accumulated Other Comprehensive Income 9-17
Summary of Stockholders' Equity 9-18
Equity Carve Outs and Convertibles 9-20
Sell-Offs 9-20
Spin-Offs 9-21
Split-Offs 9-22
Analysis of Equity Carve Outs 9-23
Mid-Module Review 4 9-23
Convertible Securities 9-23
Module-End Review 9-25

MODULE **Ten**

Reporting and Analyzing Off-Balance-Sheet Financing 10-1

Focus Company: Southwest Airlines 10-1
Introduction 10-3
Leases 10-4
Lessee Reporting of Leases 10-5
Footnote Disclosures of Leases 10-6
Capitalization of Operating Leases 10-7
Mid-Module Review 1 10-11
Pensions 10-12
Reporting of Defined Benefit Pension Plans 10-12
Balance Sheet Effects 10-12
Income Statement Effects 10-14

Footnote Disclosures - Components of Plan Assets and PBO 10-15

Footnote Disclosures and Future Cash Flows 10-16

Footnote Disclosures and Profit Implications 10-18

Other Post-Employment Benefits 10-20

Mid-Module Review 2 10-21

Special Purpose Entities (SPEs) 10-22

Applying SPEs as Financing Tools 10-23

Reporting of Consolidated SPEs 10-25

Module-End Review 10-26

Appendix 10A: Amortization Component of Pension Expense 10-27

MODULE **Eleven**
Adjusting and Forecasting Financial Statements 11-1

Focus Company: Procter & Gamble 11-1

Introduction 11-3

Adjusting Financial Statements 11-4

Adjusting the Income Statement 11-4

Adjusting the Balance Sheet 11-6

Adjusting the Statement of Cash Flows 11-7

Mid-Module Review 1 11-9

Forecasting Financial Statements 11-11

Forecasting the Income Statement 11-11

Forecasting the Balance Sheet 11-13

Forecasting the Statement of Cash Flows 11-18

Reassessing the Forecasts 11-18

Forecasting Multiple Years 11-19

Mid-Module Review 2 11-21

Parsimonious Method to Multiyear Forecasting 11-24

Module-End Review 11-25

MODULE **Twelve**
Analyzing and Valuing Equity Securities 12-1

Focus Company: Johnson & Johnson 12-1

Introduction to Security Valuation 12-3

Equity Valuation Models 12-3

Discounted Cash Flow (DCF) Model 12-4

Mid-Module Review 12-7

Residual Operating Income (ROPI) Model 12-8

Managerial Insights from the ROPI Model 12-10

Assessment of Valuation Models 12-11

Module-End Review 12-12

Appendix 12A: Johnson & Johnson Financial Statements 12-13

MODULE **Thirteen**
Comprehensive Case 13-1

Focus Company: Kimberly-Clark 13-1

Introduction 13-3

Reviewing the Financial Statements 13-4

Income Statement Reporting and Analysis 13-4

Balance Sheet Reporting and Analysis 13-11

Off-Balance-Sheet Reporting and Analysis 13-21

Statement of Cash Flows Reporting and Analysis 13-25

Independent Audit Opinion 13-26

Assessing Profitability and Creditworthiness 13-27

ROE Disaggregation 13-27

Disaggregation of RNOA—Margin and Turnover 13-27

Disaggregation of Margin and Turnover 13-27

Credit Analysis 13-28

Summarizing Profitability and Creditworthiness 13-29

Adjusting and Forecasting Financial Performance 13-29

Adjusting Accounting Numbers 13-29

Forecasting Accounting Numbers 13-30

Valuing Equity Securities 13-31

Discounted Cash Flow Valuation 13-31

Residual Operating Income Valuation 13-31

MODULE **Fourteen**
Managerial Accounting for MBAs 14-1

Focus Companies: HP, Dell, Compaq 14-1

Demand for Managerial Accounting 14-3

Managerial Accounting for Internal Decision Makers 14-4

Strategic Cost Management 14-4

Organizations: Missions, Goals, and Strategies 14-5

Strategic Position Analysis 14-7

Managerial Accounting and Goal Attainment 14-9

Planning, Organizing, and Controlling 14-10
Mid-Module Review 14-11
    Competition and its Key Dimensions 14-11
Cost Drivers 14-12
    Structural Cost Drivers 14-13
    Organizational Cost Drivers 14-13
    Activity Cost Drivers 14-14
Ethics in Managerial Accounting 14-15
Module-End Review 14-16

MODULE Fifteen

Cost Behavior, Activity Analysis, and Cost Estimation 15-1

Focus Companies: American, United, JetBlue 15-1
Cost Behavior Analysis 15-3
Four Basic Cost Behavior Patterns 15-3
    Factors Affecting Cost Behavior Patterns 15-5
    Total Cost Function for an Organization or Segment 15-5
    Additional Cost Behavior Patterns 15-6
    Committed and Discretionary Fixed Costs 15-8
Mid-Module Review 15-8
Cost Estimation 15-9
    High-Low Cost Estimation 15-9
    Scatter Diagrams 15-11
    Least-Squares Regression 15-12
Additional Issues in Cost Estimation 15-14
    Changes in Technology and Prices 15-14
    Matching Activity and Costs 15-15
    Identifying Activity Cost Drivers 15-15
Alternative Cost Driver Classifications 15-15
    Manufacturing Cost Hierarchy 15-16
    Customer Cost Hierarchy 15-18
Module-End Review 15-19

MODULE Sixteen

Cost-Volume-Profit Analysis and Planning 16-1

Focus Companies: Amazon, Webvan, Yahoo! 16-1
Profitability Analysis 16-3
    Key Assumptions 16-4
        Profit Formula 16-4
Contribution and Functional Income Statements 16-6
    Contribution Income Statement 16-6
    Functional Income Statement 16-6
    Analysis Using Contribution Margin Ratio 16-7
Break-Even Point and Profit Planning 16-8
    Determining Break-Even Point 16-8
    Profit Planning 16-8
    Cost-Volume-Profit Graph 16-9
    Profit-Volume Graph 16-10
    Impact of Income Taxes 16-11
Mid-Module Review 16-11
Multiple-Product Cost-Volume-Profit Analysis 16-14
    Sales Mix Analysis 16-14
Analysis of Operating Leverage 16-17
Module-End Review 16-19

MODULE Seventeen

Relevant Costs and Benefits for Decision Making 17-1

Focus Companies: AT&T, Microsoft, Time Warner 17-1
Identifying Relevant Costs 17-3
    Relevance of Future Revenues 17-4
    Relevance of Outlay Costs 17-4
    Irrelevance of Sunk Costs 17-5
    Sunk Costs Can Cause Ethical Dilemmas 17-5
    Relevance of Disposal and Salvage Values 17-5
    Relevance of Opportunity Costs 17-6
Differential Analysis of Relevant Costs 17-6
Mid-Module Review 17-7
Applying Differential Analysis 17-8
    Multiple Changes in Profit Plans 17-9
    Special Orders 17-10
    Outsourcing Decisions (Make or Buy) 17-12
    Sell or Process Further 17-14
Use of Limited Resources 17-15
    Single Constraint 17-16
    Multiple Constraints 17-17
    Theory of Constraints 17-18
Module-End Review 17-19

MODULE **Eighteen**
Product Costing: Job and Process Operations 18-1

Focus Companies: Ace, Home Depot, Lowes 18-1
Inventory Costs in Various Organizations 18-3
Inventory Costs for Financial Reporting 18-4
    Product Costs and Period Costs 18-4
    Three Components of Product Costs 18-5
    A Closer Look at Manufacturing Overhead 18-6
The Production Environment 18-8
    Production Files and Records 18-9
Job Costing for Products and Services 18-10
    Job Costing Illustrated 18-11
    Statement of Cost of Goods Manufactured 18-15
    Overapplied and Underapplied Overhead 18-17
    Job Costing in Service Organizations 18-18
Mid-Module Review 18-19
Process Costing 18-21
    Cost of Production Report 18-22
    Weighted Average and First-In, First-Out Process Costing 18-25
    Process Costing in Service Organizations 18-25
Module-End Review 18-26
Appendix 18A: Absorption and Variable Costing 18-27

MODULE **Nineteen**
Product Costing: Assigning Indirect Costs 19-1

Focus Companies: Oshkosh Truck, Shimano, SRAM 19-1
Allocating Indirect Costs 19-3
    Cost Objectives 19-3
    Cost Pools 19-4
    Allocation Bases 19-4
    Production and Service Department Costs 19-5
Service Department Cost Allocation 19-6
    Direct Method 19-7
    Step Method 19-8
    Linear Algebra (Reciprocal) Method 19-10
    Dual Rates 19-11
Mid-Module Review 19-11

Activity-Based Costing (ABC) 19-13
    ABC Product Costing Model 19-15
    Comparing Traditional and Activity-Based Costing 19-16
Traditional and ABC Costing Illustrated 19-17
    Applying Overhead with Plantwide Rates 19-17
    Applying Overhead with Department Rates 19-18
    Applying Overhead with Activity-Based Costing 19-19
    Limitations of ABC Illustration 19-21
ABC Implementation Issues 19-21
Module-End Review 19-23

MODULE **Twenty**
Operational Budgeting and Profit Planning 20-1

Focus Companies: 7-Eleven, Target, Wal-Mart 20-1
Reasons for Budgeting 20-3
General Approaches to Budgeting 20-4
    Output/Input Approach 20-4
    Activity-Based Approach 20-5
    Incremental Approach 20-5
    Minimum Level Approach 20-5
Mid-Module Review 20-6
Master Budget 20-7
    Sales Budget 20-9
    Purchases Budget 20-9
    Selling Expense Budget 20-10
    General and Administrative Expense Budget 20-10
    Cash Budget 20-11
    Budgeted Financial Statements 20-13
    Finalizing the Budget 20-14
Budget Development and Manager Behavior 20-15
    Employee Participation 20-15
    Budgeting Periods 20-16
    Forecasts 20-16
    Ethics 20-17
    Developing Budgets That Work 20-17
Module-End Review 20-18

MODULE **Twenty-One**

Performance Assessment: Standard Costs, Flexible Budgets, and Variance Analysis 21-1

Focus Company: Gateway 21-1
Responsibility Accounting 21-3
  Performance Reporting and Organization Structures 21-4
  Types of Responsibility Centers 21-5
Performance Reporting for Cost Centers 21-6
  Development of Flexible Budgets 21-6
  Flexible Budgets Emphasize Performance 21-8
Mid-Module Review 21-9
  Standard Costs 21-10
Variance Analysis for Variable Costs 21-11
  Materials Standards and Variances 21-12
  Labor Standards and Variances 21-14
  Overhead Standards and Variances 21-16
  Interpreting Variable Overhead Variances 21-18
Performance Reports for Revenue Centers 21-19
  Inclusion of Controllable Costs 21-20
  Revenue Centers as Profit Centers 21-21
Module-End Review 21-22

MODULE **Twenty-Two**

Segment Reporting, Transfer Pricing, and Balanced Scorecard 22-1

Focus Companies: Procter & Gamble, Verizon 22-1
Strategic Business Segments 22-3
Segment Reporting 22-4
  Multi-Level Segment Income Statements 22-4
  Interpreting Segment Reports 22-6
Mid-Module Review 22-7
Transfer Pricing 22-7
  Management Considerations 22-8
  Determining Transfer Prices 22-9
Investment Center Evaluation Measures 22-12
  Return on Investment 22-12
  Investment Center Income 22-14
  Investment Center Asset Base 22-15

  Other Valuation Issues 22-15
  Residual Income 22-15
  Which Measure Is Best? 22-16
Balanced Scorecard 22-17
  Balanced Scorecard Framework 22-17
  Balanced Scorecard and Strategy 22-19
Module-End Review 22-19

MODULE **Twenty-Three**

Pricing and Other Product Management Decisions 23-1

Focus Companies: Ford, GM, Honda, Toyota 23-1
Understanding the Value Chain 23-3
  Usefulness of a Value Chain Perspective 23-5
  Value-Added and Value Chain Perspectives 23-7
The Pricing Decision 23-7
  Economic Approaches to Pricing 23-7
  Cost-Based Approaches to Pricing 23-8
Mid-Module Review 23-11
Target Costing 23-12
  Target Costing is Proactive for Cost Management 23-12
  Target Costing Encourages Design for Production 23-13
  Target Costing Reduces Time to Introduce Products 23-14
  Target Costing Can Apply to Components 23-15
  Target Costing Requires Cost Information 23-15
  Target Costing Requires Coordination 23-15
  Target Costing is Key for Products with Short Life Cycles 23-16
  Target Costing Helps Manage Life Cycle Costs 23-16
Continuous Improvement Costing 23-17
Benchmarking 23-18
  Current Nonoperating (Financial) Liabilities 426
Module-End Review 23-20

Appendix A: Compound Interest Tables A-1
Appendix B: Constructing the Statement of Cash Flows B-1
Appendix C: Chart of Accounts with Acronyms C-1
Appendix D: Quick Review D-1
Glossary G-1
Index I-1

Financial Accounting for MBAs

LO1 Identify and discuss the users and suppliers of financial information. (p. 1-5)

LO2 Identify and explain the four financial statements, and define the accounting equation. (p. 1-8)

LO3 Explain the basics of profitability analysis. (p. 1-16)

LO4 Describe business analysis within the context of a competitive environment. (p. 1-18)

LO5 Describe the accounting principles that guide preparation of financial statements. (p. 1-23)

BERKSHIRE HATHAWAY

Berkshire Hathaway is a holding company. It owns numerous businesses that pursue diverse activities. In 2005, Berkshire Hathaway reported total assets of $198 billion, stockholders' equity of $92 billion, sales of $82 billion, net profit of $8.5 billion, operating cash flow of $9.5 billion, and employed 192,000 workers.[1]

The legendary Warren Buffett, the 'Sage of Omaha,' who studied under the renowned Benjamin Graham (a founder of modern value-investing), manages Berkshire Hathaway. Buffett's investment philosophy is to acquire and hold companies over the long run. His acquisition criteria, taken from Berkshire Hathaway's annual report, follow:

1. Large purchases (at least $75 million of pretax earnings).
2. Demonstrated consistent earning power (future projections are of *no* interest to us, nor are 'turnaround' situations).
3. Businesses earning good returns on equity while employing little or no debt.
4. Management in place (we can't supply it).
5. Simple businesses (if there's lots of technology, we won't understand it).
6. An offering price (we don't want to waste our time or that of the seller by talking, even preliminarily, about a transaction when price is unknown).

At least three of Buffett's six criteria relate to financial performance. First, he seeks businesses with large and consistent earning power. Buffett is

---

[1] Berkshire Hathaway's 2005 balance sheet includes an atypical third column of numbers labeled "pro forma" (which means "as if") that reflect a stock transaction that happened after the year end. Berkshire Hathaway provides the pro forma numbers so that financial statement readers can see the effect of the transaction and make apples-to-apples comparisons in the future. The balance sheet numbers we discuss in this module are the 2005 numbers that reflect only events that happened in 2005.

not only looking for consistent earnings, but earnings that are measured according to accounting policies that closely mirror the underlying economic performance of the business.

Second, Buffett focuses on "businesses earning good returns on equity," defined as net income divided by average stockholders' equity: "Our preference would be to reach our goal by directly owning a diversified group of businesses that generate cash and consistently earn above-average returns" (Berkshire Hathaway annual report). For management to earn a good return on equity, it must focus on both net income (financial performance) and equity (financial condition).

Third, Buffett values companies based on their ability to generate consistent earnings and cash. He focuses on *intrinsic value,* which he defines in each annual report as follows:

> Intrinsic value is an all-important concept that offers the only logical approach to evaluating the relative attractiveness of investments and businesses. Intrinsic value can be defined simply: It is the discounted value of the cash that can be taken out of a business during its remaining life.

The discounted value Buffett describes is the present (today's) value of the cash flows the company expects to generate in the future. Cash is generated when companies are well managed and operate profitably and efficiently.

Warren Buffett provides some especially useful investment guidance in his Chairman's letter from the Berkshire Hathaway annual report:

> Three suggestions for investors: First, beware of companies displaying weak accounting. If a company still does not expense options, or if its pension assumptions are fanciful, watch out. When managements take the low road in aspects that are visible, it is likely they are following a similar path behind the scenes. There is seldom just one cockroach in the kitchen.

> Second, unintelligible footnotes usually indicate untrustworthy management. If you can't understand a footnote or other managerial explanation, it's usually because the CEO doesn't want you to. Enron's descriptions of certain transactions still baffle me.

(Continued on next page)

(Continued from previous page)

Finally, be suspicious of companies that trumpet earnings projections and growth expectations. Businesses seldom operate in a tranquil, no-surprise environment, and earnings simply don't advance smoothly (except, of course, in the offering books of investment bankers).

This book will explain Buffett's references to stock option accounting and pension assumptions as well as a host of other accounting issues that affect interpretation and valuation of companies' financial performance. We will analyze and interpret the footnotes, which Buffett views as crucial to quality financial reporting and analysis. Our philosophy is simple: we must understand the intricacies and nuances of financial reporting to become critical readers and users of financial reports for company analysis and valuation. Financial statements tell a story, a business story. The task is to understand that story, to analyze and interpret it in the context of competing stories, and to apply the knowledge gleaned to business decisions.

Sources: Berkshire Hathaway *2005 10-K Report*, Berkshire Hathaway *2001–2005 Annual Reports*.

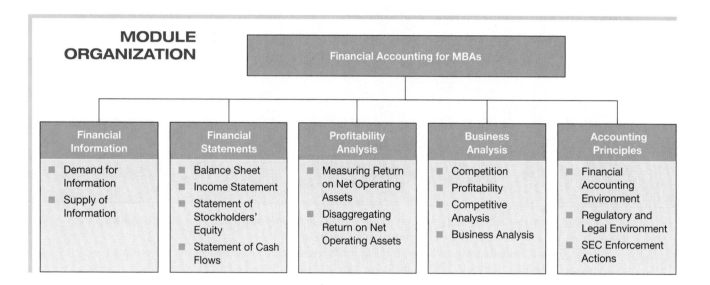

REPORTING ON BUSINESS ACTIVITIES

To effectively manage a company or infer whether it is well managed, we must understand the company's fundamental business activities. The information system called *financial accounting* helps us understand these business activities. This system reports on a company's performance and financial condition, and conveys executive management's privileged information and insights.

As managers, financial accounting information helps us to evaluate potential future strategies and ascertain the effectiveness of present and past strategies. It improves the soundness of our investment decisions, such as how to allocate resources across alternative investment projects and whether to invest additional resources in existing product lines or divisions. As managers, we also use financial accounting information to prepare client proposals, analyze the effectiveness of production processes, and evaluate the performance of management teams.

As investors, financial accounting information helps us determine which companies' stock to purchase or sell. Yet, before it is used to make decisions, the financial accounting information must be scrutinized and sometimes adjusted. This is accomplished, in part, by analyzing information contained in footnotes to companies' financial reports to determine the quality of reported figures and to make any necessary adjustments.

More generally, financial accounting satisfies the needs of different groups of users. Within firms, the *functioning* of this information system involves application of accounting standards to produce financial reports. Effectively using this information system involves making judgments, assumptions, and estimates based on data contained in the financial reports. The greatest value we derive from this system as users of financial information is the insight we gain into the business activities of the company under analysis.

To effectively analyze and use accounting information, we must consider the business context in which the information is created—see Exhibit 1.1. Without exception, all companies *plan* business activities, *finance* those activities, *invest* in those activities, and then engage in *operating* activities. Firms conduct all these activities while confronting *business forces*, including market constraints and competitive pressures. Financial accounting provides crucial input in advance of strategic planning. It also provides information about the relative success of those plans, which can be used to take corrective action or make new operating, investing, and financing decisions.

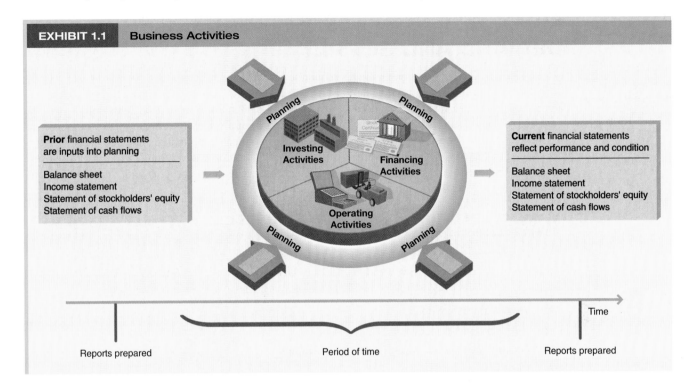

EXHIBIT 1.1   Business Activities

Exhibit 1.1 depicts the business activities for a typical company. The outer (green) ring is the planning process that reflects the overarching goals and objectives of the company within which strategic decisions are made. Those strategic decisions involve company financing, asset management, and daily operations. Apple, Inc., the focus company in Modules 2 and 3, provides the following description of its business strategy in its annual report:

> **Business Strategy**   The Company is committed to bringing the best personal computing and music experience to students, educators, creative professionals, businesses, government agencies, and consumers through its innovative hardware, software, peripherals, services, and Internet offerings. The Company's business strategy leverages its unique ability, through the design and development of its own operating system, hardware, and many software applications and technologies, to bring to its customers new products and solutions with superior ease-of-use, seamless integration, and innovative industrial design. The Company believes continual investment in research and development is critical to facilitate innovation of new and improved products and technologies. Besides updates to its existing line of personal computers and related software, services, peripherals, and networking solutions, the Company continues to capitalize on the convergence of digital consumer electronics and the computer by creating innovations like the iPod and iTunes Music Store. The Company's strategy also includes expanding its distribution network to effectively reach more of its targeted customers and provide them a high-quality sales and after-sales support experience.

A company's *strategic* (or *business*) *plan* reflects how it plans to achieve its goals and objectives. A plan's success depends on an effective analysis of market demand and supply. Specifically, a company must assess demand for its products and services, and assess the supply of its inputs (both labor and capital). The plan must also include competitive analyses, opportunity assessments, and consideration of business threats.

Historical financial statements provide valuable insight into the success of a company's strategic plan, and are an important input to the planning process. Financial statements highlight those portions of the strategic plan that proved to be effective and, thus, warrant additional capital investment. They also reveal areas that are less effective, and provide valuable information that aids in development of remedial action.

Once strategic adjustments are planned and implemented, the resulting financial statements provide input into the planning process for the following year; and this process recycles. Understanding a company's strategic plan helps focus our analysis of financial statements by placing them in proper context.

FINANCIAL ACCOUNTING INFORMATION: DEMAND AND SUPPLY

LO1 Identify and discuss the users and suppliers of financial information.

Financial accounting information facilitates economic transactions and promotes efficient resource allocations. Demand for financial reporting has existed for centuries as a means to facilitate efficient contracting and risk-sharing. Decision makers and other stakeholders demand information on a company's past and prospective returns and risks. Companies are encouraged to supply such information to lower their costs of financing and to lower some less obvious costs such as political, contracting, and labor costs.

As with all goods, the supply of information depends on companies weighing the costs of disclosure against the benefits of disclosure. Regulatory agencies intervene in this process with various disclosure requirements that establish a minimum supply of information.

BUSINESS INSIGHT   **Accounting Quality**

In the bear market that followed the bursting of the dot.com bubble, and amid a series of corporate scandals such as Enron, Tyco, and WorldCom, Congress passed the **Sarbanes-Oxley Act,** often referred to as *SOX*. SOX sought to rectify perceived problems in accounting, including:

■ Weak audit committees

■ Non-independent auditors

■ Limited management responsibility for accounting

■ Deficient internal controls

Increased scrutiny of financial reporting and internal controls has had some success. A report by Glass, Lewis and Co., a corporate-governance research firm, shows that the number of financial restatements by publicly traded companies surged to a record 1,295 in 2005—which is one restatement for each 12 public companies, and more than triple the 2002 total, the year SOX passed. The Glass, Lewis and Co. report concluded that "when so many companies produce inaccurate financial statements, it seriously calls into question the quality of information that investors relied upon to make capital-allocation decisions" (**CFO.Com**, 2006). Bottom line: we must be critical readers of financial reports.

Demand for Information

Demand for financial accounting information extends to numerous users that include:

▪ Managers and employees

▪ Investment analysts and information intermediaries

▪ Creditors and suppliers

▪ Shareholders and directors

▪ Customers and strategic partners

▪ Regulators and tax agencies

▪ Voters and their representatives

Managers and Employees

For their own well-being and future earnings potential, managers and employees demand accounting information on the financial condition, profitability, and prospects of their companies. Managers and employees also demand comparative financial information on competing companies and other business opportunities. This permits them to conduct comparative analyses to benchmark company performance and condition.

Managers and employees also demand financial accounting information for use in compensation and bonus contracts that are tied to such numbers. The popularity of employee profit sharing and stock ownership plans has further increased demand for financial information. Other sources of demand include union contracts that link wage negotiations to accounting numbers and pension and benefit plans whose solvency depends on company performance.

Investment Analysts and Information Intermediaries

Investment analysts and other information intermediaries such as financial press writers and business commentators are interested in predicting companies' future performance. Expectations about future profitability and the ability to generate cash impact the price of securities and a company's ability to borrow money at favorable terms. Financial reports reflect information about past performance and current resources available to companies. These reports also provide information on claims on those resources, including suppliers, creditors, lenders, and shareholders. This information allows analysts to make informed assessments about future financial performance and condition so they can provide stock recommendations or write commentaries.

Creditors and Suppliers

Banks and other lenders demand financial accounting information to help determine loan terms, loan amounts, interest rates, and required collateral. Loan agreements often include contractual requirements, called **covenants**, that restrict the borrower's behavior in some fashion. For example, loan covenants might require the loan recipient to maintain minimum levels of working capital, retained earnings, interest coverage, and so forth to safeguard lenders. Covenant violations can yield technical default, enabling the creditor to demand early payment or other compensation.

Suppliers similarly demand financial information to establish credit sales terms and to determine their long-term commitment to supply-chain relations. Both creditors and suppliers use financial information to monitor and adjust their contracts and commitments with a debtor company.

Shareholders and Directors

Shareholders and directors demand financial accounting information to assess the profitability and risks of companies, and to monitor the performance of their managers. Shareholders and others (including investment analysts, brokers, potential investors, etc.) look for information useful in their investment decisions. **Fundamental analysis** uses financial information to estimate company value and to form buy-sell stock strategies.

Both directors and shareholders use accounting information to evaluate managerial performance. Managers similarly use such information to request an increase in compensation and managerial power from directors. Outside directors are crucial to determining who runs the company, and these directors use accounting information to help make leadership decisions.

Customers and Strategic Partners

Customers (both current and potential) demand accounting information to assess a company's ability to provide products or services as agreed and to assess the company's staying power and reliability. Strategic partners wish to estimate the company's profitability to assess the fairness of returns on mutual transactions and strategic alliances.

Regulators and Tax Agencies

Regulators (such as the SEC, the Federal Trade Commission, and the Federal Reserve Bank) and tax agencies demand accounting information for tax policies, antitrust assessments, public protection, price setting, import-export analyses, and various other uses. Timely and reliable information is crucial to effective regulatory policy. Moreover, accounting information is often central to social and economic policy. For example, governments often grant monopoly rights to electric and gas companies serving specific areas in exchange for regulation over prices charged to consumers. These prices are mainly determined from accounting measures.

Voters and their Representatives

Voters and their representatives to national, state, and local governments demand accounting information for policy decisions. The decisions can involve economic, social, taxation, and other initiatives. Voters and their representatives also use accounting information to monitor government spending. We have all heard of the $1,000 hammer type stories that government watchdog groups uncover while sifting through accounting data. Contributors to nonprofit organizations also demand accounting information to assess the impact of their donations.

Supply of Information

In general, the quantity and quality of accounting information that firms provide are determined by managers' assessment of the benefits and costs of disclosure. Management releases information provided the benefits of disclosing that information outweigh the costs of doing so. Both *regulation* and *bargaining power* affect disclosure costs and benefits and thus play roles in determining the supply of accounting information.

Most areas of the world regulate the minimum levels of accounting disclosures. In the United States, publicly traded firms must file financial accounting information with the Securities Exchange Commission (SEC). The two main compulsory SEC filings are:

- Form **10-K**: the audited annual report that includes the four financial statements, discussed below, together with explanatory notes and the management's discussion and analysis of financial results.

- Form **10-Q**: the unaudited quarterly report that includes summary versions of the four financial statements and limited additional disclosures.

Forms 10-K and 10-Q are available electronically from the SEC Website (see Appendix 1A).

The minimum, regulated level of information is not the standard. Both the quantity and quality of information differ across companies and over time. We need only look at several annual reports to see considerable variance in the amount and type of accounting information supplied. For example, differences abound on disclosures for segment operations, product performance reports, and financing activities. Further, some stakeholders possess ample bargaining power to obtain accounting information for themselves. These typically include private lenders and major suppliers and customers.

Benefits of Disclosure

The benefits of supplying accounting information extend to a company's capital, labor, input, and output markets. Companies must compete in these markets. For example, capital markets provide debt and equity financing; the better a company's prospects, the lower is its cost of capital (as reflected in lower interest rates or higher stock prices). The same holds for a company's recruiting efforts in labor markets and its ability to establish superior supplier-customer relations in the input and output markets.

A company's performance in these markets depends on success with its business activities *and* the market's awareness of that success. Companies reap the benefits of disclosure with good news information about their products, processes, management, and so forth. That is, there are real economic incentives for companies to disclose reliable (audited) accounting information enabling them to better compete in capital, labor, input, and output markets.

What inhibits companies from providing false or misleading good news? There are several constraints. An important constraint imposed by stakeholders is that of audit requirements and legal repercussions associated with inaccurate accounting information. Another relates to reputation effects from disclosures as subsequent events either support or refute earlier news.

Costs of Disclosure

The costs of supplying accounting information include its preparation and dissemination, competitive disadvantages, litigation potential, and political costs. Preparation and dissemination costs can be substantial, but much of this cost is already borne by inside managers who need the same information for their own business decisions. The potential for information to yield competitive disadvantages is high. Companies are concerned that disclosures of their activities such as product or segment successes, strategic alliances or pursuits, technological or system innovations, and product or process quality improvements will harm their competitive advantages. Also, companies are frequently sued when disclosures create expectations that are not met. Highly visible companies often face political and public pressure, which creates "political costs." These companies often try to appear as if they do not generate excess profits. For example, government defense contractors, large software conglomerates, and oil companies are favorite targets of public scrutiny. Disclosure costs are higher for companies facing political costs.

A recent rule increased the cost of voluntary financial disclosures for all publicly traded companies. In August 2000, the SEC adopted Regulation FD, or Reg FD for short, to curb the practice of selective disclosure by public companies (called issuers by the SEC) to certain shareholders and financial analysts. In the past, many companies disclosed important information in meetings and conference calls that excluded individual shareholders. The goal of this rule is to even the playing field for all investors. Reg FD reads as follows: "Whenever an issuer discloses any material nonpublic information regarding that issuer, the issuer shall make public disclosure of that information . . . simultaneously, in the case of an intentional disclosure; and . . . promptly, in the case of a non-intentional disclosure." Reg FD increased disclosure costs and led some companies to curtail the supply of financial information to all users.

FINANCIAL STATEMENTS

Companies use four financial statements to periodically report on business activities. These statements are the: balance sheet, income statement, statement of stockholders' equity, and statement of cash flows.

Exhibit 1.2 shows how these statements are linked across time. A balance sheet reports on a company's financial position at a *point in time*. The income statement, statement of stockholders' equity, and the statement of cash flows report on performance over a *period of time*. The three statements in the middle of Exhibit 1.2 (period-of-time statements) link the balance sheet from the beginning to the end of a period.

A one-year, or annual, reporting period is common and is called the *accounting,* or *fiscal, year.* Of course, firms prepare financial statements more frequently; semi-annual, quarterly, and monthly financial statements are common. *Calendar-year* companies have reporting periods beginning on January 1 and ending on December

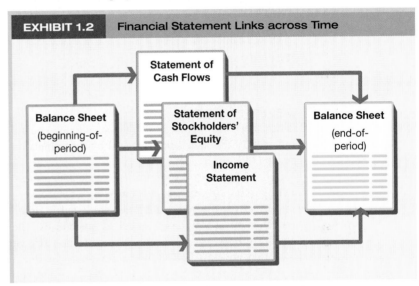

| EXHIBIT 1.2 | Financial Statement Links across Time |

31. Berkshire Hathaway is a calendar-year company. Some companies choose a fiscal year ending on a date other than December 31, such as when sales and inventory are low. For example, Best Buy's fiscal year-end is always near February 1, after the busy holiday season.

Balance Sheet

A balance sheet reports a company's financial position at a point in time. The balance sheet reports the company's *resources* (*assets*), namely what the company owns. The balance sheet also reports the *sources* of asset financing. There are two ways a company can finance its assets. It can raise money from shareholders; this is *owner financing*. It can also raise money from banks or other creditors and suppliers; this is *nonowner financing*. This means that both owners and nonowners hold claims on company assets. Owner claims on assets are referred to as *equity* and nonowner claims are referred to as *liabilities* (or debt). Since all financing must be invested in something, we obtain the following basic relation: *investing equals financing*. This equality is called the **accounting equation,** which follows:

LO2 Identify and explain the four financial statements, and define the accounting equation.

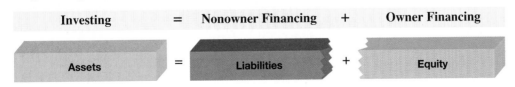

The accounting equation works for all companies at all points in time.

The balance sheet for **Berkshire Hathaway** is in Exhibit 1.3 (condensed). Refer to this balance sheet to verify the following amounts: assets = $198,325 million, liabilities = $106,025 million, and equity = $92,300 million. Assets equal liabilities plus equity, which reflects the accounting equation: investing equals financing.

EXHIBIT 1.3	**Balance Sheet ($ millions)**	
	BERKSHIRE HATHAWAY **Balance Sheet[2]** **December 31, 2005**	Report amounts at a point in time
Assets		Investing
Cash	$ 44,660	
Noncash assets	153,665	
Total assets	$198,325	Total resources
Liabilities and equity		Financing
Total liabilities	$106,025	Nonowner claim on resources
Equity		
Contributed capital	26,407	
Retained earnings	47,717	Owner claim on resources
Other stockholders' equity[3]	18,176	
Total liabilities and equity	$198,325	

Investing Activities

Balance sheets are organized like the accounting equation. Investing activities are represented by company assets. These assets are financed by a combination of nonowner financing (liabilities) and owner financing (equity).

For simplicity, Berkshire Hathaway's balance sheet in Exhibit 1.3 categorizes assets into cash and noncash assets. Noncash assets consist of several asset categories (Module 2 explains the composition of noncash assets). These categories are listed in order of their nearness to cash. For example, companies own a category of assets called inventories. These are goods that the company intends to sell to its customers. Inventories are converted into cash when they are sold within a short period of time. Hence, they are classified as short-term assets. Companies also report a category called property, plant and equipment. This category includes a company's office buildings or manufacturing facilities. Property, plant and equipment assets will be held for an extended period of time and are, therefore, generally classified as long-term assets.

The relative proportion of short-term and long-term assets is largely determined by a company's business model. This is evident in the graph to the left that depicts the relative proportion of short and long-term assets for several companies that we feature in this book. Companies such as Apple and Google require little investment in long-term assets. On the other hand, Verizon and Southwest Airlines require a large investment in long-term assets. Although managers can influence the relative amounts and proportion of assets, their flexibility is somewhat limited by the nature of their industries.

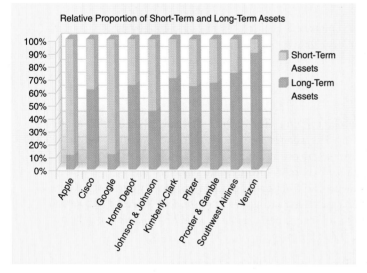

[2] Financial statement titles often begin with the word *consolidated*. This means that the financial statement includes a parent company and one or more subsidiaries, companies that the parent company owns. We discuss consolidation in Module 7.

[3] For Berkshire Hathaway, other stockholders' equity includes accumulated other comprehensive income and minority interests. These and other components of stockholders' equity are discussed in Modules 7 and 9.

Financing Activities

Assets must be paid for, and funding is provided by a combination of owner and nonowner financing. Owner (or equity) financing includes resources contributed to the company by its owners along with any profit retained by the company. Nonowner (creditor or debt) financing is borrowed money. We distinguish financing sources for an important reason: borrowed money entails a legal obligation to repay amounts owed, and failure to repay amounts borrowed can result in severe consequences for the borrower. Equity financing entails no such legal obligation for repayment.

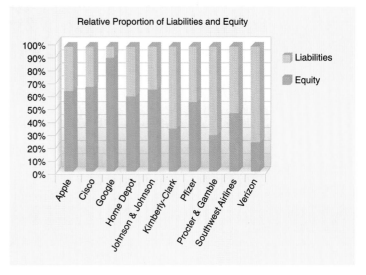

The relative proportion of nonowner (liabilities) and owner (equity) financing is largely determined by a company's business model. This is evident in the graph to the right; again citing many of the companies we feature as focus companies in this book.

Google is a relatively new company that is expanding into new markets. Its business model is, therefore, more risky than that of a more established company operating in relatively stable markets. Google, therefore, cannot afford to take on additional risk of higher nonowner financing levels. On the other hand, Proctor and Gamble competes in consumer goods markets that are largely predictable and stable. It can, therefore, operate with more nonowner financing.

Our discussion of investing and financing activities uses many terms and concepts that we explain later in the book. Our desire here is to provide a sneak preview into the interplay among financial statements, manager behavior, and economics. Some questions that we might have at this early stage regarding the balance sheet follow:

- Berkshire Hathaway reports $44.7 billion of cash on its 2005 balance sheet, which is 23% of total assets. Many investment-type companies such as Berkshire Hathaway and high-tech companies such as Cisco Systems carry high levels of cash. Why is that? Is there a cost to holding too much cash? Is it costly to carry too little cash?

- The relative proportion of short-term and long-term assets is largely dictated by companies' business models. Why is this the case? Why is the composition of assets on balance sheets for companies in the same industry similar? By what degree can a company's asset composition safely deviate from industry norms?

- What are the trade-offs in financing a company by owner versus nonowner financing? If nonowner financing is less costly, why don't we see companies financed entirely with borrowed money?

- How do shareholders influence the strategic direction of a company? How can long-term creditors influence strategic direction?

- Most assets and liabilities are reported on the balance sheet at their acquisition price, called *historical cost*. Would reporting assets and liabilities at current market values be more informative? What problems might reporting balance sheets using current market value cause?

Review the Berkshire Hathaway balance sheet summarized in Exhibit 1.3 and think about these questions. We provide answers for each of these questions as we progress through the book.

Income Statement

An **income statement** reports on a company's performance over a period of time and lists amounts for revenues (also called sales) and expenses. Revenues less expenses yield the bottom-line net income amount.

Berkshire Hathaway's income statement is in Exhibit 1.4. Refer to its income statement to verify the following: revenues = $81,663 million, expenses = $73,135 million, and net income = $8,528 million. Net income reflects the profit (also called earnings) to owners for that specific period.

EXHIBIT 1.4	Income Statement ($ millions)

BERKSHIRE HATHAWAY
Income Statement
For Year Ended December 31, 2005 ◄——— Report amounts over a period of time

Revenues	$81,663 ◄——— Goods or services provided to customers
Expenses	73,135 ◄———
Net income (loss)	$ 8,528 ——— Costs incurred to generate revenues

Manufacturing and merchandising companies typically disclose the cost of goods sold (also called cost of sales) in the income statement. This measure is reported following revenues. It is also common to report the gross profit subtotal, which is revenues less the cost of goods sold. The company's remaining expenses are then reported below gross profit. This income statement layout follows:

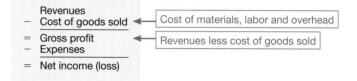

Revenues
− Cost of goods sold ◄——— Cost of materials, labor and overhead
= Gross profit ◄——— Revenues less cost of goods sold
− Expenses
= Net income (loss)

Operating Activities

Operating activities use company resources to produce, promote, and sell its products and services. These activities extend from input markets involving suppliers of materials and labor to a company's output markets involving customers of products and services. Input markets generate most *expenses* (or *costs*) such as inventory, salaries, materials, and logistics. Output markets generate *revenues* (or *sales*) to customers. Output markets also generate some expenses such as marketing and distributing products and services to customers. Net income arises when revenues exceed expenses. A loss occurs when expenses exceed revenues.

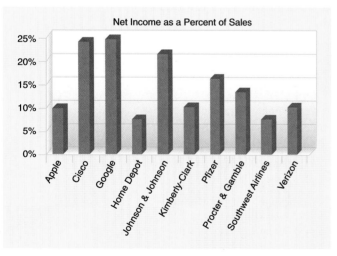

Net Income as a Percent of Sales

Differences exist in the relative profitability of companies across industries. Although effective management can increase the profitability of a company, business models play a large part in determining company profitability within an industry. These differences are highlighted in the graph (to the left) of net income as a percentage of sales for several companies we highlight in this book.

Home Depot operates in a mature industry with little ability to differentiate its products from those of its competitors. Hence, its net income as a percentage of sales is low. Southwest Airlines faces a different kind of problem: having competitors that are desperate and trying to survive. Profitability will not return to the transportation industry until weaker competitors are no longer protected by bankruptcy courts. At the other end of the spectrum are Cisco and Google. Both are dominant in their industries with products protected by patent laws. Their profitability levels are more akin to that of monopolists.

As a sneak preview, we might consider the following questions regarding the income statement:

- Assume that a company sells a product to a customer who promises to pay in 30 days. Should the seller recognize the sale when it is made or when cash is collected?

- When a company purchases a long-term asset such as a building, its cost is reported on the balance sheet as an asset. Should a company, instead, record the cost of that building as an expense when it is acquired? If not, how should a company report the cost of that asset over the course of its useful life?

- Manufacturers and merchandisers report the cost of a product as an expense when the product sale is recorded. How might we measure the costs of a product that is sold by a merchandiser? By a manufacturer?

- If an asset, such as a building, increases in value, that increase in value is not reported as income until the building is sold, if ever. What concerns arise if we record increases in asset values as part of income, when measurement of that increase is based on appraised values?

- Employees commonly earn wages that are yet to be paid at the end of a particular period. Should their wages be recognized as an expense in the period that the work is performed, or when the wages are paid?

- Companies are not allowed to report profit on transactions relating to their own stock. That is, they don't report income when stock is sold, nor do they report an expense when dividends are paid to shareholders. Why is this the case?

Review the Berkshire Hathaway income statement summarized in Exhibit 1.4 and think about these questions. We provide answers for each of these questions as we progress through the book.

RESEARCH INSIGHT   **Are Earnings Important?**

A recent study asked top finance executives of publicly traded companies to *rank the three most important measures to report to outsiders.* The study reports that:

> "[More than 50% of] CFOs state that earnings are the most important financial metric to external constituents . . . this finding could reflect superior informational content in earnings over the other metrics. Alternatively, it could reflect myopic managerial concern about earnings. The emphasis on earnings is noteworthy because cash flows continue to be the measure emphasized in the academic finance literature."

The study also reports that CFOs view year-over-year earnings to be of critical importance to outsiders. Why is that? The study provides the following insights.

> "CFOs note that the first item in a press release is often a comparison of current quarter earnings with four quarters lagged quarterly earnings . . . CFOs also mention that while analysts' forecasts can be guided by management, last year's quarterly earnings number is a benchmark that is harder, if not impossible, to manage after the 10-Q has been filed with the SEC . . . Several executives mention that comparison to seasonally lagged earnings numbers provides a measure of earnings momentum and growth, and therefore is a useful gauge of corporate performance."

Thus, are earnings important? To the majority of finance chiefs surveyed, the answer is a resounding yes. (Source: Graham, et al., *Journal of Accounting and Economics,* 2005)

Statement of Stockholders' Equity

The **statement of stockholders' equity**, or simply *statement of equity,* reports on changes in key types of equity over a period of time. For each type of equity the statement reports the beginning balance, a summary of the activity in the account during the year, and the ending balance. Berkshire Hathaway's statement of stockholders' equity is in Exhibit 1.5. During the recent period, its equity changed due to share issuances and income reinvestment. Berkshire Hathaway classifies these changes into three categories:

- Contributed capital from stockholders' net contributions to the company
- Retained earnings over the life of the company minus all dividends ever paid
- Other (see footnote 3)

Contributed capital represents the cash the company received from the sale of stock to stockholders (also called shareholders), less any funds expended for the repurchase of stock. Retained earnings (also called *earned capital* or *reinvested capital*) represent the cumulative total amount of income that the company has earned and that has been retained in the business and not distributed to shareholders in the form of dividends. The change in retained earnings links consecutive balance sheets via the income statement.

EXHIBIT 1.5	Statement of Equity ($ millions)			

BERKSHIRE HATHAWAY
Statement of Stockholders' Equity
For Year Ended December 31, 2005

Report amounts over a period of time

	Contributed Capital	Retained Earnings	Other	Total	
December 31, 2004	$26,276	$39,189	$21,193	$86,658	← Beginning period amounts
Stock issuance (repurchase)	131			131	
Net income (Loss).............		8,528		8,528	← Change in balances over a period
Dividends		0		0	
Other.......................			(3,017)	(3,017)	
December 31, 2005	$26,407	$47,717	$18,176	$92,300	← Ending period amounts

For Berkshire Hathaway, its recent year's retained earnings increases from $39,189 million to $47,717 million. This increase of $8,528 million is explained by net income of $8,528 million and no payment of dividends. (Ending retained earnings = Beginning retained earnings + Net income − Dividends; we discuss this relation further in Module 2).

Statement of Cash Flows

The **statement of cash flows** reports the change (either an increase or a decrease) in a company's cash balance over a period of time. The statement reports on cash inflows and outflows from operating, investing, and financing activities over a period of time. Berkshire Hathaway's statement of cash flows is in Exhibit 1.6. Its cash balance increased by $1,233 million in the recent period. Of this increase in cash, operating activities generated an $9,446 million cash inflow, investing activities reduced cash by $13,841 million, and financing activities yielded a cash inflow of $5,628 million.

EXHIBIT 1.6	Statement of Cash Flows ($ millions)

BERKSHIRE HATHAWAY
Statement of Cash Flows
For Year Ended December 31, 2005

Report amounts over a period of time

Operating cash flows	$ 9,446	← Net cash inflow from operating
Investing cash flows..............................	(13,841)	
Financing cash flows	5,628	← Net cash outflow from investing
Net increase in cash..............................	1,233	← Net cash inflow from financing
Cash, December 31, 2004	43,427	
Cash, December 31, 2005	$44,660	← Cash amounts per balance sheet

Berkshire Hathaway's operating cash flow of $9,446 million does not equal its $8,528 million net income. Generally, a company's net cash flow for a period does *not* equal its net income for the period. This is due to timing differences between when revenue and expense items are recognized on the income statement and when cash is received and paid. (We discuss this concept further in subsequent modules.)

Both cash flow and net income numbers are important for business decisions. Each is used in security valuation models, and both help users of accounting reports understand and assess a company's past, present, and future business activities.

As a sneak preview, we might consider the following questions regarding the statement of cash flows:

- What is the usefulness of companies providing the statement of cash flows? Do the balance sheet and income statement provide sufficient cash flow information?

- What types of information are disclosed in the statement of cash flows and why are they important?

- What kinds of activities are reported in each of the operating, investing and financing sections of the statement of cash flows? How is this information useful?

- Is it important for a company to report net cash inflows (positive amounts) relating to operating activities over the longer term? What are the implications if operating cash flows are negative for an extended period of time?

- Why is it important to know the composition of a company's investment activities? What kind of information might we look for? Are positive investing cash flows favorable?

- Is it important to know the sources of a company's financing activities? What questions might that information help us answer?

- How might the composition of operating, investing and financing cash flows change over a company's life cycle?

- Is the bottom line increase in cash flow the key number? Why or why not?

Review the Berkshire Hathaway statement of cash flows summarized in Exhibit 1.6 and think about these questions. We provide answers for each of these questions as we progress through the book.

Financial Statement Linkages

The four financial statements are linked within and across periods—see Exhibit 1.2.

- The income statement and the balance sheet are linked via retained earnings. For Berkshire Hathaway, the $8,528 million increase in retained earnings (reported on the balance sheet) equals its net income (reported on the income statement). Berkshire Hathaway did not pay dividends this year.

- Retained earnings, contributed capital, and other equity balances appear both on the statement of stockholders' equity and the balance sheet.

- The statement of cash flows is linked to the income statement as net income is a component of operating cash flow. The statement of cash flows is also linked to the balance sheet as the change in the balance sheet cash account reflects the net of cash inflows and outflows for the period.

Items that impact one financial statement ripple through the others. Linkages among the four financial statements are an important feature of the accounting system. We discuss this concept further and present a numerical example illustrating these linkages in Module 2.

BUSINESS INSIGHT   **Warren Buffett on Financial Reports**

"When Charlie and I read reports, we have no interest in pictures of personnel, plants or products. References to EBITDA [earnings before interest, taxes, depreciation and amortization] make us shudder—does management think the tooth fairy pays for capital expenditures? We're very suspicious of accounting methodology that is vague or unclear, since too often that means management wishes to hide something. And we don't want to read messages that a public relations department or consultant has turned out. Instead, we expect a company's CEO to explain in his or her own words what's happening." —Berkshire Hathaway annual report

Information Beyond Financial Statements

Important financial information about a company is communicated to various decision makers through reports other than the four financial statements. These reports include the following:

- Management Discussion and Analysis (MD&A)
- Independent Auditor Report
- Financial statement footnotes
- Regulatory filings, including proxy statements and other SEC filings

We describe and explain the usefulness of these additional information sources throughout the book.

MANAGERIAL DECISION	You Are the Product Manager

There is often friction between investors' need for information and a company's desire to safeguard competitive advantages. Assume that you are a key-product manager at your company. Your department has test-marketed a potentially lucrative new product, which it plans to further finance. You are asked for advice on the extent of information to disclose about the new product in the MD&A section of the company's upcoming annual report. What advice do you provide and why? [Answer, p. 1-30]

MID-MODULE REVIEW

The following financial information is from Allstate Corporation, a competitor of Berkshire Hathaway's GEICO Insurance, for the year ended December 31, 2005 ($ millions).

Cash, ending year	$ 313
Cash flows from operations	5,605
Revenues	35,383
Stockholders' equity	20,186
Cash flows from financing	(555)
Total liabilities	135,886
Expenses	33,618
Noncash assets	155,759
Cash flows from investing	(5,151)
Net income	1,765
Cash, beginning year	414

Required

1. Prepare an income statement, balance sheet, and statement of cash flows for Allstate at December 31, 2005.
2. Compare the balance sheet and income statement of Allstate to those of Berkshire Hathaway in Exhibits 1.3 and 1.4. What differences are observed?

Solution

1.

ALLSTATE CORPORATION
Income Statement
For Year Ended December 31, 2005

Revenues	$35,383
Expenses	33,618
Net income	$ 1,765

ALLSTATE CORPORATION
Balance Sheet
December 31, 2005

Cash asset	$ 313	Total liabilities	$135,886
Noncash assets	155,759	Stockholders' equity	20,186
Total assets.	$156,072	Total liabilities and equity . .	$156,072

ALLSTATE CORPORATION
Statement of Cash Flows
For Year Ended December 31, 2005

Cash flows from operations	$5,605
Cash flows from investing	(5,151)
Cash flows from financing	(555)
Net increase (decrease) in cash	(101)
Cash, beginning year	414
Cash, ending year	$ 313

2. Berkshire Hathaway is a larger company; its total assets are $198,325 million compared to Allstate's assets of $156,072 million. In percentage terms, Berkshire Hathaway is 27% larger. The income statements of the two companies are markedly different. Berkshire Hathaway reports more than twice as much revenue ($81,663 million compared to $35,383 million). The difference in net income is even more drastic; Berkshire Hathaway earned $8,528 million whereas Allstate reported net income of only $1,765 million. This is nearly five times more net income! The two companies are not direct competitors in that Berkshire Hathaway has a wide array of companies in its consolidated group, whereas Allstate is mainly a property and casualty insurer.

PROFITABILITY ANALYSIS

This section previews the analysis framework of this book. This framework is used extensively by market professionals who analyze financial reports to evaluate company management and value the company's debt and equity securities. Analysis of financial performance is crucial in assessing prior strategic decisions and evaluating strategic alternatives.

LO3 Explain the basics of profitability analysis.

Return on Net Operating Assets

Suppose we learn that a company reports an operating profit of $10 million. Is this company performing well? Knowing that a company reports a profit is certainly positive as it indicates that customers value its goods or services and that its revenues exceed expenses. However, we cannot assess how well it is performing. To explain, suppose we learn that this company has $500 million in operating assets. We now assess the $10 million in operating profit as low. This is because relative to the size of its asset investment, the company earned a paltry 2% return, computed as $10 million divided by $500 million. A 2% return is what a much lower-risk savings account might yield. The important point is that a company's profitability must be assessed with respect to the size of its investment. The metric we used here is known as the *return on net operating assets* (RNOA)—defined as net operating profit after tax for that period, divided by the average net operating assets for that period.

Components of Return on Net Operating Assets

We can separate return on net operating assets into two components: profitability and productivity. Profitability relates net operating profit after tax to sales, called the *net operating profit margin* (NOPM), and reflects the profit earned on each sales dollar. Management wants to earn as much profit as possible from sales.

Productivity relates sales to net operating assets. This component, called the *net operating asset turnover* (NOAT), reflects sales generated by each dollar of operating assets. Management wants to maximize asset productivity, that is, to achieve the highest possible sales level for a given level of operating assets (or to achieve a given level of sales with the smallest level of operating assets).

Exhibit 1.7 depicts the disaggregation of return on net operating assets into these two components. Profitability (NOPM) and productivity (NOAT) are multiplied to yield the return on net operating assets (RNOA).

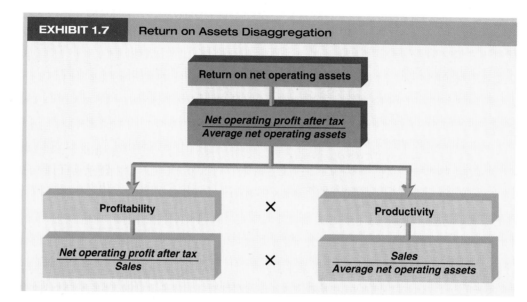

EXHIBIT 1.7   **Return on Assets Disaggregation**

There are an infinite number of combinations of net operating profit margin and net operating asset turnover that yield the same return on net operating assets. To illustrate, Exhibit 1.8 graphs actual combinations of these two components for many industries over the past 15 years. The solid line represents those profitability and productivity combinations that yield a 10.3% return on net operating assets, which is the median return for all publicly traded companies. Industries such as restaurants and retailers have low profit margins but very high asset turnovers. Asset intensive industries, such as coal and pharmaceuticals, earn a high profit margin but do not turn their assets over as frequently.

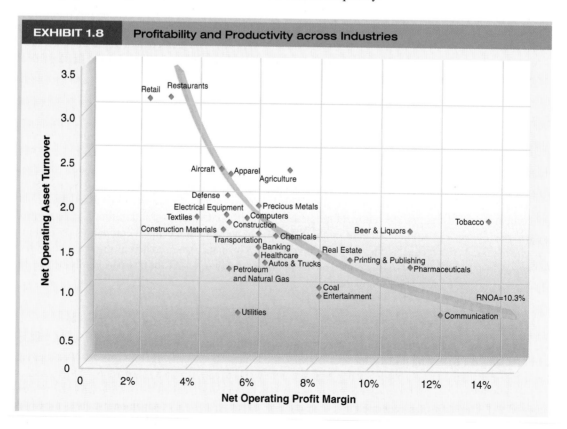

EXHIBIT 1.8   **Profitability and Productivity across Industries**

Return on Equity

Another important analysis measure is return on equity (ROE), which compares net income to average stockholders' equity. In this case, company earnings are compared to the level of stockholder (not total) investment. We further discuss ROE, RNOA, and their disaggregation in Module 4.

MANAGERIAL DECISION	You Are the Chief Financial Officer

You are reviewing your company's financial performance for the first six months of the year and are unsatisfied with the results. How can you use return on net operating assets disaggregation to identify areas for improvement? [Answer, p. 1-30]

Financial Accounting and Business Analysis

Analysis and interpretation of financial statements must consider the broader business context in which a company operates. This section describes how to systematically consider those broader business forces to enhance our analytical and interpretive skills. We can then better extract insights from financial statements and better estimate future performance and company value.

LO4 Describe business analysis within the context of a competitive environment.

Analyzing the Competitive Environment

Financial statements are influenced by five important forces that confront the company and determine its competitive intensity: (A) industry competition, (B) buyer power, (C) supplier power, (D) product substitutes, and (E) threat of entry (for further discussion, see *Porter, Competitive Strategy: Techniques for Analyzing Industries and Competitors,* 1980 and 1998). These five forces are depicted graphically in Exhibit 1.9.

EXHIBIT 1.9	Competitive Forces within the Broader Business Environment

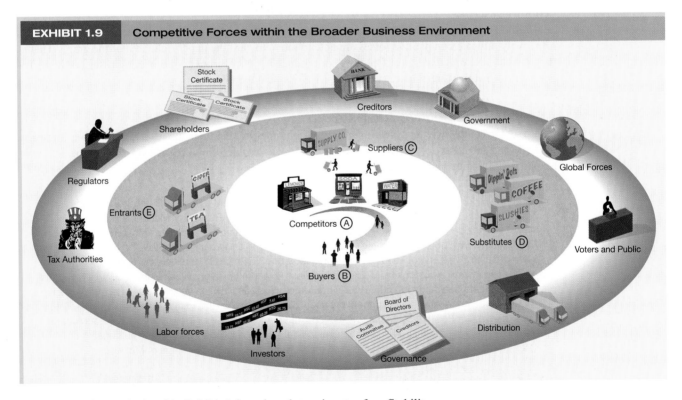

The five forces depicted in Exhibit 1.9 are key determinants of profitability.

Ⓐ **Industry competition** Competition and rivalry raises the cost of doing business as companies must hire and train competitive workers, advertise products, research and develop products, and other related activities.

Ⓑ **Bargaining power of buyers** Buyers with strong bargaining power can extract price concessions and demand a higher level of service and delayed payment terms; this force reduces both profits from sales and the operating cash flows to sellers.

Ⓒ **Bargaining power of suppliers** Suppliers with strong bargaining power can demand higher prices and earlier payments, yielding adverse effects on profits and cash flows to buyers.

Ⓓ **Threat of substitution** As the number of product substitutes increases, sellers have less power to raise prices and/or pass on costs to buyers; accordingly, threat of substitution places downward pressure on profits of sellers.

Ⓔ **Threat of entry** New market entrants increase competition; to mitigate that threat, companies expend monies on activities such as new technologies, promotion, and human development to erect *barriers to entry* and to create *economies of scale.*

This broader business environment affects the level of profitability that a company can expect to earn. Global economic forces and the quality and cost of labor affect the macroeconomy in which the company operates. Government regulation, borrowing agreements exacted by creditors, and internal governance procedures also affect the range of operating activities in which a company can engage. In addition, strategic plans are influenced by the oversight of equity markets, and investors are loathe to allow companies the freedom to manage for the longer term. Each of these external forces affects a company's strategic planning and expected level of profitability.

The relative strength of companies within their industries, and vis-à-vis suppliers and customers, is an important determinant of both their profitability and the structure of their balance sheets. As competition intensifies, profitability likely declines, and the amount of assets companies need to carry on their balance sheet likely increases. These changes in the income statement and the balance sheet can adversely impact operating performance.

Effect on RNOA and Its Components

Exhibit 1.8 plots operating profit margin (NOPM) and asset turnover (NOAT) for many industries. This graph reveals differences that exist across industries and how those differences are reflected in financial performance metrics.

Individual companies *within* an industry can be plotted in a similar manner. Generally, companies that effectively mitigate competitive forces are able to move toward the upper right area of the graph. That is, they are able to earn greater profit margins, or produce a higher turnover of operating assets, or both. The net result is that they are able to earn a higher RNOA than their peers.

Applying Competitive Analysis

We apply the competitive analysis framework to help interpret the financial results of McLane Company. McLane is a subsidiary of Berkshire Hathaway and was acquired in 2003 as explained in the following note to the Berkshire Hathaway annual report:

> On May 23, 2003, Berkshire acquired McLane Company, Inc., ("McLane") a distributor of grocery and food products to retailers, convenience stores and restaurants. Results of McLane's business operations are included in Berkshire's consolidated results beginning on that date. McLane's revenues in 2005 totaled $24.1 billion compared to $23.4 billion in 2004 and approximately $22.0 billion for the full year of 2003. Sales of grocery products increased about 5% in 2005 and were partially offset by lower sales to foodservice customers. McLane's business is marked by high sales volume and very low profit margins. Pretax earnings in 2005 of $217 million declined $11 million versus 2004. The gross margin percentage was relatively unchanged between years. However, the resulting increased gross profit was more than offset by higher payroll, fuel and insurance expenses. Approximately 33% of McLane's annual revenues currently derive from sales to Wal-Mart. Loss or curtailment of purchasing by Wal-Mart could have a material adverse impact on revenues and pre-tax earnings of McLane.

McLane is a wholesaler of food products; it purchases food products in finished and semifinished form from agricultural and food-related businesses and resells them to grocery and convenience food stores. The extensive distribution network required in this business entails considerable investment.

Industry Analysis Our business analysis of McLane's financial results includes the following observations:

▪ **Industry competitors** McLane has many competitors with food products that are difficult to differentiate.

- **Bargaining power of buyers** The note above reveals that 33% of McLane's sales are to Wal-Mart, which has considerable buying power that limits seller profits; also, the food industry is characterized by high turnover and low profit margins, which implies that cost control is key to success.

- **Bargaining power of suppliers** McLane is large ($24 billion in annual sales), which implies its suppliers are unlikely to exert forces to increase its cost of sales.

- **Threat of substitution** Grocery items are usually not well differentiated; this means the threat of substitution is high, which inhibits its ability to raise selling prices.

- **Threat of entry** High investment costs, such as warehousing and logistics, are a barrier to entry in McLane's business; this means the threat of entry is relatively low.

Our analysis reveals that McLane is a high-volume, low-margin company. Its ability to control costs is crucial to its financial performance, including its ability to fully utilize its assets. Evaluation of McLane's financial statements should focus on that dimension.

Business Analysis Quality analysis depends on an effective business analysis. Before we analyze a single accounting number, we must ask questions about a company's business environment such as the following:

- *Life cycle* At what stage in its life is this company? Is it a startup, experiencing growing pains? Is it strong and mature, reaping the benefits of competitive advantages? Is it nearing the end of its life, trying to milk what it can from stagnant product lines?

- *Outputs* What products does it sell? Are its products new, established, or dated? Do its products have substitutes? How complicated are its products to produce?

- *Buyers* Who are its buyers? Are buyers in good financial condition? Do buyers have substantial purchasing power? Can the seller dictate sales terms to buyers?

- *Inputs* Who are its suppliers? Are there many supply sources? Does the company depend on a few supply sources with potential for high input costs?

- *Competition* In what kind of markets does it operate? Are markets open? Is the market competitive? Does the company have competitive advantages? Can it protect itself from new entrants? At what cost? How must it compete to survive?

- *Financing* Must it seek financing from public markets? Is it going public? Is it seeking to use its stock to acquire another company? Is it in danger of defaulting on debt covenants? Are there incentives to tell an overly optimistic story to attract lower cost financing or to avoid default on debt?

- *Labor* Who are its managers? What are their backgrounds? Can they be trusted? Are they competent? What is the state of employee relations? Is labor unionized?

- *Governance* How effective is its corporate governance? Does it have a strong and independent board of directors? Does a strong audit committee of the board exist, and is it populated with outsiders? Does management have a large portion of its wealth tied to the company's stock?

- *Risk* Is it subject to lawsuits from competitors or shareholders? Is it under investigation by regulators? Has it changed auditors? If so, why? Are its auditors independent? Does it face environmental and/or political risks?

We must assess the broader business context in which a company operates as we read and interpret its financial statements. A review of financial statements, which reflect business activities, cannot be undertaken in a vacuum. It is contextual and can only be effectively undertaken within the framework of a thorough understanding of the broader forces that impact company performance. We should view the above questions as a sneak preview of the types we will ask and answer throughout this book when we read and interpret financial statements.

MODULE-END REVIEW

Following are selected data from Progressive Corporation's 2005 10-K.

$ millions	2005
Sales	$14,303
Net operating profit after tax	1,450
Net income	1,394
Average net operating assets	6,916
Average stockholders' equity	5,631

Required

a. Compute Progressive's return on net operating assets. Disaggregate the RNOA into its profitability and productivity components.

b. Compute Progressive's return on equity (ROE).

c. Consider Exhibit 1.8 that plots industries' RNOA components. Where does Progressive fit on the graph? How does Progressive's profitability and productivity compare to other industries?

Solution

a. RNOA = net operating profit after tax / average net operating assets = $1,450 / $6,916 = 21.0%. The profitability component is net operating profit after tax / sales = $1,450 / $14,303 = 10.1%, and the productivity component is sales / average net operating assets = $14,303 / $6,916 = 2.07. Notice that 10.1% × 2.07 = 20.9%. Thus, the two components, when multiplied yield RNOA (with a minor rounding difference).

b. ROE = net income / average stockholders' equity = $1,394 / $5,631 = 24.8%.

c. Progressive has a very high RNOA. Net operating asset turnover is 2, which is not unusual (most of the industries have turnovers between 1.5 and 2). However, with a 10.1% NOPM, Progressive is more profitable than most industries with the exception of Tobacco, Pharmaceuticals, Communications and Liquor. Thus, Progressive's high RNOA derives from its high profitability and its solid asset productivity.

APPENDIX 1A: Accessing SEC Filings using EDGAR

All publicly traded companies are required to file various reports with the SEC, two of which are the 10-Q (quarterly financial statements) and the 10-K (annual financial statements). The SEC archives these reports in a system called EDGAR, an acronym for electronic data gathering and retrieval. Following is a brief tutorial to access these electronic filings. The SEC's web site is **http://www.sec.gov**.

1. Following is the opening screen. Click on **Search for Company Filings** (highlighted below)

2. Then, click on **Companies & Other Filers**

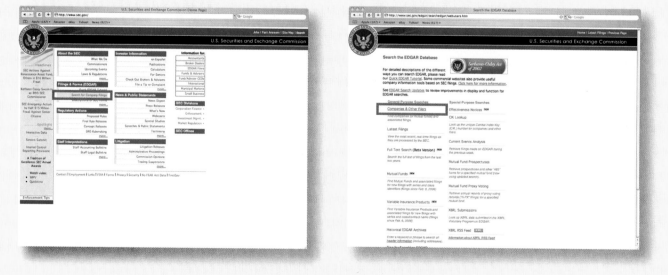

3. In **Company name**, type in the name of the company you are looking for. In this case, we are searching for Berkshire Hathaway. Then click on 'Find Companies.'

4. Several references to Berkshire appear. Click on the **CIK** (the SEC's numbering system) next to Berkshire Hathaway, Inc.

5. Find the form you want to access. In this case we are looking for its 10-K. Click on the **html** link because it's easier to read than the text file.

6. The various exhibits relating to Berkshire Hathaway's 10-K appear. Click on the **10-K** line.

7. The Berkshire Hathaway 10-K will open up. The file is searchable.

APPENDIX 1B: Accounting Principles and Governance

Financial Accounting Environment

L05 Describe the accounting principles that guide preparation of financial statements.

Information in financial statements is crucial to valuing a company's debt and equity securities. Financial statements information can affect the price the market is willing to pay for the company's equity securities and interest rates attached to its debt securities.

The importance of financial statements means that their reliability is paramount. This includes the crucial role of ethics. To the extent that financial performance and condition are accurately communicated to business decision makers, debt and equity securities are more accurately priced. When securities are mis-priced, resources can be inefficiently allocated both within and across economies. Accurate, reliable financial statements are also important for the effective functioning of many other markets such as labor, input, and output markets.

To illustrate, recall the consequences of a breakdown in the integrity of the financial accounting system at Enron. Once it became clear that Enron had not faithfully and accurately reported its financial condition and performance, the market became unwilling to purchase Enron's securities. The value of its debt and equity securities dropped precipitously and the company was unable to obtain cash needed for operating activities. Within months of the disclosure of its financial accounting irregularities, Enron, with revenues of over $100 billion and total company value of over $60 billion, the fifth largest U.S. company, was bankrupt!

Further historical evidence of the importance of financial accounting is provided by the Great Depression of the 20th century. This depression was caused, in large part, by the failure of companies to faithfully report their financial condition and performance.

Oversight of Financial Accounting

The stock market crash of 1929 and the ensuing Great Depression led Congress to pass the 1933 Securities Act. This act had two main objectives: (1) to require disclosure of financial and other information about securities being offered for public sale; and (2) to prohibit deceit, misrepresentations, and other fraud in the sale of securities. This act also

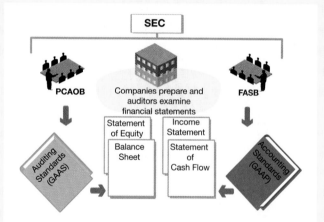

required that companies register all securities proposed for public sale and disclose information about the securities being offered, including information about company financial condition and performance. This act became and remains a foundation for contemporary financial reporting.

Congress also passed the 1934 Securities Exchange Act, which created the **Securities and Exchange Commission** (SEC) and gave it broad powers to regulate the issuance and trading of securities. The act also provided that companies with more than $10 million in assets and whose securities are held by more than 500 owners must file annual and other periodic reports, including financial statements that are available for download from the SEC's **EDGAR** database (**www.sec.gov**).

The SEC has ultimate authority over U.S. financial reporting, including setting accounting standards for preparing financial statements. Since 1939, however, the SEC has looked to the private sector to set accounting standards—the SEC retains the right to overrule or revise standards with which it disagrees. One such private sector organization is the American Institute of Certified Public Accountants (AICPA), whose two committees, the Committee on Accounting Procedure (1939–59) and the Accounting Principles Board (1959–73), authored the initial body of accounting standards.

Currently, the **Financial Accounting Standards Board (FASB)** sets U.S. financial accounting standards. The FASB is an independent body overseen by a foundation, whose members include public accounting firms, investment managers, academics, and corporate managers. The FASB has published over 150 accounting standards governing the preparation of financial reports. This is in addition to over 40 standards that were written by predecessor organizations to the FASB, numerous bulletins and interpretations, Emerging Issues Task Force (EITF) statements, AICPA statements of position (SOP), and direct SEC guidance, along with speeches made by high-ranking SEC personnel, all of which form the body of accounting standards governing financial statements. Collectively, these pronouncements, rules and guidance create what is called **Generally Accepted Accounting Principles (GAAP).**

The standard-setting process is arduous, often lasting up to a decade and involving extensive comment by the public, public officials, accountants, academics, investors, analysts, and corporate preparers of financial reports. To influence the standard-setting process, special interest groups often lobby members of Congress to pressure the SEC and, ultimately, the FASB, on issues about which constituents feel strongly. The reason for this involved process is that amendments to existing standards or the creation of new standards affect the reported financial performance and condition of companies. Consequently, given the widespread impact of financial accounting, there are considerable economic consequences as a result of accounting changes.

International Accounting Standards and Convergence

A single set of international accounting standards that is accepted in all capital markets throughout the world does not exist. In the U.S., public firms must file financial reports using U.S. generally accepted accounting principles (GAAP). Foreign firms filing with the SEC can use U.S. GAAP, their home country GAAP, or international standards—although if they use their home country GAAP or international standards, foreign issuers must reconcile their numbers to U.S. GAAP.

The International Accounting Standards Board (IASB) oversees development of international accounting standards. In 2002, the FASB and the IASB announced their commitment to minimize differences between U.S. and international accounting standards. Although the two rule-making bodies have achieved consensus on broad philosophical issues, agreement on the detailed wording of standards is more difficult to achieve.

Differences between U.S. and international accounting standards remain. One major advance, however, is that beginning in 2005, European Union companies must use IASB standards rather than their home-country GAAP. Summaries of differences between U.S. and international GAAP are available on the web. One source is the large international public accounting firms (for example, see **PWC.com** and search IFRS and GAAP).

Choices in Financial Accounting

Some people mistakenly assume that financial accounting is an exact discipline—that is, companies select the one proper accounting method to account for a transaction, and then follow the rules. The reality is that GAAP allows companies choices in preparing financial statements. The choice of methods often yields financial statements that are markedly different from one another in terms of reported income, assets, liabilities, and equity amounts.

People often are surprised that financial statements comprise numerous estimates. For example, companies must estimate the amounts that will eventually be collected from customers, the length of time that buildings and equipment will be productive, the value impairments of assets, the future costs of warranty claims, and the eventual payouts on pension plans.

Recent Accounting Scandals	
Company	**Allegations**
Adelphia Communications (ADELQ)	Founding Rigas family collected $3.1 billion in off-balance-sheet loans backed by Adelphia; overstated results by inflating capital expenses and hiding debt.
TWX Time Warner (TWX)	As the ad market faltered and AOL's purchase of Time Warner loomed, AOL inflated sales by booking revenue for barter deals and ads it sold for third parties. These questionable revenues boosted growth rates and sealed the deal. AOL also boosted sales via "round-trip" deals with advertisers and suppliers.
Bristol-Myers Squibb (BMY)	Inflated its 2001 revenue by $1.5 billion by "channel stuffing," or forcing wholesalers to accept more inventory than they could sell to get inventory off Bristol-Myers' books.
Enron	Created profits and hid debt totaling over $1 billion by improperly using off-the-books partnerships; manipulated the Texas power market; bribed foreign governments to win contracts abroad; manipulated California energy market.
Global Crossing	Engaged in network capacity "swaps" with other carriers to inflate revenue; shredded documents related to accounting practices.
Halliburton (HAL)	Improperly booked $100 million in annual construction-cost overruns before customers agreed to pay for them.
Qwest Communications International (Q)	Inflated revenue using network capacity "swaps" and improper accounting for long-term deals.
Tyco (TYC)	Ex-CEO L. Dennis Kozlowski indicted for tax evasion; Kozlowski and former CFO Mark H. Swartz, convicted of taking unauthorized loans from the company.
WorldCom	Overstated cash flow by booking $11 billion in operating expenses as capital costs; loaned founder Bernard Ebbers $400 million off-the-books.
Xerox (XRX)	Falsified financial results for five years, over-reported income by $1.5 billion.

Accounting standard setters walk a fine line regarding choice in accounting. On one hand, they are concerned that choice in preparing financial statements will lead to abuse by those seeking to gain by influencing decisions of financial statement users. On the other hand, standard setters are concerned that companies are too diverse for a "one size fits all" financial accounting system.

For example, Enron exemplifies the problems that accompany rigid accounting standards. A set of accounting standards relating to special purpose entities (SPEs) provided preparers with guidelines under which those entities were or were not to be consolidated. Unfortunately, once the SPE guidelines were set, some people worked diligently to structure SPE transactions so as to just miss the consolidation requirements and achieve *off-balance-sheet* financing. This is just one example of how, with rigid standards, companies can adhere to the letter of the rule, but not its intent. In such situations, the financial statements are not fairly presented.

For most of its existence, the FASB has promulgated standards that were quite complicated and replete with guidelines. This invited abuse of the type embodied by the Enron scandal. In recent years, the pendulum has begun to swing away from such rigidity. Now, once financial statements are prepared, company management is required to step back from the details and make a judgment on whether the statements taken as a whole 'fairly present' the financial condition of the company.

Moreover, since the enactment of the **Sarbanes-Oxley Act,** the SEC requires the chief executive officer (CEO) of the company and its chief financial officer (CFO) to personally sign a statement attesting to the accuracy and completeness of the financial statements. This requirement is an important step in restoring confidence in the integrity of financial accounting. The statements signed by both the CEO and CFO contain the following statements:

- Both the CEO and CFO have personally reviewed the annual report
- There are no untrue statements of a material fact that would make the statements misleading
- Financial statements fairly present in all material respects the financial condition of the company
- All material facts are disclosed to the company's auditors and board of directors
- No changes to its system of internal controls are made unless properly communicated

The Sarbanes-Oxley Act also imposed fines and potential jail time for executives. Presumably, the prospect of personal losses is designed to make these executives more vigilant in monitoring the financial accounting system.

Regulatory and Legal Environment

Even though key executives must personally attest to the completeness and accuracy of company financial statements, markets demand further assurances from outside parties to achieve the level of confidence necessary to warrant investment, credit, and other business decisions. The regulatory and legal environment provides further assurance that financial statements are complete and accurate.

Audit Committee

Law requires each publicly traded company to have a board of directors, where stockholders elect each director. This board represents the company owners and oversees management. The board also hires the company's executive management and regularly reviews company operations.

The board of directors usually establishes several subcommittees to focus on particular governance tasks such as compensation, strategic plans, and financial management. Exhibit 1.10 illustrates a typical organization of a company's governance structure. Corporate governance refers to the checks and balances that monitor company and manager activities. Governance committees are commonplace. One of these, the audit committee, oversees the financial accounting system.

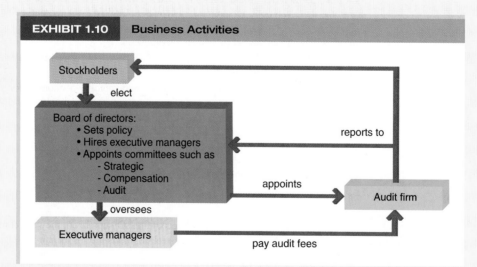

EXHIBIT 1.10 **Business Activities**

The audit committee must consist solely of outside directors, and cannot include the CEO. As part of its oversight of the financial accounting system, the audit committee focuses on **internal controls**, which are the policies and procedures used to protect assets, ensure reliable accounting, promote efficient operations, and urge adherence to company policies.

Statement of Management Responsibility

Following passage of the Sarbanes-Oxley Act, the SEC issued a ruling requiring companies "to include in their annual reports a report of management on the company's internal control over financial reporting." Many companies incorporate the rule's requirements by reference in their disclosures. Others, like Home Depot in Exhibit 1.11 make explicit reference to the rule's provisions.

EXHIBIT 1.11	Responsibility for Financial Reporting

Management's Responsibility Financial Statements

The financial statements presented in this Annual Report have been prepared with integrity and objectivity and are the responsibility of the management of The Home Depot, Inc. These financial statements have been prepared in conformity with U.S. generally accepted accounting principles and properly reflect certain estimates and judgments based upon the best available information.

The financial statements of the Company have been audited by KPMG LLP, an independent registered public accounting firm. Their accompanying report is based upon an audit conducted in accordance with the standards of the Public Company Accounting Oversight Board (United States).

The Audit Committee of the Board of Directors, consisting solely of outside directors, meets five times a year with the independent registered public accounting firm, the internal auditors and representatives of management to discuss auditing and financial reporting matters. In addition, a telephonic meeting is held prior to each quarterly earnings release. The Audit Committee retains the independent registered public accounting firm and regularly reviews the internal accounting controls, the activities of the independent registered public accounting firm and internal auditors and the financial condition of the Company. Both the Company's independent registered public accounting firm and the internal auditors have free access to the Audit Committee.

Management's Report on Internal Control over Financial Reporting

Our management is responsible for establishing and maintaining adequate internal control over financial reporting, as such term is defined in Exchange Act Rules 13a–15(f). Under the supervision and with the participation of our management, including our principal executive officer and principal financial officer, we conducted an evaluation of the effectiveness of our internal control over financial reporting based on the framework in *Internal Control—Integrated Framework* issued by the Committee of Sponsoring Organizations of the Treadway Commission (COSO). Based on our evaluation, our management concluded that our internal control over financial reporting was effective as of January 30, 2005. Our management's assessment of the effectiveness of our internal control over financial reporting as of January 30, 2005 has been audited by KPMG LLP, an independent registered public accounting firm, as stated in its report which is included herein.

Robert L. Nardelli
Chairman, President &
Chief Executive Officer

Carol B. Tomé
Executive Vice President &
Chief Financial Officer

Kelly H. Barrett
Vice Presient
Corporate Controller

The statement of responsibility contains several assertions by management:

1. Financial statements are prepared by management, which assumes responsibility for them
2. Financial statements are prepared in conformity with GAAP
3. Financial statements are audited by an external auditing firm
4. Board of directors has an audit committee to oversee the financial accounting system and the system of internal controls
5. Management is responsible for establishing and maintaining adequate internal control over financial reporting.

It is important to remember that management prepares financial statements—not the auditors who are hired to express an opinion on those statements. Moreover, remember that management's interests may or may not be aligned with those of other stakeholders.

Audit Report

Financial statements for each publicly traded company must be audited by an independent audit firm. Of the firms authorized to audit SEC clients, there are four large, international firms that dominate the others:

1. Deloitte & Touche LLP
2. Ernst & Young LLP
3. KPMG LLP
4. PricewaterhouseCoopers LLP

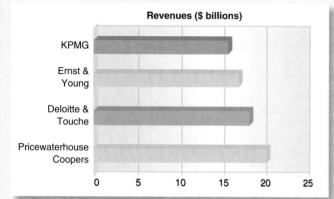

These four firms provide opinions for the majority of financial statements filed by publicly traded U.S. companies. There also are a number of regional accounting firms that provide audit services to both publicly traded and nontraded private companies.

A company's Board of Directors hires the auditors to review and express an opinion on its financial statements. The audit opinion expressed by Deloitte & Touche, LLP on the financial statements of **Berkshire Hathaway** is reproduced in Exhibit 1.12.

EXHIBIT 1.12	Audit Report for Berkshire Hathaway

To the Board of Directors and Shareholders, Berkshire Hathaway Inc.

We have audited the accompanying consolidated balance sheets of Berkshire Hathaway Inc. and subsidiaries (the "Company") as of December 31, 2005 and 2004, and the related consolidated statements of earnings, cash flows and changes in shareholders' equity and comprehensive income for each of the three years in the period ended December 31, 2005. These financial statements are the responsibility of the Company's management. Our responsibility is to express an opinion on these financial statements based on our audits.

We conducted our audits in accordance with the standards of the Public Company Accounting Oversight Board (United States). Those standards require that we plan and perform the audit to obtain reasonable assurance about whether the financial statements are free of material misstatement. An audit includes examining, on a test basis, evidence supporting the amounts and disclosures in the financial statements. An audit also includes assessing the accounting principles used and significant estimates made by management, as well as evaluating the overall financial statement presentation. We believe that our audits provide a reasonable basis for our opinion.

In our opinion, such consolidated financial statements present fairly, in all material respects, the financial position of Berkshire Hathaway Inc. and subsidiaries as of December 31, 2005 and 2004, and the results of their operations and their cash flows for each of the three years in the period ended December 31, 2005, in conformity with accounting principles generally accepted in the United States of America.

We have also audited, in accordance with the standards of the Public Company Accounting Oversight Board (United States), the effectiveness of the Company's internal control over financial reporting as of December 31, 2005, based on the criteria established in *Internal Control—Integrated Framework* issued by the Committee of Sponsoring Organizations of the Treadway Commission and our report dated March 2, 2006 expressed an unqualified opinion on management's assessment of the effectiveness of the Company's internal control over financial reporting and an unqualified opinion on the effectiveness of the Company's internal control over financial reporting.

DELOITTE & TOUCHE LLP
Omaha, Nebraska
March 2, 2006

The basic 'clean' audit report is consistent across companies and includes these assertions:

- Financial statements *present fairly, in all material respects* a company's financial condition, in conformity with GAAP.
- Financial statements are management's responsibility. Auditor responsibility is to express an opinion on those statements.
- Auditing involves a sampling of transactions, not investigation of each transaction.
- Audit opinion provides *reasonable assurance* that the statements are free of *material* misstatements, not a guarantee.
- Auditors review accounting policies used by management and the estimates used in preparing the statements.

Unless all of these conditions are met, the auditor cannot issue a clean opinion. Instead, the auditor issues a "qualified" opinion and states the reasons a clean opinion cannot be issued. Financial report readers should scrutinize with care both the qualified audit opinion and the financial statements themselves.

The audit opinion is not based on a test of each transaction. Auditors usually develop statistical samples and infer test results to other transactions. The audit report is not a guarantee that no misstatements exist. Auditors only provide reasonable assurance that the statements are free of material misstatements. Their use of the word reasonable is deliberate, as they do not want to be held to an absolute standard should problems be subsequently uncovered. The word material is used in the sense that an item must be of sufficient magnitude to change the perceptions or decisions of the financial statement user (such as a decision to purchase stock or extend credit).

The requirement of auditor independence is the cornerstone of effective auditing and is subject to debate because the company pays the auditor's fees. Regulators have questioned the perceived lack of independence of auditing firms and the degree to which declining independence compromises the ability of auditing firms to challenge a client's dubious accounting.

The Sarbanes-Oxley Act contained several provisions designed to encourage auditor independence:

1. It established the Public Company Accounting Oversight Board to oversee the development of audit standards and to monitor the effectiveness of auditors,
2. It prohibits auditors from offering certain types of consulting services, and requires audit partners to rotate clients every five years, and
3. It requires audit committees to consist of independent members.

BUSINESS INSIGHT   Warren Buffett on Audit Committees

"Audit committees can't audit. Only a company's outside auditor can determine whether the earnings that a management purports to have made are suspect. Reforms that ignore this reality and that instead focus on the structure and charter of the audit committee will accomplish little.

As we've discussed, far too many managers have fudged their company's numbers in recent years, using both accounting and operational techniques that are typically legal but that nevertheless materially mislead investors. Frequently, auditors knew about these deceptions. Too often, however, they remained silent. The key job of the audit committee is simply to get the auditors to divulge what they know.

To do this job, the committee must make sure that the auditors worry more about misleading its members than about offending management. In recent years auditors have not felt that way. They have instead generally viewed the CEO, rather than the shareholders or directors, as their client. That has been a natural result of day-to-day working relationships and also of the auditors' understanding that, no matter what the board says, the CEO and CFO pay their fees and determine whether they are retained for both auditing and other work. The rules that have been recently instituted won't materially change this reality. What will break this cozy relationship is audit committees unequivocally putting auditors on the spot, making them understand they will become liable for major monetary penalties if they don't come forth with what they know or suspect."—Warren Buffett, Berkshire Hathaway annual report

---

SEC Enforcement Actions

Companies whose securities are issued to the public must file reports with the SEC (see **www.sec.gov**). One of these reports is the 10-K, which includes the annual financial statements (quarterly statements are filed under report 10-Q). The 10-K report provides more information than the company's glossy annual report, which is partly a marketing document (although the basic financial statements are identical). You should use the 10-K because of its additional information.

The SEC has ultimate authority to accept or reject financial statements that companies submit. Should the SEC reject a company's financial statements, the company must restate and refile them. Restatements are time-consuming, publicly known, and restating companies typically see their stock market value slide. For example, in 2006, the SEC required Fannie Mae to restate its financial statements. The SEC commenced litigation, and the following excerpts come from the criminal complaint:

> The Federal National Mortgage Association engaged in a financial fraud involving multiple violations of Generally Accepted Accounting Principles ("GAAP") in connection with the preparation of its annual and quarterly financial statements. These violations had the effect, among other things, of falsely portraying stable earnings growth and reduced income statement volatility and, for year-ended 1998, of maximizing bonuses and achieving forecasted earnings. Between 1998 and 2004, Fannie Mae, a shareholder-owned government sponsored enterprise, misstated its results of operations and issued materially false and misleading financial statements in various reports and in filings with the Commission.
>
> The Company's accounting was inconsistent with GAAP. Additionally, the Company's reported financial results were smoothed through misapplications of GAAP. These practices were not disclosed to investors.
>
> As a direct result of these violations, and other errors, Fannie Mae expects to restate its historical financial statements for the years ended December 31, 2003 and 2002, and for the quarters ended June 30, 2004 and March 31, 2004. This restatement will result in at least a $1.1 billion reduction of previously reported net income.

The Commission's investigation uncovered numerous transactions over several years by which Fannie Mae management intentionally smoothed out gyrations in its earnings to show investors it was a low-risk company. In addition, the SEC charged that the company's accounting policies were created to shape the company's books in a way that made it appear that the company had reached earnings targets, thus triggering the maximum possible bonus payout for executives.

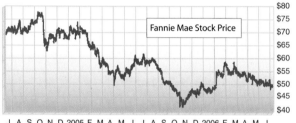

Following litigation of the above-referenced complaint, Fannie Mae fired its senior management team, including its CEO and CFO. It also agreed to pay a $400 million penalty, restate its previously issued financial reports, reform its accounting policies, and institute stricter internal controls over its accounting procedures. Fannie Mae's stock (FNM) lost a third of its market value during the proceedings—see margin graph. The SEC's power to require restatement, with its consequent damage to company reputation and company stock price, is a major deterrent to those desiring to bias their financial accounts to achieve a particular goal.

Courts

Courts provide remedies to individuals or companies that suffer damages as a result of material misstatements in financial statements. Typical court actions involve shareholders who sue the company and its auditors, alleging that the company disclosed, and the auditors attested to, false and misleading financial statements. The number of such shareholder suits has declined in the past few years. Nonetheless, shareholder suits are chronically in the news. Stanford Law School's Securities Class Action Clearinghouse commented that "Two factors are likely responsible for the decline. First, lawsuits arising from the dramatic boom and bust of U.S. equities in the late 1990s and early 2000s are now largely behind us. Second, improved governance in the wake of the Enron and WorldCom frauds likely reduced the actual incidence of fraud." The SEC and the New York District Attorney successfully brought suit against Adelphia Communications Corporation and its owners on behalf of the U.S. Government and numerous investors, creditors, employees and others affiliated with the company. The press release announcing the settlement read, in part:

> *Washington, D.C., April 25, 2005*—The Securities and Exchange Commission today announced that it and the United States Attorney's Office for the Southern District of New York (USAO) reached an agreement to settle a civil enforcement action and resolve criminal charges against Adelphia Communications Corporation, its founder John J. Rigas, and his three sons, Timothy J. Rigas, Michael J. Rigas and James P. Rigas, in one of the most extensive financial frauds ever to take place at a public company.
>
> In its complaint, the Commission charged that Adelphia, at the direction of the individual defendants: (1) fraudulently excluded billions of dollars in liabilities from its consolidated financial statements by hiding them on the books of off-balance sheet affiliates; (2) falsified operating statistics and inflated earnings to meet Wall Street estimates; and (3) concealed rampant self-dealing by the Rigas family, including the undisclosed use of corporate funds for purchases of Adelphia stock and luxury condominiums.
>
> Mark K. Schonfeld, Director of the SEC's Northeast Regional Office, said, "This settlement agreement presents a strong, coordinated approach by the SEC and the U.S. Attorney's Office to resolving one of the most complicated and egregious financial frauds committed at a public company. The

settlement provides an expedient and effective way to provide victims of Adelphia's fraud with a substantial recovery while at the same time enabling Adelphia to emerge from Chapter 11 bankruptcy."

The settlement terms of this action, and related criminal actions against the Rigas family, resulted in the following:

- Rigas family members forfeited in excess of $1.5 billion in assets derived from the fraud; the funds were used, in part, to establish a fund for the fraud victims.
- Rigas family members were barred from acting as officers or directors of a public company.
- John Rigas, the 80-year-old founder of Adelphia Communications, was sentenced to 15 years in prison.
- Timothy Rigas, the ex-finance chief, was sentenced to 20 years.

GUIDANCE ANSWERS

MANAGERIAL DECISION   You Are the Product Manager

As a manager, you must balance two conflicting objectives—namely, mandatory disclosure requirements and your company's need to protect its competitive advantages. You must comply with all minimum required disclosure rules. The extent to which you offer additional disclosures depends on the sensitivity of the information; that is, how beneficial it is to your existing and potential competitors. Another consideration is how the information disclosed will impact your existing and potential investors. Disclosures such as this can be beneficial in that they inform investors and others about your company's successful investments. Still, there are many stakeholders impacted by your disclosure decision and each must be given due consideration.

MANAGERIAL DECISION   You Are the Chief Financial Officer

Financial performance is typically measured by return on net operating assets, which can be disaggregated into the net operating profit margin (net operating profit after tax/sales) and the net operating asset turnover (sales/average net operating assets). This disaggregation might lead you to review factors affecting profitability (gross margins and expense control) and to assess how effectively your company is utilizing its assets (the turnover rates). Finding ways to increase profitability for a given level of investment or to reduce the amount of invested capital while not adversely impacting profitability contributes to improved financial performance.

Superscript $^{A(B)}$ denotes assignments based on Appendix 1A (1B).

DISCUSSION QUESTIONS

Q1-1. A firm's planning activities motivate and shape three types of business activities. List the three activities. Describe how financial accounting reports can provide useful information for each activity. How can subsequent financial accounting reports be used to evaluate the success of each of the activities?

Q1-2. The accounting equation (Assets = Liabilities + Equity) is a fundamental business concept. Explain what this equation reveals about a company's sources and uses of funds and the claims on company resources.

Q1-3. Companies prepare four primary financial statements. What are those financial statements and what information is typically conveyed in each?

Q1-4. Does a balance sheet report on a period of time or at a point in time? Explain the information conveyed in the balance sheet.

Q1-5. Does an income statement report on a period of time or at a point in time? Explain the information conveyed in the income statement.

Q1-6. Does a statement of cash flows report on a period of time or at a point in time? Explain the information and activities conveyed in the statement of cash flows.

Q1-7. Explain how a company's four primary financial statements are linked.

Q1-8. Financial statements are used by several interested stakeholders. List three or more potential external users of financial statements. Explain how each constituent on your list might use financial statement information in their decision making process.

Q1-9. What ethical issues might managers face in dealing with confidential information?

Q1-10.^{A} Access the 2006 10-K for Procter & Gamble at the SEC's EDGAR database of financial reports (www.sec.gov). Who is P&G's auditor? What specific language does the auditor use in expressing its opinion and what responsibilities does it assume?

Procter & Gamble
(PG)

Q1-11.[B]   Business decision makers external to the company increasingly demand more financial information from companies. Discuss the reasons why companies have traditionally opposed the efforts of regulatory agencies like the SEC to require more disclosure.

Q1-12.[B]   What are generally accepted accounting principles and what organizations presently establish them?

Enron   Q1-13.[B]   Corporate governance has received considerable attention since the collapse of Enron and other accounting-related scandals. What is meant by corporate governance? What are the primary means by which sound corporate governance is achieved?

Q1-14.[B]   What is the primary function of the auditor? In your own words, describe what an audit opinion says.

Q1-15.   Describe a decision that requires financial accounting information, other than a stock investment decision. How is financial accounting information useful in making this decision?

Q1-16.   Users of financial information are vitally concerned with the company's strategic direction. Despite their understanding of this need for information, companies are reluctant to supply it. Why? In particular, what costs are companies concerned about?

Q1-17.   One of Warren Buffett's acquisition criteria is to invest in businesses "earning good return on equity." The return on equity (ROE) formula uses both net income and stockholders' equity. Why is it important to relate net income to stockholders' equity? Why isn't it sufficient to merely concentrate on companies with the highest net income?

Q1-18.   One of Warren Buffett's acquisition criteria is to invest in businesses "earning good return on equity, while employing little or no debt." Why is Buffett concerned about debt?

MINI EXERCISES

Dell, Inc. (DELL)

M1-19.   Relating Financing and Investing Activities   (LO2)

In a recent year, the total assets of Dell, Inc. equal $15,470 million and its equity is $4,873 million. What is the amount of its liabilities? Does Dell receive more financing from its owners or nonowners? What percentage of financing is provided by Dell's owners?

Ford Motor Company
(F)

M1-20.   Relating Financing and Investing Activities   (LO2)

In a recent year, the total assets of Ford Motor Company equal $315,920 million and its liabilities equal $304,269 million. What is the amount of Ford's equity? Does Ford receive more financing from its owners or nonowners. What percentage of financing is provided by its owners?

M1-21.   Applying the Accounting Equation and Computing Financing Proportions   (LO2)

Use the accounting equation to compute the missing financial amounts (a), (b), and (c). Which of these companies is more owner-financed? Which of these companies is more nonowner-financed? Discuss why the proportion of owner financing might differ across these three businesses.

($ millions)	Assets	=	Liabilities	+	Equity
Hewlett-Packard........	$74,708		$ 36,962		$ (a)
General Mills...........	$18,227		$ (b)		$4,175
General Motors........	$ (c)		$365,057		$6,814

Hewlett-Packard
(HPQ)
General Mills (GIS)

General Motors (GM)

Starbucks (SBUX)

M1-22.[A] Identifying Key Numbers from Financial Statements   (LO2)

Access the October 2006 10-K for Starbucks Corporation at the SEC's EDGAR database for financial reports (www.sec.gov). What did Starbucks report for total assets, liabilities, and equity at October 1, 2006? Confirm that the accounting equation holds. What percent of Starbucks' assets is financed by nonowners?

E. I. DuPont de
Nemours (DD)

M1-23.[A] Verifying Linkages Between Financial Statements   (LO2)

Access the 2005 10-K for DuPont at the SEC's EDGAR database of financial reports (www.sec.gov). Using its December 31, 2005, consolidated statement of stockholders' equity, prepare a table to reconcile the opening and ending balances of its retained (reinvested) earnings for 2005 by showing the activity in the account during the year.

M1-24.   Identifying Financial Statement Line Items and Accounts   (LO2)

Several line items and account titles are listed below. For each, indicate in which of the following financial statement(s) we would likely find the item or account: income statement (IS), balance sheet (BS), statement of stockholders' equity (SE), or statement of cash flows (SCF).

a. Cash asset	d. Contributed capital	g. Cash inflow for stock issued
b. Expenses	e. Cash outflow for capital expenditures	h. Cash outflow for dividends
c. Noncash assets	f. Retained earnings	i. Net income

M1-25. Identifying Ethical Issues and Accounting Choices   (LO5)

Assume that you are a technology services provider and you must decide on whether to record revenue from the installation of computer software for one of your clients. Your contract calls for acceptance of the software by the client within six months of installation. According to the contract, you will be paid only when the client "accepts" the installation. Although you have not yet received your client's formal acceptance, you are confident that it is forthcoming. Failure to record these revenues will cause your company to miss Wall Street's earnings estimates. What stakeholders will be affected by your decision and how might they be affected?

M1-26.[B] Understanding Internal Controls and their Importance   (LO5)

The **Sarbanes-Oxley Act** legislation requires companies to report on the effectiveness of their internal controls. The SEC administers the Sarbanes-Oxley Act, and defines internal controls as follows:

> "A process designed by, or under the supervision of, the registrant's principal executive and principal financial officers . . . to provide reasonable assurance regarding the reliability of financial reporting and the preparation of financial statements for external purposes in accordance with generally accepted accounting principles."

Why do you think Congress believes internal controls are such an important area to monitor and report on?

EXERCISES

E1-27. Applying the Accounting Equation and Assessing Financing Contributions   (LO2)

Determine the missing amounts on lines (a), (b), and (c) below. Which of these companies is more owner-financed? Which of these companies is more nonowner-financed?

($ millions)	Assets	=	Liabilities	+	Equity	
a. Motorola, Inc.........	$31,152	=	$?		$11,239	Motorola, Inc. (MOT)
b. Kraft Foods	$?	=	$31,268		$25,832	Kraft Foods (KFT)
c. Merck & Co.........	$47,561	=	$29,361		$?	Merck & Co. (MRK)

E1-28. Applying the Accounting Equation and Assessing Financial Statement Linkages   (LO2)

Answer the following questions. (*Hint*: Apply the accounting equation.)

a. Intel had assets equal to $44,224 million and liabilities equal to $8,756 million for a recent year-end. What was Intel's total equity at year-end?   *Intel (INTC)*

b. At the beginning of a recent year, JetBlue's assets were $1,378 million and its equity was $415 million. During the year, assets increased $70 million and liabilities increased $30 million. What was JetBlue's equity at the end of the year?   *JetBlue (JBLU)*

c. At the beginning of a recent year, The Walt Disney Company's liabilities equaled $26,197 million. During the year, assets increased by $400 million, and year-end assets equaled $50,388 million. Liabilities decreased $100 million during the year. What were beginning and ending amounts for Walt Disney's equity?   *The Walt Disney Company (DIS)*

E1-29. Specifying Financial Information Users and Uses   (LO1)

Financial statements have a wide audience of interested stakeholders. Identify two or more financial statement users that are external to the company. For each user on your list, specify two questions that could be addressed with financial statement information.

E1-30. Applying Financial Statement Relations to Compute Dividends   (LO2)

Colgate-Palmolive reports the following dollar balances in its retained earnings account.   *Colgate-Palmolive (CL)*

($ millions)	2005	2004
Retained earnings	8,968.1	8,223.9

During 2005, Colgate-Palmolive reported net income of $1,351.4 million. What amount of dividends, if any, did Colgate-Palmolive pay to its shareholders in 2005? What percent of its net income did Colgate-Palmolive pay out in 2005?

E1-31. **Computing and Interpreting Financial Statement Ratios** (LO3)

Following are selected ratios of Briggs & Stratton (manufacturer of engines) for 2005 and 2004.

RNOA Component	2005	2004
Profitability (Net operating profit after tax / Sales)	4.67%	7.82%
Productivity (Sales / Average net operating assets).	2.08	1.77

   a. Was the company profitable in 2005? What evidence do you have of this?
   b. Is the change in productivity (net operating asset turnover) a positive development? Explain.
   c. Compute the company's return on net operating assets (RNOA) for 2005 (show computations).

E1-32. **Computing Return on Net Operating Assets and Applying the Accounting Equation** (LO3)

Nordstrom, Inc., reports net operating profit after tax of $477.2 million for its fiscal year ended January 2006. At the beginning of that fiscal year, Nordstrom had $2,777.3 million in net operating assets. By fiscal year-end 2006, total net operating assets had grown to $2,973.1 million. What is Nordstrom's return on net operating assets (RNOA)?

E1-33. **Discussing Accounting in Society** (LO1)

Financial accounting plays an important role in modern society and business.
   a. Identify two or more external stakeholders that are interested in a company's financial statements and what their particular interests are.
   b. What are *generally accepted accounting principles*? What organizations have primary responsibility for the formulation of GAAP?
   c. What role does financial accounting play in the allocation of society's financial resources?
   d. What are three aspects of the accounting environment that can create ethical pressure on management?

E1-34. **Computing Return on Equity** (LO3)

Starbucks reports net income for 2006 of $564 million. Its stockholders' equity is $2,229 million and $2,090 million for 2006 and 2005, respectively.
   a. Compute its return on equity for 2006.
   b. Starbucks repurchased over $850 million of its common stock in 2006. How did this repurchase affect Starbucks' ROE?
   c. Why do you think a company like Starbucks repurchases its own stock?

PROBLEMS

P1-35. **Computing Return on Equity and Return on Net Operating Assets** (LO3)

The following table contains financial statement information for Staples, Inc.

($ millions)	2006	2005	2004	2003
Net operating profit after tax	$ 853,632	$ 731,817	$ 518,887	$ 443,737
Net income.	834,409	708,388	490,211	446,000
Net operating assets	4,367,221	4,202,136	3,486,208	3,618,429
Stockholders' equity	4,425,471	4,115,196	3,662,900	2,658,892

Required
   a. Compute the return on equity (ROE) for 2004 through 2006. What trend is observed? How does Staples' ROE compare with the approximately 12% average ROE for publicly traded companies?
   b. Compute the return on net operating assets (RNOA) for 2004 through 2006. What trends are observed? How does Staples' RNOA compare with the approximate 10% average RNOA for publicly traded companies?
   c. What factors might allow a company like Staples to reap above-average returns?

P1-36. **Formulating Financial Statements from Raw Data** (LO2)

Following is selected financial information from General Mills, Inc., for its fiscal year ended May 30, 2004 ($ millions).

Cash and cash equivalents	$ 751
Net cash provided by operating activities	1,461
Net sales	11,070
Stockholders' equity	5,547
Cost of sales	6,584
Net cash used by financing activities	(943)
Total liabilities	12,901
Total expenses	3,431
Noncash assets	17,697
Net cash used by investing activities	(470)
Net income	1,055
Cash and cash equivalents beginning year	703

Required

Prepare the income statement, balance sheet, and statement of cash flows for General Mills, Inc.

P1-37. Formulating Financial Statements from Raw Data (LO2)

Following is selected financial information from Abercrombie & Fitch for its fiscal year ended January 31, 2005 ($ millions).

Abercrombie & Fitch (ANF)

Cash and equivalents	$ 350
Cash provided by operating activities	426
Sales	2,021
Stockholders' equity	669
Cost of goods sold	1,111
Cash used for financing activities	(412)
Total liabilities	679
Expenses	694
Noncash assets	998
Cash provided by investing activities	280
Net income	216
Cash and cash equivalents beginning year	56

Required

Prepare the income statement, balance sheet, and statement of cash flows for Abercrombie & Fitch.

P1-38. Formulating Financial Statements from Raw Data (LO2)

Following is selected financial information from Cisco Systems, Inc., for the year ended July 30, 2005 ($ millions).

Cisco Systems, Inc. (CSCO)

Cash and cash equivalents	$ 4,742
Cash provided by operating activities	7,568
Sales	24,801
Stockholders' equity	23,184
Cost of goods sold	8,130
Cash used in financing activities	(9,162)
Total liabilities	10,699
Expenses	10,930
Noncash assets	29,141
Cash provided by investing activities	2,614
Net income	5,741
Cash and cash equivalents beginning year	3,722

Required

Prepare the income statement, balance sheet, and statement of cash flows for Cisco Systems, Inc.

P1-39. Formulating a Statement of Stockholders' Equity from Raw Data (LO2)

Crocker Corporation began calendar-year 2005 with stockholders' equity of $100,000, consisting of contributed capital of $70,000 and retained earnings of $30,000. During 2005, it issued additional stock for total cash proceeds of $30,000. It also reported $50,000 of net income, and paid $25,000 as a cash dividend to shareholders.

Required

Prepare the 2005 statement of stockholders' equity for Crocker Corporation.

P1-40. Formulating a Statement of Stockholders' Equity from Raw Data (LO2)

EA Systems, Inc., reports the following selected information at December 31, 2005 ($ millions).

Contributed capital, December 31, 2004 and 2005....	$ 550
Retained earnings, December 31, 2004.............	2,437
Cash dividends, 2005.........................	281
Net income, 2005............................	859

Required

Use this information to prepare the statement of stockholders' equity for EA Systems, Inc., for 2005.

P1-41. Computing, Analyzing, and Interpreting Return on Equity (LO3)

Following are summary financial statement data for both Kimberly-Clark and Procter & Gamble (industry competitors) for 2004 and 2005.

Kimberly-Clark Corporation (KMB)		
($ millions)	Stockholders' Equity	Net Income
2004..................	$6,630	$1,800
2005..................	5,558	1,568

Procter & Gamble Company (PG)		
($ millions)	Stockholders' Equity	Net Income
2004..................	$18,190	$6,156
2005..................	18,475	6,923

Required

a. Compute the return on equity (net income/average stockholders' equity) for 2005.

b. Which company reports a higher return on equity for 2005? Both companies used cash to repurchase large amounts of common stock in 2005. How do these repurchases affect return on equity? Why might a company wish to repurchase its own common stock?

P1-42. Conducting Business Analysis (LO4)

Refer to the information in P1-41 to answer the following requirements.

Required

a. Discuss the possible reasons for Procter & Gamble's higher ROE in terms of its relative position in the competitive environment. (*Hint:* Review Porter's five forces analysis.)

b. Drawing on the analysis of part *a*, assess the competitive strength of Procter & Gamble.

P1-43. Computing, Analyzing, and Interpreting Return on Equity (LO3)

Nokia manufactures, markets, and sells phones and other electronics. Total stockholders' equity for Nokia is €14,576 in 2005 and €14,871 in 2004. In 2005, Nokia reported net income of €3,582 on sales of €34,191.

Required

a. What is Nokia's return on equity for 2005?

b. What are total expenses for Nokia in 2005?

c. Nokia used cash to repurchase a large amount of its common stock in 2004. What motivations might Nokia have for repurchasing its common stock?

P1-44. Comparing Abercrombie & Fitch and TJX Companies (LO3)

Following are selected financial statement data from Abercrombie & Fitch (ANF—upscale clothing retailer) and TJX Companies (TJX—value priced clothing retailer including TJ Maxx)—both dated the end of January 2006.

($ millions)	ANF	TJX
Sales.	$2,784.7	$16,057.9
Net operating profit after tax	352.8	675.3
Net operating assets—2006.	584.0	2,548.2
Net operating assets—2005.	669.3	2,321.2

Required

a. Compute the return on net operating assets for both companies for the year end January 2006.

b. Disaggregate the RNOAs for both companies into the net operating profit margin and the net operating asset turnover.

c. What differences are observed? Evaluate these differences in light of the two companies' business models. Which company has better financial performance?

P1-45.   **Computing, Analyzing, and Interpreting Return on Net Operating Assets and its Components   (LO3)**

McDonald's Corporation (MCD) reported 2005 net operating profit after tax of $2,614 million on net sales of $20,460 million. The December 31, 2005, balance sheet of MCD reports the following.

McDonald's Corporation (MCD)

($ millions)	2005	2004
Net operating assets	$23,497	$22,083

Required

a. What is MCD's return on net operating assets? Given that the average RNOA for fast-food restaurants is about 5.5%, how does MCD compare on RNOA? Explain why MCD's RNOA might be so different from the average fast-food restaurant.

b. Decompose MCD's RNOA into its net operating profit margin and its net operating asset turnover.

c. Suggest specific actions that McDonald's might take to improve (1) its net operating profit margin, and (2) its net operating asset turnover.

P1-46.   **Disaggregating Return on Net Operating Assets Over Time   (LO3)**

Following are selected financial statement data from 3M Company for 2002 through 2005.

3M Company (MMM)

($ millions)	2005	2004	2003	2002
Net sales.	$21,167	$20,011	$18,232	$16,332
Net operating profit after tax	3,256	2,976	2,413	1,980
Net operating assets	12,209	12,972	10,604	9,132

Required

a. Compute 3M Company's return on net operating assets for 2003 through 2005. What trends are observed?

b. Disaggregate 3M's RNOA into the net operating profit margin and the net operating asset turnover for 2003 through 2005.

c. Which RNOA component appears to be driving the trend observed in part a? Explain.

P1-47.[A]   **Reading and Interpreting Audit Opinions   (LO5)**

Apple, Inc.'s 2005 financial statements include the following audit report from KPMG LLP

Apple, Inc. (AAPL)

REPORT OF INDEPENDENT REGISTERED PUBLIC ACCOUNTING FIRM

The Board of Directors and Shareholders

Apple, Inc.:

We have audited the accompanying consolidated balance sheets of Apple, Inc. and subsidiaries (the Company) as of September 24, 2005 and September 25, 2004, and the related consolidated statements of operations, shareholders' equity and cash flows for each of the years in the three-year period ended September 24, 2005. These consolidated financial statements are the responsibility of the Company's management. Our responsibility is to express an opinion on these consolidated financial statements based on our audits.

Continued

We conducted our audits in accordance with the standards of the Public Company Accounting Oversight Board (United States). Those standards require that we plan and perform the audit to obtain reasonable assurance about whether the consolidated financial statements are free of material misstatement An audit includes examining, on a test basis, evidence supporting the amounts and disclosures in the consolidated financial statements. An audit also includes assessing the accounting principles used and significant estimates made by management, as well as evaluating the overall financial statement presentation. We believe that our audits provide a reasonable basis for our opinion.

In our opinion, the consolidated financial statements referred to above present fairly, in all material respects, the financial position of the Company as of September 24, 2005 and September 25, 2004, and the results of their operations and their cash flows for each of the years in the three-year period ended September 24, 2005, in conformity with U.S. generally accepted accounting principles.

We also have audited, in accordance with the standards of the Public Company Accounting Oversight Board (United States), the effectiveness of the Company's internal control over financial reporting as of September 24, 2005, based on criteria established in *Internal Control-Integrated Framework* issued by the Committee of Sponsoring Organizations of the Treadway Commission (COSO), and our report dated November 29, 2005 expressed an unqualified opinion on management's assessment of and the effective operation of internal control over financial reporting.

As discussed in Note 1 to the consolidated financial statements, the Company changed its method of accounting for asset retirement obligations and for financial instruments with characteristics of both liabilities and equity in 2003.

fs/ KPMG LLP

Mountain View, California
November 29, 2005

Required

a. To whom is the report addressed? Why?

b. In your own words, briefly describe the audit process. What steps do auditors take to determine whether a company's financial statements are free from material misstatement?

c. What is the nature of KPMG's opinion? What do you believe the word *fairly* means? Is KPMG providing a guarantee to Apple's financial statement users?

d. What other opinion is KPMG rendering? Why is this opinion important?

e. What do you believe is the purpose of the last paragraph of KPMG's audit report?

P1-48. **Reading and Interpreting CEO Certifications** (LO5)

Apple, Inc. (AAPL)

Following is the CEO Certification required by the Sarbanes-Oxley Act and signed by Apple CEO Steve Jobs. Apple's Chief Financial Officer signed a similar form.

CERTIFICATIONS

I, Steven P. Jobs, certify that:

1. I have reviewed this annual report on Form 10-K of Apple, Inc.;

2. Based on my knowledge, this report does not contain any untrue statement of a material fact or omit to state a material fact necessary to make the statements made, in light of the circumstances under which such statements were made, not misleading with respect to the period covered by this report;

3. Based on my knowledge, the financial statements, and other financial information included in this report, fairly present in all material respects the financial condition, results of operations and cash flows of the registrant as of, and for, the periods presented in this report;

4. The registrant's other certifying officer(s) and I are responsible for establishing and maintaining disclosure controls and procedures (as defined in Exchange Act Rules 13a-15(e) and 15d-15(e)) and internal control over financial reporting (as defined in Exchange Act Rules 13a-15(f) and 15d-15(f) for the registrant) and have:

    (a) Designed such disclosure controls and procedures, or caused such disclosure controls and procedures to be designed under our supervision, to ensure that material information relating to the registrant, including its consolidated subsidiaries, is made known to us by others within those entities, particularly during the period in which this report is being prepared;

    (b) Designed such internal control over financial reporting, or caused such internal control over financial reporting to be designed under our supervision, to provide reasonable assurance regarding the reliability of financial reporting and the preparation of financial statements for external purposes in accordance with generally accepted accounting principles;

    (c) Evaluated the effectiveness of the registrant's disclosure controls and procedures and presented in this report our conclusions about the effectiveness of the disclosure controls and procedures, as of the end of the period covered by this report based on such evaluation; and

    (d) Disclosed in this report any change in the registrant's internal control over financial reporting that occurred during the registrant's most recent fiscal quarter (the registrant's fourth fiscal quarter in the case of an annual report) that has materially affected, or is reasonably likely to materially affect, the registrant's internal control over financial reporting; and

Continued

> 5. The registrant's other certifying officer(s) and I have disclosed, based on our most recent evaluation of internal control over financial reporting, to the registrant's auditors and the audit committee of the registrant's board of directors (or persons performing the equivalent functions):
>
>   (a) All significant deficiencies and material weaknesses in the design or operation of internal control over financial reporting which are reasonably likely to adversely affect the registrant's ability to record, process, summarize, and report financial information; and
>
>   (b) Any fraud, whether or not material, that involves management or other employees who have a significant role in the registrant's internal control over financial reporting.
>
> Date: November 29, 2005
>
> By: /s/ STEVEN P. JOBS
>   Steven P. Jobs
>   Chief Executive Officer

Required

a. Summarize the assertions that Steve Jobs made in this certification.

b. Why did Congress feel it important that CEOs and CFOs sign such certifications?

c. What potential liability do you believe the CEO and CFO are assuming by signing such certifications?

P1-49. Assessing Corporate Governance (LO5)

Review the corporate governance section of General Electric's Website (**GE.com/en/company/investor/corp_governance.htm**). By some accounts, GE has established one of the best corporate governance structures in the world.

General Electric (GE)

Required

a. In your words, briefly describe GE's governance structure.

b. What is the main purpose of this governance structure?

CASES

C1-50. Management Application: Strategic Financing (LO2)

You and your management team are working to develop the strategic direction of your company for the next three years. One issue you are discussing is how to finance the projected increases in operating assets. Your options are to rely more heavily on operating creditors, borrow the funds, or to sell additional stock in your company. Discuss the pros and cons of each source of financing.

C1-51. Management Application: Statement Analysis (LO3)

You are evaluating your company's recent operating performance and are trying to decide on the relative weights you should put on the income statement, the balance sheet, and the statement of cash flows. Discuss the information each of these statements provides and its role in evaluating operating performance.

C1-52. Management Application: Analyst Relations (LO2)

Your investor relations department reports to you that stockholders and financial analysts evaluate the quality of a company's financial reports based on their "transparency," namely the clarity and completeness of the company's financial disclosures. Discuss the trade-offs of providing more or less transparent financial reports.

C1-53. Ethics and Governance: Management Communications (LO5)

The Business Insight box on page 1-14 quotes Warren Buffett on the use of accounting jargon. Many companies publicly describe their performance using terms such as "EBITDA" or "earnings purged of various expenses" because they believe these terms more effectively reflect their companies' performance than GAAP-defined terms such as net income. What ethical issues might arise from the use of such terms and what challenges does their use present for the governance of the company by shareholders and directors?

C1-54.ᴮ Ethics and Governance: Auditor Independence (LO5)

The SEC has been concerned with the "independence" of external auditing firms. It is especially concerned about how large non-audit (such as consulting) fees might impact how aggressively auditing firms pursue accounting issues they uncover in their audits. Congress recently passed legislation that prohibits accounting firms from providing both consulting and auditing services to the same client. How might consulting fees affect auditor independence? What other conflicts of interest might exist for auditors? How do these conflicts impact the governance process?

Introducing Financial Statements and Transaction Analysis

LEARNING OBJECTIVES

L01 Describe information conveyed by the financial statements. (p. 2-5)

L02 Explain and illustrate linkages among the four financial statements. (p. 2-21)

L03 Illustrate use of the financial statement effects template to summarize accounting transactions. (p. 2-23)

APPLE

In 1985, the board of directors of Apple along with the new CEO John Sculley, dismissed Steve Jobs, Apple's co-founder. Fast forward 12 years—Apple is struggling to survive. After a series of crippling financial losses, the company's stock price is at an all-time low. In a complete about face, the board asks Steve Jobs to return as interim CEO to begin a critical restructuring of the company's product line. True to form, Jobs shows up at his first meeting with Apple senior executives wearing shorts, sneakers, and a few days' beard growth. Sitting in a swivel chair and spinning slowly, Jobs begins quizzing the executives. "O.K., tell me what's wrong with this place," asks Jobs. Mumbled replies and embarrassed looks ensue. Jobs cuts them short and jumps up: "It's the products! So what's wrong with the products?" Again, more weak answers and again Jobs cut them off. "The products SUCK!" he roars. "There's no sex in them anymore!"

Jobs was right—Apple was mired in a sea of problems, many stemming from a weak product line. The company's decision to design proprietary software that was often incompatible with Windows had relegated Apple to a niche player in the highly competitive, low-margin PC business. Years before, Microsoft had replicated the Mac operating system and licensed the software to PC manufacturers such as Dell. Now, the Mac clung to a 3% market share. Apple reported a net loss in 2001, and its cumulative profit from 2001-2003 amounted to an anemic $109 million. Apple's prospects were dim.

That was then. This is now. Apple's 2005 iPod sales surpassed $4.5 billion, growing at over 250% per year since 2003. iPods now account for nearly three-quarters of all MP3 players sold in the U.S. In the past two years, iPods made up more than half of Apple's total sales growth, and operating profits have increased to $1.65 billion. Accompanying the meteoric rise of its music player, Apple recently announced that its iTunes Music Store had sold its two-billionth song.

Apple's shares (ticker: AAPL) now trade above $60, a staggering 15 times the $4 they fetched ten years ago when the Jobs came back on board. Indeed, Apple's stock has increased six-fold in the past two years, as the following price chart illustrates. The total stock market value of Apple stock (called the market capitalization or market cap) exceeds $50 billion.

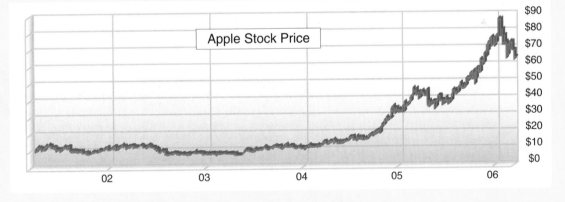

This module explains each financial statement: the balance sheet, the income statement, the statement of cash flows, and the statement of stockholders' equity. Let's begin with a sneak preview of Apple's financial statements.

Apple's balance sheet is very liquid (many of its assets can be readily converted to cash), with over 70% of its assets in cash and marketable securities. Liquidity is important for companies like Apple that must react quickly to opportunities and changing market conditions. Like other high-techs, much of Apple's production is subcontracted. Consequently, Apple's property, plant and equipment make up only 7% of its assets.

On the financing side of its balance sheet, nearly two-thirds of Apple's resources come from owner financing: from common stock sold to shareholders and from past profits reinvested in the business. Technology companies such as Apple, which have uncertain product life-cycles and highly volatile cash flows, avoid

(Continued on next page)

(Continued from previous page)

high debt levels that might cause financial problems in a business downturn. Apple's nonowner financing consists of low-cost credit from suppliers (accounts payable) and unpaid overhead expenses (accrued liabilities).

Consider Apple's income statement: driven by the popularity and high profit margins of iPods, Apple recently reported over $1.6 billion of operating income. This is impressive given that Apple spends four cents of every sales dollar on research and development and runs expensive advertising campaigns.

Yet companies cannot live by profits alone. It is cash that pays bills. Profits and cash flow are two different concepts, each providing a different perspective on company performance. Apple generated over $2.5 billion of cash flow from operating activities, nearly twice its profit level. This is due to noncash expenses included on Apple's income statement and effective management of its balance sheet. We review Apple's cash flows in this module.

Apple pays no dividends and its newly issued common stock relates primarily to executive stock options. These capital transactions are reported in the statement of stockholders' equity.

While it is important to understand what is reported in each of the four financial statements, it is also important to know what is *not* reported. To illustrate, *Fortune* reported that "Jobs cut a deal with the Big Five record companies . . . to sell songs on iTunes, but they were afraid of Internet piracy. So Jobs promised to wrap their songs in Apple's *FairPlay*—the only copy-protection software that is iPod-compatible. Other digital music services such as Yahoo Music Unlimited and Napster reached similar deals with the big record labels. But Apple refused to license *FairPlay* to them. So those companies turned to Microsoft for copy protection. That means none of the songs sold by those services can be played on the wildly popular iPod. Instead, users of the services had to rely on inferior devices made by companies like Samsung and SanDisk that supported Microsoft's Windows Media format."

Apple's copy-protection software described above creates a barrier to competition that allows iPod to earn above-average profits. This represents a valuable resource to Apple, but it is not reported on Apple's balance sheet. Consider another example. Apple's software engineers write code and create software that will generate profits for Apple in the future. While this represents a valuable resource to Apple, it is not reported on the balance sheet because Apple expensed the software engineers' salaries when the code was written. We discuss these and other issues relating to asset recognition and measurement in this module.

Sources: Apple 2005 10-K; Apple 2005 Annual Report; *BusinessWeek*, 2006; *Fortune*, 2006.

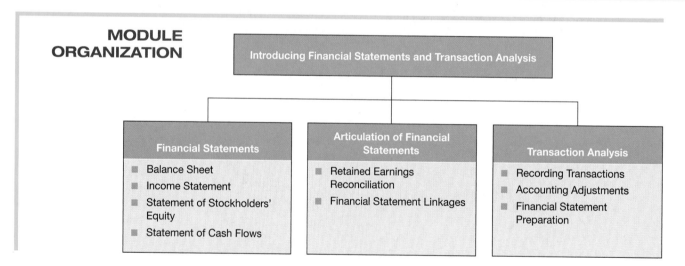

INTRODUCTION

Prior to reviewing the four financial statements, we examine how costs flow through the financial accounting system. For this purpose, we look at the balance sheet (that lists what the company owns and what it owes at a *point* in time) and the income statement (that lists the company's revenues, expenses, and income for a *period* of time).

Companies incur costs to acquire resources that will be used in operations. Every cost creates either an immediate or a future economic benefit. Determining when the company will realize the benefit from a cost is paramount. When a cost creates an immediate benefit, such as gasoline used in delivery vehicles, the company records the cost in the income statement as an expense. When a cost creates a future economic benefit, such as inventory to be resold or equipment to be later used for manufacturing, the company records the cost on the balance sheet as an asset. The definition of an asset is "a future economic benefit." An asset remains on the company's balance sheet until it is used up. When an asset is used up, the company realizes the economic benefit from the asset; that is, there is no future economic benefit left so there is no asset left. Then, the asset's cost is transferred from the balance sheet to the income statement where it is labeled as an expense. This is why assets are sometimes referred to as prepaid or deferred expenses.

Companies expense certain costs, such as research and development salaries, as they are incurred because even though the costs will likely bring future economic benefits, the related asset cannot be reliably measured. (We discuss the concept of measurement later in this module). Exhibit 2.1 illustrates how costs flow from the balance sheet to the income statement.

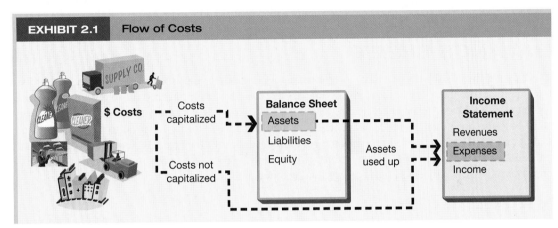

EXHIBIT 2.1   Flow of Costs

All costs are either held on the balance sheet or are transferred to the income statement. When costs are recorded on the balance sheet, assets are reported and expenses are deferred to a later period. Once the company receives benefits from the assets, the related costs are transferred from the balance sheet to the income statement. At that point, assets are reduced and expenses are recorded in the current period.

Tracking the flow of costs from the balance sheet to the income statement is an important part of accounting. If the cost transfer occurs more slowly than it should, current income is higher than it should be. If companies transfer costs too quickly, current income is lower than it should be. GAAP allows companies some flexibility in transferring costs. As such, there is potential for abuse, especially when managers confront pressures to achieve income targets.

Corporate scandals involving WorldCom and Enron regrettably illustrate improper cost transfers designed to achieve higher profit levels. Neither company transferred costs from the balance sheet to the income statement as quickly as they should have. This had the effect of overstating assets on the balance sheet and net income on the income statement. In subsequent litigation, the SEC and the Justice Department contended that these companies intentionally overstated net income to boost stock prices. A number of senior executives from both Enron and WorldCom were sentenced to lengthy jail terms as a result of their criminal actions.

The decision about whether and when to transfer costs impacts more than current period income. When costs are transferred too quickly, current period income is understated *and* future period income is overstated because once costs are removed from the balance sheet they do not impact future period income. Conversely, if costs are transferred too slowly from the balance sheet, current period income is overstated and future period income is understated. The improper transfer of costs, therefore, creates *income shifting:* increasing current period income and decreasing future period income, *or* depressing current period income and increasing future period income.

What does GAAP advise about the transfer of costs? Asset costs should transfer to the income statement when the asset no longer has any future economic benefit (i.e. it no longer meets the definition of an asset). For example, when inventories are purchased or manufactured, their cost is recorded on the balance sheet as an asset called *inventories*. When inventories are sold, they no longer have an economic benefit to the company and their cost is transferred to the income statement in an expense called *cost of goods sold*. Cost of goods sold represents the cost of inventories sold during that period. This expense is recognized in the same period as the revenue generated from the sale.

As another example, consider equipment costs. When a company acquires equipment, the cost of the equipment is recorded on the balance sheet in an asset called *equipment* (often included in the general category of property, plant, and equipment, or PPE). When equipment is used in operations, a portion of the acquisition cost is transferred to the income statement to match against the sales the equipment helped generate. To illustrate, if an asset costs $100,000, and 10% of it is used up this period in operating activities, then $10,000 of the asset's cost is transferred from the balance sheet to the income statement. This process is called *depreciation* and the expense related to this transfer of costs is called depreciation expense.

MANAGERIAL DECISION	You Are the Securities Analyst

You are analyzing the performance of a company that hired a new CEO during the current year. The current year's income statement includes an expense labeled "asset write-offs." Write-offs represent the accelerated transfer of costs from the balance sheet to the income statement. Are you concerned about the legitimacy of these expenses? Why or why not? [Answer, p. 2-32]

BALANCE SHEET

LO1 Describe information conveyed by the financial statements.

The balance sheet is divided into three sections: assets, liabilities, and stockholders' equity. It provides information about the resources available to management and the claims against those resources by creditors and shareholders. The balance sheet reports the assets, liabilities and equity at a *point* in time. Balance sheet accounts are called "permanent accounts" in that they carry over from period to period; that is, the ending balance from one period becomes the beginning balance for the next. (Income statement accounts are called "temporary accounts." They are zeroed out at the end of each accounting period so that subsequent periods show only the sales, expenses, and net income for that period.)

Assets—Reflecting Investing Activities

Companies acquire assets to yield a return for their shareholders. Assets are expected to produce economic benefits in the form of revenues, either directly such as with inventory or indirectly such as with a manufacturing plant that produces inventories for sale. To create shareholder value, assets must yield income that is in excess of the cost of the invested and borrowed funds used to acquire the assets.

The asset section of the Apple balance sheet is shown in Exhibit 2.2. Apple reports $11,551 million of total assets as of September 24, 2005, its year-end. The amounts reported on the balance sheet are at a *point in time*—that is, the close of business on the day of the report. An asset must possess two characteristics to be reported on the balance sheet:

1. It must be owned (or controlled) by the company.
2. It must possess expected future economic benefits.

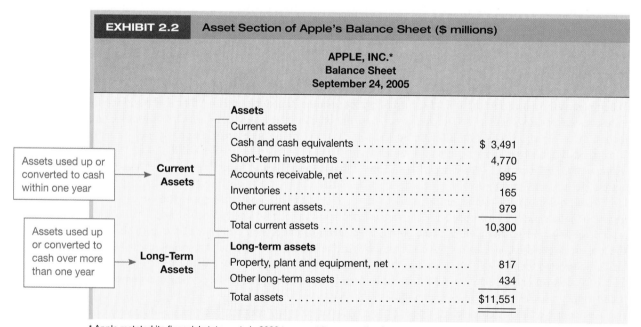

EXHIBIT 2.2	Asset Section of Apple's Balance Sheet ($ millions)

APPLE, INC.*
Balance Sheet
September 24, 2005

Assets		
Current assets		
Cash and cash equivalents		$ 3,491
Short-term investments		4,770
Accounts receivable, net		895
Inventories		165
Other current assets		979
Total current assets		10,300
Long-term assets		
Property, plant and equipment, net		817
Other long-term assets		434
Total assets		$11,551

Assets used up or converted to cash within one year → **Current Assets**

Assets used up or converted to cash over more than one year → **Long-Term Assets**

* Apple restated its financial statements in 2006 to correct its accounting for employee stock options (see Appendix 1B for a discussion of restatements and Module 9 for a discussion of employee stock options). This restatement, required by the SEC, related to back-dating stock options and impacted many companies in that year. Thus, Apple's 2005 statements included in subsequent years' filings are slightly different from its 2005 statements here. To view its financial statements used in this module, search for Apple's 10-K with a filing date of "2005-12-01" on the SEC Website.

The first requirement, owning or controlling an asset, implies that a company has legal title to the asset, such as the title to property, or has the unrestricted right to use the asset, such as a lease on the property. The second requirement implies that a company expects to realize a benefit from the asset. Benefits can be cash inflows from the sale of an asset or from sales of products produced by the asset. Benefits also can refer to the receipt of other assets such as with an account receivable from a credit sale. Or, benefits can arise from future services the company will enjoy, such as prepaying for a year-long insurance policy.

Current Assets

The balance sheet lists assets in order of decreasing **liquidity**, which refers to the ease of converting non-cash assets into cash. The most liquid assets are called **current assets** and they are listed first. A company expects to convert its current assets into cash or use those assets in operations within the coming fiscal year.[1] Typical examples of current assets follow:

Cash—currency, bank deposits, and investments with an original maturity of 90 days or less (called *cash equivalents*);

Marketable securities—short-term investments that can be quickly sold to raise cash;

Accounts receivable, net—amounts due to the company from customers arising from the sale of products on credit ("net" refers to uncollectible accounts explained in Module 6);

Inventory—goods purchased or produced for sale to customers;

Prepaid expenses—costs paid in advance for rent, insurance, advertising or other services.

Apple reports current assets of $10,300 million in 2005, which is 89% of its total assets. The amount of current assets is an important measure of liquidity. Companies require a degree of liquidity to operate effectively, as they must be able to respond to changing market conditions and take advantage of opportunities. However, current assets are expensive to hold (they must be stored, insured, monitored, financed, and so forth)—and they typically generate returns that are less than those from noncurrent assets. As a result, companies seek to maintain only just enough current assets to cover liquidity needs, but not so much so as to unnecessarily reduce income.

Long-Term Assets

The second section of the balance sheet reports long-term (noncurrent) assets. Long-term assets include the following:

Property, plant and equipment (PPE), net—land, factory buildings, warehouses, office buildings, machinery, motor vehicles, office equipment and other items used in operating activities ("net" refers to subtraction of accumulated depreciation, the portion of the assets' cost that has been transferred from the balance sheet to the income statement, which is explained in Module 6);

Long-term investments—investments that the company does not intend to sell in the near future;

Intangible and other assets—assets without physical substance, including patents, trademarks, franchise rights, goodwill and other costs the company incurred that provide future benefits.

Long-term assets are not expected to be converted into cash for some time and are, therefore, listed after current assets.

Measuring Assets

Assets are reported at their original acquisition costs, or **historical costs**, and not at their current market values. (Exceptions are marketable securities that are recorded on the balance sheet at current market values, and assets whose future economic benefits have become impaired and are written down on the balance sheet to fair market value.) The concept of historical costs is not without controversy. The controversy arises because of the trade-off between the **relevance** of current market values for many business decisions and the **reliability** of historical cost measures.

To illustrate, imagine we are financial analysts and want to determine the value of a company. The company's value equals the value of its assets less the value of its liabilities. Current market values of company

---

[1] Technically, current assets include those assets expected to be converted into cash within the upcoming year or the company's operating cycle (the cash-to-cash cycle), whichever is longer. Fortune Brands (manufacturer of Jim Beam Whiskey) provides an example of a current asset with a cash conversion cycle of longer than one year. Its inventory footnote reports: "In accordance with generally recognized trade practices, bulk whiskey inventories are classified as current assets, although the majority of such inventories, due to the duration of aging processes, ordinarily will not be sold within one year."

assets (and liabilities) are more informative and relevant to our analysis than are historic costs. But how can we determine market values? For some assets, like marketable securities, values are readily obtained from online quotes or from *The Wall Street Journal.* For other assets like property, plant, and equipment, market values are far more subjective and difficult to estimate. It would be easier for us, as analysts, if companies reported market values on their balance sheet. However, allowing companies to report estimates of asset market values would introduce potential *bias* into financial reporting. Consequently, companies continue to report historical costs because the loss in reliability from using subjective market values on the balance sheet is considered to be greater than the loss in relevance from using historical costs.

It is important to realize that balance sheets only include items that can be reliably measured. If a company cannot assign a monetary amount to an asset with relative certainty, it does not recognize an asset on the balance sheet. This means that there are, typically, considerable "assets" that are not reflected on a balance sheet. For example, the well-known apple image is absent from Apple's balance sheet. This image is called an "unrecognized intangible asset." Both requirements for an asset are met: Apple owns the brand and it expects to realize future benefits from the logo. The problem is reliably measuring the expected future benefits to be derived from the image. Intangible assets such as the Coke bottle silhouette, the iPod brand, and the Nike swoosh are not on their respective balance sheets. Companies only report intangible assets on the balance sheet when they are purchased. Any internally created intangible assets are not reported on a balance sheet. A sizable amount of resources is, therefore, potentially omitted from companies' balance sheets.

Excluded intangible assets often relate to *knowledge-based* (intellectual) assets, such as a strong management team, a well-designed supply chain, or superior technology. Although these intangible assets confer a competitive advantage to the company, and yield above-normal income (and clear economic benefits to those companies), they cannot be reliably measured. This is one reason why companies in knowledge-based industries are so difficult to analyze.

Excluded intangible assets are, however, presumably reflected in companies' market values. This can yield a large difference between the market value and the book value of a company's equity. This is illustrated in the following ratios of market value to book value: Apple is 7.6; Cisco is 5.3; IBM is 3.9; and Citigroup is 2.1. Market-to-book ratios are greater for companies with large knowledge-based assets, which are not reported on the balance sheet, but are reflected in company market value. Companies such as Citigroup have fewer of these assets. Hence, their balance sheets usually reflect a greater portion of company value.

Liabilities and Equity—Reflecting Financing Activities

Liabilities and stockholders' equity represent the sources of capital the company uses to finance the acquisition of assets. In general, liabilities represent a company's future economic sacrifices. Liabilities are

BUSINESS INSIGHT | **How Much Debt Is Reasonable?**

Apple reports total assets of $11,551 million, liabilities of $4,085 million, and stockholders' equity of $7,466 million. This reveals that it finances 35% of its assets with borrowed funds and 65% with shareholder investment. This is a lower percentage of non-owner financing than other companies such as The Gap, Target, and Procter & Gamble (P&G), but about the same as Cisco Systems. Companies must monitor their financing sources and amounts. Too much reliance on equity capital is expensive. And, too much borrowing is risky. The level of debt that a company can effectively manage depends on the stability and reliability of its operating cash flows. Companies such as P&G, Target, and The Gap can manage relatively high debt levels because their cash flows are relatively stable. Apple and Cisco, on the other hand, operate in industries that change rapidly. They cannot afford to take on too much borrowing risk.

($ millions)	Assets	Liabilities	Liabilities to Assets ratio	Equity	Equity to Assets ratio
Cisco Systems, Inc.	$33,883	$10,709	32%	$23,174	68%
Apple, Inc.	11,551	4,085	35%	7,466	65%
Gap, Inc.	10,048	5,112	51%	4,936	49%
Target Corporation	32,293	19,264	60%	13,029	40%
Procter & Gamble Co.	61,527	44,050	72%	17,477	28%

borrowed funds such as accounts payable, accrued liabilities, and obligations to lenders or bond investors. They can be interest-bearing or non-interest-bearing.

Equity represents capital that has been invested by the shareholders, either directly via the purchase of stock (net of any company repurchases of stock from its shareholders, called *treasury stock*) or indirectly in the form of *retained earnings* that reflect earnings that are reinvested in the business and not paid out as dividends. We discuss liabilities and equity in this section.

The liabilities and stockholders' equity sections of the Apple balance sheet are reproduced in Exhibit 2.3. Apple reports $4,085 million of total liabilities and $7,466 million of stockholders' equity as of its 2005 year-end.

EXHIBIT 2.3 Liabilities and Equity Sections of Apple's Balance Sheet ($ millions)

APPLE, INC.
Balance Sheet
September 24, 2005

Liabilities and Stockholders' Equity

Current liabilities	
Accounts payable	$ 1,779
Accrued liabilities	1,705
Total current liabilities	3,484
Long-term liabilities	601
Total liabilities	4,085
Stockholders' equity	
Common stock, no par value; 1.8 bil. shares authorized; 835,019,364 shares issued and outstanding	3,521
Retained earnings	4,005
Other stockholders' equity	(60)
Total stockholders' equity	7,466
Total liabilities and stockholders' equity	$11,551

Liabilities: requiring payment within one year. Liabilities not requiring payment within one year.

Why would Apple obtain capital from both borrowed funds and shareholders? Why not just one or the other? The answer lies in their relative costs and the contractual agreements that Apple has with each.

Creditors have the first claim on the assets of the company. As a result, their position is not as risky and, accordingly, their expected return on investment is less than that required by shareholders (also, interest is tax deductible whereas dividends are not). This makes debt a less expensive source of capital than equity. So, then, why should a company not finance itself entirely with borrowed funds? The reason is that borrowed funds entail contractual obligations to repay the principal and interest on the debt. If a company cannot make these payments when they come due, creditors can force the company into bankruptcy and potentially put the company out of business. Shareholders, in contrast, cannot require repurchase of their stock, or even the payment of dividends. Thus, companies take on a level of debt that they can comfortably repay at reasonable interest costs. The remaining balance required to fund business activities is financed with more costly equity capital.

Current Liabilities

The balance sheet lists liabilities in order of maturity. Obligations that are due within one year are called **current liabilities.** Examples of common current liabilities follow:

Accounts payable—amounts owed to suppliers for goods and services purchased on credit.

Accrued liabilities—obligations for expenses that have been incurred but not yet paid; examples are accrued wages payable (wages earned by employees but not yet paid), accrued interest payable (interest that is owing but has not been paid), and accrued income taxes (taxes due).

Unearned revenues—obligations created when the company accepts payment in advance for goods or services it will deliver in the future; also called advances from customers, customer deposits, or deferred revenues.

Short-term notes payable—short-term debt payable to banks or other creditors.

Current maturities of long-term debt—principal portion of long-term debt that is due to be paid within one year.

Apple reports current liabilities of $3,484 on its 2005 balance sheet.

Accounts payable arise when one company purchases goods or services from another company. Typically, sellers offer credit terms when selling to other companies, rather than expecting cash on delivery. The seller records an account receivable and the buyer records an account payable. Apple reports accounts payable of $1,779 million as of the balance sheet date. Liabilities that arise from transactions such as those making up its accounts payable are relatively uncomplicated. That is, a transaction occurs (inventory purchase), a bill is sent, and the amount owed is reported on the balance sheet as a liability.

Apple's accrued liabilities total $1,705 million. Accrued liabilities refer to incomplete transactions. For example, employees work and earn wages, but usually are not paid until later. They must be reported as expense in the period that employees earn them because those wages have been incurred by the company. Also, a liability (wages payable) must be set up on the balance sheet. This is an *accrual*. Other common accruals include the recording of liabilities such as rent and utilities payable, taxes payable, and interest payable on borrowings. All of these accruals involve recognition of expense in the income statement and a liability on the balance sheet. (We discuss accruals later in this module.)

Net working capital, or simply working capital, reflects the difference between current assets and current liabilities and is defined as follows:

Net Working Capital = Current Assets − Current Liabilities

We usually prefer to see more current assets than current liabilities to ensure that companies are liquid. That is, companies should have sufficient funds to pay their short-term debts as they mature. The net working capital required to conduct business depends on the company's **operating (or cash) cycle**, which is the time between paying cash for goods or employee services and receiving cash from customers—see Exhibit 2.4.

Companies, for example, use cash to purchase or manufacture inventories held for resale. Inventories are usually purchased on credit (accounts payable) from suppliers. This financing is called **trade credit**. Inventories are sold, either on credit (accounts receivable) or for cash. When receivables are ultimately collected, a portion of the cash received is used to repay accounts payable and the remainder goes to the cash account for the next operating cycle.

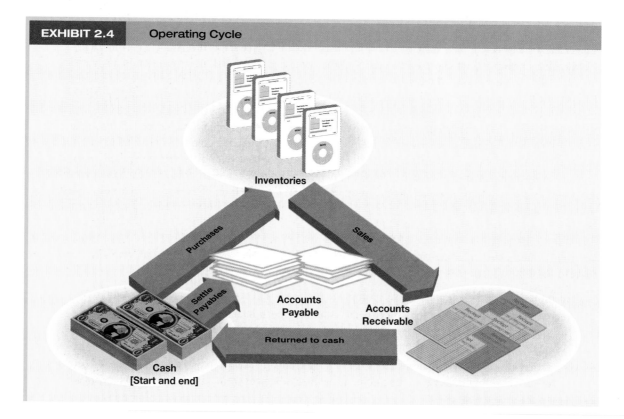

EXHIBIT 2.4   Operating Cycle

When cash is invested in inventory, the inventory can remain with the company for 30 to 90 days or more. Once inventory is sold, the resulting accounts receivable can remain with the company for another 30 to 90 days. Assets such as inventory and accounts receivable are costly to hold and, as such, companies strive to reduce operating cycles with various initiatives that aim to:

- Decrease accounts receivable by better collection procedures
- Reduce inventory levels by improved production systems and management
- Increase trade credit to minimize the cash invested in inventories

Analysts often use the "cash cycle" to evaluate company liquidity. The cash cycle is the number of days the company has its cash tied up in receivables and inventories, less the number of days of trade credit provided by company suppliers.

Noncurrent Liabilities

Noncurrent liabilities are obligations due after one year. Examples of noncurrent liabilities follow:

> **Long-term debt**—amounts borrowed from creditors that are scheduled to be repaid more than one year in the future; any portion of long-term debt that is due within one year is reclassified as a current liability called *current maturities of long-term debt*. Long-term debt includes bonds, mortgages, and other long-term loans.

> **Other long-term liabilities**—various obligations, such as pension liabilities and long-term tax liabilities, that will be settled a year or more into the future. We discuss these items in later modules.

Apple reports $601 million of noncurrent liabilities. As is typical of high-tech companies, Apple has no long-term debt. Instead, all of its noncurrent liabilities relate to deferred revenue and deferred taxes.

Deferred (unearned) revenue arises when a company receives cash in advance of providing a good or service. When cash is received, the company records a liability (deferred or unearned revenue), which represents the company's obligation to provide the good or service in the future. When the company ultimately delivers the good or provides the service, the deferred revenue account is reduced and revenues are recorded in the income statement, thus increasing net income. Deferred taxes relate to future tax liabilities resulting from differences between the income reported to shareholders and that reported to tax authorities. We discuss deferred taxes in Module 5.

Stockholders' Equity

Stockholders' equity reflects financing provided from company owners. Equity is often referred to as *residual interest*. That is, stockholders have a claim on any assets in excess of what is needed to meet company obligations to creditors. The following are examples of items typically included in equity:

> **Common stock**—par value of stock received from the original sale of common stock to investors.
> **Preferred stock**—value of stock received from the original sale of preferred stock to investors; preferred stock has fewer ownership rights compared to common stock.
> **Additional paid-in capital**—amounts received from the original sale of stock to investors in addition to the par value of common and preferred stock.
> **Treasury stock**—amount the company paid to reacquire its common stock from shareholders.

	Contributed Capital

> **Retained earnings**—accumulated net income (profit) that has not been distributed to stockholders as dividends.
> **Accumulated other comprehensive income or loss**—accumulated changes in equity that are not reported in the income statement (explained in Module 9).

	Earned Capital

The equity section of a balance sheet consists of two basic components: contributed capital and earned capital. **Contributed capital** is the net funding that a company has received from issuing and reacquiring its equity shares; that is, the funds received from issuing shares less any funds paid to repurchase such shares. Apple reports $7,466 million in total stockholders' equity. Its contributed capital is $3,521 million.

Apple's common stock is "no par." This means that Apple records all of its contributed capital in the common stock account and records no additional paid-in capital. Apple's stockholders (via its board of directors) have authorized it to issue up to 1.8 billion shares of common stock. To date, it has sold (issued) 835,019,364 shares for total proceeds of $3,521 million, or $4.22 per share, on average. Apple has repurchased no shares of stock to date. We explain these and other equity details in Module 9.

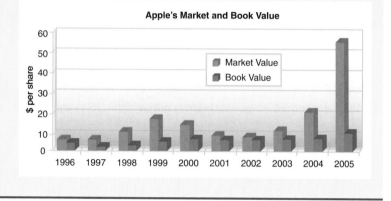

BUSINESS INSIGHT **Apple's Market and Book Values**

Apple's market value has historically exceeded its book value of equity (see graph below). Much of Apple's market value derives from intangible assets such as brand equity that are not fully reflected on its balance sheet, and from favorable expectations of future financial performance (particularly in recent years). Apple has incurred many costs such as R&D, advertising, and promotion that will probably yield future economic benefits. However, Apple expensed these costs (did not capitalize them as assets) because their future benefits were uncertain and therefore could not be reliably measured. Companies capitalize intangible assets only when those assets are purchased, and not when they are internally developed. Consequently, Apple's balance sheet and the balance sheets of many knowledge-based companies are, arguably, less informative about company value.

Earned capital is the cumulative net income (loss) that has been retained by the company (not paid out to shareholders as dividends). Apple's earned capital (titled Retained Earnings) totals $4,005 million as of its 2005 year-end.

Retained Earnings

There is an important relation for retained earnings that reconciles its beginning and ending balances as follows:

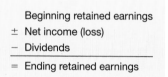

```
    Beginning retained earnings
 ±  Net income (loss)
 −  Dividends
 =  Ending retained earnings
```

This is a useful relation to remember. Apple's retained earnings increases (or decreases) each year by the amount of its reported net income (loss). If Apple paid dividends, its retained earnings would decrease further, but Apple currently pays no dividends. (There are other items that can impact retained earnings that we discuss in later modules.) After we explain the income statement, we will revisit this relation and show how retained earnings link the balance sheet and income statement.

Book Value vs Market Value Reported stockholders' equity is the "value" of the company determined by GAAP. Stockholders equity is commonly referred to as the company's **book value**. This value is different from a company's **market value** (market capitalization or market cap), which is computed by multiplying the number of outstanding common shares by the per share market value. Book value and market value can differ for several reasons, mostly related to the recognition of transactions and events in financial statements such as the following:

- GAAP generally reports assets and liabilities at historical costs, whereas the market attempts to estimate fair market values.

- GAAP excludes resources that cannot be reliably measured such as talented management, employee morale, recent innovations and successful marketing, whereas the market attempts to value these.

- GAAP does not consider market differences in which companies operate such as competitive conditions and expected changes, whereas the market attempts to factor in these differences in determining value.

■   GAAP does not usually report expected future performance, whereas the market attempts to predict and value future performance.

Presently for U.S. companies, book value is, on average, about two-thirds of market value. This means that the market has drawn on information in addition to that provided in the balance sheet and income statement in valuing equity shares. A major part of this information is in financial statement notes, but not all.

It is important to understand that, eventually, all factors determining company market value are reflected in financial statements and book value. Assets are eventually sold and liabilities are settled. Moreover, talented management, employee morale, technological innovations, and successful marketing are all eventually recognized in reported profit. The difference between book value and market value is one of timing. To the extent that market value is accurate, the change in stockholders' equity usually represents the change in company market value with a lag.

INCOME STATEMENT

The income statement reports revenues earned during a period, the expenses incurred to produce those revenues, and the resulting net income or loss. The general structure of the income statement follows:

	Revenues
−	Cost of goods sold
	Gross profit
−	Operating expenses
	Operating profit
−	Nonoperating expenses (+ Nonoperating revenues)
−	Tax expense
	Income from continuing operations
+/−	Nonrecurring items, net of tax
=	Net income

Apple's income statement from its 2005 10-K is shown in Exhibit 2.5. Apple reports net income of $1,335 million on sales of $13,931 million. As is typical of many large companies, less than $0.10 of each dollar of sales is brought down to the bottom line (many companies report less than a nickel in profit for every dollar of sales)—for Apple, it is $0.096 of each dollar, computed as $1,335 million divided by $13,931 million. The remainder of each sales dollar, $0.904 (computed as $1 minus $0.096) relates to

EXHIBIT 2.5	**Apple's Income Statement ($ millions)**

APPLE, INC.
Income Statement
For Year Ended September 24, 2005

Net sales.	$13,931
Cost of sales.	9,888
Gross margin	4,043
Operating expenses	
Research and development	534
Selling, general, and administrative	1,859
Total operating expenses	2,393
Operating profit	1,650
Other revenue and expense	
Interest and other income, net	165
Income before provision for income taxes	1,815
Provision for income taxes	480
Net income	$ 1,335

costs incurred to generate sales, such as cost of sales, wages, advertising, interest, equipment costs, research and development expenses, and taxes.

To analyze an income statement we need to understand some terminology. **Revenues** (Sales) are increases in net assets (assets less liabilities) as a result of ordinary operating activities. **Expenses** are decreases in net assets used to generate revenues, including costs of sales, operating costs like wages and advertising (usually titled selling, general, and administrative expenses or SG&A), and nonoperating costs like interest on debt. The difference between revenues and expenses is **net income** when revenues exceed expenses, or **net loss** when expenses exceed revenues. The terms income, profit, and earnings are used interchangeably (as are revenues and sales, and expenses and costs).

Operating expenses are the usual and customary costs that a company incurs to support its operating activities. These include cost of goods sold, selling expenses, depreciation expense, and research and development expense. Not all of these expenses require a cash outlay; for example, depreciation expense is a noncash expense, as are accruals of liabilities such as wages payable, that recognize the expense in advance of cash payment. **Nonoperating expenses** relate to the company's financing and investing activities, and include interest expense and interest or dividend income. Business decision makers and analysts usually segregate operating and nonoperating activities as they offer different insights into company performance and condition.

Revenue Recognition and Matching

An important consideration in preparing the income statement is *when* to recognize revenues and expenses. For many revenues and expenses, the decision is easy. When a customer purchases groceries, pays with a check, and walks out of the store with the groceries, we know that the sale is made and revenue should be recognized. Or, when companies receive and pay an electric bill with a check, they have clearly incurred an expense that should be recognized.

However, should Apple recognize revenue when it sells iPods to a retailer who does not have to pay Apple for 60 days? Should Apple recognize an expense for employees who work this week but will not be paid until the first of next month? The answer to both of these questions is yes.

Two fundamental principles guide recognition of revenues and expenses:

Revenue Recognition Principle—recognize revenues when *earned*

Matching Principle—recognize expenses when *incurred*.

These two principles are the foundation of **accrual accounting**, which is the accounting system used to prepare all GAAP-based financial statements. The general approach is this: first, recognize revenues in the time period they are earned; then, record all expenses *incurred* to generate those revenues during that same time period (this is called matching expenses to revenues). Net income is then correctly reported for that period.

Recognizing revenues when earned does not necessarily imply the receipt of cash. Revenue is *earned* when the company has done everything that it is supposed to do. This means that a sale of goods on credit would qualify for recognition as long as the revenues are earned. Likewise, companies recognize an expense when it is *incurred*, even if no cash is paid. For example, companies recognize as expenses the wages earned by employees, even though they will not be paid until the next pay period. The company records an expense but pays no cash; instead, it records an accrued liability for the wages payable. (We discuss accrual accounting later in this module, and Modules 3 and 5 review accrual accounting in more detail.)

Accrual accounting requires estimates and assumptions. Examples include estimating how much revenue has been earned on a long-term contract, the amount of accounts receivable that will not be collected,

MANAGERIAL DECISION   **You Are the Operations Manager**

You are the operations manager on a new consumer product that was launched this period with very successful sales. The Chief Financial Officer (CFO) asks you to prepare an estimate of warranty costs to charge against those sales. Why does the CFO desire a warranty cost estimate? What hurdles must you address in arriving at such an estimate? [Answer, p.2-33]

the degree to which equipment has been "used up," the cleanup costs that a company must eventually pay for environmental liabilities, and numerous other estimates. All of these estimates and assumptions affect both reported net income and the balance sheet. Judgments affect all financial statements. This is an important by-product of accrual accounting. We discuss these estimates and assumptions, and their effects on financial statements, throughout the book.

Reporting of Transitory Items

To this point, we have only considered income from continuing operations and its components. A more comprehensive income statement format is in Exhibit 2.6. The most noticeable difference involves two additional components of net income located at the bottom of the statement.

EXHIBIT 2.6	General Income Statement Format

Sales
− Cost of goods sold

Gross profit
− Operating expenses
− Nonoperating expenses (+ Nonoperating revenues)
− Tax expense ◄—————— *Tax expense applies to items comprising income from continuing operations*

Income from continuing operations
± Discontinued operations, net of tax
± Extraordinary items, net of tax   ◄—————— *Transitory items are those not expected to recur; reported 'net of tax'*

Net income

These two components are specifically segregated from the "income from continuing operations" and are defined as follows (these items are further described in Module 5):[2]

1. **Discontinued operations** Gains or losses (and net income or loss) from business segments that are being sold or have been sold in the current period.
2. **Extraordinary items** Gains or losses from events that are both *unusual* and *infrequent* and are, therefore, excluded from income from continuing operations.

These two components are segregated because they represent **transitory items**, which reflect transactions or events that are unlikely to recur. Many readers of financial statements are interested in *future* company performance. They analyze current year financial statements to gain clues to better *predict* future performance. (Stock prices, for example, are based on a company's expected profits and cash flows.)

Transitory items, by definition, are unlikely to arise in future periods. Although transitory items can help us analyze past performance, they are largely irrelevant to predicting future performance. This means that investors and other users tend to focus on income from continuing operations because it is the level of profitability that is likely to **persist** (continue) into the future. Likewise, the financial press tends to focus on income from continuing operations when it discloses corporate earnings (often described as *earnings before one-time charges*).

STATEMENT OF STOCKHOLDERS' EQUITY

The statement of stockholders' equity reconciles the beginning and ending balances of stockholders' equity accounts.

---

[2] Under current GAAP, **changes in accounting principles,** that once were included as transitory items, are applied retrospectively. That is, the company goes back and amends previous income statements to incorporate the effect of any new accounting principle. Under prior GAAP, the company made one, large cumulative adjustment to income in the period of the change. An exception to this relates to changes in depreciation methods, which are applied prospectively like a change in an estimate (retrospective adjustment is not made).

The statement of stockholders' equity for Apple is shown in Exhibit 2.7.

EXHIBIT 2.7	Apple's Statement of Stockholders' Equity

APPLE, INC.
Statement of Stockholders' Equity
For Year Ended September 24, 2005

($ millions)	Common Stock	Retained Earnings	Other Stockholders' Equity	Total Stockholders' Equity
Balance at September 25, 2004......	$2,514	$2,670	$(108)	$5,076
Common stock issued..............	1,007			1,007
Net income......................		1,335		1,335
Dividends.......................		0		0
Other...........................			48	48
Balance at September 24, 2005......	$3,521	$4,005	$ (60)	$7,466

Apple's first equity component is common stock. The balance in common stock at the beginning of the year is $2,514 million. During 2005, Apple issued $1,007 million worth of common stock to employees who exercised stock options. At the end of 2005, the common stock account reports a balance of $3,521 million.

Apple's second stockholders' equity component is retained earnings. It totals $2,670 million at the start of 2005. During the year, it increased by $1,335 million from net income. (Apple's retained earnings do not decrease for dividends because Apple pays no dividends.) The balance of retained earnings at year-end is $4,005 million.

In sum, total stockholders' equity begins the year at $5,076 million (including $108 million relating to miscellaneous accounts that reduce total stockholders' equity) and ends 2005 with a balance of $7,466 million (including $60 million relating to miscellaneous accounts that reduce total stockholders' equity) for a net increase of $2,390 million.

RESEARCH INSIGHT	Market-to-Book Ratio

The market-to-book ratio, also called price-to-book, refers to a company's market value divided by its book (equity) value—it is also computed as stock price per share divided by book value per share. Research shows that the market-to-book ratio exhibits considerable variability over time. Specifically, over the past few decades, the median (50th percentile) market-to-book ratio was less than 1.0 during the mid-1970s, over 2.0 during the mid-1990s, and often between 1.0 and 2.0 during the 1960s and 1980s.

STATEMENT OF CASH FLOWS

The balance sheet and income statement are prepared using accrual accounting, in which revenues are recognized when earned and expenses when incurred. This means that companies can report income even though no cash is received. Cash shortages—due to unexpected cash outlays or when customers refuse to or cannot pay—can create economic hardships for companies and even cause their demise.

To assess cash flows, we must assess a company's cash management. Obligations to employees, creditors, and others are usually settled with cash. Illiquid companies (those lacking cash) are at risk of failure and typically reflect poor investing activities. Given the importance of cash management, the SEC and FASB require disclosure of the statement of cash flows in addition to the balance sheet, income statement, and statement of equity.

The income statement provides information about the economic viability of the company's products and services. It tells us whether the company can sell its products and services at prices that cover its costs and that also provide a reasonable return to lenders and stockholders. On the other hand, the statement of cash flows provides information about the company's ability to generate cash from those same transactions. It tells us from what sources the company has generated its cash (so we can evaluate whether those sources are persistent or transitory) and what it has done with the cash it generated.

Statement Format and Data Sources

The statement of cash flows is formatted to report cash inflows and cash outflows by the three primary business activities:

- *Cash flows from operating activities* Cash flows from the company's transactions and events that relate to its operations.
- *Cash flows from investing activities* Cash flows from acquisitions and divestitures of investments and long-term assets.
- *Cash flows from financing activities* Cash flows from issuances of and payments toward borrowings and equity.

The combined cash flows from these three sections yield the net change in cash for the period. Preparation of these three sections of the statement of cash flows draws generally on parts of both the income statement and the balance sheet, and those sections are highlighted in blue as follows:

Cash flow section	Information from income statement	Information from balance sheet	
Net cash flows from operating activities. . . .	Revenues − Expenses = Net income	Current assets Long-term assets	Current liabilities Long-term liabilities Equity
Net cash flows from investing activities	Revenues − Expenses = Net income	Current assets Long-term assets	Current liabilities Long-term liabilities Equity
Net cash flows from financing activities	Revenues − Expenses = Net income	Current assets Long-term assets	Current liabilities Long-term liabilities Equity

Specifically, the three sections draw generally on the following information:

- **Net cash flows from operating activities** draws on the income statement and the current asset and current liabilities sections of the balance sheet.
- **Net cash flows from investing activities** uses the long-term assets section of the balance sheet.
- **Net cash flows from financing activities** draws on the long-term liabilities and stockholders' equity sections of the balance sheet.

These relations do not hold exactly, but they provide us a useful way to visualize the construction of the statement of cash flows.

In analyzing the statement of cash flows, you should not necessarily conclude that the company is better off if cash increases and worse off if cash decreases. It is not the change in cash that is most important, but the reasons behind the change. For example, what are the sources of cash inflows? Are these sources transitory? Are these sources mainly from operating activities? To what uses have cash inflows been put? Such questions and answers are key to properly using the statement of cash flows.

Exhibit 2.8 shows Apple's statement of cash flows. Apple reported $2,535 million in net cash inflows from operating activities in 2005. This is substantially greater than its net income of $1,335 million. The operating activities section of the statement of cash flows reconciles the difference between net income

EXHIBIT 2.8	Apple's Statement of Cash Flows ($ millions)

APPLE, INC.
Statement of Cash Flows
For Year Ended September 24, 2005

Operating Activities	
Net income	$1,335
Depreciation and amortization	179
Other noncash expenses, net	556
Increase in accounts receivable	(121)
Increase in inventories	(64)
Increases in other current assets	(211)
Increases in accounts payable	328
Increases in other liabilities	533
Cash generated by operating activities	2,535
Investing Activities	
Increase in short-term investments	(2,275)
Purchases of property, plant and equipment	(260)
Increase in other long-term assets	(21)
Cash used for investing activities	(2,556)
Financing Activities	
Proceeds from issuance of common stock	543
Cash generated by financing activities	543
Increase in cash and cash equivalents	$ 522
Cash and cash equivalents, beginning of year	2,969
Cash and cash equivalents, end of year	$3,491

and operating cash flow. The difference is due to the add-back of depreciation, a noncash expense in the income statement, and other noncash expenses, together with changes in operating assets and liabilities. We discuss these changes, and how to interpret them, in more detail below.

Apple reports a net cash outflow of $2,556 million for investing activities, mainly for investments in marketable securities. Apple also generated $543 million from financing activities, mainly cash received when Apple issued shares to employees who exercised their options to purchase common stock (the remaining $464 million of the $1,007 million referenced as common stock issued in Exhibit 2.7 is included in net cash flow from operating activities; the reason for this classification is discussed in Appendix B).

Overall, Apple's cash flow picture is quite strong. It is generating cash from operating activities and the sale of stock to employees, and is investing excess cash in marketable securities to ensure future liquidity.

Cash Flow Computations

It is sometimes difficult to understand why certain accounts are added to and subtracted from net income to yield net cash flows from operating activities. It often takes more than one pass through this section to grasp how this part of the cash flow statement is constructed.

A key to understanding these computations is to remember that under accrual accounting, revenues are recognized when earned and expenses when incurred. This recognition policy does not necessarily coincide with the receipt or payment of cash. The top line (net income) of the operating section of the statement of cash flows represents net (accrual) income under GAAP. The bottom line (net cash flows from operating activities) is the *cash profit* had the company constructed its income statement on a cash basis rather than an accrual basis. Computing net cash flows from operating activities begins with GAAP profit and adjusts it to compute cash profit using the following general approach:

	Add (+) or Subtract (−) from Net Income
Net income.	$ #
Add: depreciation.	+
Adjust for changes in current assets	
Subtract increases in current assets	−
Add decreases in current assets	+
Adjust for changes in current liabilities	
Add increases in current liabilities	+
Subtract decreases in current liabilities . .	−
Net cash flow from operating activities	$ #

Typically, net income is first adjusted for noncash expenses such as depreciation, and is then adjusted for changes in current assets and current liabilities to yield net cash flow from operating activities, or cash profit. The depreciation adjustment merely zeros out depreciation expense, a noncash expense, which is

BUSINESS INSIGHT   **Insights into Apple's Statement of Cash Flows**

The following provides insights into the computation of some amounts in the operating section of Apple's statement of cash flows in Exhibit 2.8 ($ millions).

Statement amount	Explanation of computation
Depreciation and amortization, $179	When buildings and equipment are acquired, their cost is recorded on the balance sheet as an asset. Subsequently, as the assets are used up to generate revenues, a portion of their cost is transferred from the balance sheet to the income statement as an expense, called *depreciation*. Depreciation expense does not involve the payment of cash (that occurs when the asset is purchased). If we want to compute *cash profit*, we must add back depreciation expense to zero it out from income. The $179 in the second line of the statement of cash flows merely zeros out (undoes) the depreciation expense that was subtracted when Apple computed GAAP net income. Likewise, the third line (other noncash expenditures of $556) uses the same concept.
Increase in accounts receivable, $(121)	When a company sells goods *on credit*, it records revenue because it is earned, even though cash is not yet received. When Apple sold $121 of goods on credit, its revenues and net income increased by that amount, but no cash was received. Apple's cash profit is, thus, $121 less than net income. The $121 is subtracted from net income in computing net cash inflows from operations.
Increase in inventories, $(64)	When Apple purchases inventories, the purchase cost is reported on its balance sheet as a current asset. When inventories are sold, their cost is removed from the balance sheet and transferred to the income statement as an expense called cost of goods sold. If some inventories acquired are not yet sold, their cost is not yet reported in cost of goods sold and net income. The subtraction of $64 relates to the increase in inventories; it reflects the fact that cost of goods sold does not include all of the cash that was spent on inventories. That is, $64 cash was spent that is not yet reflected in cost of goods sold. Thus, the $64 is deducted from net income to compute *cash profit* for the period.
Increases in accounts payable, $328	Apple purchases much of its inventories on credit. The $328 increase in accounts payable reflects inventories that have been purchased, but have not yet been paid for in cash. The add-back of this $328 to net income reflects the fact that *cash profit* is $328 higher because $328 of accounts payable are not yet paid.

deducted in computing net income. The following table provides brief explanations of adjustments for receivables, inventories, and payables and accruals:

	Change in account balance...	Means that...	Which requires this adjustment to net income to yield cash profit...
Receivables	Increase	Sales and net income increase, but cash is not yet received	Deduct increase in receivables from net income
	Decrease	More cash is received than is reported in sales and net income	Add decrease in receivables to net income
Inventories	Increase	Cash is paid for inventories that are not yet reflected in cost of goods sold	Deduct increase in inventories from net income
	Decrease	Cost of goods sold includes inventory costs that were paid for in a prior period	Add decrease in inventories to net income
Payables and accruals	Increase	More goods and services are acquired on credit, delaying cash payment	Add increase in payables and accruals to net income
	Decrease	More cash is paid than is reflected in cost of goods sold or operating expenses	Deduct decrease in payables and accruals from net income

It is also helpful to use the following decision guide, involving changes in assets, liabilities, and equity, to understand increases and decreases in cash flows.

	Cash flow increases from	Cash flow decreases from
Assets...............	Account decreases	Account increases
Liabilities and equity.....	Account increases	Account decreases

The table above applies to all sections of the statement of cash flows. To determine if a change in each asset and liability account creates a cash inflow or outflow, examine the change and apply the decision rules from the table. For example, in the investing section, cash decreases when PPE assets increase. In the financing section, borrowing from a bank increases cash. Module 3 and Appendix B near the end of the book describe the preparation of the statement of cash flows in detail.

Sometimes the cash flow effect of an item reported in the statement of cash flows does not agree with the difference in the balance sheet accounts that we observe. This can be due to several factors. One common factor is when a company uses its own stock to acquire another entity. There is no cash effect from a stock acquisition and, hence, it is not reported in the statement of cash flows. Yet, the company does increase its assets and liabilities when it adds the acquired company's assets and liabilities to its balance sheet. (We cover acquisitions in Module 7.)

Knowledge of how companies record cash inflows and outflows helps us better understand the statement of cash flows. Determining how changes in asset and liability accounts affect cash provides an analytic tool *and* offers greater insight into managing a business. For instance, reducing the levels of receivables and inventories increases cash. Similarly, increasing the levels of accounts payable and accrued liabilities increases cash. Managing cash balances by managing other accounts is called *working capital management*, which is important for all companies.

MID-MODULE REVIEW

Following are account balances ($ millions) for Dell, Inc. Using these data, prepare its income statement and statement of cash flows for the fiscal year ended February 3, 2006. Prepare its balance sheet dated February 3, 2006.

Cash and cash equivalents	$ 7,042		Inventories	$ 576
Net cash used in financing activities and other	(6,422)		Accounts payable	9,840
Long-term debt	504		Other stockholders' equity	(18,157)
Property, plant and equipment, net	2,005		Long-term Investments	2,691
Other noncurrent assets	707		Other short-term assets	2,620
Accrued and other liabilities	6,087		Retained earnings	12,746
Other noncurrent liabilities	2,549		Receivables	5,452
Short-term investments	2,016		Selling, general and administrative expenses	5,140
Income tax expense	1,002		Research and development expenses	463
Net cash provided by operating activities	4,839		Cost of revenue	45,958
Paid-in capital	9,540		Net cash provided by investing activities	3,878
Cash and cash equivalents at beginning of period	4,747		Investment and other income, net	227
Net revenue	55,908			

Solution

DELL, INC.
Balance Sheet
February 3, 2006

ASSETS		LIABILITIES AND EQUITY	
Current assets		Current liabilities	
Cash and cash equivalents	$ 7,042	Accounts payable	$ 9,840
Short-term investments	2,016	Accrued and other liabilities	6,087
Receivables	5,452	Total current liabilities	15,927
Inventories	576	Long-term debt	504
Other short-term assets	2,620	Other noncurrent liabilities	2,549
Total current assets	17,706	Total liabilities	18,980
Property, plant, and equipment, net	2,005	Stockholders' equity	
Long-term Investments	2,691	Paid-in capital	9,540
Other noncurrent assets	707	Retained earnings	12,746
		Other stockholders' equity	(18,157)
Total assets	$23,109	Total stockholders' equity	4,129
		Total liabilities and stockholders' equity	$23,109

DELL, INC.
Income Statement
For Fiscal Year Ended February 3, 2006

Net revenue	$55,908
Cost of revenue	45,958
Gross margin	9,950
Operating expenses	
Selling, general, and administrative	5,140
Research and development expenses	463
Total operating expenses	5,603
Operating income	4,347
Investment and other income, net	227
Income before income taxes	4,574
Income tax provision	1,002
Net income	$ 3,572

DELL, INC.
Statement of Cash Flows
For Fiscal Year Ended February 3, 2006

Net cash provided by operating activities	$4,839
Net cash provided by investing activities	3,878
Net cash used in financing activities and other	(6,422)
Net increase in cash and cash equivalents	2,295
Cash and cash equivalents at beginning of period	4,747
Cash and cash equivalents at end of period	$7,042

ARTICULATION OF FINANCIAL STATEMENTS

LO2 Explain and illustrate linkages among the four financial statements.

The four financial statements are linked with each other and linked across time. This linkage is called **articulation**. This section demonstrates the articulation of financial statements using Apple.

Retained Earnings Reconciliation

The balance sheet and income statement are linked via retained earnings. Recall that retained earnings is updated each period as follows:

	Beginning retained earnings
±	Net income (loss)
−	Dividends
=	Ending retained earnings

Retained earnings reflect cumulative income that has not yet been distributed to shareholders. Exhibit 2.9 shows Apple's retained earnings reconciliation for 2005.

EXHIBIT 2.9	Apple's Retained Earnings Reconciliation

APPLE, INC.
Retained Earnings Reconciliation ($ millions)
For Year Ended September 24, 2005

Retained earnings, September 25, 2004		$2,670
Add:	Net income (loss)	1,335
Less:	Dividends	0
Retained earnings, September 24, 2005		$4,005

This reconciliation of retained earnings links the balance sheet and income statement.

In the absence of transactions with stockholders—such as stock issuances and repurchases, and dividend payments—the change in stockholders' equity equals income or loss for the period. The income statement, thus, measures the change in company value as measured by *GAAP*. This is not necessarily company value as measured by the *market*. Of course, all value-relevant items eventually find their way into the income statement. So, from a macro-perspective, the income statement does measure change in company value. This is why stock prices react to reported income and to analysts' expectations about future income.

Financial Statement Linkages

Articulation of the four financial statements is shown in Exhibit 2.10. Apple begins 2005 with assets of $8,050 million, consisting of cash for $2,969 million and noncash assets for $5,081 million. These investments are financed with $2,974 million from nonowners and $5,076 million from shareholders. The owner financing consists of contributed capital of $2,514 million, retained earnings of $2,670 million, and other stockholders' equity of $(108) million.

EXHIBIT 2.10 **Articulation of Apple Financial Statements ($ millions)**

Balance Sheet
September 24, 2004

Assets	
Cash	$2,969
Noncash assets	5,081
Total assets	$8,050
Liabilities and equity	
Total liabilities	$2,974
Equity	
Contributed capital	2,514
Retained earnings	2,670
Other equity	(108)
Liabilities and equity	$8,050

Statement of Cash Flows
For Year Ended September 24, 2005

Operating cash flows	$ 2,535
Investing cash flows	(2,556)
Financing cash flows	543
Net change in cash	522
Cash balance, Sep. 25, 2004	2,969
Cash balance, Sep. 24, 2005	$ 3,491

Income Statement
For Year Ended September 24, 2005

Revenues	$13,931
Expenses	12,596
Net earnings	$ 1,335

Statement of Shareholders' Equity
For Year Ended September 24, 2005

Contributed capital, Sep. 25, 2004	$ 2,514
Stock issuance	1,007
Contributed capital, Sep. 24, 2005	$ 3,521
Retained earnings, Sep. 25, 2004	$ 2,670
Net income	1,335
Less: dividends	0
Retained earnings, Sep. 24, 2005	$ 4,005
Other equity, Sep. 25, 2004	$ (108)
Other changes in equity	48
Other equity Sep. 24, 2005	$ (60)

Balance Sheet
September 24, 2005

Assets	
Cash	$ 3,491
Noncash assets	8,060
Total assets	$11,551
Liabilities and equity	
Total liabilities	$ 4,085
Equity	
Contributed capital	3,521
Retained earnings	4,005
Other equity	(60)
Liabilities and equity	$11,551

Beginning of year — During the year — End of year

Exhibit 2.10 shows balance sheets at the beginning and end of the year on the left and right columns respectively. The middle column reflects operating activities for 2005. The statement of cash flows explains how operating, investing, and financing activities increase the cash balance by $522 million from $2,969 million at the beginning of the year to $3,491 million at year-end. The ending balance in cash is reported in the year-end balance sheet on the right.

Apple's $1,335 million net income reported on the income statement is also carried over to the statement of shareholders' equity. The net income explains the change in retained earnings reported in the statement of shareholders' equity since Apple paid no dividends in that year.

TRANSACTION ANALYSIS AND ACCOUNTING

LO3 Illustrate use of the financial statement effects template to summarize accounting transactions.

This section introduces our financial statement effects template, which is used to reflect the effects of transactions on financial statements. A more detailed explanation is in Module 3, but that module is not required to understand and apply the template.

Apple reports total assets of $11,551 million, total liabilities of $4,085 million, and equity of $7,466 million. The accounting equation for Apple follows ($ million):

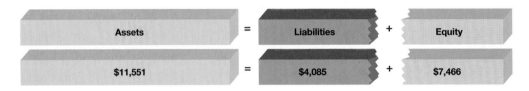

Assets	=	Liabilities	+	Equity
$11,551	=	$4,085	+	$7,466

We often draw on this relation to assess the effects of transactions and events, different accounting methods, and choices that managers make in preparing financial statements. We are interested in knowing, for example, the effects of an asset write-off (removal of an impaired asset) on the balance sheet, income statement, and cash flow statement. Or, we might want to understand how the failure to recognize a liability would understate liabilities and overstate profits and equity. To perform these sorts of analyses, we employ the following *financial statement effects template*:

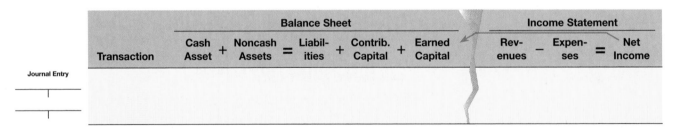

The template captures the transaction and its financial statement effects on the four financial statements: balance sheet, income statement, statement of stockholders' equity, and statement of cash flows. For the balance sheet, we differentiate between cash and noncash assets so as to identify the cash effects of transactions. Likewise, equity is separated into the contributed and earned capital components. Finally, income statement effects are separated into revenues, expenses, and net income (the updating of retained earnings is denoted with an arrow line running from net income to earned capital). This template provides a convenient means to represent relatively complex financial accounting transactions and events in a simple, concise manner for both analysis and interpretation.

In addition to using the template to show the dollar effects of a transaction on the four financial statements, we also include each transaction's *journal entry* and *T-account* representation in the margin. We explain journal entries and T-accounts in Module 3; these are part of the bookkeeping aspects of accounting. The margin entries can be ignored without any loss of insight gained from the template. (Journal entries and T-accounts use acronyms for account titles; a list of acronyms is in Appendix C near the end of the book.)

The process leading up to preparing financial statements involves two steps: (1) recording transactions during the accounting period, and (2) adjusting accounting records to reflect events that have occurred but are not yet evidenced by an external transaction. We provide a brief introduction to these two steps, followed by a comprehensive example that includes preparation of financial statements (a more detailed illustration of this process is in Module 3).

Recording Transactions

All transactions affecting a company are recorded in its accounting records. For example, assume that a company paid $100 cash wages to employees. This is reflected in the following financial statement effects template.

	Balance Sheet							Income Statement			
Transaction	Cash Asset	+	Noncash Assets	=	Liabil-ities	+	Contrib. Capital	+	Earned Capital	Rev-enues	−	Expen-ses	=	Net Income
Pay $100 cash for wages	−100 Cash			=					−100 Retained Earnings			+100 Wages Expense	=	−100

WE   100
    Cash   100
        WE
100 |
    Cash
        | 100

Cash assets are reduced by $100, and wage expense of $100 is reflected in the income statement, which reduces income and retained earnings by that amount. All transactions incurred by the company during the accounting period are recorded similarly. We show several further examples in our comprehensive illustration later in this section.

Adjusting Accounts

We must understand accounting adjustments (commonly called *accruals*) to fully analyze and interpret financial statements. In the transaction above, we record wage expense that has been earned by (and paid to) employees during the period. What if the employees were not paid for wages earned at period-end? Should the expense still be recorded? The answer is yes. The *matching principle* requires that all expenses incurred to generate, directly or indirectly, the revenues reported in the period must be recorded. This is the case even if those expenses are still unpaid at period-end. The reason is that failure to recognize wages expense would overstate net income for the period because wages have been earned and should be reported as expense in this period. Also, failure to record those wages at period-end would understate liabilities. Thus, neither the income statement nor the balance sheet would be accurate. Adjustments are, therefore, necessary to accurately portray financial condition and performance of a company.

There are four types of adjustments, which are illustrated in the following graphic.

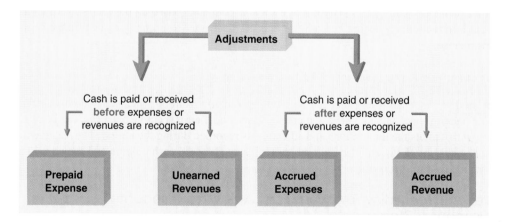

The first two adjustments (on the left) relate to the receipt or payment of cash before revenue or expense is recognized. The second two (on the right) relate to the receipt or payment of cash after revenue or expense is recognized.

Two types of adjustments arise when cash is received or paid *before* recognition of revenue or expense.

Prepaid expenses Prepaid expenses reflect advance cash payments that will ultimately become expenses; an example is the payment of radio advertising that will not be aired until sometime in the future.

Unearned revenues Unearned revenues reflect cash received from customers before any services or goods are provided; an example is cash received from patrons for tickets to an upcoming concert.

Similarly, two types of adjustments arise when cash is received or paid *after* recognition of revenue or expense.

Accrued expenses Accrued expenses are expenses incurred and recognized on the income statement, even though they are not yet paid in cash; an example is wages owed to employees who performed work but who have not yet been paid.

Accrued revenues Accrued revenues are revenues earned and recognized on the income statement, even though cash is not yet received; examples include accounts receivable and revenue earned under a long-term contract.

To illustrate the adjustment required with the wages example above, assume that the $100 of wages earned this period is paid the following period. The period-end adjustment, and subsequent payment the following period, are both reflected in the following template.

	Balance Sheet					Income Statement		
Transaction	Cash Asset	+ Noncash Assets	= Liabil-ities	+ Contrib. Capital	+ Earned Capital	Rev-enues	- Expen-ses	= Net Income
Period 1: Accrue $100 wages expense and liability			= +100 Wages Payable		-100 Retained Earnings		- +100 Wages Expense	= -100
Period 2: Pay $100 cash for wages	-100 Cash		= -100 Wages Payable					

Left margin journal entries:
WE 100
  WP 100
WE 100 | WP | 100

WP 100
  Cash 100
WP 100 | Cash | 100

Wages expense is recorded in period 1's income statement because it is incurred by the company and earned by employees in that period. Also, a liability is recorded in period 1 reflecting the company's obligation to make payment to employees. In period 2, the wages are paid, which means that both cash and the liability are reduced.

Companies make adjustments to better report their financial performance and condition. Each of these adjustments is made by company managers and accountants based on the review of financial statements and information suggesting that adjustments are necessary to properly reflect financial condition and performance.

Preparing Financial Statements

Each of the four financial statements can be prepared directly from our financial statement effects template. The balance sheet and income statement accounts, and their respective balances, can be read off the bottom row that totals the transactions and adjustments recorded during the period. The statement of cash flows and statement of stockholders' equity are represented by the cash column and the contributed and earned capital columns, respectively.

Illustration: Recording Transactions, Adjusting Accounts, and Preparing Statements

This section provides a comprehensive illustration that uses the financial statement effects template with a number of transactions related to Apple's 2005 financial statements shown earlier. These summary transactions are described in the far left column of the following template. Each column is summed to arrive at the balance sheet and income statement totals which tie to Apple's statements. Detailed explanations for each transaction are provided after the template. Then, we use the information in the template to construct Apple's financial statements.

Transaction	Cash Asset +	Noncash Assets =	Liabil- ities +	Contrib. Capital +	Earned Capital		Rev- enues −	Expen- ses =	Net Income
Balance Sept. 25, 2004	2,969	5,081 =	2,974	2,406	2,670			=	
1. Issue common stock for $1,040 cash	+1,040 Cash	=		+1,040 Common stock				=	
2. Purchase $289 of PPE, financed by $289 of long-term debt		+289 PPE, net =	+289 Long-Term Debt					=	
3. Purchase $9,952 of inventories on credit		+9,952 Inventories =	+9,952 Accounts Payable					=	
4. Sell inventories for $13,931 on credit; the cost of inventories is $9,888		+13,931 Accounts Receivable =			+13,931 Retained Earnings		+13,931 Sales	=	+13,931
		−9,888 Inventory =			−9,888 Retained Earnings			+9,888 Cost of Goods Sold =	−9,888
5. Receive $13,810 cash for accounts receivable; Pay $9,686 cash for accounts payable and other liabilities	+13,810 Cash	−13,810 Accounts Receivable =						=	
	−9,686 Cash	=	−9,686 Accounts Payable					=	
6. Pay $1,973 cash for R&D, SGA (excluding depreciation), interest, and taxes	−1,973 Cash	=			−1,973 Retained Earnings			+1,973 Operating Expenses =	−1,973
7. Accrue expenses of $556		=	+556 Accrued Liabilities		−556 Retained Earnings			+556 Operating Expenses =	−556
8. Purchase noncash assets for $2,669 cash	−2,669 Cash	+2,669 Investments in Securities =						=	
9. Record depreciation of $179		−179 PPE, net =			−179 Retained Earnings			+179 Depreciation Expense =	−179
10. Miscellaneous		+15 Other Assets =		+15 Other Accum. Comp. Income				=	
Balance, Sept. 24, 2005	3,491 +	8,060 =	4,085 +	3,461 +	4,005		13,931 −	12,596 =	1,335

Cash   1,040
    CS   1,040
        Cash
1,040 |
        CS
            | 1,040

PPE   289
    LTD   289
        PPE
289 |
        LTD
            | 289

INV   9,952
    AP   9,952
        INV
9,952 |
        AP
            | 9,952

AR   13,931
    Sales   13,931
        AR
13,931 |
        Sales
            | 13,931

COGS   9,888
    INV   9,888
        COGS
9,888 |
        INV
            | 9,888

Cash   13,810
    AR   13,810
        Cash
13,810 |
        AR
            | 13,810

AP   9,686
    Cash   9,686
        AP
9,686 |
        Cash
            | 9,686

OE   1,973
    Cash   1,973
        OE
1,973 |
        Cash
            | 1,973

OE   556
    ACC   556
        OE
556 |
        ACC
            | 556

MS   2,669
    Cash   2,669
        MS
2,669 |
        Cash
            | 2,669

DE   179
    PPE   179
        DE
179 |
        PPE
            | 179

OA   15
    AOCI   15
        OA
15 |
        AOCI
            | 15

Transaction Explanation Apple begins fiscal year 2005 with $8,050 million in total assets, consisting of $2,969 million of cash and $5,081 million of noncash assets. It also reports $2,974 million of liabilities and $5,076 million of stockholders' equity ($2,406 million of contributed capital, which includes other equity for this exhibit, and $2,670 million of earned capital). During the year, ten summary transactions occur that are described below.

1. **Owner Financing.** Companies raise funds from two sources: investing from shareholders and borrowing from creditors. Transaction 1 reflects issuance of common stock for $1,040 million. Cash is increased by that amount, as is contributed capital. Stock issuance (as well as its repurchase and any dividends paid to shareholders) does not impact income. Companies cannot record profit by trading in their own stock.

2. **Purchase PPE financed by debt.** Apple acquires $289 million of property, plant and equipment (PPE), and it finances this acquisition with a $289 million loan. Noncash assets increase by the $289 million of PPE, and liabilities increase by $289 million of long-term debt. PPE is initially reported on the balance sheet. When plant and equipment are used, a portion of the purchase cost is transferred from the balance sheet to the income statement as an expense called depreciation. Accounting for depreciation is shown in Transaction 9. The borrowing of money does not yield income, and repaying the principal amount borrowed is not an expense. Paying interest *on* liabilities, however, is an expense.

3. **Purchase inventories on credit.** Companies commonly acquire inventories from suppliers *on credit*. The phrase "on credit" means that the purchase has not yet been paid for. A purchaser is typically allowed 30 days or more during which to make payment. When acquired in this manner, noncash assets (inventories) increase by the $9,952 million cost of the acquired inventory, and a liability (accounts payable) increases to reflect the amount owed to the supplier. Although inventories (iPods, for example) normally carry a retail selling price that is higher than its cost, this eventual profit is not recognized until inventories are sold.

4. **Sell inventories on credit.** Apple subsequently sells inventories that cost $9,888 million for a retail selling price of $13,931 million *on credit*. The phrase "on credit" means that Apple has not yet received cash for the selling price; cash receipt is expected in the future. The sale of inventories is recorded in two parts: the revenue part and the expense part. First, the sale is recorded by an increase in both revenues and noncash assets (accounts receivable). Revenues increase net income which, in turn, increases earned capital. Second, the cost of inventories sold is removed from the balance sheet (Apple no longer owns those assets), and is transferred to the income statement as an expense, called *cost of goods sold,* which decreases both net income and earned capital by $9,888.

5. **Collect receivables and settle payables.** Apple receives $13,810 million cash from the collection of its accounts receivable, thus reducing noncash assets (accounts receivable) by that amount. Apple uses these proceeds to pay off $9,686 of its liabilities (accounts payable and other liabilities). There is a net increase in cash of $4,124. Collecting accounts receivable does not yield revenue; instead, revenue is recognized when *earned* (see Transaction 4). Thus, recognizing revenue when earned does not necessarily yield an immediate cash increase.

6. **Pay cash for expenses.** Apple pays $1,973 million cash for expenses. This payment increases expenses, and reduces net income (and earned capital). Expenses are recognized when incurred, regardless of when they are paid. Expenses are both incurred and paid in this transaction. Transaction 7 is a case where expenses are recognized *before* being paid.

7. **Accrue expenses.** Accrued expenses relate to expenses that are incurred but not yet paid. For example, employees often work near the end of a period but are not paid until the next period. The company must record wages expense even though employees have not yet been paid in cash. The rationale is that expenses must be *matched* against current period revenues to report the correct income for the period. In this transaction, Apple accrues $556 million of expenses, which reduces net income (and earned capital). Apple simultaneously records a $556 million increase in liabilities for its obligation to make future payment. This transaction is an accounting adjustment, or accrual.

8. **Purchase noncash assets.** Apple uses $2,669 million of its excess cash to purchase marketable securities as an investment. Thus, noncash assets increase. This is a common use of excess cash, especially for high-tech companies that desire added liquidity to take advantage of opportunities in a rapidly changing industry.

9. **Record depreciation.** Transaction 9 is another accounting adjustment. In this case, Apple recognizes that a portion of its plant and equipment is "used up" while generating revenues. Thus, it matches a portion of the PPE cost as an expense against the revenues recognized during the period. In this case, $179 million of PPE cost is removed from the balance sheet and transferred to the income statement as depreciation expense. Net income (and earned capital) is reduced by $179 million.

10. **Miscellaneous.** The final transaction is a miscellaneous adjustment to noncash assets and contributed capital.

The column totals from the financial statement effects template can be used to prepare Apple's financial statements. Apple's 2005 balance sheet and income statement are derived from the template as follows.

Balance Sheet	
Cash asset	$ 3,491
Noncash assets	8,060
Total assets	$11,551
Liabilities	$ 4,085
Contributed capital	3,461
Earned capital	4,005
Total liabilities and equity	$11,551

Income Statement	
Revenues	$13,931
Expenses	12,596
Net income	$ 1,335

A summary of Apple's cash transactions can be constructed drawing on the cash column of the template. The cash column of the financial effects template reveals that cash increases by $522 million during the year from $2,969 million to $3,491 million. Items that contribute to this net increase are identified by the cash entries in that column. Preparation of the statement of cash flows is covered in Module 3 and Appendix B.

Apple's statement of stockholders' equity summarizes the transactions relating to its equity accounts. This statement follows and is organized into its contributed capital and earned capital categories of equity.

Statement of Stockholders' Equity	Contributed Capital	Earned Capital	Total
Balance, September 25, 2004	$2,406	$2,670	$5,076
Issuance of common stock	1,040		1,040
Net income		1,335	1,335
Miscellaneous	15		15
Balance, September 24, 2005	$3,461	$4,005	$7,466

Apple's financial statements are abbreviated versions of those reproduced earlier in the module. We describe the preparation of financial statements and other accounting details at greater length in Module 3.

MODULE-END REVIEW

Part 1 At December 31, 2007, assume that the records of Hewlett-Packard show the following amounts. Use this information, as necessary, to prepare the company's 2007 income statement (ignore income taxes).

Cash	$ 3,000	Cash dividends	$ 1,000
Accounts receivable	12,000	Revenues	25,000
Office equipment	32,250	Rent expense	5,000
Land	36,000	Wages expense	8,000
Accounts payable	7,500	Utilities expense	2,000
Common stock	45,750	Other expenses	4,000

Solution

HEWLETT-PACKARD
Income Statement
For Year Ended December 31, 2007

Revenues		$25,000
Expenses		
Wages expense	$8,000	
Rent expense	5,000	
Utilities expense	2,000	
Other expenses	4,000	
Total expenses		19,000
Net income		$ 6,000

Part 2 Assume that the following is selected financial information for Hewlett-Packard for the year ended December 31, 2007.

Retained earnings, Dec. 31, 2007	$30,000	Dividends	$1,000
Net income	$6,000	Retained earnings, Dec. 31, 2006	$25,000

Reconcile its retained earnings for the 2007 fiscal year.

Solution

HEWLETT-PACKARD
Retained Earnings Reconciliation
For Year Ended December 31, 2005

Retained earnings, Dec. 31, 2006	$25,000
Add: Net income	6,000
Less: Dividends	(1,000)
Retained earnings, Dec. 31, 2007	$30,000

Part 3 Use the listing of accounts and figures reported in part 1 along with the ending retained earnings from part 2 to prepare the December 31, 2007 balance sheet for Hewlett-Packard.

Solution

HEWLETT-PACKARD Balance Sheet December 31, 2007			
Cash................	$ 3,000	Accounts payable..........	$ 7,500
Accounts receivable.....	12,000		
Office equipment	32,250	Common stock............	45,750
Land.................	36,000	Retained earnings	30,000
Total assets...........	$83,250	Total liabilities and equity.....	$83,250

APPENDIX 2A: Additional Information Sources

The four financial statements are only a part of the information available to financial statement users. Additional information, from a variety of sources, provides useful insight into company operating activities and future prospects. This section highlights additional information sources.

Form 10-K

Companies with publicly traded securities must file a detailed annual report and discussion of their business activities in their Form 10-K with the SEC (quarterly reports are filed on form 10-Q). Many of the disclosures in the 10-K are mandated by law and include the following general categories: Item 1, *Business;* Item 1A. *Risk Factors;* Item 2, *Properties;* Item 3, *Legal Proceedings;* Item 4, *Submission of Matters to a Vote of Security Holders;* Item 5, *Market for Registrant's Common Equity and Related Stockholder Matters;* Item 6, *Selected Financial Data;* Item 7, *Management's Discussion and Analysis of Financial Condition and Results of Operations;* Item 7A, *Quantitative and Qualitative Disclosures About Market Risk;* Item 8, *Financial Statements and Supplementary Data;* Item 9, *Changes in and Disagreements With Accountants on Accounting and Financial Disclosure;* Item 9A, *Controls and Procedures.*

Description of the Business (Item 1)

Companies must provide a general description of their business, including their principal products and services, the source and availability of required raw materials, all patents, trademarks, licenses, and important related agreements, seasonality of the business, any dependence upon a single customer, competitive conditions, including particular markets in which the company competes, the product offerings in those markets, and the status of its competitive environment. Companies must also provide a description of their overall strategy. Apple's partial disclosure follows:

> The Company's business strategy leverages its unique ability, through the design and development of its own operating system, hardware, and many software applications and technologies, to bring to its customers new products and solutions with superior ease-of-use, seamless integration, and innovative industrial design. The Company believes continual investment in research and development is critical to facilitate innovation of new and improved products and technologies. Besides updates to its existing line of personal computers and related software, services, peripherals, and networking solutions, the Company continues to capitalize on the convergence of digital consumer electronics and the computer by creating innovations like the iPod and iTunes Music Store. The Company's strategy also includes expanding its distribution network to effectively reach more of its targeted customers and provide them a high-quality sales and after-sales support experience.

Management's Discussion and Analysis of Financial Condition and Results of Operations (Item 7)

The management discussion and analysis (MD&A) section of the 10-K contains valuable insight into the company's results of operations. In addition to an executive overview of company status and its recent operating results, the MD&A section includes information relating to its critical accounting policies and estimates used in preparing its financial statements, a detailed discussion of its sales activity, year-over-year comparisons of operating activities, analysis of gross margin, operating expenses, taxes, and off-balance-sheet and contractual obligations, assessment of factors that affect future results and financial condition. Item 7A reports quantitative and qualitative disclosures about market risk. For example, Apple makes the following disclosure relating to its Mac operating system and its iPods.

The Company is currently the only maker of hardware using the Mac OS. The Mac OS has a minority market share in the personal computer market, which is dominated by makers of computers utilizing other competing operating systems, including Windows and Linux. The Company's future operating results and financial condition are substantially dependent on its ability to continue to develop improvements to the Macintosh platform in order to maintain perceived design and functional advantages over competing platforms. Additionally, if unauthorized copies of the Mac OS are used on other companies' hardware products and result in decreased demand for the Company's hardware products, the Company's results of operations may be adversely affected.

The Company is currently focused on market opportunities related to digital music distribution and related consumer electronic devices, including iPods. The Company faces increasing competition from other companies promoting their own digital music products, including music enabled cell phones, distribution services, and free peer-to-peer music services. These competitors include both new entrants with different market approaches, such as subscription services models, and also larger companies that may have greater technical, marketing, distribution, and other resources than those of the Company, as well as established hardware, software, and digital content supplier relationships. Failure to effectively compete could negatively affect the Company's operating results and financial position. There can be no assurance that the Company will be able to continue to provide products and services that effectively compete in these markets or successfully distribute and sell digital music outside the U.S. The Company may also have to respond to price competition by lowering prices and/ or increasing features which could adversely affect the Company's music product gross margins as well as overall Company gross margins.

Form 8-K

Another useful report that is required by the SEC and is publicly available is the Form 8-K. This form must be filed within 4 business days of any of the following events:

- Entry into or termination of a material definitive agreement (including petition for bankruptcy)
- Exit from a line of business or impairment of assets
- Change in the company's certified public accounting firm
- Change in control of the company
- Departure of the company's executive officers
- Changes in the company's articles of incorporation or bylaws

Form 8-Ks are typically used by outsiders to monitor for material adverse changes in the company.

Analyst Reports

Sell-side analysts provide their clients with objective analyses of company operating activities. Frequently, these reports include a discussion of the competitive environment for each of the company's principal product lines, strengths and weaknesses of the company, and an investment recommendation, including financial analysis and a stock price target. For example, Citigroup provides the following in its June 2006 report to clients on Apple:

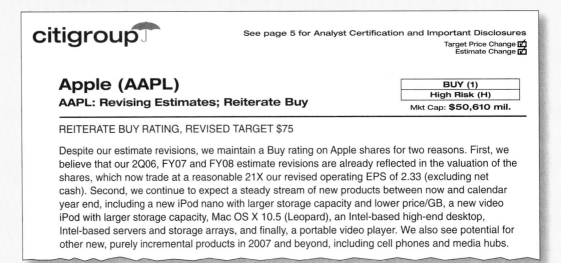

The analyst report often contains a balanced discussion of both positive and negative aspects of the company as illustrated in the following 2006 report from Bear Stearns regarding Apple.

BEAR STEARNS

IT HARDWARE

US Equity Research

June 15, 2006

Positives
- Strong brand name, fiercely loyal customer base, defensible installed base
- Innovative products and design strategies
- Incremental opportunities through "digital lifestyle" (iPod, iTunes, iDVD, iMovie, iPhoto)
- Ongoing efforts to monetize beyond-the-box revenue streams (e.g. software, paid subscription services, iTunes Store downloads) to help offset cyclicality of hardware business
- Excellent cash position and balance sheet—exited fiscal 2Q06 around $9.36 per diluted share in net cash
- Intel-based hardware and "Boot Camp" could spur upgrade cycle and new wave of demand
- Multiple growth drivers (e.g. Intel Macs, iPod nano, iPod video, iPod points of distribution)
- Ramp of flash-memory-based iPod could ignite new wave of growth for iPod business
- Improving consistency and execution (exceeded results in twelve consecutive quarters)

Concerns
- Transition risk associated with shift to Intel architecture
- Growth rates appear to be peaking and are likely to slow which can hurt a stock's P/E multiple
- Ultimate size of the music/MP3 player market is unknown along with increasing competition from multiple vendors
- Historical inability to capture a wider customer base and grow market share without a more compelling product offering to attract new users and penetrate the Wintel world, although "halo" effect appears to be playing out
- "Hit-driven" nature of business model which can produce erratic results
- Could face difficulties reconciling channel conflicts between retail stores and resellers which Apple is prepared to face to have greater control of its customer relationship

Credit Services

Several firms including Standard & Poor's (**StandardAndPoors.com**), Moody's Investors Service (**Moodys.com**), and Fitch Ratings (**FitchRatings.com**) provide credit analysis that assists potential lenders, investors, employees, and other users in evaluating a company's creditworthiness and future financial viability. Credit analysis is a specialized field of analysis, quite different from the equity analysis illustrated here. These firms issue credit ratings on publicly issued bonds as well as on firms' commercial paper.

Data Services

A number of companies supply financial statement data in easy-to-download spreadsheet formats. Thomson Corporation (**Thomson.com**) provides a wealth of information to its database subscribers, including the widely quoted *First Call* summary of analysts' earnings forecasts. Standard & Poor's provides financial data for all publicly traded companies in its *Compustat* database. This database reports a plethora of individual data items for all publicly traded companies or for any specified subset of companies. These data are useful for performing statistical analysis and making comparisons across companies or within industries.

GUIDANCE ANSWERS

MANAGERIAL DECISION   **You are the Securities Analyst**

Of special concern is the possibility that the new CEO is shifting costs to the current period in lieu of recording them in future periods. Evidence suggests that such behavior occurs when a new management team takes control. The reasoning is that the new management can blame poor current period performance on prior management and, at the same time, rid the balance sheet (and new management team) of costs that would normally be expensed in future periods.

MANAGERIAL DECISION	You are the Operations Manager

The CFO desires a warranty cost estimate that matches the sales generated from the new product. To arrive at such an estimate, you must estimate the number and types of deficiencies in your product and the costs associated with each per the warranty provisions. This is often a difficult task for product engineers because it forces them to focus on product failures and associated costs.

Superscript ^A denotes assignments based on Appendix 2A.

DISCUSSION QUESTIONS

Q2-1. The balance sheet consists of assets, liabilities, and equity. Define each category and provide two examples of accounts reported within each category.

Q2-2. Two important concepts that guide income statement reporting are the revenue recognition principle and the matching principle. Define and explain each of these two guiding principles.

Q2-3. GAAP is based on the concept of accrual accounting. Define and describe accrual accounting.

Q2-4. Analysts attempt to identify transitory items in an income statement. Define transitory items. What is the purpose of identifying transitory items?

Q2-5. What is the statement of stockholders' equity? What useful information does it contain?

Q2-6. What is the statement of cash flows? What useful information does it contain?

Q2-7. Define and explain the concept of financial statement articulation. What insight comes from understanding articulation?

Q2-8. Describe the flow of costs for the purchase of a machine. At what point do such costs become expenses? Why is it necessary to record the expenses related to the machine in the same period as the revenues it produces?

Q2-9. What are the two essential characteristics of an asset?

Q2-10. What does the concept of liquidity refer to? Explain.

Q2-11. What does the term *current* denote when referring to assets?

Q2-12. Assets are recorded at historical costs even though current market values might, arguably, be more relevant to financial statement readers. Describe the reasoning behind historical cost usage.

Q2-13. Identify three intangible assets that are likely to be *excluded* from the balance sheet because they cannot be reliably measured.

Q2-14. Identify three intangible assets that are recorded on the balance sheet.

Q2-15. What are accrued liabilities? Provide an example.

Q2-16. Define net working capital. Explain how increasing the amount of trade credit can reduce the net working capital for a company.

Q2-17. What is the difference between company *book value* and *market value*? Explain why these two amounts differ.

Q2-18. The financial statement effects template includes an arrow line running from net income to earned capital. What does this arrow line denote?

MINI EXERCISES

M2-19. **Identifying and Classifying Financial Statement Items** (LO1)

For each of the following items, indicate whether they would be reported in the balance sheet (B) or income statement (I).

a.	Net income	*d.*	Accumulated depreciation	*g.*	Interest expense
b.	Retained earnings	*e.*	Wages expense	*h.*	Interest payable
c.	Depreciation expense	*f.*	Wages payable	*i.*	Sales

M2-20. Identifying and Classifying Financial Statement Items (LO1)

For each of the following items, indicate whether they would be reported in the balance sheet (B) or income statement (I).

a.	Machinery	*e.*	Common stock	*i.*	Taxes expense
b.	Supplies expense	*f.*	Factory buildings	*j.*	Cost of goods sold
c.	Inventories	*g.*	Receivables	*k.*	Long-term debt
d.	Sales	*h.*	Taxes payable	*l.*	Treasury stock

M2-21. Computing and Comparing Income and Cash Flow Measures (LO1)

Healy Corporation recorded service revenues of $100,000 in 2007, of which $70,000 were on credit and $30,000 were for cash. Moreover, of the $70,000 credit sales for 2007, Healy collected $20,000 cash on those receivables before year-end 2007. The company also paid $25,000 cash for 2007 wages. Its employees also earned another $15,000 in wages for 2007, which were not yet paid at year-end 2007. (a) Compute the company's net income for 2007. (b) How much net cash inflow or outflow did the company generate in 2007? Explain why Healy's net income and net cash flow differ.

M2-22. Assigning Accounts to Sections of the Balance Sheet (LO1)

Identify each of the following accounts as a component of assets (A), liabilities (L), or equity (E).

a.	Cash and cash equivalents	_____	*e.*	Long-term debt	_____
b.	Wages payable	_____	*f.*	Retained earnings	_____
c.	Common stock	_____	*g.*	Additional paid-in capital	_____
d.	Equipment	_____	*h.*	Taxes payable	_____

M2-23. Computing Performance Measures Using the Accounting Equation (LO1)

Use your knowledge of accounting relations to complete the following table for Trenton Company.

	2005	2006
Beginning retained earnings.	$89,089	$?
Net income (loss)	?	48,192
Dividends	0	15,060
Ending retained earnings	69,634	?

M2-24. Reconciling Retained Earnings (LO1)

Following is financial information from Johnson & Johnson for the 2005 fiscal year ended January 1, 2006. Prepare the 2005 fiscal-year retained earnings reconciliation for Johnson & Johnson ($ millions).

Johnson & Johnson (JNJ)

Retained earnings, Jan. 2, 2005.	$35,223	Dividends.	$3,793
Net earnings.	10,411	Retained earnings, Jan. 1, 2006	?
Other retained earnings changes	(370)		

M2-25. Analyzing Transactions to Compute Net Income (LO1)

Guay Corp., a start-up company, provided services that were acceptable to its customers and billed those customers for $350,000 in 2007. However, Guay collected only $280,000 cash in 2007, and the remaining $70,000 of 2007 revenues were collected in 2008. Guay employees earned $200,000 in 2007 wages that were not paid until the first week of 2008. How much net income does Guay report for 2007? For 2008 (assuming no new transactions)?

M2-26. Analyzing Transactions using the Financial Statement Effects Template (LO3)

Report the effects for each of the following independent transactions using the financial statement effects template.

a. Issue stock for $1,000 cash.
b. Purchase inventory for $500 cash.
c. Sell inventory in transaction *b* for $2,000 on credit.
d. Receive $2,000 cash toward transaction *c* receivable.

EXERCISES

E2-27. Constructing Financial Statements from Account Data (LO1)

Barth Company reports the following year-end account balances at December 31, 2007. Prepare the 2007 income statement and the balance sheet as of December 31, 2007.

Accounts payable.	$ 16,000	Inventory	$ 36,000
Accounts receivable.	30,000	Land.	80,000
Bonds payable, long-term	200,000	Goodwill.	8,000
Buildings.	151,000	Retained earnings	60,000
Cash.	48,000	Sales revenue.	400,000
Common stock.	150,000	Supplies inventory	3,000
Cost of goods sold.	180,000	Supplies expense.	6,000
Equipment	70,000	Wages expense	40,000

E2-28. Constructing Financial Statements from Transaction Data (LO1)

Baiman Corporation commences operations at the beginning of January. It provides its services on credit and bills its customers $30,000 for January sales. Its employees also earn January wages of $12,000 that are not paid until the first of February. Complete the following statements for the month-end of January.

Income Statement			Balance Sheet		
Sales.	$		Cash.	$	
Wages expense			Accounts receivable.		
Net income (loss)	$		Total assets.	$	
			Wages payable.	$	
			Retained earnings		
			Total liabilities and equity . . .	$	

E2-29. Analyzing and Reporting Financial Statement Effects of Transactions (LO3)

L. Demers launched a professional services firm on March 1. The firm will prepare financial statements at each month-end. In March (its first month), Demers executed the following transactions. Prepare an income statement for Demers Company for the month of March.

a. Demers (owner) invested in the company, $100,000 cash and $20,000 in property and equipment. The company issued common stock to Demers.

b. The company paid $3,200 cash for rent of office furnishings and facilities for March.

c. The company performed services for clients and immediately received $4,000 cash earned.

d. The company performed services for clients and sent a bill for $14,000 with payment due within 60 days.

e. The company compensated an office employee with $4,800 cash as salary for March.

f. The company received $10,000 cash as partial payment on the amount owed from clients in transaction d.

g. The company paid $935 cash in dividends to Demers (owner).

E2-30. Analyzing Transactions Using the Financial Statement Effects Template (LO3)

Enter the effects of each of the transactions a through g from Exercise 2-29 using the financial statement effects template shown in the module.

E2-31. Identifying and Classifying Balance Sheet and Income Statement Accounts   (LO1)

Following are selected accounts for Procter & Gamble. (*a*) Indicate the appropriate classification of each account as appearing in either its balance sheet (B) or its income statement (I). (*b*) Using the following data, compute total assets and total expenses. (*c*) Compute its net profit margin (net income/sales) and its total liabilities-to-equity ratio (total liabilities/stockholders' equity).

Procter & Gamble (PG)

($ millions)	Amount	Classification
Sales.	$43,373	
Accumulated depreciation	10,438	
Depreciation expense.	1,703	
Retained earnings	11,686	
Net income.	5,186	
Property, plant & equipment, net	13,104	
Selling, general & administrative expense	13,009	
Accounts receivable.	3,038	
Total liabilities.	27,520	
Stockholders' equity	16,186	

E2-32. Identifying and Classifying Balance Sheet and Income Statement Accounts   (LO1)

Following are selected accounts for Target Corporation. (*a*) Indicate the appropriate classification of each account as appearing in either its balance sheet (B) or its income statement (I). (*b*) Using the following data, compute total assets and total expenses. (*c*) Compute its net profit margin (net income/sales) and its total liability-to-equity ratio (total liabilities/stockholders' equity).

Target Corporation (TGT)

($ millions)	Amount	Classification
Sales.	$48,163	
Accumulated depreciation	6,178	
Depreciation expense.	1,320	
Retained earnings	9,648	
Net income.	1,841	
Property, plant & equipment, net	16,969	
Selling, general & administrative expense	11,534	
Accounts receivable.	5,776	
Total liabilities.	20,327	
Stockholders' equity	11,065	

E2-33. Comparing TJX and Abercrombie & Fitch   (LO1)

Following are selected income statement and balance sheet data from two retailers: Abercrombie & Fitch (clothing retailer in the high-end market) and TJX Companies (clothing retailer in the value-priced market).

Abercrombie & Fitch (ANF)

TJX Companies (TJX)

Income Statement ($ millions)	ANF	TJX
Sales.	$2,021	$14,913
Cost of goods sold.	680	11,399
Gross profit.	1,341	3,514
Total expenses	1,125	2,904
Net income.	$ 216	$ 610

Balance Sheet ($ millions)	ANF	TJX
Current assets	$ 672	$ 2,905
Long-term assets	715	2,170
Total assets.	$1,387	$ 5,075
Current liabilities.	$429	$ 2,204
Long-term liabilities	288	1,124
Total liabilities	717	3,328
Stockholders' equity	670	1,747
Total liabilities and equity	$1,387	$ 5,075

a. Express each income statement account as a percentage of sales. Comment on any differences observed between these two companies, especially as they relate to their respective business models.

b. Express each balance sheet account as a percentage of total assets. Comment on any differences observed between these two companies, especially as they relate to their respective business models.

c. Which company has a higher proportion of stockholders' equity (and a lower proportion of debt)? What do the ratios tell us about relative riskiness of the two companies?

E2-34. **Comparing Apple and Dell** (LO1)

Apple (AAPL)
Dell (DELL)

Following are selected income statement and balance sheet data from two computer competitors: Apple and Dell.

Income Statement ($ millions)	Apple	Dell
Sales.	$13,931	$49,205
Cost of goods sold.	9,888	40,190
Gross profit.	4,043	9,015
Total expenses	2,708	5,972
Net income.	$ 1,335	$ 3,043

Balance Sheet ($ millions)	Apple	Dell
Current assets	$10,300	$16,897
Long-term assets	1,251	6,318
Total assets.	$11,551	$23,215
Current liabilities.	$ 3,484	$14,136
Long-term liabilities	601	2,594
Total liabilities	4,085	16,730
Stockholders' equity	7,466	6,485
Total liabilities and equity	$11,551	$23,215

a. Express each income statement account as a percentage of sales. Comment on any differences observed between the two companies, especially as they relate to their respective business models. (*Hint:* Apple's gross profit as a percentage of sales is considerably higher than Dell's. What aspect of Apple's business do we believe is driving its profitability?)

b. Apple has chosen to structure itself with a higher proportion of equity (and a lower proportion of debt) than Dell. What implication does this capital structure decision have for an evaluation of the relative riskiness of these two companies?

E2-35. **Comparing Income Statements and Balance Sheets of Competitors** (LO1)

Following are selected income statement and balance sheet data for two communications companies: Comcast and Verizon.

Income Statement ($ millions)	Comcast	Verizon
Sales.	$22,255	$75,112
Cost of goods sold.	7,969	25,469
Gross profit.	14,286	49,643
Total expenses	13,358	42,246
Net income.	$ 928	$ 7,397

Balance Sheet ($ millions)	Comcast	Verizon
Current assets	$ 2,954	$ 16,448
Long-term assets	100,192	151,682
Total assets.	$103,146	$168,130
Current liabilities.	$ 6,269	$ 25,063
Long-term liabilities	56,001	76,633
Total liabilities.	62,270	101,696
Stockholders' equity	40,876	66,434
Total liabilities and equity	$103,146	$168,130

a. Express each income statement account as a percentage of sales. Comment on any differences observed between the two companies, especially as they relate to their respective business models.

b. Express each balance sheet account as a percentage of total assets. Comment on any differences observed between the two companies, especially as they relate to their respective business models.

c. Both Verizon and Comcast have chosen a capital structure with a higher proportion of liabilities than equity. What implications does this capital structure decision have for our evaluation of the riskiness of these two companies? Take into consideration the large level of capital expenditures that each must make to remain competitive.

E2-36. **Comparing Financial Information Across Industries** (LO1)

Use the data and computations required in parts *a* and *b* of exercises E2-33 and E2-35 to compare TJX Companies and Verizon Communications.

a. Compare gross profit and net income as a percentage of sales for these two companies. How might differences in their respective business models explain the differences observed?

b. Compare sales versus total assets. What do observed differences indicate about the relative capital intensity of these two industries?

c. Which company has the highest percentage of total liabilities to stockholders' equity? What do differences in this percentage imply about the relative riskiness of these two companies?

d. Verizon requires large annual expenditures on new equipment to remain competitive with other companies in the communications industry. What implications does its debt level have for its ability to fund those expenditures?

e. Compare the ratio of net income to stockholders' equity for these two companies. Which business model appears to be yielding the highest returns on shareholder investment? Using answers to parts *a* through *d* above, identify the factors that appear to drive the ratio of net income to stockholders' equity.

E2-37. **Analyzing Transactions using the Financial Statement Effects Template** (LO3)

Record the effect of each of the following independent transactions using the financial statement effects template.

a. Wages of $500 are earned by employees but not yet paid.
b. $2,000 of inventory is purchased on credit.
c. Inventory purchased in transaction b is sold for $3,000 on credit.
d. Collected $3,000 cash from transaction c.
e. Equipment is acquired for $5,000 cash.
f. Recorded $1,000 depreciation expense on equipment from transaction e.
g. Paid $10,000 cash toward a note payable that came due.
h. Paid $2,000 cash for interest on borrowings.

PROBLEMS

P2-38. **Constructing and Analyzing Balance Sheet Amounts from Incomplete Data** (LO1)

3M Company (MMM)

Selected balance sheet amounts for 3M Company, a manufacturer of consumer and business products, for five recent years follow.

$ millions	Current Assets	Long-Term Assets	Total Assets	Current Liabilities	Long-Term Liabilities	Total Liabilities	Stockholders' Equity
2001	$6,296	$?	$14,606	$4,509	$?	$ 8,520	$ 6,086
2002	?	9,270	15,329	4,457	4,879	9,336	?
2003	7,720	9,880	?	?	4,633	9,715	7,885
2004	8,720	11,988	?	6,071	4,259	?	10,378
2005	?	13,398	20,513	5,238	5,175	10,413	?

Required

a. Compute the missing balance sheet amounts for each of the five years shown.
b. What types of accounts would we expect to be included in current assets? In long-term assets?

P2-39. **Analyzing, Reconstructing and Interpreting Balance Sheet Data** (LO1)

Abercrombie & Fitch (ANF)

Selected balance sheet amounts for Abercrombie & Fitch, a retailer of name-brand apparel at premium prices, for five recent years follow.

$ millions	Current Assets	Long-Term Assets	Total Assets	Current Liabilities	Long-Term Liabilities	Total Liabilities	Stockholders' Equity
2002	$?	$365	?	$164	$?	$175	$595
2003	601	394	?	211	34	245	?
2004	753	?	1,383	?	214	525	858
2005	671	716	?	429	?	?	669
2006	947	?	1,790	?	303	795	?

Required

a. Compute the missing balance sheet amounts for each of the five years shown.
b. What asset category would we expect to constitute the majority of Abercrombie's current assets?
c. Does the company appear to be conservatively financed; that is, financed by a greater proportion of equity than of debt? Explain

P2-40. **Analyzing, Reconstructing and Interpreting Balance Sheet Data** (LO1)

Selected balance sheet amounts for Albertsons Inc., a grocery company, for five recent years follow.   Albertsons Inc.

$ millions	Current Assets	Long-Term Assets	Total Assets	Current Liabilities	Long-Term Liabilities	Total Liabilities	Equity Stockholders'
2002	$4,609	$?	$15,967	$3,582	$?	$10,052	$5,915
2003	4,268	10,943	?	3,448	6,566	?	?
2004	?	10,975	15,394	3,685	6,328	10,013	?
2005	4,295	14,016	?	4,085	?	?	5,421
2006	4,355	?	17,871	?	8,284	12,164	5,707

Required

a. Compute the missing balance sheet amounts for each of the five years shown.

b. What asset category would we expect to constitute the majority of Albertsons' current assets? Of its long-term assets?

c. Is the company conservatively financed; that is, is it financed by a greater proportion of equity than of debt? Explain.

P2-41. **Comparing Operating Characteristics Across Industries** (LO1)

Following are selected income statement and balance sheet data for companies in different industries.

$ millions	Sales	Cost of Goods Sold	Gross Profit	Net income	Assets	Liabilities	Stockholders' Equity
Harley-Davidson	$ 5,342	$ 3,302	$ 2,040	$ 960	$ 5,255	$ 2,171	$ 3,084
Nike, Inc.	13,740	7,624	6,116	1,212	8,794	3,149	5,645
Starbucks Corp.	6,369	2,605	3,764	494	3,514	1,423	2,091
Target Corp.	51,271	34,927	16,344	2,408	34,995	20,790	14,205

Harley-Davidson (HOG)
Nike (NKE)
Starbucks (SBUX)
Target (TGT)

Required

a. Compute the following ratios for each company.

1. Gross profit / Sales
2. Net income / Sales
3. Net income / Stockholders' equity
4. Liabilities / Stockholders' equity

b. Comment on any differences we observe among the companies' gross profit to sales ratios and net income as a percentage of sales. Do differences in the companies' business models explain the differences observed?

c. Which company reports the highest ratio of net income to equity? Suggest one or more reasons for this result.

d. Which company has financed itself with the highest percentage of liabilities to equity? Suggest one or more reasons why this company can take on such debt levels.

P2-42. **Comparing Cash Flows Across Retailers** (LO1)

Following are selected accounts from the income statement and the statement of cash flows for several retailers.

$ millions	Sales	Net Income	Cash Flows from Operating	Cash Flows from Investing	Cash Flows from Financing
Federated Dept. Stores	$ 22,390	$ 1,406	$ 1,950	$ (2,506)	$ (58)
Home Depot, Inc.	81,511	5,838	6,484	(4,586)	(1,612)
Staples, Inc.	16,079	834	1,235	(634)	(621)
Target Corp.	52,620	2,408	4,451	(4,149)	(899)
Wal-Mart Stores	312,427	11,231	17,633	(14,183)	(2,422)

Federated (FD)
Home Depot (HD)
Staples (SPLS)
Target (TGT)
Wal-Mart (WMT)

Required

a. Compute the ratio of net income to sales for each company. Rank the companies on the basis of this ratio. Do their respective business models give insight into these differences?

b. Compute net cash flows from operating activities as a percentage of sales. Rank the companies on the basis of this ratio. Does this ranking coincide with the ratio rankings from part a? Suggest one or more reasons for any differences you observe.

c. Compute net cash flows from investing activities as a percentage of sales. Rank the companies on the basis of the absolute value of this ratio. Does this ranking coincide with the ratio rankings from part a? Suggest one or more reasons for any differences you observe.

d. Each of these companies report negative cash flows from financing activities. What does it mean for a company to have net cash *outflow* from financing?

P2-43. Interpreting the Statement of Cash Flows (LO1)

Wal-Mart (WMT)

Following is the statement of cash flows for Wal-Mart Stores, Inc.

WAL-MART STORES, INC	
Statement of Cash Flows ($ millions)	
For Year Ended January 31, 2006	
Operating activities	
Net income.	$11,231
Depreciation.	4,717
Increase in accounts receivable.	(456)
Increase in inventories	(1,733)
Increase in accounts payable.	2,390
Increase in accrued liabilities.	993
Other.	491
Net cash flows from operating activities	17,633
Investing activities	
Purchase of property and equipment.	(14,563)
Other.	380
Net cash flows from investing activities.	(14,183)
Financing activities	
Increase in debt	3,916
Purchase of company stock.	(3,580)
Dividends paid	(2,511)
Other.	(349)
Net cash flows from financing activities.	(2,524)
Net increase in cash and cash equivalents	$ 926
Cash at beginning of year	5,488
Cash at end of year	$ 6,414

Required

a. Why does Wal-Mart add back depreciation to compute net cash flows from operating activities?

b. Wal-Mart reports a cash outflow of $1,733 million from an increase in inventories and a cash inflow of $2,390 million from an increase in accounts payable. How does Wal-Mart's relative bargaining power with its suppliers affect cash outflows for inventory purchases?

c. Wal-Mart reports that it invested $14,563 million in property and equipment. Is this an appropriate amount for Wal-Mart to invest? Would our opinion change if the expenditure was to purchase another company rather than to purchase separate assets?

d. Wal-Mart indicates that it paid $3,580 million to repurchase its common stock in 2005 and, in addition, paid dividends of $2,511 million. Thus, Wal-Mart paid $6,091 million of cash to its shareholders during the year. How do we evaluate that use of cash relative to other possible uses for Wal-Mart's cash?

e. Provide an overall assessment of Wal-Mart's cash flows for 2005. In the analysis, consider the sources and uses of cash.

P2-44. **Interpreting the Statement of Cash Flows** (LO1)
Following is the statement of cash flows for Verizon.

Verizon (VZ)

VERIZON Statement of Cash Flows For Year Ended December 31, 2005 ($ millions)	
Operating activities	
Net income	$ 7,397
Depreciation	14,047
Increase in accounts receivable	(933)
Increase in inventories	(252)
Decrease in accounts payable and accrued liabilities .	(1,034)
Other.	2,787
Net cash flows from operating activities	22,012
Investing activities	
Purchase of property and equipment.	(15,324)
Other.	(3,168)
Net cash flows from investing activities.	(18,492)
Financing activities	
Increase in debt	3,616
Repayment of debt.	(3,919)
Purchase of company stock.	(304)
Dividends paid	(4,427)
Net cash flows from financing activities.	(5,034)
Net decrease in cash and cash equivalents.	$ (1,514)
Cash at beginning of year	2,290
Cash at end of year	$ 776

Required

a. Why does Verizon add back depreciation to compute net cash flows from operating activities?

b. What does the size of the depreciation add-back indicate about the relative capital intensity of this industry?

c. Verizon reports that it invested $15,324 million in property and equipment. These expenditures are necessitated by market pressures as the company faces stiff competition from other communications companies, such as Comcast. Where in the 10-K might we find additional information about these capital expenditures to ascertain whether Verizon is addressing the company's most pressing needs?

d. Verizon's statement of cash flows indicates that the company paid $3,919 million in debt payments, financed, in part, by the additional borrowing of $3,616 million on short-term notes. Is this a good strategy?

e. During the year, Verizon paid dividends of $4,427 million but did not repay a sizeable portion of its debt. How should we assess the payment of dividends? Specifically, how do dividend payments differ from debt payments?

f. Provide an overall assessment of Verizon's cash flows for 2005. In the analysis, consider the sources and uses of cash.

P2-45. **Analyzing Transactions using the Financial Statement Effects Template** (LO3)
On March 1, S. Penman (owner) launched AniFoods, Inc., an organic foods retailing company. Following are the transactions for its first month of business.

a. S. Penman (owner) contributed $100,000 cash to the company in return for common stock. Penman also lent the company $55,000. This $55,000 note is due one year hence.

b. The company purchased equipment in the amount of $50,000, paying $10,000 cash and signing a note payable to the equipment manufacturer for the remaining balance.

c. The company purchased inventory for $80,000 cash in March.

d. The company had March sales of $100,000 of which $60,000 was for cash and $40,000 on credit. Total cost of goods sold for its March sales was $70,000.

e. The company purchased future advertising time from a local radio station for $10,000 cash.

f. During March, $7,500 worth of radio spots purchased in *e* are aired. The remaining spots will be aired in April.

g. Employee wages earned and paid during March total $15,000 cash.

h. Prior to disclosing the financial statements, the company recognized that employees had earned an additional $1,000 in wages that will be paid in the next period.

i. The company recorded $2,000 of depreciation for March relating to its equipment.

Required

Record the effect of each transaction using the financial statement effects template shown in the module.

P2-46.   Preparing an Income Statement and Balance Sheet from Transaction Data   (LO1)

Use the information in Problem 2-45 to complete the following requirement.

Required

Prepare a March income statement and a balance sheet as of the end of March, for AniFoods, Inc.

P2-47.   Reconciling and Computing Operating Cash Flows from Net Income   (LO1)

Petroni Company reports the following selected results for its calendar year 2005.

Net income.	$130,000
Depreciation expense.	25,000
Accounts receivable increase. . . .	10,000
Accounts payable increase	6,000
Prepaid expenses decrease.	3,000
Wages payable decrease	4,000

Required

a. Prepare the operating section only of Petroni Company's statement of cash flows for 2005.

b. Does the positive sign on depreciation expense indicate that the company is generating cash by recording depreciation? Explain.

c. Explain why the increase in accounts receivable is a use of cash in the statement of cash flows.

d. Explain why the decrease in prepaid expense is a source of cash in the statement of cash flows.

CASES

C2-48. **Management Application: Understanding Company Operating Cycle and Management Strategy** (LO1)

Consider the operating cycle as depicted in Exhibit 2.4, to answer the following questions.

a. Why might a company want to reduce its cash cycle? (*Hint*: Consider the financial statement implications of reducing the cash cycle.)

b. How might a company reduce its cash cycle?

c. Examine and discuss the potential impacts on *customers* and *suppliers* of taking the actions identified in part *b.*

C2-49. **Ethics and Governance: Understanding Revenue Recognition and Expense Matching** (LO1)

Revenue should be recognized when it is earned and expense when incurred. Given some lack of specificity in these terms, companies have some latitude when applying GAAP to determine when to recognize revenues and expenses. A few companies use this latitude to manage reported earnings. Some have argued that it is not necessarily bad for companies to manage earnings in that, by doing so, management (1) can better provide investors and creditors with reported earnings that are closer to "core" earnings (that is, management purges earnings of components deemed irrelevant or distracting so that share prices better reflect company performance); and (2) presents the company in the best light, which benefits both shareholders and employees—a Machiavellian argument that 'the end justifies the means.'

a. Is it good that GAAP is written as broadly as it is? Explain. What are the pros and cons of defining accounting terms more strictly?

b. Assess (both pro and con) the Machiavellian argument above that defends managing earnings.

Constructing Financial Statements and Analyzing Transactions

LEARNING OBJECTIVES

LO1 Analyze and record transactions using the financial statement effects template. (p. 3-4)

LO2 Prepare and explain accounting adjustments and their financial statement effects. (p. 3-9)

LO3 Explain and construct the trial balance. (p. 3-13)

LO4 Construct financial statements from account balances. (p. 3-16)

LO5 Describe the closing process. (p. 3-21)

APPLE

In late 2001, Apple Computer launched the iPod, arguably the most important product in the company's history. A basic hard-drive-based player, the iPod was not a new concept. Yet, Apple created a durable, slim, and sexy package, paired it with ear buds, and made the iPod a fashion statement as well as a great music player. Marrying the hardware with the intuitive Apple-like software for navigation, the company had a winning combination. By the end of 2001, nearly 125,000 iPods had flown off the shelves.

The following March, Apple launched a 10 GB version of the iPod followed by a 20 GB version in July. Apple soon introduced its scroll wheel, similar to a touch pad with no moving parts. Apple sold 700,000 iPods in 2002.

The company announced even more innovations in early 2003: a 30 GB version, an improved connector that could use both FireWire and USB ports, and, the biggest coup: the iTunes music store. With that innovation, consumers could play songs on a PC, burn songs to a CD, or download them to their iPod. 2003 also witnessed the advent of the now-famous marketing campaign showcasing black silhouettes holding the blazing white iPod while dancing to its tunes. By mid-2003, Apple announced a new 40 GB version and unit sales soared to 939,000.

Apple soon introduced a smaller model, the iPod mini in five colors, and boasted more sophisticated ear buds to reduce background noise. But the major innovation was the advent of iPod video. The iPod was now a complete audio-visual phenomenon and well positioned to compete in the growing handheld communications market. 2004 unit sales were 4.4

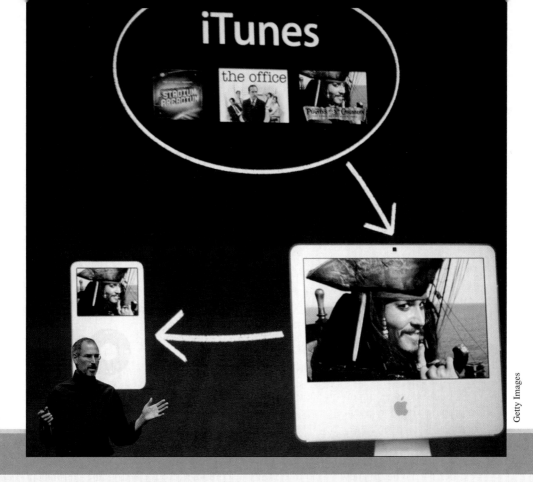

million, a 370% increase over the prior year! But the story wasn't over: in 2005, Apple sold a staggering 22 million iPods for a total of $4.5 billion. And in 2006, iTunes sold more than a billion songs.

To bring each iPod to market, Apple must purchase component parts, manufacture the iPods, hire sales personnel, pay advertisers, and distribute finished iPods. Each of these activities involves a transaction that Apple's accounting records must capture. The resulting financial statements tell the story of Apple's manufacturing and sales process in financial language.

This module explains how the accounting system captures business transactions, creates financial records, and aggregates the individual records to produce the financial reports that we read and interpret in company 10-Ks.

Sources: Apple 2005 Annual Report; osViews.com, May 03, 2005; Apple 2005 10-K; *Fortune*, January 2007.

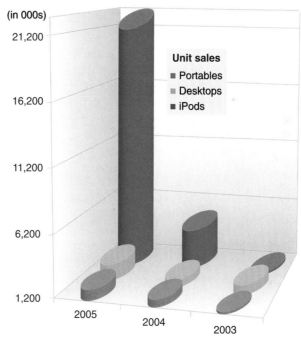

(in 000s)

Unit sales
■ Portables
■ Desktops
■ iPods

21,200
16,200
11,200
6,200
1,200

2005   2004   2003

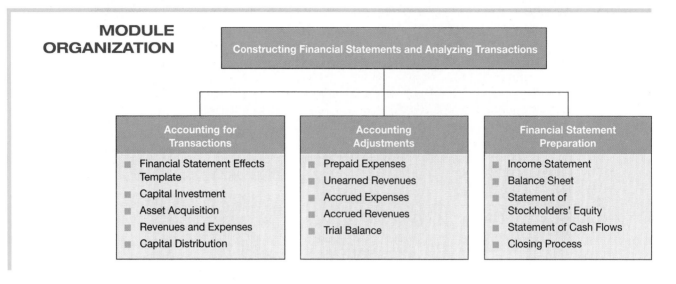

INTRODUCTION

Financial statements report on the financial performance of a business using the language of accounting. To prepare these statements, companies translate day-to-day transactions into accounting records (called journals), and then record (post) them to individual accounts. At the end of an accounting period, each of these accounts is totaled, and the resulting balances are used to prepare financial statements. After the financial statements are prepared, the temporary (income statement) accounts are 'zeroed out' so that the next period can begin anew—akin to clearing a scoreboard for the next game. Permanent (balance sheet) accounts continue to reflect financial position and carry over from period to period—akin to keeping track of wins and losses even when a particular scoreboard is cleared.

The accounting cycle is illustrated in Exhibit 3.1. Transactions are first recorded in the accounting records. Each of these transactions is, generally, the result of an external transaction, such as recording a sale to a customer or the payment of wages to employees. Once all of the transactions have been recorded during the accounting period, the company adjusts the accounting records to recognize a number of events that have occurred, but which have not yet been recorded. These might include the recognition of wage expense and the related wages payable for those employees who have earned wages, but have not yet been paid, or the recognition of depreciation expense for buildings and equipment. These adjustments are made at the end of the accounting period to properly adjust the accounting records in preparation of financial statements. Once all adjustments are made, financial statements are prepared. Details of the accounting cycle are described in this module.

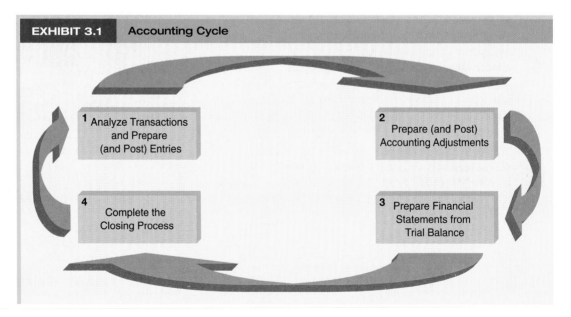

Understanding the financial statement preparation process requires an understanding of the language used to record business transactions in accounting records. The recording and statement preparation processes are readily understood once we learn that language (of financial effects) and its mechanics (entries and posting). The goal of this module is to explain that language and those mechanics.

Even if we never journalize a transaction or prepare a financial statement, understanding the accounting process aids us in analyzing and interpreting accounting reports. Understanding the accounting language also aids communication with business professionals within a company and with members of the business community outside of a company.

ACCOUNTING FOR TRANSACTIONS

This section explains how we account for and assess business transactions. We describe the financial statement effects template that we use throughout the book. We then illustrate its application to four main categories of business transactions.

LO1 Analyze and record transactions using the financial statement effects template.

Financial Statement Effects Template

Transaction analysis refers to the process of analyzing, identifying, and recording the financial statement effects of transactions. For this purpose, we use the following **financial statement effects template**.

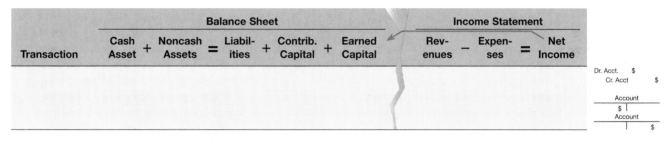

Each transaction is identified in the "Transaction" column. Then, the dollar amounts (positive or negative) of the financial statement effects are recorded in the appropriate balance sheet or income statement columns. The template also reflects the statement of cash flow effects (via the cash column) and the statement of stockholders' equity effects (via the contributed capital and earned capital columns). The retained earnings account, one of the accounts in earned capital, is immediately updated to reflect any income or loss arising from each transaction (denoted by the arrow line from net income to earned capital). This template is instructive as it reveals the financial impacts of transactions, and it provides insights into the effects of accounting choices.

T-Accounts and Journal Entries

In the margin next to the financial statement effects template are shown the related journal entry and T-account effects. The **T-Accounts,** named for their likeness to a large 'T', are used to reflect increases and decreases to individual accounts. When a transaction occurs, it is recorded (*journalized*) in the accounting books (*general ledger*) of the company, and the affected accounts are increased or decreased. This process of continuously updating individual account balances from transactions is referred to as *posting* transactions to accounts. A T-account provides a simple illustration of the financial effects of each transaction.

Specifically, one side of the T-account is used for increases and the other for decreases. A convenient way to remember which side records increases is to recall the accounting equation: **Assets = Liabilities + Equity.** Assets are on the left side of the equation. So, the left side of an asset T-account records increases in the asset—the right side records decreases. Liabilities and equity are on the right side of the accounting equation. So, the right side of a liability and an equity T-account records increases and the left side records decreases. This relation is represented graphically as follows.

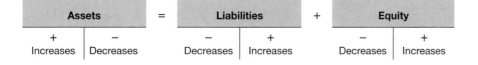

Journal entries also capture the effects of transactions. Journal entries reflect increases and decreases to accounts using the language of debits and credits. Debits and credits are "directions" that simply refer to the left or right side of a T-account, respectively. We can superimpose the descriptors of debit and credit on a T-account as follows.

Account Title	
Debit (Left side)	Credit (Right side)

The left side of the T-account is the "debit" side and the right side is the "credit" side. This holds for all T-accounts. Thus, to record an increase in an asset, we enter an amount on the left or debit side of the T-account—that is, we *debit the account*. Decreases in assets are recorded with an entry on the opposite (credit) side. To record an increase in a liability or equity account, we enter an amount on the right or credit side of the T-account—we *credit the account*. Decreases in liability or equity accounts are recorded on the opposite (debit) side.

In the margin of our financial statement effects template, we show the journal entry first, followed by the related T-accounts. In accounting jargon, this sequence relates to *journalizing* the entry and *posting* it to the affected accounts. The T-accounts represent the financial impact of each transaction on the respective asset, liability or equity accounts.

Introduction to Transaction Analysis

This section uses Apple, Inc., to illustrate the accounting for selected business transactions. The assumed time frame will be one quarter, as all public companies are required to prepare financial statements at least quarterly. We select transactions to illustrate four fundamental types of business activities: (1) capital investment in the company, (2) asset (inventory) acquisition, (3) revenue and expense recognition, and (4) dividend distribution. Next, we consider accounting adjustments, prepare the financial statements, and close the books.

Capital Investment

Assume that Apple investors contribute $300 cash to the company in exchange for common stock. Apple's cash and common stock both increase. Recall that common stock is a component of contributed capital. The financial statement effects template reflects this transaction as follows.

		Balance Sheet						Income Statement		
Transaction	Cash Asset	+	Noncash Assets	=	Liabil- ities	+	Contrib. Capital	+ Earned Capital	Rev- enues	− Expen- ses	= Net Income
Issued stock for $300 cash	+300 Cash			=			+300 Common Stock			=

Margin note:
```
Cash    300
  CS         300
     Cash
   300 |
     CS
       |  300
```

Journal Entry and T-Account

Although it is not our intent to refer to journal entries and T-accounts in this book, we will describe them for this first transaction. Specifically, the $300 debit equals the $300 credit in the journal entry: assets ($300 cash) = liabilities ($0) + equity ($300 common stock). This balance in transactions is the basis of *double-entry accounting*. For simplicity, we use acronyms (such as CS for common stock) in journal entries and T-accounts. (A listing of accounts and acronyms is located in Appendix C near the end of the book.) The journal entry for this transaction is

Cash	300	
CS (Common Stock)		300

Convention dictates that debits are listed first, followed by credits—the latter are indented.[1] The total debit(s) must always equal the total credit(s) for each transaction. The T-account representation for this transaction follows:

Cash			CS	
300				300

Cash is an asset; thus, a cash increase is recorded on the left or debit side of the T-account. Common stock is an equity account; thus, a common stock increase is recorded on the right or credit side.

Asset (Inventory) Acquisition

Assume that Apple purchases $2,000 worth of iPods from its supplier (we keep this illustration simple by ignoring Apple's manufacturing activities). When one company buys from another, it is normal to give a period of time in which to pay the obligation due, usually 30 to 60 days, or more. This purchase "on credit" (also called *on account*) means that Apple owes its supplier $2,000 for the purchase. Apple records the cost of the purchased iPods as an asset called inventories, which are goods held for resale. This acquisition of iPods on credit is recorded as follows.

	Balance Sheet						Income Statement		
Transaction	**Cash Asset** +	**Noncash Assets** =	**Liabil- ities** +	**Contrib. Capital** +	**Earned Capital**		**Rev- enues** −	**Expen- ses** =	**Net Income**
Purchase iPods for $2,000 on credit		+2,000 Inventories =	+2,000 Accounts Payable						=

INV   2,000
AP   2,000
INV
2,000
          AP
                2,000

Revenue and Expense Recognition

Assume that Apple sells iPods that cost $600 to a retailer for $700 on credit. The sale *on credit* means that the customer has not yet paid and Apple has a $700 account receivable.

Can Apple record the $700 sale as revenue even though it has not collected any cash? The answer is yes. This decision reflects an important concept in accounting, called the **revenue recognition principle,** which is part of *accrual accounting*. The revenue recognition principle prescribes that a company can recognize revenues provided that two conditions are met:

1. Revenues are *earned*, and
2. Revenues are *realized* or *realizable*.

Earned means that the company has done whatever it is required to do. In this case, it means that Apple has delivered the iPods to its retail customer. **Realized** or **realizable** means that the seller has either received cash or will receive cash at some point in the future. That is, Apple can recognize revenue if it expects to collect the $700 account receivable in the future. (We explain revenue recognition in more detail in Module 5.)

Recording the $700 sale is only half the transaction. Apple must also record the decrease in iPod inventory of $600. When a company purchases inventory, it records the cost on the balance sheet as an asset. When inventory is sold, the "asset" is used up and its cost must be transferred from the balance sheet to the income statement as an expense. In particular, the expense associated with inventory is called cost of goods sold. Thus, the second part of Apple's revenue transaction is to remove the cost of the iPods from the balance sheet and recognize the cost of goods sold (an expense) in its income statement. This will match the cost of the inventory to the related revenue.

---

[1] There can be more than one debit and one credit for a transaction. To illustrate, assume that Apple raises $300 cash, with $200 from investors and $100 borrowed from a bank. The resulting journal entry is:

Cash...	300	
CS (common stock)		200
NP (note payable).....................................		100

Matching of expenses with revenues in this manner is evidence of the **matching principle.** Once revenues are recognized (using the revenue recognition principle), we must then match all related expenses incurred to generate those revenues *in the same period* that we recognize the revenue. This yields the proper measure of income for the period and is an application of accrual accounting.

The $700 sale of Apple iPods that cost $600 is recorded as follows.

		Balance Sheet						Income Statement		
Transaction	Cash Asset	+ Noncash Assets	= Liabil- ities	+ Contrib. Capital	+ Earned Capital		Rev- enues	− Expen- ses	= Net Income
Sold $700 of iPods on credit		+700 Accounts Receivable =			+700 Retained Earnings		+700 Sales		= +700
Record $600 cost of the $700 iPod sale		−600 Inventory =			−600 Retained Earnings			+600 − Cost of Goods Sold	= −600

Left margin T-accounts:

```
AR       700
  Sales      700
      AR
  700 |
      Sales
         |    700

COGS  600
  INV        600
      COGS
  600 |
      INV
         |    600
```

The first part of this sales transaction records the $700 sale and the $700 increase in accounts receivable. Revenues are earned and therefore recognized even though no cash was received. The sale is reflected in the account receivable that will later be converted to cash. The increase in revenues increases income, which increases retained earnings.[2]

The second part of this sale transaction transfers the $600 in inventory on the balance sheet to the income statement as the cost of iPods sold. This entry increases expenses, and decreases both income and retained earnings. The transaction also reduces assets because Apple no longer owns the inventory; it is "used up."

Capital Distributions

Assume that Apple decides to pay $50 to its shareholders in the form of a cash dividend. Dividends are treated as a return of shareholders' investment. All transactions between the company and its shareholders are considered financing transactions. This includes payment of dividends, the issuance of stock, and any subsequent stock repurchase. Financing transactions affect only the balance sheet; they do not affect the income statement. Dividends are distributions of income. They represent the portion of income that the company chooses to distribute to shareholders—the portion that will no longer be retained. Thus, dividends reduce retained earnings. It is important to distinguish dividends from expenses—dividends are NOT an expense, they do not reduce net income. They are a distribution of net income; they reduce retained earnings. Apple's $50 dividend payment is reflected in the following template. (Companies typically record dividends in a separate dividends account and then later, in the closing process, this account is transferred to retained earnings. The template depicts dividends as an immediate reduction of retained earnings, which is part of earned capital. The end result of both approaches is identical.)

		Balance Sheet						Income Statement		
Transaction	Cash Asset	+ Noncash Assets	= Liabil- ities	+ Contrib. Capital	+ Earned Capital		Rev- enues	− Expen- ses	= Net Income
Paid $50 cash for dividends	−50 Cash		=		−50 Dividends				=

Left margin T-accounts:

```
DIV     50
  Cash       50
      DIV
  50 |
      Cash
         |    50
```

[2] The retained earnings account is not automatically updated in most accounting software programs as our financial effects template illustrates. Instead, accountants transfer income to retained earnings using a journal entry as part of the closing process. We briefly explain the closing process near the end of this module and more fully in Appendix 3A.

MID-MODULE REVIEW 1

Assume that Symantec Corporation experienced the following six transactions relating to a capital investment, the purchase and sale of inventory, the collection of an account receivable, and the payment of an account payable.

1. Shareholders contribute $3,000 cash to Symantec in exchange for its common shares.
2. Symantec purchases $1,000 of inventory on credit.
3. Symantec sells $300 of inventory for $500 on credit.
4. Symantec collects $300 cash owed by customers from part 3.
5. Symantec pays $400 cash toward its accounts payable to suppliers.
6. Symantec pays $20 cash for dividends to its stockholders.

Required

Record each transaction in the financial statement effects template. Include journal entries for each account in the margin and post those entries to T-accounts.

Solution

Transaction	Balance Sheet					Income Statement		
	Cash Asset +	Noncash Assets =	Liabil- ities +	Contrib. Capital +	Earned Capital	Rev- enues −	Expen- ses =	Net Income
1. Issue stock for $3,000 cash	+3,000 Cash	=		+3,000 Common Stock			=	
2. Purchase $1,000 of inventory on credit		+1,000 Inventory =	+1,000 Accounts Payable				=	
3a. Sell inventory for $500 on credit		+500 Accounts = Receivable			+500 Retained Earnings	+500 Sales	=	+500
3b. Record $300 cost of inventory sold		−300 Inventory =			−300 Retained Earnings		+300 − Cost of = Goods Sold	−300
4. Collect $300 cash owed by customers	+300 Cash	−300 Accounts = Receivable					=	
5. Pay $400 cash toward accounts payable	−400 Cash		−400 = Accounts payable				=	
6. Pay $20 cash for dividends	−20 Cash	=			−20 Dividends		=	

Cash   3,000
CS   3,000
Cash
3,000 |
CS
| 3,000

INV   1,000
AP   1,000
INV
1,000 |
AP
| 1,000

AR   500
Sales   500
AR
500 |
Sales
| 500

COGS 300
INV   300
COGS
300 |
INV
| 300

Cash   300
AR   300
Cash
300 |
AR
| 300

AP   400
Cash   400
AP
400 |
Cash
| 400

DIV   20
Cash   20
DIV
20 |
Cash
| 20

ACCOUNTING ADJUSTMENTS (ACCRUALS)

Recognizing revenue when earned (even if not received in cash), and matching expenses when incurred (even if not paid in cash), are cornerstones of **accrual accounting,** which is required under

LO2 Prepare and explain accounting adjustments and their financial statement effects.

GAAP.[3] Understanding accounting adjustments, commonly called *accruals*, is crucial to effectively analyzing and interpreting financial statements. In this module's Apple illustration, we recorded inventory as a purchase even though no cash was paid, and we recognized the sale as revenue even though no cash was received. Both of these transactions reflect accrual accounting. Some accounting adjustments affect the balance sheet alone (as with purchasing inventory on account). Other adjustments affect the balance sheet *and* the income statement (as with selling inventory on account). Accounting adjustments can affect asset, liability or equity accounts, and can either increase or decrease net income.

Companies make adjustments to more accurately report their financial performance and condition. For example, employees might not have been paid for wages earned at the end of an accounting period. Failure to recognize this labor cost would understate the company's total liabilities (because wages payable would be too low), and would overstate net income for the period (because wages expense would be too low). Thus, neither the balance sheet nor the income statement would be accurate.

Accounting adjustments yield a more accurate presentation of the economic results of a company for a period. Despite their (generally) beneficial effects, adjustments can be misused. Managers can use adjustments to bias reported income, rendering it higher or lower than it really is. Adjustments, if misused, can adversely affect business and investment decisions. Many recent accounting scandals have resulted from improper use of adjustments. Although outsiders cannot directly observe companies' specific accounting entries, their impact can be detected as changes in balance sheet and income statement accounts. Those changes provide signals for financial statement analysis. Consequently, understanding the accrual process will help us know what to look for as we analyze companies' financial reports.

BUSINESS INSIGHT | **Accounting Scandals and Improper Adjustments**

Many accounting scandals involve the improper use of adjustments to manipulate income. The following table highlights three specific adjustment manipulations by companies. These accounting scandals underscore the important role of adjustments in financial accounting and the economic impact they can have on balance sheets and income statements. When used improperly, adjustments distort financial reports and can mislead investors and other financial statement users. (Source: "Corporate Scandal Sheet," Forbes 2002.)

Company	Allegations	Accounting Adjustment
Halliburton (HAL)	Improperly booked $100 million in annual construction cost overruns before customers agreed to pay for them.	Halliburton recognized revenues before earned. Its accounting entry increased accounts receivable and revenue, thereby inflating net income. It later wrote off the receivables when customers refused to pay.
WorldCom (WCOEQ)	Improperly recorded $11 billion of operating expenses as capital costs (assets).	WorldCom recorded costs as assets on the balance sheet rather than as expenses in the income statement. This inflated both assets and income. It later wrote off the assets (and reduced income) when the transactions were uncovered.
Xerox (XRX)	Overstated net income by $1.5 billion over five years.	Customers purchased copiers and service contracts as one purchase. Xerox allocated most of the "sale" to hardware, thereby recognizing revenues before they were earned under service contracts.

Exhibit 3.2 identifies four general types of accounting adjustments which are briefly described on the next page.

---

[3] **Cash accounting** recognizes revenues when cash is received and expenses when cash is paid. This is not acceptable accounting under GAAP. However, small businesses that do not prepare financial reports for public investors and creditors, sometimes use cash accounting.

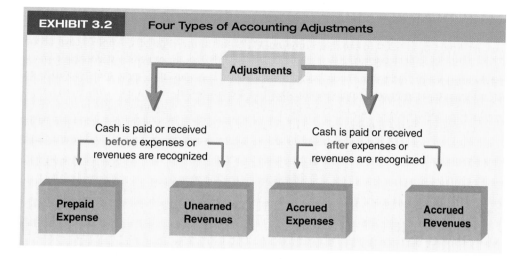

EXHIBIT 3.2   Four Types of Accounting Adjustments

Prepaid expenses   Prepaid expenses reflect advance cash payments that will ultimately become expenses. An example is the payment of radio advertising that will not be aired until sometime in the future.

Unearned revenues   Unearned revenues reflect cash received from customers before any services or goods are provided. An example is cash received from patrons for tickets to an upcoming concert.

Accrued expenses   Accrued expenses are expenses incurred and recognized on the income statement, even though they are not yet paid in cash. An example is wages owed to employees who performed work but who have not yet been paid.

Accrued revenues   Accrued revenues are revenues earned and recognized on the income statement, even though cash is not yet received. Examples include sales on credit and revenue earned under a long-term contract.

The remainder of this section illustrates how Apple's financial statements would reflect each of these four types of adjustments.

RESEARCH INSIGHT   Accruals: Good or Bad?

Accounting accruals are used to study the effects of earnings management on financial accounting. Earnings management is broadly defined as the use of accounting discretion to distort reported earnings. Managers have incentives to manage earnings in many situations. For example, managers have tendencies to accelerate revenue recognition to increase stock prices prior to equity offerings. Also, management buyouts occur when management repurchases common stock and take the company "private." In this case, research shows that managers decelerate revenue recognition to depress stock prices prior to the management buyout. Research also shows that managers use discretion when reporting special items to either meet or beat analysts' forecasts of earnings and/or to avoid reporting a loss. Not all earnings management occurs for opportunistic reasons. Research shows that managers use accruals to communicate private information about future profitability to outsiders. For example, management might signal future profitability through use of income-decreasing accruals to show investors that it can afford to apply conservative accounting. This "signaling" through accruals is found to precede stock splits and dividend increases.

To examine the information conveyed in accruals, we must determine what portion of accruals is unexpected. These accruals are referred to as "discretionary accruals" and are estimated using regression models. Total accruals are defined as the difference between net income before extraordinary items and cash flows from operations. Total accruals can be decomposed into changes in working capital accounts (such as accounts receivable, inventory, accounts payable, and accrued liabilities) and noncash income statement accounts (such as depreciation and special items). Regression is used to determine the predicted (or expected) change in total accruals that should be generated from actual changes in sales and the level of fixed assets for each firm in each year. Actual total accruals are compared with predicted total accruals and the difference is considered to be the unexpected accruals (the discretionary portion). In sum, we must look at reported earnings in conjunction with other earnings quality signals (such as levels of disclosure, degree of corporate governance, and industry performance) to interpret information in accruals.

Prepaid Expenses (Assets)

Assume that Apple pays $200 to purchase time on MTV for future iPod ads. Apple's cash account decreases by $200. Should the $200 advertising cost be recorded as an expense when Apple pays MTV, when MTV airs the ads, or at some other point? Under accrual accounting, Apple must record an expense when it is incurred. That means Apple should expense the ads when MTV airs them. When Apple pays for the advertisement, it records an asset; Apple "owns" TV time that will presumably provide future benefits when the ads air. In the interim, the cost of the ads is an asset on the balance sheet. Apple's financial statement effects template follows for this transaction. There is a decrease in cash and an increase in the advertising asset, titled prepaid advertising.

PPDA   200
  Cash   200
      PPDA
200 |
  Cash
    | 200

	Balance Sheet						Income Statement		
Transaction	Cash Asset	+ Noncash Assets	= Liabilities	+ Contrib. Capital	+ Earned Capital		Revenues	– Expenses	= Net Income
Pay $200 cash in advance for ad time	−200 Cash	+200 Prepaid Advertising	=						=

When an ad airs, the prepaid advertising asset is used up and the portion of the prepaid advertising account relating to the aired ad is reduced. The cost is transferred to the income statement as advertising expense.

Unearned Revenues (Liabilities)

Assume that Apple receives $400 cash from a customer as advance payment on a multi-unit iPod sale to be delivered next month. Apple must record cash received on its balance sheet, but cannot recognize revenue from the order until earned, which is generally when iPods are delivered to the customer. Until then, Apple must recognize a liability called unearned or deferred revenue that represents Apple's obligation to fulfill the order at some future point. The financial statement effects template for this transaction follows.

Cash   400
  UR   400
    Cash
400 |
  UR
    | 400

	Balance Sheet						Income Statement		
Transaction	Cash Asset	+ Noncash Assets	= Liabilities	+ Contrib. Capital	+ Earned Capital		Revenues	– Expenses	= Net Income
Received $400 cash in advance for iPod sale	+400 Cash		+400 = Unearned Revenue						=

Assume that Apple delivers the iPods a month later (but still within the fiscal quarter). Apple must recognize the $400 as revenue at delivery because it is now earned. Thus, net income increases by $400. The second part of this transaction is to record the cost of the iPods sold. Assuming the cost is $150, Apple reduces iPod inventory by $150 and records cost of goods sold by the same amount. These effects are reflected in the following template.

UR   400
  Sales   400
     UR
400 |
  Sales
    | 400

COGS   150
  INV   150
    COGS
150 |
  INV
    | 150

	Balance Sheet						Income Statement		
Transaction	Cash Asset	+ Noncash Assets	= Liabilities	+ Contrib. Capital	+ Earned Capital		Revenues	– Expenses	= Net Income
Delivered $400 of iPods paid in advance			−400 = Unearned Revenues		+400 Retained Earnings		+400 Sales		= +400
Record $150 cost of the $400 iPod sale		−150 Inventory =			−150 Retained Earnings			+150 – Cost of Goods Sold	= −150

Accrued Expenses (Liabilities)

Assume that Apple's sales staff earns $100 of sales commissions this period that will not be paid until next period. The sales staff earned the wages as they made the sales. However, because Apple pays its employees twice a month, the related cash payment will not occur until the next pay period. Should Apple record the wages earned by its employees as an expense even though payment has not yet been made? The answer is yes. The matching principle requires Apple to recognize wages expense when it is *incurred*, even if not paid in cash. It must record wages expense incurred as a liability (wages payable).

	Balance Sheet						Income Statement		
Transaction	Cash Asset	+ Noncash Assets	= Liabil-ities	+ Contrib. Capital	+ Earned Capital		Rev-enues	− Expen-ses	= Net Income
Incurred $100 of wages not yet paid			= +100 Wages Payable		−100 Retained Earnings			− +100 Wages Expense	= −100

```
WE    100
    WP      100
       WE
  100 |
     WP
       | 100
```

In the next period, when Apple pays the wages, it reduces both cash and wages payable. Net income is not affected by the cash payment; instead, net income decreased in the previous period when Apple accrued the wage expense.

Next assume that Apple rents office space and that it owes $25 in rent at period-end. Apple has incurred rent expense in the current period and that expense must be recorded this period. Failing to make this adjustment would mean that Apple's liabilities (rent payable) would be understated and its income would be overstated. The entry to record the accrual of rent expense for office space follows.

	Balance Sheet						Income Statement		
Transaction	Cash Asset	+ Noncash Assets	= Liabil-ities	+ Contrib. Capital	+ Earned Capital		Rev-enues	− Expen-ses	= Net Income
Incurred $25 of rent not yet paid			= +25 Rent Payable		−25 Retained Earnings			− +25 Rent Expense	= −25

```
RNTE   25
    RNTP     25
       RNTE
  25 |
     RNTP
       | 25
```

Accrued Revenues (Assets)

Assume that Apple delivers iPods to a customer in Germany who will pay next quarter. The sales price for those units is $500 and the cost is $400. Apple has completed its revenue earning process with this sale and must accrue revenue from the German customer even though Apple received no cash. Like all sales transactions, Apple must record two parts, the sales revenue and the cost of sales. The financial effects template for this two-part transaction follows.

	Balance Sheet						Income Statement		
Transaction	Cash Asset	+ Noncash Assets	= Liabil-ities	+ Contrib. Capital	+ Earned Capital		Rev-enues	− Expen-ses	= Net Income
Sold $500 of iPods on credit		+500 Accounts Receivable	=		+500 Retained Earnings		+500 Sales		= +500
Record $400 cost for $500 iPod sale		−400 Inventory	=		−400 Retained Earnings			− +400 Cost of Goods Sold	= −400

```
AR    500
    Sales    500
       AR
  500 |
     Sales
       | 500

COGS  400
    INV     400
       COGS
  400 |
     INV
       | 400
```

Summary of Accounting Adjustments

Adjustments are an important part of the accounting process and are crucial to accurate and informative financial accounting. It is through the accruals process that managers communicate information about future cash flows. For example, from accrual information, we know that Apple paid for a resource (advertising) that it has not yet used. We know that all cash advances from customers have been honored because there are no unearned revenues. We know that employees have earned wages but Apple won't pay them until a future period. We know that revenues have been earned but cash not yet received. Those accruals tell us about Apple's past performance and, perhaps more importantly, about Apple's future cash flows. When used correctly, accruals convey a wealth of information about the past and the future that is useful in our evaluation of company financial performance and condition. Thus, we can use accrual information to more precisely value companies' equity and debt securities.

Not all managers are honest; some misuse accounting accruals to improperly recognize revenues and expenses. Abuses include accruing revenue before it is earned; and accruing expenses in the wrong period or in the wrong amount. These actions are fraudulent as they deliberately overstate or understate revenues and expenses and, thus, reported net income is incorrect. Safeguards against this type of managerial behavior include corporate governance systems (internal controls, accounting policies and procedures, routine scrutiny of accounting reports, and audit committees) and external checks and balances (independent auditors, regulatory bodies, and the court system). Collectively, these safeguards aim to protect interests of companies' internal and external stakeholders. When managers abuse accounting systems, tough and swift sanctions remind others that corporate malfeasance is unacceptable. Videos of police officers leading corporate executives to jail in handcuffs (the infamous "perp walk") sends that message.

MANAGERIAL DECISION	You Are the CFO

The plant manager of your company informs you of the leakage of hazardous waste from your company's factory. It is estimated that cleanup will cost $10 million. Part 1: What effect will recording this accrual have on your company's balance sheet and its income statement? Part 2: Accounting rules require you to record the accrual if it is both probable and can be reliably estimated. Although the cleanup is relatively certain, the cost is a guess at this point. Consequently, you have some discretion whether to record the accrual. Discuss the parties that are likely affected by your decision on whether or not to record the liability and related expense, and the ethical issues involved.

[Answer 3-25]

Trial Balance Preparation and Use

LO3 Explain and construct the trial balance.

After Apple records all of its transactions, it must prepare financial statements so it can assess its financial performance and condition for the quarter. The following template shows a summary of Apple's transactions thus far.

The first step in preparing financial statements is to prepare a **trial balance,** which is a listing of all accounts and their balances at a point in time. To prepare a trial balance we compile a listing of accounts, their balances, and we determine whether that balance is a debit or credit. Its purpose is to prove the mathematical equality of debits and credits, provide a useful tool to uncover any accounting errors, and help prepare the financial statements.

	Balance Sheet					Income Statement		
Transaction	Cash Asset	+ Noncash Assets	= Liabil- ities	+ Contrib. Capital	+ Earned Capital	Rev- enues	− Expen- ses	= Net Income
Issued stock for $300 cash	+300 Cash	=		+300 Common Stock				=
Purchase $2,000 of iPods on credit		+2,000 Inventory =	+2,000 Accounts Payable					=
Sold $700 of iPods on credit		+700 Accounts = Receivable			+700 Retained Earnings	+700 Sales		= +700
Record $600 cost of $700 iPod sale		−600 Inventory =			−600 Retained Earnings		+600 − Cost of Goods Sold	= −600
Paid $50 cash for dividends	−50 Cash	=			−50 Dividends			=
Pay $200 cash in advance for ad time	−200 Cash	+200 Prepaid = Advertising						=
Received $400 cash in advance for iPod sale	+400 Cash	=	+400 Unearned Revenue					=
Delivered $400 of iPods paid in advance		=	−400 Unearned Revenues		+400 Retained Earnings	+400 Sales		= +400
Record $150 cost of $400 iPod sale		−150 Inventory =			−150 Retained Earnings		+150 − Cost of Goods Sold	= −150
Incurred $100 of wages not yet paid		=	+100 Wages Payable		−100 Retained Earnings		+100 − Wages Expense	= −100
Incurred $25 of rent not yet paid		=	+25 Rent Payable		−25 Retained Earnings		+25 − Rent Expense	= −25
Sold $500 of iPods on credit		+500 Accounts = Receivable			+500 Retained Earnings	+500 Sales		= +500
Record $400 cost of $500 iPod sale		−400 Inventory =			−400 Retained Earnings		+400 − Cost of Goods Sold	= −400
Total	450 +	2,250 =	2,125 +	300 +	275	1,600 −	1,275 =	325

Cash 300
  CS   300
    Cash
  300
    CS
         300

INV 2,000
  AP   2,000
    INV
  2,000
    AP
         2,000

AR 700
  Sales   700
    AR
  700
    Sales
         700

COGS 600
  INV   600
    COGS
  600
    INV
         600

DIV 50
  Cash   50
    DIV
  50
    Cash
         50

PPDA 200
  Cash   200
    PPDA
  200
    Cash
         200

Cash 400
  UR   400
    Cash
  400
    UR
         400

UR 400
  Sales   400
    UR
  400
    Sales
         400

COGS 150
  INV   150
    COGS
  150
    INV
         150

WE 100
  WP   100
    WE
  100
    WP
         100

RNTE 25
  RNTP   25
    RNTE
  25
    RNTP
         25

AR 500
  Sales   500
    AR
  500
    Sales
         500

COGS 400
  INV   400
    COGS
  400
    INV
         400

The trial balance for Apple, which we assume to be as of December 31, 2007, follows.

APPLE Trial Balance December 31, 2007		
	Debit	**Credit**
Cash....................	$ 450	
Accounts receivable.........	1,200	
Inventories................	850	
Prepaid advertising..........	200	
Accounts payable...........		$2,000
Wages payable.............		100
Rent payable		25
Unearned revenues		0
Common stock.............		300
Dividends	50	
Sales.....................		1,600
Cost of goods sold..........	1,150	
Wage expense	100	
Rent expense..............	25	
Totals	$4,025	$4,025

The trial balance amounts consist of the ending balance for each of the accounts. For the Apple illustration, we total all transactions for each account listed in the template. To illustrate, cash has an ending balance of $450 ($300 − $50 − $200 + $400). Also, because cash is an asset (which is on the left hand side of the balance sheet), it normally has a debit balance (which is on the left hand side of the T-accounts). We can confirm the ending cash debit balance by totalling each of the cash T-account entries. Liabilities and equity accounts normally have credit balances (because they are on the right hand side of the balance sheet), and we can confirm these ending credit balances by referring to their respective T-accounts in the template.

The trial balance shows total debits equal $4,025, which also equals total credits. Accordingly, we know that all of the template transactions balance. We do not know, however, that all required journal entries have been properly included, or if Apple recorded entries that it should not have. (An *unadjusted trial balance* is one that is prepared prior to accounting adjustments; an *adjusted trial balance* is one prepared after accounting adjustments are entered.)

MID-MODULE REVIEW 2

Refer to the transactions in Mid-Module Review 1. Assume that Symantec Corporation reports the following additional transactions.

1. Symantec pays $100 cash toward rent for the next period.
2. Symantec receives $200 cash in advance from a client for future consulting services.
3. Symantec employees earn $50 in wages that will not be paid until the next period.
4. Symantec provides $150 of services revenue and bills the client.

Required

Record each of these additional transactions using the financial statement effects template. Also record the journal entry for each transaction in the margin and post each entry to T-accounts. Prepare a trial balance for Symantec reflecting these transactions together with those of Mid-Module Review 1.

Solution

	Balance Sheet						Income Statement					
Transaction	**Cash Asset**	**+**	**Noncash Assets**	**=**	**Liabil- ities**	**+**	**Contrib. Capital**	**+**	**Earned Capital**	**Rev- enues**	**−**	**Expen- ses**	**=**	**Net Income**
Pays $100 cash for next period rent	−100 Cash		+100 Prepaid rent	=									=
Receives $200 cash advance for future services	+500 Cash			=	+500 Unearned revenues								=
Incurs $50 in wages to be paid next period				=	+50 Wages payable				−50 Retained Earnings		−	+50 Wage expense	= −50
Provides $150 of services and bills client			+150 Accounts receivable	=					+150 Retained Earnings	+150 Sales			= +150

T-accounts:
- PPRNT 100 / Cash 100
- PPRNT 100 | Cash 100
- Cash 500 / UR 500
- Cash 500 | UR 500
- WE 50 / WP 50
- WE 50 | WP 50
- AR 150 / Sales 150
- AR 150 | Sales 150

SYMANTEC
Trial Balance

	Debit	Credit
Cash	$3,280	
Accounts receivable	350	
Inventories	700	
Prepaid rent	100	
Accounts payable		$ 600
Wages payable		50
Unearned revenues		500
Common stock		3,000
Dividends	20	
Sales		650
Cost of goods sold	300	
Wage expense	50	
Totals	$4,800	$4,800

FINANCIAL STATEMENT PREPARATION

Financial statement preparation involves working with the accounts in the adjusted trial balance to properly report them in financial statements. There is an order to financial statement preparation. First, a company prepares its income statement using the income statement accounts. It then uses the net income number and dividend information to update the retained earnings account. Second, it prepares the balance sheet using the updated retained earnings account along with the remaining balance sheet accounts from the trial balance. Third, it prepares the statement of stockholders' equity. Fourth, it prepares the statement of cash flows using information from the cash account (and other sources).

L04 Construct financial statements from the trial balance.

Income Statement

Apple's income statement follows. Apple's trial balance reveals four income statement accounts. Those income statement accounts are called *temporary accounts* because they begin each accounting period with a zero balance. Apple's income statement also includes a line for gross profit because that subtotal is important to evaluate manufacturers' performance and profitability. Income for this quarterly period is $325 (we ignore taxes in this illustration).

APPLE Income Statement For Quarter Ended December 31, 2007	
Sales....................	$1,600
Cost of goods sold..........	1,150
Gross profit..............	450
Wage expense	100
Rent expense.............	25
Net income...............	$ 325

Retained Earnings Computation

Apple updates its retained earnings balance at period-end using income from the income statement and the dividends information from its trial balance. (For simplicity, we assume retained earnings is zero at the beginning of this period). This computation follows.

APPLE Retained Earnings Computation For Quarter Ended December 31, 2007	
Retained earnings, beginning of period.........	$ 0
Add: Net income (loss).................	325
Deduct: Dividends.......................	50
Retained earnings, end of period.............	$275

Balance Sheet

Once Apple computes its ending balance in retained earnings, it can prepare its balance sheet, which follows. Balance sheet accounts are called *permanent accounts* because their respective balances carry over from one period to the next. For example, the cash balance at the end of the current accounting period (ended December 31, 2007) is $450, which will be the balance at the beginning of the next accounting period (beginning January 1, 2008).

APPLE Balance Sheet December 31, 2007	
Assets	
Cash.................................	$ 450
Accounts receivable.....................	1,200
Inventories	850
Prepaid advertising.....................	200
Total assets...........................	$2,700
Liabilities and Stockholders' Equity	
Liabilities	
Accounts payable.......................	$2,000
Wages payable.........................	100
Rent payable	25
Total liabilities........................	2,125
Stockholders' equity	
Common stock.........................	300
Retained earnings	275
Total liabilities and stockholders' equity.......	$2,700

Statement of Stockholders' Equity

Apple uses the information pertaining to its contributed capital and earned capital categories to prepare the statement of stockholders' equity, as follows.

APPLE Statement of Stockholders' Equity For Quarter Ended December 31, 2007	Contributed Capital	Earned Capital	Total Stockholders' Equity
Beginning balance	$ 0	$ 0	$ 0
Stock issuance.	300		300
Net income (loss)		325	325
Dividends		(50)	(50)
Ending balance.	$300	$275	$575

Statement of Cash Flows

The statement of cash flows summarizes the cash-based transactions for the period and reports the sources and uses of cash. Each cash transaction represents an operating, investing, or financing activity. To prepare the statement, Apple uses the Cash column of the financial statement effects template, see above. The following cash flow statement for Apple is based on the *direct method* for reporting operating cash flows. The indirect method is an alternative presentation, which we discuss later. During the current period, Apple's cash increased by $450. Its increase in cash consists of a $200 net cash inflow from operating activities plus a $250 cash inflow from financing activities. There were no investing activities during this period.

APPLE Statement of Cash Flows (Direct Method) For Quarter Ended December 31, 2007	
Operating activities	
Receipts from sales contracts	$400
Payments for advertising	(200)
Net cash flows from operating activities	200
Investing activities	
Net cash flows from investing activities.	0
Financing activities	
Issuance of common stock	300
Payment of cash dividends	(50)
Net cash flows from financing activities.	250
Net change in cash	$450
Cash, beginning of period	0
Cash, end of period	$450

In practice, preparing a statement of cash flows is more complicated. Companies can have millions of transactions in the cash account and the task of classifying each transaction as operating, investing or financing would be costly and time consuming. Instead, companies prepare the statement of cash flows using the current income statement and the balance sheets for the current and prior periods. The basic approach is to adjust net income to arrive at net cash flows from operating activities (the so-called *indirect method*) and then review changes in balance sheet accounts (by comparing the opening and ending balances) to arrive at net cash flows from investing and financing activities.

As mentioned, there are two methods to display net cash flows from operating activities: the direct method and the indirect method. Both methods report the same net operating cash flow, the only difference is in presentation. Companies can choose which method to follow. Apple's simplified statement of cash flows above, is an example of the direct method. However, the **indirect method** is, by far, the most widely used method in practice today (over 98% of public companies use it). The indirect method computes operating cash flows *indirectly* by adjusting net income using the following format.

	Add (+) or Subtract (−) from Net Income
Net income............................	$ #
Add: depreciation expense	+
Adjust for changes in current assets	
Subtract increases in current assets	−
Add decreases in current assets	+
Adjust for changes in current liabilities	
Add increases in current liabilities	+
Subtract decreases in current liabilities	−
Net cash flow from operating activities	$ #

Net income is first adjusted for noncash expenses such as depreciation and amortization, and is then adjusted for changes in current assets and current liabilities to yield net cash flow from operating activities, or *cash profit*. The depreciation adjustment merely zeros out (undoes the effect of) depreciation expense, a noncash expense, which is deducted in computing net income. The following table provides brief explanations of adjustments for receivables, inventories, and payables and accruals.

	Change in account balance ...	Means that ...	Which requires this adjustment to net income to yield cash profit ...
Receivables	Increase	Sales and net income increase, but cash is not yet received	Deduct increase in receivables from net income
	Decrease	More cash is received than is reported in sales and net income	Add decrease in receivables to net income
Inventories	Increase	Cash is paid for inventories that are not yet reflected in cost of goods sold	Deduct increase in inventories from net income
	Decrease	Cost of goods sold includes inventory costs that were paid for in a prior period	Add decrease in inventories to net income
Payables and accruals	Increase	More goods and services are acquired on credit, delaying cash payment	Add increase in payables and accruals to net income
	Decrease	More cash is paid than that reflected in cost of goods sold or operating expenses	Deduct decrease in payables and accruals from net income

It is also helpful to use the following decision guide, involving changes in assets, liabilities, and equity, to understand increases and decreases in cash flows.

	Cash flow increases from	Cash flow decreases from
Assets......................	Account decreases	Account increases
Liabilities and equity...........	Account increases	Account decreases

Using this decision guide we can determine the cash flow effects of the income statement and balance sheet information and categorize them into the following table for our Apple illustration.

Financial Element	Change	Source or Use	Cash Flow Effect	Classification on SCF
Current assets				
Accounts receivable........	+ $1,200	Use	$(1,200)	Operating
Increase in inventories	+ 850	Use	(850)	Operating
Prepaid advertising.........	+ 200	Use	(200)	Operating
Noncurrent assets				
PPE....................	0		0	Investing
Accumulated depreciation ...		Neither	0*	Operating
Current liabilities				
Accounts payable..........	+ 2,000	Source	2,000	Operating
Wages payable............	+ 100	Source	100	Operating
Rent payable.............	+ 25	Source	25	Operating
Long-term liabilities	0		0	Financing
Stockholders' equity				
Common stock............	+ 300	Source	300	Financing
Retained earnings				
Net income	+ 325	Source	325	Operating
Dividends	+ 50	Use	(50)	Financing
Total (net cash flow)			$ 450	

*Depreciation, if present, is added to net income in computing cash flows from operating activities.

Increases in the three current assets reflect a use of cash, and are subtracted in the operating section of the statement of cash flows. Increases in noncurrent PPE assets are coded likewise, but are classified as an investing activity. An increase in accumulated depreciation reflects the recording of depreciation expense in the income statement, which is a noncash expense that must be zeroed out (with an addition to net income) to yield cash profit. Increases in the three current liabilities reflect sources of cash, and are recorded as positive amounts in the statement of cash flows.

Issuance of common stock is a source of cash, and the payment of dividends to shareholders is a use of cash. Both of these are reflected in the financing section of the statement of cash flows. The financing section also reflects any increases or decreases in borrowings as sources (uses), respectively. The increase in retained earnings, resulting from net income, is a source of cash, but it is reported as an operating activity. (Components of the change in retained earnings, net income less dividends, are reflected in the statement of cash flows and, consequently, the change in retained earnings is already recognized.)

The sum of these elements yields a net increase in cash of $450. This is the same result we obtained earlier using the direct method. Reporting these elements by operating, investing and financing activities yields the following familiar form of the statement of cash flows (statement shown to the right).

APPLE Statement of Cash Flows (Indirect Method) For Quarter Ended December 31, 2007	
Operating activities	
Net income..............................	$ 325
Depreciation and other noncash expenses	0
Increase in accounts receivable..............	(1,200)
Increase in inventories	(850)
Increase in prepaid advertising..............	(200)
Increase in accounts payable................	2,000
Increase in wages payable	100
Increase in rent payable	25
Net cash flows from operating activities	200
Investing activities	
Net cash flows from investing activities..........	0
Financing activities	
Issuance of common stock	300
Payment of cash dividends	(50)
Net cash flows from financing activities..........	250
Net change in cash.........................	$ 450
Cash, beginning of period	0
Cash, end of period	$ 450

Closing Process

LO5 Describe the closing process.

The **closing process** refers to the 'zeroing out' of revenue and expense accounts (the temporary accounts) by transferring their ending balances to retained earnings. (Recall, income statement accounts—revenues and expenses—and the dividend account are temporary accounts because their balances are zero at the end of each accounting period; balance sheet accounts carry over from period to period and are called permanent accounts.) The closing process is typically carried out via a series of journal entries that successively zero out each revenue and expense account, transferring those balances to retained earnings. The result is that all income statement accounts begin the next period with zero balances. The balance sheet accounts do not need to be similarly adjusted because their balances carry over from period to period. Recall the scoreboard analogy.

Our financial statement effects template makes the closing process unnecessary because the template updates retained earnings with each revenue and expense entry. The arrow that runs from net income to retained earnings (part of earned capital) highlights the continual updating. To illustrate, recall the following entries that reflect Apple's initial sale of iPods on credit.

	Balance Sheet						Income Statement		
Transaction	Cash Asset	+ Noncash Assets	= Liabil- ities	+ Contrib. Capital	+ Earned Capital		Rev- enues	− Expen- ses	= Net Income
Sold $700 of iPods on credit		+700 Accounts Receivable =			+700 Retained Earnings		+700 Sales		= +700
Record $600 cost of $700 iPod sale		−600 Inventory =			−600 Retained Earnings			+600 − Cost of Goods Sold	= −600

AR   700
   Sales   700
         AR
   700 |
      Sales
            | 700

COGS   600
   INV   600
      COGS
   600 |
      INV
            | 600

Sales of $700 increase net income by $700, which the template immediately transfers to retained earnings. Likewise, cost of goods sold reduces net income by $600, and this reduction is immediately carried to retained earnings. Consequently, the financial statement effects template always reports an updated retained earnings, making the closing process unnecessary.

It is important to distinguish our financial statement effects template from companies' accounting systems. The financial statement effects template and T-accounts are pedagogical tools that represent transactions' effects on the four financial statements. The template is highly stylized but its simplicity is instructive. In practice, managers use journal entries to record transactions and adjustments. The template captures these in summarized fashion. However, income statement transactions are not automatically transferred to retained earnings and retained earnings is not continuously updated. All companies perform the closing process—someone or some program must transfer the temporary account balances to retained earnings. Thus, it is important to understand the closing process and why companies "close" the books each period. We describe the mechanical details of the closing process in Appendix 3A.

The entire accounting process, from analysis of basic transactions to financial statement preparation to the closing process, is called the **accounting cycle.** As we discuss at the outset of this module and portray graphically in Exhibit 3.1, there are four basic processes in the accounting cycle. First, companies analyze transactions and prepare (and post) entries. Second, companies prepare (and post) adjusting entries. Third, financial statements are prepared from an adjusted trial balance. Fourth, companies perform the closing process. The analysis and posting of transactions is done regularly during each accounting period. However, the preparation of accounting adjustments and financial statements is only done at the end of an accounting period. At this point, we have explained and illustrated all aspects of the accounting cycle.

MODULE-END REVIEW

Refer to the transactions in Mid-Module Reviews 1 and 2. From those transactions, assume that Symantec Corporation prepares the following trial balance. Also assume its transactions are for the quarter ended December 31, 2007.

SYMANTEC
Trial Balance
December 31, 2007

	Debit	Credit
Cash.	$3,280	
Accounts receivable.	350	
Inventories	700	
Prepaid rent	100	
Accounts payable.		$ 600
Wages payable.		50
Unearned revenues		500
Common stock.		3,000
Dividends	20	
Sales.		650
Cost of goods sold.	300	
Wage expense	50	
Totals	$4,800	$4,800

Required

Prepare Symantec's income statement, statement of stockholders' equity, balance sheet, and statement of cash flows.

Solution

SYMANTEC
Income Statement
For Quarter Ended December 31, 2007

Sales.	$650
Cost of goods sold.	300
Gross profit.	350
Wage expense	50
Net income.	$300

SYMANTEC
Retained Earnings Computation
For Quarter Ended December 31, 2007

Retained earnings, beginning of period	$ 0
Add: Net income (loss)	300
Deduct: Dividends	(20)
Retained earnings, end of period.	$280

SYMANTEC
Balance Sheet
December 31, 2007

Assets

Cash	$3,280
Accounts receivable	350
Inventories	700
Prepaid rent	100
Total assets	$4,430

Liabilities and Stockholders' Equity

Liabilities

Accounts payable	$ 600
Wages payable	50
Unearned revenues	500
Total liabilities	1,150

Stockholders' equity

Common stock	3,000
Retained earnings	280
Total liabilities and stockholders' equity	$4,430

SYMANTEC
Statement of Stockholders' Equity
For Quarter Ended December 31, 2007

	Contributed Capital	Earned Capital	Total Stockholders' Equity
Beginning balance	$ 0	$ 0	$ 0
Stock issuance	3,000		3,000
Net income (loss)		300	
Dividends		(20)	(20)
Ending balance	$3,000	$280	$3,280

SYMANTEC
Statement of Cash Flows
For Quarter Ended December 31, 2007

Operating activities

Net income	$ 300
Depreciation and other noncash expenses	0
Gains or losses on asset sales	0
Increase in accounts receivable	(350)
Increase in inventories	(700)
Increase in prepaid rent	(100)
Increase in accounts payable	600
Increase in wages payable	50
Increase in unearned revenues	500
Net cash flows from operating activities	300

Investing activities

Net cash flows from investing activities	0

Financing activities

Issuance of common stock	3,000
Payment of cash dividends	(20)
Net cash flows from financing activities	2,980
Net change in cash	$3,280
Cash, beginning of period	0
Cash, end of period	$3,280

APPENDIX 3A: Closing Process Using Journal Entries

The idea of the closing process is to close all temporary accounts—all the income statement accounts and any dividend account. The balance in each temporary account is transferred to retained earnings leaving the temporary accounts with zero balances. That way, the temporary accounts are ready to capture transaction data for the next period. The closing process brings the retained earnings account up to date so that it is accurate and so that the balance sheet can be prepared. To illustrate, let's return to Apple's income statement.

APPLE Income Statement For Quarter Ended December 31, 2007	
Sales..	$1,600
Cost of goods sold...........................	1,150
Gross profit..................................	450
Wage expense	100
Rent expense................................	25
Net income..................................	$ 325

The closing process transfers the ending balances for each of these income statement accounts, to retained earnings. The dividend account is a temporary account and therefore, it also must be closed to retained earnings. The journal entries, and the related T-accounts, follow for this 3-step process.

1. Close all revenue accounts.

2. Close all expense accounts.

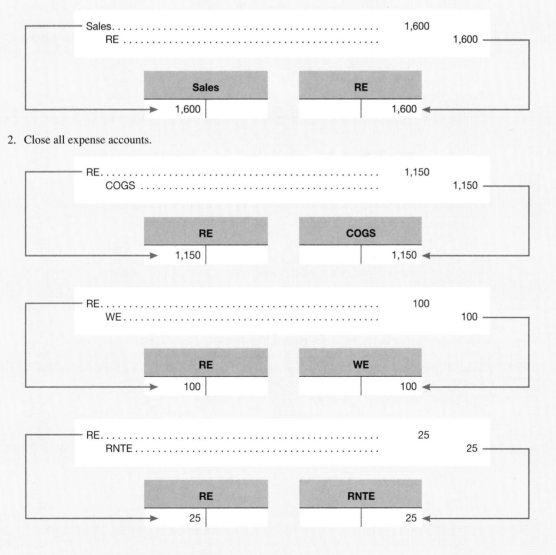

3. Close any dividend accounts.

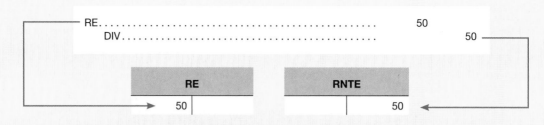

Apple must close one revenue account, three expense accounts, and a dividend account to retained earnings at the end of the period. The first closing entry transfers the $1,600 balance in the sales account to retained earnings. The closing entry debits sales for $1,600 (because the sales account has a $1,600 credit balance at period-end) and credits retained earnings. The second closing entry closes cost of good sold ($1,150), wages expense ($100), and rent expense ($25). The entry credits each of the expense accounts because their ending balances are debit balances. Third, the $50 dividend account balance is transferred to retained earnings. All the temporary accounts are now *closed*.

Retained earnings, which began the period with a zero balance, now reports a balance of $275, which equals net income for the period less the dividends paid to shareholders. This is the balance Apple reports in the stockholders' equity section of its balance sheet. Further, all of the income statement accounts (sales, cost of goods sold, wages expense, and rent expense) and the dividend account now show zero balances to begin the next period.

GUIDANCE ANSWERS

MANAGERIAL DECISION   **You Are the CFO**

Part 1: Liabilities will increase by $10 million for the estimated amount of the cleanup, an expense in that amount will be recognized in the income statement, thus reducing both income and retained earnings (equity) by $10 million. Part 2: Stakeholders affected by recognition decisions of this type are often much broader than first realized. Management is directly involved in the decision. The accrual can affect the market value of the company, its relations with lenders and suppliers, its auditors, and many other stakeholders. Further, if recording the accrual is the right accounting decision, failure to do so can foster unethical behavior throughout the company, thus affecting additional company employees.

Superscript [A] denotes assignments based on Appendix 3A.

DISCUSSION QUESTIONS

Q3-1.   What does the term *fiscal year* mean?

Q3-2.   What is the purpose of a general journal?

Q3-3.   Explain the process of posting.

Q3-4.   What four different types of adjustments are frequently necessary before financial statements are prepared at the end of an accounting period? Give at least one example of each type.

Q3-5.   On January 1, Prepaid Insurance was debited for $1,872 related to the cost of a two-year premium, with coverage beginning immediately. How should this account be adjusted on January 31 before financial statements are prepared for the current month?

Q3-6.   At the beginning of January, the first month of the accounting year, the Supplies account (asset) had a debit balance of $825. During January, purchases of $260 worth of supplies were debited to the account. At the end of January, $630 of supplies were still available. How should this account be adjusted? If no adjustment is made, describe the impact on (a) the income statement for January, and (b) the balance sheet prepared at January 31?

Q3-7.   The publisher of *Accounting View*, a monthly magazine, received $9,720 cash on January 1 for new subscriptions covering the next 24 months, with service beginning immediately. (a) Use the financial statement effects template to record the receipt of the $9,720. (b) Use the template to show how the accounts should be adjusted at the end of January before financial statements are prepared for the current month.

Q3-8. Refer to Question Q3-7. Prepare journal entries for the receipt of cash and the delivery of the magazines.

Q3-9. Trombley Travel Agency pays an employee $475 in wages each Friday for the five-day work week ending on Friday. The last Friday of January falls on January 27. How should Trombley Travel Agency adjust wages expense on January 31, its fiscal year-end?

Q3-10. The Basu Company earns interest amounting to $360 per month on its investments. The company receives the interest revenue every six months, on December 31 and June 30. Monthly financial statements are prepared. Which accounts should Basu adjust on January 31?

Q3-11. ^A What types of accounts are closed at the end of the accounting year? What are the three major steps in the closing process?

MINI EXERCISES

M3-12. Assessing Financial Statement Effects of Transactions (LO1)

DeFond Services, a firm providing art services for advertisers, began business on June 1, 2007. The following accounts are needed to record the transactions for June: Cash; Accounts Receivable; Supplies; Office Equipment; Accounts Payable; Common Stock; Retained Earnings; Service Fees Earned; Rent Expense; Utilities Expense; and Salaries Expense. Record the following transactions for June using the financial statement effects template.

June	1	M. DeFond invested $12,000 cash to begin the business in exchange for common stock.
	2	Paid $950 cash for June rent.
	3	Purchased $6,400 of office equipment on credit.
	6	Purchased $3,800 of art materials and other supplies; the company paid $1,800 cash with the remainder due within 30 days.
	11	Billed clients $4,700 for services rendered.
	17	Collected $3,250 cash from clients on their accounts billed on June 11.
	19	Paid $3,000 cash toward the account for office equipment (see June 3).
	25	Paid $900 cash for dividends.
	30	Paid $350 cash for June utilities.
	30	Paid $2,500 cash for June salaries.

M3-13. Preparing Journal Entries and Posting (LO1)

Refer to the information in M3-12. Prepare a journal entry for each transaction. Create a T-account for each account, and then post the journal entries to the T-accounts (use dates to reference each entry).

M3-14. Assessing Financial Statement Effects of Transactions (LO1)

Verrecchia Company, a cleaning services firm, began business on April 1, 2007. The company created the following accounts to record the transactions for April: Cash; Accounts Receivable; Supplies; Prepaid Van Lease; Equipment; Notes Payable; Accounts Payable; Common Stock; Retained Earnings; Cleaning Fees Earned; Wages Expense; Advertising Expense; and Van Fuel Expense. Record the following transactions for April using the financial statement effects template.

April	1	R. Verrecchia invested $9,000 cash to begin the business in exchange for common stock.
	2	Paid $2,850 cash for six months' lease on van for the business.
	3	Borrowed $10,000 cash from bank and signed note payable agreeing to repay it in 1 year plus 10% interest.
	4	Purchased $5,500 of cleaning equipment; the company paid $2,500 cash with the remainder due within 30 days.
	5	Paid $4,300 cash for cleaning supplies.
	7	Paid $350 cash for advertisements to run in the area newspaper during April.
	21	Billed customers $3,500 for services performed.
	23	Paid $3,000 cash toward the account for cleaning equipment (see April 4).
	28	Collected $2,300 cash from customers on their accounts billed on April 21.
	29	Paid $1,000 cash for dividends.
	30	Paid $1,750 cash for April wages.
	30	Paid $995 cash for gasoline used during April.

M3-15. Preparing Journal Entries and Posting (LO1)

Refer to the information in M3-14. Prepare a journal entry for each transaction. Create a T-account for each account, and then post the journal entries to the T-accounts (use dates to reference each entry).

M3-16. **Assessing Financial Statement Effects of Transactions and Adjustments** (LO1, 2)
Schrand Services offers janitorial services on both a contract basis and an hourly basis. On January 1, 2006, Schrand collected $20,100 cash in advance on a six-month contract for work to be performed evenly during the next six months.
a. Prepare the entry on January 1 to reflect the receipt of $20,100 cash for contract work; use the financial statements effect template.
b. Adjust the appropriate accounts on January 31, 2006, for the contract work done during January; use the financial statements effect template.
c. At January 31, a total of 30 hours of hourly rate janitor work was unbilled. The billing rate is $19 per hour. Prepare the accounting adjustment needed on January 31, 2006, using the financial statements effect template. (Note: The firm uses the account Fees Receivable to reflect amounts due but not yet billed.)

M3-17. **Preparing Accounting Adjustments** (LO1, 2)
Refer to the information in M3-16. Prepare a journal entry for each of parts a, b, and c.

M3-18. **Assessing Financial Statement Effects of Transactions and Adjustments** (LO2)
Selected accounts of Piotroski Properties, a real estate management firm, are shown below as of January 31, 2008, before any accounts have been adjusted.

	Debits	Credits
Prepaid Insurance	$6,660	
Supplies	1,930	
Office Equipment	5,952	
Unearned Rent Revenue		$ 5,250
Salaries Expense	3,100	
Rent Revenue		15,000

Piotroski Properties prepares monthly financial statements. Using the following information, adjust the accounts as necessary on January 31 using the financial statements effect template.
a. Prepaid Insurance represents a three-year premium paid on January 1, 2008.
b. Supplies of $850 were still available on January 31.
c. Office equipment is expected to last eight years (or 96 months).
d. On January 1, 2006, Piotroski collected $5,250 for six months' rent in advance from a tenant renting space for $875 per month.
e. Salaries of $490 have been earned by employees but yet not recorded as of January 31.

M3-19. **Preparing Accounting Adjustments** (LO2)
Refer to the information in M3-18. Prepare journal entries for each of parts *a* through *e*.

M3-20. **Inferring Transactions from Financial Statements** (LO1, 2)
Foot Locker, Inc., a retailer of athletic footwear and apparel, operates 3,921 stores in the United States, Canada, Europe and Asia Pacific. During its fiscal year ended in 2006, Foot Locker purchased merchandise inventory costing $4,047 ($ millions). Assume that Foot Locker makes all purchases on credit, and that its accounts payable is only used for inventory purchases. The following T-accounts reflect information contained in the company's fiscal 2005 and 2006 balance sheets ($ millions).

Inventories			Accounts Payable	
2005 Bal.	1,151		381	2005 Bal.
2006 Bal.	1,254		361	2006 Bal.

a. Use the financial statement effects template to record Foot Locker's 2006 purchases.
b. What amount did Foot Locker pay in cash to its suppliers during fiscal year 2006? Explain.
c. Use the financial statement effects template to record cost of goods sold for its fiscal years 2006.

M3-21. **Preparing Journal Entries and Posting** (LO1, 2)
Refer to the information in M3-20. Prepare journal entries for each of parts *a*, *b* and *c*.

M3-22. **Preparing a Statement of Stockholders' Equity** (LO4)

On December 31, 2005, the accounts of Leuz Architect Services showed credit balances in its Common Stock and Retained Earnings accounts of $30,000 and $18,000, respectively. The company's stock issuances for 2006 totaled $6,000, and it paid $9,700 cash dividends in 2006. During 2006, the company had net income of $29,900. Prepare a 2006 statement of stockholders' equity for Leuz Architect Services.

M3-23.[A] **Preparing Closing Journal Entries** (LO5)

The adjusted trial balance at December 31, 2007, for Francis Real Estate Company includes the following selected accounts.

	Debits	Credits
Commissions Earned		$84,900
Wages Expense	$36,000	
Insurance Expense.	1,900	
Utilities Expense.	8,200	
Depreciation Expense	9,800	
Retained Earnings		72,100

Assume that the company has not yet closed any accounts to retained earnings. Prepare journal entries to close the temporary accounts above. Set up the needed T-accounts and post the closing entries. After these entries are posted, what is the balance of the Retained Earnings account?

M3-24. **Inferring Transactions from Financial Statements** (LO1, 2)

Lowe's is the second-largest home improvement retailer in the world with 1,234 stores in 49 states. During its fiscal year ended in 2006, Lowe's purchased merchandise inventory at a cost of $29,238 ($ millions). Assume that all purchases were made on account and that accounts payable is only used for inventory purchases. The following T-accounts reflect information contained in the company's 2006 and 2005 balance sheets.

Lowe's Companies (LOW)

Merchandise Inventories	
2005 Bal. 5,911	
2006 Bal. 6,706	

Accounts Payable	
	2,695 2005 Bal.
	2,832 2006 Bal.

a. Use the financial statement effects template to record Lowe's purchases during fiscal 2006.
b. What amount did Lowe's pay in cash to its suppliers during fiscal-year 2006? Explain.
c. Use the financial statement effects template to record cost of goods sold for its fiscal year ended in 2006.

M3-25.[A] **Closing Journal Entries** (LO5)

The adjusted trial balance as of December 31, 2007, for Hanlon Consulting contains the following selected accounts.

	Debits	Credits
Service Fees Earned		$80,300
Rent Expense.	$20,800	
Salaries Expense	45,700	
Supplies Expense.	5,600	
Depreciation Expense	10,200	
Retained Earnings		67,000

Prepare entries to close these accounts in journal entry form. Set up T-accounts for each account and record the adjusted trial balance amount in each account. Then, post the closing entries to the T-accounts. After these entries are posted, what is the balance of the Retained Earnings account?

EXERCISES

E3-26. **Assessing Financial Statement Effects of Adjustments** (LO2)

For each of the following separate situations, prepare the necessary accounting adjustments using the financial statement effects template.

a. Unrecorded depreciation on equipment is $610.

b. The Supplies account has an unadjusted balance of $2,990. Supplies still available at the end of the period total $1,100.

c. On the date for preparing financial statements, an estimated utilities expense of $390 has been incurred, but no utility bill has yet been received or paid.

d. On the first day of the current period, rent for four periods was paid and recorded as a $2,800 debit to Prepaid Rent and a $2,800 credit to Cash.

Allstate Insurance
Company (ALL)

e. Nine months ago, Allstate Insurance Company sold a one-year policy to a customer and recorded the receipt of the premium by debiting Cash for $624. No adjusting entries have been prepared during the nine-month period. Allstate's annual financial statements are now being prepared.

f. At the end of the period, employee wages of $965 have been incurred but not paid or recorded.

g. At the end of the period, $300 of interest has been earned but not yet received or recorded.

E3-27. **Preparing Accounting Adjustments** (LO2)

Refer to the information in E3-26. Prepare journal entries for each accounting adjustment.

E3-28. **Assessing Financial Statement Effects of Adjustments Across Two Periods** (LO1, 2)

Engel Company closes its accounts on December 31 each year. The company works a five-day work week and pays its employees every two weeks. On December 31, 2006, Engel accrued $4,700 of salaries payable. On January 9, 2007, the company paid salaries of $12,000 cash to employees. Prepare entries using the financial statement effects template to (a) accrue the salaries payable on December 31; and (b) record the salary payment on January 9.

E3-29.ᴬ **Preparing Accounting Adjustments** (LO1, 2)

Refer to the information in E3-28. Prepare journal entries to accrue the salaries in December; close salaries expense for the year; and pay the salaries in January. Assume that there is no change in the pay rate during the year, and no change in the company's work force.

E3-30. **Financial Analysis using Adjusted Account Data** (LO2)

Selected T-account balances for Bloomfield Company are shown below as of January 31, 2008; accounting adjustments have already been posted. The firm uses a calendar-year accounting period but prepares *monthly* adjustments.

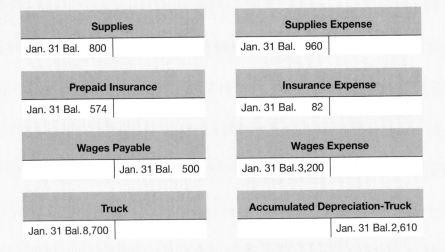

Supplies		Supplies Expense	
Jan. 31 Bal. 800		Jan. 31 Bal. 960	

Prepaid Insurance		Insurance Expense	
Jan. 31 Bal. 574		Jan. 31 Bal. 82	

Wages Payable		Wages Expense	
	Jan. 31 Bal. 500	Jan. 31 Bal. 3,200	

Truck		Accumulated Depreciation-Truck	
Jan. 31 Bal. 8,700			Jan. 31 Bal. 2,610

a. If the amount in Supplies Expense represents the January 31 adjustment for the supplies used in January, and $620 worth of supplies were purchased during January, what was the January 1 beginning balance of Supplies?

b. The amount in the Insurance Expense account represents the adjustment made at January 31 for January insurance expense. If the original insurance premium was for one year, what was the amount of the premium and on what date did the insurance policy start?

c. If we assume that no beginning balance existed in either Wages Payable or Wages Expense on January 1, how much cash was paid as wages during January?

d. If the truck has a useful life of five years (or 60 months), what is the monthly amount of depreciation expense and how many months has Bloomfield owned the truck?

E3-31. **Assessing Financial Statement Effects of Adjustments** (LO2)

T. Lys began Thomas Refinishing Service on July 1, 2007. Selected accounts are shown below as of July 31, before any adjusting entries have been made.

	Debits	Credits
Prepaid Rent	$5,700	
Prepaid Advertising	630	
Supplies	3,000	
Unearned Refinishing Fees		$ 600
Refinishing Fees Revenue		2,500

Using the following information, prepare the accounting adjustments necessary on July 31 using the financial statement effects template.

a.   On July 1, the firm paid one year's rent of $5,700 in cash.

b.   On July 1, $630 cash was paid to the local newspaper for an advertisement to run daily for the months of July, August, and September.

c.   Supplies still available at July 31 total $1,100.

d.   At July 31, refinishing services of $800 have been performed but not yet recorded or billed to customers. The firm uses the account Fees Receivable to reflect amounts due but not yet billed.

e.   In early July, a customer paid $600 in advance for a refinishing project. At July 31, the project is one-half complete.

E3-32. **Preparing Accounting Adjustments and Posting** (LO2)

Refer to the information in E3-31. Prepare adjusting journal entries for each transaction. Set up T-accounts for each of the ledger accounts and post the journal entries to them.

E3-33. **Inferring Transactions from Financial Statements** (LO1)

Harley-Davidson manufactures and sells motorcycles as well as retail parts and accessories throughout the world. The following information is taken from Harley-Davidson's fiscal 2005 annual report.

Harley-Davidson, Inc.
(HOG)

Selected Balance Sheet Data	2005	2004
Inventories	$221,418	$226,893
Accounts receivable.	$121,333	$122,087

a.   Harley-Davidson spent $3,296,240 to purchase and manufacture inventories during its 2005 fiscal year. Use the financial statement effects template to record cost of goods sold for Harley-Davidson's fiscal year ended 2005.

b.   Assume that Harley-Davidson had $1,003,881 sales on credit during fiscal year 2005. What amount did the company collect from credit customers during the year? Record this with the financial statement effects template.

E3-34. **Inferring Transactions and Preparing Journal Entries** (LO1)

Refer to the information in E3-33. Prepare journal entries for each transaction.

Harley-Davidson, Inc.
(HOG)

E3-35.[A] **Preparing Closing Journal Entries** (LO5)

The adjusted trial balance of Plumlee Corporation, dated December 31, 2007, contains the following selected accounts.

	Debit	Credit
Service Fees Earned		$92,500
Interest Income.		2,200
Salaries Expense	$41,800	
Advertising Expense.	4,300	
Depreciation Expense	8,700	
Income Tax Expense	9,900	
Retained Earnings		42,700

Prepare entries to close these accounts in journal entry form. Set up T-accounts for each of the ledger accounts and post the entries to them. After these entries are posted, what is the balance of the Retained Earnings account?

E3-36. **Inferring Transactions from Financial Statements** **(LO1, 2)**

Costco Wholesale Corporation (COST)

Costco Wholesale Corporation operates membership warehouses selling food, appliances, consumer electronics, apparel and other household goods at 471 locations across the U.S. as well as in Canada, Mexico and Puerto Rico. As of its fiscal year-end 2005, Costco had approximately 21.2 million members. Selected fiscal-year information from the company's balance sheets follow ($ thousands).

Selected Balance Sheet Data	2005	2004
Merchandise Inventories	$4,014,699	$3,643,585
Deferred membership income (liability)	500,558	453,881

a. During fiscal 2005, Costco collected $1,119,833 cash for membership fees. Use the financial statement effects template to record the cash collected for membership fees.

b. Calculate the membership fee revenue that Costco recognized during the year. Use the financial statement effects template to record this revenue.

c. Costco recorded merchandise costs (that is, cost of goods sold) of $46,346,961 in 2005. Record this transaction in the financial statements effects template.

d. Determine the value of merchandise that Costco purchased during fiscal-year 2005. Use the financial statement effects template to record these merchandise purchases. Assume all of Costco's purchases are on credit.

E3-37. **Inferring Transactions and Preparing Journal Entries** **(LO1, 2)**

Costco Wholesale Corporation (COST)

Refer to the information in E3-36. Prepare journal entries for transactions in parts a through d.

E3-38.^A **Preparing Financial Statements and Closing Entries** **(LO4, 5)**

The adjusted trial balance for Beneish Corporation is as follows.

BENEISH CORPORATION Adjusted Trial Balance December 31, 2008	Debit	Credit
Cash	$ 4,000	
Accounts Receivable	6,500	
Equipment	78,000	
Accumulated Depreciation		$ 14,000
Notes Payable		10,000
Common Stock		43,000
Retained Earnings		20,600
Dividends	8,000	
Service Fees Earned		71,000
Rent Expense	18,000	
Salaries Expense	37,100	
Depreciation Expense	7,000	
Totals	$158,600	$158,600

a. Prepare Beneish Corporation's income statement and statement of stockholders' equity for year-end December 31, 2008, and its balance sheet as of December 31, 2008. The company paid cash dividends of $8,000 and there were no stock issuances or repurchases during 2008.

b. Prepare journal entries to close Beneish's temporary accounts.

c. Set up T-accounts for each of its accounts and post the closing entries.

PROBLEMS

P3-39. **Assessing Financial Statement Effects of Transactions and Adjustments** (LO2)

The following information relates to December 31 adjustments for Koonce Kwik Print Company. The firm's fiscal year ends on December 31.

1. Weekly salaries for a five-day week total $1,800, payable on Fridays. December 31 of the current year is a Tuesday.
2. Koonce Kwik Print has $20,000 of notes payable outstanding at December 31. Interest of $200 has accrued on these notes by December 31, but will not be paid until the notes mature next year.
3. During December, Koonce Kwik Print provided $900 of printing services to clients who will be billed on January 2. The firm uses the account Fees Receivable to reflect amounts due but not yet billed.
4. Starting December 1, all maintenance work on Koonce Kwik Print's equipment is handled by Richardson Repair Company under an agreement whereby Koonce Kwik Print pays a fixed monthly charge of $400. Koonce Kwik Print paid six months' service charge of $2,400 cash in advance on December 1, and increased its Prepaid Maintenance account by $2,400.
5. The firm paid $900 cash on December 15 for a series of radio commercials to run during December and January. One-third of the commercials have aired by December 31. The $900 payment was recorded in its Prepaid Advertising account.
6. Starting December 16, Koonce Kwik Print rented 400 square feet of storage space from a neighboring business. The monthly rent of $0.80 per square foot is due in advance on the first of each month. Nothing was paid in December, however, because the neighbor agreed to add the rent for one-half of December to the January 1 payment.
7. Koonce Kwik Print invested $5,000 cash in securities on December 1 and earned interest of $38 on these securities by December 31. No interest will be received until January.
8. Annual depreciation on the firm's equipment is $2,175. No depreciation has been recorded during the year.

Required

Prepare its accounting adjustments required at December 31 using the financial statement effects template.

P3-40. **Preparing Accounting Adjustments** (LO2)

Refer to the information in P3-39. Prepare adjustments required at December 31 using journal entries.

P3-41. **Assessing Financial Statement Effects of Adjustments Across Two Periods** (LO1, 2)

The following selected accounts appear in Sloan Company's unadjusted trial balance at December 31, 2008, the end of its fiscal year (all accounts have normal balances).

Prepaid Advertising	$ 1,200	Unearned Service Fees	$ 5,400
Wages Expense	43,800	Service Fees Earned	87,000
Prepaid Insurance	3,420	Rental Income	4,900

Required

a. Prepare its accounting adjustments at December 31, 2008, using the financial statement effects template and the following additional information.
1. Prepaid advertising at December 31 is $800.
2. Unpaid wages earned by employees in December are $1,300.
3. Prepaid insurance at December 31 is $2,280.
4. Unearned service fees at December 31 are $3,000.
5. Rent revenue of $1,000 owed by a tenant is not recorded at December 31.
b. Prepare entries on January 4, 2009, using the financial statement effects template to record (1) payment of $2,400 cash in wages and (2) cash receipt from the tenant of the $1,000 rent revenue.

P3-42. **Preparing Accounting Adjustments** (LO1, 2)

Refer to the information in P3-41. Prepare journal entries for parts a and b.

P3-43. **Journalizing and Posting Transactions, and Preparing a Trial Balance and Adjustments** (LO1, 2, 3)

D. Roulstone opened Roulstone Roofing Service on April 1, 2008. Transactions for April follow.

Apr. 1 Roulstone contributed $11,500 cash to the business in exchange for common stock.
  2 Paid $6,100 cash for the purchase of a used truck.
  2 Purchased $3,100 of ladders and other equipment; the company paid $1,000 cash, with the balance due in 30 days.
  3 Paid $2,880 cash for two-year (or 24-month) premium toward liability insurance.
  5 Purchased $1,200 of supplies on credit.
  5 Received an advance of $1,800 cash from a customer for roof repairs to be done during April and May.
  12 Billed customers $5,500 for roofing services performed.
  18 Collected $4,900 cash from customers toward their accounts billed on April 12.
  29 Paid $675 cash for truck fuel used in April.
  30 Paid $100 cash for April newspaper advertising.
  30 Paid $2,500 cash for assistants' wages earned.
  30 Billed customers $4,000 for roofing services performed.

Required

a. Set up T-accounts for the following accounts: Cash; Accounts Receivable; Supplies; Prepaid Insurance; Trucks; Accumulated Depreciation–Trucks; Equipment; Accumulated Depreciation–Equipment; Accounts Payable; Unearned Roofing Fees; Common Stock; Roofing Fees Earned; Fuel Expense; Advertising Expense; Wages Expense; Insurance Expense; Supplies Expense; Depreciation Expense–Trucks; and Depreciation Expense–Equipment.
b. Record these transactions for April using journal entries.
c. Post these entries to their T-accounts (key numbers in T-accounts by date).
d. Prepare an unadjusted trial balance at April 30, 2008.
e. Prepare entries to adjust the following accounts: Insurance Expense, Supplies Expense, Depreciation Expense—Trucks, Depreciation Expense—Equipment, and Roofing Fees Earned in journal entry form. Supplies still available on April 30 amount to $400. Depreciation for April was $125 on the truck and $35 on equipment. One-fourth of the roofing fee received in advance was earned by April 30.
f. Post adjusting entries to their T-accounts.

P3-44. **Assessing Financial Statement Effects of Transactions and Adjustments** (LO1, 2)

Refer to the information in P3-43.

a. Use the financial statement effects template to record the transactions for April.
b. Use the financial statement effects template to record the adjustments at the end of April (described in part *e* of P3-43).

P3-45. **Preparing an Unadjusted Trial Balance and Accounting Adjustments** (LO2, 3)

Pownall Photomake Company, a commercial photography studio, completed its first year of operations on December 31, 2008. General ledger account balances before year-end adjustments follow; no adjustments have been made to the accounts at any time during the year. Assume that all balances are normal.

Cash.	$ 2,150	Accounts Payable.	$ 1,910
Accounts Receivable	3,800	Unearned Photography Fees	2,600
Prepaid Rent.	12,600	Common Stock.	24,000
Prepaid Insurance	2,970	Photography Fees Earned	34,480
Supplies	4,250	Wages Expense	11,000
Equipment	22,800	Utilities Expense.	3,420

An analysis of the firm's records discloses the following (business began on January 1, 2008).

1. Photography services of $925 have been rendered, but customers have not yet paid or been billed. The company uses the account Fees Receivable to reflect amounts due but not yet billed.
2. Equipment, purchased January 1, 2006, has an estimated life of 10 years.

3. Utilities expense for December is estimated to be $400, but the bill will not arrive or be paid until January of next year. (All prior months' utilities bills have been received and paid.)
4. The balance in Prepaid Rent represents the amount paid on January 1, 2008, for a 2-year lease on the studio it operates from.
5. In November, customers paid $2,600 cash in advance for photos to be taken for the holiday season. When received, these fees were credited to Unearned Photography Fees. By December 31, all of these fees are earned.
6. A 3-year insurance premium paid on January 1, 2008, was debited to Prepaid Insurance.
7. Supplies still available at December 31 are $1,520.
8. At December 31, wages expense of $375 has been incurred but not yet paid or recorded.

Required

a. Prepare Pownall Photomake's unadjusted trial balance at December 31, 2008.
b. Prepare its adjusting entries using the financial statement effects template.

P3-46. Recording Adjustments with Journal Entries and T-Accounts (LO2, 3)
Refer to the information in P3-45.
a. Prepare journal entries to record the accounting adjustments.
b. Set up T-accounts for each account and post the journal entries to them.

P3-47. Preparing an Unadjusted Trial Balance and Accounting Adjustments (LO2, 3)
BensEx, a mailing service, has just completed its first year of operations on December 31, 2008. Its general ledger account balances before year-end adjustments follow; no adjusting entries have been made to the accounts at any time during the year. Assume that all balances are normal.

Cash	$ 2,300	Accounts Payable	$ 2,700
Accounts Receivable	5,120	Common Stock	9,530
Prepaid Advertising	1,680	Mailing Fees Earned	86,000
Supplies	6,270	Wages Expense	38,800
Equipment	42,240	Rent Expense	6,300
Notes Payable	7,500	Utilities Expense	3,020

An analysis of the firm's records reveals the following (business began on January 1, 2008).

1. The balance in Prepaid Advertising represents the amount paid for newspaper advertising for one year. The agreement, which calls for the same amount of space each month, covers the period from February 1, 2008, to January 31, 2009. BensEx did not advertise during its first month of operations.
2. Equipment, purchased January 1, has an estimated life of eight years.
3. Utilities expense does not include expense for December, estimated at $325. The bill will not arrive until January 2009.
4. At year-end, employees have earned $1,200 in wages that will not be paid or recorded until January.
5. Supplies available at year-end amount to $1,520.
6. At year-end, unpaid interest of $450 has accrued on the notes payable.
7. The firm's lease calls for rent of $525 per month payable on the first of each month, plus an amount equal to 0.5% of annual mailing fees earned. The rental percentage is payable within 15 days after the end of the year.

Required

a. Prepare its unadjusted trial balance at December 31, 2008.
b. Prepare its adjusting entries using the financial statement effects template.

P3-48. Recording Accounting Adjustments with Journal Entries and T-Accounts (LO2, 3)
Refer to information in P3-47.
a. Prepare journal entries to record the accounting adjustments.
b. Set up T-accounts for each account and post the journal entries to them.

P3-49.[A] **Preparing Accounting Adjustments** (LO2, 4, 5)

Wysocki Wheels began operations on March 1, 2008, to provide automotive wheel alignment and balancing services. On March 31, 2008, the unadjusted balances of the firm's accounts follow.

WYSOCKI WHEELS Unadjusted Trial Balance March 31, 2008		
	Debit	Credit
Cash.	$ 1,900	
Accounts Receivable	3,820	
Prepaid Rent.	4,770	
Supplies	3,700	
Equipment	36,180	
Accounts Payable		$ 2,510
Unearned Service Revenue		1,000
Common Stock		38,400
Service Revenue.		12,360
Wages Expense	3,900	
	$54,270	$54,270

The following information is also available.
1. The balance in Prepaid Rent was the amount paid on March 1 to cover the first 6 months' rent.
2. Supplies available on March 31 amounted to $1,720.
3. Equipment has an estimated life of nine years (or 108 months).
4. Unpaid and unrecorded wages at March 31 were $560.
5. Utility services used during March were estimated at $390; a bill is expected early in April.
6. The balance in Unearned Service Revenue was the amount received on March 1 from a car dealer to cover alignment and balancing services on cars sold by the dealer in March and April. Wysocki Wheels agreed to provide the services at a fixed fee of $500 each month.

Required
a. Prepare its accounting adjustments at March 31, 2008 in journal entry form.
b. Set up T-accounts and post the accounting adjustments to them.
c. Prepare its income statement for March and its balance sheet at March 31, 2008.
d. Prepare entries to close its temporary accounts in journal entry form. Post the closing entries to the T-accounts.

CASES

C3-50. **Preparing Accounting Adjustments and Financial Statements** (LO1, 2, 4)

Stocken Surf Shop began operations on July 1, 2008, with an initial investment of $50,000. During the initial three months of operations, the following cash transactions were recorded in the firm's checking account.

Deposits

Initial investment by owner	$ 50,000
Collected from customers	81,000
Borrowings from bank	10,000
	$141,000

Checks drawn

Rent	$ 24,000
Fixtures and equipment	25,000
Merchandise inventory.	62,000
Salaries	6,000
Other expenses	13,000
	$130,000

Additional information:

a. Most sales were for cash, however, the store accepted a limited amount of credit sales; at September 30, 2008, customers owed the store $9,000.

b. Rent was paid on July 1 for six months.

c. Salaries of $3,000 per month are paid on the 1st of each month for salaries earned in the month prior.

d. Inventories are purchased for cash; at September 30, 2008, inventory of $21,000 was still available.

e. Fixtures and equipment were expected to last five years (or 60 months) with zero salvage value.

f. The bank charges 12% annual interest (1% per month) on its $10,000 bank loan. Stocken took the loan out July 1.

Required

a. Record all of Stocken's cash transactions and prepare any necessary adjusting entries at September 30, 2008. You may either use the financial statement effects template or journal entries combined with T-accounts.

b. Prepare the income statement for the three months ended September 30, 2008, and its balance sheet at September 30, 2008.

c. Analyze the statements from part b and assess the company's performance over its initial three months.

C3-51. **Analyzing Transactions, Impacts on Financial Ratios, and Loan Covenants** (LO2)

Kadous Consulting, a firm started three years ago by K. Kadous, offers consulting services for material handling and plant layout. Its balance sheet at the close of 2008 follows.

KADOUS CONSULTING Balance Sheet December 31, 2008					
Assets			**Liabilities**		
Cash		$ 3,400	Notes Payable		$30,000
Accounts Receivable		22,875	Accounts Payable		4,200
Supplies		13,200	Unearned Consulting Fees.		11,300
Prepaid Insurance		4,500	Wages Payable.		400
Equipment	$68,500		Total Liabilities		45,900
Less: Accumulated			**Equity**		
Depreciation.	23,975	44,525	Common Stock		8,000
Total Assets		$88,500	Retained Earnings		34,600
			Total liabilities and Equity.		$88,500

Earlier in the year Kadous obtained a bank loan of $30,000 cash for the firm. One of the provisions of the loan is that the year-end debt-to-equity ratio (ratio of total liabilities to total equity) cannot exceed 1.0. Based on the above balance sheet, the ratio at the end of 2008 is 1.08. Kadous is concerned about being in violation of the loan agreement and requests assistance in reviewing the situation. Kadous believes that she might have overlooked some items at year-end. Discussions with Kadous reveal the following.

1. On January 1, 2008, the firm paid a $4,500 insurance premium for 2 years of coverage; the amount in Prepaid Insurance has not yet been adjusted.

2. Depreciation on the equipment should be 10% of cost per year; the company inadvertently recorded 15% for 2008.

3. Interest on the bank loan has been paid through the end of 2008.

4. The firm concluded a major consulting engagement in December, doing a plant layout analysis for a new factory. The $6,000 fee has not been billed or recorded in the accounts.

5. On December 1, 2008, the firm received an $11,300 cash advance payment from Dichev Corporation for consulting services to be rendered over a 2-month period. This payment was credited to the Unearned Consulting Fees account. One-half of this fee was earned but unrecorded by December 31, 2008.

6. Supplies costing $4,800 were available on December 31; the company has made no adjustment of its Supplies account.

Required

a. What is the correct debt-to-equity ratio at December 31, 2008?

b. Is the firm in violation of its loan agreement? Prepare computations to support the correct total liabilities and total equity figures at December 31, 2008.

C3-52. Ethics, Accounting Adjustments, and Auditors (LO1, 2)

It is the end of the accounting year for Anne Beatty, controller of a medium-sized, publicly held corporation specializing in toxic waste cleanup. Within the corporation, only Beatty and the president know that the firm has been negotiating for several months to land a large contract for waste cleanup in Western Europe. The president has hired another firm with excellent contacts in Western Europe to help with negotiations. The outside firm will charge an hourly fee plus expenses, but has agreed not to submit a bill until the negotiations are in their final stages (expected to occur in another 3 to 4 months). Even if the contract falls through, the outside firm is entitled to receive payment for its services. Based upon her discussion with a member of the outside firm, Beatty knows that its charge for services provided to date will be $150,000. This is a material amount for the company.

Beatty knows that the president wants negotiations to remain as secret as possible so that competitors will not learn of the contract the company is pursuing in Europe. In fact, the president recently stated to her, "This is not the time to reveal our actions in Western Europe to other staff members, our auditors, or the readers of our financial statements; securing this contract is crucial to our future growth." No entry has been made in the accounting records for the cost of contract negotiations. Beatty now faces an uncomfortable situation. The company's outside auditor has just asked her if she knows of any year-end adjustments that have not yet been recorded.

Required

a. What are the ethical considerations that Beatty faces in answering the auditor's question?

b. How should Beatty respond to the auditor's question?

C3-53. Inferring Accounting Adjustments from Financial Statements (LO1, 2)

Coldwater Creek
(CWTR)

Coldwater Creek, Inc., a specialty retailer of women's apparel, markets its products through retail stores and catalogs. Selected information from its 2006 and 2005 balance sheets follows ($ thousands).

Selected Balance Sheet Data	2006	2005
Prepaid and deferred marketing costs asset	$10,438	$6,905
Unearned gift certificate revenue liability	13,719	9,329

The following excerpt is from Coldwater Creek's fiscal 2006 10-K report.

All direct costs associated with the development, production and circulation of catalogs are accumulated as prepaid marketing costs until such time as the related catalog is mailed. After that, these costs are reclassified as deferred marketing costs and are amortized into selling, general and administrative expenses over the expected sales realization cycle, typically several weeks. The Company's policy regarding gift certificates and gift cards is to record revenue as the gift certificates and gift cards are redeemed for merchandise. Prior to their redemption, amounts under the gift certificates and gift cards are recorded as a liability.

Required

a. Assume that Coldwater Creek spent $84,933 cash for direct costs associated with catalogs in 2006. Prepare the entry, using the financial statement effects template, to reflect these direct costs.

b. Use the financial statement effects template to adjust the balance in the prepaid and deferred marketing costs account as of its 2006 year-end.

c. Assume that Coldwater Creek sold gift certificates valued at $31,470 in 2006. Use the financial statement effects template to reflect the cash received when customers purchased gift cards.

d. Use the financial statement effects template to record the 2006 merchandise sales to customers who paid with gift certificates.

C3-54. Preparing Journal Entries and Posting (LO1, 2)

Refer to the information in C3-53. Prepare journal entries for parts *a* through *d*. Create T-accounts for the Prepaid and Deferred Marketing Costs account and for the Unearned Gift Certificate Revenue account; then post your journal entries to the relevant T-accounts.

Coldwater Creek
(CWTR)

Analyzing and Interpreting Financial Statements

LEARNING OBJECTIVES

LO1 Compute return on equity (ROE) and disaggregate it into components of operating and nonoperating returns. (p. 4-4)

LO2 Disaggregate operating return (RNOA) into its components of profitability and asset turnover. (p. 4-12)

LO3 Compute and interpret measures of liquidity and solvency. (p. 4-18)

HOME DEPOT

Home Depot measures its employee activities, everything from gross margin per labor-hour to the number of "greets" at its entry doors. It also applies several measures to assess its overall performance and financial condition. These measures include the debt-to-equity ratio, current ratio, inventory turnover, and return on invested capital. Analysts, too, use a variety of measures to capture different aspects of company performance to answer questions such as: Is it managed efficiently and profitably? Does it use assets effectively? Is performance achieved with a minimum of debt?

One fundamental measure is that which Warren Buffett, CEO of the investment firm Berkshire Hathaway, lists in his acquisition criteria cited in Module 1: "Our preference would be to reach our goal by directly owning a diversified group of businesses that generate cash and consistently earn above-average returns on capital." Buffett is referring to return on invested capital, one of the most powerful metrics in the analyst's toolkit.

All return metrics follow the same basic formula—they divide some measure of profit by some measure of investment. A company's performance is commonly judged by its profitability. Although analysis of profit is important, it is only part of the story. A more meaningful analysis is to compare level of profitability with the amount of investment in operating assets. Home Depot's return on invested capital in the past few years has gone from 18% to over 21%. Is that a good return? Well, the median return on invested capital for the S&P 500 for this past year was 10%. By that token, Home Depot is doing very well.

A variation of the return on invested capital metric is the return on equity (ROE), which focuses on shareholder investment. By focusing on the *equity* investment, ROE measures return from the perspective of the common shareholder rather than the company overall. Home Depot's ROE for 2006 was 22.9%, up from 18.4% four years ago. The 2006 median

ROE for the S&P 500 was 15.9%. Home Depot has consistently out-performed this benchmark as the graph to the side illustrates.

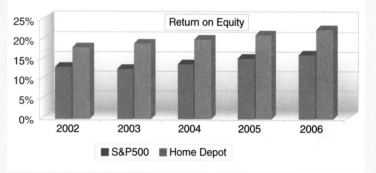

This module focuses on analysis of returns. We put special emphasis on the return on net operating assets (RNOA), computed as net operating profit after tax (NOPAT) divided by average net operating assets (NOA). RNOA focuses on operating activities—operating profit relative to investment in net operating assets. It is important to distinguish operating activities from nonoperating activities because the capital markets value each component differently, placing much greater emphasis on operations. Home Depot's RNOA rose from 16% in 2002 to over 21% in 2006.

RNOA consists of two components: profitability and asset productivity. Increasing either component increases RNOA. These components reflect on the first two questions we posed above. The profitability component of RNOA measures net operating profit after tax for each sales dollar (NOPAT/Sales), and is called the net operating profit margin (NOPM). Over the past five years, Home Depot has increased NOPM from 6% to over 7.2%. As *BusinessWeek* reports "by squeezing more out of each orange box through centralized purchasing and a $1.1 billion investment in technology, such as self-checkout aisles and in-store Web kiosks, profits have more than doubled." Home Depot cannot achieve greater profit margin by simply raising prices because the market is too competitive and there are many substitutes for its products. Instead, it must manage product costs and control overhead costs.

Asset productivity, the second component of RNOA, is reflected in net operating asset turnover (NOAT). NOAT is measured as sales divided by average net operating assets—it captures the notion of how many sales dollars are generated by each dollar of invested assets. Home Depot has increased its NOAT only slightly from 2.8 to 2.9 in the past five years. Increasing the turnover for large asset bases is difficult, and NOAT

(Continued on next page)

(Continued from previous page)

measures tend to fluctuate in a narrow band. When companies are able to make a meaningful improvement in NOAT, however, it usually has a large impact on RNOA.

RNOA is an important metric in assessing the performance of company management. We can use the RNOA components, NOPM and NOAT, to assess how effectively and efficiently management uses the company's operating assets to produce a return.

The difference between ROE and RNOA is important for our analysis. Specifically, ROE consists of a return on operating activities (RNOA) *plus* a return on nonoperating activities, where the latter reflects how well the company uses borrowed funds. Companies can increase ROE by borrowing money and effectively using those borrowed funds. However, debt can increase the company's risk—where severe consequences can result if debt is not repaid when due. This is why Warren Buffett focuses on "businesses earning good returns on equity while employing little or no debt." For those companies that do employ debt, our analysis seeks to evaluate their ability to repay the amounts owed when due. We cover that aspect of analysis using concepts of liquidity and solvency in the latter part of this module.

Over the years, analysts, creditors and others have developed hundreds of ratios to measure specific aspects of financial performance. Most of these seek answers to the root question: Can the company achieve a high return on its invested capital and, if so, is that return sustainable?

Sources: *BusinessWeek*, 2006; Home Depot 10-K, 2006; Home Depot Annual Report, 2006; Berkshire Hathaway 10-K, 2006.

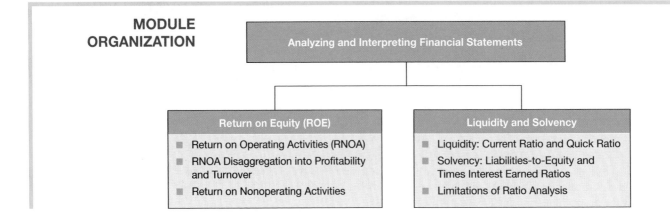

INTRODUCTION

A key aspect of any analysis is identifying the business activities that drive company success. We pursue an answer to the question: Is the company earning an acceptable rate of return on its invested capital? We also want to know the extent to which the company's return on invested capital results from its operating versus its nonoperating activities. The distinction between returns from operating and nonoperating activities is important and plays a key role in our analysis.

Operating activities are the core activities of a company. They consist of those activities required to deliver a company's products or services to its customers. A company engages in operating activities when it conducts research and development, establishes supply chains, assembles administrative support, produces and markets its products, and follows up with after-sale customer services.

The asset side of a company's balance sheet reflects resources devoted to operating activities with accounts such as cash, receivables, inventories, and property, plant and equipment (PPE). They are reflected in liabilities with accounts such as accounts payable, accrued expenses, and long-term operating liabilities such as pension and health care obligations. The income statement reflects operating activities through accounts such as revenues, costs of goods sold, and operating expenses such as selling, general, and administrative expenses that include wages, advertising, depreciation, occupancy, insurance, and research and development. Operating activities create the most long-lasting (persistent) effects on future profitability and cash flows of the company. Operations provide the primary value drivers for company stakeholders. It is for this reason that operating activities play such a prominent role in assessing profitability.

Nonoperating activities relate to the investing of excess cash in marketable securities and in other nonoperating investments. They also relate to borrowings. Nonoperating activities are reflected in a company's balance sheet though accounts such as investments and short- and long-term debt. These nonoperating assets and liabilities expand and contract to buffer fluctuations in operating asset and liability levels. When operating assets grow faster than operating liabilities, companies typically increase their nonoperating liabilities to fund the deficit. Later, these liabilities decline when operating assets decline. When companies have cash in excess of what is needed for operating activities, they often invest the cash temporarily in marketable securities or other investments to provide some return until those funds are needed for operations.

The income statement reflects nonoperating activities through accounts such as interest and dividend revenue, capital gains or losses relating to investments, and interest expense on borrowed funds. Nonoperating expenses, net of any nonoperating revenues, provide a nonoperating return for a company. Although nonoperating activities are important and must be managed well, they are not the main value drivers for company stakeholders.

We begin this module by explaining the return on equity (ROE). We then discuss in more detail how ROE consists of both an operating return (RNOA) and a nonoperating return. Next, we discuss the two RNOA components that measure profitability and asset turnover. We conclude the first half of this module with a discussion of nonoperating return, focusing on the notion that companies can increase ROE through judicious use of debt.

In the second half of this module, we expand our explanation of nonoperating return by exploring how much debt a company can reasonably manage. For this purpose, we examine a number of liquidity and solvency metrics. As part of that analysis, we identify ratios typically used by bond rating agencies, which are key determinants of bond prices and the cost of debt financing for public companies.

RETURN ON EQUITY (ROE)

Return on equity (ROE) is the principle summary measure of company performance and is defined as follows:

LO1 Compute return on equity (ROE) and disaggregate it into components of operating and nonoperating returns.

$$\text{ROE} = \frac{\text{Net income}}{\text{Average stockholders' equity}}$$

ROE relates net income to the average investment by shareholders as measured by total stockholders' equity from the balance sheet. Warren Buffett highlights this return as part of his acquisition criteria: "Businesses earning good returns on equity while employing little or no debt." The ROE formula can be rewritten in a way to better see the point Buffett is making (derivation of this ROE formula is in Appendix 4B):

$$\text{ROE} = \text{Operating return} + \text{Nonoperating return}$$

The equation above shows that ROE consists of two returns: (1) the return from the company's operating activities, linked to revenues and expenses from the company's products or services, and (2) the return from the company's use of debt, net of any return from nonoperating investments. Companies can use debt to increase their return on equity, but this increases risk as the failure to make required debt payments can yield many legal consequences, including bankruptcy. This is one reason why Warren Buffett focuses on companies whose return on equity is derived primarily from operating activities.

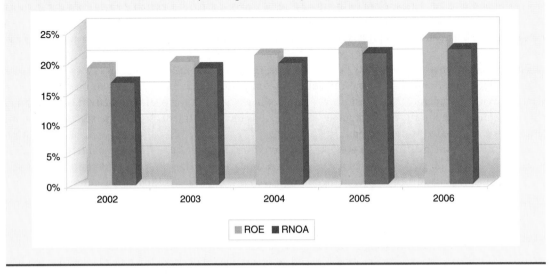

BUSINESS INSIGHT   Home Depot's ROE and RNOA

The following graph shows that Home Depot's ROE and RNOA have increased steadily in the past 5 years. ROE exceeds RNOA in all years, widening more in the most recent year as the company increased its net debt and the nonoperating return component of its ROE.

Operating Return (RNOA)

Operating returns are captured by the **return on net operating assets (RNOA),** defined as follows:

$$\text{RNOA} = \frac{\text{Net operating profit after tax (NOPAT)}}{\text{Average net operating assets (NOA)}}$$

EXHIBIT 4.1	**Operating and Nonoperating Items in the Income Statement**

Typical Income Statement Operating Items Highlighted
Revenues
Cost of sales
Gross profit
Operating expenses
Selling, general and administrative
Asset impairment expense
Gains and losses on asset disposal
Total operating expenses
Operating income
Interest expense
Interest and dividend revenue
Investment gains and losses
Total nonoperating expenses
Income before tax, minority interest and discontinued operations
Tax expense
Income before minority interest and discontinued operations
Minority interest (see Appendix 4B)
Discontinued operations (see Appendix 4B)
Net income

To implement this formula, we must first classify the income statement and balance sheet into operating and nonoperating components so that we can assess each separately. We first consider operating activities on the income statement and explain how to compute NOPAT. Second, we consider operating activities on the balance sheet and explain how to compute NOA.

Operating Items in the Income Statement—NOPAT Computed

The income statement reports both operating and non-operating activities. Exhibit 4.1 shows a typical income statement with the operating activities highlighted.

Some companies divide the income statement into operating and nonoperating sections to facilitate analysis (this division is not required by GAAP). Operating activities are those that relate to bringing a company's products or services to market and any after-sales support. The income statement in Exhibit 4.1 reflects operating activities through revenues, costs of goods sold (COGS), and other expenses. Selling, general, and administrative expense (SG&A) includes wages, advertising, occupancy, insurance, research and development, depreciation, and many other operating expenses the company incurs in the ordinary course of business (some of these are often reported as separate line items in the income statement). Companies also dispose of operating assets, and can realize gains or losses from their disposal, or write them off in full or partially when they become impaired. These, too, are operating activities. Finally, the reported tax expense on the income statement reflects both operating and nonoperating activities. Later in this section we use Home Depot's income statement to explain how to separately compute the effect of taxes on NOPAT.

Nonoperating activities relate to borrowed money that creates interest expense. Nonoperating activities also relate to investments such as marketable securities and other investments that yield interest or dividend revenue and capital gains or losses from any sales of nonoperating investments during the period.

Following is Home Depot's 2006 income statement with the operating items highlighted.

HOME DEPOT Income Statement ($ millions) For Year Ended January 29, 2006	
Revenues	$81,511
Cost of sales	54,191
Gross profit	27,320
Operating expenses	
Selling, general and administrative	16,485
Depreciation	1,472
Total operating expenses	17,957
Operating income	9,363
Interest revenue	62
Interest expense	(143)
Earnings before taxes	9,282
Tax expense	3,444
Net income	$ 5,838

Home Depot's operating items include sales, cost of sales, SG&A, and depreciation expense. Home Depot's earned pretax operating income is $9,363 million. Its nonoperating activities relate to its borrowed money (interest expense is $143 million) and its investment in marketable securities (interest revenue is $62 million). These two nonoperating items combined yield net nonoperating expense of $81 million ($143 million − $62 million).

Computing Tax on Operating Profit—Method 1 Home Depot's income statement reports net operating profit *before* tax of $9,363 million. But, the numerator of the RNOA formula, defined previously, uses net operating profit *after* tax (NOPAT). Thus, we need to subtract taxes to determine NOPAT. The tax expense of $3,444 million that Home Depot reports on its income statement pertains to both operating *and* nonoperating activities. To compute NOPAT, we need to compute the tax expense relating solely to operating profit as follows:

Tax on operating profit = Tax expense + (Net nonoperating expense × Statutory tax rate)

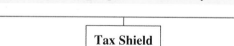

Tax Shield

The amount in parentheses is called the *tax shield*, which are the taxes that Home Depot saved by having tax-deductible nonoperating expenses (see Tax Shield box on page 4–7 for details). That tax benefit, however, does not apply to operating profit; as such, the tax shield is added back to compute tax on operating profit. (For companies with nonoperating revenue greater than nonoperating expense, so-called *net nonoperating revenue*, the tax on operating profit is computed as: Tax expense − [Net nonoperating revenue × Statutory tax rate]). Next, we subtract the tax on operating profit from the net operating profit before tax to obtain NOPAT.

Applying this method, we see that Home Depot had a tax shield of $31 million; computed as net non-operating expense of $81 million times its statutory tax rate of 38%).[1] Thus, Home Depot's net operating profit after tax is computed as follows ($ millions):

Net operating profit before tax..................		$9,363
Less tax on operating profit		
Tax expense (from income statement)	$3,444	
Tax shield ($81 × 38%)......................	+ 31	(3,475)
Net operating profit after tax (NOPAT)		$5,888

BUSINESS INSIGHT   **Tax Shield**

Those of us with a home mortgage understand well the beneficial effects of the "interest tax shield." To see how the interest tax shield works, consider two individuals, each with income of $50,000 and each with only one expense: a home. Assume that one person pays $10,000 per year in rent; the other pays $10,000 in interest on a home mortgage. Rent is not deductible for tax purposes, whereas mortgage interest (but not principal) is deductible. Each person pays taxes at 25%, the personal tax rate for this income level. Their tax payments follow.

	Renter	Home owner
Income	$50,000	$50,000
Less interest deduction	0	(10,000)
Taxable income	$50,000	$40,000
Taxes paid (25% rate).........	$12,500	$10,000

The renter reports $50,000 in taxable income and pays $12,500 in taxes. The home owner deducts $10,000 in interest, which lowers taxable income to $40,000 and reduces taxes to $10,000. By deducting mortgage interest, the home owner's tax bill is $2,500 lower. The $2,500 is called the interest tax shield, and we can compute it directly as the $10,000 interest deduction multiplied by the 25% tax rate. Similarly, we can compute the interest tax shield for corporations using the net interest expense and the statutory corporate tax rate (commonly 37% for federal and state taxes). The adjustment made to determine the tax rate on operating income adds back the tax savings from any interest deduction, since this is a nonoperating item.

Computing Tax on Operating Profit—Method 2   Alternatively, by rearranging terms, we can also compute NOPAT using the following two-step method. First, we compute the tax rate on operating profit as follows.

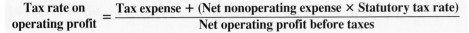

$$\text{Tax rate on operating profit} = \frac{\text{Tax expense} + (\text{Net nonoperating expense} \times \text{Statutory tax rate})}{\text{Net operating profit before taxes}}$$

---

[1] The statutory federal tax rate for corporations is 35% (per U.S. tax code). Also, each state taxes corporate income, and those state taxes are deductible for federal tax purposes. The *net* state tax rate is the statutory rate less the federal tax deduction. Home Depot's 10-K reports federal taxes of $3,249 million and net state taxes of $279 million. Its *tax rate* is, therefore, 38%, computed as ($3,249 million + $279 million)/$9,282 million [the denominator is pretax profit, which is different from operating income before tax reported on the income statement]. This is the "statutory tax rate" used in computing the tax shield to determine tax on operating profit. Most companies, however, provide both the federal and net state tax *percentages* in the income tax footnote (instead of dollars for tax expense). In this case, the tax rate on operating profit is the sum of the two. Lowe's, for example, identifies its federal rate as 35% and its net state tax rate as 3.5% in its income tax footnote. The tax rate on operating profit for Lowe's is 38.5% (35% + 3.5%). This is the rate we use in the Lowe's NOPAT example in Mid-Module Review 1. (The Business Insight on page 4-8 provides an example of this presentation format and Module 5 has additional discussion of income taxes.)

Second, we use that rate to compute NOPAT.

NOPAT = Net operating profit before tax × (1 − Tax rate on operating profit)

Home Depot's tax rate on operating profit is 37.11%, computed as $\left(\dfrac{\$3{,}444 + (\$81 \times 38\%)}{\$9{,}363}\right)$, and its NOPAT is \$5,888 million, computed as \$9,363 million × (1 − 37.11%).

BUSINESS INSIGHT   **Tax Rates for computing NOPAT**

Computing NOPAT requires the tax rate on operating profit, which in turn requires the statutory tax rate (sum of federal and state tax rates). These are disclosed in the required income tax footnote to the 10-K. Following is this footnote from General Mills' 10-K.

Fiscal Year	2005
U.S. statutory rate	35.0%
State and local income taxes, net of federal tax benefits	2.0
Divestitures, net	1.8
Other, net	(2.2)
Effective Income Tax Rate	36.6%

The federal statutory rate is 35.0%, and General Mills pays state and local taxes amounting to an additional 2.0%. It also incurred another 1.8% in tax related to divestitures, and received miscellaneous deductions that lowered its rate by 2.2%. Thus, General Mills effective tax rate for *ALL* its income is the sum of all its taxes paid less benefits received, or 36.6%. However, the interest tax shield that we add back in computing NOPAT only uses *federal and state tax rates*. For General Mills, the tax rate used to compute the tax shield is 37.0% (35.0% + 2.0%).

MID-MODULE REVIEW 1

Following is the income statement of Lowe's Companies, Inc.

LOWE'S COMPANIES, INC.
Income Statement ($ millions)
For Fiscal Year Ended February 3, 2006

Net sales	$43,243
Cost of sales	28,443
Gross margin	14,800
Expenses	
Selling, general and administrative	9,014
Store opening costs	142
Depreciation	980
Interest	158
Total expenses	10,294
Pretax earnings	4,506
Income tax provision	1,735
Net earnings	$ 2,771

Required

Compute Lowe's net operating profit after tax (NOPAT) assuming a 38.5% tax rate on operating profit.

Solution

All expenses reported in Lowe's income statement pertain to operating activities except for interest expense. Therefore, its net operating profit after tax (NOPAT) equals $2,868.4 million, computed as ($ millions) [$43,243 − $28,443 − $9,014 − $142 − $980] × [1 − 0.385]. (This computation uses method 2 as described on page 4-7.)

Operating Items in the Balance Sheet—NOA Computed

RNOA relates NOPAT to the average net operating assets (NOA) of the company. We compute NOA as follows:

Net operating assets = Operating assets − Operating liabilities

To compute NOA we must partition the balance sheet into operating and nonoperating items. Exhibit 4.2 shows a typical balance sheet and highlights the operating items.

EXHIBIT 4.2	Operating and Nonoperating Items in the Balance Sheet
Typical Balance Sheet **Operating Items Highlighted**	

Current assets	**Current liabilities**
Cash and cash equivalents	Short-term notes and interest payable
Short-term investments	Accounts payable
Accounts receivable	Accrued liabilities
Inventories	Deferred income tax liabilities
Prepaid expenses	Current maturities of long-term debt
Deferred income tax assets	
Other current assets	**Long-term liabilities**
	Bonds and notes payable
Long-term assets	Capitalized lease obligations
Long-term investments in securities	Pension and other post-employment liabilities
Property, plant and equipment, net	Deferred income tax liabilities
Capitalized lease assets	Minority Interest
Natural resources	
Equity method investments	**Stockholders' equity**
Goodwill and Intangible assets	All equity accounts
Deferred income tax assets	
Other long-term assets	

Operating assets are those assets directly linked to operating activities, the company's ongoing business operations. They typically include cash, receivables, inventories, prepaid expenses, property, plant and equipment (PPE), and capitalized lease assets, and exclude short-term and long-term investments in marketable securities. Equity investments in affiliated companies and goodwill are considered operating assets if they pertain to the ownership of stock in other firms linked to the company's operating activities (see Module 7). Deferred tax assets (and liabilities) are operating items because they relate to future tax deductions (or payments) arising from operating activities (see Module 5).

Operating liabilities are liabilities that arise from operating revenues and expenses and commonly relate to operating assets. For example, accounts payable and accrued expenses help fund inventories, wages, utilities, and other operating expenses; also, deferred revenue (an operating liability) relates to operating revenue. Similarly, pension and other post-employment obligations relate to long-term obligations for employee retirement and health care, which by definition are operating activities (see Module 10). Operating liabilities exclude bank loans, mortgages or other debt, which are nonoperating. Further, companies often use capitalized leases to finance assets, and these capitalized lease liabilities are also nonoperating (see Module 10).

The following is Home Depot's balance sheets for 2006 and 2005. Its operating assets and operating liabilities are highlighted.

HOME DEPOT Balance Sheet		
$ millions	Jan. 29, 2006	Jan. 30, 2005
Assets		
Current assets		
Cash and cash equivalents	$ 793	$ 506
Short-term investments	14	1,659
Receivables, net	2,396	1,499
Inventories	11,401	10,076
Other current assets	742	533
Total current assets	15,346	14,273
Net property and equipment	24,901	22,726
Other long-term assets	4,235	2,021
Total assets	$44,482	$39,020
Liabilities and stockholders' equity		
Current liabilities		
Short-term borrowings	$ 1,413	$ 11
Accounts payable	6,032	5,766
Accrued expenses and other current liabilities	5,456	4,678
Total current liabilities	12,901	10,455
Long-term debt	2,672	2,148
Other long-term obligations	2,000	2,259
Stockholders' equity		
Common stock	7,407	6,769
Retained earnings	28,943	23,962
Other stockholders' equity	(9,441)	(6,573)
Total stockholders' equity	26,909	24,158
Total liabilities and stockholders' equity	$44,482	$39,020

We assume that Home Depot's "other" assets and liabilities are operating. We can sometimes make a finer distinction if footnotes to financial statements provide additional information. For now, assume that these "other" items reported in balance sheets pertain to operations.

Using the highlighted balance sheet above, we compute net operating assets for Home Depot in 2006 and 2005 as follows (we use: Net operating assets (NOA) = Total operating assets − Total operating liabilities).

$ millions	Jan. 29, 2006	Jan. 30, 2005
Operating Assets		
Cash and cash equivalents	$ 793	$ 506
Receivables, net	2,396	1,499
Inventories	11,401	10,076
Other current assets.	742	533
Net property and equipment	24,901	22,726
Other long-term assets	4,235	2,021
Total operating assets	44,468	37,361
Operating Liabilities		
Accounts payable	6,032	5,766
Accrued expenses and other current liabilities	5,456	4,678
Other long-term obligations	2,000	2,259
Total operating liabilities.	13,488	12,703
Net operating assets (NOA)	$30,980	$24,658

To determine average NOA, we take a simple average of two consecutive years' numbers. Thus, return on net operating assets (RNOA) for Home Depot for 2006 is computed as follows ($ millions).

$$RNOA = \frac{NOPAT}{Average\ NOA} = \frac{\$5,888}{(\$30,980 + \$24,658)/2} = 21.2\%$$

Home Depot's 2006 RNOA is 21.2%. By comparison, Lowe's Companies' (its main competitor) RNOA is 18%, and the average for all publicly traded companies is about 10%.

Recall that RNOA is related to ROE as follows: ROE = Operating return + Nonoperating return, where RNOA is the operating return. Thus, we can ask how do Home Depot's RNOA and ROE compare? Home Depot's 2006 ROE is computed as follows ($ millions).

$$ROE = \frac{Net\ income}{Average\ stockholders'\ equity} = \frac{\$5,838}{(\$26,909 + \$24,158)/2} = 22.9\%$$

In relative terms, Home Depot's operating return is 93% (21.2%/22.9%) of its total ROE. Its nonoperating return of 1.7% (22.9% − 21.2%) makes up the remaining 7% of ROE. Home Depot's RNOA as a percent of ROE is impressive because the average publicly traded company's RNOA is only 84% of ROE (Nissim and Penman, 2001). Thus, Home Depot appears to satisfy Warren Buffett's criterion of earning good returns on equity while employing little or no debt. Indeed, Home Depot's debt accounts for only 9% of its total assets, computed as [$1,413 + $2,672]/$44,482 ($ millions).

Exhibit 4.3 provides a summary of key terms introduced to this point and their definitions.

EXHIBIT 4.3	Key Ratio Definitions

Ratio	Definition
ROE: Return on equity	Net income/Average stockholders' equity
NOPAT: Net operating profit after tax	Operating revenues less operating expenses such as cost of sales, selling, general and administrative expense, and taxes; it excludes nonoperating revenues and expenses such as interest revenue, dividend revenue, interest expense, gains and losses on investments, and minority interest.
NOA: Net operating assets	Operating assets less operating liabilities; it excludes investments in marketable securities and interest-bearing debt.
RNOA: Return on net operating assets. . .	NOPAT/Average NOA
NNE: Net nonoperating expense	NOPAT − Net income; NNE consists of nonoperating expenses and revenues, net of tax

RNOA Disaggregation into Margin and Turnover

Disaggregating RNOA into its two components, profit margin and asset turnover, yields further insights into a company's performance. This disaggregation follows.

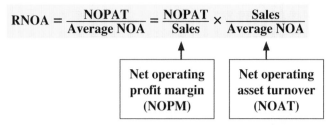

$$\text{RNOA} = \frac{\text{NOPAT}}{\text{Average NOA}} = \frac{\text{NOPAT}}{\text{Sales}} \times \frac{\text{Sales}}{\text{Average NOA}}$$

Net operating profit margin (NOPM)

Net operating asset turnover (NOAT)

LO2 Disaggregate operating return (RNOA) into its components of profitability and asset turnover.

Net operating profit margin (NOPM) reveals how much operating profit the company earns from each sales dollar. All things equal, a higher NOPM is preferable. NOPM is affected by the level of gross profit the company earns on its products (revenue minus cost of goods sold), which depends on product prices and manufacturing or purchase costs. NOPM is also affected by the level of operating expenses the company requires to support its products or services. This includes overhead costs such as wages, marketing, occupancy, and research and development. Finally, NOPM is affected by the level of competition (which affects product pricing) and the company's willingness and ability to control costs.

Home Depot's net operating profit margin is computed as follows ($ millions).

$$\text{NOPM} = \frac{\text{NOPAT}}{\text{Revenues}} = \frac{\$5,888}{\$81,511} = 7.22\%$$

This result means that for each dollar of sales at Home Depot, the company earns just over 7.2¢ profit after all operating expenses and tax. As a reference, the median NOPM for all publicly traded firms is 5.5¢ (Nissim and Penman, 2001).

BUSINESS INSIGHT   **Home Depot's NOPM**

The following chart shows that Home Depot's net operating profit margin increased from 5.8% of revenues in 2002 to 7.2% in 2006, which is a substantial increase for such a competitive industry.

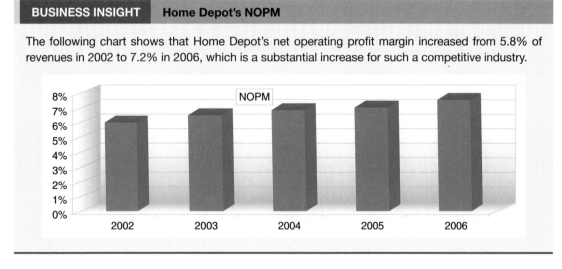

Net operating asset turnover (NOAT) measures the productivity of the company's net operating assets. This metric reveals the level of sales the company realizes from each dollar invested in net operating assets. All things equal, a higher NOAT is preferable. Home Depot's net operating asset turnover ratio follows ($ millions).

$$\text{NOAT} = \frac{\text{Revenues}}{\text{Average NOA}} = \frac{\$81,511}{(\$30,980 + \$24,658)/2} = 2.93$$

This result means that for each dollar of net operating assets, Home Depot realizes $2.93 in sales. As a reference, the median for all publicly traded companies is $1.97 (Nissim and Penman, 2001).

NOAT can be increased by either increasing sales for a given level of investment in operating assets, or by reducing the amount of operating assets necessary to generate a dollar of sales, or both. Reducing operating working capital (current operating assets less current operating liabilities) is usually easier than

BUSINESS INSIGHT Home Depot's NOAT

The following chart shows Home Depot's net operating asset turnover from 2002 to 2006. Its largest value is 3.05 in 2005 and its lowest is 2.78 in 2002. Home Depot's net operating asset turnover exceeds the 1.97 median for publicly traded firms in each of these years.

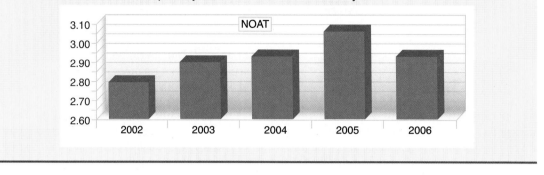

reducing net long-term operating assets. For example, companies can implement strategies to collect their receivables faster, reduce their inventories, and delay payments to their suppliers. All of these actions reduce operating working capital and, thereby, increase NOAT. These strategies must be managed, however, so as not to negatively impact sales or supplier relations. Working capital management is an important part of managing the company effectively.

It is usually more difficult to reduce the level of net long-term operating assets. The level of PPE required by the company is determined more by the demands of the products or services offered than by management action. For example, telecommunications companies require more capital investment than do retail stores. Still, there are several actions that managers can take to reduce capital investment. Some companies pursue novel approaches, such as corporate alliances, outsourcing, and use of special purpose entities; we discuss some of these approaches in Module 10.

MANAGERIAL DECISION You Are the Entrepreneur

You are analyzing the performance of your start-up company. Your analysis of RNOA reveals the following (industry benchmarks in parenthesis): RNOA is 16% (10%), NOPM is 18% (17%), and NOAT is 0.89 (0.59). What interpretations do you draw that are useful for managing your company?
[Answer, p. 4-30]

Trade-Off between Margin and Turnover

Operating profit margin and turnover of operating assets are largely affected by a company's business model. This is an important concept. Specifically, an infinite number of combinations of net operating profit margin and net operating asset turnover will yield a given RNOA. This relation is depicted in Exhibit 4.4 (where the curved line reflects the median RNOA for all publicly traded companies; from Nissim and Penman, 2001).

This exhibit reveals that some industries, like communication and pharmaceuticals, are capital intensive with relatively low operating asset turnover. Accordingly, for such industries to achieve a required RNOA (to be competitive in the overall market), they must obtain a higher profit margin. On the other hand, service companies such as retailers and restaurants hold fewer assets and, therefore, can operate on lower operating profit margins to achieve a sufficient RNOA. This is because their asset turnover is far greater.

This exhibit warns of blindly comparing the performance of companies across different industries. For instance, a higher profit margin in the Communication industry compared with the Apparel industry is not necessarily the result of better management. Instead, the Communication industry is extremely capital intensive and thus, to achieve an equivalent RNOA, Communications firms must earn a higher profit margin to offset their lower asset turnover. Basic economics suggests that all industries must earn an acceptable return on investment if they are to continue to attract investors and survive.

The trade-off between margin and turnover is obvious when comparing firms that operate in sole industries (*pure-play* firms). Analyzing conglomerates that operate in several industries is more challenging. Conglomerates' margins and turnover rates are a weighted-average of the margins and turnover

EXHIBIT 4.4	Profitability and Productivity across Industries

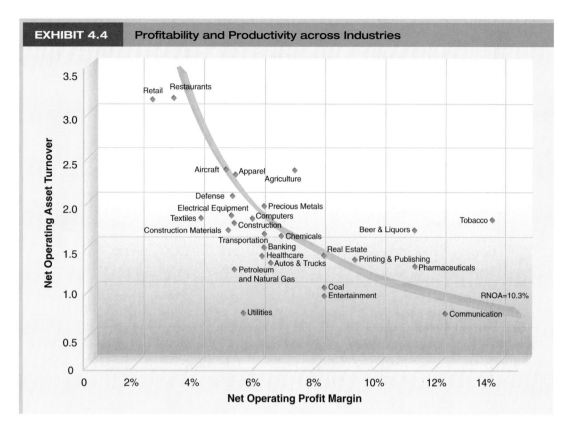

rates for the various industries in which they operate. For example, Ford Motor Company is a blend of a manufacturing company and a financial institution (Ford Motor Credit Company); thus, the margin and turnover benchmarks for Ford on a consolidated basis is a weighted average of the two industries.

To summarize, ROE is the sum of the returns from operating (RNOA) and nonoperating activities. RNOA is the product of NOPM and NOAT.

MID-MODULE REVIEW 2

Following is the balance sheet of Lowe's Companies, Inc.

LOWE'S COMPANIES, INC.
Balance Sheet

$ millions	February 3, 2006	January 28, 2005
Assets		
Cash and cash equivalents	$ 423	$ 530
Short-term investments	453	283
Accounts receivable, net	18	9
Merchandise inventory, net	6,706	5,911
Deferred income taxes, net	127	95
Other assets	104	75
Total current assets	7,831	6,903
Property, net	16,354	13,911
Long-term investments	294	146
Other assets	203	178
Total assets.	$24,682	$21,138

continued

LOWE'S COMPANIES, INC.
Balance Sheet

$ millions	February 3, 2006	January 28, 2005
Liabilities and shareholders' equity		
Current maturities of long-term debt	$ 32	$ 630
Accounts payable.	2,832	2,695
Accrued salaries and wages	424	386
Self-insurance liabilities	571	467
Deferred revenue	709	539
Other current liabilities	1,264	931
Total current liabilities.	5,832	5,648
Long-term debt	3,499	3,060
Deferred income taxes	735	736
Other long-term liabilities	277	159
Total liabilities	10,343	9,603
Shareholders' equity		
Common stock	392	387
Capital in excess of par value	1,712	1,514
Retained earnings	12,234	9,634
Other	1	—
Total shareholders' equity	14,339	11,535
Total liabilities and shareholders' equity.	$24,682	$21,138

Required

1. Compute Lowe's net operating assets for 2006 and 2005.
2. Refer to Lowe's income statement and NOPAT from Mid-Module Review 1. Compute Lowe's return on net operating assets (RNOA) for 2006.
3. Compute Lowe's 2006 ROE. What percentage of Lowe's ROE comes from operations?
4. Disaggregate Lowe's 2006 RNOA into net operating profit margin (NOPM) and net operating asset turnover (NOAT).
5. Compare and contrast Lowe's ROE, RNOA, NOPM, and NOAT with those same measures computed in this module for Home Depot. Interpret the results.

Solution ($ millions)

1.

LOWE'S COMPANIES, INC.
Balance Sheet

$ millions	February 3, 2006	January 28, 2005
Cash and cash equivalents	$ 423	$ 530
Accounts receivable, net	18	9
Merchandise inventory, net	6,706	5,911
Deferred income taxes, net	127	95
Other assets	104	75
Property, net	16,354	13,911
Other assets	203	178
Accounts payable.	(2,832)	(2,695)
Accrued salaries and wages	(424)	(386)
Self-insurance liabilities	(571)	(467)
Deferred revenue	(709)	(539)
Other current liabilities	(1,264)	(931)
Deferred income taxes	(735)	(736)
Other long-term liabilities	(277)	(159)
Net operating assets	$17,123	$14,796

2. RNOA $= \dfrac{\$2,868.4}{(\$17,123 + \$14,796)/2} = 18.0\%$

3. ROE $= \dfrac{\$2,771}{(\$14,339 + \$11,535)/2} = 21.4\%$

Lowe's RNOA makes up 84.1% of its ROE, computed as 18.0%/21.4%.

4. NOPM $= \dfrac{\$2,868.4}{\$43,243} = 6.63\%$

NOAT $= \dfrac{\$43,243}{(\$17,123 + \$14,796)/2} = 2.71$

5. Despite similar business models, Home Depot is superior on the profitability measures of ROE, RNOA, NOPM, and NOAT.

	ROE	RNOA	NOPM	NOAT
Home Depot	22.9%	21.2%	7.22%	2.93%
Lowe's	21.4	18.0	6.63	2.71

Home Depot's RNOA comprises 92.6% of its ROE (computed as 21.2%/22.9%), while Lowe's is 84.1%. Lowe's is relying on the beneficial effects of borrowing to a greater extent, but its ROE still lags behind Home Depot's. Home Depot's net operating profit margin and net operating asset turnover both exceed those for Lowe's. Additional analysis (in the next section) of gross profit margins and expense management provides further insight into the reasons for Home Depot's superior operating profitability. Further, asset management can be assessed by analyzing the control of receivables and inventories, as well as construction costs and sales per square foot.

Further RNOA Disaggregation

While disaggregation of RNOA into net operating profit margin (NOPM) and net operating asset turnover (NOAT) yields valuable insight into factors driving company performance, analysts and creditors usually disaggregate those components even further. The purpose is to better identify the specific drivers of both profitability and turnover.

To disaggregate NOPM, we examine the gross profit on products sold and the individual expense accounts that affect operating profit as a percentage of sales (such as Gross profit/Sales and SG&A/Sales). These margin ratios aid comparisons across companies of differing sizes and across different time periods for the same company. We further discuss profit margin disaggregation in Appendix 4A and in other modules that focus on operating results.

To disaggregate NOAT, we examine the individual balance sheet accounts that comprise NOA and compare them to the related income statement activity. Specifically, we compute accounts receivable turnover (ART), inventory turnover (INVT), property, plant and equipment turnover (PPET), as well as turnovers for liability accounts such as accounts payable turnover (APT). Analysts and creditors often compute the net operating working capital turnover (NOWCT) to assess a company's working capital management compared to its competitors and recent trends. These turnover rates are further discussed in other modules that focus on operating assets and liabilities. Exhibit 4.5 provides a broad overview of ratios commonly used for component disaggregation and analysis.

Nonoperating Return

This section discusses a company's nonoperating return. In simplest form, the return on nonoperating activities measures the extent to which a company is using debt to increase its return on equity. The following example provides the intuition for this return. Assume that a company has $1,000 in average assets for the current year in which it earns a 20% RNOA. It finances those assets entirely with equity investment (no debt). Its ROE is computed as follows:

$$\text{ROE} = \text{Operating return} + \text{Nonoperating return}$$
$$= \quad 20\% \quad + \quad 0\%$$
$$= \quad 20\%$$

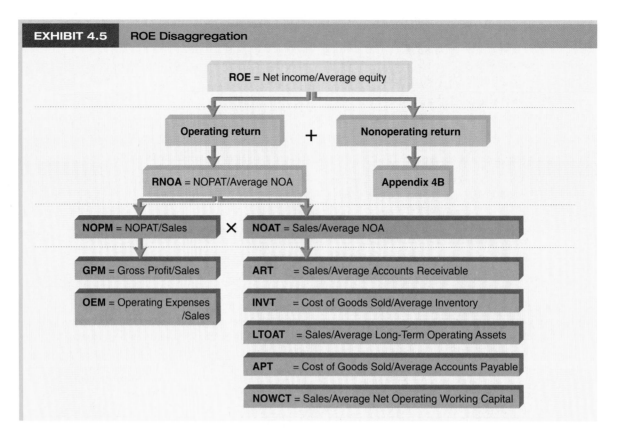

EXHIBIT 4.5   ROE Disaggregation

Next, assume that this company borrows $500 at 7% interest and uses those funds to acquire additional assets yielding the same operating return. Its average assets for the year now total $1,500, and its profit is $265, computed as follows:

Profit from assets financed with equity ($1,000 × 20%)		$200
Profit from assets financed with debt ($500 × 20%).	$100	
Less interest expense from debt ($500 × 7%)	(35)	65
Net profit.		$265

We see that this company has increased its profit to $265 (up from $200) with the addition of debt, and its ROE is now 26.5% ($265/$1,000). The reason for the increased ROE is that the company borrowed $500 at 7% (and paid $35 of interest expense) and invested those funds in assets earning 20% (which generated $100 of profits). The difference of 13% ($65 profit, computed as 13% × $500) accrues to shareholders. Stated differently, the company's ROE now consists of the following.

$$\textbf{ROE} = \textbf{Operating return} + \textbf{Nonoperating return}$$
$$= \quad 20\% \quad + \quad 6.5\%$$
$$= \quad 26.5\%$$

The company has made effective use of debt to increase its ROE. The nonoperating return is inferred as the difference between ROE and RNOA. This return can be computed directly, and we provide an expanded discussion of this computation in Appendix 4B.

We might further ask: If a higher ROE is desirable, why don't companies use the maximum possible debt? The answer is that increasing levels of debt result in successively higher interest rates charged by creditors (see Module 8). At some point, the cost of debt exceeds the return on assets that a company can acquire from the debt financing. Thereafter, further debt financing does not make economic sense. The market, in essence, places a limit on the level of debt that a company can effectively acquire. In sum, shareholders benefit from increased use of debt provided that the assets financed with the debt earn a return that exceeds the cost of the debt.

RESEARCH INSIGHT   **Ratio Behavior over Time**

How do ROE, RNOA, and NNEP (net nonoperating expense percent, defined later in this module) behave over time? Following is a graph of these ratios over a recent 34-year period (from graph B, p.134, of Nissim and Penman, 2001, *Review of Accounting Studies* 6 (1), pp. 109–154, with permission of Springer Science and Business Media). There is considerable variability in these ratios over time. The proportion of RNOA to ROE is greater for some periods of time than for others. Yet, in all periods, RNOA exceeds the net nonoperating expense percent, NNEP. This is evidence of a positive effect, on average, for ROE from financial leverage.

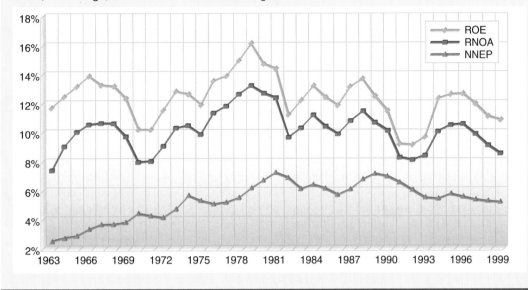

In addition, creditors usually require a company to execute a loan agreement that places varying restrictions on its operating activities. These restrictions, called *covenants*, help safeguard debtholders in the face of increased risk. This is because debtholders do not have a voice on the board of directors like stockholders do. These debt covenants impose a "cost" on the company beyond that of the interest rate, and these covenants are more stringent as a company increases its reliance on debt financing.

LIQUIDITY AND SOLVENCY

LO3 Compute and interpret measures of liquidity and solvency.

Companies can effectively use debt to increase ROE with returns from nonoperating activities. The advantage of debt is that it typically is a less costly source of financing; currently the cost of debt is about 4% versus a cost of equity of about 12%, on average. Although it reduces financing costs, debt does carry default risk: the risk that the company will be unable to repay debt when it comes due. Creditors have several legal remedies when companies default, including forcing a company into bankruptcy and possibly liquidating its assets.

The median ratio of total liabilities to stockholders' equity, which measures the relative use of debt versus equity in a company's capital structure, is about 1.0 for all publicly traded companies. This means that the average company is financed with about half debt and half equity. However, the relative use of debt varies considerably across industries as illustrated in Exhibit 4.6.

Companies in the utilities industry have among the highest proportions of debt. Since the utilities industry is regulated, profits and cash flows are relatively certain and stable and, as a result, utility companies can support a higher debt level. The transportation industry also utilizes a relatively high proportion of debt. However, this industry is not regulated, its market is more competitive and volatile and, consequently, its use of debt carries more risk. At the lower end of debt financing are pharmaceuticals and software companies. Historically, these industries have been characterized by relatively uncertain profits and cash flows. Consequently, they use less debt in their capital structures.

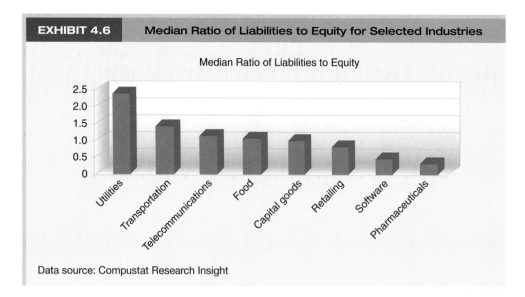

EXHIBIT 4.6 Median Ratio of Liabilities to Equity for Selected Industries

Median Ratio of Liabilities to Equity

Data source: Compustat Research Insight

The core of our analysis relating to debt is the examination of a company's ability to generate cash to *service* its debt (that is, to make required debt payments of both interest and principal). Analysts, investors and creditors are primarily concerned about whether the company either has sufficient cash available or whether it is able to generate the required cash in the future to cover its debt obligations. The analysis of available cash is called *liquidity analysis*. The analysis of the company's ability to generate sufficient cash in the future is called *solvency analysis* (so named because a bankrupt company is said to be "insolvent").

Liquidity Analysis

Liquidity refers to cash availability: how much cash a company has, and how much it can raise on short notice. Two of the most common ratios used to assess the degree of liquidity are the current ratio and the quick ratio. Both of these ratios link required near-term payments to cash available in the near-term.

Current Ratio

Current assets are those assets that a company expects to convert into cash within the next operating cycle, which is typically a year. *Current liabilities* are those liabilities that come due within the next year. An excess of current assets over current liabilities (Current assets − Current liabilities), is known as *net working capital* or simply *working capital*.[2] Positive working capital implies more expected cash inflows than cash outflows in the short run. The current ratio expresses working capital as a ratio and is computed as follows:

$$\text{Current ratio} = \frac{\text{Current assets}}{\text{Current liabilities}}$$

A current ratio greater than 1.0 implies positive working capital. Both working capital and the current ratio consider existing balance sheet data only and ignore cash inflows from future sales or other sources. The current ratio is more commonly used than working capital because ratios allow comparisons across companies of different size. Generally, companies prefer a higher current ratio; however, an excessively high current ratio indicates inefficient asset use. Furthermore, a current ratio less than 1.0 is not always bad for at least two reasons:

---

[2] Both operating assets and operating liabilities can be either current or long-term. "Current" means that the asset is expected to be used, or the liability paid, within the next operating cycle or one year, whichever is longer, which for most companies means a year. Using the current versus long-term nature of operating assets and liabilities we derive two types of net operating assets: net operating working capital (NOWC), and net long-term operating assets. Net operating working capital is defined as:

Net operating working capital (NOWC) = Current operating assets − Current operating liabilities

For Home Depot, NOWC is $3,844 million for 2006 ($15,332 million − $11,488 million).

1. A cash-and-carry company (like a grocery store) can have potentially few current assets (and a low current ratio), but consistently large operating cash inflows ensure the company will be sufficiently liquid.

2. A company can efficiently manage its working capital by minimizing receivables and inventories and maximizing payables. Dell and Wal-Mart, for example, use their buying power to exact extended credit terms from suppliers. Consequently, because both companies are essentially cash-and-carry companies, their current ratios are less than 1.0 and both are sufficiently liquid.

The aim of current ratio analysis is to discern if a company is having, or is likely to have, difficulty meeting its short-term obligations. Home Depot's current ratio for 2006 is 1.19 ($15,346 million/$12,901 million) and for 2005 it is 1.37 ($14,273 million/$10,455 million). Its current ratio has steadily declined over the past five years as shown in the margin graph.

Although, according to this measure, Home Depot's liquidity has declined, it is a cash-and-carry business as it reports only $2.4 billion of accounts receivable on $81.5 billion in sales. We would not expect Home Depot's current ratio to be as high as those companies that carry a high level of receivables. Thus, Home Depot seems sufficiently liquid.

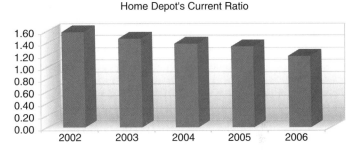

Home Depot's Current Ratio

Quick Ratio

The quick ratio is a variant of the current ratio. It focuses on quick assets, which are those assets likely to be converted to cash within a relatively short period of time. Specifically, quick assets include cash, marketable securities, and accounts receivable; they exclude inventories and prepaid assets. The quick ratio is defined as follows:

$$\text{Quick ratio} = \frac{\text{Cash + Marketable securities + Accounts receivables}}{\text{Current liabilities}}$$

The quick ratio reflects on a company's ability to meet its current liabilities without liquidating inventories that could require markdowns. It is a more stringent test of liquidity than the current ratio.

Home Depot's 2006 quick ratio is 0.25 $\left(\frac{\$793 \text{ million} + \$14 \text{ million} + \$2,396 \text{ million}}{\$12,901 \text{ million}}\right)$, compared with 0.35 $\left(\frac{\$506 \text{ million} + \$1,659 \text{ million} + \$1,499 \text{ million}}{\$10,455 \text{ million}}\right)$ in 2005, and has steadily declined over the past five years—see margin graph. It is not uncommon for a company's quick ratio to be less than 1.0. Home Depot's liquidity has declined according to the quick ratio, which is similar to the pattern of its current ratio over recent years. Although liquidity is not a major concern for Home Depot, the current decline is something financial statement users would want to monitor.

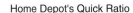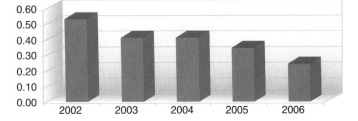

Home Depot's Quick Ratio

Solvency Analysis

Solvency refers to a company's ability to meet its debt obligations, including both periodic interest payments and the repayment of the principal amount borrowed. Solvency is crucial since an insolvent company is a failed company. There are two general approaches to measuring solvency. The first approach uses balance sheet data and assesses the proportion of capital raised from creditors. The second approach uses income statement data and assesses the profit generated relative to debt payment obligations. We discuss each approach in turn.

Liabilities-to-Equity

The liabilities-to-equity ratio is a useful tool for the first type of solvency analysis. It is defined as follows:

$$\text{Liabilities-to-equity ratio} = \frac{\text{Total liabilities}}{\text{Stockholders' equity}}$$

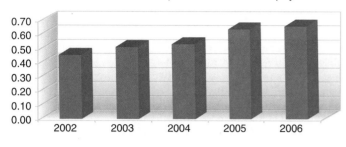

Home Depot Total Liabilities to Equity

This ratio conveys how reliant a company is on creditor financing compared with equity financing. A higher ratio indicates less solvency, and more risk. Home Depot's 2006 liabilities-to-equity ratio is 0.65 $\left(\frac{\$12,901 \text{ million} + \$2,672 \text{ million} + \$2,000 \text{ million}}{\$26,909 \text{ million}}\right)$, and for 2005 it is 0.62 $\left(\frac{\$10,455 \text{ million} + \$2,148 \text{ million} + \$2,259 \text{ million}}{\$24,158 \text{ million}}\right)$. This ratio has consistently increased for Home Depot over the past five years—see margin graph. Still, its ratio is lower than 1.0, the average for publicly traded companies.

A variant of this ratio considers a company's *long-term* debt divided by equity. This approach assumes that current liabilities are repaid from current assets (so-called self-liquidating). Thus, it assumes that creditors and stockholders need only focus on the relative proportion of long-term capital.

Times Interest Earned

The second type of solvency analysis compares profits to liabilities. This approach assesses how much operating profit is available to cover debt obligations. A common measure for this type of solvency analysis is the times interest earned ratio, defined as follows:

$$\text{Times interest earned} = \frac{\textbf{Earnings before interest and taxes}}{\textbf{Interest expense}}$$

The times interest earned ratio reflects the operating income available to pay interest expense. The underlying assumption is that only interest needs to be paid because the principal will be refinanced. This ratio is sometimes abbreviated as EBIT/I. The numerator is similar to net operating profits after tax (NOPAT), but it is *pretax* instead of after tax.

Management wants this ratio to be sufficiently high so that there is little risk of default. Although declining over the past five years, Home Depot's 2006 times interest earned ratio is a healthy 66, computed as $\left(\frac{\$9,282 \text{ million} + \$143 \text{ million}}{\$143 \text{ million}}\right)$—see margin graph. This result implies that Home Depot could suffer a

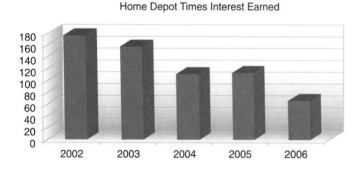

Home Depot Times Interest Earned

large decline in profitability and still be able to service its interest payments when due. Any solvency concerns we might have had relating to Home Depot's lack of liquidity are mitigated by its earning power and its relatively low level of debt in relation to its shareholder investment.

There are many variations of solvency and liquidity analysis and the ratios used. The basic idea is to construct measures that reflect a company's credit risk exposure. There is not one "best" financial leverage ratio. Instead, as financial statement users, we want to use measures that capture the risk we are most concerned with. It is also important to compute the ratios ourselves to ensure we know what is included and excluded from each ratio.

Limitations of Ratio Analysis

The quality of financial statement analysis depends on the quality of financial information. We ought not blindly analyze numbers; doing so can lead to faulty conclusions and suboptimal decisions. Instead, we need to acknowledge that current accounting rules (GAAP) have limitations, and be fully aware of the company's environment, its competitive pressures, and any structural and strategic changes. This section discusses some of the factors that limit the usefulness of financial accounting information for ratio analysis.

GAAP Limitations Several limitations in GAAP can distort financial ratios. Limitations include:

1. **Measurability.** Financial statements reflect what can be reliably measured. This results in nonrecognition of certain assets, often internally developed assets, the very assets that are most

likely to confer a competitive advantage and create value. Examples are brand name, a superior management team, employee skills, and a reliable supply chain.

2. **Non-capitalized costs.** Related to the concept of measurability is the expensing of costs relating to "assets" that cannot be identified with enough precision to warrant capitalization. Examples are brand equity costs from advertising and other promotional activities, and research and development costs relating to future products.

3. **Historical costs.** Assets and liabilities are usually recorded at original acquisition or issuance costs. Subsequent increases in value are not recorded until realized, and declines in value are only recognized if deemed permanent.

Thus, GAAP balance sheets omit important and valuable assets. Our analysis of ROE, including that of liquidity and solvency, must consider that assets can be underreported and that ratios can be distorted. We discuss many of these limitations in more detail in later modules.

Company Changes Many companies regularly undertake mergers, acquire new companies and divest subsidiaries. Such major operational changes can impair the comparability of company ratios across time. Companies also change strategies, such as product pricing, R&D, and financing. We must understand the effects of such changes on ratios and exercise caution when we compare ratios from one period to the next. Companies also behave differently at different points in their life cycles. For instance, growth companies possess a different profile than do mature companies. Seasonal effects also markedly impact analysis of financial statements at different times of the year. Thus, we must consider life cycle and cyclicality when we compare ratios across companies and over time.

Conglomerate Effects Few companies are pure-play; instead, most companies operate in several businesses or industries. Most publicly traded companies consist of a parent company and multiple subsidiaries, often pursuing different lines of business. Most heavy equipment manufacturers, for example, have finance subsidiaries (Ford Credit Corporation and Cat Financial are subsidiaries of Ford and Caterpillar respectively). Financial statements of such conglomerates are consolidated and include the financial statements of the parent and its subsidiaries. Consequently, such consolidated statements are challenging to analyze. Typically, analysts break the financials apart into their component businesses and separately analyze each component. Fortunately, companies must report financial information (albeit limited) for major business segments in their 10-Ks.

Means to an End Ratios reduce, to a single number, the myriad complexities of a company's operations. No scalar can accurately capture the qualitative aspect of company. Ratios cannot hope to capture the innumerable transactions and events that occur each day between a company and various parties. Ratios cannot meaningfully convey a company's marketing and management philosophies, its human resource activities, its financing activities, its strategic initiatives, and its product management. In our analysis we must learn to look through the numbers and ratios to better understand the operational factors that drive financial results. Successful analysis seeks to gain insight into what a company is really about and what the future portends. Our overriding purpose in analysis is to understand the past and present to better predict the future. Computing and examining ratios is just one step in that process.

MODULE-END REVIEW

Refer to the income statement and balance sheet of Lowe's Companies, Inc., from Mid-Module Reviews 1 and 2 earlier in this module.

Required
Compute the following liquidity and solvency ratios for Lowe's. Interpret and assess these ratios for Lowe's relative to those same ratios previously computed for Home Depot in the text.

1. Current ratio
2. Quick ratio
3. Liabilities-to-equity ratio
4. Times interest earned

Solution ($ millions)

Ratio	Lowe's Companies	Home Depot
Current ratio	$7,831/$5,832 = 1.34	$15,346/$12,901 = 1.19
Quick ratio	($423 + $453 + $18)/$5,832 = 0.15	($793 + $14 + $2,396)/$12,901 = 0.25
Liabilities-to-equity ratio. .	$10,343/$14,339 = 0.72	($12,901 + $2,672 + $2,000)/$26,909 = 0.65
Times interest earned. . . .	($4,506 + $158)/$158 = 29.52	($9,282 + $143)/$143 = 65.9

Interpretation: Home Depot is slightly less liquid than Lowe's. Both its current ratio and quick ratio are lower for Home Depot but the difference is not striking. Home Depot and Lowe's both have fewer liabilities than equity; the ratio is less than 1.0 for both firms. Lowe's liabilities-to-equity ratio indicates that it is slightly less solvent than Home Depot, but again, the difference is not striking. Both companies have extremely high times-interest-earned ratios. In conclusion, each company appears sufficiently liquid and each has strong solvency ratios.

APPENDIX 4A: Vertical and Horizontal Analysis

Companies come in all sizes, which presents difficulties when making inter-firm comparisons. There are several methods that attempt to overcome this obstacle.

Vertical analysis expresses financial statements in ratio form. Specifically, it is common to express income statement items as a percent of net sales, and balance sheet items as a percent of total assets. Such *common-size financial statements* facilitate comparisons *across companies* of different sizes and comparisons of accounts within a set of financial statements.

Horizontal analysis is the scrutiny of financial data *across time*. Comparing data across two or more consecutive periods assists in analyzing company performance and in predicting future performance.

Exhibits 4A.1 and 4A.2 present Home Depot's common-size balance sheet and common-size income statement. We also present data for horizontal analysis by showing three years of common-size statements.

Home Depot's total assets in dollars have increased by 29% since 2004. However, we are primarily interested in the *composition* of the balance sheet, or the proportion invested in each asset category. Specifically, liquidity has generally deteriorated as cash, short-term investments, and receivables represent 7.2% of total assets in 2006, down from 11.5% in 2004. Inventories, on the other hand, have remained at about the same percentage of total assets. Home Depot reports in the MD&A section of its 10-K that it has used some of its excess liquidity to repurchase common stock in 2006. Generally, companies repurchase their stock when they feel it is undervalued and wish to send that signal to the market. Despite the depletion of its short-term investment portfolio, Home Depot asserts that its liquidity is sufficient in this excerpt from its 2006 10-K.

> As of January 29, 2006, we had $807 million in Cash and Short-Term Investments. We believe that our current cash position and cash flow generated from operations should be sufficient to enable us to complete our capital expenditure programs and any required long-term debt payments through the next several fiscal years. In addition, we have funds available from the $2.5 billion commercial paper program and the ability to obtain alternative sources of financing for future acquisitions and other requirements.

Home Depot's property and equipment have decreased as a percentage of total assets, from 58.3% to 56%. Still, it remains a capital-intensive company. Other long-term assets have increased as a percentage of the total, from 3% in 2004 to 9.5% in 2006. This category represents goodwill arising from numerous acquisitions that it executed over the past few years.

Home Depot's short-term liabilities have increased as a percentage of total financing. This mainly results from a 1.7% percentage point increase in short-term debt. Accounts payable and accrued liabilities have decreased slightly (from 26.3% to 25.9%) in the past two years. Short-term and long-term debt have been used to fund a recent acquisition, and Home Depot indicated its intent to repay $900 million in short-term debt in fiscal 2007. The proportion of equity in its capital structure has declined from 65.1% in 2004 to 60.5% in 2006 as the company used debt to finance new-store construction and acquire other companies. It is not uncommon for companies to utilize lower-cost debt to finance expansion, especially if they feel that their stock price is not sufficiently high to fund those expenditures.

EXHIBIT 4A.1 Common-Size Comparative Balance Sheets

HOME DEPOT
Common-Size Comparative Balance Sheets

	Amounts ($ millions)			Percentages		
	2006	2005	2004	2006	2005	2004
Assets						
Cash and cash equivalents	$ 793	$ 506	$ 1,103	1.8%	1.3%	3.2%
Short-term investments	14	1,659	1,749	0.0	4.3	5.1
Receivables, net.	2,396	1,499	1,097	5.4	3.8	3.2
Inventories	11,401	10,076	9,076	25.6	25.8	26.4
Other current assets.	742	533	303	1.7	1.4	0.9
Total current assets	15,346	14,273	13,328	34.5	36.6	38.7
Net property and equipment, net.	24,901	22,726	20,063	56.0	58.2	58.3
Other long-term assets	4,235	2,021	1,046	9.5	5.2	3.0
Total assets.	$44,482	$39,020	$34,437	100.0	100.0	100.0
Liabilities and Stockholders' Equity						
Short-term borrowings.	$ 1,413	$ 11	$ 509	3.2%	0.0%	1.5%
Accounts payable.	6,032	5,766	5,159	13.6	14.8	15.0
Accrued expenses and other current liabilities . . .	5,456	4,678	3,886	12.3	12.0	11.3
Total current liabilities.	12,901	10,455	9,554	29.0	26.8	27.7
Long-term debt	2,672	2,148	856	6.0	5.5	2.5
Other long-term obligations	2,000	2,259	1,620	4.5	5.8	4.7
Stockholders' equity						
Common stock.	7,407	6,769	6,303	16.7	17.3	18.3
Retained earnings	28,943	23,962	19,694	65.1	61.4	57.2
Other stockholders' equity.	(9,441)	(6,573)	(3,590)	(21.2)	(16.8)	(10.4)
Total stockholders' equity	26,909	24,158	22,407	60.5	61.9	65.1
Total liabilities and stockholders' equity.	$44,482	$39,020	$34,437	100.0	100.0	100.0

EXHIBIT 4A.2 Common-Size Comparative Income Statements

HOME DEPOT
Common-Size Comparative Income Statements

	Amounts ($ millions)			Percentages		
	2006	2005	2004	2006	2005	2004
Revenues	$81,511	$73,094	$64,816	100.0%	100.0%	100.0%
Cost of sales	54,191	48,664	44,236	66.5	66.6	68.2
Gross profit	27,320	24,430	20,580	33.5	33.4	31.8
Operating expenses						
Selling, general and administrative	16,485	15,256	12,713	20.2	20.9	19.6
Depreciation.	1,472	1,248	1,021	1.8	1.7	1.6
Total operating expenses	17,957	16,504	13,734	22.0	22.6	21.2
Operating income.	9,363	7,926	6,846	11.5	10.8	10.6
Interest income.	62	56	59	0.1	0.1	0.1
Interest expense.	(143)	(70)	(62)	(0.2)	(0.1)	(0.1)
Earnings before taxes.	9,282	7,912	6,843	11.4	10.8	10.6
Tax expense	3,444	2,911	2,539	4.2	4.0	3.9
Net income.	$ 5,838	$ 5,001	$ 4,304	7.2	6.8	6.6

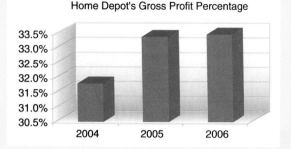

Home Depot's income statement reflects a marked increase in its gross profit percentage, increasing from 31.8% in 2004 to 33.5% in 2006—see margin graph. This is a large increase for a company operating in competitive conditions. Further, Home Depot has successfully reduced its selling, general and administrative expenses as a percentage of revenues, from 20.9% in 2005 to 20.2% in 2006. Finally, its operating income increased from 10.6% of revenues to 11.5% from 2004 to 2006, and its net income from 6.6% to 7.2%. Home Depot's increase in debt is not as threatening if profitability increases, as it has in the past year.

APPENDIX 4B: Nonoperating Return Component of ROE

In this appendix, we consider the nonoperating return component of ROE in more detail. We also provide a derivation of that nonoperating return and discuss several special topics pertaining to it. We begin by considering three special cases of capital structure financing.

Nonoperating Return With Debt Only

In the module, we infer the nonoperating return as the difference between ROE and RNOA. The nonoperating return can also be computed directly as FLEV × SPREAD, where FLEV is the degree of financial leverage.

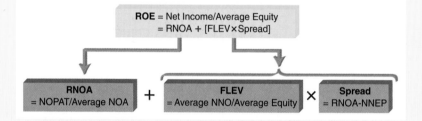

Exhibit 4B.1 provides definitions for each of the terms required in this computation.

EXHIBIT 4B.1	Nonoperating return definitions
NNO: net nonoperating obligations	Nonoperating obligations less nonoperating assets
FLEV: financial leverage	Average NNO/Average equity
NNE: net nonoperating expense	NOPAT – Net income; NNE consists of nonoperating expenses and revenues, net of tax
NNEP: net nonoperating expense percent.	NNE/Average NNO
Spread	RNOA – NNEP

To illustrate computation of the nonoperating return when the company has only debt (no investments), let's refer to our example in this module of the company which increases its ROE through use of debt. (For this first illustration, view FLEV as the relative use of debt in the capital structure, and SPREAD as the difference between RNOA and the net nonoperating expense percent). Again, assume that this company has $1,000 of equity and $500 of 7% debt invested in $1,500 of total assets earning a 20% return. The net income of this firm is $265, computed as follows:

Profit from assets financed with equity ($1,000 × 20%)		$200
Profit from assets financed with debt ($500 × 20%)	$100	
Less interest expense from debt ($500 × 7%)	(35)	65
Net profit		$265

Its ROE is 26.5%, computed as $265/$1,000 (assuming income received at year-end for simplicity; meaning average equity is $1,000). Its RNOA is 20%, FLEV is 0.50 (computed as $500 of average net nonoperating obligations divided by $1,000 average equity), and its SPREAD is 13% (computed as 20% less 7%). This company's ROE, shown with the nonoperating return being directly computed, is as follows:

$$\begin{aligned} \text{ROE} &= \text{RNOA} + [\,\text{FLEV} \times \text{SPREAD}\,] \\ &= 20\% + [\; 0.50 \times 13\% \;] \\ &= 26.5\% \end{aligned}$$

Nonoperating Return With Investments Only

When a company's nonoperating activities relate solely to the borrowing of money (no investments in marketable securities), FLEV collapses to the debt-to-equity ratio, a ratio similar to that which we explained in the solvency section of this module. However, many high-tech companies have no debt, and maintain large portfolios of marketable securities. They hold these highly liquid assets so that they can respond quickly to new opportunities or react to competitive pressures. With high levels of nonoperating assets and no nonoperating liabilities, net nonoperating obligations (NNO) has a negative sign (NNO = Nonoperating obligations − Nonoperating assets). Likewise, FLEV is negative: Average NNO (−)/Average Equity (+). Further, net nonoperating expense (NNE = NOPAT − Net income) is negative because investment *income* is a negative nonoperating expense. However, the net nonoperating expense percent (NNEP) is positive because the negative NNE is divided by the negative NNO. This causes ROE to be less than RNOA (see computations below). We use the 2005 10-K of Cisco Systems, Inc to explain this curious result.

($ millions, except percentages)	2005	2004
NOA	$ 11,871	$ 10,371
NNO	$(11,303)	$(15,455)
Stockholders' equity	$ 23,174	$ 25,826
Net income	$ 5,741	
NOPAT	$ 4,820	
NNE	$ (921)	
FLEV	(54.6)%	
RNOA	43.3%	
NNEP	6.9%	
Spread	36.4%	

Cisco's NNO is negative because its investment in marketable securities exceeds its debt. Cisco's ROE is 23.4%, and it consists of the following:

$$\begin{aligned} \text{ROE} &= \text{RNOA} + [\; \text{FLEV} \times \text{SPREAD}\,] \\ &= 43.3\% + [\; -54.6\% \times 36.4\% \;] \\ &= 43.3\% + [\qquad -19.9\% \qquad] \\ &= 23.4\% \end{aligned}$$

Cisco's ROE is lower than its RNOA because of its large investment in marketable securities. That is, its excessive liquidity is penalizing in its return on equity. The rationale for this seemingly incongruous result is this: Cisco's ROE derives from operating and nonoperating assets. Cisco's operating assets are providing an outstanding return (43.3%), much higher than the return on its marketable securities (6.9%). Holding liquid assets that are less productive means that Cisco's shareholders are funding a sizeable level of liquidity, and sacrificing returns in the process. Why? Many companies in high-tech industries feel the need to maintain excessive liquidity to gain flexibility—the flexibility to take advantage of opportunities and to react quickly to competitor maneuvers. Cisco's management, evidently, feels that the investment of costly equity capital in this manner will reap future rewards for its shareholders. Its 43.3% RNOA provides some evidence that this strategy is not necessarily misguided.

Nonoperating Return With Both Debt and Investments

Many companies report both debt and investments on their balance sheets. If that debt markedly exceeds the investment balance, their ROE will look more like our first example (with debt only). Instead, if investments predominate, their ROE will look more like Cisco's. It is important to remember that both the average NNO (and FLEV) and NNE can be either positive (debt) or negative (investments), and it is not always the case that ROE exceeds RNOA. We now compute nonoperating return for Home Depot, a company with both debt and investments.

Nonoperating Return for Home Depot

Home Depot has both debt and investments. Its debt (with interest expense) exceeds nonoperating investments (with interest income). Recall that nonoperating activities primarily relate to two activities: borrowed money that creates interest expense and nonoperating investments that yield interest revenue or dividend revenue and capital gains or losses. Combining interest expense with nonoperating income and gains or losses yields net nonoperating expense. Exhibit 4B.2 highlights the typical components of net nonoperating expense.

EXHIBIT 4B.2 Simplified Income Statement
Nonoperating Items Highlighted
Revenues
Cost of sales
Gross profit
Total operating expenses
Operating income
Interest expense
Interest and dividend revenues
Investment gains and losses
Total nonoperating expenses
Income before tax
Tax expense
Net income

The nonoperating items are reported on the income statement before tax. However, nonoperating expenses (net) create a tax shield and thus, we need to consider the after-tax value of net nonoperating expense. This is called the net nonoperating expense (NNE), which we compute as:

$$\text{Net nonoperating expense (NNE)} = \begin{bmatrix} \text{Interest expense} - \text{Interest revenue} \\ - \text{Dividend revenue} - \text{Investment} \\ \text{gains (+losses)} \end{bmatrix} \times [1 - \text{Tax rate on operating profit}]$$

The simple illustration shown earlier in this appendix ignored taxes and thus, NNE was equal to the $35 interest paid on the debt. Recall from page 4-8 that Home Depot's tax rate on operating profit is 37.11%. Thus, for Home Depot, we can compute NNE as follows ($ millions): $[\$143 - \$62] \times [1 - 37.11\%] = \$51$.

To compute operating return (RNOA) we divided NOPAT from the income statement, by NOA from the balance sheet. Similarly, to compute the net nonoperating expense percent (NNEP), we divide NNE from the income statement by net nonoperating items from the balance sheet (called net nonoperating obligations, NNO). Exhibit 4B.3 shows how a balance sheet can be reorganized into operating and nonoperating items.

EXHIBIT 4B.3 Simplified Balance Sheet		
	Assets	**Liabilities**
Net operating assets (NOA)	Current Operating Assets	Current Operating Liabilities
(assets – liabilities)	+ Long-Term Operating Assets	+ Long-Term Operating Liabilities
	= Total Operating Assets	= Total Operating Liabilities
Net nonoperating obligations (NNO).	Current Nonoperating Assets	Current Nonoperating Liabilities
(liabilities – assets)	+ Long-Term Nonoperating Assets	+ Long-Term Nonoperating Liabilities
	= Total Nonoperating Assets	= Total Nonoperating Liabilities
		Equity
Equity (NOA – NNO)		Stockholders' Equity
	Total Assets	Total Liabilities and Equity

Net nonoperating obligations are total nonoperating liabilities less total nonoperating assets. The accounting equation stipulates that Assets = Liabilities + Equity, so we can adjust the balance sheet to yield the following identity:

Net operating assets (NOA) = Net nonoperating obligations (NNO) + Stockholders' Equity

For Home Depot, we compute NNO as follows:

$ millions	2006	2005
Short-term borrowings	$1,413	$ 11
Long-term debt	2,672	2,148
Total nonoperating liabilities	4,085	2,159
Short-term investments	14	1,659
Long-term investments	0	0
Total nonoperating assets	14	1,659
Net nonoperating obligations (NNO)	$4,071	$ 500

Accordingly (drawing on NNE from the income statement and NNO from the balance sheet), we compute the net nonoperating expense percent (NNEP) as follows:

$$\text{Net Nonoperating Expense Percent (NNEP)} = \frac{\text{Net Nonoperating Expense (NNE)}}{\text{Average Net Nonoperating Obligations (NNO)}}$$

The net nonoperating expense percent (NNEP) measures the average rate of return on nonoperating activities. The denominator uses the average NNO similar to the prior return calculations we previously discussed (ROE and RNOA).

In the simple illustration from earlier in this appendix, the company's net nonoperating expense percent is 7%, computed as $35/$500, which is exactly equal to the interest rate on the loan. With real financial statements, such as Home Depot, NNEP is more complicated because NNE includes both interest on borrowed money and nonoperating income, and NNO is the net of operating liabilities less nonoperating assets. Thus NNEP reflects an average return on nonoperating activities. For Home Depot, its 2006 NNEP is 2.2%, computed as $51/[($4,071 + $500)/2], $ millions.

Home Depot's 2006 RNOA is 21.2%, which means that net operating assets generate more return than the 2.2% cost of its net nonoperating obligations. That is, Home Depot earns a SPREAD of 19%, the difference between RNOA (21.2%) and NNEP (2.2%), on each asset financed with borrowed funds compared to other assets. By borrowing funds, Home Depot creates leverage, which can be measured relative to shareholder's equity; that ratio is called financial leverage (FLEV). Total nonoperating return is computed by the following formula:

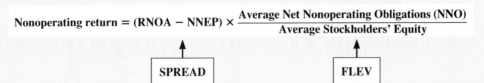

$$\text{Nonoperating return} = (\text{RNOA} - \text{NNEP}) \times \frac{\text{Average Net Nonoperating Obligations (NNO)}}{\text{Average Stockholders' Equity}}$$

For Home Depot, its 2006 spread between RNOA and NNEP is 19%. It has average NNO of $2,286 [($4,071 + $500)/2] and average equity of $25,534 [($26,909 + $24,158)/2], $ millions. Thus, Home Depot' ROE consists of the following ($ millions):

$$
\begin{aligned}
\text{ROE} &= \text{Operating return} + \text{Nonoperating return} \\
&= 21.2\% + (21.2\% - 2.2\%) \times (\$2,286/\$25,534) \\
&= 21.2\% + 1.7\% \\
&= 22.9\%
\end{aligned}
$$

Two points are immediately clear from this equation. First, ROE increases with the spread between RNOA and NNEP. The more profitable the return on operating assets, the higher the return to shareholders. Second, the higher the debt relative to equity, the higher the ROE (assuming, of course, a positive spread).

Derivation of Nonoperating Return Formula

Following is the algebraic derivation of the nonoperating return formula.

$$
\begin{aligned}
\text{ROE} &= \frac{\text{NI}}{\text{SE}} \\
&= \frac{\text{NOPAT} - \text{NNE}}{\text{SE}} \\
&= \frac{\text{NOPAT}}{\text{SE}} - \frac{\text{NNE}}{\text{SE}} \\
&= \left(\frac{\text{NOA}}{\text{SE}} \times \text{RNOA} \right) - \left(\frac{\text{NNO}}{\text{SE}} \times \text{NNEP} \right) \\
&= \left(\frac{(\text{SE} + \text{NNO})}{\text{SE}} \times \text{RNOA} \right) - \left(\frac{\text{NNO}}{\text{SE}} \times \text{NNEP} \right) \\
&= \left[\text{RNOA} \times \left(1 + \frac{\text{NNO}}{\text{SE}} \right) \right] - \left(\frac{\text{NNO}}{\text{SE}} \times \text{NNEP} \right) \\
&= \text{RNOA} + \left(\frac{\text{NNO}}{\text{SE}} \times \text{RNOA} \right) - \left(\frac{\text{NNO}}{\text{SE}} \times \text{NNEP} \right) \\
&= \text{RNOA} + \left(\frac{\text{NNO}}{\text{SE}} \right) (\text{RNOA} - \text{NNEP}) \\
&= \text{RNOA} + (\text{FLEV} \times \text{SPREAD})
\end{aligned}
$$

where NI is net income, SE is average stockholders' equity, and all other terms are as defined in Exhibit 4B.1.

Special topics

The return on equity (ROE) computation becomes a bit more complicated in the presence of discontinued operations, preferred stock, and minority (or noncontrolling) equity interest. The first of these apportions ROE between operating and nonoperating returns, and the other two affect the dollar amount included in the denominator (average equity) of the ROE computation. Recall that ROE measures the return on investment for common shareholders. The ROE numerator should include only the income available to pay common dividends, and the denominator should include common equity only, not that relating to preferred or minority shareholders.

Discontinued operations Discontinued operations are subsidiaries or business segments that the board of directors has formally decided to divest. Companies must report discontinued operations on a separate line, below income from continuing operations. The separate line item includes the net income or loss from discontinued operations along with any gains or losses on the disposal of discontinued net assets (see Module 5 for details). Although not required, many companies disclose the net assets of discontinued operations on the balance sheet to distinguish them from continuing net assets (if the net assets are not separated on the balance sheet, the footnotes provide details to facilitate a disaggregated analysis). These net assets of discontinued operations should be considered to be nonoperating (they represent an investment once they have been classified as discontinued) and their after-tax profit (loss) should be treated as nonoperating as well. Although the ROE computation is unaffected, the nonoperating portion of that return will include the contribution of discontinued operations.

Preferred stock The ROE formula takes the perspective of the common shareholder in that it relates the income available to pay common dividends to the average common shareholder investment. As such, preferred stock should not be included in average stockholders' equity in the denominator of the ROE formula. Similarly, any dividends paid on preferred stock should be subtracted from net income to yield the profit available to pay common dividends. (Dividends are not an expense in computing net income; thus, net income is available to both preferred and common shareholders. To determine net income available to common shareholders, we must subtract preferred dividends.) Thus, the presence of preferred stock requires two adjustments to the ROE formula.

1. Preferred dividends must be subtracted from net income in the numerator.
2. Preferred stock must be subtracted from stockholders' equity in the denominator.

This modified return on equity formula is more accurately labeled return on common equity (ROCE).

$$
\text{ROCE} = \frac{\text{Net income} - \text{Preferred dividends}}{\text{Average stockholders' equity} - \text{Average preferred equity}}
$$

Minority (non-controlling) Interest When a company acquires controlling interest of the outstanding voting stock of another company, the parent company must consolidate the new subsidiary in its balance sheet and income statement (see Module 7). This means that the parent company must include 100% of the subsidiary's assets, liabilities, revenues and expenses. Should the parent acquire less than 100% of the subsidiary's voting stock, the remaining claim of minority shareholders is reported on the balance sheet as a liability usually called minority interest (in a proposed amendment to current accounting standards, the FASB will require recognition of minority interest as a component of stockholders' equity, if passed).

On the consolidated income statement, the minority (non-controlling) shareholders' claim to the subsidiary's net income is reported as a separate line item called minority interest expense. This minority interest expense represents the portion of income attributable to minority interests. Reported net income is, therefore, attributable to the parent's shareholders.

If minority interest is excluded from stockholders' equity, no adjustments need be made to the ROE computation (ROE = Net income / Average stockholders' equity) as net income already excludes the income attributable to minority interests (treated as an expense). If minority interest is included in stockholders' equity (which it will be under the proposed amendment to the business combinations accounting standard), it must be subtracted from stockholders' equity before computing ROE.

It is possible to take additional steps to add back the effects of minority interest expense and minority interest equity to distinguish return to common shareholders as follows:

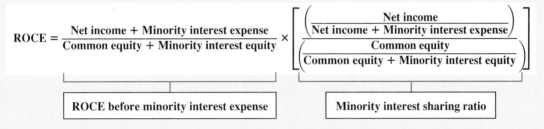

However, as the following equations show, the end result is the same because terms in the equations cancel and we are left with ROE:

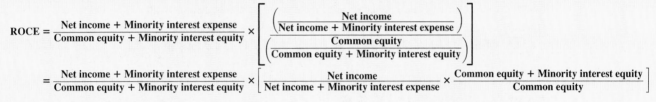

$$= \text{Net income/Common equity}$$

(Technically, this ROCE calculation should use comprehensive income rather than net income because the former includes several relevant items, which we explain in Module 5.)

Calculating RNOA involves no modifications because NOPAT is operating income before minority interest, and NOA excludes minority interest on the balance sheet. Similarly, SPREAD is computed as usual. However, we need to adjust FLEV to reflect total equity because a company's operating and nonoperating activities generate returns to both the majority (the common shareholders' equity or CSE) and minority shareholders (labelled MI). Consequently, for companies with minority interest on the balance sheet, we adjust FLEV as follows: FLEV = NNO/ (CSE + MI). An alternative way of describing this relation is:

$$\text{ROCE} = \text{RNOA} + [[\text{NNO/(CSE + MI)}] \times (\text{Spread} \times \text{MI Sharing ratio})] + [\text{RNOA} \times (\text{MI Sharing ratio} - 1)].$$

GUIDANCE ANSWERS

MANAGERIAL DECISION **You Are the Entrepreneur**

Your company is performing substantially better than its competitors. Namely, your RNOA of 16% is markedly superior to competitors' RNOA of 10%. However, RNOA disaggregation shows that this is mainly attributed to your NOAT of 0.89 versus competitors' NOAT of 0.59. Your NOPM of 18% is essentially identical to competitors' NOPM of 17%. Accordingly, you will want to maintain your NOAT as further improvements are probably difficult to achieve. Importantly, you are likely to achieve the greatest benefit with efforts at improving your NOPM of 18%, which is only marginally better than the industry norm of 17%.

Superscript ᴬ⁽ᴮ⁾ denotes assignments based on Appendix 4A (4B).

DISCUSSION QUESTIONS

Q4-1. Explain in general terms the concept of return on investment. Why is this concept important in the analysis of financial performance?

Q4-2.ᴮ (a) Explain how an increase in financial leverage can increase a company's ROE. (b) Given the potentially positive relation between financial leverage and ROE, why don't we see companies with 100% financial leverage (entirely nonowner financed)?

Q4-3. Gross profit margin (Gross profit/Sales) is an important determinant of NOPAT. Identify two factors that can cause gross profit margin to decline. Is a reduction in the gross profit margin always bad news? Explain.

Q4-4. When might a reduction in operating expenses as a percentage of sales denote a short-term gain at the cost of long-term performance?

Q4-5. Describe the concept of asset turnover. What does the concept mean and why it is so important to understanding and interpreting financial performance?

Q4-6. Explain what it means when a company's ROE exceeds its RNOA.

Q4-7.ᴮ Discontinued operations are typically viewed as a nonoperating activity in the analysis of the balance sheet and the income statement. What is the rationale for this treatment?

Q4-8. Describe what is meant by the "tax shield."

Q4-9. What is meant by the term "net" in net operating assets (NOA).

Q4-10. Why is it important to disaggregate RNOA into operating profit margin (NOPM) and net operating assets turnover (NOAT)?

Q4-11. What insights do we gain from the graphical relation between profit margin and asset turnover?

Q4-12. Explain the concept of liquidity and why it is crucial to company survival.

Q4-13. Identify at least two factors that limit the usefulness of ratio analysis.

Q4-14.ᴬ What are common-size financial statements? What role do they play in financial statement analysis?

MINI EXERCISES

M4-15. Identify and Compute Net Operating Assets and its Components   (LO2)

Target Corporation
(TGT)

Following is the balance sheet for Target Corporation. Identify and compute its fiscal year-end 2006 net operating assets.

($ millions)	January 28, 2006	January 29, 2005
Assets		
Cash and cash equivalents	$ 1,648	$ 2,245
Accounts receivable, net	5,666	5,069
Inventory	5,838	5,384
Other curret assets	1,253	1,224
Total current assets	14,405	13,922
Property and equipment		
Land	4,449	3,804
Buildings and improvements	14,174	12,518
Fixtures and equipment	3,219	2,990
Computer hardware and software	2,214	1,998
Construction-in-progress	1,158	962
Accumulated depreciation	(6,176)	(5,412)
Property and equipment, net	19,038	16,860
Other noncurrent assets	1,552	1,511
Total assets	$34,995	$32,293

continued

($ millions)	January 28, 2006	January 29, 2005
Liabilities and shareholders' investment		
Accounts payable	$ 6,268	$ 5,779
Accrued liabilities	2,193	1,633
Income taxes payable	374	304
Current portion of long-term debt and notes payable	753	504
Total current liabilities	9,588	8,220
Long-term debt	9,119	9,034
Deferred income taxes and other	851	973
Other noncurrent liabilities	1,232	1,037
Shareholders' investment		
Common stock	73	74
Additional paid-in-capital	2,121	1,810
Retained earnings	12,013	11,148
Accumulated other comprehensive income	(2)	(3)
Total shareholders' investment	14,205	13,029
Total liabilities and shareholders' investment	$34,995	$32,293

M4-16. Identify and Compute NOPAT (LO2)

Following is the income statement for Target Corporation. (*a*) Compute Target's net operating profit *before* tax. (*Hint:* Treat Target's credit card revenues and related expenses as operating.) (*b*) Assume that the combined federal and state statutory tax rate is 38.3%. Compute NOPAT for Target for 2006.

Target Corporation (TGT)

($ millions)	2006
Sales	$51,271
Net credit card revenues	1,349
Total revenues	52,620
Cost of sales	34,927
Selling, general and administrative expenses	11,185
Credit card expenses	776
Depreciation and amortization	1,409
Earnings from continuing operations before interest expense and income taxes	4,323
Net interest expense	463
Earnings from continuing operations before income taxes	3,860
Provision for income taxes	1,452
Net earnings	$ 2,408

M4-17. Compute RNOA, NOPAT Margin, and NOA Turnover (LO2)

Selected balance sheet and income statement information for Target Corporation, a department store retailer, follows.

Target Corporation (TGT)

Company ($ millions)	Ticker	2006 Revenues	2006 NOPAT	2006 Net Operating Assets	2005 Net Operating Assets
Target Corp	TGT	$52,620	$2,693	$24,077	$22,567

a. Compute its 2006 return on net operating assets (RNOA).
b. Disaggregate RNOA into net operating profit margin (NOPM) and net operating asset turnover (NOAT). Confirm that RNOA = NOPM × NOAT.

M4-18. Identify and Compute Net Operating Assets (LO2)

3M Company (MMM)

Following is the balance sheet for 3M Company. Identify and compute its net operating assets (NOA).

3M COMPANY AND SUBSIDIARIES December 31 ($ millions, except per share amount)	2005	2004
Assets		
Cash and cash equivalents	$ 1,072	$ 2,757
Accounts receivable—net of allowances of $73 and $83	2,838	2,792
Inventories		
Finished goods	1,050	947
Work in process	706	614
Raw materials and supplies	406	336
Total inventories	2,162	1,897
Other current assets	1,043	1,274
Total current assets	7,115	8,720
Investments	272	227
Property, plant and equipment	16,127	16,290
Less: Accumulated depreciation	(10,534)	(10,579)
Property, plant and equipment—net	5,593	5,711
Goodwill	3,473	2,655
Intangible assets—net	486	277
Prepaid pension and postretirement benefits	2,905	2,591
Other assets	669	527
Total assets	$20,513	$20,708
Liabilities and Stockholders' Equity		
Short-term borrowings and current portion of long-term debt	$ 1,072	$ 2,094
Accounts payable	1,256	1,168
Accrued payroll	469	487
Accrued income taxes	989	867
Other current liabilities	1,452	1,455
Total current liabilities	5,238	6,071
Long-term debt	1,309	727
Other liabilities	3,866	3,532
Total liabilities	10,413	10,330
Stockholders' equity		
Common stock, par value $.01 per share	9	9
Share outstanding—2005: 754,538,387		
Share outstanding—2004: 773,518,281		
Capital in excess of par value	287	287
Retained earnings	17,358	15,649
Treasury stock	(6,965)	(5,503)
Unearned compensation	(178)	(196)
Accumulated other comprehensive income (loss)	(411)	132
Stockholders' equity—net	10,100	10,378
Total liabilities and stockholders' equity	$20,513	$20,708

M4-19. Identify and Compute NOPAT (LO2)

3M Company (MMM)

Following is the income statement for 3M Company. Compute its 2005 net operating profit after tax (NOPAT) assuming a 36.3% total statutory tax rate.

3M COMPANY AND SUBSIDIARIES			
Year ended December 31 ($ millions)	2005	2004	2003
Net sales....................................	$21,167	$20,011	$18,232
Operating expenses			
Cost of sales..................................	10,381	9,958	9,285
Selling, general and administrative expenses	4,535	4,281	3,994
Research, development and related expenses	1,242	1,194	1,147
Other expense	—	—	93
Total	16,158	15,433	14,519
Operating income...............................	5,009	4,578	3,713
Interest expense and income			
Interest expense.............................	82	69	84
Interest income..............................	(56)	(46)	(28)
Total	26	23	56
Income before income taxes, minority interest and cumulative effect of accounting change.............	4,983	4,555	3,657
Provision for income taxes.........................	1,694	1,503	1,202
Minority interest	55	62	52
Income before cumulative effect of accounting change ...	3,234	2,990	2,403
Cumulative effect of accounting change	(35)	—	—
Net income....................................	$ 3,199	$ 2,990	$ 2,403

M4-20. Compute RNOA, NOPAT Margin, and NOA Turnover   (LO2)

Selected balance sheet and income statement information for 3M Company, a manufacturing company, follows.   3M Company (MMM)

Company ($ millions)	Ticker	2005 Sales	2005 NOPAT	2005 Net Operating Assets	2004 Net Operating Assets
3M Company	MMM	$21,167	$3,306	$12,209	$12,972

a. Compute 3M's 2005 return on net operating assets (RNOA).
b. Disaggregate RNOA into net operating profit margin (NOPM) and net operating asset turnover (NOAT). Confirm that RNOA = NOPM × NOAT.

M4-21. Compute RNOA, NOPAT Margin and NOA Turnover for Competitors   (LO2)

Selected balance sheet and income statement information from Abercrombie & Fitch and TJX Companies, clothing retailers in the high-end and value-priced segments, respectively, follows.   Abercrombie & Fitch (ANF) and TJX Companies (TJX)

Company ($ millions)	Ticker	2006 Sales	2006 NOPAT	2006 Net Operating Assets	2005 Net Operating Assets
Abercrombie & Fitch...	ANF	$ 2,784.7	$324.7	$ 615.6	$ 700.5
TJX Companies	TJX	16,057.9	708.5	2,701.5	2,508.5

Required
a. Compute the 2006 return on net operating assets (RNOA) for both companies.
b. Disaggregate RNOA into net operating profit margin (NOPM) and net operating asset turnover (NOAT) for each company. Confirm that RNOA = NOPM × NOAT.
c. Discuss differences observed with respect to NOPM and NOAT and interpret these differences in light of each company's business model.

M4-22. Compute and Interpret Liquidity and Solvency Ratios   (LO3)

Verizon (VZ)

Selected balance sheet and income statement information from Verizon follows.

($ millions)	2005	2004
Current assets	$ 16,448	$ 19,479
Current liabilities.	25,063	23,129
Total liabilities	101,696	103,345
Equity	66,434	62,613
Earnings before interest and taxes.	12,787	12,496
Interest expense.	2,180	2,384
Net cash flow from operating activities	22,012	21,820

a. Compute the current ratio for each year and discuss any trend in liquidity. What additional information about the numbers used to calculate this ratio might be useful in helping us assess liquidity? Explain.

b. Compute times interest earned, the total-liabilities-to-equity, and the net cash from operating activities to total liabilities ratios for each year and discuss any trends for each. (The median total-liabilities-to-equity ratio for the telecommunications industry is 1.13.) Do you have any concerns about the extent of Verizon's financial leverage and the company's ability to meet interest obligations? Explain.

c. Verizon's capital expenditures are expected to increase substantially as it seeks to respond to competitive pressures to upgrade the quality of its communication infrastructure. Assess Verizon's liquidity and solvency in light of this strategic direction.

M4-23. Compute Tax Rates on Operating Profit and NOPAT   (LO2)

Proctor & Gamble
McDonald's
Valero Energy
Abercrombie and Fitch

Selected income statement information is presented below for Proctor & Gamble, McDonald's, Valero Energy and Abercrombie and Fitch.

Company ($ millions)	Ticker	Net Operating Profit Before Tax	Net Nonoperating Expense (Revenue) Before Tax	Tax Expense	Statutory Tax Rate
Procter & Gamble.	PG	$10,927.0	$488.0	$3,182.0	35.0%
McDonald's	MCD	$4,021.6	$320.0	$1,099.4	36.8%
Valero Energy	VLO	$5,459.0	$172.0	$1,697.0	35.1%
Abercrombie and Fitch .	ANF	$542.7	(6.7)	$215.4	39.2%

a. Compute the tax shield for each company: Net nonoperating expense (revenue) × Statutory rate.

b. Use the following equation to compute the tax rate on net operating profit for each company.

$$\text{Tax rate on operating profit} = \frac{\text{Tax expense} + (\text{Net nonoperating expense} \times \text{Statutory tax rate})}{\text{Net operating profit before tax}}$$

c. Compute NOPAT using the tax rates from part *b*.

EXERCISES

E4-24. Compute and Interpret RNOA, Profit Margin, and Asset Turnover of Competitors   (LO2)

Target Corporation
(TGT)
Wal-Mart Stores
(WMT)

Selected balance sheet and income statement information for department store retailers Target Corporation and Wal-Mart Stores follows.

Company ($ millions)	Ticker	2006 Sales	2006 NOPAT	2006 Net Operating Assets	2005 Net Operating Assets
Target	TGT	$ 52,620	$ 2,693	$24,077	$22,567
Wal-Mart.	WMT	312,427	12,290	93,457	81,788

a. Compute the 2006 return on net operating assets (RNOA) for each company.
b. Disaggregate RNOA into net operating profit margin (NOPM) and net operating asset turnover (NOAT) for each company.
c. Discuss any differences in these ratios for each company. Your interpretation should reflect the distinct business strategies of each company.

E4-25. Compute, Disaggregate, and Interpret RNOA of Competitors (LO2)

Selected balance sheet and income statement information for the clothing retailers, Abercrombie & Fitch and The GAP, Inc., follows.

Abercrombie & Fitch (ANF)

The GAP, Inc. (GPS)

Company ($ millions)	Ticker	2006 Sales	2006 NOPAT	2006 Net Operating Assets	2005 Net Operating Assets
Abercrombie & Fitch. . .	ANF	$ 2,785	$ 324.7	$ 615.7	$ 700.5
The GAP	GPS	16,023	1,047.7	4,986.0	6,005.0

a. Compute the 2006 return on net operating assets (RNOA) for each company.
b. Disaggregate RNOA into net operating profit margin (NOPM) and net operating asset turnover (NOAT) for each company.
c. Discuss any differences in these ratios for each company. Your interpretation should reflect the distinct business strategies of each company.

E4-26. Compute, Disaggregate, and Interpret RNOA of Competitors (LO2)

Selected balance sheet and income statement information for the drug retailers CVS Corporation and Walgreen Company follows.

CVS Corporation (CVS)

Walgreen Company (WAG)

Company ($ millions)	Ticker	2006 Sales	2006 NOPAT	2006 Net Operating Assets	2005 Net Operating Assets
CVS Corp.	CVS	$37,006	$1,292	$10,520	$9,829
Walgreen Company . . .	WAG	42,202	1,539	8,395	6,888

a. Compute the 2006 return on net operating assets (RNOA) for each company.
b. Disaggregate RNOA into net operating profit margin (NOPM) and net operating asset turnover (NOAT) for each company.
c. Discuss any differences in these ratios for each company. Identify the factor(s) that drives the differences in RNOA observed from your analyses in parts a and b.

E4-27. Compute, Disaggregate, and Interpret ROE and RNOA (LO1)

Selected fiscal year balance sheet and income statement information for the computer chip maker, Intel, follows ($ millions).

Intel (INTC)

Company	Ticker	2005 Sales	2005 Net Income	2005 Net Operating Profit After Tax	2005 Net Operating Assets	2004 Net Operating Assets	2005 Stockholders' Equity	2004 Stockholders' Equity
Intel.	INTC	$38,826	$8,664	$8,487	$28,481	$27,499	$36,182	$38,579

a. Compute the 2005 return on equity (ROE) and the 2005 return on net operating assets (RNOA).
b. Disaggregate RNOA into net operating profit margin (NOPM) and net operating asset turnover (NOAT).
c. Compute the percentage of RNOA to ROE, and infer the return from nonoperating activities. How do we interpret this finding?

E4-28. **Compute, Disaggregate and Interpret ROE and RNOA** (LO1)

Staples (SPLS)

Selected balance sheet and income statement information from Staples, Inc. follows ($ millions).

Company	Ticker	2006 Sales	2006 Net Income	2006 Net Operating Profit After Tax	2006 Net Operating Assets	2005 Net Operating Assets	2006 Stockholders' Equity	2005 Stockholders' Equity
Staples	SPLS	$16,079	$834	$832	$4,367	$4,202	$4,425	$4,115

a. Compute the 2006 return on equity (ROE) and 2006 return on net operating assets (RNOA)
b. Disaggregate RNOA into net operating profit margin (NOPM) and net operating asset turnover (NOAT).
c. Compute the percentage of RNOA to ROE. What inferences do we draw from NOPM compared to NOAT?

E4-29. **Compute, Disaggregate and Interpret ROE and RNOA** (LO2)

Intuit (INTU)

Selected balance sheet and income statement information from the software company, Intuit, Inc., follows ($ millions).

Company	Ticker	2005 Sales	2005 Net Income	2005 Net Operating Profit After Tax	2005 Net Operating Assets	2004 Net Operating Assets	2005 Stockholders' Equity	2004 Stockholders' Equity
Intuit	INTU	$2,038	$382	$330	$651	$680	$1,696	$1,822

a. Compute the 2005 return on equity (ROE) and 2005 return on net operating assets (RNOA)
b. Disaggregate the RNOA from part a into net operating profit margin (NOPM) and net operating asset turnover (NOAT).
c. Compute the percentage of RNOA to ROE. What explanation can we offer for the relation between ROE and RNOA observed and for Intuit's use of stockholders' equity?

E4-30. **Compute and Interpret Liquidity and Solvency Ratios** (LO3)

Comcast Corporation (CMCSA)

Selected balance sheet and income statement information from Comcast Corporation for 2003 through 2005 follows ($ millions).

	Total Current Assets	Total Current Liabilities	Pretax Income	Interest Expense	Total Liabilities	Stockholders' Equity
2003	$5,403	$9,654	$ (137)	$2,018	$67,105	$42,054
2004	3,535	8,635	1,810	1,807	62,804	41,890
2005	2,594	6,269	1,880	1,796	62,270	40,876

a. Compute the current ratio for each year and discuss any trend in liquidity. Do you believe the company is sufficiently liquid? Explain. What additional information about the accounting numbers comprising this ratio might be useful in helping you assess liquidity? Explain.
b. Compute times interest earned and the total-liabilities-to-stockholders' equity ratio for each year and discuss any trends for each.
c. What is your overall assessment of the company's liquidity and solvency from the analyses in (a) and (b)? Explain.

E4-31. **Compute and Interpret Liquidity and Solvency Ratios** (LO3)

Selected balance sheet and income statement information from Verizon Communications, Inc., for 2003 through 2005 follows ($ millions).

Verizon Communications, Inc. (VZ)

	Total Current Assets	Total Current Liabilities	Pretax Income	Interest Expense	Total Liabilities	Stockholders' Equity
2003	$18,293	$26,570	$ 6,344	$2,797	$108,154	$57,814
2004	19,479	23,129	12,521	2,384	103,345	62,613
2005	16,448	25,063	13,652	2,180	74,942	66,434

a. Compute the current ratio for each year and discuss any trend in liquidity. Do you believe the company is sufficiently liquid? Explain. What additional information about the accounting numbers comprising this ratio might be useful in helping you assess liquidity? Explain.

b. Compute times interest earned and the total-liabilities-to-stockholders' equity ratio for each year and discuss any trends for each.

c. What is your overall assessment of the company's liquidity and solvency from the analyses in (a) and (b)? Explain.

E4-32. **Compute and Interpret Solvency Ratios for Business Segments** (LO2)

Selected balance sheet and income statement information from General Electric Company and its two principle business segments (Industrial and Financial) for 2005 follows.

General Electric (GE)

($ millions)	Pretax Income	Interest Expense	Total Liabilities	Stockholders' Equity
Industrial segment	$21,025	$ 1,432	$ 74,599	$109,354
Financial segment	10,246	14,308	487,542	50,815
Other..........................	(9,142)[1]	(553)[2]	(6,207)[2]	
General Electric Consolidated	22,129	15,187	555,934	109,354[3]

[1] Includes unallocated corporate operating activities.

[2] Includes intercompany loans and related interest expense; these are deducted (eliminated) in preparing consolidated financial statements.

[3] The consolidated equity equals the equity of the parent (industrial); this is explained in Module 7.

a. Compute times interest earned and the total-liabilities-to-stockholders' equity ratio for 2005 for its two business segments (Industrial and Financial) and the company as a whole

b. What is your overall assessment of the company's solvency? Explain. What differences do you observe between the two business segments? Do these differences correspond to your prior expectations given each company's business model?

c. Discuss the implications of the analysis of consolidated financial statements and the additional insight that can be gained from a more in-depth analysis of primary business segments.

E4-33.[B] **Direct Computation of Nonoperating Return** (LO1)

Refer to the income statement and balance sheet of Lowe's Companies, Inc., from Mid-Module Reviews 1 and 2.

Lowe's Companies, Inc. (LOW)

Required

a. Compute the FLEV and SPREAD for Lowe's for 2006.

b. Use RNOA from Mid-Module review 2, and the FLEV and SPREAD from part a, to compute ROE. Compare the ROE calculated in this exercise with the ROE we compute in the Mid-Module review 2.

E4-34.   Compute Tax Rates on Operating Profit and NOPAT   (LO1)

The income statement for The TJX Companies, Inc., follows.

THE TJX COMPANIES, INC. Consolidated Statements of Income			
Fiscal Year Ended ($ Thousands)	January 28, 2006	January 29, 2005	January 31, 2004
Net sales.....................................	$16,057,935	$14,913,483	$13,327,938
Cost of sales, including buying and occupancy costs....	12,295,016	11,398,656	10,101,279
Selling, general and administrative expenses	2,723,960	2,500,119	2,212,669
Interest expense, net	29,632	25,757	27,252
Income before provision for income taxes.............	1,009,327	988,951	986,738
Provision for income taxes........................	318,904	379,252	377,326
Net income.....................................	$ 690,423	$ 609,699	$ 609,412

a.   Compute the tax shield for 2006 and 2005. Assume that the combined statutory tax rate is 38% for both years.

b.   Use the following equation to compute TJX's tax rate on operating profit for both years.

$$\text{Tax rate on operating profit} = \frac{\text{Tax expense} + (\text{Net nonoperating expense} \times \text{Statutory tax rate})}{\text{Operating profit before taxes}}$$

c.   Compute NOPAT using the tax rate from part b, for 2006 and 2005.

PROBLEMS

P4-35.   Analysis and Interpretation of Profitability   (LO1, 2)

Balance sheets and income statements for Lockheed Martin Corporation (LMT) follow. Refer to these financial statements to answer the requirements.

Income Statement (In millions)	Year Ended December 31,		
	2005	2004	2003
Net sales			
Products	$31,518	$30,202	$27,290
Service	5,695	5,324	4,534
	37,213	35,526	31,824
Cost of sales			
Products	28,800	27,879	25,306
Services	5,073	4,765	4,099
Unallocated corporate costs	803	914	443
	34,676	33,558	29,848
	2,537	1,968	1,976
Other income and exenses, net	449	121	43
Operating profit	2,986	2,089	2,019
Interest expense..................	370	425	487
Earnings before taxes..............	2,616	1,664	1,532
Income tax expense...............	791	398	479
Net earnings.....................	$ 1,825	$ 1,266	$ 1,053

Balance Sheet (In millions)	December 31, 2005	December 31, 2004
Assets		
Cash and cash equivalents	$ 2,244	$ 1,060
Short-term investments	429	396
Receivables	4,579	4,094
Inventories	1,921	1,864
Deferred income taxes	861	982
Other current assets	495	557
Total current assets	10,529	8,953
Property, plant and equipment net	3,924	3,599
Investments in equity securities	196	812
Goodwill	8,447	7,892
Purchased intangibles, net	560	672
Prepaid pension asset	1,360	1,030
Other assets	2,728	2,596
Total assets	$27,744	$25,554
Liabilities and stockholders' equity		
Accounts payable	$ 1,998	$ 1,726
Customer advances and amounts in excess of costs incurred	4,331	4,028
Salaries, benefits and payroll taxes	1,475	1,346
Current maturities of long-term debt	202	15
Other current liabilities	1,422	1,451
Total current liabilities	9,428	8,566
Long-term debt	4,784	5,104
Accrued pension liabilities	2,097	1,660
Other postretirement benefit liabilities	1,277	1,236
Other liabilities	2,291	1,967
Stockholders' equity		
Common stock, $1 par value per share	432	438
Additional paid-in capital	1,724	2,223
Retained earnings	7,278	5,915
Accumulated other comprehensive loss	(1,553)	(1,532)
Other	(14)	(23)
Total stockholders' equity	7,867	7,021
Total liabilities and stockholders' equity	$27,744	$25,554

Required

a. Compute net operating profit after tax (NOPAT) for 2005 and 2004. Assume that combined federal and state statutory tax rates are 37.2% for 2005 and 37.9% for 2004.

b. Compute net operating assets (NOA) for 2005 and 2004.

c. Compute and disaggregate Lockheed Martin's RNOA into net operating profit margin (NOPM) and net operating asset turnover (NOAT) for 2005 and 2004; the 2003 NOA is $11,664 million. Has its RNOA improved or worsened? Explain why.

d. Compute net nonoperating obligations (NNO) for 2005 and 2004. Confirm the relation: NOA = NNO + Stockholders' equity.

e. Compute return on equity (ROE) for 2005 and 2004. (Stockholders' equity in 2003 is $6,756 million.)

f. What is Lockheed Martin's nonoperating return component of ROE for 2005 and 2004?

g. Comment on the difference between ROE and RNOA. What inference can we draw from this comparison?

Lockheed Martin
Corporation (LMT)

P4-36. **Analysis and Interpretation of Liquidity and Solvency**   **(LO3)**

Refer to the financial information of Lockheed Martin (LMT) in P4-35 to answer the following requirements.

Required

a.   Compute Lockheed Martin's current ratio and quick ratio for 2005 and 2004. Comment on any observed trends.

b.   Compute times interest earned and total-liabilities-to-stockholders' equity ratios for 2005 and 2004. Comment on any trends observed.

c.   Summarize your findings in a conclusion about the company's liquidity and solvency. Do you have any concerns about its ability to meet its debt obligations?

Lockheed Martin
Corporation (LMT)

P4-37.[B] **Direct Computation of Nonoperating Return**   **(LO1, 2)**

Refer to the financial information of Lockheed Martin (LMT) in P4-35 to answer the following requirements.

a.   Compute Lockheed Martin's financial leverage (FLEV) and Spread for 2005. Recall that NNE = NOPAT − Net income.

b.   Assume that Lockheed Martin's return on equity (ROE) for 2005 is 24.52% and its return on net operating assets (RNOA) is 17.76%. Confirm computations to yield the relation: ROE = RNOA + (FLEV × Spread).

c.   What do your computations of the nonoperating return imply about the company's use of borrowed funds?

Target Corporation
(TGT)

P4-38. **Analysis and Interpretation of Profitability**   **(LO1, 2)**

Balance sheets and income statements for Target Corporation (TGT) follow. Refer to these financial statements to answer the requirements.

Income Statement			
For Years Ended (In millions)	2006	2005	2004
Sales.	$51,271	$45,682	$40,928
Net credit card revenues	1,349	1,157	1,097
Total revenues.	52,620	46,839	42,025
Cost of sales.	34,927	31,445	28,389
Selling, general and administrative expenses	11,185	9,797	8,657
Credit card expenses.	776	737	722
Depreciation and amortization.	1,409	1,259	1,098
Earnings from continuing operations before interest expense and income taxes	4,323	3,601	3,159
Net interest expense	463	570	556
Earnings from continuing operations before income taxes	3,860	3,031	2,603
Provision for income taxes.	1,452	1,146	984
Earnings from continuing operations.	2,408	1,885	1,619
Earnings from discontinued operations, net of taxes of $6 and $116.	—	75	190
Gain on disposal of discontinued operations, net of taxes of $761.	—	1,238	—
Net earnings.	$ 2,408	$ 3,198	$ 1,809

Balance Sheet		
(In millions)	**January 28, 2006**	**January 28, 2005**
Assets		
Cash and cash equivalents	$ 1,648	$ 2,245
Accountings receivable, net	5,666	5,069
Inventory.	5,838	5,384
Other current assets.	1,253	1,224
Total current assets	14,405	13,922
Property and equipment		
Land	4,449	3,804
Buildings and improvements	14,174	12,518
Fixtures and equipment	3,219	2,990
Computer hardware and software	2,214	1,998
Construction-in-progress	1,158	962
Accumulated depreciation	(6,176)	(5,412)
Property and equipment, net	19,038	16,860
Other noncurrent assets.	1,552	1,511
Total assets.	$34,995	$32,293
Liabilities and shareholders' investment		
Accounts payable.	$ 6,268	$ 5,779
Accrued liabilities	2,193	1,633
Income taxes payable	374	304
Current portion of long-term debt		
and notes payable	753	504
Total current liabilities.	9,588	8,220
Long-term debt	9,119	9,034
Deferred income taxes	851	973
Other noncurrent liabilities	1,232	1,037
Shareholders' investment		
Common stock.	73	74
Additional paid-in-capital	2,121	1,810
Retained earnings	12,013	11,148
Accumulated other comprehensive income.	(2)	(3)
Total shareholders' investment.	14,205	13,029
Total liabilities and shareholders' investment.	$34,995	$32,293

Required

a. Compute net operating profit after tax (NOPAT) for 2006 and 2005. Assume that the combined federal and state statutory tax rates for both 2006 and 2005 are 38.3%.

b. Compute net operating assets (NOA) for 2006 and 2005.

c. Compute and disaggregate Target's RNOA into net operating profit margin (NOPM) and net operating asset turnover (NOAT) for 2006 and 2005; the 2004 NOA is $21,307 million. Comment on the drivers of the improvement in Target's RNOA.

d. Compute net nonoperating obligations (NNO) for 2006 and 2005. Confirm the relation: NOA = NNO + Stockholders' equity.

e. Compute return on equity (ROE) for 2006 and 2005; the 2004 stockholders' equity is $11,132 million.

f. Infer the nonoperating return component of ROE for both 2006 and 2005.

g. Comment on the difference between ROE and RNOA. What does this relation suggest about Target's use of equity capital?

P4-39. Analysis and Interpretation of Liquidity and Solvency (LO3)

Refer to the financial information of Target Corporation (TGT) in P4-38 to answer the following requirements.

Required

a. Compute Target's current ratio and quick ratio for 2006 and 2005. Comment on any observed trends.

b. Compute Target's times interest earned and its total-liabilities-to-stockholders' equity ratios for 2006 and 2005. Comment on any trends observed.

c. Summarize your findings in a conclusion about the company's liquidity and solvency. Do you have any concerns about Target's ability to meet its debt obligations?

P4-40.^{B} Direct Computation of Nonoperating Return (LO1)

Refer to the financial information of Target Corporation (TGT) in P4-38 to answer the following requirements.

Required

a. Compute Target's financial leverage (FLEV) and Spread for 2006; recall, NNE = NOPAT − Net income.

b. Assume that Target's return on equity (ROE) for 2006 is 17.68% and its return on net operating assets (RNOA) is 11.55%. Confirm computations to yield the relation: ROE = RNOA + (FLEV × Spread).

c. What do your computations of the nonoperating return in parts a and b imply about the company's use of borrowed funds?

P4-41. Analysis and Interpretation of Profitability (LO1, 2)

Balance sheets and income statements for Intel Corporation (INTC) follow. Refer to these financial statements to answer the requirements.

INTEL CORPORATION
Consolidated Statements of Income

Three Years Ended December 31 (In Millions)	2005	2004	2003
Net revenue	$38,826	$34,209	$30,141
Cost of sales	15,777	14,463	13,047
Gross margin	23,049	19,746	17,094
Research and development	5,145	4,778	4,360
Marketing, general and administrative	5,688	4,659	4,278
Impairment of goodwill	—	—	617
Amortization and impairment of acquisition-related intangibles and costs	126	179	301
Purchased in-process research and development	—	—	5
Operating expenses	10,959	9,616	9,561
Operating income	12,090	10,130	7,533
Losses on equity securities, net	(45)	(2)	(283)
Interest and other, net	565	289	192
Income before taxes	12,610	10,417	7,442
Provision for taxes	3,946	2,901	1,801
Net income	$ 8,664	$ 7,516	$ 5,641

INTEL CORPORATION
Consolidated Balance Sheets

December 31 (In Millions, except par value)	2005	2004
Assets		
Cash and cash equivalents	$ 7,324	$ 8,407
Short-term investments	3,990	5,654
Trading assets	1,458	3,111
Accounts receivable, net of allowance for doubtful accounts of $64 ($43 in 2004)	3,914	2,999
Inventories	3,126	2,621
Deferred tax assets	1,149	979
Other current assets	233	287
Total current assets	21,194	24,058
Property, plant and equipment, net	17,111	15,768
Marketable strategic equity securities	537	656
Other long-term investments	4,135	2,563
Goodwill	3,873	3,719
Deferred taxes and other assets	1,464	1,379
Total assets	$48,314	$48,143
Liabilities and stockholders' equity		
Short-term debt	$ 313	$ 201
Accounts payable	2,249	1,943
Accrued compensation and benefits	2,110	1,858
Accrued advertising	1,160	894
Deferred income on shipments to distributors	632	592
Other accrued liabilities	810	1,355
Income taxes payable	1,960	1,163
Total current liabilities	9,234	8,006
Long-term debt	2,106	703
Deferred tax liabilities	703	855
Other long-term liabilities	89	—
Stockholders' equity		
Perferred stock, $0.001 par value, 50 shares authorized; none issued	—	—
Common stock, $0.001 par value, 10,000 shares authorized; 5,919 issued and outstanding (6,253 in 2004) and capital in excess of par value	6,245	6,143
Acquisition-related unearned stock compensation	—	(4)
Accumulated other comprehensive income	127	152
Retained earnings	29,810	32,288
Total stockholders' equity	36,182	38,579
Total liabilities and stockholders' equity	$48,314	$48,143

Required

a. Compute net operating profit after tax (NOPAT) for 2005 and 2004. Assume that the combined federal and state statutory tax rates are 36.3% for 2005 and 34.6% for 2004.

b. Compute net operating assets (NOA) for 2005 and 2004. (*Hint:* Assume that trading assets and other long-term investments are investments in marketable securities and are therefore, nonoperating assets. Assume that marketable strategic equity securities are operating investments.)

c. Compute RNOA and disaggregate it into net operating profit margin (NOPM) and net operating asset turnover (NOAT) for 2005 and 2004; the 2003 NOA is $28,947 million. Comment on the drivers of RNOA.

d. Compute net nonoperating obligations (NNO) for 2005 and 2004. Confirm the relation: NOA = NNO + Stockholders' equity.

e. Compute return on equity (ROE) for 2005 and 2004; the 2003 stockholders' equity is $37,846 million.

f. Infer the nonoperating return component of ROE for both 2005 and 2004.

g. Comment on the difference between ROE and RNOA. What does this relation suggest about Intel's use of equity capital?

P4-42. Analysis and Interpretation of Profitability (LO1, 2)

Merck & Co. (MRK)

Balance sheets and income statements for Merck & Co. (MRK) follow. Refer to these financial statements to answer the requirements. (Note: This problem requires computation of ROCE in the presence of minority interest.)

MERCK & CO., INC. AND SUBSIDIARIES Consolidated Statement of Income			
Years Ended December 31 ($ millions, except per share amounts)	**2005**	**2004**	**2003**
Sales.	$22,011.9	$22,938.6	$22,485.9
Costs, expenses and other			
Materials and production	5,149.6	4,959.8	4,436.9
Marketing and administrative	7,155.5	7,238.7	6,200.3
Research and development	3,848.0	4,010.2	3,279.9
Restructuring costs.	322.2	107.6	194.6
Equity income from affiliates.	(1,717.1)	(1,008.2)	(474.2)
Other (income) expense, net.	(110.2)	(344.0)	(203.2)
	14,648.0	14,964.1	13,434.3
Income from continuing operations before taxes.	7,363.9	7,974.5	9,051.6
Taxes on income	2,732.6	2,161.1	2,462.0
Income from continuing operations	4,631.3	5,813.4	6,589.6
Income from discontinued operations, net of taxes.	—	—	241.3
Net income.	$ 4,631.3	$ 5,813.4	$ 6.830.9

MERCK & CO., INC. AND SUBSIDIARIES Consolidated Balance Sheet		
December 31 ($ millions)	**2005**	**2004**
Assets		
Cash and cash equivalents	$ 9,585.3	$ 2,878.8
Short-term investments	6,052.3	4,211.1
Accounts receivable.	2,927.3	3,627.7
Inventories (excludes inventories of $753.8 in 2005 and $638.7 in 2004 classified in Other assets).	1,658.1	1,898.7
Prepaid expenses and taxes	826.3	858.9
Total current assets	21,049.3	13,475.2

continued

MERCK & CO., INC. AND SUBSIDIARIES
Consolidated Balance Sheet

December 31 ($ millions)	2005	2004
Investments	1,107.9	6,727.1
Property, plant and equipment (at cost)		
Land	433.0	366.6
Buildings	9,479.6	8,874.3
Machinery, equipment and office furnishings	12,785.2	11,926.1
Construction in progress	1,015.5	1,641.6
	23,713.3	22,808.6
Less allowance for depreciation	9,315.1	8,094.9
	14,398.2	14,713.7
Goodwill	1,085.7	1,085.7
Other intangibles, net	518.7	679.2
Other assets	6,686.0	5,891.9
Total assets	$44,845.8	$42,572.8
Liabilities and Stockholders' Equity		
Loans payable and current portion of long-term debt	$ 2,972.0	$ 2,181.2
Trade accounts payable	471.1	421.4
Accrued and other current liabilities	5,381.2	5,288.1
Income taxes payable	3,649.2	3,012.3
Dividends payable	830.0	841.1
Total current liabilities	13,303.5	11,744.1
Long-term debt	5,125.6	4,691.5
Deferred income taxes and noncurrent liabilities	6,092.9	6,442.1
Minority interests	2,407.2	2,406.9
Stockholders' equity		
Common stock, one cent par value		
Authorized—5,400,000,000 shares		
Issued—2,976,223,337 shares—2005		
—2,976,230,393 shares—2004	29.8	29.8
Other paid-in capital	6,900.0	6,869 8
Retained earnings	37,918.9	36,626.3
Accumulated other comprehensive income (loss)	52.3	(45.9)
	44,901.0	43,480.0
Less treasury stock, at cost		
794,299,347 shares—2005		
767,591,491 shares—2004	26,984.4	26,191.8
Total stockholders' equity	17,916.6	17,288.2
Total liabilities and stockholders' equity	$44,845.8	$42,572.8

Required
a. Compute net operating profit after tax (NOPAT) for 2005 and 2004. Assume that the combined federal and state statutory tax rates are 37.5% for 2005 and 36.3% for 2004. Other income includes net interest expense and minority interest expense of $121.8 million in 2005 and $154.2 million in 2004.
b. Compute net operating assets (NOA) for 2005 and 2004. (*Hint:* Short- and long-term investments are investments in marketable securities.)
c. Compute RNOA and disaggregate it into net operating profit margin (NOPM) and net operating asset turnover (NOAT) for 2005 and 2004; the 2003 NOA is $15,374.4 million. Comment on the drivers of RNOA.
d. Compute net nonoperating obligations (NNO) for 2005 and 2004. Confirm the relation: NOA = NNO + Stockholders' equity + Minority interest.

e. Compute return on equity for the common shareholders (ROCE) for 2005 and 2004; the 2003 stockholders' equity is $15,576.4 million. For 2005 only, show that ROCE = ROCE before minority interest × Minority interest sharing ratio, see Appendix 4B.

f. Compute Merck's R&D as a percentage of sales and its sales growth for 2003 through 2005; its 2003 sales are $21,445.8 million. Comment on your findings.

P4-43. Analysis and Interpretation of Profitability   (LO1, 2)

United Parcel Service
(UPS)

Balance sheets and income statements for United Parcel Service (UPS) follow. Refer to these financial statements to answer the following requirements.

UNITED PARCEL SERVICE
Income Statement

Years Ended December 31 ($ millions)	2005	2004	2003
Revenue	$42,581	$36,582	$33,485
Operating expenses			
Compensation and benefits	22,517	20,823	19,251
Other	13,921	10,770	9,789
	36,438	31,593	29,040
Operating profit	6,143	4,989	4,445
Other income and (expense)			
Investment income	104	82	18
Interest expense	(172)	(149)	(121)
Gain on redemption of long-term debt	—	—	28
	(68)	(67)	(75)
Income before income taxes	6,075	4,922	4,370
Income taxes	2,205	1,589	1,472
Net income	$ 3,870	$ 3,333	$ 2,898

UNITED PARCEL SERVICE
Balance Sheet

December 31 ($ millions, except per share amounts)	2005	2004
Assets		
Cash & cash equivalents	$ 1,369	$ 739
Marketable securities & short-term investments	1,672	4,458
Accounts receivable, net	5,950	5,156
Finance receivables, net	411	524
Income tax receivable	—	371
Deferred income taxes	475	392
Other current assets	1,126	965
Total current assets	11,003	12,605
Property, plant & equipment—at cost, net of accumulated depreciation & amortization of $14,268 and $13,505 in 2005 and 2004	15,289	13,973
Prepaid pension cost	3,932	3,222
Goodwill	2,549	1,255
Intangible assets, net	684	669
Other assets	1,765	1,364
Total assets	$35,222	$33,088

continued

UNITED PARCEL SERVICE
Balance Sheet

December 31 ($ millions, except per share amounts)	2005	2004
Liabilities and shareowners' equity		
Current maturities of long-term debt and commercial paper.	$ 821	$ 1,187
Accounts payable.	2,352	2,312
Accrued wages & withholdings	1,324	1,197
Dividends payable	364	315
Income taxes payable	180	79
Other current liabilities	1,752	1,439
Total current liabilities.	6,793	6,529
Long-term debt	3,159	3,261
Accumulated postretirement benefit obligation, net	1,704	1,470
Deferred taxes, credits & other liabilities	6,682	5,450
Shareowners' equity		
Preferred stock, no par value, authorized 200 shares, none issued.	—	—
Class A common stock, par value $.01 per share, authorized 4,600 shares, issued 454 and 515 in 2005 and 2004	5	5
Class B common stock, par value $.01 per share, authorized 5,600 shares, issued 646 and 614 in 2005 and 2004	6	6
Additional paid-in capital	—	417
Retained earnings.	17,037	16,192
Accumulated other comprehensive loss	(164)	(242)
Deferred compensation obligations	161	169
	17,045	16,547
Less: Treasury stock (3 shares in 2005 and 2004)	(161)	(169)
Total shareowners' equity.	16,884	16,378
Total liabilities and shareowners' equity.	$35,222	$33,088

Required

a. Compute net operating profit after tax (NOPAT) for 2005 and 2004. Assume that the combined federal and state statutory tax rates are 37.0% for 2005 and 36.2% for 2004.

b. Compute net operating assets (NOA) for 2005 and 2004.

c. Compute RNOA and disaggregate it into net operating profit margin (NOPM) and net operating asset turnover (NOAT) for 2005 and 2004; the 2003 NOA is $15,787 million. Comment on the drivers of the improvement in RNOA.

d. Compute net nonoperating obligations (NNO) for 2005 and 2004. Confirm the relation: NOA = NNO + Stockholders' equity.

e. Compute return on equity (ROE) for 2005 and 2004; the 2003 stockholders' equity is $14,852 million.

f. Infer the nonoperating return component of ROE for both 2005 and 2004.

g. Comment on the difference between ROE and RNOA. What does this relation suggest about UPS's use of debt?

P4-44. Analysis and Interpretation of Liquidity and Solvency   (LO3)

Refer to the financial information of United Parcel Service in P4-43 to answer the following requirements. United Parcel Service (UPS)

Required

a. Compute its current ratio and quick ratio for 2005 and 2004. Comment on any observed trends.

b. Compute its times interest earned and its total-liabilities-to-stockholders' equity ratios for 2005 and 2004. Comment on any trends observed.

c. Summarize your findings in a conclusion about the company's liquidity and solvency. Do you have any concerns about its ability to meet its debt obligations?

United Parcel Service
(UPS)

P4-45.[B] **Direct Computation of Nonoperating Return** (LO1)

Refer to the financial information of United Parcel Service in P4-43 to answer the following requirements.

Required

a. Compute its financial leverage (FLEV) and Spread for 2005; recall, NNE = NOPAT − Net income.

b. Assume that UPS's NOPAT for 2005 is $3,913 million, its 2005 return on equity (ROE) is 23.27%, and its 2005 return on net operating assets (RNOA) is 22.01%. Confirm computations to yield the relation: ROE = RNOA + (FLEV × Spread). (*Hint:* Compute net nonoperating expense as NOPAT − Net income.)

c. What do your computations of the nonoperating return in parts *a* and *b* imply about the company's use of borrowed funds?

P4-46. **Analysis and Interpretation of Profit Margin, Asset Turnover, and RNOA for Several Companies** (LO2)

Net operating profit margin (NOPM) and net operating asset turnover (NOAT) for several selected companies for 2005 follow.

	NOPM	NOAT
Albertsons.................	1.99%	2.83
Caterpillar	8.25%	1.40
Home Depot	7.56%	2.69
McDonald's.................	13.04%	0.78
Merck......................	19.05%	0.74
Southwest Airlines	7.03%	0.75
Target......................	5.31%	2.07
Verizon....................	12.59%	0.52

Albertsons, Inc. (ABS)
Caterpillar, Inc. (CAT)
Home Depot, Inc. (HD)
McDonalds Corporation (MCD)
Merck (MRK)
Southwest Airlines (LUV)
Target (TGT)
Verizon (VZ)

Required

a. Graph NOPM and NOAT for each of these companies. Do you see a pattern revealed that is similar to that shown in this module? Explain. (The graph in the module is based on medians for selected industries; the graph for this problem uses fewer companies than in the module and, thus, will not be as smooth.)

b. Consider the trade-off between profit margin and asset turnover. How can we evaluate companies on the profit margin and asset turnover trade-off? Explain.

CASES

C4-47. **Management Application: Gross Profit and Strategic Management** (LO2)

One way to increase overall profitability is to increase gross profit. This can be accomplished by raising prices and/or by reducing manufacturing costs.

Required

a. Will raising prices and/or reducing manufacturing costs unambiguously increase gross profit? Explain.

b. What strategy might you develop as a manager to (i) yield a price increase for your product, or (ii) reduce product manufacturing cost?

C4-48.   Management Application: Asset Turnover and Strategic Management   (LO2)

Increasing net operating asset turnover requires some combination of increasing sales and/or decreasing net operating assets. For the latter, many companies consider ways to reduce their investment in working capital (current assets less current liabilities). This can be accomplished by reducing the level of accounts receivable and inventories, or by increasing the level of accounts payable.

Required

a.   Develop a list of suggested actions to achieve all three of these objectives as manager.

b.   Examine the implications of each. That is, describe the marketing implications of reducing receivables and inventories, and the supplier implications of delaying payment. How can a company achieve working capital reduction without negatively impacting its performance?

C4-49.   Ethics and Governance: Earnings Management

Companies are aware that analysts focus on profitability in evaluating financial performance. Managers have historically utilized a number of methods to improve reported profitability that are cosmetic in nature and do not affect "real" operating performance. These are typically subsumed under the general heading of "earnings management." Justification for such actions typically includes the following arguments:

- Increasing stock price by managing earnings benefits shareholders; thus, no one is hurt by these actions.
- Earnings management is a temporary fix; such actions will be curtailed once "real" profitability improves, as managers expect.

Required

a.   Identify the affected parties in any scheme to manage profits to prop up stock price.

b.   Do the ends (of earnings management) justify the means? Explain.

c.   To what extent are the objectives of managers different from those of shareholders?

d.   What governance structure can you envision that might prohibit earnings management?

Reporting and Analyzing Operating Income

LEARNING OBJECTIVES

LO1 Explain revenue recognition criteria and identify transactions of special concern. (p. 5-5)

LO2 Describe accounting for operating expenses, including research and development, and restructuring. (p. 5-11)

LO3 Explain and analyze accounting for income taxes. (p. 5-17)

LO4 Compute earnings per share and explain the effect of dilutive securities. (p. 5-24)

LO5 Explain how foreign currency fluctuations affect the income statement. (p. 5-26)

PFIZER

Pfizer's business is to discover, develop, manufacture and market leading prescription medicines. These endeavors define the company's operating activities and include research and development, manufacturing, advertising, sales, after-sale customer support, and all administrative functions necessary to support Pfizer's various activities.

Accounting for operating activities involves numerous estimates and choices, and GAAP often grants considerable latitude. To illustrate, consider the choice of when to recognize sales revenue. Should Pfizer recognize revenue when it receives a customer order? When it ships the drug order? Or, when the customer pays? GAAP requires that revenues be recognized when *earned*. It is up to the company to decide when that condition is met. This module identifies several revenue-recognition scenarios that are especially troublesome for companies, their auditors, regulators, and outside stakeholders.

Pfizer's key operating activity is its research and development (R&D). To protect its discoveries, Pfizer holds thousands of patents and applies for hundreds more each year. However, patents don't protect Pfizer indefinitely—patents expire or fail legal challenges and, then, Pfizer's drugs face competition from other drug manufacturers. In 2005, Pfizer's sales declined by 2%, in part because patents expired. Indeed, as the company reported in the MD&A section of its 10-K, "revenues of major products with lost exclusivity in the U.S. declined by 44% from 2004." In addition, several Pfizer products have recently come under fire, and the company's 10K reports the bad news: "uncertainty related to Celebrex and the suspension of Bextra sales have resulted in a significant decline in prescription volume in the arthritis and pain market, resulting in a 63% decline in revenues in those products from 2004." Even the company's blockbuster drug, Lipitor, with sales exceeding $12 billion in 2005 (24% of Pfizer's total revenues), is not a panacea for what ails Pfizer—the Lipitor patent expires in 2010.

Wall Street is not optimistic about Pfizer's ability to replace patents that will lapse over the next decade. While Pfizer's revenues have increased by 77% since 2001, its profits have only increased by 4%, and Pfizer's stock price has fallen 40 percent—see stock price chart below. Over that same period the American Stock Exchange Pharmaceutical index (DRG) fell by only 13 percent.

Accounting for R&D costs is controversial. Even though R&D activities generally yield future benefits and, thus, meet the criteria to be recorded as an asset, GAAP requires that companies expense all R&D costs. This creates balance sheets with significant "missing" assets. For example, the only asset that Pfizer has on its books related to Lipitor is the legal cost of filing the patent with the U.S. Patent Office. Clearly this does not capture Lipitor's full value to Pfizer. This module explains R&D accounting and the resulting financial statement implications.

Pfizer has restructured its activities several times in an attempt to maintain operating profit in light of declining sales. Restructurings typically involve two types of costs: severance costs relating to employee terminations and asset write-offs. GAAP grants leeway in how to account for restructuring activities. Should

(Continued on next page)

(Continued from previous page)

Pfizer expense the severance costs when the board of directors approves the layoffs? Or when the employees are actually paid? Or at some other point? This module discusses accounting for restructurings, including footnote disclosures that can help financial statement readers interpret restructuring activities.

A necessary part of operations is paying income taxes on profits earned. The IRS has its own rules for computing taxes owed. These rules, called the Internal Revenue Code, are different from GAAP. Thus, it is legal (and necessary) for companies to prepare two sets of financial reports, one for shareholders and one for tax authorities. In this module, we will see that tax expense reported on the income statement is not computed as a simple percentage of pretax income. The module also discusses the valuation allowance that is related to deferred tax assets, and explains how the allowance can markedly affect net income.

Earnings per share (EPS) is the most frequently quoted operating number in the financial press. It represents earnings that are available to pay dividends to common shareholders. Companies report two EPS numbers: basic and diluted. The latter represents the lower bound on that year's EPS. It is important that we understand the difference between the two, and this module describes the two EPS computations.

Pfizer does business around the world, transacting in many currencies. Indeed, many of Pfizer's subsidiaries maintain their entire financial records in currencies other than the U.S. dollar. Consequently, to prepare its financial statements in $US, Pfizer must translate each transaction from foreign currencies into $US. This module describes the effects of foreign currency translation. When the dollar strengthens and weakens against other world currencies, a company's foreign revenues and expenses increase or decrease even if unit volumes remain unchanged. It is important to understand this mechanical relation if we are to properly analyze companies with global operations. This module considers these issues.

Sources: Pfizer 2005 10-K, Pfizer 2005 Annual Report; *Fortune*, January 2007; *BusinessWeek*, January 2007.

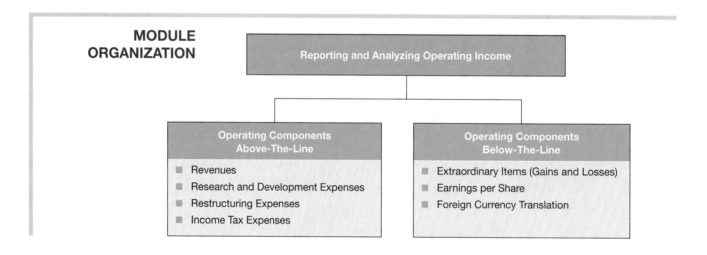

INTRODUCTION

Operating activities refer to a company's primary transactions. These include the purchase of goods from suppliers and, if a manufacturing company, the conversion of goods into finished products, the promotion and distribution of goods, the sale of goods to customers, and post-sale customer support. Operating activities are reported in the income statement under items such as sales, cost of goods sold, and selling, general, and administrative expenses. They represent a company's primary activities, and they must be executed successfully for a company to consistently succeed.

Nonoperating activities relate to the borrowing of money and the securities investment activities of a company. They are not a company's primary activities.[1] These activities are typically reported in the income statement under items such as interest revenues and expenses, dividend revenues, and gains and losses on sales of securities.

---

[1] However, income derived from investments is considered to be operating income for financial-services firms such as banks and insurance companies. Many analysts also consider as operating, the income derived from financing subsidiaries of manufacturing companies, such as Ford Motor Credit and Caterpillar Financial, because these activities can be viewed as extensions of the sales process.

Proper identification of operating and nonoperating components is important for valuation of companies' equity (stock) and debt (note and bond) securities. It is of interest, for example, to know whether company profitability results from operating activities, or whether poor operating performance is being masked by income from nonoperating activities (income from nonoperating activities usually depends on a favorable investment climate, which can be short-lived).

Exhibit 5.1 classifies several common income components as operating and nonoperating.

EXHIBIT 5.1	**Distinguishing Operating and Nonoperating Income Components**
Operating Activities	**Nonoperating Activities**
• Sales	• Interest revenues and expenses
• Cost of goods sold	• Dividend revenues
• Selling, general and administrative expenses	• Gains and losses on sales of investments
• Depreciation expense	• Gains and losses on debt retirement
• Research and development expenses	• Gains and losses on discontinued operations
• Restructuring expenses	• Minority interest expense
• Income tax expenses	• Investment write-downs
• Extraordinary gains and losses	
• Gains and losses on sales of operating assets	
• Foreign currency translation effects	
• Operating asset write-downs	
• Other income or expenses	

The list of operating activities above includes all the familiar operating items, as well as gains and losses on transactions relating to operating assets and the write-down of operating assets.[2] The list also includes "other" income statement items. We treat these as operating unless the income statement designates them as nonoperating or footnote information indicates that some or all of these "other" items are nonoperating. Footnotes are usually uninformative about "other" income statement items and "other" balance sheet items. GAAP does not require specific disclosure of such items unless they are deemed *material*.[3]

We build our discussion of operating income around the operating accounts in Pfizer's income statement (Exhibit 5.2), which includes all of the typical operating accounts. We highlight the following topics in this module:

▨ Revenues

▨ Research and development expenses

▨ Restructuring expenses

▨ Income tax expenses

▨ Extraordinary gains and losses

▨ Earnings per share (EPS)

▨ Foreign currency translation effects

---

[2] For example, a loss on the sale of equipment implies that the company did not depreciate the equipment quickly enough. Had the company recorded the "right" amount of depreciation over the years (that is, the amount of depreciation that perfectly matched the equipment's economic devaluation over time), the equipment's book value would have been exactly the same as its market value and no loss would have been recorded. Thus, we treat the loss on disposal in the same manner as depreciation expense—as operating. The same logic applies to write-downs of operating assets.

[3] *Material* is an accounting term that means that the item in question is significant enough to make a difference to someone relying on the financial statements to make a business decision. Investors, for example, might find an item material if it is large enough to change their investment decision (whether to buy or sell the stock). This *materiality* judgment is in the eye of the beholder, and this subjectivity makes materiality an elusive concept.

BUSINESS INSIGHT	Ratios Across Industries

Over time, industries evolve and reach equilibrium levels for operating activities. For example, some industries require a high level of selling, general and administrative (SG&A) expenses, perhaps due to high advertising demands or high occupancy costs. Other industries require intense research and development (R&D) expenditures to remain competitive. To a large extent, these cost structures dictate the prices that firms in the industry charge—each industry prices its product or service to yield a sufficient level of gross profit (Sales less Cost of Goods Sold) to cover the operating expenses and allow the industry to remain viable. Review the following table of selected operating margins for companies in various industries.

	Gross profit/Sales	SG&A/Sales	R&D/Sales	NOPM
Pfizer......................	88.0%	47.1%	17.7%	14.6%
Intel	70.9	27.9	13.3	20.2
Cisco Systems	70.4	36.3	13.5	19.4
Procter & Gamble	54.3	31.7	3.4	12.5
Home Depot	33.7	20.1	0.0	7.5
Dell	19.1	9.8	0.8	5.6
Target	33.6	22.8	0.0	5.3

We see that Cisco, Intel, Pfizer, and Proctor & Gamble report high gross profit margins. This does not necessarily suggest they are better managed than Dell. Instead, their industries require higher levels of gross profit to cover their high levels of SG&A and R&D. Dell, on the other hand, is in a highly price competitive segment of the computer industry. To maintain its competitive advantage Dell must control costs. Indeed, Dell reports the lowest SG&A-to-sales ratio of any of the companies listed.

OPERATING INCOME COMPONENTS

Pfizer's 2005 income statement in Exhibit 5.2 highlights the operating income components discussed in this module. We defer discussion of cost of goods sold to Module 6, which focuses on inventories and other operating assets. Modules 2 and 4 discuss items typically included in selling, general and administrative (SG&A) expenses, and Module 7 addresses the accounts related to acquisitions of other companies (such as amortization of intangible assets, merger-related in-process research and development charges, discontinued operations, and minority interest expense).

We begin by discussing revenue, including the criteria for revenue recognition that companies must employ and improper revenue recognition that the SEC has recently challenged. Next, we discuss Pfizer's research and development expenses, restructuring charges, provision for taxes, extraordinary items, and earnings per share (EPS). We finish with a discussion of the effects of foreign currency fluctuations on the income statement.

Revenues

LO1 Explain revenue recognition criteria and identify transactions of special concern.

Pfizer reports over $51 billion of revenue. This revenue represents the culmination of a process that includes the manufacture of the drugs, their promotion, the receipt of orders, delivery to the customer, billing for the sale amount, and collection of the amounts owed. At what point in this process should Pfizer recognize its revenue and the related profit? When the drugs are delivered to the customer? When payment is received? And, how should Pfizer treat sales discounts or rights of return?

GAAP specifies two **revenue recognition criteria** that must both be met for revenue to be recognized on the income statement. Revenue must be (1) **realized or realizable**, and (2) **earned**.[4] *Realized or*

---

[4] SEC provides guidance for revenue recognition in *Staff Accounting Bulletin (SAB) 101* (http://www.sec.gov/interps/account/sab101.htm), which states that revenue is realized, or realizable, and earned when *each* of the following criteria are met: (1) there is persuasive evidence that a sales agreement exists; (2) delivery has occurred or services have been rendered; (3) the seller's price to the buyer is fixed or determinable; and (4) collectibility is reasonably assured.

EXHIBIT 5.2	Pfizer Income Statement	
(Millions, Except per Common Share Data)		**2005**
Revenues		$51,298
Costs and expenses		
Cost of sales		8,525
Selling, informational and administative expenses		16,997
Research and development expenses		7,442
Amortization of intangible assets		3,409
Merger-related in-process research and development charges		1,652
Restructuring charges and merger-related costs		1,392
Other (income)/deductions—net		347
Income from continuing operations before provision for taxes on income, minority interests and cumulative effect of a change in accounting principles		11,534
Provision for taxes on income		3,424
Minority interest		16
Income from continuing operalions		8,094
Discontinued operations		
(Loss)/income from discontinued operations—net of tax		(31)
Gains on sales of discontinued operations—net of tax		47
Discontinued operations—net of tax		16
Other income (expense)		(25)
Net income		$ 8,085
Earnings per common share—basic		
Income from continuing operations before cumulative effect of a change in accounting principles		$ 1.10
Discontinued operations		—
Net income		$ 1.10
Earnings per common share—diluted		
Income from continuing operations before cumulative effect of a change in accounting principles		$ 1.09
Discontinued operations		—
Net income		$ 1.09
Weighted-average shares—basic		7,361
Weighted-average shares—diluted		7,411

realizable means that the seller's net assets (assets less liabilities) increase. That is, the seller receives an asset, such as cash or accounts receivable, or satisfies a liability, such as deferred revenue, as a result of a transaction. The company does not have to wait to recognize revenue until after it collects the accounts receivable; the increase in the account receivable (asset) means that the revenue is realizable. *Earned* means that the seller has performed its duties under the terms of the sales agreement and that title to the product sold has passed to the buyer with no right of return or other contingencies. As long as Pfizer has delivered the drugs ordered by its customers, and its customers are obligated to make payment, Pfizer can recognize revenue. The following conditions would each argue *against* revenue recognition:

- *Rights of return exist,* other than due to routine product defects covered under product warranty.
- *Consignment sales,* where products are held on consignment until ultimately sold by the consignee.
- *Continuing involvement by seller in product resale,* such as where the seller retains possession of the product until it's resold.
- *Contingency sales,* such as when product sales are contingent on product performance or further approvals by the customer.

Revenue is not recognized in these cases until the factors inhibiting revenue recognition are resolved.

Companies are required to report their revenue recognition policies in footnotes to their 10-K reports. Pfizer recognizes its revenues as follows:

> Revenue Recognition—we record revenue from product sales when the goods are shipped and title passes to the customer. At the time of sale, we also record estimates for a variety of sales deductions, such as sales rebates, discounts and incentives, and product returns.

Pfizer adopts the position that its revenues are *earned* when its products are shipped and title to the merchandise passes to its customers. At that point, Pfizer has done everything required and, thus, recognizes the sale in the income statement. Most companies recognize revenues using these criteria. Pfizer does *not* recognize revenues for the gross selling price. Instead, Pfizer deducts that portion of gross sales that is likely to be refunded to customers through sales rebates, discounts or incentives (including volume purchases). Pfizer estimates the likely cost of those price reductions and deducts that amount from gross sales. Similarly, Pfizer does not recognize revenues for those products that it estimates will be returned, possibly because the drugs hit their expiration date before they are sold by Pfizer's customers. In sum, Pfizer recognizes revenues for products delivered to customers, and for only for the sales price *net* of anticipated discounts and returns. This is why we often see "Revenues, net" on companies' income statements.

BUSINESS INSIGHT | **Cisco's Revenue Recognition**

Following is an excerpt from Cisco Systems' policies on revenue recognition as reported in footnotes to its recent annual report.

> We recognize product revenue when persuasive evidence of an arrangement exists, delivery has occurred, the fee is fixed or determinable, and collectibility is reasonably assured. In instances where final acceptance of the product, system, or solution is specified by the customer, revenue is deferred until all acceptance criteria have been met . . . Service revenue is generally deferred and, in most cases, recognized ratably over the period during which the services are to be performed . . . Contracts and customer purchase orders are generally used to determine the existence of an arrangement. Shipping documents and customer acceptance, when applicable, are used to verify delivery . . . When a sale involves multiple elements, such as sales of products that include services, the entire fee from the arrangement is allocated to each respective element based on its relative fair value and recognized when revenue recognition criteria for each element are met.

Cisco's criteria for revenue recognition mirror SEC guidance. The key components are that revenue is *earned* and that proceeds are *realized or realizable*. For Cisco, earned means that delivery to and acceptance by the customer occurs, or that Cisco is available to perform service commitments, even if not called upon.

Risks of Revenue Recognition

More than 70% of SEC accounting and auditing enforcement actions involve misstated revenues (Dechow, P., and C. Schrand. 2004. "Earnings quality," The Research Foundation of CFA Institute. Charlottesville, Virginia). The SEC is so concerned about aggressive (premature) revenue recognition that it recently issued a special *Staff Accounting Bulletin (SAB) 101* on the matter. The SEC provides the following examples of problem areas to assist companies in properly recognizing revenue:

- *Case 1: Channel stuffing.* Some sellers use their market power over customers to induce (or even require) them to purchase more goods than they actually need. This practice, called *channel stuffing*, increases period-end sales and net income. If no side agreements exist for product returns, the practice does not violate GAAP revenue recognition guidelines, but the SEC contends that revenues are misrepresented and that the practice is a violation of securities laws.

- *Case 2: Barter transactions.* Some barter transactions are concocted to create the illusion of revenue. Examples include the advertising swaps that dot-com companies engage in, and the excess capacity swaps of fiber optic communications businesses. The advertising swap relates to the simultaneous sale and purchase of advertising. The excess capacity swap relates to a company selling excess capacity to a competitor and, simultaneously, purchasing excess capacity from that competitor. Both types of swaps are equal exchanges and do not provide income or create an expense for either party. Further, these transactions do not represent a culmination of the normal earning process and, thus, the "earned" revenue recognition criterion is not met.

- *Case 3: Mischaracterizing transactions as arm's-length.* Transfers of inventories or other assets to related entities are typically not recognized as revenue until arm's-length sales occur. Sometimes, companies disguise non-arm's length transactions as sales to unrelated entities. This practice is improper when (1) the buyer is related to the seller, (2) the seller is providing financing, or (3) the buyer is a special-purpose entity that fails to meet independence requirements. Revenue should not be recognized unless the sales process is complete, that is, goods have been transferred and an asset has been created (future payment from a solvent, independent party).

- *Case 4: Pending execution of sales agreements.* Sometimes companies boost current period profits by recording revenue for goods delivered for which formal customer approval has yet to be received. The SEC's position is that if the company's practice is to obtain sales authorization, then revenue is *not* earned until such approval is obtained, even though product delivery is made and customer approval is anticipated.

- *Case 5: Gross versus net revenues.* Some companies use their distribution network to sell other companies' goods at a slight markup (i.e. for a commission). There are increasing reports of companies that inflate revenues by reporting such transactions on a gross basis (separately reporting both sales and cost of goods sold) instead of reporting only the commission (typically a percentage of sales price). The incentives for such reporting are high for some dot.com companies and start-ups that believe the market prices of their stocks are based on revenue growth and not on profitability. Reporting revenues at gross rather than net would have enormous impact on the valuations of those companies. The SEC prescribes that such sales be reported on a net basis.

- *Case 6: Sales on consignment.* Some companies deliver goods to other companies with the understanding that these goods will be ultimately sold to third parties. At the time of delivery, title does not pass to the second company, and the second company has no obligation to make payment to the seller until the product is sold. This type of transaction is called a *consignment sale*. The SEC's position is that a sale has not occurred, and revenue is *not* to be recognized by the original company, until the product is sold to a third party. Further, the middleman (consignee) cannot report the gross sale, and can only report its commission revenue.

- *Case 7: Failure to take delivery.* Some customers may not take delivery of the product by period-end. In this case, revenue is *not* yet earned. The earning process is only complete once the product is delivered and accepted. An example is a layaway sale. Even though the product is ordered, and even partially paid for, revenue is not recognized until the product is delivered and final payment is made or agreed to be made.

- *Case 8: Nonrefundable fees.* Sellers sometimes receive fees that are nonrefundable to the customer. An example is a health club initiation fee or a cellular phone activation fee. Some sellers wish to record these cash receipts as revenue to boost current sales and income. However, even though cash is received and nonrefundable, revenue is not recognized until the product is delivered or the service performed. Until that time, the company reports the cash received as a liability (deferred revenue). Once the obligation is settled, the liability is removed and revenue is reported.

In sum, revenue is only recognized when it is earned and when it is realized or realizable. This demands that the seller has performed its obligations (no contingencies exist) and the buyer is an independent party with the financial capacity to pay the amounts owed.

Percentage-of-Completion Revenue Recognition

Challenges arise in determining the point at which revenue is earned for companies with long-term sales contracts (spanning more than one period), such as construction companies and defense contractors. For these companies, revenue is often recognized using the percentage-of-completion method, which recognizes revenue by determining the costs incurred under the contract relative to its total expected costs.

To illustrate, assume that Abbott Construction signs a $10 million contract to construct a building. Abbott estimates construction will take two years and will cost $7,500,000. This means the contract yields an expected gross profit of $2,500,000 over two years. The following table summarizes construction costs incurred each year and the revenue Abbott recognizes.

	Construction costs incurred	Percentage complete	Revenue recognized
Year 1	$4,500,000	$\dfrac{\$4,500,000}{\$7,500,000} = 60\%$	$10,000,000 × 60% = $6,000,000
Year 2	$3,000,000	$\dfrac{\$3,000,000}{\$7,500,000} = 40\%$	$10,000,000 × 40% = $4,000,000

This table reveals that Abbott would report $6 million in revenue and $1.5 million ($6 million − $4.5 million) in gross profit on the construction project in the first year and $4 million in revenue and $1 million ($4 million − $3 million) in gross profit in the second year.

Next, assume that Abbott's client makes a $1 million deposit at the signing of the contract and that Abbott submits bills to the client based on the percentage of completion. The following table reflects the bills sent to, and the cash received from, the client.

	Revenue recognized	Client billed	Cash received
At signing	$ 0	$ 0	$1,000,000
Year 1	6,000,000	5,000,000	3,000,000
Year 2	4,000,000	4,000,000	6,000,000

At the signing of the contract, Abbott recognizes no revenue because construction has not begun and thus, Abbott has not earned any revenue. At the end of the second year, Abbott has recognized all of the contract revenue and the client has paid all monies owed per the accounts receivable.

The following template captures Abbott Construction's transactions over this two-year period (M indicates millions).

	Balance Sheet						Income Statement		
Transaction	Cash Asset	+ Noncash Assets	= Liabil-ities	+ Contrib. Capital	+ Earned Capital		Rev-enues	− Expen-ses	= Net Income
Start of year 1: Record $1M deposit received at contract signing	+1M Cash		+1M Unearned Revenue =					−	=
Year 1: Record $4.5M construction costs	−4.5M Cash		=		−4.5M Retained Earnings			+4.5M Cost of Sales −	= −4.5M
Year 1: Recognize $6M revenue on partly completed contract		+5M Accounts Receivable	−1M Unearned Revenue =		+6M Retained Earnings		+6M Revenue	−	= +6M
Year 1: Record $3M cash received from client	+3M Cash	−3M Accounts Receivable	=					−	=
Year 2: Record $3M construction costs	−3M Cash		=		−3M Retained Earnings			+3M Cost of Sales −	= −3M

T-accounts (left margin):

Cash 1M
UR   1M
  Cash
1M |
  UR
   | 1M

COGS 4.5M
Cash   4.5M
  COGS
4.5M |
  Cash
   | 4.5M

AR   5M
UR   1M
REV   6M
  AR
5M |
  UR
1M |
  REV
   | 6M

Cash 3M
AR   3M
  Cash
3M |
  AR
   | 3M

COGS 3M
Cash   3M
  COGS
3M |
  Cash
   | 3M

continued

	Balance Sheet						Income Statement		
Transaction	Cash Asset	+ Noncash Assets	= Liabil- ities	+ Contrib. Capital	+ Earned Capital		Rev- enues	− Expen- ses	= Net Income
Year 2: Recognize $4M revenue for completed contract		+4M Accounts Receivable =			+4M Retained Earnings		+4M Revenue −		= +4M
Year 2: Record $6M cash received from client	+6M Cash	−6M Accounts Receivable =							=

```
AR      4M
     Rev      4M
        AR
4M │
     Rev
        │      4M


Cash    6M
     AR       6M
        Cash
6M │
     AR
        │      6M
```

Revenue recognition policies for these types of contracts are disclosed in a manner typical to the following from the 2005 10-K report footnotes of **Raytheon Company**:

> Revenue Recognition—Sales under long-term contracts generally are recorded under the percentage of completion method. Incurred costs and estimated gross margins are recorded as sales when work is performed based on the percentage that incurred costs bear to the Company's estimates of total costs and contract value . . . Due to the long-term nature of many of the Company's programs, developing estimates of total costs and contract value often requires significant judgment.

The percentage-of-completion method of revenue recognition requires an estimate of total costs. This estimate is made at the beginning of the contract and is typically the one used to initially bid the contract. However, estimates are inherently inaccurate. If the estimate changes during the construction period, the percentage-of-completion is computed as the total costs incurred to date divided by the *current* estimate of total anticipated costs (costs incurred to date plus total estimated costs to complete).

If total construction costs are underestimated, the percentage-of-completion is overestimated (the denominator is too low) and revenue and gross profit to date are overstated. The estimation process inherent in this method has the potential for inaccurate or, even, improper revenue recognition. In addition, estimates of remaining costs to complete projects are difficult for the auditors to verify. This uncertainty adds additional risk to financial statement analysis.

BUSINESS INSIGHT   Disney's Revenue Recognition

The Walt Disney Company uses a method similar to percentage-of-completion to determine the amount of production cost to match against film and television revenues. Following is an excerpt from its 10-K.

> Film and television production costs are expensed based on the ratio of the current period's gross revenues to estimated remaining total gross revenues from all sources on an individual production basis. Television network series costs and multi-year sports rights are charged to expense based on the ratio of the current period's gross revenues to estimated remaining total gross revenues from such programs.

As Disney pays production costs, they record those costs on the balance sheet as inventory. Then, as film and television revenues are recognized, the company matches a portion of production costs (from inventory) against revenues in computing income. Each period, the costs recognized are equal to the proportion of total revenues recognized in the period to the total revenues expected over the life of the film or television show. Thus, estimates of both costs and income depend on the quality of its revenue estimates, which are, likely, imprecise.

Recognition of Unearned Revenue

In some industries it is common to receive cash before recording revenue. Customers might pay in advance for special orders, make deposits for future services, or buy concert tickets, subscriptions, or gift cards. In those cases, companies must record unearned revenues, a liability, and only record revenue when those products and services are provided. Specifically, deposits or advance payments are not recorded as revenue until the company performs the services owed or delivers the goods. Until then, the company's balance sheet shows the advance payment as a liability (called unearned revenue or deferred revenue) because the company is obligated to deliver those products and services.

To illustrate, assume that on January 1 a client pays Pfizer $360,000 for a guaranteed one year supply of a rare medicine. Pfizer initially records $360,000 cash and a $360,000 liability (unearned revenue). Pfizer will earn that revenue by delivering the medicine during the coming year. Revenue is computed as a proportion of medicine delivered to the total amount purchased under the contract. For example, if Pfizer prepares quarterly financial statements and it has provided one-fourth of the contracted medicine by first quarter-end, it would record one-fourth of that revenue as earned. As revenue is earned, the unearned revenue account on the balance sheet is reduced and revenue is recorded in the income statement. The following template reflects the cash received for the medicine contract and the subsequent first quarter accounting adjustment.

		Balance Sheet						Income Statement		
Transaction	Cash Asset	+ Noncash Assets	= Liabil- ities	+ Contrib. Capital	+ Earned Capital		Rev- enues	− Expen- ses	= Net Income
Jan 1: Receive $360,000 cash advance for medicine	+360,000 Cash		+360,000 Unearned Revenue						=
Mar 31: Recognize one-fourth of unearned revenue			−90,000 Unearned Revenue		+90,000 Retained Earnings		+90,000 Revenue		= +90,000

Cash 360,000
UR 360,000
Cash
360,000 |
UR
| 360,000

UR 90,000
Rev 90,000
UR
90,000 |
Rev
| 90,000

Research and Development (R&D) Expenses

LO2 Describe accounting for operating expenses, including research and development, and restructuring.

R&D activities are a major expenditure for many companies, especially for those in technology and pharmaceutical industries. Pfizer's R&D costs, for example, make up 14.5% of revenues ($7,442 million/$51,298 million). These expenses include employment costs for R&D personnel, R&D related contract services, and R&D fixed-asset costs.

Accounting for R&D activities follows a uniform method: *expense all R&D costs as incurred.* For many companies this creates unrecorded assets because R&D often yields future economic benefits to the company. Because measuring the benefits is difficult, GAAP requires all R&D to be immediately expensed. Even costs related to plant assets are expensed in certain circumstances, and this expensing of R&D fixed assets contrasts sharply with the capitalization-and-depreciation of non-R&D fixed assets. The expensing of R&D fixed assets is mandated *unless those assets have alternative future uses* (in other R&D projects or otherwise). For example, a general research facility housing multi-use lab equipment is capitalized and depreciated like any other depreciable asset. However, project-directed research buildings and equipment with no alternate uses must be expensed.

Following is a footnote excerpt from Pfizer's 2005 annual report related to its research and development expenditures:

Research and development (R&D) costs are expensed as incurred. These expenses include the costs of our proprietary R&D efforts, as well as costs incurred in connection with our third-party collaboration efforts. Pre-approval milestone payments made by us to third parties under contracted R&D arrangements are expensed when the specific milestone has been achieved. Once the product receives regulatory approval, we record any subsequent milestone payments in *Identifiable intangible assets, less accumulated amortization* and amortize them evenly over the remaining agreement term or the expected product life cycle, whichever is shorter.

Pfizer capitalizes and depreciates general research facilities (those with alternate uses). All other R&D costs are expensed as incurred.

When a company immediately expenses its R&D fixed assets, it lowers current period income, total assets, and stockholders' equity. These effects are mitigated to the extent that a company's R&D purchases are relatively constant from year to year. Specifically, after the average useful life is reached, say in 5 to 10 years, the expensing of current year purchases will approximate the depreciation that would have been reported had the assets been capitalized (thus, the effect on net income is minimal). However, the recorded assets are permanently lower than they would be if the R&D fixed assets had been capitalized and depreciated. This affects asset turnover ratios and, consequently, analysis of RNOA and ROE. In particular the ratios are biased upwards due to unrecorded assets (and equity) in the denominator. More generally, the effects of expensing R&D for financial statements is summarized in Exhibit 5.3.

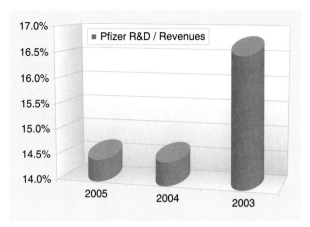

EXHIBIT 5.3	Financial Reporting of R&D Expenditures	
Balance Sheet	**Income Statement**	**Statement of Cash Flows**
• R&D assets with no alternate use are not capitalized • Unrecorded assets increase return ratios (RNOA and ROE) and asset turnover ratios • R&D expensing reduces equity, which can affect ROE	• R&D expensing (versus capitalization-and-depreciation) lowers income; more so when R&D costs are increasing	• R&D expensing (versus capitalization-and-depreciation) has no cash effect

To illustrate the effect of immediately expensing R&D plant assets, consider the following example. Assume in year 1, that Pfizer purchases equipment designed solely to develop a new drug that it anticipates selling in years 2 and 3. The equipment costs $600,000 and Pfizer realizes sales of $800,000 per year in the two subsequent years. The following template shows the effects of those transactions over these three years ($ 000s).

Transaction	Balance Sheet						Income Statement		
	Cash Asset	+ Noncash Assets	= Liabilities	+ Contrib. Capital	+ Earned Capital		Revenues	− Expenses	= Net Income
Year 1: Purchase R&D plant assets	−600 Cash		=		−600 Retained Earnings		−	+600 R&D Expense	= −600
Year 2: Record sales from newly developed drug	+800 Cash		=		+800 Retained Earnings		+800 Revenues −		= +800
Year 3: Record sales from newly developed drug	+800 Cash		=		+800 Retained Earnings		+800 Revenues −		= +800

Pfizer charges the entire cost of the plant asset to income in year 1. There are no revenues in year 1 related to the R&D expense. Then, in years 2 and 3, revenue earned from the new drug has no related expenses. This accounting treatment reports no R&D (plant) asset on the balance sheet (see that no transactions affect the Noncash Assets column in the template). Thus, analyzing the financial performance of the drug is complicated because the drug's revenues and expenses impact different years and because there is no asset on the balance sheet. Return metrics such as ROE and RNOA are inaccurate in all three years.

Next, assume that, instead, the equipment has some alternate use to Pfizer. In that case Pfizer can capitalize and depreciate the asset. Also assume that Pfizer's accounting policy is to depreciate plant assets of this nature using the straight-line method over two years and that no depreciation is taken in the acquisition year. With these facts, the template reveals the following financial effects ($ 000s).

	Transaction	Balance Sheet							Income Statement				
		Cash Asset	+	Noncash Assets	=	Liabil-ities	+	Contrib. Capital	+	Earned Capital	Rev-enues	−	Expen-ses	=	Net Income

Side Entry	Transaction	Cash Asset	Noncash Assets	Liabilities	Contrib. Capital	Earned Capital	Revenues	Expenses	Net Income
PPE 600 　Cash 600 　PPE 　600 　Cash 　600	Year 1: Purchase R&D plant assets	−600 Cash	+600 Equipment	=					=
Cash 800 　REV 800 　Cash 　800 　REV 　800	Year 2: Record sales from newly developed drug	+800 Cash		=		+800 Retained Earnings	+800 Revenues	−	= +800
RDE 300 　AD 300 　RDE 　300 　AD 　300	Year 2: Depreciate R&D plant assets		−300 Equipment (Accumulated Depreciation)	=		−300 Retained Earnings		+300 R&D Expense	= −300
Cash 800 　REV 800 　Cash 　800 　REV 　800	Year 3: Record sales from newly developed drug	+800 Cash		=		+800 Retained Earnings	+800 Revenues	−	= +800
RDE 300 　AD 300 　RDE 　300 　AD 　300	Year 3: Depreciate R&D plant assets		−300 Equipment (Accumulated Depreciation)	=		−300 Retained Earnings		+300 R&D Expense	= −300

With this accounting treatment, Pfizer reports no revenue and no expenses in the first year. Then in years 2 and 3, as Pfizer recognizes drug sales, the cost of the R&D equipment is transferred to the income statement and, thus, matched to the related revenues. This enables more accurate analysis of the drug's financial performance and yields a more accurate representation of Pfizer's R&D operations. Nonetheless, if the R&D equipment has no alternate use, then GAAP requires the first treatment (full expensing).

One last effect deserves mention: because expensing R&D assets generally depresses profits and book value of equity, the market-to-book ratios (market price per share divided by equity book value per share) for high-R&D industries tend to be higher than those for less-R&D intensive industries. This difference is driven as much by accounting conservatism as it is by fundamental differences in industry characteristics and market expectations about future performance. This emphasizes the need to compare financial ratios within industries, particularly for industries with substantial R&D activities.

BUSINESS INSIGHT **Pfizer R&D**

Pfizer spends about $7.4 billion annually for R&D compared with its revenues of $51.3 billion, or about 14.4%. This reflects a high percent of revenues devoted to R&D for the pharmaceutical industry. Following is the R&D-expense-to-sales ratio for Pfizer and some of its competitors.

	2005	2004	2003
Bristol-Meyers Squibb	14.3%	13.2%	10.9%
GlaxoSmithKline	14.2	13.9	12.9
Eli Lilly.....................	20.7	22.2	18.7
Merck	17.5	17.1	14.6
Pfizer.....................	14.4	14.6	16.7

Restructuring Expenses

Restructuring expenses are substantial in many income statements. They tend to be large in magnitude and, as a result, GAAP requires enhanced disclosure, either as a separate line item in the income statement or as a footnote. Restructuring costs typically consists of two components:

1. Employee severance or relocation costs
2. Asset write-downs

The first part, **employee severance or relocation costs**, represent accrued (estimated) costs to terminate or relocate employees as part of a restructuring program. By accruing those costs, we mean:

▪ Estimating total costs of terminating or relocating selected employees; costs might include severance pay (typically a number of weeks of pay based on the employee's tenure with the company), outplacement costs, and relocation or retraining costs for remaining employees.

▪ Reporting *total* estimated costs as an expense (and a liability) in the period the costs are estimated and the restructuring program announced; subsequent payments reduce this liability.

The second part of restructuring costs is **asset write-downs**, also called *write-offs* or *charge-offs*. Restructuring activities usually involve closure or relocation of manufacturing or administrative facilities. This can require write-down of long-term assets (such as plant assets or goodwill), and the write-down of inventories whose market value is less than book value. Recall that asset cost is first recorded on the balance sheet and is subsequently transferred from the balance sheet to the income statement as expense when the asset is used. The write-down of an asset accelerates this process for a portion, or all, of the asset cost. Write-downs have no cash flow effects unless the write-down has some potential tax benefits.

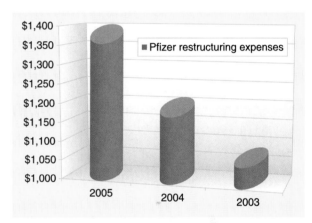

The financial statement effects of restructuring charges can be large. We must remember that management determines the amount of restructuring costs and when to recognize them. As such, it is not uncommon for a company to time recognition of restructuring costs in a period when its income is already depressed. This behavior is referred to as a **big bath**.

RESEARCH INSIGHT   **Restructuring Costs and Managerial Incentives**

Research has investigated the circumstances and effects of restructuring costs. Some research finds that stock prices increase when a company announces a restructuring as if the market appreciates the company's candor. Research also finds that many companies that reduce income through restructuring costs later reverse a portion of those costs, resulting in a substantial income boost for the period of reversal. These reversals often occur when the company would have otherwise reported an earnings decline. Whether or not the market responds favorably to trimming the fat or simply disregards restructuring costs as transitory and, thus, as uninformative, managers have incentives to exclude such income-decreasing items from operating income. These incentives often derive from contracts such as debt covenants and managerial bonus plans.

The FASB has tightened rules relating to restructuring costs in an effort to mitigate abuses. For example, a company is required to have a formal restructuring plan that is approved by its board of directors before any restructuring charges are accrued. Also, a company must identify the relevant employees and notify them of its plan. In each subsequent year, the company must disclose in its footnotes the original amount of the liability (accrual), how much of that liability is settled in the current period (such as employee payments), how much of the original liability has been reversed because of cost overestimation, any new accruals for unforeseen costs, and the current balance of the liability. This creates more transparent financial statements, which presumably deters earnings management.

BUSINESS INSIGHT	Pfizer's Restructuring

A portion of Pfizer's restructuring activities in 2005 relates to its "Adapting to Scale" (AtS) initiative. The company describes this activity in its footnotes as follows:

Pfizer management has performed a comprehensive review of our processes, organizations, systems and decision-making procedures, in a company-wide effort to improve performance and efficiency. We expect the costs associated with this multi-year effort to continue through 2008 and to total approximately $4 billion to $5 billion, on a pre-tax basis. The actions associated with the AtS productivity initiative will include restructuring charges, such as asset impairments, exit costs and severance costs. We incurred the following costs in connection with our AtS initiative, which was launched in the first quarter of 2005:

(Millions of Dollars)	Year Ended Dec. 31, 2005
Implementation costs	$330
Restructuring charges.	450
Total AtS costs.	$780

Through December 31, 2005, the restructuring charges primarily relate to employee termination costs at our manufacturing facilities in North America and in our U.S. marketing and worldwide research and development operations, and the implementation costs primarily relate to system and process standardization, as well as the expansion of shared services. The components of restructuring charges associated with AtS follow:

(Millions of Dollars)	Costs Incurred 2005	Utilization Through Dec. 31, 2005	Accrual as of Dec. 31, 2005[a]
Employee termination costs	$305	$166	$139
Asset impairments.	131	131	—
Other	14	3	11
	$450	$300	$150

(a) Included in Other current liabilities.

Financial statement effects of Pfizer's accounting for restructuring costs are illustrated in the following template ($ millions).

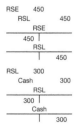

	Balance Sheet						Income Statement		
Transaction	Cash Asset	+ Noncash Assets	= Liabil- ities	+ Contrib. Capital	+ Earned Capital		Rev- enues	− Expen- ses	= Net Income
Record restructuring expense and liability			+450 = Restructuring Liability		−450 Retained Earnings			+450 − Restructuring = Expense	−450
Paid $300 cash toward liability	−300 Cash		−300 = Restructuring Liability						

When Pfizer estimated restructuring costs of $450 million, it recorded the expense and established a $450 million liability on its balance sheet. As costs are incurred, cash is paid out and the liability is reduced. GAAP requires disclosure of the initial liability, together with subsequent reductions or reversals of amounts not ultimately used. Through 2005, Pfizer spent $300 million for restructuring; the remaining $150 million is reported as a current liability on Pfizer's 2005 balance sheet.

Restructuring costs are typically large and, as such, greatly affect reported profits. Our analysis must consider whether these costs are properly chargeable to the accounting period in which they are recognized. Following are some guidelines relating to the two components of restructuring costs:

1. **Asset write-downs** Asset write-downs accelerate (or catch up) the depreciation process to reflect asset impairment. Impairment implies the loss of cash-generating capability and, likely, occurs over several years. However, the write-down expense is included in a single period's income statement when the impairment is recognized. It can be argued that the loss of cash-generating ability occurred over recent prior periods in addition to the current period. Thus, prior periods' profits are arguably not as high as reported, and the current period's profit is not as low. This measurement error is difficult to estimate and, thus, many analysts do not adjust balance sheets and income statements for write-downs. At a minimum, however, we must recognize informally the implications of restructuring costs for the profitability of recent prior periods and the current period.

2. **Employee severance or relocation costs** GAAP permits recognition of costs relating to employee separation or relocation that are *incremental* and that do not benefit future periods. Thus, accrual of these costs is treated like other liability accruals. We must, however, be aware of over- or understated costs and its effects on current and future profitability. GAAP requires a reconciliation of this restructuring accrual in future years (see Business Insight on page 5-16). Overstatements are followed by a reversal of the restructuring liability, and understatements are followed by further accruals. Should a company develop a reputation for recurring reversals or understatements, its management loses credibility.

MANAGERIAL DECISION **You Are the Financial Analyst**

You are analyzing the 10-K of a company that reports a large restructuring expense, involving both employee severance and asset write-downs. How do you interpret and treat this cost in your analysis of the company's current and future profitability? [Answer, p. 5-28]

MID-MODULE REVIEW 1

Merck & Co., Inc., reports the following income statements for 2003 through 2005.

($ in millions)	2005	2004	2003
Sales	$22,011.9	$22,938.6	$22,485.9
Costs, expenses and other			
Materials and production	5,149.6	4,959.8	4,436.9
Marketing and administrative	7,155.5	7,238.7	6,200.3
Research and development	3,848.0	4,010.2	3,279.9
Restructuring cost	322.2	107.6	194.6
Equity income from affiliates	(1,717.1)	(1,008.2)	(474.2)
Other (income) expense, net	(110.2)	(344.0)	(203.2)
	14,648.0	14,964.1	13,434.3
Income from continuing operations before taxes	7,363.9	7,974.5	9,051.6
Taxes on income	2,732.6	2,161.1	2,462.0
Income from continuing operations	4,631.3	5,813.4	6,589.6
Income from discontinued operations, net taxes	—	—	241.3
Net income	$ 4,631.3	$ 5,813.4	$ 6,830.9

Required

1. Merck's revenue recognition policy, as outlined in footnotes to its 10-K, includes the following: "Revenues from sales of products are recognized when title and risk of loss passes to the customer." What is the importance for revenue recognition of 'title and risk of loss passing to the customer'?

2. Merck's research and development (R&D) efforts require specialized equipment and facilities that cannot be used for any other purpose. How does Merck account for costs related to this specialized equipment and facilities? Would Merck account for these costs differently if they were not used for R&D? Explain.

3. Merck reports restructuring cost (expenses) each year. What are the two general categories of restructuring expenses? How do accrual accounting and disclosure requirements prevent companies from intentionally overstating restructuring expenses in one year (referred to as taking a "big bath") and reversing the unused expenses in a future year?

Solution

1. Revenues are only recognized when the earning process is complete. Merck delivers its product before the customer is obligated to make payment. Passage of title typically constitutes delivery.

2. All R&D related equipment and/or facilities that have no alternative use must be expensed under GAAP. Should the assets have other uses, they are capitalized and depreciated like other plant assets. R&D costs are aggregated into one line item (research and development expense) on Merck's income statement. Other costs are reported under materials and production and/or marketing and administrative expenses.

3. Restructuring expenses generally fall into two categories: severance costs and asset write-offs. Restructuring programs must be approved by the board of directors before they are recognized in financial statements. Further, companies are required to disclose the initial liability accrual together with the portion that was subsequently utilized and reversed, if any. Because the restructuring accrual is an estimate, overestimates and subsequent reversals are possible. Should the company develop a reputation for recurring reversals, it will lose credibility with analysts and other stakeholders.

Income Tax Expenses

LO3 Explain and analyze accounting for income taxes.

Companies maintain two sets of accounting records, one for preparing financial statements for external constituents, including current and prospective shareholders, and another for reporting to tax authorities. Two sets of accounting records are necessary because the U.S. tax code is different from GAAP. These two different sets of accounting records can report dramatically different levels of pretax income (in publicly available financial reports) and taxable income (in reports sent to taxing authorities).

One common difference between these two sets of records relates to fixed assets. Companies usually compute depreciation expense using the straight-line method for financial reporting purposes—this means they transfer the same amount of the asset's cost from the balance sheet to the income statement each year. However, for tax reporting, companies (legally) transfer more of the asset's cost from the balance sheet to the income statement in the earlier years of the asset's life (referred to as *accelerated* depreciation). This reduces taxable income and the company's tax liability and, thereby, increases cash flows during the early years of an asset's useful life. However, in the later years of the asset's useful life, the amount of depreciation expense for tax reporting declines and, consequently, taxable income and income taxes paid will be higher than for earlier years. Financial reporting (GAAP) requires that companies recognize this future tax liability. To see this, assume that Pfizer acquires office equipment for $200. The equipment has a four-year life, and zero salvage value. Further assume that Pfizer has $300 income before depreciation and a 40% tax rate. For tax purposes, assume that Pfizer uses an accelerated depreciation method that permits the company to deduct depreciation of $100, $50, $30 and $20 over the four years. Depreciation schedules for GAAP and tax accounting records follow:

	Year 1	Year 2	Year 3	Year 4	Total
Financial reporting depreciation (computed)	$ 50	$ 50	$ 50	$ 50	$ 200
Financial reporting income (assumed)	250	250	250	250	1,000
Financial reporting tax expense (40%)	100	100	100	100	400
Financial reporting net book value of asset[†]	150	100	50	0	
Tax reporting depreciation (given).	100	50	30	20	200
Tax reporting (taxable) income*	200	250	270	280	1,000
Taxes paid (40%)	80	100	108	112	400
Tax reporting net book value of asset[†]	100	50	20	0	

[†]Cost less accumulated depreciation.
*$300 − Tax depreciation expense.

The table shows that because the financial reporting (GAAP) depreciation expense differs from its tax reporting counterpart, the equipment will have a different net book value for financial and tax reporting purposes. To keep track of the tax consequences arising from the difference between financial and tax reporting net book values, companies record *deferred income taxes* on the balance sheet. In this example, the company records deferred tax liabilities because the book value for tax purposes is less than that for financial reporting purposes (we later discuss deferred tax assets and how they arise).

To illustrate a deferred tax liability, let's use the information from the preceding table. In year 1, the financial reporting net book value of the asset is $150 ($200 − $50 GAAP depreciation expense) whereas the tax reporting net book value is only $100 ($200 − $100 tax depreciation expense). The difference of $50 creates a deferred tax liability of $20 ($50 × 40% tax rate). The intuition for this is that since the two book values must eventually be equal, taxable income will be higher in the future (comparatively less depreciation expense), thus giving rise to higher taxes that must be recognized currently on the balance sheet. The following template captures these effects.

	Balance Sheet						Income Statement		
Transaction	Cash Asset	+ Noncash Assets	= Liabil- ities	+ Contrib. Capital	+ Earned Capital		Rev- enues	− Expen- ses	= Net Income
Year 1: Paid taxes of $80 cash, and reported a $20 increase in deferred tax liability and the $100 tax expense	−80 Cash		+20 = Deferred Tax Liability		−100 Retained Earnings			+ +100 Tax Expense	= −100

TE   100
   Cash   80
   DTL   20

      TE
100 |
   Cash
     | 80
   DTL
     | 20

Accounting standards require a company to first compute the taxes it owes (per its tax return), then to compute any changes in deferred tax liabilities and assets, and finally to compute tax expense reported in the income statement (as a residual figure). Tax expense is, thus, not computed as pretax income multiplied by the company's tax rate as we might initially have expected. Instead, tax expense is computed as follows:

Tax Expense = Taxes Paid − Increase (or + Decrease) in Deferred Tax Assets + Increase (or − Decrease) in Deferred Tax Liabilities

In year 2, the difference between the financial reporting net book value of the equipment ($100) and its tax reporting net book value ($50) is still $50. Thus, the deferred tax liability is unchanged. Another way of seeing this is that the company pays taxes of $100 and records $100 tax expense on the income statement, because depreciation expense in the company's tax return is the same as the depreciation on the income statement. Net book value decreased by the same amount on both sets of books. The following template shows the year 2 tax expense effects.

	Balance Sheet						Income Statement		
Transaction	Cash Asset	+ Noncash Assets	= Liabil- ities	+ Contrib. Capital	+ Earned Capital		Rev- enues	− Expen- ses	= Net Income
Year 2: Paid taxes of $100 cash and reported $100 tax expense	−100 Cash		=		−100 Retained Earnings			+ +100 Tax Expense	= −100

TE   100
   Cash   100
      TE
100 |
   Cash
     | 100

In year 3, the difference between the financial reporting net book value of the equipment ($50) and its tax reporting net book value ($20) has declined to $30. This means that the deferred tax liability decreases to $12 ($30 × 40%) from the $20 in the prior year. Pfizer must adjust the deferred tax liability account by $8 ($20 − $12) to reflect this lower value. The deferred tax liability decreases in year 3 because financial reporting depreciation expense of $50 exceeds the tax reporting depreciation expense of $30. Following the rule for computing tax expense, Pfizer reports $100 on the income statement ($108 cash paid less the decrease in deferred tax liabilities). The template below captures these effects.

	Balance Sheet						Income Statement		
Transaction	**Cash Asset** +	**Noncash Assets** =	**Liabil- ities** +	**Contrib. Capital** +	**Earned Capital**		**Rev- enues** −	**Expen- ses** =	**Net Income**
Year 3: Paid taxes of $108, reported $100 tax expense, and reduced deferred tax by $8	−108 Cash		−8 = Deferred Tax Liability		−100 Retained Earnings		−	+100 Tax Expense =	−100

```
TE     100
DTL      8
   Cash      108
       TE
   100 |
       DTL
   8 |
       Cash
       | 108
```

EXHIBIT 5.4	Sources of Deferred Tax Assets and Liabilities

Net Book Value of Assets

Financial reporting net book value	>	Tax reporting net book value	→	Deferred tax liability on balance sheet
Financial reporting net book value	<	Tax reporting net book value	→	Deferred tax asset on balance sheet

Net Book Value of Liabilities

Financial reporting net book value	<	Tax reporting net book value	→	Deferred tax liability on balance sheet
Financial reporting net book value	>	Tax reporting net book value	→	Deferred tax asset on balance sheet

The example above demonstrates how accelerated depreciation for tax purposes and straight-line for financial reporting creates deferred tax liabilities. Other differences between the two sets of books create other types of deferred tax accounts. Exhibit 5.4 shows the relation between the financial reporting and tax-reporting net book values and the resulting deferred taxes on the balance sheet.

Deferred tax assets arise when the net book value of liabilities is greater for financial reporting than for tax reporting, or when the net book value of assets is smaller for financial reporting than for tax reporting. A frequent example relates to restructuring. In the year a reorganization plan is approved, the company will accrue restructuring costs (this creates a GAAP liability) and will write down assets to their market values (this reduces the net book value of the assets for financial reporting purposes). However, tax authorities do not recognize these accrual accounting transactions. In particular, for tax purposes, restructuring costs are not deductible until paid in the future and asset write-downs are not deductible until the loss is realized when the asset is sold. As a result, the restructuring accrual is not a liability for tax reporting purposes—it has a tax-reporting net book value of $0. Moreover, the tax-reporting value of the assets remains unchanged. Both of these differences (the liability and the assets) give rise to a deferred tax asset. The deferred tax asset will be transferred to the income statement in the future when the company pays the restructuring costs and sells the assets for a loss.

Another common deferred tax asset relates to tax loss carryforwards. Specifically, when a company reports a loss for tax purposes, it can carry back that loss for up to two years to recoup previous taxes paid. Any unused losses can be carried forward for up to twenty years to reduce future taxes. This creates a benefit (an "asset") on the tax reporting books for which there is no corresponding financial reporting asset and thus the company records a deferred tax asset.

Companies are also required to establish a **deferred tax valuation** allowance for deferred tax assets when the future realization of their benefits is uncertain. The effect on financial statements is to reduce reported assets, increase tax expense, and reduce equity. These effects are reversed if the allowance is reversed in the future when realization of these tax benefits becomes more likely. Pfizer reported an allowance of $177 million in 2004, of which $35 million was then reversed in 2005 when it determined that the realization of the tax benefits was more certain. The effect of a change (increase or decrease) in the deferred tax valuation allowance on net income is dollar-for-dollar (meaning Pfizer's net income increased by $35 million in 2005).

To see how income tax expense is disclosed, Pfizer's tax footnote to its income statement is shown in Exhibit 5.5. Pfizer's $3,424 million tax expense reported in its income statement (called the *provision*) consists of the following two components (organized by federal, state and foreign):

1. *Current tax expense.* Current tax expense is determined from the company's tax returns; it is the amount payable (in cash) to tax authorities (some of these taxes have been paid during the year as the company makes installments). Pfizer labels this "Taxes currently payable."

2. *Deferred tax expense.* Effect on tax expense from changes in deferred tax liabilities and deferred tax assets (in the above example, deferred tax liabilities increase by $20 in year 1, reflecting a future

liability, which yields a higher income tax expense than taxes paid). Pfizer labels this "Deferred income taxes."

EXHIBIT 5.5	Income Tax Expense Footnote for Pfizer
(Millions of Dollars)	**2005**
United States:	
Taxes currently payable	
Federal	$1,369
State and local	122
Deferred income taxes	12
Total U.S. tax provision	1,503
International:	
Taxes currently payable	3,317
Deferred income taxes	(1,396)
Total international tax provision	1,921
Total provision for taxes on income	$3,424

Companies must disclose the components of deferred tax liabilities and assets. Pfizer's deferred tax footnote to its balance sheet (shown in Exhibit 5.6) reports total deferred tax assets of $7,070 million and total deferred tax liabilities of $15,164. Companies are permitted to net some deferred tax assets and liabilities, and Pfizer reports a net deferred tax liability of $8,094 million on its 2005 balance sheet. Many of Pfizer's deferred tax assets relate to accrued liabilities or asset write-downs arising from expenses included in financial reporting income, but not yet recognized for tax reporting (such as prepaid items, allowance for doubtful accounts, restructuring accruals, employee benefits, inventory allowances, investment provisions, and write-offs of in-process R&D expenditures). Pfizer also has a deferred tax asset from a net operating loss carryforward and has recorded a small valuation allowance. These deferred tax assets represent future reductions of the company's tax liability and are, therefore, classified as assets.

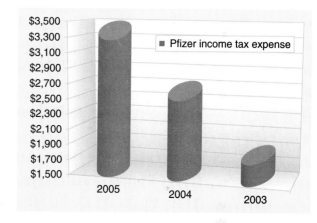

Pfizer's deferred tax liabilities relate to a number of items. Intangible assets and property plant and equipment have different tax and financial reporting net book values because Pfizer uses accelerated depreciation for tax purposes and straight-line for financial reporting. The deferred tax liability relating to employee benefits arises from pension contributions and other payments that are deductible for tax purposes but that Pfizer has not yet accrued for financial reporting purposes (thus there is no GAAP liability). The deferred tax liability relating to unremitted earnings results from consolidation of Pfizer's subsidiaries. The subsidiaries' profits are included in Pfizer's consolidated income statement and reflected in the net book value of the investment on

EXHIBIT 5.6	Deferred Taxes Footnote for Pfizer	
	2005 Deferred Tax	
(Millions of Dollars)	**Assets**	**(Liabilities)**
Prepaid/deferred items	$1,318	$ (753)
Intangibles	857	(8,748)
Inventories	583	—
Property, plant and equipment	87	(1,183)
Employee benefits	2,282	(1,376)
Restructurings and other charges	729	(118)
Net operating loss/credit carryforwards	406	—
Unremitted earnings	—	(2,651)
All other	950	(335)
Subtotal	7,212	(15,164)
Valuation allowance	(142)	—
Total deferred taxes	$7,070	$ (15,164)
Net deferred tax liability		$ (8,094)

Pfizer's balance sheet (we discuss accounting for intercompany investments in Module 7). The subsidiaries' profits are not taxable until the subsidiaries actually pay dividends to Pfizer. Thus, the net book value of the investment asset for financial reporting (related to profits from the subsidiary) is greater than its tax reporting book values. Pfizer will pay taxes on the subsidiaries' profits when the subsidiaries pay dividends in the future.

Pfizer's 2005 income before tax is $11,534 million. Its tax expense of $3,424 million represents an effective tax rate of 29.7%. The *effective tax rate* is defined as tax expense divided by pretax income ($3,424 million/$11,534 million = 29.7%).[5] By comparison, the federal *statutory tax rate* for corporations (the rate prescribed in tax regulations) is 35%. Companies must provide a schedule that reconciles the effective tax rate (29.7% for Pfizer) with the Federal statutory rate of 35%. Following is the schedule that Pfizer reports in its 10-K.

Reconciliation of the U.S. statutory income tax rate to our effective tax rate for continuing operations before the cumulative effect of a change in accounting principles follows:

Year Ended	2005	2004	2003[a]
U.S. statutory income tax rate	35.0%	35.0%	35.0%
Earnings taxed at other than U.S. statutory rate	(19.5)	(18.3)	(53.2)
U.S. research tax credit	(0.7)	(0.6)	(3.1)
Repatriation of foreign earnings	14.4	—	—
Resolution of certain tax positions	(5.1)	—	—
Acquired IPR&D	5.0	2.7	54.2
Litigation settlement provisions	—	—	13.7
All other—net	0.6	0.2	3.1
Effective tax rate for income from continuing operations before cumulative effect of a change in accounting principles	29.7%	19.0%	49.7%

(a) The large component percentages in 2003 reflect lower income from continuing operations in 2003 due to the impact of the Pharmacia acquisition.

In addition to federal taxes (paid to the IRS), companies also pay taxes to state, local, and foreign jurisdictions where they operate. These tax rates are typically lower than the statutory rate of 35%. In 2005, for example, these taxes reduced Pfizer's effective tax rate by 19.5%. In addition, Pfizer received tax credits for research (reducing the effective tax rate by another 0.7%). Repatriation of foreign earnings resulted in additional tax, raising the effective tax rate by 14.4%. (*American Jobs Creation Act of 2004* created a temporary incentive for U.S. corporations to repatriate accumulated income earned abroad by providing a deduction for certain dividends from controlled foreign corporations in 2005. Pfizer chose to repatriate earnings from its foreign subsidiaries, paying additional tax at a much lower rate than it would have otherwise paid.) Favorable settlements of tax disputes with taxing authorities reduced its effective tax rate by 5.1%, and other miscellaneous items added another 0.6% to the effective tax rate.

In sum, Pfizer's effective tax rate for 2005 is 29.7%, 5.3 percentage points below the 35% statutory rate. In 2004, however, the effective tax rate was only 19%, and in 2003 it was 49.7%, due mainly to additional taxes it incurred as a result of the Pharmacia acquisition. Fluctuations, such as these, in the effective tax rate are not uncommon and highlight the difference between income reported under GAAP and that computed using multiple tax codes under which companies operate.

Analysis of deferred taxes can yield useful insights. Generally, income is not taxable until received. Thus, revenue accruals (such as accounts receivable for percentage-of-completion contracts) increase deferred tax liabilities as GAAP assets (accounts receivable) exceeds tax-reporting assets (similar to the effect of using straight-line depreciation for financial reporting purposes and accelerated depreciation for tax returns). An increase in deferred tax liabilities indicates that a company is reporting higher GAAP income relative to taxable income and can indicate the company is managing earnings upwards.

---

[5] This is the effective tax rate for *all* of Pfizer's income. In the previous module we computed the tax rate on operating income by first deducting the taxes related to nonoperating income (or adding back the tax shield related to nonoperating expenses). The effective tax rate on total income, is a weighted average of the two (operating and nonoperating).

The difference between reported corporate profits and taxable income increased substantially in the late 1990s, just prior to huge asset write-offs. *CFO Magazine* (November 2002) implied that such differences are important for analysis and should be monitored:

> Fueling the sense that something [was] amiss [was] the growing gap between the two sets of numbers. In 1992, there was no significant difference between pretax book income and taxable net income . . . By 1996, according to IRS data, a $92.5 billion gap had appeared. By 1998 [prior to the market decline], the gap was $159 billion—a fourth of the total taxable income reported . . . If people had seen numbers showing very significant differences between book numbers for trading and tax numbers, they would have wondered if those [income] numbers were completely real.

Although an increase in deferred tax liabilities can legitimately result, for example, from an increase in depreciable assets and the use of accelerated depreciation for tax purposes, we must be aware of the possibility that such an increase is the result of improper revenue recognition in that the company may not be reporting those revenues to tax authorities.

Adequacy of Deferred Tax Asset Valuation

Analysis of the deferred tax asset valuation account provides us with additional insight. This analysis involves (1) assessing the adequacy of the valuation allowance and (2) determining how and why the valuation account changed during the period and how that change affects net income.

When a company reports a deferred tax asset, the company implies that it will more likely than not receive a future tax benefit equal to the deferred tax asset. If the company is uncertain about the future tax benefit, it records an allowance to reduce the asset. How can we gauge the adequacy of a valuation allowance account? We might assess the reasons for the valuation account (typically reported in the tax footnote). We might examine other companies in the industry for similar allowances. We might also review the MD&A for any doubt on company prospects for future profitability.

We can quantify our analysis in at least three ways. First, we can examine the allowance as a percentage of the deferred tax assets (most valuation allowances relate to tax loss carryforwards). For **Pfizer**, this 2005 percentage is 35%; see below. We also want to gather data from other pharmaceutical companies and compare the sizes of their allowance accounts relative to their related deferred tax assets. The important point is that we must be comfortable with the size of the valuation account and remember that management has control over the adequacy and reporting of the allowance account (with audit assurances).

($ millions)	2005	2004	2003
Deferred tax asset from net operating loss carryforward	$406	$353	$92
Valuation allowance.	$142	$177	$3
Valuation allowance as a percent of net operating loss carryforward.	35.0%	50.1%	3.3%

Second, we can examine changes in the allowance account. During a year, circumstances change and the company might be more or less assured of receiving the tax benefit. In that case, the company might decrease or increase its allowance account. For Pfizer, the allowance markedly declined from the prior year (from 50% in 2004 to 35% in 2005). What does such a decline denote? Perhaps Pfizer's overall economic environment has improved, rendering it more likely that it will be profitable for tax purposes. We want to determine why it reduced the allowance and assess the validity of its claims in light of industry and economy-wide factors.

Third, we can quantify how a change in the valuation allowance affects net income and its effective tax rate (see table above). To see this, recall that changes in the valuation allowance affect tax expense in the same direction, dollar for dollar. This is turn, affects net income (in the opposite direction) again, dollar for dollar. For Pfizer, its 2005 valuation allowance decreased by $35 million ($177 million − $142 million), which decreased tax expense and increased net income by $35 million. This is not a large effect on income for Pfizer, or on its effective tax rate (29.7% after the valuation allowance change versus 29.4% before). However, changes in valuation allowances can have (and have had) marked effects on net income for numerous companies. For our analysis, we must remember that a company can increase current period income by deliberately decreasing the valuation allowance. Knowing that such decreases can boost net income, companies might deliberately create too large a valuation allowance in one of more prior years and use it as a *cookie jar reserve*. We want to assess the details of the valuation account and changes therein from the footnotes and from the MD&A.

($ millions)	2005	2004	2003
Change in valuation allowance	$(35)	$ 174	
Impact of valuation allowance change on net income	$ 35	$(174)	
Income before tax	$11,534	$14,007	$3,246
Tax expense.	$ 3,424	$ 2,665	$1,614
Effective tax rate	29.7%	19.0%	49.7%
Tax expense before change in valuation account	$ 3,389	$ 2,839	
Effective tax rate before change in valuation account	29.4%	20.3%	

MID-MODULE REVIEW 2

Refer to the Merck & Co., Inc., 2005 income statement in the Mid-Module Review 1. Merck provides the following additional information in footnotes to its 10-K.

Taxes on income from continuing operations consisted of:

Years Ended December 31	2005	2004	2003
Current provision			
Federal	$1,688.1	$1,420.0	$1,464.2
Foreign	739.6	530.9	611.3
State	295.9	161.3	254.8
	2,723.6	2,112.2	2,330.3
Deferred provision			
Federal	97.0	95.6	21.3
Foreign	(134.0)	(32.3)	96.5
State	46.0	(14.4)	13.9
	9.0	48.9	131.7
	$2,732.6	$2,161.1	$2,462.0

Required
1. What is the total income tax expense that Merck reports in its income statement?
2. What amount of its total tax expense did (or will) Merck pay in cash (that is, what amount is currently payable)?
3. Explain how Merck calculates its income tax expense.

Solution
1. Total income tax expense is $2,732.6 million.
2. Of the total, $2,723.6 million is currently payable.
3. Income tax expense is the sum of current taxes (that is, currently payable as determined from the company's tax returns) plus the change in deferred tax assets and liabilities. It is a calculated figure, not a percentage that is applied to pretax income.

OPERATING COMPONENTS 'BELOW-THE-LINE'

Pfizer's income statement includes a subtotal labeled "income from continuing operations." Historically, this presentation highlighted the non-recurring (*transitory*) portions of the income statement so that they could be eliminated to facilitate the projection of future profitability. The word "continuing" was meant to imply that income was purged of one-time items, as these were presented "below-the-line," that is, below income from continuing operations. Two categories of items are presented below-the-line:[6]

1. **Discontinued operations**   Net income (loss) from business segments that have been or will be sold, and any gains (losses) on net assets related to those segments sold in the current period.
2. **Extraordinary items**   Gains or losses from events that are both *unusual* and *infrequent*.

Discontinued operations are generally viewed as nonoperating, and we discuss their accounting treatment in Module 7. Explanation of the accounting for extraordinary items follows.

Extraordinary Items

Extraordinary items refer to events that are both unusual *and* infrequent. Their effects are reported following income from continuing operations. Management determines whether an event is unusual and infrequent (with auditor approval) for financial reporting purposes. Further, management often has incentives to classify unfavorable items as extraordinary because they will be reported separately, after income from continuing operations (*below-the-line*). These incentives derive from investors who tend to focus more on items included in income from continuing operations and less on non-recurring items that are not included in continuing operations.

GAAP provides the following guidance in determining whether or not an item is extraordinary:

- *Unusual nature.* The underlying event or transaction must possess a high degree of abnormality and be clearly unrelated to, or only incidentally related to, the ordinary activities of the entity, taking into account the entity's operating environment.

- *Infrequency of occurrence.* The underlying event or transaction must be of a type that would not reasonably be expected to recur in the foreseeable future, taking into account the entity's operating environment.

The following items are generally *not reported* as extraordinary items:

- Gains and losses on retirement of debt
- Write-down or write-off of operating or nonoperating assets
- Foreign currency gains and losses
- Gains and losses from disposal of specific assets or business segment
- Effects of a strike
- Accrual adjustments related to long-term contracts
- Costs of a takeover defense
- Costs incurred as a result of the September 11, 2001, events

Extraordinary items are reported separately (net of tax) and below income from continuing operations on the income statement.[7]

Earnings Per Share

The income statement reports earnings per share (EPS) numbers. At least one, and potentially two, EPS figures are reported: basic and diluted. The difference between the two measures is shown in Exhibit 5.7.

LO4 Compute earnings per share and explain the effect of dilutive securities.

---

[6] Prior accounting standards included a third category, **changes in accounting principles.** This category included voluntary and mandated changes in accounting policies utilized by a company, such as a change in the depreciation method. Under current GAAP, changes in accounting principles are no longer reported below-the-line. Instead, they are applied retrospectively (unless it is impractical to do so, in which case they are applied at the earliest practical date). No cumulative effect adjustment is made to income as was the case in prior standards. Instead, changes in depreciation methods are now accounted for as changes in estimates, which are applied prospectively.

[7] Until recently, gains and losses on debt retirement were treated as extraordinary items. To explain, understand that debt is accounted for at historical cost, just like the accounting for equipment. The *market price* of debt, however, is determined by fluctuations in interest rates. As a result, if a company retires (pays off) its debt before maturity, the purchase price often differs from the debt amount reported on the balance sheet, resulting in gains and losses on retirement. These gains and losses were formerly treated as extraordinary. Following passage of SFAS 145, these gains and losses are no longer automatically treated as extraordinary, but instead must be unusual and infrequent to be designated as extraordinary.

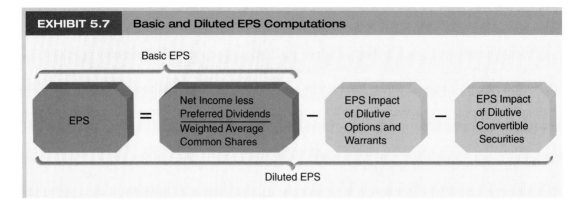

EXHIBIT 5.7   **Basic and Diluted EPS Computations**

Basic EPS is computed as: (Net income − Dividends on preferred stock)/Weighted average number of common shares outstanding during the year. The subtraction of preferred stock dividends yields the income available for dividend payments to common shareholders. Computation of **diluted EPS** reflects the additional shares that would be issued if all stock options, warrants, and convertible securities had been converted into common shares at the beginning of the year. Diluted EPS never exceeds basic EPS.

Pfizer reports Basic EPS of $1.10 in 2005 and Diluted EPS of $1.09. Given the near identical results for basic and diluted EPS, we know that Pfizer has few dilutive securities. Symantec Corporation's 2005 EPS, however, differs by 7¢ (81¢ compared to 74¢ diluted, a difference of almost 10%) as reported in the following footnote disclosure to its 2005 10-K.

(in thousands, except per share amounts)	2005
Basic net income per share	
Net income.	$536,159
Weighted average number of common shares outstanding during the period	660,631
Basic net income per share.	$ 0.81
Diluted net income per share	
Net income.	$536,159
Interest on convertible subordinated notes, net of income tax effect.	8,380
Net income, as adjusted	$544,539
Weighted average number of common shares outstanding during the period	660,631
Shares issuable from assumed exercise of options using the treasury stock method.	35,745
Shares issuable from assumed conversion of convertible subordinated notes	41,780
Restricted stock.	89
Total shares for purpose of calculating diluted net income per share.	738,245
Diluted net income per share	$ 0.74

Diluted earnings per share for Symantec is 7¢ lower than basic EPS, mainly due to convertible bonds. If the bonds had been converted to stock, Symantec would have avoided interest expense of $8.4 million (net of tax) and net income would have increased by that amount. In addition, the weighted average number of shares in the denominator would have increased by 77.5 million (35.7 million + 41.8 million), representing the shares issued in the bond conversion. The two effects reduced earnings per share from $0.81 to $0.74.[8]

In addition to convertible bonds such as Symantec's, companies might have potentially dilutive convertible preferred stock and stock options. To compute diluted EPS for convertible preferred stock, the company

---

[8] The effects of dilutive securities are only included if they are, in fact, dilutive. If they are *antidilutive,* inclusion would actually increase EPS, and they are, thus, excluded from the computation. An example of an antidilutive security is employee stock options whose exercise price is greater than the stock's current market price. These *underwater* (or out-of-the-money) options are antidilutive and are, therefore, excluded from the EPS computation. Symantec, for example, excludes 4.2 million of underwater stock options from its 2005 EPS computation. Should the market price of Symantec's common stock increase above the exercise price of the options, their effects will, once again, be included and diluted EPS will decline, all else equal.

BUSINESS INSIGHT   **Pro Forma Income and Managerial Motives**

Income from continuing operations per GAAP, once a key measure of company performance, is often supplemented or even supplanted by pro forma income in company financial statements and press releases. **Pro forma income** begins with the GAAP income from continuing operations (that excludes discontinued operations and extraordinary items), and then excludes other one-time items (most notably, restructuring charges), and some additional items such as acquisition expenses (goodwill amortization and other acquisition costs), stock-option compensation expense, and research and development expenditures.

The purported motive for reporting pro forma income is to eliminate transitory (one-time) items to enhance year-to-year comparability. Although this might be justified on the basis that pro forma income has greater predictive ability, important information is lost in the process. One role for accounting is to report how effective management has been in its stewardship of invested capital. Asset write-downs, liability accruals, and other charges that are eliminated in calculating pro forma income often reflect outcomes of poor management decisions. Our analysis must not blindly eliminate information contained in nonrecurring items by focusing solely on pro forma income. Critics of pro forma income also argue that the items excluded by managers from GAAP income are inconsistent across companies and time. They contend that a major motive for pro forma income is to mislead stakeholders. Legendary investor Warren Buffet puts pro forma in context: "When companies or investment professionals use terms such as 'EBITDA' and 'pro forma,' they want you to unthinkingly accept concepts that are dangerously flawed." (Berkshire Hathaway, Annual Report)

would add back preferred dividends previously subtracted from net income in the EPS numerator and would increase the denominator by the number of shares that would be issued to the preferred stockholders. The adjustment for stock-option exercise is a bit more complicated. The number of shares issued to the option holder upon exercise is added to the diluted EPS denominator. Then, the number of shares that the company could have repurchased with the exercise proceeds, is subtracted from the denominator.

EPS figures are often used as a method of comparing operating results for companies of different sizes under the assumption that the number of shares outstanding is proportional to the income level (that is, a company twice the size of another will report double the income and will have double the common shares outstanding, leaving EPS approximately equal for the two companies). This assumption is erroneous. Management controls the number of common shares outstanding and there is no relation between firm size and number of shares outstanding. Different companies also have different philosophies regarding share issuance and repurchase. For example, consider that most companies report annual EPS of less than $5, while Berkshire Hathaway reported EPS of $5,538 for 2005! This is because Berkshire Hathaway has so few common shares outstanding, not necessarily because it has stellar profits.

RESEARCH INSIGHT   **"Pro Forma" Income**

Transitory items such as discontinued operations, restructuring charges, and extraordinary items make it difficult for investors to predict future income. The past decade has seen more companies reporting pro forma income, which excludes nonrecurring or noncash items that companies feel are unimportant for valuation purposes. Research, however, provides no evidence that pro forma income is a better predictor of future cash flows. More important, investors appear to be misled when firms report pro forma income. Research also finds that companies reporting pro forma income tend to be young companies concentrated in technology and business services. Too often, these companies have below-average sales and income, which might explain why they choose to report pro forma income.

Foreign Currency Translation

Many companies conduct international operations and transact business in currencies other than $US. It is common for companies to purchase assets in foreign currencies, borrow money in foreign currencies, and transact business with their customers in foreign currencies. Increasingly many companies have subsidiaries whose balance sheets and income statements are prepared in foreign currencies.

Financial statements prepared according to U.S. GAAP must be reported in $US. This means that any transactions conducted in foreign currencies must be reported in $US, and the financial statements of any

L05 Explain how foreign currency fluctuations affect the income statement.

foreign subsidiaries must be translated into $US before consolidation with the U.S. parent company. This translation process can markedly alter both the balance sheet and income statement. We discuss income statement effects of foreign currency translation in this module; we discuss the effects on stockholders' equity in Module 9.

Effects of Foreign Currency Transactions on Income

A change in the strength of the $US vis-à-vis foreign currencies affects reported income in the following manner: changes in foreign currency exchange rates have a direct effect on the $US equivalent for revenues, expenses, and income of the foreign subsidiary because revenues and expenses are translated at the average exchange rate for the period. Exhibit 5.8 shows those financial effects.

EXHIBIT 5.8	Income Statement Effects from Foreign Currency Movements					
	Revenues	–	Expenses	=	Profit	
$US Weakens.	Increase		Increase		Increase	
$US Strengthens	Decrease		Decrease		Decrease	

Specifically, when the foreign currency strengthens ($US weakens), the subsidiary's revenues, expenses, and income increase. On the other hand, when the $US strengthens, the subsidiary's revenues, expenses, and income decrease. (The profit effect assumes that revenues exceed expenses; if expenses exceed revenues, a loss occurs, which increases if the $US weakens and decreases if the $US strengthens.)

Pfizer discusses how currency fluctuations affect its income statement in the following excerpt from footnotes to the company's 2005 10-K.

> 48% of our 2005 revenues were derived from international operations, including 18% from countries in the Euro zone and 7% from Japan. These international-based revenues expose our revenues and earnings to foreign currency exchange rate changes . . . Depending on the direction of change relative to the U.S. dollar, foreign currency values can increase or decrease the reported dollar value of our results of operations . . . Changes in foreign exchange rates increased total revenues in 2005 by $945 million or 1.8% compared to 2004. The foreign exchange impact on 2005 revenue growth was due to the weakening of the U.S. dollar relative to many foreign currencies, especially the Euro, which accounted for about 35% of the impact in 2005

The $US weakened against many foreign currencies for several years preceding and including 2005. Thus, each unit of foreign currency purchased more $US. Therefore, revenues and expenses denominated in foreign currencies were translated to higher $US equivalents, yielding increased revenues and profits even when unit volumes remained unchanged. Pfizer also discloses that it attempts to dampen the effect that these fluctuations have on reported profit:

> While we cannot predict with certainty future changes in foreign exchange rates or the effect they will have on us, we attempt to mitigate their impact through operational means and by using various financial instruments.

The phrase 'operational means' includes attempts to structure transactions in $US rather than a foreign currency. Foreign currency financial instruments are common and include forward and futures contracts, which lock in future currency values. We explain how these instruments (called derivatives) work in Appendix 7A. In sum, we must be cognizant of the effects of currency fluctuations on reported revenues, expenses, and profits for companies with substantial foreign-currency transactions.

MODULE-END REVIEW

Refer to the Merck & Co., Inc., 2005 income statement in the Mid-Module Review.

Required

1. Assume that during 2005 the $US weakened with respect to the currencies in which Merck conducts its business. How would that weakening affect Merck's income statement?
2. What is the difference between basic and diluted earnings per share?

Solution

1. Income statement accounts that are denominated in foreign currencies must be translated into $US before the financial statements are publicly disclosed. When the $US weakens, each foreign currency unit is worth more $US. Consequently, each account in Merck's income statement is larger because the dollar weakened.

2. Basic earnings per share is equal to net income (less preferred dividends) divided by the weighted average number of common shares outstanding during the period. Diluted EPS considers the effects of dilutive securities. In diluted EPS, the denominator increases by the additional shares that would have been issued assuming exercise of all options and conversion of all convertible securities. The numerator is also adjusted for any preferred dividends and/or interest that would not have been paid upon conversion.

GUIDANCE ANSWERS

MANAGERIAL DECISION   **You Are the Financial Analyst**

Typically, restructuring charges have two components: asset write-downs (such as inventories, property, plant, and goodwill) and severance costs. Write-downs occur when the cash-flow-generating ability of an asset declines, thus reducing its current market value below its book value reported on the balance sheet. Arguably, this decline in cash-flow-generating ability did not occur solely in the current year and, most likely, has developed over several periods. It is not uncommon for companies to delay loss recognition, such as write-downs of assets. Thus, prior period income is, arguably, not as high as reported, and the current period loss is not as great as reported. Turning to severance costs, GAAP permits restructuring expense to include only those costs that are *incremental* and will *not* benefit future periods. The accrual of severance-related expenses can be viewed like other accruals; that is, it might be over- or understated. In future periods, the required reconciliation of the restructuring accrual will provide insight into the adequacy of the accrual in that earlier period.

DISCUSSION QUESTIONS

Q5-1. What are the criteria that guide firms in recognition of revenue? What does each of the criteria mean? How are the criteria met for a company like Abercrombie & Fitch, a clothing retailer? How are the criteria met for a construction company that builds offices under long-term contracts with developers?

Abercrombie & Fitch (ANF)

Q5-2. Why are extraordinary items reported separately from continuing operations in the income statement?

Q5-3. What are the criteria for categorizing an event as an extraordinary item? Provide an example of an event that would properly be categorized as an extraordinary item and one that would not.

Q5-4. What is the difference between basic earnings per share and diluted earnings per share? Are potentially dilutive securities always included in the EPS computation?

Q5-5. What effect, if any, does a weakening $US have on reported sales and net income for companies operating outside the United States?

Q5-6. Identify the two typical categories of restructuring costs and their effects on the balance sheet and the income statement. Explain the concept of a big bath and why restructuring costs are often identified with this event.

Q5-7. What is the proper accounting treatment for research and development costs? Why are R&D costs normally not capitalized under GAAP?

Q5-8. Under what circumstances will deferred taxes likely result in a cash outflow?

Q5-9. What is the concept of pro forma income and why has this income measure been criticized?

Q5-10. What is unearned revenue? Provide three examples of unearned revenue.

MINI EXERCISES

M5-11. **Computing Percentage-of-Completion Revenues**   (LO1)

Bartov Corporation agreed to build a warehouse for a client at an agreed contract price of $2,500,000. Expected (and actual) costs for the warehouse follow: 2005, $400,000; 2006, $1,000,000; and 2007, $500,000. The company completed the warehouse in 2007. Compute revenues, expenses, and income for each year 2005 through 2007 using the percentage-of-completion method.

M5-12. Applying the Financial Statement Effects Template. (LO1)

Refer to the information for Bartov Corporation in M5-11.

a. Use the financial statement effects template to record contract revenues and expenses for each year 2005 through 2007 using the percentage-of-completion method.

b. Prepare journal entries and T-accounts to record contract revenues and expenses for each year 2005 through 2007 using the percentage-of-completion method.

M5-13. Assessing Revenue Recognition of Companies (LO1)

Identify and explain when each of the following companies should recognize revenue.

The GAP (GPS)

Merck & Company (MRK)

John Deere (DE)

Bank of America (BAC)

Johnson Controls (JCI)

a. The GAP: The GAP is a retailer of clothing items for all ages.

b. Merck & Company: Merck engages in developing, manufacturing, and marketing of pharmaceutical products. It sells its drugs to retailers like CVS and Walgreen.

c. John Deere: Deere manufactures heavy equipment. It sells equipment to a network of independent distributors, who in turn sell the equipment to customers. Deere provides financing and insurance services both to distributors and customers.

d. Bank of America: Bank of America is a banking institution. It lends money to individuals and corporations and invests excess funds in marketable securities.

e. Johnson Controls: Johnson Controls manufactures products for the government under long-term contracts.

M5-14. Assessing Risk Exposure to Revenue Recognition (LO1)

BannerAD Corporation manages a Website in which it sells products on consignment from sellers. It pays these sellers a portion of the sales price, absent its commission. Identify at least two potential revenue recognition problems relating to such sales.

M5-15. Estimating Revenue Recognition with Right of Return (LO1)

The GAP (GPS)

The GAP offers an unconditional return policy. It normally expects 2% of sales at retail selling prices to be returned before the return period expires. Assuming that The GAP records total sales of $5 million for the current period, how much in *net* sales should it record for this period?

M5-16. Assessing Research and Development Expenses (LO2)

Abbott Laboratories (ABT)

Abbott Laboratories reports the following (summary) income statement.

Year Ended December 31 ($ 000s)	2005
Net sales	$22,338
Cost of products sold	10,641
Research and development	1,821
Selling, general and administrative	5,514
Total operating cost and expenses	17,976
Pretax operating earnings	$ 4,362

a. Compute the percent of net sales that Abbott Laboratories spends on research and development (R&D). How would you assess the appropriateness of its R&D expense level?

b. Describe how accounting for R&D expenditures affects Abbott Laboratories' balance sheet and income statement.

M5-17. Interpreting Foreign Currency Translation Disclosure (LO5)

Bristol-Myers Squibb (BMY)

Bristol-Myers Squibb (BMY) reports the following footnote to its 10-K report relating to the year-over-year change in sales.

	Total Change	Analysis of % Change		
		Volume	Price	Foreign Exchange
2005 vs. 2004	(1)%	(2)%	—	1%
2004 vs. 2003	4%	—	—	4%

a. Did sales increase or decrease in 2004 and 2005? By what percentage? What amount of this change was attributable to fluctuations in the value of foreign currencies vis-a-vis the $US?

    b.   What can we infer from the table about the relative strength of the $US compared with the currencies in the countries in which BMY does business?

M5-18. **Analyzing Income Tax Disclosure** **(LO3)**

Cisco Systems reports the following footnote disclosure to its 10-K report ($ millions).

Cisco Systems
(CSCO)

Years Ended	July 30, 2005
Federal	
Current	$1,340
Deferred	497
	1,837
State	
Current	496
Deferred	(292)
	204
Foreign	
Current	404
Deferred	(150)
	254
Total	$2,295

    a.   What amount of income tax expense does Cisco report in its income statement for 2005?

    b.   How much of Cisco's income tax expense is current (as opposed to deferred)?

    c.   Why do deferred tax assets and liabilities arise? How do they impact the tax expense that Cisco reports in its 2005 income statement?

M5-19. **Defining and Computing Earnings per Share** **(LO4)**

Lucent Corporation (LU) reports the following basic and diluted earnings per share in its 2005 10-K report. (a) Describe the accounting definitions for basic and diluted earnings per share. (b) Identify the Lucent numbers that make up both EPS computations. (c) Why does Lucent add back $86 million for interest expense on the convertible debt securities in the diluted EPS calculation?

Lucent Corporation
(LU)

(in millions, except per share amounts)	2005
Net income (loss)	$1,185
Conversion and redemption cost—8.00% covertible securities	—
Preferred stock dividends and accretion	—
Net income (loss) applicable to common shareowners—basic	1,185
Adjustment for dilutive securities on net income (loss):	
Interest expense related to convertible securities	86
Net income (loss) applicable to common shareowners—diluted	$1,271
Weighted average shares outstanding—basic	4,426
Effect of dilutive securities:	
Stock options	60
Warrants	15
2.75% covertible securities	542
8.00% convertible securities	167
7.75% convertible securities	8
Weighted average shares outstanding—diluted	5,218
EPS:	
Basic	$ 0.27
Diluted	0.24

M5-20.   Assessing Revenue Recognition for Advance Payments   (LO1)

Koonce Company operates a performing arts center. The company sells tickets for its upcoming season of six Broadway musicals and receives $420,000 cash. The performances occur monthly over the next six months.

a.   When should Koonce record revenue for the Broadway musical series?

b.   Use the financial statement effects template to show the $420,000 cash receipt and recognition of the first month's revenue.

M5-21.   Reporting Unearned Revenue and its Recognition   (LO1)

Target Corporation
(TGT)

Target Corporation sells gift cards that can be used at any of the company's Target or Greatland stores. Target encodes information on the card's magnetic strip about the card's value, the date it expires (typically two years after issuance), and the store where it was purchased.

a.   How will Target's balance sheet reflect the gift card?

b.   When does Target record revenue from the gift card?

EXERCISES

E5-22.   Assessing Revenue Recognition Timing   (LO1)

Explain when each of the following businesses should recognize revenues:

Limited (LTD)

Boeing Corp. (BA)

Supervalu, Inc. (SVU)

MTV(MTV)

Bank of America (BAC)

Harley-Davidson (HOG)

Time-Warner (TW)

a.   A clothing retailer like The Limited.

b.   A contractor like Boeing Corporation that performs work under long-term government contracts.

c.   A grocery store like Supervalu.

d.   A producer of television shows like MTV that syndicates its content to television stations.

e.   A residential real estate developer who constructs only speculative houses and later sells these houses to buyers.

f.   A banking institution like Bank of America that lends money for home mortgages.

g.   A manufacturer like Harley-Davidson.

h.   A publisher of magazines such as Time-Warner.

E5-23.   Assessing Revenue Recognition Timing and Income Measurement   (LO1)

Explain when each of the following businesses should recognize revenue and identify any income measurement issues that could arise.

TheStreet.Com
(TSCM)

a.   RealMoney.Com, a division of TheStreet.Com, provides investment advice to customers for an up-front fee. It provides these customers with password-protected access to its Website where customers can download investment reports. RealMoney has an obligation to provide updates on its Website.

Oracle (ORCL)

b.   Oracle develops general ledger and other business application software that it sells to its customers. The customer pays an up-front fee for the right to use the software and a monthly fee for support services.

Intuit (INTU)

c.   Intuit develops tax preparation software that it sells to its customers for a flat fee. No further payment is required and the software cannot be returned, only exchanged if defective.

d.   A developer of computer games sells its software with a 10-day right of return period during which the software can be returned for a full refund. After the 10-day period has expired, the software cannot be returned.

E5-24.   Constructing and Assessing Income Statements Using Percentage-of-Completion   (LO1)

General Electric
Company (GE)

Assume that General Electric Company agreed in May 2006 to construct a nuclear generator for NSTAR, a utility company serving the Boston area. The contract price of $500 million is to be paid as follows: $200 million at the time of signing; $100 million on December 31, 2006; and $200 million at completion in May 2007. General Electric incurred the following costs in constructing the generator: $100 million in 2006, and $300 million in 2007.

a.   Compute the amount of General Electric's revenue, expense, and income for both 2006 and 2007 under the percentage-of-completion revenue recognition method.

b.   Discuss whether or not you believe the percentage-of-completion method provides a good measure of General Electric's performance under the contract.

E5-25. **Constructing and Assessing Income Statements Using Percentage-of-Completion**   (LO1)

On March 15, 2005, Frankel Construction contracted to build a shopping center at a contract price of $120 million. The schedule of expected (which equals actual) cash collections and contract costs follows:

Year	Cash Collections	Cost Incurred
2005	$ 30 million	$15 million
2006	50 million	40 million
2007	40 million	30 million
Total	$120 million	$85 million

a. Calculate the amount of revenue, expense, and net income for each of the three years 2005 through 2007 using the percentage-of-completion revenue recognition method.

b. Discuss whether or not the percentage-of-completion method provides a good measure of this construction company's performance under the contract.

E5-26. **Interpreting the Income Tax Expense Footnote Disclosure**   (LO3)

The income tax footnote to the financial statements of FedEx follows.   FedEx (FDX)

The components of the provision for income taxes for the years ended May 31 were as follows:

($ millions)	2005	2004	2003
Current provision			
Domestic			
Federal	$634	$371	$112
State and local	65	54	28
Foreign	103	85	39
	802	510	179
Deferred provision (benefit)			
Domestic			
Federal	67	(22)	304
State and local	(4)	(7)	25
Foreign	(1)	—	—
	62	(29)	329
Provision for income taxes	$864	$481	$508

a. What is the amount of income tax expense reported in FedEx's 2005, 2004 and 2003 income statements?

b. What percentage of total tax expense is currently payable in each of 2003, 2004, and 2005? Explain why the percentages are different each year.

c. One possible reason for the $67 million federal deferred tax expense in 2005 is that deferred tax liabilities increased during that year. Provide an example that gives rise to an increase in the deferred tax liability.

Bristol-Myers Squibb
(BMY)

E5-27. Identifying Operating and Transitory Income Components (LO3)

Following is the Bristol-Myers Squibb income statement.

a. Identify the components in its statement that you would consider operating.

b. BMY's net profit increased despite a slight decrease in sales. Identify the main reason for its profit increase and discuss whether that factor is sustainable.

Dollars in Millions	2005	2004
Net sales	$19,207	$19,380
Cost of products sold	5,928	5,989
Marketing, selling and administrative	5,106	5,016
Advertising and product promotion	1,476	1,411
Research and development	2,746	2,500
Provision for restructuring, net	32	104
Litigation charges, net	269	420
Gain on sale of business	(569)	(320)
Equity in net income of affiliates	(334)	(273)
Other expense, net	37	115
Total expenses	14,691	14,962
Earnings from continuing operations before minority interest and income taxes	4,516	4,418
Provision for income taxes	932	1,519
Minority interest, net of taxes	592	521
Earnings from continuing operations	2,992	2,378
Discontinued operations		
Net earnings	(5)	10
Net gain on disposal	13	—
	8	10
Net earnings	$ 3,000	$ 2,388

Notes:

• **Equity in net income of affiliates** refers to income BMY earned on investments in affiliated (but unconsolidated) companies.

• **Minority interest** expense relates to the claims of outside shareholders of BMY's (consolidated) subsidiaries in the income of those companies.

Excerpt from BMY's income tax footnotes in 2004 and 2005

> The effective income tax rate on earnings from continuing operations before minority interest and income taxes was 20.6% in 2005 compared with 34.4% in 2004 and 25.8% in 2003. The lower effective tax rate in 2005 was due primarily to a 2004 charge of approximately $575 million for estimated deferred income taxes related to the repatriation of approximately $9 billion in special dividends from the Company's non-U.S. subsidiaries.
>
> The AJCA, which President Bush signed into law on October 22, 2004, provides for a temporary 85 percent dividends-received deduction for certain cash distributions of the earnings of foreign subsidiaries. The deduction would result in a federal tax rate of approximately 5.25% on the repatriated earnings (assuming a marginal federal tax rate of 35% on those earnings). To qualify for the deduction, the repatriated earnings must be reinvested in the United States pursuant to a domestic reinvestment plan approved by a company's chief executive officer and subsequently by its board of directors.

E5-28. **Identifying Operating and Transitory Income Components** (LO2)

Following is the Deere & Company income statement for 2005.

($ millions)	2005
Net sales and revenues	
Net sales	$19,401.4
Finance and interest income	1,439.5
Health care premiums and fees	724.9
Other income	364.7
Total	21,930.5
Costs and expenses	
Cost of sales	15,163.4
Research and development expenses	677.3
Selling, administrative and general expenses	2,218.6
Interest expense	761.0
Health care claims and costs	573.9
Other operating expenses	380.5
Total	19,774.7
Income of consolidated group before income taxes	2,155.8
Provision for income taxes	715.1
Income of consolidated group	1,440.7
Equity in income of unconsolidated affiliates	
Credit	0.6
Other	5.5
Total	6.1
Net income	$ 1,446.8

Notes:

• Income statement includes John Deere commercial and consumer tractor segment, a finance subsidiary that provides loan and lease financing relating to the sales of those tractors, and a health care segment that provides managed health care services for the company and certain outside customers.

• **Equity in income of unconsolidated affiliates** refers to income John Deere has earned on investments in affiliated (but unconsolidated) companies. These are generally investments made for strategic purposes.

Deere provides the following description of its business segments in footnotes to its 10-K.

The company's Equipment Operations generate revenues and cash primarily from the sale of equipment to John Deere dealers and distributors. The Equipment Operations manufacture and distribute a full line of agricultural equipment; a variety of commercial and consumer equipment; and a broad range of construction and forestry equipment. The company's Financial Services primarily provide credit services and managed health care plans. The credit operations primarily finance sales and leases of equipment by John Deere dealers and trade receivables purchased from the Equipment Operations. The health care operations provide managed health care services for the company and certain outside customers.

Required

a. Identify the components in its income statement that you would consider operating.

b. Discuss your treatment of Deere's activities relating to the financing of its John Deere lawn and garden, commercial tractors, and its health care business segments.

E5-29. **Assessing the Income Tax Footnote** (LO3)

Dow Chemical reports the following income tax footnote disclosure in its 10-K report.

	2005		2004	
Deferred Tax Balances at December 31 (In millions)	**Deferred Tax Assets**	**Deferred Tax Liabilities**	**Deferred Tax Assets**	**Deferred Tax Liabilities**
Property.............................	$ 382	$(2,304)	$ 674	$(2,998)
Tax loss and credit carryforwards	2,297	—	2,514	—
Postretirement benefit obligations	1,501	(861)	2,038	(594)
Other accruals and reserves............	1,666	(437)	1,839	(625)
Inventory	160	(184)	152	(135)
Long-term debt	216	(64)	650	(71)
Investments	282	—	218	(4)
Other—net..........................	551	(643)	389	(635)
Subtotal	$7,055	$(4,493)	$8,474	$(5,062)
Valuation allowance..................	(179)	—	(165)	—
Total	$6,876	$(4,493)	$8,309	$(5,062)

Required

a. Dow reports $2,304 million of deferred tax liabilities in 2005 relating to "Property." Explain how such liabilities arise.

b. Describe how a deferred tax asset can arise from postretirement benefit (health care) obligations.

c. Dow reports $2,297 million in deferred tax assets for 2005 relating to tax loss carryforwards. Describe how these loss carryforwards arise and under what conditions these assets will be realized.

d. Dow has established a deferred tax asset valuation allowance of $179 million for 2005. What is the purpose of this allowance? How did the increase in this allowance of $14 million from 2004 to 2005 affect net income?

e. Assuming that cash paid for income tax is $918 million, compute Dow's income tax expense (as reported in its income statement) of $1,782 million for 2005 using the financial statement effects template. (*Hint*: Show the effects of changes in deferred taxes.)

E5-30. **Analyzing and Assessing Research and Development Expenses** (LO2)

Advanced Micro Devices (AMD) and **Intel (INTC)** are competitors in the high-tech computer processor industry. Following is a table ($ millions) of sales and R&D expenses for both companies.

AMD	R&D Expense	Sales		INTC	R&D Expense	Sales
2003......	$ 852.1	$3,519.2		2003......	$4,365.0	$30,141.0
2004......	934.6	5,001.4		2004......	4,778.0	34,209.0
2005......	1,144.0	5,847.6		2005......	5,145.0	38,826.0

a. What percentage of sales are AMD and INTC spending on research and development?

b. How are AMD and INTC's balance sheets and income statements affected by the accounting for R&D costs?

c. How can one evaluate the effectiveness of R&D spending? Does the difference in R&D as a percentage of sales necessarily imply that one company is more heavily invested in R&D? Why might this not be the case?

E5-31. Analyzing and Interpreting Foreign Currency Translation Effects (LO5)

Johnson Controls reports the following table and discussion in its 2005 10-K.

The company's net sales for the fiscal years ended September 30, 2005 and 2004, were as follows.

Sales (In millions)	2005	2004	% Change
Building efficiency	$ 5,717.7	$ 5,323.7	7%
Interior experience—North America	8,498.6	8,237.4	3%
Interior experience—Europe	8,935.5	7,677.6	16%
Interior experience—Asia	1,399.1	1,092.6	28%
Power solutions	2,928.5	2,271.7	29%
Total	$27,479.4	$24,603.0	12%

Consolidated net sales in the current fiscal year were $27.5 billion, increasing 12% above the prior year sales of $24.6 billion. Excluding the favorable effects of currency translation, sales increased 9% above the prior year. For fiscal 2006, management anticipates that net sales will grow to $32 billion, an increase of approximately 16% from fiscal 2005 net sales. The growth is expected to be partially offset by unfavorable effects of currency translation, as the company assumes the dollar will strengthen relative to the euro assuming a euro exchange rate of $1.20.

RISK MANAGEMENT—*Foreign Exchange* The Company has manufacturing, sales and distribution facilities around the world and thus makes investments and enters into transactions denominated in various foreign currencies. In order to maintain strict control and achieve the benefits of the Company's global diversification, foreign exchange exposures for each currency are netted internally so that only its net foreign exchange exposures are, as appropriate, hedged with financial instruments. The Company hedges 70 to 90 percent of its known foreign exchange transactional exposures. The Company primarily enters into foreign currency exchange contracts to reduce the earnings and cash flow impact of non-functional currency denominated receivables and payables. Gains and losses resulting from hedging instruments offset the foreign exchange gains or losses on the underlying assets and liabilities being hedged. The maturities of the forward exchange contracts generally coincide with the settlement dates of the related transactions. Realized and unrealized gains and losses on these contracts are recognized in the same period as gains and losses on the hedged items. The Company also selectively hedges anticipated transactions that are subject to foreign exchange exposure, primarily with foreign currency exchange contracts, which are designated as cash flow hedges in accordance with SFAS No. 133, "Accounting for Derivative Instruments and Hedging Activities," as amended by SFAS No. 137, No. 138, and No. 149.

a. How did foreign currency exchange rates affect sales for Johnson Controls in 2005?
b. In what direction does Johnson Controls expect exchange rate fluctuations to affect sales in 2006? Explain. What crucial assumption is JCI making to project 2006 operating results?
c. Describe how the accounting for foreign exchange translation affects reported sales and profits.
d. How does Johnson Controls manage the risk related to its foreign exchange exposure? Describe the financial statement effects of this risk management activity.

E5-32. Interpreting Revenue Recognition for Gift Cards (LO1)

Footnotes to the 2005 annual report of Barnes & Noble Booksellers disclose the following:

The Barnes & Noble Membership Program entitles the customer to receive a 10% discount on all purchases made during the twelve-month membership period. The annual membership fee of $25.00 is nonrefundable after the first 30 days of the membership term. Revenue is being recognized over the twelve-month membership period based upon historical spending patterns for Barnes & Noble customers. Refunds of membership fees due to cancellations within the first 30 days are minimal.

Required

a. Explain in layman terms how Barnes & Noble accounts for the cash received for its membership program. When does Barnes & Noble record revenue from this program?
b. How does Barnes & Noble's balance sheet reflect those membership fees?
c. Does the 10% discount affect Barnes & Noble's income statement when memberships fees are received?

PROBLEMS

P5-33.   **Analyzing and Interpreting Revenue Recognition Policies and Risks**   (LO1)

Amazon.com, Inc., provides the following explanation of its revenue recognition policies from its 10-K report.

> The Company generally recognizes revenue from product sales or services rendered when the following four revenue recognition criteria are met: persuasive evidence of an arrangement exists, delivery has occurred or services have been rendered, the selling price is fixed or determinable, and collectibility is reasonably assured.
>
> The Company evaluates the criteria outlined in EITF Issue No. 99-19, "Reporting Revenue Gross as a Principal versus Net as an Agent," in determining whether it is appropriate to record the gross amount of product sales and related costs or the net amount earned as commissions. Generally, when the Company is the primary obligor in a transaction, is subject to inventory risk, has latitude in establishing prices and selecting suppliers, or has several but not all of these indicators, revenue is recorded gross as a principal. If the Company is not the primary obligor and amounts earned are determined using a fixed percentage, a fixed-payment schedule, or a combination of the two, the Company generally records the net amounts as commissions earned.
>
> Product sales (including sales of products through the Company's Syndicates Stores program), net of promotional gift certificates and return allowances, are recorded when the products are shipped and title passes to customers. Return allowances are estimated using historical experience.
>
> Commissions received on sales of products from Amazon Marketplace, Auctions and zShops are recorded as a net amount since the Company is acting as an agent in such transactions. Amounts earned are recognized as net sales when the item is sold by the third-party seller and our collectibility is reasonably assured. The Company records an allowance for refunds on such commissions using historical experience.
>
> The Company earns revenues from services, primarily by entering into business-to-business strategic alliances, including providing the Company's technology services such as search, browse and personalization; permitting third parties to offer products or services through the Company's Websites; and powering third-party Websites, providing fulfillment services, or both. These strategic alliances also include miscellaneous marketing and promotional agreements. As compensation for the services the Company provides under these agreements, it receives one or a combination of cash and equity securities. If the Company receives non-refundable, up-front payments, such amounts are deferred until service commences, and are then recognized on a straight-line basis over the estimated corresponding service period. Generally, the fair value of consideration received, whether in cash, equity securities, or a combination thereof, is measured when agreement is reached, and any subsequent appreciation or decline in the fair value of the securities received does not affect the amount of revenue recognized over the term of the agreement. To the extent that equity securities received or modified after March 16, 2000 are subject to forfeiture or vesting provisions and no significant performance commitment exists upon signing of the agreements, the fair value of the securities and corresponding revenue is determined as of the date of the respective forfeiture or as vesting provisions lapse. The Company generally recognizes revenue from these services on a straight-line basis over the period during which the Company performs services under these agreements, commencing at the launch date of the service. Outbound shipping charges to customers are included in net sales.

Required

a.   Identify and discuss the main revenue recognition policies for its two primary sources of business revenues.

b.   Identify and describe at least three potential areas for revenue recognition shams in a business such as Amazon.

P5-34.   **Analyzing and Interpreting Income Tax Disclosures**   (LO3)

The 2005 income statement for **Pfizer** is reproduced in this module. Pfizer also reports the following footnote relating to its income taxes in its 2005 10-K report.

> **Deferred Taxes** Deferred taxes arise because of different treatment between financial statement accounting and tax accounting, known as "temporary differences." We record the tax effect of these temporary differences as "deferred tax assets" (generally items that can be used as a tax deduction or credit in future periods) or "deferred tax liabilities" (generally items for which we received a tax deduction,

but that have not yet been recorded in the consolidated statement of income). The tax effects of the major items recorded as deferred tax assets and liabilities as of December 31 are:

(Millions of Dollars)	2005 Deferred Tax	
	Assets	(Liabilities)
Prepaid/deferred items	$1,318	$ (753)
Intangibles	857	(8,748)
Inventories	583	—
Property, plant and equipment	87	(1,183)
Employee benefits	2,282	(1,376)
Restructructuring and other charges	729	(118)
Net operating loss/credit carryforwards	406	—
Unremitted earnings	—	(2,651)
All other	950	(335)
Subtotal	7,212	(15,164)
Valuation allowance	(142)	—
Total deferred taxes	$7,070	$ (15,164)
Net deferred tax liability		$ (8,094)

The net deferred tax liability position is primarily due to the deferred taxes recorded in connection with our acquisition of Pharmacia. We have carryforwards primarily related to net operating losses which are available to reduce future U.S. federal and state, as well as international income, expiring at various times between 2006 and 2025. Valuation allowances are provided when we believe that our deferred tax asstes are not recoverable based on an assessment of estimated future taxable income that incorporates ongoing, prudent, feasible tax planning strategies.

Required

a. Describe the terms "deferred tax liabilities" and "deferred tax assets." Include a description of how these accounts can arise.

b. Intangible assets (other than goodwill) acquired in the purchase of a company are depreciated (amortized) similar to buildings and equipment (see Module 7 for a discussion). Describe how the deferred tax liability of $8,748 million relating to intangibles arose.

c. Pfizer has many employee benefit plans, such as a long-term health plan and a pension plan. Some of these are generating deferred tax assets and others are generating deferred tax liabilities. Explain the timing of the recognition of expenses under these plans that would give rise to these different outcomes.

d. Pfizer is reporting a deferred tax liability that it labels as "unremitted earnings." This relates to an investment in an affiliated company for which Pfizer is recording income, but has not yet received dividends. Generally, investment income is taxed when received. Explain what information the deferred tax liability for unremitted earnings is conveying.

e. Pfizer reports a deferred tax asset relating to net operating loss carryforwards. Explain what loss carryforwards are.

f. Pfizer reports a valuation allowance of $142 million in 2005. Explain why Pfizer has established this allowance and its effect on reported profit. Pfizer's valuation allowance was $177 million in 2004. Compute the change in its allowance during 2005 and explain how that change affected 2005 tax expense and net income.

P5-35. Analyzing and Interpreting Income Components and Disclosures (LO2,3)

The income statement for Xerox Corporation follows.

Year ended December 31 (in millions)	2005	2004	2003
Sales	$ 7,400	$ 7,259	$ 6,970
Service, outsourcing and rentals	7,426	7,529	7,734
Finance income	875	934	997
Total revenues	15,701	15,722	15,701
Costs and expenses			
Cost of sales	4,695	4,545	4,346
Cost of service, outsourcing and rentals	4,207	4,295	4,307
Equipment financing interest	326	345	362
Research, development and engineering expenses	943	914	962
Selling, administrative and general expenses	4,110	4,203	4,249
Restructuring and asset impairment charges	366	86	176
Other expenses, net	224	369	863
Total costs and expenses	14,871	14,757	15,265
Income from continuing operations before income taxes, equity income and discontinued operations	830	965	436
Income tax (benefits) expenses	(5)	340	134
Equity in net income of unconsolidated affiliates	98	151	58
Income from continuing operations before discontinued operations	933	776	360
Income from discontinued operations, net of tax	45	83	—
Net income	$ 978	$ 859	$ 360

Notes:

- The income statement includes sales of Xerox copiers and a finance subsidiary that provides loan and lease financing relating to the sales of those copiers.

- **Equity in net income of unconsolidated affiliates** refers to income Xerox has earned on investments in affiliated (but unconsolidated) companies.

- Xerox tax expense was reduced in 2005 as a result of an audit. The company makes the following disclosure in its footnotes: "In June 2005, the 1996–1998 IRS audit was finalized. As a result, we recorded an aggregate second quarter 2005 net income benefit of $343."

Required

a. Xerox reports three main sources of income: sales, service, and finance income. How should revenue be recognized for each of these business activities? Explain.

b. Xerox reports research and development (R&D) expenses of $943 million in 2005, which is 12.7% of its sales. (1) How are R&D expenses accounted for under GAAP? (2) Why do you believe GAAP prohibits the capitalization of expenses such as R&D?

c. Xerox reports restructuring costs of $366 million in 2005. It also reports restructuring costs in each of 2004 and 2003. (1) Describe the two typical categories of restructuring costs and the accounting for each. (2) How do you recommend treating these costs for analysis purposes? (3) Should regular recurring restructuring costs be treated differently than isolated occurrences of such costs for analysis purposes?

d. Xerox's tax expense was reduced as a result of a favorable IRS ruling in 2005. How should this benefit be treated in your analysis of the company?

e. Xerox reports $224 million in expenses in 2005 labeled as 'Other expenses, net.' How can a company use such an account to potentially obscure its actual financial performance?

P5-36. Analyzing and Interpreting Income Tax Footnote (LO3)

FedEx reports the following footnote for its income taxes in its 2005 10-K report.

The components of the provision for income taxes for the years ended May 31 were as follows.

(in millions)	2005	2004	2003
Current provision			
Domestic:			
Federal	$634	$371	$112
State and local	65	54	28
Foreign	103	85	39
	802	510	179
Deferred provision (benefit)			
Domestic:			
Federal	67	(22)	304
State and local	(4)	(7)	25
Foreign	(1)	—	—
	62	(29)	329
Provision for income taxes ...	$864	$481	$508

The significant components of deferred tax assets and liabilities as of May 31 were as follows.

	2005		2004	
(in millions)	Deferred Tax Assets	Deferred Tax Liabilities	Deferred Tax Assets	Deferred Tax Liabilities
Property, equipment, leases and intangibles..	$ 301	$1,455	$ 310	$1,372
Employee benefits......................	397	453	386	406
Self-insurance accruals..................	311	—	297	—
Other	319	128	277	104
Net operating loss/credit carryforwards......	54	—	47	—
Valuation allowance.....................	(42)	—	(52)	—
Totals	$1,340	$2,036	$1,265	$1,882

Required

a. What income tax expense does FedEx report in its 2005 income statement? How much of this expense is currently payable?

b. FedEx reports deferred tax liabilities relating to property, equipment, leases and intangibles. Describe how these liabilities arise. How likely is it that these liabilities will be paid? Specifically, describe a scenario that will (i) defer these taxes indefinitely, and (ii) will result in these liabilities requiring payment within the near future.

c. FedEx reports a deferred tax asset relating to self-insurance accruals. When a company self-insures, it does not purchase insurance from a third-party insurance company. Instead, it records an expense and related liability to reflect the probable payment of losses that can occur in the future. Explain why this accrual results in a deferred tax asset.

d. FedEx reports net loss carryforwards. Explain how these arise and how they will result in a future benefit.

e. FedEx reports a valuation allowance related to its deferred tax assets. Why did FedEx set up such an allowance? How did the decrease in the allowance from 2004 to 2005 affect net income? How can a company use this allowance to meet its income targets in a particular year?

P5-37. Analyzing and Interpreting Tax Footnote (Financial Statement Effects Template) (LO3)
Benihana, Inc. (BNHN), reports the following deferred tax information in a footnote to its 10-K filing.   Benihana Inc. (BNHN)

Income Taxes Deferred tax assets and liabilities reflect the tax effect of temporary differences between amounts of assets and liabilities for financial reporting purposes and the amounts of such assets and liabilities as measured by income tax law. A valuation allowance is recognized to reduce deferred tax assets to the amounts that are more likely than not to be realized. The income tax effects of temporary differences that give rise to deferred tax assets and liabilities are as follows (in thousands):

	March 27, 2005	March 28, 2004
Deferred tax assets		
Rent straight-lining.	$1,483	$1,422
Tax credit carryforward	1,017	1,383
Gift certificate liability	870	554
Amortization of gain.	807	847
Employee benefit accruals	308	366
Tax loss carryforwards	—	301
Other.	234	161
	4,719	5,034
Deferred tax liabilities		
Property and equipment	2,501	3,307
Inventories	839	764
Goodwill	1,118	778
	4,458	4,849
Net deferred tax asset.	$ 261	$ 185

The net deferred tax asset is classified on the balance sheet as follows (in thousands):

	March 27, 2005	March 28, 2004
Current asset	$ 417	$ 185
Long-term liability	156	—
Net deferred tax asset.	$ 261	$ 185

The income tax provision consists of (in thousands):

Fiscal Year Ended	March 27, 2005	March 28, 2004	March 30, 2003
Current			
Federal	$3,037	$1,876	$2,826
State	1,559	680	1,244
Deferred			
Federal and State.	(76)	2,265	655
Income tax provision	$4,520	$4,821	$4,725

Required

a. Did Benihana's deferred tax assets increase or decrease during the most recent fiscal year? Interpret the change.

b. Did Benihana's deferred tax liabilities increase or decrease during the most recent fiscal year? Explain how the change arose (*Hint:* Look at the individual deferred tax liabilities and the most significant change during the year.)

c. Use the financial statement effects template to record Benihana's income tax expense for 2005 along with the changes in both deferred tax assets and liabilities. Your transaction should have two parts, one for the current portion of tax expense (the cash paid, or payable to the tax authorities) and one for the deferred portion of tax expense.

P5-38.   Analyzing and Interpreting Restructuring Costs and Effects   (LO2)

Dow Jones &
Company (DJ)

Dow Jones & Company reports the following footnote disclosure in its 2005 10-K relating to its restructuring programs.

Restructuring and other items included in operating expenses were as follows:

(in thousands)	2005	2004
Severance	$11,367	$6,813
Other exit costs	—	(120)
Reversal of lease obligation reserve-WFC	—	(2,761)
Total	$11,367	$3,932

The following table displays the activity and balances of the restructuring reserve (liability) accounts through December 31, 2005.

(in thousands)	December 31, 2004 Reserve	2005 Expense	Cash Payments	December 31, 2005 Reserve
Employee severance—2005	$ —	$11,367	$ (6,771)	$4,596
Employee severance—2004	7,262	—	(4,408)	2,854
Total	$7,262	$11,367	$(11,179)	$7,450

The workforce reductions related to the restructuring actions are substantially complete. The remaining reserve relates primarily to continuing payments for employees that have already been terminated and is expected to be paid over the next twelve months.

2005 In the second quarter of 2005, the company recorded a restructuring charge of $11.4 million ($6.9 million, net of taxes) primarily reflecting employee severance related to a workforce reduction of about 120 full-time employees. Most of the charge related to the Company's efforts to reposition its international print and online operations but also included headcount reductions at other parts of the business.

2004 In the fourth quarter of 2004, the Company recorded a restructuring charge of $6.7 million ($4.0 million, net of taxes) primarily reflecting employee severance related to a workforce reduction of about 100 employees. The majority of this charge was related to employee severance in connection with the Company's decision to publish Far Eastern Economic Review (FEER) as a monthly periodical beginning in December 2004, with the balance of the charge related to headcount reductions in circulation and international operations.

On September 11, 2001, the Company's headquarters at the World Financial Center (WFC) sustained damage from debris and dust as a result of the terrorist attacks on the World Trade Center. Approximately 60% of the floor space, including furniture and related equipment, had been deemed a total loss. In the fourth quarter 2001, the company recorded a charge of $32.2 million as a result of its decision to permanently re-deploy certain personnel and to abandon four of seven floors that were leased at its WFC headquarters. This charge primarily reflected the Company's rent obligation through May 2005 on this vacated space. In the first quarter of 2004, the Company decided to extend the term of its lease for one of the floors that was previously abandoned and reoccupy this floor with personnel from another of its New York locations, whose lease term was expiring. As a result, the Company reversed $2.8 million ($1.7 million, net of taxes) of the remaining lease obligation reserve for the previously abandoned floor at WFC.

Required

a. Why did DJ reverse restructuring charges in 2004? What effect did this reversal have on operating expenses and operating profit for the year? In your analysis of the DJ operating results for 2004, how might you treat this reversal?

b. Describe the circumstances relating to the 2005 restructuring expense. What were the effects on the income statement and the balance sheet when DJ initially recorded the expense? Explain why the accrual was reduced in 2005.

P5-39. Analyzing and Interpreting Restructuring Accruals (Financial Statement Effects Template)   (LO2)

Consider the footnote information for Dow Jones & Company from P5-38.

Dow Jones & Company (DJ)

Required

a. Use the financial statement effects template to record the activity in the restructuring reserve account for the year ended December 31, 2005. You should record two separate entries in the template, one for the 2005 restructuring expense accrual and one for the cash payments during the year.

b. Prepare journal entries and T-account entries for the activity in the restructuring reserve account for the year ended December 31, 2005.

P5-40. Analyzing and Interpreting Gains and Losses on Asset (Subsidiary) Sales   (LO2)

Altria Group, Inc., formerly Phillip Morris Companies, sold its Miller Brewing subsidiary. Following is a footnote to its 10-K report, which describes that transaction.

Altria Group, Inc. (MO)

On May 30, 2002, ALG announced an agreement with SAB to merge Miller into SAB. The transaction closed on July 9, 2002, and SAB changed its name to SABMiller plc ("SABMiller"). At closing, ALG received 430 million shares of SABMiller valued at approximately $3.4 billion, based upon a share price of 5.12 British pounds per share, in exchange for Miller, which had $2.0 billion of existing debt. The shares in SABMiller owned by ALG resulted in a 36% economic interest in SABMiller and a 24.9% voting interest. The transaction resulted in a pre-tax gain of approximately $2.6 billion or approximately $1.7 billion after-tax. The gain was recorded in the third quarter of 2002. Beginning with the third quarter of 2002, ALG's ownership interest in SABMiller is being accounted for under the equity method. Accordingly, ALG's investment in SABMiller of approximately $1.9 billion is included in other assets on the consolidated balance sheet at December 31, 2002. In addition, ALG records its share of SABMiller's net earnings, based on its economic ownership percentage, in minority interest in earnings and other, net, on the consolidated statement of earnings.

Required

a. Identify (1) the total value received by Altria in exchange for Miller, (2) the book value of Altria's investment in the Miller Brewing subsidiary, and (3) the pretax and after-tax gains recognized by Altria from the Miller transaction.

b. How much of the purchase price was received in cash by Altria? Explain.

c. How should the gain from this transaction be interpreted in an analysis of Altria, especially with respect to projections of Altria's future cash flows?

P5-41. Analyzing Unearned Revenue Disclosures (LO1)

Costco Wholesale (COST)

The following disclosures are from the August 28, 2005, annual report of Costco Wholesale Corporation.

Summary of Significant Accounting Policies (excerpt)

Membership fee revenue represents annual membership fees paid by substantially all of the Company's members. The Company accounts for membership fee revenue on a "unearned basis," whereby membership fee revenue is recognized ratably over the one-year term of the membership.

Current Liabilities ($ thousands)	2005	2004
Short-term borrowings	$ 54,356	$ 21,595
Accounts payable	4,213,724	3,600,200
Accrued salaries and benefits	1,025,181	904,209
Accrued sales and other taxes	263,899	223,009
Deferred membership income	500,558	453,881
Current portion long-term debt	3,225	305,594
Other current liabilities	548,031	662,062
Total current liabilities	$6,608,974	$6,170,550

Revenue ($ thousands)	2005	2004	2003
Net sales	$51,862,072	$47,145,712	$41,692,699
Membership fees	1,073,156	961,280	852,853
Total revenue	$52,935,228	$48,106,992	$42,545,552

Required

a. Explain in layman terms how Costco accounts for the cash received for its membership fees.

b. Use the balance sheet information on Costco's Deferred Membership Income liability account and its income statement revenues related to membership fees earned during 2005 to compute the cash that Costco received during 2005 for membership fees.

c. Use the financial statement effects template to show the effect of the cash Costco received during 2005 for memberships and the recognition of membership fees revenue for 2005.

P5-42. Analyzing Unearned Revenue Transactions (LO1)

Centex Corp. (CTX)

The annual report of Centex Corporation, a home builder, reveals the following information about new home sales order backlogs by geographic region. Assume that each sales order includes a $1,000 deposit from the customer.

Sales (Orders) Backlog, at the end of the period (in units):

Centex Corp. (CTX)

| | As of March 31, | | | | |
	2006	2005	2004	2003	2002
Mid-Atlantic	3,073	3,461	2,801	2,148	1,503
Southeast.	4,116	5,006	3,707	2,713	2,315
Midwest	2,755	3,273	3,392	2,920	2,093
Southwest	4,094	3,688	2,869	2,258	2,361
West Coast.	3,349	3,161	2,645	2,011	1,099
	17,387	18,589	15,414	12,050	9,371

We define backlog units as units that have been sold, as evidenced by a signed contract with the customer, but not closed. Substantially all of the orders in sales backlog as of March 31, 2006 are expected to close during fiscal year 2007. For each unit in backlog, we have received a customer deposit, which is refundable under certain circumstances. The backlog units included in the table above are net of cancellations. Cancellations occur for a variety of reasons including: a customer's inability to obtain financing, customer relocations or other customer financial hardships.

Required

a. Explain in layman terms how Centex records a customer deposit when a sale is not yet closed.
b. How does Centex's balance sheet reflect the deposits on the backlog units at the end of March 2006?
c. When, if ever, will Centex's income statement reflect the deposits on the backlog units?
d. Explain how Centex might account for deposits that are refunded to customers.

CASES

C5-43. **Management Application: Managing Foreign Currency Risk** (LO5)

Fluctuations in foreign currency exchange rates can result in increased volatility of revenues, expenses, and profits. Companies generally attempt to reduce this volatility.

a. Identify two possible solutions to reduce the volatility effect of foreign exchange rate fluctuations. (*Hint*: Examine the risk management discussion for Johnson Controls in Exercise E5-31)
b. What costs would arise if you implemented each of your solutions?

C5-44. **Ethics and Governance: Revenue Recognition** (LO1)

GAAP offers latitude in determining when revenue is earned. Assume that a company that normally required acceptance by its customers prior to recording revenue as earned, delivers a product to a customer near the end of the quarter. The company believes that acceptance is assured, but cannot obtain it prior to quarter-end. Recording the revenue would assure "making its numbers" for the quarter. Although formal acceptance is not obtained, the sales person records the sale, fully intending to obtain written acceptance as soon as possible.

a. What are the revenue recognition requirements in this case?
b. What are the ethical issues relating to this sale?
c. Assume you are on the board of directors of this company. What safeguards can you put in place to provide assurance that the company's revenue recognition policy is followed?

C5-45. **Ethics and Governance: Earnings Management** (LO2)

Assume that you are CEO of a company. Your company has reported a loss for the current year. Since it cannot carry back the entire loss to recoup taxes paid in prior years, it records a loss carryforward as a deferred tax asset. Your expectation is that future profitability will be sufficient to realize the tax benefits of the carryforward. Your chief financial officer approaches you with an idea to create a deferred tax valuation allowance that will reduce the deferred tax asset, increase tax expense for the year, and increase your reported loss. He reasons that the company's stock price will not be reduced markedly by the additional reported loss since a loss year has already been factored into the current price. Further, this deferred tax valuation allowance will create a reserve that can be used in future years to increase profit (via reversal of the allowance) if needed to meet analyst expectations.

a. What stakeholders are potentially affected by the CFO's proposal?
b. How do you respond to the proposal? Justify your response.

Reporting and Analyzing Operating Assets

LEARNING OBJECTIVES

LO1 Describe accounting for accounts receivable and the importance of the allowance for uncollectible accounts in determining profit. (p. 6-4)

LO2 Explain accounting for inventories and the effects on the balance sheet and income statement from different inventory costing methods. (p. 6-13)

LO3 Describe accounting for property, plant and equipment and explain the impacts on profit and cash flows from different depreciation methods. (p. 6-26)

CISCO SYSTEMS

Cisco Systems, Inc., manufactures and sells networking and communications products for transporting data, voice, and video within buildings, across town and around the world. Cisco's products are everywhere, here are but a few applications:

- Schoolchildren can view a virtual science experiment from a neighborhood center's Cisco-outfitted computer room.

- Airline passengers can check flight information and print boarding passes at convenient Cisco kiosks.

- Hospital nurses check medication levels at patients' bedsides using Cisco handheld devices and wireless networks.

- Auto designers in Japan, assembly technicians in the U.S., and component makers worldwide trade manufacturing data over a Cisco network in real time.

- Police rely on citywide Cisco wireless networks to deliver fingerprint files, mug shots, and voicemail to mobile units.

- Customers call their bank's Cisco Internet Protocol (IP) based center, where account profiles immediately appear to call agents.

- Companies shore up their databases with Cisco network security.

Cisco reported 2005 net income of $5.7 billion on $24.8 billion in sales, and a return on net operating assets (RNOA) of 43%. Four years earlier, Cisco reported a *loss* of $1 billion after recording $2.25 billion of restructuring costs, including costs related to the severance of 6,000 employees and the write-off of obsolete inventory and other assets.

Cisco's turnaround is remarkable. Sales have increased by 31% in the past two years, and its return on net operating assets has nearly doubled. The RNOA improvement cannot be attributed to profit increases alone. It also reflects Cisco's effective asset (balance sheet) management. Recall that RNOA comprises both a profitability component and a productivity

Getty Images

component (see Module 4). The productivity component (reflected in net operating asset turnover, NOAT) is measured as sales divided by average net operating assets. Effective management of operating assets is crucial to achieving a high RNOA. We focus on three important operating assets in this module: accounts receivable, inventories, and property, plant and equipment (PPE).

As part of their overall marketing efforts, companies extend credit to customers. At Cisco, for example, accounts receivable are a significant asset because all sales are on account. While favorable credit terms stimulate sales, the resulting accounts receivables are costly. First, accounts receivable are generally non-interest bearing and tie up a company's working capital in non-earning assets. Second, receivables expose the company to collectibility risk - the risk that some customers won't pay. Third, companies incur the administrative costs associated with billing and collection. These costs must be weighed against the costs of other marketing tools, like advertising, sales incentives, and price discounts. Management of receivables is critical to financial success.

Inventories are significant assets at many companies, particularly for manufacturers such as Cisco, where inventories consist of raw materials (the basic product inputs), work in process (the cost of partially completed products), and finished goods (completed products awaiting sale). Inventories too are costly to maintain. The cost of buying and manufacturing the goods must be financed and inventories must be stored, moved, and insured. Consequently, companies prefer lower inventory levels whenever possible. However, companies must be careful to hold enough inventory. If they reduce inventory quantities too far, they risk inventory stock-outs, that is, not having enough inventory to meet demand. Management of inventories is also a critical activity.

Property, plant and equipment (PPE) is often the largest, and usually the most important, asset on the balance sheet. Companies need administrative offices, IT and R&D facilities, regional sales and customer service offices, manufacturing and distribution facilities, vehicles, computers, and a host of other fixed assets. Fixed asset costs are substantial and are indirectly linked to sales and profits. Consequently, fixed-asset investments are often difficult to justify and, once acquired, fixed assets are often difficult to divest. Effective management of PPE assets usually requires management review of the entire value chain.

John Chambers, CEO of Cisco, recalls a conversation he once had with the legendary Jack Welch, former Chairman of GE. Following Cisco's announced restructuring program in 2001, Welch commented, "John, you'll never have a great company until you go through the really tough times. What builds a company is not just how

(Continued on next page)

(Continued from previous page)
you handle the successes, but it's the way you handle the real challenges." Cisco survived the tech bubble burst, which is as "real" a challenge as any company is likely to face. Further, Cisco is now reporting impressive financial results. To ensure future financial performance, however, Cisco must effectively manage both its income statement and its operating assets.

Sources: *BusinessWeek,* 2003 and 2006; Cisco Systems 10-K, 2006; Cisco Systems Annual Report, 2006.

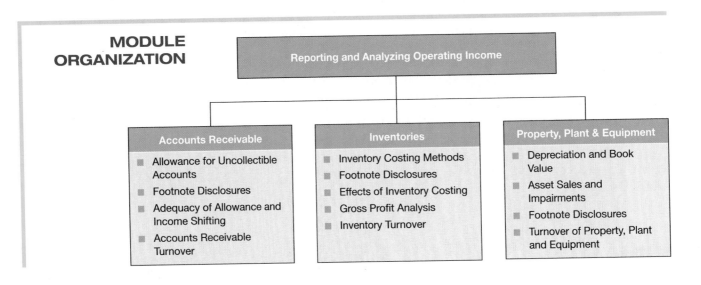

MODULE ORGANIZATION

Reporting and Analyzing Operating Income

Accounts Receivable	Inventories	Property, Plant & Equipment
■ Allowance for Uncollectible Accounts	■ Inventory Costing Methods	■ Depreciation and Book Value
■ Footnote Disclosures	■ Footnote Disclosures	■ Asset Sales and Impairments
■ Adequacy of Allowance and Income Shifting	■ Effects of Inventory Costing	■ Footnote Disclosures
■ Accounts Receivable Turnover	■ Gross Profit Analysis	■ Turnover of Property, Plant and Equipment
	■ Inventory Turnover	

INTRODUCTION

Managing net operating assets is crucial to creating shareholder value. To manage and assess net operating assets, we need to understand how they are measured and reported. This module describes the reporting and measuring of operating working capital, mainly receivables and inventories, and of long-term operating assets such as property, plant, and equipment. We do not discuss other long-term operating assets, such as equity investments in affiliated companies, investment in intangible assets, and nonoperating investments in marketable securities, as they are covered in other modules.

Receivables are usually a major part of operating working capital. They must be carefully managed as they represent a substantial asset for most companies and are an important marketing tool. GAAP requires companies to report receivables at the amount they expect to collect. This requires estimation of uncollectible accounts. The receivables reported on the balance sheet, and expenses reported on the income statement, impound management's estimate of uncollectible amounts. Accordingly, it is important that companies accurately assess uncollectible accounts and timely report them. It is also necessary that readers of financial reports understand management's accounting choices and their effects on reported balance sheets and income statements.

Inventory is another major component of operating working capital. Inventories usually constitute one of the three largest assets (along with receivables and long-term operating assets). Also, cost of goods sold, which flows from inventory, is the largest expense category for retailing and manufacturing companies. GAAP allows several methods for inventory accounting, and inventory-costing choices can markedly impact balance sheets and income statements, especially for companies experiencing relatively high inflation, coupled with slowly turning inventories.

Long-term plant assets are often the largest component of operating assets. Indeed, long-term operating assets are typically the largest asset for manufacturing companies, and their related depreciation expense is typically second only in amount to cost of goods sold in the income statement. GAAP allows different accounting methods for computing depreciation that can significantly impact the income statement and the balance sheet. When companies dispose of fixed assets, a gain or loss may result. Understanding these gains and losses on asset sales is important as we assess performance. Further, accounting for asset write-downs not only affects companies' current financial performance, but also future profitability. We must understand these effects when we assess future income statements. This module considers all of these fixed asset accounting choices and consequences.

ACCOUNTS RECEIVABLE

Our focus on operating assets begins with accounts receivable. To help frame our discussion, we refer to the following graphic as we proceed through the module:

Income Statement	Balance Sheet	
Sales	Cash	Current liabilities
Cost of goods sold	Accounts receivable, net	Long-term liabilities
Selling, general & administrative	Inventory	
Income taxes	Property, plant, and equipment, net	Shareholders' equity
Net income	Investments	

LO1 Describe accounting for accounts receivable and the importance of the allowance for uncollectible accounts in determining profit.

The graphic highlights the balance sheet and income statement effects of accounts receivable. This section explains the accounting, reporting, and analysis of these highlighted items.

Retail companies transact mostly in cash. But other companies, including those that sell to other firms, usually do not expect cash upon delivery. Instead, they offer credit terms and have *credit sales* or *sales on account*.[1] An account receivable on the seller's balance sheet is always matched by a corresponding account payable on the buyer's balance sheet. Accounts receivable are reported on the seller's balance sheet at *net realizable value*, which is the net amount the seller expects to collect.

Sellers do not expect to collect all accounts receivable; they anticipate that some buyers will be unable to pay their accounts when they come due. For example, buyers can suffer business downturns that limit the cash available to meet liabilities. Then, buyers must decide which liabilities to pay. Typically, financially distressed companies decide to pay off liabilities to the IRS, to banks, and to bondholders because those creditors have enforcement powers and can quickly seize assets and disrupt operations, leading to bankruptcy and eventual liquidation. Buyers also try to cover their payroll, as they cannot exist without employees. Then, if there is cash remaining, buyers will pay suppliers to ensure continued flow of goods.

Accounts payable are *unsecured liabilities,* meaning that buyers have not pledged collateral to guarantee payment of amounts owed. As a result, when a company declares bankruptcy, accounts payable are comingled with other unsecured creditors (after the IRS and the secured creditors), and are typically not paid in full. Consequently, there is risk in the collectibility of accounts receivable. This *collectibility risk* is crucial to analysis of accounts receivable.

Cisco reports $2,216 million of accounts receivable in the following current asset section from its 2005 balance sheet:

$ millions	July 30, 2005
Cash and cash equivalents	$ 4,742
Short-term investments	2,227
Accounts receivable, net of allowance for doubtful accounts of $162	2,216
Inventories	1,297
Deferred tax assets	1,582
Prepaid expenses and other current assets	967
Total current assets	$13,031

Cisco reports its receivables net of allowances for doubtful (uncollectible) accounts of $162 million. This means the total amount owed to Cisco is $2,378 million ($2,216 million + $162 million), but Cisco *estimates* that $162 million are uncollectible and reports on its balance sheet only the amount it expects to collect.

---

[1] An example of common credit terms are 2/10, net 30. These terms indicate that the seller offers the buyer an early-pay incentive, in this case a 2% discount off the cost if the buyer pays within 10 days of billing. If the buyer does not take advantage of the discount, it must pay 100% of the invoice cost within 30 days of billing. From the seller's standpoint, offering the discount is often warranted because it speeds up cash collections and then the seller can invest the cash to yield a return greater than the early-payment discount. The buyer often wishes to avail itself of attractive discounts even if it has to borrow money to do so. If the discount is not taken, however, the buyer should withhold payment as long as possible (at least for the full net period) so as to maximize its available cash. Meanwhile, the seller will exert whatever pressure it can to collect the amount due as quickly as possible. Thus, it is normal for there to be some tension between sellers and buyers.

We might ask why buyers would sell to companies from whom they do not expect to collect. The answer is they would not have extended credit *if* they knew beforehand which companies would eventually not pay. For example, Cisco probably cannot identify those companies that constitute the $162 million in uncollectible accounts. Yet, it knows from past experience that a certain portion of its receivables will prove uncollectible. GAAP requires companies to estimate the dollar amount of uncollectible accounts (even if it cannot identify specific accounts that are uncollectible), and to report accounts receivable at the resulting *net realizable value* (total receivables less an allowance for uncollectible accounts).

Allowance for Uncollectible Accounts

Companies typically use an *aging analysis* to estimate the amount of uncollectible accounts. This requires an analysis of receivables as of the balance sheet date. Specifically, customer accounts are categorized by the number of days that the related invoices have been unpaid (outstanding). Based on prior experience, or on other available statistics, uncollectible percentages are applied to each category, with larger percentages applied to older accounts. The result of this analysis is a dollar amount for the allowance for uncollectible accounts (also called allowance for doubtful accounts) at the balance sheet date.

Aging Analysis

To illustrate, Exhibit 6.1 shows an aging analysis for a seller with $100,000 of accounts receivable at period-end. The current accounts are those that are still within their original credit period. As an example, if a seller's credit terms are 2/10, net 30, all invoices that have been outstanding for 30 days or fewer are current. Accounts listed as 1–60 days past due are those 1 to 60 days past their due date. This would include an account that is 45 days outstanding for a net 30-day invoice. This same logic applies to all categories.

EXHIBIT 6.1	**Aging of Accounts Receivable**		
Age of Accounts	**Receivable Balance**	**Estimated Percent Uncollectible**	**Estimated Uncollectible Accounts**
Current	$ 50,000	2%	$1,000
1-60 days past due	30,000	3	900
61-90 days past due	15,000	4	600
Over 90 days past due	5,000	8	400
Total	$100,000		$2,900

Exhibit 6.1 also reflects the seller's experience with uncollectible accounts, which manifests itself in the uncollectible percentages for each aged category. For example, on average, 3% of buyers' accounts that are 1-60 days past due prove uncollectible for this seller. Hence, the company estimates a potential loss of $900 for the $30,000 in receivables one to sixty days past due.

Reporting Receivables

The seller represented in Exhibit 6.1 reports its accounts receivable on the balance sheet as follows:

Accounts receivable, net of $2,900 in allowances $97,100

Assume that, as of the end of the *previous* accounting period, the company had estimated total uncollectible accounts of $2,200 based on an aging analysis of the receivables at that time. Also assume that the company did not write off any accounts receivable during the period. The *reconciliation* of its allowance account for the period follows:

Beginning allowance for uncollectible accounts	$ 2,200
Add: Provision for uncollectible accounts	700
Less: Write-offs of accounts receivable	0
Ending allowance for uncollectible accounts	$ 2,900

The aging analysis revealed that the allowance for uncollectible accounts is $700 too low and therefore, the company increased the allowance accordingly. This adjustment affects the financial statements as follows:

1. Accounts receivable are reduced by an additional $700 on the balance sheet (receivables are reported *net* of the allowance account).
2. A $700 expense, called bad debts expense, is reported in the income statement (usually part of SG&A expense). This reduces pretax profit by the same amount.[2]

The allowance for uncollectible accounts increases with new provisions (additional bad debts expense) and decreases as accounts are written off. Individual accounts are written off when the seller identifies them as uncollectible. (A write-off reduces both accounts receivable and the allowance for uncollectible accounts as described below.) As with all permanent accounts on the balance sheet, the ending balance of the allowance account is the beginning balance for next period.

Writing Off Accounts

To illustrate the write-off of an account receivable, assume that subsequent to the period-end shown above, the seller receives notice that one of its customers, owing $500 at the time, has declared bankruptcy. The seller's attorneys believe that legal costs in attempting to collect this receivable would likely exceed the amount owed. So, the seller decides not to pursue collection and to write off this account. The write-off has the following effects:

1. Gross accounts receivable are reduced from $100,000 to $99,500.
2. Allowance for uncollectible accounts is reduced from $2,900 to $2,400.

After the write-off, the seller's balance sheet appears as follows:

> Accounts receivable, net of $2,400 in allowances $97,100

Exhibit 6.2 shows the effects of this write-off on the individual accounts.

EXHIBIT 6.2	Effects of an Accounts Receivable Write-Off		
Account	**Before Write-Off**	**Effects of Write-Off**	**After Write-Off**
Accounts receivable.	$100,000	$(500)	$99,500
Less: Allowance for uncollectible accounts	2,900	(500)	2,400
Accounts receivable, net of allowance.	$ 97,100		$97,100

The balance of net accounts receivable is the same before and after the write-off. This is always the case. The write-off of an account is a non-event from an accounting point of view. That is, total assets do not change, liabilities stay the same, and equity is unaffected as there is no net income effect. The write-off affects individual asset accounts, but not total assets.

Let's next consider what happens when additional information arrives that alters management's expectations of uncollectible accounts. To illustrate, assume that sometime after the write-off above, the seller realizes that it has underestimated uncollectible accounts and that $3,000 (not $2,400) of the remaining $99,500 accounts receivable are uncollectible. The company must increase the allowance for uncollectible accounts by $600. The additional $600 provision has the following financial statement effects:

1. Allowance for uncollectible accounts increases by $600 to the revised estimated balance of $3,000; and accounts receivable (net of the allowance for uncollectible accounts) declines by $600 from $97,100 to $96,500 (or $99,500 − $3,000).

---

[2] Companies can also estimate uncollectible accounts using the *percentage of sales* method. The percentage of sales method computes bad debts expense directly, as a percentage of sales and the allowance for uncollectible accounts is estimated indirectly. In contrast, the aging method computes the allowance balance directly and the bad debts expense is the amount required to bring the allowance account up to (or down to) the amount determined by the aging analysis. To illustrate, if a company reports sales of $100,000 and estimates the provision at 1% of sales, it would report a bad debts expense of $1,000 and an allowance balance of $3,200 instead of the $700 bad debts expense and the $2,900 allowance as determined using the aging analysis. The two methods nearly always report different values for the allowance, net accounts receivable, and bad debts expense.

2. A $600 bad debts expense is added to the income statement, which reduces pretax income. Recall that in the prior period, the seller reported $700 of bad debts expense when the allowance account was increased from $2,200 to $2,900.

Analyzing Receivable Transactions

To summarize, recording bad debts expense increases the allowance for uncollectible accounts, which affects both the *balance sheet* and *income statement*. Importantly, the financial statement effects occur when the allowance is estimated, and not when accounts are written off. In this way, sales are matched with bad debts expense, and accounts receivable are matched with expected uncollectible accounts. Exhibit 6.3 illustrates each of the transactions discussed in this section using the financial statement effects template:

EXHIBIT 6.3 Financial Statement Effects of Key Accounts Receivable Transactions

Transaction	Cash Asset	+ Noncash Assets	= Liabil- ities	+ Contrib. Capital	+ Earned Capital	Rev- enues	− Expen- ses	= Net Income
a. Credit sales of $100,000		+100,000 Accounts Receivable	=		+100,000 Retained Earnings	+100,000 Sales		= +100,000
b. Increase allowance for uncollectible accounts by $700		−700 Allowance for Uncollectible Accounts	=		−700 Retained Earnings		+700 Bad Debts Expense	= −700
c. Write off $500 in accounts receivable		−500 Accounts receivable +500 Allowance for Uncollectible Accounts	=					=
d. Increase allowance for uncollectible accounts by $600		−600 Allowance for Uncollectible Accounts	=		−600 Retained Earnings		+600 Bad Debts Expense	= −600

Footnote Disclosures

To illustrate the typical accounts receivable footnote disclosure, consider Cisco's discussion of its allowance for uncollectible accounts:

> **Allowance for Doubtful Accounts** The allowance for doubtful accounts as of July 30, 2005, was $162 million or 6.8% of the gross accounts receivable balance. This compares with $179 million or 8.9% of the gross accounts receivable balance as of July 31, 2004. The allowance is based on an assessment of the collectibility of customer accounts. Companies regularly review the allowance by considering factors such as historical experience, credit quality, the age of the accounts receivable balances, and current economic conditions that may affect a customer's ability to pay. If a major customer's creditworthiness deteriorates, or if actual defaults are higher than historical experience, or if other circumstances arise, estimates of the recoverability of amounts due could be overstated, and additional allowances are probably required.

Cisco's allowance for uncollectible accounts declined as a percentage of gross receivables from the prior year. As the level of uncollectible accounts decreases, the company recognizes less bad debts expense. The effect is to raise net income. Cisco alludes to the level of estimation required, and cautions the reader that additional allowances (provisions) could be required under certain circumstances, and that would adversely affect profit.

Cisco provides a footnote reconciliation of its allowance for uncollectible (doubtful) accounts for the past three years as shown in Exhibit 6.4.

EXHIBIT 6.4	Reconciliation of Cisco's Allowance for Uncollectible Accounts
$ millions	**Allowance for Doubtful Accounts**
Year ended July 26, 2003	
Balance at beginning of fiscal year	$335
(Credited) to expenses	(59)
Deductions for write-offs	(93)
Balance at end of fiscal year	$183
Year ended July 31, 2004	
Balance at beginning of fiscal year	$183
Charged to expenses	19
Deductions for write-offs	(23)
Balance at end of fiscal year	$179
Year ended July 30, 2005	
Balance at beginning of fiscal year	$179
Charged to expenses	—
Deductions for write-offs	(17)
Balance at end of fiscal year	$162

Reconciling Cisco's allowance account provides insight into the level of the provision (expense) each year relative to the actual write-offs. Cisco wrote off $93 million of accounts receivable in 2003, $23 million in 2004, and $17 million in 2005. This pattern is impressive especially given that gross receivables increased by 30% over this three-year period. Over the same period, Cisco reduced the allowance as a percentage of gross receivables from 10% ($183 million/$1,834 million) in 2003 to 8.9% ($179 million/$2,004 million) in 2004, and to 6.8% ($162 million/$2,378 million) in 2005. Because the allowance account was too high in 2003, Cisco *reversed* the provision by $59 million in 2003 (that is, Cisco recorded a negative bad debts expense in 2003), a minimal provision of $19 million in 2004, and no provision at all in 2005. Since 2002, Cisco as reduced its allowance for uncollectible accounts by $173 million.

Analysis Implications

This section considers analysis of accounts receivable and the provision for uncollectible accounts.

Adequacy of Allowance Account
A company makes two representations when reporting accounts receivable (net) in the current asset section of its balance sheet:

1. It expects to collect the amount reported on the balance sheet (remember, accounts receivable are reported net of allowance for uncollectible accounts).
2. It expects to collect the amount within the next year (implied by the classification of accounts receivable as a current asset).

From an analysis viewpoint, we scrutinize the adequacy of a company's provision for its uncollectible accounts. If the provision is inadequate, the cash ultimately collected will be less than the net receivables reported on the balance sheet.

How can an outsider assess the adequacy of the allowance account? One answer is to compare the allowance account to gross accounts receivable. For Cisco, the 2005 percentage is 6.8% (see above), a 24% decline from the prior year. What does such a decline signify? Perhaps the overall economic environment has improved, rendering write-offs less likely. Perhaps the company has improved its credit underwriting or receivables collection efforts. The MD&A section of the 10-K report is likely to discuss such new initiatives. Or perhaps the company's customer mix has changed and it is now selling to more creditworthy customers (or, it eliminated a risky class of customers).

The important point is that we must be comfortable with the percentage of uncollectible accounts reported by the company. We must remember that management controls the size of the allowance account—albeit with audit assurances.

Income Shifting

We noted that the financial statement effects of uncollectible accounts transpire when the allowance is increased for new bad debts expense and not when the allowance account is decreased for the write-off of uncollectible accounts. It is also important to note that management controls the amount and timing of the uncollectible provision. Although external auditors assess the reasonableness of the allowance for uncollectible accounts, they do not possess management's inside knowledge and experience. This puts the auditors at an information disadvantage, particularly if any dispute arises.

Studies show that many companies use the allowance for uncollectible accounts to shift income from one year into another. For example, a company can increase current-period income by deliberately underestimating bad debts expense. However, in the future it will become apparent that the bad debts expense was too low when the company's write-offs exceed the balance in the allowance account. Then, the company will need to increase the allowance to make up for the earlier period's underestimate. As an example, consider a company that accurately estimates that it has $1,000 of uncollectible accounts at the end of 2007. Assume that the current balance in the allowance for uncollectible accounts is $200. But instead of recording bad debts expense of $800 as needed to have an adequate ($1,000) allowance, the company records only $100 of bad debts expense and reports an allowance of $300 at the end of 2007. Now if the company's original estimate was accurate, in 2008 it will write off accounts totaling $1,000. The write-offs ($1,000) are greater than the allowance balance ($300) and the company will need to increase the allowance by recording an additional $700 in 2008. The effect of this is that the company borrowed $700 of income from 2008 in order to report higher income in 2007. This is called "income shifting."

Why would a company want to shift income from a later period into the current period? Perhaps it is a lean year and the company is in danger of missing income targets. For example, internal targets influence manager bonuses and external targets set by the market influence stock prices. Or, perhaps the company is in danger of defaulting on loan agreements tied to income levels. The reality is that income pressures are great and these pressures can cause managers to bend (or even break) the rules.

Companies can just as easily shift income from the current period to one or more future periods by overestimating the current period bad debts expense and allowance for uncollectible accounts. Why would a company want to shift income to one or more future periods? Perhaps current times are good and the company wants to "bank" some of that income for future periods; sometimes called a *cookie jar reserve*. It can then draw on that reserve, if necessary, to boost income in one or more future lean years. Another reason for a company to shift income from the current period is that it does not wish to unduly inflate market expectations for future period income. Or perhaps the company is experiencing a very bad year and it feels that overestimating the provision will not drive income materially lower than it is. Thus, it decides to take a big bath (a large loss) and create a reserve that can be used in future periods. (Sears provides an interesting case as described in the Business Insight on next page).

Use of the allowance for uncollectible accounts to shift income is a source of concern. This is especially so for banks where the allowance for loan losses is a large component of banks' balance sheets and loan loss expense is a major component of reported income. Our analysis must scrutinize the allowance for uncollectible accounts to identify any changes from past practices or industry norms and, then, to justify those changes before accepting them as valid.

Accounts Receivable Turnover and Average Collection Period

The net operating asset turnover (NOAT) is sales divided by average net operating assets. An important component of this measure is the **accounts receivables turnover (ART)**, which is defined as:[3]

$$\textbf{Accounts Receivable Turnover} = \textbf{Sales/Average Accounts Receivable}$$

---

[3] Technically, the numerator should be net credit sales because receivables arise from credit sales. Including cash sales in the numerator inflates the ratio. Typically, outsiders do not know the level of cash sales and, therefore, must use total sales to calculate the turnover ratio.

BUSINESS INSIGHT	Sears' Cookie Jar

The Heard on the Street column in *The Wall Street Journal* (1996) reported the following: "Analyst David Poneman argues that Sears' earnings growth this year of 24%, or $134 million, has been aided by a 1993 balance-sheet maneuver that softens the impact of soaring levels of bad credit-card debt among its 50 million cardholders. Wall Street got a wake-up call in the second quarter, when Sears increased its provision for bad credit-card debt by $254 million, up 73% from the year earlier. Then in the third quarter, it made another $286 million provision, a 53% increase. Yet the retailer posted a 22% gain in third-quarter net. How so? "Sears is using its superabundant balance sheet to smooth out its earnings," says Mr. Poneman. He says 'Sears has a quality-of-earnings' issue.

Poneman is referring to a $2 billion reserve for credit losses that Sears set up in 1993. As it turned out, the reserve was higher than needed. Three years later, Sears still had a nearly $1 billion reserve on its balance sheet. That was nearly twice the size of reserves at most credit-card companies as a percentage of receivables. The credit-card reserve was part of a big bath that included restructuring charges that Sears took in 1993. Such charges and reserves can be a big help for a new CEO (which Sears had) who wishes to show a pattern of improving results in future years. Poneman says the big addition to reserves "moved income out of 1992 and 1993 and into 1995 and 1996." Why is that bad? The overly large reserve allowed Sears to prop up its earnings at a time when losses in its credit-card unit were soaring. Sears' credit-card delinquencies had risen by $420 million in 1996. Poneman asserts that "Considering that increased delinquencies exceed year-to-date increased earnings, it could be argued that the increase in Sears' year-to-date earnings has depended entirely on its over-reserved condition."

Accounts receivable turnover reveals how many times receivables have turned (been collected) during the period. More turns indicate that receivables are being collected more quickly.

A companion measure to accounts receivable turnover is the **average collection period (ACP)** for accounts receivable, also called *days sales outstanding*, which is defined as:

$$\text{Average Collection Period} = \text{Accounts Receivable/Average Daily Sales}$$

where average daily sales equals sales divided by 365 days. The average collection period indicates how long, on average, the receivables are outstanding before being collected.[4]

To illustrate, assume that sales are $1,000, ending accounts receivable are $230, and average accounts receivable are $200. The accounts receivable turnover is 5, computed as $1,000/$200, and the average collection period (days sales outstanding) is 84 days, computed as $230/($1,000/365 days).

The accounts receivable turnover and the average collection period yield valuable insights on at least two dimensions:

1. *Receivables quality* Changes in receivable turnover (and collection period) speak to accounts receivable quality. If turnover slows (collection period lengthens), the reason could be deterioration in collectibility. However, there are at least three alternative explanations:

   a. *A seller can extend its credit terms*. If the seller is attempting to enter new markets or take market share from competitors, it may extend credit terms to attract buyers.

   b. *A seller can take on longer-paying customers*. For example, facing increased competition, many computer and automobile companies began leasing their products, thus reducing customers' cash outlays and stimulating sales. Moving away from cash sales and toward leasing reduced receivables turnover and increased the collection period.

---

[4] The average collection period computation in this Module uses *ending* accounts receivable. This focuses the analysis on the most current receivables. Cisco uses a variant of this approach, described in its MD&A section as follows: Accounts receivable/Average annualized 4Q sales (or AR/[(4Q Sales × 4)/365]). Arguably, Cisco's variant focuses even more on the most recent collection period because ending accounts receivable relate more closely to 4Q sales than to reported annual sales. Most analysts use the reported annual sales instead of the annualized 4Q sales because the former are easily accessed in financial statement databases. As an alternative, we could also examine average daily sales in *average* accounts receivable (Average accounts receivable/Average daily sales). The approach we use in the text addresses the average collection period of *current* accounts receivable, and the latter approach examines the average collection period of *average* accounts receivable. The "correct" ratio depends on the issue we wish to investigate. It is important to choose the formula that best answers the question we are asking.

c. *The seller can increase the allowance provision.* Receivables turnover is sometimes computed using net receivables (after the allowance for uncollectible accounts). Overestimating the provision reduces net receivables and increases the turnover ratio. Consequently, an apparent improvement in turnover could be incorrectly attributed to improved operating performance rather than a decline in the quality of the receivable portfolio.

2. *Asset utilization* Asset turnover is an important financial performance measure used both by managers for internal performance goals, as well as by the market in evaluating companies. High-performing companies must be both effective (controlling margins and operating expenses) and efficient (getting the most out of their asset base). An increase in receivables ties up cash. As well, slower-turning receivables carry increased risk of loss. One of the first "low-hanging fruits" that companies pursue in efforts to improve overall asset utilization is efficiency in receivables collection.

The following chart shows the average collection period for accounts receivable of Cisco and six peer competitors that Cisco indentifies in its 10-K.

Average Collection Period for Cisco and Competitors

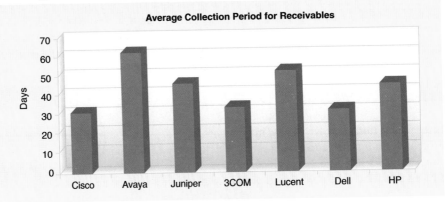

Cisco's average collection period of 33 days compares favorably with its primary competitors. Only Cisco, 3COM and Dell report collection periods less than 40 days.

To appreciate differences in average collection periods across industries, let's compare the average collection periods across a number of industries as follows:

Accounts Receivable Turnover for Different Industries

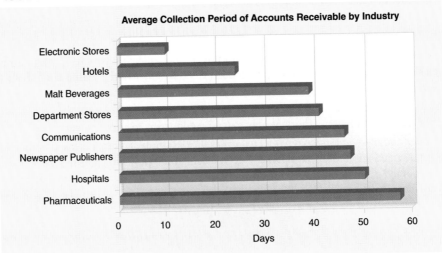

Electronic stores and hotels have the shortest collection periods. For those industries, receivables are minimal because sales are made mainly via cash, check or credit card. Most of the other industries in the table have collection periods ranging from 30 to 60 days. This corresponds with typical credit terms offered on commercial transactions. Pharmaceutical companies and hospitals have longer collection periods because they often require payment from third party insurers.

> **MANAGERIAL DECISION**   **You Are the Receivables Manager**
>
> You are analyzing your receivables turnover report for the period and you are concerned that the average collection period is lengthening. What specific actions can you take to reduce the average collection period? [Answer, p. 6-36]

MID-MODULE REVIEW 1

At December 31, 2007, assume that Lucent Technologies had a balance of $770,000 in its Accounts Receivable account and a balance of $7,000 in its Allowance for Uncollectible Accounts. The company then analyzed and aged its accounts receivable as shown below. Assume that Lucent experienced past losses as follows: 1% of current balances, 5% of balances 1-60 days past due, 15% of balances 61-180 days past due, and 40% of balances over 180 days past due. The company bases its provision for credit losses on the aging analysis.

Current	$468,000
1-60 days past due	244,000
61-180 days past due	38,000
Over 180 days past due	20,000
Total accounts receivable	$770,000

Required

1. What amount of uncollectible accounts (bad debts) expense will Lucent report in its 2007 income statement?
2. Show how Accounts Receivable and the Allowance for Uncollectible Accounts appear in its December 31, 2007, balance sheet.
3. Assume that Lucent's allowance for uncollectible accounts has maintained an historical average of 2% of gross accounts receivable. How do you interpret the current allowance percentage?

Solution

1. As of December 31, 2007:

Current	$468,000	× 1% =	$ 4,680	
1-60 days past due	244,000	× 5% =	12,200	
61-180 days past due	38,000	× 15% =	5,700	
Over 180 days past due	20,000	× 40% =	8,000	
Amount required			$ 30,580	
Unused allowance balance			7,000	
Provision			$ 23,580	2007 bad debts expense

2. Current assets section of balance sheet:

Accounts receivable, net of $30,580 in allowances . . .	$739,420

3. The information here reveals that Lucent has markedly increased the percentage of the allowance for uncollectible accounts to gross accounts receivable-from the historical 2% to the current 4% ($30,580/$770,000). There are at least two possible interpretations:

a. The quality of Lucent's receivables has declined. Possible causes include the following: (1) Sales have stagnated and the company is selling to lower quality accounts to maintain sales volume; (2) It may have introduced new products for which average credit losses are higher; and (3) Its administration of accounts receivable has become lax.

   b. The company has intentionally increased its allowance account above the level needed for expected future losses so as to reduce current period income and "bank" that income for future periods (income shifting).

INVENTORY

LO2 Explain accounting for inventories and the effects on the balance sheet and income statement from different inventory costing methods.

The second major component of operating working capital is inventory. To help frame this discussion, we refer to the following graphic that highlights inventory, a major asset for manufacturers and merchandisers. The graphic also highlights cost of goods sold on the income statement, which reflects the matching of inventory costs to related sales. This section explains the accounting, reporting, and analysis of inventory and related items.

Income Statement	Balance Sheet	
Sales	Cash	Current liabilities
Cost of goods sold	Accounts receivable, net	Long-term liabilities
Selling, general & administrative	Inventory	
Income taxes	Property, plant, and equipment, net	Shareholders' equity
Net income	Investments	

Inventory is reported on the balance sheet at its purchase price or the cost to manufacture goods that are internally produced. Inventory costs vary over time with changes in market conditions. Consequently, the cost per unit of the goods available for sale varies from period to period—even if the quantity of goods available remains the same.

When inventory is purchased or produced, it is "capitalized." That is, it is carried on the balance sheet as an asset until it is sold, at which time its cost is transferred from the balance sheet to the income statement as an expense (cost of goods sold). The process by which costs are removed from the balance sheet is important. For example, if higher cost units are transferred from the balance sheet, then cost of goods sold is higher and gross profit (sales less cost of goods sold) is lower. Conversely, if lower cost units are transferred to cost of goods sold, gross profit is higher. The remainder of this section discusses the accounting for inventory including the mechanics, reporting, and analysis of inventory costing.

Capitalization of Inventory Cost

Capitalization means that a cost is recorded on the balance sheet and is not immediately expensed on the income statement. Once costs are capitalized, they remain on the balance sheet as assets until they are used up, at which time they are transferred from the balance sheet to the income statement as expense. If costs are capitalized rather than expensed, then assets, current income, and current equity are all higher.

For purchased inventories (such as merchandise), the amount of cost capitalized is the purchase price. For manufacturers, cost capitalization is more difficult, as **manufacturing costs** consist of three components: cost of direct materials used in the product, cost of direct labor to manufacture the product, and manufacturing overhead. Direct materials cost is relatively easy to compute. Design specifications list the components of each product, and their purchase costs are readily determined. The direct labor cost per unit of inventory is based on how long each unit takes to construct and the rates for each labor class working on that product. Overhead costs are also capitalized into inventory, and include the costs of plant asset depreciation, utilities, supervisory personnel, and other costs that contribute to manufacturing activities—that is, all costs of manufacturing other than direct materials and direct labor. (How these costs are assigned to individual units and across multiple products is a *managerial accounting* topic.)

When inventories are sold, their costs are transferred from the balance sheet to the income statement as cost of goods sold (COGS). COGS is then deducted from sales to yield **gross profit**:

$$\text{Gross Profit} = \text{Sales} - \text{Cost of Goods Sold}$$

The manner in which inventory costs are transferred from the balance sheet to the income statement affects both the level of inventories reported on the balance sheet and the amount of gross profit (and net income) reported on the income statement.

Inventory Costing Methods

Exhibit 6.5 shows the computation of cost of goods sold.

EXHIBIT 6.5	Cost of Goods Sold Computation

	Beginning inventory (prior period balance sheet)
+	Inventory purchased and/or produced
	Cost of goods available for sale
−	Ending inventory (current period balance sheet)
	Cost of goods sold (current income statement)

The cost of inventory available at the beginning of a period is a carryover from the ending inventory balance of the prior period. Current period inventory purchases (or costs of newly manufactured inventories) are added to the beginning inventory balance, yielding the total cost of goods (inventory) available for sale. Then, the goods available are either sold, and end up in cost of goods sold for the period (reported on the income statement), or the goods available remain unsold and are still in inventory at the end of the period (reported on the balance sheet). Exhibit 6.6 shows this cost flow graphically.

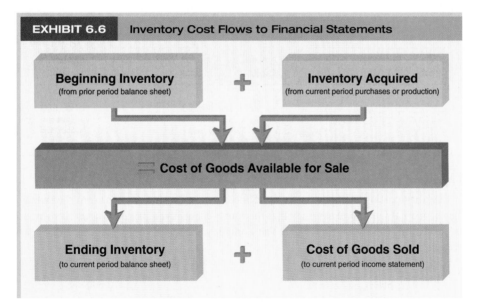

EXHIBIT 6.6   Inventory Cost Flows to Financial Statements

Understanding the flow of inventory costs is important. If all inventory purchased or manufactured during the period is sold, then COGS is equal to the cost of the goods purchased or manufactured. However, when inventory remains at the end of a period, companies must distinguish the cost of the inventories that were sold from the cost of the inventories that remain. GAAP allows for several options.

To illustrate, Exhibit 6.7 illustrates the partial inventory records of a company.

EXHIBIT 6.7	Summary Inventory Records		
Inventory on January 1, 2007.	500 units	@ $100 per unit	$ 50,000
Inventory purchased in 2007	200 units	@ $150 per unit	30,000
Total cost of goods available for sale in 2007	700 units		$ 80,000
Inventory sold in 2007	450 units	@ $250 per unit	$112,500

This company began the period with 500 units of inventory that were purchased or manufactured for $50,000 ($100 each). During the period the company purchased and/or manufactured an additional 200 units costing $30,000. The total cost of goods available for sale for this period equals $80,000.

The company sold 450 units during 2007 for $250 per unit for total sales of $112,500. Accordingly, the company must remove the cost of the 450 units sold from the inventory account on the balance sheet and match this cost against the revenues generated from the sale. An important question is which costs should management remove from the balance sheet and report as cost of goods sold in the income statement? Three inventory costing methods (FIFO, LIFO and average cost) are common and all are acceptable under GAAP.

First-In, First-Out (FIFO)

The FIFO inventory costing method transfers costs from inventory in the order that they were initially recorded. That is, FIFO assumes that the first costs recorded in inventory (first-in) are the first costs transferred from inventory (first-out). Applying FIFO to the data in Exhibit 6.7 means that the costs of the 450 units sold comes from *beginning* inventory, which consists of 500 units costing $100 each. The company's cost of goods sold and gross profit, using FIFO, is computed as follows:

Sales.	$112,500
COGS (450 @ $100 each).	45,000
Gross profit.	$ 67,500

The cost remaining in inventory and reported on the 2007 year-end balance sheet is $35,000 ($80,000 goods available for sale less $45,000 COGS). The following financial statement effects template captures the transaction.

		Balance Sheet						Income Statement		
Transaction	Cash Asset	+ Noncash Assets	= Liabil- ities	+ Contrib. Capital	+ Earned Capital		Rev- enues	− Expen- ses	= Net Income
Sold 450 units using FIFO costing (450 @ $100 each)		−45,000 Inventory =			−45,000 Retained Earnings			+45,000 − Cost of Goods Sold	= −45,000

COGS 45,000
  INV   45,000
      COGS
45,000 |
      INV
      | 45,000

Last-In, First-Out (LIFO)

The LIFO inventory costing method transfers the most recent inventory costs from the balance sheet to COGS. That is, the LIFO method assumes that the most recent inventory purchases (last-in) are the first costs transferred from inventory (first-out). The company's cost of goods sold and gross profit, using LIFO, is computed as follows:

Sales.		$112,500
COGS: 200 @ $150 per unit	$30,000	
250 @ $100 per unit	25,000	55,000
Gross profit.		$ 57,500

The cost remaining in inventory and reported on the company's 2007 balance sheet is $25,000 (computed as $80,000 − $55,000). This is reflected in our financial statements effects template as follows.

		Balance Sheet						Income Statement		
Transaction	Cash Asset	+ Noncash Assets	= Liabil- ities	+ Contrib. Capital	+ Earned Capital		Rev- enues	− Expen- ses	= Net Income
Sold 450 units using LIFO costing (200 @ $150) + (250 @ $100)		−55,000 Inventory =			−55,000 Retained Earnings			+55,000 − Cost of Goods Sold	= −55,000

COGS 55,000
  INV   55,000
      COGS
55,000 |
      INV
      | 55,000

Average Cost (AC)

The average cost method computes the cost of goods sold as an average of the cost to purchase or manufacture all of the inventories that were available for sale during the period. To calculate the average cost of $114.286 per unit the company divides the total cost of goods available for sale by the number of units available for sale ($80,000/700 units). The company's sales, cost of sales, and gross profit follow.

Sales.	$112,500
COGS (450 @ $114.286 per unit).	51,429
Gross profit.	$ 61,071

The cost remaining in inventory and reported on the company's 2007 balance sheet is $28,571 ($80,000 − $51,429). This is reflected in our financial statements effects template as follows.

	Balance Sheet						Income Statement		
Transaction	Cash Asset	+ Noncash Assets	= Liabil- ities	+ Contrib. Capital	+ Earned Capital		Rev- enues	− Expen- ses	= Net Income
Sold 450 units using average cost method (450 @ $114.286)		−51,429 Inventory	=		−51,429 Retained Earnings			+51,429 Cost of Goods Sold	− = −51,429

COGS 51,429
INV   51,429

COGS
51,429 |
          INV
          | 51,429

It is important to understand that the inventory costing method a company chooses is independent of the actual flow of inventory. The method choice determines COGS and ending inventory but not the actual physical inventory sold. For example, many grocery chains use LIFO inventory but certainly do not sell the freshest products first. (Companies do not frequently change inventory costing methods. Companies can adopt a new inventory costing method if doing so enhances the quality of the company's financial reports. Also, IRS regulations prohibit certain inventory costing method changes.)

Footnote Disclosures

Notes to financial statements describe the inventory accounting method a company uses. To illustrate, Cisco reports $1,297 million in inventory on its 2005 balance sheet as a current asset. Cisco includes a general footnote on inventory along with more specific disclosures in other footnotes. Following is an excerpt from Cisco's general footnote on inventories.

> **Inventories.** Inventories are stated at the lower of cost or market. Cost is computed on a first-in, first-out basis. The Company provides inventory allowances based on excess and obsolete inventories determined primarily by future demand forecasts. The allowance is measured as the difference between the cost of the inventory and market based upon assumptions about future demand and charged to the provision for inventory, which is a component of cost of sales. At the point of the loss recognition, a new, lower-cost basis for that inventory is established, and subsequent changes in facts and circumstances do not result in the restoration or increase in that newly established cost basis.

This footnote includes at least two items of interest for our analysis of inventory:

1. Cisco uses the FIFO method of inventory costing.
2. Inventories are reported at the lower of cost or market (LCM), which means that inventory is written down if its replacement cost, referred to as 'market,' declines below its balance sheet cost (see impairment cost discussion on the following page).

For example, if the current value of Cisco's inventories is less than its reported cost, Cisco would set up an "allowance" for inventories, similar to the allowance for uncollectible accounts. The inventory allowance reduces the reported inventory amount to the current (lower) market value.

Cisco also includes a more detailed inventory footnote as follows:

$ millions		July 30, 2005		July 31, 2004
Inventories				
Raw materials		$ 82		$ 58
Work in process		431		416
Finished goods				
Distributor inventory and deferred cost of sales. . . .	$385		$316	
Manufacturing finished goods	184		206	
Total finished goods		569		522
Service related spares		180		177
Demonstration systems		35		34
Total		$1,297		$1,207

This disclosure separately reports inventory costs by the following stages in the production cycle:

- *Raw materials and supplies* These are costs of direct materials and inputs into the production process including, for example, chemicals in raw state, plastic and steel for manufacturing, and incidental direct materials such as screws and lubricants.

- *Work in process* These are costs of partly finished products (also called work-in-progress).

- *Finished goods* These are the costs of products that are completed and awaiting sale.

Cisco's raw materials and work-in-process inventories have remained at 2004 levels despite a $2 billion increase in sales. Finished goods inventory increased slightly during the year.

Why do companies disclose such details about inventory? First, investment in inventory is typically large—markedly impacting both balance sheets and income statements. Second, risks of inventory losses are often high, due to technical obsolescence and consumer tastes. This is an important issue for a company such as Cisco that operates in a technology-sensitive industry. Indeed, Cisco reported a loss of over $2 billion in 2001 when the tech bubble burst, demand dried up, and the company had to write down obsolete inventories. Third, inventory details can provide insight into future performance—both good and bad. Fourth, high inventory levels result in substantial costs for the company, such as the following:

- Financing costs to hold inventories (when not purchased on credit)
- Storage costs (such as warehousing and related facilities)
- Handling costs (including wages)
- Insurance costs

Consequently, companies seek to minimize inventory levels provided this does not exceed the cost of holding insufficient inventory, called stock-outs. Stock-outs result in lost sales and production delays if machines and employees must be reconfigured to fill order backlogs.

Lower of Cost or Market

Cisco's inventory disclosures refer to the cost of its inventories not exceeding market value. Companies must write down the carrying amount of inventories on the balance sheet *if* the reported cost (using FIFO, for example) exceeds market value (determined by current replacement cost). This process is called reporting inventories at the **lower of cost or market** and creates the following financial statement effects:

- Inventory book value is written down to current market value (replacement cost); reducing inventory and total assets.
- Inventory write-down is reflected as an expense (part of cost of goods sold) on the income statement; reducing current period gross profit, income, and equity.

To illustrate, assume that a company has inventory on its balance sheet at a cost of $27,000. Management learns that the inventory's replacement cost is $23,000 and writes inventories down to a balance of $23,000. The following financial statement effects template shows the adjustment.

Transaction	Balance Sheet					Income Statement			
	Cash Asset +	Noncash Assets =	Liabil- ities +	Contrib. Capital +	Earned Capital	Rev- enues −	Expen- ses =	Net Income	
Write down inventory from $27,000 to $23,000.		−4,000 Inventory =			−4,000 Retained Earnings		+4,000 Cost of Goods Sold	= −4,000	

```
COGS   4,000
     INV     4,000
         COGS
4,000 |
         INV
         |  4,000
```

The inventory write-down (a noncash expense) is reflected in cost of goods sold and reduces gross profit by $4,000. Inventory write-downs are included in cost of goods sold. They are *not* reported in selling, general, and administrative expenses, which is common for other asset write-downs. The most common occurrence of inventory write-downs is in connection with restructuring activities.

The write-down of inventories can potentially shift income from one period to another. If, for example, inventories were written down below current replacement cost, future gross profit would be increased via lower future cost of goods sold. GAAP anticipates this possibility by requiring that inventories not be written down below a floor that is equal to net realizable value less a normal markup. Although this still allows some discretion (and the ability to manage income), the auditors must assess net realizable value and markups.

Financial Statement Effects of Inventory Costing

This section describes the financial statement effects of different inventory costing methods.

Income Statement Effects

The three inventory costing methods yield differing levels of gross profit as Exhibit 6.8 shows.

EXHIBIT 6.8	Income Effects from Inventory Costing Methods		
	Sales	Cost of Goods Sold	Gross Profit
FIFO	$112,500	$45,000	$67,500
LIFO	112,500	55,000	57,500
Average cost	112,500	51,429	61,071

Recall that inventory costs rose during this period from $100 per unit to $150 per unit. The higher gross profit reported under FIFO arises because FIFO matches older, lower cost inventory against current selling prices. To generalize: in an inflationary environment, FIFO yields higher gross profit than LIFO or average cost methods do.

In recent years, the gross profit impact from using the FIFO method has been minimal due to lower rates of inflation and increased management focus on reducing inventory quantities through improved manufacturing processes and better inventory controls. The FIFO gross profit effect can still arise, however, with companies subject to high inflation and slow inventory turnover.

Balance Sheet Effects

In our illustration above, the ending inventory using LIFO is less than that reported using FIFO. In periods of rising costs, LIFO inventories are markedly lower than under FIFO. As a result, balance sheets using LIFO do not accurately represent the cost that a company would incur to replace its current investment in inventories.

Caterpillar (CAT), for example, reports 2005 inventories under LIFO costing $5,224 million. As disclosed in the footnotes to its 10-K, if CAT valued these inventories using FIFO, the reported amount would be $2,345 million greater, a 45% increase. This suggests that CAT's balance sheet omits over $2,345 million in inventories.

Cash Flow Effects

Unlike for most other accounting method choices, inventory costing methods affect taxable income and, thus, taxes paid. When a company adopts LIFO in its tax filings, the IRS requires it to also use LIFO for financial reporting purposes (in its 10-K). This requirement is known as the *LIFO conformity rule*. In an inflationary economy, using FIFO results in higher taxable income and, consequently, higher taxes payable. Conversely, using LIFO reduces the tax liability.

Caterpillar, Inc. discloses the following inventory information in its 2005 10-K:

Inventories are stated at the lower of cost or market. Cost is principally determined using the last-in, first-out (LIFO) method. The value of inventories on the LIFO basis represented about 80% of total inventories at December 31, 2005, 2004 and 2003. If the FIFO (first-in, first-out) method had been in use, inventories would have been $2,345 million, $2,124 million and $1,863 million higher than reported at December 31, 2005, 2004 and 2003, respectively.

CAT uses LIFO for most of its inventories.[5] The use of LIFO has reduced the carrying amount of 2005 inventories by $2,345 million. Had it used FIFO, its inventories would have been reported at $7,569 million ($5,224 million + $2,345 million) rather than the $5,224 million that is reported on its balance sheet as of 2005. This difference, referred to as the **LIFO reserve**, is the amount that must be added to LIFO inventories to adjust them to their FIFO value.

FIFO Inventory = LIFO Inventory + LIFO Reserve

This relation also impacts cost of goods sold (COGS) as follows:

FIFO COGS = LIFO COGS − Increase in LIFO Reserve (or + Decrease)

Use of LIFO reduced CAT's inventories by $2,345 million, resulting in a cumulative increase in cost of goods sold and a cumulative decrease in gross profit and pretax profit of that same amount.[6] Because CAT also uses LIFO for tax purposes, the decrease in pretax profits reduced CAT's cumulative tax bill by about $821 million ($2,345 million × 35% assumed corporate tax rate). This had real cash-flow consequences: CAT's cumulative operating cash flow was $821 million higher because CAT used LIFO instead of FIFO. The increased cash flow from tax savings is often cited as a compelling reason for management to adopt LIFO.

Because companies use different inventory costing methods, their financial statements are often not comparable. The problem is most serious when companies hold large amounts of inventory and when prices markedly rise or fall. To compare companies using different inventory costing methods, say LIFO and FIFO, we need to adjust the LIFO numbers to their FIFO equivalents or vice versa. For example, one way to compare CAT with another company that uses FIFO, is to add CAT's LIFO reserve to its LIFO inventory. As explained above, this $2,345 million increase in 2005 inventories would have increased its cumulative pretax profits by $2,345 million and taxes by $821 million. Thus, to adjust the 2005 balance sheet we increase inventories by $2,345 million, tax liabilities by $821 million (the extra taxes CAT would have had to pay under FIFO), and equity by the difference of $1,524 million (computed as $2,345 − $821).

To adjust CAT's 2005 income statement from LIFO to FIFO, we use the change in LIFO reserve. For CAT, the LIFO reserve increased by $221 million during 2005, from $2,124 million in 2004 to $2,345 million in 2004. This means that had it been using FIFO, its COGS would have been $221 million lower, and 2005 gross profit and pretax income would have been $221 million higher. In 2005, CAT would have paid $77 million more in taxes had it used FIFO ($221 million × 35% assumed tax rate).

---

[5] Neither the IRS nor GAAP requires use of a single inventory costing method. That is, companies are allowed to, and frequently do, use different inventory costing methods for different types of inventory (such as spare parts versus finished goods).

[6] Recall: Cost of Goods Sold = Beginning Inventories + Purchases − Ending Inventories. Thus, as ending inventories decrease, cost of goods sold increases.

RESEARCH INSIGHT | **LIFO and Stock Prices**

The value-relevance of inventory disclosures depends at least partly on whether investors rely more on the income statement or the balance sheet to assess future cash flows. Under LIFO, cost of goods sold reflects current costs, whereas FIFO ending inventory reflects current costs. This implies that LIFO enhances the usefulness of the income statement to the detriment of the balance sheet. This trade-off partly motivates the required LIFO reserve disclosure (the adjustment necessary to restate LIFO ending inventory and cost of good sold to FIFO). Research suggests that LIFO-based income statements better reflect stock prices than do FIFO income statements that are restated using the LIFO reserve. Research also shows a negative relation between stock prices and LIFO reserve—meaning that higher magnitudes of LIFO reserve are associated with lower stock prices. This is consistent with the LIFO reserve being viewed as an inflation indicator (for either current or future inventory costs), which the market views as detrimental to company value.

Tools of Inventory Analysis

This section describes several useful tools for analysis of inventory and related accounts.

Gross profit analysis

The **gross profit margin (GPM)** is gross profit divided by sales. This important ratio is closely monitored by management and outsiders. Exhibit 6.9 shows the gross profit margin on Cisco's product sales for the past three years.

EXHIBIT 6.9	**Gross Profit Margin for Cisco**		
	2005	**2004**	**2003**
Product sales	$20,853	$18,550	$15,565
Product cost of goods sold	6,758	5,766	4,594
Gross profit.	$14,095	$12,784	$10,971
Gross profit margin.	67.6%	68.9%	70.5%

The gross profit margin is commonly used instead of the dollar amount of gross profit as it allows for comparisons across companies and over time. A decline in GPM is usually cause for concern since it indicates that the company has less ability to pass on increased product cost to customers or that the company is not effectively managing product costs. Some possible reasons for a GPM decline follow:

- *Product line is stale.* Perhaps it is out of fashion and the company must resort to markdowns to reduce overstocked inventories. Or, perhaps the product lines have lost their technological edge, yielding reduced demand.

- *New competitors enter the market.* Perhaps substitute products are now available from competitors, yielding increased pressure to reduce selling prices.

- *General decline in economic activity.* Perhaps an economic downturn reduces product demand. The recession of the early 2000s led to reduced gross profits for many companies.

- *Inventory is overstocked.* Perhaps the company overproduced goods and finds itself in an overstock position. This can require reduced selling prices to move inventory.

- *Manufacturing costs have increased.* This could be due to poor planning, production glitches, or unfavorable supply chain reconfiguration.

- *Changes in product mix.* Perhaps the company is selling a higher proportion of low margin goods.

Cisco's gross profit margin on product sales has declined by 2.9 percentage points over the past two years. Following is Cisco's discussion of its gross profit situation taken from its 2005 10-K:

Product Gross Margin   Product gross margin percentage decreased by 1.3%. Changes in the mix of products sold decreased product gross margin by approximately 2.5% due to higher sales of certain lower-margin switching products and increased sales of home networking products. Product pricing reductions and sales discounts decreased product gross margin by approximately 2%. In addition, a higher provision for warranty and a higher provision for inventory decreased product gross margin by approximately 0.5%. However, lower overall manufacturing costs related to lower component costs and value engineering and other manufacturing-related costs increased product gross margin by approximately 2%. Value engineering is the process by which the production costs are reduced through component redesign, board configuration, test processes, and transformation processes. Higher shipment volumes also increased product gross margin by approximately 1.5%.

Product gross margin may continue to be adversely affected in the future by: changes in the mix of products sold, including further periods of increased growth of some of our lower-margin products; introduction of new products, including products with price-performance advantages; our ability to reduce production costs; entry into new markets, including markets with different pricing and cost structures; changes in distribution channels; price competition, including competitors from Asia and especially China; changes in geographic mix; sales discounts; increases in material or labor costs; excess inventory and obsolescence charges; warranty costs; changes in shipment volume; loss of cost savings due to changes in component pricing; impact of value engineering; inventory holding charges; and how well we execute on our strategic and operating plans.

Cisco's gross profit margin declined in 2005 because product mix changed toward lower margin products, the company faced increased price competition and increased product warranty expense, and management increased the provision (expense) for inventory obsolescence. The gross profit margin decline was partially offset by reductions in the cost to manufacture and by higher shipment volumes that spread out manufacturing overhead over a greater unit volume. Cisco's report includes a general discussion of factors that can adversely affect gross profit margins: changes in product mix, introduction of new products at lower introductory prices to gain market share, increases in production costs, sales discounts, inventory obsolescence and warranty costs, and changes in production volume.

Competitive pressures mean that companies rarely have the opportunity to affect gross profit with price increases. Improvements in gross profit on existing product lines typically arise from a result of better management of supply chains, production processes, or distribution networks. Companies that succeed typically do so because of better performance on basic business processes. This is one of Cisco's primary objectives.

Inventory Turnover

Inventory turnover (INVT) reflects the management of inventory and is computed as follows:

Inventory Turnover = Cost of Goods Sold/Average Inventory

Cost of goods sold is in the numerator because inventory is reported at cost. Inventory turnover indicates how many times inventory turns (is sold) during a period. More turns indicate that inventory is being sold more quickly, which decreases the risk of obsolete inventory and increases liquidity.

Average inventory days outstanding (AIDO), also called *days inventory outstanding*, is a companion measure to inventory turnover and is computed as follows:

Average Inventory Days Outstanding = Inventory/Average Daily Cost of Goods Sold

where average daily cost of goods sold equals cost of goods sold divided by 365 days.[7]

Average inventory days outstanding indicates how long, on average, inventories are *on the shelves* before being sold. For example, if cost of goods sold is $1,200 and inventories are $300, inventories are on the shelves 91.25 days ($300/[$1,200/365 days]) on average. This performance might be an acceptable turnover for the retail fashion industry where firms need to sell out inventories each retail selling season,

---

[7] Similar to the average receivables collection period, this formula examines the average daily COGS in *ending* inventories to focus analysis on current inventories. One can also examine average daily COGS in *average* inventories (Average inventories/Average daily COGS). These two approaches address different issues: the first addresses the average days outstanding of *current ending* inventories, and the second examines the average days outstanding of *average* inventories. It is important that we first identify the issue under investigation and then choose the formula that best addresses that issue.

but it would not be acceptable for the grocery industry where perishability is a concern, or for Cisco where obsolescence is of concern.

Overall, analysis of inventory turnover and days outstanding is important for at least two reasons:

1. *Inventory quality.* Inventory turnover can be compared over time and across competitors. Higher turnover is viewed favorably, because it implies that products are salable, preferably without undue discounting (we would compare profit margins to assess discounting). Conversely, lower turnover implies that inventory is on the shelves for a longer period of time, perhaps from excessive purchases or production, missed fashion trends or technological advances, increased competition, and so forth. Our conclusions about higher or lower turnover must consider alternative explanations including the following:

   • Product mix can include more (or less) higher margin, slower turning inventories. This can occur from business acquisitions that consolidate different types of inventory.

   • A company can change its promotion policies. Increased, effective advertising is likely to increase inventory turnover. Advertising expense is in SG&A, not COGS. This means the additional advertising cost is in operating expenses, but the benefit is in gross profit and turnover. If the promotion campaign is successful, the positive effects in margin and turnover should offset the promotion cost in SG&A.

   • A company can realize improvements in manufacturing efficiency and lower investments in direct materials and work-in-process inventories. Such improvements reduce inventory and, consequently, increase inventory turnover. Although a good sign, it does not yield any information about the desirability of a company's product line.

2. *Asset utilization.* Companies strive to optimize their inventory investment. Carrying too much inventory is expensive, and too little inventory risks stock-outs and lost sales (current and future). Companies can make the following operational changes to reduce inventory.

   • Improved manufacturing processes can eliminate bottlenecks and the consequent build-up of work-in-process inventories.

   • Just-in-time (JIT) deliveries from suppliers, that provide raw materials to the production line when needed, can reduce the level of raw materials and associated holding costs.

   • Demand-pull production, in which raw materials are released into the production process when final goods are demanded by customers instead of producing for estimated demand, can reduce inventory levels. **Dell Computer**, for example, does not manufacture a computer until it receives the customer's order; thus, Dell produces for actual, rather than estimated, demand.

Reducing inventories reduces inventory carrying costs, thus improving profitability and increasing cash flows. The reduction in inventory is reflected as an operating cash inflow in the statement of cash flows.

There is normal tension between the sales side of a company, that argues for depth and breadth of inventory, and the finance side that monitors inventory carrying costs and seeks to maximize cash flow. Companies, therefore, seek to *optimize* inventory investment, not minimize it.

Following is a chart comparing Cisco's average inventory days outstanding with its peer companies.

Average Inventory Days Outstanding for Cisco and Competitors

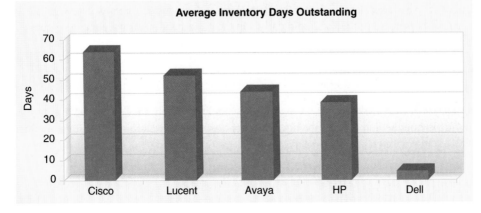

Cisco's average inventory days outstanding of 64 does not compare favorably with its peers. Cisco's 2005 10-K provides the following comments regarding inventory management :

> Inventory management remains an area of focus as we balance the need to maintain strategic inventory levels to ensure competitive lead times against the risk of inventory obsolescence because of rapidly changing technology and customer requirements. We believe the amount of our inventory is appropriate for our current revenue level.

Dell's average inventory days outstanding of 5 is markedly lower than other companies shown in this graph. Dell has traditionally focused on excellence in this area, and views this as a competitive advantage. Dell's 2005 10-K reports the following:

> Dell believes the direct business model is the most effective model for providing solutions that address customer needs. In addition, Dell's flexible, build-to-order manufacturing process enables Dell to reduce inventory levels. This allows Dell to rapidly introduce the latest relevant technology more quickly than companies with slow-moving, indirect distribution channels, and to rapidly pass on component cost savings directly to customers . . . Dell's direct business model allows the company to maintain a leading asset management system in comparison to its major competitors. Dell is capable of minimizing inventory risk while collecting amounts due from customers before paying vendors, thus allowing the company to generate annual cash flows from operating activities that typically exceed net income.

It is also instructive to compare the average inventory days outstanding for selected industries.

Inventory Turnover for Companies from Different Industries

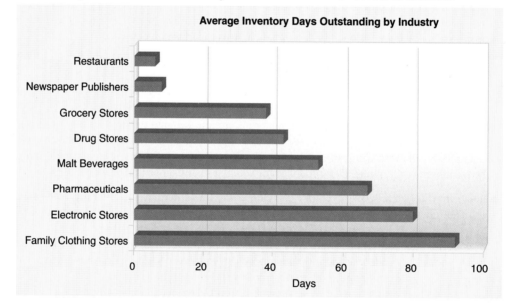

Restaurants and newspaper publishers carry only a few days' inventory at any point in time. Restaurants are mindful of the perishable nature of their food products, and inventories are low in the publishing industry because newspapers are printed and sold daily. On the other hand, pharmaceuticals, electronic stores, and family clothing stores must carry high levels of inventory to support customer demand.

MANAGERIAL DECISION   **You Are the Plant Manager**

You are analyzing your inventory turnover report for the month and are concerned that the average inventory days outstanding is lengthening. What actions can you take to reduce average inventory days outstanding? [Answer, p. 6-37]

LIFO Liquidations

When companies acquire inventory at different costs, they are required to maintain each cost level as a separate inventory pool or layer (for example, there are the $100 and $150 units in our Exhibit 6.7 illustration). When companies reduce inventory levels, older inventory costs flow to the income statement. When companies use LIFO, older costs are often markedly different than current replacement costs. Given the usual inflationary environment, sales of older pools often yield a boost to gross profit as older, lower costs are matched against current selling prices on the income statement.

The increase in gross profit resulting from a reduction of inventory quantities in the presence of rising costs is called **LIFO liquidation.** The effect of LIFO liquidation is evident in the following footnote from General Motors Corporation's 2005 10-K:

> Inventories are stated generally at cost, which is not in excess of market. The cost of approximately 67% of U.S. inventories is determined by the last-in, first-out (LIFO) method. Generally, the cost of all other inventories is determined by either the first-in, first-out (FIFO) or average cost methods.
>
> During 2005 and 2004, U.S. LIFO eligible inventory quantities were reduced. This reduction resulted in a liquidation of LIFO inventory quantities carried at lower costs prevailing in prior years as compared with the cost of 2005 and 2004 purchases, the effect of which decreased cost of goods sold by approximately $100 million, pre-tax, in both 2005 and 2004.

GM reports that reductions in inventory quantities led to the sale (at current selling prices) of products that carried very low costs from prior years. As a result of these inventory reductions, pretax income increased by $100 million from lower COGS. In this case, the inventory LIFO liquidation yielded a profit increase. We must be aware, however, of potentially different income effects from LIFO liquidations when inventory costs fluctuate.

MID-MODULE REVIEW 2

At the beginning of the current period, assume that Avaya, Inc., holds 1,000 units of its only product with a unit cost of $18. A summary of purchases during the current period follows:

		Units	Unit Cost	Cost
Beginning Inventory		1,000	$18.00	$18,000
Purchases:	#1	1,800	18.25	32,850
	#2	800	18.50	14,800
	#3	1,200	19.00	22,800
Goods available for sale		4,800		$88,450

During the current period, Avaya sells 2,800 units.

Required

1. Assume that Avaya uses the first-in, first-out (FIFO) method. Compute the cost of goods sold for the current period and the ending inventory balance.
2. Assume that Avaya uses the last-in, first-out (LIFO) method. Compute the cost of goods sold for the current period and the ending inventory balance.
3. Assume that Avaya uses the average cost (AC) method. Compute the cost of goods sold for the current period and the ending inventory balance.
4. As manager, which of these three inventory costing methods would you choose:
   a. To reflect what is probably the physical flow of goods? Explain.
   b. To minimize income taxes for the period? Explain.
5. Assume that Avaya utilizes the LIFO method and both allows its inventory level to decline *and* delays purchasing lot #3 until the next period. Compute cost of goods sold under this scenario and discuss how the LIFO liquidation affects profit.

Solution

Preliminary computation: Units in ending inventory = 4,800 available − 2,800 sold = 2,000

1. First-in, first-out (FIFO)

Cost of goods sold computation:	Units		Cost		Total
	1,000	@	$18.00	=	$18,000
	1,800	@	$18.25	=	32,850
	2,800				**$50,850**
Cost of goods available for sale..............		$88,450			
Less: Cost of goods sold...................		50,850			
Ending inventory ($22,800 + $14,800).........		**$37,600**			

2. Last-in, first-out (LIFO)

Cost of goods sold computation:	Units		Cost		Total
	1,200	@	$19.00	=	$22,800
	800	@	$18.50	=	14,800
	800	@	$18.25	=	14,600
	2,800				**$52,200**
Cost of goods available for sale..............		$88,450			
Less: Cost of goods sold...................		52,200			
Ending inventory ($18,000 + [1,000 × $18.25])...		**$36,250**			

3. Average cost (AC)

Average unit cost   = $88,450/4,800 units = $18.427
Cost of goods sold = 2,800 × $18.427 = $51,596
Ending inventory   = 2,000 × $18.427 = $36,854

4. a. FIFO is normally the method that most closely reflects physical flow. For example, FIFO would apply to the physical flow of perishable units and to situations where the earlier units acquired are moved out first because of risk of deterioration or obsolescence.
   b. LIFO results in the highest cost of goods sold during periods of rising costs (as in the Avaya case); and, accordingly, LIFO yields the lowest net income and the lowest income taxes.

5. Last-in, first-out with LIFO liquidation

Cost of goods sold computation:	Units		Cost		Total
	800	@	$18.50	=	$14,800
	1,800	@	$18.25	=	32,850
	200	@	$18.00	=	3,600
	2,800				$51,250
Cost of goods available for sale..............		$65,650			
Less: Cost of goods sold...................		51,250			
Ending inventory (800 × $18)................		$14,400			

The company's LIFO gross profit has increased by $950 ($52,200 − $51,250) because of the LIFO liquidation. The reduction of inventory quantities matched older (lower) cost layers against current selling prices. The company has, in effect, dipped into lower cost layers to boost current period profit—all from a simple delay of inventory purchases.

PROPERTY, PLANT, AND EQUIPMENT (PPE)

Many companies' largest operating asset is property, plant, and equipment. To frame our PPE discussion, the following graphic highlights long-term operating assets on the balance sheet, and selling, general and administrative expenses on the income statement. The latter includes depreciation and asset write-downs that match the assets' cost against sales derived from the assets. (Depreciation on any manufacturing facilities is included in cost of goods sold.) This section explains the accounting, reporting, and analysis of PPE and related items.

LO3 Describe accounting for property, plant and equipment and explain the impacts on profit and cash flows from different depreciation methods.

Income Statement
Sales
Cost of goods sold
Selling, general & administrative
Income taxes
Net income

Balance Sheet	
Cash	Current liabilities
Accounts receivable, net	Long-term liabilities
Inventory	
Property, plant, and equipment, net	Shareholders' equity
Investments	

Capitalization of Asset Costs

Companies capitalize costs as an asset on the balance sheet only if that asset possesses both of the following characteristics:

1. The asset is owned or controlled by the company.
2. The asset provides future expected benefits.

Owning the asset means the company has title to the asset as provided in a purchase contract. (Assets acquired under leases are also capitalized if certain conditions are met—see Module 10.) Future expected benefits usually refer to future cash inflows. Companies capitalize the full cost to acquire the asset, including the purchase price, transportation, setup, and all other costs necessary to get the asset into service. This is called the asset's acquisition cost.

Companies can only capitalize asset costs that are *directly linked* to future cash inflows, and the costs capitalized as an asset can be no greater than the related expected future cash inflows. This means that if a company reports a $200 asset, we can reasonably expect that it will derive at least $200 in expected cash inflows from the use and ultimate disposal of the asset.

The *directly linked* condition for capitalization of asset cost is important. When a company acquires a machine, it capitalizes the cost because the company expects the machine's output to yield cash inflows from the sale of product made by the machine and from the cash received when the company eventually disposes of the machine. On the other hand, when it comes to research and development (R&D) activities, it is more difficult to directly link expected cash inflows with the R&D expenditures because R&D activities are often unsuccessful. Further, companies cannot reliably estimate the future cash flows from successful R&D activities. Accordingly, GAAP requires that R&D expenditures be expensed when paid. Similar arguments are applied to advertising, promotion and wages to justify expensing of those costs.

Each of these examples relates to items or activities that we generally think of as intangible assets. That is, we reasonably expect R&D efforts and advertising campaigns to produce results. If not, companies would not pursue them. We also generally view employee activities as generating future benefits. Indeed, we often refer to the *human resources* (asset) of a company. However, the link between these items or activities and their outputs is not as direct as GAAP requires for capitalizing such costs. The nonrecognition of these assets is one reason why it is difficult to analyze and value knowledge-based companies and such companies are less suited to traditional ROE disaggregation analysis. Capitalization and noncapitalization of costs can markedly impact financial statements and, therefore, our analysis inferences and assessment of a company as an investment prospect.

BUSINESS INSIGHT	WorldCom and Improper Cost Capitalization

WorldCom's CEO, Bernie Ebbers, and chief financial officer, Scott Sullivan, were convicted in 2005 of *cooking the books* so the company would not show a loss for 2001 and subsequent quarters. Specifically, WorldCom incurred large costs in anticipation of an increase in Internet-related business that did not materialize. Instead of expensing the costs as GAAP requires and reporting a loss in the WorldCom income statement, executives shifted the costs to the balance sheet. By capitalizing these costs (recording them on the balance sheet), WorldCom was able to disguise these costs as assets, thereby inflating current profitability. Although the WorldCom case involved massive fraud, which is difficult for outsiders to detect, an astute analyst would have suspected something was amiss from analysis of WorldCom's long-term asset turnover (Sales/Average long-term assets) as shown below. The obvious decline in turnover reveals that WorldCom's assets constituted an ever increasing percent of total sales during periods leading up to 2002. This finding does not, in itself, imply fraud. It does, however, raise serious questions that analysts should have posed to WorldCom executives in analyst meetings.

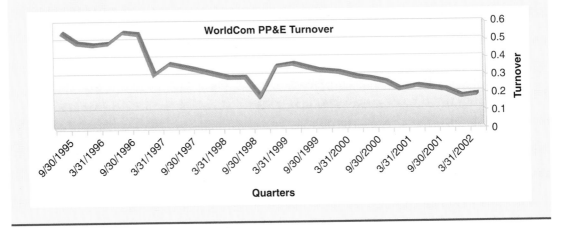

Depreciation

Once a cost is capitalized on the balance sheet as an asset, it must be systematically transferred from the balance sheet to the income statement as depreciation expense to match the asset's cost to the revenues it generates. The depreciation process requires the following estimates:

1. **Useful life.** Period of time over which the asset is expected to generate cash inflows
2. **Salvage value.** Expected disposal amount at the end of the asset's useful life
3. **Depreciation rate.** An estimate of how the asset will be used up over its useful life

Management must determine each of these factors when the asset is acquired. Depreciation commences immediately upon asset acquisition and use. Management also can revise estimates that determine depreciation during the asset's useful life.

The **depreciation base**, also called *nonrecoverable cost*, is the amount to be depreciated. The depreciation base is the acquisition cost less estimated salvage value. This means that at the end of the asset's useful life, only the salvage value remains on the balance sheet.

Depreciation rate refers to the manner in which the asset is used up. Companies make one of the following three assumptions about the depreciation rate:

1. Asset is used up by the same amount each period.
2. Asset is used up more in the early years of its useful life.
3. Asset is used up in proportion to its actual usage.

A company can depreciate different assets using different depreciation rates (and different useful lives). After a depreciation rate is chosen, however, the company must generally stick with that rate throughout the asset's useful life. This is not to say that companies can't change depreciation rates, but changes must be justified as providing more useful financial reports.

The using up of an asset generally relates to physical or technological obsolescence. *Physical obsolescence* relates to an asset's diminished capacity to produce output. *Technological obsolescence* relates to an asset's diminished efficiency in producing output in a competitive manner.

All depreciation methods have the following general formula:

Depreciation Expense = Depreciation Base × Depreciation Rate

Remembering this general formula helps us understand the depreciation process. Also, each depreciation method reports the same amount of depreciation expense *over the life of the asset*. The only difference is in the amount of depreciation expense reported *for a given period*. To illustrate, consider a machine with the following details: $100,000 cost, $10,000 salvage value, and a five-year useful life. We look at two of the most common methods of depreciation.

Straight-Line Method
Under the straight-line (SL) method, depreciation expense is recognized evenly over the estimated useful life of the asset as follows:

Depreciation Base	Depreciation Rate
Cost − Salvage value	1/Estimated useful life
= $100,000 − $10,000	= 1/5 years
= $90,000	= 20%

Depreciation expense per year for this asset is $18,000, computed as $90,000 × 20%. For the asset's first full year of usage, $18,000 of depreciation expense is reported in the income statement. (If an asset is purchased midyear, it is typically depreciated only for the portion of the year it is used. For example, had the asset in this illustration been purchased on May 1, the company would report $10,500 of depreciation in the first year, computed as 7/12 × $18,000, assuming the company has a December 31 year-end.) This depreciation is reflected in the company's financial statements as follows:

Transaction	Balance Sheet						Income Statement		
	Cash Asset	+ Noncash Assets	= Liabil- ities	+ Contrib. Capital	+ Earned Capital		Rev- enues	− Expen- ses	= Net Income
Record $18,000 straight-line depreciation		−18,000 Accumulated Depreciation			−18,000 Retained Earnings			+18,000 Depreciation Expense	= −18,000

DE 18,000
AD 18,000
DE 18,000 | AD 18,000

The accumulated depreciation (contra asset) account increases by $18,000, thus reducing net PPE by the same amount. Also, $18,000 of the asset cost is transferred from the balance sheet to the income statement as depreciation expense. At the end of the first year the asset is reported on the balance sheet as follows:

Machine, at cost..................	$100,000
Less accumulated depreciation......	18,000
Machine, net (end of year 1).........	$ 82,000

Net book value →

Accumulated depreciation is the sum of all depreciation expense that has been recorded to date. The asset **net book value (NBV)**, or *carrying value*, is cost less accumulated depreciation. Although the word value is used here, it does not refer to market value. Depreciation is a cost allocation concept (transfer of costs from the balance sheet to the income statement), not a valuation concept.

In the second year of usage, another $18,000 of depreciation expense is recorded in the income statement and the net book value of the asset on the balance sheet follows:

Machine, at cost.................	$100,000
Less accumulated depreciation......	36,000
Net book value → Machine, net (end of year 2).........	$ 64,000

Accumulated depreciation of $36,000 now includes the sum of the first and second years' depreciation, and the net book value of the asset is now reduced to $64,000. After the fifth year, a total of $90,000 of accumulated depreciation will be recorded ($18,000 per year × 5 years), yielding a net book value for the machine of $10,000. The net book value at the end of the machine's useful life is exactly equal to the salvage value that management estimated when the asset was acquired.

Double-Declining-Balance Method

GAAP also allows *accelerated* methods of depreciation, the most common being the double-declining-balance method. This method records more depreciation in the early years of an asset's useful life (hence the term *accelerated*) and less depreciation in later years. At the end of the asset's useful life, the balance sheet will still report a net book value equal to the asset's salvage value. The difference between straight-line and accelerated depreciation methods is not in the total amount of depreciation, but in the rate at which costs are transferred from the balance sheet to the income statement.

For the double-declining-balance (DDB) method, the depreciation base is net book value, which declines over the life of the asset (this is why the method is called "declining balance"). The depreciation rate is twice the straight-line (SL) rate (which explains the word "double"). The depreciation base and rate for the asset in our illustrative example are computed as follows:

Depreciation Base	Depreciation Rate
Net Book Value = Cost − Accumulated Depreciation	2 × SL rate = 2 × 20% = 40%

The depreciation expense for the first year is $40,000, computed as $100,000 × 40%. This depreciation is reflected in the company's financial statements as follows:

		Balance Sheet					Income Statement		
Transaction	**Cash Asset** +	**Noncash Assets** =	**Liabil- ities** +	**Contrib. Capital** +	**Earned Capital**		**Rev- enues** −	**Expen- ses** =	**Net Income**
Record $40,000 DDB depreciation		−40,000 Accumulated Depreciation =			−40,000 Retained Earnings			+40,000 − Depreciation = Expense	−40,000

```
DE      40,000
   AD        40,000
        DE
40,000 |
        AD
           | 40,000
```

The accumulated depreciation (contra asset) account increases by $40,000 which reduces net PPE (compare this to the $18,000 depreciation under straight-line). This means that $40,000 of the asset cost is transferred from the balance sheet to the income statement as depreciation expense. At the end of the first year, the asset is reported on the balance sheet as follows:

Machine, at cost.................	$100,000
Less accumulated depreciation......	40,000
Net book value → Machine, net (end of year 1).........	$ 60,000

In the second year, the net book value of the asset is the new depreciable base, and the company records depreciation of $24,000 ($60,000 × 40%) in the income statement. At the end of the second year, the net book value of the asset on the balance sheet is:

Machine, at cost.................	$100,000
Less accumulated depreciation......	64,000
Machine, net (end of year 2)........	$ 36,000

Net book value →

Under the double-declining-balance method, a company continues to record depreciation expense in this manner until the salvage value is reached, at which point the depreciation process is discontinued. This leaves a net book value equal to the salvage value, as with the straight-line method.[8] The DDB depreciation schedule for the life of this asset is in Exhibit 6.10.

EXHIBIT 6.10	Double-Declining-Balance Depreciation Schedule		
Year	Book Value at Beginning of Year	Depreciation Expense	Book Value at End of Year
1	$100,000	$40,000	$60,000
2	60,000	24,000	36,000
3	36,000	14,400	21,600
4	21,600	8,640	12,960
5	12,960	2,960*	10,000

*The formula value of $5,184 ($12,960 × 40%) is *not* reported because it would depreciate the asset below salvage value; only the $2,960 needed to reach salvage value is reported.

Exhibit 6.11 shows the depreciation expense and net book value for both the SL and DDB methods. During the first two years, the DDB method yields a higher depreciation expense compared to the SL method. Beginning in the third year, this pattern reverses and the SL method produces higher depreciation expense. Over the asset's life, the same $90,000 of asset cost is transferred to the income statement as depreciation expense, leaving a salvage value of $10,000 on the balance sheet under both methods.

EXHIBIT 6.11	Comparison of Straight-Line and Double-Declining-Balance Depreciation			
	Straight-Line		Double-Declining-Balance	
Year	Depreciation Expense	Book Value at End of Year	Depreciation Expense	Book Value at End of Year
1	$18,000	$82,000	$40,000	$60,000
2	18,000	64,000	24,000	36,000
3	18,000	46,000	14,400	21,600
4	18,000	28,000	8,640	12,960
5	18,000	10,000	2,960	10,000
	$90,000		$90,000	

All depreciation methods yield the same salvage value

Total depreciation over asset life is identical for all methods

Companies typically use the SL method for financial reporting purposes and an accelerated depreciation method for tax returns.[9] The reason is that in early years the SL depreciation yields higher income on shareholder reports, whereas accelerated depreciation yields lower taxable income. Even though this relation reverses in later years, companies prefer to have the tax savings sooner rather than later so that the cash savings can be invested to produce earnings. Further, the reversal may never occur—if depreciable

[8] A variant of DDB allows for a change from DDB to SL at the point when SL depreciation exceeds that for DDB.

[9] The IRS mandates the use of MACRS (Modified Accelerated Cost Recovery System) for tax purposes. This method fixes the useful life for various classes of assets, assumes no salvage value, and generally uses the double-declining-balance method.

assets are growing at a fast enough rate, the additional first year's depreciation on acquired assets more than offsets the lower depreciation expense on older assets, yielding a "permanent" reduction in taxable income and taxes paid.[10]

Asset Sales and Impairments

This section discusses gains and losses from asset sales, and the computation and disclosure of asset impairments.

Gains and Losses on Asset Sales

The gain or loss on the sale (disposition) of a long-term asset is computed as follows.

Gain or Loss on Asset Sale = Proceeds from Sale − Net Book Value of Asset Sold

An asset's net book value is its acquisition cost less accumulated depreciation. When an asset is sold, its acquisition cost and related accumulated depreciation are both removed from the balance sheet and any gain or loss is reported in income from continuing operations.

Gains and losses on asset sales can be large, and analysts must be aware that these gains are *transitory operating* income components. It is often difficult to uncover gains and losses from asset sales because, if the gain or loss is small (immaterial), companies often include the item in selling, general and administrative expenses. To illustrate, Ford Motor Company provides the following footnote disclosure to its 2005 10-K relating to the sale of its Hertz automotive leasing subsidiary ($ millions):

> **Held-for-Sale Operations** During 2005, management committed to sell Hertz as it is not core to our Automotive business. On September 12, 2005, we entered into a definitive agreement with an investor group of private equity firms under which we agreed to sell Hertz in a transaction valued at approximately $15 billion. On December 21, 2005, we completed, through our wholly-owned subsidiary Ford Holdings LLC, the sale of our 100% ownership interest in Hertz to CCMG Investor, LLC. We received $5.6 billion in cash for the sale of Hertz. As a result of the sale, we recognized in *Gain on sale of Hertz* a pre-tax gain of $1.1 billion.

Ford sold a subsidiary company, carried on its balance sheet at a net book value of $13.9 billion (computed as $15 billion sale less $1.1 billion gain), for $15 billion. The impacts on its financial statements follow:

		Balance Sheet						Income Statement		
Transaction	**Cash Asset**	**+**	**Noncash Assets**	**= Liabil-ities**	**+**	**Contrib. Capital**	**+ Earned Capital**	**Rev-enues**	**− Expen-ses**	**= Net Income**
Sale of subsidiary	15.0 Bil. Cash		−13.9 Bil. Investment in Hertz	=			1.1 Bil. Retained Earnings	1.1 Bil. Gain on Asset Sale		= 1.1 Bil.

Cash 15.0 Bil.
  Hertz 13.9 Bil.
  Gain 1.1 Bil.
    Cash
15.0 Bil.
  Hertz
      13.9 Bil.
    Gain
      1.1 Bil.

Ford reported a pretax gain of $1.1 billion from this sale, which was more than half of its total pretax income for that year.

Asset Impairments

Property, plant, and equipment (PPE) assets are reported at their net book values (original cost less accumulated depreciation). This is the case even if the market values of these assets increase subsequent to acquisition. As a result, there can be unrecognized gains *buried* in the balance sheet.

---

[10] The **units-of-production depreciation** method is also common, which depreciates assets according to use. Specifically, the depreciation base is cost less salvage value, and the depreciation rate is the units produced and sold during the year compared with the total expected units to be produced and sold. For example, if a truck is driven 10,000 miles out of a total expected 100,000 miles, 10% of its nonrecoverable cost is reflected as depreciation expense. This method is common for extractive industries like timber and coal.

On the other hand, if market values of PPE assets subsequently decrease—and the asset value is deemed as permanently impaired—then companies must write off the impaired cost and recognize losses on those assets. **Impairment** of PPE assets is determined by comparing the asset's net book value to the sum of the asset's *expected* future (undiscounted) cash flows. If the sum of expected cash flow is greater than net book value, there is no impairment. However, if the sum of the expected cash flow is less than net book value, the asset is deemed impaired and it is written down to its current market value (generally, the present value of those expected cash flows). Exhibit 6.12 depicts this impairment analysis.

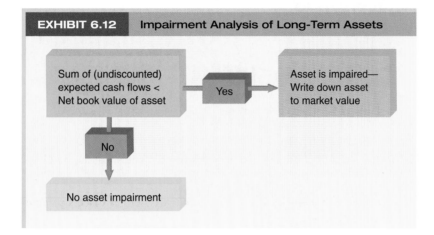

EXHIBIT 6.12   Impairment Analysis of Long-Term Assets

When a company takes an impairment charge, assets are reduced by the amount of the write-down and the loss is recognized in the income statement. To illustrate, a footnote to the 2005 10-K of Agilent Technologies, Inc., reports the following about asset impairments:

Valuation of long-lived assets. We have assessed the recoverability of our long-lived assets, by determining whether the carrying value of such assets will be recovered through undiscounted future cash flows. We incurred $26 million of investment and restructuring asset impairment charges in 2005.

Agilent's write-down of impaired assets affected its financial statements as follows:

	Balance Sheet					Income Statement			
Transaction	Cash Asset	+ Noncash Assets	= Liabil- ities	+ Contrib. Capital	+ Earned Capital	Rev- enues	− Expen- ses	= Net Income	
Write-down long-lived assets by $26 Mil.		−26 Mil. Property, Plant and Equipment =			−26 Mil. Retained Earnings		+26 Mil. Asset − Impairment Expense =	−26 Mil.	AIE 26 Mil. PPE 26 Mil.

Agilent wrote down the carrying value (net book value) of its long-lived assets by $26 million. This write-down accelerated the transfer of the asset's cost from the balance sheet to the income statement. Consequently, Agilent recognized an expense of $26 million in the current year rather than over time via the depreciation process.

It is important to note that management determines if and when to recognize asset impairments. Thus, there is room for management to opportunistically over- or under-estimate asset impairments. Write-downs of long-term assets are often recognized in connection with a restructuring program.

Analysis of asset write-downs present at least two potential challenges:

1. *Insufficient write-down.* Assets sometimes are impaired but an impairment charge is not recognized. This can arise if management is overly optimistic about future prospects or is reluctant to recognize the full impairment in income.

2. *Aggressive write-down.* This *big bath* scenario can arise if income is already very low in a given year. Management's view is that the market will not penalize the company's stock for an extra

write-off when the year was already bad. Taking a larger impairment charge purges the balance sheet of costs that would otherwise hit future years' income.

GAAP condones neither of these cases. Yet, because management must estimate future cash flows for the impairment test, it has some degree of control over the timing and amount of the asset write-off and can use that discretion to manage reported income.

Footnote Disclosures

Cisco reports the following PPE asset amounts in its balance sheet:

At December 31 ($ millions)	2005	2004
Property, Plant and Equipment, net	3,320	3,290

In addition to its balance sheet disclosure, Cisco provides two footnotes that more fully describe its PPE assets:

1. *Summary of Significant Accounting Policies.* This footnote describes Cisco's accounting for PPE assets in general terms:

   Depreciation and Amortization Property and equipment are stated at cost, less accumulated depreciation and amortization. Depreciation and amortization are computed using the straight-line method over the estimated useful lives of the assets. Estimated useful lives of 25 years are used for buildings. Estimated useful lives of 30 to 36 months are used for computer equipment and related software and five years for furniture and fixtures. Estimated useful lives of up to five years are used for production, engineering, and other equipment. Depreciation of operating lease assets is computed based on the respective lease terms, which generally range up to three years. Depreciation and amortization of leasehold improvements are computed using the shorter of the remaining lease terms or five years.

   There are a two items of interest in this disclosure: (a) Cisco, like most publicly traded companies, depreciates its PPE assets using the straight-line method (for tax purposes it uses an accelerated method). (b) Cisco provides general disclosures on the useful lives of its assets: 30 months to 25 years. We will discuss a method to more accurately estimate the useful lives in the next section.

2. *Supplemental balance sheet information.* This footnote provides a breakdown of PPE assets by category as well as the balance in the accumulated depreciation account:

Property and equipment, net (millions)	
Land, buildings and leasehold improvements	$3,492
Computer equipment and related software	1,244
Production, engineering and other equipment.	3,095
Operating lease assets.	136
Furniture and fixtures	355
. . . .	8,322
Less accumulated depreciation and amortization	(5,002)
Total	$3,320

Analysis Implications

This section explains how to measure long-term asset utilization and asset age.

PPE Turnover

A crucial issue in analyzing PPE assets is determining their productivity (utilization). For example, what level of plant assets is necessary to generate a dollar of revenues? How capital intensive is the company and its competitors? To address these and similar questions, we use **PPE turnover**, defined as follows:

> **PPE Turnover (PPET) = Sales/Average PPE Assets, net**

Cisco's 2005 PPE turnover is 7.5 times ($24,801 million/[($3,320 million + $3,290 million)/2]).[11] This turnover places Cisco solidly among its peers (see chart below). Dell's asset utilization is legendary and its PPE turnover of 30 is about four times higher than most of the other companies Cisco identifies as its peers.

PPE Turnover for Cisco and Its Peer Companies

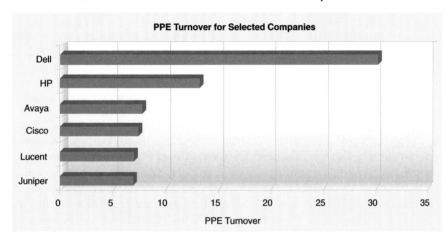

Higher PPE turnover is preferable to lower. A higher PPE turnover implies a lower capital investment for a given level of sales. Higher turnover, therefore, increases profitability because the company avoids asset carrying costs and because the freed-up assets can now generate operating cash flow.

PPE turnover is lower for capital-intensive manufacturing companies than it is for companies in service or knowledge-based industries. To this point, consider the following chart of PPE turnover for selected industries.

PPE Turnover for Selected Industries

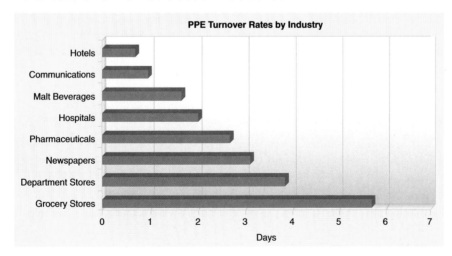

---

[11] We use Cisco's PPE, net in this example. The argument for the use of gross assets in computing PPE turnover is not as compelling as it is for receivables since accumulated depreciation is not as discretionary as the allowance for uncollected accounts and is less prone to fluctuation as a percentage of gross assets.

Hotels and communications companies are capital-intensive businesses. Their PPE turnover rates are, correspondingly, lower than for other industries. On the other hand, department stores and grocery stores require comparatively less capital investment. Their PPE turnover rates are much higher.

MANAGERIAL DECISION	You Are the Division Manager

You are the manager for a main operating division of your company. You are concerned that a declining PPE turnover is adversely affecting your division's return on net operating assets. What specific actions can you take to increase PPE turnover? [Answer, p. 6-37]

Useful Life and Percent Used Up

Cisco reports that the useful lives of its depreciable assets range from 30 months for computer equipment and up to 25 years for buildings. The longer an asset's useful life, the lower the annual depreciation expense reported in the income statement and the higher the income each year. It might be of interest, therefore, to know whether a company's useful life estimates are more conservative or more aggressive than its competitors.

If we assume straight-line (SL) depreciation and zero salvage value, we can estimate the average useful life for depreciable assets as follows:

Estimated Average Useful Life = Depreciable Asset Cost/Depreciation Expense

For Cisco, the estimated useful life for its plant assets is 8.2 years ($8,322 million/$1,009 million). Land cost is nearly always excluded from gross PPE cost because land is a nondepreciable asset. However, Cisco does not provide a breakout of land cost in its footnotes and Cisco does not report depreciation expense as a separate line item on the income statement. Therefore, we use the depreciation and amortization expense of $1,009 million (reported in the statement of cash flows). For many companies, amortization expense is synonymous with depreciation expense because it relates to tangible assets like leasehold improvements. If amortization expense relates to intangible assets (like patents, for example), however, the amortization portion of the expense should be subtracted from total depreciation and from amortization expense in computing the Estimated Average Useful Life.

We can also estimate the proportion of a company's depreciable assets that have already been transferred to the income statement. This ratio reflects the percent of depreciable assets that are no longer productive—as follows:

Percent Used Up = Accumulated Depreciation/Depreciable Asset Cost

Cisco's assets are 60% used up, computed as $5,002 million/$8,322 million. If a company replaced all of its assets evenly each year, the percent used up ratio would be 50%. Cisco's depreciable assets are slightly older than this benchmark. Knowing the degree to which a company's assets are used up is of interest in forecasting future cash flows. If, for example, depreciable assets are 80% used up, we might anticipate a higher level of capital expenditures in the near future. We also expect that older assets are less efficient and will incur higher maintenance costs.

MODULE-END REVIEW

On January 2, assume that Hewlett-Packard purchases equipment that fabricates a key-product part. The equipment costs $95,000, and its estimated useful life is five years, after which it is expected to be sold for $10,000.

Required

1. Compute depreciation expense for each year of the equipment's useful life for each of the following depreciation methods:
   a. Straight-line
   b. Double-declining-balance
2. Show how HP reports the equipment on its balance sheet at the end of the third year assuming straight-line depreciation.

3. Assume that this is the only depreciable asset the company owns and that it uses straight-line depreciation. Using the depreciation expense computed in 1a and the balance sheet presentation from 2, estimate the useful life and the percent used up for this asset at the end of the third year.

Solution

1. *a.* Straight-line depreciation expense = ($95,000 − $10,000)/5 years = $17,000 per year

   b. Double-declining-balance (note: twice straight-line rate = 2 × [100%/5 years] = 40%)

Year	Book Value × Rate	Depreciation Expense
1	$95,000 × 0.40 =	$38,000
2	($95,000 − $38,000) × 0.40 =	22,800
3	($95,000 − $60,800) × 0.40 =	13,680
4	($95,000 − $74,480) × 0.40 =	8,208
5	($95,000 − $82,688) × 0.40 =	2,312*

*The formula value of $4,925 is not reported for year 5 because doing so would depreciate the asset below the estimated salvage value; only the $2,312 needed to reach salvage value is depreciated.

2. HP reports the equipment on its balance sheet at its net book value of $44,000.

Equipment, cost......................	$95,000
Less accumulated depreciation..........	51,000
Equipment, net (end of year 3)..........	$44,000

3. The estimated useful life is computed as: Depreciable asset cost/Depreciation expense = $95,000/ $17,000 = 5.6 years. Because companies do not usually disclose salvage values (not required disclosure), the useful-life estimate is a bit high for this asset. This estimate is still informative because companies typically only provide a range of useful lives for depreciable assets in the footnotes.

   The percent used up is computed as: Accumulated depreciation/Depreciable asset cost = $51,000/ $95,000 = 53.7%. The equipment is more than one-half used up at the end of the third year. Again, the lack of knowledge of salvage value yields an underestimate of the percent used up. Still, this estimate is useful in that we know that the company's asset is over one-half used up and is likely to require replacement in about 2 years (estimated as less than one-half of its estimated useful life of 5.6 years). This replacement will require a cash outflow or financing when it arises and should be considered in our projections of future cash flows.

GUIDANCE ANSWERS

MANAGERIAL DECISION **You Are the Receivables Manager**

First, you must realize that extending credit is an important tool in the marketing of your products, often as important as advertising and promotion. Given that receivables are necessary, there are certain ways to speed their collection. (1) We can better screen the customers to whom we extend credit. (2) We can negotiate advance or progress payments from customers. (3) We can use bank letters of credit or other automatic drafting procedures that obviate billing. (4) We can make sure products are sent as ordered to reduce disputes. (5) We can improve administration of past due accounts to provide for more timely notices of delinquencies and better collection procedures.

You Are the Plant Manager

Companies need inventories to avoid lost sales opportunities; however, there are several ways to minimize inventory needs. (1) We can reduce product costs by improving product design to eliminate costly features that customers don't value. (2) We can use more cost-efficient suppliers; possibly producing in lower wage-rate parts of the world. (3) We can reduce raw material inventories with just-in-time delivery from suppliers. (4) We can eliminate bottlenecks in the production process that increase work-in-process inventories. (5) We can manufacture for orders rather than for estimated demand to reduce finished goods inventories. (6) We can improve warehousing and distribution to reduce duplicate inventories. (7) We can monitor product sales and adjust product mix as demand changes to reduce finished goods inventories.

You Are the Division Manager

PPE is a difficult asset to reduce. Since companies need long-term operating assets, managers usually try to maximize throughput to reduce unit costs. Also, many companies form alliances to share administrative, production, logistics, customer service, IT and other functions. These alliances take many forms (such as joint ventures) and are designed to spread ownership of assets among many users. The goal is to identify underutilized assets and to increase capacity utilization. Another solution might be to reconfigure the value chain from raw material to end user. Examples include the sharing of IT or manufacturing facilities, outsourcing of production or administration such as customer service centers, and the use of variable interest entities for asset securitization (see Module 9).

DISCUSSION QUESTIONS

Q6-1. Explain how management can shift income from one period into another by its estimation of uncollectible accounts.

Q6-2. Why do relatively stable inventory costs across periods reduce the importance of management's choice of an inventory costing method?

Q6-3. What is one explanation for increased gross profit during periods of rising inventory costs when FIFO is used?

Q6-4. If inventory costs are rising, which inventory costing method—first-in, first-out; last-in, first-out; or average cost—yields the (a) lowest ending inventory? (b) lowest net income? (c) largest ending inventory? (d) largest net income? (e) greatest cash flow assuming the same method is used for tax purposes?

Q6-5. Even though it may not reflect their physical flow of goods, why might companies adopt last-in, first-out inventory costing in periods when costs are consistently rising?

Kaiser Aluminum Corporation

Q6-6. In a recent annual report, Kaiser Aluminum Corporation made the following statement in reference to its inventories: "The Company recorded pretax charges of approximately $19.4 million because of a reduction in the carrying values of its inventories caused principally by prevailing lower prices for alumina, primary aluminum, and fabricated products." What basic accounting principle caused Kaiser Aluminum to record this $19.4 million pretax charge? Briefly describe the rationale for this principle.

Q6-7. Why is depreciation expense necessary to properly match revenues and expenses?

Q6-8. How might a company treat a revision of depreciation due to a change in an asset's estimated useful life or salvage value?

Q6-9. When is a PPE asset considered to be impaired? How is an impairment loss computed?

Q6-10. What is the benefit of accelerated depreciation for income tax purposes when the total depreciation taken over the asset's life is identical under any method of depreciation?

Q6-11. What factors determine the gain or loss on the sale of a PPE asset?

MINI EXERCISES

M6-12. **Estimating Uncollectible Accounts and Reporting Accounts Receivables** (LO1)
Mohan Company estimates its uncollectible accounts by aging its accounts receivable and applying percentages to various aged categories of accounts. Mohan computes a total of $2,100 in estimated

uncollectible accounts as of December 31, 2007. Its Accounts Receivable has a balance of $98,000, and its Allowance for Uncollectible Accounts has an unused balance of $500 before adjustment at December 31, 2007.

    a.   What amount of bad debts expense will Mohan report in 2007?

    b.   Determine the net amount of accounts receivable reported in current assets at December 31, 2007.

M6-13. **Interpreting the Allowance Method for Accounts Receivable** **(LO1)**

At a recent board of directors meeting of Ascot, Inc., one of the directors expressed concern over the allowance for uncollectible accounts appearing in the company's balance sheet. "I don't understand this account," he said. "Why don't we just show accounts receivable at the amount owed to us and get rid of that allowance?" Respond to the director's question, include in your response (a) an explanation of why the company has an allowance account, (b) what the balance sheet presentation of accounts receivable is intended to show, and (c) how the matching principle relates to the analysis and presentation of accounts receivable.

M6-14. **Analyzing the Allowance for Uncollectible Accounts** **(LO1)**

Following is the current asset section from the Kraft Foods, Inc., balance sheet.

Kraft Foods, Inc.
(KFT)

$ millions	2005	2004
Cash and cash equivalents	$ 316	$ 282
Receivables (less allowances of $92 in 2005 and $118 in 2004)	3,385	3,541
Inventories:		
Raw materials	1,363	1,367
Finished product	1,980	2,080
	3,343	3,447
Deferred income taxes	879	749
Assets of discontinued operations held for sale	—	1,458
Other current assets	230	245
Total current assets	$8,153	$9,722

    a.   Compute the gross amount of accounts receivable for both 2005 and 2004. Compute the percentage of the allowance for uncollectible accounts relative to the gross amount of accounts receivable for each of those years.

    b.   How do you interpret the change in the percentage computed in part *a*?

M6-15. **Evaluating Accounts Receivable Turnover for Competitors** **(LO1)**

Procter & Gamble (PG) and Colgate-Palmolive (CL) report the following sales and accounts receivable balances ($ millions).

Procter & Gamble
(PG)

Colgate-Palmolive
(CL)

	Procter & Gamble		**Colgate-Palmolive**	
	Sales	**Accounts Receivable**	**Sales**	**Accounts Receivable**
2004	$51,407	$4,062	$10,584	$1,320
2005	56,741	4,185	11,397	1,309

    a.   Compute the 2005 accounts receivable turnover for both companies.

    b.   Identify and discuss a potential explanation for the difference between these competitors' accounts receivable turnover.

M6-16. **Computing Cost of Goods Sold and Ending Inventory under FIFO, LIFO, and Average Cost** **(LO2)**

Assume that Gode Company reports the following initial balance and subsequent purchase of inventory.

Beginning inventory, 2007	1,000 units @ $100 each	$100,000
Inventory purchased in 2007	2,000 units @ $150 each	300,000
Cost of goods available for sale in 2007	3,000 units	$400,000

Assume that 1,700 units are sold during 2007. Compute the cost of goods sold for 2007 and the balance reported as ending inventory on the 2007 balance sheet under the following inventory costing methods:
a. FIFO
b. LIFO
c. Average Cost

M6-17. Computing Cost of Goods Sold and Ending Inventory (LO2)
Bartov Corporation reports the following beginning inventory and inventory purchases for 2007.

Beginning inventory, 2007	400 units @ $10 each	$ 4,000
Inventory purchased in 2007	700 units @ $12 each	8,400
Cost of goods available for sale in 2007	1,100 units	$12,400

Bartov sells 600 of its inventory units in 2007. Compute its cost of goods sold for 2007 and the ending inventory reported on its 2007 balance sheet under the following inventory costing methods:
a. FIFO
b. LIFO
c. Average Cost

M6-18. Computing and Evaluating Inventory Turnover for Two Companies (LO5)

Abercrombie and Fitch (ANF) and **TJ Maxx** (TJX) report the following information in their respective January 2006 10-K reports.

	Abercrombie & Fitch			TJ Maxx		
$ millions	Sales	Cost of Goods Sold	Inventories	Sales	Cost of Goods Sold	Inventories
2005	$2,021	$680	$211	$14,913	$11,398	$2,352
2006	2,785	933	363	16,058	12,295	2,366

a. Compute the 2006 inventory turnover for each of these two retailers.
b. Discuss any difference you observe in inventory turnover between these two companies. Does the difference confirm your expectations given their respective business models? Explain. (*Hint:* ANF is a higher-end retailer and TJX sells more value-priced clothing.)
c. Describe ways that a retailer can improve its inventory turnover.

M6-19. Computing Depreciation under Straight-Line and Double-Declining-Balance (LO3)
A delivery van costing $18,000 is expected to have a $1,500 salvage value at the end of its useful life of 5 years. Assume that the truck was purchased on January 1, 2007. Compute the depreciation expense for 2007 and 2008 (its second year) under the following depreciation methods:
a. Straight-line.
b. Double-declining-balance.

M6-20. Computing Depreciation under Straight-Line and Double-Declining-Balance for Partial Years (LO3)
A company with a calendar year-end, purchases a machine costing $145,800 on May 1, 2007. The machine is expected to be obsolete after three years (36 months) and, thereafter, no longer useful to the company. The estimated salvage value is $5,400. The company's depreciation policy is to record depreciation for the portion of the year that the asset is in service. Compute depreciation expense for both 2007 and 2008 under the following depreciation methods:
a. Straight-line.
b. Double-declining-balance.

M6-21. **Computing and Comparing PPE Turnover for Two Companies** **(LO3)**

Texas Instruments (TXN) and Intel Corporation (INTC) report the following information.

Texas Instruments
(TXN)

Intel Corporation
(INTC)

| $ millions | Intel Corp | | Texas Instruments | |
	Sales	Plant, Property and Equipment, net	Sales	Plant, Property and Equipment, net
2004	$34,209	$15,768	$12,580	$3,918
2005	38,826	17,111	13,392	3,899

a. Compute the 2005 PPE turnover for both companies. Comment on any difference you observe.

b. Discuss ways in which high-tech manufacturing companies like these can increase their PPE turnover.

EXERCISES

E6-22. **Estimating Uncollectible Accounts and Reporting Accounts Receivable** **(LO1)**

LaFond Company analyzes its accounts receivable at December 31, 2007, and arrives at the aged categories below along with the percentages that are estimated as uncollectible.

Age Group	Accounts Receivable	Estimated Loss %
0–30 days past due	$ 90,000	1%
31–60 days past due	20,000	2
61–120 days past due	11,000	5
121–180 days past due	6,000	10
Over 180 days past due	4,000	25
Total accounts receivable	$131,000	

The unused balance of the allowance for uncollectible accounts is $520 on December 31, 2007, before any adjustments.

a. What amount of bad debts expense will LaFond report for 2007?

b. Use the financial statement effects template to record LaFond's bad debts expense for 2007.

c. What is the balance of accounts receivable that it reports on its December 31, 2007, balance sheet?

E6-23. **Analyzing and Reporting Receivable Transactions and Uncollectible Accounts (using percentage of sales method)** **(LO1)**

At the beginning of 2007, Penman Company had the following account balances in its financial records.

Accounts Receivable $122,000
Allowance for Uncollectible Accounts 7,900

During 2007, Penman's credit sales were $1,173,000 and collections on accounts receivable were $1,150,000. The following additional transactions occurred during the year.

Feb. 17 Wrote off Nissim's account, $3,600.
May 28 Wrote off Weiss's account, $2,400.
Dec. 15 Wrote off Ohlson's account, $900.
Dec. 31 Recorded the bad debts expense assuming that Penman's policy is to record bad debts expense as 0.8% of credit sales. (*Hint*: The allowance account is increased by 0.8% of credit sales regardless of write-offs.)

Compute the ending balances in accounts receivable and the allowance for uncollectible accounts. Show how Penman's December 31, 2007 balance sheet reports the two accounts.

Hewlett-Packard
(HPQ)

E6-24. Interpreting the Accounts Receivable Footnote (LO1)

Hewlett-Packard Company (HP) reports the following trade accounts receivable in its 2005 10-K report.

October 31 (In millions)	2005	2004
Accounts receivable, net of allowance for doubtful accounts of $227 and $286 as of October 31, 2005 and 2004, respectively	$9,903	$10,226

HP's footnotes to its 10-K provide the following additional information relating to its allowance for doubtful accounts.

For the fiscal years ended October 31 (In millions)	2005	2004	2003
Allowance for doubtful accounts—accounts receivable			
Balance, beginning of period	$286	$347	$410
Amount acquired through acquisition.....................	—	9	—
Addition (reversal) of bad debts provision	17	(6)	29
Deductions, net of recoveries..........................	(76)	(64)	(92)
Balance, end of period	$227	$286	$347

a. What is the gross amount of accounts receivables for HP in fiscal 2005 and 2004?

b. What is the percentage of the allowance for doubtful accounts to gross accounts receivable for 2005 and 2004?

c. What amount of bad debts expense did HP report each year 2003 through 2005? How does bad debts expense compare with the amounts of its accounts receivable actually written off? (Identify the amounts and explain.)

d. Explain the changes in the allowance for doubtful accounts from 2003 through 2005. Does it appear that HP increased or decreased its allowance for doubtful accounts in any particular year beyond what seems reasonable?

E6-25. Estimating Bad Debts Expense and Reporting Receivables (LO1)

At December 31, 2007, Sunil Company had a balance of $375,000 in its accounts receivable and an unused balance of $4,200 in its allowance for uncollectible accounts. The company then aged its accounts as follows:

Current	$304,000
1–60 days past due	44,000
61–180 days past due	18,000
Over 180 days past due...........	9,000
Total accounts receivable.........	$375,000

The company has experienced losses as follows: 1% of current balances, 5% of balances 1–60 days past due, 15% of balances 61–180 days past due, and 40% of balances over 180 days past due. The company continues to base its allowance for uncollectible accounts on this aging analysis and percentages.

a. What amount of bad debts expense does Sunil report on its 2007 income statement?

b. Show how Sunil's December 31, 2007, balance sheet will report the accounts receivable and the allowance for uncollectible accounts.

E6-26. Estimating Uncollectible Accounts and Reporting Receivables over Multiple Periods (LO1)

Barth Company, which has been in business for three years, makes all of its sales on credit and does not offer cash discounts. Its credit sales, customer collections, and write-offs of uncollectible accounts for its first three years follow:

Year	Sales	Collections	Accounts Written Off
2005	$751,000	$733,000	$5,300
2006	876,000	864,000	5,800
2007	972,000	938,000	6,500

a. Barth recognizes bad debts expense as 1% of sales. (*Hint:* This means the allowance account is increased by 1% of credit sales regardless of any write-offs and unused balances.) What does Barth's 2007 balance sheet report for accounts receivable and the allowance for uncollectible accounts? What total amount of bad debts expense appears on Barth's income statement for each of the three years?

b. Comment on the appropriateness of the 1% rate used to provide for bad debts based on your analysis in part *a*.

E6-27. Applying and Analyzing Inventory Costing Methods   (LO2)

At the beginning of the current period, Chen carried 1,000 units of its product with a unit cost of $20. A summary of purchases during the current period follows:

	Units	Unit Cost	Cost
Beginning Inventory	1,000	$20	$20,000
Purchases: #1.	1,800	22	39,600
#2.	800	26	20,800
#3.	1,200	29	34,800

During the current period, Chen sold 2,800 units.

a. Assume that Chen uses the first-in, first-out method. Compute both cost of goods sold for the current period and the ending inventory balance. Use the financial statement effects template to record cost of goods sold for the period.

b. Assume that Chen uses the last-in, first-out method. Compute both cost of goods sold for the current period and the ending inventory balance.

c. Assume that Chen uses the average cost method. Compute both cost of goods sold for the current period and the ending inventory balance.

d. Which of these three inventory costing methods would you choose to:
   1. Reflect what is probably the physical flow of goods? Explain.
   2. Minimize income taxes for the period? Explain.
   3. Report the largest amount of income for the period? Explain.

E6-28. Analyzing an Inventory Footnote Disclosure   (LO2)

General Electric Company reports the following footnote in its 10-K report.

General Electric
Company (GE)

December 31 (In millions)	2005	2004
Raw materials and work in process	$ 5,527	$ 5,042
Finished goods.	5,152	4,806
Unbilled shipments.	333	402
	11,012	10,250
Less revaluation to LIFO.	(697)	(661)
	$10,315	$ 9,589

The company reports its inventories using the LIFO inventory costing method.

a. What is the balance in inventories reported on GE's 2005 balance sheet?

b. What would GE's 2005 balance sheet have reported for inventories had the company used FIFO inventory costing?

c. What *cumulative* effect has GE's choice of LIFO over FIFO had on its pretax income as of year-end 2005? Explain.

d. Assume GE has a 35% income tax rate. As of the 2005 year-end, how much has GE saved in taxes by choosing LIFO over FIFO method for costing inventory? Has the use of LIFO increased or decreased GE's cumulative tax liability?

e. What effect has the use of LIFO inventory costing had on GE's pretax income and tax liability for 2005 only (assume a 35% income tax rate)?

E6-29. Computing Cost of Sales and Ending Inventory (LO2)

Stocken Company has the following financial records for the current period.

	Units	Unit Cost
Beginning inventory	100	$46
Purchases: #1.	650	42
#2.	550	38
#3.	200	36

Ending inventory at the end of this period is 350 units. Compute the ending inventory and the cost of goods sold for the current period using (a) first-in, first out, (b) average cost, and (c) last-in, first-out.

E6-30. Analyzing an Inventory Footnote Disclosure (LO2)

Deere & Co. (DE)

The inventory footnote from the Deere & Company's 2005 10-K follows ($ millions).

Inventories Most inventories owned by Deere & Company and its United States equipment subsidiaries are valued at cost, on the "last-in, first-out" (LIFO) basis. Remaining inventories are generally valued at the lower of cost, on the "first-in, first-out" (FIFO) basis, or market. The value of gross inventories on the LIFO basis represented 61 percent of worldwide gross inventories at FIFO value on October 31, 2005 and 2004, respectively. If all inventories had been valued on a FIFO basis, estimated inventories by major classification at October 31 in millions of dollars would have been as follows:

	2005	2004
Raw materials and supplies	$ 716	$ 589
Work-in-process.	425	408
Finished machines and parts	2,126	2,004
Total FIFO value	3,267	3,001
Less adjustment to LIFO value.	1,132	1,002
Inventories	$2,135	$1,999

We notice that not all of Deere's inventories are reported using the same inventory costing method (companies can use different inventory costing methods for different inventory pools).

a. What amount does Deere report for inventories on its 2005 balance sheet?

b. What would Deere have reported as inventories on its 2005 balance sheet had the company used FIFO inventory costing for all of its inventories?

c. What *cumulative* effect has the use of LIFO inventory costing had, as of year-end 2005, on Deere's pretax income compared with the pretax income it would have reported had it used FIFO inventory costing for all of its inventories? Explain.

d. Assuming a 35% income tax rate, by what *cumulative* dollar amount has Deere's tax liability been affected by use of LIFO inventory costing as of year-end 2005? Has the use of LIFO inventory costing increased or decreased Deere's cumulative tax liability?

e. What effect has the use of LIFO inventory costing had on Deere's pretax income and tax liability for 2005 only (assume a 35% income tax rate)?

E6-31. Computing Straight-Line and Double-Declining-Balance Depreciation (LO3)

On January 2, Haskins Company purchases a laser cutting machine for use in fabrication of a part for one of its key products. The machine cost $80,000, and its estimated useful life is five years, after which the expected salvage value is $5,000. (*a*) Compute depreciation expense for each year of the machine's useful life under each of the following depreciation methods. (*b*) Use the financial statements effects template to show the effect of depreciation on the first year only for both methods.

a. Straight-line

b. Double-declining-balance

E6-32. Computing Depreciation, Asset Book Value, and Gain or Loss on Asset Sale (LO3)

Sloan Company owns an executive plane that originally cost $800,000. It has recorded straight-line depreciation on the plane for six full years, calculated assuming an $80,000 expected salvage value at the end of its estimated 10-year useful life. Sloan disposes of the plane at the end of the sixth year.

a. At the disposal date, what is the (1) cumulative depreciation expense and (2) net book value of the plane?

b. How much gain or loss is reported at disposal if the sales price is:
1. A cash amount equal to the plane's net book value.
2. $195,000 cash.
3. $600,000 cash.

E6-33. Computing Straight-Line and Double-Declining-Balance Depreciation (LO3)

On January 2, 2007, Dechow Company purchases a machine that manufactures a part for one of its key products. The machine cost $218,700 and is estimated to have a useful life of six years, with an expected salvage value of $23,400. Compute depreciation expense for 2007 and 2008 for each of the following depreciation methods.

a. Straight-line.
b. Double-declining-balance.

E6-34. Computing Depreciation, Asset Book Value, and Gain or Loss on Asset Sale (LO3)

Palepu Company owns and operates a delivery van that originally cost $27,200. Palepu has recorded straight-line depreciation on the van for three years, calculated assuming a $2,000 expected salvage value at the end of its estimated six-year useful life. Depreciation was last recorded at the end of the third year, at which time Palepu disposes of this van.

a. Compute the net book value of the van on the sale date.
b. Compute the gain or loss on sale of the van if its sales price is:
1. A cash amount equal to the van's net book value.
2. $15,000 cash.
3. $12,000 cash.

E6-35. Estimating Useful Life and Percent Used Up (LO3)

The property and equipment footnote from the Deere & Company balance sheet follows.

Deere & Co. (DE)

Property and Depreciation   A summary of property and equipment at October 31 follows:

($ millions)	Average Useful Lives (Years)	2005	2004
Equipment Operations			
Land		$ 79	$ 75
Buildings and building equipment	25	1,490	1,419
Machinery and equipment	10	2,961	2,870
Dies, patterns, tools, etc.	7	1,039	987
All other	5	589	571
Construction in progress		232	156
Total at cost		6,390	6,078
Less accumulated depreciation		4,113	3,966
Total		$2,277	$2,112

During 2005, the company reported $636.5 million of depreciation expense (this expense also includes amortization expense relating to computer software that is included with property and equipment).

a. Compute the estimated useful life of Deere's depreciable assets. (*Hint:* Exclude land and construction in progress.) How does this estimate compare with the useful lives reported in Deere's footnote disclosure?

b. Estimate the percent used up of Deere's depreciable assets. How do you interpret this figure?

E6-36. **Computing and Evaluating Receivables, Inventory and PPE Turnovers** (LO1, 2, 3)

3M Company reports the following financial statement amounts in its 2005 10-K report.

$ millions	Sales	Cost of Goods Sold	Receivables, net	Inventories	Plant, property and equipment, net
2003	$18,232	$ 9,285	$2,714	$1,816	$5,609
2004	20,011	9,958	2,792	1,897	5,711
2005	21,167	10,381	2,838	2,162	5,593

Required

a. Compute the receivables, inventory, and PPE turnover ratios for both 2004 and 2005.

b. What changes are evident in the turnover rates of 3M for these years? Discuss ways in which a company such as 3M can improve receivables, inventory, and PPE turnover ratios.

E6-37. **Computing and Assessing Plant Asset Impairment** (LO3)

On July 1, 2003, Zeibart Company purchases equipment for $225,000. The equipment has an estimated useful life of 10 years and expected salvage value of $25,000. The company uses straight-line depreciation. On July 1, 2007, economic factors cause the market value of the equipment to decline to $90,000. On this date, Zeibart examines the equipment for impairment and estimates $125,000 in undiscounted future cash inflows from this equipment.

a. Is the equipment impaired at July 1, 2007? Explain.

b. If the equipment is impaired at July 1, 2007, compute the impairment loss.

PROBLEMS

P6-38. **Evaluating Turnover Rates for Different Companies** (LO1, 2, 3)

Following are asset turnover rates for accounts receivable; inventory; and property, plant, and equipment (PPE) for Best Buy (retailer of consumer products), Carnival (vacation cruise line), Caterpillar (manufacturer of heavy equipment), Harley-Davidson (manufacturer of motorcycles), Microsoft (software company), Oracle (software company), and Sharper-Image (retailer of specialty consumer products).

Company Name	Receivables Turnover	Inventory Turnover	Plant, Property and Equipment Turnover
Best Buy Co	70.03	7.47	11.92
Carnival Corp	27.14	25.28	0.53
Caterpillar Inc	2.59	5.07	4.64
Harley-Davidson Inc.	3.67	14.28	5.57
Microsoft Corp	6.09	11.66	17.03
Oracle Corp.	4.51	n.a.	9.40
Sharper Image Corp.	32.46	3.35	8.91

Required

a. Interpret and explain differences in receivables turnover for the retailers (Best Buy and Sharper Image) vis-à-vis that for the manufacturers (Caterpillar and Harley-Davidson).

b. Interpret and explain the difference in inventory turnover for Harley-Davidson versus Sharper Image. Why is Oracle's inventory turnover reported as n.a.?

c. Interpret and explain the difference in PPE turnover for Carnival versus Microsoft.

d. What are some general observations you might draw regarding the relative levels of these turnover rates across the different industries?

P6-39.   Interpreting Accounts Receivable and its Footnote Disclosure   (LO1)

Following is the current asset section from the W.W. Grainger, Inc., balance sheet.

W.W. Grainger, Inc.
(GWW)

As of December 31 ($ 000s)	2005	2004	2003
Cash and cash equivalents	$ 544,894	$ 429,246	$ 402,824
Accounts receivable (less allowances for doubtful accounts of $18,401, $23,375 and $24,736, respectively	518,625	480,893	431,896
Inventories	791,212	700,559	661,247
Prepaid expenses and other assets.	54,334	47,086	37,947
Deferred income taxes.	88,803	96,929	99,499
Total current assets	$1,997,868	$1,754,713	$1,633,413

Grainger reports the following footnote relating to its receivables.

Allowance for Doubtful Accounts   The following table shows the activity in the allowance for doubtful accounts.

For Years Ended December 31 ($ 000s)	2005	2004	2003
Balance at beginning of period	$23,375	$24,736	$26,868
Provision for uncollectible accounts	1,326	5,159	9,263
Write-off of uncollectible accounts, less recoveries. . . .	(6,380)	(6,662)	(11,713)
Foreign currency exchange impact	80	142	318
Balance at end of period	$18,401	$23,375	$24,736

Required

a.   What amount do customers owe Grainger at each of the year-ends 2003 through 2005?

b.   What percentage of its total accounts receivable does Grainger feel are uncollectible? (*Hint:* Percentage of uncollectible accounts = Allowance for uncollectible accounts/Gross accounts receivable)

c.   What amount of bad debts expense did Grainger report in its income statement for each of the years 2003 through 2005?

d.   Explain the change in the balance of the allowance for uncollectible accounts since 2003. Specifically, did the allowance increase or decrease as a percentage of gross accounts receivable, and why?

e.   If Grainger had kept its 2005 allowance for uncollectible accounts at the same percentage of gross accounts receivable as it was in 2004, by what amount would its profit have changed (ignore taxes)? Explain.

f.   Overall, what is your assessment of Grainger's allowance for uncollectible accounts and the related expense provision?

P6-40.   Analyzing and Interpreting Receivables and Related Ratios   (LO1)

Following is the current asset section from Intuit's balance sheet.

Intuit, Inc. (INTU)

July 31 ($ 000s)	2005	2004
Cash and cash equivalents	$ 83,842	$ 25,992
Investments	910,416	991,971
Accounts receivable, net of allowance for doubtful accounts of $15,653 and $6,994, respectively.	86,125	81,615
Deferred income taxes.	54,854	31,094
Prepaid expenses and other current assets.	99,275	62,792
Current assets of discontinued operations	21,989	12,279
Current assets before funds held for payroll customers.	1,256,501	1,205,743
Funds held for payroll customers.	357,838	323,041
Total current assets	$1,614,339	$1,528,784

Total revenues were $2,038 million ($1,243 million in product sales and $795 million in service revenues and other) in 2005.

Required

a.   What are Intuit's gross accounts receivable at the end of 2005 and 2004?

b.   For both 2005 and 2004, compute the ratio of the allowance for uncollectible accounts to gross receivables. What trend do you observe?

c.   Compute the receivables turnover ratio and the average collection period for 2005 based on gross receivables computed in part *a*. Does the collection period (days sales in receivables) appear reasonable given Intuit's lines of business (Intuit's products include QuickBooks, TurboTax and Quicken, which it sells to consumers and small businesses)? Explain.

d.   Is the percentage of Intuit's allowance for uncollectible accounts to gross accounts receivable consistent with what you expect for Intuit's line of business? Explain.

e.   Intuit discloses the following table related to its allowance for uncollectible accounts from its 10-K. Comment on the change in the allowance account during 2003 through 2005.

(In thousands)	Balance at Beginning of Period	Additions Charged to Expense	Deductions	Balance at End of Period
Year ended July 31, 2005				
Allowance for doubtful accounts . . .	$6,994	$13,815	$(5,156)	$15,653
Year ended July 31, 2004				
Allowance for doubtful accounts . . .	$5,095	$5,325	$(3,426)	$6,994
Year ended July 31, 2003				
Allowance for doubtful accounts . . .	$5,535	$1,410	$(1,850)	$5,095

P6-41. **Analyzing and Interpreting Inventories and Related Ratios and Disclosures**   **(LO2)**

Dow Chemical (DOW)

The current asset section from The Dow Chemical Company's 2005 annual report follows.

December 31 (In millions)	2005	2004
Cash and cash equivalents	$ 3,806	$ 3,108
Marketable securities and interest-bearing deposits	32	84
Accounts and notes receivable		
Trade (net of allowance for doubtful receivables—2005: $169; 2004: $136)	5,124	4,753
Other	2,802	2,604
Inventories	5,319	4,957
Deferred income tax assets—current.	321	384
Total current assets	$17,404	$15,890

The Dow Chemical inventory footnote follows.

Inventories   The following provides a breakdown of inventories at December 31, 2005 and 2004.

Inventories at December 31 (In millions)	2005	2004
Finished goods.	$2,941	$2,989
Work in process	1,247	889
Raw materials.	645	605
Supplies	486	474
Total inventories	$5,319	$4,957

Inventory reserves reduce Dow's inventories from the first-in, first-out ("FIFO") basis to the last-in, first-out ("LIFO") basis. These reserves amount to $1,149 million at December 31, 2005 and $807 million at December 31, 2004.

Required

a.   What inventory costing method does Dow Chemical use? As of 2005, what is the effect on cumulative pretax income and cash flow of using this inventory costing method? (Assume a 35% tax rate.) What is the effect on 2005 pretax income and cash flow of using this inventory costing method.

b.   Compute inventory turnover and average inventory days outstanding for 2005 (2005 cost of goods sold is $38,276 million). Comment on the level of these two ratios. Is the level what you expect given Dow's industry? Explain.

c.   Dow provides the following additional disclosure in its inventory footnote: "A reduction of certain inventories resulted in the liquidation of some of the Company's LIFO inventory layers, increasing pretax income $110 million in 2005, $154 million in 2004 and $70 million in 2003." Explain why a reduction of inventory quantities increased income in 2003, 2004 and 2005.

P6-42.   Estimating Useful Life and Percent Used Up   (LO3)

The property and equipment section of the Abbott Laboratories 2005 balance sheet follows.

Abbott Laboratories
(ABT)

Property and equipment, at cost ($ thousands)	
Land	$ 370,949
Buildings	2,655,356
Equipment	8,813,517
Construction in progess	920,599
	12,760,421
Less: accumulated depreciation and amortization	6,757,280
Net property and equipment	$ 6,003,141

The company also provides the following disclosure relating to the useful lives of its depreciable assets.

Property and Equipment—Depreciation and amortization are provided on a straight-line basis over the estimated useful lives of the assets. The following table shows estimated useful lives of property and equipment.

Classification	Estimated Useful Lives
Buildings	10 to 50 years (average 27 years)
Equipment	3 to 20 years (average 11 years)

During 2005, the company reported $868,808 ($ 000s) for depreciation expense.

Required

a.   Compute the estimated useful life of Abbott Laboratories' depreciable assets. How does this compare with its useful lives footnote disclosure above?

b.   Compute the estimated percent used up of Abbott Laboratories' depreciable assets. How do you interpret this figure?

P6-43. **Interpreting and Applying Disclosures on Property and Equipment** (LO3)

Following are selected disclosures from the Rohm and Haas Company (a specialty chemical company) 2005 10-K.

Land, Building and Equipment, Net

(in millions)	2005	2004
Land	$ 139	$ 141
Buildings and improvements	1,683	1,744
Machinery and equipment	5,570	5,656
Capitalized interest.	329	320
Construction in progress	168	166
	7,889	8,027
Less: Accumulated depreciation	5,208	5,098
Total	$2,681	$2,929

The principal lives (in years) used in determining depreciation rates of various assets are: buildings and improvement (10–50); machinery and equipment (5–20); automobiles, trucks and tank cars (3–10); furniture and fixtures, laboratory equipment and other assets (5–10); capitalized software (5–7). The principle life used in determining the depreciation rate for leasehold improvements is the years remaining in the lease term or the useful life (in years) of the asset, whichever is shorter.

IMPAIRMENT OF LONG-LIVED ASSETS

Long-lived assets, other than investments, goodwill and indefinite-lived intangible assets, are depreciated over their estimated useful lives, and are reviewed for impairment whenever changes in circumstances indicate the carrying value of the asset may not be recoverable. Such circumstances would include items such as a significant decrease in the market price of a long-lived asset, a significant adverse change in the manner the asset is being used or planned to be used or in its physical condition or a history of operating or cash flow losses associated with the use of the asset . . . When such events or changes occur, we assess the recoverability of the asset by comparing the carrying value of the asset to the expected future cash flows associated with the asset's planned future use and eventual disposition of the asset, if applicable . . . We utilize marketplace assumptions to calculate the discounted cash flows used in determining the asset's fair value. In 2005, $81 million of asset impairments were recognized for the impairment of certain finite-lived intangible assets and fixed assets across several of our chemical businesses and our Electronic Materials segment.

Required

a. Compute the PPE (land, buildings and equipment) asset turnover for 2005 (Sales in 2005 are $7,994 million). Does the level of its PPE turnover suggest that Rohm and Haas is capital intensive? (*Hint:* The median PPE turnover for all publicly traded companies is approximately 1.3 in 2005.) Explain. Do you believe that Rohm and Haas' balance sheet reflects all of the company's operating assets? Explain.

b. Rohm and Haas reported depreciation expense of $422 million in 2005. Assuming that Rohm and Haas uses straight-line depreciation, estimate the useful life, on average, for its depreciable PPE assets.

c. By what percentage are Rohm and Haas' assets "used up" at year-end 2005? What implication does the assets used up computation have for forecasting cash flows?

d. Rohm and Haas reports an asset impairment charge in 2005. How do companies determine if assets are impaired? How do asset impairment charges affect Rohm and Haas' cash flows for 2005? How would we treat these charges for analysis purposes?

CASES

C6-44.   Management Application: Managing Operating Asset Reduction   (LO1, 2, 3)

Return on net operating assets (RNOA = NOPAT/Average NOA, see Module 4) is commonly used to evaluate financial performance. If managers cannot increase NOPAT, they can still increase this return by reducing the amount of net operating assets (NOA). List specific ways that managers could reduce the following assets:

a.   Receivables

b.   Inventories

c.   Plant, property and equipment

C6-45.   Ethics and Governance: Managing the Allowance for Uncollectible Accounts   (LO1)

Assume that you are the CEO of a publicly traded company. Your chief financial officer (CFO) informs you that your company will not be able to meet earnings per share targets for the current quarter. In that event, your stock price will likely decline. The CFO proposes reducing the quarterly provision for uncollectible accounts (bad debts expense) to increase your EPS to the level analysts expect. This will result in an allowance account that is less than it should be. The CFO explains that outsiders cannot easily detect a reduction in this allowance and that the allowance can be increased next quarter. The benefit is that your shareholders will not experience a decline in stock price.

a.   Identify the parties that are likely to be affected by this proposed action.

b.   How will reducing the provision for uncollectible accounts affect the income statement and the balance sheet?

c.   How will reducing the provision for uncollectible accounts in the current period affect the income statement and the balance sheet in a future period?

d.   What argument might the CFO use to convince the company's external auditors that this action is justified?

e.   How might an analyst detect this earnings management activity?

f.   How might this action affect the moral compass of your company? What repercussions might this action have?

Reporting and Analyzing Intercorporate Investments

LEARNING OBJECTIVES

LO1 Describe and illustrate accounting for passive investments. (p. 7-5)

LO2 Explain and illustrate accounting for equity method investments. (p. 7-13)

LO3 Describe and illustrate accounting for consolidations. (p. 7-18)

GOOGLE

How does Google make money? A recent *BusinessWeek* article explains: "everybody knows that Google Inc.'s innovations in search technology made it the No. 1 search engine. But Google didn't make money until it started auctioning ads that appear alongside the search results. Advertising today accounts for 99% of the revenue of a company whose market capitalization now tops $100 billion." This seems to suggest that Google is a media company. Indeed, with a market capitalization of $100 billion, (greater even than that of Time Warner), Google is the world's largest media company and among America's top 30 most valuable companies. Since its IPO in 2004, Google's (GOOG) stock price has quadrupled making Google one of the fastest growing companies on any stock exchange.

Google's operations generated nearly $2.5 billion of cash in 2005, over eight times the cash generated two years before. During 2005, Google completed its second public offering, netting $4.3 billion. By fiscal year-end 2005, Google reported nearly $3.9 billion of cash and $4.2 billion of investments in marketable securities.

Google's investments in marketable securities are *passive investments* because Google owns a relatively small percentage of the stock for a variety of companies. Google holds these investments because it has excess cash awaiting deployment in other business activities and expects to earn dividends and potentially capital gains from these securities. The accounting for these marketable securities differs markedly from the accounting for most other assets—Google's balance sheet reports these marketable securities at their current market value. As a result, the assets on Google's balance sheet fluctuate with the stock market. This causes stockholders' equity to fluctuate because, as we know from the accounting equation, assets equal liabilities plus equity.

We might wonder why Google would report these assets at market value when nearly all other assets are reported at historical cost. As well, we might ask how these fluctuations in market value affect Google's reported profit, if at all. This module answers both questions and explains the accounting for, and analysis of, such so-called passive investments in marketable securities.

To expand its business activities beyond its current search-engine and advertising base, Google has strategically invested in the stock of several other companies, which is a second category of investments. Through these strategic investments, Google has acquired substantial ownership of those companies such that Google can significantly influence their operations. The nature and purpose of these investments differs from Google's passive investment in marketable securities and, accordingly, the accounting reflects that difference. In particular, if Google owns enough voting stock to exert significant influence over another company, Google uses the *equity method* to account for those investments. Under the equity method, Google carries the investment on its balance sheet at an amount equal to its proportionate share of the investee company's equity. An equity method investment increases and decreases, not with changes in the stock's market value, but with changes in the investee company's stockholders' equity. That is, Google's share of the investee's net assets (assets less liabilities) appear on Google's balance sheet as a long-term investment

An interesting by-product of the equity method is that Google's balance sheet does not reflect the investee company's individual assets and liabilities, but only its net assets (the stockholders' equity). This is important because Google could be using the investee's assets and be responsible, to some extent, for the investee's liabilities. Yet, these are not detailed on Google's balance sheet. This creates what is called *off-balance-sheet financing*, potentially of great concern to accountants, analysts, creditors and others who rely on financial reports. This module describes the equity method of accounting for investments, including the implications of this type of off-balance-sheet financing.

When an investor company acquires a sufficiently large proportion of the voting stock of another company, it can effectively control the other company. At that point, the acquired company is *consolidated*. Most of the financial statements of public companies are titled "consolidated." Consolidation essentially adds together the financial statements of two or more companies. It is important that we understand what consolidated financial statements tell us and what they do not. This module covers consolidation along with a discussion of its implications for analysis.

(Continued on next page)

(Continued from previous page)

There was much consternation among investors when Google's stock price passed $100, then $200, then $300, then $400. At each milestone, investors became increasingly concerned that Google's stock was overvalued. That concern still abounds. But, as Google continues to make strategic investments necessary to broaden its revenue base, its share price will likely increase. Google's management believes that investments are a crucial part of the company's strategic plan. Understanding the accounting for all three types of inter-corporate investment is, thus, important to our understanding of Google's (and other companies') ongoing operations.

Sources: *Google Form 10-K*, 2006; *Google Annual Report*, 2006; *BusinessWeek*, 2006; and *Fortune*, 2006.

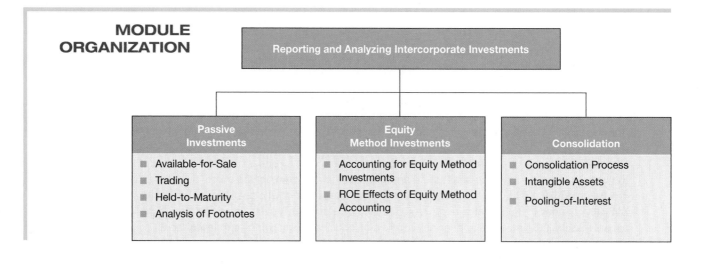

INTRODUCTION

It is common for one company to purchase the voting stock of another. These purchases, called *intercorporate investments,* have the following strategic aims:

- **Short-term investment of excess cash.** Companies might invest excess cash to use during slow times of the year (after receivables are collected and before seasonal production begins) or to maintain liquidity (such as to counter strategic moves by competitors or to quickly respond to acquisition opportunities).

- **Alliances for strategic purposes.** Companies might acquire an equity interest in other companies for strategic purposes, such as gaining access to their research and development activities, to their supply or distribution markets, or to their production and marketing expertise.

■ **Market penetration or expansion.** Companies might acquire control of other companies to achieve vertical or horizontal integration in existing markets or to penetrate new and growth markets.

Accounting for intercorporate investments follows one of three different methods, each of which affects the balance sheet and the income statement differently. These differences can be quite substantial. To help assimilate the materials in this module, Exhibit 7.1 graphically depicts the accounting for investments.

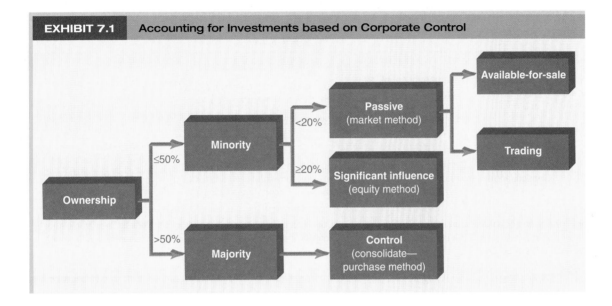

EXHIBIT 7.1   **Accounting for Investments based on Corporate Control**

The degree of influence or control that the investor company (purchaser) can exert over the investee company (the company whose securities are being purchased) determines the accounting method. GAAP identifies three levels of influence/control.

1. **Passive.** A passive investment is one where the purchasing company has a relatively small investment and cannot exert influence over the investee company. The investor's goal is to realize dividends and capital gains. Generally, the investment is considered passive if the investor company owns less than 20% of the outstanding voting stock of the investee.

2. **Significant influence.** A company can sometimes exert significant influence over, but not control, the activities of the investee company. Significant influence can result when the percentage of voting stock owned is more significant than a passive, short-term investment. However, an investment can also exhibit "significant influence" if there exist legal agreements between the investor and investee, such as a license to use technology, a formula, or a trade secret like production know-how. A significant investment also can occur when the investor company is a large supplier or customer of the investee. Generally, significant influence is presumed if the investor company owns 20% to 50% of the voting stock of the investee.

3. **Control.** When a company has control over another, it has the ability to elect a majority of the board of directors and, as a result, the ability to affect the investee company's strategic direction and the hiring of executive management. Control is generally presumed if the investor company owns more than 50% of the outstanding voting stock of the investee company. Control can sometimes occur at less than 50% stock ownership by virtue of legal agreements, technology licensing, or other contractual means.

The level of influence/control determines the specific accounting method applied and its financial statement implications as outlined in Exhibit 7.2.

EXHIBIT 7.2	Investment Type, Accounting Treatment, and Financial Statement Effects			
	Accounting	**Balance Sheet Effects**	**Income Statement Effects**	**Cash Flow Effects**
Passive	Market method	Investment account is reported at current market value	Dividends and capital gains included in income Interim changes in market value may or may not affect income depending on whether the investor actively trades the securities Sale of investment yields capital gain or loss	Dividends and sale proceeds are cash inflows Purchases are cash outflows
Significant influence	Equity method	Investment account equals percent owned of investee company's equity*	Dividends reduce investment account Investor reports income equal to percent owned of investee income Sale of investment yields capital gain or loss	Dividends and sale proceeds are cash inflows Purchases are cash outflows
Control	Consolidation	Balance sheets of investor and investee are combined	Income statements of investor and investee are combined (and sale of investee yields capital gain or loss)	Cash flows of investor and investee are combined (and sale/purchase of investee yields cash inflow/outflow)

*Investments are often acquired at purchase prices in excess of book value (on average, market prices are 1.5 times book value for public companies). In this case the investment account exceeds the proportionate ownership of the investee's equity, which we discuss later in the module.

There are two basic reporting issues with investments: (1) how investment income should be recognized in the income statement and (2) at what amount (cost or fair market value) the investment should be reported on the balance sheet. We next discuss both of these issues as we consider the three investment types.

PASSIVE INVESTMENTS

LO1 Describe and illustrate accounting for passive investments.

Short-term investments of excess cash are typically passive investments. Passive investments can involve equity or debt securities. Equity securities involve an ownership interest such as common stock or preferred stock, whereas debt securities have no ownership interest. A voting stock investment is passive when the investor does not possess sufficient ownership to either influence or control the investee company. The *market method* is used to account for passive investments.

Acquisition and Sale

When a company makes a passive investment, it records the shares acquired on the balance sheet at fair market value, that is, the purchase price. This is the same as accounting for the acquisition of other assets such as inventories or plant assets. Subsequent to acquisition, passive investments are carried on the balance sheet as current or long-term assets, depending on management's expectations about their ultimate holding period.

When investments are sold, any recognized gain or loss on sale is equal to the difference between the proceeds received and the book (carrying) value of the investment on the balance sheet as follows:

Gain or Loss on Sale = Proceeds from Sale − Book Value of Investment Sold

To illustrate the acquisition and sale of a passive investment, assume that Microsoft purchases 1,000 shares of Ask.com for $20 cash per share (this includes transaction costs such as brokerage fees). Microsoft, subsequently, sells 400 of the 1,000 shares for $22 cash per share. The following financial statement effects template shows how these transactions affect Microsoft.

	Balance Sheet						Income Statement		
Transaction	Cash Asset	+ Noncash Assets	= Liabil- ities	+ Contrib. Capital	+ Earned Capital		Rev- enues	− Expen- ses	= Net Income
1. Purchase 1,000 shares of Ask.com common stock for $20 cash per share	−20,000 Cash	+20,000 Marketable Securities	=						=
2. Sell 400 shares of Ask. com common stock for $22 cash per share	+8,800 Cash	−8,000 Marketable Securities	=		+800 Retained Earnings		+800 Gain on Sale		= +800

```
MS      20,000
  Cash       20,000
        MS
20,000 |
   Cash
        |  20,000
```

```
Cash  8,800
  MS         8,000
  GN           800
     Cash
8,800 |
   MS
        | 8,000
   GN
        |  800
```

Income statements include the gain or loss on sale of marketable securities as a component of *other income*, which is typically reported separately from operating income and often aggregated with interest and dividend revenue. Accounting for the purchase and sale of passive investments is the same as for any other asset. Further, there is no difference in accounting for purchases and sales across the different types of passive investments discussed in this section. However, there are differences in accounting for different types of passive investments between their purchase and their sale. We next address this issue.

Mark-to-Market versus Cost

If a passive investment in securities has an active market with published prices, that investment is reported on the balance sheet at market value. **Market value** is the published price (as listed on a stock exchange) multiplied by the number of shares owned. This is one of few assets that are reported at market value instead of historical cost.[1] If there exists no active market with published prices for the stock, the investment is reported at its historical cost.

Why are passive investments recorded at current market value on the balance sheet? The answer lies in understanding the trade-off between the *objectivity* of historical cost and the *relevance* of market value. All things equal, current market values of assets are more relevant in determining the market value of the company. However, for most assets, market values cannot be reliably determined. Adding unreliable "market values" to the balance sheet would introduce subjectivity into financial reports.

In the case of marketable securities, market prices result from numerous transactions between willing buyers and sellers. Market prices in this case provide an unbiased (objective) estimate of value to report on balance sheets. This reliability is the main reason GAAP allows passive investments to be recorded at market value instead of at historical cost.

This market method of accounting for securities causes asset values (the marketable securities) to fluctuate, with a corresponding change in equity (liabilities are unaffected). This is reflected in the following accounting equation:

$$\text{Assets} \uparrow = \text{Liabilities} + \text{Equity} \uparrow \qquad \text{or} \qquad \text{Assets} \downarrow = \text{Liabilities} + \text{Equity} \downarrow$$

An important issue is whether such changes in equity should be reported as income (with a consequent change in retained earnings), or whether they should bypass the income statement and directly impact equity via *other comprehensive income (OCI)*. The answer differs depending on the classification of securities, which we explain next.

---

[1] Other assets reported at market value include (1) derivative securities (such as forward contracts, options, and futures) that are purchased to provide a hedge against price fluctuations or to eliminate other business risks (such as interest or exchange rate fluctuations), and (2) inventories and long-term assets that must be written down to market when their values permanently decline.

Investments Marked to Market

For accounting purposes, marketable securities are classified into two types, both of which are reported on the balance sheet at current market value (*marked-to-market*):

1. **Available-for-sale (AFS).** These are securities that management intends to hold for capital gains and dividend revenue; although, they can be sold if the price is right.
2. **Trading (T).** These are investments that management intends to actively buy and sell for trading profits as market prices fluctuate.

Management classifies securities depending on the degree of turnover (transaction volume) it expects in the investment portfolio, which reflects management's intent to actively trade the securities or not. Available-for-sale portfolios exhibit less turnover than trading portfolios. (GAAP permits companies to have multiple portfolios, each with a different classification, and management can change portfolio classification provided it adheres to strict disclosure and reporting requirements if its expectations of turnover change.) The classification as either available-for-sale or trading determines the accounting treatment, as Exhibit 7.3 summarizes.

EXHIBIT 7.3	Accounting Treatment for Available-for-Sale and for Trading Investments	
Investment Classification	**Reporting of Market Value Changes**	**Reporting of Dividends Received and Gains and Losses on Sale**
Available-for-Sale (AFS)	Market value changes bypass the income statement and are reported in accumulated *other comprehensive income* (OCI) as part of equity	Reported as *other income* in income statement
Trading (T)	Market value changes are reported in the income statement as unrealized gains or losses; impacting equity via retained earnings	Reported as *other income* in income statement

The difference between the accounting treatment of available-for-sale and trading investments relates to how market value changes affect equity. Changes in the market value of available-for-sale securities have no income effect; changes in market value of trading securities have an income affect. The impact on total stockholders' equity is identical for both classifications. The only difference is whether the change is reflected in retained earnings or in the accumulated other comprehensive income (AOCI) component of stockholders' equity. Dividends and any gains or losses on security sales are reported in the other income section of the income statement for both classifications.

Market Adjustments

To illustrate the accounting for changes in market value subsequent to purchase (and before sale), assume that Microsoft's investment in Ask.com (600 remaining shares purchased for $20 per share) increases in value to $25 per share at year-end. The investment must be marked to market to reflect the $3,000 unrealized gain ($5 per share increase for 600 shares). The financial statement effects depend on whether the investment is classified as available-for-sale or as trading as follows:

	Balance Sheet						Income Statement		
Transaction	**Cash Asset**	**+ Noncash Assets**	**= Liabil- ities**	**+ Contrib. Capital**	**+ Earned Capital**		**Rev- enues**	**− Expen- ses**	**= Net Income**
If classified as available-for-sale									
$5 increase in market value of Ask.com investment		+3,000 Marketable Securities	=		+3,000 OCI				=

MS   3,000
   OCI   3,000
       MS
3,000 |
   OCI
      | 3,000

continued

Transaction	Balance Sheet					Income Statement				
	Cash Asset	+ Noncash Assets	= Liabil- ities	+ Contrib. Capital	+ Earned Capital		Rev- enues	− Expen- ses	= Net Income	
If classified as trading										
$5 increase in market value of Ask.com investment		+3,000 Marketable Securities =			+3,000 Retained Earnings		+3,000 Unrealized Gain		= +3,000	MS 3,000 UG 3,000 MS 3,000 UG 3,000

Under both classifications, the investment account increases by $3,000 to reflect the increase in the stock's market value. If Microsoft classifies these securities as available-for-sale, the unrealized gain increases the accumulated other comprehensive income (AOCI) account (which analysts typically view as a component of earned capital). However, if Microsoft classifies the securities as trading, the unrealized gain is recorded as income, thus increasing both reported income and retained earnings for the period. (Our illustration uses a portfolio with only one security for simplicity. Portfolios usually consist of multiple securities, and the unrealized gain or loss is computed based on the total cost and total market value of the entire portfolio.)

These market adjustments only apply if market prices are available, that is, for publicly traded securities. Thus, this mark-to-market accounting does not apply to investments in start-up companies or privately held corporations. Investments in nonpublicly traded companies are accounted for at cost as we discuss later in this section.

Financial Statement Disclosures

Companies are required to disclose cost and market values of their investment portfolios in footnotes to financial statements. Google reports the accounting policies for its investments in the following footnote to its 10-K report:

Cash and Cash Equivalents and Marketable Securities All highly liquid investments with stated maturities of three months or less from date of purchase are classified as cash equivalents; all highly liquid investments with stated maturities of greater than three months are classified as marketable securities. Our marketable debt and equity securities have been classified and accounted for as available for sale. These securities are carried at fair value, with the unrealized gains and losses, net of taxes, reported as a component of stockholders' equity

Non-Marketable Equity Securities We have accounted for non-marketable equity security investments at historical cost because we do not have significant influence over the investees. They are subject to a periodic impairment review. To the extent any impairment is considered other-than-temporary, the investment is written down to its fair value and the loss is recorded as interest income and other, net.

Google accounts for its investments in marketable securities at market value. Because Google classifies those investments as "available-for-sale," unrealized gains and losses flow to the other comprehensive income (OCI) component of stockholders' equity. When Google sells the securities, it will record any *realized* gains or losses in income together with dividend and/or interest income. Google uses historical cost to account for investments in non-marketable securities (equity investments where Google cannot exert significant influence over the investee company). Google moniters the value of these invesments and writes them down to market value if they suffer a permanent decline in value.

Following is the current asset section of Google's 2005 balance sheet reflecting these investments.

December 31 ($ 000s)	2004	2005
Cash and cash equivalents	$ 426,873	$3,877,174
Marketable securities	1,705,424	4,157,073
Accounts receivable, net of allowances of $3,962 and $14,852	311,836	687,976
Income taxes receivable	70,509	—
Deferred income taxes, net	19,463	49,341
Prepaid revenue share, expenses and other assets	159,360	229,507
Total current assets	$2,693,465	$9,001,071

Google's investments in marketable securities that are expected to mature within 90 days of the balance sheet date are recorded together with cash as cash equivalents. Its remaining investments are reported as marketable securities.

Footnotes to the Google 10-K provide further information about the composition of its investment portfolio.

As of December 31 ($ 000s)	2004	2005
Cash and cash equivalents		
Cash	$ 394,460	$1,588,515
Cash equivalents		
Municipal securities.	2,951	—
U.S. government note and agencies.	18,997	2,281,858
Money market mutual funds	10,465	6,801
Total cash and cash equivalents.	426,873	3,877,174
Marketable securities		
Municipal securities	1,616,684	1,203,209
U.S. governement notes and agencies	5,163	2,906,698
U.S. corporate securities	83,577	—
Equity security	—	47,166
Total marketable securities.	1,705,424	4,157,073
Total cash, equivalents and marketable securities.	$2,132,297	$8,034,247

The majority of Google's investments are in government debt securities such as bonds and T-bills, with a relatively small portion invested in equity securities. Google accounts for all of these investments as available-for-sale and reports them in the current asset section of the balance sheet because they mature within the coming year or can be readily sold, if necessary.

Google provides additional (required) disclosures on the costs, market values, and unrealized gains and losses for its available-for-sale investments as follows:

December 31, 2005 ($ 000s)	Adjusted Cost	Gross Unrealized Gains	Gross Unrealized Losses	Fair Value
Municipal securities	$1,219,078	$ 28	$(15,897)	$1,203,209
U.S. government notes and agencies	2,911,410	418	(5,130)	2,906,698
Equity security	5,000	42,166	—	47,166
Total marketable securities.	$4,135,488	$42,612	$(21,027)	$4,157,073

For each type investment, Google reports its cost, fair market value, and gross unrealized gains and losses; the latter reflect differences between cost and market. Google reports that the cost of its investment portfolio is $4,135,488, and that there are unrealized gains (losses) of $42,612 ($21,027) as of December 31, 2005. Google's balance sheet reports the total market value of $4,157,073 at December 31, 2005 ($ 000s).

Google' net unrealized gain of $21,585 ($42,612 − $21,027) is reported net of tax in the accumulated other comprehensive income (AOCI) section of its stockholders' equity as follows ($ 000s):

December 31 ($ 000s)	2004	2005
Class A and Class B common stock	$ 267	$ 293
Additional paid-in capital	2,582,352	7,477,792
Deferred stock-based compensation.	(249,470)	(119,015)
Accumulated other comprehensive income.	5,436	4,019
Retained earnings	590,471	2,055,868
Total stockholders' equity	$2,929,056	$9,418,957

Google does not identify the components of its 2005 accumulated other comprehensive income of $4,019 except to report that the other component, beyond the unrealized gains on available-for-sale investments, is the cumulative translation adjustment relating to subsidiaries whose balance sheets are denominated in currencies other than $US. This lack of information can be confusing because the amount of unrealized gain (loss) reported in the investment footnote and the amount reported in accumulated other comprehensive income differ. Part of this difference relates to taxes: the net unrealized gain of $21,585 reported in the investment footnote is pretax while the amount reported in the accumulated other comprehensive income section of stockholders' equity is after-tax.

Investments Reported at Cost

Companies often purchase debt securities, including bonds issued by other companies or by the U.S. government. Such debt securities have maturity dates—dates when the security must be repaid by the borrower. If a company buys debt securities, and management intends to hold the securities to maturity (as opposed to selling them early), the securities are classified as **held-to-maturity** (HTM). The cost method applies to held-to-maturity securities. Exhibit 7.4 identifies the reporting of these securities.

EXHIBIT 7.4	Accounting Treatment for Held-to-Maturity Investments	
Investment Classification	Reporting of Market Value Changes	Reporting Interest Received and the Gains and Losses on Sale
Held-to-Maturity (HTM)	Market value changes are *not* reported in either the balance sheet or income statement	Reported as *other income* in income statement

Changes in market value do not affect either the balance sheet or the income statement. The presumption is that these investments will indeed be held to maturity, at which time their market value will be exactly equal to their face value. Fluctuations in market value, as a result, are less relevant for this investment classification. Finally, any interest received, and gains and losses on the sale of these investments, are recorded in current income. Sometimes companies acquire held-to-maturity debt securities for more or less than the security's face value. This can happen if the company acquires the security from the open market (as opposed to buying it directly from the company or government agency that issued it). Because the value of debt securities fluctuates with the prevailing rate of interest, the market value of the security will be greater than its face value if current market interest rates are lower than what the security pays for interest. In that case, the acquirer will pay a premium for the security. Conversely, if current market interest rates exceed what the security pays in interest, the acquirer will purchase the security at a discount. (We cover premiums and discounts on debt securities in more detail in Module 8.) Either way, the company records the investment at its acquisition cost (like any other asset) and amortizes any discount or premium over the remaining life of the held-to-maturity investment. At any point in time, the acquirer's balance sheet carries the investment at "amortized cost," which is never adjusted for subsequent market value changes.

In addition to held-to-maturity investments, companies sometimes acquire equity interests in other companies that are not traded on an organized exchange. These might be start-ups that have never issued stock or established privately held companies. Because there is no market for such securities, they cannot be classified as marketable securities and are carried at historical cost on the balance sheet. Google references one such investment in its 2005 10-K.

> Our investment in this non-marketable equity security will be accounted for at historical cost. In addition, this investment will be subject to a periodic impairment review. To the extent any impairment is considered other-than-temporary, this investment would be written down to its fair value and the loss would be recorded in "interest income and other, net."

If such an investee company ever goes public, Google will change its accounting method. If Google's ownership percentage does not allow it to exert significant influence or control, Google will account for this investment following the procedures described above for marketable securities. However, if Google can exert influence or control, it will apply different accounting methods that we explain in the following sections of this module.

MID-MODULE REVIEW 1

Part 1: Available-for-sale securities

Using the financial statement effects template, enter the effects (amount and account) relating to the following four transactions involving investments in marketable securities classified as available-for-sale.

1. Purchased 1,000 shares of Netscape common stock for $15 cash per share.
2. Received cash dividend of $2 per share on Netscape common stock.
3. Year-end market price of Netscape common stock is $17 per share.
4. Sold all 1,000 shares of Netscape common stock for $17,000 cash in the next period.

Solution for Part 1:

		Balance Sheet						Income Statement		
Transaction	**Cash Asset**	**+ Noncash Assets**	**= Liabil- ities**	**+ Contrib. Capital**	**+ Earned Capital**		**Rev- enues**	**− Expen- ses**	**= Net Income**
1. Purchased 1,000 shares of Netscape common stock for $15 cash per share	−15,000 Cash	+15,000 Marketable Securities	=						=
2. Received cash dividend of $2 per share on Netscape common stock	+2,000 Cash		=		+2,000 Retained Earnings		+2,000 Dividend Income		= +2,000
3. Year-end market price of Netscape common stock is $17 per share		+2,000 Marketable Securities	=		+2,000 OCI				=
4. Sold 1,000 shares of Netscape common stock for $17,000 cash	+17,000 Cash	−17,000 Investments	=		−2,000 OCI +2,000 Retained Earnings		+2,000 Gain on Sale		= +2,000

Journal entry margin notes:

1.
MS   15,000
  Cash   15,000

MS	
15,000	
	Cash
	15,000

2.
Cash   2,000
  DI   2,000

Cash	
2,000	
	DI
	2,000

3.
MS   2,000
  OCI   2,000

MS	
2,000	
	OCI
	2,000

4.
Cash   17,000
OCI   2,000
  MS   17,000
  GN   2,000

Cash	
17,000	
	OCI
2,000	
	MS
	17,000
	GN
	2,000

Part 2: Trading securities

Using the financial statement effects template and the transaction information 1 through 4 from part 1, enter the effects (amount and account) relating to these transactions assuming that the investments are classified as trading securities.

Solution for Part 2:

Transaction	Balance Sheet						Income Statement		
	Cash Asset	+ Noncash Assets	= Liabil- ities	+ Contrib. Capital	+ Earned Capital		Rev- enues	− Expen- ses	= Net Income
1. Purchased 1,000 shares of Netscape common stock for $15 cash per share	−15,000 Cash	+15,000 Marketable Securities	=						=
2. Received cash dividend of $2 per share on Netscape common stock	+2,000 Cash		=		+2,000 Retained Earnings		+2,000 Dividend Income		= +2,000
3. Year-end market price of Netscape common stock is $17 per share		+2,000 Marketable Securities	=		+2,000 Retained Earnings		+2,000 Unrealized Gain		= +2,000
4. Sold all 1,000 shares of Netscape common stock for $17,000 cash	+17,000 Cash	−17,000 Investments	=						=

T-accounts (right margin):

1. MS 15,000 / Cash 15,000
   MS 15,000 | / Cash | 15,000
2. Cash 2,000 / DI 2,000
   Cash 2,000 | / DI | 2,000
3. MS 2,000 / UG 2,000
   MS 2,000 | / UG | 2,000
4. Cash 17,000 / MS 17,000
   Cash 17,000 | / MS | 17,000

Part 3: Footnote Disclosure

Yahoo! reports the following table in the footnotes to its 2005 10-K ($ millions).

December 31, 2005	Gross Amortized Costs	Gross Unrealized Gains	Gross Unrealized Losses	Estimated Fair Value
United States Government and agency securities	$1,057,960	$ 29	$(13,210)	$1,044,779
Municipal bonds	9,760	—	(166)	9,594
Corporate debt securities	1,528,282	127	(12,627)	1,515,782
Corporate equity securities	31,175	—	(1,168)	30,007
Total investments in available-for-sale securities	$2,627,177	$156	$(27,171)	$2,600,162

Required

a. What amount does Yahoo! report as investments on its balance sheet? What does this balance represent?

b. How did the net unrealized loss affect reported income in 2005? How do we know?

INVESTMENTS WITH SIGNIFICANT INFLUENCE

LO2 Explain and illustrate accounting for equity method investments.

Many companies make equity investments that yield them significant influence over the investee companies. These intercorporate investments are usually made for strategic reasons such as the following:

- **Prelude to acquisition.** Significant ownership can allow the investor company to gain a seat on the board of directors from which it can learn much about the investee company, its products, and its industry.

- **Strategic alliance.** Strategic alliances permit the investor to gain trade secrets, technical know-how, or access to restricted markets. For example, a company might buy an equity share in a company that provides inputs for the investor's production process. This relationship is closer than the usual supplier-buyer relationship and will convey benefits to the investor company.

- **Pursuit of research and development.** Many research activities in the pharmaceutical, software, and oil and gas industries are conducted jointly. The common motivation is to reduce the investor's risk or the amount of capital investment. The investment often carries an option to purchase additional shares, which the investor can exercise if the research activities are fruitful.

A crucial feature in each of these investments is that the investor company has a level of ownership that is sufficient to exert *significant influence* over the investee company. GAAP requires that such investments be accounted for using the *equity method*.

Significant influence is the ability of the investor to affect the financing, investing and operating policies of the investee. Ownership levels of 20% to 50% of the outstanding common stock of the investee typically convey significant influence. Significant influence can also exist when ownership is less than 20%. Evidence of such influence can be that the investor company is able to gain a seat on the board of directors of the investee by virtue of its equity investment, or the investor controls technical know-how or patents that are used by the investee, or the investor is able to exert significant influence by virtue of legal contracts with the investee. (There is growing pressure for determining significant influence by the facts and circumstances of the investment instead of a strict ownership percentage rule.)

Accounting for Investments with Significant Influence

GAAP requires that investors use the **equity method** when significant influence exists. The equity method reports the investment on the balance sheet at an amount equal to the percentage of the investee's equity owned by the investor; hence, the name equity method. (This assumes acquisition at book value. Acquisition at an amount greater than book value is covered later in this section.) Contrary to passive investments whose carrying amounts increase or decrease with the market value of the investee's stock, equity method investments increase (decrease) with increases (decreases) in the investee's stockholders' equity.

Equity method accounting is summarized as follows:

- Investments are recorded at their purchase cost.

- Dividends received are treated as a recovery of the investment and, thus, reduce the investment balance (dividends are not reported as income as with passive investments).

- The investor reports income equal to its percentage share of the investee's reported income; the investment account is increased by the percentage share of the investee's income or decreased by the percentage share of any loss.

- Changes in market value do not affect the investment's carrying value.

To illustrate the equity method, consider the following scenario: Assume that Google acquires a 30% interest in Mitel Networks, a company seeking to develop a new technology. This investment is a strategic alliance for Google. At the acquisition date, Mitel's balance sheet reports $1,000 of stockholders' equity, and Google purchases a 30% stake for $300. At the first year-end, Mitel reports profits of $100 and pays $20 in cash dividends to its shareholders ($6 to Google). Following are the financial statement effects for Google from this investment using the equity method:

	Balance Sheet						Income Statement		
Transaction	Cash Asset	+ Noncash Assets	= Liabil- ities	+ Contrib. Capital	+ Earned Capital		Rev- enues	− Expen- ses	= Net Income
1. Purchase 30% investment in Mitel for $300 cash	−300 Cash	+300 Investment in = Mitel							=
2. Mitel reports $100 income		+30 Investment in = Mitel			+30 Retained Earnings		+30 Investment Income		= +30
3. Mitel pays $20 cash dividends; $6 to Google	+6 Cash	−6 Investment in = Mitel							=
Ending balance of Google's investment account		324							

T-accounts (right margin):

```
EMI      300
   Cash       300
      EMI
  300 |
     Cash
          |  300

EMI       30
EI             30
      EMI
   30 |
        EI
          |  30

Cash       6
   EMI          6
      Cash
    6 |
       EMI
          |  6
```

The investment is initially reported on Google's balance sheet at its purchase price of $300, representing a 30% interest in Mitel's total stockholders' equity of $1,000. During the year, Mitel's equity increases to $1,080 ($1,000 plus $100 income and less $20 dividends). Likewise, Google's investment increases by $30 to reflect its 30% share of Mitel's $100 income, and decreases by $6, relating to its share of Mitel's dividends. After these transactions, Google's investment in Mitel is reported on Google's balance sheet at 30% of $1,080, or $324.

Google's investment in Mitel is an asset, just like any other asset. As such, it must be tested annually for impairment. If the investment is found to be permanently impaired, Google must reduce the investment amount on the balance sheet and report a loss in the income statement. If and when Google sells Mitel. any gain or loss on the sale is reported in Google's income statement. The gain or loss is computed as the difference between the sales proceeds and the balance sheet value of the Mitel investment. For example, if Google sold Mitel for $500, Google would report a gain on sale of $176 ($500 proceeds − $324 balance sheet value).

Companies often pay more than book value when they make equity investments. For example, if Google paid $400 for its 30% stake in Mitel, Google would initially report its investment at its $400 purchase price. The $400 investment consists of two parts: the $300 equity investment described above and the $100 additional investment. Google is willing to pay the higher purchase price because it believes that Mitel's reported equity is below its current market value (such as when assets are reported at costs that are below market values or when intangible assets like internally generated goodwill are not recorded on the balance sheet). The $300 portion of the investment is accounted for as described above. Management of the investor company decides on how to allocate the excess of the amount paid over the book value of the investee company's equity and accounts for the excess accordingly. For example, if management decides that the $100 relates to depreciable assets, the $100 is depreciated over the assets' estimated useful lives. Or, if it relates to identifiable intangible assets that have a determinable useful life (like patents), it is amortized over the useful lives of the intangible assets. If it relates to goodwill, however, it is not amortized and remains on the balance sheet at $100 unless and until it is deemed to have become impaired. (See Appendix 7A for an expanded illustration.)

Two final points about equity method accounting: First, there can be a substantial difference between the book value of an equity method investment and its market value. An increase in value is not recognized until the investment is sold. If the market value of the investment has permanently declined, however, the investment is deemed impaired and it is written down to that lower market value. Second, if the investee company reports income, the investor company reports its share. Recognition of equity income by the investor, however, does not mean that it has received that income in cash. Cash is only received if the investee pays a dividend. To highlight this, the investor's statement of cash flows will include a reconciling item (a deduction from net income in computing operating cash flow) for its percentage share of the investee's net income. This is typically reported net of any cash dividends received.

RESEARCH INSIGHT   **Equity Income and Stock Prices**

Under the equity method of accounting, the investor does not recognize as income any dividends received from the investee, nor any changes in the investee's market value, until the investment is sold. However, research has found a positive relation between investors' and investees' stock prices at the time of investees' earnings and dividend announcements. This suggests that the market includes information regarding investees' earnings and dividends when assessing the stock prices of investor companies, and implies that the market looks beyond the book value of the investment account in determining stock prices of investor companies.

Equity Method Accounting and ROE Effects

The investor company reports equity method investments on the balance sheet at an amount equal to the percentage owned of the investee company's equity when that investment is acquired at book value. To illustrate, consider the case of Abbott Laboratories, Inc., which owns 50% of TAP Pharmaceutical Products Inc. (TAP is a joint venture with Takeda Pharmaceutical Company, Limited of Japan). TAP Pharmaceuticals (TAP) develops and markets pharmaceutical products mainly for the U.S. and Canada. Abbott accounts for its investment in TAP using the equity method as described in the following footnote to its 2005 10-K report:

> **Equity Method Investments *($ millions)*** Abbott's 50 percent-owned joint venture, TAP Pharmaceutical Products Inc. (TAP), is accounted for under the equity method of accounting. The investment in TAP was $167, $76 and $340 at December 31, 2005, 2004 and 2003, respectively. Dividends received from TAP were $343, $638 and $606 in 2005, 2004 and 2003, respectively. Abbott performs certain administrative and manufacturing services for TAP at negotiated rates that approximate fair market value.

At the end of 2005, the TAP joint venture reported stockholders' equity of $334.0 million and net income of $882.8 million. (TAP's financial statements are included in an exhibit to Abbott's 2005 10-K; not reproduced here.) In the footnote above, Abbott reports an investment balance at December 31, 2005, of $167 million (TAP equity of $334 million × 50%). In its income statement, Abbott reports income of $441.4 million (TAP net income of $882.8 million × 50%). Provided the investment is originally acquired at book value these relations will always hold.

Let's look a bit closer at TAP. TAP's balance sheet reports assets of $1,470.2 million, liabilities of $1,136.2 million, and stockholders' equity of $334 million. TAP is a highly leveraged company with considerable assets. The $167 million investment balance on Abbott's balance sheet does not provide investors with any clue about the level of TAP's total assets nor about the substantial amount of TAP's financial obligations. It reflects only Abbott's share of TAP's net assets (assets less liabilities, or equity).

Further, although TAP reports net income of $882.8 million, it only paid out $686.2 million in dividends—$343.1 million to Abbott. This means that Abbott reports equity income relating to this investment of $441.4 million, but only receives $343.1 million in cash. Accordingly, Abbott makes the following additional disclosure in its footnotes relating to the cumulative payment of dividends by TAP:

> Undistributed earnings of investments accounted for under the equity method amounted to approximately $151 as of December 31, 2005.

Cumulatively, Abbott has recorded $151 million more of income than it has received in cash dividends from TAP. This shows that equity income does not necessarily equal cash inflow. This is particularly true for equity investments in growth-stage companies that do not pay dividends, or for foreign subsidiaries of U.S. nationals that might not pay dividends for tax reasons or other restrictions.

Another area of concern with equity method accounting relates to unreported liabilities. As described above, TAP reports total liabilities of $1,136.2 million as of 2005, none of which appear on Abbott's balance sheet (Abbott only reports its investment in TAP's equity as an asset). Pharmaceutical companies face large potential liabilities arising from drug sales. (For example, TAP reports a loss of $150 million relating to litigation that it settled in 2004.) Although Abbott might have no direct legal obligation for TAP's liabilities, it might need to fund settlement costs via additional investment or advances to maintain TAP's viability if the company is important to Abbott's strategic plan. Further, companies that routinely fund R&D activities through equity investments in other companies, a common practice in the pharmaceutical and software industries, can find themselves supporting underperforming equity investments to assure continued capital market funding for these entities. One cannot always assume, therefore, that the investee's liabilities will not adversely affect the investor.

To summarize, under equity method accounting, only the net equity owned is reported on the balance sheet (not the underlying assets and liabilities), and only the net equity in earnings is reported in the income statement (not the investee's sales and expenses). From an analysis standpoint, because the assets and liabilities are left off the balance sheet, and because the sales and expenses are omitted from the income statement, the *components* of ROE are markedly affected as follows:

- **Net operating profit margin (NOPM = NOPAT/Sales).** Most analysts include equity income (sales less expenses) in NOPAT since it relates to operating investments. However, investee's sales are not included in the NOPM denominator. The reported NOPM is, thus, *overstated.*

- **Net operating asset turnover (NOAT = Sales/Average NOA).** Investee's sales are excluded from the NOAT numerator. This means that NOAT is *understated.* (When investee assets exceed the investment balance, the impact on NOAT is *indeterminate.*)

- **Financial leverage (FLEV = Net nonoperating obligations/Average equity).** Financial leverage is understated due to the absence of investee liabilities in the numerator.

Although ROE components are affected, ROE is unaffected by equity method accounting because the correct amount of investee net income and equity *is* included in the ROE numerator and denominator, respectively. Still, the evaluation of the quality of ROE is affected. Analysis using reported equity method accounting numbers would use an overstated NOPM and an understated FLEV because the numbers are based on net balance sheet and net income statement numbers. As we discuss in a later module, analysts frequently adjust reported financial statements for these types of items before conducting analysis. One such adjustment might be to consolidate (for analysis purposes) the equity method investee with the investor company.

MANAGERIAL DECISION   **You Are the Chief Financial Officer**

You are receiving capital expenditure requests for long-term operating asset purchases from various managers. You are concerned that capacity utilization is too low. What potential courses of action can you consider? Explain. [Answer, p. 7-33]

MID-MODULE REVIEW 2

Part 1: Using the financial statement effects template, enter the effects (amount and account) relating to the following five transactions involving investments in marketable securities accounted for using the equity method.

1. Purchased 5,000 shares of LookSmart common stock at $10 cash per share; these shares reflect 30% ownership of LookSmart.
2. Received a $2 per share cash dividend on LookSmart common stock.
3. Recorded an accounting adjustment to reflect $100,000 income reported by LookSmart.
4. Year-end market price of LookSmart has increased to $12 per common share.
5. Sold all 5,000 shares of LookSmart common stock for $90,000 cash in the next period.

Solution to Part 1:

Transaction	Balance Sheet					Income Statement		
	Cash Asset	+ Noncash Assets	= Liabil- ities	+ Contrib. Capital	+ Earned Capital	Rev- enues	− Expen- ses	= Net Income
1. Purchased 5,000 shares of LookSmart common stock at $10 cash per share; these shares reflect 30% ownership	−50,000 Cash	+50,000 Investments	=					=
2. Received a $2 per share cash dividend on LookSmart stock	10,000 Cash	−10,000 Investments	=					=
3. Made an adjustment to reflect $100,000 income reported by LookSmart		+30,000 Investments	=		+30,000 Retained Earnings	+30,000 Equity Income		= +30,000
4. Market value has increased to $12 per share		NOTHING RECORDED						
5. Sold all 5,000 shares of LookSmart stock for $90,000	+90,000 Cash	−70,000 Investments	=		+20,000 Retained Earnings	+20,000 Gain on Sale		= +20,000

Transaction 1:
EMI 50,000
  Cash 50,000
EMI
50,000 |
  Cash
       | 50,000

Transaction 2:
Cash 10,000
  EMI 10,000
Cash
10,000 |
  EMI
       | 10,000

Transaction 3:
EMI 30,000
  EI 30,000
EMI
30,000 |
  EI
       | 30,000

Transaction 5:
Cash 90,000
  EMI 70,000
  GN 20,000
CASH
90,000 |
  EMI
       | 70,000
  GN
       | 20,000

Part 2: Yahoo! reports a $349.7 million equity investment in Yahoo! Japan related to its 33.5% ownership interest. Yahoo's footnotes reveal the following financial information about Yahoo! Japan ($ thousands).

Twelve Months Ended September 30	2003	2004	2005
Operating data			
Revenues	$500,091	$868,281	$1,367,247
Gross profit	462,352	810,114	1,251,599
Income from operations	262,393	470,681	656,167
Net income	145,720	290,576	382,287

September 30	2004	2005
Balance sheet data		
Current assets	$622,794	$900,149
Long-term assets	291,566	469,077
Current liabilities	192,761	306,441
Long-term liabilities	22,803	19,663

Required

a. How much income does Yahoo! report in its 2005 income statement related to this equity investment?
b. Show the computations required to yield the $349.7 million balance in the equity investment account on Yahoo!'s balance sheet.

Solution to Part 2

a. Yahoo! reports $128,066 ($382,287 × 33.5%) of equity income related to this investment in its 2005 income statement.

b. Yahoo! Japan's stockholders' equity is $1,043,519 thousand (computed as $900,149 + $469,077 − $306,044 − $19,663, in $ 000s), and Yahoo!'s investment account equals $349.7 million, computed as $1,043,519 thousand × 33.5% (difference due to rounding).

INVESTMENTS WITH CONTROL

This section discusses accounting for investments where the investor company "controls" the investee company. For example, in its footnote describing its accounting policies, Google reports the following:

LO3 Describe and illustrate accounting for consolidations.

> **Basis of Consolidations** The consolidated financial statements include the accounts of Google and wholly-owned subsidiaries. All intercompany balances and transactions have been eliminated.

This means that Google's financial statements are an aggregation (an adding up) of those of the parent company, Google, and all its subsidiary companies, less any intercompany activities.

Accounting for Investments with Control

Accounting for business combinations (acquiring a controlling interest) goes one step beyond equity method accounting. Under the equity method, the investor's investment balance represents the proportion of the investee's equity owned by the investor, and the investor company's income statement includes its proportionate share of the investee's income. Once "control" over the investee company is achieved, GAAP requires consolidation for financial statements issued to the public (not for the internal financial records of the separate companies). Consolidation accounting includes 100% of the investee's assets and liabilities on the investor's balance sheet and 100% of the investee's sales and expenses on its income statement. Specifically, the consolidated balance sheet includes the gross assets and liabilities of the investee company, and the income statement includes the investee's gross sales and expenses rather than just the investor's share of the investee company's net assets or income. All intercompany sales and expenses are eliminated in the consolidation process to avoid double counting when, for example, goods are sold from the investee (called a subsidiary) to the investor (called the parent company) for resale to the parent's ultimate customers.

To illustrate, consider the following scenario. Penman Company acquires all of the common stock of Nissim Company by exchanging newly issued Penman shares for all of Nissim's common stock. The purchase price is equal to the $3,000 book value of Nissim's stockholders' equity (contributed capital of $2,000 and retained earnings of $1,000). On its balance sheet, Penman accounts for the investment in Nissim Co. using the equity method. This is important. Even if the investor (the parent) owns 100% of the investee, it records the investment on its balance sheet using the equity method described in the previous section. That is, Penman records an initial balance in the investment account of $3,000, equal to the purchase price. The balance sheets for Penman and Nissim immediately after the acquisition, together with the consolidated balance sheet, are shown in Exhibit 7.5.

EXHIBIT 7.5	Mechanics of Consolidation Accounting (Purchased at Book Value)			
	Penman Company	Nissim Company	Consolidating Adjustments	Consolidated
Current assets	$ 5,000	$1,000		$ 6,000
Investment in Nissim	3,000	0	(3,000)	0
PPE, net	10,000	4,000		14,000
Total assets	$18,000	$5,000		$20,000
Liabilities	$ 5,000	$2,000		$ 7,000
Contributed capital	10,000	2,000	(2,000)	10,000
Retained earnings	3,000	1,000	(1,000)	3,000
Total liabilities and equity	$18,000	$5,000		$20,000

Since Penman "controls" the activities of Nissim, GAAP requires consolidation of the two balance sheets. This process, shown in Exhibit 7.5, involves summing the individual lines for each balance sheet, after eliminating any intercompany transactions (such as investments and loans, and sales and purchases), within the consolidated group. The consolidated balances for accounts such as current assets, PPE, and liabilities are computed as the sum of those accounts from each balance sheet. The equity investment account, however, represents an intercompany transaction that Penman must eliminate during the consolidation process. This is accomplished by removing the equity investment of $3,000 (from Penman's balance sheet), and removing Nissim's stockholders' equity to which Penman's investment relates.[2]

Exhibit 7.5 shows the consolidated balance sheet in the far right column. It shows total assets of $20,000, total liabilities of $7,000 and stockholders' equity of $13,000. Notice that consolidated equity equals that of the parent company—this is always the case. (Likewise, consolidated net income always equals the parent company's net income as the subsidiary's net income is already reflected in the parent's income statement as equity income from its investment.)

The illustration above assumes that the purchase price of the acquisition equals the book value of the investee company. It is more often the case, however, that the purchase price exceeds the book value. This might arise, for example, if an investor company believes it is acquiring something of value that is not reported on the investee's balance sheet—such as tangible assets whose market values have risen above book value, or unrecorded intangible assets, like patents or corporate synergies. When the acquisition price exceeds book value, all net assets acquired (both tangible and intangible) must be recognized on the consolidated balance sheet.

To illustrate, assume that Penman Company acquires Nissim Company for $4,000 instead of the $3,000 purchase price we used in the previous illustration. Also assume that in determining its purchase price, Penman paid the additional $1,000 because (1) Nissim's PPE is worth $300 more than its book value, and (2) Penman expects to realize $700 in additional value from corporate synergies (these "synergies" are an intangible asset with an unidentifiable useful life; they are classified as an asset called goodwill). The $4,000 investment account reflects two components: the book value acquired of $3,000 (as before) and an additional $1,000 of newly acquired assets. Exhibit 7.6 shows the post-acquisition balance sheets of the two companies, together with the consolidating adjustments and the consolidated balance sheet.

EXHIBIT 7.6	Mechanics of Consolidation Accounting (Purchase Price above Book Value)			
	Penman Company	Nissim Company	Consolidating Adjustments	Consolidated
Current assets	$ 5,000	$1,000		$ 6,000
Investment in Nissim	4,000	0	(4,000)	0
PPE, net	10,000	4,000	300	14,300
Goodwill			700	700
Total assets	$19,000	$5,000		$21,000
Liabilities	$ 5,000	$2,000		$ 7,000
Contributed capital	11,000	2,000	(2,000)	11,000
Retained earnings	3,000	1,000	(1,000)	3,000
Total liabilities and equity	$19,000	$5,000		$21,000

The consolidated current assets, PPE, and liabilities are the sum of those accounts on each company's balance sheet. The investment account, however, includes the $1,000 of additional newly acquired assets that

---

[2] In the event that Penman acquires less than 100% of the stock of Nissim, consolidated equity must increase to maintain the accounting equation. This equity account is titled **minority interest**. For example, assume that Penman acquires 80% of Nissim for $2,400 (80% of $3,000). The consolidating adjustments follow. The claim of noncontrolling shareholders is recognized in consolidated stockholders' equity, just like that of the majority shareholders.

	Balance Sheet					Income Statement		
Transaction	Cash Asset	+ Noncash Assets	= Liabil- ities	+ Contrib. Capital	+ Retained Earnings	Rev- enues	− Expen- ses	= Net Income
		−2,400 Investment in Nissim		−2,000 Nissim's Common Stock	−1,000 Nissim's Retained Earnings			
				+600 Minority Interest				

must be reported on the consolidated balance sheet. The consolidation process in this case has two steps. First, the $3,000 equity of Nissim Company is eliminated against the investment account as before. Then, the remaining $1,000 of the investment account is eliminated and the newly acquired assets ($300 of PPE and $700 of goodwill not reported on Nissim's balance sheet) are added to the consolidated balance sheet. Thus, the consolidated balance sheet reflects the book value of Penman and the *fair market value* of Nissim (the book value plus the excess of Nissim's market value over its book value).

To illustrate consolidation mechanics with an actual case, consider the consolidated balance sheet (parent company, subsidiary and consolidated balance sheet) that General Electric reports in a supplemental schedule to its 10-K report as shown in Exhibit 7.7.

EXHIBIT 7.7	General Electric's Consolidated Balance Sheet		
At December 31, 2005 (In millions, except share amounts)	General Electric Company and Consolidated Affiliates	GE (Parent)	GECS (Subsidiary)
ASSETS			
Cash and equivalents.	$ 9,011	$ 2,015	$ 7,316
Investment securities	53,144	461	52,706
Current receivables	14,851	15,058	—
Inventories	10,474	10,315	159
Financing receivables—net	287,639	—	287,69
Other GECS receivables.	14,767	—	19,060
Property, plant and equipment—net	67,528	16,504	51,024
Investment in GECS.	—	50,815	—
Intangible assets—net	81,726	57,839	23,887
All other assets.	87,446	36,752	52,058
Assets of discontinued operations.	46,756	—	46,756
Total assets.	$673,342	$189,759	$540,605
LIABILITIES AND EQUITY			
Short-term borrowings.	$158,156	$1,127	$157,672
Accounts payable, principally trade accounts	21,273	11,870	13,133
Progress collections and price adjustments accrued	4,456	4,456	—
Dividends payable	2,623	2,623	—
All other current costs and expenses accrued.	18,419	18,436	—
Long-term borrowings	212,281	9,081	204,397
Investment contracts, insurance liabilities and insurance annuity benefits	45,432	—	45,722
All other liabilities	40,632	23,273	17,453
Deferred income taxes.	16,330	3,733	12,597
Liabilities of and minority interest in discontinued operations.	36,332	—	36,568
Total liabilities	555,934	74,599	487,542
Minority interest in equity of consolidated affiliates	8,054	5,806	2,248
Common stock (10,484,268,000 and 10,586,358,000 shares outstanding at year-end 2005 and 2004, respectively)	669	669	1
Accumulated gains (losses)—net			
Investment securities	1,831	1,831	1,754
Currency translation adjustments.	2,532	2,532	2,287
Cash flow hedges.	(822)	(822)	(813)
Minimum pension liabilities.	(874)	(874)	(179)
Other capital.	25,227	25,227	12,386
Retained earnings	98,117	98,117	35,379
Less common stock held in treasury	(17,326)	(17,326)	—
Total shareowners' equity.	109,354	109,354	50,815
Total liabilities and equity	$673,342	$189,759	$540,605

General Electric Company (GE) owns 100% of its financial products subsidiary, General Electric Capital Services (GECS), whose stockholders' equity is $50,815 million as of 2005. The Investment in GECS account is also reported at $50,815 million on GE's (parent company) balance sheet. This investment account is subsequently removed (eliminated) in the consolidation process, together with the equity of GECS to which it relates. Following this elimination, and the elimination of all other intercompany sales and advances, the adjusted balance sheets of the two companies are summed to yield the consolidated balance sheet that is reported in GE's 10-K.

Reporting of Acquired Intangible Assets

As previously discussed, acquisitions are routinely made at a purchase price in excess of the book value of the investee company's equity. The purchase price is first allocated to the fair market values of tangible assets and liabilities (such as PPE in our example). Then, the remainder is allocated to acquired intangible assets (Goodwill in our example).

As of the acquisition date, the purchasing company values the tangible assets acquired and liabilities assumed in the purchase and records them on the consolidated balance sheet at fair market value. (In the Exhibit 7.6 example, we sum the $4,000 PPE book value of Nissim with the $300 excess of market over book value to yield the $4,300 PPE fair market value that is included among the assets on the consolidated balance sheet.) Any remaining purchase price above book value is allocated to acquired identifiable *intangible* assets, which are also valued at the acquisition date. (In the example, the consolidated balance sheet includes $700 of goodwill, which is one type of intangible asset.) A sampling of the types of intangible assets that are often recognized during acquisitions follows:

- Marketing-related assets like trademarks and Internet domain names
- Customer-related assets like customer lists and customer contracts
- Artistic-related assets like plays, books, and videos
- Contract-based assets like licensing, franchise and royalty agreements, and lease contracts
- Technology-based assets like patents, software, databases, and trade secrets

To illustrate, Hewlett-Packard reported the following allocation of its $24,170 million purchase price for Compaq Computer in the footnotes to its 10-K report ($ millions).

Tangible assets	Cash and cash equivalents	$ 3,615
	Accounts receivable	4,305
	Financing receivables	1,241
	Inventory	1,661
	Current deferred tax assets	1,475
	Other current assets	1,146
	Property, plant and equipment	2,998
	Long-term financing receivables and other assets	1,914
Acquired intangible assets	Amortizable intangible assets	
	Customer contracts and lists, distribution agreements	1,942
	Developed and core technology, patents	1,501
	Product trademarks	74
	Intangible asset with an indefinite life	1,422
	Goodwill	14,450
Liabilities assumed	Accounts payable	(2,804)
	Short- and long-term debt	(2,704)
	Accrued restructuring	(960)
	Other current liabilities	(5,933)
	Other long-term liabilities	(1,908)
IPR&D →	In-process research and development	735
	Total purchase price	$24,170

In its acquisition of Compaq, HP allocated $4,939 million ($1,942 million + $1,501 million + $74 million + $1,422 million) of its purchase price to identifiable intangible assets (before goodwill), as described in the following footnote to its 10-K:

Amortizable intangible assets   Of the total purchase price, approximately $3.5 billion [$1,942 million + $1,501 million + $74 million] was allocated to amortizable intangible assets including customer contracts and developed and core technology. . . . HP is amortizing the fair value of these assets on a straight-line basis over a weighted average estimated useful life of approximately 9 years. Developed technology, which consists of products that have reached technological feasibility, includes products in most of Compaq's product lines. . . . Core technology and patents represent a combination of Compaq processes, patents and trade secrets. . . . HP is amortizing the developed and core technology and patents on a straight-line basis over a weighted average estimated useful life of approximately 6 years.

Intangible asset with an indefinite life   The estimated fair value of the intangible asset with an indefinite life was $1.4 billion, consisting of the estimated fair value allocated to the Compaq trade name. This intangible asset will not be amortized because it has an indefinite remaining useful life based on many factors and considerations, including the length of time that the Compaq name has been in use, the Compaq brand awareness and market position and the plans for continued use of the Compaq brand.

HP allocated a portion of the purchase price to the following identifiable intangible assets:

- Customer contracts
- Customer lists and distribution agreements
- Developed technology
- Core technology and patents
- Compaq trade name

HP deemed the first four of these identifiable intangible assets as amortizable assets, which are those having a finite useful life. HP will subsequently amortize them over their useful lives (similar to depreciation). The last asset (Compaq trade name) is deemed to have an indefinite useful life. It is not amortized, but is tested annually for impairment like goodwill.

HP also allocated $735 million of the purchase price to *In-Process Research and Development*. This relates to the acquisition-date value of research projects that have not yet reached technological feasibility. HP immediately expensed this R&D asset like all other R&D costs (rather than capitalize the costs on the balance sheet). This treatment was consistent with GAAP when HP acquired Compaq.

The IPR&D write-off has been subject to abuse. Excessive allocation of the purchase price to IPR&D artificially reduces current period income and inflates income in successive periods (by the elimination of future depreciation or amortization expense). The SEC monitors purchase allocations closely and challenges those with which it disagrees. As a result of these reviews, a number of companies have subsequently been forced to restate the amounts of their initial IPR&D write-offs. As well, the FASB monitored the IPR&D write-off issue and, in 2005, proposed an amendment to accounting standards to "prohibit writing-off immediately after the business combination the fair value of in-process research and development assets acquired." Under the new standard, companies will capitalize IPR&D costs on the balance sheet, amortize them, and test the IPR&D asset annually for impairment. The standard will likely come into play in 2007.

Once the purchase price has been allocated to identifiable tangible and intangible assets (net of liabilities assumed), any remaining purchase price is allocated to goodwill. Goodwill, thus, represents the remainder of the purchase price that is not allocated to other assets. HP allocated $14.45 billion (60%) of the Compaq purchase price to goodwill. The SEC is also scrutinizing companies that assign an excessive proportion of the purchase price to goodwill (companies might do this to avoid the future earnings drag from amortization expense).

Reporting of Goodwill

Goodwill is no longer amortized, as it was prior to 2001. Instead, GAAP requires companies to test the goodwill asset annually for impairment just like any other asset. The impairment test is a two-step process:

1. The market value of the investee company is compared with the book value of the investor's equity investment account.[3]

---

[3] The fair market value of the investee company can be determined using market comparables or other valuation methods (such as the discounted cash flow model, residual operating income model, or P/E multiples—see Module 12).

2. If the market value is less than the investment balance, the *investment* is deemed impaired. Step 2, then, determines if the *goodwill* portion of the investment is impaired rather than other acquired assets. The investor estimates the goodwill value as if the subsidiary were acquired at current market value, and the imputed balance for goodwill becomes the balance in the goodwill account. If this imputed goodwill amount is less than its book value, the company writes goodwill down, resulting in an impairment loss on the consolidated income statement.

To illustrate the impairment computation, assume that an investment, currently reported at $1 million on the investor's balance sheet, has a current fair market value of $900,000 (we know, therefore, that the investment is impaired); also assume the consolidated balance sheet reports goodwill at $300,000. Management review reveals that the current fair market value of the net assets of the investee company (absent goodwill) is $700,000. This indicates that the goodwill component of the investment account is impaired by $100,000, which is computed as follows:

Fair market value of investee company	$ 900,000
Fair market value of net assets (absent goodwill)	(700,000)
Implied goodwill	200,000
Current goodwill balance	(300,000)
Impairment loss	$(100,000)

This analysis implies that goodwill must be written down by $100,000. The impairment loss is reported in the consolidated income statement. The related footnote disclosure would describe the reasons for the write-down and the computations involved.

Corning provides an example of a goodwill impairment disclosure in its 10-K report:

Impairment Charge Pursuant to SFAS No 142, "Goodwill and Other Intangible Assets," (SFAS 142) goodwill is required to be tested for impairment annually at the reporting unit level. In addition, goodwill should be tested for impairment between annual tests if an event occurs or circumstances change that would more likely than not reduce the fair value of the reporting unit below its related carrying value. In the third quarter of 2004, we identified certain factors that caused us to lower our estimates and projections for the long-term revenue growth of the Telecommunications segment, which indicated that the fair value of the Telecommunications segment reporting unit was less than its carrying value. We performed an interim impairment test of the Telecommunications segment goodwill in the third quarter of 2004 and, as a result, recorded an impairment charge of $1,420 million to reduce the carrying value of goodwill to its implied fair value at September 30, 2004 of $117 million.

Corning determined that goodwill, reported on its balance sheet at $1,537 million, had a current (implied) market value $117 million. That is, Corning's goodwill was impaired, resulting in a write-down of $1,420 million. Corning reported a pretax operating loss of $1,485 million in 2004, nearly all of this related to its goodwill write-down.

BUSINESS INSIGHT   **Pitfalls of Acquired Growth**

One of the greatest destructions of shareholder value occurred during the bull market between 1995 and 2001 when market exuberance fueled a tidal wave of corporate takeovers. Companies often overpaid as a result of overestimating the cost-cutting and synergies their planned takeovers would bring. Then, acquirers failed to quickly integrate operations. The result? Subsequent years' market returns of most acquirers fell below those of their peers and were often negative. Indeed, 61% of corporate buyers saw their shareholders' wealth *decrease* after the acquisition. Who won? The sellers; which are the target-company shareholders who sold their stock within the first week of the takeover and reaped enormous profits at the expense of the acquirers' shareholders.

Reporting Subsidiary Stock Issuances

After subsidiaries are acquired, they can, and often do, issue stock. If issued to outside investors, the result is an infusion of cash into the subsidiary and a reduction in the parent's percentage ownership. For example, Clear Channel Communications' (CCU) 10-K report discloses the following stock issuance by one of its subsidiaries.

> **Initial Public Offering ("IPO") of Clear Channel Outdoor Holdings, Inc. ("CCO")** The Company completed the IPO on November 11, 2005, which consisted of the sale of 35.0 million shares, for $18.00 per share, of Class A common stock of CCO, its indirect, wholly owned subsidiary prior to the IPO. After completion of the IPO, the Company owns all 315.0 million shares of CCO's outstanding Class B common stock, representing approximately 90% of the outstanding shares of CCO's common stock and approximately 99% of the total voting power of CCO's common stock. The net proceeds from the offering, after deducting underwriting discounts and offering expenses, were approximately $600.6 million. All of the net proceeds of the offering were used to repay a portion of the outstanding balances of intercompany notes owed to the Company by CCO. Under the guidance in SEC Staff Accounting Bulletin Topic 5H, *Accounting for Sales of Stock by a Subsidiary*, the Company has recorded approximately $120.9 million of minority interest and $479.7 million of additional paid in capital on its consolidated balance sheet at December 31, 2005 as a result of this transaction.

While the note is complicated, the gist is that CCO, a Clear Channel Communications' subsidiary, issued stock to the public (an IPO). This increased the amount that Clear Channel reports on its balance sheet for this equity investment. To illustrate, consider Parent Company that acquires 100% of Subsidiary Company at book value, and the latter has a book value for stockholders' equity of $500. The investment account on Parent's balance sheet, using the equity method, is $500. Next, Subsidiary issues shares to outsiders for $100, which reduces Parent's ownership to, say, 90%. Parent now owns 90% of Subsidiary whose book value of equity has increased to $600. The Parent's investment should therefore, have a balance sheet value of $540 (90% × $600). The value of Parent's equity method investment account rose by $40 ($540 vs. $500) because of the Subsidiary's stock sale.

Similarly, Clear Channel's equity method investment account increased by $600.6 million. This increase must be matched with a corresponding increase in Clear Channel's stockholders' equity. The question is, what stockholders' equity account ought to increase? Should Clear Channel record the $600.6 million as income (thereby affecting retained earnings) or as an increase to paid-in capital? Clear Channel did the latter. It recognized a $600.6 million increase in stockholders' equity in two parts. First, Clear Channel added $479.7 million to additional paid-in capital. Second, it recorded minority interest for $120.9 million, which represents the book value of the CCO shares that were sold to the public. Minority interest is the part of CCO not owned by Clear Channel.

Current accounting standards also allow companies the option to record this sort of equity increase as income. For example, Citigroup, Inc., reports the following stock issuance in its 10-K report by one of its subsidiaries:

> **Travelers Property Casualty Corp.** (an indirect wholly owned subsidiary of Citigroup on December 31, 2001) sold 231 million shares of its class A common stock representing approximately 23.1% of its outstanding equity securities in an initial public offering (the IPO) on March 27, 2002. In 2002, Citigroup recognized an after-tax gain of $1.158 billion as a result of the IPO.

Under proposed changes to the business combinations accounting standard, the effects of stock sales by subsidiaries will be recognized only as additional paid-in capital, and not as gains on the income statement. However, unless and until this standard is enacted, companies will be able to choose to report changes in the equity investment balance either way: as income or as additional paid-in capital. Analysts need to be mindful of this option when assessing profitability and other equity changes that arise from sales of stock by subsidiary companies.

Reporting the Sale of Subsidiary Companies

Discontinued operations refer to any separately identifiable business unit that the company sells or intends to sell. The income or loss of the discontinued operations (net of tax), and the after-tax gain or loss on sale of the unit, are reported in the income statement below income from continuing operations. The segregation of discontinued operations means that its revenues and expenses are *not* reported with revenues and expenses from continuing operations.

To illustrate, assume that Google's recent periods' results were generated by both continuing and discontinuing operations as follows:

	Continuing Operations	Discontinued Operations	Total
Revenues	$10,000	$3,000	$13,000
Expenses	7,000	2,000	9,000
Pretax Income	3,000	1,000	4,000
Tax expense (40%)	1,200	400	1,600
Net Income	$ 1,800	$ 600	$ 2,400

Its reported income statement would appear as follows—notice the separate disclosure for discontinued operations (as highlighted).

Revenues	$10,000
Expenses	7,000
Pretax Income	3,000
Tax expense (40%)	1,200
Income from continuing operations	1,800
Income from discontinued operations, net	600
Net income	$ 2,400

Revenues and expenses reflect those of the continuing operations only, and the (persistent) income from continuing operations is reported net of its related tax expense. Results from the (transitory) discontinued operations are collapsed into one line item and reported separately net of its own tax (this includes any gain or loss from sale of the discontinued unit's net assets). The net income figure is unchanged by this presentation.

Importantly, results of the discontinued operations are segregated from those of continuing operations. This presentation facilitates the prediction of results from the (persistent) continuing operations. The segregation of discontinued operations is made in the current year and for the two prior years' comparative results reported in the income statement. To illustrate, Agilent reports the following footnote to its 2005 10-K relating to the decision to divest its semiconductor products business.

Discontinued Operations In August 2005, the Board of Directors approved the divestiture of our semiconductor products business. We subsequently signed an Asset Purchase Agreement with Avago Technologies Ltd. (f/k/a Argos Acquisition Pte. Ltd.) ("Avago") providing for the sale of our semiconductor products business for approximately $2.66 billion. The purchase price is subject to adjustment based on a determination of our semiconductor products business' Adjusted EBITDA (as defined in the Asset Purchase Agreement) and working capital at closing. The sale closed in December 2005. Our consolidated financial statements reflect our semiconductor products business, including the camera module business, as a discontinued operation in accordance with SFAS No.144, "Accounting for the Impairment or Disposal of Long-Lived Assets" ("SFAS No.144"). As required under SFAS No.144, we have ceased depreciation and amortization on our assets held for sale as of August 2005. The financial position, results of operations and cash flows of our semiconductor products business have been classified as discontinued operations and prior periods have been restated.

Years Ended October 31 (Restated, in millions)	2005	2004	2003
Net revenue	$1,796	$2,021	$1,688
Costs and expenses	1,670	1,779	1,594
Income (loss) from discontinued operations	226	242	(6)
Other income (expense), net	6	—	3
Income (loss) from discontinued operations before taxes	232	242	(3)
Provision (benefit) for taxes	46	—	10
Net income (loss) from discontinued operations	$ 186	$ 242	$ (13)

The revenue and expenses of Agilent's discontinued operation are eliminated from its 2005 income statement, leaving only the revenues and expenses of continuing operations. Restated revenues, for example, are $1,796 million lower. Revenues for the other years reported are, likewise, restated. Only the net income (loss) of the discontinued operations is reported in a separate line below income from continuing operations. Also, assets and liabilities of the discontinued operation are segregated on Agilent's balance sheet as highlighted in the following current asset section of its report.

October 31 (Restated, in millions)	2005	2004
Cash and cash equivalents	$2,226	$2,315
Short term investments	25	—
Cash and cash equivalents and short term investments	2,251	2,315
Accounts receivable, net	753	788
Inventory	722	809
Other current assets	298	266
Current assets of discontinued operations	423	485
Total current assets	$4,447	$4,663

The discontinued operation is reported in this manner until it is sold, at which time its assets and liabilities are removed from the balance sheet, and a gain or loss on the sale is reported in the income statement below income from continuing operations, as illustrated in the footnote above. The reported gain or loss on sale is equal to the proceeds received less the balance of the (equity method) investment that is reported on the parent's balance sheet at the sale date.

Limitations of Consolidation Reporting

Consolidation of financial statements is meant to present a financial picture of the entire set of companies under the control of the parent. Since investors typically purchase stock in the parent company, and not in the subsidiaries, that view is more relevant than the parent company merely reporting subsidiaries as equity investments in its balance sheet. Still, we must be aware of certain limitations that the consolidation process entails:

1. Consolidated income does not imply that the parent company has received any or all of the subsidiaries' net income as cash. The parent can only receive cash from subsidiaries via dividend payments. Conversely, the consolidated cash is not automatically available to the individual subsidiaries. It is quite possible, therefore, for an individual subsidiary to experience cash flow problems even though the consolidated group has strong cash flows. Likewise, unguaranteed debts of a subsidiary are not obligations of the consolidated group. Thus, even if the consolidated balance sheet is strong, creditors of a failing subsidiary are often unable to sue the parent or other subsidiaries to recoup losses.
2. Consolidated balance sheets and income statements are a mix of the various subsidiaries, often from different industries. Comparisons across companies, even if in similar industries, are often complicated by the different mix of subsidiary companies.
3. Segment disclosures on individual subsidiaries are affected by intercorporate transfer pricing policies relating to purchases of products or services that can artificially inflate the profitability of one segment at the expense of another. Companies also have considerable discretion in the allocation of corporate overhead to subsidiaries, which can markedly affect segment profitability.

Reporting Consolidations under Pooling-of-Interests

Prior to 2001, companies had a choice in their accounting for business combinations. They could use the *purchase method* as described in this module (now required for all acquisitions), or they could use the *pooling-of-interests (pooling) method*. A large number of acquisitions were accounting for under the pooling-of-interest method, and its impact on financial statements will linger for many years.

The main difference between the pooling-of-interest and the purchase method of accounting for acquisitions is this: under the purchase method the investment account is initially recorded at the *fair market*

BUSINESS INSIGHT   **Determining the parent company in an acquisition**

Sensor, Inc. is acquiring Boston Instrument Company through an exchange of stock valued at $500 million. Sensor will survive as the continuing company, and the senior management of Boston Instrument will own 65% of the outstanding stock, reflecting a premium in the exchange ratios paid by Sensor to acquire Boston Instrument. Sensor's Chairman will remain as Chairman of the company, but the purchase agreement specifies that the board of directors will elect a new Chairman within six months of the deal's close. Boston Instrument's President and CFO will assume those same positions in the new entity. Following are the market values of the tangible and intangible net assets of both companies on the date of acquisition: Sensor, $400 million; and Boston Instrument, $200 million. Which of these two companies should be viewed as the acquiring firm (parent company) for purposes of consolidation, and how does this decision affect the amount of goodwill recorded on the consolidated balance sheet? Although Sensor is the larger firm, its name will survive, and its Chairman will serve in that capacity in the combined company, most accountants would likely conclude that Boston Instrument is the parent company for purposes of consolidation. This determination is based on the 65% ownership interest of the Boston Instrument shareholders who control the new entity. Further, these shareholders will be able to elect a new Chairman within six months. The amount of goodwill recorded following the acquisition is equal to the purchase price less the market value of the net tangible and identifiable intangible assets acquired. If Senror is the acquiring firm, $100 million ($500 million − $400 million) of goodwill will be recorded. If Boston Instrument is the acquiring firm, $300 million ($500 million − $200 million) of goodwill will be recorded. This decision will dramatically affect both the balance sheet (relative amounts of goodwill and other assets recorded) as well as the income statement (depreciation of tangible assets and amortization of identifiable intangible assets recognized vs. annual impairment testing for goodwill).

---

value of the acquired company. Under the pooling-of-interest method, the investment account is initially recorded at the *book value* (amount reported on the balance sheet) of stockholders' equity for the acquired company, regardless of the amount actually paid. As a result, the pooling method created no goodwill. Further, since goodwill amortization was required under previous GAAP, subsequent income was larger under pooling. This feature spawned widespread use of pooling-of-interest, especially for high-tech companies.

Acquisitions previously accounted for under pooling-of-interest remain unaffected under current GAAP. We must be aware of at least two points for analysis purposes:

1. Assets were usually understated with the pooling-of-interest method because the investee's assets were recorded at book rather than market value. This implies that consolidated return on net operating assets (RNOA) and asset turnover ratios are overstated.

2. Net income with the pooling-of-interest method was nearly always overstated due to elimination of goodwill amortization. This continues to create difficulties for comparative analysis when looking at companies that previously applied pooling-of-interest accounting.

MODULE-END REVIEW

On January 1 of the current year, assume that Yahoo!, Inc., purchased all of the common shares of EarthLink for $600,000 cash—this is $200,000 more than the book value of EarthLink's stockholders' equity. Assume that the balance sheets of the two companies immediately after the acquisition follow:

	Yahoo! (Parent)	EarthLink (Subsidiary)	Consolidating Adjustments	Consolidated
Current assets	$1,000,000	$100,000		
Investment in EarthLink	600,000	—		
PPE, net	3,000,000	400,000		
Goodwill	—	—		
Total assets.	$4,600,000	$500,000		
Liabilities.	$1,000,000	$100,000		
Contributed capital.	2,000,000	200,000		
Retained earnings	1,600,000	200,000		
Total liabilities and equity	$4,600,000	$500,000		

During purchase negotiations, EarthLink's PPE was appraised at $500,000, and all of EarthLink's remaining assets and liabilities were appraised at values approximating their book values. Also, Yahoo! concluded that payment of an additional $100,000 was warranted because of anticipated corporate synergies. Prepare the consolidating adjustments and the consolidated balance sheet at acquisition.

Solution

	Yahoo! (Parent)	EarthLink (Subsidiary)	Consolidating Adjustments	Consolidated
Current assets	$1,000,000	$100,000		$1,100,000
Investment in EarthLink	600,000	—	$(600,000)	
PPE, net	3,000,000	400,000	100,000	3,500,000
Goodwill	—	—	100,000	100,000
Total assets.	$4,600,000	$500,000		$4,700,000
Liabilities.	$1,000,000	$100,000		$1,100,000
Contributed capital.	2,000,000	200,000	(200,000)	2,000,000
Retained earnings	1,600,000	200,000	(200,000)	1,600,000
Total liabilities and equity	$4,600,000	$500,000		$4,700,000

Explanation: The $600,000 investment account is eliminated together with the $400,000 book value of Earth-Link's equity to which Yahoo's investment relates. The remaining $200,000 consists of the additional $100,000 in PPE assets and the $100,000 in goodwill from expected corporate synergies. Following these adjustments, the balance sheet items are summed to yield the consolidated balance sheet.

APPENDIX 7A: Equity Method Mechanics

The appendix provides a comprehensive example of accounting for an equity method investment. Assume that Petroni Company acquires a 30% interest in the outstanding voting shares of Wahlen Company on January 1, 2005. To obtain these shares, Petroni pays $126,000 cash and issues 6,000 of its $10 par value common stock. On that date, Petroni's stock has a fair market value of $18 per share, and Wahlen's book value of equity is $560,000. Petroni agrees to pay $234,000 ($126,000 plus 6,000 shares at $18 per share) for a company with a book value of equity equivalent to $168,000 ($560,000 × 30%) because it believes that (1) Wahlen's balance sheet is undervalued by $140,000 (Petroni estimates PPE with a remaining useful life of 9 years is undervalued by $50,000 and that Wahlen has unrecorded patents with remaining useful lives of 5 years, valued at $90,000) and (2) the investment will yield intangible benefits valued at $24,000. (The $140,000 by which the balance sheet is undervalued translates into an investment equivalent of $42,000 [$140,000 × 30%]; this, plus the intangible benefits valued at $24,000, comprises the $66,000 difference between the purchase price of $234,000 and the book value equivalent of $168,000.)

To record the investment, Petroni reduces cash and/or increases financing by $234,000 and creates a new asset account for the investment in Wahlen for $234,000. The investment is reported at its fair market value at acquisition, just like all other asset acquisitions, and it is reported as a noncurrent asset because investors typically expect to hold strategic equity method investments more than one year. Subsequent to this purchase there are four main aspects of equity method accounting:

1. Dividends received from the investee are treated as a return *of* the investment rather than a return *on* the investment (investor company records an increase in cash received and a decrease in the investment account). This mirrors the effect of dividends on the investee's equity—dividends decrease stockholders' equity and thus, they also decrease the equity method investment on the investor's balance sheet.
2. When the investee company reports net income for a period, the investor company reports its percentage share, typically as "Other income" in the income statement. Thus, the investor's equity and investment account both increase from equity method income. If the investee company reports a net *loss* for the period, the investor company reduces its own income as well as its investment account by its proportionate share of the loss.
3. When the purchase price exceeds the investor's share of the investee's book value of the equity, the excess is added to the investment account. To the extent it relates to identifiable assets, the excess must be depreciated (for tangible assets) and amortized (for intangibles) over the assets' lives. This reduces both the equity method income reported each year and the investment account.
4. The investment balance is not marked-to-market as with passive investments. Instead, it is recorded at its historical cost and is increased (decreased) by the investor company's proportionate share of investee income (loss) and decreased by any cash dividends received. Unrecognized gains (losses) will occur if the market value of the investment differs from this adjusted cost, but the investor will not change the balance sheet value of the investment (unless the decline in value is deemed permanent, at which time the investment is written down as with any impaired asset).

To illustrate these mechanics, assume that, subsequent to acquisition, Wahlen reports net income of $50,000 and pays $10,000 cash dividends. Petroni calculates extra depreciation of $3,000 on the additional PPE (the excess of $50,000 over the 5-year life × Petroni's 30% share of Wahlen) and extra amortization of $3,000 on the patents (the excess of $90,000 for patents with 9 year lives × 30%). Petroni reduces the equity income it reports on its income statement by a total of $6,000 and reduces its investment account on the balance sheet by $6,000. Petroni's balance sheet and income statement are impacted as follows:

Transaction	Change in Investment Account on Petroni's Balance Sheet	Equity Income on Petroni's Income Statement
Acquisition balance	$234,000	
Wahlen reports income of $50,000 (30% for Petroni)............................	15,000	$15,000
Depreciation and amortization of excess of purchase price over book value of identifiable assets.............................	(6,000)	(6,000)
Wahlen pays a $10,000 cash dividend ($3,000 to Petroni)	(3,000)*	
Total	$240,000	$ 9,000

* Accompanied by an increase in cash.

Petroni's ending investment balance is $240,000, an increase of $6,000 and its cash balance increased by the $3,000 dividend received. Corresponding to the $9,000 increase in assets from Wahlen's income (adjusted by Petroni for the depreciation and amortization of the excess paid over book value) is a $9,000 increase in Petroni's retained earnings because Petroni reports $9,000 ($15,000 − $6,000) as investment income. Cash dividends received are treated as a return of the capital that Petroni invested in Wahlen and, thus, the investment account is reduced.

There is symmetry between Petroni's investment account and Wahlen's stockholders' equity as follows:

Investment Account on Petroni's Balance Sheet		Wahlen's Stockholders' Equity	
Acquisition balance	$234,000	Acquisition balance	$560,000
Income	9,000	Income	50,000
Dividends	(3,000)	Dividends	(10,000)
Ending balance...............	$240,000	Ending balance...............	$600,000

Petroni's ending investment balance of $240,000 is 30% of Wahlen's $600,000 stockholders' equity plus the original $66,000 excess less the depreciation/amortization of the excess of $6,000. The balance of the excess is therefore $60,000 at the end of the period, and it will shrink over time as Petroni continues to depreciate and amortize it. This excess explains why the equity investment balance we see reported on a balance sheet does not always equal the percentage owned of the investee company.

APPENDIX 7B: Consolidation Accounting Mechanics

This appendix extends the example we introduced in Appendix 7A, to include the consolidation of a parent company and one wholly owned subsidiary. Assume that Petroni Company acquires 100 percent (rather than 30% as in Appendix 7A) of the outstanding voting shares of Wahlen Company on January 1, 2005. To obtain these shares, Petroni pays $420,000 cash and issues 20,000 shares of its $10 par value common stock. On this date, Petroni's stock has a fair market value of $18 per share, and Wahlen's book value of equity is $560,000. Petroni is willing to pay $780,000 ($420,000 plus 20,000 shares at $18 per share) for this company with a book value of equity of $560,000 because it believes Wahlen's balance sheet is understated by $140,000 (PPE with 5 years of remaining useful life is undervalued by $50,000 and it has unrecorded patents that expire in 9 years, valued at $90,000). The remaining $80,000 of the purchase price excess over book value is ascribed to corporate synergies and other unidentifiable intangible assets (goodwill). Thus, the purchase price consists of the following three components:

Investment ($780,000)
- Book value of Wahlen ($560,000)
- Excess fair market value over book value ($140,000)
- Goodwill ($80,000)

On its own (unconsolidated) balance sheet, Petroni uses the equity method of accounting to account for the Wahlen acquisition.[4] This means that, at acquisition, Petroni's assets (investments) increase by $780,000, cash decreases by $420,000, and contributed capital increases by $360,000 (20,000 shares $\times$ $18). The balance sheets of Petroni and Wahlen at acquisition follow, including the adjustments that occur in the consolidation process and the ultimate consolidated balance sheet.

Accounts	Petroni Company	Wahlen Company	Consolidation Adjustments*		Consolidated Balance Sheet
Cash.	$ 168,000	$ 80,000			$ 248,000
Receivables, net.	320,000	180,000			500,000
Inventory.	440,000	260,000			700,000
Investment in Wahlen	780,000	0	[S]	(560,000)	0
			[A]	(220,000)	
Land	200,000	120,000			320,000
PPE, net	1,040,000	320,000	[A]	50,000	1,410,000
Patent.	0	0	[A]	90,000	90,000
Goodwill	0	0	[A]	80,000	80,000
Totals	$2,948,000	$960,000			$3,348,000
Accounts payable.	$ 320,000	$ 60,000			$ 380,000
Long-term liabilities	760,000	340,000			1,100,000
Contributed capital.	1,148,000	80,000	[S]	(80,000)	1,148,000
Retained earnings	720,000	480,000	[S]	(480,000)	720,000
Totals	$2,948,000	$960,000			$3,348,000

*[S] refers to elimination of stockholders' equity and [A] refers to recognition of assets acquired.

---

[4] The equity method is used for all investments other than passive investments. Once "control" is achieved, the investor company is required to consolidate its financial statements. The investment account remains unchanged on the parent's books, it is merely replaced with the assets and liabilities of the subsidiaries to which it relates during the consolidation process.

The initial balance of the investment account at acquisition ($780,000) reflects the $700,000 market value of Wahlen's net tangible and intangible (patent) assets ($560,000 book value and the $140,000 undervaluation of the net assets) plus the goodwill ($80,000) acquired. Goodwill is the excess of the purchase price over the fair market of the net assets acquired. Neither the patent nor the goodwill appear on Petroni's balance sheet as explicit assets. They are, however, included in the investment balance, and will emerge as a separate asset during consolidation.

The process of completing the initial consolidated balance sheet involves eliminating the investment account and replacing it with the assets and liabilities of Wahlen Company to which it relates. Recall the investment account consists of three items: the book value of Wahlen ($560,000), the excess of market price over book value ($140,000), and goodwill ($80,000). The consolidation process eliminates each item as follows:

[S] Elimination of Wahlen's book value of equity: Investment account is reduced by the $560,000 book value of Wahlen, and each of the components of Wahlen's equity ($80,000 common stock and $480,000 retained earnings) are eliminated.

[A] Elimination of the excess of purchase price over book value: Investment account is reduced by $220,000. The remaining adjustments increase assets (A) by the additional purchase price paid. PPE is written up by $50,000, and a $90,000 patent asset and an $80,000 goodwill asset are reported.

Consolidation is similar in successive periods. To the extent that the excess purchase price has been assigned to depreciable assets, or identifiable intangible assets that are amortized over their useful lives, the new assets recognized initially are depreciated. For example, if the PPE has an estimated life of 10 years with no salvage value, Petroni would add $10,000 to depreciation expense on the consolidated income statement. This would reduce the consolidated PPE. Likewise, the $90,000 patent is amortized over its remaining life of nine years and thus, consolidated amortization expense is increased by $10,000 a year. Recall from Appendix 7A, above, that Petroni reduces its investment in Wahlen for its share of the extra depreciation and amortization each year. Here, that would be for the entire amount because Petroni owns 100% of Wahlen. Finally, since goodwill is not amortized under GAAP, it remains at its carrying amount of $80,000 on the consolidated balance sheet unless and until it is impaired and written down.

As the excess of the purchase price over book value acquired is depreciated/amortized, the investment account on Petroni's balance sheet gradually declines. Assuming goodwill is not impaired, the investment reaches a balance equal to the percentage of the investee's equity owned (100% in this case) plus the balance of goodwill. Generally, the investment account equals the percentage of the equity owned plus any remaining undepreciated/unamortized excess over purchase price.

APPENDIX 7C: Accounting for Derivatives

Derivatives refer to financial instruments that companies use to reduce various kinds of risks. Some examples follow:

- A company expects to purchase raw materials for its production process and wants to reduce the risk that the purchase price increases prior to the purchase.
- A company has an accounts receivable on its books that is payable in a foreign currency and wants to reduce the risk that exchange rates move unfavorably prior to collection.
- A company borrows funds on a floating rate of interest (such as linked to the prime rate) and wants to convert the loan to a fixed interest rate.

Companies are routinely exposed to these and many other risks. Although companies are generally willing to assume the normal market risks that are inherent in their business, financial-type risks can add variability to income because they are uncontrollable. Fortunately, commodities, currencies, and interest rates are all traded on various markets and, further, securities have been developed to manage all of these risks. These securities, called derivatives, include forward contracts, futures contracts, option contracts, and swap agreements.

Companies use derivatives to manage (hedge) financial risks. But risk reduction comes at a price: another party (called the counterparty) charges a fee to assume the company's financial risk. Most counterparties are financial institutions, and managing financial risk is their business and is a source of their profits. Although derivatives can be used effectively to manage financial risk, they can also be used for speculation with potentially disastrous results. It is for this reason that regulators passed standards regarding derivative disclosure in financial statements.

Reporting of Derivatives

Derivatives work by offsetting gains or losses on the related (hedged) assets or liabilities. Derivatives shelter the company from fluctuations in the value of the related assets or liabilities that are hedged. For example, if a company has a receivable denominated in a foreign currency, which later declines in value (due to a strengthening of the $US), the company will incur a foreign currency loss. To avoid this situation, the company can hedge the receivable with a foreign-currency derivative. When the $US strengthens, the derivative will increase in value by an amount that exactly offsets the decrease in the value of the receivable. As a result, the company's net asset position (receivable less derivative) remains unaffected and no gain or loss arises.[5]

Although accounting for derivatives is complex, it essentially boils down to this: the derivative contract, and the asset or liability to being hedged, are both reported on the balance sheet at market value. If the market value of the hedged asset or liability changes, the value of the derivative changes in the opposite direction *if* the hedge is effective and, thus, net assets and liabilities are unaffected. Likewise, the related gains and losses are largely offsetting, leaving income unaffected. Income is impacted only to the extent that the hedging activities are ineffective or result from speculative activities. It is this latter activity, in particular, that prompted regulators to formulate newer, tougher accounting standards for derivatives.

Disclosure of Derivatives

Companies must disclose both qualitative and quantitative information about derivatives in notes to their financial statements and elsewhere (usually in Management's Discussion and Analysis section). The aim of these disclosures is to inform outsiders about potential risks associated with derivative use.

Following is Southwest Airlines's disclosures from its 2005 10-K report relating to its use of derivatives:

> **Financial Derivative Instruments** The Company utilizes financial derivative instruments primarily to manage its risk associated with changing jet fuel prices, and accounts for them under Statement of Financial Accounting Standards No. 133, "Accounting for Derivative Instruments and Hedging Activities", as amended (SFAS 133) . . . SFAS 133 requires that all derivatives be marked to market (fair value) and recorded on the Consolidated Balance Sheet. At December 31, 2005, the Company was a party to over 400 financial derivative instruments, related to fuel hedging, for year 2006 and beyond. The fair value of the Company's fuel hedging financial derivative instruments recorded on the Company's Consolidated Balance Sheet as of December 31, 2005, was $1.7 billion, compared to $796 million at December 31, 2004. The large increase in fair value primarily was due to the dramatic increase in energy prices throughout 2005, and the Company's addition of derivative instruments to increase its hedge positions in future years. Changes in the fair values of these instruments can vary dramatically, as was evident during 2005, based on changes in the underlying commodity prices . . . The Company enters into financial derivative instruments with third party institutions in "over-the-counter" markets. Since the majority of the Company's financial derivative instruments are not traded on a market exchange, the Company estimates their fair values . . . To the extent that the total change in the estimated fair value of a fuel hedging instrument differs from the change in the estimated price of the associated jet fuel to be purchased, both on a cumulative and a period-to-period basis, ineffectiveness of the fuel hedge can result, as defined by SFAS 133. This could result in the immediate recording of noncash charges or income, even though the derivative instrument may not expire until a future period . . . Ineffectiveness is inherent in hedging jet fuel with derivative positions based in other crude oil-related commodities, especially considering the recent volatility in the prices of refined products. In addition, given the magnitude of the Company's fuel hedge portfolio total market value, ineffectiveness can be highly material to financial results . . . This may result in increased volatility in the Company's results.

Southwest Airlines uses derivatives mainly to hedge fuel costs. Those hedges place a ceiling on fuel cost and are used for 30% to 60% of Southwest Airlines' fuel purchases.

These derivatives are cash flow hedges. Thus, unrealized gains and losses on these derivative contracts are added to the Accumulated Other Comprehensive Income (AOCI) (part of stockholders' equity) until the fuel is purchased. Once that fuel is purchased, any unrealized gains and losses are removed from AOCI to income. The gain (loss) on the derivative contract offsets the increased (decreased) cost of fuel. In 2005, $900 million of hedging gains were used to offset fuel expense for Southwest Airlines. This use of fuel derivatives is the prime reason that soaring oil prices in that year did not affect Southwest Airlines as harshly as at other large carriers.

Although the market value of derivatives and their related assets or liabilities can be large, the net effect on stockholders' equity is usually minor. This is because companies use derivatives mainly to hedge and not to speculate. The FASB enacted SFAS 133, 'Accounting for derivative instruments and hedging activities,' to respond to concerns that speculative activities were not adequately disclosed. However, subsequent to the passage of SFAS 133, the financial effects have been minimal. Either companies were not speculating to the extent suspected, or they have since reduced their level of speculation in response to increased scrutiny from better disclosures.

---

[5] Unrealized gains and losses on derivatives classified as *cash flow hedges* (such as those relating to planned purchases of commodities) are included in accumulated other comprehensive income (OCI) and are not recognized in income until the planned transaction is complete (such as when the purchase of inventory occurs). Unrealized gains and losses on derivatives classified as *fair value hedges* (including those relating to existing assets or liabilities such as inventory or debt) are recorded in current income along with the changes in value of the hedged asset or liability.

GUIDANCE ANSWERS

Capacity utilization is important. If long-term operating assets are used inefficiently, cost per unit produced is too high. Cost per unit does not relate solely to manufacturing products, but also applies to the cost of providing services and many other operating activities. However, if we purchase assets with little productive slack, our costs of production at peak levels can be excessive. Further, the company may be unable to service peak demand and risks losing customers. In response, the company might explore strategic alliances. These take many forms. Some require a simple contract to use another company's manufacturing, service, or administrative capability for a fee (note: these executory contracts are not recorded under GAAP). Another type of alliance is that of a joint venture to share ownership of manufacturing or IT facilities. In this case, if demand can be coordinated with that of a partner, perhaps operating assets can be more effectively used. Finally, a variable interest entity (VIE) can be formed to acquire the asset for use by the company and its partner—explained in Module 10.

Superscript $^{A(B,C)}$ denotes assignments based on Appendix 7A (7B, 7C).

DISCUSSION QUESTIONS

Q7-1. What measure (fair market value or amortized cost) is on the balance sheet for (a) trading securities, (b) available-for-sale securities, and (c) held-to-maturity securities?

Q7-2. What is an unrealized holding gain (loss)? Explain.

Q7-3. Where are unrealized holding gains and losses related to trading securities reported in the financial statements? Where are unrealized holding gains and losses related to available-for-sale securities reported in the financial statements?

Q7-4. What does *significant influence* imply regarding intercorporate investments? Describe the accounting procedures used for such investments.

Q7-5. On January 1 of the current year, Yetman Company purchases 40% of the common stock of Livnat Company for $250,000 cash. This 40% ownership allows Yetman to exert significant influence over Livnat. During the year, Livnat reports $80,000 of net income and pays $60,000 in cash dividends. At year-end, what amount should appear in Yetman's balance sheet for its investment in Livnat?

Q7-6. What accounting method is used when a stock investment represents more than 50% of the investee company's voting stock and allows the investor company to "control" the investee company? Explain.

Q7-7. What is the underlying objective of consolidated financial statements?

Q7-8. Finn Company purchases all of the common stock of Murray Company for $750,000 when Murray Company has $300,000 of common stock and $450,000 of retained earnings. If a consolidated balance sheet is prepared immediately after the acquisition, what amounts are eliminated in consolidation? Explain.

Q7-9. Bradshaw Company owns 100% of Dee Company. At year-end, Dee owes Bradshaw $75,000 arising from a loan made during the year. If a consolidated balance sheet is prepared at year-end, how is the $75,000 handled? Explain.

Q7-10. What are some limitations of consolidated financial statements?

MINI EXERCISES

M7-11. Interpreting Disclosures of Available-for-Sale Securities   **(LO1)**

Pfizer Inc. (PFE)

Use the following year-end footnote disclosure from Pfizer's 10-K report to answer parts *a* and *b*.

(Millions of Dollars)	2005
Cost of available-for-sale equity securities	$270
Gross unrealized gains	189
Gross unrealized losses	(12)
Fair value of available-for-sale equity securities	$447

a.   What amount does Pfizer report on its 2005 balance sheet as available-for-sale equity securities? Explain.

b.   How does Pfizer report the net unrealized gain of $177 million ($189 million − $12 million) in its financial statements?

M7-12.   Accounting for Available-for-Sale and Trading Securities   (LO1)
Assume that Wasley Company purchases 6,000 common shares of Pincus Company for $12 cash per share. During the year, Wasley receives a cash dividend of $1.10 per common share from Pincus, and the year-end market price of Pincus common stock is $13 per share. How much income does Wasley report relating to this investment for the year if it accounts for the investment as:

a.   Available-for-sale investment
b.   Trading investment

M7-13.   Interpreting Disclosures of Investment Securities   (LO1)
Abbott Laboratories reports the following disclosure relating to its December 31 comprehensive income. How is Abbott accounting for its investment in marketable equity securities? How do you know? Explain how its 2005 financial statements are impacted by its investment in marketable equity securities.

Abbott Laboratories (ABT)

Comprehensive Income, net of tax ($ 000s)	2005
Foreign currency translation adjustments	$ (953,726)
Minimum pension liability adjustments, net of taxes of $57,219	346,172
Unrealized (losses) gains on marketable equity securities	(9,219)
Net (losses) gains on derivative instruments designated as cash flow hedges	38,574
Reclassification adjustments for realized (gains)	(35)
Other comprehensive income	(578,234)
Net earnings	3,372,065
Comprehensive income	$2,793,831

M7-14.   Analyzing and Interpreting Equity Method Investments   (LO2)
Stober Company purchases an investment in Lang Company at a purchase price of $1 million cash, representing 30% of the book value of Lang. During the year, Lang reports net income of $100,000 and pays cash dividends of $40,000. At the end of the year, the market value of Stober's investment is $1.2 million.

a.   What amount does Stober report on its balance sheet for its investment in Lang?
b.   What amount of income from investments does Stober report? Explain.
c.   Stober's $200,000 unrealized gain in the market value of the Lang investment (choose one and explain):
     (1) Is not reflected on either its income statement or balance sheet.
     (2) Is reported in its current income.
     (3) Is reported on its balance sheet only.
     (4) Is reported in its other comprehensive income.

M7-15.   Computing Income for Equity Method Investments   (LO2)
Kross Company purchases an equity investment in Penno Company at a purchase price of $5 million, representing 40% of the book value of Penno. During the current year, Penno reports net income of $600,000 and pays cash dividends of $200,000. At the end of the year, the market value of Kross's investment is $5.3 million. What amount of income does Kross report relating to this investment in Penno for the year? Explain.

M7-16.   Interpreting Disclosures on Investments in Affiliates   (LO2)
Merck's 10-K report included the following footnote disclosure:

Merck & Co., Inc. (MRK)

Joint Ventures and Other Equity Method Affiliates Investments in affiliates accounted for using the equity method . . . totaled $3 billion at December 31, 2005. These amounts are reported in Other assets. Dividends and distributions received from these affiliates were $1.1 billion in 2005.

a.   At what amount are the equity method investments reported on Merck's balance sheet? Does this amount represent Merck's adjusted cost or market value?
b.   How does Merck account for the dividends received on these investments?

M7-17. Computing Consolidating Adjustments and Minority Interest (LO3)

Philipich Company purchases 80% of Hirst Company's common stock for $600,000 cash when Hirst Company has $300,000 of common stock and $450,000 of retained earnings. If a consolidated balance sheet is prepared immediately after the acquisition, what amounts are eliminated when preparing that statement? What amount of minority interest appears in the consolidated balance sheet?

M7-18. Computing Consolidated Net Income (LO3)

Benartzi Company purchased a 90% interest in Liang Company on January 1 of the current year and the purchase price reflected 90% of Liang's net book value of equity. Benartzi Company had $600,000 net income for the current year *before* recognizing its share of Liang Company's net income. If Liang Company had net income of $150,000 for the year, what is the consolidated net income for the year?

M7-19. Computing Earnings under Pooling-of-Interest Method (LO3)

DeFond Company acquired 100% of Verduzco Company on September 1 of the current year. Why might the consolidated earnings of the two companies for the current year be higher if DeFond had treated the transaction as a pooling-of-interest (which is no longer accepted under GAAP for new acquisitions, but is allowed for acquisitions made prior to the effective date of the new business combinations standard) rather than as a purchase?

EXERCISES

E7-20. Assessing Financial Statement Effects of Trading and Available-for-Sale Securities (LO1)

a. Use the financial statement effects template to record the following four transactions involving investments in marketable securities classified as trading.

(1) Purchased 6,000 common shares of Liu, Inc., for $12 cash per share.

(2) Received a cash dividend of $1.10 per common share from Liu.

(3) Year-end market price of Liu common stock was $11.25 per share.

(4) Sold all 6,000 common shares of Liu for $66,900.

b. Using the same transaction information as above, complete the financial statement effects template (with amounts and accounts) assuming the investments in marketable securities are classified as available-for-sale.

E7-21. Assessing Financial Statement Effects of Trading and Available-for-Sale Securities (LO1)

Use the financial statement effects template to record the accounts and amounts for the following four transactions involving investments in marketable securities:

(1) Ohlson Co. purchases 5,000 common shares of Freeman Co. at $16 cash per share.

(2) Ohlson Co. receives a cash dividend of $1.25 per common share from Freeman.

(3) Year-end market price of Freeman common stock is $17.50 per share.

(4) Ohlson Co. sells all 5,000 common shares of Freeman for $86,400 cash.

a. Assume the investments are classified as trading.

b. Assume the investments are classified as available-for-sale.

E7-22. Interpreting Footnotes on Security Investments (LO1)

Berkshire Hathaway
(BRKA)

Berkshire Hathaway reports the following footnotes with its 10-K report ($ millions).

Years Ended December 31	2005	2004	2003
Accumulated Other Comprehensive Income			
Unrealized appreciation of investments..........................	$ 2,081	$ 2,599	$10,842
Applicable income taxes....................................	(728)	(905)	(3,802)
Reclassification adjustment for appreciation			
included in net earnings	(6,261)	(1,569)	(2,922)
Applicable income taxes....................................	2,191	549	1,023
Foreign currency translation adjustments	(359)	140	267
Applicable income taxes....................................	(26)	134	(127)
Minimum pension liability adjustment	(62)	(38)	1
Applicable income taxes....................................	38	3	(3)
Other, including minority interests	51	(34)	6
Other comprehensive income	(3,075)	879	5,285
Accumulated other comprehensive income at beginning of year	20,435	19,556	14,271
Accumulated other comprehensive income at end of year	$17,360	$20,435	$19,556

Data with respect to investments in equity securities are shown below. Amounts are in millions.

December 31, 2005	Cost	Unrealized Gains/losses	Fair Value
American Express Company...........	$ 1,287	$ 6,515	$ 7,802
The Coca-Cola Company	1,299	6,763	8,062
The Proctor & Gamble Company	5,963	(175)	5,788
Wells Fargo & Company..............	2,754	3,221	5,975
Other............................	10,036	9,058	19,094
	$21,339	$25,382	$46,721

American Express Company (AXP)

The Coca-Cola Company (KO)

Proctor & Gamble Company (PG)

Wells Fargo & Company (WFC)

a. At what amount does Berkshire Hathaway report its equity securities investment portfolio on its balance sheet? Does that amount include any unrealized gains or losses? Explain.

b. How is Berkshire Hathaway accounting for its equity securities investment portfolio—as an available-for-sale or trading portfolio? How do you know?

c. What does the number $2,081 represent in the Accumulated Other Comprehensive Income footnote? Is this number pretax or after-tax? Explain.

E7-23. Interpreting Footnote Disclosures for Investments (LO1)

CNA Financial Corporation provides the following footnote to its 2005 10-K report.

CNA Financial Corporation (CNA)

Valuation of investments: CNA classifies its fixed maturity securities (bonds and redeemable preferred stocks) and its equity securities as available-for-sale, and as such, they are carried at fair value. The amortized cost of fixed maturity securities is adjusted for amortization of premiums and accretion of discounts to maturity, which are included in net investment income. Changes in fair value are reported as a component of other comprehensive income. Investments are written down to fair value and losses are recognized in income when a decline in value is determined to be other-than-temporary.

Summary of Fixed Maturity and Equity Securities

December 31, 2005 (In millions)	Cost or Amortized Cost	Gross Unrealized Gains	Gross Unrealized Losses		Estimated Fair Value
			Less than 12 Months	Greater than 12 Months	
Fixed maturity securities available-for-sale					
U.S. Treasury securities and obligations of government agencies	$ 1,355	$ 119	$ 4	$ 1	$ 1,469
Asset-backed securities	12,986	43	137	33	12,859
States, municipalities and political subdivisions—tax-exempt	9,054	193	31	7	9,209
Corporate securities	5,906	322	52	11	6,165
Other debt securities	2,830	234	18	2	3,044
Redeemable preferred stock	213	4	—	1	216
Options embedded in convertible debt securities...............	1	—	—	—	1
Total fixed maturity securities	32,345	915	242	55	32,963
Total fixed maturity securities trading	271	—	—	—	271
Equity securities available-for-sale					
Common stock.................	140	150	1	—	289
Preferred stock	322	22	1	—	343
Total equity securities available-for-sale.............	462	172	2	—	632
Total equity securities trading.	49	—	—	—	49
Total	$33,127	$1,087	$244	$55	$33,915

    a.   At what amount does CNA report its investment portfolio on its balance sheet? In your answer identify the portfolio's market value, cost, and any unrealized gains and losses.

    b.   How do CNA's balance sheet and income statement reflect any unrealized gains and/or losses on the investment portfolio?

    c.   How do CNA's balance sheet and income statement reflect gains and losses realized from the sale of available-for-sale securities?

E7-24. **Assessing Financial Statement Effects of Equity Method Securities** (LO2)

Use the financial statement effects template (with amounts and accounts) to record the following transactions involving investments in marketable securities accounted for using the equity method:

    a.   Purchased 12,000 common shares of Barth Co. at $9 per share; the shares represent 30% ownership in Barth.

    b.   Received a cash dividend of $1.25 per common share from Barth.

    c.   Barth reported annual net income of $80,000.

    d.   Sold all 12,000 common shares of Barth for $120,500.

E7-25. **Assessing Financial Statement Effects of Equity Method Securities** (LO2)

Use the financial statement effects template (with amounts and accounts) to record the following transactions involving investments in marketable securities accounted for using the equity method:

    a.   Healy Co. purchases 15,000 common shares of Palepu Co. at $8 per share; the shares represent 25% ownership of Palepu.

    b.   Healy receives a cash dividend of $0.80 per common share from Palepu.

    c.   Palepu reports annual net income of $120,000.

    d.   Healy sells all 15,000 common shares of Palepu for $140,000.

E7-26. **Assessing Financial Statement Effects of Passive and Equity Method Investments** (LO1, 2)

On January 1, 2007, Ball Corporation purchased shares of Leftwich Company common stock.

    a.   Assume that the stock acquired by Ball represents 15% of Leftwich's voting stock and that Ball classifies the investment as available-for-sale. Use the financial statement effects template (with amounts and accounts) to record the following transactions:

        (1) Ball purchased 10,000 common shares of Leftwich at $15 cash per share; the shares represent a 15% ownership in Leftwich.

        (2) Leftwich reported annual net income of $80,000.

        (3) Ball received a cash dividend of $1.10 per common share from Leftwich.

        (4) Year-end market price of Leftwich common stock is $19 per share.

    b.   Assume that the stock acquired by Ball represents 30% of Leftwich's voting stock and that Ball accounts for this investment using the equity method since it is able to exert significant influence. Use the financial statement effects template (with amounts and accounts) to record the following transactions:

        (1) Ball purchased 10,000 common shares of Leftwich at $15 cash per share; the shares represent a 30% ownership in Leftwich.

        (2) Leftwich reported annual net income of $80,000.

        (3) Ball received a cash dividend of $1.10 per common share from Leftwich.

        (4) Year-end market price of Leftwich common stock is $19 per share.

E7-27. **Interpreting Equity Method Investment Footnotes** (LO2)

DuPont (DD)

DuPont's 2005 10-K report includes information relating to the company's equity method investments ($ millions). The following footnote reports summary balance sheets for affiliated companies for which DuPont uses the equity method of accounting. The information below is shown on a 100 percent basis followed by the carrying value of DuPont's investment in these affiliates.

Financial Position at December 31 (in millions)	2005	2004
Current assets	$1,292	$1,972
Noncurrent assets	1,780	2,811
Total assets	$3,072	$4,783
Short-term borrowings	$606	$734
Other current liabilities	621	932
Long-term borrowings	259	716
Other long-term liabilities	111	305
Total liabilities	$1,597	$2,687
DuPont's investment in affiliates (includes advances of $55 and $84, respectively)	$ 844	$1,034

    a.   DuPont reports its investment in equity method affiliates on its balance sheet at $844 million. Does this reflect the adjusted cost or market value of DuPont's interest in these companies?

    b.   What is the total stockholders' equity of the affiliates at the end of 2005? What is the carrying (book value) of DuPont's investment without the advances, at the end of 2005? Approximately what percentage does DuPont own, on average, of these affiliates? Explain.

    c.   DuPont reports that its equity interest in reported profits of these affiliates is approximately $108 million in 2005, and that it received $107 million in dividends from these affiliates in 2005. It also reports the sale of an affiliate with an equity investment balance of $162. Use this information, and the footnote above, to explain the change in the investment account from $950 million in 2004 to $789 million (net of advances) in 2005.

    d.   How does use of the equity method impact DuPont's ROE and its RNOA components (net operating asset turnover and net operating profit margin)?

E7-28.   **Analyzing and Interpreting Disclosures on Equity Method Investments**   **(LO2)**

    Caterpillar, Inc. (CAT) reports investments in affiliated companies, consisting mainly of its 50% ownership of Shin Caterpillar Mitsubishi, Ltd. Caterpillar reports those investments on its balance sheet at $565 million, and provides the following footnote in its 10-K report.

    Caterpillar, Inc. (CAT)

    Shin Caterpillar Mitsubishi, Ltd.

> **Investment in unconsolidated affiliated companies** Our investment in affiliated companies accounted for by the equity method consists primarily of a 50% interest in Shin Caterpillar Mitsubishi Ltd. (SCM) located in Japan. Combined financial information of the unconsolidated affiliated companies accounted for by the equity method (generally on a three-month lag, e.g., SCM results reflect the periods ending September 30) was as follows:

Years Ended December 31 (Millions of Dollars)	2005	2004	2003
Results of operations			
Sales	$4,140	$3,628	$2,946
Cost of sales	3,257	2,788	2,283
Gross profit	883	840	663
Profit	$ 161	$ 129	$ 48
Caterpillar's profit	$ 73	$ 59	$ 20

December 31 (Millions of Dollars)	2005	2004	2003
Financial position			
Assets			
Current assets	$1,714	$1,540	$1,494
Property, plant and equipment—net	1,121	1,097	961
Other assets	193	145	202
	3,028	2,782	2,657
Liabilities			
Current liabilities	1,351	1,345	1,247
Long-term debt due after one year	336	276	343
Other liabilities	188	214	257
	1,875	1,835	1,847
Ownership	$1,153	$ 947	$ 810

Caterpillar's investment in unconsolidated affiliated companies (Millions of Dollars)			
Investment in equity method companies	$ 540	$ 487	$ 432
Plus: Investment in cost method companies	25	30	368
Investment in unconsolidated affiliated companies	$ 565	$ 517	$ 800

> Certain investments in unconsolidated affiliated companies are accounted for using the cost method.

a. What assets and liabilities of unconsolidated affiliates are omitted from CAT's balance sheet as a result of the equity method of accounting for those investments?

b. Do the liabilities of the unconsolidated affiliates affect CAT directly? Explain.

c. How does the equity method impact CAT's ROE and its RNOA components (net operating asset turnover and net operating profit margin)?

E7-29. **Reporting and Interpreting Stock Investment Performance** **(LO1)**

Kasznik Company began operations in 2007 and, by year-end (December 31), had made six stock investments. Year-end information on these stock investments follows.

December 31, 2007	Cost or Equity Basis (as appropriate)	Year-End Market Value	Market Classification
Barth, Inc.	$ 68,000	$ 65,300	Trading
Foster, Inc.	162,500	160,000	Trading
McNichols, Inc.	197,000	192,000	Available-for-sale
Patell, Inc.	157,000	154,700	Available-for-sale
Ertimur, Inc.	100,000	102,400	Equity method
Soliman, Inc.	136,000	133,200	Equity method

a. What does Kaznik's balance sheet report for trading stock investments at December 31, 2007?

b. What does Kaznik's balance sheet report for available-for-sale stock investments at December 31, 2007?

c. What does Kaznik's balance sheet report for equity method stock investments at December 31, 2007?

d. What total amount of unrealized holding gains or unrealized holding losses related to stock investments appear in Kasnik's 2007 income statement?

e. What total amount of unrealized holding gains or unrealized holding losses related to stock investments appear in the stockholders' equity section of Kasnik's December 31, 2007, balance sheet?

f. What total amount of market value adjustment to stock investments appears in the December 31, 2007, balance sheet? Which category of stock investments does the market value adjustment relate to? Does the market value adjustment increase or decrease the carrying value of these stock investments?

E7-30. **Interpreting Equity Method Investment Footnotes** **(LO2)**

AT&T, Inc. (T)

AT&T reports the following footnote to its 2005 10-K report.

Equity Method Investments We account for our nationwide wireless joint venture, Cingular, and our investments in equity affiliates under the equity method of accounting. The following table is a reconciliation of our investments in and advances to Cingular as presented on our Consolidated Balance Sheets.

	2005	2004
Beginning of year	$33,687	$11,003
Contributions	—	21,688
Equity in net income......	200	30
Other adjustments	(2,483)	966
End of year	$31,404	$33,687

Undistributed earnings from Cingular were $2,711 and $2,511 at December 31, 2005 and 2004. "Other adjustments" in 2005 included the net activity of $2,442 under our revolving credit agreement with Cingular, consisting of a reduction of $1,747 (reflecting Cingular's repayment of their shareholder loan during 2005) and a decrease of $695 (reflecting Cingular's net repayment of their revolving credit balance during 2005). During 2004, we made an equity contribution to Cingular in connection with its acquisition of AT&T Wireless. "Other adjustments" in 2004 included the net activity of $972 under our revolving credit agreement with Cingular, consisting of a reduction of $30 (reflecting Cingular's repayment of advances during 2004) and an increase of $1,002 (reflecting the December 31, 2004 balance of advances to Cingular under this revolving credit agreement).

We account for our 60% economic interest in Cingular under the equity method of accounting in our consolidated financial statements since we share control equally (i.e., 50/50) with our 40% economic partner in the joint venture. We have equal voting rights and representation on the Board of Directors that controls Cingular. The following table presents summarized financial information for Cingular at December 31, or for the year then ended.

	2005	2004	2003
Income Statements			
Operating revenues ...	$34,433	$19,565	$15,577
Operating income.....	1,824	1,528	2,254
Net income	333	201	977
Balance Sheets			
Current assets........	$ 6,049	$ 5,570	
Noncurrent assets.....	73,270	76,668	
Current liabilities......	10,008	7,983	
Noncurrent liabilities...	24,333	29,719	

We have made a subordinated loan to Cingular that totaled $4,108 and $5,855 at December 31, 2005 and 2004, which matures in June 2008. This loan bears interest at an annual rate of 6.0%. During 2005, Cingular repaid $1,747 to reduce the balance of this loan in accordance with the terms of a revolving credit agreement. We earned interest income on this loan of $311 during 2005, $354 in 2004 and $397 in 2003. This interest income does not have a material impact on our net income as it is mostly offset when we record our share of equity income in Cingular.

a. At what amount is the equity investment in Cingular reported on AT&T's balance sheet? (*Hint:* the table in the footnote reports AT&T's equity investment plus its "advances" of $4,108 to Cingular plus $311 of interest accrued on the advances.) Confirm that this amount is equal to its proportionate share of Cingular's equity.

b. Did Cingular pay out any of its earnings as dividends in 2005? How do you know?

c. How much income did AT&T report in 2005 relating to this investment in Cingular?

d. Interpret the AT&T statement that "undistributed earnings from Cingular were $2,711 and $2,511 at December 31, 2005 and 2004."

e. How does use of the equity method impact AT&T's ROE and its RNOA components (net operating asset turnover and net operating profit margin)?

f. AT&T accounts for its investment in Cingular under the equity method, despite its 60% economic ownership position. Why?

g. In 2006, AT&T merged with Bell South, its joint venture partner in Cingular. What impact will this merger have on the way AT&T accounts for its investment in Cingular?

E7-31. Constructing the Consolidated Balance Sheet at Acquisition (LO3)

On January 1 of the current year, Healy Company purchased all of the common shares of Miller Company for $500,000 cash. Balance sheets of the two firms at acquisition follow:

	Healy Company	Miller Company	Consolidating Adjustments	Consolidated
Current assets	$1,700,000	$120,000		
Investment in Miller	500,000	—		
Plant assets, net..........	3,000,000	410,000		
Goodwill	—	—		
Total assets..............	$5,200,000	$530,000		
Liabilities................	$ 700,000	$ 90,000		
Contributed capital........	3,500,000	400,000		
Retained earnings	1,000,000	40,000		
Total liabilities and equity	$5,200,000	$530,000		

During purchase negotiations, Miller's plant assets were appraised at $425,000 and all of its remaining assets and liabilities were appraised at values approximating their book values. Healy also concluded that an additional $45,000 (in goodwill) demanded by Miller's shareholders was warranted because Miller's earning power was better than the industry average. Prepare the consolidating adjustments and the consolidated balance sheet at acquisition.

E7-32. Constructing the Consolidated Balance Sheet at Acquisition (LO3)

Rayburn Company purchased all of Kanodia Company's common stock for cash on January 1, at which time the separate balance sheets of the two corporations appeared as follows:

	Rayburn Company	Kanodia Company	Consolidating Adjustments	Consolidated
Investment in Kanodia	$ 600,000	—		
Other assets	2,300,000	$700,000		
Goodwill	—	—		
Total assets	$2,900,000	$700,000		
Liabilities	$ 900,000	$160,000		
Contributed capital	1,400,000	300,000		
Retained earnings	600,000	240,000		
Total liabilities and equity	$2,900,000	$700,000		

During purchase negotiations, Rayburn determined that the appraised value of Kanodia's Other Assets was $720,000; and, all of its remaining assets and liabilities were appraised at values approximating their book values. The remaining $40,000 of the purchase price was ascribed to goodwill. Prepare the consolidating adjustments and the consolidated balance sheet at acquisition.

E7-33. Assessing Financial Statement Effects from a Subsidiary Stock Issuance (LO3)

Ryan Company owns 80% of Lev Company. Information reported by Ryan Company and Lev Company as of January 1, 2007, follows:

Ryan Company

Shares owned of Lev	40,000
Book value of investment in Lev	$320,000

Lev Company

Shares outstanding	50,000
Book value of equity	$400,000
Book value per share	$8

Assume Lev Company issues 30,000 additional shares of previously authorized but unissued common stock solely to outside investors (none to Ryan Company) for $12 cash per share. Indicate the financial statement effects of this stock issuance on Ryan Company using the financial statement effect template for both of the reporting options available under GAAP. Identify and explain both options.

Ryan Company's Financial Statements

	Balance Sheet						Income Statement		
Transaction	Cash Asset	+ Noncash Assets	= Liabil- ities	+ Contrib. Capital	+ Earned Capital		Rev- enues	− Expen- ses	= Net Income
Lev Co. issues 30,000 shares (Option A)			=						=
Lev Co. issues 30,000 shares (Option B)			=						=

E7-34.   Estimating Goodwill Impairment   (LO3)

On January 1, 2007, Engel Company purchases 100% of Ball Company for $16.8 million. At the time of acquisition, the fair market value of Ball's tangible net assets (excluding goodwill) is $16.2 million. Engel ascribes the excess of $600,000 to goodwill. Assume that the market value of Ball declines to $12.5 million and that the fair market value of Ball's tangible net assets is estimated at $12.3 million as of December 31, 2007.

    a.   Determine if the goodwill has become impaired and, if so, the amount of the impairment.

    b.   What impact does the impairment of goodwill have on Engel's financial statements?

E7-35.   Allocating Purchase Price including In-Process R&D   (LO3)

Amgen, Inc., reports the following footnote to its 10-K report.   Amgen Inc. (AMGN)

> **Immunex acquisition.** On July 15, 2002, the Company acquired all of the outstanding common stock of Immunex in a transaction accounted for as a business combination. Immunex was a leading biotechnology company dedicated to developing immune system science to protect human health. The acquisition enhanced Amgen's strategic position within the biotechnology industry by strengthening and diversifying its (1) product base and product pipeline in key therapeutic areas, and (2) discovery research capabilities in proteins and antibodies. The purchase price was allocated to the tangible and identifiable intangible assets acquired and liabilities assumed based on their estimated fair values at the acquisition date. The following table summarizes the estimated fair values of the assets acquired and liabilities assumed as of the acquisition date (in millions):

Current assets, principally cash and marketable securities	$ 1,619.1
Deferred tax assets	200.2
Property, plant, and equipment	571.6
In-process research and development	2,991.8
Identifiable intangible assets, principally developed product technology and core technology	4,803.2
Goodwill	9,774.2
Other assets	26.2
Current liabilities	(579.0)
Deferred tax liabilities	(1,635.5)
Net assets	$17,771.8

> The allocation of the purchase price was based, in part, on a third-party valuation of the fair values of in-process research and development, identifiable intangible assets, and certain property, plant, and equipment. The estimated fair value of the in-process R&D projects was determined based on the use of a discounted cash flow model. For each project, the estimated after-tax cash flows were probability weighted to take into account the stage of completion and the risks surrounding the successful development and commercialization. These cash flows were then discounted to a present value using discount rates ranging from 12% to 14%.

    a.   Of the total assets acquired, what portion is allocated to tangible assets and what portion to intangible assets?

    b.   Are the assets (both tangible and intangible) of Immunex reported on the consolidated balance sheet at the book value or at the fair market value on the date of the acquisition? Explain.

    c.   How are the tangible and intangible assets accounted for subsequent to the acquisition?

    d.   Comment on the valuation of the in-process R&D. How is IPR&D accounted for under current GAAP?

    e.   If the amount allocated to in-process R&D was decreased, what effect would this have on the allocation of the purchase price to the remaining acquired assets? What effect would this have on current and future earnings?

E7-36.[B]   Constructing the Consolidated Balance Sheet at Acquisition   (LO3)

Easton Company acquires 100 percent of the outstanding voting shares of Harris Company. To obtain these shares, Easton pays $210,000 in cash and issues 5,000 of its $10 par value common stock. On this date, Easton's stock has a fair market value of $36 per share, and Harris's book value of stockholders' equity is $280,000. Easton is willing to pay $390,000 for a company with a book value for equity of $280,000 because it believes that (1) Harris's buildings are undervalued by $40,000, and (2) Harris has an unrecorded patent that Easton values at $30,000. Easton considers the remaining balance sheet items to be fairly valued (no book-to-market difference). The remaining $40,000 of the purchase price is ascribed to corporate synergies and other general unidentifiable intangible assets (goodwill). The balance sheets at the acquisition date follow:

	Easton Company	Harris Company	Consolidating Adjustments	Consolidated
Cash....................	$ 84,000	$ 40,000		
Receivables	160,000	90,000		
Inventory................	220,000	130,000		
Investment in Harris	390,000	—		
Land....................	100,000	60,000		
Buildings, net	400,000	110,000		
Equipment, net............	120,000	50,000		
Total assets..............	$1,474,000	$480,000		
Accounts payable..........	$ 160,000	$ 30,000		
Long-term liabilities	380,000	170,000		
Common stock............	500,000	40,000		
Additional paid-in capital	74,000	—		
Retained earnings	360,000	240,000		
Total liabilities & equity......	$1,474,000	$480,000		

a. Show the breakdown of the investment into the book value acquired, the excess of fair value over book value, and the portion of the investment representing goodwill.

b. Prepare the consolidating adjustments and the consolidated balance sheet on the date of acquisition. Identify the adjustments by whether they relate to the elimination of stockholders' equity [S] or the excess of purchase price over book value [A].

c. How will the excess of the purchase price over book value acquired be treated in years subsequent to the acquisition?

E7-37.^C **Reporting and Analyzing Derivatives** **(LO1)**

Hewlett Packard (HPQ)

Hewlett Packard reports the following schedule of comprehensive income (net income plus other comprehensive income) in its 2005 10-K report ($ millions):

2005 Comprehensive income (millions)	
Net earnings.....................................	$2,398
Net unrealized loss on available-for-sale securities....	(1)
Net unrealized gain on cash flow hedges	69
Minimum pension liability, net of taxes	171
Cumulative translation adjustment	(17)
Comprehensive income	$2,620

a. Describe how firms like Hewlett Packard typically use derivatives.

b. How does HP report its derivatives and the hedged assets (and/or liabilities) on its balance sheet?

c. By what amount has the unrealized gain of $69 million on the cash flow hedges affected its current income? What are the analysis implications?

PROBLEMS

P7-38. Analyzing and Interpreting Available-for-Sale Securities Disclosures (LO1)

Following is a portion of the investments footnote from MetLife's 2005 10-K report. Investment earnings are a crucial component of the financial performance of insurance companies such as MetLife, and investments comprise a large part of Metlife's assets. MetLife accounts for its bond investments as available-for-sale securities.

MetLife, Inc. (MET)

December 31, 2005 (in millions)	Cost or Amortized Cost	Gross Unrealized		Estimated Fair Value
		Gain	Loss	
U.S. corporate securities	$ 72,339	$2,814	$ 835	$ 74,318
Residential mortgaged-backed securities	47,365	353	472	47,246
Foreign corporate securities	33,578	1,842	439	34,981
U.S. treasury/agency securities	25,643	1,401	86	26,958
Commercial mortgaged-backed securities	17,682	223	207	17,698
Asset-backed securities	11,533	91	51	11,573
Foreign government securities	10,080	1,401	35	11,446
State and political subdivision securities	4,601	185	36	4,750
Other fixed maturity securities	912	17	41	888
Total bonds	223,733	8,327	2,202	229,858
Redeemable preferred stocks	193	2	3	192
Total fixed maturities	$223,926	$8,329	$2,205	$230,050

December 31, 2004 (in millions)	Cost or Amortized Cost	Gross Unrealized		Estimated Fair Value
		Gain	Loss	
U.S. corporate securities	$ 58,022	$ 3,870	$172	$ 61,720
Residential mortgaged-backed securities	31,683	612	65	32,230
Foreign corporate securities	24,972	2,582	85	27,469
U.S. treasury/agency securities	16,534	1,314	22	17,826
Commercial mortgaged-backed securities	12,099	440	38	12,501
Asset-backed securities	10,784	125	33	10,876
Foreign government securities	7,621	973	26	8,568
State and political subdivision securities	3,683	220	4	3,899
Other fixed maturity securities	887	131	33	985
Total bonds	166,285	10,267	478	176,074
Redeemable preferred stocks	326	—	23	303
Total fixed maturities	$166,611	$10,267	$501	$176,377

Required

a. At what amount does MetLife report its bond investments on its balance sheets for 2005 and 2004?

b. What are the net unrealized gains (losses) for 2005 and 2004? How did these unrealized gains (losses) affect the company's reported income in 2005 and 2004?

c. What is the difference between *realized* and *unrealized* gains and losses? Are realized gains and losses treated differently in the income statement than unrealized gains and losses?

d. MetLife reports a balance for unrealized gains (losses) on fixed maturities investments of approximately $4 billion in the equity section of its 2005 balance sheet. Explain the difference between this amount and the amount computed in part b.

P7-39.   **Analyzing and Interpreting Disclosures on Equity Method Investments**   (LO2)

General Mills invests in a number of joint ventures to manufacture and distribute its food products as discussed in the following footnote to its fiscal year 2005 10-K report:

Investments in Joint Ventrues   We have a 50 percent equity interest in Cereal Partners Worldwide (CPW), a joint venture with Nestlé that manufactures and markets ready-to-eat cereals outside the United States and Canada. We have guaranteed 50 percent of CPW's debt. We have a 50 percent equity interest in 8th Continent, LLC, a domestic joint venture with DuPont to develop and market soy foods and beverages. We have 50 percent interests in the following joint ventures for the manufacture, distribution and marketing of Häagen-Dazs frozen ice cream products and novelties: Häagen-Dazs Japan K.K., Häagen-Dazs Korea Company Limited, Häagen-Dazs Distributors (Thailand) Company Limited, and Häagen-Dazs Marketing & Distribution (Philippines) Inc. We also have a 50 percent interest in Seretram, a joint venture with Co-op de Pau for the production of Green Giant canned corn in France.

On February 28, 2005, our 40.5 percent ownership interest in the Snack Ventures Europe (SVE) joint venture was redeemed for $750 million. The redemption ended the European snack joint venture between General Mills and PepsiCo, Inc.

The joint ventures are reflected in our consolidated financial statements on the equity basis of accounting. We record our share of the earnings or losses of these joint ventures. We also receive royalty income from certain joint ventures, incur various expenses (primarily research and development) and record the tax impact of certain joint venture operations that are structured as partnerships.

Our cumulative investment in these joint ventures (including our share of earnings and losses) was $223 million, $434 million and $372 million at the end of fiscal 2005, 2004 and 2003, respectively. We made aggregate investments in the joint ventures of $15 million, $31 million and $17 million in fiscal 2005, 2004 and 2003, respectively. We received aggregate dividends from the joint ventures of $83 million, $60 million and $95 million in fiscal 2005, 2004 and 2003, respectively.

Summary combined financial information for the joint ventures on a 100 percent basis follows:

Combined Financial Information—Joint Ventures—100 Percent Basis

In Millions, Fiscal Year	2005	2004
Net sales.	$2,652	$2,625
Net Sales less Cost of Sales	1,184	1,180
Earnings before Income Taxes	231	205
Earnings after Income Taxes	184	153

In Millions, Fiscal Year Ended	2005	2004
Current assets	$604	$852
Noncurrent assets	612	972
Current liabilities.	695	865
Noncurrent liabilities.	7	14

Required

a.   How does General Mills account for its investments in joint ventures? How are these investments reflected on General Mills' balance sheet, and how generally is income recognized on these investments?

b.   General Mills reports the total of all of these investments on its May 29, 2005, balance sheet at $223 million. Approximately what percent of these joint ventures does it own, on average?

c.   Does the $223 million investment reported on General Mills' balance sheet sufficiently reflect the assets and liabilities required to conduct these operations? Explain.

d.   Do you believe that the liabilities of these joint venture entities represent actual obligations of General Mills? Explain.

e.   What potential problem(s) does equity method accounting present for analysis purposes?

P7-40.   Analyzing and Interpreting Disclosures on Consolidations   (LO3)

Caterpillar Inc. consists of two business units: the manufacturing company (parent corporation) and a   Caterpillar Inc. (CAT)
wholly owned finance subsidiary. These two units are consolidated in Caterpillar's 10-K report. Following is
a supplemental disclosure that Caterpillar includes in its 10-K report that shows the separate balance sheets
of the parent and its subsidiary, as well as consolidating adjustments and the consolidated balance sheet
presented to shareholders. This supplemental disclosure is not mandated under GAAP, but is voluntarily
reported by Caterpillar as useful information for investors and creditors. Using this disclosure, answer the
following questions:

Required

a.   Does each individual company (unit) maintain its own financial statements? Explain. Why does
GAAP require consolidation instead of separate financial statements of individual companies (units)?

b.   What is the balance of Investments in Financial Products Subsidiaries as of December 31, 2005, on
the parent's balance sheet? What is the equity balance of the financial products subsidiary to which
this relates as of December 31, 2005? Do you see a relation? Will this relation always exist?

c.   Refer to your answer for (a). How does the equity method of accounting for the investment in the
subsidiary company obscure the actual financial condition of the parent company that is revealed in
the consolidated financial statements?

d.   Refer to the Consolidating Adjustments column reported—it is used to prepare the consolidated
balance sheet. Generally, what do these adjustments accomplish?

e.   Compare the consolidated balance of stockholders' equity with the stockholders' equity of the parent
company (Machinery and Engines). Will the relation that is evident always hold? Explain.

f.   Recall that the parent company uses the equity method of accounting for its investment in the
subsidiary, and that this account is eliminated in the consolidation process. What is the relation
between consolidated net income and the net income of the parent company? Explain.

g.   What do you believe is the implication for the consolidated balance sheet if the market value of the
Financial Products subsidiary is greater than the book value of its stockholders' equity?

| December 31, 2005 (Millions of Dollars) | Consolidated | Supplemental Consolidating Data | | |
		Machinery and Engines	Financial Products	Consolidating Adjustments
Cash and short-term investments	$ 1,108	$ 951	$ 157	$ —
Receivables—trade and other	7,526	2,833	419	4,274
Receivables—finance.	6,442	—	11,058	(4,616)
Deferred and refundable income taxes	344	276	68	—
Prepaid expenses.	2,146	2,139	26	(19)
Inventories	5,224	5,224	—	—
Total current assets	22,790	11,423	11,728	(361)
Property, plant and equipment—net	7,988	5,067	2,921	—
Long-term receivables—trade and other	1,037	301	36	700
Long-term receivables—finance	10,301	—	11,036	(735)
Investments in unconsolidated affiliated companies	565	526	39	—
Investments in Financial Products subsidiaries	—	3,253	—	(3,253)
Deferred income taxes	768	1,057	32	(321)
Intangible assets	424	418	6	—
Goodwill	1,451	1,451	—	—
Other assets	1,745	491	1,254	—
Total assets.	$47,069	$23,987	$27,052	$(3,970)

(Continued on next page)

(Continued from previous page)

December 31, 2005 (Millions of Dollars)	Consolidated	Supplemental Consolidating Data		
		Machinery and Engines	Financial Products	Consolidating Adjustments
Liabilities				
Short-term borrowings.	$ 5,569	$ 871	$ 4,897	$ (199)
Accounts payable.	3,471	3,347	261	(137)
Accrued expenses	2,617	1,605	1,038	(26)
Accrued wages, salaries and employee benefits. . . .	1,845	1,826	19	—
Customer Advances.	395	395	—	—
Dividends payable	168	168	—	—
Deferred and current income taxes payable	528	448	84	(4)
Long-term debt due within one year	4,499	340	4,159	—
Total current liabilities.	19,092	9,000	10,458	(366)
Long-term debt due after one year	15,677	2,752	12,960	35
Liability for postemployment benefits	2,991	2,991	—	—
Deferred income taxes and other liabilities	877	812	381	(316)
Total liabilities	38,637	15,555	23,799	(717)
Stockholders' equity				
Common stock.	1,859	1,859	875	(875)
Treasury stock	(4,637)	(4,637)	—	—
Profit employed in the business.	11,808	11,808	2,197	(2,197)
Accumulated other comprehensive income.	(598)	(598)	181	(181)
Total stockholders' equity	8,432	8,432	3,253	(3,253)
Total liabilities and stockholders' equity.	$47,069	$23,987	$27,052	$(3,970)

CASES

C7-41.   Management Application: Determining the Reporting of an Investment   (LO1, 2, 3)

Assume that your company acquires 20% of the outstanding common stock of APEX Software as an investment. You also have an option to purchase the remaining 80%. APEX is developing software (its only activity) that it hopes to eventually package and sell to customers. You do not intend to exercise your option unless its software product reaches commercial feasibility. APEX has employed your software engineers to assist in the development efforts and you are integrally involved in its software design. Your ownership interest is significant enough to give you influence over APEX' software design specifications.

Required

a.   Describe the financial statement effects of the three possible methods to accounting for this investment (market, equity, or consolidation).

b.   What method of accounting is appropriate for this investment (market, equity, or consolidation)? Explain.

C7-42.   Ethics and Governance: Establishing Corporate Governance   (LO2, 3)

Effective corporate governance policies are a crucial component of contemporary corporate management.

Required

What provisions do you believe should be incorporated into such a policy? How do such policies impact financial accounting?

Reporting and Analyzing Nonowner Financing

LO1 Describe the accounting for current operating liabilities, including accounts payable and accrued liabilities. (p. 8-4)

LO2 Describe the accounting for current and long-term nonoperating liabilities. (p. 8-10)

LO3 Explain how credit ratings are determined and identify their effect on the cost of debt. (p. 8-21)

VERIZON COMMUNICATIONS

Verizon Communications, Inc., began doing business in 2000, when Bell Atlantic Corporation merged with GTE Corporation. Verizon is one of the world's leading providers of communications services. It is the largest provider of wireline and wireless communications in the U.S., and is the largest of the 'Baby Bells' as of 2005 with $75 billion in revenues and $168 billion in assets.

When Ivan Seidenberg became sole CEO of Verizon in mid-2002 (and its chairman in late 2003), the Internet frenzy had cooled and Verizon's stock price had plunged, falling from an all-time high of $70 in late 1999 to $27 in mid-2002. Since then, the stock has rebounded somewhat, but continues to trade below $40 per share in late 2006.

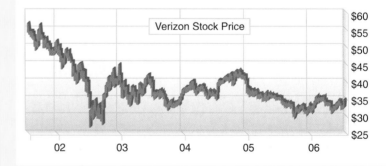

Verizon survived the Internet and telecom downturn. Now it faces a formidable new challenger: cable. Cable companies spent an estimated $75 billion in recent years upgrading their infrastructure to offer customers discounted bundled packages of local voice, high-speed Internet connec-

tions, and video. Market analysts estimate that cable companies could capture a quarter of the local voice market over the next decade as they deploy new voice over Internet protocol (VOIP) technology.

While Verizon and the other traditional phone companies see their market positions erode, they also struggle to retain their image as innovators. They face creative pressures from researchers and from companies (including Intel) who continue to develop new wireless technologies. BusinessWeek (2006) explains:

> AT&T and Verizon are rushing to build networks to deliver TV service and high-speed broadband access . . . Verizon is spending billions to roll out a next-generation phone, data, and video network called FiOS (as in "fiber optic") to give its customers faster Internet service and an alternative to cable. Indeed, over the past three years, Verizon has spent $40 billion on capital expenditures in addition to its 2006 acquisition of MCI. The demand for new capital spending is coming at an inopportune time for Verizon. Saddled with a debt load of over $36 billion as of 2005, a third of which matures over the next five years, Verizon must also pay over $4 billion in stock dividends annually plus nearly $20 billion in accumulated employee pensions and health-care costs. Verizon is concerned. Faced with a question from a stockholder about why Verizon isn't repurchasing its stock given its decline in value, Seidenberg said "our number-one priority for using free cash flow over the last two years has been reducing debt.

This module focuses on liabilities; that is, short-term and long-term obligations. Liabilities are one of two financing sources for a company. The other is shareholder financing. Bonds and notes are a major part of most companies' liabilities. In this module, we show how to price liabilities and how the issuance and subsequent payment of the principal and interest affect financial statements. We also discuss the required disclosures that enable us to effectively analyze a company's ability to pay its debts as they come due.

Verizon's current slogan is "we never stop working for you." The company is now working harder than ever to transform itself in an era of fiber optics and wireless communication. The dilemma facing Silverberg is how to allocate available cash flow between strategic investment and debt payments.

Sources: *BusinessWeek* 2003, 2004 and 2006; *TheStreet.Com* 2003; *Verizon* 2005 and 2004 Annual Reports; *Verizon* 2004 and 2005 10-Ks.

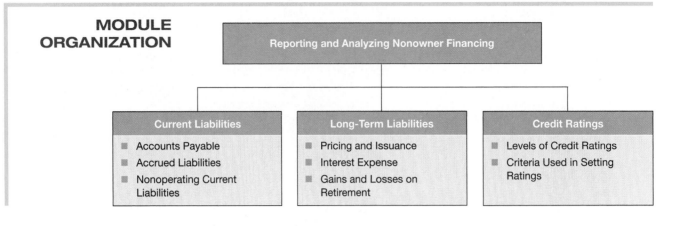

INTRODUCTION

The accounting equation (Assets = Liabilities + Equity) is a useful tool in helping us think about how the balance sheet and income statement are constructed, the linkages among the financial statements, and the effects of transactions on financial statements. The accounting equation is also useful in helping us think about the statements from another perspective, namely, how the business is financed. Consider the following representation of the accounting equation:

$$\underbrace{\textbf{Assets}}_{\textbf{Uses}} = \underbrace{\textbf{Liabilities} + \textbf{Equity}}_{\textbf{Sources}}$$

Assets represent investments (uses of funds) that management has made. It includes current operating assets such as cash, accounts receivable, and inventories. It also includes long-term operating assets such as manufacturing and administrative facilities. Most companies also invest a portion of funds in nonoperating assets (marketable securities) that provide the liquidity a company needs to conduct transactions and to react to market opportunities and changes.

Just as asset disclosures provide us with information on where a company invests its funds, liability and equity disclosures inform us as to how those assets are financed. These are the sources of funds. To be successful, a company must not only invest funds wisely, but must also be astute in the manner in which it raises funds.

Companies strive to finance their assets at the lowest possible cost. Current liabilities (such as accounts payable and accrued liabilities) are generally non-interest-bearing. As a result, companies try to maximize the financing of their assets with these sources of funds.

Current liabilities, as the name implies, are short-term in nature, generally requiring payment within the coming year. As a result, they are not a suitable source of funding for long-term assets that generate cash flows over several years. Instead, companies often finance long-term assets with long-term liabilities that require payments over several years. Generally, companies try to link the cash outflows of the financing source with the cash inflows of the related asset. As such, long-term financing is usually in the form of bonds, notes, and stock issuances.

When a company acquires assets, and finances them with liabilities, its financial leverage increases. Also, the required liability payments increase proportionally with the level of liabilities, and those larger payments imply a higher probability of default should a downturn in business occur. Increasing levels of liabilities, then, make the company riskier to investors who, consequently, demand a higher return. Assessing the appropriate level of liabilities is part of liquidity and solvency analysis.

This module describes and assesses *on-balance-sheet financing,* namely current and noncurrent liabilities that are reported on financial statements. If companies can find a way to purchase assets and have neither the asset, nor its related financing, appear on the balance sheet, they can report higher levels of asset turnover and appear less risky. This creates off-balance-sheet financing, which is the focus of Module 10.

CURRENT LIABILITIES

Current liabilities consist of both operating and nonoperating liabilities. Most *current operating liabilities* such as those related to inventory (accounts payable) or to utilities, wages, insurance, rent, and taxes (accrued liabilities), impact operating expenses such as cost of goods sold or selling, general and administrative expenses. *Current nonoperating liabilities* typically relate to short-term bank notes or the current portion of long-term debt. Verizon's balance sheet reports the following current liabilities:

LO1 Describe the accounting for current operating liabilities, including accounts payable and accrued liabilities.

At December 31 ($ millions)	2005	2004
Debt maturing within one year...................	$ 7,141	$ 3,593
Accounts payable and accrued liabilities...........	12,351	13,177
Liabilities of discontinued operations.............	—	525
Other......................................	5,571	5,834
Total current liabilities.........................	$25,063	$23,129

Verizon reports four categories of current liabilities: (1) long-term obligations that are scheduled for payment in the upcoming year, (2) accounts payable and accrued liabilities, (3) current liabilities from discontinued operations (these operations were sold in 2005, hence they are no longer reported on Verizon's balance sheet), and (4) other current liabilities, which consist mainly of customer deposits, dividends payable, and miscellaneous obligations.

Analysis and interpretation of the return on net operating assets (RNOA) requires that we separate current liabilities into operating and nonoperating components. In general, these two components consist of the following:

1. **Current operating liabilities**
   - **Accounts payable** Obligations to others for amounts owed on purchases of goods and services; these are usually non-interest-bearing.
   - **Accrued liabilities** Obligations for which there is no related external transaction in the current period. These include, for example, accruals for employee wages earned but yet unpaid, accruals for taxes (usually quarterly) on payroll and current period profits, and accruals for other liabilities such as rent, utilities, and insurance. Companies make accruals to properly reflect the liabilities owed as of the statement date and the expenses incurred for the period reported.
   - **Unearned revenue** Obligations to provide goods or services in the coming year; these arise from customers' deposits, subscriptions, or prepayments.

2. **Current nonoperating liabilities**
   - **Short-term interest-bearing debt** Short-term bank borrowings and notes expected to mature in whole or in part during the upcoming year; this item can include any accrued interest payable.
   - **Current maturities of long-term debt** Long-term borrowings that are scheduled to mature in whole or in part during the upcoming year; this current portion of long-term debt includes maturing principal payments only.

The remainder of this section describes current operating liabilities followed by a discussion of current nonoperating liabilities.

Accounts Payable

Accounts payable arise from the purchase of goods and services from others. Accounts payable are normally non-interest-bearing and are, thus, an inexpensive financing source. Verizon does not break out accounts payable on its balance sheet but, instead, reports them with other accruals. It reports $12,351 million in accounts payable and accrued liabilities. The footnotes reveal that accounts payable represent $2,827 million, or 23%, of this total amount.

The following financial statement effects template shows the accounting for a typical purchase of goods on credit and the ultimate sale of those goods. A series of four connected transactions illustrate the revenue and cost cycle.

Transaction	Balance Sheet						Income Statement		
	Cash Asset	+ Noncash Assets	= Liabil- ities	+ Contrib. Capital	+ Earned Capital		Rev- enues	− Expen- ses	= Net Income
1. Purchase $100 inventory on credit		+100 Inventory	= +100 Accounts Payable						=
2a. Sell inventory on credit for $140		+140 Accounts Receivable	=		+140 Retained Earnings		+140 Sales		= +140
2b. Record $100 cost of inventory sold in 2a		−100 Inventory	=		−100 Retained Earnings			− +100 Cost of Goods Sold	= −100
3. Receive $140 cash from accounts receivable	+140 Cash	−140 Accounts Receivable	=						=
4. Pay $100 cash for accounts payable	−100 Cash		= −100 Accounts Payable						=

T-accounts (left margin):

```
INV    100
  AP       100
      INV
100 |
   AP
      |  100

AR    140
  Sales    140
      AR
140 |
   Sales
      |  140

COGS  100
  INV      100
     COGS
100 |
    INV
      |  100

Cash  140
  AR       140
     Cash
140 |
    AR
      |  140

AP    100
  Cash     100
      AP
100 |
   Cash
      |  100
```

The financial statement effects template reveals several impacts related to the purchase of goods on credit and their ultimate sale.

- Purchase of inventory is reflected on the balance sheet as an increase in inventory and an increase in accounts payable.

- Sale of inventory involves two components—revenue and cost. The revenue part reflects the increase in sales and the increase in accounts receivable (revenue is recognized when earned, even though cash is not yet received).

- The cost part of the sales transaction reflects the decrease in inventory and the increase in cost of goods sold (COGS). COGS is reported in the income statement and matched against revenues (this expense is recognized because the inventory asset is sold, even though inventory-related payables may not yet be paid).

- Collection of the receivable reduces accounts receivable and increases cash. It is solely a balance sheet transaction and does not impact the income statement.

- Cash payment of accounts payable is solely a balance sheet transaction and does not impact income statement accounts (expense relating to inventories is recognized when the inventory is sold or used up, not when the liability is paid).

Accounts Payable Turnover (APT)

Inventories are financed, in large part, by accounts payable (also called *trade credit* or *trade payables*). Such payables usually represent interest-free financing and are, therefore, less expensive than using available cash or borrowed money to finance purchases or production. Accordingly, companies use trade credit whenever possible. This is called *leaning on the trade*.

The **accounts payable turnover** reflects management's success in using trade credit to finance purchases of goods and services. It is computed as:

Accounts Payable Turnover (APT) = Cost of Goods Sold/Average Accounts Payable

Payables reflect the cost of inventory, not its retail value. Thus, to be consistent with the denominator, the ratio uses cost of goods sold (and not sales) in the numerator. Management desires to use trade credit to the greatest extent possible for financing. This means that a lower accounts payable turnover is preferable. Verizon's accounts payable turnover rate has increased from 6.67 times per year in 2004 to 9.01 times per year in 2005. (Its APT for 2005 is computed as $25,469 million/[$2,827 million + $2,827 million/2]; by coincidence, it reports the same accounts payable balance in 2005 and 2004.) This increase in accounts payable turnover indicates that Verizon is paying its obligations more quickly, which is *not* a positive development (unless the prior year is excessively low).

A metric analogous to accounts payable turnover is the **accounts payable days outstanding**, which is defined as follows:

Accounts Payable Days Outstanding (APDO) = Accounts Payable/Average Daily Cost of Goods Sold

Since accounts payable are a source of low cost financing, management desires to extend the accounts payable days outstanding as long as possible, provided that this action does not harm supply channel relations. Verizon's accounts payable remain unpaid for 40.51 days in 2005, down from 44.54 days in the prior year. (Its 2005 APDO is computed as $2,827 million/[$25,469 million/365 days].) Verizon is, therefore, leaning on the trade less than it has in the recent past. As with APT, this is generally not a positive development.

Accounts payable reflect a source of interest-free financing. Increased payables reduce the amount of net operating working capital as payables (along with other current operating liabilities) are deducted from current operating assets in the computation of net operating working capital. Also, increased payables mean increased cash flow (as increased liabilities increase net cash from operating activities) and increased profitability (as the level of interest-bearing debt that is required to finance operating assets declines). RNOA increases when companies make use of this low-cost financing source. Yet, companies must be careful to avoid excessive 'leaning on the trade' as short-term income gains can yield long-term costs such as damaged supply channels.[1,2]

MID-MODULE REVIEW 1

Verizon's accounts payable turnover (cost of goods sold/average accounts payable) increased from 6.67 in 2004 to 9.01 in 2005.

a. Does this change indicate that accounts payable have increased or decreased relative to cost of goods sold? Explain.

b. What effect does this change have on net cash flows from operating activities?

c. What management concerns, if any, might this change in accounts payable turnover pose?

Solution

a. We know that accounts payable turnover is computed as cost of goods sold divided by average accounts payable. Thus, an increase in accounts payable turnover indicates that accounts payable have decreased relative to cost of goods sold (all else equal).

b. A decrease in accounts payable results in a decrease in net cash flows from operating activities because Verizon is using cash to pay bills more quickly.

c. Decreased accounts payable yield an increase net operating working capital (all else equal), with a consequent decline in profitability and cash flow. While detrimental to profitability and cash flow, the more timely payment of accounts payable can improve supplier relations. Analysts must be aware of the potentially damaging consequences of leaning on the trade too heavily.

---

[1] Excessive delays in payment of payables can result in suppliers charging a higher price for their goods or, ultimately, refusing to sell to certain buyers. Although a hidden "financing" cost is not interest, it is still a real cost.

[2] Accounts payable often carry credit terms such as 2/10, net 30. These terms give the buyer, for example, 2% off the invoice price of goods purchased if paid within 10 days. Otherwise the entire invoice is payable within 30 days. By failing to take a discount, the buyer is effectively paying 2% interest charge to keep its funds for an additional 20 days. Since there are approximately 18 such 20-day periods in a year (365/20), this equates to an annual rate of interest of about 36%. Thus, borrowing funds at less than 36% to pay this liability within the discount period would be cost effective.

Accrued Liabilities

Accrued liabilities reflect expenses that have been incurred during the period but not yet paid in cash. (Accruals can also be used to recognize revenue and a corresponding receivable; an example might be revenue recognition on a long-term contract that has reached a particular milestone, or for interest earned on an investment in bonds but not yet received by period-end. Accruals can also reflect unearned revenue as explained in Module 5.) **Verizon** reports details of its accrued liabilities (along with accounts payable) in the following footnote to its 2005 10-K report.

At December 31 (dollars in millions)	2005	2004
Accounts payable.	$ 2,827	$ 2,827
Accrued expenses	3,036	3,071
Accrued vacation pay.	914	842
Accrued salaries and wages	2,390	2,526
Interest payable	579	585
Accrued taxes	2,605	3,326
Total accounts payable and accrued liabilities.	$12,351	$13,177

Verizon reports one nonoperating accrual: interest payable. Its other accrued liabilities are operating accruals that include miscellaneous accrued expenses, accrued vacation pay, accrued salaries and wages, and accrued taxes. Verizon's accruals are typical. To record accruals, companies recognize a liability on the balance sheet and a corresponding expense on the income statement. This means that liabilities increase, current income decreases, and equity decreases. When an accrued liability is ultimately paid, both cash and the liability decrease (but no expense is recorded because it was recognized previously).

Accounting for Accrued Liabilities

Accounting for a typical accrued liability such as accrued wages, for two consecutive periods, follows:

	Balance Sheet							Income Statement		
Transaction	Cash Asset	+	Noncash Assets	=	Liabil- ities	+	Contrib. Capital	+	Earned Capital	
										Rev- enues	−	Expen- ses	=	Net Income

(Table structure with the following entries:)

1. Period 1: Accrued $75 for employee wages earned at period-end

- Liabilities: +75 Wages Payable
- Earned Capital: −75 Retained Earnings
- Expenses: +75 Wages Expense
- Net Income: = −75

WE 75
   WP 75
WE
75
   WP
      75

2. Period 2: Paid $75 for wages earned in prior period

- Cash Asset: −75 Cash
- Liabilities: −75 Wages Payable
- Net Income: =

WP 75
   Cash 75
WP
75
   Cash
      75

The following financial statement effects result from this accrual of employee wages:

■ Employees have worked during a period and have not yet been paid. The effect of this accrual is to increase wages payable on the balance sheet and to recognize wages expense on the income statement. Failure to recognize this liability and associated expense would understate liabilities on the balance sheet and overstate income in the current period.

■ When the company pays employees in the following period, cash and wages payable both decrease. This payment does not result in expense because the expense was recognized in the prior period when incurred.

The accrued wages illustration relates to events that are fairly certain. We know, for example, when wages are incurred but not paid. Other examples of such accruals are rental costs, insurance premiums, and taxes owed.

Contingent Accrued Liabilities Some accrued liabilities are less certain than others. Consider a company facing a lawsuit. Should it record the possible liability and related expense? The answer depends on the likelihood of occurrence and the ability to estimate the obligation. Specifically, if the obligation is *probable* and the amount *estimable* with reasonable certainty, then a company will recognize this obligation, called a **contingent liability**. If an obligation is only *reasonably possible* (or cannot be reliably estimated), the contingent liability is not reported on the balance sheet and is merely disclosed in the footnotes. All other contingent liabilities that are less than reasonably possible are not disclosed.

Management of Accrued Liabilities Management has some latitude in determining the amount and timing of accruals. This latitude can lead to misreporting of income and liabilities (unintentional or otherwise). Here's how: If accruals are underestimated, then expenses are underestimated, income is overestimated, and retained earnings are overestimated. In subsequent periods when an understated accrued liability is reversed, reported income is lower than it should be; this is because prior period income was higher than it should have been. (The reverse holds for overestimated accruals.) The misreporting of accruals, therefore, shifts income from one period into another. We must be keenly aware of this potential for income shifting as we analyze the financial condition of a company.

Experience tells us that accrued liabilities related to restructuring programs (including severance accruals and accruals for asset write-downs), or to legal and environmental liabilities, or business acquisitions are somewhat problematic. These accruals too often represent early recognition of expenses. Sometimes companies aggressively overestimate one-time accruals and record an even larger expense. This is called taking a *big bath*. The effect of a big bath is to depress current period income, which relieves future periods of these expenses (thus, shifting income forward in time). Accordingly, we must monitor any change or unusual activity with accrued liabilities and view large one-time charges with skepticism.

Estimating Accruals

Some accrued liabilities require more estimation than others. Warranty liabilities are an example of an accrual that requires managerial assumptions and estimates. Warranties are commitments that manufacturers make to their customers to repair or replace defective products within a specified period of time. The expected cost of this commitment can be reasonably estimated at the time of sale based on past experience. As a result, GAAP requires manufacturers to record the expected cost of warranties as a liability, and to record the related expected warranty expense in the income statement in the same period that the sales revenue is reported.

To illustrate, assume that a company estimates that its defective units amount to 1% of sales and that each unit costs $10 to replace. If sales during the period are $10,000, the estimated warranty cost is $1,000 ($10,000 × 1% × $10). The entries to accrue this liability and its ultimate payment follow.

Transaction	Balance Sheet						Income Statement			
	Cash Asset	+ Noncash Assets	= Liabil- ities	+ Contrib. Capital	+ Earned Capital		Rev- enues	− Expen- ses	= Net Income	
1. Period 1: Accrued $1,000 of expected warranty costs on units sold during the period			+1,000 = Warranty Payable		−1,000 Retained Earnings			+1,000 − Warranty Expense	= −1,000	WRE 1,000 WRP 1,000 WRE 1,000 WRP 1,000
2. Period 2: Delivered $1,000 in replacement products to cover warranty claims		−1,000 Inventory	−1,000 = Warranty Payable						=	WRP 1,000 INV 1,000 WRP 1,000 INV 1,000

Accruing warranty liabilities has the same effect on financial statements as accruing wages expense in the previous section. That is, a liability is recorded on the balance sheet and an expense is reported in the income statement. When the defective product is later replaced (or repaired), the liability is reduced together with the cost of the inventory or the cash paid for other costs that were necessary to satisfy the claim. (Only a portion of the products estimated to fail does so in the current period; we expect other product failures in future periods. Management monitors this estimate and adjusts it if failure is higher or lower than expected.) As in the accrual of wages, the expense and the liability are reported when incurred and not when paid.

To illustrate, Ford Motor Company reports $6,158 million of warranty liability on its 2005 balance sheet. Its footnotes reveal the following additional information:

Warranty. Estimated warranty costs and additional service actions are accrued for at the time the vehicle is sold to a dealer. Included in the warranty cost accruals are costs for basic warranty coverages on vehicles sold. Additional service actions such as product recalls and other customer service actions are not included in the warranty reconciliation below, but are also accrued for at the time of sale. Estimates for warranty costs are made based primarily on historical warranty claim experience. The following is a tabular reconciliation of the product warranty accrual.

(in millions)	2005	2004
Beginning balance	$ 5,751	$ 5,443
Payments made during the year.	(3,986)	(3,694)
Changes in accrual related to warranties issued during the year.	3,949	3,611
Changes in accrual related to pre-existing warranties	593	161
Foreign currency translation and other.	(149)	230
Ending balance.	$ 6,158	$ 5,751

Of the $5,751 million balance at the beginning of 2005, Ford incurred costs of $3,986 million to replace or repair defective automobiles during 2005. This reduced Ford's liability by that amount. These costs include cash paid to customers, or to employees as wages, and the cost of parts used for repairs. Ford accrued an additional $4,542 ($3,949 + $593) million in new warranty liabilities in 2005, and recorded additional miscellaneous adjustments amounting to a net decrease in the liability of $149 million. It is important to understand that only the increase in the liability resulting from additional accruals impacts the income statement, reducing income through additional warranty expense. Payments made to settle warranty claims do not affect current period income; they merely reduce the pre-existing liability.

GAAP requires that the warranty liability reflects the estimated amount of cost that the company expects to incur as a result of warranty claims. This is often a difficult estimate to make and is prone to error. There is also the possibility that a company might underestimate its warranty liability to report higher current income, or overestimate it so as to depress current income and create an additional liability on the balance sheet (*cookie jar reserve*) that can be used to absorb future warranty costs and, thus, to reduce future expenses. The overestimation would shift income from the current period to one or more future periods. Warranty liabilities must, therefore, be examined closely and compared with sales levels. Any deviations from the historical relation of the warranty liability to sales, or from levels reported by competitors, should be scrutinized.

MID-MODULE REVIEW 2

Assume that Verizon's employees worked during the current month and earned $10,000 in wages that Verizon will not pay until the first of next month. Must Verizon recognize any wages liability and expense for the current month? Explain with reference to the financial statement effects template.

Solution

Yes. Verizon must recognize liabilities and expenses when incurred, regardless of when payment is made. Accruing expenses as incurred will match the expenses to the revenues they helped generate. Failure to recognize the wages owed to employees for the period would understate liabilities and overstate income. Verizon must reflect the wages earned and the related expense in its financial statements as follows:

	Balance Sheet					Income Statement		
Transaction	Cash Asset	+ Noncash Assets	= Liabil- ities	+ Contrib. Capital	+ Earned Capital	Rev- enues	− Expen- ses	= Net Income
Accrue $10,000 in wages expense			+10,000 Wages Payable		−10,000 Retained Earnings		+10,000 Wages Expense	= −10,000

```
WE    10,000
      WP    10,000
      WE
10,000  |
      WP
        |  10,000
```

Current Nonoperating Liabilities

Current nonoperating liabilities include short-term bank loans, accrued interest on those loans, and the current maturities of long-term debt. Companies generally try to structure their financing so that debt service requirements (payments) coincide with the cash inflows from the assets financed. This means that current assets are usually financed with current liabilities, and that long-term assets are financed with long-term liabilities (and equity).

L02 Describe the accounting for current and long-term nonoperating liabilities.

To illustrate, a seasonal company's investment in current assets tends to fluctuate during the year as depicted in the graphic below:

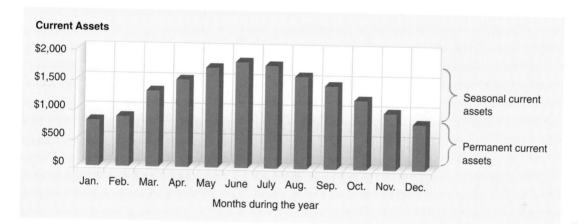

This company does most of its selling in the summer months. More inventory is purchased and manufactured in the early spring than at any other time of the year. High summer sales give rise to accounts receivable that are higher than normal during the fall. The company's working capital peaks at the height of the selling season and is lowest as the business slows in the off-season. There is a permanent level of working capital required for this business (about $750), and a seasonal component (maximum of about $1,000). Different businesses exhibit different patterns in their working capital requirements, but many have both permanent and seasonal components.

The existence of permanent and seasonal current operating assets often require that financing sources also have permanent and seasonal components. Consider again the company depicted in the graphic above. A portion of the company's assets is in inventories that are financed, in part, with accounts payable and accruals. Thus, we expect that current operating liabilities also exhibit a seasonal component that fluctuates with the level of operations. These payables are generally non-interest-bearing and, thus, provide low-cost financing that should be used to the greatest extent possible. Additional financing needs are covered by short-term interest-bearing debt.

This section focuses on current nonoperating liabilities, which include short-term debt, current maturities of long-term liabilities, and accrued interest expenses.

Short-Term Interest-Bearing Debt

Seasonal swings in working capital are often financed with a bank line of credit (short-term debt). In this case the bank provides a commitment to lend up to a maximum amount with the understanding that the amounts borrowed will be repaid in full sometime during the year. An interest-bearing note evidences any such borrowing.

When the company borrows these short-term funds, it reports the cash received on the balance sheet together with an increase in liabilities (notes payable). The note is reported as a current liability since the expectation is that it will be repaid within a year. This borrowing has no effect on income or equity. The borrower incurs (and the lender earns) interest on the note as time passes. GAAP requires the borrower to accrue the interest liability and the related interest expense each time financial statements are issued.

To illustrate, assume that **Verizon** borrows $1,000 cash on January 1. The note bears interest at a 12% annual rate, and the interest (3% per quarter) is payable on the first of each subsequent quarter (April 1, July 1, October 1, January 1). Assuming that Verizon issues calendar-quarter financial statements, this borrowing results in the following financial statement effects for January 1 through April 1.

	Balance Sheet						Income Statement		
Transaction	Cash Asset	+ Noncash Assets	= Liabil- ities	+ Contrib. Capital	+ Earned Capital		Rev- enues	− Expen- ses	= Net Income
Jan 1: Borrow $1,000 cash and issue note payable	+1,000 Cash		+1,000 Note Payable =						=
Mar 31: Accrue quarterly interest on 12%, $1,000 note payable			+30 Interest Payable =		−30 Retained Earnings			+30 Interest Expense −	= −30
Apr 1: Pay $30 cash for interest due	−30 Cash		−30 Interest Payable =						=

Cash   1,000
   NP   1,000
     Cash
1,000 |
     NP
       | 1,000

IE   30
   IP   30
     IE
30 |
     IP
       | 30

IP   30
   Cash   30
     IP
30 |
     Cash
       | 30

The January 1 borrowing increases both cash and notes payable. On March 31, Verizon issues its quarterly financial statements. Although interest is not paid until April 1, the company has incurred three months' interest obligation as of March 31. Failure to recognize this liability and the expense incurred would not fairly present the financial condition of the company. Accordingly, the quarterly accrued interest payable is computed as follows:

$$\textbf{Interest Expense} = \textbf{Principal} \times \textbf{Annual Rate} \times \textbf{Portion of Year Outstanding}$$
$$\$30 \quad\quad = \quad \$1,000 \;\times\; 12\% \;\times\; 3/12$$

The subsequent interest payment on April 1 reduces both cash and the interest payable that Verizon accrued on March 31. There is no expense reported on April 1, as it was recorded the previous day (March 31) when Verizon prepared its financial statements. (For fixed-maturity borrowings specified in days, such as a 90-day note, we use a 365-day year for interest accrual computations, see Mid-Module Review 3.)

Current Maturities of Long-Term Debt

Principal payments that must be made during the upcoming 12 months on long-term debt (such as for a mortgage), or on bonds and notes that mature within the next year, are reported as current liabilities called *current maturities of long-term debt*. All companies must provide a schedule of the maturities of their long-term debt in the footnotes to the financial statements. To illustrate, Verizon reports $7,141 million in long-term debt due within one year in the the current liability section of the balance sheet shown on page 8-4.

MID-MODULE REVIEW 3

On January 15, assume that **Verizon** borrowed $10,000 on a 90-day, 6% note payable. The bank accrues interest daily based on a 365-day year. Use the financial statement effects template to show the January 31 interest accrual.

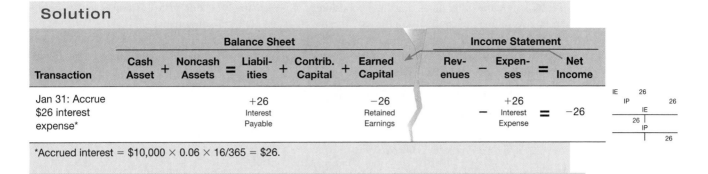

Solution

	Balance Sheet						Income Statement			
Transaction	Cash Asset	+ Noncash Assets	= Liabil-ities	+ Contrib. Capital	+ Earned Capital		Rev-enues	− Expen-ses	= Net Income	
Jan 31: Accrue $26 interest expense*			+26 Interest Payable		−26 Retained Earnings			− +26 Interest Expense	= −26	

*Accrued interest = $10,000 × 0.06 × 16/365 = $26.

LONG-TERM NONOPERATING LIABILITIES

Companies often include long-term nonoperating liabilities in their capital structure to fund long-term assets. Long-term debt in smaller amounts can be readily obtained from banks, private placements with insurance companies, and other credit sources. However, when a large amount of financing is required, the issuance of bonds (and notes) in capital markets is a cost-efficient way to raise capital. The following discussion uses bonds for illustration, but the concepts also apply to long-term notes.

Bonds are structured like any other borrowing. The borrower receives cash and agrees to pay it back with interest. Generally, the entire **face amount** (principal) of the bond is repaid at maturity (at the end of the bond's life) and interest payments are made in the interim (usually semiannually).

Companies that raise funds in the bond market normally work with an underwriter (like Merrill Lynch) to set the terms of the bond issue. The underwriter then sells individual bonds (usually in $1,000 denominations) from this general bond issue to its retail clients and professional portfolio managers (like The Vanguard Group), and receives a fee for underwriting the bond issue. These bonds are investments for individual investors, other companies, retirement plans and insurance companies.

After they are issued, the bonds can trade in the secondary market just like stocks. Market prices of bonds fluctuate daily despite the fact that the company's obligation for payment of principal and interest normally remains fixed throughout the life of the bond. Then, why do bond prices change? The answer is that the bond's fixed-rate of interest can be higher or lower than the interest rates offered on other securities of similar risk. Because bonds compete with other possible investments, bond prices are set relative to the prices of other investments. In a competitive investment market, a particular bond will become more or less desirable depending on the general level of interest rates offered by competing securities. Just as for any item, competitive pressures will cause bond prices to rise and fall.

This section analyzes and interprets the reporting for bonds. We also examine the mechanics of bond pricing and describe the accounting for and reporting of bonds.

Pricing of Debt

The following two different interest rates are crucial for pricing debt.

- **Coupon (contract** or **stated) rate** The coupon rate of interest is stated in the bond contract; it is used to compute the dollar amount of (semiannual) interest payments that are paid to bondholders during the life of the bond issue.
- **Market (yield** or **effective) rate** This is the interest rate that investors expect to earn on the investment for this debt security; this rate is used to price the bond.

The coupon (contract) rate is used to compute interest payments and the market (yield) rate is used to price the bond. The coupon rate and the market rate are nearly always different. This is because the coupon rate is fixed prior to issuance of the bond and normally remains fixed throughout its life. Market rates of interest, on the other hand, fluctuate continually with the supply and demand for bonds in the market place, general macroeconomic conditions, and the financial condition of borrowers.

The bond price, both its initial sales price and the price it trades at in the secondary market subsequent to issuance, equals the present value of the expected cash flows to the bondholder. Specifically, bondholders normally expect to receive two different types of cash flows:

1. **Periodic interest payments** (usually semiannual) during the bond's life; these payments are called an **annuity** because they are equal in amount and made at regular intervals.
2. **Single payment** of the face (principal) amount of the bond at maturity; this is called a *lump sum payment* because it occurs only once.

The bond price equals the present value of the periodic interest payments plus the present value of the single payment. If the present value of the two cash flows is equal to the bond's face value, the bond is sold at par. If the present value is less than or greater than the bond's face value, the bond sells at a discount or premium, respectively. We next illustrate the issuance of bonds at three different prices: at par, at a discount, and at a premium.

Bonds Issued at Par

To illustrate a bond sold at par, assume that a bond with a face amount of $10 million, has a 6% annual coupon rate payable semiannually (3% semiannual rate), and a maturity of 10 years. (Semiannual interest payments are typical for bonds. This means that the issuer pays bondholders two interest payments per year. Each semiannual interest payment is equal to the bond's face value times the annual rate divided by two.) Investors purchasing this issue receive the following cash flows.

	Number of Payments	Dollars per Payment	Total Cash Flows
Semiannual interest payments.....	10 years × 2 = 20	$10,000,000 × 3% = $300,000	$ 6,000,000
Principal payment at maturity......	1	$10,000,000	10,000,000
			$16,000,000

Specifically, the bond agreement dictates that the borrower must make 20 semiannual payments of $300,000 each, computed as $10,000,000 × (6%/2). At maturity, the borrower must repay the $10,000,000 face amount. To price bonds, investors identify the *number* of interest payments and use that number when computing the present value of *both* the interest payments and the principal (face) payment at maturity.

The bond price is the present value of the periodic interest payments (the annuity) plus the present value of the principal payment (the lump sum). In our example, assuming that investors desire a 3% semiannual market rate (yield), the bond sells for $10,000,000, which is computed as follows:

Present value factors are from Appendix A

	Payment	Present Value Factor[a]	Present Value
Interest.................	$ 300,000	14.87747[b]	$ 4,463,200[d]
Principal..............	$10,000,000	0.55368[c]	5,536,800
			$10,000,000

[a] Mechanics of using tables to compute present values are explained in Appendix 8A; present value factors come from Appendix A near the end of the book.

[b] Present value of an ordinary annuity for 20 periods discounted at 3% per period.

[c] Present value of a single payment in 20 periods discounted at 3% per period.

[d] Rounded.

Since the bond contract pays investors a 3% semiannual rate when investors demand a 3% semiannual market rate, given the borrower's credit rating and the time to maturity, the investors purchase those bonds at the **par (face) value** of $10 million.

Discount Bonds

As a second illustration, assume investors demand a 4% semiannual return for the 3% semiannual coupon bond, while all other details remain the same. The bond now sells for $8,640,999, computed as follows:

	Payment	Present Value Factor	Present Value
Interest	$ 300,000	13.59033[a]	$ 4,077,099
Principal	$10,000,000	0.45639[b]	4,563,900
			$ 8,640,999

[a] Present value of an ordinary annuity for 20 periods discounted at 4% per period.
[b] Present value of a single payment in 20 periods discounted at 4% per period.

Since the bond carries a coupon rate *lower* than what investors demand, the bond is less desirable and sells at a **discount**. More generally, bonds sell at a discount whenever the coupon rate is less than the market rate.

Premium Bonds

As a third illustration, assume that investors demand a 2% semiannual return for the 3% semiannual coupon bonds, while all other details remain the same. The bond now sells for $11,635,129, computed as follows:

	Payment	Present Value Factor	Present Value
Interest	$ 300,000	16.35143[a]	$ 4,905,429
Principal	$10,000,000	0.67297[b]	6,729,700
			$11,635,129

[a] Present value of an ordinary annuity for 20 periods discounted at 2% per period.
[b] Present value of a single payment in 20 periods discounted at 2% per period.

Since the bond carries a coupon rate *higher* than what investors demand, the bond is more desirable and sells at a **premium**. More generally, bonds sell at a premium whenever the coupon rate is greater than the market rate.[3] Exhibit 8.1 summarizes this relation for bond pricing.

EXHIBIT 8.1	Coupon Rate, Market Rate, and Bond Pricing
Coupon rate > market rate →	Bond sells at a **premium** (above face amount)
Coupon rate = market rate →	Bond sells at **par** (at face amount)
Coupon rate < market rate →	Bond sells at a **discount** (below face amount)

Exhibit 8.2 shows an announcement (called a *tombstone*) of a recent General Electric $5 billion debt issuance. It has a 5% coupon rate paying 2.5% semiannual interest, maturing in 2013, with an issue price of 99.626 (sold at a discount). GE's underwriters took 0.425 in fees (more than $21 million) for underwriting and selling this debt issue.[4]

---

[3] Bond prices are often stated in percent form. For example, a bond sold at par is said to be sold at 100 (that is, 100% of par). The bond sold at $8,640,999 is said to be sold at 86.41 (86.41% of par, computed as $8,640,999/$10,000,000). The bond sold for a premium is said to be sold at 116.35 (116.35% of the bond's face value).

[4] The tombstone makes clear that if we purchase any of these notes (in denominations of $1,000) after the semiannual interest date, we must pay accrued interest in addition to the purchase price. This interest is returned to us in the regular interest payment. (This procedure makes the bookkeeping easier for the issuer/underwriter because all interest payments are equal regardless of when GE actually sold the bond.)

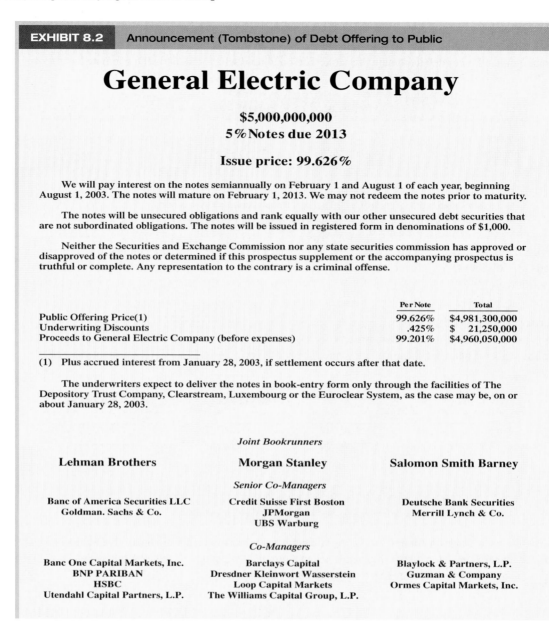

EXHIBIT 8.2	Announcement (Tombstone) of Debt Offering to Public

General Electric Company

$5,000,000,000
5% Notes due 2013

Issue price: 99.626%

We will pay interest on the notes semiannually on February 1 and August 1 of each year, beginning August 1, 2003. The notes will mature on February 1, 2013. We may not redeem the notes prior to maturity.

The notes will be unsecured obligations and rank equally with our other unsecured debt securities that are not subordinated obligations. The notes will be issued in registered form in denominations of $1,000.

Neither the Securities and Exchange Commission nor any state securities commission has approved or disapproved of the notes or determined if this prospectus supplement or the accompanying prospectus is truthful or complete. Any representation to the contrary is a criminal offense.

	Per Note	Total
Public Offering Price(1)	99.626%	$4,981,300,000
Underwriting Discounts	.425%	$ 21,250,000
Proceeds to General Electric Company (before expenses)	99.201%	$4,960,050,000

(1) Plus accrued interest from January 28, 2003, if settlement occurs after that date.

The underwriters expect to deliver the notes in book-entry form only through the facilities of The Depository Trust Company, Clearstream, Luxembourg or the Euroclear System, as the case may be, on or about January 28, 2003.

Joint Bookrunners

Lehman Brothers	**Morgan Stanley**	**Salomon Smith Barney**

Senior Co-Managers

Banc of America Securities LLC	Credit Suisse First Boston	Deutsche Bank Securities
Goldman. Sachs & Co.	JPMorgan	Merrill Lynch & Co.
	UBS Warburg	

Co-Managers

Banc One Capital Markets, Inc.	Barclays Capital	Blaylock & Partners, L.P.
BNP PARIBAN	Dresdner Kleinwort Wasserstein	Guzman & Company
HSBC	Loop Capital Markets	Ormes Capital Markets, Inc.
Utendahl Capital Partners, L.P.	The Williams Capital Group, L.P.	

Effective Cost of Debt

When a bond sells for par, the cost to the issuing company is the cash interest paid. In our first illustration above, the *effective cost* of the bond is the 6% interest paid by the issuer.

When a bond sells at a discount, the issuer must repay more (the face value when the bond matures) than the cash received at issuance (the discounted bond proceeds). This means that the effective cost of a discount bond is greater than if the bond had sold at par. A discount is a cost and, like any other cost, must eventually be transferred from the balance sheet to the income statement as an expense.

When a bond sells at a premium, the borrower received more cash at issuance than it must repay. The difference, the premium, is a benefit that must eventually find its way into the income statement as a *reduction* of interest expense. As a result of the premium, the effective cost of a premium bond is less than if the bond had sold at par.

Bonds are priced to yield the return (market rate) demanded by investors. Consequently, the effective rate of a bond *always* equals the yield (market) rate demanded by investors, regardless of the coupon rate of the bond. This means that companies cannot influence the effective cost of debt by raising or lowering the coupon rate. Doing so will only result in a bond premium or discount. We discuss the factors affecting the yield demanded by investors later in the module.

The effective cost of debt is reflected in the amount of interest expense reported in the issuer's income statement. Because of bond discounts and premiums, interest expense is usually different from the cash interest paid. The next section discusses how management reports bonds on the balance sheet and interest expense on the income statement.

REPORTING OF DEBT FINANCING

This section identifies and describes the financial statement effects of bond transactions.

Financial Statement Effects of Debt Issuance

Bonds Issued at Par

When a bond sells at par, the issuing company receives the cash proceeds and accepts an obligation to make payments per the bond contract. Specifically, cash is increased and a long-term liability (bonds payable) is increased by the same amount. There is no revenue or expense at bond issuance. Using the facts from our $10 million bond illustration above, the issuance of bonds at par has the following financial statement effects:

	Balance Sheet							Income Statement		
Transaction	**Cash Asset**	+	**Noncash Assets**	=	**Liabil- ities**	+	**Contrib. Capital**	+	**Earned Capital**		**Rev- enues**	−	**Expen- ses**	=	**Net Income**
Issue bonds at par for cash	+10 mil. Cash				+10 mil. Long-Term Debt									=	

Cash   10 mil
    LTD   10 mil
        Cash
10 mil
    LTD
       10 mil

Discount Bonds

When a bond is sold at a discount, the cash proceeds and net bond liability are recorded at the amount of the proceeds received (not the face amount of the bond). Again, using the facts above from our bond discount illustration, the financial statement effects follow:

	Balance Sheet							Income Statement		
Transaction	**Cash Asset**	+	**Noncash Assets**	=	**Liabil- ities**	+	**Contrib. Capital**	+	**Earned Capital**		**Rev- enues**	−	**Expen- ses**	=	**Net Income**
Issue bonds at discount for cash	+$8,640,999 Cash				+$8,640,999 Long-Term Debt									=	

Cash   8,640,999
    LTD   8,640,999
        Cash
8,640,999
    LTD
      8,640,999

The net bond liability reported on the balance sheet consists of two components as follows:

Bonds payable, face.	$10,000,000
Less bond discount	(1,359,001)
Bonds payable, net	$ 8,640,999

Bonds are reported on the balance sheet net of any discount (or premium). When the bond matures, however, the company is obligated to repay $10 million. Accordingly, at maturity, the bond liability needs to read $10 million, the amount that is owed. This means that between the bond issuance and its maturity, the discount must decline to zero. This reduction of the discount over the life of the bond is called **amortization**. The next section shows how discount amortization results in additional interest expense in the income statement. This amortization causes the effective interest expense to be greater than the periodic cash interest payments.

BUSINESS INSIGHT   Verizon's Zero Coupon Debt

Zero coupon bonds and notes, called *zeros,* do not carry a coupon rate. Pricing of these bonds and notes is done in the same manner as those with coupon rates—the exception is the absence of an interest annuity. This means that the price is the present value of the principal payment at maturity; hence the bond is sold at a *deep discount.* Following is an example from Verizon's 2005 10-K report:

> ***Zero-Coupon Convertible Notes***   In May 2001, Verizon . . . issued approximately $5.4 billion in principal amount at maturity of zero-coupon convertible notes due 2021, resulting in gross proceeds of approximately $3 billion. The notes are convertible into shares of our common stock at an initial price of $69.50 per share if the closing price of Verizon common stock on the NYSE exceeds specified levels or in other specified circumstances. The conversion price increases by at least 3% a year. The initial conversion price represents a 25% premium over the May 8, 2001, closing price of $55.60 per share. There are no scheduled cash interest payments associated with the notes. The zero-coupon convertible notes are callable by Verizon . . . on or after May 15, 2006. In addition, the notes are redeemable at the option of the holders on May 15th in each of the years 2004, 2006, 2011 and 2016. On May 15, 2004, $3,292 million of principal amount of the notes ($1,984 million after unamortized discount) were redeemed by Verizon. As of December 31, 2005, the remaining zero-coupon convertible notes were classified as debt maturing within one year since they are redeemable at the option of the holders on May 15, 2006.

When Verizon issued its zero-coupon convertible notes in 2001, they had a maturity value of $5.4 billion and were slated to mature in 2021. No interest is paid in the interim. The notes sold for $3 billion. The difference between the $3 billion sales proceeds and the $5.4 billion maturity value represents Verizon's interest costs, which is the return to the investor. The effective cost of the debt is the interest rate that equates the issue price and maturity value, or approximately 3%. In May 2004, Verizon redeemed almost $3.3 billion of the bonds—this constituted an early repayment.

Premium Bonds

When a bond is sold at a premium, the cash proceeds and net bond liability are recorded at the amount of the proceeds received (not the face amount of the bond). Again, using the facts above from our premium bond illustration, the financial statement effects follow:

	Balance Sheet						Income Statement		
Transaction	Cash Asset	+ Noncash Assets	= Liabil- ities	+ Contrib. Capital	+ Earned Capital		Rev- enues	− Expen- ses	= Net Income
Issue bonds at premium for cash	+$11,635,129 Cash		+$11,635,129 = Long-Term Debt						=

Cash   11,635,129
 LTD   11,635,129
          Cash
11,635,129
          LTD
            11,635,129

The bond liability amount reported on the balance sheet, again, consists of two parts:

Bonds payable, face.	$10,000,000
Add bond premium	1,635,129
Bonds payable, net	$11,635,129

The $10 million must be repaid at maturity, and the premium is amortized to zero over the life of the bond. The premium represents a *benefit,* which *reduces* interest expense on the income statement.

Effects of Discount and Premium Amortization

For bonds issued at par, interest expense reported on the income statement equals the cash interest payment. However, for bonds issued at a discount or premium, interest expense reported on the income statement also includes any amortization of the bond discount or premium as follows:

Cash interest paid	Cash interest paid
+ Amortization of discount	− Amortization of premium
——————————— or	———————————
Interest expense	Interest expense

Specifically, periodic amortization of a discount is added to the cash interest paid to get interest expense. Amortization of the discount reflects the additional cost the issuer incurs from issuing the bonds at a discount. Over the bond's life, the discount is transferred from the balance sheet to the income statement via amortization, as an increase to interest expense. For a premium bond, the premium is a benefit the issuer receives at issuance. Amortization of the premium reduces interest expense over the bond's life. In both cases, interest expense on the income statement represents the *effective cost* of debt (the *nominal cost* of debt is the cash interest paid).

Companies amortize discounts and premiums using the effective interest method. To illustrate, recall the assumptions of the discount bond above—face amount of $10 million, a 6% annual coupon rate payable semiannually (3% semiannual rate), a maturity of 10 years, and a market (yield) rate of 8% annual (4% semiannual). These facts resulted in a bond issue price of $8,640,999. Exhibit 8.3 shows the first two and final two periods of a bond discount amortization table for this bond.

EXHIBIT 8.3   Bond Discount Amortization Table

Period	[A] ([E] × market%) Interest Expense	[B] (Face × coupon%) Cash Interest Paid	[C] ([A] − [B]) Discount Amortization	[D] (Prior bal − [C]) Discount Balance	[E] (Face − [D]) Bond Payable, Net
0				$1,359,001	$ 8,640,999
1	$345,640	$300,000	$45,640	1,313,361	8,686,639
2	347,466	300,000	47,466	1,265,895	8,734,105
⋮	⋮	⋮	⋮	⋮	⋮
19	392,458	300,000	92,458	96,087	9,903,913
20	396,157*	300,000	96,157*	0	10,000,000

* Due to rounding, we must subtract $70 from both [A] and [C] in period 20 to yield the $10,000,000 face value.

The interest period is denoted in the left-most column. Period 0 is the point at which the bond is issued, and period 1 and following are successive six-month periods (recall, interest is paid semiannually). Column [A] is interest expense, which is reported in the income statement. Interest expense is computed as the bond's net balance sheet value (the carrying amount of the bond) at the beginning of the period (column [E]) multiplied by the 4% semiannual rate used to compute the bond issue price. Column [B] is cash interest paid, which is a constant $300,000 per the bond contract (face amount × coupon rate). Column [C] is discount amortization, which is the difference between interest expense and cash interest paid. Column [D] is the discount balance, which is the previous balance of the discount less the discount amortization in column [C]. Column [E] is the net bond payable, which is the $10 million face amount less the unamortized discount from column [D].

The table shows amounts for interest in periods 0, 1, 2, 19, and 20. The amortization process continues until period 20, at which time the discount balance is 0 and the net bond payable is $10 million (the maturity value). Each semiannual period, interest expense is recorded at 4%, the market rate of interest at the bond's issuance. This rate does not change over the life of the bond, even if the prevailing market interest rates change. An amortization table reveals the financial statement effects of the bond for its duration. Specifically, we see the income statement effects in column [A], the cash effects in column [B], and the balance sheet effects in columns [D] and [E]. (A fully completed amortization table is shown in Appendix 8B.)

To illustrate amortization of a premium bond, we use the assumptions of the premium bond above—$10 million face value, a 6% annual coupon rate payable semiannually (3% semiannual rate), a maturity of 10 years, and a 2% semiannual market interest rate. These parameters resulted in a bond issue price of $11,635,129. Exhibit 8.4 shows the first and last two periods of a bond premium amortization table for this bond.

	[A]	**[B]**	**[C]**	**[D]**	**[E]**
	([E] × market%)	(Face × coupon%)	([B] − [A])	(Prior bal − [C])	(Face + [D])
	Interest	**Cash**	**Premium**	**Premium**	**Bond**
Period	**Expense**	**Interest Paid**	**Amortization**	**Balance**	**Payable, Net**
0				$1,635,129	$11,635,129
1	$232,703	$300,000	$67,297	1,567,832	11,567,832
2	231,357	300,000	68,643	1,499,188	11,499,188
⋮	⋮	⋮	⋮	⋮	⋮
19	203,883	300,000	96,117	98,018	10,098,018
20	201,960*	300,000	98,040*	0	10,000,000

EXHIBIT 8.4   Bond Premium Amortization Table

* Due to rounding, we must add $22 to [A] and subtract $22 from [C] in period 20 to yield the $10,000,000 face value.

Interest expense is computed using the same process that we used for discount bonds. The difference is that the yield rate is 2% semiannual in the premium case. Also, cash interest paid follows from the bond contract (face amount × coupon rate), and the other columns' computations reflect the premium amortization. After period 20, the premium is fully amortized (equals zero) and the net bond payable balance is $10 million, the amount owed at maturity. Again, an amortization table reveals the financial statement effects of the bond—the income statement effects in column [A], the cash effects in column [B], and the balance sheet effects in columns [D] and [E].

Financial Statement Effects of Bond Repurchase

Companies report bonds payable at *historical (adjusted) cost.* Specifically, net bonds payable amounts follow from the amortization table, as do the related cash flows and income statement numbers. All financial statement relations are set when the bond is issued and do not subsequently change.

Once issued, however, bonds trade in secondary markets. The yield rate used to compute bond prices for these subsequent transactions is the market interest rate prevailing at the time. These rates change daily based on the level of interest rates in the economy and the perceived creditworthiness of the bond issuer.

Companies can and sometimes do repurchase (or *redeem*) their bonds prior to maturity. The bond indenture (contract agreement) can include provisions giving the company the right to repurchase its bonds. Or, the company can repurchase bonds in the open market. To illustrate, **Verizon**'s 2005 10-K includes the following footnote relating to its repurchase of **MCI** debt in connection with the MCI acquisition:

Redemption of MCI Debt   On January 17, 2006, Verizon announced offers to purchase two series of MCI senior notes, MCI $1,983 million aggregate principal amount of 6.688% Senior Notes Due 2009 and MCI $1,699 million aggregate principal amount of 7.735% Senior Notes Due 2014, at 101% of their par value. Due to the change in control of MCI that occurred in connection with the merger with Verizon on January 6, 2006, Verizon is required to make this offer to noteholders within 30 days of the closing of the merger of MCI and Verizon. Separately, Verizon notified noteholders that MCI is exercising its right to redeem both series of Senior Notes prior to maturity under the optional redemption procedures provided in the indentures. The 6.688% Notes were redeemed on March 1, 2006, and the 7.735% Notes were redeemed on February 16, 2006. In addition, on January 20, 2006, Verizon announced an offer to repurchase MCI $1,983 million aggregate principal amount of 5.908% Senior Notes Due 2007 at 101% of their par value. On February 21, 2006, $1,804 million of these notes were redeemed by Verizon. Verizon satisfied and discharged the indenture governing this series of notes shortly after the close of the offer for those noteholders who did not accept this offer.

When a bond repurchase occurs, a gain or loss usually results, and is computed as follows:

Gain or Loss on Bond Repurchase = Net Bonds Payable − Repurchase Payment

The net bonds payable, also referred to as the *book value,* is the net amount reported on the balance sheet. If the issuer pays more to retire the bonds than the amount carried on its balance sheet, it reports a loss on its income statement, usually called *loss on bond retirement*. The issuer reports a *gain on bond retirement* if the repurchase price is less than the net bonds payable.

GAAP dictates that any gains or losses on bond repurchases be reported as part of ordinary income unless they meet the criteria for treatment as an extraordinary item (unusual and infrequent, see Module 5). Relatively few debt retirements meet these criteria and, hence, most gains and losses on bond repurchases are reported as part of income from continuing operations.

How should we treat these gains and losses for analysis purposes? That is, do they carry economic effects? The answer is no—the gain or loss on repurchase is exactly offset by the present value of the future cash flow implications of the repurchase (Appendix 8B demonstrates this).

Another analysis issue involves assessing the market value of bonds and other long-term liabilities. This information is relevant for some investors and creditors in revealing unrealized gains and losses (similar to that reported for marketable securities). GAAP requires companies to provide information about current market values of their long-term liabilities in footnotes (see Verizon's fair value of debt disclosure in the next section). However, these market values are *not* reported on the balance sheet and changes in these market values are not reflected in net income. We must make our own adjustments to the balance sheet and income statement if we want to include changes in market values of liabilities.

Financial Statement Footnotes

Companies are required to disclose details about their long-term liabilities, including the amounts borrowed under each debt issuance, the interest rates, maturity dates, and other key provisions. Following is Verizon's disclosure for its long-term debt.

Long-Term Debt   Outstanding long-term obligations are as follows:

At December 31 ($ millions)	Interest Rates %	Maturities	2005	2004
Notes payable	4.00–8.61	2006–2035	$16,310	$17,481
Telephone subsidiaries—debentures and first/refunding mortgage bonds.....	4.63–7.00	2006–2042	11,869	12,958
	7.15–7.65	2007–2032	1,725	1,825
	7.85–9.67	2010–2031	1,926	1,930
Other subsidiaries—debentures and other ..	4.25–8.75	2006–2028	3,410	3,480
Zero-coupon convertible notes, net of unamortized discount of $790 and $830 .	3.18	2021	1,360	1,320
Employee stock ownership plan loans: NYNEX debentures.................	9.55	2010	113	145
Capital lease obligations (average rate 11.9% and 9.4%)			112	138
Property sale holdbacks held in escrow, vendor financing and other............	3.00–3.25	2006–2009	13	21
Unamortized discount, net of premium			(43)	(55)
Total long-term debt, including current maturities			36,795	39,243
Less: debt maturing within one year			(4,926)	(3,569)
Total long-term debt..................			$31,869	$35,674

Verizon reports a book value for long-term debt of $36,795 million at year-end 2005. Of this amount, $4,926 million matures in the next year and is classified as a current liability (current maturities of long-term debt). The remainder of $31,869 matures after 2006. Verizon also reports $43 million in unamortized discount (net of premium) on this debt.

In addition to long-term debt amounts, rates, and due dates, and as required under GAAP, Verizon reports aggregate maturities for the five years subsequent to the balance sheet date as follows:

Maturities of Long-Term Debt   Maturities of long-term debt outstanding at December 31, 2005 are $4.9 billion in 2006, $4.7 billion in 2007, $2.5 billion in 2008, $1.7 billion in 2009, $2.8 billion in 2010 and $20.2 billion thereafter.

This reveals that Verizon is required to make principal payments of $16.6 billion in the next five years, with $9.6 billion of that coming due in the next two years. Such maturities are important information as a company must meet its required payments, negotiate a rescheduling of the indebtedness, or refinance the debt to avoid default. Failing to repay debts (defaulting) usually has severe consequences as debtholders have legal remedies available to them that can bankrupt the company.

Verizon's disclosure on the market value of its total debt follows:

December 31, 2005 ($ millions)	Carrying Amount	Fair Value
Short- and long-term debt	$38,898	$40,313

As of 2005, indebtedness with a book value of $38,898 million had a market value of $40,313 million, resulting in an unrecognized liability (which would be realized if Verizon redeemed the debt) of $1,415 million. The increase in market value is due mainly to a decline in interest rates subsequent to the bonds' issuance. The justification for not recognizing unrealized gains and losses on the balance sheet and income statement is that such amounts can reverse with future fluctuations in interest rates. Further, since only the face amount of debt is repaid at maturity, unrealized gains and losses that arise during intervening years are not necessarily relevant. This is the same logic for nonrecognition of gains and losses on held-to-maturity debt investments (see Module 7).

CREDIT RATINGS AND THE COST OF DEBT

LO3 Explain how credit ratings are determined and identify their effect on the cost of debt.

Earlier in the module we explained that the effective cost of debt to the issuing company is the market (yield) rate of interest used to price the bond, regardless of the bond coupon rate. The market rate of interest is usually defined as the yield on U.S. Government borrowings such as treasury bills, notes, and bonds, called the *risk-free rate*, plus a *spread* (also called a risk premium).

Yield Rate = Risk-Free Rate + Spread

Both treasury yields (the so-called risk-free rates) and corporate yields vary over time as illustrated in the following graphic.

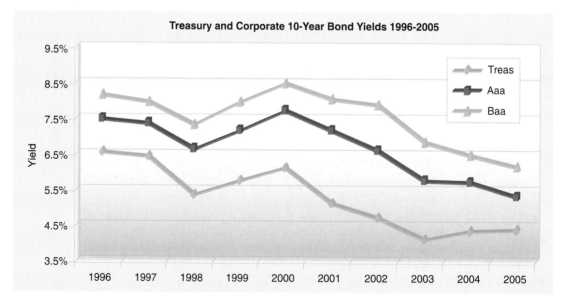

The rate of interest that investors expect for a particular bond is a function of the risk-free rate and the spread that depends on the creditworthiness of the issuing entity.

The yield increases (shifts upward) as debt quality moves from Treasury securities (generally considered to be risk free), which is the highest quality debt reflected in the line nearest to zero, to the AAA (highest) rated corporates and, finally, to the Baa (lower-rated) corporates shown in this graph. That is, higher credit-rated issuers warrant a lower rate than lower credit-rated issuers. This difference is substantial. For example, in 2005, the average 10-year treasury bond yield is 4.29%, while the AAA corporate bond yield is 5.23% and the average Baa (the lowest investment grade corporate) yield is 6.06%.

RESEARCH INSIGHT   **Accounting Conservatism and Cost of Debt**

Research indicates that companies that use more conservative accounting policies incur a lower cost of debt. Research also suggests that while accounting conservatism can lead to lower-quality accounting income (because such income does not fully reflect economic reality), creditors are more confident in the numbers and view them as more credible. Evidence also implies that companies can lower the required return demanded by creditors (the spread) by issuing high-quality financial reports that include enhanced footnote disclosures and detailed supplemental reports.

A company's credit rating, also referred to as debt rating, credit quality or creditworthiness, is related to default risk. **Default** refers to the nonpayment of interest and principal and/or the failure to adhere to the various terms and conditions (covenants) of the bond indenture. Companies seeking to obtain bond financing from the capital markets, normally first seek a rating on their proposed debt issuance from one of several rating agencies such as Standard & Poor's, Moody's Investors Service, or Fitch. The aim of rating agencies is to rate debt so that its default risk is more accurately conveyed to and priced by the market. Each rating agency uses its own rating system, as Exhibit 8.5 shows. This exhibit includes the general description for each rating class—for example, AAA is assigned to debt of prime maximum safety (maximum creditworthiness).

EXHIBIT 8.5   Corporate Debt Ratings and Descriptions

Moody's	S&P	Fitch	Description
Aaa	AAA	AAA	Prime Maximum Safety
Aa1	AA+	AA+	High Grade, High Quality
Aa2	AA	AA	
Aa3	AA−	AA−	
A1	A+	A+	Upper-Medium Grade
A2	A	A	
A3	A−	A−	
Baa1	BBB+	BBB+	Lower-Medium Grade
Baa2	BBB	BBB	
Baa3	BBB−	BBB−	
Ba1	BB+	BB+	Non-Investment Grade
Ba2	BB	BB	Speculative
Ba3	BB−	BB−	
B1	B+	B+	Highly Speculative
B2	B	B	
B3	B−	B−	
Caa1	CCC+	CCC	Substantial Risk
Caa2	CCC		In Poor Standing
Caa3	CCC−		
Ca			Extremely Speculative
C			May be in Default
		DDD	Default
		DD	
	D	D	

<table>
<tr><td>MANAGERIAL DECISION</td><td>You Are the Vice President of Finance</td></tr>
</table>

Your company is currently rated B1/B+ by the Moody's and S&P credit rating agencies, respectively. You are considering possible financial and other restructurings to increase your company's credit rating. What types of restructurings might you consider? What benefits will your company receive from those restructurings? What costs will your company incur to implement such restructurings? [Answer, p. 8-30]

Verizon bonds are rated A3/A by Moody's and S&P, respectively, as of 2006. It is this rating, in conjunction with the maturity of Verizon's bonds, that establishes the market interest rate and the bonds' selling price. There are a number of considerations that affect the rating of a bond. Standard & Poor's lists the following factors, categorized by business risk and financial risk, among its credit rating criteria:

Business Risk
- Industry characteristics
- Competitive position (marketing, technology, efficiency, regulation)
- Management

Financial Risk
- Financial characteristics
- Financial policy
- Profitability
- Capital structure
- Cash flow protection
- Financial flexibility

Debt ratings are set to convey information primarily to debt investors who are mainly interested in assessing the probability that the borrower will make interest and principal payments on time. If a company defaults on its debt, debtholders seek legal remedies, including forcing the borrower to liquidate its assets to settle obligations. However, in forced liquidations, debtholders rarely realize the entire amounts owed to them.

Standard and Poor's uses several financial ratios to assess default risk. A list of these ratios, together with median averages for various risk classes, is in Exhibit 8.6. In examining the ratios, recall that debt is increasingly more risky as we move from the first column, AAA, to the last, CCC.[5]

---

[5] Definitions for the key ratios in Exhibit 8.6 follow:

$$\text{EBIT interest coverage} = \frac{\text{Earnings from continuing operations before interest and taxes}}{\text{Gross interest incurred before subtracting (1) capitalized interest and (2) interest income}}$$

$$\text{EBITDA interest coverage} = \frac{\text{Earnings from continuing operations before interest and taxes, depreciation, and amortization}}{\text{Gross interest incurred before subtracting (1) capitalized interest and (2) interest income}}$$

$$\text{Funds from operations/total debt} = \frac{\text{Net income from continuing operations plus depreciation, amortization, deferred income taxes, and other noncash items}}{\text{Long-term debt plus current maturities, commercial paper, and other short-term borrowings}}$$

$$\text{Free operating cash flow/total debt} = \frac{\text{Funds from operations minus capital expenditures, minus (plus) the increase (decrease) in working capital (excluding changes in cash, marketable securities, and short-term debt)}}{\text{Long-term debt plus current maturities, commercial paper, and other short-term borrowings}}$$

$$\text{Return on capital} = \frac{\text{Earnings from continuing operations before interest and taxes}}{\text{Average of beginning of year and end of year capital, including short-term debt, current maturities, long-term debt, noncurrent deferred taxes, and equity}}$$

$$\text{Operating income/sales} = \frac{\text{Sales minus cost of goods manufactured (before depreciation and amortization), selling, general and administrative, and research and development costs}}{\text{Sales}}$$

$$\text{Long-term debt/capital} = \frac{\text{Long-term debt}}{\text{Long-term debt plus shareholders' equity (including preferred stock) plus minority interest}}$$

$$\text{Total debt/capital} = \frac{\text{Long-term debt plus current maturities, commercial paper, and other short-term borrowings}}{\text{Long-term debt plus current maturities, commercial paper, and other short-term borrowings plus shareholders' equity (including preferred stock) plus minority interest}}$$

EXHIBIT 8.6	**Ratio Values for Different Risk Classes of Corporate Debt***						
Three-Year Medians	**AAA**	**AA**	**A**	**BBB**	**BB**	**B**	**CCC**
EBIT interest coverage (×).	21.4	10.1	6.1	3.7	2.1	0.8	0.1
EBITDA interest coverage (×)	26.5	12.9	9.1	5.8	3.4	1.8	1.3
FFO/Total debt (%).	128.8	55.4	43.2	30.8	18.8	7.8	1.6
Free oper. cash flow/Total debt (%)	84.2	25.2	15.0	8.5	2.6	(3.2)	(12.9)
Return on capital (%)	34.9	21.7	19.4	13.6	11.6	6.6	1.0
Operating income/Sales (%)	27.0	22.1	18.6	15.4	15.9	11.9	11.9
Long-term debt/Capital (%)	13.3	28.2	33.9	42.5	57.2	69.7	68.8
Total debt/Capital (incl. STD) (%)	22.9	37.7	42.5	48.2	62.6	74.8	87.7

**Corporate Ratings Criteria—Adjusted Key Financial Ratios*, Standard & Poor's Ratings, Standard & Poor's, a division of The McGraw-Hill Companies (reproduced with permission).

A review of these ratios indicates that S&P considers the following factors relevant in evaluating a company's ability to meet its debt service requirements:

1. Liquidity (ratios 1 through 4)
2. Profitability (ratios 5 and 6)
3. Solvency (ratios 7 and 8)

Further, these ratios are variants of many of the ratios we describe in Module 4.

Other relevant debt-rating factors include the following:

- **Collateral**   Companies can provide security for debt by pledging certain assets against the bond. This is like mortgages on assets. To the extent debt is secured, the debtholder is in a preferred position vis-à-vis other creditors.

- **Covenants**   Debt agreements (indentures) can restrict the behavior of the issuing company so as to protect debtholders. For example, covenants commonly prohibit excessive dividend payment, mergers and acquisitions, further borrowing, and commonly prescribe minimum levels for key liquidity and solvency ratios. These covenants provide debtholders an element of control over the issuer's operations since, unlike equity investors, debtholders have no voting rights.

- **Options**   Options are sometimes written into debt contracts. Examples are options to convert debt into stock (so that debtholders have a stake in value creation) and options allowing the issuing company to repurchase its debt before maturity (usually at a premium).

RESEARCH INSIGHT	**Valuation of Debt Options**

Debt instruments can include features such as conversion options, under which the debt can be converted to common stock. Such conversion features are not accounted for separately under GAAP. Instead, convertible debt is accounted for just like debt with no conversion features (unless the conversion option can be separately traded). However, option-pricing models can be used to estimate the value of such debt features even when no market for those features exist. Empirical results suggest that those debt features represent a substantial part of debt value. These findings contribute to the current debate regarding the separation of compound financial instruments into debt and equity portions for financial statement presentation and analysis.

MODULE-END REVIEW

On January 1, assume that Sprint Nextel Corporation issues $300,000 of 15-year, 10% bonds payable for $351,876, yielding an effective semiannual interest rate of 4%. Interest is payable semiannually on June 30 and December 31. (1) Show computations to confirm the issue price of $351,876, and (2) complete Sprint's financial statement effects template for (a) bond issuance, (b) semiannual interest payment and premium amortization on June 30 of the first year, and (c) semiannual interest payment and premium amortization on December 31 of the first year.

Solution

1.

Issue price for $300,000, 15-year bonds that pay, 10% interest semiannually discounted at 8%:	
Present value of principal payment ($300,000 × 0.30832)	$ 92,496
Present value of semiannual interest payments ($15,000 × 17.29203).	259,380
Issue price of bonds.	$351,876

2.

Margin T-accounts:

```
Cash    351,876
   LTD      351,876
       Cash
351,876 |
   LTD
        | 351,876

IE      14,075
LTD        925
   Cash     15,000
       IE
14,075 |
   LTD
925 |
   Cash
        | 15,000

IE      14,038
LTD        962
   Cash     15,000
       IE
14,038 |
   LTD
962 |
   Cash
        | 15,000
```

	Balance Sheet						Income Statement		
Transaction	Cash Asset	+ Noncash Assets	= Liabil- ities	+ Contrib. Capital	+ Earned Capital		Rev- enues	− Expen- ses	= Net Income
January 1: Issue 10% bonds	+351,876 Cash		+351,876 = Long-Term Debt						=
June 30: Pay interest and amortize bond premium[1]	−15,000 Cash		−925 = Long-Term Debt		−14,075 Retained Earnings			− +14,075 Interest Expense	= −14,075
December 31: Pay interest and amortize bond premium[2]	−15,000 Cash		−962 = Long-Term Debt		−14,038 Retained Earnings			− +14,038 Interest Expense	= −14,038

[1] $300,000 × 0.10 × 6/12 = $15,000 cash payment; 0.04 × $351,876 = $14,075 interest expense; the difference is the bond premium amortization, which reduces the net bond carrying amount.

[2] 0.04 × ($351,876 − $925) = $14,038 interest expense. The difference between this amount and the $15,000 cash payment is the premium amortization, which reduces the net bond carrying amount.

APPENDIX 8A: Compound Interest

This appendix explains the concepts of present and future value.

Present Value Concepts

Would you rather receive a dollar now or a dollar one year from now? Most people would answer, a dollar now. Intuition tells us that a dollar received now is more valuable than the same amount received sometime in the future. Sound reasons exist for choosing the dollar now, the most obvious of which concerns risk. Since the future is uncertain, any number of events can prevent us from receiving the dollar a year from now. To avoid this risk, we choose the earlier date. Another reason is that the dollar received now could be invested. That is, one year from now, we would have the dollar and the interest earned on that dollar.

Present Value of a Single Amount

Risk and interest factors yield the following generalizations: (1) the right to receive an amount of money now, its **present value,** is worth more than the right to receive the same amount later, its **future value;** (2) the longer we must wait to receive an amount, the less attractive the receipt is; (3) the greater the interest rate the greater the amount we will receive in the future. (Putting 2 and 3 together we see that difference between the present value of an amount and its future value is a function of both interest rate and time, that is, Principal × Interest Rate × Time); and (4) the more risk associated with any situation, the higher the interest rate.

To illustrate, let's compute the amount we would need to receive today (the present value) that would be equivalent to receiving $100 one year from now if money can be invested at 10%. We recognize intuitively that, with a 10% interest rate, the present value (the equivalent amount today) will be less than $100. The $100 received in the future must include 10% interest earned for the year. Thus, the $100 received in one year (the future value) must be 1.10 times the amount received today (the present value). Dividing $100/1.10, we obtain a present value of $90.91 (rounded). This means that we would do as well to accept $90.91 today as to wait one year and receive $100. To confirm the equality of the $90.91 receipt now to a $100 receipt one year later, we calculate the future value of $90.91 at 10% for one year as follows:

$$\$90.91 \times 1.10 \times 1 \text{ year} = \$100 \text{ (rounded)}$$

To generalize, we compute the present value of a future receipt by *discounting* the future receipt back to the present at an appropriate interest rate (also called the *discount rate*). We present this schematically below:

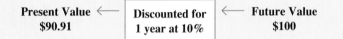

Present Value ⟵	Discounted for	⟵ Future Value
$90.91	1 year at 10%	$100

If either the time period or the interest rate were increased, the resulting present value would decrease. If more than one time period is involved, our future receipts include interest on interest. This is called *compounding*.

Time Value of Money Tables

Appendix A near the end of the book includes time value of money tables. Table 1 is a present value table that we can use to compute the present value of future amounts. A present value table provides present value factors (multipliers) for many combinations of time periods and interest rates that determine the present value of $1.

Present value tables are used as follows. First, determine the number of interest compounding periods involved (three years compounded annually are 3 periods, and three years compounded semiannually are 6 periods). The extreme left-hand column indicates the number of periods. It is important to distinguish between years and compounding periods. The table is for compounding periods (years × number of compounding periods per year).

Next, determine the interest rate per compounding period. Interest rates are usually quoted on a *per year* (annual) basis. The rate per compounding period is the annual rate divided by the number of compounding periods per year. For example, an interest rate of 10% *per year* would be 10% per period if compounded annually, and 5% *per period* if compounded semiannually.

Finally, locate the present value factor, which is at the intersection of the row of the appropriate number of compounding periods and the column of the appropriate interest rate per compounding period. Multiply this factor by the dollars that will be paid or received in the future.

All values in Table 1 are less than 1.0 because the present value of $1 received in the future is always smaller than $1. As the interest rate increases (moving from left to right in the table) or the number of periods increases (moving from top to bottom), the present value factors decline. This illustrates two important facts: (1) present values decline as interest rates increase, and (2) present values decline as the time to receipt lengthens. Consider the following two cases:

Case 1. Compute the present value of $100 to be received one year from today, discounted at 10% compounded semiannually:

> Number of periods (one year, semiannually) = 2
> Rate per period (10%/2) = 5%
> Multiplier = 0.90703
> Present value = $100.00 × 0.90703 = $90.70 (rounded)

Case 2. Compute the present value of $100 to be received two years from today, discounted at 10% compounded semiannually:

> Number of periods (two years, semiannually) = 4
> Rate per period (10%/2) = 5%
> Multiplier = 0.82270
> Present value = $100 × 0.82270 = $82.27 (rounded)

Case 3. Compute the present value of $100 to be received two years from today, discounted at 12% compounded semiannually:

> Number of periods (two years, semiannually) = 4
> Rate per period (12%/2) = 6%
> Multiplier = 0.79209
> Present value = $100 = 0.79209 = $79.21 (rounded)

In Case 2, the present value of $82.27 is less than for Case 1 ($90.70) because the time increased from one to two years—the longer we must wait for money, the lower its value to us today. Then in Case 3, the present value of $79.21 was lower than in Case 2 because, while there were still four compounding periods, the interest rate per year was higher (12% annually instead of 10%)—the higher the interest rate the more interest that could have been earned on the money and therefore the lower the value today.

Present Value of an Annuity

In the examples above, we computed the present value of a single amount (also called a lump sum) made or received in the future. Often, future cash flows involve the same amount being paid or received each period. Examples include semiannual interest payments on bonds, quarterly dividend receipts, or monthly insurance premiums. If the payment or the receipt (the cash flow) is equally spaced over time and each cash flow is the same dollar amount, we have an *annuity*. One way to calculate the present value of the annuity would be to calculate the present value of each future cash flow separately. However, there is a more convenient method.

To illustrate, assume $100 is to be received at the end of each of the next three years as an annuity. When annuity amounts occur at the *end of each period*, the annuity is called an *ordinary annuity*. As shown below, the present value of this ordinary annuity can be computed from Table 1 by computing the present value of each of the three individual receipts and summing them (assume a 5% annual rate).

Future Receipts (ordinary annuity)			PV Multiplier (Table 1)		Present Value
Year 1	Year 2	Year 3			
$100			× 0.95238	=	$ 95.24
	$100		× 0.90703	=	90.70
		$100	× 0.86384	=	86.38
			2.72325		$272.32

Table 2 in Appendix A provides a single multiplier for computing the present value of an ordinary annuity. Referring to Table 2 in the row for three periods and the column for 5%, we see that the multiplier is 2.72325. When applied to the $100 annuity amount, the multiplier gives a present value of $272.33. As shown above, the same present value (with 1 cent rounding error) is derived by summing the three separate multipliers from Table 1. Considerable computations are avoided by using annuity tables.

Bond Valuation

Recall that (1) a bond agreement specifies a pattern of future cash flows—usually a series of interest payments and a single payment of the face amount at maturity, and (2) bonds are priced using the prevailing market rate on the day the bond is sold. This is the case for the original bond issuance and for subsequent open-market sales. The market rate on the date of the sale is the rate we use to determine the bond's market value (its price). That rate is the bond's *yield*. The selling price of a bond is determined as follows:

1. Use Table 1 to compute the present value of the future principal payment at the prevailing market rate.
2. Use Table 2 to compute the present value of the future series of interest payments (the annuity) at the prevailing market rate.
3. Add the present values from steps 1 and 2.

We illustrate in Exhibit 8A.1 the price of $100,000, 8%, 4-year bonds paying interest semiannually and sold when the prevailing market rate was (1) 8%, (2) 10% or (3) 6%. Note that the price of 8% bonds sold to yield 8% is the face (or par) value of the bonds. A bond issue price of $93,537 (discount bond) yields 10%. A bond issue price of $107,019 (premium bond) yields 6%.

EXHIBIT 8A.1	Calculation of Bond Price Using Present Value Tables

Future Cash Flows	Multiplier (Table 1)	Multiplier (Table 2)	Present Values at 4% Semiannually
(1) $100,000 of 8%, 4-year bonds with interest payable semiannually priced to yield 8%.			
Principal payment, $100,000 (a single amount received after 8 semiannual periods)...............	0.73069		$ 73,069
Interest payments, $4,000 at end of each of 8 semiannual periods.........		6.73274	26,931
Present value (issue price) of bonds			$100,000

Future Cash Flows	Multiplier (Table 1)	Multiplier (Table 2)	Present Values at 5% Semiannually
(2) $100,000 of 8%, 4-year bonds with interest payable semiannually priced to yield 10%.			
Principal payment, $100,000 (a single amount received after 8 semiannual periods)...............	0.67684		$ 67,684
Interest payments, $4,000 at end of each of 8 semiannual periods.........		6.46321	25,853
Present value (issue price) of bonds			$ 93,537

Future Cash Flows	Multiplier (Table 1)	Multiplier (Table 2)	Present Values at 3% Semiannually
(3) $100,000 of 8%, 4-year bonds with interest payable semiannually priced to yield 6%.			
Principal repayment, $100,000 (a single amount received after 8 semiannual periods)...............	0.78941		$ 78,941
Interest payments, $4,000 at end of each of 8 semiannual periods.........		7.01969	28,079
Present value (issue price) of bonds			$107,020

Future Value Concepts

Future Value of a Single Amount

The **future value** of a single sum is the amount that a specific investment is worth at a future date if invested at a given rate of compound interest. To illustrate, suppose that we decide to invest $6,000 in a savings account that pays 6% annual interest and we intend to leave the principal and interest in the account for five years. We assume that interest is credited to the account at the end of each year. The balance in the account at the end of five years is determined using Table 3 in Appendix A, which gives the future value of a dollar, as follows:

$$\text{Principal} \times \text{Factor} = \text{Future Value}$$
$$\$6,000 \times 1.33823 = \$8,029$$

The factor 1.33823 is at the intersection of the row for five periods and the column for 6%.

Next, suppose that the interest is credited to the account semiannually rather than annually. In this situation, there are 10 compounding periods, and we use a 3% semiannual rate (one-half the annual rate since there are two compounding periods per year). The future value calculation follows:

$$\text{Principal} \times \text{Factor} = \text{Future Value}$$
$$\$6,000 \times 1.34392 = \$8,064$$

Future Value of an Annuity

If, instead of investing a single amount at the beginning of a series of periods, we invest a specified amount *each period,* then we have an annuity. To illustrate, assume that we decide to invest $2,000 at the end of each year for five years at an 8% annual rate of return. To determine the accumulated amount of principal and interest at the end of five years, we refer to Table 4 in Appendix A, which furnishes the future value of a dollar invested at the end of each period. The factor 5.86660 is in the row for five periods and the column for 8%, and the calculation is as follows:

$$\text{Periodic Payment} \times \text{Factor} = \text{Future Value}$$
$$\$2,000 \times 5.86660 = \$11,733$$

If we decide to invest $1,000 at the end of each six months for five years at an 8% annual rate of return, we would use the factor for 10 periods at 4%, as follows:

$$\text{Periodic Payment} \times \text{Factor} = \text{Future Value}$$
$$\$1,000 \times 12.00611 = \$12,006$$

APPENDIX 8B: Economics of Gains and Losses on Bond Repurchases

Is a reported gain or loss on bond repurchases before maturity of economic substance? The short answer is no. To illustrate, assume that on January 1, a company issues $50 million face value bonds with an 8% annual coupon rate. The interest is to be paid semiannually (4% each semiannual period) for a term of five years (10 semiannual periods), at which time the principal will be repaid. If investors demand a 10% annual return (5% semiannually) on their investment, the bond price is computed as follows:

Present value of semiannual interest ($2,000,000 × 7.72173)	=	$15,443,460
Present value of principal ($50,000,000 × 0.61391)	=	30,695,500
Present value of bond	=	$46,138,960

This bond's amortization table follows:

EXHIBIT 8B.4	Bond Premium Amortization Table				
Period	**[A]** *([E] × market%)* **Interest Expense**	**[B]** *(Face × coupon%)* **Cash Interest Paid**	**[C]** *([A] − [B])* **Discount Amortization**	**[D]** *(Prior bal − [C])* **Discount Balance**	**[E]** *(Face − [D])* **Bond Payable, Net**
0				$3,861,040	$46,138,960
1	$2,306,948	$2,000,000	$306,948	3,554,092	46,445,908
2	2,322,295	2,000,000	322,295	3,231,797	46,768,203
3	2,338,410	2,000,000	338,410	2,893,387	47,106,613
4	2,355,331	2,000,000	355,331	2,538,056	47,461,944
5	2,373,097	2,000,000	373,097	2,164,959	47,835,041
6	2,391,752	2,000,000	391,752	1,773,207	48,226,793
7	2,411,340	2,000,000	411,340	1,361,867	48,638,133
8	2,431,907	2,000,000	431,907	929,960	49,070,040
9	2,453,502	2,000,000	453,502	476,458	49,523,542
10	2,476,458	2,000,000	476,458	0	50,000,000

Next, assume we are at period 6 (three years after issuance) and the market rate of interest for this bond has risen from 10% to 12%. The firm decides to retire (redeem) the outstanding bond issue and finances the retirement by issuing new bonds. That is, it issues bonds with a face amount equal to the market value of the old bonds and uses the proceeds to retire the existing (old) bonds. The new bond issue will have a term of two years (four semiannual periods), the remaining life of the existing bond issue.

At the end of the third year, there are four $2,000,000 semiannual interest payments remaining on the old bonds, plus the repayment of the face amount of the bond due at the end of the fourth semiannual period. The present value of this cash flow stream, discounted at the current 12% annual rate (6% semiannual rate) is:

Present value of semiannual interest ($2,000,000 × 3.46511)	=	$ 6,930,220
Present value of principal ($50,000,000 × 0.79209)	=	39,604,500
Present value of bond	=	$46,534,720

This means the company pays $46,534,720 to redeem a bond that is on its books at a carrying amount of $48,226,793. The difference of $1,692,073 is reported as a gain on repurchase (also called *redemption*). GAAP requires this gain be reported in income from continuing operations unless it meets the tests for treatment as an extraordinary item (the item is both unusual and infrequent).

Although the company reports a gain in its income statement, has it actually realized an economic gain? Consider that this company issues new bonds that carry a coupon rate of 12% (6% semiannually) for $46,534,720. Since we assume that those bonds are sold with a coupon rate equal to the market rate, they will sell at par (no discount or premium). The interest expense per six-month period, therefore, equals the interest paid in cash, or $2,792,083 ($46,534,720 × 6%). Total expense for the four-period life of the bond is $11,168,333 ($2,792,083 × 4). That amount, plus the $46,534,720 face amount of bonds due at maturity, results in total bond payments of $57,703,053. Had this company not redeemed the bonds, it would have paid four additional interest payments of $2,000,000 each plus the face amount of $50,000,000 at maturity, for total bond payments of $58,000,000. On the surface, it appears that the firm is able to save $296,947 by redeeming the bonds and, therefore, reports a gain. (Also, total interest expense on the new bond issue is $3,168,333 [$11,168,333 − $8,000,000] more than it would have recorded under the old issue; so, although it is recording a present gain, it also incurs future higher interest costs which are not recognized under GAAP.)

However, this gain is misleading. Specifically, this gain has two components. First, interest payments increase by $792,083 per year ($2,792,083 − $2,000,000). Second, the face amount of the bond that must be repaid in four years decreases by $3,465,280 ($50,000,000 − $46,534,720). To evaluate whether a real gain has been realized, we must consider the present value of these cash outflows and savings. The present value of the increased interest outflow, a four-period annuity of $792,083 discounted at 6% per period, is **$2,744,655** ($792,083 × 3.46511). The present value of the reduced maturity amount, $3,465,280 in four periods hence, is **$2,744,814** ($3,465,280 × 0.79209)—note: the two amounts differ by $159, which is due to rounding. The conclusion is that the two amounts are the same.

This analysis shows there is no real economic gain from early redemption of debt. The present value of the increased interest payments exactly offsets the present value of the decreased amount due at maturity. Why, then, does GAAP yield a gain? The answer lies in use of historical costing. Bonds are reported at amortized cost, that is, the face amount less any applicable discount or plus any premium. These amounts are a function of the bond issue price and its yield rate at issuance, which are both fixed for the bond duration. Market prices for bonds, however, vary continually with changes in market interest rates. Companies do not adjust bond liabilities for these changes in market value. As a result, when companies redeem bonds, their carrying amount differs from market value and GAAP reports a gain or loss equal to this difference.

GUIDANCE ANSWERS

MANAGERIAL DECISION   **You Are the Vice President of Finance**

You might consider the types of restructuring that would strengthen financial ratios typically used to assess liquidity and solvency by the rating agencies. Such restructuring includes generating cash by reducing inventory, reallocating cash outflows from investing activities (PPE) to debt reduction, and issuing stock for cash and using the proceeds to reduce debt (an equity for debt recapitalization). These actions increase liquidity or reduce financial leverage and, thus, should improve debt rating. An improved debt rating will attract more debtholders because your current debt rating is below investment grade and is not a suitable investment for many professionally managed portfolios. An improved debt rating will also lower the interest rate on your debt. Offsetting these benefits are costs such as the following: (1) potential loss of sales from inventory stock-outs; (2) potential future cash flow reductions and loss of market power from reduced PPE investments; and (3) costs of equity issuances (equity costs more than debt because investors demand a higher return to compensate for added risk and the lack of tax deductibility of dividends vis-à-vis interest payments), which can yield a net increase in the total cost of capital. All cost and benefits must be assessed before you pursue any restructuring.

Superscript ^A(^B) denotes assignments based on Appendix 8A (8B).

DISCUSSION QUESTIONS

Q8-1. What does the term *current liabilities* mean? What assets are usually used to settle current liabilities?

Q8-2. What is an accrual? How do accruals impact the balance sheet and the income statement?

Q8-3. What is the difference between a bond's coupon rate and its market interest rate (yield)?

Q8-4. Why do companies report a gain or loss when they repurchase their bonds? Is this a real economic gain or loss.

Q8-5. How do credit (debt) ratings affect the cost of borrowing for a company?

Q8-6. How would you interpret a company's reported gain or loss on the repurchase of its bonds?

MINI EXERCISES

M 8-7.   Interpreting a Contingency Footnote   (LO1)

Altria Group, Inc.
(MO)

Altria Group, Inc., reports the following footnote to its 2005 10-K related to pending smoking-related litigation.

> **Contingencies:** Legal proceedings covering a wide range of matters are pending or threatened in various United States and foreign jurisdictions against ALG, its subsidiaries and affiliates, including PM USA and PMI, as well as their respective indemnitees. Various types of claims are raised in these proceedings, including product liability, consumer protection, antitrust, tax, contraband shipments, patent infringement, employment matters, claims for contribution and claims of competitors and distributors . . . It is not possible to predict the outcome of the litigation pending against ALG and its subsidiaries . . .
>
> *Contingencies:* (i) management has not concluded that it is probable that a loss has been incurred in any of the pending tobacco-related litigation; [and] (ii) management is unable to make a meaningful estimate of the amount or range of loss that could result from an unfavorable outcome of pending tobacco-related litigation . . .
>
> The present legislative and litigation environment is substantially uncertain, and it is possible that the business and volume of ALG's subsidiaries, as well as Altria Group, Inc.'s consolidated results of operations, cash flows or financial position could be materially affected by an unfavorable outcome or settlement of certain pending litigation or by the enactment of federal or state tobacco legislation.

a. Review the content of this footnote. In what manner do you believe Altria is reporting this potential liability on its balance sheet?

b. Altria discloses over 10 pages of discussion relating to pending litigation in its footnotes (an abnormally large disclosure). Irrespective of your answer to part *a*, what do you believe is Altria's motivation for this extended disclosure?

M8-8.   Analyzing and Computing Financial Statement Effects of Interest   (LO1)

DeFond Company signed a 90-day, 8% note payable for $7,200 on December 16. Use the financial statement effects template to illustrate the year-end December 31 accounting adjustment DeFond must make.

M8-9.   Analyzing and Determining Liability Amounts   (LO1)

For each of the following situations, indicate the liability amount, if any, that is reported on the balance sheet of Basu, Inc., at December 31, 2007.

a. Basu owes $110,000 at year-end 2007 for its inventory purchases.

b. Basu agreed to purchase a $28,000 drill press in January 2008.

c. During November and December of 2007, Basu sold products to a customer and warranted them against product failure for 90 days. Estimated costs of honoring this 90-day warranty during 2008 are $2,200.

d. Basu provides a profit-sharing bonus for its executives equal to 5% of reported pretax annual income. The estimated pretax income for 2007 is $600,000. Bonuses are not paid until January of the following year.

M8-10.   Interpreting Relations among Bond Price, Coupon, Yield, and Credit Rating   (LO2, 3)

Boston Scientific
(BSX)

The following notice appeared in *The Wall Street Journal* regarding a bond issuance by **Boston Scientific**.

> **Boston Scientific Corp.**—$500 million of notes was priced with the following terms in two parts via joint lead managers Merrill Lynch & Co., UBS Securities and Wachovia:
>
> (1) Amount: $250 million; Maturity: Jan. 12, 2011; Coupon: 4.25%; Price: 99.476; Yield: 4.349%; Ratings: Baa1 (Moody's), A2 (S&P).
>
> (2) Amount: $250 million; Maturity: Jan. 12, 2017; Coupon: 5.125%; Price: 99.926; Yield: 5.134%; Ratings: Baa1 (Moody's), A2 (S&P).

    a. Discuss the relation among the coupon rate, issuance price, and yield for the 2011 issuance.

    b. Compare the yields on the two parts of the bond issuances. Why are the yields different when the credit ratings are the same?

M8-11. Determining Gain or Loss on Bond Redemption (LO2)

On April 30, one year before maturity, Easton Company retired $200,000 of its 9% bonds payable at the current market price of 101 (101% of the bond face amount, or $200,000 × 1.01 = $202,000). The bond book value on April 30 is $197,600, reflecting an unamortized discount of $2,400. Bond interest is currently fully paid and recorded up to the date of retirement. What is the gain or loss on retirement of these bonds? Is this gain or loss a real economic gain or loss? Explain.

M8-12. Interpreting Bond Footnote Disclosures (LO2)

Bristol-Myers Squibb (BMY) reports the following in the long-term debt footnote to its 2005 10-K.

> The aggregate maturities of long-term debt for each of the next five years are as follows: 2006, $522.0 million; 2007, $351.7 million; 2008, $1.4 billion; 2009, $306.5 million; 2010, $5.4 million.

Bristol-Myers Squibb (BMY)

    a. What does the $1.4 billion in 2008 indicate about BMY's future payment obligations?

    b. What implications does this payment schedule have for our evaluation of BMY's liquidity and solvency?

M8-13. Classifying Liability-Related Accounts into Balance Sheet or Income Statement (LO2)

Indicate the proper financial statement classification (balance sheet or income statement) for each of the following liability-related accounts.

    a. Gain on Bond Retirement   *e.* Bond Interest Expense

    b. Discount on Bonds Payable   *f.* Bond Interest Payable (due next period)

    c. Mortgage Notes Payable   *g.* Premium on Bonds Payable

    d. Bonds Payable   *h.* Loss on Bond Retirement

M8-14. Interpreting Bond Footnote Disclosures (LO2)

Comcast Corporation reports the following footnote to the long-term debt section of its 2005 10-K.

Comcast Corporation (CMCSA)

> **Debt Covenants** Some of our subsidiaries' loan agreements require that we maintain financial ratios based on debt, interest and operating income before depreciation and amortization, as defined in the agreements. We were in compliance with all financial covenants for all periods presented.

    a. The financial ratios to which Comcast refers are similar to those discussed in the section on credit ratings and the cost of debt. What effects might these ratios have on the degree of freedom that management has in running Comcast?

    b. Violation of debt covenants is a serious event that typically triggers an 'immediately due and payable' provision in the debt contract. What pressures might management face if the company's ratios are near covenant limits?

M8-15. Analyzing Financial Statement Effects of Bond Redemption (LO2)

Holthausen Corporation issued $400,000 of 11%, 20-year bonds at 108 on January 1, 2003. Interest is payable semiannually on June 30 and December 31. Through January 1, 2008, Holthausen amortized $5,000 of the bond premium. On January 1, 2008, Holthausen retires the bonds at 103. Use the financial statement effects template to illustrate the bond retirement at January 1, 2008.

M8-16. Analyzing Financial Statement Effects of Bond Redemption (LO2)

Dechow, Inc., issued $250,000 of 8%, 15-year bonds at 96 on July 1, 2003. Interest is payable semiannually on December 31 and June 30. Through June 30, 2008, Dechow amortized $3,000 of the bond discount. On July 1, 2008, Dechow retired the bonds at 101. Use the financial statement effects template to illustrate the bond retirement at June 30, 2008.

M8-17. Analyzing and Computing Accrued Interest on Notes (LO1)

Compute any interest accrued for each of the following notes payable owed by Penman, Inc., as of December 31, 2007 (use a 365-day year).

Lender	Issuance Date	Principal	Coupon Rate (%)	Term
Nissim.........	11/21/07	$18,000	10%	120 days
Klein	12/13/07	14,000	9	90 days
Bildersee.......	12/19/07	16,000	12	60 days

M8-18. Interpreting Credit Ratings (LO3)

General Mills reports the following information in the Management Discussion & Analysis section of its 2005 10-K report.

> We believe that two important measures of financial strength are the ratios of fixed charge coverage and cash flows from operations to adjusted debt plus certain minority interests. Our fixed charge coverage in fiscal 2005 was 4.7 times compared to 3.8 times in fiscal 2004, and cash flows from operations to adjusted debt plus certain minority interests increased to 26 percent. We expect to pay down between $100 and $200 million of adjusted debt plus certain minority interests in fiscal 2006. Our goal is to return to a mid single-A rating for our long-term debt, and to the top tier short-term rating, that we held prior to our announcement of the Pillsbury acquisition. Currently, Standard and Poor's Corporation has ratings of BBB+ on our publicly held long-term debt and A-2 on our commercial paper. Moody's Investors Services, Inc. has ratings of Baa2 for our long-term debt and P-2 for our commercial paper. Fitch Ratings, Inc. rates our long-term debt BBB+ and our commercial paper F-2.

a. Why will debt reduction result in a higher credit rating for General Mills' bonds?

b. What effect will a higher credit rating have on General Mills' borrowing costs? Explain.

M8-19. Computing Bond Issue Price (LO2)

Bushman, Inc., issues $500,000 of 9% bonds that pay interest semiannually and mature in 10 years. Compute the bond issue price assuming that the prevailing market rate of interest is:

a. 8% per year compounded semiannually.

b. 10% per year compounded semiannually.

M8-20. Computing Issue Price for Zero Coupon Bonds (LO2)

Bushman, Inc., issues $500,000 of zero coupon bonds that mature in 10 years. Compute the bond issue price assuming that the bonds' market rate is:

a. 8% per year compounded semiannually.

b. 10% per year compounded semiannually.

M8-21. Determining the Financial Statement Effects of Accounts Payable Transactions (LO1)

Petroni Company had the following transactions relating to its accounts payable.

a. Purchases $300 of inventory on credit.

b. Sells inventory for $420 on credit.

c. Records $300 cost of sales for transaction b.

d. Receives $420 cash toward accounts receivable.

e. Pays $300 cash to settle accounts payable.

Use the financial statement effects template to identify the effects (both amounts and accounts) for these transactions.

M8-22. Computing Bond Issue Price and Preparing an Amortization Table in Excel (LO2)

On January 1, 2007, Bushman, Inc., issues $500,000 of 9% bonds that pay interest semiannually and mature in 10 years (December 31, 2016).

a. Using the Excel PRICE function, compute the issue price assuming that the bonds' market rate is 8% per year compounded semiannually. (Use 100 for the redemption value to get a price as a percentage of the face amount, and use 1 for the basis.)

b. Prepare an amortization table in Excel to demonstrate the amortization of the book (carrying) value to the $500,000 maturity value at the end of the 20th semiannual period.

EXERCISES

E8-23. Analyzing and Computing Accrued Warranty Liability and Expense (LO1)

Waymire Company sells a motor that carries a 60-day unconditional warranty against product failure. From prior years' experience, Waymire estimates that 2% of units sold each period will require repair at an average cost of $100 per unit. During the current period, Waymire sold 69,000 units and repaired 1,000 units.

a. How much warranty expense must Waymire report in its current period income statement?

b. What amount of warranty liability related to current period sales will Waymire report on its current period-end balance sheet? (*Hint:* Remember that some units were repaired in the current period.)

c. What analysis issues must we consider with respect to the amount of reported warranty liability?

E8-24. Analyzing Contingencies and Assessing Liabilities   (LO1)

The following independent situations represent various types of liabilities. Analyze each situation and indicate which of the following is the proper accounting treatment for the company: (a) record a liability on the balance sheet, (b) disclose the liability in a financial statement footnote, or (c) neither record nor disclose any liability.

1. A stockholder has filed a lawsuit against **Clinch Corporation**. Clinch's attorneys have reviewed the facts of the case. Their review revealed that similar lawsuits have never resulted in a cash award and it is highly unlikely that this lawsuit will either.
2. **Foster Company** signed a 60-day, 10% note when it purchased items from another company.
3. The Environmental Protection Agency notifies **Shevlin Company** that a state where it has a plant is filing a lawsuit for groundwater pollution against Shevlin and another company that has a plant adjacent to Shevlin's plant. Test results have not identified the exact source of the pollution. Shevlin's manufacturing process often produces by-products that can pollute ground water.
4. **Sloan Company** manufactured and sold products to a retailer that sold the products to consumers. The Sloan Company will replace the product if it is found to be defective within 90 days of the sale to the consumer. Historically, 1.2% of the products are returned for replacement.

E8-25. Recording and Analyzing Warranty Accrual and Payment   (LO1)

Refer to the discussion of and excerpt from the Ford Motor Company warranty reserve on page 8-9 to answer the following questions.

Ford Motor Company (F)

a. Using the financial statement effects template, record the accrual of warranty liability relating only to the "Changes in accrual related to warranties issued during the year" and to the "Payments made during the year."
b. Does the level of Ford's warranty accrual appear to be reasonable?
c. General Motors reports the following table relating to its warranty accrual.

December 31 ($ millions)	2005	2004
Beginning balance	$9,315	$8,832
Payments	(4,696)	(4,669)
Increase in liability (warranties issued during period)	5,159	5,065
Adjustments to liability (pre-existing warranties)	(381)	(85)
Effect of foreign currency translation	(269)	172
Ending balance	$9,128	$9,315

For both companies, compare the size of the warranty liability with the claims made. What insight does this comparison give us regarding the adequacy of the warranty accruals for both companies.

E8-26. Analyzing and Computing Accrued Wages Liability and Expense   (LO1)

Demski Company pays its employees on the 1st and 15th of each month. It is March 31 and Demski is preparing financial statements for this quarter. Its employees have earned $25,000 since the 15th of March and have not yet been paid. How will Demski's balance sheet and income statement reflect the accrual of wages on March 31? What balance sheet and income statement accounts would be incorrectly reported if Demski failed to make this accrual (for each account indicate whether it would be overstated or understated)?

E8-27. Analyzing and Reporting Financial Statement Effects of Bond Transactions   (LO2)

On January 1, Hutton Corp. issued $300,000 of 15-year, 10% bonds payable for $351,876, yielding an effective interest rate of 8%. Interest is payable semiannually on June 30 and December 31. (a) Show computations to confirm the issue price of $351,876. (b) Indicate the financial statement effects using the template for (1) bond issuance, (2) semiannual interest payment and premium amortization on June 30 of the first year, and (3) semiannual interest payment and premium amortization on December 31 of the first year.

E8-28. Analyzing and Reporting Financial Statement Effects of Mortgages   (LO2)

On January 1, Piotroski, Inc., borrowed $700,000 on a 12%, 15-year mortgage note payable. The note is to be repaid in equal semiannual installments of $50,854 (payable on June 30 and December 31). Each mortgage payment includes principal and interest. Interest is computed using the effective interest method. Indicate the financial statement effects using the template for (a) issuance of the mortgage note payable, (b) payment of the first installment on June 30, and (c) payment of the second installment on December 31.

E8-29.   **Assessing the Effects of Bond Credit Rating Changes**   (LO3)

Ford (F)   Ford reports the following footnote to its 2005 10-K report.

> *Credit Ratings.* Our short- and long-term debt is rated by four credit rating agencies designated as nationally recognized statistical rating organizations ("NRSROs") by the Securities and Exchange Commission:
>
> - Dominion Bond Rating Service Limited ("DBRS");
> - Fitch. Inc. ("Fitch");
> - Moody's Investors Service, Inc. ("Moody's"); and
> - Standard & Poor's Rating Services, a division of McGraw-Hill Companies, Inc. ("S&P").
>
> In several markets, locally recognized rating agencies also rate us. A credit rating reflects an assessment by the rating agency of the credit risk associated with particular securities we issue, based on information provided by us and other sources. Credit ratings are not recommendations to buy, sell or hold securities and are subject to revision or withdrawal at any time by the assigning rating agency. Each rating agency may have different criteria for evaluating company risk, and therefore ratings should be evaluated independently for each rating agency. Lower credit ratings generally result in higher borrowing costs and reduced access to capital markets. The NRSROs have indicated that our lower ratings are primarily a reflection of the rating agencies' concerns regarding our automotive cash flow and profitability, declining market share, excess industry capacity, industry pricing pressure and rising health care costs.
>
> *Ford.* In December 2005, Fitch lowered Ford's long-term raring to BB+ from BBB−, lowered our short-term rating to B from F2 and maintained our outlook at Negative. In January 2006, S&P lowered our long-term rating to BB− from BB+, lowered our short-term rating to B-2 from B-1 and maintained our outlook at Negative. In January 2006, Moody's lowered our long-term rating to Ba3 from Ba1 and maintained our outlook at Negative. In January 2006, DBRS lowered our long-term rating to BB (low) from BB (high), affirmed our short-term rating at R-3 (high) and maintained our trend at Negative.
>
> *Ford Credit.* In December 2005, Fitch lowered Ford Credit's long-term rating to BB+ from BBB−, lowered Ford Credit's short-term rating to B from F2 and maintained Ford Credit's outlook at Negative. In January 2006, S&P lowered Ford Credit's long-term rating to BB− from BB+, lowered Ford Credit's short-term debt rating to B-2 from B-1 and maintained Ford Credit's outlook at Negative. In January 2006, Moody's lowered Ford Credit's long-term rating to Ba2 from Baa3, lowered Ford Credit's short-term rating to Not Prime ("NP") from P3 and maintained Ford Credit's outlook at Negative. In January 2006, DBRS lowered Ford Credit's long-term rating to BB from BBB (low), lowered Ford Credit's short-term rating to R-3 (high) from R-2 (low) and maintained Ford Credit's trend at Negative.

a.   What financial ratios do credit rating companies such as the four NRSROs listed above, use to evaluate the relative riskiness of borrowers?

b.   Why might a reduction in credit ratings result in higher interest costs and restrict Ford's access to credit markets?

c.   What type of actions can Ford take to improve its credit ratings?

E8-30.   **Analyzing and Reporting Financial Statement Effects of Bond Transactions**   (LO2)

Lundholm, Inc., reports financial statements each December 31 and issues $500,000, 9%, 15-year bonds dated May 1, 2007, with interest payments on October 31 and April 30. Assuming the bonds are sold at par on May 1, 2007, complete the financial statement effects template to reflect the following events: (a) bond issuance, (b) the first semiannual interest payment, and (c) retirement of $300,000 of the bonds at 101 on November 1, 2007.

E8-31.   **Analyzing and Reporting Financial Statement Effects of Bond Transactions**   (LO2)

On January 1, 2007, McKeown, Inc., issued $250,000 of 8%, 9-year bonds for $220,776, which implies a market (yield) rate of 10%. Semiannual interest is payable on June 30 and December 31 of each year. (a) Show computations to confirm the bond issue price. (b) Indicate the financial statement effects using the template for (1) bond issuance, (2) semiannual interest payment and discount amortization on June 30, 2007, and (3) semiannual interest payment and discount amortization on December 31, 2007.

E8-32.   **Analyzing and Reporting Financial Statement Effects of Bond Transactions**   (LO2)

On January 1, 2007, Shields, Inc., issued $800,000 of 9%, 20-year bonds for $879,172, yielding a market (yield) rate of 8%. Semiannual interest is payable on June 30 and December 31 of each year. (a) Show computations to confirm the bond issue price. (b) Indicate the financial statement effects using the template for (1) bond issuance, (2) semiannual interest payment and premium amortization on June 30, 2007, and (3) semiannual interest payment and premium amortization on December 31, 2007.

E8-33. **Determining Bond Prices, Interest Rates, and Financial Statement Effects** (LO2)

Deere & Company's 2005 10-K reports the following footnote relating to long-term debt. Deere's   Deere & Co (DE)
borrowings include $200 million, 6.55% debentures (unsecured bonds), due in 2028 (highlighted below).

Long-term borrowings at October 31 consisted of the following in millions of dollars:

Notes and debentures	2005	2004
Medium-term notes:		
Average interest rate of 9.2%—2004		$ 20
5-7/8% U.S. dollar notes due 2006: ($250 principal)		
Swapped $170 to Euro at average variable		
interest rates of 3.1%—2004		250
7.85% debentures due 2010	$ 500	500
6.95% notes due 2014: ($700 principal)		
Swapped to variable interest rates		
of 5.2%—2005, 3.1%—2004	744	786
8.95% debentures due 2019	200	200
8-1/2% debentures due 2022	200	200
6.55% debentures due 2028	200	200
8.10% debentures due 2030	250	250
7.125% notes due 2031.	300	300
Other notes.	29	22
Total	$2,423	$2,728

A recent price quote (from www.BondPage.com) on Deere's 6.55% debentures follows.

Credit ratings	Issuer name I Issue	Coupon rate I Maturity	Price quote I Yield
A3/A-	Deere & Co	6.550	108.104
Industrial	Non Callable, NYBE, DE	10-01-2028	5.890

This price quote indicates that Deere's bonds have a market price of 108.104 (108.104% of face value), resulting in a yield to maturity of 5.89%.

a. Assuming that these bonds were originally issued at par value, what does the market price reveal about interest rate changes since Deere issued its bonds? (Assume that Deere's credit rating has remained the same.)

b. Does the change in interest rates since the issuance of these bonds affect the amount of interest expense that Deere reports in its income statement? Explain.

c. How much cash would Deere have to pay to repurchase the 6.55% debentures at the quoted market price of 108.104. (Assume no interest is owed when Deere repurchases the debentures.) How would the repurchase affect Deere's current income?

d. Assuming that the bonds remain outstanding until their maturity, at what market price will the bonds sell on their due date in 2028?

E8-34.[A] **Computing Present Values of Single Amounts and Annuities** (LO2)

Refer to Tables 1 and 2 in Appendix A near the end of the book to compute the present value for each of the following amounts:

a. $90,000 received 10 years hence if the annual interest rate is:
   1. 8% compounded annually.
   2. 8% compounded semiannually.

b. $1,000 received at the end of each year for the next eight years discounted at 10% compounded annually.

c. $600 received at the end of each six months for the next 15 years if the interest rate is 8% per year compounded semiannually.

d. $500,000 received 10 years hence discounted at 10% per year compounded annually.

E8-35. **Analyzing and Reporting Financial Statement Effects of Bond Transactions** (LO2)

On January 1, 2007, Trueman Corporation issued $600,000 of 20-year, 11% bonds for $554,860, yielding a market (yield) rate of 12%. Interest is payable semiannually on June 30 and December 31. (a) Confirm the bond issue price. (b) Indicate the financial statement effects using the template for (1) bond issuance, (2) semiannual interest payment and discount amortization on June 30, 2007, and (3) semiannual interest payment and discount amortization on December 31, 2007.

E8-36. **Analyzing and Reporting Financial Statement Effects of Bond Transactions** (LO2)

On January 1, 2007, Verrecchia Company issued $400,000 of 5-year, 13% bonds for $446,329, yielding a market (yield) rate of 10%. Interest is payable semiannually on June 30 and December 31. (a) Confirm the bond issue price. (b) Indicate the financial statement effects using the template for (1) bond issuance, (2) semiannual interest payment and premium amortization on June 30, 2007, and (3) semiannual interest payment and premium amortization on December 31, 2007.

PROBLEMS

P8-37. **Interpreting Term Structures of Coupon Rates and Yield Rates** (LO2)

The Pepsi Bottling Group (PBG)

The Pepsi Bottling Group reports $4,561 million of long-term debt outstanding as of December 2005 in the following schedule to its 10-K report.

Short-term Borrowings and Long-term Debt ($ millions)	2005	2004
Short-term borrowings		
Current maturities of long-term debt	$ 594	$ 53
SFAS No. 133 adjustment	(4)	—
Unamortized discount, net	(1)	—
Current maturities of long-term debt, net	589	53
Other short-term borrowings	426	155
	$1,015	$ 208

($ millions)	2005	2004
Long-term debt		
2.45% senior notes due 2006	$ 500	$ 500
5.63% senior notes due 2009	1,300	1,300
4.63% senior notes due 2012	1,000	1,000
5.00% senior notes due 2013	400	400
4.13% senior notes due 2015	250	250
7.00% senior notes due 2029	1,000	1,000
Other	111	109
	4,561	4,559
Unamortized discount, net and other	(33)	(17)
Current maturities of long-term debt, net	(589)	(53)
	$3,939	$4,489

Certain of our credit facilities and senior notes have financial covenants consisting of the following:

- Our debt to capitalization ratio should not be greater than .75 on the last day of a fiscal quarter when PepsiCo Inc.'s ratings are A by S&P and A3 by Moody's or higher. Debt is defined as total long-term and short-term debt plus accrued interest plus total standby letters of credit and other guarantees less cash and cash equivalents not in excess of $500 million. Capitalization is defined as debt plus shareholders' equity plus minority interest excluding the impact of the cumulative translation adjustment.

- Our debt to EBITDA ratio should not be greater than five on the last day of a fiscal quarter when PepsiCo Inc.'s ratings are less than A− by S&P or A3 by Moody's. EBITDA is defined as the last four quarters of earnings before depreciation, amortization, net interest expense, income taxes, minority interest, net other non-operating expenses and extraordinary items.
- New secured debt should not be greater than 10 percent of Bottling Group, LLC's net tangible assets. Net tangible assets are defined as total assets less current liabilities and net intangible assets.

We are in compliance with all debt covenants.

The price of the $1,000 million 7% senior notes due 2029 as of August 2006 is as follows (from Yahoo! Finance Bond Center; Finance.yahoo.com/Bonds):

Issue	Price	Coupon (%)	Maturity	YTM (%)	Fitch Ratings
Pepsi Bottling Group Inc.....	114.05	7.000	1-Mar-2029	5.869	A

Required

a.   PBG reports current maturities of long-term debt of $589 million as part of short-term debt. Why is this amount reported that way? PBG reports $1,300 million of long-term debt maturing in 2009. What does this mean? Is this amount important to our analysis of Pepsi Bottling Group? Explain.

b.   The $1,000 million 7% senior notes maturing in 2029 are priced at 114.05 (114.05% of face value, or $1,140.5 million) as of August 2006, resulting in a yield to maturity of 5.869%. Assuming that the credit rating of PBG has not changed, what does the pricing of this 7% coupon bond imply about interest rate changes since PBG issued the bond?

c.   PBG identifies a number of financial covenants relating to its long-term debt. Describe each of these covenants and how they affect our financial analysis.

d.   PBG reports an unamortized discount of $14 million in another disclosure to its financial statements. How does a discount arise and what effect will its amortization have on reported interest expense?

P8-38.   Interpreting Debt Footnotes on Interest Rates and Interest Expense   (LO2)

CVS Corporation discloses the following footnote in its 10-K relating to its debt.

CVS Corporation (CVS)

BORROWING AND CREDIT AGREEMENTS

Following is a summary of the Company's borrowings as of the respective balance sheet dates.

In millions	Dec. 31, 2005	Jan. 1, 2005
Commercial paper	$ 253.4	$ 885.6
5.625% senior notes due 2006	300.0	300.0
3.875% senior notes due 2007	300.0	300.0
4.0% senior notes due 2009	650.0	650.0
4.875% senior notes due 2014	550.0	550.0
8.52% ESOP notes due 2008	114.0	140.9
Mortgage notes payable	21.0	14.8
Capital lease obligations	0.7	0.8
	2,189.1	2,842.1
Less:		
Short-term debt	(253.4)	(885.6)
Current portion of long-term debt	(341.6)	(30.6)
	$1,594.1	$1,925.9

CVS also discloses the following information.

Interest expense, net—Interest expense was $117.0 million, $64.4 million and $53.9 million, and interest income was $6.5 million, $5.7 million and $5.8 million, in 2005, 2004 and 2003, respectively. Interest paid totaled $135.9 million in 2005, $70.4 million in 2004 and $64.9 million in 2003.

Required

a. What is the average coupon rate (interest paid) and the average effective rate (interest expense) on CVS' long-term debt? (*Hint:* Use the disclosure for interest expense, net.)

b. Does your computation of the coupon rate in part *a* seem reasonable given the footnote disclosure relating to specific bond issues? Explain.

c. Explain how the amount of interest paid can differ from the amount of interest expense recorded in the income statement.

P8-39. **Analyzing Bond Rates, Yields, Prices, and Credit Ratings** (LO2, 3)

Southwest Airlines
(LUV)

Reproduced below is the long-term debt footnote from the 10-K report of Southwest Airlines.

Long-Term Debt (In millions)	2005	2004
8% Notes due 2005	$ —	$ 100
Zero Coupon Notes due 2006	58	58
Pass Through Certificates	523	544
7⅞% Notes due 2007	100	100
French Credit Agreements due 2012	41	44
6½% Notes due 2012	370	377
5¼% Notes due 2014	340	348
5⅛% Notes due 2017	300	—
French Credit Agreements due 2017	106	111
7⅜% Debentures due 2027	100	100
Capital leases (Note 8)	74	80
	2,012	1,862
Less current maturities	601	146
Less debt discount and issue costs	17	16
	$1,394	$1,700

During February 2005, the Company issued $300 million senior unsecured Notes due 2017. The Notes bear interest at 5.125 percent, payable semi-annually in arrears, with the first payment made on September 1, 2005. Southwest used the net proceeds from the issuance of the notes, approximately $296 million, for general corporate purposes.

In fourth quarter 2004, the Company entered into four identical 13-year floating-rate financing arrangements, whereby it borrowed a total of $112 million from French banking partnerships. Although the interest on the borrowings is at floating rates, the Company estimates that, considering the full effect of the "net present value benefits" included in the transactions, the effective economic yield over the 13-year term of the loans will be approximately LIBOR minus 45 basis points. Principal and interest are payable semi-annually on June 30 and December 31 for each of the loans, and the Company may terminate the arrangements in any year on either of those dates, with certain conditions. The Company pledged four aircraft as collateral for the transactions.

In September 2004, the Company issued $350 million senior unsecured Notes due 2014. The notes bear interest at 5.25 percent, payable semi-annually in arrears, on April 1 and October 1. Concurrently, the Company entered into an interest-rate swap agreement to convert this fixed-rate debt to a floating rate. See Note 10 for more information on the interest-rate swap agreement. Southwest used the net proceeds from the issuance of the notes, approximately $346 million, for general corporate purposes.

In February 2004 and April 2004, the Company issued two separate $29 million two-year notes, each secured by one new 737-700 aircraft. Both of the notes are non-interest bearing and accrete to face value at maturity at annual rates of 2.9 percent and 3.4 percent, respectively. The proceeds of these borrowings were used to fund the individual aircraft purchases.

On March 1, 2002, the Company issued $385 million senior unsecured Notes due March 1, 2012. The notes bear interest at 6.5 percent, payable semi-annually on March 1 and September 1. Southwest used the net proceeds from the issuance of the notes, approximately $380 million, for general corporate purposes. During 2003, the Company entered into an interest rate swap agreement relating to these notes. See Note 10 for further information.

As of December 31, 2005, aggregate annual principal maturities for the five-year period ending December 31, 2010, were $612 million in 2006, $127 million in 2007, $28 million in 2008, $29 million in 2009, $30 million in 2010, and $1.186 billion thereafter.

Reproduced below is a summary of the market values of the Southwest Airlines' bonds maturing from 2012 to 2017 from the Yahoo! Finance bond center (Finance.yahoo.com/bonds).

Issue	Price	Coupon (%)	Maturity	YTM (%)	Current Yield (%)	Fitch Ratings
SW Air......	105.28	6.500	1-Mar-2012	5.389	6.174	A
SW Air......	97.00	5.250	1-Oct-2014	5.715	5.413	A
SW Air......	95.64	5.125	1-Mar-2017	5.678	5.358	A

Required

a. What is the amount of long-term debt reported on Southwest's 2005 balance sheet? What are the scheduled maturities for this indebtedness? Why is information relating to a company's scheduled maturities of debt useful in an analysis of its financial condition?

b. Southwest reported $122 million in interest expense in its 2005 income statement. In the note to its statement of cash flows, Southwest indicates that the cash portion of this expense is $71 million. What could account for the difference between interest expense and interest paid? Explain.

c. Southwest's long-term debt is rated "A" by Fitch and similarly by other credit rating agencies. What factors would be important to consider in attempting to quantify the relative riskiness of Southwest compared with other borrowers? Explain.

d. Southwest's $370 million 6.5% notes traded at 105.28, or 105.28% of par, as of August 2006. What is the dollar value of these notes? How is the difference between this market value and the $370 million face value reflected in Southwest's financial statements? What effect would the repurchase of this entire note issue have on Southwest's financial statements? What does the 105.28 price tell you about the general trend in interest rates since Southwest sold this bond issue? Explain.

e. Southwest's 5.25% bonds are trading at 97.00 as of August 2006. What is the market value of these bonds? Why does trading at a discount result in a yield to maturity of 5.715%, which is higher than the coupon rate of 5.25%?

f. Examine the yields to maturity of the three bonds in the table above. What relation do we observe between these yields and the maturities of the bonds? Also, explain why this relation applies in general.

P8-40   **Analyzing Notes, Bonds, and Credit Ratings**   (LO2, LO3)

Comcast Corporation reports long-term senior notes totaling over $21 billion in its 2005 10-K. A selected listing of the market values for these notes as of August 2006 follows: Comcast Corp. (CMCSA)

Borrower	Price	Coupon (%)	Maturity	YTM (%)	Fitch Ratings
COMCAST CORP.......	99.67	6.45	3/15/37	6.474	BBB
COMCAST CORP.......	105.55	6.50	1/15/17	5.784	BBB
COMCAST CORP.......	92.77	4.95	6/15/16	5.928	BBB
COMCAST CORP.......	99.67	5.90	3/15/16	5.945	BBB
COMCAST CORP.......	99.31	5.85	11/15/15	5.947	BBB
COMCAST CORP.......	104.04	6.50	1/15/15	5.885	BBB
COMCAST CORP.......	97.07	5.30	1/15/14	5.790	BBB
COMCAST CABLE COMMUNICATIONS...	107.41	7.125	6/15/13	5.799	BBB
COMCAST CORP.......	100.99	5.50	3/15/11	5.255	BBB
COMCAST CABLE COMMUNICATIONS...	105.97	6.75	1/30/11	5.237	BBB
COMCAST CORP.......	101.16	5.45	11/15/10	5.142	BBB
COMCAST CORP.......	102.79	5.85	1/15/10	4.956	BBB
COMCAST CABLE COMMUNICATIONS...	105.32	6.875	6/15/09	4.853	BBB
COMCAST CABLE COMMUNICATIONS...	103.36	6.20	11/15/08	4.621	BBB
COMCAST CABLE COMMUNICATIONS...	104.04	8.375	5/1/07	2.763	BBB

These notes have been issued by Comcast Corporation (the parent company) and its wholly-owned subsidiary, Comcast Cable Communications.

Following are selected ratios from Exhibit 8.6 computed for Comcast Corp. utilizing its 2005 data.

EBIT interest coverage	$3,690/$1,796 = 2.05
EBITDA interest coverage	($3,690 + $3,630 + $1,173)/$1,796 = 4.73
FFO/Total debt	($947 + $3,630 + $1,173 + $183)/($21,682 + $1,689) = 0.25
Free operating cash flow/Total debt . . .	($4,922 − $3,621 + $97 + $65 + $860)/($21,682 + $1,689) = 0.10
Return on capital	$1,880/[($1,689 + $3,499 + $21,682 + $20,093 + $27,370 + $26,815 + $40,219 + $41,422)/2] = .021
Operating income/Sales	$3,690/$22,255 = 16.6%
Long-term debt/Capital	$2,1682/($21,682 + $657 + $40,219) = 0.35
Total debt/Capital	($1,689 + $21,682)/($1,689 + $21,682 + $657 + $40,219) = 0.36

Required

a. Graph the yield to maturity (YTM) on the Y-axis and the maturity on the X-axis. What pattern do we observe? Explain this pattern.

b. Comcast's credit ratings for all of these bonds are BBB, which is a low medium grade. Examine Comcast's 2005 10-K (download from EDGAR or the Comcast Website) as well as the ratios provided above. What factors do you believe contribute to Comcast's credit rating being less than stellar?

c. Some of Comcast's bonds are trading at a premium and others at a discount. Why is this the case?

CASES

C8-41.   Management Application: Coupon Rate versus Effective Rate   L02

Assume that you are the CFO of a company that intends to issue bonds to finance a new manufacturing facility. A subordinate suggests lowering the coupon rate on the bond to lower interest expense and to increase the profitability of your company. Is the rationale for this suggestion a good one? Explain.

C8-42.   Ethics and Governance: Bond Covenants   (L02)

Since lenders do not have voting rights like shareholders do, they often reduce their risk by invoking various bond covenants that restrict the company's operating, financing and investing activities. For example, debt covenants often restrict the amount of debt that the company can issue (in relation to its equity) and can impose operating restrictions (such as the ability to acquire other companies or to pay dividends). Failure to abide by these restrictions can have serious consequences, including forcing the company into bankruptcy and potential liquidation. Assume that you are on the board of directors of a company that issues bonds with such restrictions. What safeguards can you identify to ensure compliance with those restrictions?

Reporting and Analyzing Owner Financing

LEARNING OBJECTIVES

LO1 Describe and illustrate accounting for contributed capital, including stock sales and repurchases. (p. 9-5)

LO2 Explain and illustrate accounting for earned capital, including cash dividends, stock dividends, and comprehensive income. (p. 9-12)

LO3 Describe accounting for equity carve outs and convertible debt. (p. 9-20)

ACCENTURE

Accenture is one of the world's leading management consulting, technology services, and outsourcing companies. With more than 120,000 employees based in 48 countries, Accenture's 2005 revenues exceeded $15 billion. Accenture explains its business model as follows:

> We use our industry and business-process knowledge, our service offering expertise and our insight into and deep understanding of emerging technologies to identify new business and technology trends and formulate and implement solutions for clients . . . We help clients identify and enter new markets, increase revenues in existing markets, improve operational performance and deliver their products and services more effectively and efficiently.

Accenture is organized into three key service areas:

- Consulting. Clients draw on Accenture's expertise in strategy, business transformation, and specialty and functional consulting.
- Technology. Accenture helps clients manage their information technology needs; it develops and deploys software to streamline and integrate business processes and systems.
- Outsourcing. Accenture's outsourcing services include business process outsourcing (BPO), application outsourcing, and infrastructure outsourcing.

Following is a listing of several clients of Accenture and the types of services they purchased from Accenture:

- Vodafone Accenture defined and executed a program to improve key functions for Vodafone Germany including its IT customer service, network development, rollout and operations, and overall technology governance.
- Staples Accenture refined Staples' "big box" retail model, helping the company to focus on operational excellence to simplify customers'

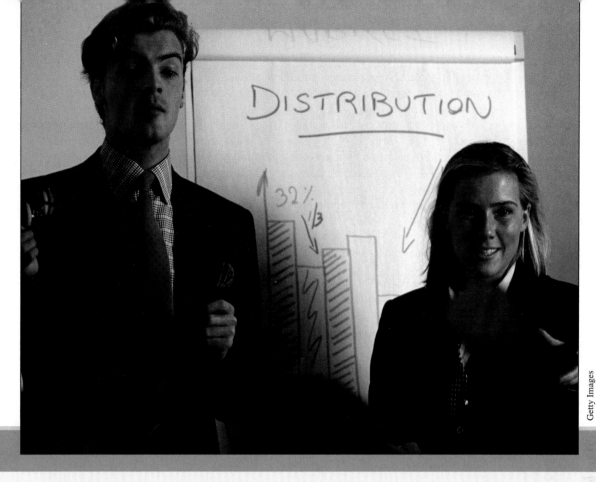

shopping experience; Accenture focused on Staples' supply chain, inventory management, retail operations, merchandising, and marketing.

- **Royal & SunAlliance** Accenture provided several outsourcing and business solutions including R&SA's UK and Ireland IT application and maintenance functions as well as UK sales and service calls.
- **KeySpan Corporation** Accenture helped KeySpan deliver a scalable operating model, build leading capabilities, optimize its cost structure, and create a performance-based culture for all employees.

The Wall Street Journal explains that:

> Accenture has no operational headquarters and no formal branches. Its chief financial officer lives in Silicon Valley. Its chief technologist is based in Germany. The head of human resources is in Chicago. And the firm's thousands of management and technology consultants are constantly on the go, often reviewing projects and negotiating new contracts in clients' offices or working temporarily in offices that Accenture leases in more than 100 locations around the world.

Accenture's value lies not in plant assets, such as land and buildings, but in the knowledge capital of its employees, most of whom are Accenture shareholders. This module considers how shareholders' investment is accounted for on the balance sheet. We consider capital stock, stock options, share issuances, share repurchases, and dividend payments.

Accenture initially operated as a collection of related partnerships located throughout the world. Then, in 2001, the partnership converted to a corporation and the partners became shareholders. Accenture's capital structure provides liquidity and incentives to its employee/owners as well as a vehicle to raise additional funds.

Accenture has three classes of stock: preferred, which has been authorized, but has yet to be issued, and two classes of common, one voting (Class A) and the other nonvoting (Class X). Only the Class A shares are entitled to dividends and Accenture issues these shares to raise new capital. The company is currently in the process of redeeming its Class X shares.

Accenture also has restricted shares. These shares are awarded to employees under the company's deferred compensation plan, which entitles the employees to convert their restricted shares into Class A common shares. Employees cannot immediately convert their restricted shares. Instead, they must wait until the shares vest in the future. In the meantime, restricted shares are included as deferred compensation in

(Continued on next page)

(Continued from previous page)

shareholders' equity. Over time, as the restricted shares vest, Accenture issues Class A shares and records compensation expense. Vesting and conversion do not increase stockholders' equity because the increase in capital stock is exactly offset by a reduction in retained earnings. Restricted stock has become a popular way to compensate employees following recent changes in accounting for employee stock options. This module covers both employee stock options and restricted stock.

Accenture has repurchased over $760 million of its common stock. Many companies routinely repurchase their common stock as it is the best use of excess cash when a company has no better outside investment opportunities. Another reason for repurchasing stock is to offset the dilutive effect of stock-based compensation programs. This module explains stock repurchases. The module also discusses a variety of equity transactions under the general heading of equity carve outs and convertibles. These transactions include a number of methods by which companies seek to unlock hidden value for the benefit of their shareholders.

Sources: Accenture 2005 Form 10-K; Accenture 2005 Annual Report; *Fortune*, January 2007; *The Wall Street Journal*, June 2006.

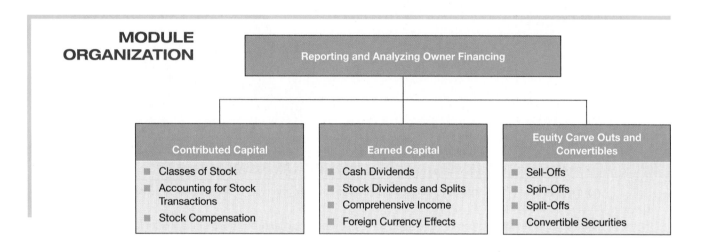

INTRODUCTION

A company finances its assets through operating cash flows or it taps one or both of the following sources: either it borrows funds or it sells stock to shareholders. On average, companies obtain about half of their external financing from borrowed sources and the other half from shareholders. This module describes the issues relating to stockholders' equity, including the accounting for stock transactions (sales and repurchases of stock, dividends, stock-based compensation, and convertible securities). We also discuss equity carve outs, a process by which companies can unlock substantial shareholder value via spin-offs and split-offs of business units into separate companies. Finally, we discuss the accumulated other comprehensive income component of stockholders' equity.

When a company issues stock to the public, it records the receipt of cash (or other assets) and an increase in stockholders' equity, representing the shareholders' investment in the company. The increase in cash and equity is equal to the market price of the stock on the issue date multiplied by the number of shares sold.

Like bonds, stockholders' equity is accounted for at *historical cost*. Consequently, the company's financial statements do not reflect fluctuations in the market price of the stock subsequent to the initial public offering. This is because these market transactions involve outside parties and not the company. However, if the company repurchases and/or resells shares of its own stock, the balance sheet will be affected because those transactions involve the company.

There is an important difference between accounting for stockholders' equity and accounting for transactions involving assets and liabilities: *there is never any gain or loss reported on the purchase and sale of a company's own stock or the payment of dividends to its shareholders.* Instead, these "gains and losses" are reflected as increases and decreases in the contributed capital component of stockholders' equity.

The typical balance sheet has two broad categories of stockholders' equity:

1. **Contributed capital** These accounts report the proceeds received by the issuing company from original stock issuances. It often includes common stock, preferred stock, and additional paid-in capital. Netted against these contributed capital accounts is treasury stock, the amounts paid to repurchase shares of the issuer's stock from its investors, less the proceeds from the resale of such shares. Collectively, these accounts are referred to as contributed capital (or *paid-in capital*).

2. **Earned capital** This section consists of (a) retained earnings, which represent the cumulative income and losses of the company, less any dividends to shareholders, and (b) accumulated other comprehensive income (AOCI), which includes changes to equity that have not yet impacted income and are, therefore, not reflected in retained earnings.

Exhibit 9.1 illustrates the stockholders' equity section of **Accenture**'s balance sheet (both contributed capital and earned capital). Accenture's balance sheet reports eight equity accounts that make up contributed capital: preferred stock, two classes of common stock, restricted share units, deferred compensation, additional paid-in capital, and two types of treasury (repurchased) stock. Accenture's balance sheet also reports two earned capital accounts: retained earnings and accumulated other comprehensive income (loss).

EXHIBIT 9.1	**Stockholders' Equity from Accenture's Balance Sheet**		
	($ 000)	**2005**	**2004**
	Preferred shares, 2,000,000,000 shares authorized, zero shares issued and outstanding	$ —	$ —
	Class A common shares, par value $0.0000225 per share, 20,000,000,000 shares authorized, 602,705,936 and 591,496,780 shares issued as of August 31, 2005 and 2004, respectively.	13	13
	Class X common shares, par value $0.0000225 per share, 1,000,000,000 shares authorized, 321,088,062 and 365,324,882 shares issued and outstanding as of August 31, 2005 and 2004, respectively	7	9
Contributed Capital	Restricted share units (related to Class A common shares) 32,180,787 and 28,278,704 units issued and outstanding as of August 31, 2005 and 2004, respectively	606,623	475,240
	Deferred compensation	(240,915)	(150,777)
	Additional paid-in capital	1,365,013	1,643,652
	Treasury shares, at cost, 32,265,976 and 6,098,122 shares at August 31, 2005 and 2004, respectively.	(763,682)	(132,313)
	Treasury shares owned by Accenture Ltd. Share Employee Compensation Trust, at cost, zero and 13,120,050 shares at August 31, 2005 and 2004, respectively.	—	(296,894)
Earned Capital	Retained earnings.	962,339	46,636
	Accumulated other comprehensive loss	(232,484)	(113,760)
	Total shareholders' equity.	$1,696,914	$1,471,806

We discuss contributed capital and earned capital in turn. For each section, we provide a graphic that displays the part of stockholders' equity in the balance sheet impacted by the discussion of that section.

CONTRIBUTED CAPITAL

Contributed capital represents the cumulative cash inflow that the company has received from the sale of various classes of stock, less the net cash that it has paid out to repurchase its stock from the market. The contributed capital of Accenture is highlighted in the following graphic:

Shareholders' Equity ($ 000)	2005	2004
Preferred shares, 2,000,000,000 shares authorized, zero shares issued and outstanding	$ —	$ —
Class A common shares, par value $0.0000225 per share, 20,000,000,000 shares authorized, 602,705,936 and 591,496,780 shares issued as of August 31, 2005 and 2004, respectively	13	13
Class X common shares, par value $0.0000225 per share, 1,000,000,000 shares authorized, 321,088,062 and 365,324,882 shares issued and outstanding as of August 31, 2005 and 2004, respectively.	7	9
Restricted share units (related to Class A common shares) 32,180,787 and 28,278,704 units issued and outstanding as of August 31, 2005 and 2004, respectively	606,623	475,240
Deferred compensation.	(240,915)	(150,777)
Additional paid-in capital.	1,365,013	1,643,652
Treasury shares, at cost, 32,265,976 and 6,098,122 shares at August 31, 2005 and 2004, respectively	(763,682)	(132,313)
Treasury shares owned by Accenture Ltd. Share Employee Compensation Trust, at cost, zero and 13,120,050 shares at August 31, 2005 and 2004, respectively.	—	(296,894)
Retained earnings	962,339	46,636
Accumulated other comprehensive loss	(232,484)	(113,760)
Total shareholders' equity	$1,696,914	$1,471,806

For Accenture, contributed capital consists of par value and additional paid-in capital for its preferred stock (if issued), common stock, and restricted share units (its stock compensation plan). Its contributed capital is reduced by the cost of shares awarded to employees as deferred compensation and by the cost of Accenture's treasury stock (repurchased shares).

Classes of Stock

LO1 Describe and illustrate accounting for contributed capital, including stock sales and repurchases.

There are two general classes of stock: preferred and common. The difference between the two lies in the legal rights conferred upon each class.

Preferred Stock

Preferred stock generally has preference, or priority, with respect to common stock. Two usual preferences are:

1. **Dividend preference** Preferred shareholders receive dividends on their shares before common shareholders do. If dividends are not paid in a given year, those dividends are normally forgone. However, some preferred stock contracts include a *cumulative provision* stipulating that any forgone dividends (dividends in *arrears*) must first be paid to preferred shareholders, together with the current year's dividends, before any dividends are paid to common shareholders.

2. **Liquidation preference** If a company fails, its assets are sold (liquidated) and the proceeds are paid to the creditors and shareholders, in that order. Shareholders, therefore, have a greater risk of loss than creditors. Among shareholders, the preferred shareholders receive payment in full before common shareholders. This liquidation preference makes preferred shares less risky than common shares. Any liquidation payment to preferred shares is normally at par value, although sometimes the liquidation is specified in excess of par; called a *liquidating value*.

To illustrate the typical provisions contained in preferred stock agreements, consider the following footnote disclosure from Chesapeake Energy Corporation (2005 10-K).

In April 2005, we issued 4,600,000 shares of 5.00% (Series 2005) cumulative convertible preferred stock, par value $0.01 per share and liquidation preference $100 per share, in a private offering, all of which were outstanding as of December 31, 2005. The net proceeds from the offering were $447.2 million. Each share of preferred stock is convertible, at the holder's option at any time, initially into approximately 3.8811 shares of our common stock based on an initial conversion price of $25.766 per share, subject to specified adjustments. At December 31, 2005, 17,853,060 shares of our common stock were reserved for issuance upon conversion. The preferred stock is subject to mandatory conversion, at our option, on or after April 15, 2010 . . . Annual cumulative cash dividends of $5.00 per share are payable quarterly on the fifteenth day of each January, April, July and October.

Following are several important features of Chesapeake's preferred stock:

▪ Each share of preferred stock is convertible into 3.8811 shares of common shares at the option of the preferred shareholder. After April 15, 2010, the company has the option of converting the preferred stock to common.

▪ The preferred stock pays an annual dividend of $5 per share, payable quarterly.

▪ The preferred stock is *cumulative*. This feature protects preferred shareholders in that unpaid dividends (called *dividends in arrears*) must be paid before any dividends are paid to common shareholders.

Chesapeake's cumulative preferred shares carry a dividend yield of 5%. This preferred dividend yield compares favorably with the $0.20 of dividends per share (1.09% yield on a $18.31 share price) paid to its common shareholders in 2005. Generally, preferred stock can be an attractive investment for shareholders seeking higher dividend yields, especially when tax laws wholly or partially exempt such dividends from taxation. (In comparison, interest payments received by debtholders are not tax exempt.)

In addition to the sorts of conversion features outlined above, preferred shares sometimes carry a *participation feature* that allows preferred shareholders to share ratably with common stockholders in dividends. The dividend preference over common shares can be a benefit when dividend payments are meager, but a fixed dividend yield limits upside potential if the company performs exceptionally well. A participation feature can overcome this limitation.

Common Stock

Accenture has two classes of common stock, Class A and Class X. The Accenture common stock has the following important characteristics:

▪ Both classes of common stock have a par value of $0.0000225 per share. **Par value** is an arbitrary amount set by company organizers at the time of formation and has no relation to or impact on the stock's market value. Generally, par value has no substance from a financial reporting or financial statement analysis perspective (there are some legal implications, which are usually minor). Its main impact is in specifying the allocation of proceeds from stock issuances between the two contributed capital accounts on the balance sheet: common stock and additional paid-in capital, as we describe below.

▪ Accenture has authorized the issuance of 20 billion class A common shares. Shareholders control the number of shares that can be issued—called *authorized shares*. The articles of incorporation set the number of shares authorized for issuance. Once that limit is reached, shareholders must approve any increase in authorized shares. As of 2005, over 602.7 million shares are issued. When shares are first issued the number of shares outstanding equals the number issued. Any shares subsequently repurchased as treasury stock are no longer "outstanding" and the number of treasury shares are deducted from issued shares to derive *outstanding shares*. Because Accenture has repurchased some Class A shares, the number outstanding is fewer than the 602.7 million issued.[1]

---

[1] Accenture has a second class of common shares (Class X) issued and outstanding. These shares have a par value $0.0000225. Footnotes reveal that Class X shares are entitled to vote but are not entitled to dividends, do not have any preference in liquidation, and cannot be sold without the company's consent. Accenture's Class X shares are not publicly traded. Accenture has issued about 321 million Class X shares and has not repurchased any (the issued and outstanding number of shares are the same).

Accounting for Stock Transactions

We cover the accounting for stock transactions in this section, including the accounting for stock issuances and repurchases.

Stock Issuance

Companies issue stock to obtain cash and other assets for use in their business. Stock issuances increase assets (cash) by the issue proceeds: the number of shares sold multiplied by the price of the stock on the issue date. Equity increases by the same amount, which is reflected in contributed capital accounts. If the stock has a par value, the common stock account increases by the number of shares sold multiplied by its par value and the additional paid-in capital account increases for the remainder. If the stock is no-par, the common stock account increases by the total cash received. (Stock can also be issued as "no-par" or as "no-par with a stated value." For no-par stock, the common stock account is increased by the entire proceeds of the sale and no amount is assigned to additional paid-in capital. For no-par stock with a stated value, the stated value is treated just like par value, that is, common stock is increased by the number of shares multiplied by the stated value, and the remainder is assigned to the additional paid-in capital account.)

To illustrate, assume that Accenture issues 100,000 shares of its $0.0000225 par value common stock at a market price of $43 cash per share. This stock issuance has the following financial statement effects:

	Balance Sheet							Income Statement		
Transaction	Cash Asset	+	Noncash Assets	=	Liabil- ities	+	Contrib. Capital	+ Earned Capital	Rev- enues	− Expen- ses	= Net Income
Issue 100,000 common shares with $0.0000225 par value for $43 cash per share	+4,300,000 Cash			=			+2 Common Stock +4,299,998 Additional Paid-In Capital				=

```
Cash    4,300,000
  CS                    2
  APIC        4,299.998
     Cash
4,300,000 |
      CS
          |        2
     APIC
          |   4,299,998
```

Specifically, the stock issuance affects the financial statements as follows:

1. Cash increases by $4,300,000 (100,000 shares × $43 per share)
2. Common stock increases by the par value of shares sold (100,000 shares × $0.0000225 par value = $2.25, rounded to $2 here)
3. Additional paid-in capital increases by the $4,299,998 difference between the issue proceeds and par value ($4,300,000 − $2)

Once shares are issued, they are traded in the open market among investors. The proceeds of those sales and their associated gains and losses, as well as fluctuations in the company's stock price subsequent to issuance, do not affect the issuing company and are not recorded in its accounting records.

Refer again to the following report of common stock on Accenture's balance sheet:

($ 000)	2005	2004
Class A common shares, par value $0.0000225 per share, 20,000,000,000 shares authorized, 602,705,936 and 591,496,780 shares issued as of August 31, 2005 and 2004, respectively	$ 13	$ 13
Additional paid-in capital	1,365,013	1,643,652

Accenture's Class A common stock, in the amount of $13 million, equals the number of shares issued multiplied by the common stock's par value: 602,705,936 × $0.0000225 = $13,561 (rounded to $13 thousand). Total proceeds from its stock issuances are $1,365,026,000, the sum of the par value and additional paid-in capital. This implies that Class A shares were sold, on average, for $2.26 per share ($1,365,026,000/602,705,936 shares).

> **RESEARCH INSIGHT** **Stock Issuance and Stock Returns**
>
> Research shows that, historically, companies issuing equity securities experience unusually low stock returns for several years following those offerings. Evidence suggests that this poor performance is partly due to overly optimistic estimates of long-term growth for these companies by equity analysts. That optimism causes offering prices to be too high. This over-optimism is most pronounced when the analyst is employed by the brokerage firm that underwrites the stock issue. There is also evidence that companies manage earnings upward prior to an equity offering. This means the observed decrease in returns following an issuance likely reflects the market's negative reaction, on average, to earnings management.

Stock Repurchase

Accenture provides the following description of its stock repurchase program in notes to its 10-K report:

> **Share Purchase Activity** Since April 2002, the Board of Directors of Accenture Ltd has authorized funding for its publicly announced open-market share purchase program for acquiring Accenture Ltd Class A common shares . . . Effective as of October 15, 2004, the Board of Directors of Accenture Ltd has authorized the purchase, redemption and exchange from time to time of up to an additional $3 billion of Accenture shares.

This footnote goes on to say that Accenture has repurchased over $2.9 billion of its common stock since the share repurchase program was approved by its board of directors. One reason a company repurchases shares is because it believes that the market undervalues them. The logic is that the repurchase sends a favorable signal to the market about the company's financial condition that positively impacts its share price and, thus, allows it to resell those shares for a "gain." Any such gain on resale is *never* reflected in the income statement. Instead, any excess of the resale price over the repurchase price is added to additional paid-in capital. GAAP prohibits companies from reporting gains and losses from stock transactions with their own shareholders.

Another reason companies repurchase shares is to offset the dilutive effects of an employee stock option program. When an employee exercises stock options, the number of shares outstanding increases. These additional shares reduce earnings per share and are, therefore, viewed as *dilutive*. In response, many companies repurchase an equivalent number of shares in a desire to keep outstanding shares constant. Of the $2.9 billion in share repurchases, $2.1 billion has been purchased from Accenture executives. Those shares were originally issued under Accenture's incentive compensation program (disclosed in footnotes not reproduced here).

A stock repurchase reduces the size of the company (cash declines and, thus, total assets decline). A repurchase has the opposite financial statement effects from a stock issuance. That is, cash is reduced by the price of the shares repurchased (number of shares repurchased multiplied by the purchase price per share), and stockholders' equity is reduced by the same amount. The reduction in equity is achieved by increasing a contra equity (negative equity) account called **treasury stock,** which reduces stockholders' equity. Thus, when the treasury stock contra equity account increases, total equity decreases.

When the company subsequently reissues treasury stock there is no accounting gain or loss. Instead, the difference between the proceeds received and the original purchase price of the treasury stock is reflected as an increase or decease to additional paid-in capital.

To illustrate, assume that 3,000 common shares of Accenture previously issued for $43 are repurchased for $40. This repurchase has the following financial statement effects:

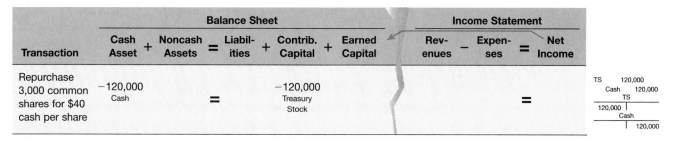

Assets (cash) and equity both decrease. Treasury stock (a contra equity account) increases by $120,000, which reduces stockholders' equity by that amount.

Assume that these 3,000 shares are subsequently resold for $42 cash per share. This resale of treasury stock has the following financial statement effects:

	Balance Sheet						Income Statement		
Transaction	Cash Asset	+ Noncash Assets	= Liabil- ities	+ Contrib. Capital	+ Earned Capital		Rev- enues	− Expen- ses	= Net Income
Reissue 3,000 treasury (common) shares for $42 cash per share	+126,000 Cash		=	+120,000 Treasury Stock +6,000 Additional Paid-In Capital					=

Cash   126,000
TS   120,000
APIC   6,000
       Cash
126,000 |
        TS
        | 120,000
        APIC
        | 6,000

Cash assets increase by $126,000 (3,000 shares × $42 per share), the treasury stock account is reduced by the $120,000 cost of the treasury shares issued, and the $6,000 excess (3,000 shares × $2 per share) is reported as an increase in additional paid-in capital. (If the reissue price is below the repurchase price, then additional paid-in capital is reduced until it reaches a zero balance, after which retained earnings are reduced.) Again, there is no effect on the income statement as companies are prohibited from reporting gains and losses from repurchases and reissuances of their own stock.

The treasury stock section of Accenture's balance sheet is reproduced below:

($ 000s)	2005	2004
Treasury shares, at cost, 32,265,976 and 6,098,122 shares at August 31, 2005 and 2004, respectively	$(763,682)	$(132,313)

Accenture has repurchased a cumulative total of 32,265,976 shares of its common stock for $763,682,000, an average repurchase price of $23.67 per share. This compares with total contributed capital of $1,730,741 ($13 + $7 + $606,623 − $240,915 + 1,365,013; all $ in 000s, see page 9-5). Thus, Accenture has repurchased about 44% of its original contributed capital. Although some of Accenture's treasury purchases were to meet stock option exercises, it appears that most of these purchases are motivated by a perceived low stock price by Accenture management.

MANAGERIAL DECISION	You Are the Chief Financial Officer

As CFO, you believe that your company's stock price is lower than its real value. You are considering various alternatives to increase that price, including the repurchase of company stock in the market. What are some factors you should consider before making your decision? [Answer, p. 9-25]

Stock Compensation Plans

Common stock has been an important component of executive compensation for decades. The general idea follows: If the company executives own stock they will have an incentive to increase its value. This aligns the executives' interests with those of other shareholders. Although the strength of this alignment is the subject of much debate, its logic compels boards of directors of most American companies to use stock-based compensation.

Common stock can be used as a performance incentive in several possible ways. One popular form is to give an employee the right to purchase common stock at a pre-specified price for a given period of time. This is called a stock option plan. Options allow employees to purchase stock at a fixed price (called the exercise price) and resell it at the prevailing (expectedly higher) market price, thus realizing an immediate gain. Because there is a good chance of future stock price increases, options are valuable to employees when they receive them, even if the exercise price is exactly equal to the stock's market price the day the options are awarded. (The fair value of the stock option to the employee can be determined using a formula developed by professors Fisher Black and Myron Scholes. The "Black-Scholes" formula is widely used to value a wide variety of options although other fair-value formulae exist.)

Under prior GAAP, companies could avoid recognizing the fair value of options in the income statement as compensation expense, and only needed to disclose that fair value in footnotes. Accounting standards were changed in 2005 and now income statements must include as compensation expense, the fair value of the options granted during the period. This eliminated one key financial reporting benefit for companies of this form of compensation.

Many companies, including Accenture, then began compensating employees with **restricted stock** instead of with stock options. Under a restricted stock plan, the company transfers shares to the employee, but the shares are restricted in that they cannot be sold until the end of a "vesting" period. (Vesting is the period of time over which an employee gains ownership of the shares, usually 5-7 years; employees commonly acquire ownership ratably over time, such as 1/5 each year over 5 years, or acquire full (100%) vesting after the vesting period ends—called *cliff vesting*.) Accounting for restricted stock is illustrated in the following template:

	Balance Sheet					Income Statement			
Transaction	Cash Asset	+ Noncash Assets	= Liabil- ities	+ Contrib. Capital	+ Earned Capital	Rev- enues	− Expen- ses	= Net Income	
Company issues 100 shares of $10 par restricted stock with a market value of $30 per share, vesting ratably over 6 years		=		+1,000 Common Stock +2,000 Additional Paid-In Capital -3,000 Deferred Compensation			=		DC 3,000 CS 1,000 APIC 2,000 DC 3,000 CS 1,000 APIC 2,000
Record compensation expense for first year (same entry for the next 5 years)		=		+500 Deferred Compensation	−500 Retained Earnings	−	+500 Wage Expense	= −500	WE 500 DC 500 WE 500 DC 500

The company records the restricted stock grants as a share issuance exactly as if the shares were sold. That is, the common stock account increases by the par value of the shares and additional paid-in capital increases for the remainder of the share value. However, instead of cash received, the company records a deferred compensation (contra equity) account for the value of the shares that have not yet been issued. This reduces equity. Thus, granting restricted shares leaves the total dollar amount of equity unaffected.

Subsequently, the value of shares given to employees is treated as compensation expense and recorded over the vesting period. Each year, the deferred compensation account is reduced by the vested shares and wage expense is recorded, thus reducing retained earnings. Total equity is unaffected by this transaction as the reduction of the deferred compensation contra equity account (thereby increasing stockholders' equity) is exactly offset by the decrease in retained earnings. The remaining deferred compensation account decreases total stockholders' equity until the end of the vesting period when the total restricted stock grant has been recognized as wage expense. Equity is, therefore, never increased when restricted stock is issued.

Accenture's restricted stock compensation program is reflected in stockholders' equity as follows:

($ 000s)	2005	2004
Restricted share units (related to Class A common shares) 32,180,787 and 28,278,704 units issued and outstanding as of August 31, 2005 and 2004, respectively.	$606,623	$475,240
Deferred compensation	(240,915)	(150,777)

As of 2005, Accenture had granted employees $606,623,000 in restricted stock, $365,708,000 of which has been reflected as compensation expense, leaving a balance in deferred compensation of $240,915,000. These restricted share units (RSU) entitle the employee to receive one share of Accenture Class A common stock under the company's vesting schedule as described in the following excerpt from its 10-K.

> **Restricted Share Units**   Under the [Share Incentive Plan], participants may be granted restricted share units without cost to the participant. Each restricted share unit awarded to a participant represents an unfunded, unsecured right, which is nontransferable except in the event of death of the participant, to receive an Accenture Ltd Class A common share on the date specified in the participant's award agreement. The restricted share units granted under this plan vest at various times, generally ranging from immediate vesting to vesting over a ten year period. For awards with graded vesting, compensation expense is recognized over the vesting term of each separately vesting portion. Compensation expense is recognized on a straight-line basis for awards with cliff vesting. A summary of information with respect to restricted share units is as follows:

	2005	2004	2003
Shares granted................................	7,335,407	4,715,894	6,908,328
Weighted average fair value of shares..............	$ 25.78	$ 22.62	$ 16.13
Pretax compensation expense charged to earnings, net of cancellations..........................	$88,341,000	$60,486,000	$51,615,000

During 2005, Accenture issued 7,335,407 RSUs, valued at $25.78 per share (the value of the Class A common traded on the NYSE: ACN), for a total value of $189,106,792. During 2005, Accenture recognized $88,341,000 as compensation expense relating to the vesting of the 2005 RSUs and previously issued RSUs. Upon exchange of the RSUs for the Class A common stock, Accenture records issuance of common stock as if it had sold the stock for the cost of the RSU. (If employees forfeit shares, perhaps as a result of employment termination, the compensation recognized to date, and the remaining deferred compensation balance is reversed and offset against the related common stock and paid-in capital accounts. Income increases by the reversal of the compensation expense recognized to date.)

To summarize, restricted stock plans do not affect the total dollar amount of equity. Retained earnings decrease over time as the company recognizes compensation when the restricted shares vest, and paid-in capital increases by the same amount. The effect is a transfer of equity from earned capital to paid-in capital.

MID-MODULE REVIEW 1

Assume that BearingPoint reported the following transactions relating to its stock accounts in 2005.

Jan 15   Issued 10,000 shares of $5 par value common stock at $17 cash per share

Mar 31   Purchased 2,000 shares of its own common stock at $15 cash per share.

June 25   Reissued 1,000 shares of its treasury stock at $20 cash per share.

Use the financial statement effects template to identify the effects of these stock transactions.

Solution

		Balance Sheet					Income Statement		
Transaction	Cash Asset	+ Noncash Assets	= Liabil- ities	+ Contrib. Capital	+ Earned Capital		Rev- enues	– Expen- ses	= Net Income
Jan. 15	+170,000 Cash		=	+50,000 Common Stock +120,000 Additional Paid-In Capital					=

Cash   170,000
   CS   50,000
  APIC   120,000

Cash
170,000 |
       CS
        | 50,000
    APIC
      | 120,000

continued

	Balance Sheet						Income Statement			
Transaction	**Cash Asset**	+ **Noncash Assets**	= **Liabil- ities**	+ **Contrib. Capital**	+ **Earned Capital**		**Rev- enues**	− **Expen- ses**	= **Net Income**	
Mar. 31	−30,000 Cash	=		−30,000 Treasury Stock						
June 25	+20,000 Cash			+15,000 Treasury Stock +5,000 Additional Paid-In Capital						

```
TS      30,000
   Cash      30,000
        TS
30,000 |
   Cash
        | 30,000
Cash    20,000
   TS        15,000
   APIC       5,000
        Cash
20,000 |
   TS
        | 15,000
   APIC
        | 5,000
```

EARNED CAPITAL

We now turn attention to the earned capital portion of stockholders' equity. Earned capital represents the cumulative profit that the company has retained. Recall that earned capital increases each period by income earned and decreases by any losses incurred. Earned capital also decreases by dividends paid to shareholders. Not all dividends are paid in the form of cash. Companies can pay dividends in many forms, including property (land, for example) or additional shares of stock. We cover both cash and stock dividends in this section. Earned capital also includes the positive or negative effects of accumulated other comprehensive income (AOCI). The earned capital of Accenture is highlighted in the following graphic:

LO2 Explain and illustrate accounting for earned capital, including cash dividends, stock dividends, and comprehensive income.

Shareholders' Equity ($ 000)	2005	2004
Preferred shares, 2,000,000,000 shares authorized, zero shares issued and outstanding	$ —	$ —
Class A common shares, par value $0.0000225 per share, 20,000,000,000 shares authorized, 602,705,936 and 591,496,780 shares issued as of August 31, 2005 and 2004, respectively	13	13
Class X common shares, par value $0.0000225 per share, 1,000,000,000 shares authorized, 321,088,062 and 365,324,882 shares issued and outstanding as of August 31, 2005 and 2004, respectively	7	9
Restricted share units (related to Class A common shares) 32,180,787 and 28,278,704 units issued and outstanding as of August 31, 2005 and 2004, respectively	606,623	475,240
Deferred compensation	(240,915)	(150,777)
Additional paid-in capital	1,365,013	1,643,652
Treasury shares, at cost, 32,265,976 and 6,098,122 shares at August 31, 2005 and 2004, respectively	(763,682)	(132,313)
Treasury shares owned by Accenture Ltd. Share Employee Compensation Trust, at cost, zero and 13,120,050 shares at August 31, 2005 and 2004, respectively.	—	(296,894)
Retained earnings	962,339	46,636
Accumulated other comprehensive loss	(232,484)	(113,760)
Total shareholders' equity	$1,696,914	$1,471,806

Cash Dividends

Many companies, but not all, pay dividends. Their reasons for dividend payments are varied. Most dividends are paid in cash on a quarterly basis. The following is a description of Accenture's dividend policy from its 10-K.

Dividend Policy From our incorporation in 2001 through the end of fiscal 2005, Accenture Ltd did not declare or pay any cash dividends on any class of equity. On October 6, 2005, Accenture Ltd declared a cash dividend of $0.30 per share on its Class A common shares for shareholders of record at the close of business on October 17, 2005. Dividends are to be payable on November 15, 2005. Future dividends on the Accenture Ltd Class A common shares, if any, will be at the discretion of the Board of Directors of Accenture Ltd and will depend on, among other things, our results of operations, cash requirements and surplus, financial condition, contractual restrictions and other factors that the Board of Directors may deem relevant.

Outsiders closely monitor dividend payments. It is generally perceived that the level of dividend payments is related to the company's expected long-term recurring income. Accordingly, dividend increases are usually viewed as positive signals about future performance and are accompanied by stock price increases. By that logic, companies rarely reduce their dividends unless absolutely necessary because dividend reductions are often met with substantial stock price declines.

Financial Effects of Cash Dividends

Cash dividends reduce both cash and retained earnings by the amount of the cash dividends paid. To illustrate, Accenture's Board of Directors authorized cash dividends of approximately $181 million to be paid in fiscal 2006 to Class A common stockholders (602,705,936 shares × $0.30 per share). The financial statement effects of this cash dividend payment are as follows:

	Balance Sheet						**Income Statement**		
Transaction	**Cash Asset** +	**Noncash Assets** =	**Liabil- ities** +	**Contrib. Capital** +	**Earned Capital**		**Rev- enues** –	**Expen- ses** =	**Net Income**
Payment of $181 million in cash dividends	−181 mil. Cash	=			−181 mil. Retained Earnings			=	

RE 181 mil.
   Cash 181 mil.
        RE
181 mil. |
   Cash
      | 181 mil.

Dividend payments do not affect net income. They directly reduce retained earnings and bypass the income statement.

Dividends on preferred stock have priority over those on common stock, including unpaid prior years' preferred dividends (dividends in arrears) when preferred stock is cumulative. To illustrate, assume that a company has 15,000 shares of $50 par value, 8% preferred stock outstanding and 50,000 shares of $5 par value common stock outstanding. During its first three years in business, assume that the company declares $20,000 dividends in the first year, $260,000 of dividends in the second year, and $60,000 of dividends in the third year. If the preferred stock is cumulative, the total amount of cash dividends paid to each class of stock in each of the three years follows:

	Preferred Stock	**Common Stock**
Year 1—$20,000 cash dividends paid		
Current year dividend ($750,000 × 8%; but only $20,000 paid, leaving $40,000 in arrears)	$20,000	
Balance to common		$ 0
Year 2—$260,000 cash dividends paid		
Dividends in arrears from Year 1 ([$750,000 × 8%] − $20,000)	40,000	
Current year dividend ($750,000 × 8%).............................	60,000	
Balance to common		160,000
Year 3—$60,000 cash dividends paid		
Current year dividend ($750,000 × 8%).............................	60,000	
Balance to common		0

MID-MODULE REVIEW 2

Assume that Electronic Data Systems (EDS) has outstanding 10,000 shares of $100 par value, 5% preferred stock and 50,000 shares of $5 par value common stock. During its first three years in business, assume that EDS declared no dividends in the first year, $300,000 of cash dividends in the second year, and $80,000 of cash dividends in the third year.

a. If preferred stock is cumulative, determine the dividends paid to each class of stock for each of the three years.

b. If preferred stock is noncumulative, determine the dividends paid to each class of stock for each of the three years.

Solution

a.

Cumulative Preferred Stock	Preferred Stock	Common Stock
Year 1—$0 cash dividends paid.	$ 0	$ 0
Year 2—$300,000 cash dividends paid		
Dividends in arrears from Year 1 ($1,000,000 × 5%).	50,000	
Current year dividend ($1,000,000 × 5%)	50,000	
Balance to common		200,000
Year 3—$80,000 cash dividends paid		
Current year dividend ($1,000,000 × 5%)	50,000	
Balance to common		30,000

b.

Noncumulative Preferred Stock	Preferred Stock	Common Stock
Year 1—$0 cash dividends paid.	$ 0	$ 0
Year 2—$300,000 cash dividends paid		
Current year dividend ($1,000,000 × 5%)	50,000	
Balance to common		250,000
Year 3—$80,000 cash dividends paid		
Current year dividend ($1,000,000 × 5%)	50,000	
Balance to common		30,000

Stock Dividends and Splits

Dividends need not be paid in cash. Many companies pay dividends in the form of additional shares of stock. Companies can also distribute additional shares to their stockholders with a stock split. We cover both of these distributions in this section.

Stock Dividends

When dividends are paid in the form of the company's stock, retained earnings are reduced and contributed capital is increased. However, the amount by which retained earnings are reduced depends on the proportion of the outstanding shares distributed to the total outstanding shares on the dividend distribution date. Exhibit 9.2 illustrates two possibilities depending on whether stock dividends are classified as either small stock dividends or large stock dividends. The break point between small and large is 20–25% of the outstanding shares. (When the number of additional shares issued as a stock dividend is so great that it could materially reduce share price, the transaction is akin to a stock split. The 20–25% guideline is used as a rule of thumb to distinguish material stock price effects.)

For *small stock dividends,* retained earnings are reduced by the *market* value of the shares distributed (dividend shares × market price per share), and par value and contributed capital together are increased by the same amount. For *large stock dividends,* retained earnings are reduced by the *par* value of the shares distributed (dividend shares × par value per share), and common stock is increased by the same amount (no change to additional paid-in capital).

EXHIBIT 9.2	Analysis of Stock Dividend Effects	
Percentage of Outstanding Shares Distributed	**Retained Earnings**	**Contributed Capital**
Less than 20-25% (*small stock dividend treated as a dividend*)	Reduce by **market value** of shares distributed	Common stock increased by: Dividend shares × Par value per share; Additional paid-in capital increased for the balance
More than 20-25% (*large stock dividend treated as a stock split*)	Reduce by **par value** of shares distributed	Common stock increased by: Dividend shares × Par value per share

To illustrate the financial statement effects of stock dividends, assume that BearingPoint has 1 million shares of $5 par common stock outstanding. It then declares a small stock dividend of 15% of the outstanding shares (1,000,000 shares × 15% = 150,000 shares) when the market price of the stock is $30 per share. This small stock dividend has the following financial statement effects:

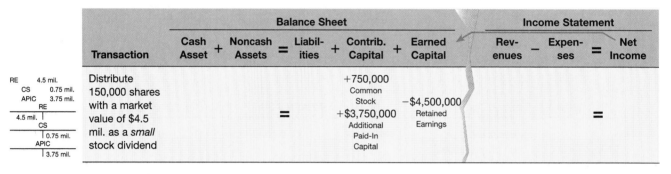

The company reduces retained earnings by $4,500,000, which equals the market value of the small stock dividend (150,000 shares × $30 market price per share). The increase in contributed capital is split between the par value of $750,000 (150,000 shares × $5 par value) and additional paid-in capital ($3,750,000). Similar to cash dividend payments, stock dividends, whether large or small, never impact income.

Next, assume that instead, BearingPoint declares a large stock dividend of 70% of the 1 million outstanding common ($5 par) shares when the market price of the stock is $30 per share. This large stock dividend is treated like a stock split and has the following financial statement effects:

	Balance Sheet						Income Statement			
Transaction	Cash Asset	+ Noncash Assets	= Liabil- ities	+ Contrib. Capital	+ Earned Capital		Rev- enues	- Expen- ses	= Net Income
Distribute 700,000 shares as a *large* stock dividend			=	+$3,500,000 Common Stock	-$3,500,000 Retained Earnings				=

RE 3.5 mil.
    CS 3.5 mil.
       RE
3.5 mil. |
    CS
      | 3.5 mil.

The company's retained earnings declines by $3,500,000, which equals the par value of the large stock dividend (700,000 shares × $5 par value per share). Common stock is increased by the par value of $3,500,000. There is no effect on additional paid-in capital since large stock dividends are reported at par value.

For both large and small stock dividends, companies are required to show comparable shares outstanding for all prior periods for which earnings per share (EPS) is reported in the statements. The reasoning is that a stock dividend has no effect on the ownership percentage of each common stockholder. As such, to show a dilution in reported EPS would erroneously suggest a decline in profitability when it is simply due to an increase in shares outstanding.

Stock Splits

A stock split is a proportionate distribution of shares and, as such, is similar in substance to a stock dividend. A typical stock split is 2-for-1, which means that the company distributes one additional share for each share owned by a shareholder. Following the distribution, each investor owns twice as many shares, so that their percentage ownership in the company is unchanged.

A stock split is not a monetary transaction and, as such, there are no financial statement effects. However, companies must disclose the new number of shares outstanding for all periods presented in the financial statements. Further, many states require that the par value of shares be proportionately adjusted as well (for example, halved for a 2-for-1 split).

If state law requires that par value not be reduced for a stock dividend, this event should be described as a *stock split affected in the form of a dividend*. The following disclosure from Adobe Systems' 2005 annual report provides such an example:

> **Stock Dividend** On March 16, 2005, our Board of Directors approved a two-for-one stock split, in the form of a stock dividend, of our common stock payable on May 23, 2005, to stockholders of record as of May 2, 2005. Share and per share data, for all periods presented, have been adjusted to give effect to this stock split.

MID-MODULE REVIEW 3

Assume that the stockholders' equity of Ceridian Corporation at December 31, 2007, follows.

5% preferred stock, $100 par value, 10,000 shares authorized; 4,000 shares issued and outstanding.	$ 400,000
Common stock, $5 par value, 200,000 shares authorized; 50,000 shares issued and outstanding	250,000
Paid-in capital in excess of par value-Preferred stock.	40,000
Paid-in capital in excess of par value-Common stock.	300,000
Retained earnings	656,000
Total stockholders' equity	$1,646,000

Use the template to identify the financial statement effects for each of the following transactions that occurred during 2008:

Apr. 1 Declared and issued a 100% stock dividend on all outstanding shares of common stock when the market value of the stock was $11 per share.

Dec. 7 Declared and issued a 3% stock dividend on all outstanding shares of common stock when the market value of the stock was $7 per share.

Dec. 31 Declared and paid a cash dividend of $1.20 per share on all outstanding shares.

Solution

		Balance Sheet						Income Statement			
Transaction	**Cash Asset** +	**Noncash Assets** =	**Liabil- ities** +	**Contrib. Capital** +	**Earned Capital**		**Rev- enues** −	**Expen- ses** =	**Net Income**	

Apr. 1		=		+250,000 Common Stock	−250,000[1] Retained Earnings				=	RE 250,000
										  CS 250,000
										RE
										250,000 |
										    CS
										     | 250,000

Dec. 7		=		+15,000 Common Stock +6,000 Additional Paid-In Capital	−21,000[2] Retained Earnings				=	RE 21,000
										  CS 15,000
										  APIC 6,000
										RE
										21,000 |
										  CS
										   | 15,000
										  APIC
										   | 6,000

Dec. 31	−123,600 Cash	=			−123,600[3] Retained Earnings				=	RE 123,600
										  Cash 123,600
										RE
										123,600 |
										  Cash
										   | 123,600

[1] This large stock dividend reduces retained earnings at the par value of shares distributed (50,000 shares × 100% × $5 par value = $250,000). Contributed capital (common stock) increases by the same amount.

[2] This small stock dividend reduces retained earnings at the market value of shares distributed (3% × 100,000 shares × $7 per share = $21,000). Contributed capital increases by the same amount ($15,000 to common stock and $6,000 to paid-in capital).

[3] At the time of the cash dividend, there are 103,000 shares outstanding. The cash paid is, therefore, 103,000 shares × $1.20 per share = $123,600.

Accumulated Other Comprehensive Income

Comprehensive income is a more inclusive notion of company performance than net income. It includes all recognized changes in equity that occur during a period except those resulting from contributions by and distributions to owners. It's important to note that comprehensive income includes both net income and other items.

Specifically, comprehensive income includes (and net income excludes) foreign currency translation adjustments, unrealized changes in market values of available-for-sale securities, pension liability adjustments, and changes in market values of certain derivative investments. Comprehensive income, therefore, includes the effects of economic events that are often outside of management's control. Accordingly, some assert that net income measures management's performance, while comprehensive income measures company performance. Each period, net income or loss is added to retained earnings so that the balance sheet maintains a running total of the company's cumulative net income and losses (less any dividends paid out). In the same way, each period, comprehensive income items that are not included in net income are added to a balance sheet account called Accumulated Other Comprehensive Income (or loss if the comprehensive items are losses). This account maintains a running balance of the cumulative differences between net income and comprehensive income.

Accenture reports the following components of its accumulated other comprehensive loss from its 10-K report:

($ 000s)	2005	2004
Foreign currency translation adjustments	$ (43,036)	$ (22,752)
Unrealized (losses) gains on marketable securities, net of reclassification adjustments	(2,219)	524
Minimum pension liability adjustments, net of taxes	(187,229)	(91,532)
Accumulated other comprehensive loss	$(232,484)	$(113,760)

Accenture's accumulated other comprehensive loss includes the three following items that affect stockholders' equity and are not reflected in net income:

1. **Foreign currency translation adjustment** ($43,036,000). This is the unrecognized loss on assets and liabilities denominated in foreign currencies. A loss implies that the $US has strengthened relative to foreign currencies; such as when assets denominated in foreign currencies translate to fewer $US. We discuss the effects of foreign currency translation adjustments on accumulated other comprehensive income in more detail below.

2. **Unrealized gains (losses) on available-for-sale securities** ($2,219,000). Unrealized gains and losses on available-for-sale securities are not reflected in net income. Instead, they are accumulated in a separate equity account until the securities are sold.

3. **Minimum pension liability** ($187,229,000). This is the additional pension liability that must be recorded under GAAP because some of Accenture's pension plans are underfunded.

We discuss accounting for available-for-sale securities and pensions in Modules 7 and 10, respectively, and the income statement effects of foreign currency translation adjustments in Module 5. In the next section, we discuss the balance sheet effects of foreign currency translation adjustments, specifically their impact on accumulated other comprehensive income.

Foreign Currency Translation Effects on Accumulated Other Comprehensive Income

Many companies have international transactions denominated in foreign currencies. They might purchase assets in foreign currencies, borrow money in foreign currencies, and transact business with their customers and suppliers in foreign currencies. Other companies might have subsidiaries whose entire balance sheets and income statements are stated in foreign currencies. Financial statements prepared according to U.S. GAAP must be reported in $US. This means that financial statements of foreign subsidiaries must be translated into $US before they are consolidated with those of the U.S. parent company. This translation process can markedly alter both the balance sheet and income statement. We discuss the income statement effects of foreign currency translation in Module 5 and the balance sheet effects in this section.

Consider a U.S. company with a foreign subsidiary that conducts its business in Euros. The subsidiary prepares its financial statements in Euros. Assume that the $US weakens vis-à-vis the Euro during the current period—that is, each Euro can now purchase more $US. When the balance sheet is translated into $US, the assets and liabilities are reported at higher $US than before the $US weakened. This result is shown in accounting equation format in Exhibit 9.3.[2]

EXHIBIT 9.3	Balance Sheet Effects of Euro Strengthening versus the Dollar				
Currency	**Assets**	**=**	**Liabilities**	**+**	**Equity**
$US weakens..............	Increase	=	Increase	+	Increase
$US strengthens...........	Decrease	=	Decrease	+	Decrease

The amount necessary to balance the accounting equation is reported in equity and is called a **foreign currency translation adjustment**. The *cumulative* foreign currency translation adjustment is included in accumulated other comprehensive income (or loss) as illustrated above for Accenture. Foreign currency translation adjustments are direct adjustments to stockholders' equity; they do not impact reported net income. Since assets are greater than liabilities for solvent companies, the cumulative translation adjustment is positive when the $US weakens and negative when the dollar strengthens.

Referring to Accenture's accumulated other comprehensive income table on p 9-17, the cumulative foreign currency translation is a loss of $22,752,000 at the beginning of 2005, which grows to a loss of $43,036,000 by year-end. The $20,284,000 increase in the loss (decrease in Accenture's equity) reflects a strengthening of the $US vis-à-vis the foreign currencies that Accenture dealt with in 2005. That is, as the $US strengthened, Accenture's foreign assets and liabilities translated into fewer $US at year-end (the opposite effect from that described above). This decreased Accenture's equity. In general, unrealized losses (or gains) remain in other accumulated comprehensive income as long as the company owns the foreign subsidiaries to which the losses relate. The translation adjustments fluctuate between positive and negative amounts as the value of the $US fluctuates. However, when a subsidiary is sold, any remaining foreign currency translation adjustment (positive or negative) is immediately recognized in current income along with other gains or losses arising from sale of the subsidiary.

Summary of Stockholders' Equity

The statement of shareholders' equity summarizes the transactions that affect stockholders' equity during the period. This statement reconciles the beginning and ending balances of important stockholders' equity accounts. Accenture's statement of stockholders' equity is in Exhibit 9.4.

---

[2] We assume that the company translates the subsidiary's financial statements using the more common **current rate method**, which is required for subsidiaries operating independently from the parent. Under the current rate method, most items in the balance sheet are translated using exchange rates in effect at the period-end consolidation date and the income statement is translated using the average exchange rate for the period. An alternative procedure is the *temporal method,* which is covered in advanced accounting courses.

EXHIBIT 9.4	Accenture's Statement of Stockholders' Equity

Line No.	($ and shares in 000s)	Class A Shares		Restricted Share Units		Deferred Compensation Expense	Additional Paid-In Capital	Treasury Stock		Retained Earnings	Accumulated Other Comprehensive Income	Other	Total
		$ 000s	Shares	$ 000s	Shares			$ 000s	Shares				
1	Balance, August 31, 2004	$13	591,497	$475,240	28,279	$(150,777)	$1,643,652	$(429,207)	(19,218)	$ 46,636	$(113,760)	$9	$1,471,806
2	Net income . . .									940,474			940,474
3	Unrealized loss on available-for-sale securities										(2,743)		(2,743)
4	Foreign currency translation adjustment . . .										(20,284)		(20,284)
5	Minimum pension liability adjustment . . .										(95,697)		(95,697)
6	Stock-based compensation						84,378						84,378
7	Contract termination . . .									134			134
8	Purchase of Class A shares		(562)				(13,286)	(503,088)	(21,497)				(516,374)
9	Grant of Restricted Share Units			177,778	6,745	(177,778)							0
10	Stock compensation expense					87,640	701						88,341
11	Redemption of SCA shares . . .						(1,095,155)					(2)	(1,095,157)
12	Employee share purchases		4,955				99,678	72,916	3,831	(4,270)			168,324
13	Employee stock options		5,008				69,193	75,538	3,582	(17,775)			126,956
14	Restricted Share Units		1,808	(46,395)	(2,843)		29,096	20,159	1,036	(2,860)			0
15	Transaction fees						3,427						3,427
16	Minority interest						543,329						543,329
17	Balance, August 31, 2005 . .	$13	602,706	$606,623	32,181	$(240,915)	$1,365,013	$(763,682)	(32,266)	$962,339	$(232,484)	$7	$1,696,914

Accenture's statement of shareholders' equity reveals the following key transactions for 2005:

- Line 2: Accenture's retained earnings increased by $940,474,000 from net income (the company paid no dividends in 2005).

- Lines 3–5: Accumulated other comprehensive income began the year with a loss balance of $113,760,000. Other comprehensive income recorded during the year included an unrecognized loss on available-for-sale securities of $2,743,000, a foreign currency translation adjustment loss of $20,284,000, and an increase in the minimum pension liability adjustment of $95,697,000. Together, these three items increased the accumulated other comprehensive loss to $232,484,000 by year-end.

- Line 6: Tax benefits arising from employee exercise of stock options are recorded as an increase in additional paid-in capital (rather than as a reduction of tax expense).

- Line 8: Repurchase of Class A common shares increased treasury stock by $503,088,000 with a small balance also reducing additional paid-in capital (reducing equity by that amount). The column for Class A shares includes both dollars and number of shares.

- Line 9: Accenture granted its employees an additional 6,745,000 restricted share units under its deferred compensation plan; market value of the shares was $177,778,000. The restricted share unit capital account increased by $177,778,000 with an offsetting increase in the deferred compensation contra equity account. There is no net increase in equity from this grant.

- Line 10: Accenture recorded $87,640,000 of stock compensation expense in 2005 relating to the restricted stock units in line 9; this represents the 2005 amortization of the deferred compensation over the vesting period.

- Line 11: Redemption of SCA shares relates to the purchase of restricted shares held by Accenture executives. In 2005, Accenture repurchased and retired $1,095,155,000 of these shares. Because Accenture retired these shares, they were not treated as treasury stock. Instead, Accenture reduced additional paid-in capital because the shares cannot be resold.

- Line 12–13: Employees purchased Accenture Class A common stock in 2005, either newly issued or from the company's treasury stock. These purchases are related to employee share purchases and to the exercise of employee stock options. These purchases increased equity by $295,280,000 ($168,324,000 + $126,956,000).

- Line 14: Employees exchanged restricted share units for Class A common stock in 2005; the exchange had no effect on total equity.

- Line 16: Accenture repurchased shares from minority shareholders at less than book value in 2005. This is similar to the effect from the sale of shares by a subsidiary (an IPO) at a price in excess of book value (see Module 7).

One final point: the financial press sometimes refers to a measure called **book value per share**. This is the net book value of the company that is available to common shareholders, defined as: stockholders' equity less preferred stock (and preferred additional paid-in capital) divided by the number of common shares outstanding (issued common shares less treasury shares). Accenture's book value per share of the Class A stock at the end of 2005 (assuming that all additional paid-in capital is related to that class of stock) is computed as: ($1,696,914,000 − $7,000)/(602,705,936 − 32,265,976) = $2.97 book value per share. In contrast, Accenture's **market price per share** ranged from $22.20 to $25.70 in the 4th quarter of 2005.

EQUITY CARVE OUTS AND CONVERTIBLES

LO3 Describe accounting for equity carve outs and convertible debt.

Corporate divestitures, or **equity carve outs**, are increasingly common as companies seek to increase shareholder value through partial or total divestiture of operating units. Generally, equity carve outs are motivated by the notion that consolidated financial statements often obscure the performance of individual business units, thus complicating their evaluation by outsiders. Corporate managers are concerned that this difficulty in assessing the performance of individual business units limits their ability to reach full valuation. Shareholder value is, therefore, not maximized. In response, conglomerates have divested subsidiaries so that the market can individually price them.

Sell-Offs

Equity carve outs take many forms. The first and simplest form of divestiture is the outright sale of a business unit, called a **sell-off**. In this case, the company sells its equity interest to an unrelated party. The sale is accounted for just like the sale of any other asset. Specifically, any excess (deficit) of cash received over the book value of the business unit sold is recorded as a gain (loss) on the sale.

To illustrate, in 2005, Accenture purchased the North American Health practice from The Capgemini Group for $175 million (€143 million). Capgemini recorded a gain on the sale of €123 million as disclosed in the following excerpt from its 2005 annual report:

> On June 16, 2005, the Group sold its US healthcare business to the Accenture Group for €143 million, generating a capital gain of €123 million.

The financial statement effects of this transaction follow:

- Capgemini received €143 million in cash.

- The North American Health practice was carried on Capgemini's balance sheet as an investment with a book value of €20 million (inferred from the proceeds less gain).

- Capgemini's gain on sale equaled the sale proceeds less the book value: €143 million − €20 million = €123 million gain on sale.

- The gain on sale is reported in Capgemini's 2005 income from continuing operations.

- Capgemini subtracts the gain from net income in its statement of cash flows to compute net cash flows from operations since the transaction generated a noncash operating gain. Instead, the €143 million cash proceeds are reported as a cash inflow from investing activities.

Spin-Offs

A **spin-off** is a second form of divestiture. In this case, the parent company distributes the subsidiary shares that it owns as a dividend to its shareholders who, then, own shares in the subsidiary directly rather than through the parent company. In recording this dividend, retained earnings are reduced by the book value of the equity method investment, and the subsidiary's investment account is removed from the parent's balance sheet.

The spin-off of the Medco Health subsidiary by its parent company, Merck & Co., Inc., is an example of this form of equity carve out. Merck described this spin-off as follows:

On August 19, 2003, Merck completed the spin-off of Medco Health. The spin-off was effected by way of a pro rata dividend to Merck stockholders. Holders of Merck common stock at the close of business on August 12, 2003, received a dividend of .1206 shares of Medco Health common stock for every one share of Merck common stock held on that date. No fractional shares of Medco Health common stock were issued. Shareholders entitled to a fractional share of Medco Health common stock in the distribution received the cash value instead. Based on a letter ruling Merck received from the U.S. Internal Revenue Service, receipt of Medco Health shares in the distribution was tax-free for U.S. federal income tax purposes, but any cash received in lieu of fractional shares was taxable . . . The following is a summary of the assets and liabilities of discontinued operations that were spun off:

August 19, 2003 ($ millions)	
Assets	
Cash and cash equivalents	$ 247.4
Other current assets	2,728.4
Property, plant and equipment, net	816.3
Goodwill	3,310.2
Other intangibles, net	2,351.9
Other assets	138.4
	$9,592.6
Liabilities	
Current liabilities	$2,176.2
Long-term debt	1,362.3
Deferred income taxes	1,195.0
	$4,733.5
Net Assets Transferred	$4,859.1

This distribution was reflected in Merck's statement of retained earnings as follows:

MERCK & CO., INC. AND SUBSIDIARIES Consolidated Statement of Retained Earnings		
Years Ended December 31 ($ millions)	2003	2002
Balance January 1	$35,434.9	$31,489.6
Net Income.	6,830.9	7,149.5
Common Stock Dividends Declared	(3,264.7)	(3,204.2)
Spin-off of Medco Health.	(4,859.1)	—
Balance, December 31.	$34,142.0	$35,434.9

The spin-off is treated as a dividend distribution of 100% of the subsidiary's stock to Merck shareholders. Merck reduced retained earnings by the book value of the Medco Health shares distributed, or $4,859.1 million in this case. Merck also removes the investment in Medco Health account (for the same amount) from its balance sheet.

Split-Offs

The **split-off** is a third form of equity carve out. In this case, the parent company buys back its own stock using the shares of the subsidiary company instead of cash. After completing this transaction, the subsidiary is an independent publicly traded company.

The parent treats the split-off like any other purchase of treasury stock. As such, the treasury stock account is increased and the equity method investment account is reduced, reflecting the distribution of that asset. The dollar amount recorded for this treasury stock depends on how the distribution is set up. There are two possibilities:

1. **Pro rata distribution.** Shares are distributed to stockholders on a pro rata basis. Namely, a shareholder owning 10% of the outstanding stock of the parent company receives 10% of the shares of the subsidiary. The treasury stock account is increased by the *book value* of the investment in the subsidiary. The accounting is similar to the purchase of treasury stock for cash, except that shares of the subsidiary are paid to shareholders instead of cash.

2. **Non pro rata distribution.** This case is like a tender offer where individual stockholders can accept or reject the distribution. The treasury stock account is recorded at the *market value* of the shares of the subsidiary distributed. Since the investment account can only be reduced by its book value, a gain or loss on distribution is recorded in the income statement for the difference. (The SEC also allows companies to record the difference as an adjustment to additional paid-in capital; the usual practice, as might be expected, is for companies to report any gain as part of income.)

AT&T's split-off of its subsidiary, AT&T Wireless (AWE), provides an example. This transaction is described in the following excerpt from footnotes to AT&T's 10-K:

> On July 9, 2001, AT&T completed the split-off of AT&T Wireless as a separate, independently traded company . . . Shares of AT&T Wireless common stock held by AT&T were [exchanged for] AT&T common. AT&T common shareowners received whole shares of AT&T Wireless and cash payments for fractional shares. The IRS ruled that the transaction qualified as tax-free for AT&T and its shareowners for U.S. federal income tax purposes, with the exception of cash received for fractional shares . . . The split-off of AT&T Wireless resulted in a noncash tax-free gain of $13.5 billion, which represented the difference between the fair value of the AT&T Wireless tracking stock at the date of the split-off and AT&T's book value in AT&T Wireless. This gain was recorded in the third quarter of 2001 as a "Gain on disposition of discontinued operations."

Key financial statement facts and effects of this transaction follow:

- AT&T Wireless was a wholly owned subsidiary of AT&T Corporation.
- The split-off resulted in a separate, publicly traded company

- AT&T received shares of its common stock from participating shareholders in exchange for shares of AT&T Wireless.

- Since the exchange was made via a tender offer, it is non pro rata as only those shareholders wishing to exchange their AT&T common stock accepted the offer.

- AT&T realized a gain on the exchange in the amount of $13.5 billion.

Three years later, as a separately traded company, AT&T Wireless was acquired by Cingular Wireless.

Analysis of Equity Carve Outs

Sell-offs, spin-offs, and split-offs all involve the divestiture of an operating segment. They are usually stock transactions and, as a result, do not involve cash. Although they are one-time occurrences, they can result in substantial gains that can markedly alter the income statement and balance sheet. Consequently, we need to interpret them carefully. This involves learning as many details about the carve out as possible from the annual report, the Management Discussion and Analysis, and other publicly available information.

Following an equity carve out, the parent company loses the cash flows (positive or negative) of the divested business unit. As such, the divestiture should be treated like any other discontinued operation. Any recognized gain or loss from divestiture is treated as a nonoperating activity. The sale price of the divested unit reflects the valuation of *future expected* cash flows by the purchaser and is best viewed as a nonoperating activity by the seller. Income (and cash flows) of the divested unit up to the date of sale, however, is part of operations, although discontinued operations are typically segregated.

MID-MODULE REVIEW 4

Assume that BearingPoint announced the split-off of its Canadian subsidiary. BearingPoint reported a gain from the split-off. (1) Describe the accounting for a split-off. (2) Why was BearingPoint able to report a gain on this transaction?

Solution

1. In a split-off, shares of the parent company owned by the shareholders are exchanged for shares of the subsidiary owned by the parent. If the distribution is non pro rata, the parent can report a gain equal to the difference between the fair market value of the subsidiary and its book value on the parent's balance sheet.
2. BearingPoint met the conditions for a split-off as described in part 1, which enabled it to report a gain.

Convertible Securities

Convertible securities are debt and equity securities that provide the holder with an option to convert those securities into other securities. Convertible debentures, for example, are debt securities that give the holder the option to convert the debt into common stock at a predetermined conversion price.

Convertible Debt Securities

Symantec Corporation had convertible debt transactions in 2005, as explained in the following excerpt from footnotes to its 10-K report:

> **Convertible Subordinated Notes** On October 24, 2001, we completed a private offering of $600 million of 3% convertible subordinated notes due November 1, 2006, the net proceeds of which were $585 million. The notes are convertible into shares of our common stock by the holders at any time before maturity at a conversion price of $17.07 per share, subject to certain adjustments. We had the right to redeem the remaining notes on or after November 5, 2004, at a redemption price of 100.75% of stated principal during the period November 5, 2004 through October 31, 2005. Interest was paid semiannually and we commenced making these payments on May 1, 2002. Debt issuance costs of $16 million related to the notes were being amortized on a straight-line basis through November 1, 2006. We had reserved 70.3 million shares of common stock for issuance upon conversion of the notes. On July 20, 2004, our Board of Directors approved the redemption of all of the outstanding

convertible subordinated notes and in September 2004 we sent notice to registered holders that all notes would be redeemed November 5, 2004. As of November 4, 2004 (the day prior to the redemption date), substantially all of the outstanding convertible subordinated notes were converted into 70.3 million shares of our common stock. The remainder was redeemed for cash. Unamortized debt issuance costs of $6 million relative to the converted notes were charged to Capital in excess of par value on the Consolidated Balance Sheet during fiscal 2005.

To summarize, in 2001, Symantec issued $600 million of 3% convertible notes. The noteholders (Symantec's creditors) could convert the notes into 34,271,000 common shares at the initial conversion price of $17.07 ($585,000,000/$17.07 per share = 34,271,000 shares). At any time before October 2005, Symantec could redeem the notes (repay them before maturity and without conversion). In July 2004, Symantec announced that it would exercise its redemption option in November that year. In response, all of the noteholders converted their notes to Symantec common stock. Symantec's statement of stockholders' equity records the effects of the conversion as follows.

| (In thousands) | Common Stock | | Capital In Excess of Par Value | Accumulated Other Comprehensive Income (Loss) | Retained Earnings | Total Stockholders' Equity |
	Shares	Amount				
Conversion of convertible debt . . .	35,142	$352	$593,182	—	—	$593,534

On the conversion date, Symantec's balance sheet carried the notes at $593,534,000. The notes were retired and Symantec issued 35,142,000 shares to the noteholders. This represented a conversion price for the stock of $16.89 a share ($593,534,000/35,142,000). The market price of Symantec common stock on November 4, 2005, (the date of conversion) was $18.63. The conversion, therefore, made economic sense for the noteholders.

When Symantec originally issued the convertible notes, the balance sheet reported their issue price without consideration of the conversion feature, because a conversion option is *not* valued on the balance sheet unless it is detachable from the security (and can be separately sold). Instead, the convertible debt was recorded just like debt that does not have a conversion feature. Accounting for the conversion of the Symantec bonds is illustrated in the following financial statement effects template.

	Balance Sheet						Income Statement			
Transaction	Cash Asset	+ Noncash Assets	= Liabil- ities	+ Contrib. Capital	+ Earned Capital		Rev- enues	− Expen- ses	= Net Income	
Conversion of Symantec notes into common stock			−593,534 = Long-Term Debt	+352 Common Stock +593,182 Additional Paid-In Capital					=	

```
LTD      593,534
     CS           352
     APIC    593,182
       LTD
593,534 |
       CS
         |    352
       APIC
         |    593,182
```

Accounting for the Symantec conversion is straightforward and yields the following effects:

▪ The debt's carrying amount is removed from the balance sheet because the debt is retired.

▪ Symantec issues 35,142,000 shares of $0.01 par value common stock for an "issue" price of $593,534,000 (book value of bonds); common stock, therefore, increases by $352 million (35,142,000 × $0.01, rounded up), and capital in excess of par value (additional paid-in capital) increases by the amount of $593,182,000.

▪ No gain or loss (or cash inflow or outflow) is recorded from the conversion.

Convertible Preferred Stock

Preferred stock can also contain a conversion privilege. Pfizer provides an example of the latter in its description of the Pharmacia acquisition:

Preferred Stock In connection with our acquisition of Pharmacia in 2003, we issued a newly created class of Series A convertible perpetual preferred stock . . . Each share is convertible, at the holder's option, into 2,574.87 shares of our common stock with equal voting rights. The conversion option is indexed to our common stock and requires share settlement, and therefore, is reported at the fair value at the date of issuance. The Company may redeem the preferred stock, at any time, at its option, in cash, in shares of common stock or a combination of both at a price of $40,300 per share.

Accounting for the conversion of preferred stock is essentially the same as that for debt that we describe above: the preferred stock account is removed from the balance sheet and common stock is issued for the dollar amount of the preferred.

Conversion privileges offer an additional benefit to the holder of a security. That is, debtholders and preferred stockholders carry senior positions as claimants in bankruptcy, and also carry a fixed or dividend yield. Thus, they are somewhat protected from losses and their annual return is guaranteed. With a conversion privilege, debtholders or preferred stockholders can enjoy the residual benefits of common shareholders should the company perform well.

A conversion option is valuable and yields a higher price for the securities than they would otherwise command. However, conversion privileges impose a cost on common shareholders. That is, the higher market price received for convertible securities is offset by the cost imposed on the subordinate (common) securities.

One final note, diluted earnings per share (EPS) takes into account the potentially dilutive effect of convertible securities. Specifically, the diluted EPS computation assumes conversion at the beginning of the year (or when the security is issued if during the year). The earnings available to common shares in the numerator are increased by any forgone after-tax interest expense or preferred dividends, and the additional shares that would have been issued in the conversion increase the shares outstanding in the denominator (see Module 5).

MODULE-END REVIEW

Assume that **IBM** has issued the following convertible debentures: each $1,000 bond is convertible into 200 shares of $1 par common. Assume that the bonds were sold at a discount, and that each bond has a current unamortized discount equal to $150. Using the financial statements effect template, illustrate the effects on the financial statements of the conversion of one of these convertible debentures.

Solution

	Balance Sheet							Income Statement		
Transaction	Cash Asset	+	Noncash Assets	=	Liabil- ities	+	Contrib. Capital	+	Earned Capital	Rev- enues − Expen- ses = Net Income
Convert a bond with $850 book value into 200 common shares with $1 par value					−850 = Long-Term Debt		+200 Common Stock +650 Additional Paid-In Capital			=

LTD 850
CS 200
APIC 650

LTD
850 |
CS
| 200
APIC
| 650

GUIDANCE ANSWERS

MANAGERIAL DECISION   **You Are the Chief Financial Officer**

Several points must be considered. (1) Treasury shares are likely to prop up earnings per share (EPS). While the EPS numerator (earnings) is likely dampened by the use of cash for the stock repurchase, EPS is likely to increase because of the reduced shares in the denominator. (2) Another motivation is that, if the shares are sufficiently undervalued (in management's opinion), the stock repurchase and subsequent resale can provide a better return than alternative investments. (3) Stock repurchases send a strong signal to the market that management feels its stock is undervalued. This is more credible than merely making that argument with analysts. On the other hand, company cash is diverted from other investments. This is bothersome if such investments are mutually exclusive either now or in the future.

DISCUSSION QUESTIONS

Q9-1. Define *par value stock*. What is the significance of a stock's par value from an accounting and analysis perspective?

Q9-2. What are the basic differences between preferred stock and common stock? What are the typical features of preferred stock?

Q9-3. What features make preferred stock similar to debt? Similar to common stock?

Q9-4. What is meant by preferred dividends in arrears? If dividends are two years in arrears on $500,000 of 6% preferred stock, and dividends are declared at the end of this year, what amount of total dividends must the company pay to preferred shareholders before paying any dividends to common shareholders?

Q9-5. Distinguish between authorized shares and issued shares. Why might the number of shares issued be more than the number of shares outstanding?

Q9-6. Describe the difference between contributed capital and earned capital. Specifically, how can earned capital be considered as an investment by the company's shareholders?

Q9-7. How does the account "additional paid-in capital" (APIC) arise? Does the amount of APIC reported on the balance sheet relative to the common stock amount provide any information about the financial condition of the company?

Q9-8. Define *stock split*. What are the major reasons for a stock split?

Q9-9. Define *treasury stock*. Why might a corporation acquire treasury stock? How is treasury stock reported in the balance sheet?

Q9-10. If a corporation purchases 600 shares of its own common stock at $10 per share and resells them at $14 per share, where would the $2,400 increase in capital be reported in the financial statements? Why is no gain reported?

Q9-11. A corporation has total stockholders' equity of $4,628,000 and one class of $2 par value common stock. The corporation has 500,000 shares authorized; 300,000 shares issued; 260,000 shares outstanding; and 40,000 shares as treasury stock. What is its book value per share?

Q9-12. What is a stock dividend? How does a common stock dividend distributed to common shareholders affect their respective ownership interests?

Q9-13. What is the difference between the accounting for a small stock dividend and the accounting for a large stock dividend?

Q9-14. Employee stock options potentially dilute earnings per share (EPS). What can companies do to offset these dilutive effects and how might this action affect the balance sheet?

Q9-15. What information is reported in a statement of stockholders' equity?

Q9-16. What items are typically reported under the stockholders' equity category of other comprehensive income (OCI)?

Q9-17. What is the difference between a spin-off and a split-off? Under what circumstances can either result in the recognition of a gain in the income statement?

Q9-18. Describe the accounting for a convertible bond. Can the conversion ever result in the recognition of a gain in the income statement?

MINI EXERCISES

M9-19. Analyzing and Identifying Financial Statement Effects of Stock Issuances (LO1)
On June 1, 2007, Beatty Company, (*a*) issues 8,000 shares of $50 par value preferred stock at $68 cash per share and (*b*) issues 12,000 shares of $1 par value common stock at $10 cash per share. Indicate the financial statement effects of these two issuances using the financial statement effects template.

M9-20. Analyzing and Identifying Financial Statement Effects of Stock Issuances (LO1)
On September 1, 2007, Magliolo, Inc., (*a*) issues 18,000 shares of $10 par value preferred stock at $48 cash per share and (*b*) issues 120,000 shares of $2 par value common stock at $37 cash per share. Indicate the financial statement effects of these two issuances using the financial statement effects template.

M9-21. Distinguishing between Common Stock and Additional Paid-in Capital (LO1)
Following is the 2005 stockholders' equity section from the Cisco Systems, Inc., balance sheet.

Cisco Systems, Inc.
(CSCO)

Shareholders' Equity (in millions, except par value)	July 30, 2005
Preferred stock, no par value: 5 shares authorized; none issued and outstanding	$ —
Common stock and additional paid-in capital, $0.001 par value: 20,000 shares authorized; 6,331 shares issued and outstanding at July 30, 2005	22,394
Retained earnings	506
Accumulated other comprehensive income.	274
Total shareholders' equity	$23,174

   a. For the $22,394 million reported as "common stock and additional paid-in capital," what portion is common stock and what portion is additional paid-in capital?

   b. Explain why Cisco does not report the two components described in part *a* separately.

M9-22. Identifying Financial Statement Effects of Stock Issuance and Repurchase (LO1)

On January 1, 2007, Bartov Company issues 5,000 shares of $100 par value preferred stock at $250 cash per share. On March 1, the company repurchases 5,000 shares of previously issued $1 par value common stock at $83 cash per share. Use the financial statement effects template to record these two transactions.

M9-23. Assessing the Financial Statement Effects of a Stock Split (LO2)

Procter & Gamble
Company (PG)

Procter & Gamble Company discloses the following footnote to its 10-K report:

> **Stock Split** In March 2004, the Company's Board of Directors approved a two-for-one stock split effective for common and preferred shareholders of record as of May 21, 2004. The financial statements, notes and other references to share and per share data have been restated to reflect the stock split for all periods presented.

What restatements has P&G made to its balance sheet as a result of the stock split?

M9-24. Reconciling Common Stock and Treasury Stock Balances (LO1)

Abercrombie & Fitch
(ANF)

Following is the stockholders' equity section from the Abercrombie & Fitch balance sheet.

Shareholders' Equity ($ thousands)	January 28, 2006	January 29, 2005
Class A common stock—$.01 par value: 150,000,000 shares authorized and 103,300,000 shares issued at January 28, 2006 and January 29, 2005, respectively	$ 1,033	$ 1,033
Paid-in capital	161,678	140,251
Retained earnings	1,357,791	1,076,023
Accumulated other comprehensive income.	(796)	—
Deferred compensation	26,206	15,048
Treasury stock at average cost: 15,573,789 and 17,262,943 shares at January 28, 2006 and January 29, 2005, respectively	(550,795)	(563,029)
Total shareholders' equity	$ 995,117	$ 669,326

   a. Show the computation to yield the $1,033 balance reported for common stock.

   b. How many shares are outstanding at its 2006 fiscal year-end?

   c. Use the common stock and paid-in capital accounts to determine the average price at which Abercrombie & Fitch issued its common stock.

   d. Use the treasury stock account to determine the average price Abercrombie & Fitch paid when it repurchased its common shares.

M9-25. Identifying and Analyzing Financial Statement Effects of Cash Dividends (LO2)

Freid Company has outstanding 6,000 shares of $50 par value, 6% preferred stock, and 40,000 shares of $1 par value common stock. The company has $328,000 of retained earnings. At year-end, the company declares and pays the regular $3 per share cash dividend on preferred stock and a $2.20 per share cash dividend on common stock. Use the financial statement effects template to indicate the effects of these two dividend payments.

M9-26. **Analyzing and Identifying Financial Statement Effects of Stock Dividends** (LO2)

Dutta Corp. has outstanding 70,000 shares of $5 par value common stock. At year-end, the company declares and issues a 4% common stock dividend when the market price of the stock is $21 per share. Use the financial statement effects template to indicate the effects of this stock dividend declaration and payment.

M9-27. **Analyzing, Identifying and Explaining the Effects of a Stock Split** (LO2)

On September 1, 2007, Weiss Company has 250,000 shares of $15 par value ($165 market value) common stock that are issued and outstanding. Its balance sheet on that date shows the following account balances relating to its common stock:

Common stock........................	$3,750,000
Paid-in capital in excess of par value.......	2,250,000

On September 2, 2007 Weiss splits its stock 3-for-2 and reduces the par value to $10 per share.

a. How many shares of common stock are issued and outstanding immediately after the stock split?
b. What is the dollar balance of the common stock account immediately after the stock split?
c. What is the likely reason that Weiss Company split its stock?

M9-28. **Determining Cash Dividends to Preferred and Common Shareholders** (LO2)

Dechow Company has outstanding 20,000 shares of $50 par value, 6% cumulative preferred stock and 80,000 shares of $10 par value common stock. The company declares and pays cash dividends amounting to $160,000.

a. If there are no preferred dividends in arrears, how much in total dividends, and in dividends per share, does Dechow pay to each class of stock?
b. If there are one year's dividends in arrears on the preferred stock, how much in total dividends, and in dividends per share, does Dechow pay to each class of stock?

M9-29. **Reconciling Retained Earnings** (LO2)

Use the following data to reconcile the 2007 retained earnings (that is, explain the change in retained earnings during the year) for Bamber Company.

Total retained earnings, December 31, 2006	$347,000
Stock dividends declared and paid in 2007.....	28,000
Cash dividends declared and paid in 2007	35,000
Net income for 2007......................	94,000

M9-30. **Interpreting a Spin-Off Disclosure** (LO3)

Bristol-Myers Squibb discloses the following in notes to its 2003 10-K report.

Bristol-Myers Squibb (BMY)

The Company spun off Zimmer Holdings, Inc. (Zimmer), in a tax-free distribution, resulting in a common stock dividend of $156 million.

a. Describe the difference between a spin-off and a split-off.
b. What effects did BMY's spin-off have on its balance sheet and its income statement?

M9-31. **Interpreting a Proposed Split-Off Disclosure** (LO3)

Viacom, Inc., reports the following footnote in its 2005 10-K.

Viacom, Inc. (VIA)

DISCONTINUED OPERATIONS In 2004, Viacom completed the exchange offer for the split-off of Blockbuster Inc. ("Blockbuster") (NYSE: BBI and BBI.B). Under the terms of the offer, Viacom accepted 27,961,165 shares of Viacom common stock in exchange for the 144 million common shares of Blockbuster that Viacom owned. Each share of Viacom Class A or Class B common stock accepted for exchange by Viacom was exchanged for 5.15 shares of Blockbuster common stock, consisting of 2.575 shares of Blockbuster class A common stock and 2.575 shares of Blockbuster class B common stock.

a. Describe the accounting for a split-off.
b. How will the proposed split-off affect the number of Viacom shares outstanding?
c. Under what circumstances will Viacom be able to report a gain for this proposed split-off?

M9-32. **Interpreting Disclosure Related to the Split-Off of AT&T Wireless** (LO3)

AT&T (T)

AT&T reports the following footnote to its 2003 10-K.

> In 2001, we realized a tax-free noncash gain on the disposition of discontinued operations of $13.5 billion, representing the difference between the fair value of the AT&T Wireless tracking stock at the date of the split-off and our book value of AT&T Wireless.

a. Describe the accounting for a split-off.
b. Describe the circumstances that allowed AT&T to recognize a gain on this split-off.
c. How should you interpret the gain from this split-off in your analysis of AT&T for 2003?

M9-33. **Analyzing Financial Statement Effects of Convertible Securities** (LO3)

JetBlue Airways Corporation (JBLU)

JetBlue Airways Corporation reports the following footnote to its 2005 10-K.

> In March 2005, we completed a public offering of $250 million aggregate principal amount of 3¾% convertible unsecured debentures due 2035, which are currently convertible into 14.6 million shares of our common stock at a price of approximately $17.10 per share.

a. Describe the effects on JetBlue's balance sheet if the convertible bonds are converted.
b. Would the conversion affect earnings? Explain.

EXERCISES

E9-34. **Identifying and Analyzing Financial Statement Effects of Stock Transactions** (LO1)

Lipe Company reports the following transactions relating to its stock accounts.

Feb 20	Issued 10,000 shares of $1 par value common stock at $25 cash per share
Feb 21	Issued 15,000 shares of $100 par value, 8% preferred stock at $275 cash per share.
Jun 30	Purchased 2,000 shares of its own common stock at $15 cash per share.
Sep 25	Sold 1,000 shares of its treasury stock at $21 cash per share.

Use the financial statement effects template to indicate the effects from each of these transactions.

E9-35. **Analyzing and Identifying Financial Statement Effects of Stock Transactions** (LO1)

McNichols Corp. reports the following transactions relating to its stock accounts in 2007.

Jan 15	Issued 25,000 shares of $5 par value common stock at $17 cash per share
Jan 20	Issued 6,000 shares of $50 par value, 8% preferred stock at $78 cash per share.
Mar 31	Purchased 3,000 shares of its own common stock at $20 cash per share.
June 25	Sold 2,000 shares of its treasury stock at $26 cash per share.
July 15	Sold the remaining 1,000 shares of treasury stock at $19 cash per share.

Use the financial statement effects template to indicate the effects from each of these transactions.

E9-36. **Analyzing and Computing Average Issue Price and Treasury Stock Cost** (LO1)

Best Buy (BBY)

Following is the stockholders' equity section from the Best Buy balance sheet.

Shareholders' Equity ($ millions)	February 25, 2006	February 26, 2005
Preferred stock, $1.00 par value: Authorized—400,000 shares; Issued and outstanding—none	$ —	$ —
Common stock, $.10 par value: Authorized—1 billion shares; Issued and outstanding—485,098,000 and 492,512,000 shares, respectively	49	49
Additional paid-in capital	643	936
Retained earnings	4,304	3,315
Accumulated other comprehensive income	261	149
Total shareholders' equity	$5,257	$4,449

Best Buy also reports the following statement of stockholders' equity.

($ and shares in millions)	Common Shares	Common Stock	Additional Paid-in Capital	Retained Earnings	Accumulated Other Comprehensive Income	Total
Balances at February 26, 2005	493	$49	$936	$3,315	$149	$4,449
Net earnings..................	—	—	—	1,140	—	1,140
Other comprehensive income, net of tax:						
Foreign currency translation adjustments...............	—	—	—	—	101	101
Other.....................	—	—	—	—	11	11
Total comprehensive income						1,252
Stock options exercised.........	9	1	256	—	—	257
Tax benefit from stock options exercised and employee stock purchase plan...........	—	—	55	—	—	55
Issuance of common stock under employee stock purchase plan...	1	—	35	—	—	35
Stock-based compensation.......	—	—	132	—	—	132
Common stock dividends, $0.31 per share..............	—	—	—	(151)	—	(151)
Repurchase of common stock.....	(18)	(1)	(771)	—	—	(772)
Balances at February 25, 2006 ...	485	$49	$643	$4,304	$261	$5,257

a. Show the computation to arrive at the $49 million in the common stock account.
b. At what average price were the Best Buy shares issued?
c. Reconcile the beginning and ending balances of retained earnings.
d. Best Buy reports $101 million in an account labeled foreign currency translation adjustments. Explain what this account represents. What effect has this account had on net earnings for the year?
e. Best Buy reports an increase in stockholders' equity relating to the exercise of stock options. This transaction involves the purchase of common stock by employees at a pre-set price. Describe how this transaction affects stockholders' equity.
f. Describe the transaction relating to the "repurchase of common stock" line in the statement of stockholders' equity.

E9-37. **Analyzing Cash Dividends on Preferred and Common Stock** (LO2)

Moser Company began business on March 1, 2005. At that time, it issued 20,000 shares of $60 par value, 7% cumulative preferred stock and 100,000 shares of $5 par value common stock. Through the end of 2007, there has been no change in the number of preferred and common shares outstanding.

a. Assume that Moser declared and paid cash dividends of $0 in 2005, another $183,000 in 2006, and $200,000 in 2007. Compute the total cash dividends and the dividends per share paid to each class of stock in 2005, 2006, and 2007.
b. Assume that Moser declared and paid cash dividends of $0 in 2005, another $84,000 in 2006, and $150,000 in 2007. Compute the total cash dividends and the dividends per share paid to each class of stock in 2005, 2006, and 2007.

E9-38. **Analyzing Cash Dividends on Preferred and Common Stocks** (LO2)

Potter Company has outstanding 15,000 shares of $50 par value, 8% preferred stock and 50,000 shares of $5 par value common stock. During its first three years in business, it declared and paid no cash dividends in the first year, $280,000 in the second year, and $60,000 in the third year.

a. If the preferred stock is cumulative, determine the total amount of cash dividends paid to each class of stock in each of the three years.
b. If the preferred stock is noncumulative, determine the total amount of cash dividends paid to each class of stock in each of the three years.

E9-39.   **Analyzing and Computing Issue Price, Treasury Stock Cost, and Shares Outstanding**   (LO1)

Altria (MO)   Following is the stockholders' equity section from Altria's 2005 balance sheet.

December 31 ($ million)	2005
Common stock, par value $0.33\frac{1}{3}$ per share (2,805,961,317 shares issued)	$ 935
Additional paid-in capital	6,061
Earnings reinvested in the business.	54,666
Accumulated other comprehensive losses (including currency translation of $1,317 in 2005) . .	(1,853)
Cost of repurchased stock (721,696,918 shares in 2005)	(24,102)
Total stockholders' equity	$35,707

a.   Show the computation to derive the $935 million for common stock.

b.   At what average price has Altria issued its common stock?

c.   How many shares of Altria common stock are outstanding as of December 31, 2005?

d.   At what average cost has Altria repurchased its treasury stock as of December 31, 2005?

e.   Why would a company such as Altria want to repurchase $24,102 million of its common stock?

E9-40.   **Analyzing Cash Dividends on Preferred and Common Stock**   (LO2)

Skinner Company began business on June 30, 2005. At that time, it issued 18,000 shares of $50 par value, 6% cumulative preferred stock and 90,000 shares of $10 par value common stock. Through the end of 2007, there has been no change in the number of preferred and common shares outstanding.

a.   Assume that Skinner declared and paid cash dividends of $63,000 in 2005, $0 in 2006, and $378,000 in 2007. Compute the total cash dividends and the dividends per share paid to each class of stock in 2005, 2006, and 2007.

b.   Assume that Skinner declared and paid cash dividends of $0 in 2005, $108,000 in 2006, and $189,000 in 2007. Compute the total cash dividends and the dividends per share paid to each class of stock in 2005, 2006, and 2007.

E9-41.   **Analyzing and Identifying Financial Statement Effects of Dividends**   (LO2)

Chaney Company has outstanding 25,000 shares of $10 par value common stock. It also has $405,000 of retained earnings. Near the current year-end, the company declares and pays a cash dividend of $1.90 per share and declares and issues a 4% stock dividend. The market price of the stock the day the dividends are declared is $35 per share. Use the financial statement effects template to indicate the effects of these two separate dividend transactions.

E9-42.   **Identifying and Analyzing Financial Statement Effects of Dividends**   (LO2)

The stockholders' equity of Revsine Company at December 31, 2006, appears below.

Common stock, $10 par value, 200,000 shares authorized; 80,000 shares issued and outstanding.	$800,000
Paid-in capital in excess of par value.	480,000
Retained earnings	305,000

During 2007, the following transactions occurred:

May 12   Declared and issued a 7% stock dividend; the common stock market value was $18 per share.

Dec. 31   Declared and paid a cash dividend of 75 cents per share.

a.   Use the financial statement effects template to indicate the effects of these transactions.

b.   Reconcile retained earnings for 2007 assuming that the company reports 2007 net income of $283,000.

E9-43. **Analyzing and Identifying Financial Statement Effects of Dividends** (LO2)

The stockholders' equity of Kinney Company at December 31, 2006, is shown below.

5% preferred stock, $100 par value, 10,000 shares authorized; 4,000 shares issued and outstanding..........................	$ 400,000
Common stock, $5 par value, 200,000 shares authorized; 50,000 shares issued and outstanding.........................	250,000
Paid-in capital in excess of par value—preferred stock.............	40,000
Paid-in capital in excess of par value—common stock.............	300,000
Retained earnings	656,000
Total stockholders' equity	$1,646,000

The following transactions, among others, occurred during 2007:

Apr. 1   Declared and issued a 100% stock dividend on all outstanding shares of common stock. The market value of the stock was $11 per share.

Dec. 7   Declared and issued a 3% stock dividend on all outstanding shares of common stock. The market value of the stock was $14 per share.

Dec. 20   Declared and paid (1) the annual cash dividend on the preferred stock and (2) a cash dividend of 80 cents per common share.

a.   Use the financial statement effects template to indicate the effects of these separate transactions.

b.   Compute retained earnings for 2007 assuming that the company reports 2007 net income of $253,000.

E9-44. **Analyzing, Identifying and Explaining the Effects of a Stock Split** (LO2)

On March 1 of the current year, Xie Company has 400,000 shares of $20 par value common stock that are issued and outstanding. Its balance sheet shows the following account balances relating to common stock.

Common stock.........................	$8,000,000
Paid-in capital in excess of par value.......	3,400,000

On March 2, Xie Company splits its common stock 2-for-1 and reduces the par value to $10 per share.

a.   How many shares of common stock are issued and outstanding immediately after the stock split?

b.   What is the dollar balance in its common stock account immediately after the stock split?

c.   What is the dollar balance in its paid-in capital in excess of par value account immediately after the stock split?

E9-45. **Analyzing and Computing Issue Price, Treasury Stock Cost, and Shares Outstanding** (LO1)

Following is the stockholders' equity section of the 2005 Caterpillar, Inc., balance sheet.

Caterpillar, Inc. (CAT)

Stockholders' Equity ($ millions)	2005	2004	2003
Common stock of $1.00 par value; Authorized shares: 900,000,000; Issued shares (2005, 2004 and 2003—814,894,624) at paid-in amount	$1,859	$1,231	$1,059
Treasury stock (2005—144,027,405 shares; 2004—129,020,726 shares; 2003—127,370,544 shares) at cost....................	(4,637)	(3,277)	(2,914)
Profit employed in the business..............................	11,808	9,937	8,450
Accumulated other comprehensive income......................	(598)	(424)	(517)
Total stockholders' equity	**$8,432**	**$7,467**	**$6,078**

CAT also provides the following schedule in its statement of stockholders' equity:

($ millions)	2005	2004	2003
Common stock			
Balance at beginning of year	$1,231	$1,059	$1,034
Common shares issued from treasury stock	290	172	25
Impact of 2-for-1 stock split	338	—	—
Balance at year-end	$1,859	$1,231	$1,059
Treasury stock			
Balance at beginning of year	$(3,277)	$(2,914)	$(2,669)
Shares issued: 2005—18,912,521; 2004—12,216,618; 2003—9,913,946.	324	176	160
Shares repurchased: 2005—33,919,200; 2004—13,866,800; 2003—10,900,000.	(1,684)	(539)	(405)
Balance at year-end	$(4,637)	$(3,277)	$(2,914)

Stock Split On June 8, 2005, Caterpillar's Board of Directors approved a 2-for-1 stock split in the form of a 100 percent stock dividend. The stock split shares were distributed on July 13, 2005, to stockholders of record at the close of business on June 22, 2005. Capital accounts, share data and profit per share data reflect the stock split, applied retroactively, to all periods presented.

a. How many shares of Caterpillar common stock are outstanding at year-end 2005?
b. What does the phrase "at paid-in amount" in the stockholders' equity section mean?
c. At what average cost has Caterpillar repurchased its stock as of year-end 2005?
d. Why would a company such as Caterpillar want to repurchase its common stock?
e. Explain how CAT's "issued shares" remains constant over the three-year period while the dollar amount of its common stock account increases.
f. Show the computation of the $338 million addition to capital as a result of the 2-for-1 stock split.

E9-46.   Analyzing Equity Changes from Convertible Preferred and Employee Stock Options (LO3)

JetBlue Airways
Corporation (JBLU)

Following is the 2002 statement of stockholders' equity for JetBlue Airways Corporation.

($ thousands)	Convertible Redeemable Preferred Stock	Common Stock	Additional Paid-in Capital	Accumulated Deficit/ Retained Earnings	Unearned Compensation	Accumulated Other Comprehensive Income	Total
Balance at December 31, 2001	$210,441	$ 65	$ 3,868	$(33,117)	$(2,983)	$ —	$ (32,167)
Net income	—	—	—	54,908	—	—	54,908
Other comprehensive income	—	—	—	—	—	187	187
Total comprehensive income							55,095
Accrued undeclared dividends on preferred stock	5,955	—	—	(5,955)	—	—	(5,955)
Proceeds from initial public offering, net of offering expenses	—	101	168,177	—	—	—	168,278
Conversion of redeemable preferred stock	(216,394)	461	215,933	—	—	—	216,394
Exercise of common stock options	—	8	1,058	—	—	—	1,066
Tax benefit of stock options exercised	—	—	6,568	—	—	—	6,568

continued

continued

($ thousands)	Convertible Redeemable Preferred Stock	Common Stock	Additional Paid-in Capital	Accumulated Deficit/ Retained Earnings	Unearned Compensation	Accumulated Other Comprehensive Income	Total
Unearned compensation on common stock options, net of forfeitures	—	—	8,144	—	(8,144)	—	—
Amortization of unearned compensation	—	—	—	—	1,713	—	1,713
Stock issued under crew member stock purchase plan	—	3	3,711	—	—	—	3,714
Other	(2)	—	12	(45)	—	—	(33)
Balance at December 31, 2002 . . .	$ —	$638	$407,471	$ 15,791	$(9,414)	$187	$414,673

Heading: **Stockholders' Equity (Deficit)** spans Common Stock, Additional Paid-in Capital, Accumulated Deficit/Retained Earnings, Unearned Compensation, and Accumulated Other Comprehensive Income.

a. Identify the line labeled, "Conversion of redeemable preferred stock." Discuss the linkage among the convertible redeemable preferred stock, common stock, and additional paid-in capital accounts for 2002.

b. During 2002, JetBlue issued 811,623 shares to employees who exercised stock options. How did these option exercises affect stockholders' equity in 2002? JetBlue's stock traded in the $20 per share range during that same period. How does this compare to per share price employees paid for the stock at exercise?

E9-47. **Analyzing and Computing Issue Price, Treasury Stock Cost, and Shares Outstanding** (LO1)

Following is the stockholders' equity and minority interest sections of the 2005 Merck & Co., Inc., balance sheet.

Merck & Co., Inc. (MRK)

Stockholders' Equity ($ millions)	2005
Common stock, one cent par value; Authorized—5,400,000,000 shares; Issued—2,976,223,337 shares—2005	$ 29.8
Other paid-in capital	6,900.0
Retained earnings	37,918.9
Accumulated other comprehensive income	52.3
	44,901.0
Less treasury stock, at cost; 794,299,347 shares—2005	26,984.4
Total stockholders' equity	$17,916.6

a. Explain the derivation of the $29.8 million in the common stock account.
b. At what average price were the Merck common shares issued?
c. At what average cost was the Merck treasury stock purchased?
d. How many common shares are outstanding as of December 31, 2005?

E9-48. **Interpreting a Split-Off Disclosure** (LO3)

IMS Health reports the following footnote to its 2003 10-K related to the split-off of its CTS subsidiary.

IMS Health (RX)

CTS Split-OFF On February 6, 2003, the Company completed an exchange offer to distribute its majority interest in CTS. The Company exchanged 0.309 shares of CTS class B common shares for each share of the Company that was tendered. Under terms of the offer, the Company accepted 36,540 IMS common shares tendered in exchange for all 11,291 CTS common shares that the Company owned. As the offer was oversubscribed, the Company accepted tendered IMS shares on a pro-rata basis in proportion to the number of shares tendered. The proration factor was 21.115717%. As a result of this exchange offer, during 2003, the Company recorded a net gain from discontinued operations of $496,887. This gain was based on the Company's closing market price on February 6, 2003 multiplied by the 36,540 shares of IMS common shares accepted in the offer, net of the Company's carrying value of CTS and after deducting direct and incremental expenses related to the exchange offer.

a. Describe the accounting procedures for a split-off.
b. Describe the circumstances that allowed IMS to recognize a gain from this split-off.
c. How should we interpret this gain in our analysis of the company for 2003?

PROBLEMS

P9-49. **Analyzing and Identifying Financial Statement Effects of Stock Transactions** **(LO1)**

The stockholders' equity section of Gupta Company at December 31, 2006, follows:

8% preferred stock, $25 par value, 50,000 shares authorized; 6,800 shares issued and outstanding.........................	$170,000
Common stock, $10 par value, 200,000 shares authorized; 50,000 shares issued and outstanding........................	500,000
Paid-in capital in excess of par value—preferred stock..............	68,000
Paid-in capital in excess of par value—common stock..............	200,000
Retained earnings	270,000

During 2007, the following transactions occurred:

Jan. 10 Issued 28,000 shares of common stock for $17 cash per share.
Jan. 23 Repurchased 8,000 shares of common stock at $19 cash per share.
Mar. 14 Sold one-half of the treasury shares acquired January 23 for $21 cash per share.
July 15 Issued 3,200 shares of preferred stock for $128,000 cash.
Nov. 15 Sold 1,000 of the treasury shares acquired January 23 for $24 cash per share.

Required
a. Use the financial statement effects template to indicate the effects from each of these transactions.
b. Prepare the December 31, 2007, stockholders' equity section of the balance sheet assuming the company reports 2007 net income of $59,000.

P9-50. **Analyzing and Identifying Financial Statement Effects of Stock Transactions** **(LO1)**

The stockholders' equity of Sougiannis Company at December 31, 2006, follows:

7% Preferred stock, $100 par value, 20,000 shares authorized; 5,000 shares issued and outstanding.........................	$ 500,000
Common stock, $15 par value, 100,000 shares authorized; 40,000 shares issued and outstanding........................	600,000
Paid-in capital in excess of par value—preferred stock..............	24,000
Paid-in capital in excess of par value—common stock..............	360,000
Retained earnings	325,000
Total stockholders' equity	$1,809,000

The following transactions, among others, occurred during the year:

Jan. 12 Announced a 3-for-1 common stock split, reducing the par value of the common stock to $5 per share. The authorized shares were increased to 300,000 shares.
Sept. 1 Repurchased 10,000 shares of common stock at $10 cash per share.
Oct. 12 Sold 1,500 treasury shares acquired September 1 at $12 cash per share.
Nov. 21 Issued 5,000 shares of common stock at $11 cash per share.
Dec. 28 Sold 1,200 treasury shares acquired September 1 at $9 cash per share.

Required
a. Use the financial statement effects template to indicate the effects from each of these transactions.
b. Prepare the December 31, 2007, stockholders' equity section of the balance sheet assuming that the company reports 2007 net income of $83,000.

P9-51. **Identifying and Analyzing Financial Statement Effects of Stock Transactions** (LO1)

The stockholders' equity of Verrecchia Company at December 31, 2006, follows:

Common stock, $5 par value, 350,000 shares authorized;	
150,000 shares issued and outstanding......................	$750,000
Paid-in capital in excess of par value..........................	600,000
Retained earnings	346,000

During 2007, the following transactions occurred:

Jan. 5   Issued 10,000 shares of common stock for $12 cash per share.

Jan. 18 Repurchased 4,000 shares of common stock at $14 cash per share.

Mar 12 Sold one-fourth of the treasury shares acquired January 18 for $17 cash per share.

July 17 Sold 500 shares of the remaining treasury stock for $13 cash per share.

Oct. 1   Issued 5,000 shares of 8%, $25 par value preferred stock for $35 cash per share. This is the first issuance of preferred shares from the 50,000 authorized preferred shares.

Required

a.   Use the financial statement effects template to indicate the effects of each transaction.

b.   Prepare the December 31, 2007, stockholders' equity section of the balance sheet assuming that the company reports net income of $72,500 for the year.

P9-52. **Identifying and Analyzing Financial Statement Effects of Stock Transactions** (LO1)

Following is the stockholders' equity of Dennis Corporation at December 31, 2006:

8% preferred stock, $50 par value, 10,000 shares authorized;	
7,000 shares issued and outstanding.........................	$ 350,000
Common stock, $20 par value, 50,000 shares authorized;	
25,000 shares issued and outstanding........................	500,000
Paid-in capital in excess of par value—preferred stock..............	70,000
Paid-in capital in excess of par value—common stock..............	385,000
Retained earnings	238,000
Total stockholders' equity	$1,543,000

The following transactions, among others, occurred during the year:

Jan. 15 Issued 1,000 shares of preferred stock for $62 cash per share.

Jan. 20 Issued 4,000 shares of common stock at $36 cash per share.

May 18 Announced a 2-for-1 common stock split, reducing the par value of the common stock to $10 per share. The authorization was increased to 100,000 shares.

June 1   Issued 2,000 shares of common stock for $60,000 cash.

Sept. 1   Repurchased 2,500 shares of common stock at $18 cash per share.

Oct. 12 Sold 900 treasury shares at $21 cash per share.

Dec. 22 Issued 500 shares of preferred stock for $59 cash per share.

Required

Use the financial statement effects template to indicate the effects of each transaction.

P9-53. **Analyzing and Interpreting Equity Accounts and Comprehensive Income** (LO2)

Following is the stockholders' equity section of the 2006 balance sheet for Procter & Gamble Company and its statement of stockholders' equity.

Procter & Gamble Company (PG)

Amounts in millions; June 30	2006	2005
Shareholders' Equity		
Convertible Class A preferred stock, stated value $1 per share (600 shares authorized)...	$ 1,451	$ 1,483
Non-Voting Class B preferred stock, stated value $1 per share (200 shares authorized)...	—	—
Common stock, stated value $1 per share (10,000 shares authorized; shares outstanding: 2006—3,975.8, 2005—2,976.6)..................	3,976	2,977
Additional paid-in capital	57,856	3,030
Reserve for ESOP debt retirement..................................	(1,288)	(1,259)
Accumulated other comprehensive income...........................	(518)	(1,566)
Treasury stock, at cost (shares held: 2006—797.0, 2005—503.7)...........	(34,235)	(17,194)
Retained earnings	35,666	31,004
Total shareholders' equity	$62,908	$18,475

Consolidated Statement of Shareholders' Equity

Dollars in millions/ Shares in thousands	Common Shares Outstanding	Common Stock	Preferred Stock	Additional Paid-in Capital	Reserve for ESOP Debt Retirement	Accumulated Other Comprehensive Income	Treasury Stock	Retained Earnings	Total	Total Comprehensive Income
Bal. June 30, 2005....	2,472,934	$2,977	$1,483	$3,030	$(1,259)	$(1,566)	$(17,194)	$31,004	$18,475	
Net earnings.........								8,684	8,684	$8,684
Other comprehensive income:										
Financial statement translation						1,316			1,316	1,316
Net investment hedges, net of $472 tax.............						(786)			(786)	(786)
Other, net of tax benefits						518			518	518
Total comprehensive income..........										$9,732
Dividends to shareholders:										
Common..........								(3,555)	(3,555)	
Preferred, net of tax benefits								(148)	(148)	
Treasury purchases ...	(297,132)			(9)			(16,821)		(16,830)	
Employee plan issuances	36,763	16		1,308			887		(319) 1,892	
Preferred stock conversions.......	3,788		(32)	5			27		—	
Gillette acquisition	962,488	983		53,522			(1,134)		53,371	
Change in ESOP debt reserve					(29)				(29)	
Bal. June 30, 2006....	3,178,841	$3,976	$1,451	$57,856	$(1,288)	$ (518)	$(34,235)	$35,666	$62,908	

Required

a. What does the term *convertible* mean?

b. How many shares of common stock did Procter & Gamble issue when convertible class A preferred stock was converted during fiscal 2006?

c. Assuming that the convertible class A preferred stock was sold at par value, at what average price were the common shares issued as of year-end 2006?

d. What is the accumulated other comprehensive income account? Explain.

    e.   What items are included in the $9,732 million 'total comprehensive income' for the year ended June 30, 2006? How do these items affect stockholders' equity? How do these items affect net income?

    f.   What cash dividends did Procter & Gamble pay in 2006 for each class of stock?

P9-54. **Analyzing and Interpreting Equity Accounts and Comprehensive Income** (LO2)

Following is the stockholders' equity section of Fortune Brands balance sheet and its statement of stockholders' equity.

Fortune Brands (FO)

December 31 (In millions, except per share amounts)	2005	2004
$2.67 Convertible preferred stock	$ 6.6	$ 7.1
Common stock, par value $3.125 per share, 229.6 shares issued	717.4	717.4
Paid-in capital	182.8	155.8
Accumulated other comprehensive (loss) income	(22.2)	6.4
Retained earnings	5,890.2	5,447.2
Treasury stock, at cost	(3,129.2)	(3,203.2)
Total stockholders' equity	$3,645.6	$3,130.7

(In millions, except per share amounts)	$2.67 Convertible Preferred Stock	Common Stock	Paid-in Capital	Accumulated Other Comprehensive Income (Loss)	Retained Earnings	Treasury Stock At Cost	Total
Balance at December 31, 2004	$ 7.1	$717.4	$155.8	$ 6.4	$5,447.2	$(3,203.2)	$3,130.7
Comprehensive income							
Net income	—	—	—	—	621.1	—	621.1
Foreign exchange adjustments, net of effect of hedging activities	—	—	—	1.7	—	—	1.7
Minimum pension liability adjustments	—	—	—	(30.3)	—	—	(30.3)
Total comprehensive Income	—	—	—	(28.6)	621.1	—	592.5
Dividends ($1.38 per share)	—	—	—	—	(201.6)	—	(201.6)
Tax benefit on exercise of stock options	—	—	26.0	—	—	—	26.0
Conversion of preferred stock (0.1 shares) and delivery of stock plan shares (1.9 shares)	(0.5)	—	1.0	—	—	74.0	74.5
Spin-off of ACCO World Corporation	—	—	—	—	23.5	—	23.5
Balance at December 31, 2005	$ 6.6	$717.4	$182.8	$(22.2)	$5,890.2	$(3,129.2)	$3,645.6

Discontinued Operation On August 16, 2005, the Company completed the spin-off of the Office products business, ACCO World Corporation (ACCO), to the Company's shareholders. In addition to retaining their shareholdings in Fortune Brands, each Fortune Brands shareholder received one share of ACCO World Corporation for each 4.255 shares of Fortune Brands stock held. Fortune Brands did not record a gain or loss on the transaction as a result of the spin-off. As a part of the spin-off, ACCO paid a cash dividend of $625 million, of which Fortune Brands received $613.3 million and the minority shareholder received $11.7 million. The statements of income and consolidated balance sheets for all prior periods have been adjusted to reflect the presentation of the spin-off of ACCO as a discontinued operation.

Required

    a.   Explain the "$2.67" component of the convertible preferred stock account title.

    b.   Show (confirm) the computation that yields the $717.4 million common stock at year-end 2005.

    c.   Assuming that the convertible preferred stock was sold at par value, at what average price were its common shares issued as of year-end 2005?

  d. What accounts are included in Fortune Brands' accumulated other comprehensive income and loss adjustments for 2005? What other accounts are typically included in accumulated other comprehensive income?

  e. Consider the "Discontinued Operation" note reproduced above from Fortune Brands footnotes. Assuming that the investment in ACCO World Corporation was carried on Fortune Brands' balance sheet at $589.8 million on the date of the spin-off, explain why the spin-off increased Fortune Brands' retained earnings by $23.5 million.

P9-55. **Interpreting Footnote Disclosure on Convertible Debentures** (LO3)

Lucent Technologies reports the following footnote to its 2005 10-K related to its convertible debentures.

> **2.75% series A and B debentures** During the third quarter of fiscal 2003, we sold 2.75% Series A Convertible Senior Debentures and 2.75% Series B Convertible Senior Debentures for an aggregate amount of $1.6 billion, net of the underwriters' discount and related fees and expenses of $46 million. The debentures were issued at a price of $1,000 per debenture and were issued under our universal shelf. The debentures rank equal in priority with all of the existing and future unsecured and unsubordinated indebtedness and senior in right of payment to all of the existing and future subordinated indebtedness. The terms governing the debentures limit our ability to create liens, secure certain indebtedness and merge with or sell substantially all of our assets to another entity. The debentures are convertible into shares of common stock only if (1) the average sale price of our common stock is at least equal to 120% of the applicable conversion price, (2) the average trading price of the debentures is less than 97% of the product of the sale price of the common stock and the conversion rate, (3) the debentures have been called for redemption by us or (4) certain specified corporate actions occur.

Required

  a. How did Lucent initially account for the issuance of the 2.75% debentures, assuming that the conversion option cannot be detached and sold separately?

  b. How will Lucent account for the conversion of the 2.75% debentures, if and when conversion occurs? Specifically, will Lucent recognize any gain or loss related to conversion? Explain.

  c. How are the convertible debentures treated in the computation of basic and diluted earnings per share (EPS)?

  d. How should we treat the convertible debentures in our analysis of Lucent?

P9-56. **Interpreting Disclosure on Convertible Preferred Securities** (LO3)

Lucent Technologies reports the following footnote to its 2003 10-K related to its convertible preferred stock.

> **Mandatorily Redeemable Convertible Preferred Stock** We have 250,000,000 shares of authorized preferred stock. During fiscal 2001, we designated and sold 1,885,000 shares of non-cumulative 8% redeemable convertible preferred stock having an initial liquidation preference of $1,000 per share, subject to accretion. The net proceeds were $1.8 billion, including fees of $54 million. . . . Holders of the preferred stock have no voting rights, except as required by law, and rank junior to our debt obligations. In addition, upon our dissolution or liquidation, holders are entitled to the liquidation preference plus any accrued and unpaid dividends prior to any distribution of net assets to common shareowners . . . Each trust preferred security is convertible at the option of the holder into 206.6116 shares of our common stock.

Required

  a. Explain the terms and phrases: *noncumulative, 8%, convertible,* and *liquidation preference.*

  b. Describe the general impact on Lucent's balance sheet when it issued the preferred shares. (*Hint:* Aggregate all equity into the contributed capital account, that is, do not break out par value and additional paid-in capital.)

  c. Describe the general impact on Lucent's balance sheet for the following transactions related to the mandatorily redeemable convertible preferred stock:

   1. The preferred stock is redeemed for cash.

   2. The preferred stock is converted into common stock

   (*Hint:* Aggregate all equity into the contributed capital account, that is, do not break out par value and additional paid-in capital).

  d. How should we treat the convertible stock for our analysis of Lucent?

CASES

C9-57.   Management Application: Convertible Debt   (LO3)

When convertible debt is issued, the conversion option is not valued, unless it can be detached and sold separately from the debt security. Since many conversion options cannot be separately sold, convertible debt is priced like any other debt (see Module 8). Explain why the accounting for convertible debt with nondetachable options can result in interest expense that is lower if the conversion option had been accounted for separately.

C9-58.   Ethics and Governance: Equity Carve Outs   (LO3)

Many companies use split-offs as a means to unlock shareholder value. The split-off effectively splits the company into two pieces, each of which can then be valued separately by the stock market. If managers are compensated based on reported profit, how might they strategically structure the split-off? What corporate governance issues does this present?

Reporting and Analyzing Off-Balance-Sheet Financing

LEARNING OBJECTIVES

LO1 Describe and illustrate the accounting for capitalized leases. (p. 10-4)

LO2 Describe and illustrate the accounting for pensions. (p. 10-12)

LO3 Explain the accounting for special purpose entities (SPEs). (p. 10-22)

SOUTHWEST AIRLINES

Southwest Airlines is one of the few air carriers to have successfully performed in the past five years. Its management makes the following claim:

> As a result of our discipline and financial conservatism, we have strengthened our balance sheet during the most difficult period in aviation history . . . our unmortgaged assets have a value of nearly $7 billion, and our debt to total capital is approximately 35 percent, including aircraft leases as debt.

Southwest Airline's debt to total capital ratio of 35%, *including aircraft leases as debt*, comes as a surprise to many. Not the ratio part, but the reference to aircraft leases. Many airlines do not own most of the planes that they fly. To a large extent, those planes are owned by commercial leasing companies like General Electric Commercial Credit (GE's financial subsidiary), and are leased to the airlines for periods of one to five years, at which time the airline can extend the leases for an additional period of time.

If structured in a specific way, neither the leased planes (the assets) nor the lease obligation (the liability) appear on Southwest's balance sheet. That non-disclosure can substantially alter investors' perceptions of the capital investment Southwest needs to operate as well as the amount of debt it carries. Including aircraft leases as debt (as Southwest did in computing its 35% ratio quoted above) is an analytical procedure that provides a more complete view of the company's investing and financing activities.

The analytical adjustment adds a huge liability to Southwest's balance sheet: lease payment obligations on aircrafts totaling $1.8 billion, which is a large amount when compared to its net operating assets of $8.4 billion. This module discusses the accounting for leases and explains this analytical adjustment and how to apply it.

Pensions and long-term health care plans are another large obligation for many large companies, including Southwest. Pension and health care liabilities can be enormous. Until recently, information about these obligations was buried in footnotes. Recent accounting rule changes now require companies to report that information on the balance sheet. In particular, the balance sheet now reports the net pension and health care liabilities (the total liability less related investments that fund the liabilities).

For Southwest, the net pension liability is not huge (about $94 million) in comparison with its $14 billion in reported liabilities and equity. However, for American Airlines, a Southwest competitor, the net pension and health care liability exceeds $6.4 billion. That amount is staggering considering American Airlines' total assets are $30 billion. This module walks through the accounting for both pensions and health care obligations. The discussion includes footnote disclosures that convey a wealth of information relating to assumptions underlying estimates of these obligations.

As the market has increased its scrutiny of balance sheets and footnotes, some companies have begun to utilize increasingly sophisticated techniques to shift liabilities (and expenses) to outside entities. This is called *off-balance-sheet financing*. Although the idea of off-balance-sheet financing has been around for decades, the techniques companies use to achieve it have become increasingly complex. One of the more popular techniques is to use special purpose entities (SPEs). Companies use SPEs to finance a wide range of activities from manufacturing facilities to consumer loans. This module discusses SPEs as a financing tool, and explains the accounting for these entities and the required footnote disclosures.

Sources: Southwest Airlines 2005 annual report; Southwest Airlines 2005 Form 10-K; American Airlines 2005 Form 10-K; *Fortune*, January 2007.

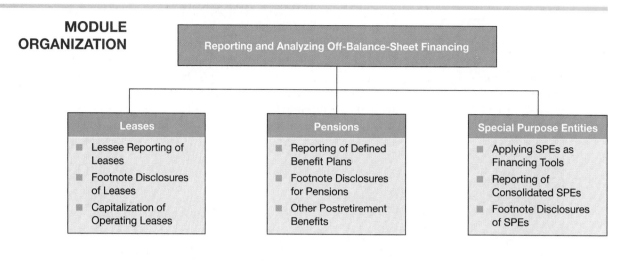

INTRODUCTION

Company stakeholders pay attention to the composition of the balance sheet and its relation to the income statement. This attention extends to their analysis and valuation of both equity and debt securities. Of particular importance in this valuation process is the analysis of return on equity (ROE) and its components: return on net operating assets (RNOA)—including its components of net operating profit margin (NOPM) and net operating asset turnover (NOAT)—and the degree of financial leverage (FLEV), which is a component of nonoperating return. (Module 4 and its appendix explain these measures.)

To value debt securities such as bonds and notes, one must consider a company's financial leverage (claims against assets) and the level of debt service (interest and principal payments), and compare them with expected cash flows. If analysis reveals that ROE and cash flows are inadequate, companies' credit ratings could decline. The resulting higher cost of debt capital could limit the number of investment projects that yield a return greater than their financing cost. This restricts the company's growth and profitability.

Financial managers are aware of the importance of how financial markets perceive their companies. They also recognize the market attention directed at the quality of their balance sheets and income statements. This reality can pressure managers to *window dress* financial statements to present the company's financial condition and performance in the best possible light. Consider the following cases:

- **Case 1.** A company is concerned that its liquidity is perceived as insufficient. Prior to the end of the current financial reporting period, it takes out a short-term bank loan and delays payment of accounts payable. The company's cash and current assets increase, yielding a balance sheet that appears more liquid.

- **Case 2.** A company's level of accounts receivable is perceived as too high, suggesting possible collection problems and reduced liquidity. Prior to the statement date, the company sells receivables to a financial institution or other third party entity. The sale of receivables increases the company's reported cash balance and presents a healthier current financial picture. Further, if inventory is too high, the company can reduce its available quantities and increase its liquidity position by delaying purchases or by inflating sales via steep price markdowns.

- **Case 3.** A company faces the maturity of a long-term liability, such as the maturity of a bond or note. The amount coming due is reported as a current liability (current maturities of long-term debt), thus reducing net working capital. Prior to the end of its accounting period, the company renegotiates the debt to extend the maturity date of the payment or refinances the indebtedness with longer-term debt. The company reports the indebtedness as a long-term liability thereby increasing net working capital.

- **Case 4.** The company's financial leverage is deemed excessive, resulting in lower credit ratings and increased borrowing costs. To remedy the problem, the company issues new common equity and utilizes the proceeds to reduce its indebtedness.

To increase reported solvency and decrease risk metrics, companies generally wish to present a balance sheet with low levels of debt. Companies that are more liquid and less financially leveraged are viewed as less likely to go bankrupt. As a result, the risk of default on their debt is less, resulting in a better credit rating and a lower interest rate.

Companies also generally wish to present a balance sheet with fewer assets. This is driven by return considerations. ROE has two components: operating return and nonoperating return. The latter is a function of the company's effective use of debt. We generally prefer a company's ROE to be derived from operations (RNOA) rather than from its use of debt. So, if a company can maintain a given level of profitability with fewer assets, the related increase in ROE is perceived to be driven by higher RNOA (asset turnover), and not by increased financial leverage.

Off-balance-sheet financing means that assets or liabilities, or both, are not reported on the balance sheet. Even though GAAP requires detailed footnote disclosures, managers generally believe that keeping such assets and liabilities off the balance sheet improves market perception of their operating performance and financial condition. This belief presumes that the market is somewhat inefficient, a notion that persists despite empirical evidence suggesting that analysts adjust balance sheets to include assets and liabilities that managers exclude.

This module explains and illustrates several types of off-balance-sheet financing. Major topics we discuss are leases, pensions, health care liabilities, and special purpose entities (SPEs). This is not an exhaustive list of the techniques that managers have invented to achieve off-balance-sheet financing, but it includes the most common methods. We must keep one point in mind: the relevant information to assess off-balance-sheet financing is mainly in footnotes. While GAAP footnote disclosures on such financing are fairly good, we must have the analytic tools to interpret them and to understand the nature and the magnitude of assets and liabilities that managers have moved off of the balance sheet. This module provides those tools.

LEASES

We begin the discussion of off-balance-sheet financing with leases. The following graphic shows that leasing impacts both sides of the balance sheet (liabilities and assets) and the income statement (leasing expenses are often reported in selling, general and administrative).

LO1 Describe and illustrate the accounting for capitalized leases.

Income Statement	Balance Sheet	
Sales	Cash	Current liabilities
Cost of goods sold	Accounts receivable	Long-term liabilities
Selling, general & administrative	Inventory	
Income taxes	Long-term operating assets	Shareholders' equity
Net income	Investments	

Footnote Disclosures—Off-Balance-Sheet Financing		
Leases	Pensions	SPEs

A lease is a contract between the owner of an asset (the **lessor**) and the party desiring to use that asset (the **lessee**). Since this is a private contract between two willing parties, it is governed only by applicable commercial law, and can include whatever provisions the parties negotiate.

Leases generally provide for the following terms:

- Lessor allows the lessee the unrestricted right to use the asset during the lease term.
- Lessee agrees to make periodic payments to the lessor and to maintain the asset.
- Title to the asset remains with the lessor, who usually takes physical possession of the asset at lease-end unless the lessee negotiates the right to purchase the asset at its market value or other predetermined price.

From the lessor's standpoint, lease payments are set at an amount that yields an acceptable return on investment, commensurate with the lessee's credit rating. The lessor has an investment, and the lessee gains use of the asset.

The lease serves as a financing vehicle, similar to a secured bank loan. However, there are several advantages to leasing over bank financing:

- Leases often require less equity investment by the lessee (borrower) compared with bank financing. Leases usually require the first lease payment be made at the inception of the lease. For a 60-month lease, this amounts to a 1/60 (1.7%) investment by the lessee, compared with a typical bank loan of 70-80% of the asset cost (thus requiring 20-30% equity by the borrower).

- Since leases are contracts between two parties, their terms can be structured to meet both parties' needs. For example, a lease can allow variable payments to match the lessee's seasonal cash inflows or have graduated payments for start-up companies.

- If the lease is properly structured, neither the lease asset nor the lease liability is reported on the balance sheet. Accordingly, leasing can be a form of off-balance-sheet financing.

Lessee Reporting of Leases

GAAP identifies two different approaches for the reporting of leases by the lessee:

- **Capital lease method.** This method requires that both the lease asset and the lease liability be reported on the balance sheet. The lease asset is depreciated like any other long-term asset. The lease liability is amortized like debt, where lease payments are separated into interest expense and principal repayment.

- **Operating lease method.** Under this method, neither the lease asset nor the lease liability is reported on the balance sheet. Lease payments are recorded as rent expense by the lessee when paid.

The financial statement effects for the lessee of these methods are summarized in Exhibit 10.1

EXHIBIT 10.1	Financial Statement Effects of Lease Type for the Lessee			
Lease Type	**Assets**	**Liabilities**	**Expenses**	**Cash Flows**
Capital	Lease asset reported	Lease liability reported	Depreciation and interest expense	Payments per lease contract
Operating	Lease asset **not** reported	Lease liability **not** reported	Rent expense	Payments per lease contract

GAAP defines criteria to determine whether a lease is capital or operating.[1] Managers seeking off-balance-sheet financing structure their leases around the GAAP rules so as to fail the "capitalization tests."

Under the operating method, lease assets and lease liabilities are *not* recorded on the balance sheet. The company merely discloses key details of the transaction in the lease footnote. The income statement reports the lease payment as rent expense. And, the cash outflows (payments to lessor) per the lease contract are included in the operating section of the statement of cash flows.

For capital leases, both the lease asset and lease liability are reported on the balance sheet. In the income statement, depreciation and interest expense are reported instead of rent expense. (Since only depreciation is an operating expense, NOPAT is higher when a lease is classified as a capital lease.) Further, although the cash payments to the lessor are identical whether or not the lease is capitalized on the balance sheet, the cash flows are classified differently for capital leases—that is, each payment is part interest (operating cash flow) and part principal (financing cash flow). Operating cash flows are, therefore, greater when a lease is classified as a capital lease.

Classifying leases as "operating" has four important benefits for the lessee:

1. The lease asset is not reported on the balance sheet. This means that net operating asset turnover (NOAT) is higher because reported operating assets are lower and revenues are unaffected.

2. The lease liability is not reported on the balance sheet. This means that balance sheet measures of financial leverage (like the total liabilities-to-equity ratio) are improved; many managers believe the

---

[1] Leases must be capitalized when one or more of the following four criteria are met: (1) The lease automatically transfers ownership of the lease asset from the lessor to the lessee at termination of the lease. (2) The lease provides that the lessee can purchase the lease asset for a nominal amount (a bargain purchase) at termination of the lease. (3) The lease term is at least 75% of the economic useful life of the lease asset. (4) The present value of the lease payments is at least 90% of the fair market value of the lease asset at inception of the lease.

reduced financial leverage will result in a better credit rating and, consequently, a lower interest rate on borrowed funds.

3. Without analytical adjustments (see later section on capitalization of operating leases), the portion of ROE derived from operating activities (RNOA) appears higher, which improves the perceived quality of the company's ROE.

4. During the early years of the lease term, rent expense reported for an operating lease is less than the depreciation and interest expense reported for a capital lease.[2] This means that net income is higher in those early years with an operating lease.[3] Further, if the company is growing and continually adding operating lease assets, the level of profits will continue to remain higher during the growth period.

The benefits of applying the operating method for leases are obvious to managers, thus leading them to avoid lease capitalization. Furthermore, the lease accounting standard includes rigid requirements relating to capitalization. Whenever accounting standards are rigidly defined, managers can structure transactions to meet the letter of the standard to achieve a desired accounting result when the essence of the transaction would suggest a different accounting treatment. This is *form over substance.*

Footnote Disclosures of Leases

Disclosures of expected payments for leases are required under both operating and capital lease methods. Southwest Airlines provides a typical disclosure from its 2005 annual report:

Leases The Company had nine aircraft classified as capital leases at December 31, 2005. The amounts applicable to these aircraft included in property and equipment were:

(In millions)	2005	2004
Flight equipment.	$164	$173
Less accumulated depreciation	113	126
	$ 51	$ 47

Total rental expense for operating leases, both aircraft and other, charged to operations in 2005, 2004, and 2003 was $409 million, $403 million, and $386 million, respectively. The majority of the Company's terminal operations space, as well as 84 aircraft, were under operating leases at December 31, 2005. Future minimum lease payments under capital leases and noncancelable operating leases with initial or remaining terms in excess of one year at December 31, 2005, were:

(In millions)	Capital Leases	Operating Leases
2006	$16	$ 332
2007	16	309
2008	16	274
2009	16	235
2010	15	219
After 2010.	12	1,164
Total minimum lease payments	91	$2,533
Less amount representing interest.	17	
Present value of minimum leases payments	74	
Less current portion	11	
Long-term portion	$63	

The aircraft leases generally can be renewed at rates based on fair market value at the end of the lease term for one to five years. Most aircraft leases have purchase options at or near the end of the lease term at fair market value, generally limited to a stated percentage of the lessor's defined cost of the aircraft.

---

[2] This is true even if the company employs straight-line depreciation for the lease asset since interest expense accrues on the outstanding balance of the lease liability, which is higher in the early years of the lease life. Total expense is the same *over the life of the lease,* regardless of whether the lease is capitalized or not. That is: Total rent expense (from operating lease) = Total depreciation expense (from capital lease) + Total interest expense (from capital lease).

[3] However, NOPAT is *lower* for an operating lease because rent expense is an operating expense whereas only depreciation expense (and not interest expense) is an operating expense for a capital lease.

Lease disclosures such as this provide information concerning current and future payment obligations. These contractual obligations are similar to debt payments and must be factored into our evaluation of the company's financial condition.

Southwest Airlines' footnote disclosure reports minimum (base) contractual lease payment obligations for each of the next five years and the total lease payment obligations that come due in year six and beyond. This is similar to disclosures of future maturities for long-term debt. The company also must provide separate disclosures for operating leases and capital leases (Southwest Airlines has both operating and capital leases outstanding).

MANAGERIAL DECISION   **You Are the Division President**

You are the president of an operating division. Your CFO recommends operating lease treatment for asset acquisitions to reduce reported assets and liabilities on your balance sheet. To achieve this classification, you must negotiate leases with shorter base terms and lease renewal options that you feel are not advantageous to your company. What is your response? [Answer, p. 10-28]

Capitalization of Operating Leases

Although not recognized on-balance-sheet, leased properties represent assets (and create liabilities) as defined under GAAP. That is, the company controls the assets and will profit from their future benefits. Also, lease liabilities represent real contractual obligations. Although the financial statements are prepared in conformity with GAAP, the failure to capitalize operating lease assets and lease liabilities for analysis purposes distorts ROE analysis—specifically:

▪ Net operating profit margin (NOPM) is understated; although, over the life of the lease, rent expense under operating leases equals depreciation plus interest expense under capital leases, only depreciation expense is included in net operating profit (NOPAT) as interest is a nonoperating expense. Operating expense is, therefore, overstated, and NOPM is understated. (While cash payments are the same whether the lease is classified as operating or capital, *operating cash flow* is higher with capital leases since depreciation is an add-back, and the reduction of the capital lease obligation is classified as a *financing* outflow. Operating cash flows are, therefore, lower with operating leases than with capital leases.)

▪ Net operating asset turnover (NOAT) is overstated due to nonreporting of lease assets.

▪ Financial leverage (FLEV) is understated by the omitted lease liabilities—recall that lease liabilities are nonoperating.

Although aggregate ROE is relatively unaffected (assuming that the leases are at their midpoint on average so that rent expense is approximately equal to depreciation plus interest) failure to capitalize an operating lease results in a balance sheet that, arguably, neither reflects all of the assets that are used in the business, nor the nonoperating obligations for which the company is liable. Such noncapitalization of leases makes ROE appear to be of higher quality since it derives from higher RNOA (due to higher NOA turnover) and not from higher financial leverage. This is, of course, the main reason why managers want to exclude leases from the balance sheet.

Lease disclosures that are required under GAAP allow us to capitalize operating leases for analysis purposes. This capitalization process involves three steps (this is the same basic process that managers would have used if the leases had been classified as capital leases):

1. Determine the discount rate.[4]

---

[4] There are at least two approaches to determine the appropriate discount rate for our analysis: (1) If the company discloses capital leases, we can infer a rate equal to the rate that yields the present value computed by the company given the future capital leases payments (see Business Insight box later in this section). (2) Use the rate that corresponds to the company's credit rating or the rate from any recent borrowings involving intermediate term secured obligations. Companies typically disclose these details in their long-term debt footnote.

2. Compute the present value of future operating lease payments.

3. Adjust the financials to include the present value from step 2 as both a lease asset and a lease liability.

To illustrate the capitalization of operating leases, we use **Southwest Airline**'s footnote. We determine the implicit rate on its capital leases (step 1) to be 7% (see Business Insight box on page 10-10). We then use this 7% discount rate to compute the present value of its operating leases in Exhibit 10.2.

EXHIBIT 10.2	Present Value of Operating Lease Payments ($ millions)		
Year	Operating Lease Payment	Discount Factor (i = 0.07)	Present Value
1	$ 332	0.93458	$ 310
2	309	0.87344	270
3	274	0.81630	224
4	235	0.76290	179
5	219	0.71299	156
>5	1,164 [$219 for ~5 years]	4.10020 × 0.71299	640
			$1,779
Remaining life	$1,164/$219 = 5.315 years		

Step 2, determining the present value of future operating lease payments, has four parts:

1. Discount each of the first five lease payments using the present value factor for that number of years.

2. Compute the number of annual payments beyond year 5. To do this we assume that the company continues to pay the same amount each year as it paid in year 5 (an annuity) and continues to do so until it exhausts the remaining payments disclosed in the lease footnote. For Southwest Airlines, if the company continues to pay $219 per year, it will take 5.315 years to exhaust the remaining payments of $1,164, computed as $1,164/$219.

3. Compute the present value of the remaining lease payment annuity. There are three ways to arrive at this present value. One way is to use the factor from the time value of money tables in the appendix near the end of the book. To do this, we first round the number of years computed (5.315) to the nearest whole year (5). The tables show an annuity factor of 4.10020 for 5 years at 7%. A second way is to include the exact number of years in the annuity formula $\frac{1 - (1 + 0.07)^{-5.315}}{0.07}$, which yields an annuity factor of 4.31498. Third, we can compute the present value of the annuity using a financial calculator with inputs: N = 5.315, I = 7%, PMT = $1, FV = 0. This also yields the present value of 4.31498. Regardless of the method used, the computed amount is the present value of the annuity at the end of year 5. We must discount that amount to the present (year 0) by multiplying it by the year 5 present value factor of a single sum (0.71299). Thus, the present value is $640 under the first computational method and $674 under methods 2 and 3. Methods 2 and 3 are more exact, but may or may not yield a material difference as compared to method 1. Exhibit 10.2 shows the results using method 1. For simplicity, we use method 1 hereafter.

4. Sum the present values for the first five years and that for years after year 5. For Southwest, this totals $1,779, computed as $310 + $270 + $224 + $179 + $156 + $640 (or $1,813 under the alternate computational methods).

Balance Sheet Effects

These steps yield the adjusted figures in Exhibit 10.3 for Southwest Airlines at year-end 2005.

EXHIBIT 10.3	Adjustments to Balance Sheet from Capitalization of Operating Leases		
($ millions)	Reported Figures	Adjustments	Adjusted Figures
Net operating assets	$8,419	$1,779	$10,198
Net nonoperating liabilities..............	1,744	1,779	3,523
Equity	6,675		6,675

The capitalization of its operating leases has a marked impact on Southwest Airline's balance sheet. For the airline and retailing industries, in particular, lease assets (airplanes and real estate) comprise a large portion of net operating assets, which are typically accounted for using the operating lease method. Thus, companies in these industries usually have sizeable off-balance-sheet assets and liabilities.

Income Statement Effects

Capital leases also affect the income statement via depreciation of the leased equipment and interest on the lease liability. Operating lease payments are reported as rent expense, typically included in selling, general and administrative expenses. The income statement adjustments relating to the capitalization of operating leases involve two steps:

1. Remove rent expense from operating expense (for simplicity, we assume that the current year rent expense is approximated by the year 1 projected lease payment of $332 million).

2. Add depreciation expense from the lease assets to operating expense and add interest expense from the lease obligation as a nonoperating expense. Lease assets are estimated at $1,779 million (see Exhibit 10.3). GAAP requires companies to depreciate capital lease assets over their useful lives or the lease terms, whichever is less. For this example, we assume that the remaining lease term is 10 years (5 years reported in the lease schedule plus 5 years after the fifth year). Using this term and zero salvage value results in estimated straight-line depreciation for lease assets of $178 million ($1,779 million/10 years). Interest expense on the $1,779 million lease liability at the 7% capitalization rate is $125 million ($1,779 million $\times$ 7%) for the first year.[5]

Southwest Airlines reports operating income of $820 million, nonoperating income of $54 million, income tax expense of $326 million, and a federal and state statutory tax rate of 36.8% in 2005. Thus, its tax rate on operating income is 37.3%, computed as ($326 million − [$54 million $\times$ 36.8%])/$820 million. The net adjustment to NOPAT, reflecting the elimination of rent expense and the addition of depreciation expense, is $97 million, computed as ($332 million − $178 million) $\times$ (1 − 37.3%). The after-tax increase in nonoperating expense is $79 million, computed as $125 million $\times$ (1 − 36.8%). Exhibit 10.4 summarizes these adjustments to some of Southwest's profitability measures.

EXHIBIT 10.4	Adjustments to Income Statement from Capitalization of Operating Leases		
($ millions)	Reported Figures	Adjustments	Adjusted Figures
NOPAT	$571	$97	$668
Nonoperating expense................	23	79	102
Net income........................	$548	$18	$566

---

[5] This approach uses the operating lease payments from year 1 of the projected payments to approximate the rent expense for operating leases and the depreciation and interest expense for capital leases. An alternative approach is to use *actual* rent expense for the year (disclosed in the leasing footnote) together with depreciation and interest computed based on capitalization of the *prior* year forecast lease payments. Although, arguably more exact, most analysts use the simplified approach illustrated here given the extent of other estimates involved (such as discount rates, depreciation lives, and salvage values).

ROE and Disaggregation Effects

Adjustments to capitalize operating leases can alter our assessment of ROE components. The impact for ROE and its components, defined in Module 4, is summarized in Exhibit 10.5 for Southwest Airlines.

EXHIBIT 10.5	Ratio Effects of Adjustments from Capitalization of Operating Leases		
($ millions)	Reported	Adjusted	Computations for Adjustments
NOPM.................................	7.5%	8.8%	$668/$7,584
NOAT	0.90	0.74	$7,584/$10,198
RNOA................................	6.8%	6.6%	$668/$10,198
Nonoperating return......................	1.4%	1.9%	(residual number)
ROE	8.2%	8.5%	$566/$6,693*

* Reported equity of $6,675 + $18.

Using year-end (reported and adjusted) data, and Southwest Airlines total revenues of $7,584 million, its adjusted RNOA is 6.6% (down from 6.8% reported). The increase in net operating profit margin (from 7.5% to 8.8% reflecting the increased operating income resulting from elimination of rent expense that is only partially offset by the increase in depreciation expense) is more than offset by a reduction of net operating asset turnover (from 0.90 to 0.74; reflecting the increase in operating lease assets).

Although Southwest's ROE increases only by 0.3%, this analysis reveals that 22% (1.9%/8.5%) of its ROE results from nonoperating activities, up from 17% (1.4%/8.2%) using reported figures. The adjusted figures reveal a greater financial leverage in the form of capital lease obligations. Specifically, its liabilities-to-equity ratio is 0.53 times equity using adjusted figures ($3,523/$6,693) versus 0.26 times using reported figures ($1,744/$6,675). Financial leverage is, therefore, revealed to play a greater role in ROE.

Adjusted assets and liabilities arguably present a more realistic picture of the invested capital required to operate Southwest Airlines and of the amount of leverage represented by its leases. Similarly, operating profitability is revealed to be higher than reported, since a portion of Southwest's rent payments represent repayment of the lease liability (a nonoperating cash outflow) rather than operating expense.

BUSINESS INSIGHT	Imputed Discount Rate for Leases

When companies report both operating and capital leases, the average rate used to discount capital leases can be imputed from disclosures in the leasing footnote. Southwest Airlines reports total undiscounted minimum capital lease payments of $91 million and a discounted value for those lease payments of $74 million in its footnote. Using Excel, we can estimate by trial and error the discount rate that yields the present value—which is about 7% (see chart below). We used this 7% discount rate to capitalize the operating lease payments for Southwest.

Year	Capital Lease Payment	Discount Factor (i = 0.07)	Present Value
1...............	$16	0.93458	$15
2...............	16	0.87344	14
3...............	16	0.81630	13
4...............	16	0.76290	12
5...............	15	0.71299	11
>5..............	12 [$15 for ~1 year]	0.93458* × 0.71299	10†
			$75

Remaining life...... $12/$15 = 0.8 years, rounded to 1 year

*The annuity factor from the tables for 1 year at 7% is 0.93458.
†$15 × 0.93458 × 0.71299 = $9.995 (or approximately $10).

MID-MODULE REVIEW 1

Following is the leasing footnote disclosure from American Airlines's 2005 10-K report.

Leases AMR's subsidiaries lease various types of equipment and property, primarily aircraft and airport facilities. The future minimum lease payments required under capital leases, together with the present value of such payments, and future minimum lease payments required under operating leases that have initial or remaining non-cancelable lease terms in excess of one year as of December 31, 2005, were (in millions):

Year Ending December 31	Capital Leases	Operating Leases
2006	$ 263	$ 1,065
2007	196	1,039
2008	236	973
2009	175	872
2010	140	815
2011 and thereafter	794	7,453
	1,804	$12,217
Less amount representing interest	716	
Present value of net minimum lease payments	$1,088	

At December 31, 2005, the Company was operating 213 aircraft and 27 turboprop aircraft under operating leases and 91 jet aircraft and three turboprop aircraft under capital leases. The aircraft leases can generally be renewed at rates based on fair market value at the end of the lease term for one to five years. Some aircraft leases have purchase options at or near the end of the lease term at fair market value, but generally not to exceed a stated percentage of the defined lessor's cost of the aircraft or a predetermined fixed amount.

1. What adjustments would you make to American Airline's balance sheet to capitalize the operating leases at the end of 2005? (*Hint:* The implicit rate on AMR's capital leases is approximately 11%.)
2. Assuming the same facts as in part 1, what income statement adjustments might you consider?

Solution

1. Using an 11% discount rate, the present value of American Airline's operating leases follows ($ millions):

Year	Operating Lease Payment	Discount Factor (i = 0.11)	Present Value
1	$ 1,065	0.90090	$ 959
2	1,039	0.81162	843
3	973	0.73119	711
4	872	0.65873	574
5	815	0.59345	484
>5	7,453 [$815 for ~9 years]	5.53705* × 0.59345	2,678†
			$6,249

Remaining life...... $7,453/$815 = 9.145 years, rounded to 9 years

*The annuity factor for 9 years at 11% is 5.53705.
†$815 × 5.53705 × 0.59345 = $2,678. (Under the alternate method the present value is $815 × 5.59034 × 0.59345 = $2,704.)

AMR's operating leases represent $6,249 million in both unreported operating assets and unreported non-operating liabilities. These amounts should be added to the balance sheet for analysis purposes.

2. Income statement adjustments relating to capitalization of operating leases involve two steps:
    a. Remove rent expense of $1,065 million from operating expense.
    b. Add depreciation expense from lease assets to operating expense and also reflect interest expense on the lease obligation as a nonoperating expense. We assume that the remaining lease term is 14 years (5 years reported in the lease schedule plus 9 years after year 5). Using this term and zero salvage value results in estimated straight-line depreciation for lease assets of $446 million ($6,249 million/14 years). Interest expense on the $6,249 million lease liability at the 11% capitalization rate is $687 million ($6,249 million × 11%).

PENSIONS

Companies frequently offer pension plans as a benefit for their employees. There are two general types of pension plans:

LO2 Describe and illustrate the accounting for pensions.

1. **Defined contribution plan.** This plan requires the company to make periodic contributions to an employee's account (usually with a third party trustee like a bank), and many plans require an employee matching contribution. Following retirement, the employee makes periodic withdrawals from that account. A tax-advantaged 401(k) account is a typical example. Under a 401(k) plan, the employee makes contributions that are exempt from federal taxes until they are withdrawn after retirement.

2. **Defined benefit plan.** This plan also requires the company to make periodic payments to a third party, which then makes payments to an employee after retirement. Payments are usually based on years of service and the employee's salary. The company may or may not set aside sufficient funds to cover these obligations (federal law does set minimum funding requirements). As a result, defined benefit plans can be overfunded or underfunded. All pension investments are retained by the third party until paid to the employee. In the event of bankruptcy, employees have the standing of a general creditor, but usually have additional protection in the form of government pension benefit insurance.

For a defined contribution plan, the company contribution is recorded as an expense in the income statement when the cash is paid or the liability accrued. For a defined benefit plan, it is not so simple. This is because while the company contributes cash or securities to the pension investment account, the pension obligation is not satisfied until the employee receives pension benefits, which may be many years into the future. This section focuses on how a defined benefit plan impacts financial statements, and how we assess company performance and financial condition when such a plan exists.

Reporting of Defined Benefit Pension Plans

There are two accounting issues concerning the reporting of defined benefit pension plans.

1. How are pension plans (assets and liabilities) reported in the balance sheet (if at all)?
2. How are pension costs and returns from pension plan assets reported in the income statement?

The following graphic shows where pensions appear on the balance sheet (liabilities and assets) and the income statement (pension expense is usually reported in SG&A).

Income Statement	Balance Sheet	
Sales	Cash	Current liabilities
Cost of goods sold	Accounts receivable	Long-term liabilities
Selling, general & administrative	Inventory	
Income taxes	Long-term operating assets	Shareholders' equity
Net income	Investments	

Footnote Disclosures—Off-Balance-Sheet Financing		
Leases	Pensions	SPEs

Balance Sheet Effects

Pension plan assets are primarily investments in stocks and bonds (mostly of other companies, but it is not uncommon for companies to invest pension funds in their own stock). Pension liabilities (called the **projected benefit obligation** or **PBO**) are the company's obligations to pay current and former employees. The difference between the market value of the pension plan assets and the projected benefit obligation is called the **funded status** of the pension plan. If the PBO exceeds the pension plan assets, the pension is **underfunded**. Conversely, if pension plan assets exceed the PBO, the pension plan is **overfunded**. Under current GAAP, companies are required to record only the funded status on their balance sheets (namely, the *net* amount, not the pension plan assets and PBO separately), either as an asset if the plan is overfunded, or as a liability if it is underfunded.

Pension plan assets consist of stocks and bonds whose value changes each period in three ways. First, the value of the investments increases or decreases as a result of interest, dividends, and gains or losses on the stocks and bonds held. Second, the pension plan assets increase when the company contributes additional cash or stock to the investment account. Third, the pension plan assets decrease by the amount of benefits paid to retirees during the period. These three changes in the pension plan assets are articulated below.

Pension Plan Assets
Pension plan assets, beginning balance
+ Actual returns on investments (interest, dividends, gains and losses)
+ Company contributions to pension plan
− Benefits paid to retirees
= Pension plan assets, ending balance

The pension liability, or PBO (projected benefit obligation), is computed as the present value of the expected future benefit payments to employees. The present value of these future payments depend on the number of years the employee is expected to work (years of service) and the employee's salary level at retirement. Consequently, companies must estimate future wage increases, as well as the number of employees expected to reach retirement age with the company and how long they are likely to receive pension benefits following retirement. Once the future retiree pool is determined, the expected future payments under the plan are discounted to arrive at the present value of the pension obligation. This is the PBO. A reconciliation of the PBO from beginning balance to year-end balance follows.

Pension Obligation
Projected benefit obligation, beginning balance
+   Service cost
+   Interest cost
+/− Actuarial losses (gains)
−   Benefits paid to retirees
=   Projected benefit obligation, ending balance

As this reconciliation shows, the balance in the PBO changes during the period for four reasons.

▪ First, as employees continue to work for the company, their pension benefits increase. The annual **service cost** represents the additional (future) pension benefits earned by employees during the current year.

▪ Second, **interest cost** accrues on the outstanding pension liability, just as it would with any other long-term liability (see the accounting for bond liabilities in Module 8). Because there are no scheduled interest payments on the PBO, the interest cost accrues each year, that is, interest is added to the existing liability.

▪ Third, the PBO can increase (or decrease) due to actuarial losses (and gains), which arise when companies make changes in their pension plans or make *changes in actuarial assumptions* (including assumptions that are used to estimate the PBO, such as the rate of wage inflation, termination and mortality rates, and the discount rate used to compute the present value of future obligations). For example, if a company increases the discount rate used to compute the present value of future pension plan payments from, say, 8% to 9%, the present value of future benefit payments declines (just like bond prices.) Conversely, if the discount rate is reduced to 7%, the present value of the PBO increases. Other actuarial assumptions used to estimate the pension liability (such as the expected wage inflation rate or the expected life span of current and former employees) can also create similar actuarial losses or gains.

▪ Fourth, pension benefit payments to retirees reduce the PBO (just as the payments reduce the pension plan assets).

Finally, the net pension liability (or asset) that is reported in a company's balance sheet, then, is computed as follows:

Net Pension Liability (or Asset)
Pension plan assets (at market value)
− Projected benefit obligation (PBO)
Funded status

If the funded status is positive (assets exceed liabilities such that the plan is overfunded), the overfunded pension plan is reported on the balance sheet as an asset, typically called prepaid pension cost. If the funded status is negative (liabilities exceed assets and the plan is underfunded), it is reported as a liability.[6,7] During the early 2000s, long-term interest rates declined drastically and many companies lowered their discount rate for computing the present value of future pension payments. Lower discount rates meant higher PBO values. This period also witnessed a bear market and pension plan assets declined in value. The combined effect of the increase in PBO and the decrease in asset values caused many pension funds to become severely underfunded. Of the 1,912 U.S. publicly traded companies reporting pension plans in 2005, a total of 1,721 (90%) were underfunded. (American Airlines, for example, reports an underfunded pension plan of $3.2 billion in 2005.)

Income Statement Effects

A company's net pension expense is computed as follows.

Net Pension Expense
Service cost
+ Interest cost
− *Expected* return on pension plan assets
± Amortization of deferred amounts
Net pension expense

The net pension expense is rarely reported separately on the income statement. Instead, it is included with other forms of compensation expense in selling, general and administrative (SG&A) expenses. However, pension expense is disclosed separately in footnotes.

The net pension expense has four components. The previous PBO section described the first two components: service costs and interest costs. The third component of pension expense relates to the return on pension plan assets, which *reduces* total pension expense. To compute this component, companies use

---

[6] Balance sheet recognition of the funded status is a new requirement. In 2006, the FASB issued new rules entitled "Employers' Accounting for Defined Benefit Pension and Other Postretirement Plans an amendment of FASB Statements No. 87, 88, 106, and 132(R)." Previously, companies' balance sheets did not recognize certain types of pension obligations. Instead, these were reported only in the footnotes. Recognizing the funded status will increase total liabilities for most companies. To balance the accounting equation, the FASB allowed companies to recognize the offsetting amount in stockholders' equity, using the Accumulated Other Comprehensive Income (OCI) account.

[7] Companies typically maintain many pension plans. Some are overfunded and others are underfunded. Current GAAP requires companies to group all of the overfunded and underfunded plans together, and to present a net asset for the overfunded plans and a net liability for the underfunded plans.

the long-term *expected* rate of return on the pension plan assets, rather than the *actual* return, and multiply that expected rate by the prior year's balance in pension plan assets account (usually the average balance in the prior year). Use of the expected return rather than actual return is an important distinction. Company CEOs and CFOs dislike income variability because they believe that stockholders react negatively to it, and so company executives intensely (and successfully) lobbied the FASB to use the more stable expected long-term investment return, rather than the actual return, in computing pension expense. Thus, the pension plan assets' expected return is deducted to compute net pension expense.[8]

Any difference between the expected and the actual return is accumulated, together with other deferred amounts, off-balance-sheet and reported in the footnotes. (Other deferred amounts include changes in PBO resulting from changes in estimates used to compute the PBO and from amendments to the pension plans made by the company.) However, if the deferred amount exceeds certain limits, the excess is recognized on-balance-sheet with a corresponding amount recognized (as amortization of deferred amounts) in the income statement.[9] This amortization is the fourth component of pension expense and can be either a positive or negative amount depending on the sign of the difference between expected and actual return on plan assets. (We discuss the amortization component of pension expense further in Appendix 10A.)

Most analysts consider the service cost portion of pension expense to be an operating expense, similar to salaries and other benefits. However, the interest cost component is generally viewed as a nonoperating (financing) cost. Similarly, the expected return on plan assets is considered nonoperating. Consequently, proper analysis of the income statement requires the parsing of pension expense into these operating and nonoperating components.

Footnote Disclosures—Components of Plan Assets and PBO

GAAP requires extensive footnote disclosures for pensions (and other postretirement benefits which we discuss later). These notes provide details relating to the net pension liability reported in the balance sheet and the components of pension expense are reported as part of SG&A expense in the income statement.

American Airlines' pension footnote indicates that the funded status of its pension plan is $(3,225) million on December 31, 2005. (Southwest Airlines has not yet funded its pension liability of $94 million, a relatively small amount compared with its total liabilities and equity of $14 billion; consequently, Southwest's pension footnote does not provide all of the information necessary for a complete illustration.) This means American's plan is underfunded. Following are the disclosures American Airlines makes in its pension footnote, $ millions.

Pension obligation at January 1, 2005	$10,022
Service cost	372
Interest cost	611
Actuarial loss	649
Benefit payments	(651)
Obligation at December 31, 2005	$11,003
Fair value of plan assets at January 1, 2005	$ 7,335
Actual return on plan assets	779
Employer contributions	315
Benefit payments	(651)
Fair value of plan assets at December 31, 2005	$ 7,778
Funded status at December 31, 2005	$ (3,225)

---

[8] The FASB has issued an exposure draft containing a proposal to further amend the pension accounting standard to eliminate the use of the expected return. If passed, this amendment will result in increased earnings volatility as changes in the market value of the pension investments will impact net pension expense (and operating profits before tax) directly.

[9] To avoid amortization, the deferred amounts must be less than 10% of the PBO or pension investments, whichever is less. The excess, if any, is amortized until no further excess remains. When the excess is eliminated (by investment returns or company contributions, for example), the amortization ceases.

American Airlines' PBO began the year with a balance of $10,022 million. It increased by the accrual of $372 million in service cost and $611 million in interest cost. During the year, American also realized an actuarial loss of $649 million, which increased the pension liability. The PBO decreased as a result of $651 million in benefits paid to retirees, leaving a balance of $11,003 million at year-end.

Pension plan assets began the year with at a fair market value of $7,335 million, which increased by $779 million from investment returns and by $315 million from company contributions. The company drew down its investments to make pension payments of $651 million to retirees. Notice that the $651 million payment reduced the PBO by the same amount, as discussed above, leaving the pension plan assets with a year-end balance of $7,778 million. The funded status of American Airlines' pension plan at year-end is $(3,225) million ($11,003 million − $7,778 million). The negative balance indicates that its pension plan is underfunded.[10] The PBO and pension plan assets accounts cannot be separated into operating and nonoperating components; thus, most analysts treat the entire funded status as an operating item (either asset or liability).

American Airlines incurred $392 million of pension expense in 2005. This is not broken out separately in its income statement. Instead, it is included in SG&A expense. Details of this expense are found in its pension footnote, which follows ($ millions):

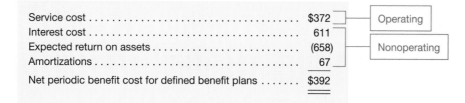

Service cost	$372	Operating
Interest cost	611	
Expected return on assets	(658)	Nonoperating
Amortizations	67	
Net periodic benefit cost for defined benefit plans	$392	

Using the information in American Airlines' footnote, we can parse the pension expense into operating and nonoperating components. Most analysts treat service cost as operating, and interest costs and expected return as nonoperating. The amortization expense of $67 million indicates that the deferred amounts have exceeded the maximum limit prescribed under GAAP, and the excess is now amortized gradually to expense so long as the deferred amount still exceeds those limits. The amortization is partly operating (pension plan changes) and partly nonoperating (changes in actuarial assumptions and discount rates). For our analysis, we will treat the entire amortization of $67 as nonoperating. Thus, the pension expense comprises $372 operating expense and $20 nonoperating expense.

RESEARCH INSIGHT	Valuation of Pension Footnote Disclosures

The FASB requires footnote disclosure of the major components of pension cost presumably because it is useful for investors. Pension-related research has examined whether investors assign different valuation multiples to the components of pension cost when assessing company market value. Research finds that the market does, indeed, attach different interpretation to pension components, reflecting differences in information about perceived permanent earnings.

Footnote Disclosures and Future Cash Flows

Companies use their pension plan assets to pay pension benefits to retirees. When markets are booming, as during the 1990s, pension plan assets can grow rapidly. However, when markets reverse, as in the bear market of the early 2000s, the value of pension plan assets can decline. The company's annual pension plan contribution is an investment decision influenced, in part, by market conditions and minimum

---

[10] American Airlines also reports deferred amounts of $2,343 million. This represents components of the PBO that were not required to be recognized on-balance-sheet under prior GAAP. Consequently, it only reported $(882) million ($3,225 million − $2,343 million) on its balance sheet as a liability in 2005. The nonrecognition of pension obligations, of concern to many financial-report users, prompted the FASB to amend the pension accounting standard in 2006 to require recognition on-balance-sheet of the *entire* funded status.

> **RESEARCH INSIGHT** **Why do Companies offer Pensions?**
>
> Research examines why companies choose to offer pension benefits. It finds that deferred compensation plans and pensions help align the long-term interests of owners and emloyees. Research also examines the composition of pension investments. It finds that a large portion of pension fund assets are invested in fixed-income securities, which are of lower risk than other investment securities. This implies that pension assets are less risky than nonpension assets.

required contributions specified by law.[11] Companies' cash contributions come from borrowed funds or operating cash flows.

American Airlines paid $651 million in pension benefits to retirees in 2005, yet it contributed only $315 million to pension assets that year. The remaining amount was paid out of available funds in the investment account. Cash contributions to the pension plan assets are the relevant amounts for an analysis of projected cash flows. Benefits paid in relation to the pension liability balance can provide a clue about the need for *future* cash contributions. Companies are required to disclose the expected benefit payments for five years after the statement date and the remaining obligations thereafter. Following is American Airlines' benefit disclosure statement:

The following benefit payments, which reflect expected future service as appropriate, are expected to be paid:

($ millions)	Pension
2006	$ 494
2007	561
2008	595
2009	698
2010	682
2011–2015	3,660

As of 2005, American Airlines pension plan assets account reports a balance of $7,778 million, as discussed above, and during the year, the plan assets generated actual returns of $779 million. The pension plan asset account is currently generating investment returns sufficient to cover the $500 million to $700 million in projected benefit payments outlined in the schedule above. Were investment returns not sufficient, the company would have to use operating cash flow or borrow money to fund the deficit.

One application of the pension footnote is to assess the likelihood that the company will be required to increase its cash contributions to the pension plan. This estimate is made by examining the funded status of the pension plan and the projected payments to retirees. For severely underfunded plans, the projected payments to retirees ($500 to $700 million per year in American's footnote disclosure) will not be covered by existing pension assets and projected investment returns. In this case, the company might need to divert operating cash flow from other prospective projects to cover its pension plan. Alternatively, if operating cash flows are not available, it might need to borrow to fund those payments. This can be especially troublesome as the debt service payments include interest, thus, effectively increasing the required pension contribution. GM's situation illustrates the problems associated with underfunded plans, as shown in the following Business Insight.

---

[11] The Pension Protection Act of 2006 mandates that companies fully fund pension obligations by 2013. The bipartisan act also shields taxpayers from assuming airline pension plan obligations, tightens funding requirements so employers make greater cash contributions to pension funds, closes loopholes that allow companies with underfunded plans to skip cash pension payments, prohibits employers and union leaders from promising extra benefits if pension plans are markedly underfunded, and strengthens disclosure rules to give workers and retirees more information about the status of their pension plan.

BUSINESS INSIGHT   Why GM's Bonds Were Rated Junk

Analysts have long been concerned with General Motors' mounting obligations to its employees stemming from generous pension and health care packages. The following graphic tracks the funded status of GM's pension and health care obligations since 1997. The unfunded obligation has exceeded $40 billion in eight out of nine years, reaching a peak of over $70 billion in 2002, and has only declined slightly since then.

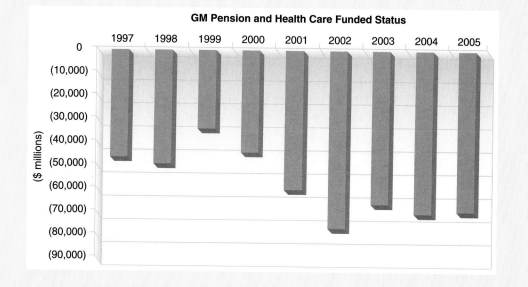

Companies can only look to two sources of funds to pay pension and health-care liabilities. Either plan investments must increase in value or the company must make additional cash contributions to the plan. The latter, of course, uses borrowed money or operating cash flows, potentially at the expense of needed capital investment, R&D, or employee wages, resulting in long-term damage to the company's market position. The bond markets also became increasingly concerned about GM's ability to generate sufficient cash flow to pay its bonds when they mature and to make the payments promised to employees. That is why GM's bonds were eventually downgraded to junk status.

Footnote Disclosures and Profit Implications

Recall the following earlier breakdown for pension expense:

Net Pension Expense
Service cost
+ Interest cost
− *Expected* return on pension plan assets
± Amortization of deferred amounts
Net pension expense

Interest cost is the product of the PBO and the discount rate. This discount rate is set by the company. The expected dollar return on pension assets is the product of the pension plan asset balance and the expected long-run rate of return on the investment portfolio. This rate is also set by the company. Further, PBO is affected by the expected rate of wage inflation, termination and mortality rates, all of which are estimated by the company.

GAAP requires disclosure of several rates used by the company in its estimation of PBO and the related pension expense. American Airlines discloses the following table in its pension footnote:

Pension Benefits	2005	2004
Weighted-average assumptions used to determine net periodic benefit cost for the years ended December 31		
Discount rate	6.00%	6.25%
Salary scale (ultimate).	3.78	3.78
Expected return on plan assets	9.00	9.00

During 2005, American Airlines reduced its discount rate (used to compute the present value of its pension obligations, or PBO) by 0.25%, while leaving unchanged its estimates of the rate of wage inflation and the expected return on plan assets.

Changes in these assumptions have the following general effects on pension expense and, thus, profitability. This table summarizes the effects of increases in the various rates. Decreases have the exact opposite effects.

Estimate change	Probable effect on pension expense	Reason for effect
Discount rate increase	Increase	While the higher discount rate reduces the PBO, the lower PBO is multiplied by a higher rate. The rate effect is larger than the discount effect, resulting in increased pension expense.*
Investment return increase	Decreases	The dollar amount of expected return on plan assets is the product of the plan assets balance and the expected long-term rate of return. Increasing the return increases the expected return on plan assets, thus reducing pension expense.
Wage inflation increase	Increases	The expected rate of wage inflation affects future wage levels that determine expected pension payments. An increase, thus, increases PBO, which increases both the service and interest cost components of pension expense.

* The effect on the PBO and interest cost is seen in the following table of the present values of an annuity of $1 for 10 and 40 years, respectively (dollar amounts are the present value factors from Appendix A; present value of an ordinary annuity, rounded to 2 decimal places).

	Discount rate	10 Years	40 Years
PBO	5%	$7.72	$17.16
	8%	6.71	11.92

As the discount rate increases, the PBO decreases. This is the discount effect. Second, the interest cost component of pension expense is computed as the PBO × Discount rate. For the four PBO amounts and related discount rates above, interest cost is computed as follows:

	Discount rate	10 Years	40 Years
Interest cost	5%	$0.39	$0.86
	8%	0.54	0.95

See that interest cost increases with increases in the discount rate, regardless of the length of the liability. This is the rate effect.

In the case of American Airlines, reduction of the discount rate, coupled with no change in the expected rate of wage inflation and return on investments, served to reduce pension costs and increase profitability in that year. It is often the case that companies reduce the expected investment returns with a lag, but increase them without a lag, to favorably impact profitability. We must be aware of the impact of these changes in assumptions in our evaluation of company profitability.

BUSINESS INSIGHT **How Pensions Confound Income Analysis**

Overfunded pension plans and boom markets can inflate income. Specifically, when the stock market is booming, pension investments realize large gains that flow to income (via reduced pension expense). Although pension plan assets do not belong to shareholders (as they are the legal entitlement of current and future retirees), the gains and losses from those plan assets are reported in income. The following graph plots the funded status of General Electric's pension plan together with pension expense (revenue) that GE reported from 1996 to 2005.

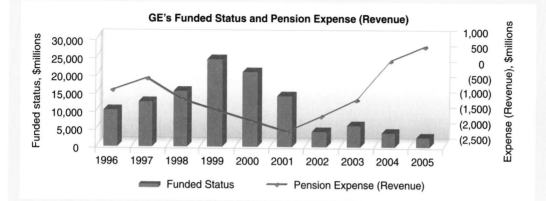

GE's funded status has consistently been positive (indicating an overfunded plan). The degree of overfunding peaked in 1999 at the height of the stock market, and began to decline during the bear market of the early 2000s. GE reported pension *revenue* (not expense) during this period. In 2001, GE's reported pension *revenue* was $2,095 million (10.6% of its pretax income). Because of the plan's overfunded status, the expected return and amortization of deferred gains components of pension expense amounted to $5,288 million, far in excess of the service and interest costs of $3,193 million. In 2004 and 2005, GE recorded pension expense (rather than revenue) as the pension plan's overfunding and expected long-term rates of return declined.

Other Post-Employment Benefits

In addition to pension benefits, many companies provide health care and insurance benefits to retired employees. These benefits are referred to as **other post-employment benefits (OPEB)**. These benefits present reporting challenges similar to pension accounting. However, companies most often provide these benefits on a "pay-as-you-go" basis and it is rare for companies to make contributions in advance for OPEB. As a result, this liability, known as the **accumulated post-employment benefit obligation (APBO)**, is largely, if not totally, unfunded. GAAP requires that the unfunded APBO liability, net of any unrecognized amounts, be reported in the balance sheet and the annual service costs and interest costs be accrued as expenses each year. This requirement is controversial for two reasons. First, future health care costs are especially difficult to estimate, so the value of the resulting APBO (the present value of the future benefits) is fraught with error. Second, these benefits are provided at the discretion of the employer and can be altered or terminated at any time. Consequently, employers argue that without a legal obligation to pay these benefits, the liability should not be reported in the balance sheet.

Other post-employment benefits can produce large liabilities. For example, American Airlines' footnotes report a funded status for the company's health care obligation of $3,223 million, consisting of an APBO liability of $3,384 million less health care plan investments with a market value of $161 million. General Motors provides an extreme OPEB example (as described in the following Business Insight box). Our analysis of cash flows related to pension obligations can be extended to other post-employment benefit obligations. For example, in addition to its pension payments, American Airlines also discloses that it is obligated to make health care payments to retirees totaling $200 million per year. Because health care obligations are rarely funded until payment is required (federal minimum funding standards do not apply to OPEB and there is no tax benefit to pre-funding), there are no investment returns to fund the payments. Our analysis of projected cash flows must consider this potential cash outflow.

RESEARCH INSIGHT   **Valuation of Nonpension Post-Employment Benefits**

The FASB requires employers to accrue the costs of all nonpension post-employment benefits; known as *accumulated post-employment benefit obligation* (APBO). These benefits consist primarily of health care and insurance. This requirement is controversial due to concerns about the reliability of the liability estimate. Research finds that the APBO (alone) is associated with company value. However, when other pension-related variables are included in the research, the APBO liability is no longer useful in explaining company value. Research concludes that the pension-related variables do a better job at conveying value-relevant information than the APBO number alone, which implies that the APBO number is less reliable.

MID-MODULE REVIEW 2

Following is the pension disclosure footnote from Midwest Airlines' 10-K report. All questions relate only to its U.S. plan.

(in $000)	2005	2004
Change in Benefit Obligation		
Net benefit obligation at beginning of year	$ 20,770	$ 17,743
Service cost	1,355	1,167
Interest cost	1,132	986
Actuarial (gain) loss	(917)	915
Gross benefits paid	(78)	(41)
Net benefit obligation at end of year	$ 22,262	$ 20,770
Change in Plan Assets		
Fair value of assets at beginning of year	$ 4,077	$ 3,383
Actual return on plan assets.	97	299
Employer contributions	1,472	436
Gross benefits paid	(78)	(41)
Fair value of plan assets at end of year	$ 5,568	$ 4,077
Funded status at end of year	$(16,694)	$(16,693)

Following is Midwest Airlines' footnote for its pension cost as reported in its income statement.

Components of Net Periodic Benefit Cost (in $000)	2005	2004	2003
Service cost	$1,355	$1,167	$924
Interest cost	1,132	986	838
Expected return on assets	(372)	(319)	(233)
Amortization of:			
Prior service cost	310	310	310
Actuarial loss (gain).	353	329	199
Total net periodic benefit cost	$2,778	$2,473	$2,038

Required

1. In general, what factors impact a company's pension benefit obligation during a period?
2. In general, what factors impact a company's pension plan investments during a period?
3. What amount is reported on the balance sheet relating to the Midwest Airlines pension plan?
4. How does the expected return on plan assets affect pension cost?
5. How does Midwest Airlines' expected return on plan assets compare with its actual return (in $s) for 2005?

6. How much net pension cost is reflected in Midwest Airlines' 2005 income statement?

7. Assess Midwest Airlines' ability to meet payment obligations to retirees.

Solution

1. A pension benefit obligation increases primarily by service cost, interest cost, and actuarial losses (which are increases in the pension liability as a result of changes in actuarial assumptions). It is decreased by the payment of benefits to retirees and by any actuarial gains.

2. Pension investments increase by positive investment returns for the period and cash contributions made by the company. Investments decrease by benefits paid to retirees and by investment losses.

3. Midwest Airlines' funded status is $(16,694,000) as of 2005. The negative amount indicates that the plan is underfunded. Consequently, this amount is reflected as a liability on its balance sheet.

4. Expected return on plan assets acts as an offset to service cost and interest cost in computing net pension cost. As the expected return increases, net pension cost decreases.

5. Midwest Airlines' expected return of $372,000 is greater than its actual return of $97,000 in 2005.

6. Midwest Airlines reports a net pension cost of $2,778,000 in its 2005 income statement.

7. Midwest Airlines' funded status is negative, indicating a severely underfunded plan. In 2005, the company contributed $1,472,000 to the pension plan, up from $436,000 in the prior year. It is likely that the company will need to increase its future funding levels to cover the plan's requirements. This might have negative repercussions for its ability to fund other operating needs, and can eventually damage its competitive position.

SPECIAL PURPOSE ENTITIES (SPEs)

Special purpose entities (SPEs) allow companies to structure projects or transactions with a number of financial advantages. SPEs have long been used and are an integral part of corporate finance. The SPE concept is illustrated by the following graphic that summarizes information taken from Ford's 2005 10-K relating to the SPE structure it uses to securitize the receivables of Ford Credit (its financing sibsidiary):

LO3 Explain the accounting for special purpose entities (SPEs).

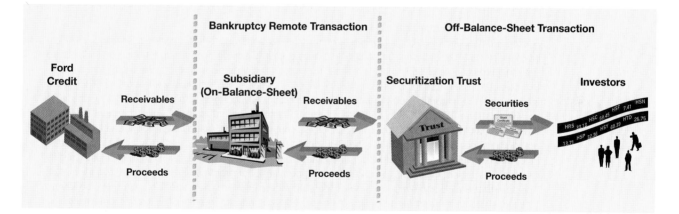

This graph is typical of many SPEs and has the following characteristics of all SPEs:

- A sponsoring company (here, Ford Credit) forms a subsidiary that is capitalized entirely with equity; this creates a *bankruptcy remote transaction*, which reduces the likelihood of bankruptcy for subsequent investors.

- The subsidiary purchases assets from the sponsoring company and sells them to a securitization (off-balance-sheet) trust (the SPE), which purchases the assets using borrowed funds (here, the SPE purchases receivables from Ford Credit's subsidiary).

- Cash flows from the acquired assets are used by the SPE to repay its debt (here, the SPE collects receivables and uses the funds to repay any borrowings).

The sponsoring company benefits in two ways. First, SPEs create direct economic benefits by improving the company's operating cash flows and by mitigating certain types of risk. Second, SPEs create indirect economic benefits by providing financial reporting benefits and alternatives. These indirect benefits derive from having assets, and their related debt, moved off-balance-sheet. The SPE owns the sponsoring company's former assets. Thus, the sponsoring company enjoys an improved asset turnover ratio (assets are less in the denominator of the turnover ratio) and an improved financial leverage ratio (liabilities are less in the numerator of the liabilities-to-equity ratio).

The following graphic shows that SPEs impact both the balance sheet (liabilities and assets) and the income statement of the sponsoring company.

Income Statement	Balance Sheet	
Sales	Cash	Current liabilities
Cost of goods sold	Accounts receivable	Long-term liabilities
Selling, general & administrative	Inventory	
Income taxes	Long-term operating assets	Shareholders' equity
Net income	Investments	

Footnote Disclosures—Off-Balance-Sheet Financing		
Leases	Pensions	SPEs

Applying SPEs as Financing Tools

This section describes two common means of using SPEs as financing tools.

Asset Securitization

Consumer finance companies, retailers, and financial subsidiaries of manufacturing companies commonly use SPEs to securitize (sell) their financial assets. Ford Credit, the finance subsidiary of Ford Motor Company, provides a common example as illustrated in the footnotes to Ford's 2005 10-K report:

> **Sales of Receivables by Ford Credit**
>
> *Securitization.* Ford Credit sells receivables in securitizations and other structured financings and in whole-loan sale transactions. Some of these arrangements satisfy accounting sale treatment and are not reflected on Ford Credit's balance sheet in the same way as debt funding. Securitization involves the sale of a pool of receivables to a special purpose entity ("SPE"), typically a trust. The SPE issues interest-bearing securities, commonly called asset-backed securities, that are backed by the sold receivables. The SPE uses proceeds from the sale of these securities to pay the purchase price for the sold receivables. The SPE may only purchase the receivables, issue asset-backed securities and make payments on the securities. The SPE has a limited duration and generally is dissolved when investors holding the asset-backed securities have been paid all amounts owed to them. Ford Credit's use of SPEs in securitizations is consistent with conventional practices in the securitization industry. The sale to the SPE achieves isolation of the sold receivables for the benefit of securitization investors and protects them from the claims of Ford Credit's creditors. The use of SPEs combined with the structure of these transactions means that the payment of the asset-backed securities is based on the creditworthiness of the underlying finance receivables . . . and not Ford Credit's creditworthiness. As a result, the senior asset-backed securities issued by the SPEs generally receive the highest short-term credit ratings and among the highest long term credit ratings from the credit rating agencies that rate them and are sold to securitization investors at cost-effective pricing.
>
> Ford Credit's typical U.S. retail securitization is a two-step transaction. Ford Credit sells a pool of its retail installment sale contracts to a wholly owned, bankruptcy-remote special purpose subsidiary that establishes a separate SPE, usually a trust, and transfers the receivables to the SPE in exchange for the proceeds from securities issued by the SPE. The securities issued by the trust, usually notes of various maturities and interest rates, are paid by the SPE from collections on the pool of receivables it owns. These securities are usually structured into senior and subordinated classes. The senior classes have priority over the subordinated classes in receiving collections from the sold receivables. The receivables acquired by the SPE and the asset-backed securities issued by the SPE are assets and obligations of the SPE.

Ford Credit's use of SPEs is typical. As Ford Credit finances the purchases of autos by customers of Ford Motor Company, it accumulates the receivables on its balance sheet. Periodically, through a subsidiary, it packages certain receivables and sells them to its SPE, which funds the purchase by selling certificates entitling the holder to a portion of the cash receipts from eventual collection of receivables. Ford Credit does not provide any other form of protection to the outside certificate holders (its footnote indicates that the receivables are sold "without recourse," meaning without collection rights against Ford Credit or its parent, Ford Motor Company). Nonrecourse is required if Ford Credit wants to account for the sale of receivables as a sale. If Ford Credit has ongoing responsibilities for the receivables, the transfer is not deemed a sale and the transferred assets would remain on Ford Credit's balance sheet.

Ford Motor Company's credit ratings have declined in recent years, thus making its unsecured borrowings more costly and limiting its availability to borrowed funds. In response, it has increased its use of SPEs as a financing source. This funding mechanism is now an important source of liquidity for the company, as highlighted in the following excerpt from the liquidity analysis section of its 10-K.

> Ford Credit's funding strategy is to maintain liquidity and access to diverse funding sources that are cost effective. As a result of lower credit ratings, Ford Credit's unsecured borrowing costs have increased, its access to the unsecured debt market has become more restricted, and its outstanding short- and long-term unsecured debt balances have declined. In response, Ford Credit has increased its use of securitization and other asset-related sources of liquidity, and will continue to expand and diversify its asset-backed funding by asset class, region and channel . . . During 2005, Ford Credit continued to meet a significant portion of its funding requirements through securitizations because of their lower relative costs given our credit ratings (as described below), the stability of the market for asset-backed securities, and the diversity of funding sources that they provide. Securitized funding (both on- and off-balance sheet, net of retained interests) as a percent of total managed receivables was as follows at the end of each of the last three years: 2005–38%, 2004–26%, 2003–25% . . .
>
> The cost of both debt and funding in securitizations is based on a margin or spread over a benchmark interest rate, such as interest rates paid on U.S. Treasury securities of similar maturities. Ford Credit's unsecured spreads have been very volatile over the last three years, as a result of market perception and its lower credit ratings, whereas its securitized funding spreads (which are based on the underlying finance receivables and credit enhancements) have not. In 2005, Ford Credit's unsecured long-term debt funding spreads fluctuated between 165 and 660 basis points above comparable U.S. Treasury securities, while its spreads on securitized funding fluctuated between 42 and 58 basis points above comparable U.S. Treasury securities.

Ford's use of SPEs as a funding source provides necessary liquidity and also provides capital at a substantially lower interest rate. Due to the SPEs limited scope of operations, and its isolation from the general business risk of the parent company, lenders to the SPE face lower risk of default and can, therefore, charge a comparatively lower rate of interest on its borrowings.

Project and Real Estate Financing

Another common use of SPEs is to finance construction projects. For example, a sponsoring company desires to construct a manufacturing plant. It establishes a SPE and executes a contract with the SPE to build the plant and to later purchase output from the plant. The SPE uses the contract, and the newly constructed manufacturing plant assets, to collateralize debt that it issues to finance the plant's construction. The sponsoring company obtains the benefits of the plant, but does not recognize either the PPE asset or the related liability on its balance sheet. The sponsoring company has commitments with the SPE, labeled executory contracts, but GAAP currently does not require such contracts be recognized in the balance sheet, nor does it even require footnote disclosure of these contracts.

Clothing retailers such as Gap and Abercrombie & Fitch use these types of executory contracts involving outside manufacturers. The manufacturing assets, and related liabilities, of these SPEs are consequently kept off the balance sheet.

A slight variation is to add leasing to this transaction. To illustrate, assume a company desires to construct an office building. It establishes a SPE to construct and finance the building and then lease it back to the company under an operating lease. As we explained earlier in this module, if the lease is structured as an operating lease, neither the lease asset nor the lease obligation is reported on the company's balance sheet. Thus, the company obtains the use and benefit of the building without recording either the building or the related debt on its balance sheet.

Rationale for SPE Financing

Each of the cases in this section demonstrates the financing capabilities of SPEs. There are two main reasons for the popularity of SPEs.

1. **Lower cost of capital.** SPEs can provide lower cost financing for a company. Since the SPE is not burdened with the myriad of business risks that can affect a company (for example, in Ford's case, the SPE only has the risk of uncollectibility), its investors do not need to be compensated for additional risk. Further, because the SPEs are formed by an all-equity (no debt) subsidiary of the parent company, it is generally perceived that SPEs are protected from the bankruptcy of the sponsoring company, thus further reducing investment risk.

2. **Nonconsolidation.** SPEs can provide a mechanism for off-balance-sheet financing if unconsolidated with the sponsoring company. As we discuss in the next section, however, recent accounting standards have made it more difficult to avoid consolidation.

Reporting of Consolidated SPEs

Nonconsolidation of SPEs allows assets and liabilities related to the business to be reported off-balance-sheet. This improves the sponsoring company's net operating asset turnover (Sales/NOA), which in turn improves return on net operating assets (RNOA), an important metric of financial performance.[12]

In recent years, regulators have passed legislation making it difficult to conduct SPE-related transactions off-balance-sheet. For instance, in 2001 the FASB published *SFAS 140,* that prescribed the conditions for asset securitization to be treated as a sale; that is, conditions under which the company can consider the securitized assets as sold and remove them from the balance sheet. To account for a securitization as a sale, the SPE must be an independent entity with sufficient equity capital to finance its ongoing operations without the support of the sponsoring company. These SPEs are called Qualifying Special Purpose Entities (QSPEs). Many previously existing SPEs did not meet these independence and capitalization conditions and, as a result, the sponsoring companies were forced to consolidate the SPE balance sheets. By consolidating the SPE, the sponsoring company includes the SPE's assets and liabilities on-balance-sheet, thus negating any financial reporting benefits of the off-balance-sheet financing. Since the passage of this standard, companies have been careful to structure their SPEs as QSPEs to avoid consolidation, and to be able to treat the transfer of securitized assets as sales and to remove the asset from the balance sheet. (Ford Credit's SPEs are structured as QSPEs to avoid consolidation.)

Subsequent to passage of *SFAS 140,* the FASB issued Interpretation Number 46R (FIN 46R), *Consolidation of Variable Interest Entities, an Interpretation of ARB No. 51* in 2003. (FASB issues Interpretations, FINs, periodically to modify or extend existing accounting standards.) This interpretation identified a new class of SPEs, called Variable Interest Entities (VIEs) and the characteristics of VIEs that require consolidation. Generally, any SPE that lacks independence from the sponsoring company (that is, does not qualify as a QSPE) and lacks sufficient capital to conduct its operations apart from the sponsoring company, must be consolidated with the entity that bears the greatest risk of loss and stands to reap the greatest rewards from the SPE's activities. That entity is called the *primary beneficiary*. VIEs can only be consolidated with the primary beneficiary, defined as the entity that bears most of the risk and enjoys most of the potential return. In a joint venture, entities typically share risks and rewards equally. As a result, no primary beneficiary exists. These joint ventures are accounted for under the equity method (see Module 7). As such, the investor company's balance sheet shows only the net investment in the VIE, thereby moving substantial assets and liabilities off-balance-sheet. This structure presents a different set of analysis issues as we discuss in Module 7.

We have witnessed a marked increase in the use of QSPEs in recent years. These entities are structured with the degree of independence and capital investment necessary to avoid consolidation. Ford discloses that the securitization of its consumer loans is a substantial source of liquidity. This is true for many companies that utilize this method of financing.

---

[12] RNOA is improved so long as the increase in asset turnover (NOAT) is not offset by a reduction in operating profit margin (NOPM) due to the increased cost of using the SPE structure (such as from purchasing goods in a finished state from wholesalers rather than manufacturing those goods, selling receivables at a discount, or leasing property from outside investors). This is a reasonable assumption; because, otherwise, the sponsoring company would likely not have created the SPE and transferred assets.

Unfortunately, GAAP does not mandate disclosure of summary balance sheets and income statements of QSPEs. Therefore, consolidation of these entities for analysis purposes is not possible. Nevertheless, in our analysis of companies, we must be aware of this financing source and assess its continued viability, just as we must assess a company's access to other sources of capital to meet liquidity needs.

Following are two analysis implications related to SPEs.

- **Cost of capital.** As discussed, SPEs reduce business risk and bankruptcy risk for their lenders. Consequently, the sponsoring company is able to obtain capital at a lower cost. Ford Motor Company (the manufacturer), for example, has witnessed a reduction in its credit ratings and a consequent increase in its cost of borrowed funds. Ordinarily, its negative credit rating would be ascribed to its subsidiaries as well, including its finance subsidiary. Using SPEs, however, the finance subsidiary, Ford Credit, is able to obtain financing at lower interest rates, which allows it to pass along that lower cost in the form of lower interest rates on auto and other loans to its customers. Without that financing source, Ford Credit would be less competitive in the market place vis-à-vis other, financially stronger, financial institutions.

- **Liquidity.** Financial institutions, and finance subsidiaries of manufacturing companies, rely on a business model of generating a high volume of loans, each of which carries a relatively small profit (spread of the interest rate over the cost of the funds). If they were forced to hold all of those loans on their own balance sheets, they would eventually need to raise costly equity capital to balance the increase in debt financing. That would also serve to reduce their competitiveness in the marketplace. These companies must, therefore, be able to package loans for sale, a crucial source of liquidity.

Given the importance of the cash flows to Ford Motor Company contributed by its Ford Credit financing subsidiary, analysts would become concerned about the welfare of the overall entity were there indications that its SPE financing sources would no longer be available (say, if further accounting standards limited Ford's ability to remove these loans from its consolidated balance sheet and record their transfer to the SPE as a sale). Analysts would also become concerned if the credit markets no longer favored this SPE structure as a financing mechanism (say, if the presumed bankruptcy protection of the SPEs was ultimately proven to be false following the bankruptcy of the sponsoring company and the consequent bankruptcy of an SPE that it sponsored). Neither of these events has occurred, and lenders rely on legal opinions that SPEs are "bankruptcy remote." Analysts must always assess these risks when assessing the financial strength of companies that rely on the SPE financial structure.

MODULE-END REVIEW

Following is the footnote disclosure relating to General Motors' receivable securitization program from its 2005 10-K report.

> GM and GMAC use off-balance sheet arrangements where the economics and sound business principles warrant their use. GM's principal use of off-balance sheet arrangements occurs in connection with the securitization and sale of financial assets generated or acquired in the ordinary course of business by GMAC and its subsidiaries and, to a lesser extent, by GM . . . The Corporation securitizes automotive and mortgage financial assets as a funding source. GMAC sells retail finance receivables, wholesale loans, residential mortgage loans, commercial mortgage loans and commercial mortgage securities.

1. Why does GM securitize its receivables?
2. What are the requirements for the transfer of these receivables to be recorded as a sale with consequent removal from the balance sheet?
3. What are the financial reporting implications if GM does not structure the transaction as a sale?

Solution

1. Companies in the financial sector typically securitize receivables as a source of liquidity. Their business model is to realize comparatively low margins on a high volume of assets. As receivables are sold, the proceeds are reinvested into new loans that are, likewise, sold. GM realizes a small interest spread on each of these loans.
2. To account for the transfer as a sale, GM must sell the assets without recourse. That means that GM must "surrender control" of the assets transferred. On that point, "the transferee has the right to pledge

> or exchange the assets" and GM has "surrendered control over the rights and obligations of the receivables."
>
> 3. If GM does not structure the transaction as a sale, the transferred assets remain on GM's balance sheet and no gain on sale is reported on GM's income statement. Such a transaction, thus, amounts to a secured borrowing. This would potentially compromise the liquidity goals of GM's securitization program.

APPENDIX 10A: Amortization Component of Pension Expense

One of the more difficult aspects of pension accounting relates to the issue of what is recognized on-balance-sheet and what is disclosed in the footnotes off-balance-sheet. This is an important distinction, and the FASB is moving toward more on-balance-sheet recognition and less off-balance-sheet disclosure in two important initiatives that will result in new pension accounting rules. The first of these is to recognize on-balance-sheet the funded status of pension plans as described in the text. This first initiative has been enacted. The second initiative, which we discuss below, is to eliminate deferred gains and losses, and to require recognition in the income statement of *all* changes to pension assets and liabilities. This second initiative is still under discussion. Until this standard is enacted, deferred gains and losses will only impact reported pension expense via their amortization (the fourth component of pension expense described on page 10-14).

There are three sources of *unrecognized gains and losses*:

1. The difference between actual and expected return on pension investments.

2. Changes in actuarial assumptions such as expected wage inflation, termination and mortality rates, and the discount rate used to compute the present value of the projected benefit obligation.

3. Amendments to the pension plan to provide employees with additional benefits (called **prior service costs**).

Accounting for gains and losses resulting from these three sources is the same; specifically:

- Balance sheets report the net pension asset (overfunded status) or liability (underfunded status) irrespective of the magnitude of deferred gains and losses; that is, based solely on the relative balances of the pension assets and PBO accounts.

- Cumulative unrecognized gains and losses from all sources are recorded in one account, called deferred gains and losses, which is only disclosed in the footnotes, not on-balance-sheet.

- When the balance in the deferred gains and losses account exceeds prescribed levels, companies transfer a portion of the deferred gain or loss onto the balance sheet, with a matching expense on the income statement. This is the amortization process described in the text.

Recall that a company reports the *estimated* return on pension investments as a component (reduction) of pension expense. The pension assets, however, increase (decrease) by the *actual* return (loss). The difference between the two returns is referred to as a deferred (unrecognized) gain or loss. To illustrate, let's assume that the pension plan is underfunded at the beginning of the year by $200, with pension assets of $800, a PBO of $1,000, and no deferred gains or losses. Now, let's assume that actual returns for the year of, say, $100 exceed the long-term expected return of $70. We can illustrate the accounting for the deferred gain as follows:

	On-Balance-Sheet			Off-Balance-Sheet (Footnotes)		
Year 1	Liabilities	Earned Capital	Income Statement	Pension Assets	PBO	Deferred Gains (Losses)
Balance, Jan. 1.	$200		$ 0	$800	$1,000	$ 0
Return.	(100)	$70 (Retained Earnings) 30 (AOCI)	70	100		30
Balance, Dec. 31	$100	$70 (Retained Earnings) 30 (AOCI)	$70	$900	$1,000	$30

The balance sheet at the beginning of the year reports the funded status of the pension plan as a $200 liability, reflecting the underfunded status of the pension plan. Neither the $800 pension asset account, nor the $1,000 PBO appear on-balance-sheet. Instead, their balances are only disclosed in a pension footnote.

During the year, pension assets (off-balance-sheet) increase by the actual return of $100 with no change in the PBO, thus decreasing the pension liability (negative funded status) by $100. The pension expense on the income statement, however, only reflects the expected return of $70, and retained earnings increase by that amount. The remaining $30 is recognized in accumulated other comprehensive income (AOCI), a component of earned capital.

These deferred gains and losses do not affect reported profit until they exceed prescribed limits, after which the excess is gradually recognized in income.[13] For example, assume that in the following year, $5 of the $30 deferred gain is amortized (recognized on-balance-sheet). This amortization would result in the following effects:

| Year 2 | On-Balance-Sheet | | | Off-Balance-Sheet (Footnotes) | | |
	Liabilities	Earned Capital	Income Statement	Pension Assets	PBO	Deferred Gains (Losses)
Balance, Jan. 1.......	$100	$70 (Retained Earnings) 30 (AOCI)	$ 0	$900	$1,000	$30
Amortization.........		$ 5 (Retained Earnings)	5			(5)
Balance, Dec. 31	$100	$ 75 (Retained Earnings) 25 (AOCI)	$ 5	$900	$1,000	$25

The deferred gain is reduced by $5 and is now recognized in reported income as a reduction of pension expense. (This amortization is the fourth line of the Net Pension Expense computation table from page 10-18.) This is the only change, as the pension assets still report a balance of $900 and the PBO reports a balance of $1,000, for a funded status of $(100) that is reported as a liability on the balance sheet.

In addition to the difference between actual and expected gains (losses) on pension assets, the deferred gains (losses) account includes increases or decreases in the PBO balance that result from changes in assumptions used to compute it, namely, the expected rate of wage inflation, termination and mortality rates for employees, and changes in the discount rate used to compute the present value of the pension obligations. Some of these can be offsetting, and all accumulate in the same deferred gains (losses) account. Justification for off-balance-sheet treatment of these items was the expectation that their offsetting nature would combine to keep the magnitude of deferred gains (losses) small. It is only in relatively extreme circumstances that this account becomes large enough to warrant amortization and, consequently, on-balance-sheet recognition. Further, the amortization effect on reported pension expense is usually small.

GUIDANCE ANSWERS

MANAGERIAL DECISION **You are the Division President**

Lease terms that are not advantageous to your company but are structured merely to achieve off-balance-sheet financing can destroy shareholder value. Long-term shareholder value is created by managing your operation well, including negotiating leases with acceptable terms. Lease footnote disclosures also provide sufficient information for skilled analysts to undo the operating lease treatment. This means that you can end up with effective capitalization of a lease with lease terms that are not in the best interests of your company and with few benefits from off-balance-sheet financing. There is also the potential for lost credibility with stakeholders.

---

[13] The upper (lower) bound on the deferred gains (losses) account is 10% of the PBO or Plan Asset account balance, whichever is greater, at the beginning of the year. Once this limit is exceeded, the excess is amortized until the account balance is below that threshold, irrespective of whether such reduction results from amortization, or changes in the PBO or Pension Asset accounts (from changes in actuarial assumptions, company contributions, or positive investment returns).

DISCUSSION QUESTIONS

Q10-1. What are the financial reporting differences between an operating lease and a capital lease? Explain.

Q10-2. Are footnote disclosures sufficient to overcome nonrecognition on the balance sheet of assets and related liabilities for operating leases? Explain.

Q10-3. Is the expense of a lease over its entire life the same whether or not it is capitalized? Explain.

Q10-4. What are the economic and accounting differences between a defined contribution plan and a defined benefit plan?

Q10-5. Under what circumstances will a company report a net pension asset? A net pension liability?

Q10-6. What are the components of pension expense that are reported in the income statement?

Q10-7. What effect does the use of expected returns on pension investments and the deferral of unexpected gains and losses on those investments have on income?

Q10-8. What is a special purpose entity (SPE)? Provide an example of the use of a SPE as a financing vehicle.

Q10-9. What effect does FIN 46R have on both accounting for SPEs and the balance sheets of companies that sponsor them?

MINI EXERCISES

M10-10. Analyzing and Interpreting Lease Footnote Disclosures (LO1)

YUM! Brands, Inc.
(YUM)

YUM! Brands, Inc., discloses the following schedule to its 2005 10-K report relating to its leasing activities.

Future minimum commitments and amounts to be received as lessor or sublessor under non-cancelable leases are set forth below:

Commitments ($ millions)	Capital	Operating
2006	$ 16	$ 362
2007	15	326
2008	14	286
2009	14	258
2010	13	230
Thereafter	91	1,218
	$163	$2,680

a. Yum reports both capital and operating leases. In general, what effects does each of these lease types have on Yum's balance sheet and its income statement?

b. What types of adjustments might we consider to Yum's balance sheet and income statement for analysis purposes?

M10-11. Analyzing and Capitalizing Operating Lease Payments Disclosed in Footnotes (LO1)

Continental Airlines,
Inc. (CAL)

Continental discloses the following in the footnotes to its 10-K report relating to its leasing activities.

Year ending December 31 ($ millions)	Capital Leases	Aircraft Operating Leases
2006	$ 39	$ 1,003
2007	40	966
2008	46	955
2009	16	910
2010	16	924
Later years	457	6,310
Total minimum lease payments	614	$11,068
Less: amount representing interest	341	
Present value of capital leases	273	
Less: current maturities of capital leases	22	
Long-term capital leases	$251	

Operating leases are not reflected on-balance-sheet. In our analysis of a company, we often desire to capitalize these operating leases, that is, add the present value of the future operating lease payments to both the reported assets and liabilities. (*a*) Compute the present value of Continental's operating lease payments assuming a 7% discount rate (the approximate implicit rate on the capitalized leases). (*b*) What effect does capitalization of operating leases have on Continental's total liabilities (it reported total liabilities of $10,303 million for 2005).

M10-12. Analyzing and Interpreting Pension Disclosures—Expenses and Returns   (LO2)

American Express discloses the following pension footnote in its 10-K report.

American Express (AXP)

(Millions)	2005
Service cost	$104
Interest cost	117
Expected return on plan assets	(141)
Other	32
Net periodic pension benefit cost	$112

a. How much pension expense does American Express report in its 2005 income statement?
b. Explain, in general, how expected return on plan assets affects reported pension expense. How did expected return affect American Express' 2005 pension expense?
c. Explain use of the word 'expected' as it relates to pension plan investments.

M10-13. Analyzing and Interpreting Pension Disclosures—Expenses and Returns   (LO2)

YUM! Brands, Inc., discloses the following pension footnote in its 10-K report.

YUM! Brands, Inc. (YUM)

Pension Benefits ($ millions)	2005	2004
Benefit obligation at beginning of year	$700	$629
Service cost	33	32
Interest cost	43	39
Plan amendments	—	1
Curtailment gain	(2)	(2)
Settlement loss	1	—
Benefits and expenses paid	(33)	(26)
Actuarial (gain) loss	73	27
Benefit obligation end of year	$815	$700

a. Explain the terms "service cost" and "interest cost."
b. How do actuarial losses arise?
c. The fair market value of YUM!'s plan assets is $610 million as of 2005. What is the funded status of the plan, and how will this be reflected on YUM!'s balance sheet?

M10-14. Analyzing and Interpreting Pension Plan Benefit Footnote   (LO2)

YUM! Brands, Inc. discloses the following pension footnote in its 10-K report.

YUM! Brands, Inc. (YUM)

Pension Benefits ($ millions)	2005	2004
Change in plan assets		
Fair value of plan assets at beginning of year	$518	$438
Actual return on plan assets	63	53
Employer contributions	64	54
Benefits paid	(33)	(26)
Administrative expenses	(2)	(1)
Fair value of plan assets end of year	$610	$518

    a. How does the "actual return on plan assets" of $63 million affect YUM!'s reported profits for 2005?

    b. What are the cash flow implications of the pension plan for YUM! in 2005?

    c. YUM!'s pension plan paid out $33 million in benefits during 2005. Where else is this payment reflected?

M10-15. Analyzing and Interpreting Retirement Benefit Footnote (LO2)

Abercrombie and Fitch (ANF)

Abercrombie and Fitch discloses the following footnote relating to its retirement plans in its 2005 10-K report.

> **RETIREMENT BENEFITS** The Company maintains a qualified defined contribution retirement plan and a nonqualified retirement plan. Participation in the qualified plan is available to all associates who have completed 1,000 or more hours of service with the Company during certain 12-month periods and attained the age of 21. Participation in the nonqualified plan is subject to service and compensation requirements. The Company's contributions to these plans are based on a percentage of associates' eligible annual compensation. The cost of these plans was $10.5 million in Fiscal 2005, $9.9 million in Fiscal 2004 and $7.0 million in Fiscal 2003.

    a. Does Abercrombie have a defined contribution or defined benefit pension plan? Explain.

    b. How does Abercrombie account for its contributions to its retirement plan?

    c. How does Abercrombie report its obligation for its retirement plan on the balance sheet?

M10-16. Analyzing and Interpreting Disclosure on Variable Interest Entities (VIEs) (LO3)

Dow Chemical Company (DOW)

Dow Chemical Company provided the following footnote in its 2002 10-K report relating to special purpose entities, which would now be classified as variable interest entities (VIEs).

> Dow has operating leases with various special purpose entities. Nine of these entities qualify as variable interest entities ("VIEs") under *FIN No. 46,* "Consolidation of Variable Interest Entities." Based on the current terms of the lease agreements and the residual value guarantees Dow provides to the lessors, the Company expects to be the primary beneficiary of the VIEs. As a result, if the facts and circumstances remain the same, Dow would be required to consolidate the assets and liabilities held by these VIEs in the third quarter of 2003.

Three years later, in its 2005 10-K report, Dow Chemical provided the following update.

> In the second quarter of 2003, Dow terminated its lease of an ethylene facility in The Netherlands with a variable interest entity ("VIE") and entered into a lease with a new owner trust, which is also a VIE. However, Dow is not the primary beneficiary of the owner trust and, therefore, is not required to consolidate the owner trust. Based on the valuation completed in mid-2003, the facility was valued at $394 million. Upon expiration of the lease, which matures in 2014, Dow may purchase the facility for an amount based upon a fair market value determination. At December 31, 2005, Dow had provided to the owner trust a residual value guarantee of $363 million, which represents Dow's maximum exposure to loss under the lease. Given the productive nature of the facility, it is probable that the facility will have continuing value to Dow or the owner trust in excess of the residual value guarantee.

    a. In general, what business reason(s) prompted Dow to establish these VIEs?

    b. How does Dow account for these VIEs in 2002? In 2005?

    c. What would have been the effect on Dow's balance sheet had consolidation of its VIEs been required under FIN 46R?

    d. Why do you suppose Dow restructured its lease of an ethylene facility as reported in 2005?

M10-17. Analyzing and Interpreting Disclosure on Contract Manufacturers (LO3)

Nike, Inc. (NKE)

Nike reports the following information relating to its manufacturing activities in footnotes to its 2005 10-K report.

> **Manufacturing** Virtually all of our footwear is produced outside of the United States. In fiscal 2005, contract suppliers in China, Vietnam, Indonesia and Thailand manufactured 36 percent, 26 percent, 22 percent and 15 percent of total NIKE brand footwear, respectively. We also have manufacturing agreements with independent factories in Argentina, Brazil, India, Italy, Mexico and South Africa to manufacture footwear for sale primarily within those countries. Our largest single footwear supplier accounted for approximately 7 percent of total fiscal 2005 footwear production.

    a. What effect does the use of contract manufacturers have on Nike's balance sheet?

    b. How does Nike's use of contract manufacturers affect Nike's return on net operating assets (RNOA) and its components? Explain.

    c. Nike executes agreements with its contract manufacturers to purchase their output. How are such "executory contracts" reported under GAAP? Does your answer suggest a possible motivation for the use of contract manufacturing?

M10-18. Analyzing and Interpreting Pension Plan Benefit Footnotes (LO2)

Lockheed Martin Corporation discloses the following funded status for its defined benefit pension plans in its 10-K report.

Lockheed Martin Corp. (LMT)

Defined Benefit Pension Plans (In millions)	2005	2004
Unfunded status of the plans.......	$(4,989)	$(4,876)

The company also reports that it is obligated for the following expected payments to retirees in the next five years.

(In millions)	Pension Benefits
2006	$1,380
2007	1,430
2008	1,490
2009	1,550
2010	1,610

Lockheed contributed $1,054 million to its pension plan assets in 2005, up from $505 million in the prior year.

a. How is this funded status reported in Lockheed's balance sheet under current GAAP?

b. How should we interpret this funded status in our analysis of the company?

c. Lockheed reports total assets of $27.7 billion and stockholders' equity of $7.9 billion. How does this funded status, and the projected benefit payments, impact our evaluation of Lockheed's financial condition?

d. Lockheed reports $3.2 billion of net cash inflows from operating activities and $900 million in capital expenditures for 2005. How does this information impact our evaluation of Lockheed's financial condition?

EXERCISES

E10-19. Analyzing and Interpreting Leasing Footnote (LO1)

Fortune Brands, Inc., reports the following footnote relating to its leased facilities in its 2005 10-K report.

Fortune Brands, Inc. (FO)

Future minimum rental payments under noncancelable operating leases as of December 31, 2005 are as follows:

(In millions)	
2006	$ 45.6
2007	33.5
2008	26.9
2009	20.2
2010	15.7
Remainder	37.3
Total minimum rental payments	$179.2

a. Assuming that this is the only information available about its leasing activities, does Fortune Brands classify its leases as operating or capital? Explain.

b. What effect has its lease classification had on Fortune Brands' balance sheet? Over the life of the lease, what effect does this classification have on net income?

c. Compute the present value of these operating leases using a discount rate of 7%. How might we use this information in our analysis of the company?

E10-20. Analyzing and Interpreting Footnote on Operating and Capital Leases (LO1)

Verizon
Communications,
Inc. (VZ)

Verizon Communications, Inc., provides the following footnote relating to its leasing activities in its 10-K report.

The aggregate minimum rental commitments under noncancelable leases for the periods shown at December 31, 2005, are as follows:

Years (dollars in millions)	Capital Leases	Operating Leases
2006	$ 37	$1,184
2007	28	791
2008	21	652
2009	13	504
2010	12	316
Thereafter	55	1,050
Total minimum rental commitments	166	$4,497
Less interest and executory costs	(54)	
Present value of minimum lease payments	112	
Less current installments	(17)	
Long-term obligation at December 31, 2005	$ 95	

a. Assuming that this is the only available information relating to its leasing activities, what amount does Verizon report on its balance sheet for its lease obligations? Does this amount represent its total obligation to lessors? How do you know?

b. What effect has its lease classification as capital or operating had on Verizon's balance sheet? Over the life of its leases, what effect does this lease classification have on its net income?

c. Compute the present value of Verizon's operating leases, assuming a 10% discount rate (the approximate implicit rate on the capitalized leases). How might we use this additional information in our analysis of the company?

E10-21. Analyzing, Interpreting and Capitalizing Operating Leases (LO1)

Staples, Inc. (SPLS)

Staples, Inc., reports the following footnote relating to its capital and operating leases in its 2005 10-K report ($ thousands).

Future minimum lease commitments due for retail and support facilities (including lease commitments for 54 retail stores not yet opened at January 28, 2006) and equipment leases under non-cancelable operating leases are as follows (in thousands):

Fiscal Year	Total
2006	$ 617,021
2007	593,176
2008	558,355
2009	526,981
2010	491,310
Thereafter	2,460,031
	$5,246,874

a. What dollar adjustment(s) might we consider to Staples' balance sheet and income statement given this information and assuming that Staples intermediate-term borrowing rate is 7%? Explain.

b. Would the adjustment from part a make a substantial difference to Staples' total liabilities? (Staples reported total liabilities of $3,251,118 ($ 000s) for 2005.)

E10-22. Analyzing, Interpreting and Capitalizing Operating Leases (LO1)

YUM! Brands, Inc., reports the following footnote relating to its capital and operating leases in its 2005 10-K report ($ millions).

YUM! Brands, Inc. (YUM)

Future minimum commitments under non-cancelable leases are set forth below:

Commitments	Capital	Operating
2006	$ 16	$ 362
2007	15	326
2008	14	286
2009	14	258
2010	13	230
Thereafter	91	1,218
	$163	$2,680

a. What adjustment(s), assuming a discount rate of 7%, might we consider making to Yum's balance sheet and income statement given this information? Explain.

b. Would the adjustment from part *a* make a sizeable difference to Yum's total liabilities? Yum reported total liabilities of $4,249 million for 2005.

E10-23. Analyzing, Interpreting and Capitalizing Operating Leases (LO1)

Nordstrom reports the following footnote relating to its capital and operating leases in its fiscal 2005 10-K report.

Nordstrom (JWN)

Leases   Future minimum lease payments as of January 28, 2006 are as follows:

Fiscal Year ($000)	Capital Leases	Operating Leases
2006	$ 1,946	$ 73,389
2007	1,946	73,296
2008	1,946	70,525
2009	1,376	67,892
2010	1,270	63,524
Thereafter	6,990	332,016
Total minimum lease payments	15,474	$680,642
Less amount representing interest..............	(6,137)	
Present value of net minimum lease payments	$ 9,337	

What adjustment(s) might we consider to Nordstrom's balance sheet and income statement given this information and assuming that Nordstrom's discount rate is 12% (the approximate implicit rate in its capital leases)? Explain.

E10-24. Analyzing and Interpreting Pension Disclosures (LO2)

Ford Motor Company reports the following pension footnote in its 10-K report.

($ millions)	Pension Benefits	
	U.S. Plans 2005	Non-U.S. Plans 2005
Change in Benefit Obligation		
Benefit obligation at January 1............	$43,077	$29,452
Service cost	734	630
Interest cost	2,398	1,408
Amendments	—	218
Separation programs	179	422
Plan participant contributions	41	146
Benefits paid	(2,856)	(1,355)
Foreign exchange translation............	—	(2,936)
Divestiture..........................	(400)	(163)
Actuarial (gain) loss	722	2,878
Benefit obligation at December 31.........	$43,895	$30,700
Change in Plan Assets		
Fair value of plan assets at January 1	$39,628	$20,595
Actual return on plan assets..............	3,922	3,239
Company contributions	1,432	1,355
Plan participant contributions	41	150
Benefits paid	(2,856)	(1,355)
Foreign exchange translation.............	—	(1,924)
Divestiture..........................	(309)	(95)
Other...............................	(1)	(38)
Fair value of plan assets at December 31 ...	$41,857	$21,927

Ford also discloses the following expected payments to its retirees.

	Pension Benefits	
	U.S. Plans	Non-U.S. Plans
	Benefit Payments	Benefit Payments
2006	$ 2,870	$1,370
2007	2,940	1,230
2008	3,010	1,250
2009	3,050	1,290
2010	3,070	1,330
2011–2015	15,410	7,340

a. Describe what is meant by *service cost* and *interest cost*.
b. What is the total amount paid to retirees during fiscal 2005 for its U.S. and non-U.S. plans? What is the source of funds to make these payments to retirees?
c. Compute the 2005 funded status for Ford's pension plan.
d. What are actuarial gains and losses? What are the plan amendment adjustments, and how do they differ from the actuarial gains and losses?
e. In 2005, Ford contributed $2,787 million ($1,432 million + $1,355 million) to its pension plan in 2005. Ford reports $21.7 billion of net cash inflows from operating activities and $7.5 billion in capital expenditures for 2005. How does this information impact our evaluation of Ford's financial condition given the pension disclosures discussed above?

E10-25. Analyzing and Interpreting Pension and Health Care Footnote (LO2)

Xerox reports the following pension footnote as part of its 2005 10-K report.

Xerox Corporation
(XRX)

(in millions)	Pension Benefits		Other Benefits	
	2005	2004	2005	2004
Change in Benefit Obligation				
Benefit obligation, January 1	$10,028	$8,971	$1,662	$1,579
Service cost	234	222	19	22
Interest cost	581	660	90	89
Plan participants' contributions	11	14	15	18
Plan amendments	30	232	44	—
Actuarial loss (gain)	527	272	(54)	70
Currency exchange rate changes	(486)	356	4	6
Curtailments	(5)	(2)	—	—
Special termination benefits	—	2	—	—
Benefits paid/settlements	(618)	(699)	(127)	(122)
Benefit obligation, December 31	$10,302	$10,028	$1,653	$1,662
Change in Plan Assets				
Fair value of plan assets, January 1	$ 8,110	$ 7,301	$ —	$ —
Actual return on plan assets	933	772	—	—
Employer contribution	388	409	112	104
Plan participants' contributions	11	14	15	18
Currency exchange rate changes	(418)	311	—	—
Transfers/divestitures	38	2	—	—
Benefits paid/settlements	(618)	(699)	(127)	(122)
Fair value of plan assets, December 31	$ 8,444	$ 8,110	$ —	$ —

(in millions)	Pension Benefits			Other Benefits		
	2005	2004	2003	2005	2004	2003
Components of Net Periodic Benefit Cost						
Defined benefit plans						
Service cost	$234	$222	$197	$ 20	$ 22	$ 26
Interest cost	581	660	934	90	89	91
Expected return on plan assets	(622)	(678)	(940)	—	—	—
Recognized net actuarial loss	98	104	53	31	24	13
Amortization of prior service cost	(3)	(1)	—	(24)	(24)	(18)
Recognized net transition (asset) obligation	1	(1)	—	—	—	—
Recognized curtailment/settlement loss (gain)	54	44	120	—	—	(4)
Net periodic benefit cost	343	350	364	117	111	108
Special termination benefits	—	2	—	—	—	—
Defined contribution plans	71	69	62	—	—	—
Total	$414	$421	$426	$117	$111	$108

a. Describe what is meant by *service cost* and *interest cost* (the service and interest costs appear both in the reconciliation of the PBO and in the computation of pension expense).

b. What is the actual return on pension and health care plan investments in 2005? Was Xerox's profitability impacted by this amount?

c. Provide an example under which an "actuarial loss," such as the $527 million charge in 2005 that Xerox reports, might arise.

    d. What is the source of funds to make payments to retirees?

    e. How much cash did Xerox contribute to its pension and health care plans in 2005?

    f. How much cash did retirees receive in 2005? How much cash did Xerox pay retirees?

    g. Show the computation of its 2005 funded status for the pension and health care plans.

E10-26. **Analyzing and Interpreting Pension and Health Care Disclosures** **(LO2)**

Verizon (VZ)

Verizon reports the following pension and health care benefits footnote as part of its 10-K report.

Obligations At December 31 (dollars in millions)	Pension		Health Care and Life	
	2005	2004	2005	2004
Change in Benefit Obligation				
Beginning of year	$37,395	$40,968	$27,077	$24,581
Service cost	721	712	373	282
Interest cost	2,070	2,289	1,519	1,479
Plan amendments	181	(65)	59	248
Actuarial loss, net	390	2,467	520	2,017
Benefits paid	(2,977)	(2,884)	(1,706)	(1,532)
Termination benefits	11	4	1	2
Settlements	(35)	(6,105)	—	—
Acquisitions and divestitures, net	(194)	—	(34)	—
Other	(1)	9	—	—
End of year	$37,561	$37,395	$27,809	$27,077
Change in Plan Assets				
Beginning of year	$39,106	$42,776	$ 4,549	$ 4,467
Actual return on plan assets	4,246	4,874	348	471
Company contributions	852	443	1,085	1,143
Benefits paid	(2,977)	(2,884)	(1,706)	(1,532)
Settlements	(35)	(6,105)	—	—
Acquisitions and divestitures, net	(202)	2	—	—
End of year	$40,990	$39,106	$ 4,276	$ 4,549

Net Periodic Cost Years Ended December 31 (dollars in millions)	Pension			Health Care and Life		
	2005	2004	2003	2005	2004	2003
Service cost	$ 721	$ 712	$ 785	$ 373	$ 282	$ 176
Interest cost	2,070	2,289	2,436	1,519	1,479	1,203
Expected return on plan assets	(3,348)	(3,709)	(4,150)	(353)	(414)	(430)
Amortization of transition asset	—	(4)	(41)	2	2	2
Amortization of prior service cost	45	60	23	285	234	(9)
Actuarial loss (gain), net	146	57	(337)	278	187	130
Net periodic benefit (income) cost	$ (366)	$ (595)	$(1,284)	$2,104	$1,770	$1,072

    a. Describe what is meant by *service cost* and *interest cost*.

    b. What payments did retirees receive during fiscal 2005 from the pension and from the health care plans? What is the source of funds to make payments to retirees?

    c. Show the computation of Verizon's 2005 funded status for both the pension and health care plans.

    d. What expense does Verizon's income statement report for both its pension and health care plans?

    e. Explain the difference between the actuarial loss of $390 million that Verizon reported in its reconciliation of the PBO, and the loss relating to plan amendments of $181 million.

E10-27. **Analyzing and Interpreting Disclosure on Off-Balance-Sheet Financing** (LO3)

Harley-Davidson provides the following footnote in its 10-K report relating to the securitization of receivables by its finance subsidiary, Harley-Davidson Financial Services (HDFS).

Harley-Davidson,
Inc. (HOG)

> **OFF-BALANCE-SHEET ARRANGEMENTS:** As part of its securitization program, HDFS transfers retail motorcycle loans to a special purpose bankruptcy-remote wholly-owned subsidiary. The subsidiary sells the retail loans to a securitization trust in exchange for the proceeds from asset-backed securities issued by the securitization trust. The asset-backed securities, usually notes with various maturities and interest rates, are secured by future collections of the purchased retail installment loans. Activities of the securitization trust are limited to acquiring retail loans, issuing asset-backed securities and making payments on securities to investors. Due to the nature of the assets held by the securitization trust and the limited nature of its activities, the securitization trusts are considered QSPEs as defined by SFAS No. 140. In accordance with SFAS No. 140, assets and liabilities of the QSPEs are not consolidated in the financial statements of the Company.
>
> HDFS does not guarantee payments on the securities issued by the securitization trusts or the projected cash flows from the related loans purchased from HDFS. Investors also do not have recourse to assets of HDFS for failure of the obligors on the retail loans to pay when due.

a. Describe in your own words, the securitization process employed by HDFS.

b. What is the importance of the characterization of its SPE as a Qualifying Special Purpose Entity (QSPE)?

c. What is the importance of the statement that HDFS does not guarantee obligations of its QSPE?

d. What is the importance of "bankruptcy remote." How is this achieved?

e. What are the analysis implications of the use of QSPEs?

PROBLEMS

P10-28. **Analyzing, Interpreting and Capitalizing Operating Leases** (LO1)

The Abercrombie & Fitch 10-K report contains the following footnote relating to its leasing activities. This is the only information it discloses relating to its leasing activity.

Abercrombie & Fitch
(ANF)

> At January 28, 2006, the Company was committed to non-cancelable leases with remaining terms of one to 15 years. A summary of operating lease commitments under non-cancelable leases follows (thousands):

2006	$187,674
2007	$187,397
2008	$178,595
2009	$169,856
2010	$155,670
Thereafter	$538,635

Required

a. What lease assets and lease liabilities does Abercrombie report on its balance sheet? How do we know?

b. What effect has the operating lease classification have on A&F's balance sheet? Over the life of the lease, what effect does this classification have on its net income?

c. Using a 7% discount rate, estimate the assets and liabilities that A&F fails to report as a result of its off-balance-sheet lease financing.

d. Assuming that its operating leases relate to real estate, and that A&F depreciated such assets on a straight-line basis with no salvage value and useful life of 8 years, estimate the effect on the company's operating profit before tax of capitalizing these operating leases.

e. How are the financial ratios from the ROE disaggregation (such as margin, turnover, and leverage) affected and in what direction (increased or decreased) if A&F's operating leases are capitalized?

P10-29. Analyzing, Interpreting and Capitalizing Operating Leases (LO1)

Best Buy (BBY)

The Best Buy 10-K report has the following footnote related to its leasing activities.

The future minimum lease payments under our capital and operating leases by fiscal year at February 25, 2006, are as follows ($ millions):

Fiscal Year	Capital Leases	Operating Leases
2007	$ 5	$ 602
2008	4	605
2009	4	582
2010	3	546
2011	3	513
Thereafter	20	3,080
Subtotal	39	$5,928
Less: imputed interest	(12)	
Present value of lease obligations	$27	

Required

a. What is the balance of the lease liabilities reported on Best Buy's balance sheet?

b. What effect has the operating lease classification had on its balance sheet? Over the life of the lease, what effect does this classification have on its net income?

c. Compute the imputed rate on Best Buy's capital leases.

d. Use a 7% discount rate to estimate the assets and liabilities that Best Buy fails to report as a result of its off-balance-sheet lease financing.

e. Assuming that the operating leases relate to real estate, and that Best Buy depreciated such assets on a straight-line basis with no salvage value and a useful life of 11 years, estimate the effect on the company's operating profit before tax of capitalizing these operating leases.

f. How are financial ratios from the ROE disaggregation (such as margins, turnover, and leverage) affected and in what direction (increased or decreased) if Best Buy's operating leases are capitalized?

P10-30. Analyzing, Interpreting and Capitalizing Operating Leases (LO1)

FedEx (FDX)

FedEx reports total assets of $20,404 and total liabilities of $10,816 for 2005 ($ millions). Its 10-K report has the following footnote related to its leasing activities.

A summary of future minimum lease payments under capital leases at May 31, 2005 is as follows (in millions):

2006	$121
2007	22
2008	99
2009	11
2010	96
Thereafter	130
	479
Less amount representing interest	78
Present value of net minimum lease payments	$401

A summary of future minimum lease payments under non-cancelable operating leases (principally aircraft, retail locations and facilities) with an initial or remaining term in excess of one year at May 31, 2005 is as follows (in millions):

	Aircraft and Related Equipment	Facilities and Other	Total
2006	$ 607	$1,039	$ 1,646
2007	606	912	1,518
2008	585	771	1,356
2009	555	636	1,191
2010	544	501	1,045
Thereafter	4,460	2,789	7,249
	$7,357	$6,648	$14,005

Required

a. What is the balance of lease assets and lease liabilities as reported on FedEx's balance sheet? Explain.

b. Impute the discount rate that FedEx is using to compute the present value of its capital leases.

c. Assuming a 3% discount rate, estimate the amount of assets and liabilities that FedEx fails to report as a result of its off-balance-sheet lease financing.

d. Assuming that the operating leases relate to real estate, and that FedEx depreciated such assets on a straight-line basis with no salvage value and a useful life of 12 years, estimate the effect on the company's operating profit before tax of capitalizing these operating leases.

e. How are financial ratios from the ROE disaggregation (such as margin, turnover, and leverage) affected and in what direction (increased or decreased) if FedEx's operating leases are capitalized?

f. What portion of total lease liabilities did FedEx report on-balance-sheet and what portion is off-balance-sheet?

g. Based on your analysis, do you believe that FedEx's balance sheet adequately reports its aircraft and facilities assets and related obligations? Explain.

P10-31. Analyzing and Interpreting Pension Disclosures (LO2)

DuPont's 10-K report has the following disclosures related to its retirement plans ($ millions).

DuPont (DD)

($ millions)	Pension Benefits	
	2005	2004
Change in benefit obligation		
Benefit obligation at beginning of year	$21,757	$21,196
Service cost	349	351
Interest cost	1,160	1,198
Plan participants' contributions	11	12
Actuarial loss (gain)	1,537	1,409
Foreign currency exchange rate changes . . .	(402)	275
Benefits paid	(1,503)	(1,528)
Amendments	3	6
Net effects of acquisitions/divestitures	23	(1,162)
Benefit obligation at end of year	$22,935	$21,757
Change in plan assets		
Fair value of plan assets at beginning of year	$18,250	$17,967
Actual gain on plan assets	2,038	2,182
Foreign currency exchange rate changes . . .	(261)	187
Employer contributions	1,253	709
Plan participants' contributions	11	12
Benefits paid	(1,503)	(1,528)
Net effects of acquisitions/divestitures	4	(1,279)
Fair value of plan assets at end of year	$19,792	$18,250

Components of net periodic benefit cost (credit)	Pension Benefits		
	2005	2004	2003
Service cost	$ 349	$ 351	$ 342
Interest cost	1,160	1,198	1,223
Expected return on plan assets	(1,416)	(1,343)	(1,368)
Amortization of transition asset	(1)	(5)	(8)
Amortization of unrecognized loss	304	306	237
Amortization of prior service cost	37	42	51
Curtailment/settlement (gain) loss	(1)	448	77
Net periodic benefit cost	$ 432	$ 997	$ 554

Weighted-average assumptions used to determine net periodic benefit cost for years ended December 31	Pension Benefits	
	2005	2004
Discount rate	5.58%	6.06%
Expected return on plan assets	8.74%	8.85%
Rate of compensation increase	4.29%	4.29%

The following benefit payments, which reflect future service, as appropriate, are expected to be paid:

(In millions)	Pension Benefits
2006	$1,449
2007	1,432
2008	1,420
2009	1,417
2010	1,417
Years 2011–2015	7,360

Required

a. How much pension expense (revenue) does DuPont report in its 2005 income statement?

b. DuPont reports a $1,416 million expected return on pension plan assets as an offset to 2005 pension expense. Approximately, how is this amount computed? What is DuPont's actual gain or loss realized on its 2005 pension plan assets? What is the purpose of using this estimated amount instead of the actual gain or loss?

c. What factors affected DuPont's pension liability during 2005? What factors affected its pension plan assets during 2005?

d. What does the term *funded status* mean? What is the funded status of the 2005 DuPont pension plans?

e. DuPont reduced its discount rate from 6.06% to 5.58% in 2005. What effect(s) does this reduction have on its balance sheet and its income statement?

f. How did DuPont's pension plan affect the company's cash flow in 2005?

g. In 2005, DuPont contributed $1.253 billion to its pension plan.

(1) DuPont reports total assets of $33.3 billon and stockholders' equity of $8.9 billion. How does this funded status, and the projected benefit payments, impact our evaluation of DuPont's financial condition.

(2) DuPont reports $2.5 billion of net cash inflows from operating activities and $1.3 billion in capital expenditures for 2005. How does this information impact our evaluation of DuPont's financial condition.

P10-32. Analyzing and Interpreting Pension Disclosures (LO2)

Dow Chemical provides the following footnote disclosures in its 10-K report relating to its defined benefit pension plans and its other postretirement benefits.

Dow Chemical (DOW)

Net Periodic Benefit Cost (Credit) for All Significant Plans						
	Defined Benefit Pension Plans			Other Postretirement Benefits		
In millions	2005	2004	2003	2005	2004	2003
Service cost	$ 279	$ 260	$ 242	$ 24	$ 24	$ 31
Interest cost	815	804	773	124	125	134
Expected return on plan assets	(1,056)	(1,092)	(1,082)	(27)	(23)	(19)
Amortization of prior service cost (credit). . .	24	8	21	(7)	(11)	(9)
Amortization of unrecognized loss	123	39	13	10	8	8
Special termination/curtailment cost	2	42	5	6	37	—
Net periodic benefit cost (credit)	$ 187	$ 61	$ (28)	$130	$160	$145

Change in Projected Benefit Obligation, Plan Assets and Funded Status of All Significant Plans				
	Defined Benefit Pension Plans		Other Postretirement Benefits	
In millions	2005	2004	2005	2004
Change in projected benefit obligation				
Benefit obligation at beginning of year.	$15,004	$13,443	$2,167	$2,134
Service cost	279	260	24	24
Interest cost	815	804	124	125
Plan participants' contributions	18	18	—	—
Amendments	26	6	—	21
Actuarial changes in assumptions and experience	698	917	28	37
Acquisition/divestiture activity	—	7	—	(5)
Benefits paid	(808)	(779)	(179)	(208)
Currency impact.	(401)	303	4	6
Special termination/curtailment cost (credit)	(14)	25	—	33
Benefit obligation at end of year	$15,617	$15,004	$2,168	$2,167
Change in plan assets				
Market value of plan assets at beginning of year.	$12,206	$11,139	$ 368	$ 343
Actual return on plan assets.	877	1,428	25	32
Employer contributions	1,031	399	—	33
Plan participants' contributions	18	19	—	—
Acquisition/divestiture activity	—	—	—	(6)
Benefits paid	(808)	(779)	(16)	(34)
Market value of plan assets at end of year	$13,324	$12,206	$ 377	$ 368

U.S. Plan Assumptions for Other Postretirement Benefits	Net Periodic Costs for the Year	
	2005	2004
Discount rate	5.875%	6.25%
Expected long-term rate of return on plan assets	8.75%	9.00%
Initial health care cost trend rate	10.16%	6.70%
Ultimate health care cost trend rate, assumed to be reached in 2011 . . .	6.00%	6.70%

Required

a. How much pension expense does Dow Chemical report in its 2005 income statement?

b. Dow reports a $1,056 million expected return on pension plan assets as an offset to 2005 pension expense. Approximately, how is this amount computed? What is the actual gain or loss realized on Dow's 2005 pension plan assets? What is the purpose of using this estimated amount instead of the actual gain or loss?

c. What factors affected Dow's pension liability during 2005? What factors affected its pension plan assets during 2005?

d. What does the term *funded status* mean? What is the funded status of the 2005 Dow pension plans and postretirement benefit plans?

e. Dow reduced its discount rate from 6.25% to 5.875% in 2005. What effect(s) does this reduction have on its balance sheet and its income statement?

f. Dow decreased its estimate of expected returns on plan assets from 9% to 8.75% in 2005. What effect(s) does this decrease have on its income statement? Explain.

g. How did Dow's pension plan affect the company's cash flow in 2005?

CASES

C10-33. Management Application and Ethics: Structuring Leases   (LO1)

You are the CEO of a company. Your CFO is concerned about certain covenants in your debt agreement that specify a maximum ratio of liabilities to stockholders' equity. He proposes to structure your leases as "operating" so as to avoid capitalization. In order to do so, he proposes to structure the lease with an initial term of 5 years, and with three 5-year renewal options instead of a flat 20-year lease. That way, the lease term will not exceed 75% of the useful life of the leased assets, and the present value of the lease payments will not exceed 90% of the fair market value of the leased assets. The CFO explains that these two requirements usually trigger lease capitalization. He asks for your input into this decision.

a. What are the management issues that you feel are relevant for this decision? That is, how might this lease structure impact your company?

b. What are the ethical issues that are raised by the CFO's proposal? Explain.

Adjusting and Forecasting Financial Statements

LEARNING OBJECTIVES

LO1 Describe and illustrate adjustments to financial statements. (p. 11-4)

LO2 Explain and illustrate the forecasting of financial statements. (p. 11-11)

LO3 Describe and illustrate a parsimonious method for multiyear forecasting of net operating profit and net operating assets. (p. 11-24)

PROCTER & GAMBLE

Procter & Gamble (P&G) has successfully reinvented itself . . . again. It has shed its image as the "lumbering giant" of its industry with new products and directed marketing. Its annual sales now exceed $68 billion, following its acquisition of Gillette. P&G has also focused on its higher margin products such as those in beauty care. This has improved its profit margin and provided much needed dollars for marketing activities. Its advertising budget is nearly 10% of sales, which is nearly double the budget of some of its key competitors. P&G also spends over $2 billion per year (3% of sales) on R&D. *BusinessWeek* (2006) reported that "P&G had to tear apart and re-stitch much of its research organization. It created new job classifications, such as 70 worldwide 'technology entrepreneurs,' or TEs, who act as scouts, looking for the latest breakthroughs from places such as university labs." P&G's goal is for 50% of its new products to come from outside of the company.

P&G's financial performance has been impressive. In 2006, it generated over $11 billion of operating cash flow, and the company has only begun to fully exploit the resources acquired in the Gillette acquisition. Its abundant cash flow allows it to fund the level of advertising and R&D necessary to remain a dominant force in the consumer products industry as well as to pay over $3.5 billion in dividends to shareholders. *Business-Week* (2006) asserts that "P&G long has been the largest household-

Getty Images

products company in the world, and under (CEO) Lafley's six-year tenure, it may have become the best operator in its group."

P&G's product list is impressive. It consists of numerous well-recognized household brands. Total sales of Procter & Gamble products are distributed across its three business segments as illustrated in the chart to the side. A partial listing of its brands follows:

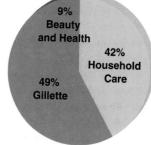

- **Beauty and Health.** Always, Head & Shoulders, Olay, Pantene, Wella, Cover Girl, Herbal Essences, Hugo Boss, Nice 'n Easy, Old Spice, Safeguard, Secret, Tampax, Crest, Oral-B, Fixodent, Metamucil, Pepto-Bismol, Prilosec OTC, PUR, Scope, ThermaCare, Vicks

- **Household Care.** Ariel, Dawn, Downy, Tide, Bold, Bounce, Cascade, Cheer, Dash, Febreze, Gain, Mr. Clean, Swiffer, Bounty, Charmin, Pampers, Luvs, Puffs, Folgers, Iams, Pringles

- **Gillette.** MACH3, Fusion, Gillette, Duracell, Braun

P&G's recent successes have coincided with strong leadership. A.G. Lafley's innovations and market savvy have consistently propelled P&G. *BusinessWeek* (2004) explains: "From its Swiffer mop to battery-powered Crest SpinBrush toothbrushes and Whitestrip tooth whiteners, P&G has simply done a better job than rivals." Since assuming the top job, Lafley has guided P&G to successive increases in sales, income, and cash flows. Such increases have driven impressive gains in its stock price as follows.

(Continued on next page)

(Continued from previous page)

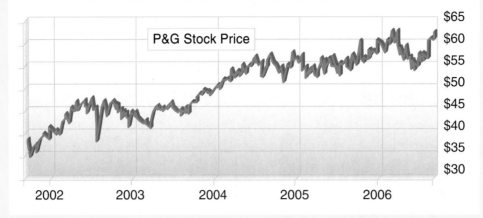

Forecasts of financial performance drive stock price. Historical financial statements are relevant to the extent that they provide information useful to forecast financial performance. Accordingly, considerable emphasis is placed on generating reliable forecasts.

This module explains the forecasting process, which typically involves two steps: (1) Historical financial statements are adjusted, if needed, to yield an income statement and statement of cash flows that identifies recurring operating income and cash flows, and an adjusted balance sheet that reflects all of the assets used in the business and the total amounts for which the company is liable. (2) Future financial performance is forecasted using the adjusted financial statements. The steady increase in P&G's stock price reflects increased optimism about its future financial performance and condition.

Sources: *Procter & Gamble* 2005–2006 10-K and Annual Reports; *BusinessWeek,* April 2006; *Barron's*, November 2006; *The Wall Street Journal,* January 2005.

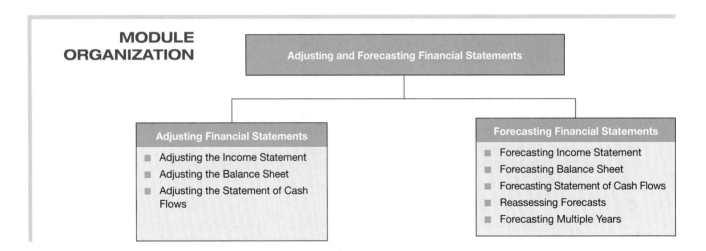

INTRODUCTION

Forecasting financial performance is integral to a variety of business decisions ranging from investing to managing a company effectively. We might, for example, wish to value a company's common stock before purchasing its shares. To that end, we might use one of the valuation models we discuss in Module 12. Or, we might be interested in evaluating the creditworthiness of a prospective borrower. In that case, we forecast the borrower's cash flows to estimate its ability to repay its obligations. We might also be interested in evaluating alternative strategic investment decisions. In this case, we can use our forecasts to evaluate the shareholder value that the investment will create.

The forecasting process begins with a retrospective analysis. That is, we analyze current and prior years' statements to be sure that they accurately reflect the company's financial condition and performance. If we believe that they do not, we adjust those statements to better reflect economic reality. Once we've adjusted the historical results, we are ready to forecast future results.

Why would we need to adjust historical results? The answer resides in the fact that financial statements prepared in conformity with GAAP do not always accurately reflect the "true" financial condition and performance of the company. This situation can arise for several reasons including the following:

▪ The income statement might include transitory items, such as an asset write-down or the accrual of expected restructuring costs; thus, current period income does not provide an accurate forecast of future income as we expect one-time (transitory) items to not recur.

▪ The balance sheet might include nonoperating assets and liabilities such as those from discontinued operations; by definition, such assets do not generate future profits. Conversely, the balance sheet might exclude operating assets and liabilities such as those from operating leases or from investments accounted for using the equity method. Forecasts would be less accurate if they failed to take these excluded assets and liabilities into account.

▪ The statement of cash flows might include operating cash inflows from excessive inventory reductions, from securitization of accounts receivable, or from tax benefits on the exercise of employee stock options. Adjustments to the current statement of cash flows might be necessary before projecting future cash flows.

These are just a few examples of how GAAP financial statements might not accurately reflect a company's true economic performance and condition. Consequently, we want to adjust GAAP financial statements before using them to forecast future financial statements.

ADJUSTING FINANCIAL STATEMENTS

LO1 Describe and illustrate adjustments to financial statements.

We begin by discussing how to adjust financial statements for purposes of forecasting. This *adjusting process,* also referred to as recasting or reformulating, is not "black and white." It requires judgment and estimation. Our discussion of adjusting (and forecasting) financial statements is meant to introduce a reasonable and reliable, but not the only, process for these tasks. It is important to distinguish between the purposes of GAAP-based financial statements and the adjusting process of this module for purposes of forecasting. Specifically, GAAP-based statements provide more than just information for forecasting. For example, financial statements are key inputs into contracts among business parties. This means that historical results, including any transitory activities, must be reported to meet management's fiduciary responsibilities. On the other hand, to forecast future performance, we need to create a set of financial statements that focus on those items that we expect to persist, with a special emphasis on persistent operating activities.

Adjusting the Income Statement

This section describes how to adjust the income statement for forecasting purposes. Adjustments generally consist of the following three steps:

1. **Separate persistent and transitory items.** The aim of forecasting is to project financial results. Since transitory items are, by definition, nonrecurring, we exclude them from current operating results. Common transitory items include gains and losses from asset sales, the results of discontinued operations, and one-time legal judgments. The purpose of these adjustments is to determine persistent earnings, that is, earnings we expect to recur in the future. Restructuring costs are often considered transitory. Alternatively, we might consider allocating restructuring costs to past and/or future income statements. Assume that a loss on an asset disposal in the current period arises because depreciation in prior periods was too low; that is, depreciation expense failed to match the asset's economic depreciation. Rather than exclude from the income statement the (transitory) loss on disposal, we might adjust prior years' depreciation expense upward. Some other restructuring costs might be better viewed as expenses for future periods. Assume that a firm incurs restructuring costs in the current period with the expectation of increasing future profit via streamlined productions or more efficient work force. Since the benefits of restructuring accrue in the future, we might allocate the restructuring charge to future periods (say, the next three to five). The implications of these adjustments are: current period's profit is usually not as low, and prior

and future periods' profits are typically not as high, because absent these adjustments, the costs are recorded in one period rather than spread over all affected periods. As we see, adjusting earnings requires in-depth knowledge of a company's competitive strategy and how its accounting data reflect its underlying economics. For simplicity only, we simply exclude restructuring costs rather than allocate them (in some ad hoc manner) over past or future periods.

2. **Separate operating and nonoperating items.** Operating activities have the most long-lasting (persistent) effects on future profitability and cash flows and, thus, are the primary value drivers for company stakeholders. It is important to separate operating items from nonoperating items for effective profitability analysis.

3. **Include (or exclude) operating expenses that GAAP-based income excludes (or includes).** We review the types and levels of operating expenses to determine their reasonableness. To the extent a company fails to recognize expenses, whether due to underaccrual of reserves or liabilities, or due to reduced expenditures for key operating activities, reported income is overstated for forecasting purposes. On the other hand, certain expenses can be temporarily high, at levels that the company does not plan to sustain. Our adjustment process includes assessment of both understated and overstated expenses.

Exhibit 11.1 lists some typical adjustments. The list is not exhaustive, it only indicates the types of adjustments that are commonly made.

EXHIBIT 11.1	Common Income Statement Adjustments

1. Separate persistent and transitory items; examples of items to exclude:
   a. Gains and losses relating to
      - Asset sales of long-term assets and investments
      - Asset write-downs of long-term assets and inventories
      - Stock issuances by subsidiaries
      - Debt retirements
   b. Transitory items reported after income from continued operations
      - Discontinued operations
      - Extraordinary items
   c. Restructuring expenses
   d. Merger costs
   e. LIFO liquidation gains
   f. Liability accruals deemed excessive
   g. Lawsuit gains and losses
   h. Revenue or expense from short-term fluctuations in tax rates and from changes in deferred tax valuation allowance
2. Separate operating and nonoperating items; examples:
   a. Treating interest revenue and expense, and investment gains and losses, as nonoperating
   b. Treating pension service cost as operating, and pension interest costs and expected returns as nonoperating
   c. Treating debt retirement gains and losses as nonoperating
   d. Treating income and losses from discontinued operations as nonoperating
3. Include expenses not reflected in net income; examples:
   a. Inadequate (or excessive) reserves for bad debts or asset impairment
   b. Reductions in R&D, advertising, and other discretionary expenses that were made to achieve short-term income targets; conversely, exclude excessive expenses related to product or market development
   c. Employee stock option expense (for financial statements issued before 2006)

The first category in Exhibit 11.1 includes gains and losses from asset sales and asset write-downs, and the financial gains and losses from debt retirements and subsidiary stock sales. To the extent that these items are transitory, they should be excluded when forecasting operating results. GAAP-based income statements help by identifying two types of transitory items that are reported net of tax and below income from continuing operations: discontinued operations and extraordinary items. We exclude other transitory items including restructuring expenses, merger and acquisition costs, LIFO liquidation gains and losses, excessive liability accruals, lawsuit gains or losses, and increases and decreases in tax expense from changes in the deferred tax asset valuation account. Another adjustment relates to tax expense. If the current period's tax expense is too high or too low because of one-time events such as short-lived tax law changes, the resulting tax rate will not persist. Such temporary swings in tax expense should be excluded.

The second step in the adjustment process is to separate operating and nonoperating items. Common nonoperating items are interest revenue and expense, the gains and losses from sales of investments, and pension interest costs and expected returns. Nonoperating components also include gains and losses on debt retirements and income or losses related to discontinued operations.

The third category of adjustments commonly involves adding expenses excluded from current income. Some omitted expenses arise because GAAP does not require their inclusion (such as employee stock option expenses before 2006). Other omitted expenses reflect management's accounting choices, estimates and predictions, which may not coincide with our conclusions about the company's true economic condition. This might include inadequate reserves for uncollectible accounts receivable or contingent liabilities such as warranties, and unrecognized asset impairment costs. We also might adjust income to include additional amounts for R&D, advertising, and other operating expenses that undo discretionary reductions of operating activities to achieve short-term income targets, or exclude those expenses incurred to help achieve the target such as new product development or other discretionary increases.

MANAGERIAL DECISION	You Are a Corporate Analyst

You are a corporate analyst working in the finance department for a company that is preparing its financial statements. You must make a decision regarding the format of its income statement. Specifically, should you subtotal to *pretax operating profit* and segregate nonoperating items? Or, should you subtotal to *pretax profit* and include operating and nonoperating items together? GAAP permits you to report either way. [Answer, p. 11-25]

Adjusting the Balance Sheet

There are two reasons to adjust the balance sheet for forecasting purposes. First, we must separate (exclude) nonoperating assets and liabilities that are reported on the balance sheet. Second, we must include operating assets and liabilities that are *not* reported on the balance sheet. Both types of adjustments typically require use of footnote disclosures to properly assess the nature of the company's assets and liabilities and to determine the nature and size of any excluded assets and liabilities.

Exhibit 11.2 lists several common balance sheet adjustments, but this listing is not exhaustive.

EXHIBIT 11.2	Common Balance Sheet Adjustments

1. Exclude nonoperating assets and liabilities
   a. Eliminate assets and liabilities from discontinued operations
   b. Write-down of assets, including goodwill, that is judged to be impaired
2. Include operating assets and liabilities not reflected in balance sheet; examples:
   a. Capitalize operating assets from operating leases; nonoperating capitalized lease liabilities are also increased
   b. Consolidate off-balance-sheet investments:
      • Equity method investments
      • Special purpose entities (SPEs)
   c. Accrue understated liabilities and assets

The first category in Exhibit 11.2 involves separating (excluding) nonoperating assets and liabilities on the balance sheet. The income statement segregates the gains and losses from discontinued operations (see Exhibit 11.1). Likewise, the assets and liabilities related to discontinued operations are excluded since, by definition, neither those assets and liabilities, nor the sales and expenses of discontinued operations, remain in continuing operations. Other adjustments to the balance sheet include the write-down of impaired assets. Adjustments to reduce assets are difficult judgment calls that benefit from information outside of the financial statements such as financial reports of competitors and analyst reports of the state of the industry. Seeking additional information can refine our opinion about such potential asset impairments.

The second category of adjustments seeks to include operating assets and liabilities not reported in the balance sheet per GAAP. One example is operating leases that are prevalent in several industries, including the retailing and airline industries. Lease disclosures mandated under GAAP provide sufficient information for us to effectively capitalize these operating leases for forecasting purposes (by including both the operating lease assets and the nonoperating lease liabilities, as detailed in Module 10). We also need to consider whether to adjust the balance sheet for unconsolidated investments. When a company exerts significant influence over an investee company (but not control), the equity method of accounting is used. (The equity method of accounting is used for investments in partnerships, joint ventures, and trusts in addition to minority interest in corporations.) Under the equity method, the company's balance sheet has a single investment (asset) account equal to the percentage of the equity in the investee company that the company owns, rather than the full amount of the assets and liabilities of the investee company that would be recognized on-balance-sheet if the entity were consolidated. This means that many unconsolidated assets and liabilities are unreported. Unfortunately, footnote disclosures about equity method investments are insufficient to estimate the full value of the assets and liabilities (and risk) of the investee companies. To the extent that sufficient information is provided in the footnotes, the adjustment process replaces the investment account with the related assets and liabilities using the consolidation mechanics discussed in Module 7.

Other adjustments to the balance sheet include the accrual of understated liabilities. Common accruals such as those relating to operating activities like warranties, premiums, and coupons are somewhat easier to assess and estimate from prior balance sheet data. Accruals for contingent liabilities such as environmental and litigation exposure are more difficult and require use of information outside of the financial statements.

RESEARCH INSIGHT | **Earnings Quality and Accounting Conservatism**

Accounting researchers commonly measure *earnings quality* in terms of sustainability, meaning that the income items persist in future periods. Sustainability is important because persistent income items are better indicators of future earnings than are transitory items. One factor that affects earnings quality is accounting conservatism. Research finds that conservative accounting leads to transitory earnings changes when the levels of investment within the firm changes. Researchers have constructed a conservatism index to study the effect conservatism and growth have on earnings changes. The index is defined as the level of estimated reserves created by conservative accounting (such as LIFO versus FIFO, and expensing of R&D and advertising) divided by the level of net operating assets. Earnings quality is then a function of changes in the conservatism index for each firm, and it is a function of the difference between the firm-specific and industry-specific conservatism index. Poor earnings quality occurs when the firm's accounting accruals grow more quickly or more slowly than net operating assets. A firm-specific conservatism index that substantially differs from that of the firm's industry is one sign of poor earnings quality. This is because a firm's profitability reverts toward the industry mean. While the conservatism index appears to indicate whether or not a firm's earnings are sustainable, market participants do not appear to fully consider the information contained in this index when determining stock prices.

Adjusting the Statement of Cash Flows

The focus of cash flow adjustments is threefold: (1) to adjust operating cash flows for any transitory (abnormal) items, (2) to adjust (exclude) transitory items from investing cash flows, and (3) to reclassify cash flows into their proper sections—operating, investing, or financing. These adjustments typically require use of the other financial statements, including footnote disclosures, and sometimes information from outside the financial statements. It's important to remember why we are adjusting GAAP-based financial statements. It is not because the financials are wrong; the auditor's report provides some assurance that those statements are free of material misstatement. Instead, we are adjusting the cash flow statement to better forecast future cash flows. By including all cash expenditures that we expect to persist, and by excluding transitory items, we obtain cash flows that better reflect the company's future cash flows than the cash flows reported in GAAP-based financial statements.

Exhibit 11.3 lists several common statement of cash flow adjustments, but this listing is not exhaustive. The first category in Exhibit 11.3 involves adjusting operating cash flows for transitory items. These transitory items commonly involve discretionary activities whose amounts are determined by management and sometimes are not in line with reasonable norms. To better understand, recall that operating cash flows increase with an increase in operating income and/or a decrease in net operating working capital (the

EXHIBIT 11.3	Common Statement of Cash Flow Adjustments

1. Adjust operating cash flows for transitory items; examples of adjustments that potentially impact operating cash flows:
   a. Adjust discretionary costs (advertising, R&D, maintenance) to normal, expected levels
   b. Adjust current operating assets (receivables, inventory) to normal, expected levels
   c. Adjust current operating liabilities (payables, accruals) to normal, expected levels
2. Adjust investing cash flows for transitory items, such as cash proceeds from asset disposals (including disposals of discontinued operations) and from tax benefits due to exercise of stock options
3. Review cash flows and reassign them, if necessary, to operating, investing, or financing sections; examples:
   a. Reclassify operating cash inflows from asset securitization to the financing section
   b. Reclassify interest payments from the operating section to the financing section

latter occurs from either or both a decrease in current operating assets or an increase in current operating liabilities). Although higher operating cash flows are generally viewed favorably, it is necessary to understand the drivers of that increase to discern whether or not future cash flows are expected to exhibit similar behavior. Following are several common adjustments to operating cash flows for nonoperating items:

- **Cost decreases.** Transitory, abnormal reductions of necessary, expected operating costs related to discretionary expenditures on advertising, promotion, R&D, and maintenance. Such reductions increase income and operating cash flows, which usually yield short-term benefits at long-term costs.

- **Current asset decreases.** Transitory, abnormal reductions in current operating assets, such as accounts receivable and inventory, increase net cash flows from operations. Such reductions are generally desirable. However, if such reductions are the result of overly restrictive credit policies or depressed inventories below what is necessary to conduct operations, then increased (short-term) operating cash flows likely result in long-term costs as customers leave or face stock-outs causing the company's image to deteriorate.

- **Current liability increases.** Transitory, abnormal increases in current operating liabilities such as accounts payable and other accrued liabilities increase operating cash flows. After some point, however, the cash inflows from extending the payment of accounts payable or other liabilities come at the cost of supplier and creditor relations.

The second category involves adjusting investing cash flows for transitory items. One example is cash proceeds from asset disposals that are greater than normal levels. To determine the normal level of operating cash flows from asset disposals, we must look at trends over time and asset growth patterns.

BUSINESS INSIGHT	What is eBay's Operating Cash Flow?

Steve Milunovich of **Merrill Lynch** believes that operating cash flow should exclude what companies spend to buy back stock to offset employee stock option-related dilution. This gets tricky in **eBay**'s case because it, unlike many others, hasn't bought back any stock to offset the dilutive effects of additional stock issuances following the exercise of stock options. This means that, even if you're a stockholder who never sold a share, you own less of eBay now than you did five years ago. It is estimated that had eBay bought back shares to enable stockholders to maintain their ownership stake rather than seeing it decline, the cash outflow would have been $1.2 billion, which is huge relative to eBay's five-year cumulative operating cash flow of $1.8 billion. (*Fortune* 2004)

The third category involves the proper categorization of cash flows into operating, investing, and financing sections. One example is cash inflows from asset securitizations, which are reported as operating cash flows per GAAP. However, companies commonly sell accounts receivable to a special purpose entity (see Module 10). The cash flow from the sale is categorized as an operating cash inflow in the year of sale, but is better viewed as a financing cash inflow (similar to borrowing against the receivables). Another example is cash flows from discontinued operations that should be reclassified from operating to investing.

BUSINESS INSIGHT | **Tyco Buys Operating Cash Flow**

Corporate management is aware of the market's focus on operating cash flow, which is a main driver of free cash flow and is used in many stock valuation models. In 2001, Tyco touted its free cash flows in a press release: *Free Cash Flow Reaches $1.7 Billion for the Fourth Quarter and $4.75 Billion for the Fiscal Year.* Said L. Dennis Kozlowski, then chairman and CEO of Tyco, "Strong cash flow generation throughout all of our businesses funds further investment in these businesses and provides the means to opportunistically expand them as circumstances allow." Tyco eventually admitted to spending $830 million to purchase roughly 800,000 individual customer contracts for its security-alarm business from a network of independent dealers. Cash outflows relating to this purchase were reported in the *investing* section of its statement of cash flows. However, fees paid by these new customers were reported in net income and immediately added to its *operating* cash flow. *The Wall Street Journal* (March 2002) declared that Tyco effectively bought earnings and operating cash flow with its contract purchases.

MID-MODULE REVIEW 1

Part 1 Income Statement Adjustments.

Following is the income statement of Time Warner, Inc.

Years ended December 31 ($ millions)	2005	2004	2003
Revenues			
Subscriptions	$22,222	$21,605	$20,448
Advertising	7,612	6,955	6,180
Content	12,615	12,350	11,446
Other	1,203	1,179	1,489
Total revenues	43,652	42,089	39,563
Costs of revenues	(25,075)	(24,449)	(23,422)
Selling, general and administrative	(10,478)	(10,274)	(9,778)
Amortization of intangible assets	(597)	(626)	(640)
Amounts related to securities litigation and government investigations	(2,865)	(536)	(56)
Merger-related and restructuring costs	(117)	(50)	(109)
Asset impairments	(24)	(10)	(318)
Gains on disposal of assets, net	23	21	14
Operating income	4,519	6,165	5,254
Interest expense, net	(1,266)	(1,533)	(1,734)
Other income, net	1,124	521	1,210
Minority interest expense, net	(285)	(246)	(214)
Income before income taxes, discontinued operations and cumulative effect of accounting change	4,092	4,907	4,516
Income tax provision	(1,187)	(1,698)	(1,370)
Income before discontinued operations and cumulative effect of accounting change	2,905	3,209	3,146
Discontinued operations, net of tax	—	121	(495)
Other revenues (expenses)	—	34	(12)
Net income	$ 2,905	$ 3,364	$ 2,639

Required

Identify and discuss any items that you would adjust in the income statement of Time Warner to forecast its future earnings.

Solution

Time Warner's income statement should be adjusted in several ways to forecast future earnings. Consider the following potential adjustments:

1. *Separate persistent and transitory items*
   a. Time Warner faces litigation every year; so, while the $2,865 million line item relating to securities litigation is a persistent item, the amount has increased substantially over this three year period. We want to know the reasons for this litigation and whether the trend will continue. The portion of the expense that is deemed to be transitory should be eliminated for forecasting purposes.
   b. Although Time Warner has reported merger and restructuring costs, each year over this period, these costs are considered transitory for our purposes. Further, Time Warner is not a typical *roll-up company* (achieving growth via acquisitions). Thus, we treat these costs as nonrecurring and we want to know more details about these costs. The portion of the expense that is deemed to be transitory should be eliminated for forecasting purposes.
   c. Asset impairments have been recurring, but declining as a proportion of revenue; we want to know if this trend will continue. The portion of the expense that is deemed to be transitory should be eliminated for forecasting purposes.
   d. Its net gain on disposal of assets, although a minor amount in this case, warrants attention. We must watch for recognition of gains and losses on asset sales, especially when the gain allows a company to achieve earnings targets or the loss is taken in a year of excessive income (or losses). This gain should be eliminated in our forecasts as it is likely transitory.
   e. Its income (loss) from discontinued operations is, by definition, eliminated from the income statement once the operations are disposed of; thus, this item is transitory and we exclude it.
2. *Separate operating and nonoperating items*
   a. Time Warner classifies $1,124 million of income as nonoperating, which is 23% of its pretax income. We would read the financial statement footnotes and the MD&A from the 10-K to learn more about this nonoperating income. We will use the Time Warner classification, unless further information in the footnotes or otherwise leads us to consider it as operating.
3. *Include expenses not reflected in net income*
   a. Time Warner has written off a substantial amount of goodwill since its merger with AOL. Yet, goodwill remains a third of its total assets at 2005 year-end. We want to know if further impairment will be recognized. If so, we should recognize the goodwill impairment before commencing our projections.

Part 2 Balance Sheet Adjustments.

DuPont's 2005 10-K report includes information relating to the company's equity method investments. The following footnote reports summary balance sheet amounts for its affiliated companies for which DuPont uses the equity method of accounting. The information below is shown on a 100 percent basis followed by the carrying value of DuPont's investment in these affiliates.

Financial Position at December 31 (in millions)	2005	2004
Current assets	$1,292	$1,972
Noncurrent assets	1,780	2,811
Total assets	$3,072	$4,783
Short-term borrowings	$ 606	$ 734
Other current liabilities	621	932
Long-term borrowings	259	716
Other long-term liabilities	111	305
Total liabilities	$1,597	$2,687
DuPont's investment in affiliates (includes advances of $55 and $84, respectively)	$ 844	$1,034

Required

What adjustments to DuPont's net operating assets are necessary to incorporate the footnote information above assuming that we conclude these equity method investments are integral to DuPont's operating activities (each of the investee companies' assets are operating, as are "other" liabilities)?

Solution

The equity of the investee companies is $1,475 million ($3,072 million − $1,597 million). These investments must have been acquired at an amount greater than book value since the investment balance represents 53% of the equity ([$844 million − $55 million] / $1,475 million). Assuming that these investments are 50% owned, the required adjustments to DuPont's NOA follow ($ millions):

Elimination of equity method investment from DuPont's NOA ($844 million − $55 million) ..	$ (789)
Add NOA of equity method investees ($3,072 million − $621 million − $111 million)	2,340
Net increase in DuPont's NOA...	$1,551

DuPont's NOA, therefore, increased by $1,551 million. (*Note:* The minority interest of outside investors is accounted for as a Minority Interest account, a nonoperating liability.)

FORECASTING FINANCIAL STATEMENTS

LO2 Explain and illustrate the forecasting of financial statements.

Stock valuation models typically use forecasted financial information to estimate stock price. Creditors also utilize forecasted financial information to evaluate the cash flows available to repay indebtedness. Knowing how to forecast financial information is, therefore, an important skill to master. In this section, we introduce the most common method to forecast the income statement, balance sheet, and statement of cash flows. It is important to forecast the income statement first, then the balance sheet, and then the statement of cash flows in that order since each succeeding statement uses forecast information from the previous forecasted statement(s). Our description, therefore, proceeds in that same order.

We use **Procter & Gamble**'s fiscal 2006 financial statements for illustration. In practice, the forecasting process begins with the adjusted financial statements resulting from the adjusting process explained in the prior section. P&G is generally free from needed adjustments with one exception. Comparing P&G sales for 2005 and 2006, we see a 20.2% increase ([$68,222/$56,741] − 1). This sales growth is high and we question its persistence. Further analysis reveals P&G's 2006 sales include eight months of sales from Gillette after its acquisition by P&G during 2006. P&G's 2005 sales do not include those from Gillette. Thus, comparing 2005 to 2006 is not a valid comparison. Footnotes reveal pro forma sales that show what the income statement would have reported had Gillette's full-year sales been included in both 2005 and 2006, P&G's sales growth would have been 4.4%, which is more realistic and is the forecasted sales growth we use. Although this item does not require us to actually adjust P&G's income statement, it does necessitate an adjustment to our assumptions before we can forecast future income.

Forecasting the Income Statement

Procter & Gamble's fiscal year income statement is shown in Exhibit 11.4.

EXHIBIT 11.4	Procter & Gamble Income Statement		
Years ended June 30 (in millions)	**2006**	**2005**	**2004**
Net sales.....................................	**$68,222**	$56,741	$51,407
Cost of products sold...........................	**33,125**	27,872	25,143
Selling, general and administrative expense	**21,848**	18,400	16,882
Operating income..............................	**13,249**	10,469	9,382
Interest expense...............................	**1,119**	834	629
Other nonoperating income, net	**283**	346	152
Earnings before income taxes	**12,413**	9,981	8,905
Income taxes	**3,729**	3,058	2,749
Net earnings..................................	**$ 8,684**	$ 6,923	$ 6,156

Assuming that we have made all necessary adjustments (see prior section), we can use the adjusted (persistent) income statement numbers to forecast future earnings.

The first step is to forecast sales.[1] As explained, we expect P&G's sales growth rate to be 4.4%. The second step in the forecasting process is to identify several key relations among the income statement line items. These key relations capture associations between specific income statement items; associations that we *assume* will persist at the same level in the future. Exhibit 11.5 lists these key relations using the Procter & Gamble income statement from Exhibit 11.4.

EXHIBIT 11.5 Procter & Gamble Key Income Statement Relations	
$ millions	**2006**
Net sales growth (see text explanation using pro forma numbers)	4.4%
Cost of products sold margin ($33,125/$68,222).	48.6%
Selling, general and administrative expense/Net sales ($21,848/$68,222)	32.0%
Interest expense.	no change
Other nonoperating income, net	no change
Income taxes/Earnings before income taxes ($3,729/$12,413)*	30.0%

* Exhibit 11.5 uses P&G's average tax rate of 30%, computed as total tax expense divided by total pretax income. This is a simplification that usually works well, yields reasonable forecasts, and is used throughout Module 11. A refinement uses the tax rate on operating profit as discussed in Module 4. Under that method, we compute tax expense on net nonoperating expense using the firm's statutory rate (which averages 36.5% for U.S. companies), and then determine the tax rate on operating profit:

$$\text{Tax rate on operating profit} = \frac{\text{Tax expense} + (\text{Net nonoperating expense} \times \text{Statutory tax rate})}{\text{Net operating profit before taxes}}$$

In this case, income statement forecasts use both rates—the statutory rate for nonoperating items and the computed rate for operating items. With a statutory tax rate of 36.5% on P&G's net nonoperating expense of $836 ($1,119 − $283), we find a tax rate on nonoperating profit of 30.49%, slightly higher than the 30% used here. Thus, the simplification works well for P&G and, in general, works well when we do not expect marked changes over time in the proportions of operating and nonoperating profits.

We use these key income statement relations to forecast future amounts. In practice, we would also review the MD&A section, footnotes, and nonfinancial information to assess whether these historical income statement relations represent persistent operating performance and, if not, adjust these income statement relations accordingly. Following are examples of how we can use additional information to enhance our income statement relations and measures.

Company Scenario	Forecasting Implications
McDonalds reports an 8% increase in 2005 sales; its MD&A reports that sales increased by 2% from a weakened $US	We might forecast a less than 8% future sales growth if we do not expect the $US to further weaken (or strengthen)
Target reports a 2005 sales increase of 12%; most of this is from new store openings as comparable store growth is 5%	Growth via acquisition or construction requires capital outlays, and is different from *organic growth;* if we forecast continuation of a 12% growth, we also must forecast the required capital outlays
Ford reports a $1.1 billion gain on sale of its Hertz subsidiary	This is a transitory item and we do not want to forecast its recurrence; we also do not want to include any operating results from this discontinued subsidiary in our forecasting process
CBS Corp. reports a 2005 goodwill impairment charge of $9.5 billion reducing the carrying values of its television and radio investments	This is a transitory item that we should not forecast as it is nonrecurring (assuming remaining goodwill is not further impaired)

---

[1] A key to financial statement forecasting is the sales forecast. Although there is no perfect method, the more information we can gather and assimilate, the more accurate the forecast will be. Using the current sales growth rate to forecast future sales is simple, and usually reasonable, and is the approach we typically take in this module and its assignments. Many other forecasting methods are employed, with varying success. For example, we could use a time series of sales and fit a trend line using statistical modeling techniques. We also could use additional company, industry, and economic variables and build a multivariate forecast model. There is no guarantee, however, that the benefits of such forecasts are worth the costs.

The forecasting mechanics in this module assume that key financial statement relations will continue to hold in the future. In practice, analysts and investors carefully review these relations and modify them as necessary. This is the *art* of forecasting. We use the income statement relations from Exhibit 11.5, to derive P&G's forecasted income statement, shown in Exhibit 11.6. We assume that the nonoperating items remain constant as we do not forecast any changes to the investing and financing activities of the company (at this point).

EXHIBIT 11.6	Procter & Gamble Forecasted Income Statement
Year ended June 30 (in millions)	**2007 Est.**
Net sales ($68,222 × 1.044)..	$71,224
Cost of products sold ($71,224 × 48.6%).............................	34,615
Gross profit (subtotal)..	36,609
Selling, general and administrative expense ($71,224 × 32.0%)..........	22,792
Operating income (subtotal)...	13,817
Interest expense (no change assumed)..................................	1,119
Other nonoperating income, net (no change assumed)...................	283
Earnings before income taxes (subtotal)..............................	12,981
Income taxes ($12,981 x 30.0%).......................................	3,894
Net earnings (total)..	$ 9,087

Forecasting the Balance Sheet

Forecasting the balance sheet requires information from our forecasted income statement as well as historical financial and nonfinancial information. Therefore, we forecast the balance sheet *after* forecasting the income statement. P&G's historical balance sheet is reproduced in Exhibit 11.7.

Forecasting of the balance sheet proceeds in two steps:

1. Forecast each asset account (*other than cash*) and each liability and equity account
2. Compute the cash amount needed to balance the forecasted accounting equation
   (Assets = Liabilities + Equity)

There are several ways to obtain forecasts of specific asset, liability, and equity accounts:

- Assume no change in balance sheet amounts.
- Use computed relations, such as capital expenditures to sales, and predicted events for accounts with more complex relations, such as scheduled payments of long-term debt and dividend policies drawn from information gleaned from MD&A and footnote disclosures.
- Use turnover rates and simple assumptions to forecast balance sheet amounts.

The first method is straightforward, but unlikely to yield accurate forecasts. The second method requires estimates and assumptions beyond the scope of this book. The third method is the one we use. It relies on plausible assumptions and typically yields reasonable forecasts. This method also uses key turnover rates. To illustrate use of turnover rates to forecast balance sheet amounts, recall the following definition of a generic turnover rate *based on year-end account balances:*

Turnover Rate = Sales (or Cost of Goods Sold)/Year-End Account Balance

Rearranging terms, we get the forecasted *year-end* account balance as

$$\textbf{Forecasted Year-End Account Balance} = \frac{\textbf{Forecasted Sales (or Cost of Goods Sold)}}{\textbf{Estimated Turnover Rate}}$$

We use year-end amounts in the denominator of the turnover rate because we are trying to estimate year-end account balances (and not the average balance). While this form of the turnover ratio can seem inconsistent with the turnover definitions in Module 4, it is because the purpose here is to forecast a year-end account balance, and not an average account balance. The forecasted year-end balance is, thus,

| EXHIBIT 11.7 | Procter & Gamble Balance Sheet |

June 30 (in millions)	2006	2005
Assets		
Cash and cash equivalents	$ 6,693	$ 6,389
Investment securities	1,133	1,744
Accounts receivable	5,725	4,185
Inventories		
Materials and supplies	1,537	1,424
Work in process	623	350
Finished goods	4,131	3,232
Total inventories	6,291	5,006
Deferred income taxes	1,611	1,081
Prepaid expenses and other receivables	2,876	11,924
Total current assets	24,329	20,329
Property, plant and equipment		
Buildings	5,871	5,292
Machinery and equipment	25,140	20,397
Land	870	636
	31,881	26,325
Accumulated depreciation	(13,111)	(11,993)
Net property, plant and equipment	18,770	14,332
Goodwill and other intangible assets		
Goodwill	55,306	19,816
Trademarks and other intangible assets, net	33,721	4,347
Net goodwill and other intangible assets	89,027	24,163
Other noncurrent assets	3,569	2,703
Total assets	$135,695	$61,527
Liabilities and Shareholders' Equity		
Accounts payable	$ 4,910	$ 3,802
Accrued and other liabilities	9,587	7,531
Taxes payable	3,360	2,265
Debt due within one year	2,128	11,441
Total current liabilities	19,985	25,039
Long-term debt	35,976	12,887
Deferred income taxes	12,354	1,896
Other noncurrent liabilities	4,472	3,230
Total liabilities	72,787	43,052
Shareholders' equity		
Convertible Class A preferred stock, stated value $1 per share (600 shares authorized)	1,451	1,483
Non-Voting Class B preferred stock, stated value $1 per share (200 shares authorized)	—	—
Common stock, stated value $1 per share (10,000 shares authorized; shares issued: 2006—3,975.8, 2005—2,976.6)	3,976	2,977
Additional paid-in capital	57,856	3,030
Reserve for ESOP debt retirement	(1,288)	(1,259)
Accumulated other comprehensive income	(518)	(1,566)
Treasury stock, at cost (shares held: 2006—797.0, 2005—503.7)	(34,235)	(17,194)
Retained earnings	35,666	31,004
Total shareholders' equity	62,908	18,475
Total liabilities and shareholders' equity	$135,695	$61,527

forecasted sales (or forecasted cost of goods sold) divided by the turnover rate estimated from prior year-end balances.

Assuming that we have made all necessary adjustments (see adjusting section), we identify and estimate several key turnover relations and other measures from information in the P&G balance sheet and income statement. We use these relations and measures (reported in Exhibit 11.8) to forecast the balance sheet.

EXHIBIT 11.8	P&G Key Relations using Income Statement and Balance Sheet†

$ millions	2006
Net sales/Year-end accounts receivable ($68,222/$5,725)	11.92
Cost of products sold/Year-end inventories ($33,125/$6,291).	5.27
Cost of products sold/Year-end accounts payable ($33,125/$4,910)	6.75
Net sales/Year-end net PPE ($68,222/$18,770).	3.64
Net sales/Year-end accrued and other liabilities ($68,222/$9,587)	7.12
Taxes payable/Income taxes ($3,360/$3,729)	90.1%
Dividends to shareholders (from statement of cash flows in Exhibit 11.11)	$3,703
Dividends/Net earnings ($3,703/$8,684)	42.6%
Depreciation and amortization expense/SG&A expense (from footnotes not reproduced in book)*	9.3%
Forecasted long-term debt = Long-term debt − Current maturities ($35,976 − $2,128).	$33,848

* For use in the statement of cash flows, not the balance sheet

† No change is assumed for the following accounts: investment securities, deferred income taxes, prepaid expenses and other receivables, net goodwill and other intangible assets, other noncurrent assets, debt due within one year, deferred income taxes, other noncurrent liabilities, and all shareholders' equity accounts with the exception of retained earnings.

The relations and amounts in Exhibit 11.8 are intuitively appealing. For example, accounts receivable and accrued liabilities are typically related to sales levels (because receivables are at selling prices and accruals typically include operating costs that relate to sales volume). Also, inventories and accounts payable are both logically related to cost of goods sold (because payables typically relate to inventory volume). Capital expenditures and dividends are taken from the statement of cash flows (see Exhibit 11.11). We assume no change in P&G capital expenditures from the prior year.

Using the income statement and balance sheet relations from Exhibit 11.8, the P&G forecasted balance sheet is shown in Exhibit 11.9; detailed computations are shown in parentheses. We should confirm each of the computations to understand the forecasted balance sheet.

The final step in forecasting the balance sheet is computing the cash balance, which equals total assets less all noncash assets. Since this is computed as a residual amount, it can be unusually high, low, or even negative. The residual cash balance is an indicator of whether the company is accumulating too much or too little cash from its operating activities less its capital expenditures (we are holding financing activities constant at this point). The following table presents two possible adjustments to the cash balance that we would consider at this point in the forecasting process.

Forecasted Cash	Possible Adjustments to Forecasted Balance Sheet and Income Statement
Too low	• Liquidate marketable securities (then adjust forecasted investment income) • Raise cash by increasing long-term debt and/or equity (then adjust forecasted interest expense and/or expected dividends)
Too high	• Invest excess cash in marketable securities (then adjust investment income) • Repay debt or pay out to shareholders as repurchased (treasury) stock or dividends (then adjust forecasted interest expense and/or expected dividends)

Determining whether the resulting cash balance is too high or too low is a judgment call. We choose to use the historical cash balance as a percentage of total assets as a benchmark (computed for the company under analysis or the industry). When adjusting the final cash balance, we must take care to not inadvertently change the financial leverage of the company. Financial leverage is an important consideration in both the

EXHIBIT 11.9	Procter & Gamble Forecasted Balance Sheet

June 30 (in millions)	2007 Est.
Assets	
Cash and cash equivalents (total forecasted liabilities and equity less all noncash assets)	$ 9,240
Investment securities (no change assumed)	1,133
Accounts receivable ($71,224/11.92).	5,975
Inventories ($34,615/5.27)	6,568
Deferred income taxes (no change assumed)	1,611
Prepaid expenses and other receivables (no change assumed)	2,876
Total current assets (subtotal)	27,403
Net property, plant and equipment ($71,224/3.64)	19,567
Net goodwill and other intangible assets (no change assumed)	89,027
Other noncurrent assets (no change assumed)	3,569
Total assets (subtotal).	$139,566
Liabilities and Shareholders' Equity	
Accounts payable ($34,615/6.75).	$ 5,128
Accrued and other liabilities ($71,224/7.12).	10,003
Taxes payable ($3,894 × 90.1%).	3,509
Debt due within one year (no change assumed)	2,128
Total current liabilities (subtotal).	20,768
Long-term debt ($35,976 − $2,128)	33,848
Deferred income taxes (no change assumed)	12,354
Other noncurrent liabilities (no change assumed)	4,472
Total liabilities (subtotal)	71,442
Preferred stock (no change assumed)	1,451
Common stock (no change assumed)	3,976
Additional paid-in capital (no change assumed)	57,856
Reserve for ESOP debt retirement (no change assumed)	(1,288)
Accumulated other comprehensive income (no change assumed).	(518)
Treasury stock (no change assumed).	(34,235)
Retained earnings (computed*)	40,882
Total shareholders' equity (subtotal).	68,124
Total liabilities and shareholders' equity (subtotal).	$139,566

* Estimated retained earnings = Prior year retained earnings of $35,666 + Forecasted net income of $9,087 − Dividends of $3,871, where Dividends = Forecasted net income of $9,087 × Dividend payout rate (Dividends/Net income) of 42.6%.

analysis and forecasting of company financials (see Module 4 for a discussion). Accordingly, we must adjust the proportion of debt and equity, if necessary, to avoid an inadvertent shift in financial leverage.

To illustrate, the projected cash balance for P&G of $9,240 million is 6.62% of total assets. In 2005, PG's cash level was approximately 5% of total assets. This suggests that P&G will accumulate excess cash in 2006 and will not require additional financing. In our forecasted balance sheet, we can take the computed excess cash and (1) invest it in securities, in which case we must adjust the forecasted investment returns, or (2) assume that P&G repays some of its debt and/or repurchases some of its stock to maintain the existing total liabilities-to-equity ratio. (At December 31, 2005, P&G's liabilities-to-equity ratio was 1.16, computed as $72,787/$62,908.)

How we determine the adjustment to cash depends on whether we will adjust marketable securities or adjust a liability or equity account such as long-term debt or treasury stock. Adjusting the marketable securities account is straightforward and is the approach we take. We first compute the desired level of cash as: Prior year cash-to-total assets ratio × Forecasted total assets. This amount is then subtracted from the forecasted cash and the difference added to or subtracted from marketable securities. Adjusting a liability or equity account involves an additional calculation so that the final cash balance yields the same proportionate [common size] balances as the prior year given that total assets will be reduced by the excess cash. Specifically, we use the following equation:

$$\text{Cash adjustment} = \frac{\text{Forecasted cash balance} - (\text{Prior year cash-to-total-assets ratio} \times \text{Forecasted total assets})}{1 - \text{Prior year cash-to-total-assets ratio}}$$

P&G's cash-to-total-assets in 2006 is 5%. Using the initial forecasted cash balance of $9,240 million and the forecasted total assets of $139,566 million from our forecasted balance sheet (Exhibit 11.9), we determine that reducing cash by $2,262 million (and increasing investment securities by a like amount) yields a 5% ratio of cash-to-total-assets ratio. (If we had instead decided to adjust either long-term debt or an equity account, we would have reduced the cash balance by $2,380; computed as $\frac{\$9,240 - (5\% \times \$139,566)}{1 - 5\%}$.)

Exhibit 11.10 shows the new projected balances after the cash reduction of $2,262 million. Again, this approach assumes that P&G invests any excess cash in marketable securities. (Low-risk marketable securities presently yield about 2%; the excess cash of $2,262 will yield about $45 of additional investment income for P&G's fiscal 2008.) Exhibit 11.10 shows the revised balance sheet that invests the excess cash in marketable securities. (Alternatively, using the excess cash to retire long-term debt would reduce the cash level to 5% of forecasted total assets, and the total liabilities-to-equity ratio to 1.01; a leverage ratio of 1.01 is markedly different from 1.16 and so this alternative is problematic.)

EXHIBIT 11.10	P&G Forecasted Balance Sheet with Excess Cash Invested in Securities		
June 30, 2007 (in millions)	**Initial Est.**	**Adjustment**	**Final Est.**
Assets			
Cash and cash equivalents	$ 9,240	$(2,262)	$ 6,978
Investment securities	1,133	2,262	3,395
Accounts receivable.	5,975		5,975
Inventories	6,568		6,568
Deferred income taxes	1,611		1,611
Prepaid expenses and other receivables	2,876		2,876
Total current assets	27,403		27,403
Net property, plant and equipment	19,567		19,567
Net goodwill and other intangible assets.	89,027		89,027
Other noncurrent assets.	3,569		3,569
Total assets.	$139,566		$139,566
Liabilities and Shareholders' Equity			
Accounts payable.	$ 5,128		$ 5,128
Accrued and other liabilities.	10,003		10,003
Taxes payable.	3,509		3,509
Debt due within one year	2,128		2,128
Total current liabilities.	20,768		20,768
Long-term debt	33,848		33,848
Deferred income taxes	12,354		12,354
Other noncurrent liabilities	4,472		4,472
Total liabilities.	71,442		71,442
Preferred stock.	1,451		1,451
Common stock.	3,976		3,976
Additional paid-in capital	57,856		57,856
Reserve for ESOP debt retirement.	(1,288)		(1,288)
Accumulated other comprehensive income.	(518)		(518)
Treasury stock	(34,235)		(34,235)
Retained earnings	40,882		40,882
Total shareholders' equity	68,124		68,124
Total liabilities and shareholders' equity.	$139,566		$139,566

Forecasting the Statement of Cash Flows

Procter & Gamble's 2006 statement of cash flows is shown in Exhibit 11.11. We forecast the statement of cash flows using the forecasted income statement and cash-adjusted forecasted balance sheet (in Exhibit 11.10). We refer to the historical statement of cash flows primarily to check the reasonableness of our forecasts. We draw on the mechanics behind the preparation of the statement of cash flows, which we discuss in Module 3 and Appendix B. Specifically, once we have forecasts of the balance sheet and income statement, we can compute the forecasted statement of cash flows just as we would its historical counterpart. In particular, we compute changes in each of the balance sheet accounts and determine what type of cash flow arises from the change (operating, investing, or financing). The forecasted statement of cash flows for P&G, and its related computations, is in Exhibit 11.12.

EXHIBIT 11.11	**Procter & Gamble Statement of Cash Flows**		
Years ended June 30 (in millions)	**2006**	**2005**	**2004**
Cash and cash equivalents, beginning of year	$ 6,389	$ 4,232	$ 5,428
Operating activities			
Net earnings	8,684	6,923	6,156
Depreciation and amortization	2,627	1,884	1,733
Share-based compensation expense	585	524	491
Deferred income taxes	(112)	564	342
Change in accounts receivable	(524)	(86)	(159)
Change in inventories	383	(644)	56
Change in accounts payable, accrued and other liabilities	230	(101)	597
Change in other operating assets and liabilities	(508)	(498)	(88)
Other	10	113	227
Total operating activities	11,375	8,679	9,355
Investing activities			
Capital expenditures	(2,667)	(2,181)	(2,024)
Proceeds from asset sales	882	517	230
Acquisitions, net of cash acquired	171	(572)	(7,476)
Change in investment securities	884	(100)	(874)
Total investing activities	(730)	(2,336)	(10,144)
Financing activities			
Dividends to shareholders	(3,703)	(2,731)	(2,539)
Change in short-term debt	(8,627)	2,016	4,911
Additions to long-term debt	22,545	3,108	1,963
Reductions of long-term debt	(5,282)	(2,013)	(1,188)
Impact of stock options and other	1,319	521	562
Treasury purchases	(16,830)	(5,026)	(4,070)
Total financing activities	(10,578)	(4,125)	(361)
Effect of exchange rate changes on cash and cash equivalents	237	(61)	(46)
Change in cash and cash equivalents	304	2,157	(1,196)
Cash and cash equivalents, end of year	$ 6,693	$ 6,389	$ 4,232

Reassessing the Forecasts

After preparing the forecasted financial statements, it is useful to reassess whether they are reasonable in light of current economic and company conditions. This task is subjective and benefits from your knowledge of company, industry, and economic factors.

Many analysts and managers prepare "what-if" forecasted financial statements. Specifically, they change key assumptions, such as the forecasted sales growth or key cost ratios and then recompute the forecasted financial statements. These alternative forecasting scenarios indicate the sensitivity of a set of predicted outcomes to different assumptions about future economic conditions. Such sensitivity estimates can be useful for setting contingency plans and in identifying areas of vulnerability for future company performance and condition.

EXHIBIT 11.12	Procter & Gamble Forecasted Statement of Cash Flows

Year ended June 30 (in millions)	2007 Est.
Cash and cash equivalents, beginning of year (from prior year balance sheet)............	$ 6,693
Operating activities	
Net earnings...	9,087
Depreciation ($22,792 × 9.3%)*.....................................	2,120
Share-based compensation expense (assumed to be zero)	0
Change in deferred income taxes (assumed to be zero)	0
Change in accounts receivable ($5,725 − $5,975)	(250)
Change in inventories ($6,291 − $6,568).................................	(277)
Change in accounts payable ($4,910 − $5,128)	218
Change in accrued and other liabilities ($9,587 − $10,003)	416
Change in taxes payable ($3,360 − $3,509)	149
Total operating activities (subtotal)...................................	11,463
Investing activities	
Increase in marketable securities (from excess cash)	(2,262)
Capital expenditures, net of proceeds from asset sales ($18,770 − $19,567 − $2,120)	(2,917)
Acquisitions, net of cash acquired (assumed to be zero)	0
Change in investment securities (assumed to be zero)	0
Total investing activities (subtotal)	(5,179)
Financing activities	
Dividends to shareholders (Est. net income $9,087 × Dividend payout rate 42.6%)	(3,871)
Change in short-term debt (assumed to be zero)	0
Additions to long-term debt (assumed to be zero)...........................	0
Reductions of long-term debt ($35,976 − $33,848)	(2,128)
Total financing activities (subtotal)	(5,999)
Change in cash and cash equivalents (subtotal)	285
Cash and cash equivalents, end of year (total)	$ 6,978

* For simplicity in this case, amortization is assumed to be zero.

Forecasting Multiple Years

Many business decisions require forecasted financial statements for more than one year ahead. For example, managerial and capital budgeting, security valuation, and strategic analyses all benefit from reliable multiyear forecasts. Module 12 uses multiyear forecasts of financial results to estimate stock price for investment decisions.

Although there are different methods to achieve multiyear forecasts, we apply a straightforward approach: we repeat the forecasting procedure we used to forecast one-year ahead numbers. To illustrate, using the same forecasting assumptions we use to forecast 2007 results (shown in Exhibit 11.6), we can forecast P&G's 2008 sales as $74,358 million, computed as $71,224 million × 1.044. The remainder of the income statement can be forecasted from this sales level using the methodology we discuss above for one-year-ahead forecasts. Similarly for the balance sheet, and assuming a continuation of the current asset (and liability) turnover rates, we can forecast current assets and liabilities using the same methodology for one-year-ahead forecast. For example, 2008 accounts receivable are forecasted as $6,238 million, computed as $74,358 million/11.92.

Exhibit 11.13 illustrates two-year-ahead (2008) forecasting for P&G's income statement, balance sheet, and statement of cash flows; the 2007 forecasts are shown in the first column for reference. To reiterate, the two-year-ahead forecast is prepared using the same forecast assumptions we employed previously. As with the one-year-ahead forecast, we must adjust the final cash balance because residual cash will build up during the 2008 fiscal year. The projected cash of $9,758 million represents 6.8% of total assets whereas the historical relation (from 2005) is 5%. We adjust the cash for the residual amount by reducing cash by $2,570 million to $7,188 million, the latter computed as $143,759 million × 5%. The excess cash causes marketable securities to increase from $3,395 million to $5,965 million.

Any forecast assumptions (such as cost percentages and turnover rates) can be changed in future years as necessary. For example, we might reduce expected sales growth if we feel that the market is becoming saturated or reduce the accounts receivable turnover rate if we expect the economy to slow. We can replicate the process for any desired forecast horizon.

EXHIBIT 11.13	Procter & Gamble Two-Year-Ahead Forecasted Income Statement	
2007 Est.	**($ millions)**	**2008 Est.**
$ 71,224	Net sales ($71,224 × 1.044)	$ 74,358
34,615	Cost of products sold ($74,358 × 48.6%).	36,138
36,609	Gross profit ($74,358 × 51.4%).	38,220
22,792	Selling, general and administrative expense ($74,358 × 32.0%)	23,795
13,817	Operating income (subtotal).	14,425
1,119	Interest expense (no change assumed)	1,119
283	Other nonoperating income, net ($283 + $45)*.	328
12,981	Earnings before income taxes (subtotal)	13,634
3,894	Income taxes ($13,634 × 30.0%)	4,090
$ 9,087	Net earnings (total).	$ 9,544

*Includes $45 interest income from excess cash invested in 2% marketable securities, computed as $2,262 × 2%.

	Procter & Gamble Two-Year-Ahead Forecasted Balance Sheet	
2007 Est.	**($ millions)**	**2008 Est.**
$ 6,978	Cash and cash equivalents (total liabilities and equity less all noncash assets)	$ 7,188
3,395	Investment securities (adjusted for excess cash)	5,965
5,975	Accounts receivable ($74,358/11.92).	6,238
6,568	Inventories ($36,138/5.27)	6,857
1,611	Deferred income taxes (no change assumed)	1,611
2,876	Prepaid expenses and other receivables (no change assumed)	2,876
27,403	Total current assets (subtotal)	30,735
19,567	Net property, plant and equipment ($74,358/3.64)	20,428
89,027	Net goodwill and other intangible assets (no change assumed)	89,027
3,569	Other noncurrent assets (no change assumed).	3,569
$139,566	Total assets (total)	$143,759
$ 5,128	Accounts payable ($36,138/6.75)	$ 5,354
10,003	Accrued and other liabilities ($74,358/7.12).	10,444
3,509	Taxes payable ($4,090 × 90.1%).	3,685
2,128	Debt due within one year (no change assumed)	2,128
20,768	Total current liabilities (subtotal).	21,611
33,848	Long-term debt ($38,848 − $2,128)	31,720
12,354	Deferred income taxes (no change assumed)	12,354
4,472	Other noncurrent liabilities (no change assumed)	4,472
71,442	Total liabilities (subtotal).	70,157
1,451	Preferred stock (no change assumed).	1,451
3,976	Common stock (no change assumed).	3,976
57,856	Additional paid-in capital (no change assumed)	57,856
(1,288)	Reserve for ESOP debt retirement (no change assumed)	(1,288)
(518)	Accumulated other comprehensive income (no change assumed).	(518)
(34,235)	Treasury stock (no change assumed)	(34,235)
40,882	Retained earnings ($40,882 + $9,544 − [$9,544 × 42.6%]).	46,360
68,124	Total shareholders' equity (subtotal)	73,602
$139,566	Total liabilities and shareholders' equity (total)	$143,759

Procter & Gamble Two-Year-Ahead Forecasted Statement of Cash Flows		
2007 Est.	**($ millions)**	**2008 Est.**
$ 6,693	Cash and cash equivalents, beginning of year	$ 6,978
	Operating activities	
9,087	Net earnings.	9,544
2,120	Depreciation and amortization ($23,795 × 9.3%)	2,213
0	Share-based compensation expense (assumed to be zero)	0
0	Deferred income taxes (assumed to be zero)	0
(250)	Change in accounts receivable ($5,975 − $6,238)	(263)
(277)	Change in inventories ($6,568 − $6,857).	(289)
218	Change in accounts payable ($5,354 − $5,128)	226
416	Change in accrued and other liabilities ($10,444 − $10,003)	441
149	Change in taxes payable ($3,685 − $3,509)	176
11,463	Total operating activities (subtotal)	12,048
	Investing activities	
(2,262)	Increase in marketable securities (excess cash)	(2,570)
(2,917)	Capital expenditures, net of proceeds from asset sales	
	($19,567 − $20,428 − $2,213)	(3,074)
0	Acquisitions, net of cash acquired (assumed to be zero)	0
(5,179)	Total investing activities (subtotal)	(5,644)
	Financing activities	
(3,871)	Dividends to shareholders ($9,544 × 42.6%)	(4,066)
	Change in short-term debt (assumed to be zero)	0
	Additions to long-term debt (assumed to be zero)	0
(2,128)	Reductions of long-term debt ($35,976 − $31,348).	(2,128)
(5,999)	Total financing activities (subtotal).	(6,194)
285	Change in cash and cash equivalents (subtotal)	210
$ 6,978	Cash and cash equivalents, end of year (total)	$ 7,188

The two-year-ahead forecasts in Exhibit 11.13 illustrate the technique used to forecast an additional year. To simplify exposition, we have not altered any of the forecast assumptions, and focus solely on the forecasting mechanics. However, it is often appropriate to modify these assumptions. For example, we might wish to increase the forecasted depreciation expense due to the forecasted acquisition of depreciable long-term operating assets in 2007, and to reduce the forecasted interest expense for 2007 in consideration of the repayment of long-term debt.

MID-MODULE REVIEW 2

Following is financial statement information from Colgate-Palmolive Company.

Income Statement For years ended December 31 ($ millions)	2005	2004
Net sales.	$11,396.9	$10,584.2
Cost of sales.	5,191.9	4,747.2
Gross profit.	6,205.0	5,837.0
Selling, general and administrative expenses	3,990.0	3,714.9
Operating profit	2,215.0	2,122.1
Interest expense, net	136.0	119.7
Income before income taxes	2,079.0	2,002.4
Provision for income taxes.	727.6	675.3
Net income.	$ 1,351.4	$ 1,327.1

Balance Sheet As of December 31 ($ millions)	2005	2004
Assets		
Cash and cash equivalents	$ 340.7	$ 319.6
Receivables (less allowances of $41.7 and		
$47.2, respectively)	1,309.4	1,319.9
Inventories	855.8	845.5
Other current assets	251.2	254.9
Total current assets	2,757.1	2,739.9
Property, plant, and equipment, net	2,544.1	2,647.7
Goodwill	1,845.7	1,891.7
Other intangible assets, net	783.2	832.4
Other assets	577.0	561.2
Total assets	$8,507.1	$8,672.9
Liabilities and Shareholders' Equity		
Notes and loans payable	$ 171.5	$ 134.3
Current portion of long-term debt	356.7	451.3
Accounts payable	876.1	864.4
Accrued income taxes	215.5	153.1
Other accruals	1,123.2	1,127.6
Total current liabilities	2,743.0	2,730.7
Long-term debt	2,918.0	3,089.5
Deferred income taxes	554.7	509.6
Other liabilities	941.3	1,097.7
Shareholders' equity		
Preference stock	253.7	274.0
Common stock, $1 par value (1,000,000,000 shares		
authorized, 732,853,180 shares issued)	732.9	732.9
Additional paid-in capital	1,064.4	1,093.8
Retained earnings	8,968.1	8,223.9
Accumulated other comprehensive income	(1,804.7)	(1,806.2)
	9,214.4	8,518.4
Unearned compensation	(283.3)	(307.6)
Treasury stock, at cost	(7,581.0)	(6,965.4)
Total shareholders' equity	1,350.1	1,245.4
Total liabilities and shareholders' equity	$8,507.1	$8,672.9

Forecast the Colgate-Palmolive balance sheet and income statement for 2006 using the following additional information (cost of goods sold margin can be inferred as sales minus gross profit margin; assume no change for all other accounts not listed below).

Key Financial Relations and Measures ($ millions)	2005
Net sales growth ([$11,396.9/$10,584.2] − 1)	7.7%
Gross profit margin ($6,205.0/$11,396.9)	54.4%
Selling, general and administrative expenses/ Net sales ($3,990.0/$11,396.9)	35.0%
Depreciation / Selling, general and administrative expenses* ($329.3/$3,990.0)	8.3%
Provision for income taxes/ Income before income taxes ($727.6/$2,079.0))	35.0%
Net sales/ Year-end receivables ($11,396.9/$1,309.4)	8.70
Cost of sales/ Year-end inventories ($5,191.9/$855.8)	6.07
Cost of sales/ Year-end accounts payable ($5,191.9/$876.1)	5.93
Net sales/ Year-end property, plant and equipment, net ($11,396.9/$2,544.1)	4.48
Net sales/ Year-end other accruals ($11,396.9/$1,123.2)	10.15
Accrued income taxes/ Provision for income taxes ($215.5/$727.6)	29.6%
Dividends paid (provided in statement of cash flows; not reproduced here)	$607.2
Current maturities of long-term debt	$356.7

*Depreciation expense of $329 is reported in the statement of cash flows (not reproduced here) and is included in selling, general and administrative expenses. All other accounts are assumed to remain constant.

Solution

Forecasted 2006 financial statements for Colgate-Palmolive follow.

Forecasted Income Statement	
($ millions)	**2006 Est.**
Net sales ($11,396.9 × 1.077)	$12,274.5
Cost of sales ($12,274.5 × 45.6%)	5,597.2
Gross profit ($12,274.5 × 54.4%)	6,677.3
Selling, general, administrative, and other expenses ($12,274.5 × 35.0%)	4,296.1
Operating profit (subtotal)	2,381.2
Interest expense, net (no change assumed)	136.0
Income before income taxes (subtotal)	2,245.2
Provision for income taxes ($2,245.2 × 35%)	785.8
Net income (total)	$ 1,459.4

Forecasted Balance Sheet	
($ millions)	**2006 Est.**
Assets	
Cash and cash equivalents (total forecasted liabilities and equity less all noncash assets)	$ 643.7
Receivables ($12,274.5/8.70)	1,410.9
Inventories ($5,597.2/6.07)	922.1
Other current assets (no change assumed)	251.2
Total current assets (subtotal)	3,227.9
Property, plant and equipment, net ($12,274.5/4.48)	2,739.8
Goodwill and other intangible assets, net (no change assumed)	2,628.9
Other assets (no change assumed)	577.0
Total assets (total)	$9,173.6
Liabilities and Shareholders' Equity	
Notes and loans payable (no change assumed)	$ 171.5
Current portion of long-term debt (no change assumed)	356.7
Accounts payable ($5,597.2/5.93)	943.9
Accrued income taxes ($785.8 x 29.6%)	232.6
Other accruals ($12,274.5/10.15)	1,209.3
Total current liabilities (subtotal)	2,914.0
Long-term debt (Prior year long-term debt of $2,918 − Prior year debt due within one year $356.7)	2,561.3
Deferred income taxes (no change assumed)	554.7
Other liabilities (no change assumed)	941.3
Total liabilities (subtotal)	6,971.3
Preference stock (no change assumed)	253.7
Common stock (no change assumed)	732.9
Additional paid-in capital (no change assumed)	1,064.4
Retained earnings (Prior year retained earnings, $8,968.1 + Forecasted net income, $1,459.4 − Dividends, $607.2)	9,820.3
Accumulated other comprehensive income (no change assumed)	(1,804.7)
Unearned compensation (no change assumed)	(283.3)
Treasury stock (no change assumed)	(7,581.0)
Total shareholders' equity (subtotal)	2,202.3
Total liabilities and shareholders' equity (total)	$9,173.6

Note: To compute the residual cash balance, we initially assume no change in the capital accounts and the level of debt (other than repayment of $356.7 in current maturities of long-term debt). This yields a forecasted cash balance of $643.7 million, which is 7% of projected total assets. In 2005, Colgate-Palmolive reported cash at 4% of total assets. The forecasting process suggests an accumulation of excess cash; that is, more cash than necessary to efficiently operate. One additional forecasting adjustment would be to assume either the investment of the excess cash in securities or the use of it to retire long-term debt and equity (in a manner to maintain the historic leverage ratio).

Parsimonious Method to Multiyear Forecasting

The forecasting process described above uses a considerable amount of available information to derive accurate forecasts. We can, however, simplify the process by using less information without seriously impairing accuracy. Stock valuation models commonly use more parsimonious methods to compute multiyear forecasts for an initial screening of prospective securities. For example, in Module 12 we introduce two stock valuation models that use parsimonious methods. One model utilizes forecasted free cash flows and the other uses forecasted net operating profits after tax (NOPAT) and net operating assets (NOA); see Module 4 for descriptions of these variables. Since free cash flows are equal to net operating profits after tax (NOPAT) less the change in net operating assets (NOA), we can accommodate both stock valuation models with forecasts of NOPAT and NOA.

LO3 Describe and illustrate a parsimonious method for multiyear forecasting of net operating profit and net operating assets.

One approach is to forecast NOPAT and NOA using the methodology outlined in this Module. A second approach is to use a more parsimonious method that requires three crucial inputs:

1. Sales growth
2. Net operating profit margin (NOPM); defined in Module 4 as NOPAT divided by sales
3. Net operating asset turnover (NOAT); defined in Module 4 as sales divided by average NOA, but using year-end NOA rather than average NOA to forecast year-end amounts.

To illustrate, we use P&G's 2006 income statement, from Exhibit 11.4, and its 2006 balance sheet, from Exhibit 11.7, to determine the following measures (assuming a statutory tax rate of 36.5% on nonoperating revenues and expenses):

Sales	$68,222
Sales growth rate	4.4%
Net operating profit *before* tax	$13,249
Tax rate on operating profit* {$3,729 + [($1,119 − $283) × 0.365)]}/$13,249	30.4%
NOPAT ($13,249 × [1 − 0.304])	$9,221
NOA ($135,695 − $1,133) − ($4,910 + $9,587 + $3,360 + $12,354 + $4,472)	$99,879
NOPM ($9,221/$68,222)	13.5%
NOAT ($68,222/$99,879)	0.68

* See Exhibit 11.5 for an explanation.

Using these inputs, we forecast P&G's sales, NOPAT and NOA. Each year's forecasted sales is the prior year sales multiplied successively by (1+ Growth rate), or 1.044 in this case, and then rounded to whole digits. NOPAT is computed using forecasted (and rounded) sales each year times the 2006 NOPM of 13.5%; and NOA is computed using forecasted (and rounded) sales divided by the 2006 NOAT of 0.68. Forecasted numbers for 2007 through 2010 are in Exhibit 11.14; supporting computations are in parentheses.

EXHIBIT 11.14	Procter & Gamble Multiyear Forecasts of Sales, NOPAT and NOA				
($ millions)	2006	2007 Est.	2008 Est.	2009 Est.	2010 Est.
Net sales	$68,222	**$71,224** ($68,222 × 1.044)	**$74,358** ($71,224 × 1.044)	**$77,629** ($74,358 × 1.044)	**$81,045** ($77,629 × 1.044)
NOPAT	$9,221 ($13,249 × [1 − 0.304])	**$9,615** ($71,224 × 13.5%)	**$10,038** ($74,358 × 13.5%)	**$10,480** ($77,629 × 13.5%)	**$10,941** ($81,045 × 13.5%)
NOA	$99,879	**$104,741** ($71,224/0.68)	**$109,350** ($74,358/0.68)	**$114,160** ($77,629/0.68)	**$119,184** ($81,045/0.68)

This forecasting process can be continued for any desired forecast horizon. Also, the forecast assumptions such as sales growth, NOPM, and NOAT can be varied by year, if desired. This alternative, parsimonious method is much simpler than the primary method illustrated in this module. However, its simplicity does forgo information that can impact forecast accuracy.

MODULE-END REVIEW

Johnson & Johnson (J&J) reports 2005 sales of $50,514 million, net operating profit after tax (NOPAT) of $10,134 million, and net operating assets (NOA) of $40,453 million. J&J's NOPM is computed as 20% ($10,134 million/$50,514 million). In a review of J&J's 10-K, we see in its tax footnote that its effective tax rate for 2005 is 23.8%, compared with 33.7% in 2004 and 30.2% in 2003. Analysis reveals that its 2005 effective tax rate is lower due to foreign tax credits and a reversal of a tax liability tied to a technical correction with the American Jobs Creation Act of 2004. We view the tax credits and technical correction as transitory. As a result, we view J&J's NOPM as abnormally high. Accordingly, in our projection of its financial information, we decide to use 32% as J&J's effective tax rate, an average of its 2004 and 2003 effective tax rates.

Required

1. Assume that J&J's pretax GAAP income for 2005 is $13,656 million, and its reported tax expense is $3,245 million. Compute J&J's adjusted NOPAT and NOPM using the adjusted 32% tax rate.
2. Compute J&J's NOAT for 2005.
3. Use the parsimonious forecast model to project J&J's sales, NOPAT and NOA for 2006 through 2009. Use the NOPAT and NOAT computed in parts *1* and *2*, and assume a sales growth rate of 6.5%.

Solution

1. If we apply 32% to J&J's $13,656 million pretax GAAP income for 2005 we get tax expense of $4,370 million, an increase of $1,125 million. J&J's adjusted 2005 NOPAT is, therefore, reduced by that amount to $9,009 million ($10,134 million − $1,125 million). The adjusted NOPM is, therefore, 18% ($9,009/$50,514), a reduction of 2 percentage points from the reported NOPM. This adjusted NOPM is the one we use in our projections.
2. NOAT = Sales/NOA = $50,514/$40,453 = 1.25
3. Projections for 2006 through 2009 using the parsimonious model follow.

	2005	2006	2007	2008	2009
Sales......	$50,514	$53,797	$57,294	$61,018	$64,985
		($50,514 × 1.065)	($53,797 × 1.065)	($57,294 × 1.065)	($61,018 × 1.065)
NOPAT	$9,009	$9,683	$10,313	$10,983	$11,697
	(given)	($53,797 × 0.18)	($57,294 × 0.18)	($61,018 × 0.18)	($64,985 × 0.18)
NOA	$40,453	$43,038	$45,835	$48,814	$51,988
	(given)	($53,797/1.25)	($57,294/1.25)	($61,018/1.25)	($64,985/1.25)

GUIDANCE ANSWERS

MANAGERIAL DECISION   **You Are a Corporate Analyst**

GAAP allows considerable flexibility in the format of the income statement, as long as all of the required elements are present. Although combining operating and nonoperating items and subtotaling to pretax profit is common in practice, many companies subtotal to pretax operating profit, which segregates nonoperating items. The argument to break with tradition and subtotal to pretax operating profit rests on the concept of *transparency*. Transparency in financial reporting means that the financial statements are clear and understandable to the reader. Many believe that greater transparency results in more trust and credibility by users of financial information. Empirical evidence supports the positive benefits of financial statement transparency. Since analysts are concerned with operating profits, your company might reap intangible benefits by being up-front in its presentation. Conversely, seeking to mask operating results, especially if misleading to outsiders, can damage management credibility.

DISCUSSION QUESTIONS

Q11-1. Describe the process of *adjusting* financial statements in preparation for forecasting them.

Q11-2. Identify three types of adjustments (for forecasting purposes) that relate to the income statement and provide two examples of each.

Q11-3. What is the objective of the adjusting process as it relates to forecasting of the balance sheet?

Q11-4. What are the main types of adjustments (for forecasting purposes) that relate to the statement of cash flows? Provide two examples of each.

Q11-5. Identify at least two applications that use forecasted financial statements.

Q11-6. What procedures must normally take place before the forecasting process begins?

Q11-7. In addition to recent trends, what other types and sources of information can be brought to bear in the forecasting of sales?

Q11-8. Describe the rationale for use of year-end balances in the computation of turnover rates that are used to forecast selected balance sheet accounts.

Q11-9. Identify and describe the steps in forecasting the income statement.

Q11-10. Describe the two-step process of forecasting and adjusting the residual cash balance when forecasting the balance sheet.

MINI EXERCISES

M11-11. Forecasting an Income Statement (LO2)

Abercrombie & Fitch reports the following fiscal year income statements.

Abercrombie & Fitch (ANF)

Income Statement ($ thousands)	2006	2005	2004
Net sales.	$2,784,711	$2,021,253	$1,707,810
Cost of goods sold.	933,295	680,029	624,640
Gross profit.	1,851,416	1,341,224	1,083,170
Stores and distribution expense.	1,000,755	738,244	597,416
Marketing, general and administrative expense.	313,457	259,835	155,553
Other operating income, net	(5,534)	(4,490)	(979)
Operating income.	542,738	347,635	331,180
Interest income, net	(6,674)	(5,218)	(3,708)
Income before income taxes	549,412	352,853	334,888
Provision for income taxes.	215,426	136,477	130,058
Net Income.	$ 333,986	$ 216,376	$ 204,830

Forecast Abercrombie & Fitch's 2007 income statement assuming the following income statement relations ($ 000s); cost of goods sold can be inferred as sales minus gross profit, and assume no change for all other accounts not listed below.

Net sales.	37.8%
Gross profit margin.	66.5%
Stores and distribution expense/Net sales	35.9%
Marketing, general and administrative expense/Net sales	11.3%
Other operating income, net/Net sales	−0.2%
Provision for income taxes/Income before income taxes	39.2%
Interest income, net	no change

M11-12. Forecasting an Income Statement (LO2)

Best Buy reports the following fiscal year income statements.

Income Statement For the Fiscal Years Ended ($ millions)	February 25, 2006	February 26, 2005	February 28, 2004
Revenue	$30,848	$27,433	$24,548
Cost of goods sold	23,122	20,938	18,677
Gross profit	7,726	6,495	5,871
Selling, general and administrative expenses	6,082	5,053	4,567
Operating income	1,644	1,442	1,304
Net interest income (expense)	77	1	(8)
Earnings from continuing operations before income tax expense	1,721	1,443	1,296
Income tax expense	581	509	496
Earnings from continuing operations	1,140	934	800
Loss from discontinued operations, net of tax	—	—	(29)
Gain (loss) on disposal of discontinued operations, net of tax	—	50	(66)
Net earnings	$ 1,140	$ 984	$ 705

Forecast Best Buy's fiscal year 2007 income statement assuming the following income statement relations; cost of goods sold can be inferred as sales minus gross profit, and assume no change for all other accounts not listed below.

Revenue growth	12.4%
Gross profit margin	25.0%
Selling, general and administrative expense/Revenue	19.7%
Income tax expense/Earnings from continuing operations before income tax	33.8%

M11-13. Forecasting an Income Statement (LO2)

General Mills reports the following fiscal year income statements.

Income Statement Fiscal year ended (in millions, except per share data)	May 28, 2006	May 29, 2005	May 30, 2004
Net sales	$11,640	$11,244	$11,070
Costs and expenses			
Cost of sales	6,966	6,834	6,584
Selling, general and administrative	2,678	2,418	2,443
Interest, net	399	455	508
Restructuring and other exit costs	30	84	26
Divestitures (gain)	—	(499)	—
Debt repurchase costs	—	137	—
Total costs and expenses	10,073	9,429	9,561
Earnings before income taxes and after-tax earnings from joint ventures	1,567	1,815	1,509
Income taxes	541	664	528
After-tax earnings from joint ventures	64	89	74
Net earnings	$ 1,090	$ 1,240	$ 1,055
Earnings per share—basic	$ 3.05	$ 3.34	$ 2.82
Earnings per share—diluted	$ 2.90	$ 3.08	$ 2.60
Dividends per share	$ 1.34	$ 1.24	$ 1.10

Forecast General Mill's fiscal year 2007 income statement assuming the following income statement relations (assume no change for Interest, net).

Net sales growth.	3.5%
Cost of sales margin.	59.8%
Selling, general and administrative/Net sales	23.0%
Restructuring and other exit costs/Net sales.	0.3%
After-tax earnings from joint ventures/Net sales	−0.5%
Income taxes/Earnings before income taxes and after-tax earnings from joint ventures	34.5%

M11-14. Analyzing, Forecasting, and Interpreting Working Capital **(LO2)**

Harley-Davidson reports 2005 net operating working capital of $2,384 million and 2005 long-term operating assets of $812 million.

Harley-Davidson (HOG)

a. Forecast Harley-Davidson's 2006 net operating working capital assuming forecasted revenues of $6,051 million, net operating working capital turnover of 2.38 times, and long-term operating asset turnover of 6.99 times. (Both turnover rates are computed here using year-end balances. Finance receivables and related debt are considered operating under the assumption that they are an integral part of Harley's operating activities).

b. Most of Harley's receivables arise from its financing activities relating to purchases of motorcycles by consumers and dealers. What effect will these receivables have on Harley's operating working capital turnover rate?

M11-15. Analyzing, Forecasting, and Interpreting Working Capital **(LO2)**

Nike reports 2005 net operating working capital of $3,992 million and 2005 long-term operating assets of $1,980 million.

Nike (NKE)

a. Forecast Nike's 2006 net operating working capital assuming forecasted sales of $15,389 million, net operating working capital turnover of 3.44 times, and long-term operating asset turnover of 6.94 times. (Both turnover rates are computed here using year-end balances.)

b. Does it seem reasonable that Nike's operating working capital turnover is less than its long-term operating asset turnover? Explain.

M11-16. Interpreting and Adjusting Balance Sheet Forecasts for a Negative Cash Balance **(LO2)**

Assume that your initial forecast of a balance sheet yields a negative cash balance.

a. What does a forecasted negative cash balance imply?

b. Given a negative cash balance, what would be your next step in forecasting the balance sheet? Explain.

M11-17. Forecasting the Balance Sheet and Operating Cash Flows **(LO2)**

Refer to the General Mills information in M11-13. General Mills reports the following current assets and current liabilities from its 2006 fiscal year-end balance sheet.

General Mills (GIS)

(In millions)	May 28, 2006	May 29, 2005
Current assets		
Cash and cash equivalents.	$ 647	$ 573
Receivables	1,076	1,034
Inventories	1,055	1,037
Prepaid expenses and other current assets.	216	203
Deferred income taxes	182	208
Total current assets.	$3,176	$3,055
Current liabilities		
Accounts payable.	$1,151	$1,136
Current portion of long-term debt	2,131	1,638
Notes payable.	1,503	299
Other current liabilities	1,353	1,111
Total current liabilities	$6,138	$4,184

Using your forecasted income statement from M11-13, and the following information on General Mills' financial statement relations, forecast General Mill's accounts receivable, inventories, and accounts payable as of the end of May 2007.

Year-end turnover rates	2006
Net sales/Year-end receivables	10.82
Cost of sales/Year-end inventories.	6.60
Cost of sales/Year-end accounts payable	6.05

M11-18. Adjusting the Balance Sheet (LO1)

Prizer, Inc. (PFE)

Prizer, Inc. (PFE) reports the following footnote to its 2005 10-K:

> In the third quarter of 2005, we sold the last of three European generic pharmaceutical businesses which we had included in our Human Health segment and had become a part of Pfizer in April 2003 in connection with our acquisition of Pharmacia, for 4.7 million euro (approximately $5.6 million) and recorded a loss of $3 million ($2 million, net of tax) in *Gains on sales of discontinued operations—net of tax* in the consolidated statement of income for 2005.

What adjustment(s) might we consider before we forecast Pfizer's income for 2006? How would we treat the cash proceeds that Pfizer realized on such a sale?

EXERCISES

E11-19. Analyzing, Forecasting, and Interpreting both Income Statement and Balance Sheet (LO2)

Whole Foods Market, Inc. (WFMI)

Following are the fiscal year income statement and balance sheet of Whole Foods Market, Inc.

Income Statement (in $ 000s)	2005	2004	2003
Sales.	$4,701,289	$3,864,950	$3,148,593
Cost of goods sold and occupancy costs	3,052,184	2,523,816	2,070,334
Gross profit.	1,649,105	1,341,134	1,078,259
Direct store expenses.	1,223,473	986,040	794,422
General and administrative expenses	158,864	119,800	100,693
Pre-opening and relocation costs	37,035	18,648	15,765
Operating income.	229,733	216,646	167,379
Other income expense			
Interest expense.	(2,223)	(7,249)	(8,114)
Investment and other income.	9,623	6,456	5,593
Income before income taxes	237,133	215,853	164,858
Provision for income taxes.	100,782	86,341	65,943
Net income.	$ 136,351	$ 129,512	$ 98,915

Balance Sheet (in $000s)	2005	2004
Assets		
Cash and cash equivalents	$308,524	$194,747
Restricted cash	36,922	26,790
Trade accounts receivable	66,682	64,972
Merchandise inventories	174,848	152,912
Prepaid expenses and other current assets.	45,965	16,702
Deferred income taxes.	39,588	29,974
Total current assets	672,529	486,097

continued

Balance Sheet (in $000s)	2005	2004
Property and equipment, net of accumulated depreciation and amortization	1,054,605	873,397
Goodwill	112,476	112,186
Intangible assets, net of accumulated amortization	21,990	24,831
Deferred income taxes	22,452	4,193
Other assets	5,244	20,302
Total assets	$1,889,296	$1,521,006
Liabilities and shareholders' equity		
Current installment of long-term debt	$ 5,932	$ 5,973
Trade accounts payable	103,348	90,751
Accrued payroll, bonus and other benefits due to team members	126,981	100,536
Dividends payable	17,208	9,361
Other current liabilities	164,914	128,329
Total current liabilities	418,383	334,950
Long-term debt, less current installments	12,932	164,770
Deferred rent liabilities	91,775	70,067
Other long-term liabilities	530	1,581
Total liabilities	523,620	571,368
Shareholders' equity		
Common stock, no par value, 300,000 and 150,000 shares authorized, 68,009 and 62,771 shares issued, 67,954 and 62,407 shares outstanding in 2005 and 2004, respectively	874,972	535,107
Accumulated other comprehensive income	4,405	2,053
Retained earnings	486,299	412,478
Total shareholders' equity	1,365,676	949,638
Total liabilities and shareholders' equity	$1,889,296	$1,521,006

a. Forecast Whole Food Market's 2006 income statement and year-end balance sheet using the following relations (cost of goods sold and occupancy costs can be inferred as sales minus gross profit; and assume no change for all other accounts not listed below).

Sales growth	21.6%
Gross profit margin	35.1%
Direct store expenses	26.0%
General and administrative expenses	3.4%
Pre-opening and relocation costs	0.8%
Depreciation/Prior year property and equipment, net	15.3%
Provision for income taxes/Income before income taxes	42.6%
Sales/Year-end trade accounts receivable	70.16
Cost of goods sold and occupancy costs/Year-end merchandise inventories	17.54
Sales/Year-end property and equipment, net	4.46
Cost of goods sold and occupancy costs/Year-end trade accounts payable	29.63
Sales/Year-end accrued payroll, bonus and other benefits due team members	37.02
Dividends/Net income	40.2%
Dividends/Dividends payable	3.22

b. What does the forecasted cash balance from part *a* reveal to us about the forecasted financing needs of the company? Explain.

E11-20 **Forecasting the Statement of Cash flows** (LO2)

Refer to the Whole Foods Market, Inc., financial information from Exercise 11-19. Prepare a forecast of its fiscal year 2006 statement of cash flows.

E11-21. **Analyzing, Forecasting, and Interpreting both Income Statement and Balance Sheet** (LO2)

Following are the fiscal year income statements and balance sheets of Abercrombie & Fitch.

Consolidated Statements of Net Income			
For Fiscal Year Ended (Thousands)	2006	2005	2004
Net sales.	$2,784,711	$2,021,253	$1,707,810
Cost of goods sold.	933,295	680,029	624,640
Gross profit.	1,851,416	1,341,224	1,083,170
Stores and distribution expense.	1,000,755	738,244	597,416
Marketing, general and administrative expense.	313,457	259,835	155,553
Other operating income, net	(5,534)	(4,490)	(979)
Operating income.	542,738	347,635	331,180
Interest income, net	(6,674)	(5,218)	(3,708)
Income before income taxes	549,412	352,853	334,888
Provision for income taxes.	215,426	136,477	130,058
Net income.	$ 333,986	$ 216,376	$ 204,830

Consolidated Balance Sheets		
(Thousands, except per share amounts)	January 28, 2006	January 29, 2005
Assets		
Cash and equivalents.	$ 50,687	$ 338,735
Marketable securities.	411,167	—
Receivables	41,855	37,760
Inventories	362,536	211,198
Deferred income taxes.	29,654	39,090
Other current assets.	51,185	44,001
Total current assets	947,084	670,784
Property and equipment, net.	813,603	687,011
Other assets.	29,031	28,996
Total assets.	$1,789,718	$1,386,791
Liabilities and shareholders' equity		
Accounts payable.	$ 86,572	$ 83,760
Outstanding checks.	58,741	53,577
Accrued expenses	215,034	205,153
Deferred lease credits	31,727	31,135
Income taxes payable	99,480	55,587
Total current liabilities.	491,554	429,212
Deferred income taxes.	38,496	50,032
Deferred lease credits	191,225	177,923
Other liabilities.	73,326	60,298
Total long-term liabilities.	303,047	288,253

continued

Consolidated Balance Sheets		
(Thousands, except per share amounts)	**January 28, 2006**	**January 29, 2005**
Shareholders' equity		
Class A common stock—$.01 par value: 150,000,000 shares authorized and 103,300,000 shares issued at January 28, 2006 and January 29, 2005, respectively	1,033	1,033
Paid-in capital	161,678	140,251
Retained earnings	1,357,791	1,076,023
Accumulated other comprehensive income	(796)	—
Deferred compensation	26,206	15,048
Treasury stock, at average cost 15,573,789 and 17,262,943 shares at January 28, 2006 and January 29, 2005, respectively	(550,795)	(563,029)
Total shareholders' equity	995,117	669,326
Total liabilities and shareholders' equity	$1,789,718	$1,386,791

a. Forecast its fiscal year 2007 income statement and its 2007 fiscal year-end balance sheet using the following relations (cost of goods sold can be inferred as sales minus gross profit; assume no change for all other accounts not listed on next page).

Net sales growth	37.8%
Gross profit margin	66.5%
Stores and Distribution expense/Net sales	35.9%
Marketing, general and administrative expense/Net sales	11.3%
Other operating income, net/Net sales	−0.2%
Depreciation/Prior year property and equipment, net	18.1%
Provision for income taxes/Income before income taxes	39.2%
Interest income, net	no change
Net sales/Year-end receivable	66.53
Cost of goods sold/Year-end inventories	2.57
Cost of goods sold/Year-end accounts payable	10.78
Net sales/Year-end property and equipment, net	3.42
Net sales/Year-end accrued expenses	12.95
Income taxes payable/Provision for income taxes	46.2%
Dividends	$52,218

b. What does the forecasted cash balance from part *a* reveal to us about the forecasted financing needs of the company? Explain.

E11-22. **Forecasting the Statement of Cash flows** **(LO2)**

Refer to the Abercrombie & Fitch financial information in Exercise 11-21. Prepare a forecast of its fiscal year 2007 statement of cash flows.

Abercrombie & Fitch
(ANF)

E11-23. **Analyzing, Forecasting, and Interpreting both Income Statement and Balance Sheet** (LO2)

Best Buy, Co., Inc.
(BBY)

Following are the fiscal year income statements and balance sheets of Best Buy, Co., Inc.

Balance Sheet ($ millions, except per share amounts)	February 25, 2006	February 26, 2005
Assets		
Cash and cash equivalents	$ 681	$ 354
Short-term investments	3,051	2,994
Receivables	506	375
Merchandise inventories	3,338	2,851
Other current assets	409	329
Total current assets	7,985	6,903
Property and equipment		
Land and buildings	580	506
Leasehold improvements	1,325	1,139
Fixtures and equipment	2,898	2,458
Property under master and capital lease	33	89
	4,836	4,192
Less accumulated depreciation	2,124	1,728
Net property and equipment	2,712	2,464
Goodwill	557	513
Tradename	44	40
Long-term investments	218	148
Other assets	348	226
Total assets	$11,864	$10,294
Liabilities and shareholders' equity		
Accounts payable	$ 3,234	$ 2,824
Unredeemed gift card liabilities	469	410
Accrued compensation and related expenses	354	234
Accrued liabilities	878	844
Accrued income taxes	703	575
Current portion of long-term debt	418	72
Total current liabilities	6,056	4,959
Long-term liabilities	373	358
Long-term debt	178	528
Shareholders' equity		
Preferred stock, $1.00 par value: Authorized—400,000 shares; Issued and outstanding-none	—	—
Common stock, $.10 par value: Authorized—1 billion shares; Issued and outstanding—485,098,000 and 492,512,000 shares, respectively	49	49
Additional paid-in capital	643	936
Retained earnings	4,304	3,315
Accumulated other comprehensive income	261	149
Total shareholders' equity	5,257	4,449
Total liabilities and shareholders' equity	$11,864	$10,294

Income Statement Fiscal years ended ($ millions)	February 25, 2006	February 26, 2005	February 28, 2004
Revenue	$30,848	$27,433	$24,548
Cost of goods sold	23,122	20,938	18,677
Gross profit	7,726	6,495	5,871
Selling, general and administrative expenses . . .	6,082	5,053	4,567
Operating income	1,644	1,442	1,304
Net interest income (expense)	77	1	(8)
Earnings from continuing operations before income tax expense	1,721	1,443	1,296
Income tax expense	581	509	496
Earnings from continuing operations	1,140	934	800
Loss from discontinued operations, net of tax. . .	—	—	(29)
Gain (loss) on disposal of discontinued operations, net of tax	—	50	(66)
Net earnings	$ 1,140	$ 984	$ 705

a. Forecast Best Buy's fiscal year 2007 income statement and its 2007 fiscal year-end balance sheet using the following relations (cost of goods sold can be inferred as revenue minus gross profit; and assume no change for all other accounts not listed below).

Revenue growth	12.4%
Gross profit margin	25.0%
Selling, general and administrative expenses/Revenue	19.7%
Depreciation (included in SG&A expense)/Prior year net property and equipment	18.5%
Income tax expense/Earnings from continuing operations before income taxes	33.8%
Revenue/Year-end receivables	60.96
Cost of goods sold/Year-end merchandise inventories	6.93
Cost of goods sold/Year-end accounts payable	7.15
Revenue/Year-end net property and equipment	11.38
Revenue/Year-end accrued compensation and related expenses and accrued liabilities	25.04
Accrued income taxes/Income taxes expense	121.0%
Dividends/Net earnings	13.2%
Long term debt due in next fiscal year (February 2007)	$16

b. What does the forecasted cash balance from part *a* reveal to us about the forecasted financing needs of the company? Explain.

E11-24. Forecasting the Statement of Cash flows (LO2)

Refer to the Best Buy Co. , Inc., financial information from Exercise 11-23. Prepare a forecast of its fiscal year 2007 statement of cash flows.

Best Buy Co., Inc.
(BBY)

General Mills, Inc.
(GIS)

E11-25. Analyzing, Forecasting, and Interpreting Both Income Statement and Balance Sheet (LO2)

Following are the fiscal year income statements and balance sheets of General Mills, Inc..

Income Statement Fiscal year ended (In millions)	May 28, 2006	May 29, 2005	May 30, 2004
Net sales.	$11,640	$11,244	$11,070
Costs and expenses			
Cost of sales.	6,966	6,834	6,584
Selling, general and administrative.	2,678	2,418	2,443
Interest, net.	399	455	508
Restructuring and other exit costs	30	84	26
Divestitures (gain)	—	(499)	—
Debt repurchase costs	—	137	—
Total costs and expenses	10,073	9,429	9,561
Earnings before income taxes and after-tax earnings from joint ventures	1,567	1,815	1,509
Income taxes	541	664	528
After-tax earnings from joint ventures	64	89	74
Net earnings.	$ 1,090	$ 1,240	$ 1,055

Balance Sheet (In millions)	May 28, 2006	May 29, 2005
Assets		
Cash and cash equivalents	$ 647	$ 573
Receivables	1,076	1,034
Inventories	1,055	1,037
Prepaid expenses and other current assets.	216	203
Deferred income taxes	182	208
Total current assets	3,176	3,055
Land, buildings and equipment	2,997	3,111
Goodwill	6,652	6,684
Other intangible assets.	3,607	3,532
Other assets.	1,775	1,684
Total assets.	$18,207	$18,066
Liabilities and equity		
Accounts payable.	$ 1,151	$ 1,136
Current portion of long-term debt	2,131	1,638
Notes payable	1,503	299
Other current liabilities	1,353	1,111
Total current liabilities.	6,138	4,184
Long-term debt	2,415	4,255
Deferred income taxes	1,822	1,851
Other liabilities	924	967
Total liabilities.	11,299	11,257
Minority interests	1,136	1,133

continued

Balance Sheet (In millions)	May 28, 2006	May 29, 2005
Stockholders' equity		
Cumulative preference stock, none issued.	—	—
Common stock, 502 shares issued	50	50
Additional paid-in capital	5,737	5,691
Retained earnings.	5,107	4,501
Common stock in treasury, at cost, shares of 146 in 2006 and 133 in 2005	(5,163)	(4,460)
Unearned compensation	(84)	(114)
Accumulated other comprehensive income.	125	8
Total stockholders' equity	5,772	5,676
Total liabilities and equity.	$18,207	$18,066

a. Forecast General Mill's fiscal year 2007 income statement and its 2007 fiscal year-end balance sheet using the following relations (cost of goods sold can be inferred as sales minus gross profit; assume no change for all other accounts not listed below).

Net sales growth.	3.5%
Cost of sales / Net sales	59.8%
Selling, general and administrative / Net sales	23.0%
Restructuring and other exit costs / Net sales.	0.3%
Other revenues (expenses) / Net sales.	−0.5%
Depreciation (included in SG&A expense) / Prior year land, buildings and equipment	14.1%
Income taxes/ Earnings before income taxes	34.5%
Net sales/Year-end receivables	10.82
Cost of sales/ Year-end inventories	6.60
Cost of sales/ Year-end accounts payable.	6.05
Net sales/ Year-end land, buildings and equipment.	3.88
Net sales/ Year-end other current liabilities	8.60
Dividends / Net earnings	44.5%
Current maturities of long-term debt for year-end May 2007	$854

b. What does the forecasted cash balance from part *a* reveal to us about the forecasted financing needs of the company? Explain.

E11-26. Forecasting the Statement of Cash flows   (LO2)
Refer to the General Mills, Inc. financial information from Exercise 11-25. Prepare a forecast of its fiscal year 2007 statement of cash flows.

General Mills, Inc. (GIS)

E11-27. Adjusting the Balance Sheet for Operating Leases   (LO1)
Southwest Airlines reports total net operating assets of $8,419 million, liabilities of $1,744 million, and equity of $6,675 in its 2005 10-K. Footnotes reveal the existence of operating leases that have a present value of $1,779 million (see Module 10 for computations). (a) What balance sheet adjustment(s) might we consider relating to those leases in anticipation of forecasting its financial statements? (*Hint:* Consider the distinction between operating and nonoperating assets and liabilities.) (b) What income statement adjustment(s) might we consider? (*Hint:* Reflect on the operating and nonoperating distinction for lease-related expenses.)

Southwest Airlines (LUV)

E11-28. Adjusting the Balance Sheet for Equity Method Investments (LO1)

Abbott Laboratories, Inc., reports its 50% joint venture investment in TAP Pharmaceutical Products Inc. using the equity method of accounting. The Abbott balance sheet reports an investment balance of $167 million. TAP has total assets of $1,470.2 million, liabilities of $1,136.2 million, and equity of $334 million. Abbott's investment balance is, thus, equal to its 50% interest in TAP's equity ($334 million × 50% = $167 million). What adjustment(s) might we consider to Abbott's balance sheet in anticipation of forecasting its financial statements? (*Hint:* Consider the distinction between operating and nonoperating assets and liabilities.) What risks might Abbott Laboratories face that are not revealed on the face of its balance sheet?

E11-29. Projecting NOPAT and NOA using Parsimonious Forecasting Model (LO3)

Following are Intel's sales, net operating profit after tax (NOPAT), and net operating assets (NOA) for its year ended December 31, 2005 ($ millions).

Sales.	$38,826
Net operating profit after tax (NOPAT)	8,333
Net operating assets (NOA)	29,018

Forecast Intel's sales, NOPAT and NOA for years 2006 through 2009 using the following assumptions:

Sales growth per year.	13.50%
Net operating profit margin (NOPM).	21.46%
Net operating asset turnover (NOAT), based on NOA at December 31, 2005. . .	1.34

E11-30. Projecting NOPAT and NOA using Parsimonious Forecasting Model (LO3)

Following are Oracle's sales, net operating profit after tax (NOPAT), and net operating assets (NOA) for its fiscal year ended May 31, 2006 ($ millions).

Sales.	$14,380
Net operating profit after tax (NOPAT)	3,245
Net operating assets (NOA)	19,960

Forecast Oracle's sales, NOPAT and NOA for fiscal years 2007 through 2010 using the following assumptions:

Sales growth per year.	21.90%
Net operating profit margin (NOPM).	22.57%
Net operating asset turnover (NOAT), based on NOA at May 31, 2006.	0.72

PROBLEMS

P11-31. Forecasting the Income Statement, Balance Sheet, and Statement of Cash Flows (LO2)

Following are fiscal year financial statements of Oracle Corporation.

Oracle Corporation
(ORCL)

Consolidated Balance Sheets		
May 31 (in millions, except per share data)	2006	2005
Assets		
Cash and cash equivalent	$ 6,659	$ 3,894
Marketable securities	946	877
Trade receivables, net of allowances of $329 and $269	3,022	2,570
Other receivables	398	330
Deferred tax assets	714	486
Prepaid expenses and other current assets	235	291
Total current assets	11,974	8,448
Non-current assets		
Property, net	1,391	1,442
Intangible assets, net	4,528	3,373
Goodwill	9,809	7,003
Other assets	1,327	421
Total non-current assets	17,055	12,239
Total assets	$29,029	$20,687
Liabilities and stockholders' equity		
Short-term borrowings and current portion of long-term debt	$ 159	$ 2,693
Accounts payable	268	230
Income taxes payable	810	904
Accrued compensation and related benefits	1,172	923
Accrued restructuring	412	156
Deferred revenues	2,830	2,289
Other current liabilities	1,279	868
Total current liabilities	6,930	8,063
Non-current liabilities		
Notes payable and long-term debt, net of current portion	5,735	159
Deferred tax liabilities	564	1,010
Accrued restructuring	273	120
Deferred revenues	114	126
Other long-term liabilities	401	372
Total non-current liabilities	7,087	1,787
Stockholders' equity		
Preferred stock, $0.01 par value-authorized: 1.0 shares; outstanding: none	—	—
Common stock, $0.01 par value and additional paid in capital— authorized: 11,000 shares; outstanding: 5,232 shares at May 31, 2006 and 5,145 shares at May 31, 2005	9,246	6,596
Retained earnings	5,538	4,043
Deferred compensation	(30)	(45)
Accumulated other comprehensive income	258	243
Total stockholders' equity	15,012	10,837
Total liabilities and stockholders' equity	$29,029	$20,687

Consolidated Statements of Operations

Year ended May 31 (in millions)	2006	2005	2004
Revenues			
New software licenses	$ 4,905	$ 4,091	$ 3,541
Software license updates and product support	6,636	5,330	4,529
Software revenues	11,541	9,421	8,070
Services	2,839	2,378	2,086
Total revenues	14,380	11,799	10,156
Operating expenses			
Sales and marketing	3,177	2,511	2,123
Software license updates and product support	719	618	547
Cost of services	2,516	2,033	1,770
Research and development	1,872	1,491	1,254
General and administrative	555	550	508
Amortization of intangible assets	583	219	36
Acquisition related	137	208	54
Restructuring	85	147	—
Total operating expenses	9,644	7,777	6,292
Operating income	4,736	4,022	3,864
Interest expense	(169)	(135)	(21)
Nonoperating income, net			
Interest income	170	185	118
Net investment gains	25	2	29
Other	48	(23)	(45)
Total nonoperating income, net	243	164	102
Income before provision for income taxes	4,810	4,051	3,945
Provision for income taxes	1,429	1,165	1,264
Net income	$ 3,381	$ 2,886	$ 2,681

Required

Forecast its fiscal year 2007 income statement, balance sheet, and statement of cash flows. (*Note*: Oracle's long-term debt footnote reports that current maturities of long-term debt are $159 million and $4 million for May 2006 and 2007, respectively; Oracle includes the current portion due with short-term borrowings on its balance sheet.) Identify all financial statement relations estimated and assumptions made. What do the forecasts imply about the financing needs of Oracle?

P11-32. Forecasting the Income Statement, Balance Sheet, and Statement of Cash Flows (LO2)

Intuit, Inc. (INTU)

Following are the fiscal year financial statements of Intuit, Inc.

Consolidated Statements of Operations

Twelve months ended July 31 (in thousands)	2006	2005	2004
Net revenue			
Product	$1,351,636	$1,242,693	$1,179,101
Service	910,506	724,049	555,496
Other	80,161	70,961	67,627
Total net revenue	2,342,303	2,037,703	1,802,224

continued

Consolidated Statements of Operations			
Twelve months ended July 31 (in thousands)	2006	2005	2004
Costs and expenses			
Cost of revenue			
Cost of product revenue	176,188	164,551	170,769
Cost of service revenue.	229,435	183,969	158,083
Cost of other revenue	20,566	24,133	24,179
Amortization of purchased intangible assets . . .	9,902	10,251	10,186
Selling and marketing.	664,056	583,408	541,387
Research and development	398,983	305,241	276,049
General and administrative.	270,292	225,507	178,653
Acquisition-related charges	13,337	16,545	23,435
Total costs and expenses	1,782,759	1,513,605	1,382,741
Operating income from continuing operations.	559,544	524,098	419,483
Interest and other income	43,038	26,636	30,400
Gains on marketable equity securities and other investments, net	7,629	5,225	1,729
Income from continuing operations before taxes. . . .	610,211	555,959	451,612
Income tax provision	232,090	181,074	128,290
Minority interest, net of tax.	691	(98)	—
Net income from continuing operations.	377,430	374,983	323,322
Net income (loss) from discontinued operations	39,533	6,644	(6,292)
Net income.	$ 416,963	$ 381,627	$ 317,030

Consolidated Balance Sheets		
July 31 (in thousands, except par value)	2006	2005
Assets		
Cash and cash equivalents	$ 179,601	$ 83,842
Investments	1,017,599	910,416
Accounts receivable, net of allowance for doubtful accounts of $12,328 and $15,653	97,797	86,125
Income taxes receivable.	64,178	38,665
Deferred income taxes	47,199	54,854
Prepaid expenses and other current assets.	53,357	60,610
Current assets of discontinued operations	—	21,989
Current assets before funds held for payroll customers.	1,459,731	1,256,501
Funds held for payroll customers.	357,299	357,838
Total current assets.	1,817,030	1,614,339
Property and equipment, net	194,434	208,548
Goodwill, net	504,991	509,499
Purchased intangible assets, net	59,521	69,678
Long-term deferred income taxes	144,697	118,475
Loans to executive officers and other employees	8,865	9,245
Other assets	40,489	30,078
Long-term assets of discontinued operations	—	156,589
Total assets.	$2,770,027	$2,716,451

continued

Consolidated Balance Sheets		
July 31 (in thousands, except par value)	2005	2005
Liabilities and stockholders' equity		
Accounts payable.	$ 70,808	$ 65,812
Accrued compensation and related liabilities	171,903	144,823
Deferred revenue	293,113	279,382
Income taxes payable	33,560	30,423
Other current liabilities	89,291	103,131
Current liabilities of discontinued operations.	—	21,995
Current liabilities before payroll customer fund deposits.	658,675	645,566
Payroll customer fund deposits	357,299	357,838
Total current liabilities	1,015,974	1,003,404
Long-term obligations	15,399	17,308
Long-term obligations of discontinued operations	—	240
Total long-term obligations.	15,399	17,548
Commitments and contingencies		
Minority interest	568	—
Stockholders' equity		
Preferred stock, $0.01 par value	—	—
Authorized - 1,345 shares total; 145 shares designated Series A; 250 shares designated Series B Junior Participating Issued and outstanding-None		
Common stock, $0.01 par value	3,442	1,793
Authorized - 750,000 shares		
Issued and outstanding - 344,171 post-split shares at July 31, 2006 and 179,270 pre-split shares at July 31, 2005		
Additional paid-in capital	2,089,472	1,976,161
Treasury stock, at cost.	(1,944,036)	(1,557,833)
Deferred compensation	—	(16,283)
Accumulated other comprehensive income.	1,084	174
Retained earnings	1,588,124	1,291,487
Total stockholders' equity	1,738,086	1,695,499
Total liabilities and stockholders' equity.	$2,770,027	$2,716,451

Required

Forecast Intuit's fiscal year 2007 income statement, balance sheet, and statement of cash flows. Identify all financial statement relations estimated and assumptions made. (*Note*: Intuit's PPE footnote reveals that depreciation for 2006 was $94 million.) What do the forecasts imply about Intuit's financing needs for the upcoming year?

P11-33. Adjusting the Income Statement Prior to Forecasting (LO1)

CBS Corporation (CBS)

Following is the income statement of CBS Corporation, along with an excerpt from its MD&A section.

Income Statement Year ended December 31 ($ millions)	2005	2004	2003
Revenues	$14,536.4	$14,547.3	$13,554.5
Expenses			
Operating	8,671.8	8,643.6	8,165.4
Selling, general and administrative.	2,699.4	2,552.5	2,376.1
Impairment charges	9,484.4	17,997.1	—
Depreciation and amortization	498.7	508.6	501.7
Total expenses	21,354.3	29,701.8	11,043.2
Operating income (loss)	$ (6,817.9)	$(15,154.5)	$ 2,511.3

Operating Expenses: Table below presents consolidated operating expenses by type

Operating expenses by type, Year ended December 31	2005	2004	Increase (Decrease) 2005 vs. 2004		2003	Increase (Decrease) 2004 vs. 2003	
Programming	$3,453.2	$3,441.8	$ 11.4	—%	$3,080.3	$361.5	12%
Production	2,453.5	2,584.7	(131.2)	(5)	2,661.9	(77.2)	(3)
Outdoor operations	1,134.2	1,102.7	31.5	3	1,012.6	90.1	9
Publishing operations.	525.0	517.6	7.4	1	486.3	31.3	6
Parks operations	243.8	232.7	11.1	5	212.2	20.5	10
Other.	862.1	764.1	98.0	13	712.1	52.0	7
Total operating expenses	$8,671.8	$8,643.6	$ 28.2	—%	$8,165.4	$478.2	6%

For 2005, operating expenses of $8.67 billion increased slightly over $8.64 billion in 2004. For 2004, operating expenses of $8.64 billion increased 6% over $8.17 billion in 2003. The major components and changes in operating expenses were as follows:

- Programming expenses represented approximately 40% of total operating expenses in 2005 and 2004 and 38% in 2003, and reflect the amortization of acquired rights of programs exhibited on the broadcast and cable networks, and television and radio stations. Programming expenses increased slightly to $3.45 billion in 2005 from $3.44 billion in 2004 principally reflecting higher costs for Showtime Networks theatrical titles. Programming expenses increased 12% to $3.44 billion in 2004 from $3.08 billion in 2003 reflecting higher program rights expenses for sports events and primetime series at the broadcast networks.

- Production expenses represented approximately 28% of total operating expenses in 2005, 30% in 2004 and 33% in 2003, and reflect the cost and amortization of internally developed television programs, including direct production costs, residuals and participation expenses, and production overhead, as well as television and radio costs including on-air talent and other production costs. Production expenses decreased 5% to $2.45 billion in 2005 from $2.58 billion in 2004 principally reflecting lower network costs due to the absence of *Frasier* partially offset by increased costs for new network series. Production expenses decreased 3% to $2.58 billion in 2004 from $2.66 billion in 2003 reflecting fewer network series produced in 2004 partially offset by higher news costs for political campaign coverage.

- Outdoor operations costs represented approximately 13% of total operating expenses n 2005 and 2004, and 12% in 2003, and reflect transit and billboard lease, maintenance, posting and rotation expenses. Outdoor operations expenses increased 3% to $1.13 billion in 2005 from $1.10 billion in 2004 principally reflecting higher billboard lease costs and maintenance costs associated with the impact of hurricanes in 2005. Outdoor operations costs increased 9% to $1.10 billion in 2004 from $1.01 billion in 2003 primarily reflecting higher transit and billboard lease costs.

- Publishing operations costs, which represented approximately 6% of total operating expenses in each of the years 2005, 2004 and 2003, reflect cost of book sales, royalties and other costs incurred with respect to publishing operations. Publishing operations expenses for 2005 increased 1% to $525.0 million and increased 6% to $617.6 million in 2004 from $486.3 million in 2003 primarily due to higher revenues.

- Parks operations costs, which represented approximately 3% of total operating expenses in each of the years 2005, 2004 and 2003, increased 5% to $243.8 million in 2005 from $232.7 million in 2004 principally reflecting the cost of fourth quarter 2005 winter events held at the parks and the impact of foreign currency translation. In 2004, Parks operations costs increased 10% to $232.7 million from $212.2 million in 2003 primarily from the impact of foreign currency translation.

- Other operating expenses, which represented approximately 10% of total operating expenses in 2005 and 9% in 2004 and 2003, primarily include distribution costs incurred with respect to television product, costs associated with digital media and compensation. Other operating expenses increased 13% to $862.1 million in 2005 from $764.1 million in 2004 primarily reflecting a 10% increase in distribution costs due to the DVD release of *Charmed* and increased costs associated with digital media from the inclusion of SportsLine.com, Inc. ("SportsLine.com") since its acquisition in December 2004. Other operating expenses for 2004 increased 7% to $764.1 million in 2004 from $712.1 million in 2003 principally reflecting 15% higher distribution costs due to additional volume of DVD releases of the *Star Trek* series and higher compensation.

Impairment Charges SFAS 142 requires the Company to perform an annual fair value-based impairment test of goodwill. The Company performed its annual impairment test as of October 31, 2005 concurrently with its annual budgeting process which begins in the fourth quarter each year. The first step of the test examines whether or not the book value of each of the Company's reporting units exceeds its fair value. If the book value for a reporting unit exceeds its fair value, the second step of the test is required to compare the implied fair value of that reporting unit's goodwill with the book value of the goodwill. The Company's reporting units are generally consistent with or one level below the operating segments underlying the reportable segments. As a result of the 2005 annual impairment test, the Company recorded an impairment charge of $9.48 billion in the fourth quarter of 2005. The $9.48 billion reflects charges to reduce the carrying value of goodwill at the CBS Television reporting unit of $6.44 billion and the Radio reporting unit of $3.05 billion. As a result of the annual impairment test performed for 2004, the Company recorded an impairment charge of $18.0 billion in the fourth quarter of 2004. The $18.0 billion reflects charges to reduce the carrying value of goodwill at the Radio reporting unit of $10.94 billion and the Outdoor reporting unit of $7.06 billion as well as the reduction of the carrying value of intangible assets of $27.8 million related to the FCC licenses at the Radio segment. Several factors led to a reduction in forecasted cash flows and long-term growth rates for both the Radio and Outdoor reporting units. Radio and Outdoor both fell short of budgeted revenue and operating income growth targets in 2004. Competition from other advertising media, including Internet advertising and cable and broadcast television reduced Radio and Outdoor growth rates. Also, the emergence of new competitors and technologies necessitated a shift in management's strategy for the Radio and Outdoor businesses, including changes in composition of the sales force and operating management as well as increased levels of investment in marketing and promotion.

Required

Identify and explain any income statement line items over the past three years that you believe should be considered for potential adjustment in preparation for forecasting the income statement of CBS.

P11-34. **Adjusting the Income Statement Prior to Forecasting** (LO1)

Xerox Corporation
(XRX)

Following are the income statements of Xerox Corporation.

Income Statement Year ended December 31 (in millions)	2005	2004	2003
Revenues			
Sales.	$ 7,400	$ 7,259	$ 6,970
Service, outsourcing and rentals	7,426	7,529	7,734
Financial income	875	934	997
Total revenues.	15,701	15,722	15,701
Costs and expenses			
Cost of sales.	4,695	4,545	4,346
Cost of service, outsourcing and rentals	4,207	4,295	4,307
Equipment financing and interest.	326	345	362
Research, development and engineering expenses	943	914	962
Selling, administrative and general expenses	4,110	4,203	4,249
Restructuring and asset impairment charges	366	86	176
Gain on affiliate's sale of stock.	—	—	(13)
Other expenses, net.	224	369	876
Total costs and expenses.	14,871	14,757	15,265
Income from continuing operations before income taxes, equity income, discontinued operations and cumulative effect of change in accounting principal.	830	965	436
Income tax (benefits) expenses	(5)	340	134
Equity in net income of unconsolidated affiliates.	98	151	58
Income from continuing operations before discontinued operations and cumulative effect of change in accounting principal.	933	776	360
Income from discontinued operations, net of tax	53	83	—
Cumulative effect of change in accounting principal, net of tax	(8)	—	—
Net income.	$ 978	$ 859	$ 360

Required

Identify and explain any income statement line items over the past three years that you believe should be considered for potential adjustment in preparation for forecasting the income statement of Xerox.

CASES

C11-35. **Adjusting the Income Statement and Forecasting the Income Statement, Balance Sheet, and Statement of Cash Flows** (LO1, 2)

Following are the income statements and balance sheets of Cisco Systems, Inc.

Cisco Systems, Inc. (CSCO)

Income Statement Years ended ($ millions)	July 29, 2006	July 30, 2005	July 31, 2004
Net sales			
Product	$23,917	$20,853	$18,550
Service	4,567	3,948	3,495
Total net sales	28,484	24,801	22,045
Cost of sales			
Product	8,114	6,758	5,766
Service	1,623	1,372	1,153
Total cost of sales	9,737	8,130	6,919
Gross margin	18,747	16,671	15,126
Operating expenses			
Research and development	4,067	3,322	3,192
Sales and marketing	6,031	4,721	4,530
General and administrative	1,169	959	867
Amortization of purchased intangible assets	393	227	242
In-process research and development	91	26	3
Total operating expenses	11,751	9,255	8,834
Operating income	6,996	7,416	6,292
Interest income, net	607	552	512
Other income, net	30	68	188
Interest and other income, net	637	620	700
Income before provision for income taxes and cumulative effect of accounting change	7,633	8,036	6,992
Provision for income taxes	2,053	2,295	2,024
Income before cumulative effect of accounting change	5,580	5,741	4,968
Cumulative effect of accounting change, net of tax	—	—	(567)
Net income	$ 5,580	$ 5,741	$ 4,401

Balance sheet ($ millions)	July 29, 2006	July 30, 2005
Assets		
Cash and cash equivalents	$3,297	$4,742
Investments	14,517	11,313
Accounts receivable, net of allowance for doubtful accounts of $175 at July 29, 2006 and $162 at July 30, 2005	3,303	2,216
Inventories	1,371	1,297
Deferred tax assets	1,604	1,475
Prepaid expenses and other current assets	1,584	967
Total current assets	25,676	22,010
Property and equipment, net	3,440	3,320
Goodwill	9,227	5,295
Purchased intangible assets, net	2,161	549
Other assets	2,811	2,709
Total assets	$43,315	$33,883
Liabilities and shareholders' equity		
Accounts payable	$ 880	$ 735
Income taxes payable	1,744	1,511
Accrued compensation	1,516	1,317
Deferred revenue	4,408	3,854
Other accrued liabilities	2,765	2,094
Total current liabilities	11,313	9,511
Long-term debt	6,332	—
Deferred revenue	1,241	1,188
Other long-term liabilities	511	—
Total liabilities	19,397	10,699
Commitments and contingencies		
Minority interest	**6**	10
Shareholders' equity		
Preferred stock, no par value: 5 shares authorized; none issued and outstanding	—	—
Common stock and additional paid-in capital, $0.001 par value: 20,000 shares authorized; 6,059 and 6,331 shares issued and outstanding at July 29, 2006 and July 30, 2005, respectively	24,257	22,394
Retained earnings (Accumulated deficit)	(617)	506
Accumulated other comprehensive income	272	274
Total shareholders' equity	23,912	23,174
Total liabilities and shareholders' equity	$43,315	$33,883

Excerpts from the Cisco Systems MD&A follow:

Acquisition of Scientific-Atlanta, Inc. On February 24, 2006, Cisco completed the acquisition of Scientific-Atlanta, Inc., a provider of set-top boxes, end-to-end video distribution networks, and video system integration. Cisco believes video is emerging as the key strategic application in the service provider "triple play" bundle of consumer entertainment, communications, and online services. Cisco believes the combined entity creates an end-to-end solution for carrier networks and the digital home and delivers large-scale video systems to extend Cisco's commitment to and leadership in the service provider market.

Stock-Based Compensation Expense On July 31, 2005, we adopted SFAS 123(R), which requires the measurement and recognition of compensation expense for all share-based payment awards made to employees and directors including employee stock options and employee stock purchases based on estimated fair values. Stock-based compensation expense related to employee stock options and employee stock purchases under SFAS 123(R) for fiscal 2006 was allocated as follows (in millions):

	Amount
Cost of sales-product.	$ 50
Cost of sales-service	112
Stock-based compensation expense included in cost of sale	162
Research and development	346
Sales and marketing.	427
General and administrative.	115
Stock-based compensation expense included in operating expense	888
Total stock-based compensation expense related to employee stock options and employee stock purchases	1,050
Tax benefit	(294)
Stock-based compensation expense related to employee stock options and employee stock purchases, net of tax.	$ 756

Gross Margin The decrease in gross margin percentage compared to fiscal 2005 was primarily related to the acquisition of Scientific-Atlanta. Other factors contributing to the decrease in gross margin percentage were the sales mix of certain switching and routing products, and the effect of stock-based compensation expense under SFAS 123(R). These factors were partially offset by lower manufacturing costs related to lower component costs and value engineering, and other manufacturing-related costs and higher volume.

Research and Development, Sales and Marketing, and General and Administrative Expenses R&D expenses increased for fiscal 2006 compared to fiscal 2005 primarily due to higher headcount-related expenses reflecting our continued investment in R&D efforts in routers, switches, advanced technologies, and other product technologies; the effect of stock-based compensation expense related to employee stock options and employee stock purchases under SFAS 123(R); and the acquisition of Scientific-Atlanta.

Sales and marketing expenses for fiscal 2006 increased compared to fiscal 2005 primarily due to an increase in sales expenses of approximately $1.1 billion. Sales expenses increased primarily due to an increase in headcount-related expenses, an increase in sales program expenses, and the acquisition of Scientific-Atlanta, which added approximately $30 million of sales expenses. Sales expenses also include stock-based compensation expense related to employee stock options and employee stock purchases under SFAS 123(R) of $337 million during fiscal 2006. Marketing expenses include $90 million of stock-based compensation expense related to employee stock options and employee stock purchases under SFAS 123(R) during fiscal 2006. Scientific-Atlanta added approximately $20 million of marketing expenses.

G&A expenses for fiscal 2006 increased compared to fiscal 2005 primarily because of stock-based compensation expense related to employee stock options and employee stock purchases under SFAS 123(R), and the acquisition of Scientific-Atlanta. G&A expenses include $115 million of stock-based compensation expense related to employee stock options and employee stock purchases under SFAS 123(R) and Scientific-Atlanta contributed approximately $40 million of G&A expenses.

Accounts Receivable, Net The increase in accounts receivable was due to increased sales and the addition of approximately $240 million of accounts receivable related to Scientific-Atlanta. Days sales outstanding in accounts receivable (DSO) as of July 29, 2006 and July 30, 2005 was 38 days and 31 days, respectively. Our DSO is primarily impacted by shipment linearity and collections performance. A steady level of shipments and good collections performance will result in reduced DSO compared with a higher level of shipments toward the end of a quarter, which will result in a shorter amount of time to collect the related accounts receivable and increased DSO.

Inventories Annualized inventory turns were 8.5 in the fourth quarter of fiscal 2006 compared to 6.6 in the fourth quarter of fiscal 2005...In the third quarter of fiscal 2006, we began the initial implementation of the lean manufacturing model. Lean manufacturing is an industry-standard model that seeks to drive efficiency and flexibility in manufacturing processes and in the broader supply chain. Over time, consistent with what we have experienced thus far, we expect this process will result in incremental increases in purchase commitments with contract manufacturers and suppliers and corresponding decreases in manufacturing inventory. Inventory management remains an area of focus as we balance the need to maintain strategic inventory levels to ensure competitive lead times with the risk of inventory obsolescence because of rapidly changing technology and customer requirements. We believe the amount of our inventory is appropriate for our revenue levels.

Required

a. Compute the ratios in the following table for fiscal years 2005 and 2006 using the financial statements provided and the following additional information:

1. Total net sales for 2004 is $22,045 million
2. 2006 depreciation expense is $900 (included in G&A expense); and 2005 depreciation divided by prior year property and equipment (net) equals 23.3%
3. Dividends are $0 in 2005 and 2006

(Ratios should reveal a marked decline in gross profit margin and marked increases in operating expense items from 2005 to 2006.)

b. For the following table, compute and enter assumptions for the forecasting of Cisco's financial statements. Do you believe that margins and operating expenses will continue at 2006 percentages? Or, are they likely to revert to 2005 levels? Explain.

	Projected	2006 Actual	2005 Actual
Gross margin/Total net sales			
Research and development/Total net sales			
Sales and marketing/Total net sales.			
General and administrative/Total net sales			
(Amortization of purchased intangibles + In-process research and development)/Total net sales			
Depreciation (in G&A)/Prior year property and equipment, net			
Provision for income taxes/Income before provision for income taxes			
Total net sales/Year-end accounts receivable, net			
Total cost of sales/Year-end inventories.			
Total net sales/Year-end property and equipment, net			
Total cost of sales/Year-end property and equipment, net . . .			
Total net sales/Year-end accrued compensation			
Income taxes payable/Provision for income taxes.			
Total net sales/Year-end deferred revenue			
Dividends/Net income			

c. Prepare one-year-ahead forecasts of Cisco's income statement, balance sheet, and statement of cash flows using your assumptions from part *b* and the information provided.

d. What does the projected cash balance reveal about Cisco's need for external financing in 2007?

Analyzing and Valuing Equity Securities

LEARNING OBJECTIVES

LO1 Describe and illustrate the discounted free cash flow model to value equity securities. (p. 12-4)

LO2 Describe and illustrate the residual operating income model to value equity securities. (p. 12-8)

LO3 Explain how equity valuation models can aid managerial decisions. (p. 12-10)

JOHNSON & JOHNSON

Pharmaceutical companies have long been the growth stocks of choice for many investors. Their income was steady and climbing, their stocks grew in value, and their growth appeared limitless as the population aged. Stockholders pushed them to grow by acquiring competitors, and encouraged them to further market existing drugs and pursue new product development. All looked rosy. The high profit margins from successful drug products fueled further expansion. Meanwhile, many pharmaceutical companies sold off their lower-growth business segments such as those manufacturing and distributing medical instruments and devices. For example, Pfizer sold off segments that manufactured surgical devices, heart valves, and orthopedic implants, while Eli Lilly sold off many of its medical device segments, including Guidant.

A few pharmaceutical companies bucked the trend to reorganize and consolidate. One of those was Johnson & Johnson (J&J). In contrast with the operating strategies of other pharmaceutical companies, and anticipating a gradual decline in pharmaceutical operating profits, J&J has been steadily increasing its investment in its medical devices and instruments segment. That segment now accounts for 40% of J&J's operating profit, up from 31% in 2004.

As expected, the pharmaceutical segment's proportion of J&J's operating profit has decreased from 58% to 48% in the past two years, while pharmaceutical sales have declined by only 2% to 44.1% of total sales. The following graphics, using data from J&J's 10-K report, reflect these trends.

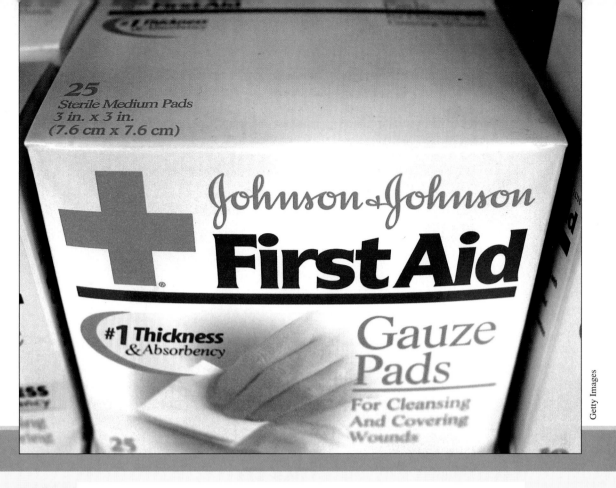

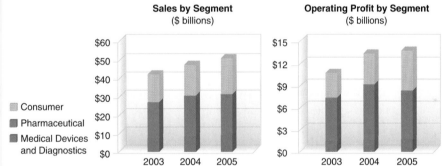

Sales by Segment
($ billions)

Operating Profit by Segment
($ billions)

- Consumer
- Pharmaceutical
- Medical Devices and Diagnostics

J&J is currently riding high while many other pharmaceutical companies are struggling. A drug-industry consultant asserts that J&J is ". . . casting a broader net for innovation, it's not just blockbuster drugs. They've held their value or grown, and the pure pharma plays that everyone thought could grow forever are the companies that have lost their luster."

Supported by its more diversified operations and fueled by a steady increase in operating profits, J&J's stock price has climbed since late 2004, as shown here.

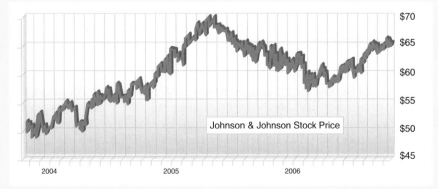

Johnson & Johnson Stock Price

(Continued on next page)

12-2

(Continued from previous page)

Despite the run-up in stock price, analysts remain bullish, continuing to rate the J&J stock a "BUY."

This raises several questions. What factors drive the J&J stock price? Why do analysts expect its price to continue to rise? How do accounting measures of performance and financial condition impact stock price? This module provides insights and answers to these questions. It explains how we can use forecasts of operating profits and cash flows to price equity securities such as J&J's stock.

Sources: *Johnson & Johnson* 2003-2005 10-K and Annual Reports; *The Wall Street Journal*, December 2004; Fortune, January 2007.

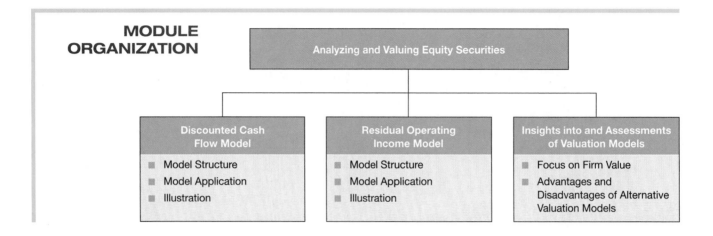

MODULE ORGANIZATION

Analyzing and Valuing Equity Securities

Discounted Cash Flow Model	Residual Operating Income Model	Insights into and Assessments of Valuation Models
▪ Model Structure	▪ Model Structure	▪ Focus on Firm Value
▪ Model Application	▪ Model Application	▪ Advantages and Disadvantages of Alternative Valuation Models
▪ Illustration	▪ Illustration	

INTRODUCTION TO SECURITY VALUATION

This module focuses on valuing equity securities (we explain the valuation of debt securities in Module 8). We describe two approaches: the discounted free cash flow model (DCF) and residual operating income model (ROPI). We then conclude by discussing the management implications from an increased understanding of the factors that impact values of equity securities. It is important that we understand the determinants of equity value to make informed decisions. Employees at all levels of an organization, whether public or private, should understand the factors that create shareholder value so that they can work effectively toward that objective. For many senior managers, stock value serves as a scorecard. Successful managers are those who better understand the factors affecting that scorecard.

Equity Valuation Models

Module 8 explains that the value of a debt security is the present value of the interest and principal payments that the investor *expects* to receive in the future. The valuation of equity securities is similar in that it is also based on expectations. The difference lies in the increased uncertainty surrounding the payments from equity securities.

There are many equity valuation models in use today. Each of them defines the value of an equity security in terms of the present value of future forecasted amounts. They differ primarily in terms of what is forecasted.

The basis of equity valuation is the premise that the value of an equity security is determined by the payments that the investor can expect to receive from the investment. Equity investments involve two types of payoffs: (1) dividends received during the holding period and (2) capital gains when the security is sold.[1] The value of an equity security is, then, based on the present value of expected dividends plus the value of the security at the end of the forecasted holding period. This **dividend discount model** is appealing in its simplicity and its intuitive focus on dividend distribution. As a practical matter, however, the model is not useful because many companies that have a positive stock price have never paid a dividend, and are not expected to pay a dividend in the foreseeable future.

---

[1] The future stock price is, itself, also assumed to be related to the expected dividends that the new investor expects to receive; as a result, the expected receipt of dividends is the sole driver of stock price under this type of valuation model.

A more practical approach to valuing equity securities focuses, instead, on the company's operating and investing activities; that is, on the *generation* of cash rather than the *distribution* of cash. This approach is called the **discounted cash flow (DCF)** model. The focus of the forecasting process for this model is the company's expected *free cash flows to the firm*, which are defined as operating cash flows net of the expected new investments in net operating assets that are required to support the business.

A second practical approach to equity valuation also focuses on operating and investing activities. It is known as the **residual operating income (ROPI)** model. This model uses both net operating profits after tax (NOPAT) and the net operating assets (NOA) to determine equity value; see Module 4 for complete descriptions of the NOPAT and NOA measures. This approach highlights the importance of return on net operating assets (RNOA), and the disaggregation of RNOA into net operating profit margin and NOA turnover. We discuss the implications of this insight for managers later in this module.

DISCOUNTED CASH FLOW (DCF) MODEL

The discounted cash flow (DCF) model defines firm value as follows:

LO1 Describe and illustrate the discounted free cash flow model to value equity securities.

Firm Value = Present Value of Expected Free Cash Flows to Firm

The expected free cash flows to the firm include cash flows arising from the operating side of the firm; that is, cash generated from the firm's operating activities (but not from nonoperating activities such as interest paid on debt or dividends received on investments), and do not include the cash flows from financing activities. More specifically, **free cash flows to the firm** (FCFF) equal net operating profit after tax that is not used to grow net operating assets.[2] Using the terminology of Module 4

FCFF = NOPAT − Increase in NOA

where

NOPAT = Net operating profit after tax
NOA = Net operating assets

Net operating profit after tax is normally positive and net cash flows from increases in net operating assets are normally negative. The sum of the two (positive or negative) represents the net cash flows available to creditors and shareholders. Positive FCFF imply that there are funds available for distribution to creditors and shareholders, either in the form of debt repayments, dividends, or stock repurchases (treasury stock). Negative FCFF imply that the firm requires additional funds from creditors and/or shareholders, in the form of new loans or equity investments, to support its business activities.

The DCF valuation model requires forecasts of *all* future free cash flows; that is, free cash flows for the remainder of the company's life. Generating such forecasts is not realistic. Consequently, analysts typically estimate FCFF over a horizon period, often 4 to 10 years, and then make simplifying assumptions about the FCFF subsequent to that horizon period.

Application of the DCF model to equity valuation involves five steps:

1. Forecast and discount FCFF for the **horizon period**.[3]
2. Forecast and discount FCFF for the post-horizon period, called **terminal period**.[4]

---

[2] FCFF is sometimes approximated by net cash flows from operating activities less capital expenditures. This is not exact because operating cash flows from the statement of cash flows include interest paid and received, which are not part of NOPAT. However, for most companies, the approximation is fairly accurate.

[3] When discounting FCFF, the appropriate discount rate (r_w) is the **weighted average cost of capital (WACC)**, where the weights are the relative percentages of debt (d) and equity (e) in the capital structure applied to the expected returns on debt (r_d) and equity (r_e), respectively: WACC $= r_w = (r_d \times \%$ of debt$) + (r_e \times \%$ of equity$)$.

[4] For an assumed growth, g, the terminal period (T) present value of FCFF in perpetuity (beyond the horizon period) is given by, $\frac{FCFF_T}{r_w - g}$, where $FCFF_T$ is the free cash flow to the firm for the terminal period, r_w is WACC, and g is the assumed long-term growth rate of those cash flows. The resulting amount is then discounted back to the present using the horizon-end period discount factor.

3. Sum the present values of the horizon and terminal periods to yield firm (enterprise) value.

4. Subtract net nonoperating obligations (NNO) from firm value to yield firm equity value. NNO can be either positive or negative; either way, we subtract NNO in step 4. (For most companies, NNO is a positive number because nonoperating liabilities exceed nonoperating assets.)

5. Divide firm equity value by the number of shares outstanding to yield stock value per share.

To illustrate, we apply the DCF model to Johnson & Johnson. J&J's recent financial statements are reproduced in Appendix 12A. Forecasted financials for J&J (forecast horizon of 2006–2009 and terminal period of 2010) are in Exhibit 12.1.[5] The forecasts (in bold) are for sales, NOPAT, and NOA. These forecasts assume an annual 6.5% sales growth during the horizon period, a terminal period sales growth of 1%, net operating profit margin (NOPM) of 18%, and a year-end net operating asset turnover (NOAT) of 1.25 (which is the 2005 turnover rate based on year-end NOA; year-end amounts are used because we are forecasting year-end account balances, not average balances).[6,7]

EXHIBIT 12.1	**Application of Discounted Cash Flow Model**					
(In millions, except per share values and discount factors)	**2005**	**Horizon Period**				**Terminal Period**
		2006	**2007**	**2008**	**2009**	
Sales.........................	$ 50,514	**$53,797**	**$57,294**	**$61,018**	**$64,985**	**$65,634**
NOPAT*......................	10,134	**9,683**	**10,313**	**10,983**	**11,697**	**11,814**
NOA**........................	40,453	**43,038**	**45,835**	**48,814**	**51,988**	**52,507**
Increase in NOA		2,585	2,797	2,979	3,174	519
FCFF (NOPAT − Increase in NOA)		7,098	7,516	8,004	8,523	11,295
Discount factor [1/(1 + r_w)^t]		0.94340	0.89000	0.83962	0.79209	
Present value of horizon FCFF		6,696	6,689	6,720	6,751	
Cum present value of horizon FCFF...	26,856					
Present value of terminal FCFF	178,933					
Total firm value	205,789					
Less (plus) NNO[†]	2,582					
Firm equity value	$203,207					
Shares outstanding	2,975					
Stock value per share.............	$ 68.30					

*Given its combined federal and state statutory tax rate of 36%, NOPAT for 2005 is computed as follows ($ mil.): $50,514 − $13,954 − $16,877 − $6,312 − $362 + $214 − ($3,245 − 0.36 × [$487 − $54]) = $10,134, which is 20% of sales ($10,134 million/$50,514 million). Footnotes to J&J's 10-K reveal that its effective tax rate for 2005 is 23.8%, compared with 33.7% in 2004 and 30.2% in 2003. Analysis reveals that its 2005 effective tax rate is lower due to foreign tax credits and a reversal of a tax liability tied to a technical correction with the American Jobs Creation Act of 2004. The credits and reversal are *transitory* and should not be included in our projections. Accordingly, we *project* its tax rate to be 32%, the average of its 2004 and 2003 rates. If we apply 32% to its $13,656 million pretax GAAP income for 2005 we get an adjusted NOPAT of $9,009 million, computed as ($ mil.): $50,514 − $13,954 − $16,877 − $6,312 − $362 + 214 − ([$13,656 × 32%] − [0.36 × {$487 − $54}]). This adjusted NOPAT yields a NOPM of 18% ($9,009 million/$50,514 million) and is the rate we use in forecasts of NOPAT. A note on rounding: Sales are forecasted using current period sales multiplied successively by (1 + Growth rate), without rounding; next, NOPAT and NOA are computed from each period's sales forecast rounded to the whole unit.

**NOA computations for 2005 follow ($ mil.): ($58,025 − $83 − $20) − ($4,315 − $3,529 − $2,017 − $1,166 − $940 − $211 − $3,065 − $2,226) = $40,453.

[†]NNO is the difference between NOA and total shareholders' equity, which is NNO ($ mil.) = $40,453 − $37,871 = $2,582.

---

[5] We use a four-period horizon in the text and assignments to simplify the exposition and to reduce the computational burden. In practice, analysts use spreadsheets to forecast future cash flows and value the equity security, and typically have a forecast horizon of seven to ten periods.

[6] **NOPAT** equals revenues less operating expenses such as cost of goods sold, selling, general, and administrative expenses, and taxes. NOPAT excludes any interest revenue and interest expense and any gains or losses from financial investments. NOPAT reflects the operating side of the firm as opposed to nonoperating activities such as borrowing and security investment activities. **NOA** equals operating assets less operating liabilities. (See Module 4.)

[7] NOPAT and NOA are typically forecasted using the detailed forecasting procedures discussed in Module 11. In this module we use the parsimonious method to multiyear forecasting (see Module 11) to focus attention on the valuation process.

The bottom line of Exhibit 12.1 is the estimated J&J equity value of $203,207 million, or a per share stock value of $68.30. The present value computations use a 6% WACC(r_w) as the discount rate.[8] Specifically, we obtain this stock valuation as follows:

1. **Compute present value of horizon period FCFF.** We compute the forecasted 2006 FCFF of $7,098 million from the forecasted 2006 NOPAT less the forecasted increase in 2006 NOA. The present value of this $7,098 million as of 2005 is $6,696 million, computed as $7,098 million × 0.94340 (the present value factor for one year discounted at 6%).[9] Similarly, the present value of 2007 FCFF (2 years from the current date) is $6,689 million, computed as $7,516 million × 0.89000, and so on through 2009. The sum of these present values (*cumulative present value*) is $26,856 million.

2. **Compute present value of terminal period FCFF.** The present value of the terminal period

   FCFF is $178,933 million, computed as $\dfrac{\left(\dfrac{\$11{,}295 \text{ million}}{0.06 - 0.01}\right)}{(1.06)^4}$, or ($11,295/0.05) × 0.79209.

3. **Compute firm equity value.** Sum present values from the horizon and terminal period FCFF to get firm (enterprise) value of $205,789 million. Subtract the value of J&J's net nonoperating obligations of $2,582 million to get firm equity value of $203,207. Dividing firm equity value by the 2,975 million shares outstanding yields the estimated per share valuation of $68.30.

This valuation would be performed in early 2006 (because J&J's 10-K was released in mid-March 2006). J&J's stock closed at $60.25 at year-end 2005. Our valuation estimate of $68.30 indicates that its stock is undervalued. In December 2006 (roughly one year later) J&J stock traded at near $67, and analysts continued to recommend it as a BUY with a target share price in the high $60s.

| BUSINESS INSIGHT | Analysts' Earnings Forecasts |

Estimates of earnings and cash flows are key to security valuation. Following are earnings estimates at the beginning of 2006 for Johnson & Johnson by Thomson First Call analysts' reports, a division of Thomson Financial™:

Period	Ending	Mean EPS	High EPS	Low EPS	Median EPS
Fiscal Year	Dec. 2006	$3.69	$3.72	$3.65	$3.69
Fiscal Year	Dec. 2007	$4.01	$4.11	$3.88	$4.01
Long-term growth (%)	—	10.06%	13.00%	7.00%	10.07%

The mean (consensus) EPS estimate for 2006 (one year ahead) is $3.69 per share, with a high of $3.72 and a low of $3.65. For 2007, the mean (consensus) EPS estimate is $4.01, with a high of $4.11 and a low of $3.88. The estimated long-term growth rate for EPS (similar to our terminal year growth rate) ranges from 7% to 13%, with a mean (consensus) estimate of 10.06%. Since the terminal year valuation is such a large proportion of total firm valuation, especially for the DCF model, the variability in stock price estimates across analysts covering Johnson & Johnson is due more to variation in estimates for long-term growth rates than to one- and two-year-ahead earnings forecasts.

---

[8] The weighted average cost of capital (WACC) for J&J is computed using the following three-step process:

1. The cost of equity capital is given by the capital asset pricing model (CAPM): $r_e = r_f + \beta\,(r_m - r_f)$, where β is the beta of the stock (an estimate of stock price variability that is reported by several services such as Standard and Poors), r_f is the risk free rate (commonly assumed as the 10-year government bond rate), and r_m is the expected return to the entire market. The expression $(r_m - r_f)$ is the "spread" of equities over the risk free rate, often assumed to be around 5%. For J&J, given its beta of 0.24 and a 10-year treasury bond rate of 4.42% (r_f) as of January 2006, r_e is estimated as 5.62%, computed as 4.42% + (0.24 × 5%).

2. Given J&J's AAA bond rating, its cost of debt capital is its after-tax rate on AAA bonds as of January 1, 2006 (5.29%) multiplied by 1-36%, the federal and state statutory tax rate from its tax footnote, yielding 3.39% (its after-tax cost of debt).

3. WACC is the weighted average of the cost of equity capital and the cost of debt capital. J&J capital structure is 95% equity and 5% debt. Thus, J&J's weighted average cost of capital is (95% × 5.62%) + (5% × 3.39%) = 5.51%. We have rounded this WACC up to 6% to facilitate use of the present value tables from Appendix A.

[9] Horizon period discount factors follow: $1/(1.06)^1 = 0.94340$; $1/(1.06)^2 = 0.89000$; $1/(1.06)^3 = 0.83962$; $1/(1.06)^4 = 0.79209$.

MANAGERIAL DECISION   **You Are the Division Manager**

Assume that you are managing a division of a company that has a large investment in plant assets and sells its products on credit. Identify steps you can take to increase your company's cash flow and hence, your company's firm value. [Answer p. 12-15]

MID-MODULE REVIEW

Following are forecasts of Procter & Gamble's sales, net operating profit after tax (NOPAT), and net operating assets (NOA). These are taken from our forecasting process in Module 11 and now include a terminal period forecast that reflects a long-term growth rate of 2%.

(In millions)	2006	Horizon Period 2007	2008	2009	2010	Terminal Period
Sales............	$68,222	$ 71,224	$ 74,358	$ 77,629	$ 81,045	$ 82,666
NOPAT	9,221	9,615	10,038	10,480	10,941	11,160
NOA	99,879	104,741	109,350	114,160	119,184	121,568

Drawing on these forecasts, compute P&G's free cash flows to the firm (FCFF) and an estimate of its stock value using the DCF model. Make the following assumptions: discount rate (WACC) of 5%, shares outstanding of 3,178.8 million, and net nonoperating obligations (NNO) of $35,816 million.

Solution

The following DCF results yield a P&G stock value estimate of $70.49 as of June 30, 2006. P&G's stock closed at $55.60 on that date. This estimate suggests that P&G's stock is undervalued on that date. P&G stock traded at around $63 in December 2006.

(In millions, except per share values and discount factors)	2006	Horizon Period 2007	2008	2009	2010	Terminal Period
Increase in NOA[a]		$ 4,862	$ 4,609	$ 4,810	$ 5,024	$ 2,384
FCFF (NOPAT − Increase in NOA).....		4,753	5,429	5,670	5,917	8,776
Discount factor $[1/(1 + r_w)^t]$		0.95238	0.90703	0.86384	0.82270	
Present value of horizon FCFF........		4,527	4,924	4,898	4,868	
Cum present value of horizon FCFF....	$ 19,217					
Present value of terminal FCFF	240,667[b]					
Total firm value....................	259,884					
Less NNO.......................	35,816					
Firm equity value	$224,068					
Shares outstanding	3,178.8					
Stock value per share..............	$ 70.49					

[a] NOA increases are viewed as a cash outflow.

[b] Computed as $\dfrac{\left(\dfrac{\$8,776 \text{ million}}{0.05 - 0.02}\right)}{(1.05)^4}$, or ($8,776/0.03) × 0.82270, where 5% is WACC and 2% is the long-term growth rate subsequent to the horizon period that is used to estimate terminal period FCFF.

RESIDUAL OPERATING INCOME (ROPI) MODEL

The residual operating income (ROPI) model focuses on net operating profit after tax (NOPAT) and net operating assets (NOA). This means it uses key measures from both the income statement and balance sheet in determining firm value. The ROPI model defines firm value as the sum of two components:

LO2 Describe and illustrate the residual operating income model to value equity securities.

Firm Value = NOA + Present Value of Expected ROPI

where

> **NOA = Net operating assets**
> **ROPI = Residual operating income**

Net operating assets (NOA) are the foundation of firm value under the ROPI model. This is potentially problematic because we measure NOA using the balance sheet, which is unlikely to fully and contemporaneously capture the true (or intrinsic) value of all of a firm's operating assets.[10] However, the ROPI model adds an adjustment that corrects for the undervaluation or overvaluation of NOA. This adjustment is the present value of expected residual operating income, and is defined as follows:

$$\text{ROPI} = \underbrace{\text{NOPAT} - (\text{NOA}_{\text{Beg}} \times r_w)}$$

Expected NOPAT

where

> **NOA_{Beg} = Net operating assets at beginning (*Beg*) of period**
> **r_w = Weighted average cost of capital (WACC)**

Residual operating income (ROPI) is the net operating profit a firm earns over and above the return that the operating assets are expected to earn given the firm's WACC.

Understanding the ROPI model helps us reap the benefits from the disaggregation of return on net operating assets (RNOA) in Module 4. In addition, the ROPI model is the foundation for many internal and external performance evaluation and compensation systems marketed by management consulting and accounting services firms.[11]

Application of the ROPI model to equity valuation involves five steps:

1. Forecast and discount ROPI for the horizon period.[12]

2. Forecast and discount ROPI for the terminal period.[13]

3. Sum the present values from both the horizon and terminal periods; then add this sum to current NOA to get firm (enterprise) value.

---

[10] If the assets earn more than expected, it could be because NOA does not capture all of the firms' assets. For example, R&D and advertising are not fully and contemporaneously reflected on the balance sheet as assets though they likely produce future cash inflows. Likewise, internally generated goodwill is not fully reflected on the balance sheet as an asset. Similarly, assets are generally not written up to reflect unrealized gains. Conversely, sometimes the balance sheet overstates the true value of NOA. For example, companies can delay the write-down of impaired assets and, thus, overstate their book values. These examples, and a host of others, can yield reported values of NOA that differs from the market value of the operating assets.

[11] Examples are economic value added (EVA™) from Stern Stewart & Company, the economic profit model from McKinsey & Co., the cash flow return on investment (CFROI™) from Holt Value Associates, the economic value management from KPMG, and the value builder from PricewaterhouseCoopers (PwC).

[12] The present value of expected ROPI uses the weighted average cost of capital (WACC) as its discount rate; same as with the DCF model.

[13] As with the DCF model, for an assumed growth, *g*, the present value of the perpetuity of ROPI beyond the horizon period is given by $\frac{\text{ROPI}_{\text{T}}}{r_w - g}$, where ROPI_{T} is the residual operating income for the terminal period, r_w is WACC for the firm, and *g* is the assumed growth rate of ROPI_{T} following the horizon period. The resulting amount is then discounted back to the present using the WACC computed over the length of the horizon period.

4. Subtract net nonoperating obligations (NNO) from firm value to yield firm equity value.
5. Divide firm equity value by the number of shares outstanding to yield stock value per share.

To illustrate application of the ROPI model, we again use Johnson & Johnson. Forecasted financials for J&J (forecast horizon of 2006–2009 and terminal period of 2010) are in Exhibit 12.2. The forecasts (in bold) are for sales, NOPAT, and NOA, and are the same forecasts from the illustration of the DCF model. Recall that forecasts assume an annual 6.5% sales growth for the horizon period, a terminal period sales growth of 1%, net operating profit margin (NOPM) of 18%, and a year-end net operating asset turnover (NOAT) of 1.25.

EXHIBIT 12.2	**Application of Residual Operating Income Model**					
(In millions, except per share values and discount factors)	**2005**	**Horizon Period**				**Terminal Period**
		2006	**2007**	**2008**	**2009**	
Sales.	$ 50,514	**$53,797**	**$57,294**	**$61,018**	**$64,985**	**$65,634**
NOPAT*.	10,134	**9,683**	**10,313**	**10,983**	**11,697**	**11,814**
NOA**.	40,453	**43,038**	**45,835**	**48,814**	**51,988**	**52,507**
ROPI (NOPAT − [NOA$_{Beg}$ × r_w])		7,256	7,731	8,233	8,768	8,695
Discount factor [1/(1 + r_w)^t]		0.94340	0.89000	0.83962	0.79209	
Present value of horizon ROPI		6,845	6,881	6,913	6,945	
Cum present value of horizon ROPI. . .	27,584					
Present value of terminal ROPI	137,744					
NOA	40,453					
Total firm value	205,781					
Less NNO.	2,582					
Firm equity value	$203,199					
Shares outstanding	2,975					
Stock value per share.	$ 68.30					

*Given its combined federal and state statutory tax rate of 36%, NOPAT for 2005 is computed as follows ($ mil.): $50,514 − $13,954 − $16,877 − $6,312 − $362 + $214 − ($3,245 − 0.36 × [$487 − $54]) = $10,134, which is 20% of sales ($10,134 million/$50,514 million). Footnotes to J&J's 10-K reveal that its effective tax rate for 2005 is 23.8%, compared with 33.7% in 2004 and 30.2% in 2003. Analysis reveals that its 2005 effective tax rate is lower due to foreign tax credits and a reversal of a tax liability tied to a technical correction with the American Jobs Creation Act of 2004. The credits and reversal are *transitory* and should not be included in our projections. Accordingly, we *project* its tax rate to be 32%, the average of its 2004 and 2003 rates. If we apply 32% to its $13,656 million pretax GAAP income for 2005 we get an adjusted NOPAT of $9,009 million, computed as ($ mil.): $50,514 − $13,954 − $16,877 − $6,312 − $362 + 214 − ([$13,656 × 32%] − [0.36 × {$487 − $54}]). This adjusted NOPAT yields a NOPM of 18% ($9,009 million/$50,514 million) and is the rate we use in forecasts of NOPAT. A note on rounding: Sales are forecasted using current period sales multiplied successively by (1 + Growth rate), without rounding; next, NOPAT and NOA are computed from each period's sales forecast rounded to the whole unit.

**NOA computations for 2005 follow ($ mil.): ($58,025 − $83 − $20) − ($4,315 − $3,529 − $2,017 − $1,166 − $940 − $211 − $3,065 − $2,226) = $40,453.

†NNO is the difference between NOA and total shareholders' equity, which is NNO ($ mil.) = $40,453 − $37,871 = $2,582.

The bottom line of Exhibit 12.2 is the estimated J&J equity value of $203,199 million, or a per share stock value of $68.30. As before, present value computations use a 6% WACC as the discount rate. Specifically, we obtain this stock valuation as follows:

1. **Compute present value of horizon period ROPI.** The forecasted 2006 ROPI of $7,256 million is computed from the forecasted 2006 NOPAT ($9,683) less the product of beginning period NOA ($40,453) and WACC (0.06). The present value of this ROPI as of 2005 is $6,845 million, computed as $7,256 million × 0.94340 (the present value 1 year hence discounted at 6%). Similarly, the present value of 2007 ROPI (2 years hence) is $6,881 million, computed as $7,731 million × 0.89000, and so on through 2009. The sum of these present values (cumulative present value) is $27,584 million.

2. **Compute present value of terminal period ROPI.** The present value of the terminal period ROPI

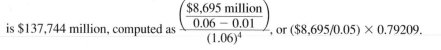
is $137,744 million, computed as $\dfrac{\left(\dfrac{\$8,695 \text{ million}}{0.06 - 0.01}\right)}{(1.06)^4}$, or ($8,695/0.05) × 0.79209.

3. **Compute firm equity value.** We must sum the present values from the horizon period ($27,584 million) and terminal period ($137,744 million), plus NOA ($40,453 million), to get firm (enterprise) value of $205,781 million. We then subtract the value of its net nonoperating obligations of $2,582 million to get firm equity value of $203,199 (the small difference from the DCF value is due to rounding). Dividing firm equity value by the 2,975 million shares outstanding yields the estimated per share valuation of $68.30.

J&J's stock closed at $60.25 at year-end 2005. The ROPI model estimate of $68.30 indicates that its stock is undervalued. In December 2006 (roughly one year later) J&J stock traded at near $67.

The ROPI model estimate is equal to that computed using the DCF model. This is the case so long as the firm is in a steady state, that is, NOPAT and NOA are growing at the same rate (for example, when RNOA is constant).

RESEARCH INSIGHT   **Power of NOPAT Forecasts**

Discounted cash flow (DCF) and residual operating income (ROPI) models yield identical estimates when the expected payoffs are forecasted for an infinite horizon. For practical reasons, we must use horizon period forecasts and a terminal period forecast. This truncation of the forecast horizon is a main cause of any difference in value estimates for these models. Importantly, if we can forecast (GAAP-based) NOPAT and NOA more accurately than forecasts of cash inflows and outflows, we will obtain more accurate estimates of firm value given a finite horizon.

MANAGERIAL INSIGHTS FROM THE ROPI MODEL

The ROPI model defines firm value as the sum of NOA and the present value of expected residual operating income as follows:

LO3 Explain how equity valuation models can aid managerial decisions.

$$\textbf{Firm Value} = \textbf{NOA} + \textbf{Present Value of } [\underbrace{\textbf{NOPAT} - (\textbf{NOA}_{\textbf{Beg}} \times r_w)}_{\textbf{ROPI}}]$$

Increasing ROPI, therefore, increases firm value. Managers can increase ROPI in two ways:

1. Decrease the NOA required to generate a given level of NOPAT (improve efficiency)
2. Increase NOPAT with the same level of NOA investment (improve profitability)

These are two very important observations. It means that achieving better performance requires effective management of *both* the balance sheet and the income statement. Most operating managers are accustomed to working with income statements. Further, they are often evaluated on profitability measures, such as achieving desired levels of sales and gross profit or efficiently managing operating expenses. The ROPI model focuses management attention on the balance sheet as well.

The two points above highlight two paths to increase ROPI and, accordingly, firm value. First, let's consider how management can reduce the level of NOA while maintaining a given level of NOPAT. Many managers begin by implementing procedures that reduce net operating working capital, such as:

- Reducing receivables through:
  - Better assessment of customers' credit quality
  - Better controls to identify delinquencies and automated payment notices
  - More accurate and timely invoicing
- Reducing inventories through:
  - Use of less costly components (of equal quality) and production with lower wage rates
  - Elimination of product features not valued by customers
  - Outsourcing to reduce product cost
  - Just-in-time deliveries of raw materials
  - Elimination of manufacturing bottlenecks to reduce work-in-process inventories
  - Producing to order rather than to estimated demand

▧ Increasing payables through:

⦿ Extending the payment of low or no-cost payables (so long as the supplier relationship is unharmed)

Management would next look at its operating long-term assets for opportunities to reduce unnecessary operating assets, such as the:

▧ Sale of unnecessary long-term assets

▧ Acquisition of production and administrative assets in partnership with other entities for greater throughput

▧ Acquisition of finished or semifinished goods from suppliers to reduce manufacturing assets

The second path to increase ROPI and, accordingly, firm value is to increase NOPAT with the same level of NOA investment. Management would look to strategies that maximize NOPAT, such as:

▧ Increasing gross profit dollars through:

⦿ Better pricing and mix of products sold

⦿ Reduction of raw material and labor cost without sacrificing product quality, perhaps by outsourcing, better design, or better manufacturing

⦿ Increase of throughput to minimize overhead costs per unit (provided inventory does not build up)

▧ Reducing selling, general, and administrative expenses through:

⦿ Better management of personnel

⦿ Reduction of overhead

⦿ Use of derivatives to hedge commodity and interest costs

⦿ Minimization of tax expense

Before undertaking any of these actions, managers must consider both short- and long-run implications for the company. The ROPI model helps managers assess company performance (income statement) relative to the net operating assets committed (balance sheet).

MANAGERIAL DECISION	You Are the Operations Manager

The residual operating income (ROPI) model highlights the importance of increasing NOPAT and reducing net operating assets, which are the two major components of the return on net operating assets (RNOA). What specific steps can you take to improve RNOA through improvement of its components: net operating profit margin and net operating asset turnover? [Answer, p. 12-16]

ASSESSMENT OF VALUATION MODELS

Exhibit 12.3 provides a brief summary of the advantages and disadvantages of the DCF and ROPI models. Neither model dominates the other, and both are theoretically equivalent. Instead, professionals must choose the model that performs best under practical circumstances.

There are numerous other equity valuation models in practice. Many require forecasting, but several others do not. A quick review of selected models follows:

The **method of comparables** (often called *multiples*) **model** predicts equity valuation or stock value using price multiples. Price multiples are defined as stock price divided by some key financial statement number. That financial number varies across investors but is usually one of the following: net income, net sales, book value of equity, total assets, or cash flow. The method then compares companies' multiples to those of their competitors to assign value.

The **net asset valuation model** draws on the financial reporting system to assign value. That is, equity is valued as reported assets less reported liabilities. Some investors adjust reported assets and liabilities for several perceived shortcomings in GAAP prior to computing net asset value. This method is commonly applied when valuing privately held companies.

The **dividend discount model** predicts that equity valuation or stock values equal the present value of expected cash dividends. This model is founded on the dividend discount formula and depends on the reliability of forecasted cash dividends.

| EXHIBIT 12.3 | Advantages and Disadvantages of DCF and ROPI Valuation Models | | |

Model	Advantages	Disadvantages	Performs Best

DCF	• Popular and widely accepted model
	• Cash flows are unaffected by accrual accounting
	• FCFF is intuitive
		• Cash investments in plant assets are treated as cash outflows, even though they create shareholder value
		• Value not recognized unless evidenced by cash flows
		• Computing FCFF can be difficult as operating cash flows are affected by
		   – Cutbacks on investments (receivables, inventories, plant assets); can yield short-run benefits at long-run cost
		   – Securitization, which GAAP treats as an operating cash flow when many view it as a financing activity
			• When the firm reports positive FCFF
			• When FCFF grows at a relatively constant rate

ROPI	• Focuses on value drivers such as profit margins and asset turnovers • Uses both balance sheet and income statement, including accrual accounting information • Reduces weight placed on terminal period value	• Financial statements do not reflect all company assets, especially for knowledge-based industries (for example, R&D assets and goodwill) • Requires some knowledge of accrual accounting	• When financial statements reflect all assets and liabilities; including those items often reported off-balance-sheet

There are additional models applied in practice that involve dividends, cash flows, research and development outlays, accounting rates of return, cash recovery rates, and real option models. Further, some practitioners, called *chartists* and *technicians,* chart price behavior over time and use it to predict equity value.

RESEARCH INSIGHT **Using Models to Identify Mispriced Stocks**

Implementation of the ROPI model can include parameters to capture differences in growth opportunities, persistence of ROPI, and the conservatism in accounting measures. Research finds differences in how such factors, across firms and over time, affect ROPI and changes in NOA. This research also hints that investors do not entirely understand the properties underlying these factors and, consequently, individual stocks can be mispriced for short periods of time. Other research contends that the apparent mispricing is due to an omitted valuation variable related to riskiness of the firm.

MODULE-END REVIEW

Following are forecasts of Procter & Gamble's sales, net operating profit after tax (NOPAT), and net operating assets (NOA). These are taken from our forecasting process in Module 11 and now include a terminal period forecast that reflects a long-term growth rate of 2%.

(In millions)	2006	Horizon Period				Terminal Period
		2007	2008	2009	2010	
Sales............	$68,222	$ 71,224	$ 74,358	$ 77,629	$ 81,045	$ 82,666
NOPAT	9,221	9,615	10,038	10,480	10,941	11,160
NOA	99,879	104,741	109,350	114,160	119,184	121,568

Drawing on these forecasts, compute P&G's residual operating income (ROPI) and an estimate of its stock value using the ROPI model. Assume the following: discount rate (WACC) of 5%, shares outstanding of 3,178.8 million, and net nonoperating obligations (NNO) of $35,816 million.

Solution

Results from the ROPI model below yield a P&G stock value estimate of $70.49 as of December 31, 2005 (small difference from DCF estimate due to rounding). P&G's stock closed at a split-adjusted price of $55.60 on that date. This estimate suggests that P&G's stock is undervalued on that date. P&G stock traded at around $63 in December 2006 as shown in the stock price chart below.

(In millions, except per share values and discount factors)	2006	Horizon Period				Terminal Period
		2007	2008	2009	2010	
ROPI (NOPAT − [NOA$_{Beg}$ × r_w])		$4,621	$4,801	$5,013	$5,233	$5,201
Discount factor [1/(1 + r_w)^t]		0.95238	0.90703	0.86384	0.82270	
Present value of horizon ROPI........		4,401	4,355	4,330	4,305	
Cum present value of horizon ROPI....	$ 17,391					
Present value of terminal ROPI	142,629[a]					
NOA	99,879					
Total firm value	259,899					
Less NNO.......................	35,816					
Firm equity value	$224,083					
Shares outstanding	3,178.8					
Stock value per share..............	$ 70.49					

[a] Computed as $\dfrac{\left(\dfrac{\$5{,}201 \text{ million}}{0.05 - 0.02}\right)}{(1.05^4)}$, or ($5,201/0.03) × 0.82270.

The P&G stock price chart, extending from late 2004 through late 2006, follows.

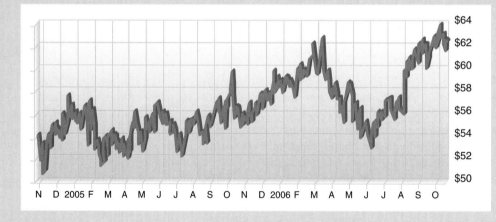

APPENDIX 12A: Johnson & Johnson Financial Statements

Balance Sheet At Fiscal Year End ($ millions, except share and per share data)	2005	2004
Assets		
Cash and cash equivalents	$16,055	$ 9,203
Marketable securities.....................................	83	3,681
Accounts receivable trade, less allowances for doubtful accounts $164 (2004, $206)......................	7,010	6,831
Inventories	3,959	3,744
Deferred taxes on income	1,845	1,737
Prepaid expenses and other receivables.....................	2,442	2,124
Total current assets	31,394	27,320

continued

Balance Sheet At Fiscal Year End ($ millions, except share and per share data)	2005	2004
Market securities, noncurrent.	$ 20	$ 46
Property, plant and equipment, net	10,830	10,436
Intangible assets, net	6,185	5,979
Goodwill, net	5,990	5,863
Deferred taxes on income	385	551
Other assets	3,221	3,122
Total assets.	$58,025	$53,317
Liabilities and Shareholders' Equity		
Loans and notes payable	$ 668	$ 280
Accounts payable.	4,315	5,227
Accrued liabilities	3,529	3,523
Accrued rebates, returns and promotions	2,017	2,297
Accrued salaries, wages and commissions	1,166	1,094
Accrued taxes on income.	940	1,506
Total current liabilities.	12,635	13,927
Long-term debt	2,017	2,565
Deferred taxes on income	211	403
Employee related obligations.	3,065	2,631
Other liabilities	2,226	1,978
Total liabilities	20,154	21,504
Shareholders equity		
Preferred stock—without par value (authorized and unissued 2,000,000 shares)	—	—
Common stock—par value $1.00 per share (authorized 4,320,000,000 shares; issued 3,119,842,000 shares)	3,120	3,120
Note receivable from employee stock ownership plan	—	(11)
Accumulated other comprehensive income.	(755)	(515)
Retained earnings	41,471	35,223
	43,836	37,817
Less: common stock held in treasury, at cost (145,364,000 shares and 148,819,000 shares).	5,965	6,004
Total shareholders' equity	37,871	31,813
Total liabilities and shareholders' equity.	$58,025	$53,317

Income Statement ($ millions, except per share figures)	2005	2004	2003
Sales to customers.	$50,514	$47,348	$41,862
Cost of products sold.	13,954	13,422	12,176
Gross profit.	36,560	33,926	29,686
Selling, marketing and administrative expenses	16,877	15,860	14,131
Research expense	6,312	5,203	4,684
Purchased in-process research and development.	362	18	918
Interest income.	(487)	(195)	(177)
Interest expense, net of portion capitalized	54	187	207
Other (income) expense, net	(214)	15	(385)
	22,904	21,088	19,378
Earnings before provision for taxes on income	13,656	12,838	10,308
Provision for taxes on income	3,245	4,329	3,111
Net earnings.	$10,411	$ 8,509	$ 7,197
Basic net earnings per share	$3.50	$2.87	$2.42
Diluted net earnings per share	$3.46	$2.84	$2.40

Statement of Cash Flows ($ millions)	2005	2004	2003
Cash flows from operating activities			
Net earnings.	$10,411	$ 8,509	$ 7,197
Adjustments to reconcile net earnings to cash flows:			
Depreciation and amortization of property and intangibles	2,093	2,124	1,869
Purchased in-process research and development.	362	18	918
Deferred tax provision.	(46)	(498)	(720)
Accounts receivable allowances.	(31)	3	6
Changes in assets and liabilities, net of effects from acquisitions:			
Increase in accounts receivable	(568)	(111)	(691)
(Increase) decrease in inventories.	(396)	11	39
(Decrease) increase in accounts payable and accrued liabilities	(911)	607	2,192
Decrease (increase) in other current and non-current assets.	620	(395)	(746)
Increase in other current and non-current liabilities	343	863	531
Net cash flows from operating activities	11,877	11,131	10,595
Cash flows from investing activities			
Addition to property, plant and equipment.	(2,632)	(2,175)	(2,262)
Proceeds from the disposal of assets	154	237	335
Acquisitions, net of cash acquired.	(987)	(580)	(2,812)
Purchases of investments	(5,660)	(11,617)	(7,590)
Sales of investments	9,187	12,061	8,062
Other (primarily intangibles).	(341)	(273)	(259)
Net cash used by investing activities.	(279)	(2,347)	(4,526)
Cash flows from financing activities			
Dividends to shareholders	(3,793)	(3,251)	(2,746)
Repurchase of common stock.	(1,717)	(1,384)	(1,183)
Proceeds from short-term debt	1,215	514	3,062
Retirement of short-term debt	(732)	(1,291)	(4,134)
Proceeds from long-term debt.	6	17	1,023
Retirement of long-term debt.	(196)	(395)	(196)
Proceeds from the exercise of stock options.	696	642	311
Net cash used by financing activities.	(4,521)	(5,148)	(3,863)
Effect of exchange rate changes on cash and cash equivalents.	(225)	190	277
Increase in cash and cash equivalents.	6,852	3,826	2,483
Cash and cash equivalents, beginning of year	9,203	5,377	2,894
Cash and cash equivalents, end of year	$16,055	$ 9,203	$ 5,377

GUIDANCE ANSWERS

MANAGERIAL DECISION   **You Are the Division Manager**

Cash flow can be increased by reducing assets. For example, receivables can be reduced by the following:

- Encouraging up-front payments or progress billings on long-term contracts
- Increasing credit standards to avoid slow-paying accounts before sales are made
- Monitoring account age and sending reminders to past due customers
- Selling accounts receivable to a financial institution or special purpose entity

As another example, plant assets can be reduced by the following:

- Selling unused or excess plant assets
- Forming alliances with other companies to share specialized plant assets
- Owning assets in a special purpose entity with other companies
- Selling production facilities to a contract manufacturer and purchasing the output

MANAGERIAL DECISION	You Are the Operations Manager

RNOA can be disaggregated into its two key drivers: NOPAT margin and net operating asset turnover. NOPAT margin can be increased by improving gross profit margins (better product pricing, lower cost manufacturing, etc.) and closely monitoring and controlling operating expenses. Net operating asset turnover can be increased by reducing net operating working capital (better monitoring of receivables, better management of inventories, extending payables, etc.) and making more effective use of plant assets (disposing of unused assets, forming corporate alliances to increase plant asset capacity, selling productive assets to contract producers and purchasing the output, etc). The ROPI model effectively focuses managers on the balance sheet *and* income statement.

DISCUSSION QUESTIONS

Q12-1. Explain how information contained in financial statements is useful in pricing securities. Are there some components of earnings that are more useful than others in this regard? What nonfinancial information might also be useful?

Q12-2. In general, what role do expectations play in pricing equity securities? What is the relation between security prices and expected returns (the discount rate, or WACC, in this case)?

Q12-3. What are free cash flows to the firm (FCFF) and how are they used in the pricing of equity securities?

Q12-4. Define the weighted average cost of capital (WACC).

Q12-5. Define net operating profit after tax (NOPAT).

Q12-6. Define net operating assets (NOA).

Q12-7. Define the concept of residual operating income. How is residual operating income used in pricing equity securities?

Q12-8. What insight does disaggregation of RNOA into profit margin and asset turnover provide for managing a company?

MINI EXERCISES

M12-9. Interpreting Earnings Announcement Effects on Stock Prices (LO2)

In a recent quarterly earnings announcement, Starbucks announced that its earnings had markedly increased (up 7 cents per share over the prior year) and were 1 cent higher than analyst expectations. Starbucks' stock "edged higher," according to *The Wall Street Journal,* but did not markedly increase. Why do you believe that Starbucks' stock price did not markedly increase given the good news?

Starbucks (SBUX)

M12-10. Computing Residual Operating Income (ROPI) (LO2)

3M Company reports net operating profit after tax (NOPAT) of $3,305 million in 2005. Its net operating assets at the beginning of 2005 are $12,972 million. Assuming a 6.66% weighted average cost of capital (WACC), what is 3M's residual operating income for 2005? Show computations.

3M Company (MMM)

M12-11. Computing Free Cash Flows to the Firm (FCFF) (LO1)

3M Company reports net operating profit after tax (NOPAT) of $3,305 million in 2005. Its net operating assets at the beginning of 2005 are $12,972 million and are $12,209 million at the end of 2005. What are 3M's free cash flows to the firm (FCFF) for 2005? Show computations.

3M Company (MMM)

M12-12. Computing, Analyzing and Interpreting Residual Operating Income (ROPI) (LO2)

In its 2005 fiscal year annual report, PepsiCo reports 2005 net operating income after tax (NOPAT) of $4,140 million. As of the beginning of fiscal year 2005 it reports net operating assets of $18,908 million.
a. Did PepsiCo earn positive residual operating income (ROPI) in 2005 if its weighted average cost of capital (WACC) is 5.78%? Explain.
b. At what level of WACC would PepsiCo not report positive residual operating income for 2005? Explain.

PepsiCo (PEP)

EXERCISES

E12-13. Estimating Share Value using the DCF and ROPI Models (LO1, 2)

Following are forecasts of Target Corporation's sales, net operating profit after tax (NOPAT), and net operating assets (NOA) as of January 31, 2006.

Target Corporation (TGT)

(In millions)	Reported 2006	Horizon Period				Terminal Period
		2007	2008	2009	2010	
Sales............	$51,271	$57,526	$64,544	$72,418	$81,253	$82,878
NOPAT	2,694	2,876	3,227	3,621	4,063	4,144
NOA	24,077	27,008	30,302	33,999	38,147	38,910

Answer the following requirements assuming a terminal period growth rate of 2%, discount rate (WACC) of 7%, shares outstanding of 874.1 million, and net nonoperating obligations (NNO) of $9,872 million.

a. Estimate the value of a share of Target common stock using the (1) discounted cash flow (DCF) model and (2) residual operating income (ROPI) model as of January 31, 2006.

b. Target Corporation (TGT) stock closed at $54.75 on January 31, 2006. How does your valuation estimate compare with this closing price? What do you believe are some reasons for the difference?

E12-14. Estimating Share Value using the DCF and ROPI Models (LO1, 2)

Abercrombie & Fitch (ANF)

Following are forecasts of Abercrombie & Fitch's sales, net operating profit after tax (NOPAT), and net operating assets (NOA) as of January 31, 2006.

(In millions)	Reported 2006	Horizon Period				Terminal Period
		2007	2008	2009	2010	
Sales............	$2,785	$3,838	$5,289	$7,288	$10,043	$10,244
NOPAT	325	448	617	850	1,172	1,195
NOA	616	849	1,170	1,612	2,221	2,266

Answer the following requirements assuming a discount rate (WACC) of 13%, common shares outstanding of 103.3 million, and net nonoperating obligations (NNO) of $(379) million (negative NNO reflects net investments rather than net obligations).

a. Estimate the value of a share of Abercrombie & Fitch common stock using the (1) discounted cash flow (DCF) model and (2) residual operating income (ROPI) model as of January 31, 2006.

b. Abercrombie & Fitch (ANF) stock closed at $66.39 on January 31, 2006. How does your valuation estimate compare with this closing price? What do you believe are some reasons for the difference?

E12-15. Estimating Share Value using the DCF and ROPI Models (LO1, 2)

CVS Corp. (CVS)

Following are forecasts of sales, net operating profit after tax (NOPAT), and net operating assets (NOA) as of December 31, 2005 for CVS Pharmacy.

(In millions)	Reported 2005	Horizon Period				Terminal Period
		2006	2007	2008	2009	
Sales............	$37,006	$44,777	$54,180	$65,558	$79,325	$80,912
NOPAT	1,292	1,563	1,891	2,288	2,768	2,824
NOA	10,520	12,721	15,392	18,624	22,536	22,986

Answer the following requirements assuming a discount rate (WACC) of 8%, common shares outstanding of 814.3 million, and net nonoperating obligations (NNO) of $2,189 million.

a. Estimate the value of a share of CVS' common stock using the (1) discounted cash flow (DCF) model and (2) residual operating income (ROPI) model as of December 31, 2005.

b. CVS Corp. (CVS) stock closed at $26.58 on December 29, 2005. How does your valuation estimate compare with this closing price? What do you believe are some reasons for the difference?

E12-16. **Identifying and Computing Net Operating Assets (NOA) and Net Nonoperating Obligations (NNO)**   **(LO1, 2)**
Following is the balance sheet for 3M Company.

3M Company (MMM)

Balance Sheet At December 31 ($ millions, except per share amount)	2005	2004
Assets		
Cash and cash equivalents	$ 1,072	$ 2,757
Accounts receivable—net of allowances of $73 and $83	2,838	2,792
Inventories		
Finished goods	1,050	947
Work in process	706	614
Raw materials and supplies	406	336
Total inventories	2,162	1,897
Other current assets	1,043	1,274
Total current assets	7,115	8,720
Investments	272	227
Property, plant and equipment	16,127	16,290
Less: Accumulated depreciation	(10,534)	(10,579)
Property, plant and equipment—net	5,593	5,711
Goodwill	3,473	2,655
Intangible assets—net	486	277
Prepaid pension and postretirement benefits	2,905	2,591
Other assets	669	527
Total assets	$20,513	$20,708
Liabilities and Stockholders' Equity		
Short-term borrowings and current portion of long-term debt	$ 1,072	$ 2,094
Accounts payable	1,256	1,168
Accrued payroll	469	487
Accrued income taxes	989	867
Other current liabilities	1,452	1,455
Total current liabilities	5,238	6,071
Long-term debt	1,309	727
Other liabilities	3,866	3,532
Total liabilities	10,413	10,330
Stockholders' equity		
Common stock, par value $.01 per share: Shares outstanding—2005: 754,538,387; Shares outstanding—2004: 773,518,281	9	9
Capital in excess of par value	287	287
Retained earnings	17,358	15,649
Treasury stock	(6,965)	(5,503)
Unearned compensation	(178)	(196)
Accumulated other comprehensive income (loss)	(411)	132
Stockholders' equity—net	10,100	10,378
Total liabilities and stockholders' equity	$20,513	$20,708

a. Compute net operating assets (NOA) and net nonoperating obligations (NNO) for 2005.
b. For 2005, show that: NOA = NNO + Stockholders' equity.

E12-17. Identifying and Computing Net Operating Profit after Tax (NOPAT) and Net Nonoperating Expense (NNE) (LO1, 2)

3M Company (MMM)

Following is the income statement for 3M Company.

Income Statement Year Ended December 31 (millions)	2005	2004	2003
Net sales.	$21,167	$20,011	$18,232
Operating expenses			
Cost of sales.	10,381	9,958	9,285
Selling, general and administrative expenses	4,535	4,281	3,994
Research, development and related expenses	1,242	1,194	1,147
Other expense	—	—	93
Total	16,158	15,433	14,519
Operating income.	5,009	4,578	3,713
Interest expense and income			
Interest expense	82	69	84
Interest income.	(56)	(46)	(28)
Total	26	23	56
Income before income taxes, minority interest and cumulative effect of accounting change	4,983	4,555	3,657
Provision for income taxes.	1,694	1,503	1,202
Minority interest	55	62	52
Income before cumulative effect of accounting change	3,234	2,990	2,403
Cumulative effect of accounting change	(35)	—	—
Net income.	$ 3,199	$ 2,990	$ 2,403

Compute net operating profit after tax (NOPAT) for 2005, assuming a federal and state statutory tax rate of 36.3%. (*Hint:* Other expense is an operating item for 3M.)

E12-18. Estimating Share Value Using the DCF and ROPI Models (LO1, 2)

3M Company (MMM)

Following are forecasts of 3M Company's sales, net operating profit after tax (NOPAT), and net operating assets (NOA) as of December 31, 2005.

(In millions)	Reported 2005	Horizon Period				Terminal Period
		2006	2007	2008	2009	
Sales.	$21,167	$22,395	$23,694	$25,068	$26,522	$26,787
NOPAT	3,306	3,498	3,701	3,916	4,143	4,184
NOA	12,209	12,945	13,696	14,490	15,331	15,484

Answer the following requirements assuming a discount rate (WACC) of 7%, common shares outstanding of 754.5 million, and net nonoperating obligations (NNO) of $2,109 million.

a. Estimate the value of a share of 3M's common stock using the (1) discounted cash flow (DCF) model and (2) residual operating income (ROPI) model as of December 31, 2005.

b. 3M (MMM) stock closed at $78.29 on December 31, 2005. How does your valuation estimate compare with this closing price? What do you believe are some reasons for the difference?

E12-19. Explaining the Equivalence of Valuation Models and the Relevance of Earnings (LO1, 2)

This module focused on two different valuation models: the discounted cash flow (DCF) model and the residual operating income (ROPI) model. The models focus on free cash flows to the firm and on residual operating income, respectively. We stressed that these two models are theoretically equivalent.

a. What is the *intuition* for why these models are equivalent?

b. Some analysts focus on cash flows as they believe that companies manage earnings, which presumably makes earnings less relevant. Are earnings relevant? Explain.

E12-20. Applying and Interpreting Value Driver Components of RNOA (LO3)

The net operating profit margin and the asset turnover components of net operating assets are often termed *value drivers,* which refers to their positive influence on stock value by virtue of their role as components of return on net operating assets (RNOA).

a. How do profit margins and asset turnover ratios influence stock values?

b. Assuming that profit margins and asset turnover ratios are value drivers, what insight does this give us about managing companies if the goal is to create shareholder value?

PROBLEMS

P12-21. Forecasting and Estimating Share Value Using the DCF and ROPI Models (LO1, 2)

Following are the income statement and balance sheet for Intel Corporation.

Intel Corporation
(INTC)

Income Statement Year Ended December 31 (In millions)	2005	2004	2003
Net revenue	$38,826	$34,209	$30,141
Cost of sales	15,777	14,463	13,047
Gross margin	23,049	19,746	17,094
Research and development	5,145	4,778	4,360
Marketing, general and administrative	5,688	4,659	4,278
Impairment of goodwill	—	—	617
Amortization and impairment of acquisition- related intangibles and costs	126	179	301
Purchased in-process research and development	—	—	5
Operating expenses	10,959	9,616	9,561
Operating income	12,090	10,130	7,533
Losses on equity securities, net	(45)	(2)	(283)
Interest and other, net	565	289	192
Income before taxes	12,610	10,417	7,442
Provision for taxes	3,946	2,901	1,801
Net income	$ 8,664	$ 7,516	$ 5,641

Balance Sheet December 31 (In millions, except par value)	2005	2004
Assets		
Cash and cash equivalents	$ 7,324	$ 8,407
Short-term investments	3,990	5,654
Trading assets	1,458	3,111
Accounts receivable, net of allowance for doubtful accounts of $64 ($43 in 2004)	3,914	2,999
Inventories	3,126	2,621
Deferred tax assets	1,149	979
Other current assets	233	287
Total current assets	21,194	24,058

continued

Balance Sheet December 31 (In millions, except par value)	2005	2004
Property, plant and equipment, net	17,111	15,768
Marketable strategic equity securities	537	656
Other long-term investments	4,135	2,563
Goodwill	3,873	3,719
Deferred taxes and other assets	1,464	1,379
Total assets	$48,314	$48,143
Liabilities and stockholders' equity		
Short-term debt	$ 313	$ 201
Accounts payable	2,249	1,943
Accrued compensation and benefits	2,110	1,858
Accrued advertising	1,160	894
Deferred income on shipments to distributors	632	592
Other accrued liabilities	810	1,355
Income taxes payable	1,960	1,163
Total current liabilities	9,234	8,006
Long-term debt	2,106	703
Deferred tax liabilities	703	855
Other long-term liabilities	89	—
Stockholders' equity		
Preferred stock, $0.001 par value, 50 shares authorized; none issued	—	—
Common stock, $0.001 par value, 10,000 shares authorized; 5,919 issued and outstanding (6,253 in 2004) and capital in excess of par value	6,245	6,143
Acquisition-related unearned stock compensation	—	(4)
Accumulated other comprehensive income	127	152
Retained earnings	29,810	32,288
Total stockholders' equity	36,182	38,579
Total liabilities and stockholders' equity	$48,314	$48,143

Required

a. Compute Intel's net operating assets (NOA) for year end 2005.

b. Compute net operating profit after tax (NOPAT) for 2005, assuming a federal and state statutory tax rate of 36.3%.

c. Forecast Intel's sales, NOPAT, and NOA for years 2006 through 2009 using the following assumptions:

Sales growth	13.5%
Net operating profit margin (NOPM)	21.46%
Net operating asset turnover (NOAT) at year end	1.34

Forecast the terminal period (2010) values assuming a 2% terminal year growth and using the NOPM and NOAT assumptions above.

d. Estimate the value of a share of Intel common stock using the (1) discounted cash flow (DCF) model, and (2) residual operating income (ROPI) model as of December 31, 2005; assume a discount rate (WACC) of 12%, common shares outstanding of 5,919 million, and net nonoperating obligations (NNO) of $(7,164) million (NNO is negative which means that Intel has net nonoperating investments).

e. Intel (INTC) stock closed at $25.07 on December 29, 2005. How does your valuation estimate compare with this closing price? What do you believe are some reasons for the difference? What investment position is suggested from your results?

P12-22. **Forecasting and Estimating Share Value Using the DCF and ROPI Models** (LO1, 2)

Following are the income statement and balance sheet for Oracle Corporation.

Balance Sheet May 31 (in millions, except per share data)	2006	2005
Assets		
Cash and cash equivalents	$ 6,659	$ 3,894
Marketable securities	946	877
Trade receivables, net of allowances of $325 and $269	3,022	2,570
Other receivables	398	330
Deferred tax assets	714	486
Prepaid expenses and other current assets	235	291
Total current assets	11,974	8,448
Property, net	1,391	1,442
Intangible assets, net	4,528	3,373
Goodwill	9,809	7,003
Other assets	1,327	421
Total non-current assets	17,055	12,239
Total assets	$29,029	$20,687
Liabilities and stockholders' equity		
Short-term borrowings and current portion of long-term debt	$ 159	$ 2,693
Accounts payable	268	230
Income taxes payable	810	904
Accrued compensation and related benefits	1,172	923
Accrued restructuring	412	156
Deferred revenues	2,830	2,289
Other current liabilities	1,279	868
Total current liabilities	6,930	8,063
Notes payable and long-term debt, net of current portion	5,735	159
Deferred tax liabilities	564	1,010
Accrued restructuring	273	120
Deferred revenues	114	126
Other long-term liabilities	401	372
Total non-current liabilities	7,087	1,787
Stockholders' equity		
Preferred stock, $0.01 par value-authorized: 1.0 shares; outstanding: none	—	—
Common stock, $0.01 par value and additional paid in capital-authorized: 11,000 shares; outstanding: 5,232 shares at May 31, 2006 and 5,145 shares at May 31, 2005	9,246	6,596
Retained earnings	5,538	4,043
Deferred compensation	(30)	(45)
Accumulated other comprehensive income	258	243
Total stockholders' equity	15,012	10,837
Total liabilities and stockholders' equity	$29,029	$20,687

Income Statement Year Ended May 31 (in millions)	2006	2005	2004
Revenues			
New software licenses	$ 4,905	$ 4,091	$ 3,541
Software license updates and product support	6,636	5,330	4,529
Software revenues	11,541	9,421	8,070
Services	2,839	2,378	2,086
Total revenues	14,380	11,799	10,156
Operating expenses			
Sales and marketing	3,177	2,511	2,123
Software license updates and product support	719	618	547
Cost of services	2,516	2,033	1,770
Research and development	1,872	1,491	1,254
General and administrative	555	550	508
Amortization of intangible assets	583	219	36
Acquisition related	137	208	54
Restructuring	85	147	—
Total operating expenses	9,644	7,777	6,292
Operating income	4,736	4,022	3,864
Interest expense	(169)	(135)	(21)
Nonoperating income, net			
Interest income	170	185	118
Net investment gains	25	2	29
Other	48	(23)	(45)
Total nonoperating income, net	243	164	102
Income before provision for income taxes	4,810	4,051	3,945
Provision for income taxes	1,429	1,165	1,264
Net income	$ 3,381	$ 2,886	$ 2,681

Required

a. Compute net operating assets (NOA) for fiscal year end 2006.

b. Compute net operating profit after tax (NOPAT) for fiscal year 2006, assuming a federal and state statutory tax rate of 36.4%.

c. Forecast Oracle's sales, NOPAT, and NOA for fiscal years 2007 through 2010 using the following assumptions:

Sales growth	21.9%
Net operating profit margin (NOPM)	23.19%
Net operating asset turnover (NOAT) at fiscal year-end	0.72

Forecast the terminal period (fiscal year 2011) values assuming a 2% terminal year growth and using the NOPM and NOAT assumptions above.

d. Estimate the value of a share of Oracle common stock using the (1) discounted cash flow (DCF) model and (2) residual operating income (ROPI) model as of May 31, 2006; assume a discount rate (WACC) of 8%, common shares outstanding of 5,232 million, and net nonoperating obligations (NNO) of $4,948 million.

e. Oracle Corp. (ORCL) stock closed at $14.22 on May 31, 2006. How does your valuation estimate compare with this closing price? What do you believe are some reasons for the difference?

P12-23. Forecasting and Estimating Share Value Using the DCF and ROPI Models **(LO1, 2)**
Following are the income statement and balance sheet for Abbott Laboratories (ABT).

Income Statement Year Ended December 31 ($ 000s)	2005	2004	2003
Net sales.	$22,337,808	$19,680,016	$17,280,333
Cost of products sold.	10,641,111	8,884,157	7,774,239
Research and development	1,821,175	1,696,753	1,623,752
Acquired in-process research and development	17,131	279,006	100,240
Selling, general, and administrative	5,496,123	4,921,780	4,808,090
Total operating cost and expenses	17,975,540	15,781,696	14,306,321
Operating earnings.	4,362,268	3,898,320	2,974,012
Net interest expense	153,662	149,087	146,365
(Income) from TAP Pharmaceutical Products joint venture	(441,388)	(374,984)	(580,950)
Net foreign exchange (gain) loss	21,804	29,059	57,048
Other (income) expense, net	8,270	(30,442)	(35,602)
Earnings from continuing operations before taxes	4,619,920	4,125,600	3,387,151
Taxes on earnings from continuing operations	1,247,855	949,764	882,426
Earnings from continuing operations	3,372,065	3,175,836	2,504,725
Earnings from discontinued operations, net of taxes.	—	60,015	248,508
Net earnings.	$ 3,372,065	$ 3,235,851	$ 2,753,233

Balance Sheet December 31 ($ 000s)	2005	2004	2003
Assets			
Cash and cash equivalents	$ 2,893,687	$ 1,225,628	$ 995,124
Investment securities, primarily time deposits and certificates of deposit	62,406	833,334	291,297
Trade receivables, less allowances of—2005: $203,683; 2004: $231,704; 2003: $259,514	3,576,794	3,696,115	3,313,377
Inventories			
Finished products.	1,203,557	1,488,939	1,467,441
Work in process	630,267	582,787	545,977
Materials.	708,155	548,737	725,021
Total inventories	2,541,979	2,620,463	2,738,439
Deferred income taxes.	1,248,569	1,031,746	1,165,259
Other prepaid expenses and receivables.	932,691	1,080,143	1,110,885
Assets held for sale	129,902	247,056	—
Total current assets	11,386,028	10,734,485	9,614,381
Investment securities, primarily equity securities.	134,013	145,849	406,357
Property and equipment, at cost:			
Land.	370,949	338,428	356,757
Buildings.	2,655,356	2,519,492	2,662,023
Equipment	8,813,517	8,681,655	9,479,044
Construction in progress	920,599	962,114	792,923
	12,760,421	12,501,689	13,290,747
Less: accumulated depreciation and amortization	6,757,280	6,493,815	7,008,941
Net property and equipment	6,003,141	6,007,874	6,281,806

continued

Balance Sheet December 31 ($ 000s)	2005	2004	2003
Intangible assets, net of amortization	4,741,647	5,171,594	4,089,882
Goodwill	5,219,247	5,685,124	4,449,408
Other long-term assets and investments in joint ventures	1,624,201	952,929	1,197,474
Assets held for sale	32,926	69,639	—
Total assets	$29,141,203	$28,767,494	$26,039,308
Liabilities and Shareholders' Investment			
Short-term borrowings	$ 212,447	$ 1,836,649	$ 828,092
Trade accounts payable	1,032,516	1,054,464	1,078,333
Salaries, wages and commissions	625,254	637,333	625,525
Other accrued liabilities	2,722,685	2,491,956	2,180,098
Dividends payable	423,335	405,730	383,352
Income taxes payable	488,926	156,417	158,836
Current portion of long-term debt	1,849,563	156,034	1,709,265
Liabilities of operations held for sale	60,788	87,061	—
Total current liabilities	7,415,514	6,825,644	6,963,501
Long-term debt	4,571,504	4,787,934	3,452,329
Post-employment obligations and other long-term liabilities	2,154,775	2,606,410	2,551,220
Liabilities of operations held for sale	1,062	1,644	—
Deferred income taxes	583,077	220,079	—
Shareholders' investment			
Preferred shares, one dollar par value, Authorized—1,000,000 shares, none issued	—	—	—
Common shares, without par value, Authorized—2,400,000,000 shares; Issued at stated capital amount—Shares: 2005: 1,553,769,958; 2004: 1,575,147,418; 2003: 1,580,247,227	3,523,766	3,239,575	3,034,054
Common shares held in treasury, at cost—Shares: 2005: 14,534,979; 2004: 15,123,800; 2003: 15,729,296	(212,255)	(220,854)	(229,696)
Unearned compensation—restricted stock awards	(46,306)	(50,110)	(56,336)
Earnings employed in the business	10,404,568	10,033,440	9,691,484
Accumulated other comprehensive income (loss)	745,498	1,323,732	632,752
Total shareholders' investment	14,415,271	14,325,783	13,072,258
Total liabilities and shareholders' investment	$29,141,203	$28,767,494	$26,039,308

Required

a. Compute net operating assets (NOA) for year end 2005.

b. Compute net operating profit after tax (NOPAT) for 2005 assuming a federal and state statutory tax rate of 36.2%.

c. Forecast Abbott Laboratories' sales, NOPAT, and NOA for 2006 through 2009 using the following assumptions:

Sales growth	13.5%
Net operating profit margin (NOPM)	15.53%
Net operating asset turnover (NOAT), year-end	1.05

Forecast the terminal period (2010) values assuming a 2% terminal year growth and using the NOPM and NOAT assumptions above.

d. Estimate the value of a share of Abbott Laboratories' common stock using the (1) discounted cash flow (DCF) model, and (2) residual operating income (ROPI) model as of December 31, 2005; assume a discount rate (WACC) of 7%, common shares outstanding of 1,539 million, and net nonoperating obligations (NNO) of $6,759 million.

e. Abbott Laboratories (ABT) stock closed at $39.43 on December 30, 2005. How does your valuation estimate compare with this closing price? What do you believe are some reasons for the difference? What investment position is suggested from your results?

P12-24. Forecasting and Estimating Share Value Using the DCF and ROPI Models (LO1, 2)

Following are the income statement and balance sheet for Harley-Davidson, Inc..

Harley-Davidson, Inc. (HOG)

Income Statement Year Ended December 31 (in thousands)	2005	2004	2003
Net revenue	$5,342,214	$5,015,190	$4,624,274
Cost of goods sold	3,301,715	3,115,655	2,958,708
Gross profit	2,040,499	1,899,535	1,665,566
Financial services income	331,618	305,262	279,459
Financial services expense	139,998	116,662	111,586
Operating income from financial services	191,620	188,600	167,873
Selling, administrative and engineering expense	762,108	726,644	684,175
Income from operations	1,470,011	1,361,491	1,149,264
Investment income, net	22,797	23,101	23,088
Other, net	(5,049)	(5,106)	(6,317)
Income before provision for income taxes	1,487,759	1,379,486	1,166,035
Provision for income taxes	528,155	489,720	405,107
Net income	$ 959,604	$ 889,766	$ 760,928

Balance Sheet December 31 (In thousands, except share amounts)	2005	2004
Assets		
Cash and cash equivalents	$ 140,975	$ 275,159
Marketable securities	905,197	1,336,909
Accounts receivable, net	122,087	121,333
Finance receivables held for sale	299,373	456,516
Finance receivables held for investment, net	1,342,393	1,167,522
Inventories	221,418	226,893
Deferred income taxes	61,285	60,517
Prepaid expenses and other current assets	52,509	38,337
Total current assets	3,145,237	3,683,186
Finance receivables held for investment, net	600,831	488,262
Property, plant and equipment, net	1,011,612	1,024,665
Prepaid pension costs	368,165	133,322
Goodwill	56,563	59,456
Other assets	72,801	94,402
Total assets	$5,255,209	$5,483,293

continued

Balance Sheet December 31 (In thousands, except share amounts)	2005	2004
Liabilities and Shareholders' Equity		
Accounts payable.	$ 270,614	$ 244,202
Accrued expenses and other liabilities.	397,525	433,053
Current portion of finance debt	204,973	495,441
Total current liabilities.	873,112	1,172,696
Finance debt.	1,000,000	800,000
Deferred income taxes	155,236	51,432
Postretirement healthcare benefits.	60,975	149,848
Other long-term liabilities	82,281	90,846
Shareholders' equity		
Series A Junior participating preferred stock, none issued	—	—
Common stock, 330,961,869 and 329,908,165 shares issued in 2005 and 2004, respectively	3,310	3,300
Additional paid-in capital	596,239	533,068
Retained earnings	4,630,390	3,844,571
Accumulated other comprehensive income (loss)	58,653	(12,096)
	5,288,592	4,368,843
Less: Treasury stock (56,960,213 and 35,597,360 shares in 2005 and 2004, respectively) at cost	(2,204,987)	(1,150,372)
Total shareholders' equity	3,083,605	3,218,471
Total liabilities and shareholders' equity.	$5,255,209	$5,483,293

Required

a. Compute net operating assets (NOA) for year end 2005. (*Hint:* Treat Harley-Davidson's financial services assets, revenues, and expenses as operating under the assumption that these are directly related to its sales activities; however, its finance debt, both long-term and current maturities, is nonoperating.)

b. Compute net operating profit after tax (NOPAT) for 2005, assuming a federal and state statutory tax rate of 37.3%. (*Hint:* Treat financial services revenue and expense as well as "other expense" as operating.)

c. Forecast Harley-Davidson's sales, NOPAT, and NOA for 2006 through 2009 using the following assumptions:

Sales growth.	6.5%
Net operating profit margin (NOPM).	17.7%
Net operating asset turnover (NOAT), year-end	1.58

Forecast the terminal period (2010) values assuming a 2% terminal year growth and using the NOPM and NOAT assumptions above.

d. Estimate the value of a share of Harley-Davidson common stock using the (1) discounted cash flow (DCF) model, and (2) residual operating income (ROPI) model; assume a discount rate (WACC) of 7%, common shares outstanding of 274 million, and net nonoperating obligations (NNO) of $299 million.

e. Harley-Davidson (HOG) stock closed at $51.49 on December 30, 2005. How does your valuation estimate compare with this closing price? What do you believe are some reasons for the difference?

CASES

C12-25. Management Application: Operating Improvement versus Financial Engineering (LO3)

Assume that you are the CEO of a small publicly traded company. The operating performance of your company has fallen below market expectations, which is reflected in a depressed stock price. At your direction, your CFO provides you with the following recommendations that are designed to increase your company's return on net operating assets (RNOA) and its operating cash flows, both of which will, presumably, result in improved financial performance and an increased stock price.

1. To improve net cash flow from operating activities, the CFO recommends that your company reduce inventories (raw material, work-in-progress, and finished goods) and receivables (through selective credit granting and increased emphasis on collection of past due accounts)

2. The CFO recommends that your company sell and lease back its office building. The lease will be structured so as to be classified as an operating lease under GAAP. The assets will, therefore, not be included in the computation of net operating assets (NOA), thus increasing RNOA.

3. The CFO recommends that your company lengthen the time taken to pay accounts payable (lean on the trade) to increase net cash flows from operating activities.

4. Since your company's operating performance is already depressed, the CFO recommends that you take a "big bath;" that is, write off all assets deemed to be impaired and accrue excessive liabilities for future contingencies. The higher current period expense will, then, result in higher future period income as the assets written off will not be depreciated and your company will have a liability account available to absorb future cash payments rather than recording them as expenses.

5. The CFO recommends that your company increase its expected return on pension investments. This will reduce pension expense and increase operating profit, a component of net operating profit after tax (NOPAT) and, thus, of RNOA.

6. The CFO recommends that your company share ownership of its outbound logistics (trucking division) with another company in a joint venture. This would have the effect of increasing throughput, thus spreading overhead over a larger volume base, and would remove the assets from your company's balance sheet since the joint venture would be accounted for as an equity method investment.

Evaluate each of the CFO's recommendations. In your evaluation, consider whether each recommendation will positively impact the operating performance of your company or whether it is cosmetic in nature.

Comprehensive Case

LEARNING OBJECTIVES

L01 Explain and illustrate a review of financial statements and their components. (p. 13-4)

L02 Assess company profitability and creditworthiness. (p. 13-27)

L03 Adjust and forecast financial statements. (p. 13-29)

L04 Describe and illustrate the valuation of firm equity and stock. (p. 13-31)

KIMBERLY-CLARK

The past decade has seen a shift in the competitive landscape for consumer products companies. Gone are numerous competitors. Many were gobbled up in the industry's consolidation trend. Also gone is media control. Now, hundreds of different media outlets and venues compete for promotion space and scarce consumer time.

Another development is in-store branding. Companies such as Costco, with its Kirkland Signature brand on everything from candy to apparel, threaten the powerhouse brands from Kimberly-Clark, Procter & Gamble, Colgate-Palmolive, and other consumer products companies.

Five years ago, when Thomas J. Falk assumed the top spot at Kimberly-Clark, the nation's largest disposable diaper producer, he inherited some extra baggage: a company in the throes of an identity crisis, a decades-long rivalry with consumer-products behemoth Procter & Gamble, and a group of investors short on patience following a series of earnings misses.

In a move aimed at boosting its stock price and its return on equity, Kimberly-Clark spun off its paper and pulp businesses in 2004, and began a strategic investment and streamlining initiative in 2005. Under Falk's leadership, the company has steadily improved its focus on its health and hygiene segments.

Kimberly-Clark has also moved to shore up its brand images across its immense product line. With sales of $16 billion, the company manufactures such well-recognized brands as Huggies and Pull-Ups disposable diapers, Kotex and Lightdays feminine products, Kleenex facial tissue, Viva paper towels, and Scott bathroom tissue.

The rocky ride that Kimberly-Clark investors have endured over the past few years is unlikely to subside—see the following stock price chart.

Competition is fierce and well-armed, and the purchase of Gillette by Procter & Gamble further muddies the future of the industry.

On the positive side, Kimberly-Clark's earnings performance is consistent, and its financial position is solid. Kimberly-Clark's RNOA for 2005 was 17.6%, and its nonoperating return increased RNOA to yield a robust 25.7% in return on equity. It also reported $16.3 billion in assets, nearly 46% of which is concentrated in plant, property, and equipment, and another 16.5% in intangible assets.

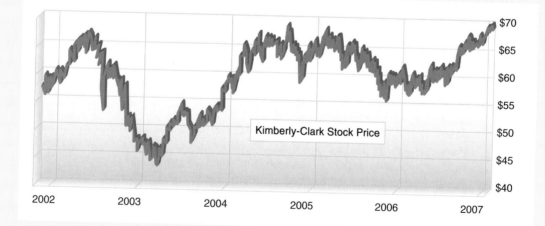

This module presents a financial accounting analysis and interpretation of Kimberly-Clark. It is intended to illustrate the key financial reporting topics covered in the book. We begin with a detailed review of Kimberly-Clark's financial statements and notes, followed by the forecasting of key accounts that we use to value its common stock.

Sources: *Kimberly-Clark* 2003 through 2005 10-K Reports; *BusinessWeek*, 2004; *The Wall Street Journal*, 2002.

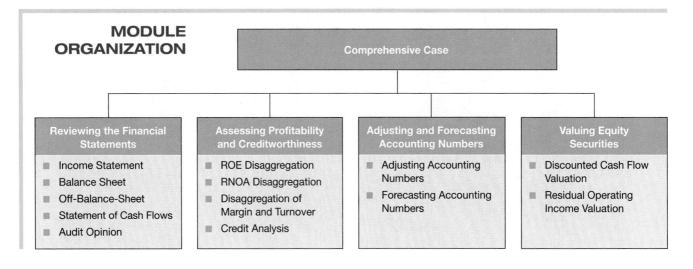

MODULE ORGANIZATION

Comprehensive Case

Reviewing the Financial Statements	Assessing Profitability and Creditworthiness	Adjusting and Forecasting Accounting Numbers	Valuing Equity Securities
■ Income Statement ■ Balance Sheet ■ Off-Balance-Sheet ■ Statement of Cash Flows ■ Audit Opinion	■ ROE Disaggregation ■ RNOA Disaggregation ■ Disaggregation of Margin and Turnover ■ Credit Analysis	■ Adjusting Accounting Numbers ■ Forecasting Accounting Numbers	■ Discounted Cash Flow Valuation ■ Residual Operating Income Valuation

INTRODUCTION

Kimberly-Clark is one of the largest consumer products companies in the world. It is organized into three general business segments (percentages are for 2005):

■ **Personal Care (40% of sales)**—manufactures and markets disposable diapers, training and youth pants and swim pants, feminine and incontinence care products, and other related products. Products in this segment are primarily for household use and are sold under a variety of brand names, including Huggies, Pull-Ups, GoodNites, Kotex, Lightdays, Depend, and Poise.

■ **Consumer Tissue (36% of sales)**—manufactures and markets facial and bathroom tissue, paper towels and napkins for household use, wet wipes, and related products. Products in this segment are sold under the Kleenex, Scott, Cottonelle, Viva, Andrex, Scottex, Hakle, Page, and other brand names.

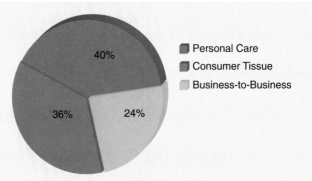

■ **Business-to-Business (24% of sales)**—manufactures and markets (1) facial and bathroom tissue, paper towels, wipes and napkins for away-from-home use; (2) health care products such as surgical gowns, drapes, infection control products, sterilization wraps, disposable face masks and exam gloves, respiratory products, and other disposable medical products; (3) printing, premium business and correspondence papers; (4) specialty and technical papers; and other products. Products in this segment are sold under the Kimberly-Clark, Kleenex, Scott, Kimwipes, WypAll, Surpass, Safeskin, Tecnol, Ballard, and other brand names.

Approximately 59% of Kimberly-Clark's sales are in North America, 18% in Europe and 23% in Asia, Latin America, and other areas. Shown below are its U.S. market shares for key categories for each of the years 2003 through 2005:

Product Category	2005	2004	2003
Personal care	39.6%	39.1%	39.9%
Consumer tissue	36.4%	35.0%	35.6%
Business-to-business.	24.1%	25.9%	24.5%

In addition, approximately 13% of Kimberly-Clark's sales are made to Wal-Mart, primarily in the personal care and consumer tissue businesses (source: Kimberly-Clark 2005 10-K).

In the MD&A section of its 10-K, Kimberly-Clark describes its competitive environment as follows:

> The Corporation competes for customers in intensely competitive markets against well-known, branded products and private label products both domestically and internationally. Inherent risks in the Corporation's competitive strategy include uncertainties concerning trade and consumer acceptance, the effects of recent consolidations of retailers and distribution channels, and competitive reaction. Some of the Corporation's major competitors have undergone consolidation, which could result in increased competition and alter the dynamics of the industry. Such consolidation may give competitors greater financial resources and greater market penetration and enable competitors to offer a wider variety of products and services at more competitive prices, which could adversely affect the Corporation's financial results. In addition, the Corporation incurs substantial development and marketing costs in introducing new and improved products and technologies. There is no guarantee that the Corporation will be successful in developing new and improved products and technologies necessary to compete successfully in the industry or that the Corporation will be successful in advertising, marketing and selling its products.

Beyond the competitive business risks described above, Kimberly-Clark faces fluctuating prices for cellulose fiber, the company's principle raw material, uncertain energy costs for manufacturing operations, foreign currency translation risks, and risks resulting from fluctuating interest rates.

Given this background, we begin the accounting analysis of Kimberly-Clark with a discussion of its financial statements.

REVIEWING THE FINANCIAL STATEMENTS

This section reviews and analyzes the financial statements of Kimberly-Clark.

LO1 Explain and illustrate a review of financial statements and their components.

Income Statement Reporting and Analysis

Kimberly-Clark's income statement is reproduced in Exhibit 13.1. The remainder of this section provides a brief review and analysis for Kimberly-Clark's income statement line items.

Net Sales

Exhibit 13.1 reveals that sales increased 5.43% in 2005 to $15,903 million, following a 7.54% sales increase in the prior year. In its MD&A report, management attributes 37% of the 2003 increase (2% of the 5.43%) to favorable currency effects resulting from the weak $US (foreign currency denominated sales were translated into a higher $US equivalent than in previous years). In addition, volume increases amounted to approximately 3% of this 5.43% increase. Price increases of approximately 1% accounted for the remainder of the sales growth (source: Kimberly-Clark 2005 10-K).

Kimberly-Clark describes its revenue recognition policy as follows:

> Sales revenue for the Corporation and its reportable business segments is recognized at the time of product shipment or delivery, depending on when title passes, to unaffiliated customers, and when all of the following have occurred: a firm sales agreement is in place, pricing is fixed or determinable, and collection is reasonably assured. Sales are reported net of estimated returns, consumer and trade promotions, rebates and freight allowed.

Its revenue recognition conditions are taken directly from GAAP and SEC guidelines, which recognize revenues when "earned and realizable." For Kimberly-Clark, *earned* means when title to the goods passes to the customer, and *realizable* means an account receivable whose collection is reasonably assured.

Sales for retailers and manufacturers are straight forward: revenue is recognized when the product is transferred to the buyer, an obligation for payment exists and collection of that payment is reasonable assured. In that case, the revenue is deemed to have been "earned." The primary issue for retailers and manufacturers relates to sales return allowances. These allowances pertain to product return or sales discounts (sometimes called *mark-downs*). Companies can only report sales when earned, that is, past the return allowance period. Further, companies can only report *net* sales as revenue (i.e., gross sales less any

EXHIBIT 13.1	Kimberly-Clark Income Statement

KIMBERLY-CLARK CORPORATION AND SUBSIDIARIES
Consolidated Income Statement

Year Ended December 31 (Millions of dollars, except per share amounts)	2005	2004	2003
Net sales.	$15,902.6	$15,083.2	$14,026.3
Cost of products sold.	10,827.4	10,014.7	9,231.9
Gross profit.	5,075.2	5,068.5	4,794.4
Marketing, research and general expenses	2,737.4	2,510.9	2,350.3
Other (income) expense, net	27.2	51.2	112.5
Operating profit	2,310.6	2,506.4	2,331.6
Nonoperating expense.	(179.0)	(158.4)	(105.5)
Interest	27.5	17.9	18.0
Interest expense.	(190.2)	(162.5)	(167.8)
Income before income taxes, equity interests, discontinued operations and cumulative effect of accounting change	1,968.9	2,203.4	2,076.3
Provision for income taxes.	(438.4)	(483.9)	(484.1)
Share of net income of equity companies	136.6	124.8	107.0
Minority owners' share of subsidiaries' net income.	(86.5)	(73.9)	(55.6)
Income from continuing operations	1,580.6	1,770.4	1,643.6
Income from discontinued operations, net of income taxes	—	29.8	50.6
Income before cumulative effect of accounting change	1,580.6	1,800.2	1,694.2
Cumulative effect of accounting change, net of income taxes	(12.3)	—	—
Net income.	$ 1,568.3	$ 1,800.2	$ 1,694.2
Per share basis			
Basic			
Continued operations.	$ 3.33	$ 3.58	$ 3.24
Discontinued operations.	—	.06	.10
Cumulative effect of accounting change	(.03)	—	—
Net income	$ 3.30	$ 3.64	$ 3.34
Diluted			
Continuing operations	$ 3.31	$ 3.55	$ 3.23
Discontinued operations.	—	.06	.10
Cumulative effect of accounting change	(.03)	—	—
Net income	$ 3.28	$ 3.61	$ 3.33

sales discounts, including volume discounts). K-C's footnotes provide the following table relating to sales allowances:

		Additions		Deductions	
December 31, 2005 ($ millions)	Balance at Beginning of Period	Charged to Costs and Expenses	Charged to Other Accounts	Write-offs and Reclassifications	Balance at End of Period
Allowances for sales discounts	20.1	249.5	(.7)	247.3	21.6

K-C's balance sheet includes a contra-asset related to sales discounts. The table indicates that the company had $20.1 million in sales discounts at the start of the year that came from sales in the prior year. During 2005, K-C granted its customers $249.5 million in additional sales discounts, $247.3 million of which had been taken by the customers by the end of the year. The remaining amount of $21.6 million, relates to discounts granted, but not yet taken, and is held over to the following year. These year-end amounts typically relate to discounts given toward the end of the year that are ultimately taken in the first quarter of the following year.

The sales discount process affects net sales and, thus, profit. This allowance works just like any other allowance. If K-C underestimated the sales discount allowance, net sales and profit in the current year would be increased. Overestimation of the sales discount allowance would have the opposite effect: current sales and profit would be depressed. K-C's allowance has not changed appreciably in 2005 and is, therefore, not of concern.

Revenue recognition in service industries and those industries that use the percentage-of-completion method can be problematic. Often, determining when a service contract has been "earned" can be difficult and revenue can easily be mis-estimated, either intentionally or not. Sanjay Kumar, former CEO of Computer Associates, was sentenced to 12 years in jail for his role in an accounting scandal relating primarily to misrepresentation of revenues and profit for the computer services company he headed up. The percentage-of-completion method is difficult to implement because it requires estimates of total costs or revenues of the project. Underestimation of costs results in overestimation of revenues. These estimation errors are often hidden from view because details in footnote disclosures are often vague or completely missing.

Cost of Products Sold and Gross Profit

Kimberly-Clark's 2005 gross profit margin is 31.9% ($5,075.2/$15,902.6), which is about 2.3 percentage points below what it was in 2003 (34.2%). As a benchmark, Proctor & Gamble, the company's principle competitor, recently reported sales of $68.2 billion, over four times the level of K-C's sales, and a gross profit margin of 51.4%, up from 50.9% in the prior year. This comparison highlights the intense competition that K-C faces from its much larger rival.

The choice of inventory costing method affects cost of goods sold. K-C uses the LIFO method to cost its inventory. In 2005, the company's LIFO reserve increased by $17 million (see inventory discussion later in this Module). This increased cost of goods sold and reduced gross profit by $17 million. COGS can also be increased by inventory write-downs, typically related to restructuring efforts. For example, Cicso Systems, Inc. reported a $2.1 billion inventory write-down in 2001 when the tech bubble burst. This write-down increased COGS and reduced gross profit by that amount.

Marketing, Research and General Expenses

Kimberly-Clark's marketing, research and general expenses have increased to 17.2% of sales from 16.7% in the prior year. This increase resulted from general cost inflation as well as from the company's restructuring efforts designed to improve long-run manufacturing and operating costs. K-C reports 2005 net operating profit after taxes (NOPAT) of $1,949.9 million [($2,310.6 + $136.6) − ($438.4 + ($190.2 − $27.5) × 36.2%)] and a net operating profit margin (NOPM) of 12.3% ($1,949.9 million/$15,902.6 million) of sales.[1] P&G, by contrast, is able to use its higher gross profit margin to fund a higher level of advertising and other SGA expenditures, resulting in a NOPM of 13.4%.

Pension Costs. Kimberly-Clark's marketing, research and general expenses include $157 million of pension expense. This is reported in the following table in the pension footnote:

| | Components of Net Periodic Benefit Cost | | | | | |
| | Pension Benefits | | | Other Benefits | | |
Year Ended December 31 (Millions of dollars)	**2005**	**2004**	**2003**	**2005**	**2004**	**2003**
Service cost	$ 81.4	$ 87.4	$ 76.1	**$17.4**	$17.8	$16.2
Interest cost	294.6	296.2	288.0	**47.1**	48.2	48.9
Expected return on plan assets	(322.6)	(324.0)	(286.3)	—	—	—
Amortization of prior service cost (benefit) and transition amount	6.3	7.3	8.7	**(.2)**	(.7)	(1.5)
Recognized net actuarial loss	92.7	83.3	74.0	**3.9**	4.0	1.9
Other	4.4	4.6	5.4	—	(1.5)	—
Net periodic benefit cost	**$156.8**	$154.8	$165.9	**$68.2**	$67.8	$65.5

---

[1] We include equity income of $136.6 million (labeled as "share of net income of equity companies" in K-C's income statement) as operating because it relates to investments in paper-related companies and it, therefore, aligns with K-C's primary operating activities. This amount is reported by K-C net of tax, and therefore, no tax adjustment is necessary when computing NOPAT. We consider K-C's Minority owners' share of subsidiaries' net income, as a non-operating expense.

For 2005, the expected return on pension investments ($322.6 million) provides an offset to the company's pension service and interest costs ($81.4 million and $294.6 million, respectively). Footnotes reveal that Kimberly-Clark's pension investments realized an *actual* return of $359.5 million in 2005 (from the pension footnote in its 10-K report). So, for 2005, use of the expected return results in an unrecognized *gain* that is deferred, along with other unrecognized gains and losses, in the computation of reported profit.

Kimberly-Clark describes how it determines the expected return in its footnotes. It is instructive to review the company's rationale and, thus, the footnote follows:

> The expected long-term rate of return on pension fund assets was determined based on several factors, including input from pension investment consultants and projected long-term returns of broad equity and bond indices. The Corporation also considered the U.S. plan's historical 10-year and 15-year compounded annual returns of 9.36 percent and 10.28 percent, respectively, which have been in excess of these broad equity and bond benchmark indices. The Corporation anticipates that on average the investment managers for each of the plans comprising the Principal Plans will generate annual long-term rates of return of at least 8.5 percent. The Corporation's expected long-term rate of return on the assets in the Principal Plans is based on an asset allocation assumption of about 70 percent with equity managers, with expected long-term rates of return of approximately 10 percent, and 30 percent with fixed income managers, with an expected long-term rate of return of about 6 percent. The Corporation regularly reviews its actual asset allocation and periodically rebalances its investments to the targeted allocation when considered appropriate. Also, when deemed appropriate, the Corporation executes hedging strategies using index options and futures to limit the downside exposure of certain investments by trading off upside potential above an acceptable level. The Corporation last executed this hedging strategy for 2003. No hedging instruments are currently in place. The Corporation will continue to evaluate its long-term rate of return assumptions at least annually and will adjust them as necessary.

The expected return on pension assets offsets service and interest costs, and serves to reduce pension expense. In general, increasing (decreasing) the expected return on pension assets, increases (decreases) profit. In 2005, K-C reduced its expected return from 8.32% to 8.29%. The discount rate (used to compute the PBO and the interest cost component of pension expense) declined by 24 basis points (5.92% to 5.68%). It is not uncommon for the expected return rate to be "stickier" on the downside (thus propping up profits) and more quickly adjusted on the upside (to take advantage of increasing returns). We need to be mindful of these effects when assessing operating profits.

Transitory versus Persistent Line Items

Expenses relating to restructuring activities have become increasingly common in the past two decades. Kimberly-Clark pursued its own restructuring activities in 2005 and recorded charges of $228.6 million relating to Competitive Improvement Initiatives. These initiatives are designed to further improve the company's competitive position by accelerating investments in targeted growth opportunities and strategic cost reductions to streamline manufacturing and administrative operations, primarily in North America and Europe.

Classification of these charges as transitory or persistent is a judgment call. In K-C's case, these charges relate to a multi-year program that is expected to continue through 2008. Therefore, we classify these expenses as persistent. Our review of the financial statements did not identify any other transitory items and thus, we classified all other activity as persistent.

Earnings per Share

Net income for Kimberly-Clark has decreased from $1,694.2 million in 2003 to $1,568.3 million in 2005. Basic (diluted) earnings per share, however, has only declined from $3.34 ($3.33) to $3.30 ($3.28). The small relative decline in EPS is a result of K-C's share repurchase program (see the financing section in Exhibit 13.5). Following is Kimberly-Clark's computation of earnings per share:

> **Earnings Per Share** A reconciliation of the average number of common shares outstanding used in the basic and diluted EPS computations follows:

Average Common Shares Outstanding (Millions)	2005	2004	2003
Basic.	474.0	495.2	507.0
Dilutive effect of stock options	2.6	3.4	1.2
Dilutive effect of restricted share awards	.8	.6	.4
Diluted	477.4	499.2	508.6

Options outstanding that were not included in the computation of diluted EPS because their exercise price was greater than the average market price of the common shares are summarized below:

Description	2005	2004	2003
Average number of share equivalents (millions).	9.1	5.4	20.5
Weighted-average exercise price.	$66.58	$70.13	$60.19
Expiration date of options	2007 to 2015	2007 to 2012	2006 to 2013
Options outstanding at year-end	8.8	5.4	20.2

The number of common shares outstanding as of December 31, 2005, 2004 and 2003 was 461.5 million, 482.9 million and 501.6 million, respectively.

Most of the difference between basic and diluted earnings per share usually arises from the dilutive effects of employee stock options. For K-C, such effects were absent in 2005 as its stock options were *under water,* meaning that K-C's stock price was lower than the exercise price of the options. The stock options, therefore, are considered *antidilutive,* meaning that including them would increase EPS. Accordingly, they are excluded in the diluted EPS computation, but remain potentially dilutive if K-C's stock price subsequently rises above the exercise price of the options. (Although not present for Kimberly-Clark, convertible debt and preferred shares are also potentially dilutive for many companies.)

Income Taxes

Kimberly-Clark's net income was positively affected by a reduction of its effective tax rate. K-C describes this tax effect in the following footnote:

> The Corporation's effective income tax rate was 22.3 percent in 2005 compared with 22.0 percent in 2004. The most significant factors causing the increase were the taxes on the dividends received under the American Jobs Creation Act partially offset by increased synthetic fuel credits.

The American Jobs Creation Act taxed funds repatriated from foreign subsidiaries at a lower tax rate to stimulate investment. Although the tax *rate* was lower, the *dollar amount* of taxes paid increased, resulting in an increase in the effective tax rate (provision for income taxes/income before income taxes). This is a transitory increase and should not be factored into our projections. We discuss this synthetic fuel partnership in our discussion of variable interest entities (VIEs) later in this Module.

Common-Size Income Statement

It is useful for analysis purposes to prepare common-size statements. Exhibit 13.2 shows Kimberly-Clark's common-size income statement covering the three most recent years.

The gross profit margin declined in 2005; specifically, from 34.2% in 2003 to 31.9%. This reflects the very competitive environment in which K-C operates. Companies typically offset a declining gross profit margin with reductions in SG&A expense. K-C has been unable to do that, however, as its marketing, research and general (SG&A) expense in 2005 actually exceeds its 2003 level as a percentage of sales. Accordingly, 2005 income before taxes declined by 2.4 percentage points relative to 2003. Further, income from equity companies (reported net of tax) increased only slightly as a percentage of sales from 0.8% to 0.9% from 2003 to 2005. Yet, despite the 2.4 percentage point reduction in pretax profit, income from continuing operations declined by only 1.8 percentage points, from 11.7% in 2003 to 9.9% in 2005. This is due to reduced tax expense as a percent of taxable income (lower tax rate).

EXHIBIT 13.2	Kimberly-Clark Common-Size Income Statement		
Year Ended December 31	**2005**	**2004**	**2003**
Net sales.	100.0%	100.0%	100.0%
Cost of products sold.	68.1	66.4	65.8
Gross profit.	31.9	33.6	34.2
Marketing, research, and general expenses	17.2	16.6	16.8
Other (income) expense, net	0.2	0.3	0.8
Operating profit	14.5	16.6	16.6
Nonoperating expense.	(1.1)	(1.1)	(0.8)
Interest income.	0.2	0.1	0.1
Interest expense.	(1.2)	(1.1)	(1.2)
Income before income taxes, equity interests, discontinued operations and cumulative effect of accounting change	12.4	14.6	14.8
Provision for income taxes.	(2.8)	(3.2)	(3.5)
Share of net income of equity companies	0.9	0.8	0.8
Minority owners' share of subsidiaries' net income.	(0.5)	(0.5)	(0.4)
Income from continuing operations	9.9	11.7	11.7
Income from discontinued operations, net of income taxes	0.0	0.2	0.4
Income before cumulative effect of accounting change	9.9	11.9	12.1
Cumulative effect of accounting change, net of income taxes	(0.1)	0.0	0.0
Net income.	9.9%	11.9%	12.1%

Note: All percentages are computed by dividing each income statement line item by that year's net sales.

Management Discussion and Analysis

The Management Discussion and Analysis section of a 10-K is usually informative for interpreting company financial statements and for additional insights into company operations. To illustrate, Kimberly-Clark provides the following analysis of its operating results in the MD&A section of its 2005 10-K:

Consolidated net sales increased 5.4 percent from 2004. Sales volumes rose more than 3 percent with each of the business segments contributing to the increase. Currency effects added nearly 2 percent to the increase primarily due to strengthening of the South Korean won, the Brazilian real, the Canadian dollar and the Australian dollar. Net selling prices increased 1 percent offset by a reduction in net sales due to the divestiture of the pulp operations as part of the spin-off of Neenah Paper on November 30, 2004.

Consolidated operating profit decreased 7.8 percent. Significant factors that negatively affected operating profit were approximately $229 million of charges related to the Competitive Improvement Initiatives that are not included in the business segments (as discussed later in this MD&A and in Item 8, Note 3 to the Consolidated Financial Statement), cost inflation of about $400 million and higher marketing, research and general expenses. Those factors were partially offset by gross cost savings of nearly $210 million, increased sales volumes and higher net selling prices. Operating profit as a percent of net sales declined to 14.5 percent from 16.6 percent for 2004.

- Operating profit for personal care products decreased .9 percent. Cost savings, higher sales volumes and favorable currency effects were offset by materials cost inflation—particularly for polymer resins and superabsorbants, lower net selling prices and increased costs for marketing and research activities. The year-over-year change in operating profit was also affected by about $37 million of costs in 2004 to improve the efficiency of the Corporation's diaper operations.

  Operating profit in North America declined about 3 percent as materials cost inflation, lower net selling prices and higher distribution costs more than offset savings and the higher sales volumes. In Europe, operating profit decreased primarily due to the lower net selling prices. Operating profit in the developing and emerging markets increased nearly 16 percent due to the higher sales volumes, higher net selling prices and favorable currency effects, tempered by higher marketing and administrative costs.

- Operating profit for consumer tissue products was essentially even with last year, an increase of .3 percent. The higher net selling prices, higher sales volumes and cost savings were offset by cost inflation for materials, energy and distribution, and higher marketing and research expenses.

  In North America, operating profit grew almost 8 percent because the higher net selling prices and increased sales volumes more than offset the cost inflation. Operating profit in Europe decreased principally due to the effects of the competitive lower net selling prices. In the developing and emerging markets, operating profit advanced approximately 19 percent on the strength of the higher sales volumes and a favorable product mix.

- Operating profit for business-to-business products increased 2.5 percent. The higher sales volumes and higher net selling prices combined with cost savings and the absence of operating losses related to the divested pulp operations allowed the segment to overcome materials and energy related cost inflation.

Business Segments

Generally accepted accounting principals require that companies disclose the composition of their operating profit by business segment. Segments are investment centers (those having both income statement and balance sheet data) that the company routinely evaluates at the chief executive level.

We outlined and discussed Kimberly-Clark's business segments at the beginning of the module: personal care, consumer tissue, and business-to-business. Following are its GAAP disclosures for each of its business segments:

Consolidated Operations by Business Segment

(Millions of dollars)	Personal Care	Consumer Tissue	Business-to-Business	Intersegment Sales	Corporate & Other	Consolidated Total
Net Sales						
2005	$6,287.4	$5,781.3	$3,821.8	$ (19.3)	$ 31.4	$15,902.6
2004	5,975.1	5,343.0	3,957.9	(217.1)	24.3	15,083.2
2003	5,652.9	5,046.7	3,477.7	(154.7)	3.7	14,026.3
Operating Profit						
2005	1,242.2	805.8	673.2	—	(410.6)	2,310.6
2004	1,253.2	803.1	656.6	—	(206.5)	2,506.4
2003	1,221.0	728.2	602.8	—	(220.4)	2,331.6
Depreciation and Amortization						
2005	267.4	301.0	188.1	—	88.0	844.5
2004	286.9	310.7	194.0	—	8.7	800.3
2003	264.4	300.2	178.2	—	2.5	745.3
Assets						
2005	4,650.7	5,672.9	4,578.9	—	1,400.7	16,303.2
2004	4,813.3	5,881.5	4,745.2	—	1,578.0	17,018.0
2003	4,781.9	5,796.5	4,850.1	—	1,351.4	16,779.9
Capital Spending						
2005	297.9	296.6	115.0	—	0.1	709.6
2004	242.5	202.3	89.4	—	0.8	535.0
2003	344.4	366.6	141.0	—	20.9	872.9

Given these data, it is possible for us to perform a rudimentary return analysis for each segment. This analysis provides insight into a company's dependence on any one segment. Following is a brief summary analysis of K-C's segment return disaggregation for 2005:

Segment ($ millions)	Net Sales	Operating Profit	Assets	Operating Profit Margin	Year-End Asset Turnover	Operating Profit Divided by Year-End Assets
Personal care	$6,287.4	$1,242.2	$4,650.7	19.8%	1.35	26.7%
Consumer tissue	5,781.3	805.8	5,672.9	13.9%	1.02	14.2%
Business-to-business	3,821.8	673.2	4,578.9	17.6%	0.83	14.7%

The intensely competitive nature of the consumer tissue market is evident in its low profit margin (13.9%) and low return on ending operating assets (14.2%). K-C relies, to a great extent, on its personal care segment to generate income. Many analysts cite the pricing pressure in the consumer tissue segment as a negative factor in their valuations of K-C.

Balance Sheet Reporting and Analysis

Kimberly-Clark's balance sheet is reproduced in Exhibit 13.3.

EXHIBIT 13.3	Kimberly-Clark Balance Sheet

KIMBERLY-CLARK CORPORATION AND SUBSIDIARIES
Consolidated Balance Sheet

December 31 (Millions of dollars)	2005	2004
Assets		
Cash and cash equivalents	$ 364.0	$ 594.0
Accounts receivable, net	2,101.9	2,038.3
Inventories	1,752.1	1,670.9
Deferred income taxes	223.4	278.2
Other current assets	341.7	380.5
Total current assets	4,783.1	4,961.9
Property, plant and equipment, net	7,494.7	7,990.5
Investments in equity companies	457.8	444.4
Goodwill	2,685.6	2,702.9
Other assets	882.0	918.3
Total assets	$16,303.2	$17,018.0
Liabilities and Stockholders' Equity		
Debt payable within one year	$ 1,222.5	$ 1,214.7
Trade accounts payable	1,055.5	983.2
Other payables	298.8	265.5
Accrued expenses	1,399.6	1,431.6
Accrued income taxes	457.9	448.0
Dividends payable	208.6	194.2
Total current liabilities	4,642.9	4,537.2
Long-term debt	2,594.7	2,298.0
Noncurrent employee benefit and other obligations	1,782.6	1,621.7
Deferred income taxes	572.9	840.3
Minority owners' interests in subsidiaries	394.5	368.4
Preferred securities of subsidiary	757.4	722.9
Stockholders' equity		
Preferred stock—no par value—authorized 20.0 million shares, none issued	—	—
Common stock—$1.25 par value—authorized 1.2 billion shares; issued 568.6 million shares at December 31, 2005 and 2004	710.8	710.8
Additional paid-in capital	324.6	348.6
Common stock held in treasury, at cost—107.1 million and 85.7 million shares at December 31, 2005 and 2004	(6,376.1)	(5,047.5)
Accumulated other comprehensive income (loss)	(1,669.4)	(1,226.0)
Retained earnings	12,581.4	11,865.9
Unearned compensation on restricted stock	(13.1)	(22.3)
Total stockholders' equity	5,558.2	6,629.5
Total liabilities and stockholders' equity	$16,303.2	$17,018.0

Kimberly-Clark reports total assets of $16,303.2 million in 2005. Its net working capital is relatively illiquid because a large proportion of current assets is tied up in accounts receivable and inventories, and its cash is only 2.2% ($364 million/$16,303.2 million) of total assets at year-end 2005, down from 3.5% in 2004. It also reports no marketable securities that can serve as another source of liquidity, if needed. The lack of liquidity is usually worrisome, but is not a serious concern in this case given Kimberly-Clark's moderate financial leverage and high level of free cash flow (see later discussion in this section).

Following is a brief review and analysis for each of Kimberly-Clark's balance sheet line items.

Accounts Receivable

Kimberly-Clark reports $2,101.9 million in net accounts receivable at year-end 2005. This represents 12.9% ($2,101.9 million/$16,303.2 million) of total assets, up from 12% in the previous year. Footnotes reveal the following additional information:

Summary of Accounts Receivable ($ millions), December 31	2005	2004
Accounts Receivable		
From customers..	$1,930.6	$1,905.4
Other...	228.8	195.5
Less allowance for doubtful accounts and sales discounts	(57.5)	(62.6)
Accounts receivable, net	$2,101.9	$2,038.3

Most accounts receivables are from customers. This means we must consider the following two issues:

1. **Magnitude**—Receivables are generally non-interest-bearing and, therefore, do not earn a return. Further, the company incurs costs to finance them. Accordingly, a company wants to optimize its level of investment in receivables—that is, keep them as low as possible while still meeting industry specific credit policies to meet customer demands.

2. **Collectibility**—Receivables represent unsecured loans to customers. It is critical therefore, to understand the creditworthiness of these borrowers. Receivables are reported at net realizable value, that is, net of the allowance for doubtful accounts. Kimberly-Clark reports an allowance of $35.8 million. In addition, the footnotes reveal the following history of the company's allowance versus its write-offs:

		Additions		Deductions	
Description (December 31, 2005)	Balance at Beginning of Period	Charged to Costs and Expenses	Charged to Other Accounts	Write-Offs and Reclassifications	Balance at End of Period
Allowance for doubtful accounts	$42.5	$8.9	$(.6)	$15.0	$35.8

The company reported a balance in the allowance for doubtful accounts of $42.5 million at the beginning of 2005, which is 2.4% of receivables [$42.5/($2,038.3 million + $42.5 million)]. During 2005 it increased this allowance account by $8.9 million. This is the amount of bad debt expense that is reported in the income statement. The company also decreased the allowance by $0.6 million (see table above) by reallocating reserves to other accounts. Write-offs and reclassifications of uncollectible accounts amounted to $15 million during the year, yielding a $35.8 million balance at year-end, which is 1.7% of receivables [$35.8 million/($2,101.9 million + $35.8 million)]. It appears, therefore, that the company's receivables were less adequately reserved at year-end relative to the beginning of the year.

Following is Kimberly-Clark's explanation of its allowance policy:

Allowance for Doubtful Accounts   The allowance for doubtful accounts represents the Corporation's best estimate of the accounts receivable that will not be collected. The estimate is based on, among other things, historical collection experience, a review of the current aging status of customer receivables, and a review of specific information for those customers that are deemed to be higher risk. At the time the Corporation becomes aware of a customer whose continued operating success is questionable, collection of their receivable balance is closely monitored and the customer may be required to prepay for shipments. If a customer enters a bankruptcy action, the progress of that action is monitored to determine when and if an additional provision for non-collectibility is warranted. The adequacy of the allowance for doubtful accounts at December 31, 2005 and 2004 was $35.8 million and $42.5 million, respectively, and the write-off of uncollectible accounts was $15.0 million and $13.6 million in 2005 and 2004, respectively.

The allowance for doubtful accounts should always reflect the company's best estimate of the potential loss in its accounts receivable. This amount should not be overly conservative (which would understate profit), and it should not be inadequate (which would overstate profit). K-C's estimate of its potential losses results from its own (unaudited) review of the age of its receivables (older receivables are at greater risk of uncollectibility).

Inventories

Kimberly-Clark reports $1,752.1 million in inventories as of 2005. Footnote disclosures reveal the following inventory costing policy:

> **Inventories and Distribution Costs** For financial reporting purposes, most U.S. inventories are valued at the lower of cost, using the Last-In, First-Out (LIFO) method or market. The balance of the U.S. inventories and inventories of consolidated operations outside the U.S. are valued at the lower of cost, using either the First-In, First-Out (FIFO) or weighted-average cost methods, or market. Distribution costs are classified as Cost of Products Sold.

Most of its U.S. inventories are reported on a LIFO basis. Some of its U.S. inventories, as well as those outside of the U.S., are valued at FIFO or weighted-average. The use of multiple inventory costing methods for different pools of inventories is common and acceptable under GAAP.

Kimberly-Clark provides the following footnote disclosure relating to the composition of its inventories:

Summary of Inventories ($ millions), December 31	2005	2004
Inventories by major class		
At the lower of cost on the FIFO or weighted-average cost methods or market		
Raw materials	$ 338.9	$ 332.7
Work in process	236.7	225.9
Finished goods	1,128.9	1,044.6
Supplies and other	232.3	235.4
	1,936.8	1,838.6
Excess of FIFO or weighted-average cost over LIFO cost	(184.7)	(167.7)
Total	$1,752.1	$1,670.9

Companies aim to optimize their investment in inventories because inventory is a non-income-producing asset until sold. Inventories must also be financed, stored, moved, and insured at some cost. Kimberly-Clark reports $338.9 million of raw materials, which is 17.5% of the total of $1,936.8 million inventories (see table above). Work-in-process inventories amount to another $236.7 million, and supplies and other amount to $232.3 million. The bulk of its inventories, or $1,128.9 million (58.3% of total inventories), is in finished goods.

Kimberly-Clark reports its total inventory cost *at FIFO* is $1,936.8 million then subtracts $184.7 million from this amount (the *LIFO reserve*) to yield the inventories balance of $1,752.1 million at LIFO as reported on the balance sheet. This means that, over time, Kimberly-Clark has reduced gross profit and pretax operating profit by $184.7 million. This has also reduced pretax income and saved federal income tax, and generated cash flow, of approximately $64.6 million (assuming a 35% statutory federal tax rate and computed as $184.7 million $\times$ 35%). During 2005, its LIFO reserve increased by $17 million, resulting in a $17 million decrease in gross profit and pretax operating profit, and a $5.95 million ($17 million $\times$ 35%) reduction in cash flow from decreased federal income taxes.

Property, Plant, and Equipment

Kimberly Clark reports Property, Plant, and Equipment, net, of $7,494.7 million at year-end 2005; PPE makes up 45.9% of total assets and is the largest single asset category. Given the cost of depreciable assets of $14,616 million and accumulated depreciation of $7,121.5 million (not reported here), PPE is 48.7% depreciated assuming straight-line depreciation ($7,121.5 million/ $14,616 million) as of 2005. This suggests these assets are about the average age that we would expect assuming a regular replacement policy. Footnotes reveal a useful life range of 40 years for buildings and 16 to 20 years for machinery as follows:

> **Property and Depreciation** For financial reporting purposes, property, plant and equipment are stated at cost and are depreciated principally on the straight-line method. Buildings are depreciated over their estimated useful lives, primarily 40 years. Machinery and equipment are depreciated over

their estimated useful lives, primarily ranging from 16 to 20 years. For income tax purposes, accelerated methods of depreciation are used. Purchases of computer software are capitalized. External
costs and certain internal costs (including payroll and payroll-related costs of employees) directly associated with developing significant computer software applications for internal use are capitalized.
Training and data conversion costs are expensed as incurred. Computer software costs are amortized
on the straight-line method over the estimated useful life of the software, which generally does not
exceed five years.

Again, assuming straight-line depreciation, Kimberly-Clark's 2005 depreciation expense of $818.5
million ($844.5 depreciation and amortization expense reported in its statement of cash flows, Exhibit
13.5, less $26 million reported as amortization expense in footnotes not reproduced in the text) reveals
that its long-term depreciable assets, as a whole, are being depreciated over an average useful life of about
17.1 years, computed as $14,616.2 million − $257.4 million of nondepreciable land and $391.3 million
of construction in progress divided by $818.5 million depreciation expense.

Each year, Kimberly-Clark tests PPE for impairment and records a write down to net realizable value
if the PPE is deemed to be impaired. Following is Kimberly-Clark's discussion relating to its impairment
testing:

Estimated useful lives are periodically reviewed and, when warranted, changes are made to them.
Long-lived assets, including computer software, are reviewed for impairment whenever events or
changes in circumstances indicate that their cost may not be recoverable. An impairment loss would
be recognized when estimated undiscounted future cash flows from the use and eventual disposition
of an asset group, which are identifiable and largely independent of other asset groups, are less than
the carrying amount of the asset over its fair value. Fair value is measured using discounted cash flows
or independent appraisals, as appropriate. When property is sold or retired, the cost of the property
and the related accumulated depreciation are removed from the balance sheet and any gain or loss on
the transaction is included in income.

The company did not report any impairment losses in the periods covered by its recent 10-K.

If present, impairment losses should be treated as a transitory item. Further, we must consider the effects of such losses on current and future income statements. An impairment loss depresses current period
income. Further, depreciation expense in future years is decreased because it is computed based on the
asset's lower net book value (cost less accumulated depreciation) following the write-down. This will increase future period profitability. The net effect of an impairment charge, therefore, is to shift profit from
the current period into future periods.

Investments in Equity Companies

K-C's balance sheet reports equity investments of $457.8 million at year-end 2005. This amount rep-
resents the book value of its investments in affiliated companies over which Kimberly-Clark can exert
significant influence, but not control. Footnotes reveal investments in the following companies:

At December 31, 2005, the Corporation's equity companies and ownership interest were as follows:
Kimberly-Clark Lever, Ltd. (India) (50%), Kimberly-Clark de Mexico S.A. de C.V. and subsidiaries
(47.9%), Olayan Kimberly-Clark Arabia (49%), Olayan Kimberly-Clark (Bahrain) WLL (49%), PT Kimsari
Paper Indonesia (50%) and Tecnosur S.A. (34%).

Consolidation is not required unless the affiliate is "controlled." Generally, control is presumed at an
ownership level of more than 50%. By this rule, Kimberly-Clark does not control any of these companies.
Thus, the company uses the equity method to account for these investments. This means that only the net
equity owned of these companies is reported on the balance sheet. We further discuss these investments in
the section on off-balance-sheet financing.

Goodwill

Kimberly-Clark reports $2,685.6 million of goodwill at year-end 2005. This amount represents the ex-
cess of the purchase price for acquired companies over the fair market value of the acquired tangible and
identifiable intangible assets (net of liabilities assumed). Under GAAP, goodwill is not systematically
amortized, but is annually tested for impairment.

Prior to 2001, GAAP required goodwill amortization. Accordingly, Kimberly-Clark last reported
goodwill amortization in 2001. Since that time its annual net income is higher by approximately $94 mil-
lion per year as a result of this mandated accounting change that eliminated goodwill amortization.

Other Assets

Kimberly-Clark reports $882 million as "other assets." There is no table detailing what assets are included in this total, but footnotes reveal the following: $2 million of long-term marketable securities, $45.7 million of assets related to discontinued operations, $276.8 million of acquired patents and trademarks that are being amortized, and $228.1 million of noncurrent deferred income tax assets. No information is given on the remaining $329.4 million of other assets, most likely because this amount represents several assets each of which is not determined to be material and, therefore, subject to disclosure.

Concerning the deferred income tax assets, Kimberly-Clark provides the following disclosure relating to its composition ($ millions):

December 31 (Millions of dollars)	2005	2004
Net current deferred income tax asset attributable to:		
Other accrued expenses.	$145.5	$162.0
Pension, postretirement and other employee benefits.	94.8	86.9
Inventory.	(27.5)	(14.6)
Prepaid royalties.	—	27.2
Other.	19.0	24.1
Valuation allowances	(8.4)	(7.4)
Net current deferred income tax asset.	(223.4)	(278.2)
Net noncurrent deferred income tax asset attributable to:		
Income tax loss carryforwards	$235.8	$304.1
State tax credits	96.0	67.6
Pension and other postretirement benefits.	22.2	37.3
Accumulated depreciation	3.7	32.6
Other.	94.8	71.5
Valuation allowances	(224.4)	(219.7)
Net noncurrent deferred income tax asset included in other assets	$228.1	$293.4

Most of this deferred tax asset (benefit) results from tax loss carryforwards. The IRS allows companies to carry forward losses to offset future taxable income, thereby reducing future tax expense. This benefit can only be realized if the company expects taxable income in the specific entity that generated the tax losses before the carryforwards expire. If the company deems it more likely than not that the carryforwards will *not* be realized, a valuation allowance for the unrealizable portion is required (this is similar to establishing an allowance for uncollectible accounts receivable). As of 2005, Kimberly-Clark has such a valuation allowance (of $224.4 million). Following is its discussion relating to this allowance:

> Valuation allowances increased $221.6 million and $4.5 million in 2005 and 2004, respectively. the increase in 2005 was related to an increase in excess foreign tax credits that are potentially not usable in the U.S. during the 2006 through 2015 carryover period. Valuation allowances at the end of 2005 primarily relate to excess foreign tax credits in the U.S. and income tax loss carryforwards of $916.7 million, that potentially are not usable primarily in jurisdictions outside the U.S. If not utilized against taxable income, $425.7 million of the loss carryforwards will expire from 2006 through 2025. The remaining $491.0 million has no expiration date.
>
> Realization of income tax loss carryforwards is dependent on generating sufficient taxable income prior to expiration of these carryforwards. Although realization is not assured, management believes it is more likely than not that all of the deferred tax assets, net of applicable valuation allowances, will be realized. The amount of the deferred tax assets considered realizable could be reduced or increased if estimates of future taxable income change during the carryforward period.

Tax loss carryforwards reduce income tax expense in the year they are recognized, similar to tax loss carry-backs. However, companies often establish a deferred tax asset valuation allowance which increases tax expense. It is common that companies establish both the loss carryforward and the valuation allowance concurrently. The net effect is to leave tax expense (and net income) unchanged. In future years, however, a reduction of the deferred tax asset valuation account, in anticipation of utilization of the tax carry-forwards (and not as a result of their expiration), reduces tax expense and increases net income. This is a transitory increase in profit and should not be factored into projections.

Current Liabilities

Kimberly-Clark reports current liabilities of $4,642.9 million at year-end 2005. Accrued expenses make up the largest single amount at $1,399.6 million. Footnotes reveal that accrued expenses consist of the following:

Summary of Accrued Expenses ($ millions), December 31	2005	2004
Accrued advertising and promotion.	$ 260.3	$ 286.3
Accrued salaries and wages	377.1	389.6
Other.	762.2	755.7
Total	$1,399.6	$1,431.6

Footnotes reveal that the "other" includes accrued benefit costs from the company's pension plans.

The remaining items in current liabilities arise from common external transactions, such as trade accounts payable and taxes payable. These transactions are less prone to management reporting bias. We must, however, determine the presence of excessive "leaning on the trade" as a means to boost operating cash flow. K-C's trade accounts payable have increased as a percentage of total liabilities and equity from 5.8% ($983.2 million/$17,018.0 million) in 2004 to 6.5% ($1,055.5 million/ $16,303.2 million) in 2005. While this change is not drastic, and the level is not excessive, we need to monitor K-C's balance sheet for a continuation of this trend.

The possibility of management reporting bias is typically greater for accrued liabilities, which are often estimated (and difficult to audit), involve no external transaction, and can markedly impact reported balance sheet and income statement amounts. One of Kimberly-Clark's accrued liabilities involves promotions and rebates, estimated at $395.5 million ($235.3 million + $160.2 million) as of 2005. Following is the description of its accrual policy in this area:

Promotion and Rebate Accruals Among those factors affecting the accruals for promotions are estimates of the number of consumer coupons that will be redeemed and the type and number of activities within promotional programs between the Corporation and its trade customers. Rebate accruals are based on estimates of the quantity of products distributors have sold to specific customers. Generally, the estimates for consumer coupon costs are based on historical patterns of coupon redemption, influenced by judgments about current market conditions such as competitive activity in specific product categories. Estimates of trade promotion liabilities for promotional program costs incurred, but unpaid, are generally based on estimates of the quantity of customer sales, timing of promotional activities and forecasted costs for activities within the promotional programs. Settlement of these liabilities sometimes occurs in periods subsequent to the date of the promotion activity. Trade promotion programs include introductory marketing funds such as slotting fees, cooperative marketing programs, temporary price reductions, favorable end of aisle or in-store product displays and other activities conducted by the customers to promote the Corporation's products. Promotion accruals as of December 31, 2005 and 2004 were $235.3 million and $263.3 million, respectively. Rebate accruals as of December 31, 2005 and 2004 were $160.2 million and $163.0 million, respectively.

The company also reports accruals relating to its insurance risks, obsolete inventories, and environmental risks as described in the following footnote:

Retained Insurable Risks Selected insurable risks are retained, primarily those related to property damage, workers' compensation, and product, automobile and premises liability based upon historical loss patterns and management's judgment of cost effective risk retention. Accrued liabilities for incurred but not reported events, principally related to workers' compensation and automobile liability, are based upon loss development factors provided to the Corporation by external insurance brokers and are not discounted.

Excess and Obsolete Inventory All excess, obsolete, damaged or off-quality inventories including raw materials, in-process, finished goods, and spare parts are required to be adequately reserved for or to be disposed of. This process requires an ongoing tracking of the aging of inventories to be reviewed in conjunction with current marketing plans to ensure that any excess or obsolete inventories are identified on a timely basis. This process also requires judgments be made about the salability of existing stock in relation to sales projections. The evaluation of the adequacy of provision for obsolete and excess inventories is performed on at least a quarterly basis. No provisions for future obsolescence, damage or off-quality inventories are made.

Environmental Expenditures Environmental expenditures related to current operations that qualify as property, plant, and equipment or which substantially increase the economic value or extend the useful life of an asset are capitalized, and all other such expenditures are expensed as incurred. Environmental expenditures that relate to an existing condition caused by past operations are expensed as incurred. Liabilities are recorded when environmental assessments and/or remedial efforts are probable and the costs can be reasonably estimated. Generally, the timing of these accruals coincides with completion of a feasibility study or a commitment to a formal plan of action. At environmental sites in which more than one potentially responsible party has been identified, a liability is recorded for the estimated allocable share of costs related to the Corporation's involvement with the site as well as an estimated allocable share of costs related to the involvement of insolvent or unidentified parties. At environmental sites in which the Corporation is the only responsible party, a liability for the total estimated costs of remediation is recorded. Liabilities for future expenditures for environmental remediation obligations are not discounted and do not reflect any anticipated recoveries from insurers.

All of these accruals have similar effects on the financial statements: when the accrual is established the company recognizes both an expense in the income statement and a liability on the balance sheet. The company subsequently reduces the liability as payments are made. Companies can (and do) use accruals to shift income from one period to another, say by over-accruing in one period to intentionally depress current period profits, and later reducing the liability account, rather than recording an expense, to increase future period profits. Accruals are sometimes referred to as "pads." They represent a cost that has previously been charged to the income statement. They also represent an account that can absorb future costs. We need to monitor accrual accounts carefully for evidence of earnings management.

Long-Term Debt

Kimberly-Clark reports $2,661.9 million of long-term debt as of 2005. Footnotes reveal the following:

Long-term debt is composed of the following:

($ millions)	Weighted-Average Interest Rate	Maturities	December 31 2005	December 31 2004
Notes and debentures	5.78%	2007–2038	**$2,149.5**	$2,309.8
Industrial development revenue bonds	3.74%	2006–2037	**299.8**	300.7
Bank loans and other financing in various currencies	8.97%	2006–2031	**212.6**	272.9
Total long-term debt.			2,661.9	2,883.4
Less current portion			67.2	585.4
Long-term portion			**$2,594.7**	$2,298.0

Most of its long-term financing is in the form of notes and debentures, $2,149.5 million in 2005, which mature over the next 25 years. GAAP requires disclosure of scheduled maturities for each of the five years subsequent to the balance sheet date. Kimberly-Clark's five-year maturity schedule follows:

Scheduled maturities of long-term debt for the next five years are $67.2 million in 2006, $337.5 million in 2007, $49.1 million in 2008, $8.0 million in 2009 and $33.1 million in 2010.

Our concern with debt maturity dates is whether or not a company is able to repay debt as it comes due. Alternatively, a company can refinance the debt. If a company is unable or unwilling to repay or refinance its debt, it must approach creditors for a modification of debt terms for those issuances coming due. Creditors are often willing to oblige but will likely increase interest rates or impose additional debt covenants and restrictions. However, if creditors deny default waivers, the company might face the prospect of bankruptcy. This highlights the importance of long-term debt maturity disclosures.

We have little concern about Kimberly-Clark's debt maturity schedule as the company has strong cash flows. Still, it is worth noting that **Standard & Poor's** (S&P) lowered K-C's debt rating from AA to AA−. This rating is still strong (described as lower "high grade" debt), but lower nonetheless. Following is Kimberly-Clark's explanation of this downgrade disclosed in its 2003 10-K:

In July 2003, Standard & Poor's ("S&P") revised the Corporation's credit rating for long-term debt from AA to AA−. Moody's Investor Service maintained its short- and long-term ratings but changed the Corporation's outlook to negative from stable, indicating that a ratings downgrade could be possible within the next 12 months. These changes were primarily based on the Corporation's business performance in the heightened competitive environment and because S&P changed the way in which it evaluates liabilities for pensions and other postretirement benefits. Management believes that these actions will not have a material adverse effect on the Corporation's access to credit or its borrowing costs since these credit ratings remain strong and are in the top eight percent of companies listed in S&P's ranking of the 500 largest companies. The Corporation's commercial paper continues to be rated in the top category.

Noncurrent Employee Benefit and Other Obligations

Kimberly-Clark reports a (negative) funded status of its pension plan of $(1,383.0) million at year-end 2005 (disclosed in footnotes). This means that the company's pension plans are underfunded by that amount. This underfunding is computed as the difference between the pension benefit obligation (PBO) of $5,509.2 million and the fair market value of the company's pension assets of $4,126.2 million (these amounts are also reported in the pension footnote not reproduced here).

The central issue with respect to pensions and other post-retirement obligations is the potential demand they present on operating cash flows. Companies can tap cash from two sources to pay pension and other post-retirement obligations: from the returns on plan assets (i.e., the cumulative contributions and investment returns that have not yet been paid out to beneficiaries) and/or from operating cash flow. To the extent that plan assets are insufficient to meet retirement obligations, companies must divert operating cash flows from other investment activities, potentially reducing the dollar amount of capital projects that can be funded.

We can gain insight into potential cash flow issues by comparing expected future benefit payments to the funds available to make those payments. Companies must provide these disclosures in a schedule to the pension footnotes. K-C provides the following schedule of expected payments in the footnotes to its 10-K:

Estimated Future Benefit Payments The following benefit payments, which reflect expected future service, as appropriate, are anticipated to be paid:

(Millions of dollars)	Pension Benefits	Other Benefits
2006	$ 317	$ 84
2007	305	86
2008	308	87
2009	310	89
2010	315	92
Years 2011–2015	$1,719	$485

The schedule shows that K-C expects to pay out $317 million in benefits to pension beneficiaries and $84 million in health care and other post-retirement benefits (OPEB) to its former employees in 2006. The schedule also reveals that the company expects these amounts to remain fairly constant over the next five years.

K-C also reports the following table relating to its pension and other post-retirement benefit plans' assets:

Change in Plan Assets Year Ended December 31 (Millions of dollars)	Pension Benefits		Other Benefits	
	2005	2004	2005	2004
Fair value of plan assets at beginning of year	$4,044.2	$4,027.9	—	—
Actual gain on plan assets	359.5	332.8	—	—
Employer contributions	116.5	200.0	66.5	59.4
Currency and other	(97.2)	103.1	8.5	8.4
Benefit payments	(296.8)	(296.3)	(75.0)	(67.8)
Spin-off Neenah Paper	—	(323.3)	—	—
Fair value of plan assets at end of year	$4,126.2	$4,044.2	—	—

In 2005, K-C contributed $116.5 million to its pension plan. That amount, when combined with investment returns of $359.5 million, was more than sufficient to cover 2005 benefit payments of $296.8 million (K-C expects this amount to be $317 million in 2006). Should pension assets decline markedly as a result of severe underfunding or investment losses, K-C will need to divert operating cash flows from other investment activities into pension contributions, or to borrow funds to meet its pension obligations. Although K-C's pension obligations are under-funded (as represented by the negative funded status), its current contribution levels and investment returns are sufficient to meet its anticipated pension obligations, at least in the near future.

Other post-retirement benefit obligations (future health care payments) present a different picture. Because federal law does not require minimum funding of these plans, and companies do not receive a tax deduction for such contributions, companies rarely fund OPEB plans. All of the OPEB payments to beneficiaries, therefore, must be funded by concurrent company contributions. These payments amounted to $75 million in 2005. Given K-C's $2.3 billion in operating cash flow for 2005, the $75 million cash requirement is not material. However, OPEB funding requirements have been a burden for many companies, most notably General-Motors (see Business Insight in Module 10).

Deferred Income Taxes

Kimberly-Clark reports a net noncurrent deferred tax liability of $572.9 million at year-end 2005. Footnote disclosures reveal this amount consists of the following ($ millions):

Year Ended December 31 (Millions of dollars)	2005	2004
Net noncurrent deferred income tax liability attributable to:		
Accumulated depreciation	$(1,103.1)	$(1,312.7)
Pension, postretirement and other employee benefits	548.1	521.9
Foreign tax credits and loss carryforwards	484.1	160.1
Installment sales	(192.0)	(188.1)
Other	(70.2)	3.8
Valuation allowances	(239.8)	(25.3)
Net noncurrent deferred income tax liability	$ (572.9)	$ (840.3)

Most of the noncurrent deferred tax liability ($1,103.1 million) arises from K-C's use of straight-line depreciation for GAAP reporting and accelerated depreciation for tax reporting. As a result, tax depreciation expense is higher in the early years of the assets' lives. This will reverse in later years for individual assets, resulting in higher taxable income and tax liability. The deferred tax liability account reflects this future expected tax.

Although depreciation expense for an individual asset declines over time, thus increasing taxable income and tax liability, if K-C adds new assets at a sufficient rate, the additional first-year depreciation on those assets will more than offset the reduction of depreciation expense on older assets, resulting in a long-term reduction of tax liability. That is, the deferred tax liability is unlikely to reverse in the aggregate. For this reason, many analysts treat the deferred tax liability as a "quasi-equity" account.

Still, while deferred taxes can be postponed, they cannot be eliminated. If the company's asset growth slows markedly, it will realize higher taxable income and tax liability. We need to be mindful of the potential for a "real" tax liability (requiring cash payment) when companies begin to downsize.

K-C also reports a long-term deferred tax asset valuation allowance of $239.8 million for 2005, an increase of $214.5 million over the prior year. This valuation allowance is related to deferred tax assets that arise from the company's tax loss carry-forwards. The valuation allowance indicates that the company does not expect to fully realize tax loss carry-forwards before their scheduled expiration. Changes in the deferred tax asset valuation allowance impact tax expense, and, thus, net income, dollar for dollar. K-C's net income (and net operating income after tax or NOPAT) was, reduced by $214.5 million in 2005 as a result of the increase in this valuation allowance. This increased tax expense more than likely offset a reduction of tax expense when the loss carryforwards were recorded, leaving net income unaffected in this year. In future years, we need to be aware that profit can increase if and when the allowance account is reversed with no offsetting expense.

Minority Owner's Interests in Subsidiaries

K-C's reports $394.5 million for the equity interests of minority shareholders in subsidiaries. Minority interests are shareholder claims against the net assets and cash flows of the company (after all senior claims are settled). Consequently, we treat minority interest as a component of stockholders' equity (a current FASB proposal will result in formal classification of minority interest liability as a component of stockholders' equity).

Preferred Securities of Subsidiary

The preferred securities represent the sale of preferred stock by a subsidiary of Kimberly-Clark to outside interests. This account is treated like all other contributed capital accounts.

Stockholders' Equity

Kimberly-Clark reports the following statement of stockholders' equity for 2005:

(Dollars in millions, shares in thousands)	Common Stock Issued Shares	Common Stock Issued Amount	Additional Paid-in Capital	Treasury Stock Shares	Treasury Stock Amount	Unearned Compensation on Restricted Stock	Retained Earnings	Accumulated Other Comprehensive Income (Loss)	Comprehensive Income
Balance at Dec. 31, 2004	568,597	$710.8	$348.6	85,694	$(5,047.5)	$(22.3)	$11,865.9	$(1,226.0)	
Net income	—	—	—	—	—	—	1,568.3	—	$1,568.3
Other comprehensive income:									
Unrealized translation loss	—	—	—	—	—	—	—	(412.6)	(412.6)
Minimum pension liability	—	—	—	—	—	—	—	(58.6)	(58.6)
Other	—	—	—	—	—	—	—	27.8	27.8
Total comprehensive income									$1,124.9
Options exercised and other awards	—	—	(39.2)	(3,040)	181.9	—	—	—	
Option and restricted share income tax benefits	—	—	15.1	—	—	—	—	—	
Shares repurchased	—	—	—	24,463	(1,511.2)	—	—	—	
Net issuance of restricted stock, less amortization	—	—	0.1	(9)	0.7	9.2	—	—	
Dividends declared	—	—	—	—	—	—	(852.8)	—	
Balance at Dec. 31, 2005	568,597	$710.8	$324.6	107,108	$(6,376.1)	$(13.1)	$12,581.4	$(1,669.4)	

K-C has issued 568.597 million shares of its $1.25 par value common stock. The common stock account is, therefore, equal to $710.746 million (rounded to $710.8 million), computed as 568,597 million shares × $1.25. The additional paid-in capital (APIC) represents the excess of proceeds from stock issuance over par value. It also includes three other components for 2005: (1) the difference between the cash K-C received per share of treasury stock and its original purchase cost is added or deducted from APIC; in this case APIC was reduced by $39.2 million when K-C issued shares to option holders and other employees and the cash received was less than the cost of the shares issued, and (2) the tax benefits received by K-C relating to the value of stock options exercised by employees is reported as an increase in APIC; it is not reflected as a component of net income, and (3) APIC is increased by $0.1 million related to the issuance of restricted stock (see below).

Kimberly-Clark's stockholders' equity is reduced by $6,376.1 million relating to repurchases of common stock, less the reissuance of those securities. These treasury shares are the result of a stock purchase plan approved by K-C's board of directors, and evidences K-C's conviction that its stock is undervalued by the marketplace. The repurchased shares are held in treasury and reduce stockholders' equity by the purchase price until such time as they are reissued, perhaps to fund an acquisition or to compensate employees under a stock purchase or stock option plan (treasury shares can also be retired).

K-C compensates employees via restricted stock in addition to other forms of compensation. Under its restricted stock plan, eligible employees are issued stock, which is restricted as to sale until fully vested (owned). When issued, the market value of the restricted stock is deducted from stockholders' equity. As the employees gain ownership of the shares (that is, the restricted stock vests), a portion of this account is transferred to the income statement as compensation expense. The consequent reduction in retained earnings offsets the reduction (and increase in equity) of the restricted stock account. Stockholders' equity is, therefore, unaffected in total, although its components change.

Retained earnings reflect a $1,568.3 million increase relating to net income and a $852.8 million decrease from declaration of dividends. Accumulated other comprehensive income (AOCI), which is often aggregated with retained earnings for analysis purposes, began 2005 with a balance of $(1,226.0) million; this negative balance reduces stockholders' equity. During the period, this AOCI account was further reduced by $412.6 million relating to the decrease in the $US value of net assets of foreign subsidiaries. This decrease in net asset value resulted from a strengthened $US vis-à-vis other currencies in which the company conducts its operations in 2005. In addition, the AOCI account was reduced by $58.6 million relating to the recognition of a minimum pension liability and increased (made less negative) by $27.8 million for activities designated as "other." Finally, K-C's comprehensive income equals net income plus (minus) the components of other comprehensive income.

Common-Size Balance Sheet

Similar to our analysis of the income statement, it is useful to compute common-size balance sheets. Such statements can reveal changes or relations masked by other analyses. Kimberly-Clark's common-size balance sheet covering its recent two years is shown in Exhibit 13.4.

K-C is somewhat less liquid in 2005 than in 2004 as evidenced by the decreased level of cash to 2.23% of total assets in 2005 from 3.49% in 2004. (Later in the module the statement of cash flows reveals that this is the result of reduced profitability and the repurchase of common stock.) Aside from receivables and inventories, which both increased by approximately one percentage point, the remaining assets and liabilities exhibit little variation from the prior year. There is a marked increase in retained earnings, from 69.73% of assets to 77.17%, but it is more than offset by the increase in treasury stock as K-C continues to draw on its operating cash flow to repurchase its common stock. At year-end 2005, stockholders provide 34.09% of its total capital, down from 38.96% in 2004.

Off-Balance-Sheet Reporting and Analysis

There are numerous assets and liabilities that do not appear on the balance sheet. Some are excluded because managers and accounting professionals only report what they can reliably measure. Others are excluded because of the rigidity of accounting standards. Following are some areas we might consider in our evaluation and adjustment of the Kimberly-Clark balance sheet.

Internally Developed Intangible Assets

Many brands and their corresponding values are excluded from the balance sheet. For example, consider the brand "Kleenex." Many individuals actually refer to facial tissues as Kleenex-that is successful branding! So, is the Kleenex brand reported and valued on Kimberly-Clark's balance sheet? No. That brand value cannot be reliably measured and, hence, is not included on K-C's balance sheet.

Likewise, other valuable assets are excluded from the company's balance sheet. Examples are the value of a competent management team, high employee morale, innovative production know-how, a superior supply chain, customer satisfaction, and a host of other assets.

R&D activities often create internally generated intangible assets that are mostly excluded from the balance sheet. Footnotes reveal that Kimberly-Clark spends over $319.5 million (2% of sales) on R&D to remain competitive—and, this is for an admittedly non-high-tech company. Further, K-C reveals that it spends $451 million (nearly 3% of sales) on advertising. Both R&D and advertising costs are expensed under GAAP as opposed to being capitalized on the balance sheet as tangible assets. These unrecognized intangible assets often represent a substantial part of a company's market value.

EXHIBIT 13.4	Kimberly-Clark Common-Size Balance Sheet		
December 31		**2005**	**2004**
Assets			
Current assets			
Cash and cash equivalents		2.23%	3.49%
Accounts receivable, net		12.89	11.98
Inventories		10.75	9.82
Deferred income taxes		1.37	1.63
Other current assets		2.10	2.24
Total current assets		29.34	29.16
Property, plant and equipment, net		45.97	46.95
Investments in equity companies		2.81	2.61
Goodwill		16.47	15.88
Other assets		5.41	5.40
Total assets		100.00%	100.00%
Liabilities and stockholders' equity			
Current liabilities			
Debt payable within one year		7.50%	7.14%
Trade accounts payable		6.47	5.78
Other payables		1.83	1.56
Accrued expenses		8.58	8.41
Accrued income taxes		2.81	2.63
Dividends payable		1.28	1.14
Total current liabilities		28.48	26.66
Long-term debt		15.92	13.50
Noncurrent employee benefit and other obligations		10.93	9.53
Deferred income taxes		3.51	4.94
Minority owners interests in subsidiaries		2.42	2.16
Preferred securities of subsidiary		4.65	4.25
Stockholders equity			
Preferred stock—no par value—authorized 20.0 million shares, none issued		0.00	0.00
Common stock—$1.25 par value—authorized 1.2 billion shares; issued 568.6 million shares at December 31, 2005 and 2004		4.36	4.18
Additional paid-in capital		1.99	2.05
Common stock held in treasury, at cost—107.1 million and 85.7 million shares at December 31, 2005 and 2004		(39.11)	(29.66)
Accumulated other comprehensive income (loss)		(10.24)	(7.20)
Retained earnings		77.17	69.73
Unearned compensation on restricted stock		(0.08)	(0.13)
Total stockholders' equity		34.09	38.96
Total liabilities and stockholders' equity		100.00%	100.00%

Note: All percentages are computed by dividing each balance sheet line item by that year's total assets.

Equity Method Investments

Kimberly-Clark reports equity investments of $457.8 million at year-end 2005. These are unconsolidated affiliates over which K-C can exert significant influence (but not control) and, hence, are accounted for using the equity method. The amount reported on the balance sheet represents the initial cost of the investment, plus (minus) the percentage share of investee earnings and losses, and minus any cash dividends received. Consequently, the investment balance equals the percentage owned of the affiliates' stockholders' equity (plus any unamortized excess purchase price).

Footnotes reveal that, in sum, these K-C affiliates have total assets of $1,861.8 million, liabilities of $1,078.0 million, and stockholders' equity of $783.8 million. K-C's reported investment balance of $457.8 in the balance sheet does not reveal the extent of the investment (assets) required to manage these companies, nor the level of potential liability exposure. For instance, if one of these affiliates falters financially, K-C might have to invest additional cash to support it rather than let it fail. Failure of an important affiliate might affect K-C's ability to finance another such venture in the future.

These investments are reported at cost, not at fair market value as are passive investments. This means that unrecognized gains and losses can be buried in such investment accounts. For example, K-C footnotes reveal the following:

> Kimberly-Clark de Mexico, S.A. de C.V. is partially owned by the public and its stock is publicly traded in Mexico. At December 31, 2005, the Corporation's investment in this equity company was $396.3 million, and the estimated fair value of the investment was $2.0 billion based on the market price of publicly traded shares.

Thus, for at least one of its investments, there is an unrecognized gain of $1,603.7 million.

Operating Leases

Kimberly-Clark has leases classified as "operating" for financial reporting purposes. As a result, neither the lease asset nor the lease obligation are reported on its balance sheet. For example, K-C reports the following disclosure relating to its operating leases:

> The Corporation has entered into operating leases for certain warehouse facilities, automobiles and equipment. The future minimum obligations under operating leases having a noncancelable term in excess of one year as of December 31, 2005, are as follows:

Year Ending December 31 (Millions of dollars):	Amount
2006	$ 85.7
2007	47.4
2008	34.1
2009	26.4
2010	17.1
Thereafter	47.0
Future minimum obligations	$257.7

These leases represent an unreported asset and an unreported liability; both amounting to $220 million. This amount is computed as follows and assumes a 6% discount rate ($ millions):

Year	Operating Lease Payment	Discount Factor (i = 0.06)	Present Value
1	$86	0.94340	$ 81
2	47	0.89000	42
3	34	0.83962	29
4	26	0.79209	21
5	17	0.74726	13
>5	47 [$17 for ~3 years]	2.67301* × 0.74726	34**
			$220

Remaining life = $47/$17 = 2.749 years rounded to 3 years
*The annuity factor for 3 years at 6% is 2.67301.
**2.67301 × 0.74726 × $17 = $34.

The classification of leases as operating for financial reporting purposes often involves a rigid application of accounting rules that depend solely on the structure of the lease. A large amount of assets and liabilities is excluded from many companies' balance sheets because leases are structured as operating leases. For K-C, these excluded assets amount to $220 million. The valuation of K-C common stock (shown later) uses net operating assets (NOA) as one of its inputs. Our adjustment to the K-C balance sheet, then, would entail the addition of these assets to NOA and the inclusion of $220 million in *non*operating liabilities.

Pensions

Kimberly-Clark's pension plan is underfunded as described earlier in the module. Total pension obligations amount to $5,509.2 million and pension assets have a market value of $4,126.2 million at year-end

2005. Neither of these amounts appears on the balance sheet, but are reported in the footnotes. In fact, neither does the $1,383.0 million ($5,509.2 million − $4,126.2 million) shortfall because in 2005 GAAP permitted the deferment (nonrecognition) of $1,018.4 million of increased pension liabilities resulting from the reduction in the discount rate in 2005 and the consequent increase in the present value of the pension obligation.

In 2006, the Financial Accounting Standards Board amended the pension accounting standard. Companies now must recognize the funded status on the face of the balance sheet with no deferral (off-balance sheet recognition). Under the new standard, K-C would have recognized a liability of $1,383.0 (the negative funded status), resulting in an increase in liabilities of $364.6 million and a reduction of pension-related assets of $442.3 million, with a consequent reduction in stockholders' equity (AOCI) of $806.9 million. These adjustments affect only the balance sheet and not the income statement.

Variable Interest Entities

Footnotes reveal that Kimberly-Clark has two categories of special purpose entities (SPEs) that have been classified as variable interest entities (VIEs). The first relates to two entities that the company established to securitize (sell) $617 million of notes receivable relating to asset sales. K-C sold the notes to the VIEs, which financed the purchase with debt sold to the public. K-C maintains an equity interest in these entities, but their voting control rests with an independent party (bank) that provides credit guarantees for a fee. The bank is deemed to be the primary beneficiary for financial reporting purposes. As a result, K-C can continue to account for the investment under the equity method and is not required to consolidate the VIE.

The second entity is a synthetic fuel partnership in which K-C has a 49.5% interest. This partnership provides tax credits to K-C, amounting to $234.3 million in 2005 (from its 10-K footnote 12). Since K-C is not the primary beneficiary of the partnership's cash flows, it is not required to consolidate its financial statements as of 2005. K-C asserts that consolidation, if required, will not have a material effect on its consolidated financial statements. As a result, it does not provide detailed disclosures of the financial statements of the VIE.

Derivatives

Kimberly-Clark is exposed to a number of market risks as outlined in the following footnote to its 10-K:

> As a multinational enterprise, the Corporation is exposed to risks such as changes in foreign currency exchange rates, interest rates and commodity prices. The Corporation employs a variety of practices to manage these risks, including operating and financing activities and, where deemed appropriate, the use of derivative instruments. These derivative instruments, including some that are not designated as either fair value or cash flow hedges, are used only for risk management purposes and not for speculation or trading. Foreign currency derivative instruments are either exchange traded or are entered into with major financial institutions. The Corporation's credit exposure under these arrangements is limited to those agreements with a positive fair value at the reporting date. Credit risk with respect to the counterparties is considered minimal in view of the financial strength of the counterparties.

The company hedges these risks using derivatives, including forwards, options, and swap contracts. This hedging process transfers risk from K-C to another entity (called the counterparty), which assumes that risk for a fee.

The accounting for derivatives is summarized in an appendix to Module 7. In brief, the derivative contracts, and the assets or liabilities to which they relate, are reported on the balance sheet at fair market value. Any unrealized gains and losses are ultimately reflected in net income, although they can be accumulated in AOICI for a short time. To the extent that a company's hedging activities are effective, the market values of the derivatives and the assets or liabilities to which they relate are largely offsetting, as are the net gains or losses on the hedging activities. As a result, the effect of derivative activities is generally minimal on both income and equity.[2]

---

[2] It is generally only when companies use derivatives for speculative purposes that these investments markedly affect income and equity. The aim of the derivatives standard was to highlight these speculative activities and we need to read risk footnotes carefully to assess whether companies are hedging or speculating with derivatives.

Statement of Cash Flows Reporting and Analysis

The statement of cash flows for Kimberly-Clark is shown in Exhibit 13.5.

EXHIBIT 13.5	Kimberly-Clark Statement of Cash Flows

KIMBERLY-CLARK CORPORATION AND SUBSIDIARIES
Consolidated Cash Flow Statement

Year Ended December 31 (Millions of dollars)	2005	2004	2003
Operating Activities			
Income from continuing operations	$1,580.6	$1,770.4	$ 1,643.6
Depreciation and amortization	844.5	800.3	745.3
Asset impairments	80.1	—	—
Deferred income taxes	(142.7)	(19.4)	(50.8)
Net losses on asset dispositions	45.8	45.5	35.0
Equity companies' earnings in excess of dividends paid	(23.8)	(30.1)	(9.6)
Minority owners' share of subsidiaries' net income	86.5	73.9	55.6
(Increase) decrease in operating working capital	(156.0)	103.6	111.8
Postretirement benefits	40.9	(54.4)	(59.9)
Other	(44.1)	36.4	81.2
Cash provided by operations	2,311.8	2,726.2	2,552.2
Investing Activities			
Capital spending	(709.6)	(535.0)	(872.9)
Acquisitions of businesses, net of cash acquired	(17.4)	—	(258.5)
Investments in marketable securities	(2.0)	(11.5)	(10.8)
Proceeds from sales of investments	27.3	38.0	29.4
Net decrease (increase) in time deposits	75.5	(22.9)	(149.0)
Proceeds from dispositions of property	46.8	30.7	7.6
Other	(16.8)	5.3	(5.9)
Cash used for investing	(596.2)	(495.4)	(1,260.1)
Financing Activities			
Cash dividends paid	(838.4)	(767.9)	(671.9)
Net increase (decrease) in short-term debt	524.3	(54.7)	424.2
Proceeds from issuance of long-term debt	397.7	38.7	540.8
Repayments of long-term debt	(599.7)	(199.0)	(481.6)
Issuance of preferred securities of subsidiary	—	125.0	—
Proceeds from exercise of stock options	142.7	290.0	31.0
Acquisitions of common stock for the treasury	(1,519.5)	(1,598.0)	(546.7)
Other	(36.8)	(9.0)	(18.3)
Cash used for financing	(1,929.7)	(2,174.9)	(1,570.9)
Effect of exchange rate changes on cash and cash equivalents	(15.9)	4.1	18.6
Cash (used for) provided by continuing operations	(230.0)	60.0	(260.2)
Discontinued operations			
Cash provided by discontinued operations	—	30.0	56.3
Cash payment from Neenah Paper,Inc.	—	213.4	—
Cash provided by discontinued operations	—	243.4	56.3
(Decrease) increase in cash and cash equivalents	(203.0)	303.4	(203.9)
Cash and cash equivalents, beginning of year	594.0	290.6	494.5
Cash and cash equivalents, end of year	$ 364.0	$ 594.0	$ 290.6

In 2005, K-C generated $2,311.8 million of operating cash flow, primarily from income (net income plus the depreciation add-back amounts to $2,425.1 million). This amount is well in excess of K-C's capital expenditures and business acquisitions of $727.0 million ($709.6 million + $17.4 million). K-C used this excess cash to pay dividends to shareholders ($838.4 million), and to repurchase stock ($1,519.5 million).

Kimberly-Clark offers the following commentary regarding its 2005 operating cash flow:

Cash provided by operations decreased $414.4 million, or 15.2 percent, primarily due to an increased investment in working capital and higher income tax payments, partially offset by lower cash contributions to the U.S. defined benefit pension plan.

Overall, the cash flow picture for Kimberly-Clark is strong: operating cash flows are more than sufficient to cover capital expenditures and acquisitions, leaving excess cash that is being returned to the shareholders in the form of dividends and share repurchases. The strength of its operating cash flows mitigates any concerns we might have regarding its relative lack of liquidity on the balance sheet.

Independent Audit Opinion

Kimberly-Clark is subject to various audit requirements. Its independent auditor is Deloitte & Touche LLP, which issued the following clean opinion on K-C's 2005 financial statements:

REPORT OF INDEPENDENT REGISTERED PUBLIC ACCOUNTING FIRM

To the Board of Directors and Stockholders of Kimberly-Clark Corporation:

We have audited the accompanying consolidated balance sheets of Kimberly-Clark Corporation and subsidiaries as of December 31, 2005 and 2004, and the related consolidated statements of income, stockholders' equity, and cash flows for each of the three years in the period ended December 31, 2005. Our audits also included the financial statement schedule listed in the Index at Item 15. These financial statements and financial statement schedule are the responsibility of the Corporation's management. Our responsibility is to express an opinion on the financial statements and the financial statement schedule based on our audits.

We conducted our audits in accordance with standards of the Public Company Accounting Oversight Board (United States). Those standards require that we plan and perform the audit to obtain reasonable assurance about whether the financial statements are free of material misstatement. An audit includes examining, on a test basis, evidence supporting the amounts and disclosures in the financial statements. An audit includes examining, on a test basis, evidence supporting the amounts and disclosures in the financial statements. An audit also includes assessing the accounting principles used and significant estimates made by management, as well as evaluating the overall financial statement presentation. We believe that our audits provide a reasonable basis for our opinion.

In our opinion, such consolidated financial statements present fairly, in all material respects, the financial position of Kimberly-Clark Corporation and subsidiaries at December 31, 2005 and 2004, and the results of their operations and their cash flows for each of the three years in the period ended December 31, 2005, in conformity with accounting principles generally accepted in the United States of America. Also, in our opinion, the financial statement schedule, when considered in relation to the basic consolidated financial statements taken as a whole, presents fairly, in all material respects, the information set forth therein.

As discussed in Note 1 to the consolidated financial statements, on December 31, 2005, the Corporation changed its method of determining conditional asset retirement obligations.

We have also audited, in accordance with the standards of the Public Company Accounting Oversight Board (United States), the effectiveness of the Corporation's internal control over financial reporting as of December 31, 2005, based on the criteria established in *Internal Control-Integrated Framework* issued by the Committee of Sponsoring Organizations of the Treadway Commission and our report dated February 21, 2006 axpressed an unqualified opinion on management's assessment of the effectiveness of the Corporation's internal control over financial reporting and an unqualified opinion on the effectiveness of the Corporation's internal control over financial reporting.

Deloitte & Touche LLP

Although this report is a routine disclosure, it should not be taken for granted. Exceptions to a clean audit report must be scrutinized. Also, any disagreements between management and the independent auditor must be documented in an SEC filing. If this occurs, it is a "red flag" that must be investigated. Management activities and reports that cannot meet usual audit standards raise serious concerns about integrity and credibility. At a minimum, the riskiness of investments and relationships with such a company markedly increases.

ASSESSING PROFITABILITY AND CREDITWORTHINESS

LO2 Assess company profitability and creditworthiness.

This section reports a profitability analysis of Kimberly-Clark. We begin by computing several key measures that are used in the ROE disaggregation, which is the overriding focus of this section. The ROE disaggregation process is defined in Module 4, and a listing of the ratio acronyms and definitions is in the review section at the end of the book.)

K-C's 2005 net operating profit after-tax (NOPAT) is $1,949.9 million, computed as $2,310.6 million + $136.6 million − ($438.4 million + [($190.2 million − $27.5 million) × 36.2%]), where 36.2% is the combined federal and state statutory income tax rate as disclosed in its tax footnote. In 2005, K-C's net operating assets (NOA) are $10,735.9 million, computed as $(16,303.2 −1,055.5 − 298.8 − 1,399.6 − 457.9 − 1,782.6 − 572.9) million.

ROE Disaggregation

Our first step is to compute the ROE and, then, disaggregate it into its operating (return on net operating assets or RNOA) and nonoperating components. Using the computations in the previous section, the 2005 disaggregation analysis of ROE for Kimberly-Clark follows:[3]

$$\textbf{ROE} = \textbf{RNOA} + \textbf{Nonoperating return}$$
$$25.74\% = 17.60\% + 8.14\%$$

where

$$\textbf{ROE} = \$1,568.3 \text{ million}/[(\$5,558.2 \text{ million} + \$6,629.5 \text{ million})/2]$$
$$\textbf{RNOA} = \$1,949.9 \text{ million}/[(\$10,735.9 \text{ million} + \$11,427.7 \text{ million})/2]$$

RNOA accounts for 68% (17.60%/25.74%) of K-C's ROE. K-C successfully uses its nonoperating activities to increase its 17.60% RNOA to a 25.74% ROE.

Disaggregation of RNOA—Margin and Turnover

The next level analysis of ROE focuses on RNOA disaggregation. Kimberly-Clark's net operating profit margin (NOPM) and net operating asset turnover (NOAT) are as follows:

RNOA = NOPAT/Average Net Operating Assets = NOPAT/Sales × Sales/Average Net Operating Assets

		NOPM	NOAT
17.6%	=	12.26% ×	1.44

where

$$\textbf{NOPM} = \$1,949.9 \text{ million}/\$15,902.6 \text{ million}$$
$$\textbf{NOAT} = \$15,902.6 \text{ million}/([\$10,735.9 \text{ million} + \$11,427.7 \text{ million}]/2)$$

Kimberly-Clark's RNOA of 17.6% consists of a net operating profit margin of 12.26% and a net operating asset turnover of 1.44 times.

Disaggregation of Margin and Turnover

This section focuses on the disaggregation of profit margin and asset turnover to better understand the drivers of RNOA. Again, understanding the drivers of financial performance (RNOA) is key to predicting

---

[3] Many of these ratios require computation of averages, such as average assets. If we wanted to compute ratios for years prior to 2005, then we would obtain information from prior 10-Ks to compute the necessary averages for these ratios.

future company performance. Our analysis of the drivers of operating profit margin and asset turnover for Kimberly-Clark follows:

Disaggregation of NOPM

Gross profit margin (GPM) ($5,075.2 mil./$15,902.6 mil.) 31.9%

Marketing, research and general expense margin [($2,737.4 mil)/$15,902.6 mil] 17.2%

Disaggregation of NOAT

Accounts receivable turnover (ART) { $15,902.6 mil./[($2,101.9 mil. + $2,038.3 mil.)/2]} 7.68

Inventory turnover (INVT) { $10,827.4 mil./[($1,752.1 mil. + $1,670.9 mil.)/2]} 6.33

Long-term operating asset turnover (LTOAT) { $15,902.6 mil./[($11,520.1 mil. + $12,056.1 mil.)/2]} 1.35

Accounts payable turnover (APT) {$10,827.4 mil./[($1,055.5 mil. + $983.2 mil.)/2]} 10.62

Related turnover measures

Average collection period [$2,101.9 mil./($15,902.6 mil./365)] .... 48.24 days

Average inventory days outstanding [$1,752.1 mil./($10,827.4 mil./365)] .... 59.06 days

Average payable days outstanding [$1,055.5 mil./($10,827.4 mil./365)] .... 35.58 days

First, let's look at the disaggregation of NOPM. K-C reports a gross profit margin of 31.9%. A schedule to its 2005 10-K indicates that this important measure has declined by 2 percentage points in the past four years, a marked decline. K-C provides the following explanation in its MD&A:

Competitive Environment The Corporation experiences intense competition for sales of its principal products in its major markets, both domestically and internationally. The Corporation's products compete with widely advertised, well-known, branded products, as well as private label products, which are typically sold at lower prices. The Corporation has several major competitors in most of its markets, some of which are larger and more diversified than the Corporation.

Declines in gross profit margin are usually countered with reductions in operating expenses to maintain a company's operating profit margin. K-C's marketing, research, and general expenses for 2005 increased by $228.6 million as a result of the company's restructuring efforts. Absent these additional costs, marketing, research and general expense would have been 15.8% of sales, compared with 16.7% and 16.8% of sales in the previous two years, respectively. The company appears to be focusing on future cost reduction (obtained via current restructuring charges) as a way to remain competitive.

Bottom line, K-C's NOPM has not fully reflected the intense competitive environment of its markets because of the decline in its effective tax rate over the past three years. This tax rate decline is mainly due to its synthetic fuel partnership. Although a laudable activity, we prefer to see cost reductions from improvements in operating activities. In addition, tax benefits are often transitory.

Next, we consider the disaggregation of NOAT. K-C's receivables turnover rate of 7.68 times corresponds to an average collection period of 48.2 days, which is reasonable considering normal credit terms. However, the more important issue here is asset productivity (turnover) instead of credit quality. This is because most of K-C's sales are to large retailers; for example, 13% of Kimberly-Clark's sales are to Wal-Mart.

Inventories turn over 6.33 times a year, resulting in an average inventory days outstanding of 59.1 days in 2005. Inventories are an important (and large) asset for companies like Kimberly-Clark. Improved turnover is always a goal so long as the company maintains sufficient inventories to meet market demand.

K-C's long-term operating assets are turning over 1.35 times a year, which is about average for publicly traded companies. The issue with respect to LTOAT is throughput, and K-C does not discuss this aspect of its business in its financial filings.

K-C's trade accounts payable turnover is 10.62, resulting in an average payable days outstanding of 35.6 days. Since payables represent a low cost source of financing, we would prefer to see its days payable lengthened so long as K-C is not endangering its relationships with suppliers.

Credit Analysis

Credit analysis is an important part of a complete company analysis. Following is a selected set of measures for 2005 that can help us gauge the relative credit standing of Kimberly-Clark ($ millions):

Current ratio ($4,783.1/$4,642.9)	1.03
Quick ratio ([$364 + $2,101.9]/$4,642.9)	0.53
Total liabilities/Equity* ([$4,642.9 + $2,594.7 + $1,782.6 + $572.9]/[$394.5 + $757.4 + $5,558.2])	1.43
Long-term debt/Equity ($2,594.7/[$394.5 + $757.4 + $5,558.2])	0.39
Earnings before interest and taxes/Interest expense ($2,310.6 − $179.0 + $190.2)/$190.2	12.21
Net operating cash flows/Total liabilities ($2,311.8/[$4,642.9 + $2,594.7 + $1,782.6 + $572.9])	0.24

* Minority interest and preferred securities of subsidiary treated as equity.

K-C's current and quick ratios are not particularly high, and both have decreased slightly over the past two years (not shown here). These ratios do not imply any excess liquidity, and probably do not suggest any room for a further decrease in liquidity.

K-C's financial leverage, as reflected in both the liability-to-equity and long-term-debt-to-equity ratios, is slightly above the median for all publicly traded companies. Normally, this is cause for some concern. However, Kimberly-Clark has strong operating and free cash flows that mitigate this concern.

K-C's times interest earned ratio of 12.21 is healthy, indicating a sufficient buffer to protect creditors if earnings decline. It also has relatively little off-balance-sheet exposure. Thus, we do not have any serious concerns about K-C's ability to repay its maturing debt obligations.

Summarizing Profitability and Creditworthiness

An increasingly competitive environment has diminished Kimberly-Clark's gross profit margin. Operating expense reductions have not offset this decline. However, the company has been able to maintain its NOPAT as a result of a decline in its effective tax rate (which is not likely to be persistent). Its level of net operating asset turnover is acceptable, although not stellar. K-C does not provide sufficient information for us to further assess the throughput performance of its operating assets. Finally, its leverage, although higher than average, is not of great concern given K-C's strong cash flows.

ADJUSTING AND FORECASTING FINANCIAL STATEMENT NUMBERS

L03 Adjust and forecast financial statements.

The valuation of K-C's common stock requires forecasts of NOPAT and NOA over a forecast horizon period and a forecast terminal period. One possible approach is to project individual income statement and balance sheet items using the methodology we discuss in Module 11. However, in this section, we employ the parsimonious method of forecasting NOPAT and NOA using only sales forecasts, profit margins, and asset turnover rates-described in a latter section of Module 11. We first consider some possible adjustments to the financial statements before commencing the forecasting process.

Adjusting Accounting Numbers

The two main targets of our parsimonious forecasting process are NOPAT and NOA. This means that we are primarily concerned with income statement and balance sheet adjustments that affect these two financial statements. Some adjustments we might consider for this purpose are shown in Exhibit 13.6 for **Kimberly-Clark.**

1. K-C reduced its allowance for uncollectible accounts from 2.4% to 1.7% of gross receivables. In 2005, bad debt expense was $8.9 million, compared with write-offs of uncollectible accounts amounting to $15 million. Our adjustment recognizes an additional $6.1 million so that the allowance for uncollectible accounts will not be further eroded.[4]

2. K-C recognized $20.7 million of expense relating to stock options under prior GAAP. Footnotes reveal that new accounting standards related to stock options will require K-C to recognize an additional $36.4 million.

---

[4] Technically, the increase in the projected bad debt expense will result in an increase in the allowance for uncollectible accounts and a consequent reduction in accounts receivable, net. We have not made this adjustment to the balance sheet so as not to overcomplicate the exposition.

3. Capitalization of operating leases will remove rent expense and substitute depreciation expense (an operating item that affects NOPAT) and interest expense (a nonoperating item that does not affect NOPAT). The $220 million leased asset will be depreciated over the remaining 8 years of the lease life, resulting in depreciation expense of $27.5 million. The operating lease adjustment removes the company's $85.7 million of projected minimum rent payments, and substitutes the $27.5 million of depreciation expense. This increases NOPAT by $58.2 million.

EXHIBIT 13.6	Kimberly-Clark Adjustments for NOPAT and NOA	
Adj.	**($ millions)**	
	Reported NOPAT	$ 1,949.9
1	Bad debt expense	(6.1)
2	Stock option expense.	(36.4)
3	Rent expense, net of depreciation expense.	58.2
4	AJCA tax adjustment	53.2
5	Synthetic fuel partnerships.	(55.3)
	Adjusted NOPAT.	$ 1,963.5
	Reported NOA	$10,735.9
6	Capitalization of operating leases	220.0
7	Funded status of pension.	(806.9)
8	Equity method investments	539.4
	Adjusted NOA.	$10,688.4

4. The American Jobs Creation Act (AJCA) increases income taxes by 2.8 percentage points (as a percent of pre-tax income). This is a transitory item. NOPAT has been increased by 2.7% of pre-tax income for 2005, which amounts to $53.2 million ($1,968.9 million × .027 = $53.2).

5. The synthetic fuel partnerships increase NOPAT by $55.3 million. The company discloses that, due to the expected rise in oil prices, K-C does not expect these benefits to continue. Our adjustment reduces NOPAT by that amount.

6. The capitalization of operating leases adds $220 million to net operating assets (the lease obligation is a nonoperating liability).

7. Recognition of the funded status of K-C's pension plan will decrease NOA by $806.9 million (consisting of a $364.6 increase in pension liability and a $442.3 million decrease in pension assets). Pension obligations are an operating liability.

8. K-C reports $457.8 million relating to equity investments in companies that have assets of $1,561.8 million and current liabilities of $564.6 million (we assume that the long-term liabilities of these companies are nonoperating such as long-term notes and bonds). Upon consolidation, these companies would add $539.4 million ($1,561.8 million − $564.6 million − $457.8 million) of net operating assets (NOPAT will be unaffected as these investments are already accounted for using the equity method and this income is included in our NOPAT calculation).

Forecasting Accounting Numbers

The adjusted NOPAT and NOA amounts become the starting point for our forecasts that are used to estimate the value of K-C common stock. The simplified forecast process uses three inputs: sales growth, NOPAT margin, and NOA turnover. Our adjusted net operating profit margin (NOPM) is 12.35% ($1,963.5 million/$15,902.6 million) and the adjusted net operating asset turnover based on year-end NOA (NOAT) is 1.49 ($15,902.6 million/$10,688.4 million). (Note: For forecasting, turnover metrics use year-end figures; see Module 11.)

The sales growth forecast is complicated by the foreign currency exchange effects that we discussed earlier. K-C's sales increased by 5.4% in 2005, down from 7.5% the previous year, but 2% of this increase resulted from the weaker $US. The "real" increase was just over 3% in 2005, which is the growth rate we use in our sales projections during the horizon period. We assume a 1% growth rate in the terminal period. Both of these rates are on the conservative side. We also use a NOPM of 12.35% and a NOAT of 1.49 consistent with actual 2005 rates (as adjusted).

Exhibit 13.7 shows forecasts of Kimberly-Clark's sales, net operating profit after tax (NOPAT), and net operating assets (NOA)-these follow from our forecasting process explained in Module 11 and include the terminal year forecast assuming a terminal growth rate of 1%.

EXHIBIT 13.7	Kimberly-Clark Forecasts of Sales, NOPAT, and NOA					
	Current	Horizon Period				Terminal
(In millions)	2005	2006	2007	2008	2009	Year
Sales..........	$15,902.6	$16,380	$16,871	$17,377	$17,899	$18,078
NOPAT	1,963.5	2,023	2,084	2,146	2,210	2,233
NOA	10,688.4	10,993	11,323	11,662	12,013	12,133

VALUING EQUITY SECURITIES

L04 Describe and illustrate the valuation of firm equity and stock.

This section estimates the values of Kimberly-Clark's equity and common stock per share.

Discounted Cash Flow Valuation

Exhibit 13.8 shows the discounted cash flow (DCF) model results. In addition to the forecast assumptions from the prior section, these results assume a discount (WACC) rate of 6.5%, a terminal growth rate of 1%, shares outstanding of 461.5 million, and net nonoperating obligations (NNO) of $4,327.4 million.[5]

EXHIBIT 13.8	Kimberly-Clark Discounted Cash Flow (DCF) Valuation					
(In millions, except per share values and discount factors)	Current 2005	Horizon Period				Terminal Period
		2006	2007	2008	2009	
Increase in NOA...................		$ 304.6	$ 330.0	$ 339.0	$ 351.0	$ 120.0
FCFF (NOPAT − Increase in NOA).....		1,718.4	1,754.0	1,807.0	1,860.0	2,113.0
Discount factor [$1/(1 + r_w)^t$]		0.93897	0.88166	0.82785	0.77732	
Present value of horizon FCFF........		1,613.5	1,546.4	1,495.9	1,445.8	
Cum. present value of horizon FCFF ...	$ 6,101.7					
Present value of terminal FCFF	29,863.2[a]					
Total firm value	35,964.9					
Less NNO......................	4,327.4					
Firm equity value	$31,637.5					
Shares outstanding	461.5					
Stock value per share.............	$ 68.55					

[a] Computed as $\dfrac{\left|\dfrac{\$2{,}113.0\ \text{million}}{0.065 - 0.01}\right|}{(1.065)^4}$

Residual Operating Income Valuation

Exhibit 13.9 reports estimates of the values of Kimberly-Clark's equity and common stock per share using the residual operating income (ROPI) model.

---

[5] NNO can be inferred from NOA minus equity. Kimberly-Clark's reported and adjusted balance sheet (reflecting the adjustments from Exhibit 13.6) is shown below. The consolidation of equity method investee companies (EMI) requires recognition of the minority interest, $457.8 million, relating to the proportion of the EMI net assets not owned by K-C; and equity is reduced by the $806.9 million reduction of AOCI resulting from recognition of the pension liability ($ millions).

	Reported	Adjustments	Adjusted
NOA	$10,735.9	− $47.5 (net)**	$10,688.4
Equity*	6,710.1	+$457.8 (EMI) − $806.9 (Pension)	6,361.0
NNO	$ 4,025.8		$ 4,327.4

* Includes stockholders' equity, minority interest and preferred stock of subsidiary.

** From Exhibit 13.6.

EXHIBIT 13.9	Kimberly-Clark Residual Operating Income (ROPI) Valuation					
(In millions, except per share values and discount factors)	**Current 2005**	**Horizon Period**				**Terminal Period**
		2006	**2007**	**2008**	**2009**	
ROPI [NOPAT − (NOA$_{Beg}$ × r_w)]		$ 1,328.3	$ 1,369.5	$ 1,410.0	$ 1,453.0	$1,452.0
Discount factor [1/(1 + r_w)^t]		0.93897	0.88166	0.82785	0.77732	
Present value of horizon ROPI		1,247.2	1,207.4	1,167.3	1,129.4	
Cum. present value of horizon ROPI . . .	$ 4,751.3					
Present value of terminal ROPI[a]	20,521.2					
NOA	10,688.4					
Total firm value	35,960.9					
Less NNO	4,327.4					
Firm equity value	$ 31,633.5					
Shares outstanding	461.5					
Stock value per share	$ 68.55					

[a] Computed as $\dfrac{\left(\dfrac{\$1{,}452.0 \text{ million}}{0.065 - 0.01}\right)}{(1.065)^4}$.

We estimate Kimberly-Clark's equity value at $31,633.5 million as of December 2005, which is equivalent to a per share value estimate of $69.55. As expected, equity value estimates are identical (difference due to rounding) for both models (because K-C is assumed to be in a steady state, that is, NOPAT and NOA growing at the same rate and, therefore, RNOA is constant).

The closing stock price on December 31, 2005, for Kimberly-Clark (KMB) was $59.65 per share. Our model's estimates, therefore, suggest that K-C stock is undervalued as of that date. As it turns out, this valuation proved prophetic as its stock price increased to the mid- to upper-$60s subsequent to that date as shown in the following graph:

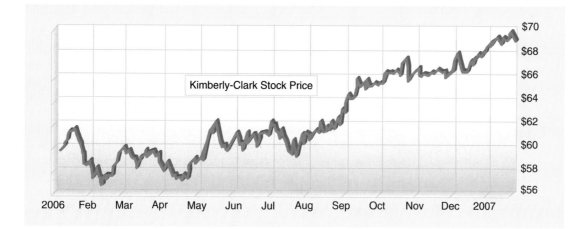

Overall, this module presents a financial accounting analysis and interpretation of Kimberly-Clark's performance and position. It illustrates many of the key financial reporting topics covered in the book. We review the company's financial statements and notes, forecast key accounts, and conclude with estimates of K-C's equity value.

The Kimberly-Clark case provides an opportunity for us to apply many of the procedures conveyed in the book in a comprehensive manner. With analyses of additional companies, we become more comfortable with, and knowledgeable of, variations in financial reporting, which enhances our analysis and business decision-making skills. Our analysis of a company must go beyond the accounting numbers to include competitor and economic factors, and we must appreciate that estimation and judgment are key ingredients in financial accounting. This comprehensive case, textbook, and course provide us with skills necessary to effectively use financial accounting and to advance our business and career opportunities.

Managerial Accounting for MBAs

LEARNING OBJECTIVES

LO1 Contrast financial and managerial accounting and explain how managerial accounting is used by internal decision makers. (p. 14-3)

LO2 Explain how an organization's mission, goals, and strategies affect managerial accounting. (p. 14-5)

LO3 Discuss the factors determining changes in the nature of business competition. (p. 14-11)

LO4 Differentiate among structural, organizational, and activity cost drivers. (p. 14-12)

LO5 Explain the nature of the ethical dilemmas managers and accountants confront. (p. 14-15)

STRATEGIC COST MANAGEMENT

A corporate chief executive officer recently observed, "If you don't have competition, you're in the wrong business." This observation captures an essential element of the modern manager's environment. No matter how well a manager's organization serves customers, manages costs, or innovates, another firm is trying to do all of those things better. Firms employ various strategies to compete in product or service markets. The strategies employed by the technology firms Hewlett-Packard and Dell Computer in the past few years illustrate two contrasting competitive approaches.

The chief executives of Hewlett-Packard (HP) and Compaq announced in 2001 that their firms planned to merge in a $25 billion deal. At the time the proposed merger was announced, the combined firms held market share leadership positions in personal computers, servers, and printers. The merged firm would become the largest computer hardware firm in the world. HP management intended to rely on the efficiencies of size to provide an array of contemporary hardware, software, and service solutions for clients. HP managers stressed the importance of research and development expenditures to support a stream of product and service innovations.

Citing the benefits of being first to market with an innovative product, former CEO Carly Fiorina discussed HP's success in the high-margin handheld computer appliance market. In her view, a business model without innovation was not sustainable. However, several powerful HP shareholders opposed the merger. These shareholders commented that Compaq's position and profitability in PCs was in jeopardy since Dell had

made the PC market "a cost game." They also felt that the merger would dilute HP's successful printer business. Nevertheless, the HP-Compaq merger went forward.

With a personal computer market share of about 15 percent, Dell relentlessly pursues market share with a high-volume, low-margin strategy. Managers at Dell periodically cut prices in the personal computer market—a competitive strategy based on the firm's cost and efficiency advantage. Since rivals typically match Dell's price cuts, these reduced prices take their toll on firms' profitability. Within this overall business model, Dell constantly refines it's operating polices to enhance efficiency. By taking orders directly from customers—the majority of whom order online; limiting operating expenses; holding little inventory; and spending little revenue on research and development, Dell has solidified its position as the personal computer market's cost leader.

Competitors comment that Dell is playing a dangerous game in a market where profit margins don't rebound since customers are accustomed to constantly lower-cost technology. Dell's managers respond with their intention to extend this business model to the markets for networking, storage, and computer services.

The competition between Hewlett-Packard and Dell continues to test both management teams' abilities to succeed with their respective business models: innovation and differentiation versus low cost and efficiency. Managers at these and other firms often employ an array of managerial accounting tools to assist them in making these strategic decisions.

Sources: *10-K Reports, The Economist, Business Week,* and *Fortune.*[1]

---

[1] Based on: 10-K reports from Hewlett-Packard, Dell Computer, and Compaq; "Sheltering from the Storm," *The Economist,* September 8, 2001, p. 34; Peter Burrows and Andrew Park, "Where's the Upside?" *Business Week,* September 17, 2001, pp. 40–43; Eric Nee, "The Hard Truth Behind a Shotgun Wedding," *Fortune,* October 1, 2001, pp. 109–114; Andrew Park and Peter Burrows, "Dell the Conqueror," *Business Week,* September 24, 2001, pp. 92–102, and "A Stunning Reversal for HP's Marriage Plans," *Business Week,* November 19, 2001, p. 42; and Janice Revell, "A Marriage Only Dell Could Love," *Fortune,* October 1, 2001, p. 184.

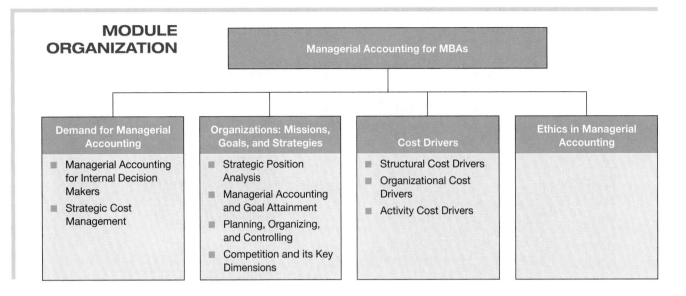

This module provides an overview of the factors that make managerial accounting increasingly important to successful businesses. We begin by distinguishing between financial and managerial (also called *management*) accounting and by investigating how competitive strategy affects the way organizations, such as Hewlett-Packard and Dell, use managerial accounting information. Next, we explore how the emergence of global competition and changes in technology have increased the need to understand managerial accounting concepts. We also provide an overview of factors that influence costs in an organization and how these factors have changed in recent years. Finally, we consider how managerial accounting assists employees in making better decisions, and we examine the interrelationships among measurement, management, and ethics.

DEMAND FOR MANAGERIAL ACCOUNTING

LO1 Contrast financial and managerial accounting and explain how managerial accounting is used by internal decision makers.

As discussed in the previous Modules of this text, **financial accounting** is an information-processing system that generates general-purpose reports of financial operations (income statement and statement of cash flows) and financial position (balance sheet) for an organization. Although financial accounting is used by decision makers inside and outside the firm, financial accounting typically emphasizes external users, such as security investors, analysts and lenders. Adding to this external orientation are external financial reporting requirements determined by law and generally accepted accounting principles.

Managers often use income statements and balance sheets as a starting point in evaluating and planning the firm's overall activities. Managers learn a great deal by performing a comparative analysis of their firm and competing firms. Corporate goals are often stated using financial accounting numbers such as net income, or ratios such as return on investment and earnings per common share.

Despite financial accounting's importance, internal decision makers often find it of limited value in managing day-to-day operating activities. They often complain that financial accounting information is too aggregated, prepared too late, based on irrelevant past costs, and not action oriented. For example, the costs of all items produced and sold or all services rendered are summarized in a single line in most financial statements, making it impossible to determine the costs of individual products or services. Financial accounting procedures, acceptable for costing inventories as a whole, often produce misleading information when applied to individual products. Even when they are accurately determined, the costs of individual products or services are rarely detailed enough to provide the information needed for decisions concerning the factors that influence costs. Financial accounting reports, seldom prepared more than once a month, are not timely enough for use in the management of day-to-day activities that cause excess costs. Finally, financial accounting reports are mainly based on historical costs rather than on current or future costs. Managers are more interested in future costs than in historical costs such as last year's depreciation. While financial accounting information is useful in making some management decisions, its primary emphasis is not on internal decision making.

Managerial Accounting for Internal Decision Makers

Managerial accounting provides an information framework to organize and evaluate data in light of an organization's goals. This information is directed to managers and other persons inside the organization. Managerial accounting reports can be designed to meet the information needs of internal decision makers. Top management may need only summary information prepared once a month for each business unit. An engineer responsible for hourly production scheduling may need continuously updated and detailed information concerning the cost of alternative ways of producing a product.

Because of the intensity of competition and the shorter life cycles of new products and services, many influential business executives believe managerial accounting is crucial to company success. **Managerial accounting** is concerned with obtaining and analyzing relevant information to help achieve organizational goals. Every manager must understand the financial implications of decisions. While accountants are available to assist in obtaining and evaluating relevant information, individual managers are responsible for requesting information, analyzing it, and making the final decisions. The increased use of accounting information is further examined in Research Insight that follows.

RESEARCH INSIGHT   **Managerial Accounting Is a Key to Success**

After studying several highly competitive, world-class companies, noted managerial accounting guru Robin Cooper observed that "with the emergence of the lean enterprise and increased global competition, companies must learn to be more proactive in the way they manage costs. For many, survival is dependent upon their abilities to develop sophisticated cost management systems that create intense pressure to reduce costs." He also observed that "as cost management becomes more critical to a company's survival, two trends emerge. First, new forms of cost management are required, and second, more individuals in the firm become actively involved in the cost management process." Cooper suggests that with the growing number of managers involved in the cost management process, there is an increased need for managerial accounting information (and people who know how to use it).[2]

Managerial accounting information exists to serve the needs of management. Hence, it is subject to a cost-benefit analysis and should be developed only if the perceived benefits exceed the costs of development and use. Also, while financial measures are often used in managerial accounting, they are not used to the exclusion of other measures. Money is simply a convenient way of expressing events in a form suitable to summary analysis. When this is not possible or appropriate, nonfinancial measures are used. Time, for example, is often an important element of quality or service. Hence, many performance measures focus on time, for example:

- **Federal Express** keeps detailed information on the time required to make deliveries.
- Fire departments and police departments measure the response time to emergency calls.
- **American Air Lines** monitors the number of on-time departures and arrivals.

No external standards (such as requirements of the Securities and Exchange Commission) are imposed on information provided to internal users. Consequently, managerial accounting information may be quite subjective. In developing a budget, management is more interested in a subjective prediction of next year's sales than in an objective report on last year's sales. The significant differences between financial and managerial accounting are summarized in Exhibit 14.1.

Strategic Cost Management

During recent years, the rapid introduction of improved products has shortened the market lives of products. Some products, such as personal computers, can be obsolete within two or three years after introduction. At the same time, the increased use of complex automated equipment makes it difficult to change

---

[2] Robin Cooper, "Look Out, Management Accountants," *Management Accounting,* May 1996, pp. 20–26.

EXHIBIT 14.1	Differences Between Financial and Managerial Accounting
Financial Accounting	**Managerial Accounting**
Reporting system for business activities	Information system for decision making
Information for internal *and* external users	Information for internal users
General-purpose financial statements	Special-purpose information and reports
Statements are highly aggregated	Information is aggregated or detailed, depending on need
Relatively long reporting periods	Reporting periods are long or short, depending on need
Report on past decisions	Oriented toward current and future decisions
Adheres to legal requirements	Not required by law
Follows generally accepted accounting principles	Not constrained by generally accepted accounting principles
Must conform to external standards	No external standards
Emphasizes objective data	Encourages subjective data, if relevant

production procedures after production begins. Combining short product life cycles with automated production results in an environment where most costs are determined by decisions made before production begins (decisions concerning product design and production procedures).

To ensure providing products and services that the customers want at the lowest possible price, businesses are working more closely with customers and suppliers. In examining challenges and opportunities, Hewlett-Packard routinely brings customers and suppliers together to discuss "business ecosystems" for products or services. "Most of the business managers are so busy minding their current businesses that it's hard to step out and see threats or opportunities," says Srinivas Sukumar, director of strategic planning for HP Labs. "By looking at the entire ecosystem, it provides a broad perspective to them. It gets people out of their boxes."[3]

In response to these trends, a strategic approach to managerial accounting, referred to as *strategic cost management* has emerged. Strategic cost management is a blending of three themes:

1. **Cost driver analysis**—the study of factors that cause or influence costs.
2. **Strategic position analysis**—an examination of an organization's basic way of competing to sell products or services.
3. **Value chain analysis**—the study of value-producing activities, stretching from basic raw materials to the final consumer of a product or service.[4]

We define **strategic cost management** as making decisions concerning specific cost drivers within the context of an organization's business strategy, internal value chain, and position in a larger value chain stretching from the development and use of resources to final consumers. Cost driver analysis and business strategy, including strategic position analysis, are introduced in this module. Value chain analysis is discussed in Module 23.

ORGANIZATIONS: MISSIONS, GOALS, AND STRATEGIES

LO2 Explain how an organization's mission, goals, and strategies affect managerial accounting.

An organization's **mission** is the basic purpose toward which its activities are directed. Organizations vary widely in their missions. According to the former chairman and CEO, the mission of The Coca-Cola Company is "to create value over time for the owners of our business." He went on to say:

Our society is based on democratic capitalism. In such a society, people create specific institutions to help meet specific needs. Governments are created to help meet social needs. . . Businesses such as ours are created to meet economic needs. The common thread between these institutions is that they can flourish only when they stay focused on the specific need they were created to fulfill. When institu-

---

[3] John A. Bryne, "Strategic Planning," *Business Week,* August 26, 1996, p. 50.

[4] John K. Shank, "Strategic Cost Management: New Wine, or Just New Bottles?" *Journal of Management Accounting Research,* Fall 1989, p. 50.

tions try to broaden their scope beyond their natural realms, when for example they try to become all things to all people, they fail.[5]

The CEO of Coca-Cola believed that Coca-Cola best contributes to society and helps government and other organizations fulfill their missions by staying focused on its shareholders. He believed this keeps a company financially healthy, and a healthy company fills its responsibilities. Conversely, a bankrupt company is incapable of paying taxes, employing people, serving customers, supporting charitable institutions, or making other contributions to society.

We frequently distinguish between organizations on the basis of profit motive. **For-profit organizations** have profit as a primary mission, whereas **not-for-profit organizations** do not have profit as a primary mission. Clearly, the Coca-Cola Company is a for-profit organization, whereas the City of Chicago and the Red Cross are not-for-profit organizations. (The term *nonprofit* is frequently used to refer to what we have identified as not-for-profit organizations.) Regardless of whether a profit motive exists, organizations must use resources wisely. Every dollar United Way spends for administrative salaries is a dollar that cannot be used to support charitable activities. Not-for-profit organizations, including governments, can go bankrupt if they are unable to meet their financial obligations. All organizations, for-profit and not-for-profit, should use managerial accounting concepts to ensure that resources are used wisely.

A **goal** is a definable, measurable objective. Based on the organization's mission, management sets a number of goals. The mission of a paper mill located in a small town is to provide quality paper products in order to earn a profit for its owners. The paper mill's goals might include earning an annual profit equal to 10 percent of average total assets, maintaining annual dividends of $2 per share of common stock, developing a customer reputation for above-average quality and service, providing steady employment for area residents, and meeting or exceeding environmental standards.

A clear statement of mission and well-defined goals provides an organization with an identity and unifying purpose, thereby ensuring that all employees are heading in the same direction. Having developed a mission and a set of goals, employees are more apt to make decisions that move the organization toward its defined purpose.

A **strategy** is a course of action that will assist in achieving one or more goals. Much of this text will focus on the financial aspects of selecting strategies to achieve goals. For example, if an organization's goal is to improve product quality, possible strategies for achieving this goal include investing in new equipment, implementing additional quality inspections, prescreening suppliers, reducing batch size, redesigning products, training employees, and rearranging the shop floor. Managerial accounting information will assist in determining which of the many alternative strategies for achieving the goal of quality improvement are cost effective. The distinction between mission, goals, and strategies is illustrated in Exhibit 14.2.

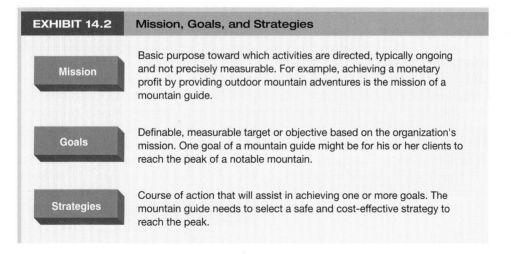

EXHIBIT 14.2   Mission, Goals, and Strategies

Mission
Basic purpose toward which activities are directed, typically ongoing and not precisely measurable. For example, achieving a monetary profit by providing outdoor mountain adventures is the mission of a mountain guide.

Goals
Definable, measurable target or objective based on the organization's mission. One goal of a mountain guide might be for his or her clients to reach the peak of a notable mountain.

Strategies
Course of action that will assist in achieving one or more goals. The mountain guide needs to select a safe and cost-effective strategy to reach the peak.

[5] Roberto Goizueta, "Why Shareholder Value?" *CEO Series Issue No. 13,* February 1997, Center for the Study of American Business, Washington University in St. Louis, p. 2.

Strategic Position Analysis

In competitive environments, managers must make a fundamental decision concerning their organization's goal for positioning itself in comparison to competitors. This goal is referred to as the organization's **strategic position.** Much of the organization's strategy depends on this strategic positioning goal. Michael Porter, a highly regarded expert on business strategy, has identified three possible strategic positions that lead to business success:[6]

1. Cost leadership
2. Product or service differentiation
3. Market niche

According to Porter, cost leadership

> requires aggressive construction of efficient-scale facilities, vigorous pursuit of cost reductions from experience, tight cost and overhead control, avoidance of marginal customer accounts, and cost minimization in areas like R&D [research and development], service, sales force, advertising, and so on. A great deal of managerial attention to cost control is necessary to achieve these aims. Low cost relative to competitors becomes the theme running through the entire strategy, though quality, service, and other areas cannot be ignored.[7]

Achieving cost leadership allows an organization to achieve higher profits selling at the same price as competitors or by allowing the firm to aggressively compete on the basis of price while remaining profitable. One of the first companies to successfully use a cost leadership strategy was **Carnegie Steel Company**.

> Carnegie's operating strategy was to push his own direct costs below his competitors so that he could charge prices that would always ensure enough demand to keep his plants running at full capacity. This strategy prompted him to require frequent information showing his direct costs in relation to those of his competitors. Possessing that information and secure in the knowledge that his costs were the lowest in the industry, Carnegie then mercilessly cut prices during economic recessions. While competing firms went under, he still made profits. In periods of prosperity, when customers' demands exceeded the industry's capacity to produce, Carnegie joined others in raising prices.[8]

Southwest Airlines and **Dell** are current examples of successful businesses competing with a strategy of cost leadership. Although **Amazon.com** uses the Internet to differentiate itself from traditional booksellers, its primary strategic position is price leadership.

Product or service differentiation involves creating something that is perceived as unique and worth a premium price. Possible approaches to differentiation include a market image (the **Aflac** duck and the **Coca-Cola** bottle), technological leadership (**Hewlett-Packard** printers), and customer service (**Nordstrom** and **Lands' End**).

Even when differentiation is a strategic theme, costs must be managed. For this strategy to succeed, the resulting price premium must exceed the seller's cost of differentiation yet not exceed the differential value to the buyer. Although **Barnes & Noble's** strategic position is product differentiation achieved by providing customers with product availability, a knowledgeable staff, and a pleasant shopping environment, management must ensure that prices do not rise too far above those of **Amazon.com**.

Conversely, while an organization might compete primarily on the basis of price, management must take care to ensure their product or service remains attuned to changing customer needs and preferences. In the early twentieth century, **General Motors** employed a differentiation strategy, focusing on the rapid introduction of technological change in new automobile designs to overcome the market dominance of the Model T produced by **Ford Motor Company**. While successfully following a cost leadership strategy for years, Ford made the mistake of excluding other considerations such as vehicle performance and customer desires for different colors.[9] The Business Insight on the following page reports on the success

---

[6] Michael E. Porter, *Competitive Strategy* (New York: The Free Press, 1980), p. 35.

[7] Porter, p. 35.

[8] H. Thomas Johnson and Robert S. Kaplan, *Relevance Lost: The Rise and Fall of Management Accounting* (Boston: Harvard Business School Press, 1987), pp. 33–34.

[9] William J. Abernathy and Kenneth Wayne, "Limits of the Learning Curve," *Harvard Business Review,* September–October 1974, pp. 109–119.

of a Massachusetts textile mill that has become a world-class competitor through a product differentiation strategy with attention to competition on the basis of quality and service.

BUSINESS INSIGHT   **Product Differentiation and Loyalty**

Most textile makers fled Massachusetts long ago due to scarce land, strict government regulation, high taxes, and high labor costs. While Malden Mills was tempted to move, management elected instead to follow a strategy of producing high-tech specialty fabrics rather than one of producing low-margin "commodity" products such as plain polyester sheets. Management believed that this strategy would allow them to pay higher labor costs while utilizing the skills of loyal employees.

Malden's first breakthrough came from working with outdoor garment-maker Patagonia to improve Polarfleece®, a double-faced fleece material originally developed by Patagonia. While the success of the new Polarfleece® attracted imitations, Malden Mills stayed ahead of the competition by continuing to develop new products, including Polartec®, an active-wear fabric used in high-priced clothing.

To improve quality and control costs, profits have been reinvested in the business. The business has gone from labor intensive to capital intensive and semiautomatic. Automation allows Malden to produce more fabric in more styles and colors. Even with automation, financial success, reflected in an increase in its sales, has also resulted in an increase in its labor force.

Illustrative of company and employee loyalty is the response to a fire that destroyed a significant portion of Malden Mills' factory complex and left 1,400 workers fearing for their jobs. The company president indicated Malden Mills would continue paychecks and health benefits and rebuild the plant. When asked why, he responded, "It was the right thing to do." To which an employee commented, "And that is the kind of man I want to work for."[10]

The third possible strategic position according to Porter, focuses on a specific market niche such as a buyer group, segment of the product line, or geographic market and

> rests on the premise that the firm is thus able to serve its narrow strategic target more effectively or efficiently than competitors who are competing more broadly. As a result, the firm achieves either differentiation from better meeting the needs of the particular target, or lower costs in serving the target, or both. Even though the focus strategy does not achieve low costs or differentiation for the market as a whole, it does achieve one or both of these positions vis-à-vis its narrow market target.[11]

Following a focused strategy, regional breweries that cater to local taste preferences, such as Iron City Beer® in Pittsburgh, have prospered, while Miller®, Coors®, and Budweiser® dominate the U.S. market. Learjet follows a focused strategy in designing and building corporate aircraft, leaving the market for larger passenger aircraft to firms such as Boeing and the market for smaller private planes to firms such as Piper Aircraft.

According to Porter, firms that do not set one of these competitive strategies as a goal or that try to be all things to all people are doomed to be "stuck in the middle." Unable to effectively compete on the basis of price or differentiation in the market as a whole or in a particular market niche, firms stuck in the middle are doomed to low profitability.

The bankruptcy of Montgomery Ward is an example of the consequences of being stuck in the middle. Two decades ago, Montgomery Ward and Sears Roebuck were America's largest mall-based retailers. In response to low-cost competitors such as Wal-Mart and "category killers" such as Circuit City, Sears decided to emphasize established brands, service, and pleasant surroundings. Wards elected to reduce prices and costs by stocking a lower grade of merchandise. Unfortunately, Ward ended up "stuck in the middle," unable to compete with the low prices of Wal-Mart or the higher grade of merchandise and service offered by retailers such as Sears and J.C. Penney.[12]

The Research Insight on the following page considers cost leadership and product or service differentiation among the working principles for twenty-first century corporations.

---

[10] Susan Diesenhouse, "A Textile Mill Thrives by Breaking All the Rules," *The New York Times,* July 24, 1994, p. F5, and a CBS news report of December 25, 1995.

[11] Porter, pp. 38–39.

[12] Kevin Mundt, "Why Sears Survived—and Ward and Woolworth's Didn't," *The Wall Street Journal,* July 28, 1997, p. A18.

A *Business Week* editorial reinforced the importance of competing on the basis of a business strategy of price or differentiation. However, recognizing the transitory nature of differentiation in a competitive environment, the editorial used the term "innovation" in place of "differentiation." According to Business Week, the first three working principles of the twenty-first century corporation follow:[13]

1. *Everything gets cheaper faster.* "The Net destroys corporate pricing power. It allows customers, suppliers, and partners to compare prices from 100 or 1,000 sources, not just two or three, and erases market inefficiencies. It rapidly commoditizes all that is new, reducing prices fast."

2. *Cutting costs is the answer.* "In an economic universe of downward pressure on margins, one path to profitability will be to reduce expenses."

3. *Innovation builds profits.* "There is one way for corporations to circumvent principle No. 1 and raise prices. In an information economy, companies can gain an edge through new ideas and products." This advantage is temporary, so corporations following this strategy must innovate rapidly and continuously.

The editorial asserts that human capital is the only asset. In a twenty-first century corporation, creativity is the sole source of growth and wealth. Consequently, the "value of education raises exponentially in an economy based on ideas and analytic thinking."

Managerial Accounting and Goal Attainment

A major purpose of managerial accounting is to support the achievement of goals. Hence, determining an organization's strategic position goal has implications for the operation of an organization's managerial accounting system.

Careful budgeting and cost control with frequent and detailed performance reports are critical with a goal of cost leadership. When the product is difficult to distinguish from that of competitors, price is the primary basis of competition. Under these circumstances, everyone in the organization should continuously apply managerial accounting concepts to achieve and maintain cost leadership. The managerial accounting system should constantly compare actual costs with budgeted costs and signal the existence of significant differences. A simplified version of a *performance report* for costs during a budget period is as follows:

Budgeted (planned) Costs	Actual Costs	Deviation from Budget	Percent Deviation
$560,000	$595,000	$35,000 unfavorable	6.25

Frequent and detailed comparisons of actual and budgeted costs are less important when a differentiation strategy is followed. This is especially true when products have short life cycles or production is highly automated. In these situations, most costs are determined before production begins and there is little opportunity to undertake cost reduction activities thereafter.

With short product lives or automated manufacturing, exceptional care must go into the initial design of a product or service and the determination of how it will be produced or delivered. Here, detailed cost information assists in design and scheduling decisions. A simplified version of the predicted costs of producing a specialty product is as follows:

Engineering and scheduling (12 hours @ $70)	$ 840
Materials (detail omitted)	3,500
Equipment setup (2.5 hours @ $100)	250
Machine operation (9.5 hours @ $90)	855
Materials movement	150
Packing and shipping	675
Total	$6,270

---

[13] Based on "The Twenty-First Century Corporation," *Business Week,* August 28, 2000, p. 278.

When a differentiation strategy is followed, it often pays to work closely with customers to find ways to enhance the perceived value of a product or service. This leads to an analysis of costs from the customer's viewpoint. The customer may not want a costly feature. Alternatively, the customer may be willing to pay more for an additional feature that will reduce subsequent operating costs.

In designing its 777 aircraft, Boeing invited potential customers to set up offices in Boeing plants and to work with Boeing employees designing the aircraft. Many design changes were made to reduce customer costs. United Airlines, for example, convinced Boeing to move the location of the 777's fuel tanks to reduce servicing costs.

Planning, Organizing, and Controlling

The process of selecting goals and strategies to achieve these goals is often referred to as **planning.** The implementation of plans requires the development of subgoals and the assignment of responsibility to achieve subgoals to specific individuals or groups within an organization. This process of making the organization into a well-ordered whole is called **organizing.** In organizing, the authority to take action to implement plans is delegated to other managers and employees.

Developing an **organization chart** illustrating the formal relationships that exist between the elements of an organization is an important part of organizing. An organization chart for Crown Department Stores is illustrated in Exhibit 14.3. The blocks represent organizational units, and the lines represent relationships between the units. Authority flows down through the organization. Top management delegates authority to use resources for limited purposes to subordinate managers who, in turn, delegate to their subordinates more limited authority for accomplishing more structured tasks. Responsibility flows up through the organization. People at the bottom are responsible for specific tasks, but the president is responsible for the operation of the entire organization.

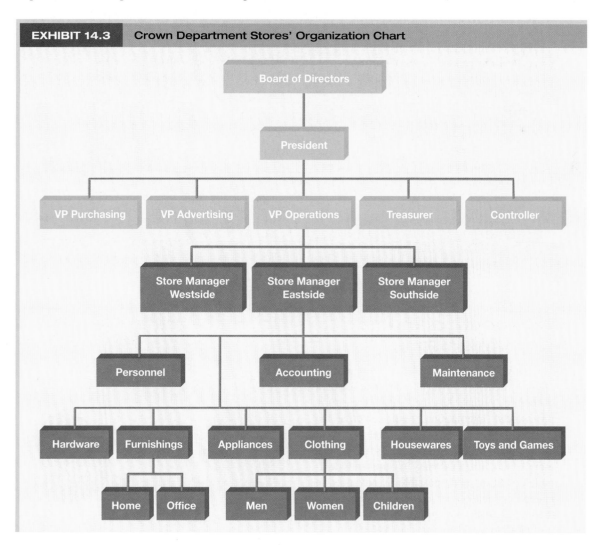

EXHIBIT 14.3   Crown Department Stores' Organization Chart

A distinction is often made between line and staff departments. *Line departments* engage in activities that create and distribute goods and services to customers. *Staff departments* exist to facilitate the activities of line departments. In Exhibit 14.3, we see that Crown Department Stores has two levels of staff organizations—corporate and store. The corporate staff departments are Purchasing, Advertising, Treasurer, and Controller. Staff departments at the store level are Personnel, Accounting, and Maintenance. All other units are line departments. A change in plans can necessitate a change in the organization. For example, Crown's plan to discontinue the sale of hardware and add an art department during the coming year will necessitate an organizational change.

Controlling is the process of ensuring that results agree with plans. A brief example of a performance report for costs was presented previously. In the process of controlling operations, actual performance is compared with plans.

With a cost leadership strategy and long-lived products, if actual results deviate significantly from plans, an attempt is made to bring operations into line with plans, or the plans are adjusted. The original plan is adjusted if it is deemed no longer appropriate because of changed circumstances.

With a differentiation strategy and short-lived products, design and scheduling personnel will consider previous errors in predicting costs as they plan new products and services. Hence, the process of controlling feeds forward into the process of planning to form a continuous cycle coordinated through the management accounting system. This cycle is illustrated in the diagram below.

MID-MODULE REVIEW

The previous discussion has focused on understanding the difference between financial and managerial accounting and the broader context of managerial accounting within a company.

Required:
Identify the statements and phrases from the following list that are primarily relevant to managerial accounting, as opposed to financial accounting:
1. Preparing periodic financial statements
2. A company's strategic position
3. Calculates earnings per share for stockholders
4. Summarizes information about past events
5. Is not based on generally accepted accounting principles
6. Must conform to external standards
7. Helping managers make decisions is its primary purpose
8. Encourages use of selective data, if relevant
9. Is tailored to the needs of the company and its managers
10. Cost driver analysis

Solution
2, 5, 7, 8, 9, and 10

Competition and its Key Dimensions

LO3 Discuss the factors determining changes in the nature of business competition.

The move away from isolated national economic systems toward an interdependent global economic system has become increasingly pronounced. International treaties, such as the North American Free Trade Agreement and the General Agreement on Tariffs and Trade, merely recognize an already existing and inevitable condition made possible by advances in telecommunications (to move data), computers (to process data into information), and transportation (to move products and people).

The labels of origins on goods (Japan, Germany, Canada, Taiwan, China, and so forth) only scratch the surface of existing global relationships. Behind labels designating a product's final assembly point are components from all over the world.

The move toward a global economy has heightened competition and reduced selling prices to such an extent that there is little or no room for error in managing costs or pricing products. Moreover, customers are not just looking for the best price. Well-informed buyers routinely search the world for the product or service that best fits their needs on the three interrelated dimensions of price/cost, quality, and service; hence, these are the three key dimensions of competition.

To customers, *price/cost* includes not only the initial purchase price but also subsequent operating and maintenance costs. To compete on the basis of price, the seller must carefully manage costs. Otherwise, reduced prices might squeeze product margins to such an extent that a sale becomes unprofitable. Hence, price competition implies cost competition.

Quality refers to the degree to which products or services meet the customer's needs. *Service* includes things such as timely delivery, helpfulness of sales personnel, and subsequent support. The Business Insight below takes a look at how Federal Express and United Parcel Service compete on the basis of quality, service, and price.

Managers of successful companies know they compete in a global market with instant communications. Because the competition is hungry and always striving to gain a competitive advantage, world-class companies must continuously struggle to improve performance on these three interrelated dimensions: price/cost, quality, and service. Throughout this text, we examine how firms successfully compete on these three dimensions.

BUSINESS INSIGHT   **FedEx and UPS Stage Battle—Customer Is Sure to Win**

To increase customer service in the express delivery business, Federal Express introduced a personal computer-based system that lets even its smallest customers go online to order pickups, print shipping labels, and track deliveries. "We have to stay ahead of the competition" was the theme of remarks describing this service by FedEx's chief information officer. Almost immediately, United Parcel Service announced a similar service. Responding to a reporter's question, the vice president of marketing at UPS, commented, "There's no question we track FedEx, just like they track us."

Both companies invest heavily in equipment and infrastructure to continue to meet increasingly tight delivery deadlines. This includes sorting hubs for air shipments and investments in new aircraft. FedEx even entered into an arrangement with the U.S. Postal Service to ship some USPS packages while the USPS placed FedEx boxes in selected Post Office buildings. A recent article in *Business Week* reports that UPS gained at least a temporary advantage by utilizing information technology to integrate its traditional strengths in ground transportation with its overnight air transportation system. According to the article, "UPS, like FedEx, still uses planes to make most (overnight) deliveries. But in the past two years, its logisticians have also figured out how to make quick mid-distance deliveries—as far as 500 miles in one night—by truck, which is much less expensive than by air." While both companies battle to improve or at least maintain profitability, customers benefit from continuously improving quality and service at lower and lower costs.[14]

COST DRIVERS

An **activity** is a unit of work. To serve a customer at a restaurant such as Outback Restaurants, a waiter or waitress might perform the following units of work:

▓ Seat customer and offer menu

▓ Take customer order

▓ Send order to kitchen

▓ Bring food to customer

LO4 Differentiate among structural, organizational, and activity cost drivers.

---

[14] Based on David Greising, "Watch Out for Flying Packages," *Business Week* (November 14, 1994), p. 40; and Charles Haddad, "Ground Wars: UPS's Rapid Ascent Leaves FedEx Scrambling," *Business Week,* May 21, 2001.

- Serve and replenish beverages
- Determine and bring bill to customer
- Collect money and give change
- Clear and reset table

Each of these is an activity, and the performance of each activity consumes resources that cost money. To manage activities and their costs, it is necessary to understand how costs respond to **cost drivers**, which are the factors that cause or influence costs.

The most basic cost driver is customer demand. Without customer demand for products or services, the organization cannot exist. To serve customers, managers and employees make a variety of decisions and take numerous actions. These decisions and actions, undertaken to satisfy customer demand, drive costs. While these cost drivers may be classified in a variety of ways, we believe that dividing them into the three categories of structural, organizational, and activity cost drivers, as summarized in Exhibit 14.4, provides a useful foundation for the study of managerial accounting.

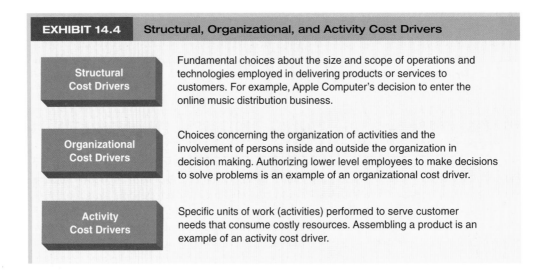

EXHIBIT 14.4	Structural, Organizational, and Activity Cost Drivers
Structural Cost Drivers	Fundamental choices about the size and scope of operations and technologies employed in delivering products or services to customers. For example, Apple Computer's decision to enter the online music distribution business.
Organizational Cost Drivers	Choices concerning the organization of activities and the involvement of persons inside and outside the organization in decision making. Authorizing lower level employees to make decisions to solve problems is an example of an organizational cost driver.
Activity Cost Drivers	Specific units of work (activities) performed to serve customer needs that consume costly resources. Assembling a product is an example of an activity cost driver.

Structural Cost Drivers

The types of activities and the costs of activities performed to satisfy customer needs are influenced by an organization's size, its location, the scope of its operations, and the technologies used. Decisions affecting structural cost drivers are made infrequently, and once made, the organization is committed to a course of action that will be difficult to change. For a chain of discount stores such as Target, possible structural cost drivers include:

- *Determining the size of stores.* This affects the variety of merchandise that can be carried and operating costs.
- *Determining the type of construction.* While a lean warehouse type of construction is less expensive, it is not an appropriate setting for selling high-fashion clothing.
- *Determining the location of stores.* Locating in a shopping mall can cost more and subject the store to mall regulations but provides for more customer traffic and shared advertising.
- *Determining types of technology to employ in stores.* A computerized system for maintaining all inventory and sales data requires a large initial investment and fixed annual operating costs while providing more current information. However, the computerized inventory and sales systems can be less expensive at high sales volumes than a less costly system relying more on clerks taking physical inventory.

Organizational Cost Drivers

Like structural cost drivers, organizational cost drivers influence costs by affecting the types of activities and the costs of activities performed to satisfy customer needs. Decisions that affect organizational cost drivers are made within the context of previous decisions affecting structural cost drivers. In a manufacturing organization, previous decisions about plant, equipment, and location are taken as a given when decisions impacting organizational cost drivers are made. Examples of organizational cost drivers at a manufacturing organization such as Harley-Davidson include making decisions regarding:

- *Working closely with a limited number of suppliers.* This can help achieve proper materials in the proper quantities at the optimal time. Developing linkages with suppliers can also result in suppliers' initiatives that improve the profitability of both organizations.

- *Providing employees with cost information and authorizing them to make decisions.* This helps improve decision speed and reduce costs while making employees more customer oriented. Production employees may, for example, offer product design suggestions that reduce manufacturing costs or reduce defects.

- *Reorganizing the existing equipment in the plant so that sequential operations are closer.* This more efficient layout reduces the cost of moving inventory between workstations.

- *Designing components of a product so they can fit together only in the correct manner.* This can reduce defects as well as assembly time and cost.

- *Manufacturing a low-volume product on low-speed, general-purpose equipment rather than high-speed, special-purpose equipment.* Assuming the special-purpose equipment is more difficult and costly to set up for a new job, this decision can increase operating time and operating cost while reducing setup time and setup cost.

Activity Cost Drivers

Activity cost drivers are specific units of work (activities) performed to serve customer needs that consume costly resources. Several examples of activities in a restaurant were mentioned previously. The customer may be outside the organization, such as a client of an advertising firm, or inside the organization, such as an accounting office that receives maintenance services. Because the performance of activities consumes resources and resources cost money, the performance of activities drives costs as illustrated in the following diagram.

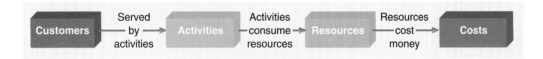

The basic decisions concerning which available activities will be used to respond to customer requests precede the actual performance of activities. At the activity level, execution of previous plans and following prescribed activities are important. All of the examples of structural and organizational cost drivers involved making decisions. In the following list of activity cost drivers for a manufacturing organization, note the absence of the decision-oriented words.

- *Placing a purchase order for raw materials*
- *Inspecting incoming raw materials*
- *Moving items being manufactured between workstations*
- *Setting up a machine to work on a product*
- *Spending machine time working on a product*
- *Spending labor time working on a product*
- *Hiring and training a new employee*
- *Packing an order for shipment*
- *Processing a sales order*
- *Shipping a product*

In managing costs, management makes choices concerning structural and organizational cost drivers. These decisions affect the types of activities required to satisfy customer needs. Because different types of activities have different costs, management's decisions ultimately affect activity costs and profitability.

| MANAGERIAL DECISION | You are the CEO |

How can you use information about structural, organizational, and activity cost drivers to help you in impementing the organization's strategy? [Answer, p. 14-17]

ETHICS IN MANAGERIAL ACCOUNTING

LO5 Explain the nature of the ethical dilemmas managers and accountants confront.

Ethics deals with the moral quality, fitness, or propriety of a course of action that can injure or benefit people. Ethics goes beyond legality, which refers to what is permitted under the law, to consider the moral quality of an action. Because situations involving ethics are not guided by well-defined rules, they are often subjective.

Although some actions are clearly ethical (working a full day in exchange for a full day's pay) and others are clearly unethical (pumping contaminants into an underground aquifer used as a source of drinking water), managers are often faced with situations that do not fall clearly into either category such as the following:

- Accelerating shipments at the end of the quarter to improve current earnings.
- Keeping inventory that is unlikely to be used so as to avoid recording a loss.
- Purchasing supplies from a relative or friend rather than seeking bids.
- Basing a budget on an overly optimistic sales forecast.
- Assigning some costs of Contract A to Contract B to avoid an unfavorable performance report on Contract A.

Many ethical dilemmas involve actions that are perceived to have desirable short-run consequences and highly probable undesirable long-run consequences. The ethical action is to face an undesirable situation now to avoid a worse situation later, yet the decision maker prefers to believe that things will work out in the long run, be overly concerned with the consequences of not doing well in the short run, or simply not care about the future because the problem will then belong to someone else. In a situation that is clearly unethical, the future consequences are known to be avoidable and undesirable. In situations involving questionable ethics, there is some hope that things will work out:

- Next year's sales will more than make up for the accelerated shipments.
- The obsolete inventory can be used in a new nostalgia line of products.
- The relative or friend may charge more but provides excellent service.
- A desire to have more confidence in the sales staff.
- Making up for the cost shift by working extra hard and more efficiently with the remaining work on Contract B.

When forced to think about the situation, most employees want to act in an ethical manner. The problem faced by personnel involved in measurement and reporting is that while they may question the propriety of a proposed action, and the arguments may be plausible, they want to be team players, and their careers can be affected by "whistle-blowing." Of course, careers are also affected when individuals are identified as being involved in unethical behavior. The careers of people who fail to point out unethical behavior are also affected, especially if they have a responsibility for measurement and reporting.

Major ethical dilemmas often evolve from a series of small compromises, none of which appears serious enough to warrant taking a stand on ethical grounds. WorldCom is such a case. Unfortunately, these small compromises establish a pattern of behavior that is increasingly difficult to reverse. The key to avoiding these situations is recognizing the early warning signs of situations that involve questionable ethical behavior and taking whatever action is appropriate.

Codes of ethics are developed by professional organizations to increase members' awareness of the importance of ethical behavior and to provide a reference point for resisting pressures to engage in actions of questionable ethics. These professional organizations include the American Bar Association, the American Institute of Certified Public Accountants, the American Medical Association, and the Institute of Management Accountants (IMA).

Many corporations have established codes of ethics. One of the important goals of corporate codes of ethics is to provide employees with a common foundation for addressing ethical issues. A survey conducted by two members of the IMA's Ethics Committee found that 56 percent of the responding companies have corporate codes of conduct. Unfortunately, the same survey also reported that although senior management and middle management usually received copies of the code, only 57 percent of the responding companies with corporate codes of conduct provided copies of the code to all employees.[15] More important than a published code of ethics is the ethical tone set by top management. If employees perceive top management as capable of taking unethical actions or as less than 100 percent committed to high ethical standards, they will be less inclined to make the difficult decisions often required to maintain ethics.

A basic rule used by General Motors Corporation is that employees should never do anything they would be ashamed to explain to their families or to see in the front page of the local newspaper. The former GM chairman and CEO added that:

> Ethical conduct in business goes beyond this, however. For example, one of the basic needs of top management is to receive reliable data and honest opinions from people throughout the organization. Too often, subordinates are reluctant to tell all the details of a project or assignment that has failed or is in trouble. This very human trait occurs in all walks of life, whether personal, business, or governmental, and contributes to the making of bad decisions. In short, ethics is an essential element of success in business.[16]

MODULE-END REVIEW

Classify each of the following as a structural, organizational, or activity cost driver.
a. Meals served to airplane passengers aboard Northwest Airlines.
b. General Motors' decision to manufacture the Saturn® automobile in completely new facilities.
c. Zenith's decision to sell its computer operations and focus on the core television business.
d. Number of tax returns filed electronically by H&R Block.
e. Number of passenger cars in a Via train.
f. Coors' decision to expand its market area east from the Rocky Mountains.
g. Boeing's decision to invite airlines to assist in designing the model 777 airplane.
h. DaimlerChrysler's decision to use cross-disciplinary teams to design the Neon® automobile.
i. St.Jude Hospital's decision to establish review committees on the appropriateness and effectiveness of medical procedures for improving patient care.
j. Harley-Davidson's efforts to restructure production procedures to reduce inventories and machine setup times.

Solution
a. Activity cost driver
b. Structural cost driver
c. Structural cost driver
d. Activity cost driver
e. Activity cost driver
f. Structural cost driver
g. Organizational cost driver
h. Organizational cost driver
i. Organizational cost driver
j. Organizational cost driver

---

[15] Robert B. Sweeney and Howard L. Siers, "Survey: Ethics and Corporate America," Management Accounting, June 1990, pp. 34–40.

[16] Roger B. Smith, "Ethics in Business: An Essential Element of Success," *Management Accounting,* June 1990, p. 50.

GUIDANCE ANSWER

MANAGERIAL DECISION	**You are the CEO**

It is important that an organization's cost structure be aligned with its strategy. If your goal is to be a cost leader (such as Wal-Mart or Costco), you will want to make sure that the structural cost drivers, such as the type of buildings acquired and the displays used are consistent with this strategy. As the CEO of Wal-Mart you would not permit many of the costs that would be incurred in an organization such as Tiffany's or Nordstrom's.

DISCUSSION QUESTIONS

Q14-1. Contrast financial and managerial accounting on the basis of user orientation, purpose of information, level of aggregation, length of time period, orientation toward past or future, conformance to external standards, and emphasis on objective data.

Q14-2. What three themes are a part of strategic cost management?

Q14-3. Distinguish between a mission and a goal.

Q14-4. Describe the three strategic positions that Porter views as leading to business success.

Q14-5. Distinguish between how managerial accounting would support the strategy of cost leadership and the strategy of product differentiation.

Q14-6. Why are the phases of planning, organizing, and controlling referred to as a *continuous cycle*?

Q14-7. Identify three advances that have fostered the move away from isolated national economic systems toward an interdependent global economy.

Q14-8. What are the three interrelated dimensions of today's competition?

Q14-9. Differentiate among structural, organizational, and activity cost drivers.

Q14-10. What is the link between performing activities and incurring costs?

Q14-11. How can top management establish an ethical tone in an organization?

Q14-12. Describe how pressures to have desirable short-run outcomes can lead to ethical dilemmas.

MINI EXERCISES

M14-13. Management Accounting Terminology (LO1-LO5)

Match the following terms with the best descriptions. Each description is used only once.

Terms

1.	Ethics	9.	Organizational cost driver
2.	Mission	10.	Financial accounting
3.	Controlling	11.	Activity cost driver
4.	Goal	12.	Structural cost driver
5.	Not-for-profit organization	13.	Managerial accounting
6.	Quality	14.	Resources
7.	Balance sheet	15.	Product differentiation
8.	Income statement		

Description

a. Designing components so they are easily assembled

b. The Starlight Foundation raising money to grant wishes for terminally ill children

c. Prepared as of a point in time

d. Accounting for external users

e. Increase year 2008 sales by 10 percent over year 2007 sales

f. Shows the results of operations for a period of time

g. Packing an order for shipment

h. Deciding to build a factory away from a highway but near a railroad

i. The degree to which a new television meets a buyer's expectations

j. Used internally to make decisions

k. Consumed by activities

l. The propriety of taking some action

m. Reduces customer price sensitivity

n. Basic purpose toward which activities are directed

o. Comparing the budget with the actual results

M14-14. Financial and Managerial Accounting (LO1)

Indicate whether each phrase is more descriptive of financial accounting or managerial accounting.

a. May be subjective

b. Often used to state corporate goals

c. Typically prepared quarterly or annually

d. May measure time or customer satisfaction

e. Future oriented

f. Subject to cost-benefit analysis

g. Keeps records of assets and liabilities

h. Highly aggregated statements

i. Must conform to external standards

j. Special-purpose reports

k. Decision-making tool

l. Income statement, balance sheet, and statement of cash flows

M14-15. Missions, Goals, and Strategies (LO2)

Identify each of the following as a mission, goal, or strategy.

a. Budget time for study, sleep, and relaxation

b. Provide shelter for the homeless

c. Provide an above-average return to investors

d. Protect the public

e. Locate fire stations so that the average response time is less than five minutes

f. Overlap police patrols so that there are always police cars on major thoroughfares

g. Achieve a 12 percent market share

h. Lower prices and costs

i. Select the most scenic route to drive between Las Vegas and Denver

j. Graduate from college

M14-16. Line and Staff Organization (LO2)

Presented are the names of several departments often found in a merchandising organization such as Kohl's Department Store.

a.	Maintenance	*d.*	Payroll
b.	Home Furnishings	*e.*	Human Resources
c.	Store Manager	*f.*	Advertising

Kohl's Department Store (KSS)

Required

Identify each as a line or a staff department.

M14-17. Line and Staff Organization (LO2)

Presented are the names of several departments often found in a manufacturing organization such as Kimberly-Clark.

a.	Manager, Plant 2	*d.*	Controller
b.	Design Engineering	*e.*	Property Accounting
c.	President	*f.*	Sales Manager, District 1

Kimberly-Clark (KMB)

Required

Identify each as a line or a staff department.

M14-18. Classifying Cost Drivers (LO4)

Classify each of the following as structural, organizational, or activity cost drivers.

a. Oneida Silversmiths reorganizes production facilities from a layout in which all similar types of machines are grouped together to one in which a set of machines is designated for the production of a particular product and that set of machines is grouped together.

b. A cable television company decides to start offering telephone service.

c. Xerox Corporation decides to stop making personal computers.

d. Canon decides to start making high-volume photocopy equipment to compete head-to-head with Xerox.

Xerox Corporation (XRX)

Canon (CAJ)

e. The number of meals a cafeteria serves.

f. The number of miles a taxi is driven.

g. A company eliminates the position of supervisor and has each work group elect a team leader.

h. Toyota empowers employees to halt production if a quality problem is identified.

i. The number of tons of grain a ship loads.

j. Crossgate Mall decides to build space for 80 additional stores.

M14-19. Classifying Cost Drivers (LO4)

Mesa Construction managers provide design and construction management services for various commercial construction projects. Senior managers are trying to apply cost driver concepts to their firm to better understand Mesa's costs.

Required

Classify each of the following actions or decisions as structural, organizational, or activity cost drivers.

a. The decision to be a leader in computer-assisted design services.

b. The decision to allow staff architects to follow a specific project through to completion.

c. The daily process of inspecting the progress on various construction projects.

d. The process of conducting extensive client interviews to assess the exact needs for Mesa services.

e. The decision to expand the market area by establishing an office in another state.

f. The decision to begin building projects with Mesa staff rather than relying on subcontractors.

g. The process of receiving approval from government authorities along with appropriate permits for each project.

h. The decision to organize the workforce into project teams.

i. The decision to build a new headquarters facility with areas for design and administration as well as storage and maintenance of construction equipment.

j. The process of grading building sites and preparing forms for foundations.

EXERCISES

E14-20. Financial and Managerial Accounting (LO1)

Assume Michelle Jones has just been promoted to product manager at Procter & Gamble. Although she is an accomplished sales representative and well versed in market research, her accounting background is limited to reviewing her paycheck, balancing her checkbook, filing income tax returns, and reviewing the company's annual income statement and balance sheet. She commented that while the financial statements are no doubt useful to investors, she just doesn't see how accounting can help her be a good product manager.

Required

Based on her remarks, it is apparent that Michelle's view of accounting is limited to financial accounting. Explain some of the important differences between financial and managerial accounting and suggest some ways managerial accounting can help Michelle be a better product manager.

E14-21. Developing an Organization Chart (LO1)

Develop an organization chart for a three-outlet bakery chain with a central baking operation and deliveries every few hours. Assume the business is incorporated and that the president has a single staff assistant. Also assume that the delivery truck driver reports to the bakery manager.

E14-22. Identifying Monetary and Nonmonetary Performance Measures (LO2)

Identify possible monetary and nonmonetary performance measures for each of the following situations. One nonmonetary measure should relate to quality, and one should relate to time.

a. Cornell University wishes to evaluate the success of last year's graduating class.

b. Cook County Hospital wishes to evaluate the performance of its emergency room.

c. L.L. Bean wishes to evaluate the performance of its telephone order–filling operations.

d. Hilton Hotels wishes to evaluate the performance of registration activities at one of its hotels.

e. United Parcel Service wishes to evaluate the success of its operations in Knoxville.

E14-23. **Identifying Monetary and Nonmonetary Performance Measures** (LO2)

Identify possible monetary and nonmonetary performance measures for each of the following situations. One nonmonetary measure should relate to quality, and one should relate to time.

   a. **AOL**'s evaluation of the performance of its Internet service in Huntsville.

   b. **Time Warner Cable**'s evaluation of the performance of new customer cable installations in Rochester.

   c. **Dell Computer**'s evaluation of the performance of its logistical arrangements for delivering computers to residential customers.

   d. **Amazon.com**'s evaluation of the performance of its Web site.

   e. **Emory University**'s evaluation of the success of its freshman admissions activities.

AOL

Time Warner Cable (TWTC)

Dell Computer (DELL)

Amazon.com (AMZN)

Emory University

E14-24. **Identifying Information Needs of Different Managers** (LO2)

Jerry Damson operates a number of auto dealerships for **Acura** and **Honda**. Identify possible monetary and nonmonetary performance measures for each of the following situations. One nonmonetary measure should relate to quality, and one should relate to time.

   a. An individual sales associate.

   b. The sales manager of a single dealership.

   c. The general manager of a particular dealership.

   d. The corporate chief financial officer.

   e. The president of the corporation.

Acura

Honda (HMC)

CASES

C14-25. **Goals and Strategies** (LO2)

   a. What is your instructor's goal for students in this course? What strategies has he or she developed to achieve this goal?

   b. What is your goal in this course? What strategies will help you achieve this goal?

   c. What is your goal for this semester or term? What strategies will help you achieve this goal?

   d. What is your employment goal? What strategies will help you achieve this goal?

C14-26. **Product Differentiation** (LO3)

You are the owner of Lobster's Limited. You have no trouble catching lobsters, but you have difficulty in selling all that you catch. The problem is that all lobsters from all vendors look the same. You do catch high-quality lobsters, but you need to be able to tell your customers that your lobsters are better than those sold by other vendors.

Required

   a. What are some possible ways of distinguishing your lobsters from those of other vendors?

   b. Explain the possible results of this differentiation.

C14-27. **Ethics and Short-Term Borrowing** (LO5)

Ethel, a secretary, is in charge of petty cash for a local law firm. Normally, about $200 is kept in the petty cash box. When Ethel is short on cash and needs some for lunch or to pay her babysitter, she sometimes takes a few dollars from the box. Since she is in charge of the box, nobody knows that she takes the money, and she always replaces it within a few days.

Required

   a. Is Ethel's behavior ethical?

   b. Assume that Ethel has recently had major problems meeting her bills. She also is in charge of purchasing supplies for the office from petty cash. Last week when she needed $12 for the babysitter, she falsified a voucher for the amount of $12. Is this behavior ethical?

C14-28. Ethics and Travel Reimbursement (LO5)

Scott takes many business trips throughout the year. All of his expenses are paid by his company. Last week he traveled to Rio De Janeiro, Brazil, and stayed there on business for five days. He is allowed a maximum of $28 per day for food and $100 per day for lodging. To his surprise, the food and accommodations in Brazil were much less than he expected. Being upset about traveling last week and having to sacrifice tickets he'd purchased to a Red Sox baseball game, he decided to inflate his expenses a bit. He increased his lodging expense from $50 per day to $75 per day and his food purchased from $10 per day to $20 per day. Therefore, for the five-day trip, he overstated his expenses by $175 total. After all, the allowance was higher than the amount he spent.

Required

Assume that the company would never find out that he had actually spent less. Are Scott's actions ethical? Are they acceptable?

C14-29. Ethics and False Claims Act (LO5)

The U.S. Government passed the Federal False Claims Act to encourage persons to bring forward evidence of fraudulent charges on government contracts. Under the provisions of the Act, whistle-blowers receive up to 25 percent of any money recovered as a result of evidence they bring forth. To date, the largest settlement under the terms of the Act was a $7.5 million reward to a former employee of a defense contractor who filed a suit after leaving his former employer to accept a position as a price analyst for the Department of Defense.

Required

Evaluate the likely impact of the Federal False Claims Act on corporations doing business with the U.S. government. Do you believe the Act is a good idea?

C14-30. Expected Values of Questionable Decisions (LO5)

Exxon Mobil (XOM)

Royal Dutch/Shell (RDS-B)

The members of the jury had to make a decision in a lawsuit brought by the State of Alabama against Exxon Mobil. The suit revolved around natural-gas wells that Exxon drilled in state-owned waters. After signing several leases obligating Exxon to share revenues with Alabama, company officials started questioning the terms of the agreement that prohibited deducting several types of processing costs before paying the state royalties.

During the course of the trial, a memo by an in-house attorney of Exxon Mobil came to light. The memo noted that Royal Dutch/Shell, which had signed a similar lease, interpreted it "in the same manner as the state." The memo then presented arguments the company might use to claim the deduction, estimated the probability of the arguments being successful (less than 50 percent), and proceeded to consider whether Exxon should obey the law using a cost-benefit analysis. According to the memo, "If we adopt anything beyond a 'safe' approach, we should anticipate a quick audit and subsequent litigation." The memo also observed that "our exposure is 12 percent interest on underpayments calculated from the due date, and the cost of litigation." Deducting the questionable costs did, indeed, result in an audit and a lawsuit. Source: *Business Week.*[17]

Required

If you were a member of the jury, what would you do? Why?

C14-31. Management Decisions Affecting Cost Drivers (LO4)

An avid bicycle rider, you have decided to use an inheritance to start a new business to sell and repair bicycles. Two college friends have already accepted offers to work for you.

Required

a. What is the mission of your new business?
b. Suggest a strategic positioning goal you might strive for to compete with area hardware and discount stores that sell bicycles.
c. Identify two items that might be long-range goals.
d. Identify two items that might be goals for the coming year.
e. Mention two decisions that will be structural cost drivers.
f. Mention two decisions that will be organizational cost drivers.
g. Identify two activity cost drivers.

---

[17] Mike France, "When Big Oil Gets Too Slick," *Business Week,* April 9, 2001, p. 70.

C14-32. Success Factors and Performance Measurement (LO2)

Three years ago, Vincent Chow completed his college degree. The economy was in a depressed state at the time, and Vincent managed to get an offer of only $35,000 per year as a bookkeeper. In addition to its relatively low pay, this job had limited advancement potential. Since Vincent was an enterprising and ambitious young man, he instead started a business of his own. He was convinced that because of changing lifestyles, a drive-through coffee establishment would be profitable. He was able to obtain backing from his parents to open such an establishment close to the industrial park area in town. Vincent named his business The Cappuccino Express and decided to sell only two types of coffee: cappuccino and decaffeinated.

As Vincent had expected, The Cappuccino Express was very well received. Within three years, Vincent had added another outlet north of town. He left the day-to-day management of each site to a manager and turned his attention toward overseeing the entire enterprise. He also hired an assistant to do the record keeping and other selected chores.[18]

Required

a. Develop an organization chart for The Cappuccino Express.
b. What factors can be expected to have a major impact on the success of The Cappuccino Express?
c. What major tasks must Vincent undertake in managing The Cappuccino Express?
d. What are the major costs of operating The Cappuccino Express?
e. Vincent would like to monitor the performance of each site manager. What measure(s) of performance should he use?
f. If you suggested more than one measure, which of these should Vincent select if he could use only one?
g. Suppose that last year, the original site had yielded total revenues of $146,000, total costs of $120,000, and hence, a profit of $26,000. Vincent had judged this profit performance to be satisfactory. For the coming year, Vincent expects that due to factors such as increased name recognition and demographic changes, the total revenues will increase by 20 percent to $175,200. What amount of profit should he expect from the site? Discuss the issues involved in developing an estimate of profit.

---

[18] Based on Chee W. Chow, "Instructional Case: Vincent's Cappuccino Express—A Teaching Case to Help Students Master Basic Cost Terms and Concepts Through Interactive Learning," *Issues in Accounting Education,* Spring 1995, pp. 173–190.

Cost Behavior, Activity Analysis, and Cost Estimation

LEARNING OBJECTIVES

LO1 Identify basic patterns of how costs respond to changes in activity cost drivers. (p. 15-3)

LO2 Determine a linear cost estimating equation. (p. 15-9)

LO3 Identify and discuss problems encountered in cost estimation. (p. 15-14)

LO4 Describe and develop alternative classifications for activity cost drivers. (p. 15-15)

COST BEHAVIOR ANALYSIS

Along with decisions about markets, products, and operating policies, managers must focus on cost issues to build profitable firms. Decisions about costs often arise from an ongoing and detailed knowledge of both the firm's cost structure and management competitive strategy. Cost issues faced by managers of major airlines, low-cost airlines, and regional airlines exemplify the interrelationship between ongoing competitive strategy and cost management issues.

Major airlines such as United, American, Delta, and Northwest compete on a variety of full-service attributes such as convenient scheduling, varying classes of service, frequent flyer programs, and airport executive clubs. Although the elimination or restructuring of frequent flyer programs and executive clubs could lower operating costs, these programs represent important customer services. Managers at these airlines usually look elsewhere to find targets for cost reduction. At United, the increase in fuel costs prompted a change in asset management strategy. United management had planned to phase out the use of older 727, 747, and DC-10 aircraft over several years. These planes, however, are both fuel and labor intensive, and in the current environment, the airline could lower its operating cost by replacing those planes ahead of the original schedule.

Using a different competitive strategy, managers of airlines such as Southwest, Air Tran, and JetBlue rely on a cost leadership approach that emphasizes different cost categories than do the full-service airlines. Since Southwest, Air Tran, and Jet Blue already have lower costs due to their "no-frills" approach to air travel, managers at these airlines focus on such cost-reducing strategies as using regional airports where costs are lower, building the fleet with only one type of aircraft to lower maintenance costs, and flying with higher load factors—a higher percentage of filled seats.

Managers at regional airlines such as SkyWest, Mesa Air, and Comair face a different cost challenge—the introduction of the regional jet. Made by firms such as Bombardier, Embraer, and Fairchild-Dornier, these planes are about half the size of regular commercial passenger jets. Carrying between 40 and 70 passengers, these planes are well suited to the medium-distance, low-density routes flown by regional carriers. The regional jets—or RJs—typically fly faster and provide more comfort than the turboprop planes that have traditionally dominated the fleets of regional airlines. The RJs add flexibility to air travel by providing more point-to-point flights and permitting passengers to bypass congested hub airports. A major issue for managers of regional airlines is the RJs' cost. While a turboprop plane might cost about $14 million, an RJ costs about $21 million. The turboprop is more fuel efficient on shorter trips while the RJ uses less fuel on trips of 400 miles or more. Although some of the regional carriers have collective marketing and operating agreements with major airlines and have received financial assistance to improve their fleets, managers at all regional carriers must analyze the impact of these potentially higher costs on the cost structure of their organizations.

In each case, managers at these three types of airlines rely on specific cost analysis to contribute to their firm's profitability. Although the firms all compete in the same industry, each group operates in a different market segment with a different competitive strategy. Because of these differences in both segment and strategy, the specific approaches to cost analysis differ. The common theme, however, is that a detailed knowledge of cost behavior is an important key to success.

Sources: *The Wall Street Journal, Business Week, Forbes,* and *Fortune.*[1]

[1]Based on: "Small is Beautiful," *The Economist,* March 20, 2001, p. 65; "Business Focus: United Airlines Speeds Its Plans to Retire Gas-Guzzling Planes," *The Wall Street Journal-Interactive Edition,* June 4, 2001; Michael Arndt, "A Simple and Elegant Flight Plan," *Business Week,* June 11, 2001, p. 118; Martha Brannagan and Melanie Trottman, "Southwest Air Tops Profit Forecasts, Benefits from Robust Flight Demand," *The Wall Street Journal-Interactive Edition,* October 18, 2000; Nicholas Stein, "Regional Jets Join the Jet Set," *Forbes,* September, 14, 2000, pp. 287-290; Alex Taylor III, "Little Jets Are Huge," *Fortune,* September 4, 2000, pp. 275-282.

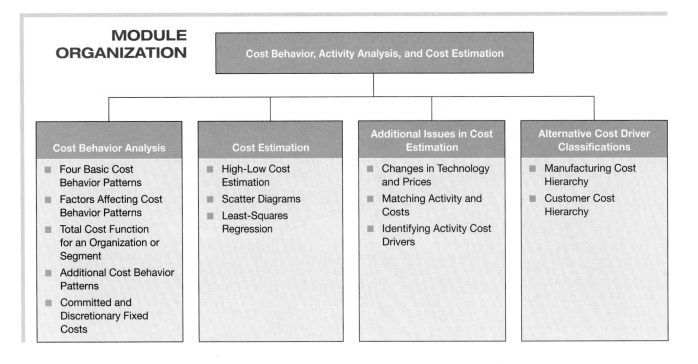

MODULE ORGANIZATION

Cost Behavior, Activity Analysis, and Cost Estimation

Cost Behavior Analysis
- Four Basic Cost Behavior Patterns
- Factors Affecting Cost Behavior Patterns
- Total Cost Function for an Organization or Segment
- Additional Cost Behavior Patterns
- Committed and Discretionary Fixed Costs

Cost Estimation
- High-Low Cost Estimation
- Scatter Diagrams
- Least-Squares Regression

Additional Issues in Cost Estimation
- Changes in Technology and Prices
- Matching Activity and Costs
- Identifying Activity Cost Drivers

Alternative Cost Driver Classifications
- Manufacturing Cost Hierarchy
- Customer Cost Hierarchy

COST BEHAVIOR ANALYSIS

This module introduces **cost behavior**, which refers to the relationship between a given cost item and the quantity of its related cost driver. Cost behavior, therefore, explains how the total amount for various costs respond to changes in activity volume. Understanding cost behavior is essential for estimating future costs. In this module we examine several typical cost behavior patterns and methods for developing cost equations that are useful for predicting future costs.

Four Basic Cost Behavior Patterns

LO1 Identify basic patterns of how costs respond to changes in activity cost drivers.

Although there are an unlimited number of ways that costs can respond to changes in cost drivers, as a starting point it is useful to classify cost behavior into four categories: variable, fixed, mixed, and step. Graphs of each are presented in Exhibit 15.1. Observe that total cost (the dependent variable) is measured on the vertical axis, and total activity for the time period (the independent variable) is measured on the horizontal axis.

1. **Variable costs** change in total in direct proportion to changes in activity. Their total amount increases as activity increases, equaling zero dollars when activity is zero and increasing at a constant amount per unit of activity. The higher the variable cost per unit of activity, the steeper the slope of the line representing total cost. With the number of pizzas served as the activity cost driver for Pizza Hut restaurants, the cost of cheese is an example of a variable cost.

2. **Fixed costs** do not change in response to a change in activity volume. Hence, a line representing total fixed costs is flat with a slope (incline) of zero. With the number of Pizza Hut pizzas sold as the cost driver, annual depreciation, property taxes, and property insurance are examples of fixed costs. While fixed costs may respond to structural and organizational cost drivers over time, they do not respond to short-run changes in activity cost drivers.

3. **Mixed costs** (sometimes called **semivariable costs**) contain a fixed and a variable cost element. Total mixed costs are positive (like fixed costs) when activity is zero, and they increase in a linear fashion (like total variable costs) as activity increases. With the number of pizzas sold as the cost driver, the cost of electric power is an example of a mixed cost. Some electricity is required to provide basic lighting, while an increasing amount of electricity is required to prepare food as the number of pizzas served increases.

EXHIBIT 15.1 **Cost Behavior Patterns**

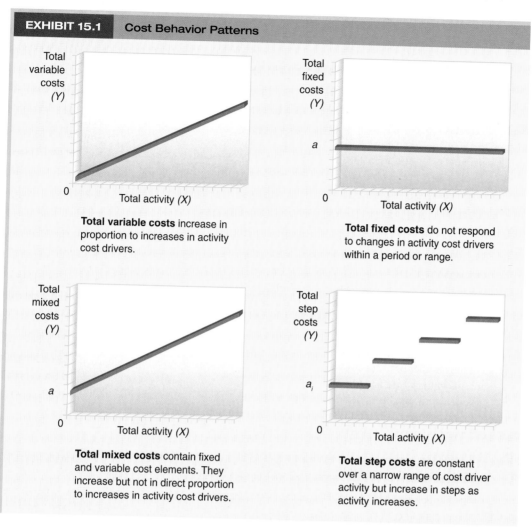

Total variable costs increase in proportion to increases in activity cost drivers.

Total fixed costs do not respond to changes in activity cost drivers within a period or range.

Total mixed costs contain fixed and variable cost elements. They increase but not in direct proportion to increases in activity cost drivers.

Total step costs are constant over a narrow range of cost driver activity but increase in steps as activity increases.

4. **Step costs** are constant within a narrow range of activity but shift to a higher level when activity exceeds the range. Total step costs increase in a steplike fashion as activity increases. With the number of pizzas served as the cost driver, employee wages is an example of a step cost. Up to a certain number of pizzas, only a small staff needs to be on duty. Beyond that number, additional employees are needed for quality service and so forth.

The relationship between total cost (Y axis) and total activity (X axis) for the four cost behavior patterns is mathematically expressed as follows:

$$\text{Variable cost: } Y = bX$$

where

b = the variable cost per unit, sometimes referred to as the slope of the cost function.

$$\text{Fixed cost: } Y = a$$

where

a = total fixed costs. The slope of the fixed cost function is zero because fixed costs do not change with activity.

$$\text{Mixed cost: } Y = a + bX$$

where

a = total fixed cost element

b = variable cost element per unit of activity.

$$\text{Step cost: } Y = a_i$$

where

a_i = **the step cost within a specific range of activity, identified by the subscript i.**

The total cost function of most organizations has shifted in recent years toward more fixed costs and fewer variable costs, making it increasingly important for organizations to manage their fixed costs. Some organizations have done this by outsourcing activities rather than performing the activities internally. This avoids the many fixed costs of infrastructure in exchange for a variable cost per unit of activity. The Business Insight below considers how an alliance between the United States Postal Service and Federal Express (FedEx) helps keep down the cost of postage by shifting fixed costs.

Factors Affecting Cost Behavior Patterns

The four cost behavior patterns presented are based on the fundamental assumption that a unit of final output is the primary cost driver. The implications of this assumption are examined later in this module.

Another important assumption is that the time period is too short to incorporate changes in strategic cost drivers such as the scale of operations. Although this assumption is useful for short-range planning, for the purpose of developing plans for extended time periods, it is more appropriate to consider possible variations in one or more strategic cost drivers. When this is done, many costs otherwise classified as fixed are better classified as variable.

Even the cost of depreciable assets can be viewed as variable if the time period is long enough. Assuming that the number of pizzas served is the cost driver, for a single month the depreciation on all Pizza Hut restaurants in the world is a fixed cost. Over several years, if sales are strong, a strategic decision will be made to open additional restaurants; if sales are weak, strategic decisions will likely be made to close some restaurants. Hence, over a multiple-year period, the number of restaurants varies with sales volume, making depreciation appear as a variable cost with sales revenue as the cost driver.

BUSINESS INSIGHT   **Alliance Alters USPS Cost Structure**

"The Postal Service delivers Main Street, and FedEx provides an air fleet," proclaimed the Postmaster General when announcing an alliance between the United States Postal Service (USPS) and FedEx. Under terms of the alliance, FedEx transports express mail, priority mail, and some first-class mail on its fleet of over 650 aircraft. The projected costs to the USPS are approximately $6.3 billion over the seven-year contract period. FedEx will also locate overnight service collection boxes at selected post offices across the United States.

It is predicted that USPS will save a billion dollars in transportation costs over the life of the contract. A major aspect of the alliance is that it moves USPS from a fixed-cost transportation network toward a variable cost network. "This is a unique opportunity to turn some fixed costs into variable costs," said the president of the Association for Postal Commerce. "It is using someone else's fixed costs." The chairman and chief executive officer of FedEx added that the system allows "the Postal Service to grow unconstrained without having to put in big [transportation] networks."[2]

Total Cost Function for an Organization or Segment

To obtain a general understanding of an organization, to compare the cost structures of different organizations, or to perform preliminary planning activities, managers are often interested in how total costs respond to a single measure of overall activity such as units sold or sales revenue. This overview can be useful, but presenting all costs as a function of a single cost driver is seldom accurate enough to support decisions concerning products, services, or activities. Doing so implies that all of an organization's costs can be manipulated by changing a single cost driver. This is seldom true.

In developing a total cost function, the independent variable usually represents some measure of the goods or services provided customers, such as total student credit hours in a university, total sales revenue

---

[2]"USPS-FedEx Alliance Could Save $1 Billion in Transportation Costs," *Federal Times,* January 15, 2001, p. 4.

in a store, total guest-days in a hotel, or total units manufactured in a factory. The resulting cost function is illustrated in Exhibit 15.2.

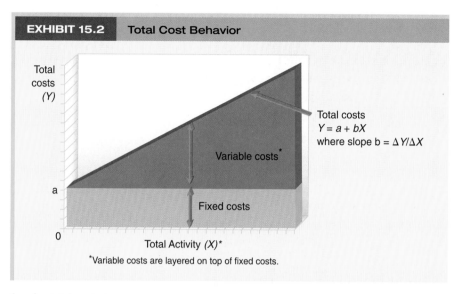

EXHIBIT 15.2   Total Cost Behavior

The equation for total costs is:

$$Y = a + bX$$

where

Y = total costs
a = vertical axis intercept (an approximation of fixed costs)
b = slope (an approximation of variable costs per unit of X)
X = value of independent variable

In situations where the variable, fixed, and mixed costs, and the related cost functions, can be determined, a total cost equation can be useful in predicting future costs for various activity levels. However, generally, a total cost equation is useful for predicting costs in only a limited range of activity. The **relevant range** of a total cost equation is that portion of the range associated with the fixed cost of the current or expected capacity. For example, assume that a Dairy Queen ice cream shop's only fixed cost is the depreciation on its ice cream making machines, and that it is able to produce a maximum of 50 gallons of ice cream per day with a single ice cream making machine. If it has four machines in operation, and if it can readily adjust its fixed capacity cost by increasing or decreasing the number of ice cream machines, the relevant range of activity for the shop's current total cost equation is 151 to 200 gallons. In the future, if the shop expects to operate at more than 200 gallons per day, the current total cost equation would not predict total cost accurately, because fixed costs would have to be increased for additional machines. Conversely, if it expects to operate at 150 gallons or less, it may reduce the number of machines in the shop, thereby reducing total fixed costs.

Additional Cost Behavior Patterns

Although we have considered the most frequently used cost behavior patterns, remember that there are numerous ways that costs can respond to changes in activity. Avoid the temptation to automatically assume that the cost in question conforms to one of the patterns discussed in this module. Think through each situation and then select a behavior pattern that seems logical and fits the known facts.

Particular care needs to be taken with the vertical axis. So far, all graphs have placed *total* costs on the vertical axis. Miscommunication is likely if one party is thinking in terms of *total* costs while the other is thinking in terms of *variable* or *average* costs. Consider the following cost function:

$$\text{Total costs} = \$3,000 + \$5X$$

where

X = customers served

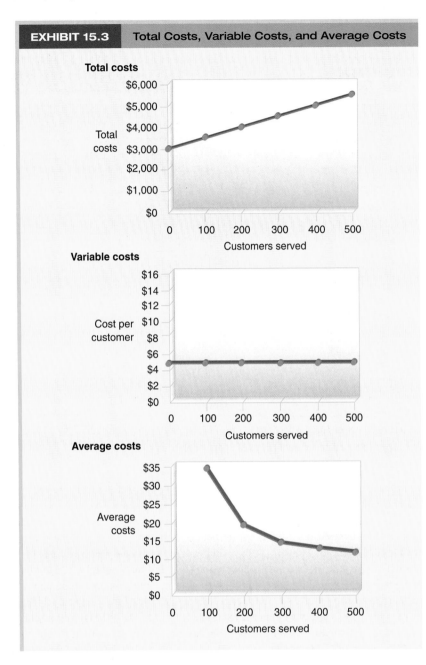

EXHIBIT 15.3	Total Costs, Variable Costs, and Average Costs

The total, variable, and average costs at various levels of activity are computed here and graphed in Exhibit 15.3. As the number of customers served increases, total costs increase, the variable costs of each unit remain constant, and the average cost decreases because fixed costs are spread over a larger number of units.

Customers Served	Total Costs	Average Cost*	Variable Costs per Customer
100......	$3,500	$35.00	$5.00
200......	4,000	20.00	5.00
300......	4,500	15.00	5.00
400......	5,000	12.50	5.00
500......	5,500	11.00	5.00

*Total costs/customers served

		Number of Shipments	Packaging Costs
(Low activity period)	January	6,000	$17,000
	February	9,000	26,000
(High activity period)	March	12,000	32,000
	April.	10,000	20,000

Equations for total costs for the packaging department in January and March (the periods of lowest and highest activity) follow:

January: $17,000 = a + b (6,000 shipments)

March: $32,000 = a + b (12,000 shipments)

where

a = fixed costs per month

b = variable costs per shipment

Solving for the estimated variable costs:

$$b = \frac{\text{Difference in total costs}}{\text{Difference in activity}}$$

$$b = \frac{\$32,000 - \$17,000}{12,000 - 6,000}$$

$$= \$2.50$$

Next, the estimated monthly fixed costs are determined by subtracting variable costs from total costs of *either* the January or March equation:

a = Total costs − Variable costs

January: a = $17,000 − ($2.50 per shipment × 6,000 shipments)

= $2,000

or

March: a = $32,000 − ($2.50 per shipment × 12,000 shipments)

= $2,000

The cost estimating equation for total packaging department costs is

Y = $2,000 + $2.50X

where

X = number of shipments

Y = total costs for the packing department

The concepts underlying the high-low method of cost estimation are illustrated in Exhibit 15.4.

Cost prediction, the forecasting of future costs, is a common purpose of cost estimation. The Business Insight on the following page examines why and how law firms are engaging in cost prediction. Previously developed estimates of cost behavior are often the starting point in predicting future costs. Continuing the mail-order example, if 5,000 shipments are budgeted for June 2007, the predicted June 2007 packaging department costs are $14,500 [$2,000 + ($2.50 per shipment × 5,000 shipments)].

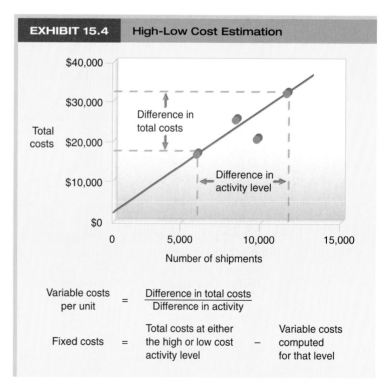

EXHIBIT 15.4   High-Low Cost Estimation

$$\text{Variable costs per unit} = \frac{\text{Difference in total costs}}{\text{Difference in activity}}$$

$$\text{Fixed costs} = \begin{array}{c}\text{Total costs at either}\\\text{the high or low cost}\\\text{activity level}\end{array} - \begin{array}{c}\text{Variable costs}\\\text{computed}\\\text{for that level}\end{array}$$

BUSINESS INSIGHT	Management Software Helps Law Firms Predict Costs

In the past, law firms made little attempt to predict the cost of a case for a large corporate client. When asked, the partner in charge of a case would likely respond, "It all depends on what the other side does." With accounting firms now doing almost everything short of courtroom briefings, and promising to do it cheaper, law firms are facing new cost-based competitive pressures. In response to such competitive pressures, Glidden Partners, a Texas law firm, has developed software intended for litigation project management. "The theory," according to Craig Glidden, "is that any piece of litigation should be viewed as a self-contained project with distinct phases." The software outlines the tasks and costs of each phase, allowing the firm to develop a budget for each case. The software even recommends ways to accomplish each task in a cost-effective manner. For example, if a task can be performed by a paralegal, the software will not recommend a lawyer.[3]

Scatter Diagrams

A **scatter diagram** is a graph of past activity and cost data, with individual observations represented by dots. Plotting historical cost data on a scatter diagram is a useful approach to cost estimation, especially when used in conjunction with other cost-estimating techniques. As illustrated in Exhibit 15.5, a scatter diagram helps in selecting high and low activity levels representative of normal operating conditions. The periods of highest or lowest activity may not be representative because of the cost of overtime, the use of less efficient equipment, strikes, and so forth. If the goal is to develop an equation to predict costs under normal operating conditions, then the equation should be based on observations of normal operating conditions. A scatter diagram is also useful in determining whether costs can be reasonably approximated by a straight line.

EXHIBIT 15.5	Selecting High and Low Activity Levels with a Scatter Diagram

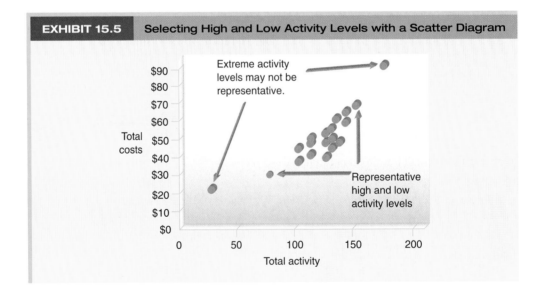

Scatter diagrams are sometimes used alone as a basis of cost estimation. This requires the use of professional judgment to draw a representative straight line through the plot of historical data. Typically, the analyst tries to ensure that an equal number of observations are on either side of the line while minimizing the total vertical differences between the line and actual cost observations at each value of the independent variable. Once a line is drawn, cost estimates at any representative volume are made by studying the line. Alternatively, an equation for the line may be developed by applying the high-low method to any two points on the line.

---

[3] Kimberly Reeves, "Project Management Software Helps Assure the Price Is Right," *Houston Business Journal,* January 9, 1998, pp. 25-26.

Least-Squares Regression

Least-squares regression analysis uses a mathematical technique to fit a cost-estimating equation to the observed data. The technique mathematically accomplishes what the analyst does visually with a scatter diagram. The least-squares technique creates an equation that minimizes the sum of the vertical squared differences between the estimated and the actual costs at each observation. Each of these differences is an estimating error. Using the packaging department example, the least-squares criterion is illustrated in Exhibit 15.6. Estimated values of total monthly packaging costs are represented by the straight line, and the actual values of total monthly packaging costs are represented by the dots. For each dot, such as the one at a volume of 10,000 shipments, the line is fit to minimize the vertical squared differences.

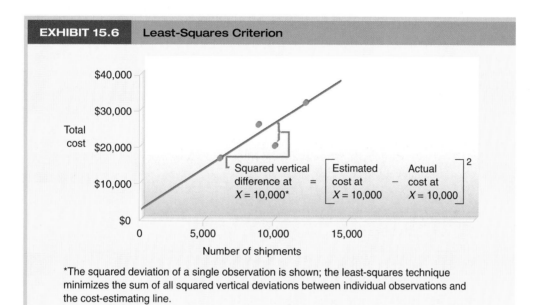

| EXHIBIT 15.6 | Least-Squares Criterion |

$$\text{Squared vertical difference at } X = 10{,}000^* = \left[\text{Estimated cost at } X = 10{,}000 - \text{Actual cost at } X = 10{,}000 \right]^2$$

*The squared deviation of a single observation is shown; the least-squares technique minimizes the sum of all squared vertical deviations between individual observations and the cost-estimating line.

Values of a and b can be manually calculated using a set of equations developed by mathematicians or by using spreadsheet software packages such as Microsoft Excel®. Many calculators also have built-in functions to compute these coefficients. The least-squares equation for monthly packaging costs is:

$$Y = \$3{,}400 + \$2.20X$$

Using the least-squares equation, the predicted June 2007 packaging department costs with 5,000 budgeted shipments are $14,400 [$3,400 + ($2.20 per shipment × 5,000 shipments)]. Recall that the high-low method predicted June 2007 costs of $14,500. Although this difference is small, we should consider which prediction is more reliable.

Advantage of Least-Squares Regression

Mathematicians regard least-squares regression analysis as superior to both the high-low and the scatter diagram methods. It uses all available data, rather than just two observations, and does not rely on subjective judgment in drawing a line. Statistical measures are also available to determine how well a least-squares equation fits the historical data. These measures are often contained in the output of spreadsheet software packages.

In addition to the vertical axis intercept and the slope, least-squares regression calculates the coefficient of determination. The **coefficient of determination** is a measure of the percent of variation in the dependent variable (such as total packaging department costs) that is explained by variations in the independent variable (such as total shipments). Statisticians often refer to the coefficient of determination as R-squared and represent it as R^2.

The coefficient of determination can have values between zero and one, with values close to zero suggesting that the equation is not very useful and values close to one indicating that the equation explains most of the variation in the dependent variable. When choosing between two cost-estimating equations, the one with the higher coefficient of determination is generally preferred. The coefficient of determination for the packaging department cost estimation equation, determined using least-squares regression analysis, is 0.68. This means that 68 percent of the variation in packaging department costs is explained by the number of shipments.

Managers, Not Models, Are Responsible

Although computers make least-squares regression easy to use, the generated output should not merely be accepted as correct. Statistics and other mathematical techniques are tools to help managers make decisions. Managers, not mathematical models, are responsible for decisions. Judgment should always be exercised when considering the validity of the least-squares approach, the solution, and the data. If the objective is to predict future costs under normal operating conditions, observations reflecting abnormal operating conditions should be deleted. Also examine the cost behavior pattern to determine whether it is linear. Scatter diagrams assist in both of these judgments. Finally, the results should make sense. When the relationships between total cost and several activity drivers are examined, it is possible to have a high R-squared purely by chance. Even though the relationship has a high R-squared, if it "doesn't make sense" there is probably something wrong.

Simple and Multiple Regression

Least-squares regression analysis is identified as "simple regression analysis" when there is only one independent variable and as "multiple regression analysis" when there are two or more independent variables. The general form for simple regression analysis is:

$$Y = a + bX$$

The general form for multiple regression analysis is:

$$Y = a + \Sigma b_i X_i$$

In this case, the subscript i is a general representation of each independent variable. When there are several independent variables, i is set equal to 1 for the first, 2 for the second, and so forth. The total variable costs of each independent variable is computed as $b_i X_i$, with b_i representing the variable cost per unit of independent variable X_i. The Greek symbol sigma, Σ, indicates that the costs of all independent variables are summed in determining total variable costs.

As an illustration, assume that Walnut Desk Company's costs are expressed as a function of the unit sales of its two products: executive desks and task desks. Fixed costs are $18,000 per month and the variable costs are $250 per executive desk and $120 per task desk. The mathematical representation of monthly costs with two variables is:

$$Y = a + b_1 X_1 + b_2 X_2$$

where

$$a = \$18,000$$
$$b_1 = \$250$$
$$b_2 = \$120$$
$$X_1 = \text{unit sales of executive desks}$$
$$X_2 = \text{unit sales of task desks}$$

During a month when 105 executive desks and 200 task desks are sold, Walnut Desk Company's estimated total costs are:

$$Y = \$18,000 + \$250(105) + \$120(200)$$
$$= \$68,250$$

In addition to estimating costs, multiple regression analysis can be used to determine the effect of individual product features on the market value of a product or service. The Research Insight on the following page reports a study that estimated the impact of mature trees on the selling price of single-family homes.

| RESEARCH INSIGHT | Regression Finds "Big Tree" Premium |

While most real estate professionals believe that, all else being equal, homes with mature trees (defined as having a diameter of nine inches or more) are preferred to homes without mature trees, it is difficult to estimate the value of mature trees. The Council of Tree and Landscape Appraisers recommends a cost-based approach for the valuation of trees. While this is possible for small trees, it is difficult to value mature trees. To better determine the market value of mature trees, a recent study used multiple regression analysis to analyze the impact of mature trees on the selling prices of homes in Baton Rouge, Louisiana. Independent variables included the size and age of the house, the presence of other house amenities such as a garage, porch, or fireplace, days on the market, location, and the presence of mature trees. The study revealed that the presence of mature trees increased the selling price of a home by 1.856 percent. The researchers conclude that an appraiser "would be supported in adding approximately 2 percent to the value of a single-family house that has mature trees."[4]

| MANAGERIAL DECISION | You are the Purchasing Manager |

Your department has been experiencing increased activity in recent periods as the company has grown, and you have observed that the average cost per purchase order processed has been declining, but not at a constant rate. You have been given an estimate by the production manager of the number of purchase orders that will be processed next period and have been asked by the accounting department to provide within one hour an estimate of the cost to process those orders. How can the scatter diagram method help you to meet this deadline? [Answer, p. 15-20]

ADDITIONAL ISSUES IN COST ESTIMATION

LO3 Identify and discuss problems encountered in cost estimation.

We have mentioned several items to be wary of when developing cost estimating equations:

- Data that are not based on normal operating conditions.
- Nonlinear relationships between total costs and activity.
- Obtaining a high R-squared purely by chance.

Additional items of concern include:

- Changes in technology or prices.
- Matching activity and cost within each observation.
- Identifying activity cost drivers.

Changes in Technology and Prices

Changes in technology and prices make cost estimation and prediction difficult. When telephone companies changed from using human operators to using automated switching equipment to place long-distance telephone calls, cost estimates based on the use of human operators were of little or no value in predicting future costs. Care must be taken to make sure that data used in developing cost estimates are based on the existing technology. When this is not possible, professional judgment is required to make appropriate adjustments.

Only data reflecting a single price level should be used in cost estimation and prediction. If prices have remained stable in the past but then uniformly increase by 20 percent, cost-estimating equations based on data from previous periods will not accurately predict future costs. In this case, all that is required

---

[4] Jonathan Dombrow, Mauricio Rodriguez, and C. F. Sirmans, "The Market Value of Mature Trees in Single-Family Housing Markets," *Appraisal Journal*, January 2000, p. 39.

is a 20 percent increase in the prediction. Unfortunately, adjustments for price changes are seldom this simple. The prices of various cost elements are likely to change at different rates and at different times. Furthermore, there are probably several different price levels included in the past data used to develop cost-estimating equations. If data from different price levels are used, an attempt should be made to restate them to a single price level.

Matching Activity and Costs

The development of accurate cost-estimating equations requires the matching of the activity to related costs within each observation. This accuracy is often difficult to achieve because of the time lag between an activity and the recording of the cost of resources consumed by the activity. Current activities usually consume electricity, but the electric bill won't be received and recorded until next month. Driving an automobile requires routine maintenance for items such as lubrication and oil, but the auto can be driven several weeks or even months before the maintenance is required. Consequently, daily, weekly, and perhaps even monthly observations of miles driven and maintenance costs are unlikely to match the costs of oil and lubrication with the cost-driving activity, miles driven.

In general, the shorter the time period, the higher the probability of error in matching costs and activity. The cost analyst must carefully review the database to verify that activity and cost are matched within each observation. If matching problems are found, it may be possible to adjust the data (perhaps by moving the cost of electricity from one observation to another). Under other circumstances, it may be necessary to use longer periods to match costs and activity.

Identifying Activity Cost Drivers

Identifying the appropriate activity cost driver for a particular cost requires judgment and professional experience. In general, the cost driver should have a logical, causal relationship with costs. In many cases, the identity of the most appropriate activity cost driver, such as miles driven for the cost of automobile gasoline, is apparent. In other situations, where different activity cost drivers might be used, scatter diagrams and statistical measures, such as the coefficient of determination, are helpful in selecting the activity cost driver that best explains past variations in cost. When scatter diagrams are used, the analyst can study the dispersion of observations around the cost-estimating line. In general, a small dispersion is preferred. If regression analysis is used, the analyst considers the coefficient of determination. In general, a higher coefficient of determination is preferred. The relationship between the activity cost driver and the cost must seem logical, and the activity data must be available.

ALTERNATIVE COST DRIVER CLASSIFICATIONS

LO4 Describe and develop alternative classifications for activity cost drivers.

So far we have examined cost behavior and cost estimation using only a unit-level approach, which assumes changes in costs are best explained by changes in the number of units of product or service provided customers. This approach may have worked for **Carnegie Steel Company**, but it is inappropriate for multiproduct organizations, such as **General Electric**. The unit-level approach becomes increasingly inaccurate for analyzing cost behavior when organizations experience the following types of changes:

▪ From labor-based to automated manufacturing,

▪ From a limited number of related products to multiple products, with variations in product volume and complexity (and related costs), and

▪ From a set of similar customers to a diverse set of customers.

Exhibit 15.7 illustrates the composition of total manufacturing costs for the past century, illustrating changes in the percentage of manufacturing costs for three major cost categories.

1. **Direct materials,** the cost of primary raw materials converted into finished goods, have increased slightly as organizations purchase components they formerly fabricated. The word "direct" is used to indicate costs that are easily or directly traced to a finished product or service.

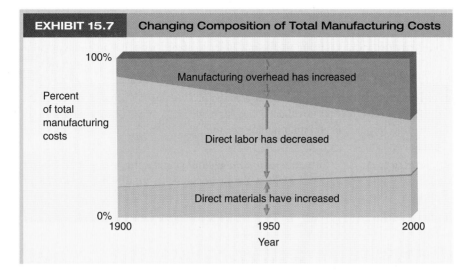

EXHIBIT 15.7 Changing Composition of Total Manufacturing Costs

2. **Direct labor,** the wages earned by production employees for the time they spend converting raw materials into finished products, has decreased significantly as employees spend less time physically working on products and more time supporting automated production activities.

3. **Manufacturing overhead,** which includes all manufacturing costs other than direct materials and direct labor, has increased significantly due to automation, product diversity, and product complexity.

Changes in the composition of manufacturing costs have implications for the behavior of total costs and the responsiveness of costs to changes in cost drivers. Because direct materials and direct labor vary directly with the number of units, they are easy to measure. In the past, when manufacturing overhead was relatively small, it was possible to assume units of product or service was the primary cost driver. This is no longer true. Units of final product is no longer an adequate explanation of changes in manufacturing overhead for many organizations.

The past tendency to ignore overhead, while focusing on direct materials and direct labor, led one researcher to describe overhead causing activities as "the hidden factory."[5] To better understand the hidden factory, several researchers have developed frameworks for categorizing cost-driving activities. The crucial feature of these frameworks is the inclusion of nonunit cost drivers. Depending on the characteristics of a particular organization, as well as management's information needs, there are an almost unlimited number of cost driver classification schemes. We consider two frequently applied cost driver classification schemes: one based on a manufacturing cost hierarchy and a second based on a customer cost hierarchy. We also illustrate variations of each.

Manufacturing Cost Hierarchy

The most well-known framework, developed by Cooper[6] and Cooper and Kaplan[7] for manufacturing situations, classifies activities into the following four categories.

1. A **unit-level activity** is performed *for each unit* of product produced. Oneida Silversmiths manufactures high-quality eating utensils. In the production of forks, the stamping of each fork into the prescribed shape is an example of a unit-level cost driver.

---

[5] Jeffrey G. Miller and Thomas E. Vollmann, "The Hidden Factory," *Harvard Business Review,* September-October 1985, pp. 142–150.

[6] Robin Cooper, "Cost Classification in Unit-Based and Activity-Based Manufacturing Cost Systems," *The Journal of Cost Management,* Fall 1990, pp. 4–14.

[7] Robin Cooper and Robert S. Kaplan, "Profit Priorities from Activity-Based Costing," *Harvard Business Review,* May-June 1991, pp. 130–135.

2. A **batch-level activity** is performed *for each batch* of product produced. At Oneida Silversmiths, a batch is a number of identical units (such as a fork of a specific design) produced at the same time. Batch-level activities include setting up the machines to stamp each fork in an identical manner, moving the entire batch between workstations (i.e., molding, stamping, and finishing), and inspecting the first unit in the batch to verify that the machines are set up correctly.

3. A **product-level activity** is performed *to support* the production of *each different type of product*. At Oneida Silversmiths, product-level activities for a specific pattern of fork include initially designing the fork, producing and maintaining the mold for the fork, and determining manufacturing operations for the fork.

4. A **facility-level activity** is performed *to maintain* general manufacturing capabilities. At Oneida Silversmiths, facility-level activities include plant management, building maintenance, property taxes, and electricity required to sustain the building.

Several additional examples of the costs driven by activities at each level are presented in Exhibit 15.8.

EXHIBIT 15.8	Hierarchy of Activity Costs	
Activity Level	**Reason for Activity**	**Examples of Activity Cost**
1. Unit level	Performed for each unit of product produced or sold	• Cost of raw materials • Cost of inserting a component • Utilities cost of operating equipment • Some costs of packaging • Sales commissions
2. Batch level	Performed for each batch of product produced or sold	• Cost of processing sales order • Cost of issuing and tracking work order • Cost of equipment setup • Cost of moving batch between workstations • Cost of inspection (assuming same number of units inspected in each batch)
3. Product level	Performed to support each different product that can be produced	• Cost of product development • Cost of product marketing such as advertising • Cost of specialized equipment • Cost of maintaining specialized equipment
4. Facility level	Performed to maintain general manufacturing capabilities	• Cost of maintaining general facilities such as buildings and grounds • Cost of nonspecialized equipment • Cost of maintaining nonspecialized equipment • Cost of real property taxes • Cost of general advertising • Cost of general administration such as the plant manager's salary

When using a cost hierarchy for analyzing and estimating costs, total costs are broken down into the different cost levels in the hierarchy, and a separate cost driver is determined for each level of cost. For example, using the above hierarchy, the costs that are related to the number of units produced (such **as** direct materials or direct labor) may have direct labor hours or machines hours as the cost driver; whereas, batch costs may be driven by the number of setups of production machines or the number of times materials are move from one machine to another. Other costs may be driven by the number of different products produced. Facility-level costs are generally regarded as fixed costs and do not vary unless capacity is increased or decreased. This will be discussed further and illustrated in Module 19.

Customer Cost Hierarchy

The manufacturing hierarchy presented is but one of many possible ways of classifying activities and their costs. Classification schemes should be designed to fit the organization and meet user needs. A merchandising organization or the sales division of a manufacturing organization might use the following hierarchy.

1. Unit-level activity: performed for each unit sold.
2. **Order-level activity:** performed for each sales order.
3. **Customer-level activity:** performed to obtain or maintain each customer.
4. Facility-level activity: performed to maintain the general marketing function

This classification scheme assists in answering questions concerning the cost of individual orders or individual customers.

If an organization sells to distinct market segments (for profit, not for profit, and government), the cost hierarchy can be modified as follows:

1. Unit-level activity
2. Order-level activity
3. Customer-level activity
4. **Market-segment-level activity:** performed to obtain or maintain operations in a segment.
5. Facility-level activity

The market-segment-level activities and their related costs differ with each market segment. This classification scheme assists in answering questions concerning the profitability of each segment.

Finally, an organization that completes unique projects for different market segments (such as buildings for IBM and the U.S. Department of Defense) can use the following hierarchy to determine the profitability of each segment:

1. **Project-level activity:** performed to support the completion of each project.
2. Market-segment-level activity
3. Facility-level activity

The possibilities are endless. The important point is that both the cost hierarchy and the costs included in the hierarchy be tailored to meet the specific circumstances of an organization and the interests of management.[8] The following Business Insight considers actions at USAir to reduce product-level cost drivers.

BUSINESS INSIGHT	USAir's Strategic Cost Management

USAir Group Inc. purchased 120 new aircraft with a list price of $5.3 billion from Airbus. The primary goal of the acquisition was to reduce the types of aircraft in USAir's fleet from nine to four. The fleet, while not old, had been called a "hodgepodge." This diversity, similar to having an unnecessary number of product-level cost drivers, raises costs for pilot training, maintenance, and spare parts inventory while limiting scheduling flexibility. Industry experts note that reducing the number of aircraft types allows USAir to get more hours out of its planes and pilots. The resulting efficiency increases and cost reductions are important as USAir faces increased competition from low-cost competitors, such as Southwest Airlines.[9]

---

[8] George Foster and Mahendra Gupta, "Marketing Cost Management and Management Accounting," *Journal of Management Accounting Research,* 6, Fall 1994, pp. 43-77.

[9] "USAir Weighs Ordering Up to 120 Jets to Simplify Its Fleet and Reduce Costs," *The Wall Street Journal,* October 14, 1996, pp. A2, A5.

MODULE-END REVIEW

Assume a local Subway reported the following results for April and May:

	April	May
Unit sales	2,100	2,700
Cost of food sold	$1,575	$2,025
Wages and salaries	1,525	1,675
Rent on building	1,500	1,500
Depreciation on equipment	200	200
Utilities	710	770
Supplies	225	255
Miscellaneous.	113	131
Total	$5,848	$6,556

Required

a. Identify each cost as being fixed, variable, or mixed.
b. Using the high-low method, estimate an equation for the cost of food, wages and salaries, rent on building, and total monthly costs.
c. Predict total costs for monthly volumes of 1,000 and 2,000 units.
d. Predict the average cost per unit at monthly volumes of 1,000 and 2,000 units. Explain why the average costs differ at these two volumes.

Solution

a. Fixed costs are easily identified. They are the same at each activity level. Variable and mixed costs are determined by dividing the total costs for an item at two activity levels by the corresponding units of activity. The quotients of the variable cost items will be identical at both activity levels. The quotients of the mixed costs will differ, being lower at the higher activity level because the fixed costs are being spread over a larger number of units.

Cost	Behavior
Cost of food sold	Variable
Wages and salaries	Mixed
Rent on building	Fixed
Depreciation on equipment	Fixed
Utilities	Mixed
Supplies	Mixed
Miscellaneous.	Mixed

b. The cost of food sold was classified as a variable cost. Hence, the cost of food may be determined by dividing the total costs at either observation by the corresponding number of units.

$$b = \frac{\$1{,}575 \text{ total variable costs}}{2{,}100 \text{ units}}$$
$$= \$0.75X$$

Wages and salaries were previously classified as a mixed cost. Hence, the cost of wages and salaries is determined using the high-low method.

(variable cost) $b = \dfrac{\$1{,}675 - \$1{,}525}{2{,}700 - 2{,}100}$
$= 0.25X$

(fixed cost) $a = \$1{,}525 \text{ total cost} - (\$0.25 \times 2{,}100) \text{ variable cost}$
$= \$1{,}000$

Rent on building was classified as a fixed cost.

$$a = \$1{,}500$$

Total monthly costs most likely follow a mixed cost behavior pattern. Hence, they can be determined using the high-low method.

$$b = \frac{\$6,556 - \$5,848}{2,700 - 2,100}$$
$$= \$1.18X$$
$$a = \$5,848 - (\$1.18 \times 2,100)$$
$$= \$3,370$$
$$\text{Total costs} = \$3,370 + \$1.18X$$

where

$$X = \text{unit sales}$$

c. and d.

Volume	Total Costs	Average Cost per Unit
1,000	$3,370 + ($1.18 × 1,000) = $4,550	$4,550/1,000 = $4.550
2,000	$3,370 + ($1.18 × 2,000) = $5,730	$5,730/2,000 = $2.865

The average costs differ at 1,000 and 2,000 units because the fixed costs are being spread over a different number of units. The larger the number of units, the smaller the average fixed cost per unit.

GUIDANCE ANSWER

MANAGERIAL DECISION **You are the Purchasing Manager**

One of the quickest methods for gaining a general understanding of the relationship between a given cost and its cost driver is to graph the relationship using data from several recent periods. As purchasing manager you could probably quickly obtain information about the amount of the total purchasing department costs and number of purchase orders processed for each of the most recent eight or ten periods. By graphing these data with costs on the vertical axis and number of purchase orders on the horizontal axis, you should be able to visually determine if there is an obvious behavioral pattern (variable, fixed, or mixed). Since costs have been declining as volume has increased, this would suggest that there are some fixed costs, and that they have been declining on a per unit basis as they are spread over an increasing number of purchase orders. Using two representative data points in the scatter diagram, you can plot a cost curve on the graph, and then use the data for those two points to calculate the estimated fixed and variable costs using the high-low cost estimation method. Using these cost estimates, you can predict the total cost for next period. This method may not give you a precise estimate of the cost, but coupled with your subjective estimate of cost based on your experience as manager of the department, it should give you more confidence than merely making a best guess. Hopefully, you will have an opportunity before presenting your budget for the next period to conduct additional analyses using more advanced methods.

DISCUSSION QUESTIONS

Q15-1. Briefly describe variable, fixed, mixed, and step costs and indicate how the total cost function of each changes as activity increases within a time period.

Q15-2. Why is presenting all costs of an organization as a function of a single independent variable, although useful in obtaining a general understanding of cost behavior, often not accurate enough to make specific decisions concerning products, services, or activities?

Q15-3. Explain the term "relevant range" and why it is important in estimating total costs.

Q15-4. How are variable and fixed costs determined using the high-low method of cost estimation?

Q15-5. Distinguish between cost estimation and cost prediction.

Q15-6. Why is a scatter diagram helpful when used in conjunction with other methods of cost estimation?

Q15-7. Identify two advantages of least-squares regression analysis as a cost estimation technique.

Q15-8. Why is it important to match activity and costs within a single observation? When is this matching problem most likely to exist?

Q15-9. During the past century, how have direct materials, direct labor, and manufacturing overhead changed as a portion of total manufacturing costs? What is the implication of the change in manufacturing overhead for cost estimation?

Q15-10. Distinguish between the unit-, batch-, product-, and facility-level activities of a manufacturing organization.

MINI EXERCISES

M15-11. Classifying Cost Behavior (LO1)

Classify the total costs of each of the following as variable, fixed, mixed, or step. Sales volume is the cost driver.

- *a.* Salary of the department manager
- *b.* Memory chips in a computer assembly plant
- *c.* Real estate taxes
- *d.* Salaries of quality inspectors when each inspector can evaluate a maximum of 1,000 units per day
- *e.* Wages paid to production employees for the time spent working on products
- *f.* Electric power in a factory
- *g.* Raw materials used in production
- *h.* Automobiles rented on the basis of a fixed charge per day plus an additional charge per mile driven
- *i.* Sales commissions
- *j.* Depreciation on office equipment

M15-12. Classifying Cost Behavior (LO1)

Classify the total costs of each of the following as variable, fixed, mixed, or step.

- *a.* Straight-line depreciation on a building
- *b.* Maintenance costs at a hospital
- *c.* Rent on a photocopy machine charged as a fixed amount per month plus an additional charge per copy
- *d.* Cost of goods sold in a bookstore
- *e.* Salaries paid to temporary instructors in a college as the number of course sessions varies
- *f.* Lumber used by a house construction company
- *g.* The costs of operating a research department
- *h.* The cost of hiring a dance band for three hours
- *i.* Laser printer paper for a department printer
- *j.* Electric power in a restaurant

M15-13. Classifying Cost Behavior (LO1)

For each of the following situations, select the most appropriate cost behavior pattern (as shown in the illustrations on the next page) where the lines represent the cost behavior pattern, the vertical axis represents costs, the horizontal axis represents total volume, and the dots represent actual costs. Each pattern may be used more than once.

- *a.* Variable costs per unit
- *b.* Total fixed costs
- *c.* Total mixed costs
- *d.* Average fixed costs per unit
- *e.* Total current manufacturing costs
- *f.* Average variable costs
- *g.* Total costs when employees are paid $10 per hour for the first 40 hours worked each week and $15 for each additional hour.
- *h.* Total costs when employees are paid $10 per hour and guaranteed a minimum weekly wage of $200.
- *i.* Total costs per day when a consultant is paid $200 per hour with a maximum daily fee of $1,000.
- *j.* Total variable costs
- *k.* Total costs for salaries of social workers where each social worker can handle a maximum of 20 cases
- *l.* A water bill where a flat fee of $800 is charged for the first 100,000 gallons and additional water costs $0.005 per gallon
- *m.* Total variable costs properly used to estimate step costs
- *n.* Total materials costs
- *o.* Rent on exhibit space at a convention

M15-14. Classifying Cost Behavior (LO1)

For each of the following situations, select the most appropriate cost behavior pattern (as shown in the illustrations on page 15-23) where the lines represent the cost behavior pattern, the vertical axis represents

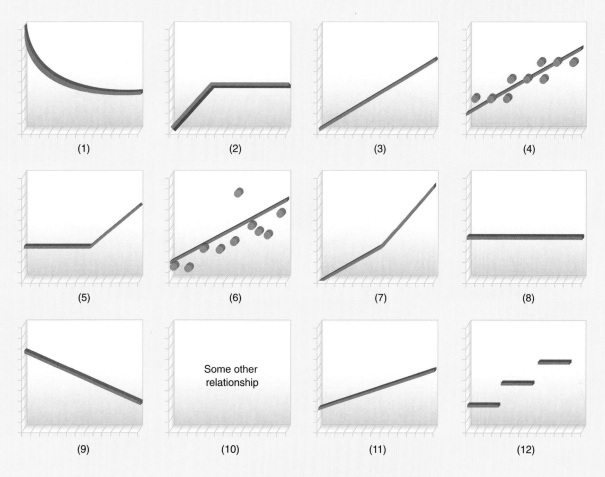

(1)　　　　(2)　　　　(3)　　　　(4)

(5)　　　　(6)　　　　(7)　　　　(8)

(9)　　　　(10) Some other relationship　　　　(11)　　　　(12)

total costs, the horizontal axis represents total volume, and the dots represent actual costs. Each pattern may be used more than once.

a. A cellular telephone bill when a flat fee is charged for the first 200 minutes of use per month and additional use costs $0.45 per minute
b. Total selling and administrative costs
c. Total labor costs when employees are paid per unit produced
d. Total overtime premium paid production employees
e. Average total cost per unit
f. Salaries of supervisors when each one can supervise a maximum of 10 employees
g. Total idle time costs when employees are paid for a minimum 40-hour week
h. Materials costs per unit
i. Total sales commissions
j. Electric power consumption in a restaurant
k. Total costs when high volumes of production require the use of overtime and obsolete equipment
l. A good linear approximation of actual costs
m. A linear cost estimation valid only within the relevant range

EXERCISES

E15-15. Computing Average Unit Costs   (LO2)

The total monthly operating costs of Chili To Go are:

$$\$10,000 + \$0.40X$$

where

$$X = \text{servings of chili}$$

Required

a. Determine the average cost per serving at each of the following monthly volumes: 100; 1,000; 5,000; and 10,000
b. Determine the monthly volume at which the average cost per serving is $0.60.

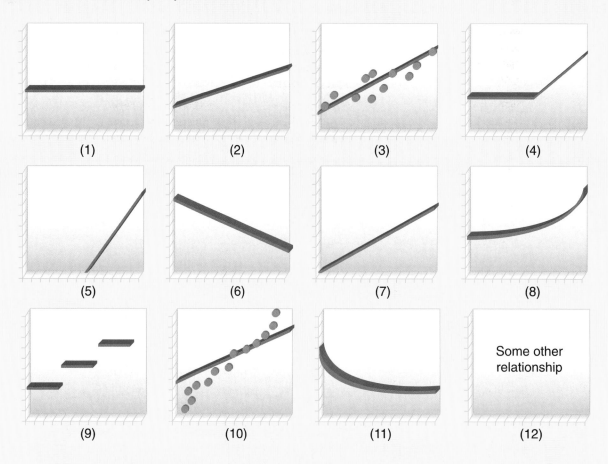

(1) (2) (3) (4)

(5) (6) (7) (8)

(9) (10) (11) (12) Some other relationship

E15-16. Automatic versus Manual Processing (LO2)

Photo Station Company operates a printing service for customers with digital cameras. The current service, which requires employees to download photos from customer cameras, has monthly operating costs of $5,000 plus $0.20 per photo printed. Management is evaluating the desirability of acquiring a machine that will allow customers to download and make prints without employee assistance. If the machine is acquired, the monthly fixed costs will increase to $10,000 and the variable costs of printing a photo will decline to $0.04 per photo.

Required

a. Determine the total costs of printing 20,000 and 50,000 photos per month:
  1. With the current employee-assisted process.
  2. With the proposed customer self-service process.
b. Determine the monthly volume at which the proposed process becomes preferable to the current process.

E15-17. Automatic versus Manual Processing (LO2)

Mid-Town Copy Service processes 1,800,000 photocopies per month at its mid-town service center. Approximately 50 percent of the photocopies require collating. Collating is currently performed by high school and college students who are paid $8 per hour. Each student collates an average of 5,000 copies per hour. Management is contemplating the lease of an automatic collating machine that has a monthly capacity of 5,000,000 photocopies, with lease and operating costs totaling $1,550, plus $0.05 per 1,000 units collated.

Required

a. Determine the total costs of collating 500,000 and 1,500,000 per month:
  1. With student help.
  2. With the collating machine.
b. Determine the monthly volume at which the automatic process becomes preferable to the manual process.
c. Should Mid-Town Copy lease the automatic collating machine at this time?

DHL (DHL)

E15-18. High-Low Cost Estimation (LO2)

Assume the local DHL delivery service hub has the following information available about fleet miles and operating costs:

Year	Miles	Operating Costs
2006	556,000	$177,000
2007	684,000	209,000

Required

Use the high-low method to develop a cost-estimating equation for total annual operating costs.

E15-19. Scatter Diagrams and High-Low Cost Estimation   (LO2, 3)

Assume the local LensCrafters has the following information on the number of sales orders received and order-processing costs.

LensCrafters

Month	Sales Orders	Order-Processing Costs
1.	3,000	$40,000
2.	1,500	28,000
3.	4,000	65,000
4.	2,800	39,000
5.	2,300	32,000
6.	1,000	20,000
7.	2,000	30,000

Required

a.   Use information from the high- and low-volume months to develop a cost-estimating equation for monthly order-processing costs.

b.   Plot the data on a scatter diagram. Using the information from representative high- and low- volume months, develop a cost-estimating equation for monthly production costs.

c.   What factors might have caused the difference in the equations developed for requirements (a) and (b)?

E15-20. Scatter Diagrams and High-Low Cost Estimation   (LO2, 3)

From April 1 through October 31, Santa Cruz County Highway Department hires temporary employees to mow and clean the right of way along county roads. The County Road Commissioner has asked you to help her in determining the variable labor cost of mowing and cleaning a mile of road. The following information is available regarding current year operations:

Month	Miles Mowed and Cleaned	Labor Costs
April	350	$7,500
May.	300	7,000
June	400	8,500
July.	250	5,000
August	375	8,000
September	200	4,500
October	100	4,300

Required

a.   Use the information from the high- and low-volume months to develop a cost-estimating equation for monthly labor costs.

b.   Plot the data on a scatter diagram. Using the information from representative high- and low-volume months, use the high-low method to develop a cost-estimating equation for monthly labor costs.

c.   What factors might have caused the difference in the equations developed for requirements (a) and (b)?

d.   Adjust the equation developed in requirement (b) to incorporate the effect of an anticipated 7 percent increase in wages.

E15-21   Cost Behavior Analysis in a Restaurant: High-Low Cost Estimation   (LO2)

Assume a Papa John's restaurant has the following information available regarding costs at representative levels of monthly sales:

Papa John's (PZZA)

	Monthly sales in units		
	5,000	**8,000**	**10,000**
Cost of food sold	$10,000	$16,000	$20,000
Wages and fringe benefits	4,250	4,400	4,500
Fees paid delivery help.	1,250	2,000	2,500
Rent on building	1,200	1,200	1,200
Depreciation on equipment	600	600	600
Utilities	500	560	600
Supplies (soap, floor wax, etc.)	150	180	200
Administrative costs.	1,300	1,300	1,300
Total	$19,250	$26,240	$30,900

Required

a. Identify each cost as being variable, fixed, or mixed.

b. Use the high-low method to develop a schedule identifying the amount of each cost that is fixed per month or variable per unit. Total the amounts under each category to develop an equation for total monthly costs.

c. Predict total costs for a monthly sales volume of 9,500 units.

E15-22. Developing an Equation from Average Costs (LO2)

The America Dog and Cat Hotel is a pet hotel located in Las Vegas. Assume that in March, when dog-days (occupancy) were at an annual low of 500, the average cost per dog-day was $21. In July, when dog-days were at a capacity level of 4,000, the average cost per dog-day was $7.

Required

a. Develop an equation for monthly operating costs.

b. Determine the average cost per dog-day at an annual volume of 24,000 dog-days.

E15-23. Selecting an Independent Variable: Scatter Diagrams (LO2, 3)

Valley Production Company produces backpacks that are sold to sporting goods stores throughout the Rocky Mountains. Presented is information on production costs and inventory changes for five recent months:

	January	**February**	**March**	**April**	**May**
Finished goods inventory in units:					
Beginning	30,000	40,000	50,000	30,000	60,000
Manufactured	60,000	90,000	80,000	90,000	100,000
Available.	90,000	130,000	130,000	120,000	160,000
Sold	(50,000)	(80,000)	(100,000)	(60,000)	(120,000)
Ending	40,000	50,000	30,000	60,000	40,000
Manufacturing costs. . .	$300,000	$500,000	$450,000	$450,000	$550,000

Required

a. With the aid of scatter diagrams, determine whether units sold or units manufactured is a better predictor of manufacturing costs.

b. Prepare an explanation for your answer to requirement (a).

c. Which independent variable, units sold or units manufactured, should be a better predictor of selling costs? Why?

E15-24. Selecting a Basis for Predicting Shipping Expenses (Requires Computer Spreadsheet*) (LO2, 3)

Pitt Company assembles and sells computer boards in western Pennsylvania. In an effort to improve the planning and control of shipping expenses, management is trying to determine which of three variables-units shipped, weight shipped, or sales value of units shipped-has the closest relationship with shipping expenses. The following information is available:

---

* This exercise and several subsequent assignments require the use of a computer spreadsheet such as Excel® to solve. This assignment assumes previous knowledge of computer spreadsheets.

Month	Units Shipped	Weight Shipped (lbs.)	Sales Value of Units Shipped	Shipping Expenses
May.	3,000	6,200	$100,000	$ 5,000
June	5,000	8,000	110,000	7,000
July	4,000	8,100	80,000	6,000
August	7,000	10,000	114,000	10,000
September	6,000	7,000	140,000	8,000
October	4,500	8,000	160,000	7,600

Required

a. With the aid of a spreadsheet program, determine whether units shipped, weight shipped, or sales value of units shipped has the closest relationship with shipping expenses.

b. Using the independent variable that appears to have the closest relationship to shipping expenses, develop a cost-estimating equation for total monthly shipping expenses.

c. Use the equation developed in requirement (b) to predict total shipping expenses in a month when 5,000 units, weighing 7,000 lbs., with a total sales value of $114,000 are shipped.

PROBLEMS

P15-25. High-Low and Scatter Diagrams with Implications for Regression (LO2, 3)

Glaze Donut Shop produces and sells donuts at each of its restaurants. Presented is monthly cost and sales information for one of Glaze's restaurants.

Month	Sales (Dozens)	Total Costs
January.	8,000	$24,000
February	6,500	22,000
March	4,500	17,000
April	2,000	16,000
May.	5,500	18,000
June	6,000	19,500

Required

a. Using the high-low method, develop a cost-estimating equation for the donut shop

b. 1. Plot the equation developed in requirement (a).
   2. Using the same graph, develop a scatter diagram of all observations for the donut shop. Select representative high and low values and draw a second cost-estimating equation.

c. Which is a better predictor of future costs? Why?

d. If you decided to develop a cost-estimating equation using least squares regression analysis, should you include all the observations? Why or why not?

e. Mention two reasons that the least-squares regression is superior to the high-low and scatter diagram methods of cost estimation.

P15-26. Multiple Cost Drivers (LO4)

Scottsdale Ltd. manufactures a variety of high-volume and low-volume products to customer demand. Presented is information on 2007 manufacturing overhead and activity cost drivers.

Level	Total Cost	Units of Cost Driver
Unit	$500,000	20,000 machine hours
Batch	100,000	1,000 customer orders
Product	200,000	50 products

Product X1 required 2,000 machine hours to fill 10 customer orders for a total of 8,000 units.

Required

a. Assuming all manufacturing overhead is estimated and predicted on the basis of machine hours, determine the predicted total overhead costs to produce the 8,000 units of product X1.

b. Assuming manufacturing overhead is estimated and predicted using separate rates for machine hours, customer orders, and products (a multiple-level cost hierarchy), determine the predicted total overhead costs to produce the 8,000 units of product X1.

c. Calculate the error in predicting manufacturing overhead using machine hours versus using multiple cost drivers. Indicate whether the use of only machine hours results in overpredicting or underpredicting the costs to produce 8,000 units of product X1.

d. Determine the error in the prediction of X1 batch-level costs resulting from the use of only machine hours. Indicate whether the use of only machine hours results in overpredicting or underpredicting the batch-level costs of product X1.

e. Determine the error in the prediction of X1 product-level costs resulting from the use of only machine hours. Indicate whether the use of only machine hours results in overpredicting or underpredicting the product-level costs of product X1.

P15-27. Unit- and Batch-Level Cost Drivers (LO4)

KC, a fast-food restaurant, serves fried chicken, fried fish, and French fries. The managers have estimated the costs of a batch of fried chicken for KC's all-you-can-eat Friday Fried Fiesta. Each batch must be 100 pieces. The chicken is precut by the chain headquarters and sent to the stores in 10-piece bags. Each bag costs $3. Preparing a batch of 100 pieces of chicken with KC's special coating takes one employee two hours. The current wage rate is $8 per hour. Another cost driver is the cost of putting fresh oil into the fryers. New oil, costing $5, is used for each batch.

Required

a. Determine the cost of preparing one batch of 100 pieces.

b. If management projects that it will sell 300 pieces of fried chicken, determine the total batch and unit costs.

c. If management estimates the sales to be 350 pieces, determine the total costs.

d. How much will the batch costs increase if the government raises the minimum wage to $10 per hour?

e. If management decided to reduce the number of pieces in a batch to 50, determine the cost of preparing 350 pieces. Assume that the batch would take half as long to prepare, and management wants to replace the oil after 50 pieces are cooked.

f. Refer to your solutions to requirements (c) and (e). Would management be wise to reduce the batch size to 50?

CASES

C15-28. Negative Fixed Costs (LO3)

"This is crazy!" exclaimed the production supervisor as he reviewed the work of his new assistant. "You and that computer are telling me that my fixed costs are negative! Tell me, how did you get these negative fixed costs, and what am I supposed to do with them?"

Required

Explain to the supervisor the meaning of the negative "fixed costs" and what can be done with them.

C15-29. Significance of High R-Squared (LO3)

Oliver Morris had always been suspicious of "newfangled mathematical stuff," and the most recent suggestion of his new assistant merely confirmed his belief that schools are putting a lot of useless junk in students' heads. It seems that after an extensive analysis of historical data, the assistant suggested that the number of pounds of scrap was the best basis for predicting manufacturing overhead. In response to Mr. Morris's rage, the slightly intimidated assistant indicated that of the 35 equations he tried, pounds of scrap had the highest coefficient of determination with manufacturing overhead.

Required

Comment on Morris's reaction. Is it justified? Is it likely that the number of pounds of scrap is a good basis for predicting manufacturing overhead? Is it a feasible basis for predicting manufacturing overhead?

C15-30. Estimating Machine Repair Costs (LO3)

In an attempt to determine the best basis for predicting machine repair costs, the production supervisor accumulated daily information on these costs and production over a one-month period. Applying simple regression analysis to the data, she obtained the following estimating equation:

$$Y = \$800 - \$2.601X$$

where

$$Y = \text{total daily machine repair costs}$$
$$X = \text{daily production in units}$$

Because of the negative relationship between repair costs and production, she was somewhat skeptical of the results, even though the R-squared was a respectable 0.765.

Required

a.   What is the most likely explanation of the negative variable costs?

b.   Suggest an alternative procedure for estimating machine repair costs that might prove more useful.

C15-31.   Ethical Problem Uncovered by Cost Estimation   (LO3)

Phoenix Management Company owns and provides management services for several shopping centers. After five years with the company, Mike Moyer was recently promoted to the position of manager of X-Town, an 18-store mall on the outskirts of a downtown area. When he accepted the assignment, Mike was told that he would hold the position for only a couple of years because X-Town would likely be torn down to make way for a new sports stadium. Mike was also told that if he did well in this assignment, he would be in line for heading one of the company's new 200-store operations that were currently in the planning stage.

While reviewing X-Town's financial records for the past few years, Mike observed that last year's oil consumption was up by 8 percent, even though the number of heating degree days was down by 4 percent. Somewhat curious, Mike uncovered the following information:

- X-Town is heated by forced-air oil heat. The furnace is five years old and has been well maintained.
- Fuel oil is kept in four 5,000-gallon underground oil tanks. The oil tanks were installed 25 years ago.
- Replacing the tanks would cost $80,000. If pollution was found, cleanup costs could go as high as $2,000,000, depending on how much oil had leaked into the ground and how far it had spread.
- Replacing the tanks would add more congestion to X-Town's parking situation.

Required

What should Mike do? Explain.

C15-32.   Activity Cost Drivers and Cost Estimation   (LO3, 4)

Blue Ridge Ice Cream Company produces ten varieties of ice cream in large vats, several thousand gallons at a time. The ice cream is distributed to several categories of customers. Some ice cream is packaged in large containers and sold to college and university food services. Some is packaged in half-gallon or small containers and sold through wholesale distributors to grocery stores. Finally, some is packaged in a variety of individual servings and sold directly to the public from trucks owned and operated by Blue Ridge. Management has always assumed that costs fluctuated with the volume of ice cream, and cost-estimating equations have been based on the following cost function:

$$\text{Estimated costs} = \text{Fixed costs} + \text{Variable costs per gallon} \times \text{Production in gallons}$$

Lately, however, this equation has not been a very accurate predictor of total costs. At the same time, management has noticed that the volumes and varieties of ice cream sold through the three distinct distribution channels have fluctuated from month to month.

Required

a.   What *relevant* major assumption is inherent in the cost-estimating equation currently used by Blue Ridge?

b.   Why might Blue Ridge wish to develop a cost-estimating equation that recognizes the hierarchy of activity costs? Explain.

c.   Develop the general form of a more accurate cost-estimating equation for Blue Ridge. Clearly label and explain all elements of the equation, and provide specific examples of costs for each element.

C15-33.   Multiple Regression Analysis for a Special Decision (Requires Computer Spreadsheet)   (LO2, 3)

For billing purposes, Central City Health Clinic classifies its services into one of four major procedures, X1 through X4. A local business has proposed that Central City provide health services to its employees and their families at the following set rates per procedure:

X1	$ 45
X2	90
X3	60
X4	105

Because these rates are significantly below the current rates charged for these services, management has asked for detailed cost information on each procedure. The following information is available for the most recent 12 months.

		Number of Procedures			
Month	Total Cost	X1	X2	X3	X4
1	$23,000	30	100	205	75
2	25,000	38	120	180	90
3	27,000	50	80	140	150
4	19,000	20	90	120	100
5	20,000	67	50	160	80
6	27,000	90	75	210	105
7	25,500	20	110	190	110
8	21,500	15	120	175	80
9	26,000	60	85	125	140
10	22,000	20	90	100	140
11	22,800	20	70	150	130
12	26,500	72	60	200	120

Required

a. Use multiple regression analysis to determine the unit cost of each procedure. How much variation in monthly cost is explained by your cost-estimating equation?

b. Evaluate the rates proposed by the local business. Assuming Central City has excess capacity and no employees of the local business currently patronize the clinic, what are your recommendations regarding the proposal?

c. Evaluate the rates proposed by the local business. Assuming Central City is operating at capacity and would have to turn current customers away if it agrees to provide health services to the local business, what are your recommendations regarding the proposal?

C15-34. Cost Estimation, Interpretation, and Analysis (Requires Computer Spreadsheet) (LO2, 3)

Carolina Table Company produces two styles of tables, dining room and kitchen. Presented is monthly information on production volume and manufacturing costs:

Period	Total Manufacturing Costs	Total Tables Produced	Dining Room Tables Produced	Kitchen Tables Produced
June 2006.	$31,100	250	50	200
July	33,925	205	105	100
August	40,420	285	105	180
September	26,495	210	40	170
October	28,080	175	75	100
November.	35,050	210	110	100
December.	35,245	245	90	155
January 2007	31,550	250	50	200
February	31,490	220	70	150
March	29,650	180	80	100
April	65,200	315	180	135
May.	39,955	280	105	175
June	34,695	255	75	180
July	36,920	235	110	125
August	30,815	195	85	110
September	40,290	260	120	140
October	35,805	250	90	160
November.	38,400	270	100	170
December.	25,100	165	60	105

Required

a. Use the high-low method to develop a cost-estimating equation for total manufacturing costs. Interpret the meaning of the "fixed" costs and comment on the results.

b. Use the chart feature of a spreadsheet to develop a scatter graph of total manufacturing costs and total units produced. Use the graph to identify any unusual observations.

c. Excluding any unusual observations, use the high-low method to develop a cost-estimating equation for total manufacturing costs. Comment on the results, comparing them with the results in requirement (a).

d. Use simple regression analysis to develop a cost-estimating equation for total manufacturing costs. What advantages does simple regression analysis have in comparison with the high-low method of cost estimation? Why must analysts carefully evaluate the data used in simple regression analysis?

e. A customer has offered to purchase 50 dining room tables for $180 per table. Management has asked your advice regarding the desirability of accepting the offer. What advice do you have for management? Additional analysis is required.

C15-35. Simple and Multiple Regression (Requires Computer Spreadsheet) (LO2, 3)

Wanda Sable is employed by a mail-order distributor and reconditions used tuner/amplifiers, tape decks, and compact disk (CD) players. Wanda is paid $12 per hour, plus an extra $6 per hour for work in excess of 40 hours per week. The distributor just announced plans to outsource all reconditioning work. Because the distributor is pleased with the quality of Wanda's work, she has been asked to enter into a long-term contract to recondition used CD players at a rate of $30 per player, plus all parts. The distributor also offered to provide all necessary equipment at a rate of $200 per month. She has been informed that she should plan on reconditioning as many CD players as she can handle, up to a maximum of 20 CD players per week.

Wanda has room in her basement to set up a work area, but she is unsure of the economics of accepting the contract, as opposed to working for a local Radio Stuff store at $8 per hour. Data related to the time spent and the number of units of each type of electronic equipment Wanda has reconditioned in recent weeks is as follows:

Week	Tuner Amplifiers	Tape Decks	Compact Disk (CD) Players	Total Units	Total Hours
1	4	5	5	14	40
2	0	7	6	13	42
3	4	3	7	14	40
4	0	2	12	14	46
5	11	6	4	21	48
6	5	8	3	16	44
7	5	8	3	16	44
8	5	6	5	16	43
9	2	6	10	18	53
10	8	4	6	18	46
Total				160	446

Required

Assuming she wants to work an average of 40 hours per week, what should Wanda do?

Cost-Volume-Profit Analysis and Planning

LEARNING OBJECTIVES

LO1 Identify the uses and limitations of traditional cost-volume-profit analysis. (p. 16-3)

LO2 Prepare and contrast contribution and functional income statements. (p. 16-6)

LO3 Apply cost-volume-profit analysis to find a break-even point and for preliminary profit planning. (p. 16-8)

LO4 Analyze the profitability and sales mix of a multiple-product firm. (p. 16-14)

LO5 Apply operating leverage ratio to assess opportunities for profit and the risks of loss. (p. 16-17)

COST STRUCTURE AND FIRM PROFITABILITY

The slowing of commercial activity and technology investments in the early 2000s radically altered the income projections of many firms. These economic changes and their resulting impacts demonstrate a valuable managerial lesson about the impact of cost structure on profitability.

Managers at firms such as Inktomi, Microsoft, Yahoo, Cisco Systems, Amazon.com, and Webvan spent heavily on new product development in years leading up to the downturn of the early 2000s. These investments financed projects such as software development, new hardware technologies, Internet marketing, Web site development, and automated warehouses. The investments generated additional productive and service capacity, but their cost structures were dominated by high fixed costs. These fixed costs resulted from both the need to maintain the technology supporting existing systems and the investment necessary to develop the next generation of hardware and software.

In an expanding market, managers take advantage of fixed costs to generate profitable growth since additional customers do not add much additional cost. In this case, a cost structure dominated by fixed costs is a smart managerial decision.

In an unstable or declining economy, however, a high fixed-cost structure is harmful. Just as adding new customers does not markedly increase costs when a firm has a high fixed-cost structure, reducing the number of customers does not lower costs very much. For example, as sales declined at Inktomi—a developer of software to manage Web

content—profits fell sharply. High fixed-cost structures are profitable when sales grow but result in rapid deterioration of profits when sales decline.

The online grocer Webvan is a striking case of the relation between cost, volume, and profit. With $1 billion of financing, Webvan's well-respected management team embarked on a strategy to use automated warehouses to service customers. These high fixed-cost fulfillment centers held the promise of substantial profitability, but *only* if Webvan could reach a high customer volume level. Other online grocery firms adopted strategies requiring less technology and more labor in the fulfillment process. Since labor costs are variable rather than fixed, rival firms would break even at about 40 percent of the customer volume that Webvan required to break even.

Although Webvan supporters correctly stated that it would be much more profitable than its rivals once the firm had covered its costs, sales never reached that level. When Webvan ceased operations after exhausting its financing, an observer commented that while demand does exist for an online, home-delivery grocery business, management must use great care in deciding its business model and cost structure.

High fixed costs can yield huge profits in the right circumstances. Yet, the recent experiences of some firms illustrate that such cost structures have some inherent risks. The relations among possible cost structures, potential volumes, and opportunities for profit provide a conceptual basis for profitability analysis and planning. This is the focus of this module.

Source: *Business Week, The Wall Street Journal, 10-K Reports.*[1]

---

[1]Peter Elstrom, "The End of Fuzzy Math," *Business Week,* December 11, 2000, p. EB100; Linda Himelstein, "Webvan Left the Basics on the Shelf," *Business Week,* July 23, 2001, p. 43; Greg Ip, "As Profits Swoon, Companies Blame a Market Change in Cost Structure," *The Wall Street Journal,* Interactive Edition, May 16, 2001; and 10-K reports for Webvan and Inktomi.

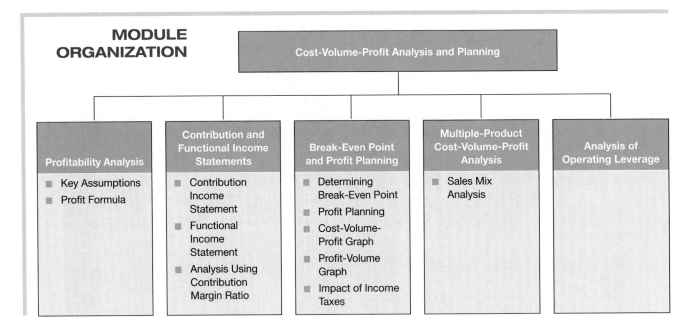

`This module introduces basic approaches to profitability analysis and planning. We consider single-product, multiple-product, and service organizations; income taxes, sales mix, and the effects of cost structure on the relation between profit potential and the risk of loss.

PROFITABILITY ANALYSIS

LO1 Identify the uses and limitations of traditional cost-volume-profit analysis.

Profitability analysis involves examining the relationships among revenues, costs, and profits. Performing profitability analysis requires an understanding of selling prices and the behavior of activity cost drivers. Profitability analysis is widely used in the economic evaluation of existing or proposed products or services. Typically, it is performed before decisions are finalized in the operating budget for a future period.

Cost-volume-profit (CVP) analysis is a technique used to examine the relationships among the total volume of an independent variable, total costs, total revenues, and profits for a time period (typically a quarter or year). With CVP analysis, volume refers to a single activity cost driver, such as unit sales, that is assumed to correlate with changes in revenues, costs, and profits.

Cost-volume-profit analysis is useful in the early stages of planning because it provides an easily understood framework for discussing planning issues and organizing relevant data. CVP analysis is widely used by for-profit as well as not-for-profit organizations. It is equally applicable to service, merchandising, and manufacturing firms.

In for-profit organizations, CVP analysis is used to answer such questions as these: How many photocopies must the local Kinko's produce to earn a profit of $80,000? At what dollar sales volume will Burger King's total revenues and total costs be equal? What profit will General Electric earn at an annual sales volume of $60 billion? What will happen to the profit of Red Lobster if there is a 20 percent increase in the cost of food and a 10 percent increase in the selling price of meals? The Research Insight on the following page indicates how the concepts discussed in this and other modules are important to the success of new businesses.

In not-for-profit organizations, CVP analysis is used to establish service levels, plan fund-raising activities, and determine funding requirements. How many meals can the downtown Salvation Army serve with an annual budget of $600,000? How many tickets must be sold for the benefit concert to raise $20,000? Given the current cost structure, current tuition rates, and projected enrollments, how much money must Cornell University raise from other sources?

Key Assumptions

CVP analysis is subject to a number of assumptions. Although these assumptions do not negate the usefulness of CVP models, especially for a single product or service, they do suggest the need for further analysis before plans are finalized. Among the more important assumptions are:

1. *All costs are classified as fixed or variable.* This assumption is most reasonable when analyzing the profitability of a specific event (such as a concert) or the profitability of an organization that produces a single product or service on a continuous basis.

2. *The total cost function is linear within the relevant range.* This assumption is often valid within a relevant range of normal operations, but over the entire range of possible activity, changes in efficiency are likely to result in a nonlinear cost function.

3. *The total revenue function is linear within the relevant range.* Unit selling prices are assumed constant over the range of possible volumes. This implies a purely competitive market for final products or services. In some economic models in which demand responds to price changes, the revenue function is nonlinear. In these situations, the linear approximation is accurate only within a limited range of activity.

4. *The analysis is for a single product, or the sales mix of multiple products is constant.* The **sales mix** refers to the relative portion of unit or dollar sales derived from each product or service. If products have different selling prices and costs, changes in the mix affect CVP model results.

5. *There is only one cost driver: unit or sales dollar volume.* In a complex organization it is seldom possible to represent the multitude of factors that drive cost with a single cost driver.

When applied to a single product (such as pounds of potato chips), service (such as the number of pages printed), or event (such as the number of tickets sold to a concert), it is reasonable to assume the single independent variable is the cost driver. The total costs associated with the single product, service, or event during a specific time period are often determined by this single activity cost driver.

Although cost-volume-profit analysis is often used to understand the overall operations of an organization or business segment, accuracy decreases as the scope of operations being analyzed increases.

RESEARCH INSIGHT   **Want to Finance a New Business?**

About 80 percent of all new businesses fail in the first five years. A major reason for their failure is the lack of equity financing. To obtain financing for a new business, it is necessary to show how the business will make a profit. Five simple steps to help convince cautious investors to risk funds in a new business follow:

1. Project start-up costs and operating budgets.
2. Project income statements.
3. Project cash flow statements.
4. Determine the business's break-even point.
5. Develop "Plan B."

The last step is important. Plan B includes "what if" statements offering solutions to potential problems.[2]

Profit Formula

The profit associated with a product, service, or event is equal to the difference between total revenues and total costs as follows:

$$\pi = R - Y$$

---

[2] "Five Simple Steps to Help Your Business Build Financial Success," *Hudson Valley Business Journal,* January 19, 1998, p. 20.

where

$$\pi = \text{Profit}$$
$$R = \text{Total revenues}$$
$$Y = \text{Total costs}$$

The revenues are a function of the unit sales volume and the unit selling price, while total costs for a time period are a function of the fixed costs per period and the unit variable costs as follows:

$$R = pX$$
$$Y = a + bX$$

where

$$p = \text{Unit selling price}$$
$$a = \text{Fixed costs}$$
$$b = \text{Unit variable costs}$$
$$X = \text{Unit sales}$$

The equation for profit can then be expanded to include the above details of the total revenue and total cost equations as follows:

$$\pi = pX - (a + bX)$$

Using information on the selling price, fixed costs per period, and variable costs per unit, this formula is used to predict profit at any specified activity level.

To illustrate, assume that Benchmark Paper Company's only product is high-quality photocopy paper that it manufactures and sells to wholesale distributors at $8.00 per carton. Applying inventory minimization techniques, Benchmark does not maintain inventories of raw materials or finished goods. Instead, newly purchased raw materials are delivered directly to the factory, and finished goods are loaded directly onto trucks for shipment. Benchmark's variable and fixed costs follow.

1. **Direct materials** refer to the cost of the primary raw materials converted into finished goods. Because the consumption of raw materials increases as the quantity of goods produced increases, *direct materials represents a variable cost.* Benchmark's raw materials consist primarily of paper purchased in large rolls and packing supplies such as boxes. Benchmark also treats the costs of purchasing, receiving, and inspecting raw materials as part of the cost of direct materials. All together, these costs are $1.00 per carton of finished product.

2. **Direct labor** refers to wages earned by production employees for the time they spend working on the conversion of raw materials into finished goods. Based on Benchmark's manufacturing procedures, *direct labor represents a variable cost.* These costs are $0.25 per carton.

3. **Variable manufacturing overhead** includes all other variable costs associated with converting raw materials into finished goods. Benchmark's variable manufacturing overhead costs include the costs of lubricants for cutting and packaging machines, electricity to operate these machines, and the cost to move materials between receiving and shipping docks and the cutting and packaging machines. These costs are $1.25 per carton.

4. **Variable selling and administrative costs** include all variable costs other than those directly associated with converting raw materials into finished goods. At Benchmark, these costs include sales commissions, transportation of finished goods to wholesale distributors, and the cost of processing the receipt and disbursement of cash. These costs are $0.50 per carton.

5. **Fixed manufacturing overhead** includes all fixed costs associated with converting raw materials into finished goods. Benchmark's fixed manufacturing costs include the depreciation, property taxes, and insurance on buildings and machines used for manufacturing, the salaries of manufacturing supervisors, and the fixed portion of electricity used to light the factory. These costs are $5,000.00 per month.

6. **Fixed selling and administrative costs** include all fixed costs other than those directly associated with converting raw materials into finished goods. These costs include the salaries of Benchmark's president and many other staff personnel such as accounting and marketing.

Also included are depreciation, property taxes, insurance on facilities used for administrative purposes, and any related utilities costs. These costs are $10,000.00 per month.

Benchmark's variable and fixed costs are summarized here.

Variable Costs per Carton			Fixed Costs per Month	
Manufacturing			Manufacturing overhead	$ 5,000.00
Direct materials.	$1.00		Selling and administrative	10,000.00
Direct labor	0.25		Total	$15,000.00
Manufacturing overhead. . .	1.25	$2.50		
Selling and administrative . . .		0.50		
Total		$3.00		

The cost estimation techniques discussed in Module 15 can be used to determine many detailed costs. Least-squares regression, for example, might be used to determine the variable and monthly fixed amount of electricity used in manufacturing. Benchmark manufactures and sells a single product on a continuous basis with all sales to distributors under standing contracts. Therefore, it is reasonable to assume that in the short run, Benchmark's total monthly costs respond to a single cost driver, cartons sold. Combining all this information, Benchmark's profit equation is:

$$\text{Profit} = \$8.00X - (\$15,000.00 + \$3.00X)$$

where

$$X = \text{cartons sold}$$

Using this equation, Benchmark's profit at a volume of 5,400 units is $12,000.00, computed as ($8.00 × 5,400) − [$15,000.00 + ($3.00 × 5,400)].

CONTRIBUTION AND FUNCTIONAL INCOME STATEMENTS

Contribution Income Statement

LO2 Prepare and contrast contribution and functional income statements.

To provide more detailed information on anticipated or actual financial results at a particular sales volume, a contribution income statement is often prepared. Benchmark's contribution income statement for a volume of 5,400 units is in Exhibit 16.1. In a **contribution income statement,** costs are classified according to behavior as variable or fixed, and the **contribution margin** (the difference between total revenues and total variable costs) that goes toward covering fixed costs and providing a profit is emphasized.

Functional Income Statement

Contrast the contribution income statement in Exhibit 16.1 with the income statement in Exhibit 16.2 (next page). This statement is called a **functional income statement** because costs are classified according to function (rather than behavior), such as manufacturing, selling, and administrative. This is the type of income statement typically included in corporate annual reports.

EXHIBIT 16.1	Contribution Income Statement	
BENCHMARK PAPER COMPANY		
Contribution Income Statement		
For a Monthly Volume of 5,400 Cartons		
Sales (5,400 × $8.00).		$43,200
Less variable costs		
Direct materials (5,400 × $1.00).	$ 5,400	
Direct labor (5,400 × $0.25)	1,350	
Manufacturing overhead (5,400 × $1.25).	6,750	
Selling and administrative (5,400 × $0.50). . . .	2,700	(16,200)
Contribution margin		27,000
Less fixed costs		
Manufacturing overhead.	5,000	
Selling and administrative.	10,000	(15,000)
Profit.		$12,000

EXHIBIT 16.2	Functional Income Statement

BENCHMARK PAPER COMPANY
Functional Income Statement
For a Monthly Volume of 5,400 Cartons

Sales (5,400 × $8.00)...............................		$43,200
Less cost of goods sold		
Direct materials (5,400 × $1.00)......................	$ 5,400	
Direct labor (5,400 × $0.25)........................	1,350	
Variable manufacturing overhead (5,400 × $1.25).........	6,750	
Fixed manufacturing overhead.......................	5,000	(18,500)
Gross margin		24,700
Less other expenses		
Variable selling and administrative (5,400 × $0.50)........	2,700	
Fixed selling and administrative.....................	10,000	(12,700)
Profit...		$12,000

A problem with a functional income statement is the difficulty of relating it to the profit formula in which costs are classified according to behavior rather than function. The relationship between sales volume, costs, and profits is not readily apparent in a functional income statement. Consequently, we emphasize contribution income statements because they provide better information to internal decision makers.

Analysis Using Contribution Margin Ratio

While the contribution income statement (shown in Exhibit 16.1) presents information on total sales revenue, total variable costs, and so forth, it is sometimes useful to present information on a per-unit or portion of sales basis.

	Total	Per Unit	Ratio to Sales
Sales (5,400 units)	$43,200	$8	1.000
Variable costs.............	(16,200)	(3)	(0.375)
Contribution margin	27,000	$5	0.625
Fixed costs...............	(15,000)		
Profit....................	$12,000		

The per-unit information assists in short-range planning. The **unit contribution margin** is the difference between the unit selling price and the unit variable costs. It is the amount, $5.00 in this case, that each unit contributes toward covering fixed costs and earning a profit.

The contribution margin is widely used in **sensitivity analysis** (the study of the responsiveness of a model to changes in one or more of its independent variables). Benchmark's income statement is an economic model of the firm, and the unit contribution margin indicates how sensitive Benchmark's income model is to changes in unit sales. If, for example, sales increase by 100 cartons per month, the increase in profit is readily determined by multiplying the 100-carton increase in sales by the $5 unit contribution margin as follows:

100 (carton sales increase) × $5 (unit contribution margin) = $500 (profit increase)

There is no increase in fixed costs, so the new profit level becomes $12,500 ($12,000 + $500) per month.

When expressed as a ratio to sales, the contribution margin is identified as the **contribution margin ratio.** It is the portion of each dollar of sales revenue contributed toward covering fixed costs and earning a profit. In the abbreviated income statement above, the portion of each dollar of sales revenue contributed toward covering fixed costs and earning a profit is $0.625 ($27,000 ÷ $43,200). This is Benchmark's contribution margin ratio. If sales revenue increases by $800 per month, the increase in profits is computed as follows:

$800 (sales increase) × 0.625 (contribution margin ratio) = $500 (profit increase)

The contribution margin ratio is especially useful in situations involving several products or when unit sales information is not available.

BREAK-EVEN POINT AND PROFIT PLANNING

The **break-even point** occurs at the unit or dollar sales volume when total revenues equal total costs. The break-even point is of great interest to management. Until break-even sales are reached, the product, service, event, or business segment of interest operates at a loss. Beyond this point, increasing levels of profits are achieved. Also, management often wants to know the **margin of safety,** the amount by which actual or planned sales exceed the break-even point. Other questions of interest include the probability of exceeding the break-even sales volume and the effect of some proposed change on the break-even point.

LO3 Apply cost-volume-profit analysis to find a break-even point and for preliminary profit planning.

Determining Break-Even Point

In determining the break-even point, the equation for total revenues is set equal to the equation for total costs and then solved for the break-even unit sales volume. Using the general equations for total revenues and total costs, the following results are obtained. Setting total revenues equal to total costs:

$$\text{Total revenues} = \text{Total costs}$$
$$pX = a + bX$$

Solving for the break-even sales volume:

$$pX - bX = a$$
$$(p - b)X = a$$
$$X = a/(p - b)$$

In words:

$$\text{Break-even unit sales volume} = \frac{\text{Fixed costs}}{\text{Selling price per unit} - \text{Variable costs per unit}}$$

Because the denominator is the unit contribution margin, the break-even point is also computed by dividing fixed costs by the unit contribution margin:

$$\text{Break-even unit sales volume} = \frac{\text{Fixed costs}}{\text{Unit contribution margin}}$$

With a $5 unit contribution margin and fixed costs of $15,000 per month, Benchmark's break-even point is 3,000 units per month ($15,000 ÷ $5). Stated another way, at a $5 per-unit contribution margin, 3,000 units of contribution are required to cover $15,000 of fixed costs. With a break-even point of 3,000 units, the monthly margin of safety and expected profit for a sales volume of 5,400 units are 2,400 units (5,400 expected unit sales − 3,000 break-even sales) and $12,000 (2,400 unit margin of safety × $5 unit contribution margin), respectively.

Profit Planning

Establishing profit objectives is an important part of planning in for-profit organizations. Profit objectives are stated in many ways. They can be set as a percentage of last year's profits, as a percentage of total assets at the start of the current year, or as a percentage of owners' equity. They might be based on a profit trend, or they might be expressed as a percentage of sales. The economic outlook for the firm's products as well as anticipated changes in products, costs, and technology are also considered in establishing profit objectives.

Before incorporating profit plans into a detailed budget, it is useful to obtain some preliminary information on the feasibility of those plans. Cost-volume-profit analysis is one way of doing this. By manipulating cost-volume-profit relationships, management can determine the sales volume corresponding to a desired profit. Management might then evaluate the feasibility of this sales volume. If the profit plans are feasible, a complete budget might be developed for this activity level. The required sales volume might be infeasible because of market conditions or because the required volume exceeds production or service capacity, in which case management must lower its profit objective or consider other ways of achieving it. Alternatively, the required sales volume might be less than management believes the firm is capable of selling, in which case management might raise its profit objective.

Assume that Benchmark's management desires to know the unit sales volume required to achieve a monthly profit of $18,000. Using the profit formula, the required unit sales volume is determined by setting profits equal to $18,000 and solving for X, the unit sales volume.

$$\textbf{Profit} = \textbf{Total revenues} - \textbf{Total costs}$$
$$\$18{,}000 = \$8X - (\$15{,}000 + \$3X)$$

Solving for X

$$\$8X - \$3X = \$15{,}000 + \$18{,}000$$
$$X = (\$15{,}000 + \$18{,}000) \div \$5$$
$$= \textbf{6{,}600 units}$$

The total contribution must cover the desired profit as well as the fixed costs. Hence, the target sales volume required to achieve a desired profit is computed as the fixed costs plus the desired profit, all divided by the unit contribution margin.

$$\textbf{Target unit sales volume} = \frac{\textbf{Fixed costs + Desired Profit}}{\textbf{Unit contribution margin}}$$

The previous Business Insight considers CVP analysis for *The American,* a small newspaper whose strategic position focuses on a market niche. In contrast, the Business Insight on the following page considers CVP analysis for **Hewlett-Packard**, a large manufacturer whose strategic position for personal computers focuses on cost leadership.

Cost-Volume-Profit Graph

A **cost-volume-profit graph** illustrates the relationships among activity volume, total revenues, total costs, and profits. Its usefulness comes from highlighting the break-even point and depicting revenue, cost, and profit relationships over a range of activity. This representation allows management to view the relative amount of important variables at any graphed volume. Benchmark's monthly CVP graph is in

---

[3]Jerry Useem, "American Hopes to Conquer World—From Long Island," *Inc.,* December 1996, p. 23.

BUSINESS INSIGHT | **HP's High-Volume, Low-Price Break-Even Point**

"The wealthiest 1 billion people in the world are pretty well served by IT companies," says HP's director of its e-inclusion program. "We're targeting the next 4 billion." The goal of e-inclusion is for HP to be the leader in satisfying a demand for simple and economical computer products for technology-excluded regions of the world. HP already derives 60 percent of its sales overseas, and it plans to build on these beachheads to develop what may be the greatest marketing frontier of the coming decades. With worldwide operations and a low selling price, the HP strategy combines high fixed costs and a low contribution margin, leading to a high break-even point. While the final payoff is unclear, one HP official observed, "You don't get a harvest until you start planting."[4]

Exhibit 16.3. Total revenues and total costs are measured on the vertical axis, with unit sales measured on the horizontal axis. Separate lines are drawn for total variable costs, total costs, and total revenues. The vertical distance between the total revenue and the total cost lines depicts the amount of profit or loss at a given volume. Losses occur when total revenues are less than total costs; profits occur when total revenues exceed total costs.

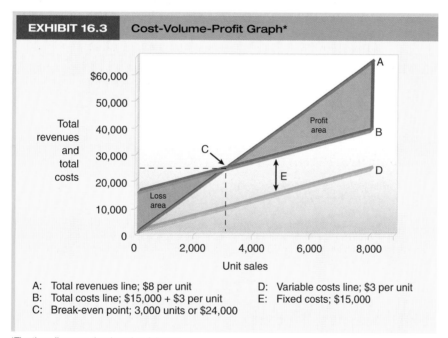

EXHIBIT 16.3 | **Cost-Volume-Profit Graph***

A: Total revenues line; $8 per unit
B: Total costs line; $15,000 + $3 per unit
C: Break-even point; 3,000 units or $24,000
D: Variable costs line; $3 per unit
E: Fixed costs; $15,000

*The three lines are developed as follows:

1. Total variable costs line, D, is drawn between the origin and total variable costs at an arbitrary sales volume. At 8,000 units, total variable costs are $24,000.
2. Total revenues line, A, is drawn through the origin and a point representing total revenues at some arbitrary sales volume. At 8,000 units, Benchmark's total revenues are $64,000.
3. Total cost line, B, is computed by layering fixed costs, $15,000 in this case, on top of total variable costs. This gives a vertical axis intercept of $15,000 and total costs of $39,000 at 8,000 units.

The total contribution margin is shown by the difference between the total revenue and the total variable cost lines. Observe that as unit sales increase, the contribution margin first goes to cover the fixed costs. Beyond the break-even point, any additional contribution margin provides a profit.

Profit-Volume Graph

In cost-volume-profit graphs, profits are represented by the difference between total revenues and total costs. When management is primarily interested in the impact of changes in sales volume on profits and less interested in the related revenues and costs, a **profit-volume graph** is sometimes used. A profit-volume

---

[4]Pete Engardio and Geri Smith, "Hewlett-Packard," *Business Week,* August 27, 2001, p. 137.

graph illustrates the relationship between volume and profits; it does not show revenues and costs. Profits are read directly from a profit-volume graph, rather than being computed as the difference between total revenues and total costs. Profit-volume graphs are developed by plotting either unit sales or total revenues on the horizontal axis.

Benchmark's monthly profit-volume graph, is presented in Exhibit 16.4. Profit or loss is measured on the vertical axis, and volume (total revenues) is measured on the horizontal axis, which intersects the vertical axis at zero profit. A single line, representing total profit, is drawn intersecting the vertical axis at zero sales volume with a loss equal to the fixed costs. The profit line crosses the horizontal axis at the break-even sales volume. The profit or loss at any volume is depicted by the vertical difference between the profit line and the horizontal axis. The slope of the profit line is determined by the contribution margin. The greater the contribution margin ratio or the unit contribution margin, the steeper the slope of the profit line.

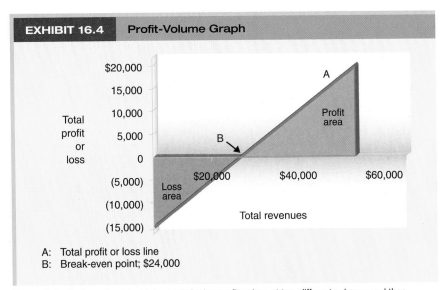

EXHIBIT 16.4   **Profit-Volume Graph**

A: Total profit or loss line
B: Break-even point; $24,000

The profit line is drawn by determining and plotting profit or loss at two different volumes and then drawing a straight line through the plotted values. Perhaps the easiest values to select are the loss at a volume of zero (with a loss equal to the fixed costs) and the volume at which the profit line crosses the horizontal axis (this is the break-even volume).

Impact of Income Taxes

Income taxes are imposed on individuals and for-profit organizations by government agencies. The amount of an individual's or organization's income tax is determined by laws that specify the calculation of taxable income (the income subject to tax) and the calculation of the amount of tax on taxable income. Income taxes are computed as a percentage of taxable income, with increases in taxable income usually subject to progressively higher tax rates. The laws governing the computation of taxable income differ in many ways from the accounting principles that guide the computation of accounting income. Consequently, taxable income and accounting income are seldom the same.

In the early stages of profit planning, income taxes are sometimes incorporated in CVP models by assuming that taxable income and accounting income are identical and that the tax rate is constant. Although these assumptions are seldom true, they are useful for assisting management in developing an early prediction of the sales volume required to earn a desired after-tax profit. Once management has developed a general plan, this early prediction should be refined with the advice of tax experts.

Assuming taxes are imposed at a constant rate per dollar of before-tax profit, income taxes are computed as before-tax profit multipled by the tax rate. After-tax profit is equal to before-tax profit minus income taxes.

$$\text{After-tax profit} = \text{Before-tax profit} - (\text{Before-tax profit} \times \text{Tax rate})$$

After-tax profit can also be expressed as before-tax profit times 1 minus the tax rate.

$$\text{After-tax profit} = \text{Before-tax profit} \times (1 - \text{Tax rate})$$

This formula can be rearranged to isolate before-tax profit as follows:

$$\text{Before-tax profit} = \frac{\text{After-tax profit}}{(1 - \text{Tax rate})}$$

Since all costs and revenues in the profit formula are expressed on a before-tax basis, the most straightforward way of determining the unit sales volume required to earn a desired after-tax profit is to:

1. Determine the required before-tax profit.
2. Substitute the required before-tax profit into the profit formula.
3. Solve for the required unit sales volume.

To illustrate, assume that Benchmark is subject to a 40 percent tax rate and that management desires to earn an after-tax profit of $18,000 for November 2007. The required before-tax profit is $30,000 ($18,000 ÷ (1 − 0.40)), and the unit sales volume required to earn this profit is 9,000 units (($15,000 + $30,000) ÷ $5).

Income taxes increase the sales volume required to earn a desired after-tax profit. A 40 percent tax rate increased the sales volume required for Benchmark to earn a profit of $18,000 from 6,600 to 9,000 units. These amounts are verified in Exhibit 16.5.

EXHIBIT 16.5	Contribution Income Statement with Income Taxes		
BENCHMARK PAPER COMPANY			
Contribution Income Statement			
Planned for the Month of November 2007			
Sales (9,000 × $8.00).		$72,000	
Less variable costs			
Direct materials (9,000 × $1.00).	$ 9,000		
Direct labor (9,000 × $0.25)	2,250		
Manufacturing overhead (9,000 × $1.25).	11,250		
Selling and administrative (9,000 × $0.50). . . .	4,500	(27,000)	
Contribution margin		45,000	
Less fixed costs			
Manufacturing overhead.	5,000		
Selling and administrative.	10,000	(15,000)	
Before-tax profit		30,000	100%
Income taxes ($30,000 × 0.40)		(12,000)	(40)%
After-tax profit		$18,000	60%

Another way to remember the computation of before-tax profit is shown on the right side of Exhibit 16.5. The before-tax profit represents 100 percent of the pie, with 40 percent going to income taxes and 60 percent remaining after taxes. Working back from the remaining 60 percent ($18,000), we can determine the 100 percent (before-tax profit) by dividing after-tax profit by 0.60.

MID-MODULE REVIEW

Memorabilia Cup Company produces keepsake 16-ounce beverage containers for educational institutions. Memorabilia sells the cups for $40 per box of 50 containers. Variable and fixed costs follow:

	Variable Costs per Box			Fixed Costs per Month	
Manufacturing			Manufacturing overhead	$15,000	
Direct materials.	$15		Selling and administrative	10,000	
Direct labor	3		Total	$25,000	
Manufacturing overhead. . .	10	$28			
Selling and administrative . . .		2			
Total		$30			

In September 2007, Memorabilia produced and sold 3,000 boxes of beverage containers.

Required

a.   Prepare a contribution income statement for September 2007.

b.   Prepare a cost-volume-profit graph with unit sales as the independent variable. Label the revenue line, total costs line, fixed costs line, loss area, profit area, and break-even point. The recommended scale for the horizontal axis is 0 to 5,000 units, and the recommended scale for the vertical axis is $0 to $200,000.

c.   Determine Memorabilia's unit contribution margin and contribution margin ratio.

d.   Determine Memorabilia's monthly break-even point in units.

e.   Determine the monthly dollar sales required for a monthly profit of $5,000 (ignoring taxes).

f.   Assuming Memorabilia is subject to a 40 percent income tax, determine the monthly unit sales required to produce a monthly after-tax profit of $4,500.

Solution

a.

MEMORABILIA CUP COMPANY
Contribution Income Statement
For the Month of September 2007

Sales (3,000 × $40)		$120,000
Less variable costs		
Direct materials (3,000 × $15)	$45,000	
Direct labor (3,000 × $3).	9,000	
Manufacturing overhead (3,000 × $10)	30,000	
Selling and administrative (3,000 × $2)	6,000	(90,000)
Contribution margin		30,000
Less fixed costs		
Manufacturing overhead.	15,000	
Selling and administrative.	10,000	(25,000)
Profit.		$ 5,000

b.

c.

Selling price	$40 per unit
Variable costs	(30) per unit
Contribution margin	$10 per unit

$$\text{Contribution margin ratio} = \frac{\text{Unit contribution margin}}{\text{Unit selling price}}$$
$$= \$10 \div \$40$$
$$= 0.25$$

d.
$$\text{Break-even point} = \frac{\text{Fixed costs}}{\text{Unit contribution margin}}$$
$$= \$25,000 \div \$10$$
$$= 2,500 \text{ units}$$

e.
$$\text{Required dollar sales} = \frac{\text{Fixed costs} + \text{Desired profit}}{\text{Contribution margin ratio}}$$
$$= (\$25,000 + \$5,000) \div 0.25$$
$$= \$120,000$$

f.
$$\text{Required unit sales} = \frac{\text{Fixed costs} + \text{Desired before-tax profit}}{\text{Contribution margin per unit}}$$
$$\text{Desired before-tax profit} = \$4,500 \div (1 - .40) = \$7,500$$
$$\text{Required units sales} = (\$25,000 + \$7,500) \div \$10$$
$$= 3,250 \text{ units}$$

MULTIPLE-PRODUCT COST-VOLUME-PROFIT ANALYSIS

LO4 Analyze the profitability and sales mix of a multiple-product firm.

Unit cost information is not always available or appropriate when analyzing cost-volume-profit relationships of multiple-product firms. Assuming the sales mix is constant, the contribution margin ratio (the portion of each sales dollar contributed toward covering fixed costs and earning a profit) can be used to determine the break-even dollar sales volume or the dollar sales volume required to achieve a desired profit. Treating a dollar of sales revenue as a unit, the break-even point in dollars is computed as fixed costs divided by the contribution margin ratio (the number of cents from each dollar of revenue contributed to covering fixed costs and providing a profit).

$$\text{Dollar break-even point} = \frac{\text{Fixed costs}}{\text{Contribution margin ratio}}$$

If unit selling price and cost information were not available, Benchmark's dollar break-even point could be computed as $24,000 ($15,000 ÷ 0.625).

Corresponding computations can be made to find the dollar sales volume required to achieve a desired profit as follows.

$$\text{Target dollar sales volume} = \frac{\text{Fixed costs} + \text{Desired profit}}{\text{Contribution margin ratio}}$$

To achieve a desired profit of $12,000, Benchmark needs sales of $43,200 (($15,000 + $12,000) ÷ 0.625).

These relationships can be graphed by placing sales dollars, rather than unit sales, on the horizontal axis. The slope of the variable and total cost lines, identified as the **variable cost ratio,** presents variable costs as a portion of sales revenue. It indicates the number of cents from each sales dollar required to pay variable costs. The Business Insight on the following page demonstrates how CVP information can be developed from the published financial statements of a multiple-product firm.

Sales Mix Analysis

Sales mix refers to the relative portion of unit or dollar sales that are derived from each product. One of the limiting assumptions of the basic cost-volume-profit model is that the analysis is for a single product

BUSINESS INSIGHT   **CVP Analysis Using Financial Statements**

Condensed data from Wal-Mart's 2002 and 2003 income statements ($ millions) follow:

	2003	2002
Revenues	$231,577	$205,823
Operating Expenses	(218,282)	(194,244)
Operating Income	$ 13,295	$ 11,579

We can determine Wal-Mart's cost-volume-profit relationships by applying the high-low cost estimation method. First, we determine variable costs as a portion of each sales dollar as follows ($ million):

$$\text{Variable cost ratio} = \frac{\$218,282 - \$194,244}{\$231,577 - \$205,823} = 0.93337$$

Next, annual fixed costs are determined by subtracting the variable costs for either period (the product of revenues and the variable cost ratio) from the corresponding total costs.

$$\text{Annual fixed costs} = \$218,282 - (\$231,577 \times 0.93337) = \underline{\$2,134.976 \text{ million}}$$

The contribution margin ratio (1 minus the variable cost ratio) is 0.06663 (1 − 0.93337). Wal Mart's annual break even point in sales dollars is now computed as $32,042.263 million ($2,134.976 million/0.06663).

In 2004 Wal-Mart reported an operating income of $15,025 million with revenues of $258,681 million. For this level of revenues, the model developed from 2002 and 2003 data predicts an operating profit of $15,100.94 ($258,681 million − [($258,681 million × 0.93337) + 2,134.976 million]). In this case, because of it's stable cost structure, the model error is less than one percent.

or the sales mix is constant. When the sales mix is constant, managers of multiple-product organizations can use the average unit contribution margin, or the average contribution margin ratio, to determine the break-even point or the sales volume required for a desired profit. Often, however, management is interested in the effect of a change in the sales mix rather than a change in the sales volume at a constant mix. In this situation, it is necessary to determine either the average unit contribution margin or the average contribution margin ratio for each alternative mix.

Unit Sales Analysis

Assume the Eagle Card Company sells two kinds of greeting cards, regular and deluxe. At a 1:1 (one-to-one) unit sales mix in which Eagle sells one box of regular cards for every box of deluxe cards, the following revenue and cost information is available:

	Regular Box	Deluxe Box	Average Box*
Unit selling price	$4	$12	$8
Unit variable costs	(3)	(3)	(3)
Unit contribution margin	$1	$ 9	$5
Fixed costs per month			$15,000

*At a 1:1 sales mix, the average unit contribution margin is
$5[{($1 × 1 unit) + ($9 × 1 unit)} ÷ 2 units].

At a 1:1 mix, Eagle's current monthly break-even sales volume is 3,000 units ($15,000 ÷ $5), consisting of 1,500 boxes of regular cards and 1,500 boxes of deluxe cards. The top line in Exhibit 16.6 represents the current sales mix. Management wants to know the break-even sales volume if the unit sales mix became 3:1; that is, on average, a sale of 4 units contains 3 regular units and 1 deluxe unit. With no changes in the selling prices or variable costs of individual products, the average contribution margin becomes $3[\{(\$1 \times 3 \text{ units}) + (\$9 \times 1 \text{ unit})\} \div 4 \text{ units}]$, and the revised break-even sales volume is 5,000 units ($15,000 ÷ $3). The revised break-even sales volume includes 3,750 regular cards [5,000 × $\frac{3}{4}$] and 1,250 deluxe cards [5,000 × $\frac{1}{4}$].

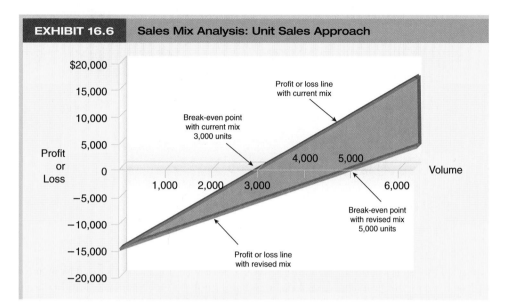

EXHIBIT 16.6	Sales Mix Analysis: Unit Sales Approach

The bottom line in Exhibit 16.6 represents the revised sales mix. Because a greater portion of the revised mix consists of lower contribution margin regular cards, the shift in the mix increases the break-even point.

Sales Dollar Analysis

The proceeding analysis focused on units and the unit contribution margin. An alternative approach focuses on sales dollars and the contribution margin ratio. Following this approach, the sales mix is expressed in terms of sales dollars.

Eagle's current sales dollars are 25 percent from regular cards and 75 percent from deluxe cards. The following display indicates the contribution margin ratios at the current sales mix and monthly volume of 5,400 units.

	Regular	Deluxe	Total
Unit sales	2,700	2,700	
Selling price	$4.00	$12.00	
Sales.	$10,800	$32,400	$43,200
Variable costs	8,100	8,100	16,200
Contribution margin	$ 2,700	$24,300	$27,000
Contribution margin ratio	0.25	0.75	0.625

With monthly fixed costs of $15,000, Eagle's current break-even sales volume is $24,000 ($15,000 ÷ 0.625), consisting of $6,000 from regular cards ($24,000 × 0.25) and $18,000 from Deluxe cards ($24,000 × 0.75). The top line in Exhibit 16.7 illustrates the current sales mix.

Management wants to know the break-even sales volume if the unit sales mix became 70 percent regular and 30 percent deluxe. With no changes in the selling prices or variable costs of individual products, the contribution margin ratio becomes 0.40 [(0.25 × 0.70) + (0.75 × 0.30)], and the revised break-even sales volume is $37,500 ($15,000 ÷ 0.40). The revised break-even sales volume includes $26,250 from regular cards ($37,500 × 0.70) and $11,250 from deluxe cards (37,500 × 0.30).

The bottom line in Exhibit 16.7 represents the revised sales mix. Because a greater portion of the revised mix consists of lower contribution ratio regular cards, the shift in the mix increases the break-even point.

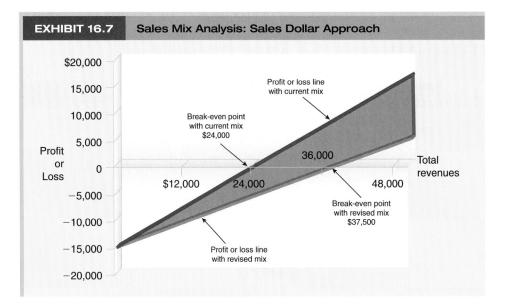

EXHIBIT 16.7 Sales Mix Analysis: Sales Dollar Approach

Sales mix analysis is important in multiple-product or service organizations. Management is just as concerned with the mix of products as with the total unit or dollar sales volume. A shift in the sales mix can have a significant impact on the bottom line. Profits may decline, even when sales increase, if the mix shifts toward products or services with lower unit margins. Conversely, profits may increase, even when sales decline, if the mix shifts toward products or services with higher unit margins. Other things being equal, managers of for-profit organizations strive to increase sales of high-margin products or services.

ANALYSIS OF OPERATING LEVERAGE

LO5 Apply operating leverage ratio to assess opportunities for profit and the risks of loss.

Operating leverage refers to the extent that an organization's costs are fixed. The **operating leverage ratio** is computed as the contribution margin divided by before-tax profit as follows.

$$\text{Operating leverage ratio} = \frac{\text{Contribution margin}}{\text{Before-tax profit}}$$

The rationale underlying this computation is that as fixed costs are substituted for variable costs, the contribution margin as a percentage of income before taxes increases. Hence, a high degree of operating leverage signals the existence of a high portion of fixed costs. As noted in Module 15 and illustrated in Exhibit 15.7, the shift from labor-based to automated activities has resulted in a decrease in variable costs and an increase in fixed costs, producing an increase in operating leverage.

Operating leverage is a measure of risk and opportunity. Other things being equal, the higher the degree of operating leverage, the greater the opportunity for profit with increases in sales. Conversely, a higher degree of operating leverage also magnifies the risk of large losses with a decrease in sales.

	Operating Leverage	
	High	**Low**
Profit opportunity with sales increase	High	Low
Risk of loss with sales decrease	High	Low

In addition to indicating the relative amount of fixed costs in the overall cost structure of a company, the operating leverage ratio can be used to measure the expected change in net income resulting from a change in sales. The operating leverage ratio multiplied times the percentage change in sales equals the percentage change in income before taxes. For example, if Benchmark Paper Company currently has an operating leverage ratio of 4.0, a change in sales of 12.5 percent will result in a 50 percent change in income before taxes; whereas, High-Fixed Paper Company, which has an operating leverage ratio of 5.2 will have an increase in sales of 65%.

	Current		Projected	
	Benchmark	High-Fixed	Benchmark	High-Fixed
Unit selling price...........................	$ 8.00	$ 8.00	$ 8.00	$ 8.00
Unit variable costs	(3.00)	(1.50)	(3.00)	(1.50)
Unit contribution margin.....................	5.00	6.50	5.00	6.50
Unit sales..................................	× 4,000	× 4,000	× 4,500	× 4,500
Contribution margin	20,000	26,000	22,500	29,250
Fixed costs................................	(15,000)	(21,000)	(15,000)	(21,000)
Before-tax profit...........................	$ 5,000	$ 5,000	$ 7,500	$ 8,250
Contribution margin	$20,000	$26,000		
Before-tax profit...........................	÷ 5,000	÷ 5,000		
Operating leverage ratio....................	4.0	5.2		
Percent increase in sales			12.5%	12.5%
Percent increase in income before sales			50%	65%

Although both companies have identical before-tax profits at a sales volume of 4,000 units, High-Fixed has a higher degree of operating leverage and its profits vary more with changes in sales volume.

If sales are projected to increase by 12.5 percent, from 4,000 to 4,500 units, the percentage of increase in each firm's profits is computed as the percent change in sales multiplied by the degree of operating leverage.

	Benchmark	High-Fixed
Increase in sales..................	12.5%	12.5%
Degree of operating leverage........	× 4.0	× 5.2
Increase in profits.................	50.0%	65.0%

The Research Insight below considers the importance of reducing operating leverage during periods of economic stress.

RESEARCH INSIGHT   **Lower Operating Leverage When in Crisis**

Bankruptcy experts recommend that companies facing sales declines take proactive measures to reduce their operating leverage and the associated risks. If the erosion in market size is permanent, firms must reduce facilities and equipment, and the reductions must be permanent. What's more, to reduce the associated risk of insolvency, firms with high operating leverage should not rely heavily on borrowed funds to acquire property, plant, and equipment assets.[5]

Management is interested in measures of operating leverage to determine how sensitive profits are to changes in sales. Risk-averse managers strive to maintain a lower operating leverage, even if this results in some loss of profits. One way to reduce operating leverage is to use more direct labor and less automated equipment. Another way is to contract outside organizations to perform tasks that could be done internally. This approach to reducing operating leverage is further considered in Module 17, where we examine the

---

[5] Gerald P. Buccino and Kraig S. McKinley, "The Importance of Operating Leverage in a Turnaround," *Secured Lender,* September/ October, 1997, pp. 64–66.

external acquisition of goods and services. While operating leverage is a useful analytic tool, long-run success comes from keeping the overall level of costs down, while providing customers with the products or services they want at competitive prices.

MANAGERIAL DECISION	You are the Division Manager

As manager of a division responsible for both production and sales of products and, hence, division profits, you are looking for ways to leverage the profits of your division to a higher level. You are considering changing your cost structure to include more fixed costs and less variable costs by automating some of the production activities currently performed by people. What are some of the considerations that you should keep in mind as you ponder this decision? [Answer, p. 16-20]

MODULE-END REVIEW

Joe's Brews is a new shop in Cambridge village shopping center that sells high-end teas and coffees. Recently, they have added smoothie drinks to their product line. Below are sales and cost data for the company:

	Coffee	Tea	Smoothie
Sales price per (12 oz.) serving	$1.35	$1.25	$1.95
Variable cost per serving	0.60	0.45	0.75
Fixed costs per month $8,000			

Currently the company sells each month an average of 6,000 servings of coffee, 3,750 servings of tea, and 2,250 servings of smoothies.

Required:
a. Calculate the current pre-tax profit, contribution margin ratio, and sales mix based on sales dollars.
b. Using a sales dollar analysis, calculate the monthly break-even point assuming the sales mix does not change.
c. Calculate Joe's operating leverage ratio. If sales increase by 20 percent, by how much will pre-tax income be expected to change? If sales decrease by 20 percent, by how much will pre-tax income be expected to change?

Solution

a.

	Coffee	Tea	Smoothies	Total
Monthly unit sales	6,000	3,750	2,250	
Selling price	$1.35	$1.25	$1.95	
Sales	$8,100.00	$4,687.50	$4,387.50	$17,175.00
Variable cost	3,600.00	1,687.50	1,687.50	6,975.00
Contribution margin	$4,500.00	$3,000.00	$2,700.00	10,200.00
Fixed cost				8,000.00
Pre-tax profit				$ 2,200.00
Contribution margin (CM) ratio	0.5556	0.640	0.6154	0.5939
Current sales mix (based on sales dollars)	47.16%	27.29%	25.55%	

b.

$$\text{Break-even} = \text{Fixed costs/Total contribution margin ratio}$$
$$= \$8,000/0.5939$$
$$= \$13,470$$

Proof:			Sales		C/M Ratio		
Coffee:	$13,470 × 47.16%	=	$ 6,352.45	×	0.5556	=	$3,529.42
Tea:	$13,470 × 27.29%	=	3,675.96	×	0.640	=	2,352.62*
Smoothies:	$13,470 × 25.55%	=	3,441.59	×	0.6154	=	2,117.96*
			$13,470.00				
Total contribution margin							8,000.00
Fixed costs							8,000.00
Pre-tax profit							–0–

*Amounts adjusted to correct for minor rounding error.

c. Joe's Brews has an operating leverage of 4.636, calculated as a contribution margin of $10,200 divided by pre-tax profit of $2,200. Therefore, if sales dollars increase by 20% to $20,610, before-tax profit should increase by 4.636 times 20%, or 92.72%, to $4,240. Because of the leverage caused by fixed costs, a 20% increase in sales results in a 92.72% increase in before-tax profit. Conversely, a 20% decrease in sales would result in a 92.72% decrease in before-tax profits to $160.

Proof:	20% Sales Increase	20% Sales Decrease
Sales.	$20,610	$13,740
CM %.	× 0.5939	× 0.5939
Total CM.	12,240	8,160
Fixed costs.	8,000	8,000
Pre-tax profit	$ 4,240	$ 160

Current pre-tax profit of $2,200 × (1 + .9272) = $4,240
Current pre-tax profit of $2,200 × (1 − .9272) = $160

GUIDANCE ANSWERS

MANAGERIAL DECISION   **You are the Division Manager**

Fixed costs represent a two-edged sword. When a company is growing its sales, fixed costs cause profits to grow faster than sales; however, if a company should experience declining sales, the rate of reduction in profits is greater than the rate of reduction in sales. When sales decline, variable costs decline proportionately, while fixed costs continue. For this reason, when a company faces serious declines that are expected to continue, one of the first steps its top management should consider is reducing capacity in order to reduce fixed costs. The automobile companies in the U.S. have been employing this technique in recent years to try to offset the effect of sales lost to importers.

DISCUSSION QUESTIONS

Q16-1. What is cost-volume-profit analysis and when is it particularly useful?

Q16-2. Identify the important assumptions that underlie cost-volume-profit analysis.

Q16-3. When is it most reasonable to use a single independent variable in cost-volume-profit analysis?

Q16-4. Distinguish between a contribution and a functional income statement.

Q16-5. What is the unit contribution margin? How is it used in computing the unit break-even point?

Q16-6. What is the contribution margin ratio and when is it most useful?

Q16-7. How is the break-even equation modified to take into account the sales required to earn a desired profit?

Q16-8. How does a profit-volume graph differ from a cost-volume-profit graph? When is a profit-volume graph most likely to be used?

Q16-9. What impact do income taxes have on the sales volume required to earn a desired after-tax profit?

Q16-10. How are profit opportunities and the risk of losses affected by operating leverage?

MINI EXERCISES

M16-11. Multiple-Product Profitability Analysis   (LO2)

Assume a local Cost Cutters provides cuts, perms, and hairstyling services. Annual fixed costs are $120,000, and variable costs are 40 percent of sales revenue. Last year's revenues totaled $240,000.

Required

a. Determine its break-even point in sales dollars.
b. Determine last year's margin of safety in sales dollars.
c. Determine the sales volume required for an annual profit of $70,000.

M16-12. Cost-Volume-Profit Graph: Identification and Sensitivity Analysis   (LO3)

A typical cost-volume-profit graph is presented below.

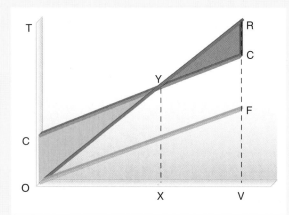

Required

a. Identify each of the following:
   1. Line OF
   2. Line OR
   3. Line CC
   4. The difference between lines OF and OV
   5. The difference between lines CC and OF
   6. The difference between lines CC and OV
   7. The difference between lines OR and OF
   8. Point X
   9. Area CYO
   10. Area RCY
b. Indicate the effect of each of the following independent events on lines CC, OR, and the break-even point:
   1. A decrease in fixed costs
   2. An increase in unit selling price
   3. An increase in the variable costs per unit
   4. An increase in fixed costs and a decrease in the unit selling price
   5. A decrease in fixed costs and a decrease in the unit variable costs

M16-13. Profit-Volume Graph: Identification and Sensitivity Analysis   (LO3)

A typical profit-volume graph follows.

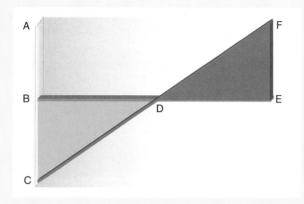

Required

a. Identify each of the following:
1. Area *BDC*
2. Area *DEF*
3. Point *D*
4. Line *AC*
5. Line *BC*
6. Line *EF*

b. Indicate the effect of each of the following on line *CF* and the break-even point:
1. An increase in the unit selling price
2. An increase in the variable costs per unit
3. A decrease in fixed costs
4. An increase in fixed costs and a decrease in the unit selling price
5. A decrease in fixed costs and an increase in the variable costs per unit

M16-14. Preparing Cost-Volume-Profit and Profit-Volume Graphs   (LO3)

Assume a Papa John's Pizza shop has the following monthly revenue and cost functions:

Papa John's Pizza
(PZZA)

$$\text{Total revenues} = \$12.00X$$
$$\text{Total costs} = \$18,000 + \$3.00X$$

Required

a. Prepare a graph (similar to that in Exhibit 16-3) illustrating Papa John's cost-volume-profit relationships. The vertical axis should range from $0 to $72,000, in increments of $12,000. The horizontal axis should range from 0 units to 6,000 units, in increments of 2,000 units.

b. Prepare a graph (similar to that in Exhibit 16-4) illustrating Papa John's profit-volume relationships. The horizontal axis should range from 0 units to 6,000 units, in increments of 2,000 units.

c. When is it most appropriate to use a profit-volume graph?

M16-15. Preparing Cost-Volume-Profit and Profit-Volume Graphs   (LO3)

Big Dog Company is a hot dog concession business operating at five baseball stadiums. It sells hot dogs, with all the fixings, for $5.00 each. Variable costs are $4.50 per hot dog, and fixed operating costs are $250,000 per year.

Required

a. Determine the annual break-even point in hot dogs.

b. Prepare a cost-volume-profit graph for the company. Use a format that emphasizes the contribution margin. The vertical axis should vary between $0 and $5,000,000 in increments of $1,000,000. The horizontal axis should vary between 0 hot dogs and 1,000,000 hot dogs, in increments of 250,000 hot dogs. Label the graph in thousands.

c. Prepare a profit-volume graph for the company. The vertical axis should vary between $(300,000) and $300,000 in increments of $100,000. The horizontal axis should vary as described in requirement (b). Label the graph in thousands.

d. Evaluate the profit-volume graph. In what ways is it superior and in what ways is it inferior to the traditional cost-volume-profit graph?

M16-16. Multiple Product Break-Even Analysis (LO4)

Presented is information for Stafford Company's three products.

	A	B	C
Unit selling price..........	$5	$7	$6
Unit variable costs	(4)	(5)	(3)
Unit contribution margin....	$1	$2	$3

With monthly fixed costs of $112,500, the company sells two units of A for each unit of B and three units of B for each unit of C.

Required

Determine the unit sales of product A at the monthly break-even point.

EXERCISES

E16-17. Contribution Income Statement and Cost-Volume-Profit Graph (LO2, 3)

Manitoba Company produces a product that is sold for $50 per unit. The company produced and sold 6,000 units during May 2007. There were no beginning or ending inventories. Variable and fixed costs follow.

Variable Costs per Unit			Fixed Costs per Month	
Manufacturing:			Manufacturing overhead	$40,000
Direct materials...........	$ 5		Selling and administrative ...	20,000
Direct labor..............	10		Total	$60,000
Factory overhead	10	$25		
Selling and administrative		5		
Total		$30		

Required

a. Prepare a contribution income statement for May.
b. Prepare a cost-volume-profit graph. Label the horizontal axis in units with a maximum value of 10,000. Label the vertical axis in dollars with a maximum value of $400,000. Draw a vertical line on the graph for the current (6,000) unit sales level, and label total variable costs, total fixed costs, and total profits at 6,000 units.

E16-18. Contribution Margin Concepts (LO3, 4)

The following information is taken from the 2007 records of Navajo Art Shop.

	Fixed	Variable	Total
Sales............			$750,000
Costs			
Goods sold		$300,000	
Labor..........	$160,000	60,000	
Supplies	2,000	5,000	
Utilities	12,000	13,000	
Rent	24,000	—	
Advertising	6,000	24,500	
Miscellaneous...	6,000	10,000	
Total costs......	$210,000	$412,500	(622,500)
Net income.......			$127,500

Required

a.   Determine the annual break-even dollar sales volume.

b.   Determine the current margin of safety in dollars.

c.   Prepare a cost-volume-profit graph for the art shop. Label both axes in dollars with maximum values of $1,000,000. Draw a vertical line on the graph for the current ($750,000) sales level, and label total variable costs, total fixed costs, and total profits at $750,000 sales.

d.   What is the annual break-even dollar sales volume if management makes a decision that increases fixed costs by $35,000?

E16-19.   Multiple Product Planning with Taxes   (LO3, 4)

In the year 2006, Wiggins Processing Company had the following contribution income statement:

WIGGINS PROCESSING COMPANY		
Contribution Income Statement		
For the Year 2006		
Sales.		$1,000,000
Variable costs		
Cost of goods sold	$420,000	
Selling and administrative.	200,000	(620,000)
Contribution margin		380,000
Fixed costs		
Factory overhead	205,000	
Selling and administrative.	80,000	(285,000)
Before-tax profit		95,000
Income taxes (36%)		(34,200)
After-tax profit		$ 60,800

Required

a.   Determine the annual break-even point in sales dollars.

b.   Determine the annual margin of safety in sales dollars.

c.   What is the break-even point in sales dollars if management makes a decision that increases fixed costs by $57,000?

d.   With the current cost structure, including fixed costs of $285,000, what dollar sales volume is required to provide an after-tax net income of $200,000?

e.   Prepare an abbreviated contribution income statement to verify that the solution to requirement (d) will provide the desired after-tax income.

E16-20.   Not-for-Profit Applications   (LO3)

Determine the solution to each of the following independent cases:

a.   Hillside College has annual fixed operating costs of $12,500,000 and variable operating costs of $1,000 per student. Tuition is $8,000 per student for the coming academic year, with a projected enrollment of 1,500 students. Expected revenues from endowments and federal and state grants total $250,000. Determine the amount the college must obtain from other sources.

b.   The Hillside College Student Association is planning a fall concert. Expected costs (renting a hall, hiring a band, etc.) are $30,000. Assuming 3,000 people attend the concert, determine the break-even price per ticket. How much will the association lose if this price is charged and only 2,700 tickets are sold?

c.   City Hospital has a contract with the city to provide indigent health care on an outpatient basis for $25 per visit. The patient will pay $5 of this amount, with the city paying the balance ($20). Determine the amount the city will pay if the hospital has 10,000 patient visits.

d.   A civic organization is engaged in a fund-raising program. On Civic Sunday, it will sell newspapers at $1.25 each. The organization will pay $0.75 for each newspaper. Costs of the necessary permits, signs, and so forth are $500. Determine the amount the organization will raise if it sells 5,000 newspapers.

e.   Christmas for the Needy is a civic organization that provides Christmas presents to disadvantaged children. The annual costs of this activity are $5,000, plus $10 per present. Determine the number of presents the organization can provide with $20,000.

E16-21. **Alternative Production Procedures and Operating Leverage** (LO3, 5)

Paper Mate

Assume Paper Mate is planning to introduce a new executive pen that can be manufactured using either a capital-intensive method or a labor-intensive method. The predicted manufacturing costs for each method are as follows:

	Capital Intensive	Labor Intensive
Direct materials per unit..........................	$ 5.00	$ 6.00
Direct labor per unit	$ 5.00	$12.00
Variable manufacturing overhead per unit	$ 4.00	$ 2.00
Fixed manufacturing overhead per year.............	$2,440,000.00	$700,000.00

Paper Mate's market research department has recommended an introductory unit sales price of $30. The incremental selling costs are predicted to be $500,000 per year, plus $2 per unit sold.

Required

a. Determine the annual break-even point in units if Paper Mate uses the:
  1. Capital-intensive manufacturing method.
  2. Labor-intensive manufacturing method.
b. Determine the annual unit volume at which Paper Mate is indifferent between the two manufacturing methods.
c. Management wants to know more about the effect of each alternative on operating leverage.
  1. Explain operating leverage and the relationship between operating leverage and the volatility of earnings.
  2. Compute operating leverage for each alternative at a volume of 250,000 units.
  3. Which alternative has the higher operating leverage? Why?

E16-22. **Contribution Income Statement and Operating Leverage** (LO3, 5)

Florida Berry Basket harvests early-season strawberries for shipment throughout the eastern United States in March. The strawberry farm is maintained by a permanent staff of 10 employees and seasonal workers who pick and pack the strawberries. The strawberries are sold in crates containing 100 individually packaged one-quart containers. Affixed to each one-quart container is the distinctive Florida Berry Basket logo inviting buyers to "Enjoy the berry best strawberries in the world!" The selling price is $90 per crate, variable costs are $80 per crate, and fixed costs are $275,000 per year. In the year 2007, Florida Berry Basket sold 45,000 crates.

Required

a. Prepare a contribution income statement for the year ended December 31, 2007.
b. Determine the company's 2007 operating leverage.
c. Calculate the percentage change in profits if sales decrease by 10 percent.
d. Management is considering the purchase of several berry-picking machines. This will increase annual fixed costs to $375,000 and reduce variable costs to $77.50 per crate. Calculate the effect of this acquisition on operating leverage and explain any change.

E16-23. **Multiple Product Break-Even Analysis** (LO4)

Yuma Tax Service prepares tax returns for low- to middle-income taxpayers. Its service operates January 2 through April 15 at a counter in a local department store. All jobs are classified into one of three categories: standard, multiform, and complex. Following is information for last year. Also, last year, the fixed cost of rent, utilities, and so forth were $45,000.

	Standard	Multiform	Complex
Billing rate......................	$50	$125	$250
Average variable costs............	(30)	(75)	(150)
Average contribution margin	$20	$50	$100
Number of returns prepared........	1,750	500	250

Required

a. Determine Yuma's break-even dollar sales volume.
b. Determine Yuma's margin of safety in sales dollars.
c. Prepare a profit-volume graph for Yuma's Tax Service.

E16-24. Cost-Volume-Profit Relations: Missing Data   (LO3)
Following are data from 4 separate companies.

	Case 1	Case 2	Case 3	Case 4
Unit sales	1,000	800	?	?
Sales revenue.	$20,000	?	?	$60,000
Variable cost per unit	$10	$1	$12	?
Contribution margin	?	$800	?	?
Fixed costs.	$8,000	?	$80,000	?
Net income.	?	$400	?	?
Unit contribution margin.	?	?	?	$15
Break-even point (units)	?	?	4,000	2,000
Margin of safety (units).	?	?	300	1,000

Required
Supply the missing data in each independent case.

E16-25. Cost-Volume-Profit Relations: Missing Data   (LO3)
Following are data from 4 separate companies.

	Case A	Case B	Case C	Case D
Sales revenue.	$100,000	$80,000	?	?
Contribution margin	$40,000	?	$20,000	?
Fixed costs.	$30,000	?	?	?
Net income.	?	$5,000	$10,000	?
Variable cost ratio.	?	0.50	?	0.20
Contribution margin ratio	?	?	0.40	?
Break-even point (dollars)	?	?	?	$25,000
Margin of safety (dollars)	?	?	?	$20,000

Required
Supply the missing data in each independent case.

PROBLEMS

P16-26. Profit Planning with Taxes   (LO3)
Chandler Manufacturing Company produces a product that it sells for $35 per unit. Last year, the company
manufactured and sold 20,000 units to obtain an after-tax profit of $54,000. Variable and fixed costs follow.

Variable Costs per Unit		Fixed Costs per Year	
Manufacturing	$18	Manufacturing	$ 80,000
Selling and administrative	7	Selling and administrative . . .	30,000
Total	$25	Total	$110,000

Required

a.   Determine the tax rate the company paid last year.

b.   What unit sales volume is required to provide an after-tax profit of $90,000?

c.   If the company reduces the unit variable cost by $2.50 and increases fixed manufacturing costs by $20,000, what unit sales volume is required to provide an after-tax profit of $90,000?

d.   What assumptions are made about taxable income and tax rates in requirements (a) through (c)?

P16-27.   **High-Low Cost Estimation and Profit Planning**   (LO3, 4)

Comparative 2006 and 2007 income statements for Dakota Products Inc. follow:

DAKOTA PRODUCTS INC. Comparative Income Statements For Years Ending December 31, 2006 and 2007		
	2006	**2007**
Unit sales	5,000	8,000
Sales revenue.	$65,000	$104,000
Expenses	(70,000)	(85,000)
Profit (loss)	$ (5,000)	$ 19,000

Required

a.   Determine the break-even point in units.

b.   Determine the unit sales volume required to earn a profit of $10,000.

P16-28.   **CVP Analysis and Special Decisions**   (LO3, 4)

Sweet Grove Citrus Company buys a variety of citrus fruit from growers and then processes the fruit into a product line of fresh fruit, juices, and fruit flavorings. The most recent year's sales revenue was $4,200,000. Variable costs were 60 percent of sales and fixed costs totaled $1,300,000. Sweet Grove is evaluating two alternatives designed to enhance profitability.

*   One staff member has proposed that Sweet Grove purchase more automated processing equipment. This strategy would increase fixed costs by $300,000 but decrease variable costs to 54 percent of sales.

*   Another staff member has suggested that Sweet Grove rely more on outsourcing for fruit processing. This would reduce fixed costs by $300,000 but increase variable costs to 65 percent of sales.

Required

a.   What is the current break-even point in sales dollars?

b.   Assuming an income tax rate of 34 percent, what dollar sales volume is currently required to obtain an after-tax profit of $500,000?

c.   In the absence of income taxes, at what sales volume will both alternatives (automation and outsourcing) provide the same profit?

d.   Briefly describe one strength and one weakness of both the automation and the outsourcing alternatives.

P16-29.   **Break-Even Analysis in a Not-for-Profit Organization**   (LO3)

Melford Hospital operates a general hospital but rents space to separately owned entities rendering specialized services such as pediatrics and psychiatry. Melford charges each separate entity for patients' services (meals and laundry) and for administrative services (billings and collections). Space and bed rentals are fixed charges for the year, based on bed capacity rented to each entity. Melford charged the following costs to Pediatrics for the year ended June 30, 2007:

	Patient Services (Variable)	Bed Capacity (Fixed)
Dietary	$ 600,000	
Janitorial........................		$ 70,000
Laundry	300,000	
Laboratory	450,000	
Pharmacy.......................	350,000	
Repairs and maintenance............		30,000
General and administrative...........		1,300,000
Rent		1,500,000
Billings and collections.............	300,000	
Total	$2,000,000	$2,900,000

In addition to these charges from Melford Hospital, Pediatrics incurred the following personnel costs:

	Annual Salaries*
Supervising nurses.....	$100,000
Nurses	200,000
Assistants............	180,000
Total	$480,000

*These salaries are fixed within the ranges of annual
patient-days considered in this problem.

During the year ended June 30, 2007, Pediatrics charged each patient $300 per day, had a capacity of 60 beds, and had revenues of $6,000,000 for 365 days. Pediatrics operated at 100 percent capacity on 90 days during this period. It is estimated that during these 90 days, the demand exceeded 80 beds. Melford has 20 additional beds available for rent for the year ending June 30, 2008. This additional rental would proportionately increase Pediatrics' annual fixed charges based on bed capacity.

Required

a.   Calculate the minimum number of patient-days required for Pediatrics to break even for the year ending June 30, 2008, if the additional beds are not rented. Patient demand is unknown, but assume that revenue per patient-day, cost per patient-day, cost per bed, and salary rates for the year ending June 30, 2008, remain the same as for the year ended June 30, 2007.

b.   Assume Pediatrics rents the extra 20-bed capacity from Melford. Determine the net increase or decrease in earnings by preparing a schedule of increases in revenues and costs for the year ending June 30, 2008. Assume that patient demand, revenue per patient-day, cost per patient-day, cost per bed, and salary rates remain the same as for the year ended June 30, 2007.

(CPA adapted)

P16-30.   Cost-Volume-Profit Analysis of Alternative Products   (LO3)

Siberian Ski Company recently expanded its manufacturing capacity to allow production of up to 15,000 pairs of the Mountaineering or the Touring models of cross-country skis. The sales department assures management that it can sell between 9,000 and 13,000 of either product this year. Because the models are very similar, Siberian Ski will produce only one of the two models. The Accounting Department compiled the following information:

	Model	
	Mountaineering	Touring
Selling price per unit...........	$88.00	$80.00
Variable costs per unit	$52.80	$52.80

Fixed costs will total $369,600 if the Mountaineering model is produced but only $316,800 if the Touring model is produced. Siberian Ski Company is subject to a 40 percent income tax rate.

Required

a. Determine the contribution margin ratio of the Touring model.

b. If Siberian Ski Company desires an after-tax profit of $24,000, how many pairs of Touring model skis will the company have to sell? (Round answer to the nearest unit.)

c. Determine the unit sales volume at which Siberian Ski Company would make the same before-tax profit or loss regardless of the ski model it decides to produce. Also determine the resulting before-tax profit or loss.

d. Determine the dollar sales volume at which Siberian Ski Company would make the same before-tax profit or loss regardless of the ski model it decides to produce. Also determine the resulting before-tax profit or loss. (*Hint:* Work with contribution margin ratios.)

e. What action should Siberian Ski Company take if the annual sales of either model were guaranteed to be at least 12,000 pairs? Why?

f. Determine how much the unit variable costs of the Touring model would have to change before both models would have the same break-even point in units. (Round calculations to the nearest cent.)

g. Determine the new unit break-even point of the Touring model if its variable costs per unit decrease by 10 percent and its fixed costs increase by 10 percent. (Round answer to nearest unit.)

(CMA adapted)

P16-31. CVP Analysis Using Published Financial Statements (LO1, 2, 3, 4)

JetBlue (JBLU)
Southwest Airlines (LUV)

Condensed data from the 2003 and 2002 financial statements of JetBlue and Southwest Airlines follow.

	2003	2002
JetBlue (thousands)*		
Revenues	$ 998	$ 635
Operating expenses	(829)	(530)
Operating profit	$ 169	$ 105
Southwest Airlines (millions)*		
Revenues	$5,937	$5,522
Operating expenses	(5,454)	(5,105)
Operating profit	$ 483	$ 417

*Data are from 2003 10-K reports of Jet Blue and Southwest Airlines.

Required

a. Develop a cost-estimating equation for annual operating expenses for each company.

b. Determine the break-even point for each airline.

c. Evaluate and interpret the equations estimated in requirement (a) and the results in requirement (b).

P16-32. Multiple-Product Profitability Analysis, Project Profitability Analysis (LO3, 4)

University Bookstore sells new college textbooks at the publishers' suggested retail prices. It then pays the publishers an amount equal to 75 percent of the suggested retail price. The store's other variable costs average 5 percent of sales revenue and annual fixed costs amount to $300,000.

Required

a. Determine the bookstore's annual break-even point in sales dollars.

b. Assuming an average textbook has a suggested retail price of $60, determine the bookstore's annual break-even point in units.

c. University Bookstore is planning to add used book sales to its operations. A typical used book costs the store 25 percent of the suggested retail price of a new book. The bookstore plans to sell used books for 75 percent of the suggested retail price of a new book. What is the effect on bookstore profitability of shifting sales toward more used and fewer new textbooks?

d. College Publishing produces and sells new textbooks to college and university bookstores. Typical project-level costs total $260,000 for a new textbook. Production and distribution costs amount to 20 percent of the net amount the publisher receives from the bookstores. Textbook authors are paid a royalty of 15 percent of the net amount received from the bookstores. Determine the dollar sales volume required for College Publishing to break even on a new textbook.

e. For a project with predicted sales of 15,000 new books at $60 each, determine:
1. The bookstores' contribution.
2. The publisher's contribution.
3. The author's royalties.

P16-33. Multiple-Product Profitability Analysis   (LO3, 4)

Hearth Manufacturing Company produces two models of wood-burning stoves, Cozy Kitchen and All-House. Presented is sales information for the year 2007.

	Cozy Kitchen	All-House	Total
Units manufactured and sold	1,000	1,500	2,500
Sales revenue	$300,000	$750,000	$1,050,000
Variable costs	(200,000)	(450,000)	(650,000)
Contribution margin	$100,000	$300,000	400,000
Fixed costs			(240,000)
Before-tax profit			160,000
Income taxes (40 percent)			(64,000)
After-tax profit			$ 96,000

Required

a. Determine the current break-even point in sales dollars.
b. With the current product mix and break-even point, determine the average unit contribution margin and unit sales.
c. Sales representatives believe that the total sales will increase to 3,000 units, with the sales mix likely shifting to 80 percent Cozy Kitchen and 20 percent All-House over the next few years. Evaluate the desirability of this projection.

P16-34. Multiple-Product Break-Even Analysis   (LO3, 4)

Currently, Corner Lunch Counter sells only Super Burgers for $2.50 each. During a typical month, the Counter reports a profit of $9,000 with sales of $50,000 and fixed costs of $21,000. Management is considering the introduction of a new Super Chicken Sandwich that will sell for $3 and have variable costs of $1.80. The addition of the Super Chicken Sandwich will require hiring additional personnel and renting additional equipment. These actions will increase monthly fixed costs by $7,760.

In the short run, management predicts that Super Chicken sales will average 10,000 sandwiches per month. However, almost all short-run sales of Super Chickens will come from regular customers who switch from Super Burgers to Super Chickens. Consequently, management predicts monthly sales of Super Burgers will decline by 10,000 units to $25,000. In the long run, management predicts that Super Chicken sales will increase to 15,000 sandwiches per month and that Super Burger sales will increase to 30,000 burgers per month.

Required

a. Determine each of the following:
1. The current monthly break-even point in sales dollars.
2. The short-run monthly profit and break-even point in sales dollars subsequent to the introduction of Super Chickens.
3. The long-run monthly profit and break-even point in sales dollars subsequent to the introduction of Super Chickens.
b. Based on your analysis, what are your recommendations?

CASES

C16-35. Ethics and Pressure to Improve Profit Plans   (LO1)

Art Conroy is the assistant controller of New City Muffler, Inc., a subsidiary of New City Automotive, which manufactures tailpipes, mufflers, and catalytic converters at several plants throughout North America. Because of pressure for lower selling prices, New City Muffler has had disappointing financial performance in recent years. Indeed, Conroy is aware of rumblings from corporate headquarters threatening to close the plant.

One of Conroy's responsibilities is to present the plant's financial plans for the coming year to the corporate officers and board of directors. In preparing for the presentation, Conroy was intrigued to note that the focal point of the budget presentation was a profit-volume graph projecting an increase in profits and a reduction in the break-even point.

Curious as to how the improvement would be accomplished, Conroy ultimately spoke with Paula Mitchell, the plant manager. Mitchell indicated that a planned increase in productivity would reduce variable costs and increase the contribution margin ratio.

When asked how the productivity increase would be accomplished, Mitchell made a vague reference to increasing the speed of the assembly line. Conroy commented that speeding up the assembly line could lead to labor problems because the speed of the line was set by union contract. Mitchell responded that she was afraid that if the speedup were opened to negotiation, the union would make a big "stink" that could result in the plant being closed. She indicated that the speedup was the "only way to save the plant, our jobs, and the jobs of all plant employees." Besides, she did not believe employees would notice a 2 or 3 percent increase in speed. Mitchell concluded the meeting observing, "You need to emphasize the results we will accomplish next year, not the details of how we will accomplish those results. Top management does not want to be bored with details. If we accomplish what we propose in the budget, we will be in for a big bonus."

Required

What advice do you have for Art Conroy?

C16-36. **CVP Analysis with Changing Cost Structure** (LO1, 3, 5)

Homestead Telephone was formed in the 1940s to bring telephone services to remote areas of the U.S. Midwest. The early equipment was quite primitive by today's standards. All calls were handled manually by operators, and all customers were on party lines. By the 1970s, however, all customers were on private lines, and mechanical switching devices handled routine local and long distance calls. Operators remained available for directory assistance, credit card calls, and emergencies. In the 1990s Homestead Telephone added local Internet connections as an optional service to its regular customers. It also established an optional cellular service, identified as the Home Ranger.

Required

a. Using a unit-level analysis, develop a graph with two lines, representing Homestead Telephones' cost structure (1) in the 1940s and (2) in the late 1990s. Be sure to label the axes and lines.

b. With sales revenue as the independent variable, what is the likely impact of the changed cost structure on Homestead Telephone's (1) contribution margin percent and (2) break-even point?

c. Discuss how the change in cost structure affected Homestead's operating leverage and how this affects profitability under rising or falling sales scenarios.

C16-37. Cost Estimation and CVP Analysis   (LO2, 3, 4)

Presented are the 2006 and 2007 functional income statements of Regional Distribution, Inc.:

	2006		2007	
REGIONAL DISTRIBUTION, INC.				
Functional Income Statements				
For Years Ending December 31, 2006 and 2007				
Sales.		$5,520,000		$5,000,000
Expenses				
Cost of goods sold	$4,140,000		$3,750,000	
Shipping	215,400		200,000	
Sales order processing. . . .	52,500		50,000	
Customer relations	120,000		100,000	
Depreciation	80,000		80,000	
Administrative.	250,000	(4,857,900)	250,000	(4,430,000)
Before-tax profit		662,100		570,000
Income taxes (40%)		(264,840)		(228,000)
After-tax profit		$ 397,260		$ 342,000

Required

a.   Determine Regional Distribution's break-even point in sales dollars.

b.   What dollar sales volume is required to earn an after-tax profit of $480,000?

c.   Assuming budgeted 2008 sales of $6,000,000, prepare a 2008 contribution income statement.

d.   Discuss the reliability of the calculations in requirements *a-c*, including the limitations of the CVP model and how they affect the reliability of the model.

Relevant Costs and Benefits for Decision Making

LEARNING OBJECTIVES

LO1 Distinguish between relevant and irrelevant revenues and costs. (p. 17-3)

LO2 Analyze relevant costs and indicate how they differ under alternative decision scenarios. (p. 17-6)

LO3 Apply differential analysis to decision scenarios, including whether to change plans; to accept a special order; to make, buy, or outsource; and to sell or further process a product. (p. 17-9)

LO4 Allocate limited resources for purposes of maximizing short-run profit. (p. 17-15)

COSTS AND BENEFITS OF OUTSOURCING

Contracting with other firms to obtain necessary goods and services—called *outsourcing*—emerged as a key management strategy in the past decade. Through outsourcing, managers intend to take advantage of specialization, better focus attention on core activities, decrease costs, and increase flexibility. Cunningham Motor Company and StarTek Inc. illustrate outsourcing from the perspectives of the purchaser and provider, respectively, of outsourcing services.

Cunningham Motor Company's product and operating strategy depends entirely on its purchasing of outsourced products and services. The Cunningham C-7 is designed as a super-exclusive American sports car. Cunningham plans to sell each car for about $250,000 with volumes between 400 and 1,000 units per year. In addition to the 500-horsepower engine and sports car styling, the C-7 differs from other autos in one other major way—it will be the product of outsourcing efforts.

Managers at Cunningham want to outsource the entire production process with one subcontractor acting as the final assembler of the car. Cunningham will own no fabrication or assembly plants but will be a virtual

manufacturer. This is no small task and the risks are high. Current activities are on hold as it tries to resolve financing hurdles.

On the other side of the outsourcing business is StarTek, a global provider of outsourcing services. StarTek packs and ships products for Microsoft, provides technical support for customers of AOLTime Warner, and maintains AT&T's communications system. The activity level of a firm like StarTek, however, entirely depends on the success of its clients' products and services. Since contract work for Microsoft provides about 40 percent of StarTek revenue, any drop in Microsoft sales directly impacts StarTek.

In response to recent declines in technology-related sales, StarTek managers expanded the breadth of business activities it provides. Further, its managers have invested in a Web retailer and discussed other related ventures. Facing a decline in its core business of providing outsourcing services, StarTek management stated they will consider "anything that's intelligent and represents a chance to enhance the value of the company."

The business of purchasing and providing outsourced products and services has its own risks and rewards. As with any firm, managers must focus on relevant revenues and costs, examine alternative economic scenarios, make decisions on a course of action, and allocate resources to maximize profits. This module focuses on each of these managerial tasks.

Source: *Forbes, The Wall Street Journal, Business Week*.[1]

[1] "Ghost Cars, Ghost Brands," *Forbes*, April 30, 2001, pp. 106–12; Michael Selz, "StarTek Expands Beyond Its Core Services As Falling Demand Halts Financial Growth," *The Wall Street Journal, Interactive Edition*, June 26, 2001; and David Welch, "Bob Lutz: The First Virtual Carmaker," *Business Week*, June 18, 2001, pp. 66, 70.

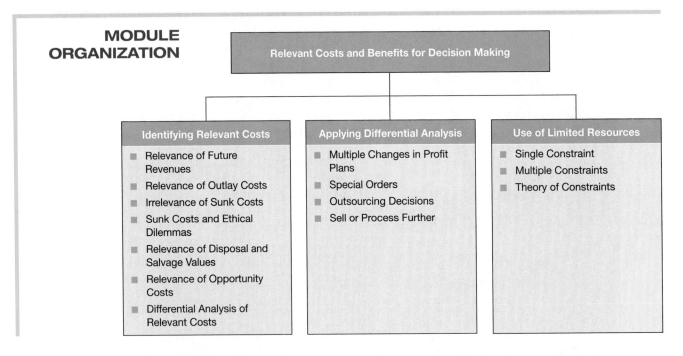

The purpose of this module is to examine approaches to identifying and analyzing revenue and cost information for specific decisions, such as the decision to outsource. Our emphasis is on identifying **relevant costs** (future costs that differ among competing decision alternatives) and distinguishing relevant costs from **irrelevant costs** that do not differ among competing decision alternatives. We consider a number of frequently encountered decisions: to make multiple changes in profit plans, to accept or reject a special order, to acquire a component or service internally or externally, to sell a product or process it further, and how to best use limited capacity. These decision situations are not exhaustive; they only illustrate relevant cost concepts. Once we understand these concepts, we can apply them to a variety of decision scenarios.

Although our focus in this module is on profit maximization, decisions should not be based solely on this criterion, especially maximizing profit in the short run. Managers must consider the implications decisions have on long-run profit, as well as legal, ethical, social, and other nonquantitative factors. These factors can lead management to select a course of action other than that selected by financial information alone.

IDENTIFYING RELEVANT COSTS

LO1 Distinguish between relevant and irrelevant revenues and costs.

For a specific decision, the key to differential cost analysis is first to identify the relevant costs (and revenues) and then to organize them in a manner that clearly indicates how they differ under each alternative. Consider the following equipment replacement decision.

Ace Welding Company manufactures frames for Mountain and Touring bicycles. Mountain bicycle frames have a unit selling price of $20 and annual production and sales total 10,000 bicycle frames. Each product is manufactured with separate equipment in a shared building. Selected cost information follows:

Mountain Bicycle Costs:	
Direct materials	$3.00 per unit
Conversion	5.00 per unit
Selling and distribution	1.00 per unit
Inspection and adjustment	$500 per batch (1,000 units)
Depreciation on welding machines	$15,000 per year
Machine maintenance	$200 per month
Advertising	$5,000 per year
Common Mountain and Touring Bicycle Costs:	
Administrative salaries	$65,000 per year
Building operations	23,000 per year
Building rent	24,000 per year

The Model I welding machine used in the manufacture of Mountain bicycle frames is two years old and has a remaining useful life of four years. Its purchase price was $90,000 (new), and it has an estimated salvage value of zero dollars at the end of its useful life. Its current book value (original cost less accumulated depreciation) is $60,000, but its current disposal value is only $35,000.

Management is evaluating the desirability of replacing the Model I welding machine with a new Model II welding machine. The new machine costs $80,000, has a useful life of four years, and a predicted salvage value of zero dollars at the end of its useful life. Although the new machine has the same production capacity as the old machine, its predicted operating costs are lower because it consumes less electricity. Further, because of a computer control system, the Model II machine allows production of twice as many units between inspections and adjustments, and the cost of inspections and adjustments is lower. The Model II machine requires only annual, rather than monthly, overhauls. Hence, machine maintenance costs are lower. The new conversion, inspection and adjustment, and machine maintenance costs are predicted as follows:

Conversion costs	$4.00 per unit
Inspection and adjustment.	$300 per batch (2,000 units)
Machine maintenance	$200 per year

All other costs and all revenues remain unchanged.

The decision alternatives are to keep the old Model I welding machine or to replace it with a new Model II welding machine. An analysis of how costs and revenues differ under each alternative assists management in making the best choice. The first objective of this module is to study the distinction between relevant and irrelevant items. After evaluating the relevance of each item, we develop an analysis of relevant costs.

Relevance of Future Revenues

Revenues, which are inflows of resources from the sale of goods and services, are relevant if they differ between alternatives. In this example, revenues are not relevant because they are identical under each alternative. They would be relevant if the new machine had greater capacity that would be used or if management intended to change the selling price should it acquire the new machine. (The $35,000 disposal value of the Model I machine is an inflow. However, *revenues* refer to resources from the sale of goods and services to customers in the normal course of business. We include the sale of the Model I machine under disposal and salvage values.)

The keep-or-replace decision facing Ace's management might be called a **cost reduction proposal** because it is based on the assumption that the organization is committed to an activity and that management desires to minimize the cost of activities. Here, the two alternatives are either to continue operating with the old machine or to replace it with a new machine.

Although this approach is appropriate for many activities, managers of for-profit organizations should remember that they have another alternative—discontinue operations. To simplify the analysis, managers normally do not consider the alternative to discontinue when operations appear to be profitable. However, if there is any doubt about an operation's profitability, this alternative should be considered. Because revenues change if an operation is discontinued, revenues are relevant whenever this alternative is considered.

Relevance of Outlay Costs

Outlay costs are costs that require future expenditures of cash or other resources. Outlay costs that differ under the decision alternatives are relevant; outlay costs that do not differ are irrelevant. Ace Welding Company's relevant and irrelevant outlay costs for the equipment replacement decision follow.

Relevant Outlay Costs	Irrelevant Outlay Costs
Mountain frame conversion costs	Mountain frame direct materials
Mountain frame inspection and adjustment costs	Mountain frame selling and distributon
Cost of new Model II machine	Mountain frame advertising
Mountain frame machine maintenance	Common outlay costs

Irrelevance of Sunk Costs

Sunk costs result from past decisions that cannot be changed. Suppose we purchased a car for $15,000 five years ago. Today we must decide whether to purchase another car or have major maintenance performed on our current car. In making this decision, the purchase price of our current car is a sunk cost.

Although the relevance of outlay costs is determined by the decision scenario, sunk costs (aside from possible tax consequences) are never relevant. The cost of the Model I machine is a sunk cost, not a future cost. This cost, and the related depreciation, results from the past decision to acquire the old machine. Even though all the outlay costs discussed earlier would be relevant to a decision to continue or discontinue operations, the sunk cost of the Model I machine is not relevant even to this decision.

If management elects to keep the old machine, its book value will be depreciated over its remaining useful life of four years. However, if management elects to replace the old machine, its book value is written off when it is replaced. Even if management elects to discontinue operations, the book value of the old machine must be written off.

Sunk Costs Can Cause Ethical Dilemmas

Although the book value of the old machine has no economic significance, the accounting treatment of past costs may make it psychologically difficult for managers to regard them as irrelevant. If management replaces the old machine, a $25,000 accounting loss is recorded in the year of replacement:

Book value	$60,000
Disposal value	(35,000)
Loss on disposal	$25,000

The possibility of recording an accounting loss can place managers in an ethical dilemma. Although an action may be desirable from the long-run viewpoint of the organization, in the short run, choosing the action may result in an accounting loss. Fearing the loss will lead superiors to question his or her judgment, a manager might prefer to use the old machine (with lower total profits over the four-year period) as opposed to replacing it and being forced to record a loss on disposal. Although this action may avoid raising troublesome questions, the cumulative effect of many decisions of this nature is harmful to the organization's long-run economic health.

From an economic viewpoint, the analysis should focus on future costs and revenues that differ. The decision should not be influenced by sunk costs. Although there is no easy solution to this behavioral and ethical problem, managers and management accountants should be aware of its potential impact.

> **MANAGERIAL DECISION** **You are the Vice President of Manufacturing**
>
> You recently made the decision to purchase a very expensive machine for your manufacturing plant that used technology that was well established over several years. The purchase of this machine was a major decision supported by the Chief Financial Officer, based solely on your recommendation. Shortly after making the purchase, you were attending a trade convention where you learned of new technology that was now available that essentially renders obsolete the machine you recently purchased. You feel that it may be best for the company to acquire the new technology since most of your competitors will be using it soon; however, you feel that this cannot be done now that you have recently purchased the new machine. What should you do? [Answer, p.17-21]

Relevance of Disposal and Salvage Values

Ace Welding Company's revenues (inflows of resources from operations) from the sale of bicycle frames were discussed earlier. The sale of fixed assets is also a source of resources. Because the sale of fixed assets is a nonoperating item, cash inflows obtained from these sales are discussed separately.

The disposal value of the Model I welding machine is a relevant cash inflow. It is obtained only if the replacement alternative is selected. Any salvage value available at the end of the useful life of either machine is also relevant. A loss on disposal can have a favorable tax impact if the loss can be offset against taxable gains or taxable income. In this case, although the book value of the old asset remains irrelevant, the expected tax reduction is relevant.

Relevance of Opportunity Costs

When making a decision between alternative courses of action, accepting one alternative results in rejecting the other alternative(s). Any benefits foregone as a result of rejecting one opportunity in favor of another opportunity is described as an **opportunity cost** of the accepted alternative. For example, if you are employed at a salary of $40,000 per year and you have the opportunity to continue to work or the opportunity to go back to school full-time for two years to earn a graduate degree, the cost of getting the degree includes not only all the outlay costs for tuition, books, and so forth, it also includes the salary forgone (or opportunity cost) of $40,000 per year. So, if your tuition and other outlay costs are going to be $25,000 per year for two years, the cost of earning the degree will be $50,000 of outlay costs and $80,000 of opportunity costs, for a total cost of earning the degree of $130,000. Opportunity costs are always relevant in making decisions among competing alternatives.

The following is a summary of all the relevant and irrelevant costs discussed in this section.

Relevant Costs		Irrelevant Costs	
Future costs that differ among competing alternatives		Future costs that do not differ among competing alternatives	

Opportunity Costs	Outlay Costs		Sunk Costs
Net benefits foregone of rejected alternatives	Future costs requiring future expenditures that differ	Future costs requiring future expenditures that do not differ	Historical costs resulting from past decisions

DIFFERENTIAL ANALYSIS OF RELEVANT COSTS

Differential cost analysis is an approach to the analysis of relevant costs that focuses on the costs that differ under alternative actions. A differential analysis of relevant costs for Ace Welding Company's equipment replacement decision is in Exhibit 17.1. Replacement provides a net advantage of $17,800 over the life of both machines.

An alternative analysis to that presented in Exhibit 17.1 is to present all revenues and costs (relevant and irrelevant) for each alternative in separate columns, such that the bottom line of the analysis is the total profit or loss for each alternative. This method is preferred if the goal is to determine the total profitability of each alternative. If the goal is to determine which of the two alternatives is most profitable, then a differential analysis is preferred.

Assuming the organization is committed to providing a particular product or service, a differential analysis of relevant costs (as shown in Exhibit 17.1) is preferred to a complete analysis of all costs and revenues for a number of reasons:

▪ A differential analysis focuses on only those items that differ, providing a clearer picture of the impact of the decision. Management is less apt to be confused by this analysis than by one that combines relevant and irrelevant items.

▪ A differential analysis contains fewer items, making it easier and quicker to prepare.

▪ A differential analysis can help to simplify complex situations (such as those encountered by multiple-product or multiple-plant firms), when it is difficult to develop complete firmwide statements to analyze all decision alternatives.

LO2 Analyze relevant costs and indicate how they differ under alternative decision scenarios.

EXHIBIT 17.1	Differential Analysis of Relevant Costs			
		Differential Analysis of Four-Year Totals		
		(1) Replace with New Model II Machine	(2) Keep Old Model I Machine	(1) – (2) Difference (effect of replacement on income)
Conversion:				
Mountain, Model I (10,000 units × $5 × 4 years). . . .			$200,000	
Mountain, Model II (10,000 units × $4 × 4 years) . . .		$160,000		$40,000
Inspection and adjustment:				
Mountain, Model I (10* setups × $500 × 4 years) . . .			20,000	
Mountain, Model II (5* setups × $300 × 4 years) . . .		6,000		14,000
Machine maintenance:				
Mountain, Model I ($200 × 12 months × 4 years) . . .			9,600	
Mountain, Model II ($200 × 4 years)		800		8,800
Disposal of Model I.		(35,000)		35,000
Cost of Model II		80,000		(80,000)
Total costs		$211,800	$229,600	$17,800
Advantage of replacement.			$17,800	

*Model I: 10,000 units ÷ 1,000 units per batch
 Model II: 10,000 units ÷ 2,000 units per batch

Before preparing a differential analysis, it is always desirable to reassess the organization's commitment to a product or service. This helps avoid "throwing good money after bad." If Ace Welding Company currently had large annual losses, acquiring the Model II machine would merely reduce total losses over the next four years by $17,800. In this case, discontinuing operations (a third alternative) should also be considered.

MID-MODULE REVIEW

Tigertec Company manufactures golf clubs using a traditional process involving significant hand tooling and finishing. A European machine company has proposed to sell Tigertec a new highly automated machine that would reduce significantly the labor cost of producing its golf clubs. The cost of the machine is $1,000,000, and would have an expected life of 5 years, at the end of which it would have a residual value of $100,000. It has an estimated operating cost of $10,000 per month. The direct labor cost savings per club from using the machine is estimated to be $5 per club. In addition, one monthly salaried manufacturing manager, whose salary is $6,000 per month would no longer be needed. The Vice President of Manufacturing earns $10,000 per month. Also, the new machine would free up about 5,000 square feet of space from the displaced workers. Tigertec's building is held under a 10-year lease that has eight years remaining. The current lease cost is $1 per square foot per month. Tigertec may be able to use the space for other purposes, and it has received an offer to rent it to a nearby related company for $3,500 per month.

Required:
a. Identify all of the costs described above as either "relevant" or "irrelevant" to the decision to acquire the new machine.
b. Assuming the new machine would be used to produce an average of 5,000 clubs per month, prepare a differential analysis of the relevant costs of buying the machine and using it for the next five years, versus continuing to use hand labor.
c. In addition to the quantitative analysis in requirement b., what qualitative considerations are important for making the right decision?

Solution

a.

Relevant costs:	Irrelevant costs:
Cost of machine	Building lease cost
Residual value of machine	Vice President's salary
Operating cost of machine	
Direct labor savings	
Cost of manager	
Opportunity cost of renting released space	

b.

	(1) Purchase Machine	(2) Use Labor	(1) – (2) Difference (in total cost of purchasing machine)
Cost of new machine	$1,000,000		$1,000,000
Residual value of machine	(100,000)		(100,000)
Operating cost of machine ($10,000 × 60 months)	600,000		600,000
Cost of direct laborers (5,000 clubs × $5 × 60 months)		$1,500,000	(1,500,000)
Cost of one manager ($6,000 × 60 months)		360,000	(360,000)
Rental value of freed up space ($3,500 × 60 months)		210,000	(210,000)
Total costs	$1,500,000	$2,070,000	$ (570,000)
Advantage of purchasing machine.		$570,000	

Alternatively, the residual value of the machine could have been shown as an opportunity cost of using labor instead of a negative cost of purchasing the machine.

c. Even though the new machine would save an estimated cost of $570,000 over the next five years, there are several qualitative questions that should be answered, including the following:
- Will the new machine provide the same quality product as the current workers?
- How important is it to have a cost structure that includes variable labor costs versus more fixed machine costs? If a business decline should occur, variable costs are often easier to eliminate than fixed costs.
- What is the expected effect on worker morale and community image of eliminating a significant number of jobs in the plant?
- How important is it for the sales staff to be able to promote the product as primarily handmade, versus machine made?

APPLYING DIFFERENTIAL ANALYSIS

Differential analysis is used to provide information for a variety of planning and decision-making situations. This section illustrates some of the more frequently encountered applications of differential analysis. To focus on differential analysis concepts, we will use a simple example involving the production of one product on a continuous basis with all output sold to distributors. From the viewpoint of our single-product firm, all costs can be classified as either (1) costs that vary with units produced and sold or (2) costs that are fixed in the short run.

Multiple Changes in Profit Plans

LO3 Apply differential analysis to decision scenarios, including whether to change plans; to accept a special order; to make, buy, or outsource; and to sell or further process a product.

Mind Trek, Limited, located in Lancaster, England, manufactures an electronic game sold to distributors for £22 per unit (a pound sterling, represented by the symbol £, is the basic unit of currency of the United Kingdom). Variable costs per unit and fixed costs per month follow:

Variable Costs per Unit		Fixed Costs per Month	
Direct materials	£ 5	Manufacturing overhead	£30,000
Direct labor.............	3	Selling and administrative ...	15,000
Manufacturing overhead ...	2	Total	£45,000
Selling.................	2		
Total	£12		

The unit contribution margin (UCM) is £10 (£22 selling price − £12 variable costs). Mind Trek's contribution income statement for April 2007 is presented in Exhibit 17.2. The April 2007 operations are typical. Monthly production and sales average 5,000 units, and monthly profits average £5,000.

Management wants to know the effect that each of the following three mutually exclusive alternatives would have on monthly profits.

1. Increasing the monthly advertising budget by £4,000, which should result in a 1,000-unit increase in monthly sales.
2. Increasing the selling price by £3, which should result in a 2,000-unit decrease in monthly sales.
3. Decreasing the selling price by £2, which should result in a 2,000-unit increase in monthly sales. However, because of capacity constraints, the last 1,000 units would be produced during overtime with the direct labor costs increasing by £1 per unit.

It is possible to develop contribution income statements for each alternative and then determine the profit impact of the proposed change by comparing the new income with the current income. A more direct approach is to use differential analysis and focus on only those items that differ under each alternative.

Alternative 1
Profit increase from increased sales
  (1,000 additional unit sales × £10 UCM) £10,000
Profit decrease from increased advertising expenditures .... (4,000)
Increase in monthly profit .... £ 6,000

Alternative 2
Profit decrease from reduced sales given no changes in prices or costs
  (2,000 lost unit sales × £10 UCM) .... £(20,000)
Profit increase from increased selling price
  [(5,000 current unit sales − 2,000 lost unit sales)
    × £3 increase in unit selling price] 9,000
Decrease in monthly profit .... £(11,000)

Alternative 3
Profit increase from increased sales given no changes in prices or costs
  (2,000 increased unit sales × £10 UCM) £20,000
Profit decrease from reduced selling price of all units
  [(5,000 current unit sales + 2,000 additional unit sales)
    × £2 decrease in unit selling price].................................... (14,000)
Profit decrease from increased direct labor costs of the last 1,000 units
  (1,000 units × £1 increase in unit labor costs) .... (1,000)
Increase in monthly profit .... £ 5,000

Alternative 2 is undesirable because it would result in a decrease in monthly profit. Because Alternative 1 results in a larger increase in monthly profit, it is preferred to Alternative 3.

Special Orders

Assume a Brazilian distributor offered to place a special, one-time order for 1,000 units at a reduced price of £12 per unit. The Brazilian distributor will contract for a common carrier to handle all packing and transportation. Mind Trek has sufficient production capacity to produce the additional units without reducing sales to its regular distributors. Management desires to know the profit impact of accepting the order. The following analysis focuses on those costs and revenues that will differ if the order is accepted.

Increase in revenues (1,000 units × £12)		£12,000
Increase in costs		
Direct materials (1,000 units × £5)	£5,000	
Direct labor (1,000 units × £3)	3,000	
Variable manufacturing overhead (1,000 units × £2)	2,000	(10,000)
Increase in profits		£ 2,000

Accepting the special order will result in a profit increase of £2,000.

If management were unaware of relevant cost concepts, it might be tempted to compare the special order price to average unit cost information developed from accounting reports. Based on Mind Trek's April 2007 contribution income statement in Exhibit 17.2, the average cost of all manufacturing, selling, and administrative expenses was £21 per unit as follows.

Variable costs	£ 60,000
Fixed costs	45,000
Total costs	£105,000
Unit production and sales	÷ 5,000
Average unit cost	£ 21

EXHIBIT 17.2	Contribution Income Statement

MIND TREK, LIMITED
Contribution Income Statement
For the Month of April 2007

Sales (5,000 units × £22)		£110,000
Less variable costs		
Direct materials (5,000 units × £5)	£25,000	
Direct labor (5,000 units × £3)	15,000	
Manufacturing overhead (5,000 units × £2)	10,000	
Selling and administrative (5,000 units × £2)	10,000	(60,000)
Contribution margin		50,000
Less fixed costs		
Manufacturing overhead	30,000	
Selling and administrative	15,000	(45,000)
Profit		£ 5,000

Comparing the special order price of £12 per unit to the average unit cost of £21, management might conclude the order would result in a loss of £9 per unit.

It is apparent that the £21 figure encompasses variable costs of £12 per unit (including irrelevant selling and administrative costs of £2 per unit) and irrelevant fixed costs of £45,000 spread over 5,000 units. But remember, management may not have detailed cost information. To obtain appropriate information for decision-making purposes, management must ask its accounting staff for the specific information needed. Different configurations of cost information are provided for different purposes. In the absence of special instructions, the accounting staff might supply some average cost information.

Importance of Time Span and Opportunity Costs

The special order is a one-time order for 1,000 units that will use current excess capacity. Because no special setups or equipment are required to produce the order, it is appropriate to consider only variable costs in computing the order's profitability.

But what if the Brazilian distributor wanted Mind Trek to sign a multiyear contract to provide 1,000 units per month at £12 each? Under these circumstances, management would be well advised to reject the contract because there is a high probability that cost increases would make the order unprofitable in later years. At the very least, management should insist that a cost escalation clause be added to the purchase agreement, specifying that the selling price would increase to cover any cost increases and detailing the cost computation.

Of more concern is the variable nature of all long-run costs. Given adequate time, management must replace fixed assets and may adjust both the number of machines as well as the size of machines used in the manufacturing process. Accordingly, *in the long run, all costs (including costs classified as fixed in a given period) are relevant*. To remain in business in the long run, Mind Trek must replace equipment, pay property taxes, pay administrative salaries, and so forth. Consequently, management should consider *all costs* (fixed and variable, manufacturing and nonmanufacturing) in evaluating a long-term contract.

Full costs include all costs, regardless of their behavior pattern or activity level. The average full cost per unit is sometimes used to approximate long-run variable costs. If accepting a long-term contract increases the monthly production and sales volume to 6,000 units, the average full cost per unit will be £19.5.

Direct materials	£ 5.0
Direct labor	3.0
Variable manufacturing overhead	2.0
Variable selling and administrative	2.0
Fixed manufacturing overhead (£30,000/6,000 units)	5.0
Fixed selling and administrative (£15,000/6,000 units)	2.5
Average full cost per unit	£19.5

If the Brazilian distributor agrees to separately pay all variable selling and administrative expenses associated with the contract, the estimated long-run variable costs are £17.5 per unit (£19.5 − £2). Many managers would say this is the minimum acceptable selling price, especially if the order extends over a long period of time.

Because Mind Trek has excess productive capacity, no opportunity cost is associated with accepting the Brazilian distributor's one-time order. There is no alternative use of the productive capacity in the short run, so there is no opportunity cost.

But what if Mind Trek were operating at capacity? In this case, accepting the special order would require reducing regular sales (assume overtime production is not possible). With an alternative use of the production capacity, an opportunity cost is associated with its use to fill the special order.

Each unit sold to the Brazilian distributor could otherwise generate a £10 contribution from regular customers. Accepting the special order would cause Mind Trek to incur an opportunity cost of £10,000, the net benefit of the most desirable alternative action, selling to regular customers.

Lost sales to regular customers (units)	1,000
Regular unit contribution margin	× £10
Opportunity cost of accepting special order	£10,000

Because this opportunity cost exceeds the £2,000 contribution derived from the special order, management should reject the special order. Accepting the order will reduce profits by £8,000 (£2,000 contribution − £10,000 opportunity cost).

Qualitative Considerations

Although an analysis of cost and revenue information may indicate that a special order is profitable in the short run, management might still reject the order because of qualitative considerations. Any concerns regarding the order's impact on regular customers might lead management to reject the order even if there is excess capacity. If the order involves a special low price, regular customers might demand a similar price reduction and threaten to take their business elsewhere. Alternatively, management might accept the special order while operating at capacity if they believed there were long-term benefits associated with penetrating a new market. Legal factors must also be considered if the special order is from a buyer who competes with regular customers.

Outsourcing Decisions (Make or Buy)

Organizations often have external opportunities to acquire services or components of products they manufacture rather than providing the service or manufacturing the component internally. The external acquisition of services or components is called **outsourcing.** There are three major reasons for outsourcing: (1) to focus on the key aspects of the business by outsourcing noncore activities, (2) to improve the quality of support activities, and (3) to better control costs. The first two points are considered in the following Business Insight, which examines the benefits Med Resorts International obtained by outsourcing accounts receivable and collections. Addressing the third point, the CEO of TeleTech Holdings (which handles customer service calls for companies such at AT&T), notes that "we show companies how to turn fixed costs into variable costs."[2]

On college campuses, Marriott and ARA Food operate many university dining halls, and Barnes & Noble manages many university bookstores. Some organizations are even outsourcing employees. SCP Enterprises of Ann Arbor Michigan, for example, laid off all 65 employees and had them rehired by a professional employer organization that is now responsible for handling all payroll and employee benefit issues and complying with employment laws.[3]

To illustrate outsourcing, suppose a Canadian manufacturer offers a one-year contract to supply Mind Trek with an electronic component at a cost of £2 per unit. Mind Trek is now faced with the decision to

---

BUSINESS INSIGHT   **Surprising Benefits of Outsourcing**

Med Resorts sells vacation programs in the leisure-time industry. Paralleling its growth in revenues, the services staff (responsible for billing, collecting, and maintaining accounts receivable records) had grown to 12 employees by the time Med Resorts made the decision to outsource this function. Outsourcing provided several expected benefits, including improved cash flows, reductions in the age of accounts receivable, and related cost reductions of $75,000 per year. Interestingly, Med Resorts reported a number of unexpected benefits.[4]

- Management no longer had to worry that invoices were not sent out on time.
- Because of a higher capacity, the external service provider eliminated delays in processing transactions during peak periods. This improved cash flows and provided more accurate customer records.
- The vendor's state-of-the-art system and experienced staff were able to inexpensively develop specialized reports.
- Med Resorts no longer needed to invest in software and hardware for billing and collections, nor in related employee training.
- The improved performance of the accounts receivable portfolio and the investor contacts provided by the vendor enabled Med Resorts to obtain more favorable financing.
- Med Resorts reduced the hassles that arise when dissatisfied customers refuse to pay their bills.

---

[2] John A. Byrne, "Has Outsourcing Gone Too Far?" *BusinessWeek*, April 1, 1996, pp. 26–28.

[3] Rick Haglund (Newhouse News Service), "More Companies Are Farming Out Payrolls," *Huntsville Times*, January 4, 1997, pp. A21, A24.

[4] Kathleen A. Cormier, "Outsourcing Accounts Receivable and Other Serendipitus Benefits," *Management Accounting*, September 1996, pp. 16–18.

continue to make the electronic component internally or to buy the component from the Canadian company. This is often called a *make or buy* decision. An analysis of the materials and operations required to manufacture the component internally reveals that if Mind Trek accepts the offer, it will be able to reduce the following:

- Materials costs by 10 percent per unit.
- Direct labor and variable factory overhead costs by 20 percent per unit.
- Fixed manufacturing overhead by £20,000 per year.

A differential analysis of Mind Trek's make or buy decision is presented in Exhibit 17.3. Continuing to make the component has a net advantage of £10,000.

EXHIBIT 17.3	Differential Analysis of Make or Buy Decision		
	(1) Cost to Make	**(2)** Cost to Buy	**(1) − (2)** Difference (income effect of buying)
Cost to buy (£2 × 60,000* units)		£120,000	£(120,000)
Cost to make			
Direct materials (£5 × 0.10 × 60,000 units).	£ 30,000		30,000
Direct labor (£3 × 0.20 × 60,000 units)	36,000		36,000
Variable manufacturing overhead (£2 × 0.20 × 60,000 units)	24,000		24,000
Fixed manufacturing overhead.	20,000		20,000
Total	£110,000	£120,000	£ (10,000)
Advantage of making		£10,000	

*5,000 units per month × 12 months

But what if the space currently used to manufacture the electronic component can be rented to a third party for £40,000 per year? In this case, the production capacity has an alternative use, and the net cash flow from this alternative use is an opportunity cost of making the component. Treating the rent Mind Trek will not receive if it continues to make the component as an opportunity cost, the analysis in Exhibit 17.4 indicates that buying now has a net advantage of £30,000.

EXHIBIT 17.4	Differential Analysis of Make or Buy Decision with Opportunity to Rent Facilities		
	(1) Cost to Make	**(2)** Cost to Buy	**(1) − (2)** Difference (income effect of buying)
Cost to buy (£2 × 60,000* units)		£120,000	£(120,000)
Cost to make			
Direct materials (£5 × 0.10 × 60,000 units).	£ 30,000		30,000
Direct labor (£3 × 0.20 × 60,000 units)	36,000		36,000
Variable manufacturing overhead (£2 × 0.20 × 60,000 units)	24,000		24,000
Fixed manufacturing overhead.	20,000		20,000
Opportunity cost of lost rent income	40,000		40,000
Total	£150,000	£120,000	£ 30,000
Advantage of buying		£30,000	

*5,000 units per month × 12 months

Even if outsourcing appears financially advantageous in the short run, management should not decide to outsource before considering a variety of qualitative factors. Is the outside supplier interested in developing a long-term relationship or merely attempting to use some temporarily idle capacity? If so, what will happen at the end of the contract period? What impact would a decision to outsource have on the morale of Mind Trek's employees? Will Mind Trek have to rehire laid-off employees after the contract expires? Will the outside supplier meet delivery schedules? Does the supplied part meet Mind Trek's quality standards? Will it continue to meet them? Organizations often manufacture products or provide services they can obtain elsewhere in order to control quality, to have an assured supply source, to avoid dealing with a potential competitor, or to maintain a core competency.

The movement toward outsourcing has grown to include many units of government, where elected officials have concluded that a profit motive in a competitive environment often leads to higher quality at lower costs. Consider the following examples:

- **California Private Transportation Company** is building toll roads.
- **BFI** provides waste collection and disposal services for many communities.
- **Rural/Metro** is contracting to run fire departments and provide medical services.
- **Corrections Corporation of America** and **Wackenhut** build, finance, and operate jails.[5]

According to the chief financial officer of Rural/Metro, his company provides better service at a fraction of the cost of traditional government-run services by focusing on the bottom line. He cites Scottsdale, Arizona, where fire losses have declined 84 percent since 1985, as an example. Some politicians have even proposed that package carriers, such as **Federal Express** and **United Parcel Service**, should be allowed to compete with the **U.S. Postal Service** in delivering first-class mail. Experts estimate that the increased competition would reduce the cost of first-class mail by 25 percent.[6]

Sell or Process Further

When a product is salable at various stages of completion, management must determine the product's most advantageous selling point. As each stage is completed, management must determine whether to sell the product then or to process it further. We consider two types of sell or process further decisions: (1) for a single product and (2) for joint products.

Single Product Decisions

Assume that Boston Rocking Company manufactures rocking chairs from precut and shaped wood. Although the chairs are salable once they are assembled, Boston Rocking sands and paints all chairs before they are sold. Management wishes to know if this is the optimal selling point.

A complete listing of unit costs and revenues for the alternative selling points follows:

	Per Chair		
	Sell after Assembly	Sell after Painting	Difference (income effect of painting)
Selling price	$40	$75	$35
Assembly costs	(25)	(25)	
Sanding and painting costs	___	(12)	(12)
Contribution margin	$15	$38	$23
Advantage of painting		$23	

---

[5] Gail DeGeorge and Julia Flynn, "Go Directly to Jail," *Business Week*, December 15, 1997, pp. 139–42.

[6] Eric Schine, Richard S. Dunham, and Christopher Farrell, "America's New Watchword: If It Moves, Privatize It," *Business Week*, December 12, 1994, p. 39.

The sanding and painting operation has an additional contribution of $23 per unit. The chairs should be sold after they are painted.

The assembly costs are the same under both alternatives. This illustrates that *all costs incurred prior to the decision point are irrelevant.* Given the existence of an assembled chair, the decision alternatives are to sell it now or to process it further. A differential analysis for the decision to sell or process further should include only revenues and the incremental costs of further processing as follows.

Increase in revenues		
Sell after painting	$75	
Sell after assembly	(40)	$35
Additional costs of sanding and painting.		(12)
Advantage of sanding and painting		$23

The identical solution is obtained if the selling price without further processing is treated as an opportunity cost as follows.

Revenues after painting		$75
Additional costs of sanding and painting.	$12	
Opportunity cost of not selling after assembly . .	40	(52)
Advantage of sanding and painting		$23

By processing a chair further, Boston Rocking has forgone the opportunity to receive $40 from its sale. Since the chair is already made, this $40 is the net cash inflow from the most desirable alternative; it is the opportunity cost of painting.

Joint Product Decisions

Two or more products simultaneously produced by a single process from a common set of inputs are called **joint products.** Joint products are often found in basic industries that process natural raw materials such as dairy, chemical, meat, petroleum, and wood products. In the petroleum industry, crude oil is refined into fuel oil, gasoline, kerosene, lubricating oil, and other products.

The point in the process where the joint products become separately identifiable is called the **split-off point.** Materials and conversion costs incurred prior to the split-off point are called **joint costs.** For external reporting purposes, a number of techniques are used to allocate joint costs among joint products. We do not discuss these techniques here (interested students should consult a cost accounting textbook), except to note that none of the methods provide information useful for determining what to do with a joint product once it is produced. Because joint costs are incurred prior to the decision point, they are sunk costs. Consequently, *joint costs are irrelevant to a decision to sell a joint product or to process it further.* The only relevant factors are the alternative costs and revenues subsequent to the split-off point.

USE OF LIMITED RESOURCES

LO4 Allocate limited resources for purposes of maximizing short-run profit.

All of us have experienced time as a limiting or constraining resource. With two exams the day after tomorrow and a paper due next week, our problem is how to allocate limited study time. The solution depends on our objectives, our current status (grades, knowledge, skill levels, and so forth), and available time. Given this information, we devise a work plan to best meet our objectives.

Managers must also decide how to best use limited resources to accomplish organizational goals. A supermarket may lose sales because limited shelf space prevents stocking all available brands of soft drinks. A manufacturer may lose sales because limited machine hours or labor hours prevent filling all orders. Managers of for-profit organizations will likely find the problems of capacity constraints less troublesome than the problems of excess capacity; nonetheless, these problems are real. The Business Insight below is an illustration of the efforts organizations will make to overcome production delays or to provide additional capacity as quickly as possible.

BUSINESS INSIGHT   Russian Aircraft Becomes Capitalist Tool

The Russian Antonov 124, built to move military cargo, burns 3.3 tons of fuel to taxi on a runway. Some of its engines need replacement after 1,000 hours (as opposed to the 8,000 to 10,000 hours before maintenance is required on a typical jet engine). It has a crew of nearly 20 so emergency repairs can be made promptly. Compared to a Boeing 747-400 cargo jet, this plane is a gas-guzzling clunker. Yet this relic of the Cold War is an important tool of capitalists trying to compete on the basis of time. The secret to the Antonov's success is not high technology. It is massive capacity and raw power. At 330,639 pounds, its maximum payload is almost 70,000 pounds more than a Lockheed C-5B. Plus, with a cargo tunnel 14 feet high, 20 feet wide, and 134 feet long, the Antonov can handle cargo that won't fit into a Boeing 747-400.

   When production delays jeopardized General Motors Corporation's sale of locomotives to an Irish railroad, an Antonov carried a 240,000-pound locomotive across the Atlantic. When Pepsi wanted to get an Italian-manufactured bottling line to Mexico as soon as possible, Pepsi's management called upon an Antonov. This allowed a new 1,200-cans-a-minute line to begin operations one month sooner than would have been possible if the next feasible method of transportation, a cargo ship, were used.[7]

If the limited resource is not a core business activity, such as manufacturing computer chips at Intel, it may be appropriate to acquire additional units of the limited resource externally. For example, many organizations have a small legal staff to handle routine activities; if the internal staff becomes fully committed, the organization seeks outside legal counsel. The external acquisition of such resources was discussed previously.

The long-run solution to the problem of limited resources to perform core activities may be to expand capacity. However, this is usually not feasible in the short run. Economic models suggest that another solution is to reduce demand by increasing the price. Again, this may not be desirable. The supermarket, for example, may want to maintain competitive prices. The manufacturer might want to maintain a long-run price to retain customer goodwill, to avoid attracting competitors, or to prevent accusations of "price gouging."

Single Constraint

The allocation of limited resources should be made only after a careful consideration of many qualitative factors. The following rule provides a useful starting point in making short-run decisions of how to best use limited resources: *To achieve short-run profit maximization, a for-profit organization should allocate limited resources in a manner that maximizes the contribution per unit of the limited resource.* The application of this rule is illustrated in the following example.

Delta Manufacturing Company produces three products: A, B, and C. A limitation of 120 machine hours per week for its finishing machine prevents Delta from meeting the sales demand for these products. Product information is as follows:

	A	B	C
Unit selling price.	$100	$80	$50
Unit variable costs	(90)	(50)	(25)
Unit contribution margin.	$ 10	$30	$25
Machine hours per unit.	2	2	1

---

[7] Douglas Lavin, "The Mighty Antonov Is the Only Way to Fly Your Locomotive," *The Wall Street Journal*, December 29, 1994, pp. 1, 4.

Product A has the highest selling price and Product B has the highest unit contribution margin. Product C is shown here to have the highest contribution per machine hour.

	A	B	C
Unit contribution margin...........	$10	$30	$25
Machine hours per unit............	÷ 2	÷ 2	÷ 1
Contribution per machine hour	$ 5	$15	$25

Following the rule of maximizing the contribution per unit of a constraining factor, Delta should use its limited machine hours to produce Product C. As shown in the following analysis, any other plan would result in lower profits:

	A	B	C
	Highest Selling Price	Highest Contribution per Unit	Highest Contribution per Unit of Constraining Factor
Machine hours available...........	120	120	120
Machine hours per unit............	÷ 2	÷ 2	÷ 1
Weekly production in units.........	60	60	120
Unit contribution margin...........	× $10	× $30	× $25
Total weekly contribution margin	$600	$1,800	$3,000

Despite this analysis, management may decide to produce some units of A or B or both to satisfy the requests of some "good" customers or to offer a full product line. However, such decisions sacrifice short-run profits.

When there is a single constraint, it is very often related to time. However, as noted in the following Research Insight, space is often the single most important constraint in the retail industry.

RESEARCH INSIGHT   More Ice Cream Yields Cool Profits

Food stores have traditionally determined the gross profit (selling price less cost of goods sold) of individual products. With limited space, they often determine each product's gross profit per square foot of aisle-facing shelf space per store per week. While a useful guide, such an analysis is incomplete in that it fails to consider operating costs, such as unloading, storing, refrigeration, and so forth.

Modern Costing Methods, for the first time, provided retail management tools to accurately determine the contribution margin of individual products and to evaluate the contribution margin per square foot of facing, per store per week. Using these techniques, a recent study of frozen foods at more than 250 grocery stores found that the overall contribution margin was $1.67 per square foot of facing per week. The contribution margins ranged from a low of $1.23 for dry goods to $2.19 for refrigerated foods and $2.32 for frozen foods. The most profitable product was ice cream, which yielded a cool contribution of $5.85 per square foot per week. With space as the constraining resource, the study concluded that ice cream is "underspaced."[8]

Multiple Constraints

Continuing our illustration, assume the weekly demand for C is only 80 units although the company is capable of producing 120 units of C each week. In this case, the production capacity of the finishing machine

---

[8] Warren Thayer, "ABCs of Ice Cream Profitability," *Frozen Food Age,* March 1997, pp. 7–10.

should first be used to satisfy the demand for Product C, with any remaining capacity going to produce Product B, which has the next highest contribution per unit of constraining factor. This allocation provides a total weekly contribution of $2,600 as follows.

Available hours.	120
Required for C (80 units × 1 machine hour).	(80)
Hours available for B	40
Machine hours per unit.	÷ 2
Production of B in units	20
Unit contribution margin of B.	× $30
Contribution from B	$ 600
Contribution from C ($25 per unit × 80 units)	2,000
Total weekly contribution margin	$2,600

When an organization has alternative uses for several limited resources, the optimal use of those resources cannot be determined using the rule for short-run profit maximization. In these situations, techniques such as linear programming can be used to assist in determining the optimal mix of products or services.

Theory of Constraints

The **theory of constraints** states that every process has a bottleneck (constraining resource) and that production cannot take place faster than it is processed through that bottleneck. The goal of the theory of constraints is to maximize **throughput** (defined as sales revenue minus direct materials costs) in a constrained environment.[9] The theory has several implications for management.

- Management should identify the bottleneck. This is often difficult when several different products are produced in a facility containing many different production activities. One approach is to walk around and observe where inventory is building up in front of workstations. The bottleneck will likely have the largest piles of work that have been waiting for the longest time.

- Management should schedule production to maximize the efficient use of the bottleneck resource. Efficiently using the bottleneck resource might necessitate inspecting all units before they reach the bottleneck rather than after the units are completed. The bottleneck resource is too valuable to waste on units that may already be defective.

- Management should schedule production to avoid a buildup of inventory. Reducing inventory lowers the cost of inventory investments and the cost of carrying inventory. It also assists in improving quality by making it easier to identify quality problems that might otherwise be hidden in large piles of inventory. Reducing inventory will require a change in the attitude of managers who like to see machines and people constantly working. To avoid a buildup of inventory in front of the bottleneck, it may be necessary for people and equipment to remain idle until the bottleneck resource calls for additional input.

- Management should work to eliminate the bottleneck, perhaps by increasing the capacity of the bottleneck resource, redesigning products so they can be produced with less use of the bottleneck resource, rescheduling production procedures to substitute nonbottleneck resources, or outsourcing work performed by bottleneck resources.

The theory of constraints has implications for management accounting performance reports. Keeping people and equipment working on production full-time is often a goal of management. To support this goal, management accounting performance reports have traditionally highlighted underutilization as an unfavorable variance (see Module 21). This has encouraged managers to have people and equipment producing inventory, even if the inventory is not needed or cannot be further processed because of bottlenecks. The theory of constraints suggests that it is better to have nonbottleneck resources idle than it is to have them fully utilized. To support the theory of constraints, performance reports should:

---

[9] *The Goal*, by Elijah M. Goldratt and Jeff Cox, presents the concepts underlying the theory of constraints in the form of a novel.

- Measure the utilization of bottleneck resources
- Measure factory throughput
- Not encourage the full utilization of nonbottleneck resources
- Discourage the buildup of excess inventory

While the theory of constraints is *similar* to our general rule for how to best use limited resources, it emphasizes throughput (selling price minus direct materials) rather than contribution (selling price minus variable costs) in allocating the limited resource. The exclusion of direct labor and variable manufacturing overhead yields larger unit margins, and it may affect resource allocations based on throughput rankings. The result will likely be a reduction in profits from those that could be achieved using our general rule for how to allocate limited resources.

It is easy to develop a textbook example demonstrating the weaknesses of this incomplete measure of contribution, and it is easy to envision situations in which the theory of constraints will produce a significant improvement in performance, even if optimal performance is not attained. Consider a situation in which management is finding it difficult to meet sales orders and the only cost information available is that used for financial reporting. Management needs a place to start in its efforts to control operations in a manner that will enhance profits. The determination of direct materials costs is relatively easy. Under these circumstances, a simple and incomplete measurement of the unit margin (computed as selling price less direct materials) may be a useful and pragmatic starting point in managing production constraints. The following Business Insight illustrates how a small business utilized the theory of constraints to improve profit planning.

BUSINESS INSIGHT | **Theory of Constraints Hooks Profits**

Daufel Enterprises is a small business that produces high-quality, hand-tied fishing flies from feathers, fur, and synthetics placed on a hook and seamed with thread. By its very nature, producing hand-tied fishing flies is labor intensive, and recruiting qualified personnel is difficult. Because of product quality and the popularity of fly-fishing, Daufel was operating at capacity, and management was wrestling with tough decisions regarding the use of limited resources.

Daufel had been charging the same price, $12.00 per dozen, for all five of its flies: Hare's Ear, Pheasant Tail, Compara Dun, Thorax Dun, and Woolly Bugger. Analysis revealed differences in materials costs, ranging from $1.95 for a dozen Compara Duns to $3.09 for a dozen Thorax Duns. With labor time as the limiting factor, management determined the time required to produce a dozen of each type of fly and computed the throughput per labor hour. Results revealed a wide variation in throughput, with the throughput of Pheasant Tail $29.30 per labor hour and of Thorax Duns $14.85 per hour. Although management decided to keep all five products for the benefit of having a complete product line, they used the throughput cost analysis to (1) shift production toward more profitable products and (2) increase prices on less profitable products.[10]

MODULE-END REVIEW

Final Copy Company produces color cartridges for inkjet printers. The cartridges are sold to mail-order distributors for $4.80 each. Manufacturing and other costs are as follows:

Variable Costs per Unit		Fixed Costs per Month	
Direct materials	$2.00	Factory overhead	$15,000
Direct labor	0.20	Selling and administrative	5,000
Factory overhead	0.25	Total	$20,000
Distribution	0.05		
Total	$2.50		

---

[10] J. Gregory Bushong, John C. Talbot, and John F. Burke, "An Application of the Theory of Constraints," *The CPA Journal*, April 1999, p. 53.

The variable distribution costs are for transportation to mail-order distributors. The current monthly production and sales volume is 15,000. Monthly capacity is 20,000 units.

Required
Determine the effect of the following independent situations on monthly profits.
a.   A $1.50 increase in the unit selling price should result in an 1,800 unit decrease in monthly sales.
b.   A $1.80 decrease in the unit selling price should result in a 6,000 unit increase in monthly sales. However, because of capacity constraints, the last 1,000 units would be produced during overtime, when the direct labor costs increase by 50 percent.
c.   A New Zealand distributor has proposed to place a special, one-time order for 4,000 units next month at a reduced price of $4.00 per unit. The distributor would pay all transportation costs. There would be additional fixed selling and administrative costs of $500.00
d.   An Australian distributor has proposed to place a special, one-time order for 8,000 units at a special price of $4.00 per unit. The distributor would pay all transportation costs. There would be additional fixed selling and administrative costs of $500.00. Assume overtime production is not possible.
e.   A Mexican manufacturer has offered a one-year contract to supply ink for the cartridges at a cost of $1.00 per unit. If Final Copy accepts the offer, it will be able to reduce variable manufacturing costs by 40 percent and rent some currently used space for $1,000.00 per month.
f.   The cartridges are currently unpackaged; that is, they are sold in bulk. Individual packaging would increase costs by $0.10 per unit. However, the units could then be sold for $5.05.

Solution

Unit selling price	$4.80
Unit variable costs	(2.50)
Unit contribution margin	$2.30

a.

Profit decrease from reduced sales given no changes in prices or costs (1,800 units × $2.30)	$ (4,140)
Profit increase from increase in selling price [(15,000 units − 1,800 units) × $1.50]	19,800
Increase in monthly profit	$15,660

b.

Profit increase from increased sales given no changes in prices or costs (6,000 units × $2.30)	$13,800
Profit decrease from reduced selling price of all units [(15,000 units + 6,000 units) × $1.80]	(37,800)
Profit decrease from increased direct labor costs for the last 1,000 units [1,000 units × ($0.20 × 0.50)]	(100)
Decrease in monthly profit	$(24,100)

c.

Increase in revenues (4,000 units × $4.00)		$16,000
Increase in costs		
Direct materials (4,000 units × $2.00)	$ 8,000	
Direct labor (4,000 units × $0.20)	800	
Factory overhead (4,000 units × $0.25)	1,000	
Selling and administrative	500	(10,300)
Increase in profits		$ 5,700

d.

Increase in revenues (8,000 units × $4.00)		$32,000
Increase in costs		
Direct materials (8,000 units × $2.00)	$16,000	
Direct labor (8,000 units × $0.20).	1,600	
Factory overhead (8,000 units × $0.25).	2,000	
Selling and administrative.	500	
Opportunity cost of lost regular sales		
[(15,000 units + 8,000 units −		
20,000 unit capacity) × $2.30]	6,900	(27,000)
Increase in profits.		$ 5,000

e.

	Cost to Make	Cost to Buy	Difference (income effect of buying)
Cost to buy (15,000 units × $1.00)		$15,000	$(15,000)
Cost to make			
Direct materials			
(15,000 units × $2.00 × 0.40).	$12,000		12,000
Direct labor			
(15,000 units × $0.20 × 0.40).	1,200		1,200
Factory overhead			
(15,000 units × $0.25 × 0.40).	1,500		1,500
Opportunity cost.	1,000		1,000
Totals.	$15,700	$15,000	$ 700
Advantage of buying		$700	

f.

Increase in revenues		
Package individually (15,000 units × $5.05)	$75,750	
Sell in bulk (15,000 units × $4.80)	(72,000)	$3,750
Additional packaging costs (15,000 units × $0.10).		(1,500)
Advantage of individual packaging		$2,250

GUIDANCE ANSWER

MANAGERIAL DECISION | **You are the Vice President of Manufacturing**

This is a decision that has both economic and ethical dimensions. Economically, the cost of the old machine is a sunk cost, since the expenditure for it has already been made. If it can be sold to another company to recover part of the initial cost, that amount would be relevant to the decision regarding the new technology. However, you should ignore the cost of the recently purchased machine and consider only the outlay costs that will differ between keeping the recently purchased machine and purchasing the new technology, plus any opportunity costs that may be involved with disposing of the existing machine and acquiring the new machine. From an ethical standpoint, managers are often hesitant to recommend an action that reflects poorly on their past decisions. The temptation is to try to justify the past decision. If you have evaluated all of the relevant costs and have considered all of the qualitative issues associated with upgrading the machine, these should be the basis for making your recommendation, not what it will do to your reputation with your superiors.

DISCUSSION QUESTIONS

Q17-1. Distinguish between relevant and irrelevant costs.

Q17-2. In evaluating a cost reduction proposal, what three alternatives are available to management?

Q17-3. When are outlay costs relevant and when are they irrelevant?

Q17-4. When are product-level activity costs relevant and when are they irrelevant?

Q17-5. Why is a differential analysis of relevant items preferred to a detailed listing of all costs and revenues associated with each alternative?

Q17-6. How can cost predictions be made when the acquisition of new equipment results in a technological change?

Q17-7. When are opportunity costs relevant to the evaluation of a special order?

Q17-8. Identify some important qualitative considerations in evaluating a decision to make or buy a part.

Q17-9. In a decision to sell or to process further, of what relevance are costs incurred prior to the decision point? Explain your answer.

Q17-10. How should limited resources be used to achieve short-run profit maximization?

Q17-11. What should performance reports do in support of the theory of constraints?

MINI EXERCISES

M17-12. Relevant Cost Terms: Matching (LO1)

A company that produces three products, M, N, and O, is evaluating a proposal that will result in doubling the production of N and discontinuing the production of O. The facilities currently used to produce O will be devoted to the production of N. Furthermore, additional machinery will be acquired to produce N. The production of M will not be affected. All products have a positive contribution margin.

Required

Presented are a number of phrases related to the proposal. For each phrase, select the most appropriate cost term. Each term is used only once.

Phrases
1. Increased revenues from the sale of N
2. Increased variable costs of N
3. Property taxes on the new machinery
4. Revenues from the sale of M
5. Cost of the equipment used to produce O
6. Contribution margin of O
7. Variable costs of M
8. Company president's salary

Cost terms
a. Opportunity cost
b. Sunk cost
c. Irrelevant variable outlay cost
d. Irrelevant fixed outlay cost
e. Relevant variable outlay cost
f. Relevant fixed outlay cost
g. Relevant revenues
h. Irrelevant revenues

M17-13. Relevant Cost Terms: Matching (LO1)

A company that produces and sells 4,000 units per month, with the capacity to produce 5,000 units per month, is evaluating a one-time, special order for 2,000 units from a large chain store. Accepting the order will increase variable manufacturing costs and certain fixed selling and administrative costs. It will also require the company to forgo the sale of 1,000 units to regular customers.

Required

Presented are a number of statements related to the proposal. For each statement, select the most appropriate cost term. Each term is used only once.

Statements
1. Cost of existing equipment used to produce special order

2. Lost contribution margin from forgone sales to regular customers
3. Increased revenues from special order
4. Variable cost of 4,000 units sold to regular customers
5. Increase in fixed selling and administrative expenses
6. Revenues from 4,000 units sold to regular customers
7. Salary paid to current supervisor who oversees manufacture of special order
8. Increased variable costs of special order

Cost terms
a. Irrelevant variable outlay cost
b. Irrelevant fixed outlay cost
c. Sunk cost
d. Relevant variable outlay cost
e. Relevant fixed outlay cost
f. Opportunity cost
g. Relevant revenues
h. Irrelevant revenues

M17-14. Identifying Relevant Costs and Revenues   (LO1)

The village of Twin Falls operates a hydroelectric plant on the west side of a river that flows through town. The village uses some of this generated electricity to operate a water treatment plant and sells the excess electricity to a local utility. The village council is evaluating two alternative proposals:

- *Proposal 1* calls for replacing the generators used in the plant with more efficient generators that will produce more electricity and have lower operating costs. The salvage value of the old generators is higher than their removal cost.
- *Proposal 2* calls for raising the level of the dam to retain more water for generating power and increasing the force of water flowing through the dam. This will significantly increase the amount of electricity generated by the plant. Operating costs will not be affected.

Required
Presented are a number of cost and revenue items. Indicate in the appropriate columns whether each item is relevant or irrelevant to proposals 1 and 2.

	Proposal 1	Proposal 2
1. Cost of new fire engine		
2. Cost of old generators		
3. Cost of new generators		
4. Operating cost of old generators		
5. Operating cost of new generators		
6. Mayor's salary		
7. Depreciation on old generators		
8. Salvage value of old generators		
9. Removal cost of old generators		
10. Cost of raising dam		
11. Maintenance costs of water plant		
12. Revenues from sale of electricity		

M17-15. Classifying Relevant and Irrelevant Items   (LO1)

The law firm of Taylor, Taylor, and Tower has been asked to represent a local client. All legal proceedings will be held out of town in Washington, D.C.

Required
Classify each of the following items on the basis of their relationship to this engagement. Items may have multiple classifications.

	Relevant costs		Irrelevant costs	
	Opportunity	Outlay	Outlay	Sunk
1. The case will require three attorneys to stay four nights in a Washington hotel. The predicted hotel bill is $1,200.				
2. Taylor, Taylor, and Tower's professional staff is paid $2,000 per day for out-of-town assignments.				
3. Last year, depreciation on Taylor, Taylor, and Tower's office was $12,000.				

(Continued)

	Relevant costs		Irrelevant costs	
	Opportunity	Outlay	Outlay	Sunk

4. Round-trip transportation to Washington is expected to cost $250 per person.
5. The firm has recently accepted an engagement that will require partners to spend two weeks in Atlanta. The predicted out-of-pocket costs of this trip are $8,500.
6. The firm has a maintenance contract on its computer equipment that will cost $2,200 next year.
7. If the firm accepts the client and sends attorneys to Washington, it will have to decline a conflicting engagement in Hilton Head that would have provided a net cash inflow of $7,200.
8. The firm's variable overhead is $80 per client hour.
9. The firm pays $250 per year for Mr. Tower's subscription to a law journal.
10. Last year the firm paid $3,500 to increase the insulation in its building.

M17-16. Relevant Costs for Equipment Replacement Decision (LO2, 3)

Health Center paid $50,000 for X-ray equipment four years ago. The equipment was expected to have a useful life of 10 years from the date of acquisition with annual operating costs of $40,000. Technological advances have made the machine purchased four years ago obsolete with a zero salvage value. An improved X-ray device incorporating the new technology is available at an initial cost of $55,000 and annual operating costs of $26,000. The new machine is expected to last only six years before it, too, is obsolete. Asked to analyze the financial aspects of replacing the obsolete but still functional machine, Health Center's accountant prepared the following analysis. After looking over these numbers, the Center's manager rejected the proposal.

Six-year savings [($40,000 − $26,000) × 6]	$84,000
Cost of new machine	(55,000)
Undepreciated cost of old machine	(30,000)
Advantage (disadvantage) of replacement	$ (1,000)

Required

Perform an analysis of relevant costs to determine whether the manager made the correct decision.

M17-17. Special Order (LO2, 3)

Tobitzu TV produces wall mounts for television sets. The forecasted income statement for 2007 is as follows:

TOBITZU TV
Budgeted Income Statement
For the Year 2007

Sales ($11 per unit).	$4,400,000
Cost of good sold ($8.00 per unit)	(3,200,000)
Gross profit.	1,200,000
Selling expenses ($0.75 per unit)	(300,000)
Net income.	$ 900,000

Additional Information

(1) Of the production costs and selling expenses, $800,000 and $100,000, respectively, are fixed. (2) Tobitzu TV received a special order from a hospital supply company offering to buy 50,000 wall mounts for $7.50. If it accepts the order, there will be no additional selling expenses, and there is currently sufficient excess capacity to fill the order. The company's sales manager argues for rejecting the order because "we are not in the business of paying $8 to make a product to sell for $7.50."

Required

Do you think the company should accept the special order? Explain.

EXERCISES

E17-18. Special Order   (LO2, 3)

Old River Farms Company grows vegetables and sells them to local restaurants after processing. The firm's leading product is Salad-in-a-Bag, which is a mixture of green salad ingredients prepared and ready to serve. The company sells a large bag to restaurants for $20. It calculates the variable cost per bag at $16 (including $1.50 for local delivery). The average cost per bag is $17.50. Because the vegetables are perishable and Old River is experiencing a large crop, the firm has extra capacity. A representative of a restaurant association in another city has offered to buy fresh salad stock from the company to augment its regular supply during an upcoming international festival. The restaurant association wants to buy 2,500 bags during the next month for $18 per bag. Delivery to restaurants in the other city will cost the company $2 per bag. It can meet most of the order with excess capacity but would sacrifice 400 bags of regular sales to fill this special order. Please assist Old River's management by answering the following questions.

Required

a.   Using differential analysis, what is the impact on profits of accepting this special order?

b.   What nonquantitative issues should management consider before making a final decision?

c.   How would the analysis change if the special order were for 2,500 bags per month for the next five years?

E17-19. Special Order   (LO2, 3)

Organic Garden, a new health-food restaurant situated on a busy highway in Pomona, California, specializes in a chef's salad dinner selling for $7. Daily fixed costs are $1,500, and variable costs are $4 per meal. With a capacity of 800 meals per day, the restaurant serves an average of 750 meals each day.

Required

a.   Determine the current average cost per meal.

b.   A busload of 40 Girl Scouts stops on its way home from the San Bernardino National Forest. The leader offers to bring them in if the scouts can all be served a meal for a total of $180. The owner refuses, saying he would lose $1.50 per meal if he accepted this offer. Comment on the owner's reasoning.

c.   A local businessman on a break overhears the conversation with the leader and offers the owner a one-year contract to feed 300 of the businessman's employees one meal each day at a special price of $4.50 per meal. Should the restaurant owner accept this offer? Why or why not?

E17-20. Special Order: High-Low Cost Estimation   (LO2, 3)

Montezuma Company produces seat belts that it sells to North American automobile manufacturers. Although the company has a capacity of 300,000 belts per year, it is currently producing at an annual rate of 180,000 belts. Montezuma has received an order from a German manufacturer to purchase 60,000 belts at $9.00 each. Budgeted costs for 180,000 and 240,000 units are as follows:

	180,000 Units	240,000 Units
Manufacturing costs		
Direct materials.	$ 450,000	$ 600,000
Direct labor	315,000	420,000
Factory overhead	1,215,000	1,260,000
Total	1,980,000	2,280,000
Selling and administrative	765,000	780,000
Total	$2,745,000	$3,060,000
Costs per unit		
Manufacturing.	$11.00	$ 9.50
Selling and administrative.	4.25	3.25
Total	$15.25	$12.75

Sales to North American manufacturers are priced at $20 per unit, but the sales manager believes the company should aggressively seek the German business even if it results in a loss of $3.75 per unit. She believes obtaining this order would open up several new markets for the company's product. The general manager commented that the company cannot tighten its belt to absorb the $225,000 loss ($3.75 × 60,000) it would incur if the order is accepted.

Required

a. Determine the financial implications of accepting the order.

b. How would your analysis differ if the company were operating at capacity? Determine the advantage or disadvantage of accepting the order under full-capacity circumstances.

E17-21. Make or Buy (LO2, 3)

Assume a division of **Hewlett-Packard** currently makes 10,000 circuit boards per year used in producing diagnostic electronic instruments at a cost of $32 per board, consisting of variable costs per unit of $24 and fixed costs per unit of $8. Further assume **Sanmina-SCI** offers to sell Hewlett-Packard the 10,000 circuit boards for $32 each. If Hewlett-Packard accepts this offer, the facilities currently used to make the boards could be rented to one of Hewlett-Packard's suppliers for $25,000 per year. In addition, $5 per unit of the fixed overhead applied to the circuit boards would be totally eliminated.

Hewlett-Packard (HPQ)

Sanmina-SCI (SANM)

Required

What alternative (make or buy) is more desirable and by what amount is it more desirable?

E17-22. Make or Buy (LO2, 3)

Mountain Air Limited manufactures a line of room air fresheners. Management is currently evaluating the possible production of an air freshener for automobiles. Based on an annual volume of 10,000 units, the predicted cost per unit of an auto air freshener follows.

Direct materials	$ 8.00
Direct labor.	1.50
Factory overhead	7.00
Total	$16.50

These cost predictions include $50,000 in facility-level fixed factory overhead averaged over 10,000 units.

One of the component parts of the auto air freshener is a battery-operated electric motor. Although the company does not currently manufacture these motors, the preceding cost predictions are based on the assumption that it will assemble such a motor. Mini Motor Company has offered to supply an assembled battery-operated motor at a cost of $5.00 per unit, with a minimum annual order of 5,000 units. If Mountain Air accepts this offer, it will be able to reduce the variable labor and variable overhead costs of the auto air freshener by 50 percent. The electric motor's components will cost $2.00 if Mountain Air assembles the motors.

Required

a. Determine whether Mountain Air should make or buy the electric motor.

b. If it could otherwise rent the motor-assembly space for $20,000 per year, should it make or buy this component?

c. What additional factors should it consider in deciding whether to make or buy the electric motors?

E17-23. Make or Buy (LO2, 3)

Rashad Rahavy, M.D., is a general practitioner whose offices are located in the South Falls Professional Building. In the past, Dr. Rahavy has operated his practice with a nurse, a receptionist/secretary, and a part-time bookkeeper. Dr. Rahavy, like many small-town physicians, has billed his patients and their insurance companies from his own office. The part-time bookkeeper, who works 10 hours per week, is employed exclusively for this purpose.

North Falls Physician's Service Center has offered to take over all of Dr. Rahavy's billings and collections for an annual fee of $10,000. If Dr. Rahavy accepts this offer, he will no longer need the bookkeeper. The bookkeeper's wages and fringe benefits amount to $12 per hour, and the bookkeeper works 50 weeks per year. With all the billings and collections done elsewhere, Dr. Rahavy will have two additional hours available per week to see patients. He sees an average of three patients per hour at an average fee of $30 per visit. Dr. Rahavy's practice is expanding, and new patients often have to wait several weeks for an appointment. He has resisted expanding his office hours or working more than 50 weeks per year. Finally, if Dr. Rahavy signs on with the center, he will no longer need to rent a records storage locker in the basement of the Professional Building. The locker rents for $100 per month.

Required

Determine whether or not Dr. Rahavy should subscribe to the service.

E17-24. Sell or Process Further (LO2, 3)

Great Lakes Boat Company manufactures sailboat hulls at a cost of $4,200 per unit. The hulls are sold to boat yards for $5,000. The company is evaluating the desirability of adding masts, sails, and rigging to the hulls prior to sale at an additional cost of $1,500. The completed sailboats could then be sold for $6,000 each.

Required

Determine whether the company should sell sailboat hulls or process them further into complete sailboats. Assume sales volume will not be affected.

E17-25. Sell or Process Further (LO2, 3)

Port Allen Chemical Company processes raw material D into joint products E and F. Raw material D costs $5 per liter. It costs $100 to convert 100 liters of D into 60 liters of E and 40 liters of F. Product F can be sold immediately for $5 per liter or processed further into Product G at an additional cost of $4 per liter. Product G can then be sold for $12 per liter.

Required

Determine whether Product F should be sold or processed further into Product G.

E17-26. Limited Resources (LO4)

Tempe Manufacturing Company, Ltd., produces three products: X, Y, and Z. A limitation of 200 labor hours per week prevents the company from meeting the sales demand for these products. Product information is as follows:

	X	Y	Z
Unit selling price.............	$160	$100	$210
Unit variable costs	(100)	(50)	(180)
Unit contribution margin.......	$ 60	$ 50	$ 30
Labor hours per unit..........	4	2	4

Required

a. Determine the weekly contribution from each product when total labor hours are allocated to the product with the highest
    1. Unit selling price.
    2. Unit contribution margin.
    3. Contribution per labor hour.
    (*Hint:* Each situation is independent of the others.)
b. What generalization can be made regarding the allocation of limited resources to achieve short-run profit maximization?
c. Determine the opportunity cost the company will incur if management requires the weekly production of 10 units of Z.

E17-27. Limited Resources (LO4)

Jo Peña, a regional sales representative for Byte Computer Supply Company, has been working more than 80 hours per week calling on a total of 140 regular customers each month. Because of family and health considerations, she has decided to spend no more than 40 hours per week (160 per month) with customers. Unfortunately, this cutback will require Jo to turn away some of her regular customers or, at least, serve them less frequently than once a month. Jo has developed the following information to assist her in determining how to best allocate time:

	Customer Classification		
	Large Business	Small Business	Individual
Number of customers...............	10	50	80
Average monthly sales per customer....	$2,000	$1,000	$500
Commission percentage	5%	8%	10%
Hours per customer per monthly visit ...	4.0	2.0	2.5

Required

a. Develop a monthly plan that indicates the number of customers Jo should call on in each classification to maximize her monthly sales commissions.
b. Determine the monthly commissions Jo will earn if she implements this plan.

PROBLEMS

P17-28. Multiple Changes in Profit Plans (LO2, 3)

In an attempt to improve profit performance, Apache Company's management is considering a number of alternative actions. An April 2008 contribution income statement for Apache Company follows.

APACHE COMPANY Contribution Income Statement For Month of April 2008		
Sales (10,000 units × $40)		$400,000
Less variable costs		
Direct materials (10,000 units × $5)	$ 50,000	
Direct labor (10,000 units × $14)	140,000	
Variable factory overhead (10,000 units × $6)	60,000	
Selling and administrative (10,000 units × $5)	50,000	(300,000)
Contribution margin (10,000 units × $10)		100,000
Less fixed costs		
Factory overhead	50,000	
Selling and administrative.	60,000	(110,000)
Net income (loss)		$ (10,000)

Required

Determine the effect of each of the following independent situations on monthly profit.

a. Purchasing automated assembly equipment, which should reduce direct labor costs by $6 per unit and increase variable overhead costs by $2 per unit and fixed factory overhead by $22,000 per month.

b. Reducing the selling price by $5 per unit. This should increase the monthly sales by 5,000 units. At this higher volume, additional equipment and salaried personnel would be required. This will increase fixed factory overhead by $3,000 per month and fixed selling and administrative costs by $2,500 per month.

c. Buying rather than manufacturing a component of Apache's final product. This will increase direct materials costs by $15 per unit. However, direct labor will decline $4 per unit, variable factory overhead will decline $1 per unit, and fixed factory overhead will decline $10,000 per month.

d. Increasing the unit selling price by $3 per unit. This action should result in a 1,000-unit decrease in monthly sales.

e. Combining alternatives (a) and (d).

P17-29. Multiple Changes in Profit Plans: Multiple Products (LO2, 3)

Information on Guadalupe Ltd.'s three products follows:

	A	B	C
Unit sales per month	900	1,400	900
Selling price per unit.	$ 5.00	$7.50	$4.00
Variable costs per unit	(5.20)	(6.00)	(2.00)
Unit contribution margin.	$(0.20)	$1.50	$2.00

Required

Determine the effect each of the following situations would have on monthly profits. Each situation should be evaluated independently of all others.

a. Product A is discontinued.

b. Product A is discontinued, and the subsequent loss of customers causes sales of Product B to decline by 100 units.

c. The selling price of A is increased to $5.50 with a sales decrease of 200 units.

d. The price of Product B is increased to $8.00 with a resulting sales decrease of 200 units. However, some of these customers shift to Product A; sales of Product A increase by 100 units.

e. Product A is discontinued, and the plant in which A was produced is used to produce D, a new product. Product D has a unit contribution margin of $0.30. Monthly sales of Product D are predicted to be 700 units.

f. The selling price of Product C is increased to $5.00, and the selling price of Product B is decreased to $7.00. Sales of C decline by 200 units, while sales of B increase by 300 units.

P17-30. Relevant Costs and Differential Analysis (LO2, 3)

First National Bank paid $50,000 for a check-sorting machine in January 2003. The machine had an estimated life of 10 years and annual operating costs of $40,000, excluding depreciation. Although management is pleased with the machine, recent technological advances have made it obsolete. Consequently, as of January 2007, the machine has a book value of $30,000, a remaining operating life of 6 years, and a salvage value of $0.

The manager of operations is evaluating a proposal to acquire a new optical scanning and sorting machine. The new machine would cost $90,000 and reduce annual operating costs to $20,000, excluding depreciation. Because of expected technological improvements, the manager believes the new machine will have an economic life of 6 years and no salvage value at the end of that life. Prior to signing the papers authorizing the acquisition of the new machine, the president of the First National Bank prepared the following analysis:

Six-year savings [($40,000 − $20,000) × 6 years]......	$120,000
Cost of new machine...........................	(90,000)
Loss on disposal of old machine..................	(30,000)
Advantage (disadvantage) of replacement...........	$ 0

After looking at these numbers, he rejected the proposal and commented that he was "tired of looking at marginal projects. This bank is in business to make a profit, not to break even. If you want to break even, go work for the government."

Required

a. Evaluate the president's analysis.

b. Prepare a differential analysis of six-year totals for the old and the new machines.

P17-31. Special Order (LO2, 3)

Thousand Islands Propulsion Company produces a variety of electric trolling motors. Management follows a pricing policy of manufacturing cost plus 60 percent. In response to a request from Northern Sporting Goods, the following price has been developed for an order of 300 Minnow Motors (the smallest motor Thousand Island produces):

Manufacturing costs	
Direct materials........	$10,000
Direct labor...........	12,000
Factory overhead......	18,000
Total..................	40,000
Markup (60%)..........	24,000
Selling price...........	$64,000

Mr. Bass, the president of Northern Sporting Goods, rejected this price and offered to purchase the 300 Minnow Motors at a price of $44,000. The following additional information is available:

- Thousand Islands has sufficient excess capacity to produce the motors.
- Factory overhead is applied on the basis of direct labor dollars.
- Budgeted factory overhead is $400,000 for the current year. Of this amount, $100,000 is fixed. Of the $18,000 of factory overhead assigned to the Minnow Motors, only $13,500 is driven by the special order; $3,500 is a fixed cost.
- Selling and administrative expenses are budgeted as follows:

Fixed......	$90,000 per year
Variable....	$20 per unit manufactured and sold

Required

a. The president of Thousand Islands Propulsion wants to know if he should allow Mr. Bass to have the Minnows for $44,000. Determine the effect on profits of accepting Mr. Bass's offer.

b. Briefly explain why certain costs should be omitted from the analysis in requirement (a).

c. Assume Thousand Islands is operating at capacity and could sell the 300 Minnows at its regular markup.

   1. Determine the opportunity cost of accepting Mr. Bass's offer.

   2. Determine the effect on profits of accepting Mr. Bass's offer.

P17-32. Special Order (LO2, 3)

Every Halloween, Glacier Ice Cream Shop offers a trick-or-treat package of 20 coupons for $3. The coupons are redeemable by children 12 years or under, for a single-scoop cone, with a limit of one coupon per child per visit. Coupon sales average 500 books per year. The printing costs are $60. A single-scoop cone of Glacier ice cream normally sells for $0.60. The variable costs of a single-scoop cone are $0.40.

Required

a. Determine the loss if all coupons are redeemed without any other effect on sales.

b. Assume all coupons will not be redeemed. With regular sales unaffected, determine the coupon redemption rate at which Glacier will break even on the offer.

c. Assuming regular sales are not affected and one additional single-scoop cone is sold at the regular price each time a coupon is redeemed, determine the coupon redemption rate at which Glacier will break even on the offer.

d. Determine the profit or loss incurred on the offer if the coupon redemption rate is 60 percent and:

   1. One-fourth of the redeemed coupons have no effect on sales.

   2. One-fourth of the redeemed coupons result in additional sales of two single-scoop cones.

   3. One-fourth of the redeemed coupons result in additional sales of three single-scoop cones.

   4. One-fourth of the redeemed coupons come out of regular sales of single-scoop cones.

P17-33. Applications of Differential Analysis (LO2, 3)

Bird Station produces squirrel-proof bird feeders that it sells to mail-order distributors for $25. Manufacturing and other costs follow:

Variable Costs per Unit		Fixed Costs per Month	
Direct materials	$ 8	Factory overhead	$10,000
Direct labor	7	Selling and administrative	5,000
Factory overhead	2	Total	$15,000
Distribution	3		
Total	$20		

The variable distribution costs are for transportation to mail-order distributors. The current monthly production and sales volume is 5,000 units. Monthly capacity is 6,000 units.

Required

Determine the effect of each of the following independent situations on monthly profits.

a. A $2.00 increase in the unit selling price should result in a 1,000-unit decrease in monthly sales.

b. A $2.50 decrease in the unit selling price should result in a 2,000-unit increase in monthly sales. However, because of capacity constraints, the last 1,000 units would be produced during overtime with the direct labor costs increasing by 60 percent.

c. A British distributor has proposed to place a special, one-time order for 1,000 units at a reduced price of $20 per unit. The distributor would pay all transportation costs. There would be additional fixed selling and administrative costs of $1,000.

d. A Dutch distributor has proposed to place a special, one-time order for 2,500 units at a special price of $20 per unit. The distributor would pay all transportation costs. There would be additional fixed selling and administrative costs of $1,500. Assume overtime production is not possible.

e. A Canadian manufacturer has offered a one-year contract to supply the squirrel guard attached to the bottom of the feeder at a cost of $5 per unit. If Bird Station accepts the offer, it will be able to reduce variable manufacturing costs by 10 percent, reduce fixed costs by $500 per month, and rent out some currently used space for $1,200 per month.

f. The bird feeders are currently sold assembled and ready for mounting. Selling the feeders unassembled would reduce costs by $5 per unit and reduce the selling price to only $18.

g. Bird Station produces a variety of bird feeders. The given information is for an average unit. Determine the variable cost markup required to earn a monthly profit of $20,000.

P17-34. **Applications of Differential Analysis** (LO2, 3)

Bushwhack Expeditions offers guided back-country hiking/camping trips in British Columbia. Bushwhack provides a guide and all necessary food and equipment at a fee of $50 per person per day. Bushwhack currently provides an average of 600 guide-days per month in June, July, August, and September. Based on available equipment and staff, maximum capacity is 800 guide-days per month. Monthly variable and fixed operating costs (valued in Canadian dollars) are as follows:

Variable Costs per Guide-Day		Fixed Costs per Month	
Food	$ 5	Equipment rental	$ 5,000
Guide salary	25	Administration	5,000
Supplies	2	Advertising	2,000
Insurance	8	Total	$12,000
Total	$40		

Required

Determine the effect of each of the following situations on monthly profits. Each situation is to be evaluated independently of all others.

a.   A $12 increase in the daily fee should result in a 200-unit decrease in monthly sales.

b.   A $5 decrease in the daily fee should result in a 300-unit increase in monthly sales. However, because of capacity constraints, the last 100 guide-days would be provided by subcontracting to another firm at a cost of $46 per guide-day.

c.   A French tour agency has proposed to place a special, one-time order for 80 guide-days at a reduced fee of $45 per guide-day. The agency would pay all insurance costs. There would be additional fixed administrative costs of $200.

d.   An Italian tour agency has proposed to place a special, one-time order for 300 guide-days next month at a special fee of $45 per guide-day. The agency would pay all insurance costs. There would be additional fixed administrative costs of $200. Assume additional capacity beyond 800 guide-days is not available.

e.   An Alberta outdoor supply company has offered to supply all necessary food and camping equipment at $7.50 per guide-day. This eliminates the current food costs and reduces the monthly equipment rental costs to $1,500.

f.   Clients must currently carry a backpack and assist in camp activities such as cooking. Bushwhack is considering the addition of mules to carry all food and equipment and the hiring of college students to perform camp activities such as cooking. This will increase variable costs by $10 per guide-day and fixed costs by $1,200 per month. However, 600 full-service guide-days per month could now be sold at $75 each.

g.   Bushwhack provides a number of different types of wilderness experiences. The given information is for an average tour. Determine the variable cost markup required to earn a monthly profit of $6,000.

CASES

C17-35. **Continue or Discontinue** (LO1, 3)

Peachtree Eye Clinic primarily performs three medical procedures: cataract removal, corneal implants, and keratotomy. At the end of the first quarter of this year, Dr. Hartsfield, president of Peachtree, expressed grave concern about the cataract sector because it had reported a loss of $10,000. He rationalized that "since the cataract market is losing $10,000, and the overall practice is making $40,000, if we eliminate the cataract market, our total profits will increase to $50,000."

Required

a.   Is the president's analysis correct?

b.   Will total profits increase if the cataract section is dropped?

c.   Is it possible total profits will decline?

C17-36. **Ethics of Frequent-Flyer Mile Incentives** (LO1, 2, 3)

In an attempt to attract and retain loyal customers, many organizations offer frequent-flyer miles. Consider the following examples:

- Airlines offer frequent-flyer miles, sometimes with a minimum of 500 or 750 miles per flight segment.
- Major automobile rental agencies award frequent-flyer mile credits on cooperating airlines.
- Many hotel chains award frequent-flyer mile credits on cooperating airlines, sometimes at the rate of 1,000 miles per night.
- A few credit cards have even joined in, offering frequent-flyer miles on cooperating selected airlines at the rate of one mile per dollar charged.

In exchange for accumulated frequent-flyer miles, airlines offer free tickets, free upgrades, and membership in airport clubs. Cooperating hotels offer free lodging for the exchange of frequent-flyer miles. Frequent-flyer programs are structured so that frequent-flyer miles can accrue only to the traveler. Hence, organizations paying for employee travel cannot accumulate frequent-flyer miles as an asset. Some frequent-flyer programs are structured so that travelers can reassign their unused frequent-flyer miles to a charitable purpose sponsored by the airline. The charity can then pool these miles to accomplish its goals.

Required

a. Discuss the potential impact of frequent-flyer incentive programs on the travel costs of organizations.

b. Discuss why the programs are structured so that organizations paying for employee travel cannot accumulate frequent-flyer miles.

c. Discuss the ethics of frequent-flyer programs. Are there any circumstances when taking advantage of frequent-flyer incentives is clearly ethical or clearly unethical? Are the administrators of frequent-flyer programs encouraging unethical behavior by not allowing organizations that pay for employee travel to accumulate frequent-flyer miles?

C17-37. Ethics of Markups on Service Charges **(LO1, 2, 3)**

Resellers of a variety of products (such as computers) often perform marketing services for manufacturers. In billing manufacturers, there is some question about the ethics and legality of adding a markup to the out-of-pocket cost of marketing services. Consider the following statements by executives in manufacturing and reselling organizations:[11]

- Paul Thomas, a marketing executive for Apple (a major computer manufacturer), said that Apple allows "no scope for profit-making on any Apple [marketing] program."   Apple (AAPL)
- Robert Sutis, in-house counsel for Hewlett-Packard (a major manufacturer of computer printers), noted that H-P bases marketing reimbursements on "claim forms that have documentation attached," such as "invoices or tear sheets or other paperwork."   Hewlett-Packard (HPQ)
- Curtis J. Scheel, a vice president of MicroAge, Inc. (a computer reseller), commented that to the extent that a company charges more than it spends, it does so to offset costs of running its marketing operations. He added that if vendors discovered that marketing money was going to the bottom line, "they might stop funding."   MicroAge, Inc.

Susan Thompson just accepted a position with Digital Distributors (DD), a regional computer wholesale company, as the new marketing director. In reviewing company records, she determined that DD was charging manufacturers much more than it spent on marketing activities. Big Pear Computing, for example, was charged $2.9 million this year for advertising, but only $1.5 million was recorded as advertising expenses on Big Pear's account. The cumulative effect of these markups was very significant to DD's overall profitability. After asking a few questions and analyzing some data with a spreadsheet program, Susan determined that marketing took in $15 million more from charges to manufacturers this year than it spent for all marketing operations.

Concerned about the situation, Susan spoke with Mike Murdstone, DD's controller. He immediately commented that DD had done nothing wrong. Mike observed that DD sends invoices to vendors with a simple statement, such as, "For marketing services, $235,000." Mike continued with the following advice: "We do not claim to bill for only actual outlay costs. If manufacturers feel we are overcharging, they could do business with someone else. In the meantime, I recommend you not kill the goose that lays the golden egg."

Required

Discuss the ethics and legality of DD's billing practices for marketing services. What advice do you have for Susan?

---

[11] Raju Narisetti, "Intelligent Electronics Made Much of Its Profit at Suppliers' Expense," *The Wall Street Journal,* December 6, 1994, pp. A1, A17.

Product Costing: Job and Process Operations

LEARNING OBJECTIVES

LO1 Describe inventory requirements and measurement issues for service, merchandising, and manufacturing organizations. (p. 18-3)

LO2 Explain the framework of inventory costing for financial reporting. (p. 18-4)

LO3 Describe the production environment as it relates to product costing systems. (p. 18-8)

LO4 Explain the operation of a job costing system. (p. 18-10)

LO5 Explain the operation of a process costing system. (p. 18-21)

COST COMPETITION AND COMPANY SUCCESS

Financial reporting is the process of preparing a firm's financial statements—income statement, balance sheet, and statement of cash flows—in accordance with generally accepted accounting principles (GAAP). GAAP requires that companies producing products measure the cost of products sold and the cost of ending inventory for each period. USG Corporation, Navistar Corporation, and Roto Zip Corporation present very different environments in which both the cost of products sold and ending inventory costs must be determined.

USG Corporation makes the *Sheetrock* brand of wallboard—also called *drywall*—and controls one-third of the wallboard market. Panels of *Sheetrock* command a 10 percent premium price over competitors because of their ease of use and handling. To maintain this premium, USG spends about $20 million on research and development each year. In 2004, USG earned $312 million on sales of $4.5 billion. As leading manufacturers of a classic commodity product, USG managers have improved efficiency in production plants and have a cost advantage over competitors.

Navistar International Corporation manufactures heavy-duty trucks. Its large, long-haul trucks—commonly called *18-wheelers*—represent 30 percent of its sales. Navistar competes with Paccar and Freightliner—a division of DaimlerChrysler. In 2004, it earned $247 million on sales of

$9.5 billion. Each unit sold can cost $100,000 and include many custom options to meet the needs of both fleet owners and individual owner-operators. To develop a competitive edge, Navistar managers focus on production efficiency. This emphasis has paid off with Navistar recording a 14 percent gross margin percentage compared with lower percents for rivals.

RotoZip Tool Corporation manufactures a unique power jigsaw that cuts easily through tile, aluminum, wood, Plexiglas, and other common building materials. The firm ships about 10,000 units per day to buyers such as Sears, Home Depot, Lowe's and Ace Hardware. Annual sales exceed $250 million. Depending on the model, RotoZip's revenue per unit ranges from $60 to $200. RotoZip recently joined with Robert Bosch Tool Corporation.

These three firms represent very different cost measurement environments. The volumes and products range from several hundred million units of an inexpensive commodity to thousands of highly customized, very expensive items. Although the specific accounting techniques and approaches differ for these three firms, the intent of these accounting efforts is the same. That is, each product costing system must accumulate and assign the costs of the direct and indirect activities involved in manufacturing its products.

Source: *Forbes*, 10-K Reports.[1]

---

[1] Brandon Copple, "Runaway Rig," *Forbes*, April 2, 2001, pp. 68–70; Stephanie Fitch, "The Gypsum King," *Forbes*, February 5, 2001, pp. 68–70; Kemp Powers, "Upward Spiral," *Forbes*, August 8, 2001, pp. 104–105; and 10-K reports.

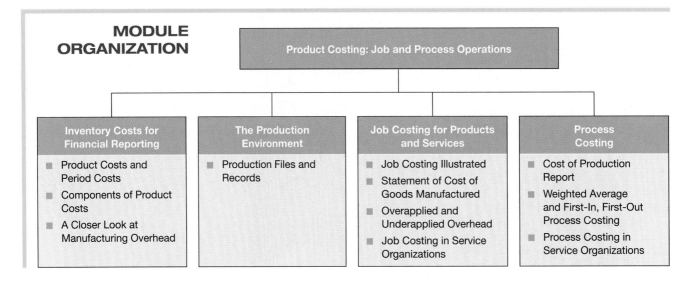

This module provides an overview of product costing systems and a framework for understanding costs in a production environment. It also examines aspects of the production environment that can affect product costing systems and discusses costing issues related to the production of physical products versus the production of services.

INVENTORY COSTS IN VARIOUS ORGANIZATIONS

LO1 Describe inventory requirements and measurement issues for service, merchandising, and manufacturing organizations.

Organizations can be classified as service, merchandising, or manufacturing. **Service organizations** perform work for others. Included in this category are Bank of America, Supercuts hair salons, Shriners Children's Hospitals, Cracker Barrel restaurants, United Artists movie theaters, Consolidated Edison electric utility, the City of New York, CSX Railroad, and Delta Air Lines. **Merchandising organizations** buy and sell goods and include companies such as Safeway grocery stores, L. L. Bean, Ace Hardware, and Wal-Mart. **Manufacturing organizations** process raw materials into finished products for sale to others and include General Motors, Birmingham Steel, and Georgia Pacific.

In general, service organizations have a low percentage of their total assets invested in inventory, which usually consists only of the supplies needed to facilitate their operations. In contrast, merchandising organizations usually have a high percentage of their total assets invested in inventory. Their largest inventory investment is merchandise purchased for resale, but they also have supplies inventories.

Manufacturing organizations, like merchandisers, often have a high percentage of their total assets invested in inventories. However, rather than just one major inventory category, manufacturing organizations typically have three: raw materials, work-in-process, and finished goods. **Raw materials inventories** contain the physical ingredients and components that will be converted by machines and/or human labor into a finished product. **Work-in-process inventories** are the partially completed goods that are in the process of being converted into a finished product. **Finished goods inventories** are the completely manufactured products held for sale to customers. In 2005, General Motors reported the following inventories:

Materials, work-in-process, and supplies	$ 5.5 billion
Finished goods.	9.9
Total	$15.4 billion

Manufacturing organizations also have supplies inventories used to facilitate production and selling and administrative activities. Exhibit 18.1 illustrates the flow of inventory costs in service, merchandising, and manufacturing organizations. In all three types of organizations, the financial accounting system initially records costs of inventories as assets; when they are eventually consumed or sold, inventory costs are recorded as expenses.

The formalized inventory costing systems in use today were developed to provide accountants with the necessary information for preparing company financial statements. Before the balance sheet and income statement could be prepared, accountants needed to know both the cost of inventory at the end of the year and the cost of inventory sold during the year.

Product cost information is crucial to business success. Managers use it to evaluate product profitability (since price minus cost equals profit) and organizational performance (since lower costs mean higher profit and higher profit means a better performance). It also affects the product mix as managers strive to replace low-profit products with high-profit products. Unreliable cost information can lead to disastrous results such as noncompetitive pricing of goods and services, wrong conclusions about performance, and bad decisions regarding product mix.

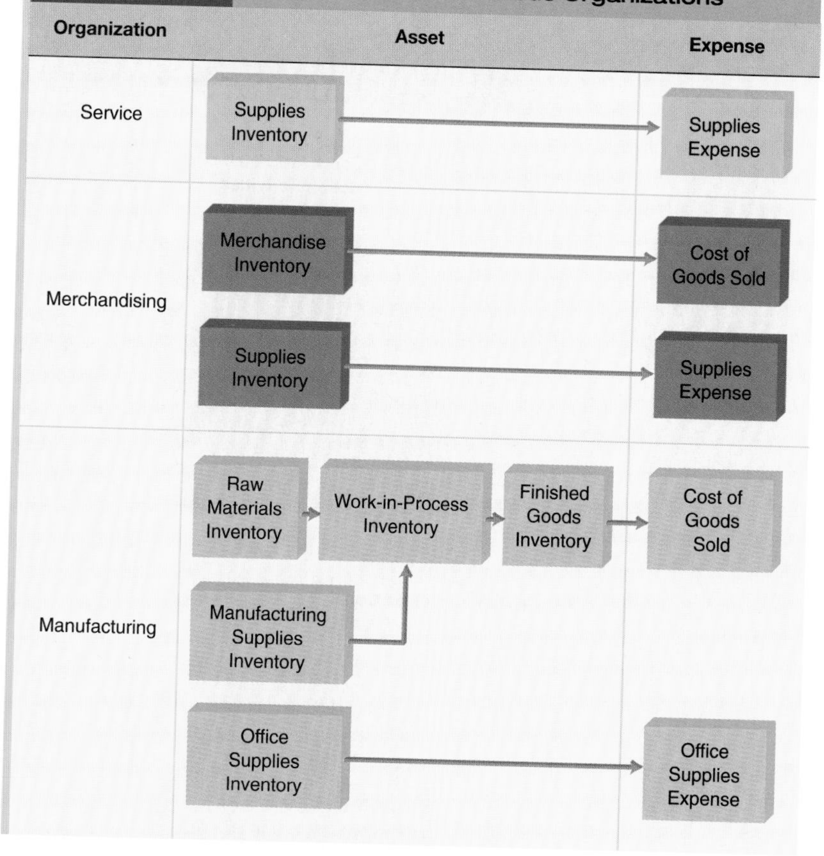

Although first developed in manufacturing organizations, costing systems are becoming increasingly important to service organizations. Whereas the term *product* was once used only to indicate a physical product, it has taken on a much broader meaning to include both physical products and services. In many cases, it is now difficult to determine whether a company is primarily a producer of goods or services. Is McDonald's producing food products or providing a service?

EXHIBIT 18.1   Inventory Costs in Various Organizations

All organizations need information about the cost of their goods and services. Besides being used for preparing external financial reports, this information aids in good decision making on a day-to-day basis that ultimately leads to a strong and progressively improving balance sheet and income statement. The profit motive and the need to produce favorable financial statements are closely linked with the need for managers to have reliable and timely cost information. Throughout the book we discuss various costing systems, pointing out strengths and weaknesses of these systems in meeting management's information needs.

INVENTORY COSTS FOR FINANCIAL REPORTING

Financial reporting makes an important distinction between the cost of *producing* products and the cost of all other activities such as selling and administration. In general, inventory values for financial reporting purposes include only the costs of producing products. Costs related to *selling* inventories (such as marketing, distribution, customer service, and so forth) are all important for managerial decision-making purposes, but they are specifically excluded from product costs in the corporate financial statements.

LO2 Explain the framework of inventory costing for financial reporting.

Product Costs and Period Costs

For financial reporting, all costs incurred in the *manufacturing* of products are called **product costs;** these costs are carried in the accounts as an asset (inventory) until the product is sold, at which time they are recognized as an expense (cost of goods sold). Product costs include the costs of raw materials, plant employee salaries and wages, and all other *manufacturing* costs incurred to transform raw materials into finished products. Expired costs (other than those related to manufacturing inventory) are called **period costs** and are recognized as expenses when incurred. Period costs include the president's salary, sales commissions, advertising costs, and all other *nonmanufacturing* costs. Product and period costs are illustrated in Exhibit 18.2.

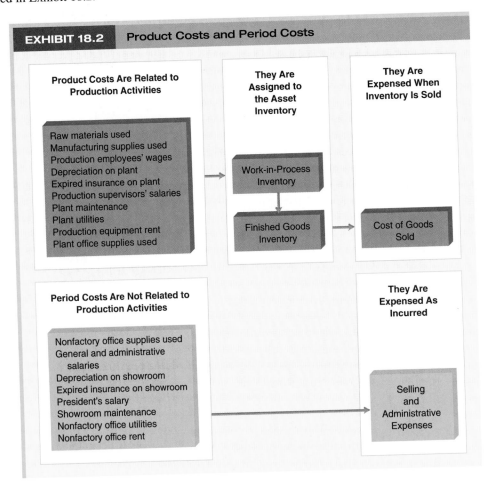

EXHIBIT 18.2 Product Costs and Period Costs

Costs such as research and development, marketing, distribution, and customer service are important for strategic analyses; however, since these costs are not incurred in the production process, they are not product costs for *financial reporting purposes.* For *internal managerial purposes,* accountants and managers often use the term *product costing* to embrace all costs incurred in connection with a product or service throughout the value chain.

To summarize, in the *product cost* versus *period cost* framework of *financial reporting,* costs are classified based on whether or not they are related to the production process. If they are related to the production process, they are product costs; otherwise, they are period costs. In this framework, costs that seem very similar may be treated quite differently. For example, note in Exhibit 18.2 that the expired cost of insurance on the *plant* is a *product cost,* but the expired cost of insurance on the *showroom* is a *period cost.* The reason is that the plant is used in production, but the showroom is not. This method of accounting for inventory that assigns all production costs to inventory is sometimes referred to as the **absorption cost (or full absorption cost)** method because all production costs are said to be fully absorbed into the cost of the product.

Three Components of Product Costs

The manufacture of even a simple product, such as a small wooden table, requires three basic ingredients: materials (wood), labor (the skill of a worker) and production facilities (a building to work in, a saw, and other tools). Corresponding to these three basic ingredients of any product are three basic categories of product costs: direct materials, direct labor, and manufacturing overhead.

Direct materials are the costs of the primary raw materials that are converted into finished goods. Examples of primary raw materials include iron ore to a steel mill, coiled aluminum to a manufacturer of aluminum siding, cow's milk to a dairy, logs to a sawmill, and lumber to a builder. The finished product of one firm may be the raw materials of another firm down the value chain. For example, rolled steel is a finished product of Bethlehem Steel Company, but it is the raw material of the Maytag Company for the manufacture of washers and dryers. **Direct labor** consists of wages earned by *production employees for the time they actually spend working on a product,* and **manufacturing overhead** includes all manufacturing costs other than direct materials and direct labor. (Manufacturing overhead is also called *factory overhead, burden, manufacturing burden,* and just *overhead.* Merchandising organizations occasionally refer to administrative costs as *overhead.*) **Conversion cost** consists of the combined costs of direct labor and manufacturing overhead incurred to convert raw materials into finished goods.

Examples of manufacturing overhead are manufacturing supplies, depreciation on manufacturing buildings and equipment, and the costs of plant taxes, insurance, maintenance, security, and utilities. Also included are production supervisors' salaries and all other manufacturing-related labor costs for employees who do not work directly on the product (such as maintenance, security, and janitorial personnel).

Just as raw materials, labor, and production facilities are combined to produce a finished product, direct materials costs, direct labor costs, and manufacturing overhead costs are accumulated to obtain the total cost of goods produced. Exhibit 18.3 illustrates that these product costs are accumulated in the general ledger in Work-in-Process Inventory (or just Work-in-Process) as production takes place and then are transferred to Finished Goods Inventory when production is completed. Product costs are finally assigned to Cost of Goods Sold when the finished goods are sold. (Account titles are capitalized to make it easier to determine when reference is being made to a physical item, such as work-in-process inventory, or to the account, Work-in-Process Inventory, in which costs assigned to the work-in-process inventory are accumulated.)

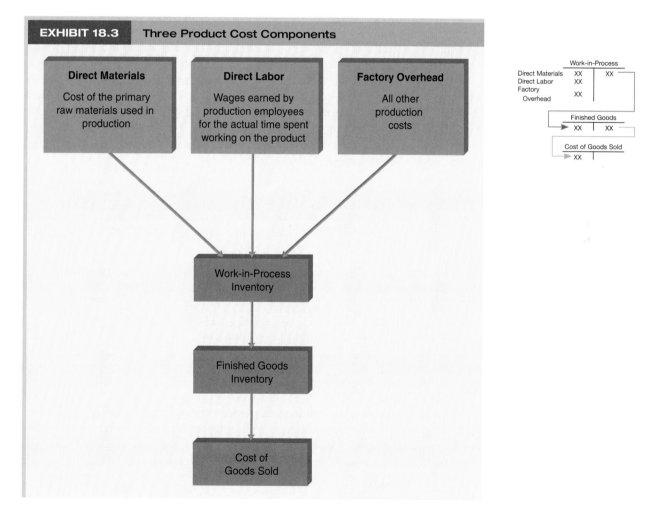

EXHIBIT 18.3   Three Product Cost Components

A Closer Look at Manufacturing Overhead

Possibly the biggest challenge in measuring the cost of a product is determining the amount of overhead incurred to produce it. Direct materials cost is driven by the number of raw materials units used; hence, its cost is simply the number of units of raw materials used multiplied by the related cost per unit. Direct labor cost is driven by the number of directly traceable labor hours worked on the product; so its cost is the number of direct labor hours used times the appropriate rate per hour. But what about manufacturing overhead? Manufacturing overhead often consists of dozens of different cost elements, potentially with many different cost drivers. Electricity cost is based on kilowatt-hours and water cost on gallons used; depreciation is usually measured in years of service and insurance in premium dollars per thousand dollars of coverage; and supervisors' salaries are a fixed amount per month.

Historically, accountants have believed that, even when possible, it is not cost effective to try to separately measure the cost incurred for each manufacturing overhead item to produce a unit of finished product. Instead of identifying separate cost drivers for each individual cost component in manufacturing overhead, all overhead costs for a department or plant are frequently placed in a cost pool and a single unit-level cost driver is used to assign (or apply) overhead to products.

If a company produced only one product, it would be simple to assign (or apply) overhead to the units produced because it would merely involve dividing total manufacturing overhead cost incurred by the number of units produced to get a cost per unit. For example, if total manufacturing overhead costs were $100,000 for a period when 20,000 units of product were produced, the overhead cost assigned to each unit would be $5.

Selecting a Basis (or Cost Driver) for Assigning Overhead

When multiple products are manufactured in the same facilities, using a simple average of manufacturing overhead cost per unit seldom provides a good estimate of the overhead costs incurred to produce each product. Units requiring extensive manufacturing activity will have too little cost assigned to them, while others requiring only a small amount of manufacturing effort will absorb too much cost. In these cases, units of production is not an appropriate cost driver for manufacturing overhead.

To solve this allocation problem, an overhead application base (or cost driver) other than number of units produced is usually used. The overhead application base selected is typically a unit-level activity that is common to all products but varies in quantity for each product, depending on the amount of manufacturing effort that went into making the product. For example, *machine hours* may be used to assign manufacturing overhead costs if the *number of machine hours used* is believed to be the primary cause of manufacturing overhead cost incurred.

Using Predetermined Overhead Rates

Although some organizations assign actual manufacturing overhead to products at the end of each period (normally a month), three problems often result from measuring product cost using "actual" manufacturing overhead costs:

1. Actual manufacturing overhead cost may not be known until days or weeks after the end of the period, delaying the calculation of unit product cost.

2. Some costs that are seasonal, such as property taxes, are not incurred each period, thus making the actual cost of a product produced in one month greater than that of another, even though nonseasonal costs may have been identical for both months.

3. When there is a significant amount of fixed manufacturing overhead, the costs assigned to each unit of product will vary from period to period, depending on the overall volume of activity for the period.

To overcome these problems, most firms use a **predetermined manufacturing overhead rate** to assign manufacturing overhead costs to products. A predetermined rate is established at the start of each year by dividing the *predicted overhead costs for the year* by the *predicted volume of activity in the overhead base* for the year. A predetermined manufacturing overhead rate based on direct labor hours is computed as follows:

$$\text{Predetermined manufacturing overhead rate per direct labor hour} = \frac{\text{Predicted total manufacturing overhead cost for the year}}{\text{Predicted total direct labor hours for the year}}$$

If management believed machine hours had a greater influence on the consumption of overhead, the denominator would change to predicted machine hours.

Using a predetermined manufacturing overhead rate based on direct labor hours, we compute the assignment of overhead to Work-in-Process Inventory as follows:

Manufacturing overhead assigned to Work-in-Process Inventory	=	Actual direct labor hours	×	Predetermined manufacturing overhead rate per direct labor hour

To illustrate, late in 2007, Harmon Manufacturing Company predicted a 2008 activity level of 25,000 direct labor hours with manufacturing overhead totaling $187,500. Using this information, its 2008 predetermined overhead rate per direct labor hour was computed as follows:

$$\text{Predetermined overhead rate} = \frac{\$187,500}{25,000 \text{ direct labor hours}}$$

$$= \$7.50 \text{ per direct labor hour}$$

If 2,000 direct labor hours were used in September 2008, the applied overhead for September would be $15,000, as shown here:

$$2,000 \times \$7.50 = \$15,000$$

When a predetermined rate is used, monthly variations between actual and applied manufacturing overhead are expected because of the seasonality in costs and the variations in monthly activity. Hence, in some months overhead will be "overapplied" as applied overhead exceeds actual overhead; in other months overhead will be "underapplied" as actual overhead exceeds applied overhead. If the beginning-of-the-year estimates are accurate for annual overhead costs and annual activity in the application base, monthly over- and underapplied amounts during the year should offset each other by the end of the period. During the year, the cumulative balance should be monitored to identify an excessive over- or underapplied balance and to determine whether the estimate of the overhead rate should be revised before year-end. Later in this module, we consider methods for accounting for any over- or underapplied manufacturing overhead balance that may exist at the end of the year.

Changing Cost Structures Affect the Basis of Overhead Application

By using a single overhead rate, we assume that overhead costs are primarily caused by a single cost driver. Historically, a single plantwide overhead application rate based on direct labor hours was widely used when direct labor was the predominant cost factor in production and manufacturing overhead costs were driven by the utilization of direct labor.

Technological progress has caused changes in the factors of manufacturing costs, resulting in major shifts in costs in many industries from direct labor to manufacturing overhead. An example of this shift is the worldwide automobile industry where firms such as DaimlerChrysler, Toyota, and Volvo have spent billions of dollars on robotics and other technologies, thereby reducing direct labor in the production process. In many cases, these technological changes mean that direct labor hours are no longer an appropriate basis for assigning manufacturing costs to products. In others, these changes mean there is no longer a single cost driver that is appropriate for assigning manufacturing overhead to products.

Although some companies continue to use a single (actual or predetermined) manufacturing overhead rate because it is convenient, many companies no longer use this approach. Instead, they have adopted multiple overhead rates based on either major departments or activities within the organization. One method for using multiple overhead rates is activity-based costing, which is discussed in Module 19.

THE PRODUCTION ENVIRONMENT

Production personnel need to know the specific products to produce on specific machines on a daily or even hourly basis. The detailed scheduling of products on machines is performed by production scheduling personnel. Exactly how production is scheduled depends on whether process manufacturing or job production is used and whether production is in response to a specific customer sales order or for the company's inventory in anticipation of future sales.

LO3 Describe the production environment as it relates to product costing systems.

In **process manufacturing,** production of identical units is on a *continuous* basis; a production facility may be devoted exclusively to one product or to a set of closely related products. Companies where you would likely find a process manufacturing environment include Exxon Mobil and Bowater Incorporated (which makes rolled paper for the printing of daily newspapers such as the *Chicago Tribune*). Process manufacturing is discussed later in this module.

In **job production,** also called **job order production,** products are manufactured in single units or in batches of identical units. Of course, the products included in different jobs may vary considerably. Examples of single-unit jobs are found at Hallco Builders, a builder of custom-designed homes; Metric Constructors Inc., which builds skyscrapers; and Riverwood International, which designs, produces, and installs packaging systems for food processors. Examples of multiple-unit jobs are found at Hartmarx, a clothing manufacturer; Steelcase Furniture Company, a large producer of office furnishings; and Intermet Corporation, a foundry company that makes parts for the automobile industry.

In a job production environment, when a customer's order is received, the marketing department forwards the order to production scheduling, where employees determine when and how the product is to be produced. Important scheduling considerations include the overall workload, raw materials availability, specific equipment or labor requirements, and the delivery date(s) of the finished product.

Important staff groups involved in production planning and control include engineering, scheduling, expediting, quality control, and accounting. Engineering is primarily concerned with determining how a product should be produced. Based on an engineering analysis and cost data, engineering personnel develop manufacturing specifications for each product. These manufacturing specifications are often summarized in two important documents: a bill of materials and an operations list. Each product's **bill of materials** specifies the kinds and quantities of raw materials required for one unit of product. The **operations list** (sometimes called an **activities list**) specifies the manufacturing operations and related times required for one unit or batch of product. The operations list should also include information on any machine setup time, movements between work areas, and other scheduled activities, such as quality inspections.

Scheduling personnel prepare a production order for each job. The **production order** contains a job's unique identification number and specifies such details as the quantity to be produced, raw materials requirements, manufacturing operations and other activities to be performed, and perhaps even the time when each manufacturing operation should be performed. In preparing a production order, scheduling personnel use the product's bill of materials and operations list to determine the materials, operations, and manufacturing times required for the job.

A **job cost sheet** is a document used to accumulate the costs for a specific job. The job cost sheet serves as the basic record for recording actual progress on the job. As production takes place, the materials, labor, and machine resources utilized are recorded on the job cost sheet along with the related costs. When a job is completed, the final cost of the job is determined by totalling the costs on the job cost sheet. See the following Business Insight for a discussion of a new software product that supports job costing in the construction industry.

BUSINESS INSIGHT	**Software for Job Costing**

A challenge of maintaining job cost systems with detailed cost sheets is capturing cost data in a timely manner. Job costing systems software is now available for the construction industry that enables job managers to automatically update and calculate job costs, projected job costs and profits, percentage of completion, and other information vital to completing jobs on budget. To provide greater timeliness, the software developer has created a linked program for handheld computers that allows users to enter information into the office system from the field. The software developer noted that "foremen are picking it up more quickly than we expected. They're using it for time and materials because they can immediately get feedback on their job."[2]

Production Files and Records

Certain files in the cost system (typically in a computer database) provide the necessary detail for amounts maintained in total in the general ledger. For example, the raw materials inventory file contains separate

---

[2] Tom Sawyer, "Taking the Back Office to the Jobsite," *Engineering News Report,* May 7, 2001, p. 27; and http: www.construction-software.com.

records for each type of raw materials, indicating increases, decreases, and the available balance for both units and costs. Every time there is a change in the Raw Materials Inventory general ledger account, there must be an equal change in one or more individual inventory records. Therefore, at any given time, the total of the balances in the raw materials inventory file for all raw materials inventory items should equal the balance in the Raw Materials Inventory general ledger account. Because of this relationship between the raw materials inventory file and Raw Materials Inventory in the general ledger, Raw Materials Inventory is called a *control account* and the raw materials file of detailed records is called a *subsidiary ledger*. Other general ledger accounts related to the product cost system that have subsidiary files are Work-in-Process, Finished Goods Inventory, and Cost of Goods Sold.

Other records required to operate a job cost system include production orders, job cost sheets, materials requisition forms, and work tickets. Production orders and job cost sheets were previously discussed. The production order serves as authorization for production supervisors to obtain materials from the storeroom and to issue work orders to production employees, and the job cost sheet accumulates the cost of the job.

A **materials requisition form** indicates the type and quantity of each raw material issued to the factory. This form is used to record the transfer of responsibility for materials and to record materials changes on raw materials and job cost sheet records. The materials requisition form has a place to record the job number; the job cost sheet has a place to record the requisition number. If a question arises regarding the issuance of materials, the requisition number and job number provide a trail for tracing the destination and the source of the materials. The materials requisition form also identifies the materials warehouse employee who issued the materials and the production employee who received them.

A **work ticket** is used to record the time a job spends in a specific manufacturing operation. Each manufacturing operation performed on a job is documented by a work ticket. The completed work tickets for a job should correspond to the operations specified on the job production order. Time information on the work tickets is used by production scheduling or expediting personnel to determine whether the job is on schedule, and to assign costs to the job.

A production operation can involve a single employee, a group of employees, a machine, or even heating, cooling, or aging processes. When the operation involves a single employee, the rate recorded on the work ticket is simply the employee's wage rate. When it involves a group of employees, the rate is composed of the wage rates of all employees in the group. When the work involves a machine operation, the rate includes a charge for machine time, as well as the time of any machine operators. Other operations, such as heating, cooling, or aging, will also have a rate for each unit of time.

JOB COSTING FOR PRODUCTS AND SERVICES

Exhibit 18.4 shows how inventory costs in a manufacturing organization flow in a logical pattern through the financial accounting system. Pay particular attention to the major inventory accounts (Raw Materials, Work-in-Process, and Finished Goods Inventory), Manufacturing Overhead, and the flow of costs through the inventory accounts. Each of the numbered items, representing a cost flow affecting an inventory account or Manufacturing Overhead, is explained here:

L04 Explain the operation of a job costing system.

1. The costs of purchased raw materials and manufacturing supplies are recorded in Raw Materials and Manufacturing Supplies, respectively. An increase in Accounts Payable typically offsets these increases.

2. As primary raw materials are requisitioned to the factory, direct materials costs are transferred from Raw Materials to Work-in-Process.

3. Direct labor costs are assigned to Work-in-Process on the basis of the time devoted to processing raw materials. Indirect labor costs associated with production employees are initially assigned to Manufacturing Overhead.

4.–6. Other production related costs are also assigned to Manufacturing Overhead. Other Payables represents the incurrence of a variety of costs such as repairs and maintenance, utilities, and property taxes.

7. Costs assigned to Manufacturing Overhead are periodically reassigned (applied) to Work-in-Process, preferably with the use of a predetermined overhead rate such as direct labor hours, machine hours, or some other cost assignment base.

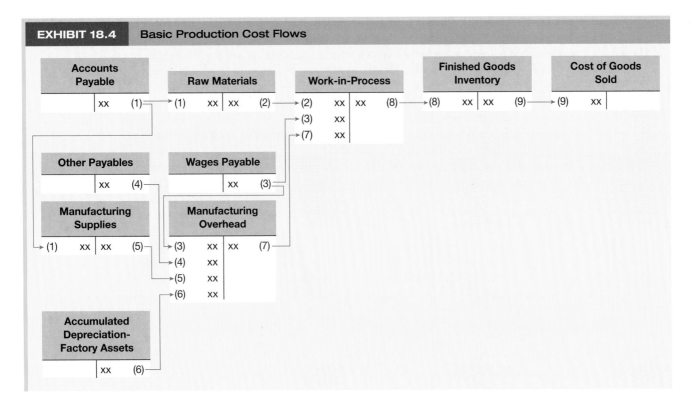

EXHIBIT 18.4   Basic Production Cost Flows

8. When products are completed, their accumulated product costs are totaled on a job cost sheet and transferred from Work-in-Process to Finished Goods Inventory.

9. When the completed products are sold, their costs are transferred from Finished Goods Inventory to Cost of Goods Sold.

Job Costing Illustrated

Even though data can be processed using manual or computerized systems, data processing procedures are best illustrated within the context of a paper-based manual system. Fox Brothers, Inc., manufactures a line of wool sports jackets for men and women. Because there are significant differences in materials costs and a need to carefully control inventories, detailed records are kept concerning the raw materials assigned to specific jobs. Raw materials consist of different styles of wool fabric, interfacing fabric, liner fabric, and button sets.

Total inventory accounts at the beginning of August 2007 included Raw Materials, $36,100; Work-in-Process, $109,900; and Finished Goods, $75,000. In addition, there were manufacturing supplies of $1,600, consisting of various items such as thread, needles, shears, and machine lubricant. The August 1 balance in Manufacturing Overhead was $0.

Raw Materials			
Description	Quantity	Unit Cost	Total Cost
Wool fabric W09	3,000 yards	$ 7	$21,000
Wool fabric W12	500 yards	12	6,000
Interfacing	1,500 yards	1	1,500
Liner	2,000 yards	3	6,000
Buttons	400 sets	4	1,600
Total			$36,100

Manufacturing Supplies	
Item	**Total Cost**
Various	$1,600

Work-in-Process	
Job	**Total Cost**
425	$ 58,600
426	51,300
Total	$109,900

Finished Goods Inventory	
Job	**Total Cost**
424	$75,000

To illustrate manufacturing cost flows in a job cost system, "T" accounts are presented in the margin for the cost system transactions for Fox Brothers, Inc., for August 2007. Each cost assignment is supported by documented information that is recorded in subsidiary cost system records. The manufacturing cost transactions for Fox Brothers for August 2007 are discussed here.

1. Raw materials and manufacturing supplies are purchased on account. The vendor's invoice totals $31,000, including $1,000 of manufacturing supplies and $30,000 of raw materials. The cost of the raw materials must be assigned to specific raw materials inventory records:

Wool fabric W12.	1,000 yards × $12 =	$12,000
Liner	2,000 yards × $ 3 =	6,000
Buttons.	3,000 sets × $ 4 =	12,000
Total		$30,000

Raw Materials Inventory
Beg. Bal. 36,100
(1) 30,000

Manufacturing Supplies
Beg. Bal. 1,600
(1) 1,000

Accounts Payable
31,000 (1)

2. Materials needed to complete Jobs 425 and 426 are requisitioned. Two new jobs, 427 and 428, were also started and direct materials were requisitioned for them. A total of $54,300 of raw materials was requisitioned:

	Job 425	Job 426	Job 427	Job 428	Total
Buttons:					
1,200 sets × $4	$4,800				$ 4,800
900 sets × $4		$3,600			3,600
500 sets × $4			$ 2,000		2,000
Wool fabric W09:					
2,400 yds. × $7				$16,800	16,800
Wool fabric W12:					
1,500 yds. × $12			18,000		18,000
Interfacing:					
500 yds. × $1.			500		500
800 yds. × $1.				800	800
Liner:					
1,000 yds. × $3			3,000		3,000
1,600 yds. × $3				4,800	4,800
Total	$4,800	$3,600	$23,500	$22,400	$54,300

Work-in-Process Inventory
Beg. Bal. 109,900
(2) 54,300

Raw Materials Inventory
Beg. Bal. 36,100 | 54,300 (2)
(1) 30,000

Work-in-Process Inventory
Beg. Bal. 109,900
(2) 54,300
(3) 34,450

Manufacturing Overhead
Beg. Bal. –0–
(3) 7,200

Wages Payable
41,650 (3)

3. The August payroll liability was $41,650, including $34,450 for direct labor and $7,200 for indirect labor. Direct labor was assigned to the jobs as follows:

	Job 425	Job 426	Job 427	Job 428	Total
Labor hours	600	900	1,000	945	
Labor rate.	× $10	× $10	× $10	× $10	
Total	$6,000	$9,000	$10,000	$9,450	$34,450

Note: The $7,200 of indirect labor costs is assigned to products as part of applied overhead.

Manufacturing Overhead
Beg. Bal. –0–
(3) 7,200
(4) 950
(5) 2,400
(6) 3,230

Manufacturing Supplies
Beg. Bal. 1,600 | 950 (4)
(1) 1,000

Accumulated Depreciation
2,400 (5)

Other Payables
3,230 (6)

4.-6. In addition to indirect labor, Fox Brothers incurred the following manufacturing overhead costs:

Manufacturing Supplies	$ 950
Accumulated Depreciation—Factory Assets	2,400
Miscellaneous (Other Payables)	3,230

Work-in-Process Inventory
Beg. Bal. 109,900
(2) 54,300
(3) 34,450
(7) 13,780

Manufacturing Overhead
Beg. Bal. –0– | 13,780 (7)
(3) 7,200
(4) 950
(5) 2,400
(6) 3,230

7. Manufacturing overhead is applied to jobs using a predetermined rate of $4 per direct labor hour. Assignments to individual jobs are as follows:

	Job 425	Job 426	Job 427	Job 428	Total
Labor hours	600	900	1,000	945	
Labor rate.	× $4	× $4	× $4	× $4	
Total	$2,400	$3,600	$4,000	$3,780	$13,780

8. Jobs 425, 426, and 427 are completed with the following costs:

	Job 425	Job 426	Job 427	Total
Beginning balance	$58,600	$51,300	$ 0	$109,900
Current costs:				
Direct materials (entry 2).	4,800	3,600	23,500	31,900
Direct labor (entry 3)	6,000	9,000	10,000	25,000
Applied overhead (entry 7)	2,400	3,600	4,000	10,000
Total	$71,800	$67,500	$37,500	$176,800

Finished Goods Inventory
Beg. Bal. 75,000
(8) 176,800

Work-in-Process Inventory
Beg. Bal. 109,900 | 176,800 (8)
(2) 54,300
(3) 34,450
(7) 13,780

Additional analysis for the completed jobs indicates the following:

	Job 425	Job 426	Job 427
Total cost of job	$71,800	$67,500	$37,500
Units in job	÷ 1,200	÷ 900	÷ 500
Unit cost.	$ 59.83	$ 75.00	$ 75.00

9. Jobs 424, 425, and 426 are delivered to customers for a sales price of $400,000. Determining the costs transferred from Finished Goods Inventory to Cost of Goods Sold requires summing the total cost of jobs sold.

Cost of Goods Sold
(9) 214,300

Finished Goods Inventory
Beg. Bal. 75,000 | 214,300 (9)
(8) 176,800

Job 424	$ 75,000
Job 425	71,800
Job 426	67,500
Total	$214,300

At this point we can determine the gross profit on the completed jobs:

Sales.	$400,000
Cost of goods sold.	(214,300)
Gross profit.	$185,700

If inventory were produced in anticipation of future sales rather than in response to specific customer orders, it is likely that not all units in a job would be sold at the same time. In this case, the unit cost information is used to determine the amount transferred from Finished Goods Inventory to Cost of Goods Sold.

Exhibit 18.5 shows the cost system records supporting the ending balances in the major inventory accounts and Cost of Goods Sold. Note the importance of the job cost sheets for determining cost transfers affecting Work-in-Process and Finished Goods Inventory. The job cost sheets are also used in determining the ending balances of these accounts.

Fox Brothers' product costing system is probably adequate for determining the cost for each job for purposes of valuing ending inventories and cost of goods sold in its external financial statements. It recognizes the differences in materials costs by carefully tracking each type of material as a separate cost pool. Because all direct labor employees are paid the same rate, it is necessary to maintain only one labor cost pool. Although there are three distinct operations in making sports coats (cutting, sewing, and finishing), the various styles of coats likely require the same proportionate times on each operation. Hence, with only one plantwide manufacturing overhead cost pool applied on the basis of direct labor hours, individual product costs are reasonably accurate.

Although the Fox Brothers' costing system may be adequate for inventory costing for financial statement purposes, the data it routinely generates do not provide management with information required for many management decisions. To evaluate product or customer profitability, management needs additional information concerning marketing, distributing, selling, and customer service costs, which are not included in the product cost system. Also, the cost system does not provide information for decisions concerning individual operations, such as cutting. A comparison of budgeted and planned cutting hours may be useful in evaluating the cutting operation. The system also does not provide the detailed information required for special decisions such as subcontracting cutting operations rather than performing them internally. To answer these questions, Fox Brothers' accountants should perform a special cost study to obtain activity-cost information (see Module 19). In spite of these limitations, this system may be adequate for the purposes it was designed. Management probably will continue to operate the system if the costs of improving and modifying the cost system exceed the perceived benefits. The Business Insight that follows provides an example of how advances in technology are influencing costing models in the commercial printing industry.

BUSINESS INSIGHT   **Weaknesses in the Job Cost Business Model**

The printing industry has long been one of the classic examples of job cost accounting. One can readily visualize the large envelope on which is printed the job cost sheet, which follows each printing job through the various processes. The time and materials records are placed in the envelope, and at the completion of the job, all costs are added and then a markup is applied to determine what the customer should pay for the job. The job cost envelope represents the cost accounting system. The problem with a job-focused business model is that it tends to overlook the efficiency of the processes that go into completing the job. Statistical print production management (SPPM) is a process model that offers improved decision support as well as better harmonization with general ledger costs. It recognizes that any activity consuming time or materials in the print process that does not result in value-added product in the hands of a customer is a loss. Changeovers, stops, trashed materials, waiting, and idle time are misuse and nonuse; they are process loss that must not be hidden away in job envelopes. They must be openly measured and managed. As a supplement to traditional job costing, SPPM is providing valuable decision support information for managers in an increasingly competitive industry.[3]

---

[3] Roger V. Dickeson, "Goodbye Job Cost Accountancy," *Printing Impressions,* January 2001, pp. 67–68.

EXHIBIT 18.5	General Ledger Accounts and Subsidiary Records for Inventory Categories and Cost of Goods Sold

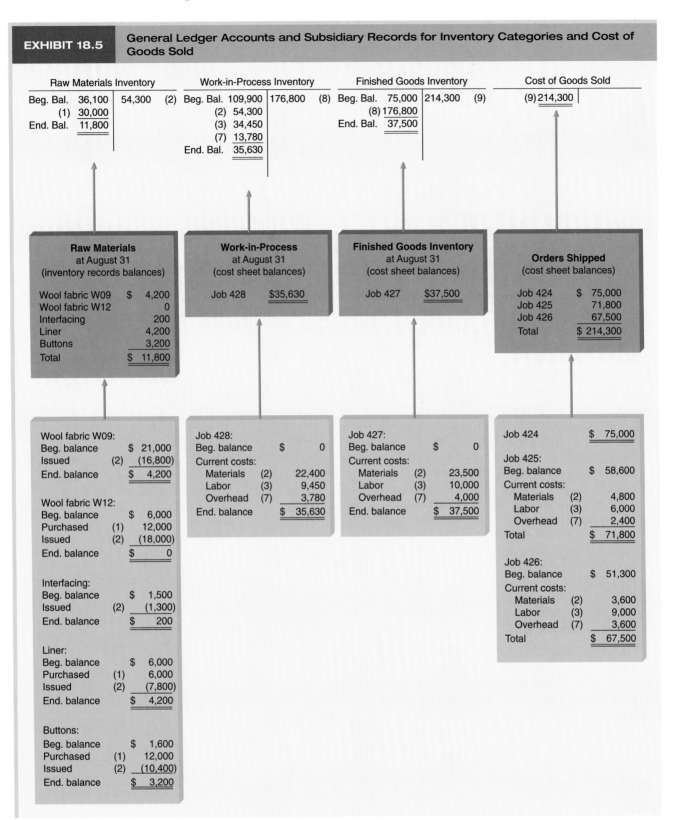

Statement of Cost of Goods Manufactured

The income statement for a merchandising organization, which purchases products ready to sell, normally includes the following calculation of cost of goods sold:

Sales.		$X,XXX
Less cost of goods sold		
Beginning inventory	$X,XXX	
Plus purchases	X,XXX	
Goods available for sale	X,XXX	
Less ending inventory.	(X,XXX)	
Cost of goods sold.		(X,XXX)
Gross profit.		X,XXX
Less selling and administrative expenses		(X,XXX)
Net income.		$X,XXX

Manufacturing organizations modify only one line of this income statement format, changing Purchases to Cost of goods manufactured. Since a manufacturer acquires finished goods from the factory, its cost of finished goods completed is the total cost transferred from Work-in-Process to Finished Goods Inventory during the period.

For internal reporting purposes, most companies prepare a separate **statement of cost of goods manufactured,** which summarizes the cost of goods completed and transferred into Finished Goods Inventory during the period. A statement of cost of goods manufactured and an income statement for Fox Brothers, Inc., are presented in Exhibit 18.6 for August 2007.

EXHIBIT 18.6	Statement of Cost of Goods Manufactured and Income Statement

FOX BROTHERS, INC.
Statement of Cost of Goods Manufactured
For Month Ending August 31, 2007

Current manufacturing costs			
Cost of materials placed in production			
Raw materials, 8/1/07	$36,100		
Purchases	30,000		
Total available	66,100		
Raw materials, 8/31/07	(11,800)	$ 54,300	
Direct labor		34,450	
Manufacturing overhead.		13,780	$102,530
Work-in-process, 8/1/07.			109,900
Total costs in process.			212,430
Work-in-process, 8/31/07.			(35,630)
Cost of goods manufactured			$176,800

FOX BROTHERS, INC.
Income Statement
For Month Ending August 31, 2007

Sales.		$400,000
Cost of goods sold		
Finished goods inventory, 8/1/07	$ 75,000	
Cost of goods manufactured	176,800	
Total goods available for sale	251,800	
Finished goods inventory, 8/31/07	(37,500)	214,300
Gross profit.		185,700
Selling and administrative expenses*		(90,000)
Net income		$ 95,700

*Selling and administrative expenses for Fox Brothers are assumed to be $90,000.

Overapplied and Underapplied Overhead

In the Fox Brothers' example, assume that the predetermined manufacturing overhead rate of $4 per direct labor hour was based on predicted manufacturing overhead for the year of $100,000 and predicted direct labor hours of 25,000. Assume further that it was determined that the company actually incurred $100,000 in manufacturing overhead during the year and that actual direct labor hours for the year were 25,000, resulting in applied overhead of $100,000 (25,000 hours × $4). The activity in Manufacturing Overhead is summarized as follows:

Manufacturing Overhead	
Beginning balance	$ 0
Actual overhead	100,000
Total	100,000
Applied overhead	(100,000)
Ending balance.	$ 0

With identical amounts of actual and applied overhead, the ending balance in Manufacturing Overhead is zero. However, if either the actual overhead cost or the actual level of the production activity base differed from its predicted value, there would be a balance in Manufacturing Overhead representing overapplied or underapplied overhead.

Assume, for example, that the prediction of 25,000 direct labor hours was correct but that actual overhead cost was $105,000. In this case, Manufacturing Overhead shows a $5,000 positive balance, representing underapplied manufacturing overhead:

Manufacturing Overhead	
Beginning balance	$ 0
Actual overhead	105,000
Total	105,000
Applied overhead	(100,000)
Ending balance.	$ 5,000*

*Underapplied; actual exceeds applied.

If actual manufacturing overhead were only $98,000, Manufacturing Overhead would be overapplied and show a $2,000 negative balance.

If the *prediction* of total manufacturing overhead cost is not accurate, there will be an underapplied or overapplied balance in Manufacturing Overhead at the end of the year. A similar result occurs when the *predicted* activity level used in computing the predetermined rate differs from the actual activity level. It is not uncommon for such differences to occur. Predictions are exactly that—predictions.

Month-to-month balances in Manufacturing Overhead are usually allowed to accumulate during the year. In the absence of evidence to the contrary, it is assumed that such differences result from seasonal variations in production or costs or both. However, any year-end balance in Manufacturing Overhead must be eliminated.

Theoretically, the disposition of any year-end balance in Manufacturing Overhead should be accomplished in a manner that adjusts every account to what its balance would have been if an actual, rather than a predetermined, overhead rate had been used. This involves adjusting the ending balances in Work-in-Process, Finished Goods Inventory, and Cost of Goods Sold. Procedures to do this are examined in cost accounting textbooks.

In most situations, the simple procedure of treating the remaining overhead as an adjustment to Cost of Goods Sold may be used. Unless there are large ending balances in inventories and a large year-end balance in Manufacturing Overhead, this simple procedure produces acceptable results. Underapplied overhead indicates that the assigned costs are less than the actual costs, understating Cost of Goods Sold. Hence, disposing of an underapplied balance in Manufacturing Overhead increases the balance in Cost of Goods Sold.

Manufacturing Overhead	
Beginning balance	$ 0
Actual overhead	105,000
Total	105,000
Applied overhead	(100,000)
Ending balance.	$ 5,000* ← Increase Cost of Goods Sold

*Underapplied; actual exceeds applied.

Conversely, overapplied overhead indicates that the assigned costs are more than the actual costs, overstating Cost of Goods Sold. Hence, disposing of an overapplied balance in Manufacturing Overhead decreases Cost of Goods Sold.

Job Costing in Service Organizations

Service costing, the assignment of costs to services performed, uses job costing concepts to determine the cost of filling customer service orders in organizations such as automobile repair shops, charter airlines, CPA firms, hospitals, and law firms. Many of these organizations bill clients on the basis of resources consumed. Consequently, they maintain detailed records for billing purposes. On the invoice sent to the client, the organization itemizes any materials consumed on the job at a selling price per unit, the labor hours worked on the job at a billing rate per hour, and the time special facilities were used at a billing rate per unit of time. Employees with different capabilities and experience often have different billing rates. In a CPA firm, for example, a partner or a senior manager has a higher billing rate than a staff accountant.

The prices and rates must be high enough to cover costs not assigned to specific jobs and to provide for a profit. To evaluate the contribution to common costs and profit from a job, a comparison must be made between the price charged the customer and the actual cost of the job. This is easily done when the actual cost of resources itemized on the customer's invoice is presented on a job cost sheet. A CPA firm, for example, should accumulate the actual hardware and software costs of an accounting system installed for a client, along with the actual wages earned by employees while working on the job and any related travel costs. Comparing the total of these costs with the price charged, the client indicates the total contribution of the job to common costs and profit.

Although service organizations may identify costs with individual jobs for management accounting purposes, there is considerable variation in the way job cost information is presented in financial statements. Some organizations report the cost of jobs completed in their income statements using an account such as Cost of Services Provided. They use procedures similar to those outlined in Exhibit 18.4; the only major change involves replacing Cost of Goods Sold with Cost of Services Provided.

BUSINESS INSIGHT   **Hospital Uses Cost System to Evaluate Treatments**

Thomas Jefferson University Hospital (TJUH) uses its costing system to determine the relative costs of different treatments for a given illness. In effect, the system is a job cost system with each patient being a separate job. One objective of the system is to evaluate the financial impact and the clinical impact of new treatments simultaneously. For example, TJUH used the system to evaluate the cost of using the pharmaceutical product, Zofran, developed to prevent severe episodes of nausea and vomiting associated with cancer chemotherapy treatments. Chemotherapy patients were divided into three different groups (job cost categories) for the study: those who received Zofran therapy, those who received traditional therapy to prevent nausea and vomiting, and those who received both. The results showed that even though Zofran was a more expensive drug, it did not cost more to use because patients using it had shorter hospital stays. As health care cost containment pressures increase, the need for this type of cost analysis is more critical; good cost accounting systems can help hospitals produce more reliable cost data for these studies.[4]

---

[4] Carly E. Carpenter, Linda C. Weitzel, Nelda E. Johnson, and David B. Nash, "Cost Accounting Supports Clinical Evaluations," *Healthcare Financial Management,* April 1994, pp. 40–45.

More often, however, service organizations do not formally establish detailed procedures to trace the flow of service costs. Instead, service job costs are left in their original cost categories such as materials expense, salaries and wages expense, travel expense, and so forth. Because all service costs are typically regarded as expenses rather than product costs, either procedure is acceptable for financial reporting. Regardless of the formal treatment of service costs in financial accounting records and statements, the managers of a well-run service organization have a need for information regarding job cost and contribution. The previous Business Insight discusses how one hospital used product cost information to improve managerial decisions.

MANAGERIAL DECISION	You are the Chief Financial Officer

You have asked the accounting staff to provide you with cost information on each of the products manufactured by your company so you can conduct profitability analysis on each product. Accounting provided you with the costs that are used in the company's external financial statements. What additional information are you going to need before you can conduct a complete profitability analysis? [Answer p 18-32]

All preceding examples of service costing involve situations in which the order is filled in response to a specific customer request. Job order costing can also be used to determine the cost of making services available even when the names of specific customers are not known in advance and the service is being provided on a speculative basis. A regularly scheduled airline flight, for example, could be regarded as a job. Management is interested in knowing the cost of the job in order to determine its profitability. This is but another example of the versatility of job order costing.

MID-MODULE REVIEW

Tri-Star Printing Company prints sales fliers for retail and mail-order companies. Production costs are accounted for using a job cost system. At the beginning of June 2007, raw materials inventories totaled $7,000; manufacturing supplies amounted to $800; two jobs were in process—Job 225 with assigned costs of $13,750, and Job 226 with assigned costs of $1,800—and there were no finished goods inventories. There was no underapplied or overapplied manufacturing overhead on June 1. The following information summarized June manufacturing activities:

- Purchased raw materials costing $40,000 on account.
- Purchased manufacturing supplies costing $9,000 on account.
- Requisitioned materials needed to complete Job 226. Started two new jobs, 227 and 228, and requisitioned direct materials for them as follows:

Job 226	$ 2,600
Job 227	18,000
Job 228	14,400
Total	$35,000

- Incurred June salaries and wages as follows:

Job 225 (500 hours × $10 per hour)	$ 5,000
Job 226 (1,500 hours × $10 per hour).	15,000
Job 227 (2,050 hours × $10 per hour).	20,500
Job 228 (800 hours × $10 per hour)	8,000
Total direct labor.	48,500
Indirect labor	5,000
Total	$53,500

- Used manufacturing supplies costing $5,500.
- Recognized depreciation on factory fixed assets of $5,000.
- Incurred miscellaneous factory overhead cost of $10,750 on account.
- Applied factory overhead at the rate of $5 per direct labor hour.
- Completed Jobs 225, 226, and 227.
- Delivered Jobs 225 and 226 to customers.

Required

a. Prepare "T" accounts showing the flow of costs through the Work-in-Process, Finished Goods and Cost of Goods Sold accounts.

b. Show the job cost details to support the June 30, 2007, balances in Work-in-Process, Finished Goods and Cost of Goods Sold.

c. Prepare a statement of cost of goods manufactured for June 2007.

Solution

a.

Work-in-Process

Balance, June 1, 2007	15,550	96,900	Cost of Goods Manufactured in June
Direct materials	35,000		
Direct labor	48,500		
Applied overhead	24,250		
Balance, June 30, 2007	26,400		

Finished Goods Inventory

Balance, June 1, 2007	–0–	48,150	Cost of jobs sold in June 2007
Cost of goods manufactured in June	96,900		
Balance, June 30, 2007	48,750		

Cost of Goods Sold

Cost of jobs sold in June 2007	48,150	

b. Job in Work-in-Process at June 30, 2007:

Job 228	
Direct materials	$14,400
Direct labor.	8,000
Applied overhead (800 × $5)	4,000
Total	$26,400

Job in Finished Goods at June 30, 2007:

Job 227	
Direct materials	$18,000
Direct labor.	20,500
Applied overhead (2,050 × $5)	10,250
Total	$48,750

Jobs sold in June 2007:

	Job 225	Job 226	Total
Costs assigned from prior period.	$13,750	$ 1,800	$15,550
June Costs: Direct materials	–0–	2,600	2,600
Direct labor	5,000	15,000	20,000
Applied overhead (500 & 1,500 × $5)	2,500	7,500	10,000
Total	$21,250	$26,900	$48,150

c. Statements of cost of goods manufactured for June 2007.

TRI-STAR PRINTING COMPANY
Statement of Cost of Goods Manufactured
For Month Ending June 30, 2007

Current manufacturing costs			
Cost of materials placed in production			
Raw materials, 6/1/07	$ 7,000		
Purchases	40,000		
Total available	47,000		
Raw materials, 6/30/07	(12,000)	$35,000	
Direct labor		48,500	
Manufacturing overhead applied		24,250	$107,750
Work-in-process, 6/1/07.			15,550
Total costs in process.			123,300
Work-in-process, 6/30/07.			(26,400)
Cost of goods manufactured			$ 96,900

PROCESS COSTING

L05 Explain the operation of a process costing system.

A job costing system works well when products are made one at a time (building houses) or in batches of identical items (making blue jeans). However, if products are produced in a continuous manufacturing environment, where production does not have a distinct beginning and ending (refining fossil fuels such as gasoline or diesel), companies usually use a process costing system.

In job costing, the unit cost is the total cost of the "job" divided by the units produced in the job. Costs are accumulated for each job on a job cost sheet, and those costs remain in Work-in-Process until the job is completed, regardless of how long the job is in progress. A multiple-unit job is not considered completed until all units in the job are finished. The cost is not determined until the job is completed, which will not necessarily coincide with the end of an accounting period. Large jobs (such as construction projects) and jobs started near the end of the period frequently overlap two or more accounting periods.

In process costing, the cost of a single unit is equal to the total product costs assigned to a "process" or "department" during the accounting period (frequently a month) divided by the number of units produced. Since goods in the beginning and ending work-in-process inventory are only partially processed during the period, it is necessary to determine the total production for the period in terms of the equivalent number of completed units. For example, if 300 units were started and completed through 40 percent of the process during the period, then the equivalent of 120 fully completed units (300 units × 0.40) were produced. The average cost per unit is computed as total product costs divided by the number of equivalent units produced.

A good example of a process costing environment involving continuous production is the soft drink bottling process. At Coca-Cola's bottling facility in Atlanta, more than 2,000 twelve-ounce cans of Coca-Cola are produced per minute in a continuous process. The process adds the ingredients (concentrate syrup, water, sweetener, and the carbonation agent) at various points in the process and blends the ingredients in the can. At the end of the process, the cans are automatically wrapped in either 6-pack or 12-pack sizes. For another example, see the following Business Insight for a discussion of the process costing environment at a large Japanese chemicals producer.

BUSINESS INSIGHT | **Process Costing in a Japanese Dyestuffs Plant**

Nippon Kayaku is a large industrial company in Japan that produces a wide range of products, including industrial explosives, pharmaceuticals, agrochemicals, sophisticated products (resins, flame retardants, etc.) and dyestuffs. Nippon Kayaku's dyestuff division produces dyes that are particularly targeted to the polyester and cotton-blended textiles market.

The Fukuyama plant manufactures about 600 products for the sophisticated products and dyestuffs divisions, some of which are produced in continuous processes and others in batches. The costing system accumulates costs separately for the more than 1,000 processes, and product costs are determined for a particular product merely by adding the unit costs of the processes used to make that product. For example, the cost of the dyestuff product, Kayaset, consists of the costs of five processes: condensation, filtration, drying, grinding, and packaging. Nippon Kayaku uses these product costs for inventory valuation purposes and for managerial decision-making purposes.

In a job cost system, job cost sheets are used to collect cost information for each and every job. In a process costing system, cost accumulation requires fewer records because each department's production is treated as the only job worked on during the period. In a department that has just one manufacturing process, process costing is particularly straightforward because the Work-in-Process account is, in effect, the departmental cost record. If a department has more than one manufacturing process, separate records should be maintained for each process.

Cost of Production Report

To illustrate process costing procedures, consider Micro Systems Co., which manufactures memory chips for microcomputers in a one-step process using sophisticated machinery. Each finished unit requires one unit of raw materials added at the beginning of the manufacturing process. The production and cost data for the month of July 2007 for Micro Systems are as follows:

July Production Data	
Units in process, beginning of period (75% converted)	4,000
Units started.	36,000
Completed and transferred to finished goods	35,000
Units in process, end of period (20% converted).	5,000

July Cost Data		
Beginning work-in-process		
Materials costs		$ 16,000
Conversion costs		9,000
Total		$ 25,000
Current manufacturing costs		
Direct materials (36,000 × $4)		$144,000
Conversion costs		
Direct labor	$62,200	
Manufacturing overhead applied	46,700	108,900
Total		$252,900

Developing a cost of production report is a useful way of organizing and accounting for costs in a process costing environment. A **cost of production report,** which summarizes unit and cost data for each department or process for each period, consists of the following sections:

- Summary of units in process.
- Equivalent units.
- Total cost to be accounted for and cost per equivalent unit.
- Accounting for total costs.

The cost of production report for Micro Systems Co. is shown in Exhibit 18.7, and its four sections are discussed below.

EXHIBIT 18.7	Cost of Production Report for Process Costing

MICRO SYSTEMS CO.
Cost of Production Report
For the Month Ending July 31, 2007

Summary of units in process

Beginning	4,000	
Units started	36,000	
In process	40,000	
Completed	(35,000)	
Ending	5,000	

Equivalent units in process	Materials	Conversion
Units completed	35,000	35,000
Plus equivalent units in ending inventory	5,000	1,000*
Equivalent units in process	40,000	36,000

Total cost to be accounted for and cost per equivalent unit in process	Materials	Conversion	Total
Beginning work-in-process	$ 16,000	$ 9,000	$ 25,000
Current cost	144,000	108,900**	252,900
Total cost in process	$160,000	$117,900	$277,900
Equivalent units in process	÷ 40,000	÷ 36,000	
Cost per equivalent unit in process	$ 4.00	$ 3.275	$ 7.275

Accounting for total costs

Transferred out (35,000 × $7.275)		$254,625
Ending work-in-process		
Materials (5,000 × $4.00)	$20,000	
Conversion (1,000 × $3.275)	3,275	23,275
Total cost accounted for		$277,900

*5,000 units, 20% converted
**Includes direct labor of $62,200 and applied manufacturing overhead of $46,700

Summary of Units in Process

This section of the cost of production report provides a summary of all units in the department during the period—both from an input and an output perspective—regardless of their stage of completion. From an input perspective, total units in process during the period consisted of the following:

- Units in process at the beginning of the period, plus
- Units started during the period.

From an output perspective, these units in process during the period were either

■ Completed and transferred out of the department, or

■ Still on hand at the end of the period.

In the summary of units in process, all units are treated as the same, regardless of the amount of processing that took place on them during the period. The objective here is to account for all discrete units of product in process at any time during the period. In the summary of units in process in Exhibit 18.7, 40,000 individual units were in process, including 4,000 partially completed units in the beginning inventory and 36,000 new units started during the month. During the period, 35,000 units were completed, and the remaining 5,000 were still in process at the end of the month.

Equivalent Units in Process

This section of the report translates the number of units in process during the period into equivalent completed units of production. The term **equivalent completed units** refers to the number of completed units that is equal, in terms of production effort, to a given number of partially completed units. For example, 80 units for which 50 percent of the expected total processing cost has been incurred is the equivalent of 40 completed units (80×0.50).

Frequently, direct materials costs are incurred largely, if not entirely, at the beginning of the process, whereas direct labor and manufacturing overhead costs are added throughout the production process. If direct labor and manufacturing costs are added to the process simultaneously, it is common to treat them jointly as conversion costs. Micro Systems Co. adds all materials at the beginning of the process; all conversion costs are added evenly throughout the process. Therefore, separate computations are made for equivalent units of materials and equivalent units of conversion. Although the department worked on 40,000 units during the period, the total number of equivalent units in process with respect to conversion costs was only 36,000 units, consisting of 35,000 finished units plus 1,000 equivalent units in ending inventory (5,000 units 20 percent converted). Because all materials are added at the start of the process, 40,000 equivalent units (35,000 finished and 5,000 in process) were in process with respect to materials costs.

Total Cost to Be Accounted for and Cost per Equivalent Unit in Process

This section of the report summarizes total costs in Work-in-Process during the period and calculates the cost per equivalent unit for materials, conversion, and in total. Total cost consists of the beginning Work-in-Process balance (if any) plus current costs incurred. For Micro Systems, the total cost to be accounted for during July was $277,900, consisting of $25,000 in Work-in-Process at the beginning of the period plus current costs of $252,900 incurred in July. Exhibit 18.7 shows these amounts broken down between materials costs and conversion costs.

To compute cost per equivalent unit, divide total cost in process by the equivalent units in process. This is done separately for materials cost and conversion cost. The total cost per equivalent unit is the sum of the unit costs for materials and conversion. Because the number of equivalent units in process was different for materials and conversion, it is not possible to get the total cost per unit by dividing total costs of $277,900 by some equivalent unit amount.

Accounting for Total Costs

This section shows the disposition of the total costs in process during the period divided between units completed (and sent to finished goods) and units still in process at the end of the period. As noted in the previous section, total cost in process is $277,900 and each equivalent unit in process has $4.00 of materials cost and $3.275 of conversion costs for a total of $7.275.

The first step in assigning total costs is to calculate the cost of units transferred out by multiplying the units completed during the period by the total cost per unit (35,000 units $\times$ $7.275). This assigns $254,625 of the total cost to units transferred out, leaving $23,275 ($277,900 − $254,625) to be assigned to ending Work-in-Process. To verify that $23,275 is the correct amount of cost remaining in ending Work-in-Process, the materials and conversion costs in ending Work-in-Process are calculated separately. Recall that the 5,000 units in process at the end of the period are 100 percent completed with materials costs, but only 20 percent completed with conversion costs. Therefore, in ending Work-in-Process, the materials cost component is $20,000 (5,000 $\times$ 1.00 $\times$ $4.00), the conversion cost component is $3,275 (5,000 $\times$ 0.20 $\times$ $3.275), and the total cost of ending Work-in-Process is $23,275 ($20,000 + $3,275).

The cost of production report summarizes manufacturing costs assigned to Work-in-Process during the period and provides information for determining the transfer of costs from Work-in-Process to Finished Goods Inventory. The supporting documents are similar to those previously illustrated for job costing, except that the single cost of production report replaces all the job cost sheets that flow through a department or process. The flow of costs through Work-in-Process is as follows:

Work-in-Process		
Beginning balance		$ 25,000
Current manufacturing costs		
Direct materials.	$144,000	
Direct labor	62,200	
Applied overhead	46,700	252,900
Total		277,900
Cost of goods manufactured		(254,625)
Ending balance.		$ 23,275

The reduction in Work-in-Process for the units completed during the period is determined in the cost of production report (see Exhibit 18.7). This amount is transferred to Finished Goods Inventory. The $23,275 ending balance in Work-in-Process is also determined in the cost of production report as the amount assigned to units in ending Work-in-Process.

Weighted Average and First-In, First-Out Process Costing

Because the costs of materials, labor, and overhead are constantly changing, unit costs are seldom exactly the same from period to period. Hence, if a unit is manufactured partially in one period and partially in the following period, its actual cost is seldom equal to the unit cost of units produced in either period.

In the cost of production report in Exhibit 18.7, we made no attempt to account separately for the completed units that came from beginning inventory and those that were started during the current period. The method illustrated in Exhibit 18.7 is called the **weighted average method,** and it simply spreads the combined beginning inventory cost and current manufacturing costs (for materials, labor, and overhead) over the units completed and those in ending inventory on an average basis. For example, the total cost in process for conversion ($117,900) included both beginning inventory cost and current costs; the 36,000 equivalent units in process for conversion included both units from beginning inventory and units started during the current period. Hence, the average cost per unit of $3.275 (or $117,900 ÷ 36,000) is a weighted average cost of the partially completed units in beginning inventory (prior period costs) and units started during the current period. It is not a precise cost per unit for the current period's production activity but an average cost that includes the cost of partially completed units in beginning inventory carried over from the previous period.

An alternative, more precise process costing method is the **first-in, first-out (FIFO) method.** It accounts for unit costs of beginning inventory units separately from those started during the current period. Under this method, the first costs incurred each period are assumed to have been used to complete the unfinished units carried over from the previous period. Hence, the cost of the beginning inventory is partially based on the prior period's unit costs and partially based on the current period's unit costs.

If unit costs are changing from period to period and beginning inventories are large in relation to total production for the period, the FIFO method is more accurate. However, with the current trend toward smaller inventories, the additional effort and cost of the FIFO method may not be justified. Detailed coverage of the FIFO method is included in cost accounting textbooks.

Process Costing in Service Organizations

There are many applications of process costing for service organizations. Process costing in service organizations is similar to that in manufacturing organizations, the primary purpose being to assign costs to cost objectives. Generally, the use of process costing techniques for service organizations is easier than for manufacturing organizations because the raw materials element is not necessary. The applications for the labor and overhead costs are similar, if not identical, to those of a manufacturing firm.

Process costing for services is similar to job costing for batches in that an average cost for similar or identical services is determined. There are important differences, though, between batch and process costing. In a batch environment, a discrete group of services is identified, but in a process environment, services are performed on a continuous basis. Batch costing accumulates the cost for a specific group of services as the batch moves through the various activities that make up the service. Process service costing measures the average cost of identical or similar services performed each period (each month) in a department. An example of batch service costing is determining the cost of registering a student at your college during the fall term registration period; an example of process service costing is determining the cost each month of processing a check by a bank. If continuously performed services involved multiple processes, the total cost of the service would be the sum of the costs for each process.

After it is determined that process costing would be appropriate for a service activity, the actual decision to use it is generally contingent on two important factors about the items being evaluated. First, is average cost per unit acceptable as an input item to the decision process? For some activities, the answer is obvious. For instance, tracking the actual cost of processing each check through a bank would probably not be as useful as determining the average cost of processing checks for a given period; therefore, average cost is acceptable. For other activities, the answer is more difficult to determine. Should the decision model include average cost per patient-day or actual cost per individual patient?

The second issue relates to the benefits versus the costs of the resulting information. Normally, it is easier to track and record the cost of an activity or process than it is to track and record the cost of each individual item in the activity. Often actual cost tracking is impossible for practical reasons (the actual cost of processing a check through a banking system, for example). Although process costing will not work in every situation, it has many applications in service organizations. As illustrated in this text, there are many possibilities for applying either job or process costing to activities in service organizations.

MODULE-END REVIEW

Magnetic Media, Inc. manufactures data disks that are used in the computer industry. Since there is little product differentiation between Magnetic's products, it uses a process costing system to determine inventory costs. Production and manufacturing cost data for 2007 are as follows:

Production data (units)

Units in process, beginning of period (60% converted)	3,000,000
Units started.	27,000,000
Completed and transferred to finished goods	25,000,000
Units in process, end of period (30% converted).	5,000,000

Manufacturing costs

Work-in-Process, beginning of period (materials, $468,000; conversion, $252,000)	$ 720,000
Current manufacturing costs:	
Raw materials transferred to processing	6,132,000
Direct labor for the period.	1,550,000
Overhead applied for the period.	3,498,000

Required:

Prepare a cost of production report for Magnetic Media, Inc. for 2007.

Solution

MAGNETIC MEDIA, INC.
Cost of Production Report
For the Year 2007

Summary of units in process:

Beginning	3,000,000
Units started	27,000,000
In process	30,000,000
Completed.	−25,000,000
Ending	5,000,000

Equivalent units in process:	Materials	Conversion
Units completed	25,000,000	25,000,000
Plus equivalent units in ending inventory . . .	5,000,000	1,500,000
Equivalent units in process	30,000,000	26,500,000

Total costs to be accounted for and cost per equivalent unit in process:	Materials	Conversion	Total
Work-in-Process, beginning	$ 468,000	$ 252,000	$ 720,000
Current cost.	6,132,000	5,048,000	11,180,000
Total cost in process	$ 6,600,000	$ 5,300,000	$11,900,000
Equivalent units in process	÷ 30,000,000	÷26,500,000	
Cost per equivalent unit in process.	$0.22	$0.20	$0.42
Accounting for total costs:			
Transferred out (25,000,000 × $0.42)			$10,500,000
Work-in-Process, ending:			
Materials (5,000,000 × $0.22)		$ 1,100,000	
Conversion (1,500,000 × $0.20)		300,000	1,400,000
Total cost accounted for			$11,900,000

APPENDIX 18A:

Absorption and Variable Costing

Product costing for inventory valuation is the link between financial and managerial accounting. Product costing systems determine the cost-based valuation of the manufactured inventories used in making key financial accounting measurements (net income on the income statement and financial position on the balance sheet). On the other hand, product costing systems also provide vital information for managers in setting prices, controlling costs, and evaluating management performance. The influence of financial accounting on product costing systems is apparent in the design of traditional job order and process costing systems. These systems reflect the requirement of financial accounting (i.e., generally accepted accounting principles) that all manufacturing costs be included in inventory valuations for external financial reporting purposes. In these systems, all other costs incurred, such as selling, general, and administrative costs, are treated as expenses of the period.

Basic Concepts

A debate exists over how to treat fixed overhead costs in the valuation of inventory. The debate centers around whether fixed overhead, such as machine depreciation, should be considered an *inventoriable product cost* and treated as an asset cost until the inventory is sold, or as a *period cost* and recorded immediately as an operating expense. **Absorption costing** (also called **full costing**) treats fixed manufacturing overhead as a product cost, whereas **variable costing** (also called **direct costing**) treats it as a period cost. Therefore, fixed manufacturing overhead is recorded initially as an asset (inventory) under absorption costing but as an operating expense under variable costing.

Suppose a company leases a manufacturing facility for a fixed amount of $25,000 per month. Absorption costing assigns the $25,000 to the asset, inventory, and spreads it over the units produced in calculating the cost of each unit, whereas variable costing excludes this cost from the inventory cost valuation, recording it immediately as an expense.

Since fixed product costs are eventually recorded as expenses under both variable and absorption costing by the time the inventory is sold, why does it matter whether fixed overhead is treated as a product cost or a period cost? It matters because the way it is treated affects the measurement of income for a particular period as well as the valuation assigned to inventory on the balance sheet at the end of the period. It could also have a behavioral effect on management decisions.

Inventory Valuations

To illustrate the difference in inventory valuations between absorption and variable costing, consider the following cost data for Nutech Company at a monthly volume of 4,000 units:

Direct materials	$7 per unit
Direct labor.	5 per unit
Variable manufacturing overhead.	4 per unit
Total variable cost.	$16 per unit
Fixed manufacturing overhead.	$8,000 per month

To determine the unit cost of inventory using absorption costing, an average fixed overhead cost of $2 per unit is calculated by dividing the monthly fixed manufacturing overhead ($8,000) by the monthly volume (4,000 units). Even though fixed manufacturing overhead is not a variable cost, under absorption costing it is applied to inventory on a per-unit basis, the same as variable costs. At a monthly volume of 4,000 units, Nutech's total inventory cost per unit, therefore, is $16 under variable costing, and $18 under absorption costing.

The $2 difference in total unit cost is attributed to the treatment of fixed overhead. The difference in the total inventory valuation on the balance sheet between absorption and variable costing is the number of units in ending inventory times $2. So if 1,000 units are on hand at the end of the month, they are valued at $18,000 if absorption costing is used but at only $16,000 with variable costing.

The $2 fixed cost per unit depends on the assumptions of $8,000 in total fixed overhead cost and 4,000 units of production per month. As illustrated later, if either total fixed overhead cost or the production volume is different, the fixed overhead per unit will change.

Income Under Absorption and Variable Costing

The income statement formats used for variable and absorption costing are not the same. One benefit of variable costing is that it separates costs into variable and fixed costs, making it possible to present the income statement in a contribution format. As illustrated in Module 16, in a contribution income statement, variable costs are subtracted from revenues to compute contribution margin; fixed costs are then subtracted from contribution margin to calculate net income, also called profit or earnings.

When absorption costing is used, the income statement is usually formatted using the functional format, which classifies costs based on cost function, such as manufacturing, selling, or administrative. The functional income statement, also illustrated in Module 16, subtracts manufacturing costs (represented by cost of goods sold) from revenues to get gross profit; selling and administrative costs are then subtracted from gross profit to get net income.

The contribution format provides information for determining the contribution margin ratio, which is calculated as total contribution margin divided by total sales. It also provides the total amount of fixed costs. These are the primary items of data needed to determine the break-even point and to conduct other cost-volume-profit analysis (see Module 16).

Not only is the income statement format usually different for absorption and variable costing methods, but also as illustrated in the following examples for Nutech Company, the amount of income reported on the income statement might not be the same because of the difference in the treatment of fixed manufacturing overhead. The following additional information is necessary for the Nutech Company examples:

Selling price	$30 per unit
Variable selling and administrative expenses. . .	$3 per unit
Fixed selling and administrative expenses.	$10,000 per month

Sales Vary but Production is Constant

Nutech has no inventory on June 1. Production remains constant at 4,000 units per month for June, July, and August, while sales are 4,000, 2,500, and 5,500 units, respectively for these months. Therefore, both total production and total sales are 12,000 units for this three-month period. A summary of inventory changes is presented at the top of Exhibit 18.8. Absorption and variable costing income statements for June, July, and August are also presented. Recall that the total manufacturing unit cost is $18 using absorption costing and $16 using variable costing, the $2 differential caused by the difference in accounting for fixed overhead costs.

In June (the first month of operation), when 4,000 units were produced and sold, no units remained in inventory, which means that all fixed manufacturing overhead cost was deducted as an expense during the current period under both methods. Under absorption costing, $8,000 of fixed overhead was deducted as part of cost of goods sold (4,000 units × $2 per unit). Under variable costing, $8,000 was deducted as a period cost from contribution margin. No costs were assigned to ending inventory under either method since all units produced were sold.

In July, the 4,000 units produced exceeded the 2,500 units sold by 1,500 units. Because variable costing treats fixed manufacturing overhead as a period cost, the full $8,000 was deducted in July. Absorption costing assigned $5,000 (2,500 units sold × $2) to cost of goods sold and $3,000 (1,500 units remaining × $2) to ending inventory. Because absorption costing deducted only $5,000 of manufacturing overhead cost on the July income statement while variable costing deducted $8,000, net income was $3,000 more under absorption costing than variable costing. Furthermore, since absorption costing assigned $2 more to each unit produced as a product cost than did variable costing, ending inventory was $3,000 more (1,500 units × $2) under absorption costing than variable costing.

In August, just the opposite of July's situation occurred: sales of 5,500 units exceeded production of 4,000 units by 1,500 units. These extra units came from the beginning inventory left from July. As in the two previous months, variable costing deducted $8,000 for fixed manufacturing overhead as a period cost. Since 5,500 units were sold in August, however, absorption costing deducted $11,000 (5,500 units × $2) for fixed manufacturing overhead. Stated another way, because absorption costing assigned $3,000 more cost to the July ending inventory, when those units were then sold in August, they had $3,000 more cost. Hence, August net income was $3,000 more under variable costing than absorption costing.

What can we conclude from this analysis? As long as the number of units produced equals units sold, the two methods will deduct the same total costs on the income statement. However, net income is higher under absorption costing when production exceeds sales (in periods when inventories are increasing), and net income is higher under variable costing when sales exceed production (when inventories are decreasing). This is logical because when inventories increase, absorption costing defers some of the current period's fixed overhead costs in inventories as an asset on the balance sheet. When inventories decrease, however, those costs are moved from the balance sheet and placed on the income statement as an expense. Absorption costing assumes that fixed overhead costs do not expire until the product is sold, whereas variable costing assumes that these costs expire as incurred each period.

Sales are Constant but Production Varies

Assume that Nutech's unit variable and monthly fixed costs remain the same for the months of October, November, and December when 4,000 units per month were sold, but 4,000, 5,000, and 3,200, respectively, were produced per month. Under this scenario, total variable costs deducted on the income statement under both variable and absorption costing will be the same each year, since the same number of units were sold each year. Under Variable costing, total fixed costs will also be the same each year, therefore, net income will be $26,000 for October, November, and December, which is the amount it was for June, when 4,000 units were both produced and sold.

Under absorption costing, however, even though 4,000 units are sold monthly in October, November, and December, net income is not the same for each of the three months because the manufacturing fixed cost per unit is different. Unlike the previous illustration in which production was constant and fixed manufacturing overhead cost was $2 per unit for absorption costing, this illustration has the following fixed manufacturing overhead costs per unit for absorption costing:

EXHIBIT 18.8	Absorption and Variable Costing Income (Production Constant)

Nutech Company: Summary of Unit Inventory Changes

	June	July	August
Beginning inventory	0	0	1,500
Production	4,000	4,000	4,000
Total available	4,000	4,000	5,500
Sales	4,000	2,500	5,500
Ending inventory	0	1,500	0

NUTECH COMPANY
Absorption Costing Income Statements
For June, July, and August

	(Sales Equal Production) June	(Production Exceeds Sales) July	(Sales Exceed Production) August
Unit sales	4,000	2,500	5,500
Sales ($30 per unit)	$120,000	$75,000	$165,000
Cost of goods sold ($18 per unit)	(72,000)	(45,000)	(99,000)
Gross profit	48,000	30,000	66,000
Selling and administrative expenses			
Variable ($3 per unit)	12,000	7,500	16,500
Fixed	10,000	10,000	10,000
Total	(22,000)	(17,500)	(26,500)
Net income	$ 26,000	$12,500	$ 39,500

NUTECH COMPANY
Variable Costing Income Statements
For June, July, and August

	June	July	August
Unit sales	4,000	2,500	5,500
Sales ($30 per unit)	$120,000	$75,000	$165,000
Less variable expenses			
Cost of goods sold ($16 per unit)	64,000	40,000	88,000
Selling and administrative ($3 per unit)	12,000	7,500	16,500
Total	(76,000)	(47,500)	(104,500)
Contribution margin	44,000	27,500	60,500
Less fixed expenses			
Manufacturing overhead	8,000	8,000	8,000
Selling and administrative	10,000	10,000	10,000
Total	(18,000)	(18,000)	(18,000)
Net income	$ 26,000	$ 9,500	$ 42,500

	October	November	December
Fixed manufacturing overhead.........	$8,000	$8,000	$8,000
Units produced.....................	÷ 4,000	÷ 5,000	÷ 3,200
Fixed cost per unit	$ 2.00	$ 1.60	$ 2.50

As a result of the varying fixed manufacturing costs per unit, the amount deducted each month on the absorption costing income statement as part of cost of goods sold expense varies and, hence, profit varies. Exhibit 18.9 shows the absorption income statements for October, November, and December. In October, when 4,000 units were both produced and sold, net income was the same as in June, when the identical situation occurred, which was the same amount of profit for each month under variable costing.

EXHIBIT 18.9	Absorption Costing (Sales Constant With Varying Production)

NUTECH COMPANY
Absorption Costing Income Statements
For October, November, and December

	October	November	December
Units sold	4,000	4,000	4,000
Units produced.....................	4,000	5,000	3,200
Sales ($30 per unit)..................	$120,000	$120,000	$120,000
Cost of goods sold			
Variable ($16 per unit)...............	64,000	64,000	64,000
Fixed ($2.00 per unit)	8,000		
(1.60 per unit)		6,400	
(1,000 units × $1.60			
plus 3,000 × $2.50)			9,100
Total	(72,000)	(70,400)	(73,100)
Gross Profit	48,000	49,600	46,900
Selling and administrative expenses			
Variable.........................	12,000	12,000	12,000
Fixed...........................	10,000	10,000	10,000
Total	(22,000)	(22,000)	(22,000)
Net income.........................	$ 26,000	$ 27,600	$ 24,900

Exhibit 18.9 also illustrates that although unit sales are constant and manufacturing cost behavior is unchanged, net income can vary under the absorption method simply by changing the number of units produced.

Sales did not change from October to November, but net income increased by $1,600 merely by increasing the number of units produced. By producing more units and spreading the fixed over-head cost over more units, total fixed cost included in cost of goods sold decreased from $8,000 to $6,400, and unit fixed cost decreased from $2.00 to $1.60, thereby increasing net income by $1,600 (4,000 × $0.40 per unit). On the other hand, from November to December, the number of units produced decreased to 3,200 and the total fixed cost increased from $6,400 to $9,100, or by $0.90 per unit. Under a first-in, first-out assumption, the 1,000 units in beginning inventory with a unit fixed cost of $1.60 were sold first, followed by 3,000 of the units produced in December at a unit fixed cost of $2.50. The other 200 units produced in December remained in ending inventory. Hence, the decrease in net income from November to December was $2,700 (3,000 units × $0.90 per unit).

Exhibits 18.8 and 18.9 reveal several important relationships between absorption costing net income and variable costing net income, as well as the way net income responds to changes in sales and production under both methods.

For each period, the income differences between absorption and variable costing can be explained by analyzing the change in inventoried fixed manufacturing overhead under absorption costing net income. In general, the following relationship exists:

$$\begin{array}{ccccc} \text{Variable} & & \text{Increase (or minus decrease)} & & \text{Absorption} \\ \text{costing} & + & \text{in inventoried fixed} & = & \text{costing} \\ \text{net income} & & \text{manufacturing overhead} & & \text{net income} \end{array}$$

Using Nutech's November information, the equation is as follows:

$$\$26{,}000 + (1{,}000 \times \$1.60) = \$27{,}600$$

For any given time period, regardless of length, if total units produced equals total units sold, net income is the same for absorption costing and variable costing, all other things being equal. Under absorption costing, all fixed manufacturing overhead is released as a product cost through cost of goods sold when inventory is sold. Under variable costing, all fixed manufacturing overhead is reported as a period cost and expensed in the period incurred. Consequently, over the life of a product, the income differences within periods are offset since they occur only because of the timing of the release of fixed manufacturing overhead to the income statement.

Evaluating Alternatives to Inventory Valuation

The issue in the variable costing debate is whether or not fixed manufacturing costs add value to products. Proponents of variable costing argue that these costs do not add value to a product. They believe that fixed costs are incurred to provide the capacity to produce during a given period, and these costs expire with the passage of time regardless of whether the related capacity was used. Variable manufacturing costs, on the other hand, are incurred only if production takes place. Consequently, these costs are properly assignable to the units produced.

Proponents of variable costing also argue that inventories have value only to the extent that they avoid the necessity of incurring costs in the future. Having inventory available for sale avoids the necessity of incurring some future variable costs, but the availability of finished goods inventory does not avoid the incurrence of future fixed manufacturing costs. Proponents conclude that inventories should be valued at their variable manufacturing cost, and fixed manufacturing costs should be expensed as incurred.

Opponents of variable costing argue that fixed manufacturing costs are incurred for only one purpose, namely, to manufacture the product. Because they are incurred to manufacture the product, they should be assigned to the product. It is also argued that in the long run all costs are variable. Consequently, by omitting fixed costs, variable costing understates long-run variable costs and misleads decision makers into underestimating true production costs.

On a pragmatic level, the central arguments for variable costing center around the fact that use of variable costing facilitates the development of contribution income statements and cost-volume-profit analysis. With costs accumulated on an absorption costing basis, contribution income statements are difficult to develop, and cost-volume-profit analysis becomes very complicated unless production and sales are equal.

Proponents of activity-based costing typically do not favor variable costing because ABC is based on the assumption that, in the long run, all costs are variable and that fixed costs should be assigned to products or services to represent long-run variable costs. Hence, inventory valuation using an ABC approach will tend to be closer to absorption costing values than variable costing values.

As modern manufacturing techniques have led to major reductions in inventory levels in many companies, the significance of the debate over absorption versus variable costing has declined. If a company has no inventories, all its costs are deducted as expenses (either as operating expenses or cost of goods sold expense) during the current period whether it uses absorption or variable costing. Hence, from an income determination standpoint, it does not matter in such cases whether fixed costs are considered a product or period cost. Despite the emergence of inventory management techniques that substantially reduce inventory levels, few companies have been able to *completely* eliminate inventories.

GUIDANCE ANSWER

MANAGERIAL DECISION   **You are the Chief Financial Officer**

Inventory costs that are provided for financial statement purposes for external stockholders and lenders are required by generally accepted accounting principles to include only the manufacturing costs of the product for direct materials, direct labor, and factory overhead. To conduct a complete profitability analysis, the CFO will need to gather data for all other costs that relate to the marketing, sales, and distribution of each product, as well as any costs related to providing service to customers who buy the products.

DISCUSSION QUESTIONS

Q18-1. Distinguish among service, merchandising, and manufacturing organizations on the basis of the importance and complexity of inventory cost measurement.

Q18-2. Distinguish between product costing and service costing.

Q18-3. When is depreciation a product cost? When is depreciation a period cost?

Q18-4. What are the three major product cost elements?

Q18-5. How are predetermined overhead rates developed? Why are they widely used?

Q18-6. Briefly distinguish between process manufacturing and job order production. Provide examples of products typically produced under each system.

Q18-7. Briefly describe the role of engineering personnel and production scheduling personnel in the production planning process.

Q18-8. Identify the primary records involved in the operation of a job cost system.

Q18-9. Describe the flow of costs through the accounting system of a labor-intensive manufacturing organization.

Q18-10. Identify two reasons that a service organization should maintain detailed job cost information.

Q18-11. What are the four major elements of a cost of production report?

Q18-12. What are equivalent completed units?

Q18-13. Under what conditions will equivalent units in process be different for materials and conversion costs?

MINI EXERCISES

M18-14. Classification of Product and Period Costs (LO2)

Classify the following costs incurred by a manufacturer of golf clubs as product costs or period costs. Also classify the product costs as direct materials or conversion costs.

a. Depreciation on computer in president's office
b. Salaries of legal staff
c. Graphite shafts
d. Plant security department
e. Electricity for the corporate office
f. Rubber grips
g. Golf club heads
h. Wages paid assembly line maintenance workers
i. Salary of corporate controller
j. Subsidy of plant cafeteria
k. Wages paid assembly line production workers
l. National sales meeting in Orlando
m. Overtime premium paid assembly line workers
n. Advertising on national television
o. Depreciation on assembly line

M18-15. Developing and Using a Predetermined Overhead Rate (LO2)

Milliken & Company

Assume that the following predictions were made for 2008 for one of the plants of Milliken & Company:

Total manufacturing overhead for the year.	$40,000,000
Total machine hours for the year	2,000,000

Actual results for February 2008 were as follows:

Manufacturing overhead	$5,520,000
Machine hours	310,000

Required

a. Determine the 2008 predetermined overhead rate per machine hour.

  b.   Using the predetermined overhead rate per machine hour, determine the manufacturing overhead applied to Work-in-Process during February.

  c.   As of February 1, actual overhead was underapplied by $400,000. Determine the cumulative amount of any overapplied or underapplied overhead at the end of February.

M18-16. Job Order Costing and Process Costing Applications   (LO4, 5)

For each of the following manufacturing situations, indicate whether job order or process costing is more appropriate and why.

  a.   Peanut butter manufacturer

  b.   Chemical plant that produces household cleaners

  c.   Shoe manufacturer

  d.   Modular home builder

  e.   Company that makes windshields for automobile manufacturers

M18-17. Job Order Costing and Process Costing Applications   (LO4, 5)

For each of the following situations, indicate whether job order or process costing is more appropriate and why.

  a.   Building contractor for residential dwellings

  b.   Manufacturer of nylon yarn that sells to fabric-making textile companies

  c.   Clothing manufacturer that makes suits in several different fabrics, colors, styles, and sizes

  d.   Hosiery mill that manufactures a one-size-fits-all product

  e.   Vehicle battery manufacturer that has just received an order for 400,000 identical batteries to be delivered as completed over the next 12 months

M18-18. Process Costing   (LO5)

Tempe Manufacturing Company makes a single product that is produced on a continuous basis in one department. All materials are added at the beginning of production. The total cost per equivalent unit in process in March 2007 was $4.60, consisting of $3.00 for materials and $1.60 for conversion. During the month, 8,500 units of product were transferred to finished goods inventory; on March 31, 3,500 units were in process, 10 percent converted. The company uses weighted average costing.

Required

  a.   Determine the cost of goods transferred to finished goods inventory.

  b.   Determine the cost of the ending work-in-process inventory.

  c.   What was the total cost of the beginning work-in-process inventory plus the current manufacturing costs?

M18-19.[A]Absorption and Variable Costing; Inventory Valuation

Intel, Inc., has a highly automated assembly line that uses very little direct labor. Therefore, direct labor is part of variable overhead. For October, assume that it incurred the following unit costs:

Direct materials	$200
Variable overhead.	180
Fixed overhead.	60

The 100 units of beginning inventory for October had an absorption costing value of $38,000 and a variable costing value of $32,000. For October, assume that Intel produced 500 units and sold 540 units.

Required

Compute the amount of ending inventory under both absorption and variable costing if the FIFO inventory method was used.

M18-20.[A]Absorption and Variable Costing; Cost of Goods Sold

Use data from Mini Exercise 18-19A.[A]

Required

Compute the Cost of Goods Sold using both the variable and absorption costing methods.

EXERCISES

E18-21.   Analyzing Activity in Inventory Accounts   (LO2, 4)

Selected data concerning operations of Cascade Manufacturing Company for the past fiscal year follow:

Raw materials used	$300,000
Total manufacturing costs charged to production during the year (includes raw materials, direct labor, and manufacturing overhead applied at a rate of 60 percent of direct labor costs)	681,000
Cost of goods available for sale.	826,000
Selling and general expenses.	30,000

	Inventories	
	Beginning	**Ending**
Raw materials.	$70,000	$ 80,000
Work-in-process.	85,000	30,000
Finished goods.	90,000	110,000

Required

Determine each of the following:

a. Cost of raw materials purchased
b. Direct labor costs charged to production
c. Cost of goods manufactured
d. Cost of goods sold

E18-22. Statement of Cost of Goods Manufactured and Income Statement (LO4)

Information from the records of the Jackson Hole Manufacturing Company for August 2007 follows:

Sales.	$205,000
Selling and administrative expenses	83,000
Purchases of raw materials	25,000
Direct labor.	15,000
Manufacturing overhead	32,000

	Inventories	
	August 1	**August 31**
Raw materials.	$ 7,000	$ 5,000
Work-in-process.	14,000	11,000
Finished goods.	15,000	19,000

Required

Prepare a statement of cost of goods manufactured and an income statement for August 2007.

E18-23. Statement of Cost of Goods Manufactured from Percent Relationships (LO4)

Information about NuWay Products Company for the year ending December 31, 2007, follows:

- Sales equal $450,000.
- Direct materials used total $64,000.
- Manufacturing overhead is 150 percent of direct labor dollars.
- The beginning inventory of finished goods is 20 percent of the cost of goods sold.
- The ending inventory of finished goods is twice the beginning inventory.
- The gross profit is 20 percent of sales.
- There is no beginning or ending work-in-process.

Required

Prepare a statement of cost of goods manufactured for 2007. (*Hint:* Prepare an analysis of changes in Finished Goods Inventory.)

E18-24. Developing and Using a Predetermined Overhead Rate: High-Low Cost Estimation (LO2)

For years, Daytona Parts Company has used an actual plantwide overhead rate and based its prices on cost plus a markup of 25 percent. Recently the marketing manager, Jan Arton, and the production manager, Sue Yount, confronted the controller with a common problem. The marketing manager expressed a concern that Daytona's prices seem to vary widely throughout the year. According to Arton, "It seems irrational to charge higher prices when business is bad and lower prices when business is good. While we get a lot of business during high-volume months because we charge less than our competitors, it is a waste of time to even call on customers during low-volume months because we are raising prices while our competitors are lowering them." Yount also believed that it was "folly to be so pushed that we have to pay overtime in some months and then lay employees off in others." She commented, "While there are natural variations in customer demand, the accounting system seems to amplify this variation."

Required

a. Evaluate the arguments presented by Arton and Yount. What suggestions do you have for improving the accounting and pricing procedures?

b. Assume that the Daytona Parts Company had the following total manufacturing overhead costs and direct labor hours in 2007 and 2008:

	2007	2008
Total manufacturing overhead	$200,000	$237,500
Direct labor hours.	20,000	27,500

Use the high-low method to develop a cost estimating equation for total manufacturing overhead.

c. Develop a predetermined rate for 2009, assuming 25,000 direct labor hours are budgeted for 2009.

d. Assume that the actual level of activity in 2009 was 30,000 direct labor hours and that the total 2009 manufacturing overhead was $250,000. Determine the underapplied or overapplied manufacturing overhead at the end of 2009.

e. Describe two ways of handling any underapplied or overapplied manufacturing overhead at the end of the year.

E18-25. Manufacturing Cost Flows with Machine Hours Allocation (LO4)

On November 1, 2007, Robotics Manufacturing Company's beginning balances in manufacturing accounts and finished goods inventory were as follows:

Raw Materials.	$ 9,000
Manufacturing Supplies	500
Work-in-Process.	5,000
Manufacturing Overhead	0
Finished Goods	25,000

During November, Robotics Manufacturing completed the following manufacturing transactions:

1. Purchased raw materials costing $58,000 and manufacturing supplies costing $3,000 on account.
2. Requisitioned raw materials costing $40,000 to the factory.
3. Incurred direct labor costs of $27,000 and indirect labor costs of $4,800.
4. Used manufacturing supplies costing $3,000.
5. Recorded manufacturing depreciation of $15,000.
6. Miscellaneous payables for manufacturing overhead totaled $3,600.
7. Applied manufacturing overhead, based on 2,250 machine hours, at a predetermined rate of $10 per machine hour.
8. Completed jobs costing $85,000.
9. Finished goods costing $96,000 were sold.

Required

a Prepare "T" accounts showing the flow of costs through all manufacturing accounts, Finished Goods Inventory, and Cost of Goods Sold.

b. Calculate the balances at the end of November for Work-in-Process Inventory and Finished Goods Inventory.

E18-26. **Service Cost Flows** **(LO4)**

Viva Marketing, Ltd., produces television advertisements for businesses that are marketing products in the western provinces of Canada. To achieve cost control, Viva Marketing uses a job cost system similar to that found in a manufacturing organization. It uses some different account titles:

Account	Replaces
Videos-in-Process	Work-in-Process
Video Supplies Inventory	Manufacturing Supplies Inventory
Cost of Videos Completed	Cost of Goods Sold
Accumulated Depreciation, Studio Assets	Accumulated Depreciation, Factory Assets
Studio Overhead	Manufacturing Overhead

Viva Marketing does not maintain Raw Materials or Finished Goods Inventory accounts. Materials, such as props needed for videos, are purchased as needed from outside sources and charged directly to Videos-in-Process and the appropriate job. Videos are delivered directly to clients upon completion. The October 1, 2007, balances were as follows:

Video Supplies	$ 300	
Videos-in-Process	1,000	
Studio Overhead	250	underapplied

During October, Viva Marketing completed the following production transactions:

1. Purchased video supplies costing $1,475 on account.
2. Purchased materials for specific jobs costing $27,000 on account.
3. Incurred direct labor costs of $65,000 and indirect labor costs of $3,200.
4. Used production supplies costing $850.
5. Recorded studio depreciation of $3,000.
6. Incurred miscellaneous payables for studio overhead of $1,800.
7. Applied studio overhead at a predetermined rate of $18 per studio hour, with 480 studio hours.
8. Completed jobs costing $100,000 and delivered them directly to clients.

Required

a. Prepare "T" accounts showing the flow of costs through all service accounts and Cost of Videos Completed.

b. Calculate the cost incurred as of the end of October for the incomplete jobs still in process.

E18-27. **Cost of Production Report: No Beginning Inventories** **(LO5)**

Oregon Paper Company produces newsprint paper through a special recycling process using scrap paper products. Production and cost data for October 2007, the first month of operations for the company's new Portland plant, follow:

Units of product started in process during October	90,000 tons
Units completed and transferred to finished goods.	75,000 tons
Machine hours operated	10,000
Direct materials costs incurred.	$486,000
Direct labor costs incurred.	$190,530

Raw materials are added at the beginning of the process for each unit of product produced, and labor and manufacturing overhead are added evenly throughout the manufacturing process. Manufacturing overhead is applied to Work-in-Process at the rate of $24 per machine hour. Units in process at the end of the period were 65 percent converted.

Required

Prepare a cost of production report for Oregon Paper Company for October.

E18-28. **Cost of Production Report: No Beginning Inventories**   (LO5)

Quality Paving Products Company manufactures asphalt paving materials for highway construction through a one-step process in which all materials are added at the beginning of the process. During October 2007, the company accumulated the following data in its process costing system:

Production data	
Work-in-process, 10/1/07	0 tons
Raw materials transferred to processing	25,000 tons
Work-in-process, 10/31/07 (75% converted)	5,000 tons
Cost data	
Raw materials transferred to processing	$625,000
Conversion costs	
Direct labor cost incurred	$38,000
Manufacturing overhead applied	?

Manufacturing overhead is applied at the rate of $2 per equivalent unit (ton) processed.

Required

Prepare a cost of production report for October 2007.

E18-29.[A] **Absorption and Variable Costing Comparisons: Production Equals Sales**

Assume that Heinz manufactures and sells 15,000 cases of catsup each quarter. The following data are available for the third quarter of 2007.

Total fixed manufacturing overhead	$30,000
Fixed selling and administrative expenses	10,000
Sales price per case	30
Direct materials per case	12
Direct labor per case	6
Variable manufacturing overhead per case	3

Required

a. Compute the cost per case under both absorption costing and variable costing.

b. Compute net income under both absorption costing and variable costing.

c. Reconcile any differences in income. Explain.

E18-30.[A] **Absorption and Variable Costing Income Statements: Production Exceeds Sales**

Glendale Company sells its product at a unit price of $12.00. Unit manufacturing costs are direct materials, $2.00; direct labor, $3.00; and variable manufacturing overhead, $1.50. Total fixed manufacturing costs are $20,000 per year. Selling and administrative expenses are $1.00 per unit variable and $10,000 per year fixed. Though 25,000 units were produced during 2006, only 22,000 units were sold. There was no beginning inventory.

Required

a. Prepare an income statement using absorption costing.

b. Prepare an income statement using variable costing.

E18-31.[A] **Absorption and Variable Costing Comparisons: Sales Exceed Production**

Eskew Development sells commercial building lots. During 2007, the company bought 1,000 acres of land for $5,000,000 and divided it into 200 sites of equal size. As the lots are sold, they are cleared at an average cost of $2,500. Storm drains and driveways are then installed at an average cost of $4,000 per site. Selling costs are 10 percent of sales price. Administrative costs are $425,000 per year. The average selling price per site was $80,000 during 2007 when 50 sites were sold. During 2008, the company purchased and developed another 1,000 acres, divided into 200 sites, with all costs remaining constant. Sales totaled 300 sites in 2008 at an average price of $80,000.

Required

Compute net income for 2007 and 2008 under both absorption costing and variable costing.

PROBLEMS

P18-32. Cost of Goods Manufactured and Income Statement (LO4)

Following is information from the records of the Calgary Company for July 2007.

Purchases	
Raw materials	$ 80,000
Manufacturing supplies	3,500
Office supplies	1,200
Sales	425,700
Administrative salaries	12,000
Direct labor	117,500
Production employees' fringe benefits*	4,000
Sales commissions	50,000
Production supervisors' salaries	7,200
Plant depreciation	14,000
Office depreciation	20,000
Plant maintenance	10,000
Plant utilities	35,000
Office utilities	8,000
Office maintenance	2,000
Production equipment rent	6,000
Office equipment rent	1,300

*Classified as manufacturing overhead

Inventories	July 1	July 31
Raw materials	$17,000	$25,000
Manufacturing supplies	1,500	3,000
Office supplies	600	1,000
Work-in-process	51,000	40,000
Finished goods	35,000	27,100

Required

Prepare a statement of cost of goods manufactured and an income statement. Actual overhead costs are assigned to products.

P18-33. Cost of Goods Manufactured and Income Statement with Predetermined Overhead and Labor Cost Classifications (LO2, 4)

Callaway Golf Company (ELY)

Assume information pertaining to Callaway Golf Company for April 2007 follows.

Sales	$200,000
Purchases	
Raw materials	37,000
Manufacturing supplies	800
Office supplies	500
Salaries (including fringe benefits)	
Administrative	6,000
Production supervisors	3,600
Sales	15,000
Depreciation	
Plant and machinery	8,000
Office and office equipment	4,000
Utilities	
Plant	5,250
Office	890

Inventories	April 1	April 30
Raw materials.	$3,000	$3,500
Manufacturing supplies	1,000	1,100
Office supplies	900	800
Work-in-process.	2,000	2,300
Finished goods.	8,000	9,000

Additional information follows:
- Manufacturing overhead is applied to products at 85 percent of direct labor dollars.
- Employee base wages are $12 per hour.
- Employee fringe benefits amount to 40 percent of the base wage rate. They are classified as manufacturing overhead.
- During April, production employees worked 5,600 hours, including 4,800 regular hours and 200 overtime hours spent working on products. There were 600 indirect labor hours.
- Employees are paid a 50 percent overtime premium. Any overtime premium is treated as manufacturing overhead.

Required
a. Prepare a statement of cost of goods manufactured and an income statement for April.
b. Determine underapplied or overapplied overhead for April.
c. Recompute direct labor and actual manufacturing overhead assuming employee fringe benefits for direct labor hours are classified as direct labor.

P18-34. Actual and Predetermined Overhead Rates (LO2, 4)
Allison's Engines, which builds high performance auto engines for race cars, started operations on January 1, 2007. During the month, the following events occurred:
- Materials costing $6,500 were purchased on account.
- Direct materials costing $3,000 were placed in process.
- A total of 380 direct labor hours was charged to individual jobs at a rate of $15 per hour.
- Overhead costs for the month of January were as follows:

Depreciation on building and equipment	$ 500
Indirect labor	1,500
Utilities	600
Property taxes on building	650
Insurance on building.	550

- On January 31, only one job (A06) was in process with materials costs of $600, direct labor charges of $450 for 30 direct labor hours, and applied overhead.
- The building and equipment were purchased before operations began and the insurance was prepaid. All other costs will be paid during the following month.

Note: Predetermined overhead rates are used throughout the module. An alternative is to accumulate actual overhead costs for the period in Manufacturing Overhead, and apply actual costs at the close of the period to all jobs in process during the period.

Required
a. Assuming Allison's Engines assigned actual monthly overhead costs to jobs on the basis of actual monthly direct labor hours, prepare an analysis of Work-in-Process for the month of January.
b. Assuming Allison's Engines uses a predetermined overhead rate of $10.50 per direct labor hour, prepare an analysis of Work-in-Process for the month of January. Describe the appropriate treatment of any overapplied or underapplied overhead for the month of January.
c. Review the overhead items and classify each as fixed or variable in relation to direct labor hours. Next, predict the actual overhead rates for months when 200 and 1,000 direct labor hours are used. Assuming jobs similar to A06 were in process at the end of each month, determine the costs assigned to these jobs. (*Hint:* Determine a variable overhead rate.)
d. Why do you suppose predetermined overhead rates are preferred to actual overhead rates?

Herman Miller, Inc.
(MLHR)

P18-35. Job Costing with Predetermined Overhead Rate (LO2, 4)

Herman Miller, Inc. manufactures desks, chairs, file cabinets, and similar office products in batches for inventory stock. Assume that Herman Miller's production costs are accounted for using a job cost system. At the beginning of April 2007, raw materials inventories totaled $8,500,000, manufacturing supplies amounted to $1,200,000 and finished goods inventories totaled $6,000,000. Two jobs were in process: Job 522 with assigned costs of $5,640,000 and Job 523 with assigned costs of $2,400,000. The following information summarizes April manufacturing activities:

- Purchased raw materials costing $25,000,000 on account.
- Purchased manufacturing supplies costing $3,000,000 on account.
- Requisitioned materials needed to complete Job 523. Started two new jobs, 524 and 525, and requisitioned direct materials for them.

Direct materials	
Job 523.............	$ 3,000,000
Job 524.............	12,900,000
Job 525.............	9,600,000
Total	$25,500,000

- Recorded April salaries and wages as follows:

Direct labor	
Job 522 (300,000 hours × $12 per hour).......	$ 3,600,000
Job 523 (800,000 hours × $12 per hour).......	9,600,000
Job 524 (1,200,000 hours × $12 per hour).....	14,400,000
Job 525 (1,000,000 hours × $12 per hour).....	12,000,000
Total direct labor............................	39,600,000
Indirect labor	6,400,000
Total	$46,000,000

- Used manufacturing supplies costing $2,250,000.
- Recognized depreciation on factory fixed assets of $4,000,000.
- Incurred miscellaneous manufacturing overhead costs of $5,500,000 on account.
- Applied manufacturing overhead at the rate of $6 per direct labor hour.
- Completed Jobs 522, 523, and 524.

Required

Prepare a complete analysis of all activity in Work-in-Process. Be sure to show the beginning and ending balances, all increases and decreases, and label each item. Provide support information on decreases with job cost sheets.

P18-36. Job Costing with Predetermined Overhead Rate (LO2, 4)

TruCut Mower Company manufactures a variety of gasoline-powered mowers for discount hardware and department stores. TruCut uses a job cost system and treats each customer's order as a separate job. The primary mower components (motors, chassis, and wheels) are purchased from three different suppliers under long-term contracts that call for the direct delivery of raw materials to the production floor as needed. When a customer's order is received, a raw materials purchase order is electronically placed with suppliers. The purchase order specifies the scheduled date that production is to begin as the delivery date for motors and chassis; the scheduled date production is to be completed is specified as the delivery date for the wheels. As a consequence, there are no raw materials inventories; raw materials are charged directly to Work-in-Process upon receipt. Upon completion, goods are shipped directly to customers rather than transferred to finished goods inventory. At the beginning of July 2007, TruCut had the following work-in-process inventories:

Job 365	....	$20,000
Job 366	....	16,500
Job 367	....	15,000
Job 368	....	9,000
Total	....	$60,500

During July, the following activities took place:
- Started Jobs 369, 370, and 371.
- Ordered and received the following raw materials for specified jobs:

Job	Motors	Chassis	Wheels	Total
366	$ 0	$ 0	$ 800	$ 800
367	0	0	1,200	1,200
368	0	0	1,600	1,600
369	12,000	4,000	1,000	17,000
370	9,000	3,500	900	13,400
371	8,500	3,800	0	12,300
Total	$29,500	$11,300	$5,500	$46,300

- Incurred July manufacturing payroll:

Direct labor

Job 365	$ 500	
Job 366	3,200	
Job 367	3,400	
Job 368	4,160	
Job 369	1,300	
Job 370	2,620	
Job 371	2,000	
Total	17,180	
Indirect labor	3,436	
Total	$20,616	

- Incurred additional manufacturing overhead costs for July:

Manufacturing supplies purchased on account and used	$ 2,800
Depreciation on factory fixed assets	6,000
Miscellaneous payables	5,100
Total	$13,900

- Applied manufacturing overhead using a predetermined rate based on predicted annual overhead of $190,000 and predicted annual direct labor of $200,000.
- Completed and shipped Jobs 365 through 370.

Required

Prepare a complete analysis of all activity in Work-in-Process. Be sure to show the beginning and ending balances, all increases and decreases, and label each item. Provide support information on decreases with job cost sheets.

P18-37. Weighted Average Process Costing (LO5)

Minot Processing Company manufactures one product on a continuous basis in two departments, Processing and Finishing. All materials are added at the beginning of work on the product in the Processing Department. During December 2007, the following events occurred in the Processing Department:

Units started..	16,000 units
Units completed and transferred to Finishing Department	15,000 units

Costs assigned to processing	
Raw materials (one unit of raw materials for each unit of product started)........................	$142,900
Manufacturing supplies used	18,000
Direct labor costs incurred	51,000
Supervisors' salaries.....................................	12,000
Other production labor costs	14,000
Depreciation on equipment	6,000
Other production costs...................................	18,000

Additional information follows:
- Minot uses weighted average costing and applies manufacturing overhead to Work-in-Process at the rate of 100 percent of direct labor cost.
- Ending inventory in the Processing Department consists of 3,000 units that are one-third converted.
- Beginning inventory contained 2,000 units, one-half converted, with a cost of $27,300 ($17,300 for materials and $10,000 for conversion).

Required

a. Prepare a cost of production report for the Processing Department for December.
b. Prepare an analysis of all changes in Work-in-Process.

P18-38. Weighted Average Process Costing (LO5)

JIF
J.M. Smucker
Company (SJM)

Assume that JIF, which is part of J.M. Smucker Company, processes its only product, 12-ounce jars of peanut butter, in a single process and uses weighted average process costing to account for inventory costs. All materials are added at the beginning of production. The following inventory, production, and cost data are provided for June 2007:

Production data	
Beginning inventory (25% converted)...................	210,000 units
Units started.......................................	650,000 units
Ending inventory (50% converted).....................	180,000 units

Manufacturing costs	
Beginning inventory in process:	
Materials cost	$146,000
Conversion cost	88,000
Raw materials cost added at beginning of process...........	739,800
Direct labor cost incurred..............................	410,000
Manufacturing overhead applied	333,600

Required

a. Prepare a cost of production report for June.
b. Prepare a statement of cost of goods manufactured for June.

P18-39.[A] **Absorption and Variable Costing Comparisons**

Never Quit Shoe Company is concerned with changing to the variable costing method of inventory valuation for making internal decisions. The absorption costing income statements for January and February follow.

NEVER QUIT SHOE COMPANY Absorption Costing Income Statements For January and February 2007		
	January	February
Sales (8,000 units)	$160,000	$160,000
Cost of goods sold.	(99,200)	(108,800)
Gross profit.	60,800	51,200
Selling and administrative expenses	(30,000)	(30,000)
Net income	$ 30,800	$ 21,200

Production data follow.

Production units.	10,000	6,000
Variable costs per unit	$10	$10
Fixed overhead costs.	$24,000	$24,000

The preceding selling and administrative expenses include variable costs of $1 per unit sold.

Required

a. Compute the absorption cost per unit manufactured in January and February.
b. Explain why the net income for January was higher than the net income for February when the same number of units was sold in each month.
c. Prepare income statements for both months using variable costing.
d. Reconcile the absorption costing and variable costing net income figures for each month. (Start with variable costing net income.)

P18-40.[A] **Absorption and Variable Costing Comparisons**

Peachtree Company manufactures peach jam. Because of bad weather, its peach crop was small. The following data have been gathered for the summer quarter of 2007:

Beginning inventory (cases)	0
Cases produced.	10,000
Cases sold	9,400
Sales price per case.	$60
Direct materials per case	$8
Direct labor per case	$9
Variable manufacturing overhead per case	$3
Total fixed manufacturing overhead.	$400,000
Variable selling and administrative cost per case	$2
Fixed selling and administrative cost.	$48,000

Required

a. Prepare an income statement for the quarter using absorption costing.
b. Prepare an income statement for the quarter using variable costing.
c. What is the value of ending inventory under absorption costing?
d. What is the value of ending inventory under variable costing?
e. Explain the difference in ending inventory under absorption costing and variable costing.

CASES

C18-41.   Cost Data for Financial Reporting and Special Order Decisions   (LO2, 4)

Friendly Greeting Card Company produces a full range of greeting cards sold through pharmacies and department stores. Each card is designed by independent artists. A production master is then prepared for each design. The production master has an indefinite life. Product designs for popular cards are deemed to be valuable assets. If a card sells well, many batches of the design will be manufactured over a period of years. Hence, Friendly Greeting maintains an inventory of production masters so that cards may be periodically reissued. Cards are produced in batches that may vary in sizes of 1,000 units. An average batch consists of approximately 10,000 cards. Producing a batch requires placing the production master on the printing press, setting the press for the appropriate paper size, and making other adjustments for colors and so forth. Following are facility-, product-, batch-, and unit-level cost information:

Product design and production master per new card	$ 1,500.00
Batch setup (typically per 10,000 cards)	150.00
Materials per 1,000 cards.	100.00
Conversion per 1,000 cards.	80.00
Shipping	
Per batch	20.00
Per card	0.01
Selling and administrative	
Companywide.	200,000.00
Per product design marketed	500.00

Information from previous year:

Product designs and masters prepared for new cards	90
Product designs marketed.	120
Batches manufactured.	500
Cards manufactured and sold	5,000,000

Required

You may need to review materials in Modules 15 and 16 to complete the requirements.

a.   Describe how you would determine the cost of goods sold and the value of any ending inventory for financial reporting purposes. (No computations are required.)

b.   You have just received an inquiry from Mall-Mart department stores to develop and manufacture 20 special designs for sale exclusively in Mall-Mart stores. The cards would be sold for $1.50 each, and Mall-Mart would pay Friendly Greeting $0.30 per card. The initial order is for 20,000 cards of each design. If the cards sell well, Mall-Mart plans to place additional orders for these and other designs. Because of the preestablished sales relationship, no marketing costs would be associated with the cards sold to Mall-Mart. How would you evaluate the desirability of the Mall-Mart proposal?

c.   Explain any differences between the costs considered in your answer to requirement (a) and the costs considered in your answer to requirement (b).

C18-42. Continue or Discontinue: Plantwide Overhead with Labor- and Machine-Intensive Operations (LO2, 4)

When Dart Products started operation five years ago, its only product was a radar detector known as the Bear Detector. The production system was simple, with Bear Detectors manually assembled from purchased components. With no ending work-in-process inventories, unit costs were calculated once a month by dividing current manufacturing costs by units produced.

Last year, Dart Products began to manufacture a second product, code-named the Lion Tamer. The production of Lion Tamers involves both machine-intensive fabrication and manual assembly. The introduction of the second product necessitated a change in the firm's simple accounting system. Dart Products now separately assigns direct material and direct labor costs to each product using information contained on materials requisitions and work tickets. Manufacturing overhead is accumulated in a single cost pool and assigned on the basis of direct labor hours, which is common to both products. Following are last year's financial results by product:

		Bear Detector		Lion Tamer
Sales				
Units		5,000		2,000
Dollars.		$ 500,000		$ 300,000
Cost of goods sold				
Direct materials.	$110,000		$65,000	
Direct labor	150,000		45,000	
Applied overhead	270,000		81,000	
Total		(530,000)		(191,000)
Gross profit.		$ (30,000)		$ 109,000

Management is concerned about the mixed nature of last year's financial performance. It appears that the Lion Tamer is a roaring success. The only competition, the Nittney Company, has been selling a competing product for considerably more than Dart's Lion Tamer; this company is in financial difficulty and is likely to file for bankruptcy. The management of Dart Products attributes the Lion Tamer's success to excellent production management. Management is concerned, however, about the future of the Bear Detector and is likely to discontinue that product unless its profitability can be improved. You have been asked to help with this decision and have obtained the following information:

- The labor rate is $15 per hour.
- Dart has two separate production operations, fabrication and assembly. Bear Detectors undergo only assembly operations and require 2.0 assembly hours per unit. Lion Tamers undergo both fabrication and assembly and require 1.0 fabrication hour and 0.5 assembly hour per unit.
- The annual Fabricating Department overhead cost function is:

$$\$200,000 + \$5 \text{ (labor hours)}$$

- The annual Assembly Department overhead cost function is:

$$\$20,000 + \$11 \text{ (labor hours)}$$

Required

You may need to review materials in Modules 15-17 to complete this case. Evaluate the profitability of Dart's two products and make any recommendations you believe appropriate.

Product Costing: Assigning Indirect Costs

LEARNING OBJECTIVES

LO1 Define and explain key elements of an indirect cost allocation system. (p. 19-3)

LO2 Describe allocation of service department costs, including that for interdepartment services. (p. 19-6)

LO3 Compare and contrast activity-based costing (ABC) and traditional costing systems. (p. 19-13)

LO4 Compute overhead rates under three methods based on plantwide, department, or activity-based rates. (p. 19-17)

LO5 Describe the implementation of an activity-based costing system. (p. 19-21)

INDIRECT COSTS OF TRACKS, TRUCKS, AND TREES

Effective management of costs is a hallmark of sound management. Indirect costs are the most challenging to manage. Direct costs such as direct materials and direct labor can be traced to a job, product, or other unit of work. Indirect costs are not so easily traced to specific units or projects. Indirect costs, including both production overhead costs and general administrative costs, have increased from under 10 percent of sales a century ago to over 35 percent currently. We describe the circumstances of three diverse firms—SRAM Corporation, Oshkosh Truck Corporation, and Enviro-Recovery Corporation—to demonstrate the managerial challenges of measuring and controlling indirect costs.

SRAM Corporation makes bicycle components such as gear shifts, brakes, and handlebars. Its Chicago headquarters office includes an indoor test track. SRAM pioneered the handgrip gear shift mechanism that allows bicycle riders to change gears without taking their hands off the handgrips. To stay a step ahead of competitors such as **Shimano**, SRAM management introduced a series of new products including SmartBars and SparcDrive. SmartBars are handlebars that allow a rider to quickly adjust the height and reach. SparcDrive is a small electric motor that provides an extra boost to riders when they travel uphill. Both products have been designed for the "comfort rider" segment of the bicycle market.

Oshkosh Truck Corporation specializes in fire, concrete-mixing, garbage, and military trucks. Military trucks make up 17 percent of sales, fire

engines 27 percent, and concrete and garbage trucks 56 percent. Using modern manufacturing techniques, Oshkosh produces a fire truck in 28 days rather than the 50 days it formerly took. As a result, the firm has saved 1.5 acres of floor space that once held inventory. Oshkosh also offers thousands of different options that can customize a rig for the needs of any customer.

Enviro-Recovery Corporation pulls up old logs from the bottom of Lake Superior and mills them for restoration projects, musical instruments, and antique furniture. It can provide custom orders of 16-inch board width, which is rarely available in modern lumber. Demand for these older pine, oak, and maple planks and beams has increased as more dealers begin to stock environmentally friendly lumber.

These three firms have two common characteristics. First, they have common indirect costs that must be assigned to their products. Costs of the indoor test track, truck production floor, and mill and drying kiln represent such common costs. Second, each firm's product line includes a group of similar but not identical products. The various bicycle components, fire truck options, and sizes and species of logs likely mean that these different products consume differing amounts of the firm's common costs. Management of these three companies must carefully consider common cost assignment in designing their product cost systems.

Source: *Forbes, Fortune, Company Web Sites.*[1]

[1] David Armstrong, "A Stick in the Spokes," *Forbes,* March 5, 2001, pp. 148–49; Tom Post, "Waterlogged," *Forbes,* March 6, 2000, pp. 132–34; Thomas A. Stewart, "Yikes! Deadwood Is Coming Back," *Fortune,* August 18, 1997, pp. 221–22; and Mark Tatge, "Red Bodies, Black Ink," *Forbes,* March 18, 2000, pp. 114–15.

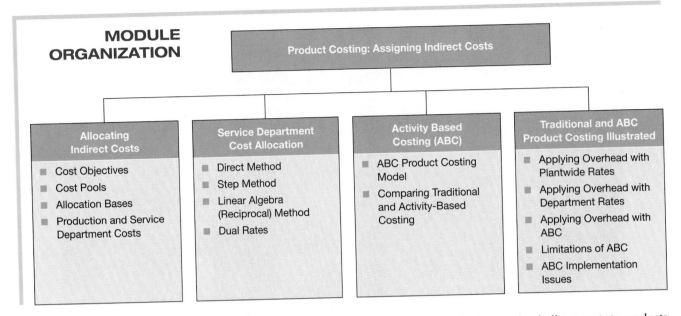

This module describes indirect costs and the frequently used methods to assign indirect costs to products or services. We begin by considering the relation between indirect costs and cost objectives such as products or services. Next, we introduce some of the traditional approaches for assigning indirect costs to cost objectives, noting the strengths and weaknesses of each. We then compare and contrast traditional and activity-based approaches to cost assignment. The module concludes with a discussion of issues involved in implementing activity-based costing.

ALLOCATING INDIRECT COSTS

LO1 Define and explain key elements of an indirect cost allocation system.

To manage costs, we must be able to measure them. Hence, a major theme of this book is cost measurement, which involves determining the costs appropriately assigned to or associated with a particular cost objective. Costs are generally assignable to a particular cost objective if they were incurred for its benefit or if the costs were caused by the existence of that cost objective. For a shipping department, the wages of the department's employees, clearly, are department costs. They can be directly traced to, or associated with, the shipping department, and they are incurred for the direct benefit of that department.

On the other hand, the cost of electricity is usually incurred for the common benefit of all occupants of the building. Hence, it is an indirect cost, or **common cost,** for all the departments occupying the building. Other indirect costs that benefited the shipping department include those for security, maintenance of the grounds and parking areas, and cleaning supplies. But what about the cost of operating the payroll department, the computer processing department, or the legal department? Should some of these costs be allocated to the shipping department if it receives services or benefits from these departments? What about the president's salary? Since the president is responsible for the whole company, should this cost be allocated to all departments in the company? What about the cost of operating the company airplane? Should this cost be combined with the president's salary (since the president is the primary user of the plane) and be allocated to all departments?

These are just a few examples of the many difficult questions concerning the allocation of indirect costs. To provide some structure for the discussion of these and other questions, it is necessary to examine the three basic elements of any indirect cost allocation system:

- Cost objectives
- Cost pools
- Allocation bases

Cost Objectives

A **cost objective** is anything to which costs are assigned. Although the most traditional cost objectives are departments, products, or services, managers' needs for cost information are quite varied. A cost objective can be anything for which management desires cost information. Examples of useful cost objectives include (1) the cost of moving materials between work stations (used in evaluating the desirability of rearranging equipment), (2) the cost of inspecting incoming raw materials and returning raw materials that do not meet quality specifications (used in rating vendors and negotiating with them), and (3) the firmwide cost of long distance telephone service (used to evaluate the desirability of switching carriers and/or subscribing to wide-area telephone service).

Cost Pools

A **cost pool** is a collection of related costs, such as manufacturing overhead, that is assigned to one or more cost objectives. It is not feasible in many situations to assign each item of cost separately. Instead, several similar costs are combined into a cost pool, and the entire pool is allocated as a single item. Indirect costs are often pooled along organization lines, such as costs for the payroll department, computing center, or maintenance department. All building-related costs, or other closely related costs, are also frequently pooled. Sometimes these functional cost pools are referred to as *departments* even though they are not real departments. For example, all building-related costs (depreciation, insurance, repairs, etc.) are often pooled together to form building department costs, which are then allocated to the various users of the building.

The key consideration in establishing cost pools is that the items pooled together should be relatively homogeneous and have a logical cause-and-effect relationship to the allocation base. For instance, a building cost pool would include all costs related to the maintenance and operation of the building and might be allocated on the basis of square footage occupied. The costs in this pool, such as insurance, property taxes, and depreciation, have a logical cause-and-effect relationship to the amount of square footage provided. As the square footage increases, these costs are usually expected to increase.

Allocation Bases

The **cost allocation base** is the factor, or characteristic, common to the cost objectives that determines how much of the cost pool is assigned to each cost objective. The allocation base is the link between cost objective and cost pool. For example, labor-related costs may be allocated according to some measure (or estimate) of the labor time devoted to the various cost objectives. Depreciation and other building-related costs are often allocated on the basis of square footage occupied. Other examples of indirect costs and frequently used allocation bases include the following:

Indirect Cost Category	Allocation Base
Employee health services	Number of employees or visits
Personnel	Number of employees or new hires
Maintenance and repairs	Number of repair orders or service hours
Purchasing	Number of orders placed or dollar value of orders placed
Warehouse	Amount of square footage used or value of materials stored

The most important consideration in selecting an allocation base is ensuring that a logical association exists between the base selected and the costs incurred. For instance, it is logical to allocate personnel department costs according to the number of employees because the function of the personnel department is to provide employee-related services to the various departments. Thus, personnel costs are incurred as these services are provided. It follows that departments with a large number of employees should receive a larger allocation of personnel department costs than departments with fewer employees.

Selecting allocation bases are not always simple and straightforward. For example, it might be necessary when allocating building costs to differentiate among various areas of the building. Some areas of the building could be more costly to operate than other areas, or some space, because of its preferred location within the building might be more valuable. For the allocation of indirect costs to be fair, these types of differences should be reflected in the choice of the allocation base, as illustrated in the next Business Insight featuring **Bellcore.**

Bellcore (which stands for Bell Communications Research) is a joint venture organization that provides scientific and engineering research services to several regional telephone companies in the United States. Bellcore was set up to provide services on a cost charge-back basis to seven regional companies. It was necessary for all support costs incurred at Bellcore to be assigned, along with direct costs, to the services performed by Bellcore engineers and scientists for the various telephone companies. This created a service cost allocation problem.

Cost cross-subsidization was strictly forbidden at Bellcore, making it important to have equitable bases for allocating support function costs to operating departments. A problem emerged almost immediately, when the service and operating departments were allocated unusually large costs for support services such as graphics, secretarial/clerical, and technical publications. Feeling that support service costs were being unfairly allocated, some managers declined to use such services, either forgoing them entirely or going outside Bellcore to less expensive vendors. The problem was caused by inappropriate cost allocation bases. For example, landlord (or building) services costs were being assigned based on square footage without regard to the nature of the space occupied; this caused secretarial/clerical to be assigned the same square footage cost for very basic building space as was charged to the applied research department, which had much more technically sophisticated space. In effect, secretarial/clerical was subsidizing applied research.[2]

Production and Service Department Costs

In product costing, all manufacturing costs (direct and indirect) ultimately must be assigned to products. Some companies accumulate all overhead costs for an entire plant in a single overhead cost pool and then allocate (reassign) those costs to products using a plantwide overhead rate based on direct labor hours, machine hours, or some other basis. This is sometimes referred to as the "peanut butter" approach that spreads all overhead costs evenly among products based on a general volume-based cost driver without any effort to differentiate among products. This approach results in an accurate product cost measurement if the plant manufactures only one product. However, when a plant utilizes multiple processes to make two or more products, it might be desirable to accumulate overhead costs by production departments to capture the unique overhead cost characteristics of the various production processes. In such cases, product costs are calculated using multiple department overhead rates reflecting the amount of work done on the products in each department.

For example, assume that Mitsubishi Company has a plant that produces both DVD players and VCRs, each of which requires work in two production departments (A and B) but not in the same proportions. Department A is a highly automated department that uses robotics; Department B relies more heavily on manual procedures. DVDs are produced 70 percent in Department A and 30 percent in Department B, and VCRs are produced 40 percent in Department A and 60 percent in Department B. This is a situation in which more accurate product cost measurements are likely to result from using department overhead rates than using a plantwide overhead rate.

In addition to multiple *production* departments, many companies have several production *support* departments such as maintenance, facilities, engineering, and administration. These departments, which provide support services to production and/or other support departments, are called **service departments.** Typically, service department costs are allocated (reassigned) to the production (and/or other service) departments that utilize their services. Production department overhead rates, therefore, include the overhead costs incurred directly by the department plus any allocated service department costs. A **direct department cost** is a cost assigned directly to a department (production or service) when it is incurred; an **indirect department cost** is a cost assigned to a department as a result of an indirect allocation, or reassignment, from another department or cost objective.

---

[2] Edward J. Kovac and Henry P. Troy, "Getting the Transfer Prices Right: What Bellcore Did," *Harvard Business Review,* September–October 1989, pp. 148–54.

SERVICE DEPARTMENT COST ALLOCATION

Service departments (maintenance, administration, security, etc.) provide a wide range of support functions, primarily for one or more production departments. These departments, which are considered essential elements in the overall manufacturing process, do not work directly on the "product" but provide auxiliary support to the producing departments. In addition to providing support for the various producing departments, some service departments also provide services to *other service departments.* For example, the payroll and personnel departments may provide services to all departments, and maintenance may provide services to the producing departments as well as to the medical center and food services. Services provided by one service department to other service departments are called **interdepartment services.**

To illustrate service department cost allocations, consider the Manufacturing Division of Krown Drink Company, which has two producing departments, three service departments, and two products. The service departments and their respective service functions and cost allocation bases are as follows:

LO2 Describe allocation of service department costs, including that for interdepartment services.

Department	Service Functions	Allocation Base
Support Services	Receiving and inventory control	Total amount of department capital investment
Engineering Resources	Production setup and engineering and testing	Number of employees
Building and Grounds	Machinery maintenance and depreciation	Amount of square footage occupied

Difficulty in choosing an allocation base for service department costs is not uncommon. For example, Krown Drink may have readily determined the appropriate allocation bases for the Engineering Resources and the Building and Grounds Departments but may have found the choice for Support Services to be less clear. Perhaps after conducting correlation studies, the most equitable base for allocating Support Services costs to other departments was determined to be total capital investment in the departments because they included expensive computer-tracking equipment, both manual and automated forklifts, and other material moving equipment.

Direct department costs and allocation base information used to illustrate Krown Drink's July service department cost allocations are summarized as follows:

	Direct Department Costs	Number of Employees		Amount of Square Footage Occupied		Total Amount of Department Capital Investment	
Service departments							
Support Services	$ 27,000	15	15%	4,000	8%	—	—
Engineering Resources......	20,000	—	—	2,000	4	$ 45,000	8%
Building and Grounds.......	10,000	5	5	—	—	50,000	9
Producing departments							
Mixing..................	40,000*	24	24	11,000	22	180,000	33
Bottling.................	90,000*	56	56	33,000	66	270,000	50
	$187,000	100	100%	50,000	100%	$545,000	100%

*Direct department overhead

The preceding information omitted the amount of capital investment in the Support Services Department, the number of employees in the Engineering Resources Department, and the amount of square footage used by the Building and Grounds Department. These data were omitted because a department normally does not allocate costs to itself; it allocates costs only to the departments it serves. The three methods commonly used for service department cost allocations—direct, step, and linear algebra—are discussed next.

Direct Method

The **direct method** allocates all service department costs based only on the amount of services provided to the producing departments. Exhibit 19.1 shows the flow of costs using the direct method. All arrows depicting the cost flows extend directly from service departments to producing departments; there are no cost allocations between the service departments.

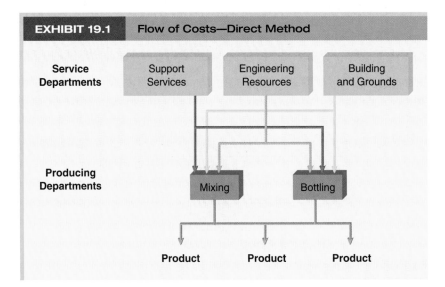

EXHIBIT 19.1	Flow of Costs—Direct Method

Exhibit 19.2 shows the service department cost allocations for the direct method. Notice the allocation base used to allocate Engineering Resources costs; only the employees in the producing departments

EXHIBIT 19.2	Service Department Cost Allocations—Direct Method

	Total	Mixing	Bottling
Support Services Department			
Allocation base (capital investment)........	$450,000	$180,000	$270,000
Percent of total base..................	100%	40%	60%
Cost allocations	$ 27,000	$ 10,800	$ 16,200
Engineering Resources Department			
Allocation base (number of employees)	80	24	56
Percent of total base..................	100%	30%	70%
Cost allocations	$ 20,000	$ 6,000	$ 14,000
Building and Grounds Department			
Allocation base (square footage occupied) ..	44,000	11,000	33,000
Percent of total base..................	100%	25%	75%
Cost allocations	$ 10,000	$ 2,500	$ 7,500

Cost Allocation Summary

	Support Services	Engineering Resources	Building and Grounds	Mixing	Bottling	Total
Department cost before allocations..........	$27,000	$20,000	$10,000	$40,000	$ 90,000	$187,000
Cost allocations						
Support Services.....................	(27,000)			10,800	16,200	—
Engineering Resources................		(20,000)		6,000	14,000	—
Building and Grounds.................			(10,000)	2,500	7,500	—
Department costs after allocations.........	$ 0	$ 0	$ 0	$59,300	$127,700	$187,000

are considered in computing the allocation percentages—24 in Mixing and 56 in Bottling, for a total of 80 employees in the allocation base. Thirty percent (24 ÷ 80) of the producing department employees work in Mixing; therefore, 30 percent of Engineering Resources costs are allocated to Mixing. Applying the same reasoning, 70 percent of Engineering Resources costs are allocated to Bottling. Similar logic is followed in computing the cost allocations for Building and Grounds and Support Services.

The cost allocation summary at the bottom of Exhibit 19.2 shows that all service department costs have been allocated, decreasing the service department costs to zero and increasing the producing department overhead balances by the amounts of the respective allocations. Also, total costs are not affected by the allocations; the total of $187,000 was merely redistributed so that all costs are reassigned to the producing departments. Total department overhead costs of the producing departments after allocation of service costs are $59,300 for Mixing and $127,700 for Bottling.

The advantage of the direct method of allocating service department costs is that it is easy and convenient to use (see the Business Insight that follows). Its primary disadvantage is that it does not recognize the costs for interdepartment services provided by one service department to another. Instead, any costs incurred to provide services to other service departments are passed directly to the producing departments. The step method improves on the allocation procedure by redirecting some of the costs to other service departments before they are finally allocated to the production departments.

BUSINESS INSIGHT   **Cost Allocations for College Services**

Service department cost allocation using the direct method is applied at many colleges. The producing departments of a college are its academic departments and professional schools; its support service departments are those such as student services (which includes housing, dining, and student life activities), facilities management (which is responsible for the physical campus), academic support (such as libraries and computer centers), and administration (such as the president's office, fundraising activities, and the legal department). Commonly used bases for allocating these service department costs are the number of students for student services and academic support, square footage of space occupied for facilities management, and total revenues for administration.

The allocation of these support service costs are often major budget line items in the operating budgets for deans and department heads. These costs greatly affect the amount of money left for direct operating needs such as faculty salaries, research support, and professional development. It is important that the cost allocation method be perceived as fair and appropriate by those whose budgets are charged with these allocated costs. Using the direct allocation method is appropriate in allocating some college service costs, such as student services; it would probably not be appropriate in allocating others, such as computer services, which are used by both academic departments and other service departments.

Step Method

The **step method** gives partial recognition of interdepartmental services by using a methodology that allocates the service department costs *sequentially* both to the remaining service departments and the producing departments. Any indirect costs allocated to a service department in this process are added to that department's direct costs to determine the total costs for allocation to the remaining departments. All service department costs will be assigned to the production departments and ultimately to the products.

To illustrate the problem that can result from using the direct method, assume that Ramso Company has two service departments, S1 and S2, and two producing departments, P1 and P2, that provide services as follows:

Provider of Services......	Receiver of Services			
	S1	S2	P1	P2
S1..............	0%	0%	70%	30%
S2.............	50%	0%	25%	25%

If the direct method is used to allocate service department costs to the producing departments, S2 total costs will be allocated equally to the producing departments because they use the same amount of S2 services (25 percent each). Is this an equitable allocation of S2 costs? S2 actually provides half of its services to the other service department (S1), which, in turn, provides the majority of its services to P1. Assume that S2 has total direct department costs of $100,000. If the direct method is used to allocate service department costs, the entire $100,000 will be divided equally among the two producing departments, each being allocated $50,000, with no allocation to S1.

	S1	S2	P1	P2
Direct allocation of S2 to P1 and P2	$0	$(100,000)	$50,000	$50,000

Consider the following alternative allocation of the $100,000 of S2 costs that takes into account inter-department services. First, 25 percent, or $25,000, is allocated to each of the producing departments, and 50 percent, or $50,000, is allocated to S1. Next, the $50,000 allocated to S1 from S2 is reallocated to the producing departments in proportion to the amount of services provided to them by S1: 70 percent and 30 percent, respectively. In this scenario, the $100,000 of S2 costs is ultimately allocated $60,000 to P1 and $40,000 to P2 as follows:

	S1	S2	P1	P2
Step 1:				
Allocate S2 costs to S1, P1, and P2....	$50,000	$(100,000)	$25,000	$25,000
Step 2:				
Reallocate S1 costs to P1 and P2	(50,000)	0	35,000	15,000
Total allocation of S2				
costs via step method	$ 0	$ 0	$60,000	$40,000

This calculation shows only the ultimate allocation of S2 costs. Of course, any S1 direct department costs would also have to be allocated to P1 and P2 on a 70:30 basis. If interdepartmental services are ignored, P1 is allocated only $50,000 of S2 costs; by considering interdepartment services, P1 is allocated $60,000. Certainly, a more accurate measure of both the direct and indirect services received by P1 from S2 is $60,000, not $50,000.

As long as all producing departments use approximately the same percentage of services of each service department, the direct method provides a reasonably accurate cost assignment. In this example, the percentages of services used by the producing departments were quite different: 70 percent and 30 percent for S1, and 50 percent and 50 percent for S2. In such situations, the direct method can result in significantly different allocations.

The step method is illustrated graphically in Exhibit 19.3 for the Krown Drink Company. Notice the sequence of the allocations: Engineering Resources, Support Services, and Building and Grounds.

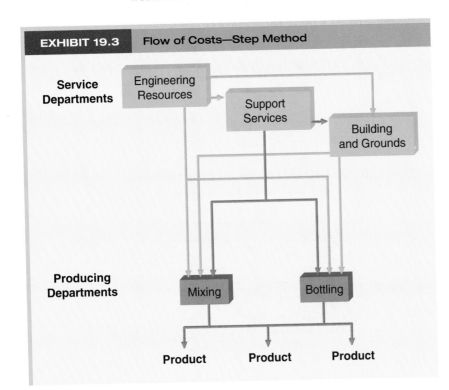

EXHIBIT 19.3 Flow of Costs—Step Method

When using the step method, the sequence of allocation is typically based on the relative percentage of services provided to other service departments, with the largest provider of interdepartment services allocated first and the smallest provider of interdepartment services allocated last. For Krown Drink, Engineering Resources is allocated first because, of the three service departments, it provides the largest percentage (20 percent) of its services to other service departments: 15 percent to Support Services and 5 percent to Building and Grounds (see previous cost allocation data). Building and Grounds is allocated last because it provides the least amount (12 percent) of its services to other service departments: 8 percent to Support Services and 4 percent to Engineering Resources. The service department cost allocations for Krown Drink using the step method are shown in Exhibit 19.4.

EXHIBIT 19.4	Service Department Cost Allocations—Step Method				
	Total	Support Services	Building and Grounds	Mixing	Bottling
Engineering Resources Department					
Allocation base (number of employees)	100	15	5	24	56
Percent of total base.	100%	15%	5%	24%	56%
Cost allocations	$20,000	$3,000	$1,000	$4,800	$11,200
Support Services Department					
Allocation base (capital investment)	$500,000		$50,000	$180,000	$270,000
Percent of total base.	100%		10%	36%	54%
Cost allocations	$30,000 ←		$3,000	$10,800	$16,200
Building and Grounds Department					
Allocation base (square footage occupied) .	44,000			11,000	33,000
Percent of total base.	100%			25%	75%
Cost allocations	$14,000 ←			$3,500	$10,500

Cost Allocation Summary						
	Engineering Resources	Support Services	Building and Grounds	Mixing	Bottling	Total
Department costs before allocations	$ 20,000	$ 27,000	$ 10,000	$40,000	$ 90,000	$187,000
Cost allocations						
Engineering Resources	(20,000)	3,000	1,000	4,800	11,200	—
Support Services.		(30,000)←	3,000	10,800	16,200	—
Building and Grounds			(14,000)	3,500	10,500	—
Department costs after allocations.	$ 0	$ 0	$ 0	$59,100	$127,900	$187,000

Linear Algebra (Reciprocal) Method

The disadvantage of the step method is that it provides only partial recognition of interdepartment services. For Krown Drink, the step method recognizes Engineering Resources services provided to the other two service departments; however, no services received by Engineering Resources from the other two departments are recognized. Similarly, services from Support Services to Building and Grounds are recognized, but not the reverse. To achieve the most mathematically accurate service department cost allocation, there should be full recognition of services between service departments as well as between service and producing departments. This requires using the linear algebra method, sometimes called the *reciprocal method*. The **linear algebra (reciprocal) method** uses a series of linear algebraic equations, which are solved simultaneously, to allocate service department costs both interdepartmentally and to the producing departments. This method is illustrated graphically in Exhibit 19.5 for a company that has two service departments and two producing departments. The cost allocation arrows run from each service department to the other service department as well as to the producing departments. Further discussion of this method can be found in Cost Accounting texts. Whether a company should use the direct method, step method, or linear algebra method depends on the extensiveness of interdepartment services and how evenly services are used by the producing departments.

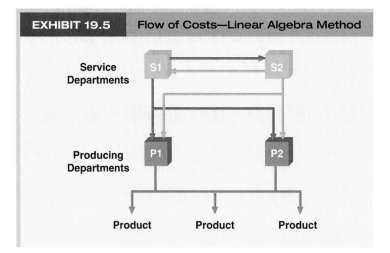

EXHIBIT 19.5 **Flow of Costs—Linear Algebra Method**

Dual Rates

When pooling costs for subsequent reassignment or allocation, it can be useful to provide separate pools for fixed costs and variable costs. This will result in cost allocations that more accurately reflect the factors that drive costs. The capacity provided most often drives fixed costs, whereas some type of actual activity usually drives variable costs. Dual rates involve establishing separate bases for allocating fixed and variable costs. Dual rates may be used for one or all service departments, depending on the size and nature of the costs in each service department. They may also be used in conjunction with the direct, step, or linear algebra methods.

It is important to remember the relationship between capacity and cost when selecting the allocation method. Total variable costs change as activity changes. Fixed costs, however, are the same whether the activity is at or below capacity. Fixed costs should usually be allocated based on the relative capacity provided the benefiting department, while variable costs should be allocated on the basis of actual usage. The allocation methods and bases also may be different for variable and fixed costs.

Fixed costs based on capacity provided eliminates the possibility that the amount of the cost allocation to one department is affected by the level of services utilized by other departments. When fixed service department costs are allocated based on the capacity provided to the user department, managers of the user departments are charged for that capacity whether they use it or not, and their use of services has no effect on the amount of costs allocated to other departments. A benefit of this allocation system is that it reduces the temptation for managers to avoid or delay services to minimize fixed cost allocations to their departments. Dual rates are examined in more detail in most cost accounting texts.

MID-MODULE REVIEW

Cotswald's Clothiers Inc. is organized into four departments: Women's Apparel, Men's Apparel, Administrative Services, and Facilities Services. The first two departments are the primary producing departments; the last two departments provide services to the producing departments as well as to each other. Top management has decided that, for internal reporting purposes, the cost of service department operations should be allocated to the producing departments. Administrative Services costs are allocated on the basis of the number of employees, and Facilities Services costs are allocated based on the amount of square footage of floor space occupied. Data pertaining to the cost allocations for February 2007 are as follows:

Department	Direct Department Cost	Number of Employees	Square Footage Occupied
Women's Apparel	$ 60,000	15	15,000
Men's Apparel.	50,000	9	7,500
Administrative Services	18,000	3	2,500
Facilities	12,000	2	1,000
Total	$140,000	29	26,000

Required

a. Determine the amount of service department costs to be allocated to the producing departments under both the *direct method* and the *step method* of service department cost allocation.

b. Discuss the *linear algebra method* of service department cost allocation, explaining circumstances when it should be considered over the direct and step methods.

c. Should Cotswald's Clothier Inc. consider using the linear algebra method?

Solution

Service Department Cost Allocation

a. *Direct Method*

	Total	Women's	Men's
Administrative Services Department			
Allocation base (number of employees)	24	15	9
Percent of total base.	100%	62.5%	37.5%
Cost allocation	$18,000	$11,250	$6,750
Facilities Services Department			
Allocation base (square footage)	22,500	15,000	7,500
Percent of total base.	100%	66.7%	33.3%
Cost allocation	$12,000	$ 8,000	$4,000

Cost Allocation Summary

	Administrative	Facilities	Women's	Men's	Total
Departmental costs before allocation	$18,000	$12,000	$60,000	$50,000	$140,000
Cost allocations					
Administrative	(18,000)	—	11,250	6,750	0
Facilities	—	(12,000)	8,000	4,000	0
Departmental costs after allocation	$ 0	$ 0	$79,250	$60,750	$140,000

Step Method

Allocation Sequence

	Administrative	Facilities
Allocation base.	Number of employees	Amount of square footage
Total base for other service and producing departments (a)	26	25,000
Total base for other service departments (b)	2	2,500
Percent of total services provided to other service departments (b ÷ a)	7.7%	10.0%
Order of allocation	Second	First

Step Allocations

	Total	Administrative	Women's	Men's
Facilities Services Department				
Allocation base (square footage)	25,000	2,500	15,000	7,500
Percent of total base.	100%	10%	60%	30%
Cost allocation	$12,000	$1,200	$ 7,200	$3,600
Administrative Services Department				
Allocation base (number of employees)	24	—	15	9
Percent of total base.	100%	—	62.5%	37.5%
Cost allocation ($18,000 + 1,200)	$19,200	—	$12,000	$7,200

Cost Allocation Summary

	Facilities	Administrative	Women's	Men's	Total
Departmental costs before allocation	$12,000	$18,000	$60,000	$50,000	$140,000
Cost allocations					
Facilities	(12,000)	1,200	7,200	3,600	0
Administrative.	—	(19,200)	12,000	7,200	0
Departmental costs after allocations	$ 0	$ 0	$79,200	$60,800	$140,000

b. Another service department cost allocation method is the *linear algebra method*. This method simultaneously allocates service department costs both to other service departments and to the producing departments. It has an advantage over the *step method* in that it fully recognizes interdepartmental services.

c. If Cotswald's Clothiers wants the most precise allocation of service department costs to the producing departments, considering both direct services and indirect services, it must use the linear algebra method of service department allocation. As indicated in the Allocation sequence section of the step method in (a), Facilities provides 10 percent of its services to Administrative, and Administrative provides 7.7 percent of its services to Facilities. The step method recognized the Facilities services provided to Administrative, but it did not recognize the Administrative services provided to Facilities.

In this case, the producing departments are using approximately the same proportion of services from each of the service departments (60.0 percent to 62.5 percent for the Women's Department and 30.0 percent to 37.5 percent for the Men's Department). Hence, using a more precise measure of cost allocation is not likely to produce significantly different results, especially since the interdepartmental services are so close (7.7 percent versus 10.0 percent). Just as the step method allocation results were quite close to the direct method results, the linear method results would likely be quite close to both the direct and step method results. Use of the linear algebra method is not recommended in this case. On the basis of simplicity and convenience, the direct method is probably the best method for Cotswald's to use.

ACTIVITY-BASED COSTING (ABC)

LO3 Compare and contrast activity-based costing (ABC) and traditional costing systems.

The manufacturing overhead cost pool has been referred to as a "blob" of common costs. The constant growth of costs classified as overhead has forced us to search for increasingly detailed methods to analyze these costs. If overhead costs are low in comparison with other costs and if factories produce few products in large production runs, the use of an overhead rate based on direct labor hours or machine hours may be adequate. However, as the amount of overhead costs continues to grow, as manufacturing facilities produce a wider variety of products, and as competition intensifies, the inadequacies of a single overhead rate become evident. These conditions shift attention to ways to improve overhead rates and the reassignment of service department costs. One method often used to improve product costing is to adopt multiple department overhead rates, as mentioned earlier in this module.

Fortunately, advances in information technology and the declining costs of computerized information systems have facilitated the development and maintenance of increasingly detailed databases. These and other factors (such as declining inventory levels that make product costing less significant for financial reporting) have led to the emergence and continuing development of activity-based costing.

Activity-based costing (ABC) involves determining the cost of activities and tracing their costs to cost objectives on the basis of the cost objective's utilization of units of activity.

The concepts underlying ABC can be summarized in the following two statements and illustrations:

1. Activities performed to fill customer needs consume resources that cost money.

2. The cost of resources consumed by activities should be assigned to cost objectives on the basis of the units of activity consumed by the cost objective.

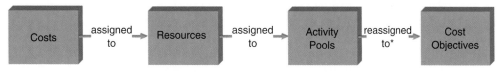

*Based on units of activity utilized by the cost objective.

The cost objective is typically a product or service provided to a customer. Depending on the information needs of decision makers, the cost objective might be the customer. The following Business Insight describes how a soap manufacturer with 5,000 different products used ABC to manage costs and profits.

BUSINESS INSIGHT   Soap Manufacturer Cleans Up with ABC

Original Bradford Soap Works is a manufacturer of 5,000 private-label soap products. A combination of the following factors brought the company to a crisis point several years ago: an increased variety of products, an increased volume of all product types, new customers with unique service requirements, and full production capacity of current plant facilities. Within this setting, the company decided to fully integrate ABC into its financial and management reporting system. It developed an ABC database of cost pools and cost drivers, and then it recast the general ledger to match this database so that the cost estimates being used to make management decisions would correspond to those reflected in the financial reports of operations.

The result was a management accounting system that tracked the job costs of products based on activities used to produce the products. Managers started using the ABC system for bidding new products since it provided them with detailed estimates of activities and expected costs needed to manufacture the proposed products. Bradford's ABC system has provided the flexibility to organize data into useful information to "identify products and customers that provide an optimal mix of business to ensure long-term profitability." The new system helped employees identify opportunities for improvement on the plant floor, reinforcing the total quality process.[3]

To summarize, activity-based costing involves determining the cost of activities and then tracing these costs to cost objectives on the basis of the cost objectives' utilization of units of activity. It is based on the premise that activities drive costs and that costs should be assigned to products (or other cost objectives) in proportion to the volume of activities they consume. Applied to product costing, ABC traces costs to products on the basis of the activities used to produce them.

---

[3] Frances Gammell and C. J. McNair, "Jumping the Growth Threshold Through Activity-Based Cost Management," *Management Accounting,* September 1994, pp. 37–46.

ABC Product Costing Model

Traditional costing considers the cost of a product to be its direct costs for materials and labor plus some allocated portion of factory overhead, using plantwide or departments overhead rates typically based on direct labor or machine hours. Activity-based costing is based on the notion that companies incur costs because of the activities they conduct in pursuit of their goals and objectives. For example, various activities take place to produce a particular product, such as setting up, maintaining, or monitoring the machines to make the product, physically moving raw materials and work in process, and so forth. Each of these activities has a cost; therefore, the total cost of producing a product using ABC is the sum of the direct materials and direct labor costs of that product, plus the cost of other activities conducted to produce that product.

The general two-stage ABC product cost model is illustrated in Exhibit 19.6. The first stage includes the assignment of resource costs, such as indirect labor, depreciation, utilities, and so on, to activity cost pools for the key activities identified. The second stage includes the assignment of those activity cost pools to products or other ultimate cost objectives. In Exhibit 19.6, costs are assigned to activity pools from the various accounts of departments that incurred the costs; hence, the costs in a particular activity pool may have been incurred in one of several different departments.

It may be possible to directly assign certain resource costs to a cost objective. The cost of lumber might be directly assigned to a house. Other costs, such as the cost of the contractor's supervisor, may be assigned to various activity pools based on the amount of time the supervisor spends supervising the various activities. Notice in Exhibit 19.6 that direct product costs, such as direct materials and direct labor, are directly assigned to products and are excluded from the activity cost pools. Only indirect product costs (manufacturing overhead) are assigned to products via activity cost pools. (In highly automated companies, direct labor is often small; thus, it is not treated as a direct cost. Instead, it is pooled with related activity costs and allocated to products.)

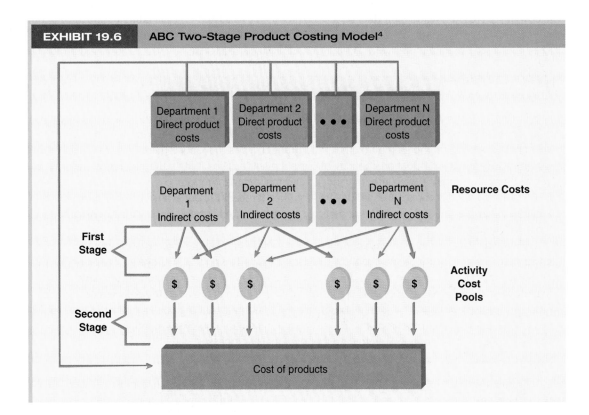

EXHIBIT 19.6	ABC Two-Stage Product Costing Model[4]

Probably the most critical step in ABC is identifying cost drivers. The activity cost driver for a particular cost (or cost pool) is the characteristic selected for measuring the quantity of the activity for a particular period of time. For example, if an activity cost pool is established for machine setup, it is necessary

---

[4] Adapted from Gary Cokins, Alan Stratton, and Jack Helbling, *An ABC Manager's Primer* (Montvale, NJ: Institute of Management Accountants, 1993).

to select some basis for measuring the quantity of machine setup activity associated with the costs in the pool. The quantity of setup activity could be measured by the number of different times machines are set up to produce a different product, the amount of time used in completing machine setups, the number of staff working on setups, or some other measure. It is critical that the activity measure used has a logical causal relationship to the costs in the pool and that the quantity of the activity is highly correlated with the amount of cost in the pool. Statistical methods, such as regression analysis and correlation analysis, can be very useful in selecting activity cost drivers.

Once the total cost in the activity pool and the activity cost driver have been determined, the cost per unit of activity is calculated as the total cost divided by the total amount of activity. For example, if total costs assigned to the setup activity pool in July is $100,000 and 200 setups were completed in July, the cost per setup for the month is $500. If during July machines were set up 10 times to make product JX2, the total setup cost that would be assigned to product JX2 would be $5,000 ($500 × 10).

Comparing Traditional and Activity-Based Costing

Procedurally, ABC is not a new method for assigning costs to cost objectives. Traditional costing systems have used a two-stage allocation model (similar to the ABC model) to assign costs to cost pools (such as departments) and subsequently assign those cost pools to products using an allocation base. In most traditional costing systems, overhead is assigned to one or more cost pools based on departments and functional characteristics (such as labor-related, machine-related, and space-related costs) and then reassigned to products using a general allocation base such as direct labor hours or machine hours. ABC is different in that it divides the overall manufacturing processes into activities. ABC accumulates costs in cost pools for the major activities and then assigns the costs of these activities to products or other cost objectives that benefit from these activities. *Conceptually,* ABC is different because of the way it views the operations of the company; *procedurally,* it uses a methodology that has been around for a long time.

The challenge in using ABC is specifying the model, that is, determining how many activity pools should be established for a given cost measurement purpose, which costs should be assigned to each activity pool, and the appropriate activity driver for each pool. Specifying the model also includes determining the resource cost drivers for assigning indirect resource costs to the various activity cost pools.

The following three scenarios help illustrate the differences between activity-based and traditional costing systems.

1. Using traditional allocation, maintenance department costs are typically allocated to production departments based on the number of repair orders or the number of service hours associated with repairs made in each production department. These costs become a part of the production department overhead rates used for assigning cost to products. Using ABC, the organization would attempt to determine whether maintenance is a key activity that can be associated with products based on an activity cost driver. For instance, in a job cost system, it might be possible to identify the maintenance activity costs associated with each job by measuring the maintenance service hours (the activity driver) used while each job was in production. Alternatively, the resource costs associated with the maintenance department might be assigned to other activity cost pools, such as setup costs, processing costs, and finishing costs, all of which are subsequently assigned to products based on the activity cost drivers for those cost pools.

2. In a traditional allocation system, purchasing department costs may be allocated to production departments based on the dollar value of raw materials issued to each department. Using ABC, the purchasing activity might represent a key activity that is assigned to products using an activity cost driver such as the dollar value of the materials used in producing a given amount of product. Alternatively, if purchasing consists of three key activities (processing, follow-up on purchase orders, and processing receipt of ordered goods), a cost pool for each of these activities is assigned to products using a separate activity cost driver. For example, processing could be assigned using the number of purchase orders as the cost driver, follow-up costs could be assigned based on the number of parts per product, and the cost of processing receipt of goods could be assigned to products based on the dollar value of the raw materials used to make the product.

3. A traditional cost system allocates service department costs first to the producing departments using the direct, step, or linear algebra method. Total overhead costs of the producing

departments (*direct department overhead costs* plus allocated *indirect department overhead costs*) are combined and allocated to products using a single cost driver for each department, such as labor hours or machine hours. In its purest form, ABC assigns all overhead costs from both service and production departments to products using ABC. Another possibility is to use ABC to assign service department costs to production departments, with subsequent assignment of production departments' costs to products, also using ABC. Often companies combine traditional costing and ABC, making some cost assignments using traditional methods and others using ABC. For example, service department costs (1) are assigned to production departments using ABC, with subsequent allocation of production department costs to products using a single department overhead rate, or (2) are allocated to production departments using a traditional allocation method, with subsequent allocation of production department costs to products using ABC.

Several important conclusions about activity-based costing emerge from the preceding discussion:

- ABC normally uses more cost pools than traditional allocation methods use.

- ABC does not use the established departmental structure for pooling costs unless that structure happens to coincide with key activities for which appropriate activity cost drivers can be determined.

- Although traditional costing procedures generally attempt to find causal bases for cost allocation, ABC insists even more on the use of causal factors in assigning costs based on activity cost "drivers."

- By definition, ABC assigns costs based on their activity cost drivers, and if cost drivers cannot be identified and measured, ABC cannot be used to assign those costs. In these cases, if full allocation of costs is required (such as for financial reporting purposes), a traditional cost allocation approach must be used.

- Implementation of ABC requires an understanding of the production process, the activities that occur in the production process, and the cost drivers that generate the costs of those activities. Hence, a team approach is useful in designing and implementing an ABC system. The team typically includes accountants, engineers, production personnel, and information systems specialists.

- Implementation and operation of ABC requires the use of judgment in identifying key activities, determining which costs should be assigned to each activity cost pool, and identifying the cost drivers for allocating each cost pool. Making these judgments is often based on observation and interviews with personnel involved in the various processes and activities. Resorting to "most common practice" is not acceptable in ABC; each application must be tailored to the specific situation—and that requires using judgement.

TRADITIONAL AND ABC PRODUCT COSTING ILLUSTRATED

LO4 Compute overhead rates under three methods based on plantwide, department, or activity-based rates.

This section illustrates for Krown Drink Company three approaches to factory overhead cost allocation using a plantwide rate, department rates, and ABC rates. The plantwide rate system is the simplest to apply but provides the least precise allocation of cost; ABC is the most complex system and provides the most precise allocation of costs.

Applying Overhead with Plantwide Rates

Recall that Krown produces two products, a carbonated drink and a fruit drink, in two departments, Mixing and Bottling. Assume that the most common element of all products is machine hours in both Mixing and Bottling. Carbonated drink takes 3 machine hours per barrel and Fruit drink takes 2 machine hours per barrel. For July, Krown Drink produced 232 barrels of Carbonated drink and 400 barrels of Fruit drink. If the total manufacturing overhead of $187,000 is divided by total machine hours of 1,496, the plantwide overhead rate will be $125 per hour. This is the simplest method and provides a total cost per unit (barrel) of $610 for Carbonated and $400 for Fruit.

	Unit Costs	
	Carbonated	**Fruit**
Direct materials	$125	$120
Direct labor...............................	110	30
Manufacturing overhead		
Carbonated: 3 machine hours × $125.........	375	
Fruit: 2 machine hours × $125..............		250
Total unit cost.............................	$610	$400

A plantwide overhead allocation method is often used in situations where companies produce only one product in a plant, or where multiple products are very similar in regard to the use of activities, such as machine or labor hours, that drive most of the overhead costs. If multiple products are produced that consume varying levels of activities in multiple production departments, departmental overhead allocation rates will produce a more accurate allocation of overhead costs to the various products.

Applying Overhead with Department Rates

For Krown Drink to establish overhead allocation rates for the two production departments, it is necessary first to assign the $187,000 of total overhead costs for the plant to the two production departments. Some of the $187,000 is directly assignable to the departments. For example, the departmental supervisors' salaries could be directly assignable to the departments. Assume that service department costs for support services, engineering services, and buildings and grounds are allocated to the production departments using the step method discussed earlier in this module (see Exhibit 19.4), and after service department costs were allocated, the total departmental costs for Mixing and Bottling were $59,100 for Mixing and $127,900 for Bottling.

Once service department costs are allocated to the producing departments, the next step in the product costing process is to apply those costs to the next level of cost objectives. Assume that the manufacturing process at Krown Drink is labor intensive in Mixing and machine intensive in Bottling and that manufacturing overhead is applied to products as follows:

Department	Manufacturing Overhead Application Base
Mixing	Direct labor hours
Bottling	Machine hours

During the month of July, 500 direct labor hours were worked in Mixing, and Bottling used 800 machine hours. The department manufacturing overhead rates based on actual costs for July are calculated as follows:

Overhead costs per unit for July	Mixing	Bottling
Total department manufacturing overhead (direct department costs plus allocated costs).........	$59,100	$127,900
Quantity of overhead application base		
Direct labor hours...............................	÷ 500	
Machine hours		÷ 800
Department manufacturing overhead rates	$118.20	$159.875
	Per direct labor hour	Per machine hour

Total costs per unit for July using department rates	Unit Costs per Barrel	
	Carbonated	Fruit
Direct materials	$125	$120
Direct labor	110	30
Manufacturing overhead		
Mixing: 1 labor hr. × $118.20	118*	
0.67 labor hrs. × $118.20		79*
Bottling: 1 machine hr. × $159.875	160*	
1.42 machine hrs. × $159.875		227*
Total costs	$513	$456

*Rounded

Allocating factory overhead costs based on department rates (rather than on a plantwide rate of $125 per machine hour) causes a shift in costs from Carbonated to Fruit drinks because Carbonated's overhead activity is incurred evenly in both Mixing and Bottling (1.00 hour each) while Fruit incurs more of its overhead activity in Bottling (1.42 hours versus 0.67 hour).

The per-unit costs with multiple allocations are substantially different from the per-unit costs when using plantwide rates and, in fact, show the cost of carbonated beverages to be slightly below a competitor's bid of $525 that was offered to one of Krown's customers. Based on the plantwide rate, the cost of $610 for carbonated was higher than the competitor's price.

By creating separate manufacturing overhead cost allocation pools, allocation bases, and overhead application rates for Mixing and Bottling, it is possible to recognize overhead cost differences in various products based on differences in Mixing Department labor hours used and Bottling Department machine hours used for each product. In most multiproduct manufacturing environments, this approach represents a cost system improvement over using a single, plantwide overhead rate, and it reduces the likelihood of cost cross-subsidization, which occurs when one product is assigned too much cost as a result of another being assigned too little cost. While department overhead rates may improve product costing results for many organizations, and in fact may be satisfactory, this method does not attempt to reflect the actual activities used in producing the different product.

Applying Overhead with Activity-Based Costing

An even more precise method of measuring the cost of products than plantwide or departmental rates is the activity-based costing method. As stated earlier, activity-based costing involves determining the cost of activities associated with a particular cost objective. ABC for product costing identifies and measures the cost of activities used to produce the various products and sums the cost of those activities to determine the cost of the products.

For Krown Drink, Mixing and Bottling have overhead costs of $59,100 and $127,900, respectively. The overhead rates for each department were determined in the last section as $118.20 and $159.875, respectively, per relevant hour of use. The easiest way to assign these costs to products is by using one base and one rate for all products going through a given process (e.g., mixing). However, different products typically use different amounts of resources from a given process and using the same base and overhead rate for all may distort the cost for some or all products.

Krown's accountants determined that the *direct* department overhead costs in Mixing were driven primarily by labor hours, whereas *direct* department overhead costs in Bottling were driven primarily by machine hours. It was also determined that each component of engineering, support, and building and grounds represents a separate activity cost pool and that these costs should be assigned to the products based on specific cost drivers.

The following is a detailed analysis of overhead cost data for July's operations:

Overhead Activity	Total Activity Cost	Activity Cost Driver (number of)	Quantity of Activity	Unit Activity Rates
Direct departmental overhead costs				
Mixing	$ 40,000	Labor hours	500	$ 80.00
Bottling	90,000	Machine hours	800	112.50
Common overhead costs				
Support Services				
Receiving.	14,000	Purchase orders	100	140.00
Inventory control	13,000	Units produced.	632	20.57*
Engineering Resources				
Production setup.	12,000	Production runs	20	600.00
Engineering and testing	8,000	Machine hours	800	10.00
Building and Grounds				
Maintenance, machines	4,000	Machine hours	800	5.00
Depreciation, machines.	6,000	Units produced.	632	9.49*
Total	$187,000			

*Rounded

The amounts of activity attributed to Carbonated and Fruit drinks and the factory overhead cost per unit based on ABC costs are as follows:

Activity (cost per unit of driver activity)	Carbonated Quantity of Activity	Carbonated Cost of Activity	Fruit Quantity of Activity	Fruit Cost of Activity
Mixing ($80.00 per labor hour)	232	$18,560	268	$ 21,440
Bottling ($112.50 per machine hour)	174	19,575	626	70,425
Receiving ($140.00 per order)	40	5,600	60	8,400
Inventory control ($20.57 per unit produced)	232	4,772*	400	8,228
Production setup ($600.00 per run)	5	3,000	15	9,000
Engineering and testing ($10.00 per machine hour)	174	1,740	626	6,260
Maintenance, machines ($5.00 per machine hour)	174	870	626	3,130
Depreciation, machines ($9.49 per unit produced)	232	2,202*	400	3,796
Total factory overhead product cost.		$56,319		$130,679
Units produced.		÷ 232		÷ 400
Factory overhead cost per unit of product*		$ 243*		$327*
Direct materials cost per unit of product		125		120
Direct labor cost per unit of product		110		30
Total unit product cost using ABC		$ 478		$ 477

*Rounded

ABC costing of Krown Drink's products presents a very different cost picture from plantwide or departmental costing. The following table summarizes the total product costs for Krown's two products using the three different overhead cost assignment methods:

	Carbonated	Fruit
Plantwide overhead rate............	$610	$400
Departmental overhead rates........	513	456
ABC	478	477

Obviously, the effect of adopting ABC is not always as significant as it was for Krown Drink in this example. However, even with less dramatic differences among the various cost methods, inaccurate costing can affect management's assessment of product profitability and its decisions regarding which products to continue to produce and which products to discontinue. Flawed product costing information can cause management mistakenly to decide to keep products that are losing money, while discontinuing products that are profitable. Using a plantwide overhead allocation method could have led Krown Management to shift its emphasis from Carbonated Drink to Fruit Drink, a decision that could have been devastating to the company.

MANAGERIAL DECISION   **You are the Controller**

You have heard about companies that have adopted ABC and experienced significant differences in product costs compared with previous costs calculations using traditional costing methods. Consequently, you were surprised when your newly implemented ABC system provided product costs that were almost identical to those from the old costing system. You are, therefore, thinking about abandoning the ABC system, since it is quite costly to maintain. Should you abandon your ABC system?

[Answer, p. 19-26]

Limitations of ABC Illustration

Several limitations of the Krown Drink illustration should be mentioned. For the sake of simplicity, the example was limited to manufacturing cost considerations. A complete analysis would also require considerations of nonmanufacturing costs, such as marketing, distribution, and customer service, before a final determination of product profitability could be made. Also, the illustrated costs represent mainly unit- and batch-level costs, with limited product-level (engineering and testing) and facility-level (maintenance and depreciation) costs. Most organizations have additional cost categories that must be considered. Finally, in calculating the activity cost per unit of activity, it is necessary to decide how to measure the total quantity of activity. For example, for Krown Drink, the receiving cost per purchase order was calculated as $140.00 based on the actual quantity of 100 purchase orders for the period. Alternatively, the receiving cost could have been calculated based on **practical capacity,** which is the maximum possible volume of activity, while allowing for normal downtime for repairs and maintenance. If the plant has a practical capacity to prepare 140 purchase orders per period, the cost per purchase order based on the practical capacity is $100 per purchase order, or $14,000 ÷ 140. Using this overhead rate in costing product, only $10,000 would have been assigned to Carbonated and Fruit Drink, which required only 100 purchase orders, and the remaining $4,000 for the 40 purchase orders of excess (or idle) capacity not used would be written off as an operating expense of the period as underapplied overhead. Practical capacity is generally regarded as better than actual capacity for calculating activity costs because it does not hide the cost of idle capacity within product costs, and it gives a truer cost of the activities used to produce the product.

ABC IMPLEMENTATION ISSUES

L05 Describe the implementation of an activity-based costing system.

The distortions in product costs for Krown Drink from using traditional cost systems based on plantwide or departmental rates, while hypothetical, is not uncommon. Studies have shown that distortions of this type occur regularly in traditional systems in which a significant variation exists in the volume and complexity of products and services produced.[5] Traditional systems tend to overcost high-volume, low-complexity

[5] Gary Cokins, Alan Stratton, and Jack Helbling, *An ABC Manager's Primer* (Montvale, NJ: Institute of Management Accountants, 1993).

products, and they tend to undercost low-volume, high-complexity products. These studies indicate that the typical amount of overcosting is up to 200 percent for high-volume products with low complexity and that the typical undercosting can be more than 1,000 percent for low-volume, highly complex products. In companies with a large number of different products, traditional costing can show that most products are profitable. After changing to ABC, however, these companies might find that 10 to 15 percent of the products are profitable while the remainder are unprofitable. Adopting ABC often leads to increased profits merely by changing the product mix to minimize the number of unprofitable products.

Most companies initially do not abandon their traditional cost system and move to a system that uses ABC for management and financial reporting purposes because financial statements must withstand the scrutiny of auditors and tax authorities. This scrutiny typically implies more demands on the cost accounting system for consistency, objectivity, and uniformity than required when the system is used only for management purposes. In addition, ABC systems must be built facility by facility rather than being embedded in a software program that can be used by all facilities within the company.[6] Most companies maintain traditional costing for external reporting purposes and ABC for pricing and other internal decision-making purposes.

Once an ABC system has been developed for a production facility, including an activities list (sometimes called an activities dictionary), identification of activity cost drivers, and calculation of cost per unit of driver activity, the activity costs of a current or proposed product can be readily determined. In ABC, as illustrated for Krown Drink, manufacturing a product is viewed simply as the combination of activities selected to make it; therefore, the activity cost of a product or service is the sum of the costs of those activities. This approach to viewing a product enables management to evaluate the importance of each of the activities consumed in making a product. Possibly some activities can be eliminated or a lower cost activity substituted for a more costly one without reducing the quality or performance of the product. The Coca-Cola Company used ABC to determine that it was less costly—and thus, more profitable—to deliver soft drink concentrate to some fountain drink retailers (such as fast-food restaurants) in nonreturnable, disposable containers rather than in returnable stainless steel containers, which had been standard in the industry for many years.

Although an ABC system may be complex, it merely mirrors the complexity of an organization's design, manufacturing, and distribution systems. If a firm's products are diverse and its production and distribution procedures complex, the ABC system will also be complex; however, if its products are homogeneous and its production environment relatively simple, its ABC system should also be relatively simple. Even in highly complex manufacturing environments, ABC systems usually have no more than 10 to 20 cost pools. Many ABC experts in practice have observed that creating a large number of activity cost pools for a given costing application normally does not significantly improve cost accuracy above that of a smaller number of cost pools. As with any information system design, the costs of developing and maintaining the system must not exceed its benefits; hence, although adding more activity cost pools may result in some small amount of increased accuracy, it may be so small as not to be cost effective. The Business Insight that follows lists ten practical tips when implementing an ABC system.

ABC is not just a product costing system used to provide data for external financial reports. If that were its only use, its cost of implementation would seldom be justifiable. ABC's primary benefit is that it provides more accurate cost data for internal decision-making purposes. Companies that sell virtually everything they produce obviously have little or no inventories. Consequently, they do not need a product costing system for external reporting purposes because all manufacturing costs are expensed as cost of goods sold each period. However, even these companies need a good cost system for evaluating product profitability, tracking changes in costs over time, and benchmarking against their competitors.

Using ABC information to better manage business processes and activities is the essence of **Activity-Based Management (ABM)**, which is defined as the identification and selection of activities to maximize the value of activities while minimizing their cost from the perspective of the final consumer. In other words, ABM is concerned with how to efficiently and effectively manage activities and processes to provide value to the final consumer. Even if adopting an ABC product costing model does not produce a significant difference in the calculation of product costs, ABC, coupled with ABM, provides a powerful model for improving the management of the activities of an organization.

In addition to using ABC for product costing purposes, other important uses for ABC have also been found. One of the most useful applications for ABC is in evaluating customer costs and distribution channel costs. Other applications include costing administrative functions such as processing accounts

---

[6] Robert S. Kaplan and Robin Cooper, *Cost and Effect* (Boston: Harvard Business School Press, 1998), p. 105.

BUSINESS INSIGHT	Top Ten Tips for Implementing ABC

An expert offered ten tips to design and install an ABC system:[7]

1. *Capture attention of top management.* ABC represents a substantial change that must be driven and supported by top management.
2. *Don't shoot the customer.* If ABC reveals that a group of customers is unprofitable, a top priority must be to find a way to meet the needs of those customers, even if it means finding another supplier for the customer.
3. *Decide the form ABC will take.* Will it be a special study, a decision model, or a real-time system?
4. *Supplement ABC measures creatively when appropriate.* Other measures such as bottleneck accounting and value-added analysis can supplement ABC for managerial decisions.
5. *Take care in costing bottlenecks that create excess capacity.* Pricing at full capacity cost could result in underpricing with possible end-game results, and pricing at current utilization can lead to a death spiral by overpricing.
6. *Challenge managers who believe their costs are fixed.* In the long run, virtually all costs are avoidable.
7. *Compute costs top-down and bottom-up.* Costs should be calculated based on both individual activities within a process (bottom-up) and the total process (top-down) as a check back to the accounting system.
8. *Account for cost of capital.* Although traditional accounting does not consider costs of capital, modern management should include these opportunity costs in decision making.
9. *Use multi-functional teams.* Empowered multi-functional teams must be compelled to deal with problems that are critical to the business as a whole.
10. *Do not underestimate the need for managing change.* ABC needs to be led, not managed, and this must be done from the top.

receivable or accounts payable; costing the process of hiring and training employees; and costing such menial tasks as processing a letter or copying a document. Any process, function, or activity performed in an organization, whether it is related to production, marketing and sales, finance and accounting, human resources, or even research and development, is a candidate for ABC analysis. In short, almost any cost objective that has more than an insignificant amount of indirect costs can be more effectively measured using ABC.

MODULE-END REVIEW

Slack Corporation has the following predicted indirect costs and cost drivers for 2007 for the given activity cost pools:

	Fabrication Department	Finishing Department	Cost Driver
Maintenance.	$ 20,000	$10,000	Machine hours
Materials handling	30,000	15,000	Material moves
Machine setups	70,000	5,000	Machine setups
Inspections.	—	25,000	Inspection hours
	$120,000	$55,000	

---

[7] Michael Gering, "Activity-Based Costing Lessons Learned from Implementing ABC," *Management Accounting,* May 1999, pp. 26–27.

The following activity predictions were also made for the year:

	Fabrication Department	Finishing Department
Machine hours	10,000	5,000
Materials moves	3,000	1,500
Machine setups	700	50
Inspection hours	—	1,000

It is assumed that the cost per unit of activity for a given activity does not vary between departments.

Slack's president, Charles Slack, is trying to evaluate the company's product mix strategy regarding two of its five product models, ZX300 and SL500. The company has been using a plantwide overhead rate based on machine hours but is considering switching to either department rates or activity-based rates. The production manager has provided the following data for the production of a batch of 100 units for each of these models:

	ZX300	SL500
Direct materials cost.	$12,000	$18,000
Direct labor cost	$5,000	$4,000
Machine hours (Fabrication) . . .	500	700
Machine hours (Finishing)	200	100
Materials moves	30	50
Machine setups	5	9
Inspection hours	30	60

Required

a. Determine the cost of one unit each of ZX300 and SL500, assuming a plantwide overhead rate is used based on total machine hours.

b. Determine the cost of one unit of ZX300 and SL500, assuming department overhead rates are used. Overhead is assigned based on machine hours in both departments.

c. Determine the cost of one unit of ZX300 and SL500, assuming activity-based overhead rates are used for maintenance, materials handling, machine setup, and inspection activities.

d. Comment on the results of these cost calculations.

Solution

a. **Plantwide overhead rate = Total manufacturing overhead ÷ Total machine hours**
$$= (\$120{,}000 + \$55{,}000) \div (10{,}000 + 5{,}000)$$
$$= \$175{,}000 \div (15{,}000)$$
$$= \$11.67 \text{ per machine hour}$$

	ZX300	SL500
Product costs per unit		
Direct materials.	$12,000	$18,000
Direct labor	5,000	4,000
Manufacturing overhead		
700 machine hours × $11.67	8,169	
800 machine hours × $11.67		9,336
Total cost per batch	$25,169	$31,336
Number of units per batch	÷ 100	÷ 100
Cost per unit.	$251.69	$313.36

b. **Departmental overhead rates = Total departmental overhead ÷ Dept. allocation base**
Fabricating = $120,000 ÷ 10,000 machine hours
= $12 per machine hour
Finishing = $55,000 ÷ 5,000 machine hours
= $11 per machine hour

	ZX300	SL500
Product costs per unit		
Direct materials...............	$12,000	$18,000
Direct labor..................	5,000	4,000
Manufacturing overhead		
Fabricating Department		
500 machine hours × $12.....	6,000	
700 machine hours × $12.....		8,400
Finishing Department		
200 machine hours × $11.....	2,200	
100 machine hours × $11.....		1,100
Total cost per batch..............	$25,200	$31,500
Number of units per batch........	÷ 100	÷ 100
Cost per unit....................	$252.00	$315.00

c. **Activity-based overhead rates = Activity cost pool ÷ Activity cost driver**
Maintenance = $30,000 ÷ 15,000 machine hours
= $2 per machine hour
Materials handling = $45,000 ÷ 4,500 materials moves
= $10 per materials move
Machine setups = $75,000 ÷ 750 setups
= $100 per machine setup
Inspections = $25,000 ÷ 1,000 inspection hours
= $25 per inspection hour

	ZX300	SL500
Product costs per unit		
Direct materials...............	$12,000	$18,000
Direct labor..................	5,000	4,000
Manufacturing overhead		
Maintenance activity		
700 machine hours × $2......	1,400	
800 machine hours × $2......		1,600
Materials handling activity		
30 materials moves × $10.....	300	
50 materials moves × $10.....		500
Machine setups activity		
5 machine setups × $100.....	500	
9 machine setups × $100.....		900
Inspections activity		
30 inspection hours × $25	750	
60 inspection hours × $25		1,500
Total cost per batch..............	$19,950	$26,500
Number of units per batch........	÷ 100	÷ 100
Cost per unit....................	$199.50	$265.00

d. Following is a summary of product costs for ZX300 and SL500 assigning overhead costs based on a plantwide rate, department rates, and activity-based rates:

	ZX300	SL500
Plantwide rate.	$251.69	$313.36
Department rates	$252.00	$315.00
Activity rates.	$199.50	$265.00

Changing from a plantwide rate to department rates had little effect on unit costs because the department rates per machine hour are close to the plantwide rate per machine hour. Based on machine hours, both departments have similar cost structures.

When using activity rates, however, the cost of these two products drops dramatically because they use only a small portion (less than 2 percent) of the activities of setup (14 of 750) and materials moves (80 of 4,500). Neither a plantwide rate nor department rates recognize this fact, resulting in a large amount of cost cross-subsizidation of other products by ZX300 and SL500 for these costs. Although this problem did not include cost analysis of the other three products, it shows that one or more are less profitable and that ZX300 and SL500 are much more profitable than management previously thought.

GUIDANCE ANSWER

MANAGERIAL DECISION **You are the Controller**

It probably is not the right decision to abandon the ABC system because there are many benefits to using ABC other than just calculating product costs. Indeed, in cases where companies produce multiple products that are fairly homogeneous in terms of the use of resources, ABC may not produce more accurate costs than traditional methods; however, there are many uses of ABC information beyond just calculating the cost of products. Having detailed information about activities and their costs can significantly improve the management of those activities. Identifying key activities and measuring their costs often causes companies to seek more efficient processes, possibly considering outsourcing activities that are currently performed internally, or even looking for ways to eliminate activities altogether. Activity cost information can also be used to identify best practices within an organization, or to benchmark internal activity costs with other organizations.

DISCUSSION QUESTIONS

Q19-1. Distinguish between the following terms:
  a. Direct product costs and indirect product costs.
  b. Direct department costs and indirect department costs.
  c. Product costs and period costs.

Q19-2. Can any generalized distinctions be made about direct and indirect costs? Explain.

Q19-3. Explain the difference between cost assignment and cost allocation. What alternative term can be used to refer to cost allocation?

Q19-4. Can a cost item be both a direct cost and an indirect cost? Explain.

Q19-5. Why might cost allocations developed for financial reporting or tax purposes not be adequate for other purposes that require the accurate determination of individual product costs?

Q19-6. What is a cost objective? Give several examples of cost objectives that may be of interest to managers.

Q19-7. Why are cost pools used in allocating direct costs?

Q19-8. What is the primary advantage of separately allocating fixed and variable indirect costs?

Q19-9. To what extent are interdepartment services recognized under the direct, step, and linear algebra methods of service department cost allocation?

Q19-10. What is the premise of activity-based costing for product costing purposes?

Q19-11. In what ways does ABC differ from traditional product cost assignment?

Q19-12. Explain why ABC often reveals existing product cost cross-subsidization problems.

Q19-13. How can ABC be used to improve cost analysis other than for product costing?

Q19-14. Define activity cost pool, activity cost driver, and cost per unit of activity.

Q19-15. Name two possible activity cost drivers for each of the following activities: maintenance, materials movement, machine setup, inspection, materials purchases, and customer service.

Q19-16. Explain activity-based management and how it differs from activity-based costing.

MINI EXERCISES

M19-17. Allocating Service Department Costs: Allocation Basis Alternatives (LO2)

Korning Glassworks has two producing departments, P1 and P2, and one service department, S1. Estimated direct overhead costs per month are as follows:

P1......	$100,000
P2......	200,000
S1......	66,000

Other data follow:

	P1	P2
Number of employees	75	25
Production capacity (units).	50,000	30,000
Space occupied (square feet).	2,500	7,500
Five-year average percent of		
S1's service output used	65%	35%

Required

a. For each of the following allocation bases, determine the total estimated overhead cost for P1 and P2 after allocating S1 cost to the producing departments.
1. Number of employees
2. Production capacity in units
3. Space occupied
4. Five-year average percentage of S1 services used
5. Estimated direct overhead costs. (Round your answer to the nearest dollar.)

b. For each of the five allocation bases, explain the circumstances (including examples) under which each allocation base might be most appropriately used to allocate service department cost in a manufacturing plant such as Korning Glassworks. Also, discuss the advantages and disadvantages that might result from using each of the allocation bases.

M19-18. Indirect Cost Allocation: Direct Method (LO2)

Sprint Manufacturing Company has two production departments, Melting and Molding. Direct general plant management and plant security costs benefit both production departments. Sprint allocates general plant management costs on the basis of the number of production employees and plant security costs on the basis of space occupied by the production departments. In November, the following overhead costs were recorded:

Melting Department direct overhead	$150,000
Molding Department direct overhead.	300,000
General plant management	100,000
Plant security	35,000

Other pertinent data follow:

	Melting	Molding
Number of employees	25	45
Space occupied (square feet).	10,000	40,000
Machine hours	10,000	2,000
Direct labor hours.	4,000	20,000

Required

a. Prepare a schedule allocating general plant management costs and plant security costs to the Melting and Molding Departments.

b. Determine the total departmental overhead costs for the Melting and Molding Departments.

c. Assuming the Melting Department uses machine hours and the Molding Department uses direct labor hours to apply overhead to production, calculate the overhead rate for each production department.

M19-19. Plantwide versus Department Allocation (LO4)

Refer to Mini-Exercise M19-18 for Sprint Manufacturing Company. In addition to the facts given, assume that Sprint produces a product, Q45, that uses 5 direct labor hours per unit (2 hours in the Melting Department and 3 hours in the Molding Department) and 2 machine hours (1 hour in each department).

Required

a. Calculate the total overhead cost to produce one unit of Q45 using the department overhead rates calculated in Mini-Exercise M19-18.

b. Calculate the manufacturing overhead rate assuming that Sprint uses a single plantwide rate based on direct labor hours to allocate both producing and service department costs to products.

c. Calculate the total overhead cost to produce one unit of Q45 using the plantwide overhead rate.

d. Comment on the cost of one unit of Q45 using departmental overhead rates versus a plantwide overhead rate.

M19-20. Interdepartment Services: Direct Method (LO2)

Tucson Manufacturing Company has five operating departments, two of which are producing departments (P1 and P2) and three of which are service departments (S1, S2, and S3). All costs of the service departments are allocated to the producing departments. The following table shows the distribution of services from the service departments.

Services provided from	Services Provided to				
	S1	S2	S3	P1	P2
S1	—	5%	25%	50%	20%
S2	10%	—	5	45	40
S3	15	5	—	20	60

The direct operating costs of the service departments are as follows:

S1	$42,000
S2	85,000
S3	19,000

Required

Using the direct method, prepare a schedule allocating the service department costs to the producing departments.

M19-21. Activities and Cost Drivers (LO5)

For each of the following activities, select the most appropriate cost driver. Each cost driver may be used only once.

Activity	Cost Driver
1. Pay vendors	*a.* Number of different kinds of raw materials
2. Evaluate vendors	*b.* Number of classes offered
3. Inspect raw materials	*c.* Number of tables
4. Plan for purchases of raw materials	*d.* Number of employees
5. Packaging	*e.* Number of operating hours
6. Supervision	*f.* Number of units of raw materials received
7. Employee training	*g.* Number of moves
8. Clean tables	*h.* Number of vendors
9. Machine maintenance	*i.* Number of checks issued
10. Move patients to and from surgery	*j.* Number of customer orders

M19-22. Stage 1 ABC at a College: Assigning Costs to Activities (LO5)

An economics professor at State College devotes 65 percent of her time to teaching, 20 percent of her time to research and writing, and 15 percent of her time to service activities such as committee work and student advising. The professor teaches two semesters per year. During each semester, she teaches two sections of an introductory economics course (with a maximum enrollment of 80 students each) and one section of a graduate economics course (with a maximum enrollment of 30 students). Including course preparation, classroom instruction, and appointments with students, each course requires an equal amount of time. The economics professor is paid $78,000 per year.

Required

Determine the activity cost of instruction per student in both the introductory and the graduate economics courses.

M19-23. Stage 1 ABC for a Machine Shop: Assigning Costs to Activities (LO5)

As the chief engineer of a small fabrication shop, Brenda Tanner refers to herself as a "jack-of-all-trades." When an order for a new product comes in, Brenda must do the following:

1. Design the product to meet customer requirements.
2. Prepare a bill of materials (a list of materials required to produce the product).
3. Prepare an operations list (a sequential list of the steps involved in manufacturing the product).

Each time the foundry manufactures a batch of the product, Brenda must perform these activities:

1. Schedule the job.
2. Supervise the setup of machines that will work on the job.
3. Inspect the first unit produced to verify that it meets specifications.

Brenda supervises the production employees who perform the actual work on individual units of product. She is also responsible for employee training, ensuring that production facilities are in proper operating condition, and attending professional meetings. Brenda's estimates (in percent) of time spent on each of these activities last year are as follows:

Designing product	15%
Preparing bills of materials	5
Preparing operations lists	10
Scheduling jobs	18
Supervising setups	5
Inspecting first units	2
Supervising production	20
Training employees	15
Maintaining facility	7
Attending professional meetings	3
	100%

Required

Assuming Brenda Tanner's salary is $120,000 per year, determine the dollar amount of her salary assigned to unit-, batch-, product-, and facility-level activities. (You may need to review Module 15 before answering this question.)

M19-24. Stage 2 ABC for a Wholesale Company: Reassigning Costs to Cost Objectives   (LO5)

Information is presented on the activity costs of Cambridge Wholesale Company:

Activity	Activity Cost
Customer relations	$100.00 per customer per month
Selling.	0.06 per sales dollar
Accounting	5.00 per order
Warehousing.	0.50 per unit shipped
Packing.	0.25 per unit shipped
Shipping	0.10 per pound shipped

The following information pertains to Cambridge Wholesale Company's activities in Vermont for the month of March 2007:

Sales orders	235
Sales revenue.	$122,200
Cost of goods sold.	$73,320
Customers	25
Units shipped	4,700
Pounds shipped	70,500

Required

Determine the profitability of sales in Vermont for March 2007.

M19-25. Stage 2 ABC for Manufacturing: Reassigning Costs to Cost Objectives   (LO5)

Regal Products has developed the following activity cost information for its manufacturing activities:

Activity	Activity Cost
Machine setup	$60.00 per batch
Movement	15.00 per batch move
	0.10 per pound
Drilling.	3.00 per hole
Welding.	4.00 per inch
Shaping	25.00 per hour
Assembly	18.00 per hour
Inspection.	2.00 per unit

Filling an order for a batch of 40 fireplace inserts that weighed 150 pounds each required the following:
1. Three batch moves
2. Two sets of inspections
3. Drilling five holes in each unit
4. Completing 80 inches of welds on each unit
5. Thirty minutes of shaping for each unit
6. One hour of assembly per unit

Required

Determine the activity cost of converting the raw materials into 40 fireplace inserts.

M19-26. Two-Stage ABC for Manufacturing   (LO5)

Columbus Foundry, a large manufacturer of heavy equipment components, has determined the following activity cost pools and cost driver levels for the year:

Activity Cost Pool	Activity Cost	Activity Cost Driver
Machine setup	$600,000	12,000 setup hours
Material handling	120,000	2,000 tons of materials
Machine operation	500,000	10,000 machine hours

The following data are for the production of single batches of two products, C23 Cams and U2 Shafts:

	C23 Cams	U2 Shafts
Units produced.	500	300
Machine hours	4	5
Direct labor hours.	200	400
Direct labor cost.	$5,000	$10,000
Direct materials cost.	$25,000	$18,000
Tons of materials	12.5	8
Setup hours	3	7

Required

Determine the unit costs of C23 Cams and U2 Shafts using ABC.

M19-27. Two-Stage ABC for Manufacturing (LO5)

Sherwin-Williams
(SHW)

Assume Sherwin-Williams Company, a large paint manufacturer, has determined the following activity cost pools and cost driver levels for the latest period:

Activity Cost Pool	Activity Cost	Activity Cost Driver
Machine setup	$950,000	2,500 setup hours
Material handling	820,000	5,000 moves of materials
Machine operation	200,000	20,000 machine hours

The following data are for the production of single batches of two products, Mirlite and Subdue:

	Mirlite	Subdue
Gallons produced.	52,000	30,000
Direct labor hours.	400	250
Machine hours	800	250
Direct labor cost.	$10,000	$7,500
Direct materials cost.	$350,000	$150,000
Setup hours	15	12
Material moves.	60	35

Required

Determine the batch and unit costs per gallon of Mirlite and Subdue using ABC.

EXERCISES

E19-28. Interdepartment Services: Step Method (LO2)

Refer to the data in Mini-Exercise 19-20. Using the step method, prepare a schedule for Tucson Manufacturing Company allocating the service department costs to the producing departments. (Round calculations to the nearest dollar.)

E19-29. **Interdepartment Services: Step Method** (LO2)

O'Brian's Department Stores allocates the costs of the Personnel and Payroll departments to three retail sales departments, Housewares, Clothing, and Furniture. In addition to providing services to the operating departments, Personnel and Payroll provide services to each other. O'Brian's allocates Personnel Department costs on the basis of the number of employees and Payroll Department costs on the basis of gross payroll. Cost and allocation information for June is as follows:

	Personnel	Payroll	Housewares	Clothing	Furniture
Direct department cost.	$6,900	$3,200	$12,200	$20,000	$15,750
Number of employees	5	3	8	15	4
Gross payroll	$6,000	$3,300	$11,200	$17,400	$8,100

Required

a. Determine the percentage of total Personnel Department services that was provided to the Payroll Department.

b. Determine the percentage of total Payroll Department services that was provided to the Personnel Department.

c. Prepare a schedule showing Personnel Department and Payroll Department cost allocations to the operating departments, assuming O'Brian's uses the step method. (Round calculations to the nearest dollar.)

E19-30. **Calculating Manufacturing Overhead Rates** (LO4)

Goldratt Company, accumulated the following data for 2007:

Milling Department manufacturing overhead.	$344,000
Finishing Department manufacturing overhead.	$100,000
Machine hours used	
Milling Department	10,000 hours
Finishing Department	2,000 hours
Labor hours used	
Milling Department	1,000 hours
Finishing Department	1,000 hours

Required

a. Calculate the plantwide manufacturing overhead rate using machine hours as the allocation base.

b. Calculate the plantwide manufacturing overhead rate using direct labor hours as the allocation base.

c. Calculate department overhead rates using machine hours in Milling and direct labor hours in Finishing as the allocation bases.

d. Calculate department overhead rates using direct labor hours in Milling and machine hours in Finishing as the allocation bases.

e. Which of these allocation systems seems to be the most appropriate? Explain.

E19-31. **Calculating Activity-Based Costing Overhead Rates** (LO3, 4)

Assume that manufacturing overhead for Ratner, Inc. consisted of the following activities and costs:

Setup (1,000 setup hours)	$144,000
Production scheduling (400 batches).	60,000
Production engineering (60 change orders)	120,000
Supervision (2,000 direct labor hours)	56,000
Machine maintenance (12,000 machine hours)	84,000
Total activity costs	$464,000

The following additional data were provided for Job 845:

Direct materials costs.	$7,000
Direct labor cost (5 Milling direct labor hours;	
35 Finishing direct labor hours)	$1,000
Setup hours	5 hours
Production scheduling	1 batch
Machine hours used (25 Milling machine hours;	
5 Finishing machine hours).	30 hours
Production engineering	3 change orders

Required

a. Calculate the cost per unit of activity driver for each activity cost category.
b. Calculate the cost of Job 845 using ABC to assign the overhead costs.
c. Calculate the cost of Job 845 using the plantwide overhead rate based on machine hours calculated in the previous exercise.
d. What additional cost data will management need for Job 845 to adequately evaluate its price and profitability?

E19-32. Activity-Based Costing and Conventional Costs Compared (LO3, 4)

Chef Grill Company manufactures two types of cooking grills: the Gas Cooker and the Charcoal Smoker. The Cooker is a premium product sold in upscale outdoor shops; the Smoker is sold in major discount stores. Following is information pertaining to the manufacturing costs for the current month.

	Gas Cooker	**Charcoal Smoker**
Units.	1,000	5,000
Number of batches.	50	10
Number of batch moves.	80	20
Direct materials	$40,000	$100,000
Direct labor.	$20,000	$25,000

Manufacturing overhead follows:

Activity	**Cost**	**Cost Driver**
Materials acquisition and inspection	$30,000	Amount of direct materials cost
Materials movement.	16,200	Number of batch moves
Scheduling	36,000	Number of batches
	$82,200	

Required

a. Determine the total and per-unit costs of manufacturing the Gas Cooker and Charcoal Smoker for the month, assuming all manufacturing overhead is assigned on the basis of direct labor dollars.
b. Determine the total and per-unit costs of manufacturing the Gas Cooker and Charcoal Smoker for the month, assuming manufacturing overhead is assigned using activity-based costing.
c. Comment on the differences between the solutions to requirements (a) and (b). Which is more accurate? What errors might managers make if all manufacturing overhead costs are assigned on the basis of direct labor dollars?
d. Comment on the adequacy of the preceding data to meet management's needs.

E19-33. Traditional Product Costing versus Activity-Based Costing (LO3, 4)

Panasonic Company

Assume that Panasonic Company has determined its estimated total manufacturing overhead cost for one of its plants to be $198,000, consisting of the following activity cost pools for the current month:

Activity Centers	Activity Costs	Cost Drivers	Activity Level
Machine setups	$ 45,000	Setup hours..............	1,500
Materials handling	15,000	Number of moves	300
Machining..............	120,000	Machine hours	12,000
Maintenance............	18,000	Maintenance hours	1,200

Total direct labor hours used during the month were 8,000. Panasonic produces many different electronic products, including the following two products produced during the current month:

	Model X301	Model Z205
Units produced..............	1,000	1,000
Direct materials costs.........	$15,000	$15,000
Direct labor costs............	$12,500	$12,500
Direct labor hours............	500	500
Setup hours	50	100
Materials moves.............	25	50
Machine hours	800	800
Maintenance hours...........	10	40

Required

a. Calculate the total per-unit cost of each model using direct labor hours to assign manufacturing overhead to products.

b. Calculate the total per-unit cost of each model using activity-based costing to assign manufacturing overhead to products.

c. Comment on the accuracy of the two methods for determining product costs.

E19-34. Traditional Product Costing versus Activity-Based Costing (LO3, 4)

Outback Luggage, Inc., makes backpacks for large sporting goods chains that are sold under the customers' store brand names. The accounting department has identified the following overhead costs and cost drivers for next year:

Overhead Item	Expected Costs	Cost Driver	Maximum Quantity
Setup costs	$ 900,000	Number of setups............	7,200
Ordering costs	240,000	Number of orders	60,000
Maintenance.........	1,200,000	Number of machine hours	96,000
Power.............	120,000	Number of kilowatt hours......	600,000

Total predicted direct labor hours for next year is 60,000. The following data are for two recently completed jobs:

	Job 201	Job 202
Cost of direct materials	$13,500	$15,000
Cost of direct labor................	$18,000	$71,250
Number of units completed	1,125	900
Number of direct labor hours........	270	330
Number of setups.................	18	22
Number of orders.................	24	45
Number of machine hours	540	450
Number of kilowatt hours...........	270	360

Required

a. Determine the unit cost for each job using a traditional plantwide overhead rate based on direct labor hours.

b. Determine the unit cost for each job using ABC. (Round answers to two decimal places.)

c. As the manager of Outback, is there additional information that you would want to help you evaluate the pricing and profitability of Jobs 201 and 202?

PROBLEMS

P19-35. Selecting Cost Allocation Bases and Direct Method Allocations   **(LO2)**

Ohio Company has three producing departments (P1, P2, and P3) for which direct department costs are accumulated. In January, the following indirect costs of operation were incurred.

Plant manager's salary and office expense	$ 9,600
Plant security	2,400
Plant nurse's salary and office expense.	3,000
Plant depreciation	4,000
Machine maintenance	4,800
Plant cafeteria cost subsidy.	2,400
	$26,200

The following additional data have been collected for the three producing departments:

	P1	P2	P3
Number of employees	10	15	5
Space occupied (square feet).	2,000	5,000	3,000
Direct labor hours.	1,600	4,000	750
Machine hours	4,800	8,000	3,200
Number of nurse office visits	20	45	10

Required

a. Group the indirect cost items into cost pools based on the nature of the costs and their common basis for allocation. Identify the most appropriate allocation basis for each cost pool and determine the total January costs in the pool. (*Hint:* A cost pool may consist of one or more cost items.)

b. Allocate the cost pools directly to the three producing departments using the allocation bases selected in requirement (a).

c. How much indirect cost would be allocated to each producing department if Ohio Company were using a plantwide rate based on direct labor hours? Based on machine hours?

d. Comment on the benefits of allocating costs in pools compared with using a plantwide rate.

P19-36. Evaluating Allocation Bases and Direct Method Allocations   **(LO2)**

Cheyenne Company has two service departments, Maintenance and Cafeteria, that serve two producing departments, Mixing and Packaging. The following data have been collected for these departments for the current year:

	Cafeteria	Maintenance	Mixing	Packaging
Direct department costs	$176,000	$112,000	$465,000	$295,000
Number of employees			50	30
Number of meals served			9,000	7,000
Number of maintenance hours used			800	600
Number of maintenance orders			180	170

Required

a. Using the direct method, allocate the service department costs under the following independent assumptions:

1. Cafeteria costs are allocated based on the number of employees, and Maintenance costs are allocated based on the number of maintenance hours used.

2. Cafeteria costs are allocated based on the number of meals served, and Maintenance costs are allocated based on the number of maintenance orders.

b. Comment on the reasonableness of the bases used in the calculations in requirement (a). What considerations should determine which bases to use for allocating Cafeteria and Maintenance costs?

P19-37.   Cost Reimbursement and Step Allocation Method   (LO2)

Community Clinic is a not-for-profit outpatient facility that provides medical services to both fee-paying patients and low-income government supported patients. Reimbursement from the government is based on total actual costs of services provided, including both direct costs of patient services and indirect operating costs. Patient services are provided through two producing departments, Medical Services and Ancillary Services (includes X-ray, therapy, etc.). In addition to the direct costs of these departments, the clinic incurs indirect costs in two service departments, Administration and Facilities. Administration costs are allocated based on the number of full-time employees, and Facilities costs are allocated based on space occupied. Costs and related data for the current month are as follows:

	Administration	Facilities	Medical Services	Ancillary Services
Direct costs	$18,000	$6,000	$121,400	$37,200
Number of employees	5	4	12	8
Amount of space occupied (square feet)	1,500	—	8,000	2,000
Number of patient visits	—	—	4,000	1,500

Required

a. Using the step method, prepare a schedule allocating the common service department costs to the producing departments.

b. Determine the amount to be reimbursed from the government for each low-income patient visit.

P19-38.   Budgeted Service Department Cost Allocation: Pricing a New Product   (LO2)

Trimco Products Company is adding a new diet food concentrate called Body Trim to its line of bodybuilding and exercise products. A plant is being built for manufacturing the new product. Management has decided to price the new product based on a 100 percent markup on total manufacturing costs. A direct cost budget for the new plant projects that direct department costs of $2,100,000 will be incurred in producing an expected normal output of 700,000 pounds of finished product. In addition, indirect costs for Administration and Technical Support will be shared by Body Trim with the two exercise products divisions, Commercial Products and Retail Products. Budgeted annual data to be used in making the allocations are summarized here.

	Administration	Technical Support	Commercial Products	Retail Products	Body Trim
Number of employees	5	5	50	30	20
Amount of technical support time (hours)	500	—	1,500	1,250	750

Direct costs are budgeted at $135,000 for the Administration Department and $240,000 for the Technical Support Department.

Required

a. Using the step method, determine the total direct and indirect costs of Body Trim.

b. Determine the selling price per pound of Body Trim. (Round calculations to the nearest cent.)

P19-39.   Allocation and Responsibility Accounting   (LO2)

Assume that Timberland Company uses a responsibility accounting system for evaluating its managers, and that abbreviated performance reports for the company's three divisions for the month of March are as presented on the following page (amounts in thousands).

Timberland Company (TBL)

	Total	East	Central	West
Income	$165,000	$60,000	$75,000	$30,000
Less allocated costs:				
Computer Services	(66,000)	(22,000)	(22,000)	(22,000)
Personnel	(72,000)	(28,000)	(32,000)	(12,000)
Division income	$ 27,000	$10,000	$21,000	$ (4,000)

The West Division manager is very disturbed over his performance report and recent rumors that his division may be closed because of its failure to report a profit in recent periods. He believes that the reported profit figures do not fairly present operating results because his division is being unfairly burdened with service department costs. He is particularly concerned over the amount of Computer Services costs charged to his division. He believes that it is inequitable for his division to be charged with one-third of the total cost when it is using only 20 percent of the services. He believes that the Personnel Department's use of the Computer Services Department should also be considered in the cost allocations. Cost allocations were based on the following distributions of service provided:

		Services Receiver			
Services Provider	Personnel	Computer Services	East	Central	West
Computer Services	40%	—	20%	20%	20%
Personnel	—	10%	35	40	15

Required

a. What method is the company using to allocate Personnel and Computer Services costs?
b. Recompute the cost allocations using the step method. (Round calculations to the nearest dollar.)
c. Revise the performance reports to reflect the cost allocations computed in requirement (b).
d. Comment on the complaint of the West Division's manager.

P19-40. Allocating Service Department Costs: Direct and Step Methods; Department and Plantwide Overhead Rates (LO2, 4)

Pennington Group

Assume that Pennington Group, a manufacturer of fine casual outdoor furniture, allocates Human Resources Department costs to the producing departments (Cutting and Welding) based on number of employees; Facilities Department costs are allocated based on the amount of square footage occupied. Direct department costs, labor hours, and square footage data for the four departments for October are as follows:

	Human Resources	Facilities	Cutting	Welding
Direct department				
overhead costs	$60,000	$120,000	$800,000	$350,000
Number of employees	5	5	35	60
Number of direct labor hours	—	—	8,000	10,000
Amount of square footage	10,000	3,000	100,000	50,000

Assume that two jobs, A1 and A2, were completed during October and that each job had direct materials costs of $1,200. Job A1 used 80 direct labor hours in the Cutting Department and 20 direct labor hours in the Welding Department. Job A2 used 20 direct labor hours in the Cutting Department and 80 direct labor hours in the Welding Department. The direct labor rate is $50 in both departments.

Required

a. Find the cost of each job using a plantwide rate based on direct labor hours.
b. Find the cost of each job using department rates with *direct* service department cost allocation.
c. Find the cost of each job using department rates with *step* service department cost allocation.

d. Explain the differences in the costs computed in requirements (a)–(c) for each job. Which costing method is better for product pricing and profitability analysis?

P19-41. Product Costing: Plantwide Overhead versus Activity-Based Costing (LO3, 4)

Sconti, Inc., produces machine parts as a contract provider for a large manufacturing company. Sconti produces two particular parts, shafts and gears. The competition is keen among contract producers, and Sconti's top management realizes how vulnerable its market is to cost-cutting competitors. Hence, having a very accurate understanding of costs is important to Sconti's survival.

Sconti's president, Joe Disharoon, has observed that the company's current cost to produce shafts is $21.24, and the current cost to produce gears is $12.62. He indicated to the controller that he suspects some problems with the cost system because Sconti is suddenly experiencing extraordinary competition on shafts, but it seems to have a virtual corner on the gears market. He is even considering dropping the shaft line and converting the company to a one-product manufacturer of gears. He asked the controller to conduct a thorough cost study and to consider whether changes in the cost system are necessary. The controller collected the following data about the company's costs and various manufacturing activities for the most recent month:

	Shafts	Gears
Production units.	50,000	10,000
Selling price	$31.86	$24
Overhead per unit (based on direct labor hours)	$12.71	$6.36
Materials and direct labor cost per unit	$8.53	$6.26
Number of production runs	10	20
Number of purchasing and receiving orders processed	40	100
Number of machine hours	12,500	6,000
Number of direct labor hours	25,000	2,500
Number of engineering hours.	5,000	5,000
Number of material moves	50	40

The controller was able to summarize the company's total manufacturing overhead into the following pools:

Setup costs	$ 24,000
Machine costs	175,000
Purchasing and receiving costs	210,000
Engineering costs.	200,000
Materials handling costs	90,000
Total	$699,000

Required

a. Calculate Sconti's current plantwide overhead rate based on direct labor hours.
b. Verify Sconti's calculation of overhead cost per unit of $12.71 for shafts and $6.36 for gears.
c. Calculate the manufacturing overhead cost per unit for shafts and gears using activity-based costing, assuming each of the five cost pools represents a separate activity pool. Use the most appropriate activity driver for assigning activity costs to the two products.
d. Comment on Sconti's current cost system and the reason the company is facing fierce competition for shafts but little competition for gears.

CASES

C19-42. Product Costing: Department versus Activity-Based Costing for Overhead (LO3, 4)

Advertising Services Company (ASCO), a wholly owned subsidiary of Bell-of-the-South Telecommunications, Inc. (BOST), specializes in providing published and on-line advertising services for the business marketplace. The company monitors its costs based on the cost per column inch of published space printed in the advertising book ("The Peach Pages") and based on the cost per minute of telephone advertising time delivered on "The Peach Line," a computer-based, on-line advertising service. ASCO has one major competitor, Atlantatec, in the teleadvertising market; with increased competition, ASCO has seen a decline in sales of on-line advertising in recent years. ASCO's president, Andrea Remington, believes that predatory pricing by Atlantatec has caused the problem. The following is a recent conversation between Andrea and Jim Tate, director of marketing for ASCO.

Jim: I just received a call from one of our major customers concerning our advertising rates on "The Peach Line" who said that a sales rep from another firm (it had to be Atlantatec) had offered the same service at $1 per minute, which is $1.50 per minute less than our price.

Andrea: It's costing about $1.27 per minute to produce that product. I don't see how they can afford to sell it so cheaply. I'm not convinced that we should meet the price. Perhaps the better strategy is to emphasize producing and selling more published ads, which we're more experienced with and where our margins are high and we have virtually no competition.

Jim: You may be right. Based on a recent survey of our customers, I think we can raise the price significantly for published advertising and still not lose business.

Andrea: That sounds promising; however, before we make a major recommitment to publishing, let's explore other possible explanations. I want to know how our costs compare with our competitors. Maybe we could be more efficient and find a way to earn a good return on teleadvertising.

After this meeting, Andrea and Jim requested an investigation of production costs and comparative efficiency of producing published versus on-line advertising services. The controller, Joanna Turner, indicated that ASCO's efficiency was comparable to that of its competitors and prepared the following cost data:

	Published Advertising	On-Line Advertising
Estimated number of production units.	200,000	10,000,000
Selling price	$200	$2.50
Direct product costs.	$21,000,000	$5,000,000
Overhead allocation*	$9,800,000	$7,700,000
Overhead per unit.	$49	$0.77
Direct costs per unit	$105	$0.50
Number of customers.	180,000	25,000
Number of salesperson days	28,000	2,000
Number of art and design hours	35,000	5,000
Number of creative services subcontract hours	100,000	25,000
Number of customer service calls	72,000	8,000

*Based on direct labor costs

Upon examining the data, Andrea decided that she wanted to know more about the overhead costs since they were such a high proportion of total production costs. She was provided the following list of overhead costs and told that they were currently being assigned to products in proportion to direct product costs.

Selling costs.	$7,500,000
Visual and audio design costs	3,000,000
Creative services costs	5,000,000
Customer service costs	2,000,000

Required
Using the data provided by the controller, prepare analyses to help Andrea and Jim in making their decisions. (*Hint:* Prepare cost calculations for both product lines using ABC to see whether there is any significant difference in their unit costs). Should ASCO switch from the fast-growing, on-line advertising market back into the well-established published advertising market? Does the charge of predatory pricing seem valid? Why are customers likely to be willing to pay a higher price to get published services? Do traditional costing and activity-based costing lead to the same conclusions?

C19-43. **Cost Allocation and Performance Evaluation** (LO1)

The Village Branch of First Bank is managed by Ron Short, who has full responsibility for the bank's operations. The Village Branch is treated as a profit center within the company's responsibility accounting system; according to rumors throughout the company, if The Village Branch does not become more profitable, it is likely to be closed. Ron is upset with the corporate accounting department because of the number of different indirect costs that are allocated to his branch each period. He believes that many of these costs provide no direct benefits to his branch and that they are not relevant to an evaluation of his performance or that of The Village Branch. An income statement for The Village Branch for February follows:

Branch revenues		$450,000
Direct branch costs		(345,000)
Branch margin		$105,000
Allocated costs		
Computer operations	$14,500	
Personnel	15,000	
Payroll.	23,800	
Maintenance.	6,000	
Accounting	5,200	
Legal and audit.	4,200	
Transportation.	9,000	
Administrative overhead.	22,000	(99,700)
Branch net income.		$ 5,300

An investigation of Mr. Short's complaint by the controller's office provided the following additional information:

- Computer operations costs are billed based on actual CPU and computer connection time used by the branch.
- Personnel and payroll costs, primarily fixed, are allocated to the various operating departments based on the number of employees in each division.
- Maintenance costs are charged to the operating departments based on the standard hours actually worked in each department plus the actual cost of materials and supplies used.
- Accounting costs are allocated based on the number of transactions processed by the computer for each branch.
- Legal and audit costs are allocated based on the total revenues of the operating departments. The Village Branch has been involved in only one lawsuit, which was about five years ago. Mr. Short receives a copy of the company audit report each year but seldom reads it.
- Transportation costs consist primarily of the costs of operating the company helicopter and the company airplane. The helicopter is used to deliver checks to the local clearing center and for local executive transportation; the airplane is used primarily for executive travel out of town. Transportation costs are allocated to the operating departments based on revenues. Mr. Short has never flown in the corporate airplane.
- Administrative overhead consists of all other administrative costs including home office salaries and office expenses. These costs are allocated to the operating departments based on revenues. Mr. Short seldom sees anyone from the home office.

Required

a. Evaluate each cost allocation to determine whether it seems appropriate to allocate it to the operating divisions. Also evaluate the basis on which each cost is allocated to the operating departments.

b. Prepare a revised income statement for The Village Branch based on your evaluations in requirement (a).

c. Do you agree with Mr. Short's complaint? How do the cost allocations affect the decision to continue or discontinue The Village Branch?

Operational Budgeting and Profit Planning

LEARNING OBJECTIVES

LO1 Discuss the importance of budgets. (p. 20-3)

LO2 Describe basic approaches to budgeting. (p. 20-4)

LO3 Explain the relations among elements of a master budget and develop a basic budget. (p. 20-7)

LO4 Describe the relationship between budget development and manager behavior. (p. 20-15)

THE FUTURE OF BUDGETING

Managers use budgeting to integrate the various components of the firm and provide insights into the appropriate scale of operations for future months or years. By linking marketing, operations, and financial information, an effective budget aids managers in their planning activities.

The sales forecast is a key starting point in the budget process. Managers estimate the volume of goods and/or services that customers will purchase. These volumes, in turn, drive the level of activities and resulting costs the firm will incur.

To effectively forecast sales, managers must evaluate leading economic indicators, potential changes in consumer preferences, and possible changes in competition. Macroeconomic variables such as income levels and interest rates provide basic information for sales forecasters. Many firms and industry segments rely on specialized economic indicators that signal upcoming activity levels. The volume of corrugated boxes is one such leading indicator.

During a recent economic expansion, corrugated box production increased 27 percent. Known commonly as cardboard boxes, these corrugated boxes lead expansionary times because manufacturers usually increase their box orders before expanding production. Although 1,500 firms make these boxes, four firms dominate the industry: Smurfit-Stone (with 20 percent market share), Weyerhaeuser (12 percent), International Paper (10 percent), and Georgia Pacific (9 percent). Industry associations track the volumes of corrugated boxes shipped by these firms, and managers monitor this leading indicator.

Getty Images

Over time, consumers' preferences change. As a result, some product volumes soar while others slide. One shift in consumer tastes concerned the relative demand for carbonated versus noncarbonated drinks. Consumers have shifted their interest from carbonated soda to noncarbonated juice drinks and water, and the latter market has grown 15 times faster than the traditional soda market. Industry estimates suggest that water and juice drinks will make up more than 50 percent of soft-drink growth in the next 5 years. At 7-Eleven stores, two-thirds of the cooler space reserved for nonalcoholic drinks is devoted to noncarbonated juice and bottled water. This trend impacts the budgets of bottlers of all types within the industry.

The competitive environment can also change. As one example, many nonprofit charities and civic organizations rely on Christmas tree sales as a major fundraising activity. In recent years, retailers such as Wal-Mart, Home Depot, Target, and many supermarkets have added Christmas trees to their garden centers during the holiday season. These stores offer expanded shopping hours and prices that often beat the nonprofit organizations by $10–$15 per tree. Although nonprofit managers complain, retailers contend that nonprofits have a natural advantage because of the public's appreciation for their services.

Overall, budgets benefit managers by providing insight into the impact of the inevitable adjustments required as circumstances change. The budget, however, is no better than the quality of the sales forecast upon which the budget is built. Managerial accounting helps managers with the general relations within a budget and provides guidelines to assess the quality of the sales forecast.

Source: *The Wall Street Journal, 10-K Reports.*[1]

---

[1] Based on Kelly Greene, "Boy Scout Troops Face Stiff Competition from Big Retailers Selling Cheap Trees," *The Wall Street Journal* (Interactive Edition), December 19, 2000; Carol Hymowitz, "Managers Must Adjust Quickly in Changing Economic Environment," *The Wall Street Journal* (Interactive Edition) January 9, 2001; Betsy McKay, "Consumers' Appetite for Soda Is Going Flat," *The Wall Street Journal* (Interactive Edition), September 19, 2000; and Dan Morse, "Sales of Corrugated Boxes Offer One Measure of Economy's Health," *The Wall Street Journal* (Interactive Edition), February 12, 2001.

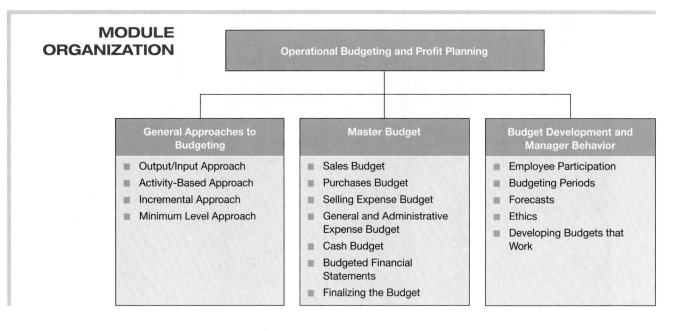

The process of projecting the operations of an organization and their financial impact into the future is called **budgeting.** A **budget** is a formal plan of action expressed in monetary terms. The purpose of this module is to examine the concepts, relationships, and procedures used in budgeting. Our emphasis is on **operating budgets,** which concern the development of detailed plans to guide operations throughout the budget period. We consider the reasons that organizations budget and alternative approaches to budget development. We also examine budget assembly and consider issues related to manager behavior and the budgeting process.

REASONS FOR BUDGETING

LO1 Discuss the importance of budgets.

Operating managers frequently regard budgeting as a time-consuming task that diverts attention from current problems. Indeed, the development of an effective budget is a difficult job. It is also a necessary one. Organizations that do not plan are likely to wander aimlessly and ultimately succumb to the swirl of current events. The formal development of a budget helps to ensure both success and survival. As discussed below, budgeting compels planning; it improves communications and coordination among organizational elements; it provides a guide to action; and it provides a basis of performance evaluation.

Formal budgeting procedures require people to think about the future. Without the discipline of formal planning procedures, busy operating managers would not find time to plan. Immediate needs would consume all available time. Formal budgeting procedures, with specified deadlines, force managers to plan for the future by making the completion of the budget another immediate need. Budgeting moves an organization from an informal "reactive" style to a formal "proactive" style of management. As a result, management and other employees spend less time solving unanticipated problems and more time on positive measures and preventative actions.

When operating responsibilities are divided, it is difficult to synchronize activities. Production must know what marketing intends to sell. Purchasing and personnel must know the factory's material and labor requirements. The treasurer must plan to ensure the availability of the cash to support receivables, inventories, and capital expenditures. Budgeting forces the managers of these diverse functions to communicate their plans and coordinate their activities. It helps ensure that plans are feasible (Can purchasing obtain adequate inventories to support projected sales?) and that they are synchronized (Will inventory be available in advance of an advertising campaign?). The final version of the budget emerges after an extensive (often lengthy) process of communication and coordination. As examined in the Research Insight that follows, recent advances in computer software allow organizations to better coordinate budget development.

Once the budget has been finalized, the various operating managers know what is expected of them, and they can set about doing it. If employees do not have a guide to action, their efforts could be wasted on unproductive or even counterproductive activities.

RESEARCH INSIGHT	Data Warehousing Gives Managers Control

A multi-user budgeting system provides shared access to a single database (data warehouse) through which all involved in the budgeting process can access common revenue and expense definitions, use similar layouts, use the same encoding and decoding structures, and share budget projections. This type of budgeting system allows the budget manager more control over the process while providing executives with better overviews. Characteristics of a good multi-user budgeting system include:

1. Support for changes to hierarchy so that different levels of budgets can be examined.
2. Shared access to common data warehouses.
3. Automatic mapping of imported data for use in multiple applications.
4. Numerous "what-if" functions.

This system is effective only if the data warehouse is well designed and managed. The design team for and management of a data warehouse should include the following technical personnel who are available to monitor and maintain the system:

1. Technical data warehouse designer (creates the database and maintains it).
2. Systems analyst/programmer (continually evaluates and creates new programs as needed).
3. End-user analyst (evaluates and monitors user needs).
4. Database administrator (creates physical database and monitors performance).
5. Technical support (maintains system integrity and reliability).

A successful data warehouse consists of a group of technologies that integrates the operational information of all budget centers into a single database. This allows managers access to the data and gives them the ability to generate budgets to their own specifications.[2]

After employees accept the budget as a guide to action, they can be held responsible for their portion of the budget. When results do not agree with plans, managers attempt to determine the cause of the divergence. This information is then used to adjust operations or to modify plans. More generally, budgeting is an important part of **management by exception,** whereby management directs attention only to those activities not proceeding according to plan. Without the budget, management might spend an inordinate amount of time seeking explanation of past activities and not enough time planning future activities. The process of developing a budgeting system could produce unexpected benefits.

GENERAL APPROACHES TO BUDGETING

Before an organization can develop operating budgets, management must decide which approaches to budget planning will be used for the various revenue and expenditure activities and organizational units. Widely used planning approaches to budgeting include the input/output, activity-based, incremental, and minimum level approaches.

LO2 Describe basic approaches to budgeting.

Output/Input Approach

The **output/input approach** budgets physical inputs and costs as a function of planned unit-level activities. This approach is often used for service, merchandising, manufacturing, and distribution activities that have defined relationships between effort and accomplishment. If each unit produced requires 2 pounds of direct materials that cost $5 each, and the planned production volume is 25 units, the budgeted inputs and costs for direct materials are 50 pounds (25 units $\times$ 2 pounds per unit) and $250 (50 pounds $\times$ $5 per pound).

The budgeted inputs are a function of the planned outputs. The output/input approach starts with the planned outputs and works backward to budget the inputs. It is difficult to use this approach for costs that do not respond to changes in unit-level cost drivers.

---

[2] Guy Haddleton, "10 Rules for Selecting Budget Management Software," *Management Accounting,* January 1998, pp. 24, 26–27; and Marc Levine and Joel Siegel, "What the Accountant Must Know about Data Warehousing," *The CPA Journal,* January 2001, pp. 37, 39–42.

Activity-Based Approach

The **activity-based approach** is a type of input/output method, but it reduces the distortions in the transformation through emphasis on the expected cost of the planned *activities* that will be consumed for a process, department, service, product, or other budget objective. Overhead costs are budgeted on the basis of the cost objective's anticipated consumption of activities, not based only on some broad-based cost driver such as direct labor hours or machine hours.

The amount of each activity cost driver used by each budget objective (for example, product or service) is determined and multiplied by the cost per unit of the activity cost driver. The result is an estimate of the costs of each product or service based on cost drivers such as assembly line setup or inspections, as well as the traditional volume-based drivers such as direct labor hours or units of direct materials consumed. Activity-based budgeting predicts costs of budget objectives by adding all costs of the activity cost drivers that each product or service is budgeted to consume. In evaluating the proposed budget, management would focus their attention on identifying the optimal set of activities rather than just the input/output relationships.

Incremental Approach

The **incremental approach** budgets costs for a coming period as a dollar or percentage change from the amount budgeted for (or spent during) some previous period. This approach is often used when the relationships between inputs and outputs are weak or nonexistent. For example, it is difficult to establish a clear relationship between sales volume and advertising expenditures. Consequently, the budgeted amount of advertising for a future period is often based on the budgeted or actual advertising expenditures in a previous period. If budgeted advertising expenditures for 2006 were $200,000, the budgeted expenditures for 2007 would be some increment, say 5 percent, above $200,000. In evaluating the proposed 2007 budget, management would accept the $200,000 base and focus attention on justifying the increment.

The incremental approach is widely used in government and not-for-profit organizations. In seeking a budget appropriation, a manager using the incremental approach need only justify proposed expenditures in excess of the previous budget. The primary advantage of the incremental approach is that it simplifies the budget process by considering only the increments in the various budget items. A major disadvantage is that existing waste and inefficiencies could escalate year after year.

Minimum Level Approach

As the portion of non-variable costs increased for most companies throughout the twentieth century, an increasing portion of costs was budgeted using the less precise incremental approach. This lack of good budgetary control led to further increases in costs. Management attempted to better control costs by employing a number of variations on the incremental approach. The minimum level approach is representative of these attempts to control the growth of costs not responding to unit-level drivers.

Using the **minimum level approach,** an organization establishes a base amount for budget items and requires explanation or justification for any budgeted amount above the minimum (base). This base is usually significantly less than the base used in the incremental approach. It likely is the minimum amount necessary to keep a program or organizational unit viable. For example, the corporate director of product development would need some basic amount to avoid canceling ongoing projects. Additional increments might also be included, first to support the current level of product development and second to undertake desirable new projects.

Some organizations, especially units of government, employ a variation of the minimum level approach, identified as *zero-based budgeting*. Under **zero-based budgeting** every dollar of expenditure must be justified. The essence of zero-based budgeting is breaking an organizational unit's total budget into program packages with related costs. Management then ranks all program packages on the basis of the perceived benefits in relationship to their costs. Program packages are then funded for the budget period using this ranking. High-ranking packages are most likely to be funded and low-ranking packages are least likely to be funded.

The minimum level approach improves on the incremental approach by questioning the necessity for costs included in the base of the incremental approach, but it is very time consuming. All three approaches are often used within the same organization. A manufacturing firm might use the output/input or the activity-based approach to budget distribution expenditures, the incremental approach to budget administrative salaries, and the minimum level approach to budget research and development.

MID-MODULE REVIEW

To illustrate the various approaches to budgeting discussed above, assume that Alpha Company manufactures two products, Beta and Gamma. Last period, Alpha produced 18,000 units of Beta and 45,000 units of Gamma at a total unit cost of $38 for Beta and $32 for Gamma. During the current period, overall costs are expected to rise about 3.5 percent over the last period. Total estimated overhead costs of $408,500 for the next period include the cost of assembly line setups, engineering and maintenance, and inspections. Total estimated assembly hours is 50,000 hours; therefore, the estimated overhead cost per assembly hour is $8.17. Other predicted data for the next period follow:

	Beta	Gamma
Direct materials (per unit)	$20.00	$14.50
Direct labor hours of assembly time (per unit)	0.5	0.8
Assembly labor cost (per hour)	$18	$18
Total estimated production (in units)	20,000	50,000
Total setup hours	1,000	1,500
Total engineering and maintenance hours	500	600
Total Inspections	650	580
Setup cost (per setup hour)	$25	$25
Engineering and Maintenance (per hour)	$35	$35
Inspection cost (per inspection)	$250	$250

Required

a. Calculate Alpha's budgeted cost per unit to produce Beta and Gamma during the next period, assuming it uses an output/input approach and budgets overhead cost based only on assembly hours.

b. Repeat a., assuming Alpha uses an activity-based approach and budgets overhead cost based on budgeted activity costs.

c. Repeat a., assuming Alpha uses an incremental approach for budgeting overhead cost.

d. Explain how the minimum level approach differs from the above methods.

Solution

a. Under the output/input approach, the output of units dictates the expected cost inputs. Here budgeted overhead costs are based on the number of budgeted assembly hours.

	Beta	Gamma
Direct materials (20,000 × $20)	$400,000	
(50,000 × $14.50).		$ 725,000
Direct assembly labor (20,000 × 0.5 × $18)	180,000	
(50,000 × 0.8 × $18)		720,000
Overhead (20,000 × 0.5 × $8.17)	$81,700	
(50,000 × 0.8 × $8.17)		326,800
Total budgeted cost	$661,700	$1,771,800
Unit Cost	$33.085	$35.436

b. Under the activity-based approach, budgeted overhead costs are based on expected activities to produce the products, not only on assembly hours.

Direct materials (20,000 × $20)	$400,000	
(50,000 × $14.50)		$ 725,000
Direct assembly labor (20,000 × 0.5 × $18)	180,000	
(50,000 × 0.8 × $18)		720,000
Setup (1,000 hours × $25)........................	25,000	
(1,500 hours × $25)........................		37,500
Engineering and Maintenance (500 hours × $35)	17,500	
(600 hours × $35)		21,000
Inspections (650 inspections × $250)...............	162,500	
(580 inspections × $250)...............		145,000
Total budgeted cost	$785,000	$1,648,500
Unit cost......................................	$39.25	$32.97

c. Under the incremental approach to budgeting, the cost per unit would be budgeted at last period's cost, plus in increment for expected additional costs in the current period. Based on last period's actual cost of $38 for Beta and $32 for Gamma, and using the 3.5 percent overall expected increase in costs, the current period's budgeted cost would be $39.33 for Beta and $33.12 for Gamma.

d. Under the minimum level approach, the company begins with either a zero or very low cost estimate, and then requires all additional costs beyond this minimum to be justified by the production mangers. This approach forces managers to evaluate thoroughly all elements of cost each period.

MASTER BUDGET

LO3 Explain the relations among elements of a master budget and develop a basic budget.

The culmination of the budgeting process is the preparation of a master budget for the entire organization that considers all interrelationships among organization units. The **master budget** groups together all budgets and supporting schedules and coordinates all financial and operational activities, placing them into an organization wide set of budgets for a given time period.

Because it explicitly considers organizational interrelationships, the master budget is more complex than budgets developed for products, services, organization units, or specific processes. The elements of the master budget depend on the nature of the business, its products or services, processes and organization, and management needs.

A major goal of developing a master budget is to ensure the smooth functioning of a business throughout the budget period and the organization's operating cycle. As shown in Exhibit 20.1, the operating cycle involves the conversion of cash into other assets, which are intended to produce revenues in excess of their costs. The cycle generally follows a path from cash, to inventories, to receivables (via sales or services), and back to cash. There are, of course, intermediate processes such as the purchase or manufacture of inventories, payments of accounts payable, and the collection of receivables. The master budget is merely a detailed model of the firm's operating cycle that includes all internal processes.

Most for-profit organizations begin the budgeting process with the development of the sales budget and conclude with the development of budgeted financial statements. Exhibit 20.2 depicts the annual budget

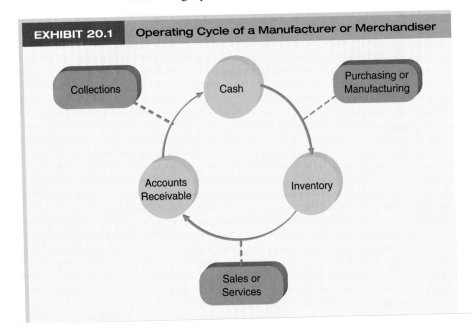

EXHIBIT 20.1 Operating Cycle of a Manufacturer or Merchandiser

assembly process in a retail merchandising organization. Most of the budget data flow from sales toward cash and then toward the budgeted financial statements.

To illustrate the procedures involved in budget assembly, a quarterly budget for the year 2008 is developed for Backpacks Galore Inc. (BGI), a retail organization that sells backpacks. Although BGI sells many types of backpacks, for our purposes they are classified as either school or hiking. The assembly sequence follows the overview illustrated in Exhibit 20.2. Each element of the budget process in Exhibit 20.2 is illustrated in a separate exhibit. Because of the numerous elements in the budget process illustrated for BGI, you will find it useful to refer to Exhibit 20.2 often.

The activities of a business can be summarized under three broad categories: operating activities, financing activities, and investing activities. To simplify the illustration, assume that Backpacks Galore engaged in no investing activities during the budget period and that the only financing activity was short-term borrowing. Normal profit-related activities performed in conducting the daily affairs of an organization are called **operating activities.** The operating activities of Backpacks Galore include the following:

1. Purchasing inventory intended for sale.
2. Selling goods or services.
3. Purchasing and using goods and services classified as selling expenses.
4. Purchasing and using goods and services classified as general and administrative expenses.

In addition to preparing the budget for each operating activity, companies prepare a cash budget for cash receipts and disbursements related to their operating activities as well as for financing and investing activities. The importance of cash planning makes this budget a vital part of the total budget process. Management must, for example, be aware in advance of the need to borrow and have some idea when borrowed funds can be repaid.

The balance sheet at the end of 2007, presented in Exhibit 20.3, contains information used as a starting point in preparing the various budgets. To reduce complexity, we use the output/input approach to budget variable costs and assume that the budgets for other costs were previously developed

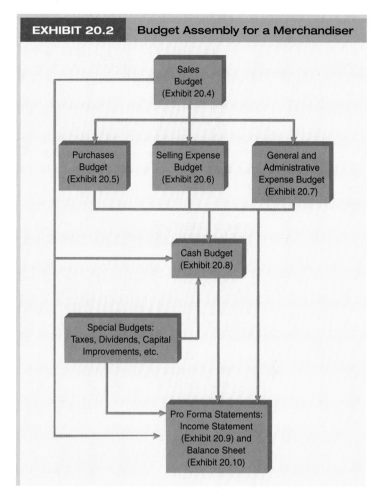

EXHIBIT 20.2   **Budget Assembly for a Merchandiser**

EXHIBIT 20.3   **Initial Balance Sheet**

BACKPACKS GALORE INC.
Balance Sheet
December 31, 2007

Assets			
Current assets			
Cash		$ 15,000	
Accounts receivable, net		21,600	
Inventory			
School backpacks (5,000 × $10)	$ 50,000		
Hiking backpacks (1,600 × $60).	96,000	146,000	$182,600
Property and equipment			
Land		60,000	
Buildings and equipment	260,000		
Less accumulated depreciation	(124,800)	135,200	195,200
Total assets.			$377,800
Liabilities and Stockholders' Equity			
Current liabilities			
Accounts payable.			$ 40,000
Stockholders' equity			
Capital stock.		$150,000	
Retained earnings.		187,800	337,800
Total liabilities and stockholders' equity.			$377,800

using the incremental approach. Budgets to be prepared include those for sales, purchases, selling expense, general and administrative expense, and cash.

Sales Budget

The **sales budget** includes a forecast of unit sales volume and sales revenue, and it can also contain a forecast of sales collections. Because sales drive almost all other activities in a for-profit organization, developing a sales budget is the starting point in the budgeting process. Managers use the best available information to accurately forecast future market conditions. These forecasts, when considered along with merchandise available, promotion and advertising plans, and expected pricing policies, should lead to the most dependable sales budget. The sales budget of BGI is in Exhibit 20.4.

EXHIBIT 20.4	Sales Budget				
BACKPACKS GALORE INC.					
Sales Budget					
For Year Ending December 31, 2008					
	First Quarter	Second Quarter	Third Quarter	Fourth Quarter	Year Total
Sales (units)					
School backpacks	4,000	3,400	3,650	3,950	15,000
Hiking backpacks.	1,100	1,600	2,500	1,300	6,500
Sales (dollars)					
School backpacks (unit sales × $20)	$ 80,000	$ 68,000	$ 73,000	$ 79,000	$300,000
Hiking backpacks (unit sales × $100)	110,000	160,000	250,000	130,000	650,000
Total	$190,000	$228,000	$323,000	$209,000	$950,000

The information in the sales budget and the predictions of the expected portion of cash sales and the timing of collections from credit sales are used to calculate cash receipts. In the event of a projected cash shortfall, management could consider ways to increase cash sales or to accelerate the collection of receipts from credit sales.

Purchases Budget

The **purchases budget** indicates the merchandise that must be acquired to meet sales needs and ending inventory requirements. It can be referred to as a *merchandise budget* if it contains only purchases of merchandise for sale. However, for a manufacturer it would include purchase of raw materials. For simplicity, BGI's purchases budget, shown in Exhibit 20.5, includes only purchases of merchandise.

In reviewing BGI's purchases budget, note the following:

- Management desires to have all inventory needed to fill the following quarter's sales in stock at the end of the previous quarter.

- To provide for a possible delay in the receipt of inventory, BGI also carries a safety stock of 1,000 school backpacks and 500 hiking backpacks.

- The total inventory needs equal current sales plus desired ending inventory, including safety stock.

- Budgeted purchases are computed as total inventory needs less the beginning inventory.

If BGI's suppliers were willing to make more frequent deliveries, BGI could adopt an inventory system that would no longer require BGI to begin each quarter with enough inventory to satisfy the quarter's entire sales. This would reduce inventory investment and the space needed to store the inventory.

EXHIBIT 20.5	Purchases Budget

BACKPACKS GALORE INC.
Purchases Budget
For Year Ending December 31, 2008

	First Quarter	Second Quarter	Third Quarter	Fourth Quarter	Year Total
Purchase units					
School backpacks					
Current sales	4,000	3,400	3,650	3,950	
Desired ending inventory*	4,400	4,650	4,950	5,100†	
Total needs.	8,400	8,050	8,600	9,050	
Less beginning inventory	(5,000)	(4,400)	(4,650)	(4,950)	
Purchases	3,400	3,650	3,950	4,100	15,100
Hiking backpacks					
Current sales	1,100	1,600	2,500	1,300	
Desired ending inventory*	2,100	3,000	1,800	1,700†	
Total needs.	3,200	4,600	4,300	3,000	
Less beginning inventory	(1,600)	(2,100)	(3,000)	(1,800)	
Purchases	1,600	2,500	1,300	1,200	6,600
Purchase dollars					
School backpacks (@ $10)** . . .	$ 34,000	$ 36,500	$ 39,500	$ 41,000	$151,000
Hiking backpacks (@ $60)	96,000	150,000	78,000	72,000	396,000
Total.	$130,000	$186,500	$117,500	$113,000	$547,000

*Next quarter's sales plus base inventory of 1,000 school backpacks and 500 hiking backpacks.
†Projected sales for the first quarter of 2009 are 4,100 school backpacks and 1,200 hiking backpacks.
**BGI's suppliers of backpacks have indicated no expected price increases in 2008.

The information in the purchases budget and the information on expected timing of payments for purchases are used to budget cash disbursements for purchases. In the event of a projected cash shortfall, management can consider ways to delay the purchase of inventory or the payment for inventory purchases.

Selling Expense Budget

The **selling expense budget** presents the expenses the organization plans to incur in connection with sales and distribution. In the selling expense budget, Exhibit 20.6, the budgeted variable selling expenses are determined as a percentage of budgeted sales dollars. The budgeted fixed selling expenses are based on amounts obtained from the manager of the sales department. To simplify the presentation of the cash budget, assume that BGI pays its selling expenses in the quarter they are incurred.

General and Administrative Expense Budget

The **general and administrative expense budget** presents the expenses the organization plans to incur in connection with the general administration of the organization. Included are expenses for the accounting department, the computer center, and the president's office, for example. BGI's general and administrative expense budget is presented in Exhibit 20.7.

The depreciation of $2,000 per quarter is a noncash item and is not carried forward to the cash budget. No variable general and administrative costs are included because most expenditures categorized as general and administrative are related to top-management operations that do not vary with unit-level cost drivers. To simplify the presentation of the cash budget, assume that BGI's general and administrative expenses, except depreciation, are paid in the quarter they are incurred.

EXHIBIT 20.6	Selling Expense Budget

BACKPACKS GALORE INC.
Selling Expense Budget
For Year Ending December 31, 2008

	First Quarter	Second Quarter	Third Quarter	Fourth Quarter	Year Total
Budgeted sales (from Exhibit 20.4)............	$190,000	$228,000	$323,000	$209,000	$950,000
Selling costs and disbursements					
Variable costs					
Setup/Display (1% sales)........	$ 1,900	$ 2,280	$ 3,230	$ 2,090	$ 9,500
Commissions (2% sales)........	3,800	4,560	6,460	4,180	19,000
Miscellaneous (1% sales).......	1,900	2,280	3,230	2,090	9,500
Total.....................	7,600	9,120	12,920	8,360	38,000
Fixed costs					
Advertising..................	2,250	2,250	2,250	2,250	9,000
Office expenses..............	1,250	1,250	1,250	1,250	5,000
Miscellaneous................	1,000	1,000	1,000	1,000	4,000
Total.....................	4,500	4,500	4,500	4,500	18,000
Total selling expenses...........	$ 12,100	$ 13,620	$ 17,420	$ 12,860	$ 56,000

EXHIBIT 20.7	General and Administrative Expense Budget

BACKPACKS GALORE INC.
General and Administrative Expense Budget
For Year Ending December 31, 2008

	First Quarter	Second Quarter	Third Quarter	Fourth Quarter	Year Total
Costs and disbursements					
Compensation................	$20,000	$20,000	$20,000	$20,000	$ 80,000
Research and development.....	5,000	5,000	5,000	5,000	20,000
Insurance...................	2,000	2,000	2,000	2,000	8,000
Depreciation.................	2,000	2,000	2,000	2,000	8,000
Property taxes................	3,000	3,000	3,000	3,000	12,000
Miscellaneous................	1,000	1,000	1,000	1,000	4,000
Total general and administrative expenses........	$33,000	$33,000	$33,000	$33,000	$132,000

Cash Budget

The **cash budget** summarizes all cash receipts and disbursements expected to occur during the budget period. Cash is critical to survival. Income is like food and cash is like water. Food is necessary to survive and prosper over time, but you can get along without food for a short period of time. You cannot survive very long without water. Hence, cash budgeting is very important, especially in a small business, such as the one considered in the following Business Insight.

After it makes sales predictions, an organization uses information regarding credit terms, collections policy, and prior collection experience to develop a cash collections budget. Collections on sales normally include receipts from the current period's sales and collections from sales of prior periods. An allowance for bad debts, which reduces each period's collections, is also predicted. Other items often included are

> ### BUSINESS INSIGHT | Going Broke Getting Rich
>
> Frank used his own cash plus some borrowed from his bank to start a business. In the first two years, Frank's company showed a small operating loss that he considered acceptable. In the third year, it showed a profit of more than $100,000. Frank thought this was great until the accountant told him that the company did not have enough cash to pay income taxes. Frank did not believe his accountant until the differences between income and cash flow were explained and the accountant showed him a cash flow statement for his business. Because income is not the same as cash inflow, cash budgets are critical to all businesses, especially small ones. Managers who do not understand cash flow can really have problems, even when profits are evident. Cash can be tied up in inventory purchased in anticipation of sales growth. When sales are on account, additional cash is tied up in receivables rather than being available to pay bills. Worse, the money Frank borrowed to start the business might come due just as the business starts to turn a profit. Managers must understand the operating cycle and relationship between income and cash flows. For Frank, a cash budget would show the cash generated by operations, the cash outflow needed for paying back his loan, and the amount of cash tied up in inventory and receivables.[3]

cash sales, sales discounts, allowances for volume discounts, and seasonal changes of sales prices and collections. BGI's cash budget is in Exhibit 20.8. Note the following important points:

▪ Management estimates that one-half of all sales are for cash and the other half are on the company's credit card. (When sales are on bank credit cards, the collection is immediate, less any bank user fee; however, charges using BGI's credit card are collected by the company from the customer.) Seventy-five percent of the BGI credit card sales are collected in the quarter of sale, and 24 percent are collected in the following quarter. Bad debts are budgeted at 1 percent of credit sales. This resource flow is graphically illustrated as follows:

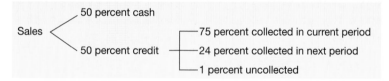

▪ Payments for purchases are made 50 percent in the quarter purchased and 50 percent in the next quarter.

▪ Information on cash expenditures for selling expenses and for general and administrative expenses is based on budgets for these items. The quarterly cash expenditures for general and administrative expenses are $31,000 rather than $33,000. The $2,000 difference relates to depreciation, which does not require use of cash.

▪ BGI's accountant provided tax information. Income taxes are determined on the basis of predicted taxable income following IRS rules.

▪ Dividend information is provided by BGI's board of directors.

▪ The cash budget shows cash operating deficiencies and surpluses expected to occur at the end of each quarter; this is used to plan for borrowing and loan payment.

▪ The cash maintenance policy for Backpacks Galore specifies that a minimum balance of $15,000 is to be maintained.

▪ BGI has a line of credit with a bank, with any interest on borrowed funds computed at the simple interest rate of 12.0 percent per year, or 1.0 percent per month. All necessary borrowing is assumed to occur at the start of each quarter in increments of $1,000. Repayments are assumed to occur at the end of the quarter. Interest is paid when loans are repaid.

▪ The cash budget indicates that BGI will need to borrow $3,000 at the beginning of the first quarter and $22,000 at the beginning of the second quarter. At the end of the third quarter, BGI will be able to repay both loans.

---

[3] Gary Gibbs, "Managing Cash Flow: A Constant Business Challenge," *Wichita Business Journal*, December 1997, pp. 8b–14b.

EXHIBIT 20.8	Cash Budget

BACKPACKS GALORE INC.
Cash Budget
For Year Ending December 31, 2008

	First Quarter	Second Quarter	Third Quarter	Fourth Quarter	Year Total
Cash balance, beginning	$ 15,000	$ 15,750	$ 15,180	$ 56,155	$ 15,000
Collections on sales					
Cash sales	95,000	114,000	161,500	104,500	475,000
Credit sales					
Current quarter	71,250	85,500	121,125	78,375	356,250
Prior quarter	21,600*	22,800	27,360	38,760	110,520
Total.	187,850	222,300	309,985	221,635	941,770
Total available from operations.	202,850	238,050	325,165	277,790	956,770
Less budgeted disbursements					
Purchasing (Exhibit 20.5)					
Current quarter (50%)	65,000	93,250	58,750	56,500	273,500
Previous quarter (50%)	40,000†	65,000	93,250	58,750	257,000
Total.	105,000	158,250	152,000	115,250	530,500
Selling (Exhibit 20-6).	12,100	13,620	17,420	12,860	56,000
General and administrative					
(Exhibit 20.7)	31,000‡	31,000	31,000	31,000	124,000
Other					
Income taxes.	22,000	22,000	22,000	11,200	77,200
Dividends	20,000	20,000	20,000	30,000	90,000
Total disbursements	(190,100)	(244,870)	(242,420)	(200,310)	(877,700)
Excess (deficiency) cash					
available over disbursements	12,750	(6,820)	82,745	77,480	79,070
Short-term financing§					
New loans.	3,000	22,000			25,000
Repayments			(25,000)		(25,000)
Interest#.			(1,590)		(1,590)
Net cash flow from financing	3,000	22,000	(26,590)		(1,590)
Cash balance, ending.	$ 15,750	$ 15,180	$ 56,155	$ 77,480	$ 77,480

* This is based on the fourth quarter 2007 credit sales.

† Unpaid balance at December 31, 2007, reflects prior year payment terms.

‡ Amounts for cash flow exclude depreciation.

§ Loans are obtained in $1,000 increments to maintain cash at a minimum balance of $15,000 at all times. New loans required are budgeted for the beginning of the quarter, and repayments are budgeted for the end of the quarter. Loan repayments are made on a first-borrowed, first-repaid basis, and interest is paid only at the time of repayment.

\# Interest for $25,000 is $1,590 ($3,000 × 9 months × 0.01 = $270) + ($22,000 × 6 months × 0.01 = $1,320).

Note: The Accounts Receivable balance on December 31, 2008, is $25,080 ($104,500 − $78,375 − $1,045); and the Accounts Payable balance is equal to one-half of fourth quarter purchases, of $56,500.

Budgeted Financial Statements

The preparation of the master budget culminates in the preparation of budgeted financial statements. **Budgeted financial statements** are pro forma statements that reflect the "as-if" effects of the budgeted activities on the actual financial position of the organization. That is, the statements reflect the results of operations assuming all budget predictions are correct. Spreadsheets that permit the user to immediately determine the impact of any assumed changes facilitate developing budgeted financial statements. The budgeted income statement can follow the functional format traditionally used for financial accounting or the contribution format introduced in Module 16. In either case, the balance sheet amounts reflect the corresponding budgeted entries.

Exhibit 20.9 presents the budgeted income statement for the year ending December 31, 2008. If all predictions made in the operating budget are correct, Backpacks Galore will produce a net income of $138,460 for the year. Almost every item on the budgeted income statement comes from one of the budget schedules.

EXHIBIT 20.9	Budgeted Income Statement

BACKPACKS GALORE INC.
Budgeted Income Statement (Functional Format)
For Year Ending December 31, 2008

Sales (Exhibit 20.4)			$950,000
Expenses			
Cost of goods sold			
Beginning inventory (Exhibit 20.3)	$146,000		
Purchases (Exhibit 20.5)	547,000		
Cost of merchandise available	693,000		
Ending inventory*	(153,000)	$540,000	
Selling operations (Exhibit 20.6)		56,000	
General and administrative (Exhibit 20.7)		132,000	
Bad debt expense†		4,750	(732,750)
Income from operations			217,250
Other expenses			
Interest expense (Exhibit 20.8)			(1,590)
Net income before taxes			215,660
Allowance for income taxes			(77,200)
Net income			$138,460

*(School backpacks, 5,100 × $10 = $51,000) + (Hiking backpacks, 1,700 × $60 = $102,000) = $153,000 (Exhibit 20.5).

†Bad debt is 1 percent of credit sales ($475,000 × 0.01).

The budgeted balance sheet, presented in Exhibit 20.10, shows the anticipated financial position of BGI at 2008 year-end, assuming that all budget predictions are correct. Sources of the budgeted balance sheet data are included as part of the exhibit.

Finalizing the Budget

After studying the BGI example, you might conclude that developing the master budget is a mechanical process. That is not the case. Understanding the basics of budget assembly is not the end; it is a tool to assist in efficient and effective budgeting. Before finalizing the budget, the following two questions must be addressed:

- Is the proposed budget feasible?
- Is the proposed budget acceptable?

To be feasible, the organization must be able to actually implement the proposed budget. Without the line of credit, BGI's budget is not feasible because the company would run out of cash by the end of the second quarter. Knowing this, management can take timely corrective action. Possible actions include obtaining equity financing, issuing long-term debt, reducing the amount of inventory on hand at the end of each quarter, or obtaining a line of credit. Other constraints that would make the budget infeasible include the availability of merchandise and, in the case of a manufacturing organization, production capacity.

Once management determines that the budget is feasible, they still need to determine if it is acceptable. To evaluate acceptability, management might consider various financial ratios, such as return on

EXHIBIT 20.10	Budgeted Balance Sheet		

BACKPACKS GALORE INC.
Budgeted Balance Sheet
December 31, 2008

Assets			
Current assets			
Cash (Exhibit 20-8)............................		$ 77,480	
Accounts receivable (net) (Exhibit 20-8)..............		25,080	
Merchandise inventory (Exhibit 20-9)...............		153,000	$255,560
Property and equipment			
Land......................................		60,000	
Buildings and equipment..............	$260,000		
Less accumulated depreciation.........	(132,800)	127,200	187,200
Total assets..			$442,760
Liabilities and Stockholders' Equity			
Current liabilities			
Accounts payable (Exhibit 20-8)...............................			$ 56,500
Stockholders' equity			
Capital stock....................................		$150,000	
Retained earnings..............................		236,260	386,260
Total liabilities and stockholders' equity...........................			$442,760

Sources of data:
1. The accounts receivable balance is 24 percent of fourth quarter credit sales ($104,500 × 0.24).
2. Land and buildings and equipment are unchanged from the prior year's balances.
3. Accumulated depreciation is equal to the balance at the end of 2007 increased by the 2008 depreciation ($124,800 + $8,000) (Exhibit 20-7).
4. The accounts payable balance is 50 percent of fourth quarter purchases ($113,000 × 0.50).
5. Capital stock is the same as its prior year balance.
6. Retained earnings is equal to the prior year-end balance plus budgeted net income less dividends ($90,000) reported in the cash budget.

assets. They might compare the return provided by the proposed budget with past returns, industry averages, or some organizational goal.

BUDGET DEVELOPMENT AND MANAGER BEHAVIOR

LO4 Describe the relationship between budget development and manager behavior.

Organizations are composed of individuals who perform a wide variety of activities in pursuit of the organization's goals. To accomplish these goals, management must recognize the effects that budgeting and performance evaluation methods have on the behavior of the organization's employees.

Employee Participation

Budgeting should be used to promote productive employee behavior directed toward meeting the organization's goals. While no two organizations use exactly the same budgeting procedures, two approaches to employee involvement in budgeting represent possible end points on a continuum. These approaches are sometimes referred to as *top-down* and *bottom-up* methods.

With a **top-down** or **imposed budget,** top management identifies the primary goals and objectives for the organization and communicates them to lower management levels. Because relatively few people are involved in top-down budgeting, an imposed budget saves time. It also minimizes the slack that managers at lower organizational levels are sometimes prone to build into their budgets. However, this nonparticipative approach to budgeting can have undesirable motivational consequences. Personnel who do not participate in budget preparation might lack a commitment to achieve their part of the budget.

With a **bottom-up** or **participative budget,** managers at all levels—and in some cases, even nonmanagers—are involved in budget preparation. Budget proposals originate at the lowest level of management possible and are then integrated into the proposals for the next level, and so on, until the proposals reach the top level of management, which completes the budget.

Participation helps ensure that important issues are considered and that employees understand the importance of their roles in meeting the organization's goals. It also provides opportunities for problem solving and fosters employee commitment to agreed-upon goals. Hence, budget predictions are likely to be more accurate, and the people responsible for the budget are more likely to strive to accomplish its objectives. These *self-imposed budgets* reinforce the concept of participative management and should strengthen the overall budgeting process.

Participative approaches to budgeting have a few disadvantages. Because they require the involvement of many people, the preparation period is longer than that for an imposed budget. Another disadvantage is the tendency of some managers to intentionally understate revenues or overstate expenses to provide **budgetary slack.** A manager might do this to reduce his or her concern regarding unfavorable performance reviews or to make it easier to obtain favorable performance reviews. If a department consistently produces favorable variances (actual results versus budget) with little apparent effort, this might be a symptom of budgetary slack.

> **MANAGERIAL DECISION**   **You are the Chief Financial Officer**
>
> As the CFO of a relatively new and fast-growing entrepreneurial enterprise, you and the other top managers have previously emphasized technical and marketing innovation and creativity over planning and budgeting. But now with growing competition and the maturing of the company's products, you recognized that a culture of better financial planning must be established if the company is to succeed in the long run. You feel that the financial staff have the best expertise and understanding of the business to prepare effective budgets, but you are concerned about the motivational effects of excluding the lower level managers from the process and are seeking advice. (Answer p. 20-20)

Budgeting Periods

Although most organizations use a one-year budget period, some organizations budget for shorter or longer periods. In addition to fixed-length budget periods, two other types of budget periods commonly used are life cycle budgeting and continuous budgeting.

When a fixed time period is not particularly relevant to planning, an organization can use **life cycle budgeting,** which involves developing a budget for a project's entire life. An ice cream vendor at the beach might develop a budget for the season. A general contractor might budget costs for the entire (multiple-year) time required to construct a building.

Under **continuous budgeting,** the budget (sometimes called a **rolling budget**) is based on a moving time frame. For example, an organization on a continuous four-quarter budget system adds a quarter to the budget at the end of each quarter of operations, thereby always maintaining a budget for four quarters into the future. Under this system, plans for a full year into the future are always available, whereas under a fixed annual budget, operating plans for a full year ahead are available only at the beginning of the budget year. Because managers are constantly involved in this type of budgeting, the budget process becomes an active and integral part of the management process. Managers are forced to be future oriented throughout the year rather than just once each year.

Forecasts

Budget preparation requires the development of a variety of forecasts. The sales forecast is based on a variety of interrelated factors such as historical trends, product innovation, general economic conditions, industry conditions, and the organization strategic position for competing on the basis of price, product differentiation, or market niche. Many organizations first determine the industry forecast for a given product or service and then extract from it their sales estimations.

Although the sales forecast is primary to most organizations, there are many other forecasts of varying importance that must be made, including (a) the collection period for sales on account, (b) percent of uncollectable sales on account, (c) cost of materials, supplies, utilities, and so forth, (d) employee turn-over, (e) time required to perform activities, (f) interest rates, and (g) development time for new products or services.

Ethics

Because most wrongful activities related to budgeting are unethical, rather than illegal, organizations often have difficulty dealing with them. However, when managers' actions cross the gray area between ethical and fradulent behavior, organizations are not reluctant to dismiss employees or even pursue legal actions against them.[4]

Although most managers have a natural inclination to be conservative in developing their budgets, at some level the blatant padding or building slack into the budget becomes unethical. In an extreme case, it might even be considered theft if an inordinate level of budgetary slack creates favorable performance variances that lead to significant bonuses or other financial gain for the manager. Another form of falsifying budgets occurs when managers include expense categories in their budgets that are not needed in their operations and subsequently use the funds to pad other budget categories. The deliberate falsification of budgets is unethical behavior and is grounds for dismissal in most organizations.

Ethical issues might also arise in the reporting of performance results, which usually compares actual data with budgeted data. Examples of unethical reporting of actual performance data include misclas-sification of expenses, overstating revenues or understating expenses, postponing or accelerating the re-cording of activities at the end of the accounting period, or creating fictitious activities. The views of the former CEO of Phillips Petroleum on this type of behavior and the competitive environment from which it is often motivated are summarized in the following Business Insight.

BUSINESS INSIGHT **The Heart of Every Decision**

The retired CEO of Phillips Petroleum stated, "What we are all called upon to do, whatever profes-sional field we have chosen, is to make ethics the heart of every decision we make, from boardroom to the mailroom." He cites several examples of managers making the wrong decisions, one involving a budget-related situation. Specifically, a plant manager at a glass container plant, inflated the results of operations, not slightly, but by 33 percent over actual levels. When the plant manager confessed to his wrongdoings, he stated that the actual results were so unfavorable that he "was afraid the company would close the aging plant, throwing [him] and 300 employees out of work." The former CEO admitted, "It's a lot harder to resist temptation when honesty and integrity could mean the end of your job, your company, even your town." Still, he says that organizations must establish policies of operations that do not cause direct conflicts with managers' decisions, a concept he labeled "the moral dimension of competitiveness." An example is an executive order to a manager to cut costs but not to cut customer satisfaction. Organizations should provide guidelines and expectations of actions, not blatant orders for which the means and goals seem to conflict.[5]

Developing Budgets that Work

It is important for management to understand that budgets are not perfect. Mistakes in prediction and judgment are made, and unforeseen circumstances often develop, necessitating modification of the bud-get. Unless top management is willing to recognize that changes in the budget are needed, support for the budget at lower levels will quickly erode. If an organization is to receive maximum benefit from the budget process, support for the budget at the top management level, as well as at lower levels, must be maintained. Achieving this support could be the most difficult challenge facing an organization undertak-ing budgeting for the first time. Lower-level managers are not likely to respect the budget and the related performance reports if they perceive a lack of commitment by top management. Disregard for the budget by top management can quickly destroy the effectiveness of the budget throughout the organization.

---

[4] *Fraud Survey Results 1993*, (New York: KPMG Peat Marwick, 1993).

[5] C. J. Silas, "The Moral Dimension of Competitiveness," *Management Accounting*, December 1994, p. 72. Reprinted with permis-sion of the Ethics Resource Center, Inc.

Managers who follow the suggestions listed here are more likely to be successful in using budgets as a positive motivational tool for accomplishing organizational goals through people.

1. Emphasize the importance of budgeting as a planning device.
2. Encourage wide participation in budget preparation at all levels.
3. Demonstrate that the budget has the complete support of top management.
4. Recognize that the budget is alterable; modifications may be required if conditions change.
5. Use budget performance reports to identify poor performers *and* to recognize good performance.
6. Conduct budget training to provide managers information about the purposes of budgets and to dispel any erroneous misconceptions.

Properly used, an operating budget is an effective mechanism for motivating employees to higher levels of performance and productivity. Improperly developed and administered, budgets can foster feelings of animosity toward management and the budget process. Behavioral research has generally concluded that when employees participate in the preparation of budgets and believe that the budgets represent fair standards for evaluating their performance, they receive personal satisfaction from accomplishing the goals set in the budgets.

MODULE-END REVIEW

Stumphouse Cheese Company is a wholesale distributor of blue cheese and ice cream. The following information is available for April 2008.

Estimated sales

Blue cheese	160,000 hoops at $10 each
Ice cream	240,000 gallons at $5 each

Estimated costs

Blue cheese	$8 per hoop
Ice cream	$2 per gallon

	Beginning	Ending
Desired inventories		
Blue cheese	10,000	12,000
Ice cream	4,000	5,000

Financial information follows:
- Beginning cash balance is $400,000.
- Purchases of merchandise are paid 60 percent in the current month and 40 percent in the following month. Purchases totaled $1,800,000 in March and are estimated to be $2,000,000 in May.
- Employee wages, salaries, and commissions are paid for in the current month. Employee expenses for April totaled $156,000.
- Overhead expenses are paid in the next month. The accounts payable amount for these expenses from March is $80,000 and for May will be $90,000. April's overhead expenses total $80,000.
- Sales are on credit and are collected 70 percent in the current period and the remainder in the next period. March's sales were $3,000,000, and May's sales are estimated to be $3,200,000. Bad debts average 1 percent of sales.
- Selling and administrative expenses are paid monthly and total $450,000, including $40,000 of depreciation.
- All unit costs for April are the same as they were in March.

Required
Prepare the following for April:
a. Sales budget in dollars.
b. Purchases budget.

c. Cash budget.
d. Budgeted income statement.

Solution

a.

STUMPHOUSE CHEESE COMPANY
Sales Budget
For Month of April 2008

	Units	Price	Sales
Blue cheese	160,000	$10	$1,600,000
Ice cream	240,000	5	1,200,000
Total			$2,800,000

b.

STUMPHOUSE CHEESE COMPANY
Purchases Budget
For Month of April 2008

	Blue Cheese	Ice Cream	Total
Units			
Sales needs	160,000	240,000	
Desired ending inventory	12,000	5,000	
Total	172,000	245,000	
Less beginning inventory	(10,000)	(4,000)	
Purchases.	162,000	241,000	
Dollars			
Sales needs	$1,280,000	$480,000	
Desired ending inventory	96,000	10,000	
Total	1,376,000	490,000	
Less beginning inventory	(80,000)	(8,000)	
Purchases needed	$1,296,000	$482,000	$1,778,000

c.

STUMPHOUSE CHEESE COMPANY
Cash Budget
For Month of April 2008

Cash balance, beginning		$ 400,000
Collections on sales		
Current month's sales ($2,800,000 × 0.70)	$1,960,000	
Previous month's sales ($3,000,000 × 0.29).	870,000	2,830,000
Cash available from operations		3,230,000
Less budgeted disbursements		
March purchases ($1,800,000 × 0.40)	720,000	
April purchases ($1,778,000 × 0.60)	1,066,800	
Labor.	156,000	
Overhead (March)	80,000	
Selling and administrative		
($450,000 − $40,000 depreciation).	410,000	(2,432,800)
Cash balance, ending.		$ 797,200

d.

STUMPHOUSE CHEESE COMPANY
Budgeted Income Statement
For Month of April 2008

Sales (sales budget)			$2,800,000
Allowance for bad debts			(28,000)
Net sales			2,772,000
Costs of merchandise sold			
Blue cheese (160,000 × $8)	$1,280,000		
Ice cream (240,000 × $2)	480,000	$1,760,000	
Wages and salaries	156,000		
Overhead	80,000		
Selling and administrative	450,000	686,000	(2,446,000)
Net income			$ 326,000

GUIDANCE ANSWERS

MANAGERIAL DECISION **You are the Chief Financial Officer**

You seem to be leaning toward using a top-down approach to budgeting. While this method may produce an effective set of benchmarks for planning and evaluation, it does not maximize the benefits of budgeting. A key element in any effective budgeting system is that it must be embraced by the managers whose performance will be evaluated by it. If the budget is imposed from the top down, it is far less likely to be embraced by managers than if they have participated from the beginning of the budget development process. The most effective budgeting systems are those that are strongly embraced by managers at all levels, which is most readily achieved through a participative (bottom-up) approach.

DISCUSSION QUESTIONS

Q20-1. What are the primary phases in the planning and control cycle?

Q20-2. Does budgeting require formal or informal planning? What are some advantages of this style of management?

Q20-3. Identify the advantages and disadvantages of the incremental approach to budgeting.

Q20-4. Explain the minimum level approach to budgeting.

Q20-5. How does activity-based budgeting predict a cost objective's budget?

Q20-6. Explain the continuous improvement concept of budgeting.

Q20-7. Which budget brings together all other budgets? How is this accomplished?

Q20-8. What budgets are normally used to support the cash budget? What is the net result of cash budget preparations?

Q20-9. Define *budgeted financial statements*.

Q20-10. Contrast the top-down and bottom-up approaches to budget preparation.

Q20-11. Is budgetary slack a desirable feature? Can it be prevented? Why or why not?

Q20-12. Why are annual budgets not always desirable? What are some alternative budget periods?

Q20-13. Explain how continuous budgeting works.

Q20-14. In addition to the sales forecast, what forecasts are used in budgeting?

Q20-15. Why should motivational considerations be a part of budget planning and utilization? List several ways to motivate employees with budgets.

MINI EXERCISES

M20-16. Department Budget Using Output/Input Approach (LO2)

The following data are from the general records of Department 16 for October.

- Each unit of product requires 6 direct labor hours, 20 liters of direct materials, and 1 container.
- Each unwasted liter of material processed requires $13 of manufacturing overhead.
- Average wages for direct laborers are $15 per hour.
- Direct materials currently cost $3 per liter.
- Containers cost $9 each.
- Direct material waste amounts to 10 percent of materials started in process.

Required

Prepare an October department budget for Department 16 if planned production is 2,000 units of output.

M20-17. Department Budget Using Incremental Approach (LO2)

Assume that the Assembly Department of Applied Materials' Texas plant prepares its budget using the incremental approach for both fixed and variable costs. For 2007 assume that the following costs were incurred for the production of 100,000 units.

Direct materials	$240,000
Direct labor.............................	600,000
Supervision..............................	90,000
Depreciation, equipment (straight line)........	34,000
Variable overhead ($1.20 per unit)	120,000

Assume that each unit takes one-half hour to assemble.

Required

Prepare a budget for the Assembly Department that allows for a 4 percent inflation rate if the Texas plant sets a production level of 140,000 for 2008.

M20-18. Purchases Budget in Units and Dollars (LO3)

Budgeted sales of The Music Shop for the first six months of 2008 are as follows:

Month	Unit Sales	Month	Unit Sales
January...........	130,000	April..............	210,000
February..........	160,000	May..............	180,000
March............	200,000	June	240,000

Beginning inventory for 2008 is 40,000 units. The budgeted inventory at the end of a month is 40 percent of units to be sold the following month. Purchase price per unit is $5.

Required

Prepare a purchases budget in units and dollars for each month, January through May.

M20-19. Cash Budget (LO3)

Wilson's Retail Company is planning a cash budget for the next three months. Estimated sales revenue is as follows:

Month	Sales Revenue	Month	Sales Revenue
January..........	$300,000	March............	$200,000
February.........	225,000	April	175,000

All sales are on credit; 60 percent is collected during the month of sale, and 40 percent is collected during the next month. Cost of goods sold is 80 percent of sales. Payments for merchandise sold are made in the month following the month of sale. Operating expenses total $41,000 per month and are paid during the month incurred. The cash balance on February 1 is estimated to be $30,000.

Required

Prepare monthly cash budgets for February, March, and April.

EXERCISES

E20-20. Activity-Based Budget (LO2)

Merrit Industries Inc. has the following budget information available for February:

Administration	$40,000
Advertising	$15,000
Assembly	½ hour per unit × $8
Direct materials	2 pounds per unit × $3
Inspection	$200 per batch of 1,000 units
Manufacturing overhead	$2 per unit
Manufactured units	20,000
Product development	$15,000
Sales units	20,000 units × $30
Setup cost	$10 per batch of 1,000 units

Required

Prepare a February activity-based budgeted income statement.

E20-21. Product and Department Budgets Using Activity-Based Approach (LO2)

The following data are from the general records of the Loading Department of Bowman Freight Company for November.

- Cleaning incoming trucks, 20 minutes.
- Obtaining and reviewing shipping documents for loading truck and instructing loaders, 30 minutes.
- Loading truck, 1 hour and 30 minutes.
- Cleaning shipping dock and storage area after each loading, 10 minutes.
- Employees perform both cleaning and loading tasks and are currently averaging $16 per hour in wages and benefits.
- The supervisor spends 10 percent of her time overseeing the cleaning activities; 60 percent overseeing various loading activities; and the remainder of her time making general plans and managing the department. Her current salary is $4,000 per month.
- Other overhead of the department amounts to $10,000 per month, 20 percent for cleaning and 80 percent for loading.

Required

Prepare an activities budget for cleaning and loading in the Loading Department for November, assuming 20 working days and the loading of an average of 14 trucks per day.

E20-22. Activity-Based Budgeting (LO2)

St. Mary's Hospital is preparing its budget for the coming year. It uses an activity-based approach for all costs except physician care. Its emergency room has three activity areas with cost drivers as follows:
1. *Reception*—paperwork of incoming patients. Cost driver is the number of forms completed.
2. *Treatment*—initial diagnosis and treatment of patients. Cost driver is the number of diagnoses treated.
3. *Cleaning*—general cleaning plus preparing treatment facilities for next patient. Cost driver is the number of people visiting emergency room (patients plus person(s) accompanying them).

Activity Area	Cost Driver Rates	Budgeted Amount of Cost Driver	
		Outpatients	Admitted Patients
Reception	$30	7,400 forms	5,500 forms
Treatment	90	7,000 diagnoses	4,400 diagnoses
Cleaning	12	6,400 people	2,400 people

Required

a. Prepare the total budgeted cost for each activity.
b. How might you adjust the budget approach if you found that outpatients were kept in the emergency room for one hour on average while admitted patients remained for two hours?
c. What advantage does an activity-based approach have over the hospital's former budgeting method of basing the next year's budget on the last year's actual amount plus a percentage increase?

E20-23. Sales Budget (LO3)

Summer Fun T-Shirt Shop has very seasonal sales. For 2008, management is trying to decide whether to establish a sales budget based on average sales or on sales estimated by quarter. The unit sales for 2008 are expected to be 10 percent higher than 2007 sales. Unit shirt sales by quarter for 2007 were as follows:

	Children's	Women's	Men's	Total
Winter quarter.	200	200	100	500
Spring quarter	200	250	200	650
Summer quarter	400	300	200	900
Fall quarter	200	250	100	550
Total	1,000	1,000	600	2,600

Children's T-shirts sell for $5 each, women's sell for $9, and men's sell for $10.

Required

Assuming a 10 percent increase in sales, prepare a sales budget for each quarter of 2008 using the following:
a. Average quarterly sales. (*Hint:* Winter quarter children's shirts are 275 [1,000 × 1.10 ÷ 4].)
b. Actual quarterly sales. (*Hint:* Winter quarter children's shirts are 220 [200 × 1.10].)
c. Suggest advantages of each method.

E20-24. Sales Budget (LO3)

Datek

Assume that Datek, a leader in on-line stock trading, is preparing for a surge in growth with a new set of stock trading fees. The following information is available:

Category	Number of Shares	Current Fee	New Fee as of July	Revenue
A	0–10,000	$ 11	$ 10	$1,210,000
B	10,001–50,000	50	40	50,000
C	50,001 and above	200	150	20,000

With the new fees, Datek expects to take many big volume traders from its competitors. Anticipated monthly growth is expected to be 10 percent, 20 percent, and 30 percent, respectively, for each category for the first three months after the new rates go into effect.

Required
a. What are the anticipated revenues per month for July and August?
b. Is the new fee structure satisfactory? Explain.

E20-25. Cash Budget (LO3)

Peruvian Tea Company began July with a cash balance of $145,000. A cash receipts and payments budget for each six-month period is prepared in advance. Sales have been estimated as follows:

Month	Sales Revenue	Month	Sales Revenue
May.	$120,000	September	$ 80,000
June	140,000	October	100,000
July.	80,000	November	100,000
August	60,000	December	110,000

All sales are on credit with 75 percent collected during the month of sale, 20 percent collected during the next month, and 5 percent collected during the second month following the month of sale. Cost of goods sold averages 70 percent of sales revenue. Ending inventory is one-half of the next month's predicted cost of sales. The other half of the merchandise is acquired during the month of sale. All purchases are paid for in the month after purchase. Operating costs are estimated at $20,000 each month and are paid for during the month incurred.

Required

Prepare monthly cash budgets for the six months from July to December. (*Hint:* Prepare monthly purchases budgets for June through November.)

E20-26. Cash Receipts (LO3)

The sales budget for Perrier Inc. is forecasted as follows:

Month	Sales Revenue
May.	$120,000
June	160,000
July.	180,000
August	120,000

To prepare a cash budget, the company must determine the budgeted cash collections from sales. Historically, the following trend has been established regarding cash collection of sales:

*   60 percent in the month of sale.
*   20 percent in the month following sale.
*   15 percent in the second month following sale.
*   5 percent uncollectible.

The company gives a 2 percent cash discount for payments made by customers during the month of sale. The accounts receivable balance on April 30 is $24,000, of which $7,000 represents uncollected March sales and $17,000 represents uncollected April sales.

Required

Prepare a schedule of budgeted cash collections from sales for May, June, and July. Include a three-month summary of estimated cash collections.

E20-27. Cash Disbursements (LO3)

Montana Timber Company is in the process of preparing its budget for next year. Cost of goods sold has been estimated at 70 percent of sales. Lumber purchases and payments are to be made during the month preceding the month of sale. Wages are estimated at 15 percent of sales and are paid during the month of sale. Other operating costs amounting to 10 percent of sales are to be paid in the month following the month of sale. Additionally, a monthly lease payment of $12,000 is paid to BMI for computer services. Sales revenue is forecast as follows:

Month	Sales Revenue
February	$100,000
March	160,000
April	180,000
May.	210,000
June	180,000
July.	230,000

Required

Prepare a schedule of cash disbursements for April, May, and June.

E20-28. Cash Disbursements (LO3)

Assume that Waycross Manufacturing manages its cash flow from its home office. Waycross controls cash disbursements by category and month. In setting its budget for the next six months, beginning in July, it used the following managerial guidelines:

Category	Guidelines
Accounts payable	Pay half in current and half in following month.
Payroll	Pay 80 percent in current month and 20 percent in following month.
Loan payments	Pay total amount due each month.

Predicted balances and due amounts for selected months follow:

Category	May	June	July	August	September	October
Accounts payable.....	$ 30,000	$ 44,000	$ 48,000	$ 50,000	$ 44,000	$ 50,000
Payroll.............	100,000	110,000	120,000	100,000	108,000	112,000
Notes payable	10,000	10,000	15,000	15,000	15,000	15,000

Required

Prepare a schedule showing cash disbursements by account for July and August.

E20-29. Budgeted Income Statement (LO3)

Pendleton Company, a merchandising company, is developing its master budget for 2008. The income statement for 2007 is as follows:

PENDLETON COMPANY
Income Statement
For Year Ending December 31, 2007

Gross sales.............................	$750,000
Less estimated uncollectible accounts	(7,500)
Net sales..............................	742,500
Cost of goods sold......................	(430,000)
Gross profit...........................	312,500
Operating expenses (including $25,000 depreciation)...........	(200,500)
Net income............................	$112,000

The following are management's goals and forecasts for 2008:
1. Selling prices will increase by 8 percent, and sales volume will increase by 5 percent.
2. The cost of merchandise will increase by 4 percent.
3. All operating expenses are fixed and are paid in the month incurred. Price increases for operating expenses will be 10 percent. The company uses straight-line depreciation.
4. The estimated uncollectibles are 1 percent of budgeted sales.

Required

Prepare a budgeted traditional income statement for 2008.

E20-30. Budgeted Income Statement (LO3)

Dakota Mfg. is planning a budget for the next fiscal year. The estimate of sales revenue is $1,000,000 and of cost of goods sold is 70 percent of sales revenue. Depreciation on the office building and fixtures is budgeted at $50,000. Salaries and wages should amount to 15 percent of sales revenue. Advertising has been budgeted at $80,000, and utilities should amount to $25,000. Income tax is estimated at 40 percent of operating income.

Required

Prepare a budgeted income statement for the next fiscal year.

PROBLEMS

P20-31. Cash Budget (LO3)

Cash budgeting for Carolina Apple, a merchandising firm, is performed on a quarterly basis. The company is planning its cash needs for the third quarter of 2007, and the following information is available to assist in preparing a cash budget. Budgeted income statements for July through October 2007 are as follows:

	July	August	September	October
Sales.....................	$18,000	$24,000	$28,000	$36,000
Cost of goods sold........	(10,000)	(14,000)	(16,000)	(20,000)
Gross profit..............	8,000	10,000	12,000	16,000
Less other expenses				
Selling..................	2,300	3,000	3,400	4,200
Administrative..........	2,600	3,000	3,200	3,600
Total	(4,900)	(6,000)	(6,600)	(7,800)
Net income..............	$ 3,100	$ 4,000	$ 5,400	$ 8,200

Additional information follows:
1. Other expenses, which are paid monthly, include $1,000 of depreciation per month.
2. Sales are 30 percent for cash and 70 percent on credit.
3. Credit sales are collected 20 percent in the month of sale, 70 percent one month after sale, and 10 percent two months after sale.
4. May sales were $15,000, and June sales were $16,000. Merchandise is paid for 50 percent in the month of purchase; the remaining 50 percent is paid in the following month. Accounts payable for merchandise at June 30 totaled $6,000.
5. The company maintains its ending inventory levels at 25 percent of the cost of goods to be sold in the following month. The inventory at June 30 is $2,500.
6. An equipment note of $5,000 per month is being paid through August.
7. The company must maintain a cash balance of at least $5,000 at the end of each month. The cash balance on June 30 is $5,100.
8. The company can borrow from its bank as needed. Borrowings and repayments must be in multiples of $100. All borrowings take place at the beginning of a month, and all repayments are made at the end of a month. When the principal is repaid, interest on the repayment is also paid. The interest rate is 12 percent per year.

Required
a. Prepare a monthly schedule of budgeted operating cash receipts for July, August, and September.
b. Prepare a monthly purchases budget and a schedule of budgeted cash payments for purchases for July, August, and September.
c. Prepare a monthly cash budget for July, August, and September. Show borrowings from the company's bank and repayments to the bank as needed to maintain the minimum cash balance.

P20-32. Cash Budget (LO3)
The Peoria Supply Company sells for $30 one product that it purchases for $20. Budgeted sales in total dollars for next year are $720,000. The sales information needed for preparing the July budget follows:

Month	Sales Revenue
May..............	$30,000
June	42,000
July..............	48,000
August	50,000

Account balances at July 1 include these:

Cash.........................	$20,000
Merchandise inventory............	16,000
Accounts receivable (sales)	23,000
Accounts payable (purchases)......	15,000

The company pays for one-half of its purchases in the month of purchase and the remainder in the following month. End-of-month inventory must be 50 percent of the budgeted sales in units for the next month. A

2 percent cash discount on sales is allowed if payment is made during the month of sale. Experience indicates that 50 percent of the billings will be collected during the month of sale, 40 percent in the following month, 8 percent in the second following month, and 2 percent will be uncollectible. Total budgeted selling and administrative expenses (excluding bad debts) for the fiscal year are estimated at $186,000, of which one-half is fixed expense (inclusive of a $20,000 annual depreciation charge). Fixed expenses are incurred evenly during the year. The other selling and administrative expenses vary with sales. Expenses are paid during the month incurred.

Required

a. Prepare a schedule of estimated cash collections for July.
b. Prepare a schedule of estimated July cash payments for purchases. (Round calculations to the nearest dollar.)
c. Prepare schedules of all July selling and administrative expenses and of those requiring cash payments.
d. Prepare a cash budget in summary form for July.

P20-33. Budgeted Financial Statements (LO3)

Ottawa Butter Company is preparing a budget for January and February of next year. The balance sheet as of December 31, 2007 follows:

OTTAWA BUTTER COMPANY Balance Sheet December 31, 2007			
Assets		**Liabilities and Stockholders' Equity**	
Cash.	$100,000	Accounts payable.	$125,000
Accounts receivable.	60,000	Operating expenses payable	10,000
Inventory.	30,000	Miscellaneous payable.	20,000
Equipment leasehold	60,000	Capital stock	25,000
		Retained earnings	70,000
Total assets.	$250,000	Total liabilities and equity	$250,000

Monthly sales data for the current year and the budgeted data for the next year are as follows:

November 2007	$180,000	February 2008	$250,000
December 2007	100,000	March 2008	260,000
January 2008	240,000	April 2008	280,000

For 2008, the following are expected:
*   Forty percent of the sales revenue is collected during the month of sale, with the balance collected during the following month.
*   Cost of goods sold is 60 percent of sales. Merchandise inventory sufficient for 20 percent of the next month's sales is to be maintained at the end of each month. All butter purchased for resale is paid for in the month following the month of purchase.
*   Operating expenses for each month are estimated at 10 percent of sales revenue. All operating expenses are paid for during the following month.
*   Income taxes are estimated at 40 percent of income before taxes. Income taxes are paid 15 days after the end of the quarter. There were no taxes payable on December 31, 2007. The miscellaneous payables at December 31, 2007, are to be paid during January 2008.

Required

a. Prepare a contribution budgeted income statement for the quarter ending March 31, 2008. Do not prepare monthly statements.
b. Prepare a budgeted balance sheet as of March 31, 2008. (*Hint:* Prepare purchases and cash budgets.)

P20-34. Developing a Master Budget (LO3)

Peyton Department Store prepares budgets quarterly. The following information is available for use in planning the second quarter budgets for 2007.

PEYTON DEPARTMENT STORE
Balance Sheet
March 31, 2007

Assets		Liabilities and Stockholders' Equity	
Cash..................	$ 3,000	Accounts payable...............	$26,000
Accounts receivable.....	25,000	Dividends payable	17,000
Inventory..............	30,000	Rent payable	2,000
Prepaid insurance.......	2,000	Stockholders' equity	40,000
Fixtures..............	25,000		
Total assets...........	$85,000	Total liabilities and equity.........	$85,000

Actual and forecasted sales for selected months in 2007 are as follows:

Month	Sales Revenue
January...........	$60,000
February..........	50,000
March............	40,000
April	50,000
May..............	60,000
June	70,000
July.............	90,000
August	80,000

Monthly operating expenses are as follows:

Wages and salaries	$25,000
Depreciation....................	100
Utilities	1,000
Rent	2,000

Cash dividends of $17,000 are declared during the third month of each quarter and are paid during the first month of the following quarter. Operating expenses, except insurance, rent, and depreciation are paid as incurred. Rent is paid during the following month. The prepaid insurance is for five more months. Cost of goods sold is equal to 50 percent of sales. Beginning inventories are sufficient for 120 percent of the next month's sales. Purchases during any given month are paid in full during the following month. All sales are on account, with 50 percent collected during the month of sale, 40 percent during the next month, and 10 percent during the month thereafter. Money can be borrowed and repaid in multiples of $1,000 at an interest rate of 12 percent per year. The company desires a minimum cash balance of $3,000 on the first of each month. At the time the principal is repaid, interest is paid on the portion of principal that is repaid. All borrowing is at the beginning of the month, and all repayment is at the end of the month. Money is never repaid at the end of the month it is borrowed.

Required
a. Prepare a purchases budget for each month of the second quarter ending June 30, 2007.
b. Prepare a cash receipts schedule for each month of the second quarter ending June 30, 2007. Do not include borrowings.
c. Prepare a cash disbursements schedule for each month of the second quarter ending June 30, 2007. Do not include repayments of borrowings.
d. Prepare a cash budget for each month of the second quarter ending June 30, 2007. Include budgeted borrowings and repayments.
e. Prepare an income statement for each month of the second quarter ending June 30, 2007.
f. Prepare a budgeted balance sheet as of June 30, 2007.

CASES

C20-35. Behavioral Implications of Budgeting (LO4)

Andrea Rawls, controller of Data Scientific, believes that effective budgeting greatly assists in meeting the organization's goals and objectives. She argues that the budget serves as a blueprint for the operating activities during each reporting period, making it an important control device. She believes that sound management evaluations can be based on the comparisons of performance and budgetary schedules and that employees respond more favorably when they participate in the budgetary process. Jeff Cooke, treasurer of Data Scientific, agrees that budgeting is essential for overall organization success, but he argues that human resources are too valuable to spend much time planning and preparing the budgetary process. He thinks that the roles people play in budgetary preparation are not important in the final analysis of a budget's effectiveness.

Required

Contrast the participative versus imposed budgeting concepts and indicate how the ideas of Rawls and Cooke fit the two categories.

C20-36. Behavioral Considerations and Budgeting (LO4)

Scott Weidner, the controller in the Division of Social Services for the state, recognizes the importance of the budgetary process for planning, control, and motivation purposes. He believes that a properly implemented participative budgeting process for planning purposes and a management by exception reporting procedure based on that budget will motivate his subordinates to improve productivity within their particular departments. Based on this philosophy, Weidner has implemented the following budget procedures.

- An appropriation target figure is given to each department manager. This amount is the maximum funding that each department can expect to receive in the next fiscal year.
- Department managers develop their individual budgets within the following spending constraints as directed by the controller's staff.
    1. Expenditure requests cannot exceed the appropriation target.
    2. All fixed expenditures should be included in the budget; these should include items such as contracts and salaries at current levels.
    3. All government projects directed by higher authority should be included in the budget in their entirety.
- The controller consolidates the departmental budget requests from the various departments into one budget that is to be submitted for the entire division.
- Upon final budget approval by the legislature, the controller's staff allocates the appropriation to the various departments on instructions from the division manager. However, a specified percentage of each department's appropriation is held back in anticipation of potential budget cuts and special funding needs. The amount and use of this contingency fund are left to the discretion of the division manager.
- Each department is allowed to adjust its budget when necessary to operate within the reduced appropriation level. However, as stated in the original directive, specific projects authorized by higher authority must remain intact.
- The final budget is used as the basis of control for a management by exception form of reporting. Excessive expenditures by account for each department are highlighted on a monthly basis. Department managers are expected to account for all expenditures over budget. Fiscal responsibility is an important factor in the overall performance evaluation of department managers.

Weidner believes that his policy of allowing the department managers to participate in the budget process and then holding them accountable for their performance is essential, especially during these times of limited resources. He also believes that department managers will be positively motivated to increase the efficiency and effectiveness of their departments because they have provided input into the initial budgetary process and are required to justify any unfavorable performances.

Required

a. Explain the operational and behavioral benefits that generally are attributed to a participative budgeting process.

b. Identify deficiencies in Weidner's participative budgetary policy for planning and performance evaluation purposes. For each deficiency identified, recommend how the deficiency can be corrected.

(CMA Adapted)

C20-37. Budgetary Slack with Ethical Considerations (LO4)

Alene Adams was promoted to department manager of a production unit in Dallas Industries three years ago. She enjoys her job except for the evaluation measures that are based on the department's budget. After three years of consistently poor annual evaluations based on a set annual budget, she has decided to improve the evaluation situation. At a recent budget meeting of junior-level managers, the topic of budgetary slack was discussed as a means to maintain some consistency in budgeting matters. As a result of this meeting, Adams decided to take the following steps in preparing the upcoming year's budget:

1. Use the top quartile for all wage and salary categories.
2. Select the optimistic values for the estimated production ranges for the coming year. These are provided by the marketing department.
3. Use the average of the three months in the current year with poorest production efficiency as benchmarks of success for the coming year.
4. Base equipment charges (primarily depreciation) on replacement values furnished by the purchasing department.
5. Base other fixed costs on current cost plus an inflation rate estimated for the coming year.
6. Use the average of the ten newly hired employees' performance as a basis of labor efficiency for the coming year.

Required

a. For each item on Adams' list, explain whether it will create budgetary slack. Use numerical examples as necessary to illustrate.

b. Given the company's use of static budgets as one of the performance evaluation measures of its managers, can the managers justify the use of built-in budgetary slack?

c. What would you recommend as a means for Adams to improve the budgeting situation in the company? Provide some specific examples of how the budgeting process might be improved.

C20-38. Budgetary Slack with Ethical Considerations (LO4)

Norton Company, a manufacturer of infant furniture and carriages, is in the initial stages of preparing the annual budget for next year. Scott Ford recently joined Norton's accounting staff and is interested to learn as much as possible about the company's budgeting process. During a recent lunch with Marge Atkins, sales manager, and Pete Granger, production manager, Ford initiated the following conversation:

Ford: Since I'm new around here and am going to be involved with the preparation of the annual budget, I'd be interested to learn how the two of you estimate sales and production numbers.

Atkins: We start out very methodically by looking at recent history, discussing what we know about current accounts, potential customers, and the general state of consumer spending. Then we add that usual dose of intuition to come up with the best forecast we can.

Granger: I usually take the sales projections as the basis for my projections. Of course, we have to make an estimate of what this year's closing inventories will be, which is sometimes difficult.

Ford: Why does that present a problem? There must have been an estimate of closing inventories in the budget for the current year.

Granger: Those numbers aren't always reliable since Marge makes some adjustments to the sales numbers before passing them on to me.

Ford: What kind of adjustments?

Atkins: Well, we don't want to fall short of the sales projections, so we generally give ourselves a little breathing room by lowering the initial sales projection anywhere from 5 to 10 percent.

Granger: So, you can see why this year's budget is not a very reliable starting point. We always have to adjust the projected production rates as the year progresses; of course, this changes the ending inventory estimates. By the way, we make similar adjustments to expenses by adding at least 10 percent to the estimates; I think everyone around here does the same thing.

Required

a. Marge Atkins and Pete Granger have described the use of budgetary slack.
1. Explain why Atkins and Granger behave in this manner, and describe the benefits they expect to realize from the use of budgetary slack.
2. Explain how the use of budgetary slack can adversely affect Atkins and Granger.

b. As a management accountant, Scott Ford believes that the behavior described by Marge Atkins and Pete Granger could be unethical and that he might have an obligation not to support this behavior. Explain why the use of budgetary slack could be unethical.

(CMA Adapted)

Performance Assessment: Standard Costs, Flexible Budgets, and Variance Analysis

LEARNING OBJECTIVES

LO1 Explain responsibility accounting. (p. 21-3)

LO2 Differentiate between static and flexible budgets for performance reporting. (p. 21-6)

LO3 Determine and interpret direct materials, direct labor, and overhead cost variances. (p. 21-11)

LO4 Calculate Revenue variances and prepare a performance report for a revenue center. (p. 21-19)

STANDARDS GONE WILD

Managers use standards, benchmarks, and various metrics to assess organizational performance. These standards and benchmarks also carry significant motivational content.

Motivational impacts of standards and benchmarks are evident at Gateway Corporation. Over the past two decades, Gateway grew into the fourth largest seller of personal computers with a low-cost-high-volume strategy. At one point, the firm had 20,000 employees, 300 stores, 15 call centers, and 5 domestic and international plants. However, a slowing economy and falling personal computer sales proved a challenge. Within 5 years, the firm's sales declined by over 50 percent, and income turned to losses.

A close look at Gateway operations reveal much more than a response to a changing economy. When founder Ted Waitt began to disengage from active involvement with the firm and ceded executive authority to a hand-picked successor and a new management team, the firm went from a rather freewheeling management style to one of rules and procedures.

Illustrative of this change was a new policy that impacted service representatives who answered technical questions for customers. The new policy stated that service reps would not receive their monthly bonus if they spent more than 13 minutes with a caller. The management goal was to better control overall service costs.

The motivational impact on employees and the ultimate results were predictable. Service reps emphasized solving service problems quickly to preserve their bonus. Their strategies included sending out new parts for

customers to install themselves, replacing entire computers if problems could not be diagnosed quickly, or simply hanging up in the middle of a call claiming phone trouble.

As a result of this and other management decisions, Gateway's selling, general, and administrative costs rose as a percent of revenues. The 13-minute standard (and others like it) had just the opposite effect from what was intended.

Management also began to emphasize the sale of expensive add-on products and services rather than the computers themselves. By raising commissions on the add-on items, management encouraged sales reps to be casual about selling the basic computers that are the firm's mainstay. As a result of these changes, customer satisfaction slumped, and referrals fell from 50 percent of sales to 30 percent.

Gateway called on Ted Waitt to resume his active management of the company. Emphasizing a back-to-basics approach, he eliminated numerous rules—including the 13-minute standard—and raised commissions on basic computers. He also cut prices to match industry leaders, eliminated noncore business operations, and rewarded employees for cost saving ideas.

While not all of Gateway's management challenges resulted from its revised standards and benchmarks, they did profoundly impact operations of the firm and its customer satisfaction ratings. Managerial accounting provides a multidimensional lens that emphasizes the technical, motivational, and strategic implications of standards, benchmarks, and metrics so that a Gateway-like situation never occurs.

[Source: *Fortune, Business Week, 10-K Reports.*][1]

---

[1]Katrina Brooker, "I Built This Company, I Can Save It," *Fortune,* April 30, 2001, pp. 94–102; and Arlene Weintraub and Andrew Park, "Can Gateway Survive in a Smaller Pasture?" *Business Week,* September 10, 2001.

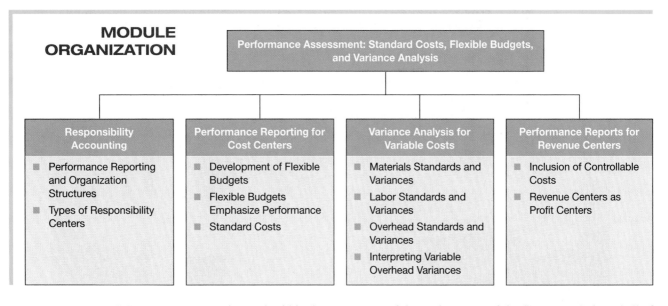

Management accounting tools aid in the assessment of the performance of the firm as a whole and all of its various components. Feedback in the form of performance reports is essential if the benefits of budgeting and other types of planning are to be fully realized. Managers must know how actual results compare with current budgets and standards to control current operations and to improve future operations. These performance reports should be prepared in accordance with the concept of **responsibility accounting,** which is the task of structuring performance reports addressed to individual (or group) members of an organization that emphasizes the factors they are able to control.

This module focuses on responsibility accounting and performance assessment. We examine responsibility accounting and identify various types of responsibility centers. We then take a close look at performance assessment for cost centers. We conclude the module by considering performance reports for revenue centers. (Responsibility accounting for major business segments is considered in Module 22.)

RESPONSIBILITY ACCOUNTING

LO1 Explain responsibility accounting.

Performance reports that include comparisons of actual results with plans or budgets serve as assessment tools and attention-directors to help managers determine and control activities. According to the concept of *management by exception,* the absence of significant differences indicates that activities are proceeding as planned whereas the presence of significant differences indicates a need to either take corrective action or revise plans. These evaluations and actions are made within the framework of an organization's overall mission, goals, and strategies as discussed in Module 14.

Responsibility accounting may focus on specific organization components or various aspects of the value chain that are accountable for the accomplishment of specific activities or objectives. Performance reports are customized to emphasize the activities of each specific organizational unit or value chain element. For example, a financial performance report addressed to the head of a production department contains manufacturing costs controllable by the department head; it does not contain costs (such as advertising, sales commissions, or the president's salary) that the head of the production department cannot control. Including noncontrollable costs in the report distracts the manager's attention from the controllable costs, thereby diluting a manager's efforts to deal with controllable items. Lower-level managers could also become frustrated with the entire performance reporting system if they believe upper-level managers expect them to control costs they cannot influence. However, some companies insist on reporting all related revenues and expenses (controllable and non-controllable) in the same report. When this is the case, the noncontrollable items should be clearly labeled.

A poorly designed responsibility accounting system can lead to unethical practices by managers in key positions. If too much pressure is placed on managers to meet performance targets, they sometimes take actions that are not in the best interest of the organization. The Business Insight that follows presents examples of such actions involving a vice president of Bausch & Lomb and the CEO of Sunbeam who forced sales into one year to the detriment of the companies' sales the following year. The designers of an organization's responsibility accounting system need to be aware of the potential pressures that such a system can place on managers. The decision-making model of the organization should be such that managers are not influenced to make undesirable decisions just to receive bonuses or promotions.

BUSINESS INSIGHT	Ethics and Responsibility Accounting

A few years ago, the contact lens division of Bausch & Lomb, Inc., was experiencing lower-than-anticipated sales levels. The head of the division called a meeting of its independent distributors and told them that the company had changed its sales strategy. Effective immediately, each distributor would have to boost its inventory of contact lenses if it wanted to remain a distributor of Bausch & Lomb products. The strategy was for distributors to buy only in very large quantities (some as much as a two-year supply) with prices increased by amounts up to 50 percent. Also, the distributors had to place these large orders by year-end. As one distributor stated, "When your No. 1 vendor says you'd better take it or else, what're you going to do?" All but two of Bausch & Lomb's distributors complied with the new sales strategy demands; and those two were subsequently dropped as customers.

Initially the strategy paid off; the sales in the last few days of the year totaled about $25 million and amounted to one-half of the division's profit for the entire year. The division manager was delighted. However, the long-term results were not favorable. By the following mid-year, the company announced that the high inventories of its distributors would severely reduce sales and profits for that year. The profit decline was approximately 37 percent. After the announcement, the company's stock fell from $50 to $32. The manager was forced to step down, and stockholders filed a class-action lawsuit accusing the company of falsely inflating sales and earnings.

History repeated itself when the CEO of Sunbeam followed the Bausch & Lomb plan to force sales to show how well his management style (firing employees and closing plants) was working. Sunbeam instituted a "bill and hold" plan that called for products to be produced in large quantities and sold to customers for delivery at a later date. While this made the financial report for that first year very favorable, it had a detrimental effect on the next year's report. In late March of that following year, Sunbeam acknowledged that first quarter income would be below expectations, and in fact, a loss. Stockholders quickly filed lawsuits charging deception, and the CEO was fired.[2]

Performance Reporting and Organization Structures

Before implementing a responsibility accounting system, all areas of authority and responsibility within an organization must be clearly defined. Organization charts and other documents should be examined to determine an organization's authority and responsibility structure. **Organization structure** is the arrangement of lines of responsibility within the organization. These structures vary widely. Some companies have functional-based structures along the lines of marketing, production, research, and so forth; other companies use products, services, customers, or geography as the basis of organization. When an attempt is made to implement a responsibility accounting system, management could find instances of overlapping duties, authority not commensurate with responsibility, and expenditures for which no one appears responsible. These circumstances can make the development of a responsibility accounting system difficult. General Electric overcame many of these problems with the use of teams and a new measurement tool as explained in the next Business Insight. (For discussions and examples of organization structures, consult a basic principles of management text.)

---

[2] "Numbers Game at Bausch & Lomb?" *Business Week,* December 19, 1994, pp. 108–10; and "How Al Dunlap Self-Destructed," *Business Week,* July 6, 1998, pp. 58–61, 64.

BUSINESS INSIGHT **GE's Six Sigma**

General Electric strives to improve quality without ignoring costs and its managers are responsible for controlling the combination of quality and costs. Its responsibility accounting program, called Six Sigma, has increased its annual productivity by over 200 percent and its operating margin by 4 percentage points. Six Sigma, is a means of measuring quality (through errors or defects) for any activity. For each activity, a target for improvement is set and a manager is assigned the responsibility to achieve the target. The reporting system centers on the rate of improvement as measured by reduced defects or errors. The program has five basic steps:

1. *Define:* Teams work to define problems related to a process or service.
2. *Measure:* Determine what is wrong with the existing process or service.
3. *Analyze:* Determine reasons for what is wrong.
4. *Improve:* Define and develop a plan of action.
5. *Control:* Ensure changes are installed and used effectively; keep problems from recurring.

GE is pleased with the system because it improved quality *and* saved millions in operating expenses.[3]

Although performance reports can be developed for areas of responsibility as narrow as a single worker, the basic responsibility unit in most organizations begins with the department and progresses to division and corporate levels. In manufacturing plants, separate performance reports can be used for responsibility centers comprising production or service departments or manufacturing cells. In large universities, separate responsibility centers are set up for individual academic departments (such as accounting, psychology, and mathematics) and staff and service departments (such as human resources, food service, and maintenance). When a large department performs a number of diverse and significant activities, responsibility accounting can be further refined so that a single department contains several responsibility centers with performance reports prepared for each.

Types of Responsibility Centers

Under responsibility accounting, performance reports are prepared for departments, segments of departments, or groupings of departments that operate under the control and authority of a responsible manager. Each organization unit for which performance reports are prepared is identified as a responsibility center. For the purpose of evaluating their financial performance, responsibility centers can be classified as cost centers, revenue centers, profit centers, or investment centers.

Cost Center

A **cost center** is a responsibility center whose manager is responsible for managing only costs; there is no revenue responsibility. A cost center can be as small as a segment of a department or large enough to include a major aspect of the organization, such as all manufacturing activities. Typical examples of cost centers include the following:

Organization	Cost Center
Manufacturing plant	Tooling department Assembly activities
Retail store	Inventory control function Maintenance department
TV station	Audio and video engineering Buildings and grounds
College	History department Registrar's office
City government	Public safety (police and fire) Road maintenance

---

[3]Sridhar Seshadri and Gregory T. Lucier, "GE Takes Six Sigma beyond the Bottom Line," *Strategic Finance,* May 2001, pp. 40–46.

Revenue Center

A **revenue center** is a responsibility center whose manager is responsible for the generation of sales revenues. Even though the basic performance report of a revenue center emphasizes sales, revenue centers are likely to be assigned responsibility for the controllable costs they incur in generating revenues. If revenues and costs are evaluated separately, the center has dual responsibility as a revenue center and as a cost center. If controllable costs are deducted from revenues to obtain some bottom-line contribution, the center is, in fact, being treated more like a profit center than a revenue center.

Profit Center

A **profit center** is a responsibility center whose manager is responsible for revenues, costs, and resulting profits. It could be an entire organization, but it is more frequently a segment of an organization such as a product line, marketing territory, or store. In the context of performance evaluation, the word "profit" does not necessarily refer to the bottom line of an income statement; instead, it likely refers to the profit center's contribution to common corporate costs and profit. Profit is computed as the center's revenues less all costs associated with operating the center. In addition to a center's profits, other measures of performance can include quality assessments, service ratings, and operating efficiencies. Having limited authority regarding the size of total assets, the profit center manager is not held responsible for the relationship between profits and assets.

Investment Center

An **investment center** is a responsibility center whose manager is responsible for the relationship between its profits and the total assets invested in the center. Investment center managers have a high degree of organization autonomy. In general, the management of an investment center is expected to earn a target profit per dollar invested. Investment center managers are evaluated on the basis of how well they use the total resources entrusted to their care to earn a profit. An investment center is the broadest and most inclusive type of responsibility center. Managers of these centers have more authority and responsibility than other managers and are primarily responsible for planning, organizing, and controlling firm activities. Because of their authority regarding the size of corporate assets, they are held responsible for the relationship between profits and assets. (Investment centers are discussed further in Module 22.)

PERFORMANCE REPORTING FOR COST CENTERS

Financial performance reports for cost centers should always include a comparison of actual and budgeted (or allowed) costs and should always identify the difference as a **variance.** *Allowed costs* in performance reports are the flexible budget amounts for the actual level of activity. The variance is favorable if actual costs are less than budgeted (or allowed) costs and unfavorable if actual costs are more than budgeted (or allowed) costs. These comparisons are made in total and individually for each type of controllable cost assigned to the cost center.

LO2 Differentiate between static and flexible budgets for performance reporting.

Development of Flexible Budgets

A budget that is based on a prediction of sales and production is called a *static budget.* The operating budget explained in Module 20 is a **static budget.** Budgets can also be set for a series of possible production and sales volumes, or budgets can be adjusted to a particular level of production after the fact. These budgets, based on cost-volume relationships, are called **flexible budgets;** they are used to determine what costs should have been for an attained level of activity. For example, if the college cafeteria budgets $10,000 for food during April for 5,000 meals but provides 6,000 meals, the budget needs to be adjusted by the original food budget rate of $2 ($10,000 ÷ 5,000 meals). Otherwise, the amount spent on food will not be a fair evaluation of the cost per the original budget. If $11,500 was spent on food during the month, the analysis might appear as follows:

Budget Item	Actual	Budget	Difference
Static analysis			
Food.............	$11,500	$10,000 (5,000 meals × $2)	$1,500 over budget
Flexible analysis			
Food.............	$11,500	$12,000 (6,000 meals × $2)	$500 under budget

The cafeteria manager is better evaluated based on what actually happened with the flexible budget than with the static budget, especially if the manager had no control over how many student meals were requested.

Before developing a flexible budget, management must understand how costs respond to changes in activity. Some costs respond to unit or volume activity; others respond to batch activity. There are always fixed costs that generally do not respond to either units or volume. The following Research Insight demonstrates how the advantages of multiple drivers can often be realized when only one or two drivers do not properly explain what is taking place.

RESEARCH INSIGHT   **System Fails to Identify Resource Use**

A large equipment manufacturer's machining shop was operating under some confusion. Its managers could not understand how they kept winning bids for simple, low-volume parts that made heavy demands of support resources. This was especially confusing since the facility was designed to be competitive on bidding for complex, high-volume parts. The manufacturer had been using a traditional standard cost accounting system in the machining department that used a three-level base composed of direct materials dollars, direct labor dollars, and machine hours. Investigation of actual cost drivers led to the development of five new cost drivers: setup time, number of production runs, materials movements, active parts numbers maintenance, and facility management. The first three related to how many batches were produced, the fourth to the number of different types of products produced; and the fifth, to the facility as a whole. The five new drivers provided managers with a different view of how the department operated. The old system failed to show the different demands that the orders placed on company resources, whereas the new system was closer to how the parts utilized company resources.[4]

For an in-depth example, assume that McMillan Company, which produces leather compact disk carrying cases, has three departments: Production, Sales, and Administration. The focus in this section is on the development of financial performance reports for the Production Department. The flexible budget cost-estimating equations for total monthly production costs of cases are based on production standards for unit- and batch-level variable costs and fixed costs. The standards follow:

Unit level cost
    Direct materials—2 pounds per unit at $5 per pound, or $10 per unit
    Direct labor—0.25 hour per unit at $24 per hour, or $6 per unit
    Waterproofing and inspection—$8 per unit
Batch level cost
    Setup costs—$400 per batch of 1,000 units, or $0.40 per unit
    Test run—$100 per batch of 1,000 units, or $0.10 unit
Fixed costs—$52,000

---

[4] Robin Cooper and Robert S. Kaplan, "Profit Priorities from Activity-Based Costing," *Harvard Business Review* (May–June 1991), pp. 130–35.

If management plans to produce 10,000 cases (10 batches of 1,000 cases) in July, requiring 4,000 machine hours and 20,000 pounds of materials, the budgeted manufacturing costs for the month will amount to $297,000 as shown below:

McMILLAN COMPANY Manufacturing Budget For Month of July	
Manufacturing costs	
Unit level costs	
Direct materials (10,000 × 2 pounds × $5)	$100,000
Direct labor (10,000 × 0.25 hours × $24).........	60,000
Waterproofing and inspection (10,000 × $8)	80,000
Batch level costs	
Setup (10 batches × $400)....................	4,000
Test run (10 batches × $100)	1,000
Fixed costs	52,000
Total	$297,000

Flexible Budgets Emphasize Performance

If actual production happened to equal 10,000 units produced in 10 batches, the performance of the Production Department in controlling costs could be based on a comparison of actual and budgeted manufacturing costs. If production was at some volume other than that planned in the original manufacturing budget, however, it would be inappropriate to compare actual manufacturing costs with the costs predicted in the original static budget. Doing so would intermix two separate Production Department responsibilities, namely, the manufacturing responsibility for production volume and the financial responsibility for cost control.

The original budget for production volume was set on the basis of predicted needs for sales and inventory requirements, taking into consideration materials, labor, and facilities constraints. In the absence of any changes in these needs, the Production Department's manufacturing responsibility for production volume is evaluated by comparing the actual and budgeted production volumes. If, however, production needs change, perhaps due to an unexpected increase or decrease in sales volume, the Production Department should attempt to make appropriate changes in its production volume. When the actual production volume is anything other than the originally budgeted amount, the Production Department's financial responsibility for cost control should be based on the actual level of production or an adjustment to the level of planned production.

For the purpose of evaluating the financial performance of cost centers, a flexible budget is tailored, after the fact, to the actual level of activity. A **flexible budget variance** is computed for each cost as the difference between the actual cost and the flexible budget cost of producing a given quantity of product or service. Assume that actual production for July totaled 11,000 units in 11 batches rather than the 10,000 units that were budgeted. Examples of a performance report for July manufacturing costs based on static and flexible budgets are presented in Exhibit 21.1. When the Production Department's financial performance is evaluated using the static budget, the actual cost of producing 11,000 units is compared to the budgeted cost of producing 10,000 units. The result is a series of unfavorable static budget variances totaling $20,600.

When the Production Department's financial performance is evaluated by comparing actual costs with costs allowed in a flexible budget drawn up for the actual production volume, however, the results are mixed. Direct materials have a $2,000 favorable flexible budget variance. Direct labor has a $4,000 unfavorable flexible budget variance. The unit-level waterproofing and inspection variance is $7,000 favorable. The batch-level costs have a $100 unfavorable variance, and the fixed overhead variance has not changed since the static and flexible fixed budgets stay the same. The net flexible budget variance is $3,900 favorable, a substantial change from the static variance of $20,600 unfavorable.

Flexible budget variances provide a much better indicator of performance than do static budget variances, which do not consider the increased level of production (11,000 units rather than 10,000 units).

EXHIBIT 21.1	Flexible Budgets and Performance Evaluation

McMILLAN COMPANY
Production Department Performance Report
For Month of July

	Based on Static Budget			Based on Flexible Budget		
	Actual	Original Budget	Static Budget Variance	Actual	Flexible Budget*	Flexible Budget Variance
Volume	11,000	10,000		11,000	11,000	
Unit level costs						
Direct materials.	$108,000	$100,000	$ 8,000 U	$108,000	$110,000	$2,000 F
Direct labor	70,000	60,000	10,000 U	70,000	66,000	4,000 U
Waterproofing and inspection.	81,000	80,000	1,000 U	81,000	88,000	7,000 F
Batch level costs						
Setup		4,000			4,400	
Test runs		1,000			1,100	
Total	5,600	5,000	600 U	5,600	5,500	100 U
Fixed costs.	53,000	52,000	1,000 U	53,000	52,000	1,000 U
Totals	$317,600	$297,000	$20,600 U	$317,600	$321,500	$3,900 F

*Flexible budget manufacturing costs: (Actual level × Budgeted unit cost)
Direct materials (11,000 units × 2 pounds × $5)
Direct labor (11,000 units × 0.25 labor hour × $24)
Waterproofing and inspection (11,000 units × $8)
Setup (11 batches × $400)
Test runs (11 batches × $100)

When production increases by, say, 10 percent, the static budget variances would be unfavorable. Likewise, when actual production is substantially below the planned level of activity, the static variances are usually favorable. While it is important to isolate variances and explain their causes, the financial-based performance report is not the appropriate place to mix volume-created variances with those related to the actual production levels.

MID-MODULE REVIEW

Ron Gilette received the following performance report from the accounting department for his first month as plant manager for a new company. Ron's supervisor, the vice president of manufacturing, has concerns that the report does not provide an accurate picture of Ron's performance in the area of cost control.

	Actual	Budgeted	Variance
Units.	10,000	12,000	2,000 U
Costs			
Direct materials	$ 299,000	$ 360,000	$ 61,000 F
Direct labor.	345,500	432,000	86,500 F
Variable factory overhead.	180,000	216,000	36,000 F
Fixed factory overhead	375,000	360,000	15,000 U
Total costs	$1,199,500	$1,368,000	$168,500 F

Required

Prepare a revised budget that better reflects Ron Gilette's performance.

Solution

The performance report prepared by the accounting department was based on a "static" budget. A better basis for evaluating Ron Gilette's performance is to compare actual performance with a flexible budget. By dividing the budgeted sales and variable costs amounts by 12,000 units, the budgeted unit variable costs amounts can be determined as follows:

Direct materials cost...........	$360,000 ÷ 12,000 units = $30 per unit
Direct labor..................	$432,000 ÷ 12,000 units = $36 per unit
Variable factory overhead.......	$216,000 ÷ 12,000 units = $18 per unit

Using these budgeted unit values, a flexible budget can be prepared as follows:

	Actual	Flexible Budget	Variance
Units.....................	10,000	10,000	
Costs			
Direct materials	$ 299,000	$ 300,000	$ 1,000 F
Direct labor................	345,500	360,000	14,500 F
Variable factory overhead.....	180,000	180,000	
Fixed factory overhead.......	375,000	360,000	15,000 U
Total plant costs............	$1,199,500	$1,200,000	$ 500 F

The plant did not produce the number of units originally budgeted. Therefore, from a cost control standpoint, a flexible budget is a better basis for evaluating Ron's performance because it compares the actual cost of producing 10,000 units with a budget also based on 10,000 units. Based on the flexible budget, his performance is still quite good; however, it is much less favorable than it appeared using a static budget.

Standard Costs

A **standard cost** indicates what it should cost to provide an activity or produce one batch or unit of product under planned and efficient operating conditions. In a standard costing environment, the flexible budget is based on standard unit costs. Traditionally, standard costs have been developed from an engineering analysis or from an analysis of historical data adjusted for expected changes in the product, production technology, or costs. When standards are developed using historical data, management must be careful to ensure that past inefficiencies are excluded from current standards.

To obtain the full benefit of standard costs, the standards must be based on realistic expectations. The standard variable product cost for direct labor for McMillan Company is $6.00 per unit. Some organizations intentionally set "tight" standards to motivate employees toward higher levels of production. The management of McMillan Company might set their standards for direct labor at 0.22 hours per unit rather than at the expected 0.25 hours per unit, hoping that employees will strive toward the lower time and, consequently, the lower cost of $5.28 ($24 × 0.22). The use of tight standards often causes planning and behavioral problems. Management expects them to result in unfavorable variances. Accordingly, tight standards should not be used to budget input requirements and cash flows because management expects to incur more labor costs than the standards allow. The use of tight standards can have undesirable behavioral effects if lower-level managers and employees find that a second set of standards is used in the "real" budget or if they are constantly subject to unfavorable performance reports. These employees could come to distrust the entire budgeting and performance evaluation system, or they may quit trying to achieve any of the organization's standards.

Tight standards are more likely to occur in an imposed budget and less likely to occur in a participation budget for which employees are actively involved in preparing. In a participation budget, the problems may be to avoid loose standards that are easily attained and to avoid overstating the costs required to produce a product. Loose standards may fail to properly motivate employees and can make the company uncompetitive due to costs and prices that are higher than those of competitors.

VARIANCE ANALYSIS FOR VARIABLE COSTS

LO3 Determine and interpret direct materials, direct labor, and overhead cost variances.

To use and interpret standard cost variances properly, managers must understand both the standard-setting process and the framework for computing and analyzing standard cost variances. While these are preliminary tools for decision analysis regarding activities and operations, they nevertheless give managers a starting point as to the general movement toward efficiency (or lack thereof) of the defined activities being evaluated. The variances alone do not explain, however, why the activity is different from expectations. Underlying causes of variances must always be investigated before final judgment is passed on the effectiveness and efficiency of an operation or activity. Later sections consider possible explanations as to why variances occur in each area.

Standard cost variance analysis provides a system for examining the flexible budget variance, which is the difference between the actual cost and flexible budget cost of producing a given quantity of product or service. Actual cost is determined from the organization's financial transactions. Flexible budget cost is determined by multiplying standard quantities allowed for the output times the standard price per unit. In other words, the flexible budget can be computed as actual output times the standard unit cost. Recall that standard unit cost represents what it *should* cost to produce a completed unit of product or service under efficient operating conditions. To determine standard unit cost, management establishes separate quantity and price (or rate) standards for each input production component. For a company using activity-based costing, each manufacturing activity could have its own standard costs that focus on underlying concepts and cost drivers, and companies even develop their own set of variances as discussed in the following Business Insight.

BUSINESS INSIGHT **Flexibility in Standard Costing**

The variances in this book are not the only ones used by managers. Many companies develop their own variances to meet the needs of their managers when confronted with unusual activities. Such is the case with **Parker Brass**. Two concerns of the production managers at Parker Brass are the timing of product cost information and providing an effective cost control system. As managers were struggling with new and different decisions, they decided that additional information was needed. They developed three new variances: standard run quantity variance, materials substitution variance, and method variance.

The *standard run quantity variance* measures the amount of setup cost that was not recovered because the batch size was smaller than the predetermined optimal batch size. Because the company had been including setup cost with labor, the managers were having difficulty explaining all of the labor variances. By pulling out the amounts related to batch sizes, the remainder of the analysis became easier to explain. The *materials substitute variance* is relevant when the standard materials have to be substituted because of lack of inventory or because a customer wants something different than normal. This often helps explain both materials price variances and usage variances so these two variances do not have to be used to justify all differences between standard and actual cost. The *method variance* is used when different machines or processes can be used to produce the same output. For example, if a process requires three labor hours and two machine hours but due to machine demand by other products, the process can be completed with seven labor hours and one machine hour, the resulting standard versus actual cost variances will be different even when all costs are perfectly controlled.

When managers know that the accounting system is flexible, there is more coordination between those who develop the system and those who use it. Parker Brass modified its standard costing system to better meet the needs of its managers without disrupting the traditional cost accounting system.[5]

---

[5] David Johnsen and Parvez Sopariwala, "Standard Costing Is Alive and Well at Parker Brass, *Management Accounting Quarterly*, Winter 2000, pp. 12–20.

Standard cost variance analysis identifies the general causes of the total flexible budget variance by breaking it into separate price and quantity variances for each production component. Two possible reasons that actual cost could differ from flexible budget cost for a given amount of output produced are (1) a difference between actual and standard prices paid for the production components—the price variance—and (2) a difference between the actual quantity and the standard quantity allowed for the production components—the quantity variance. Variances have different names for different cost categories as follows:

Cost Component	Price Variance Name	Quantity Variance Name
Direct materials	Materials price variance	Materials quantity variance
Direct labor	Labor rate variance	Labor efficiency variance
Variable overhead	Variable overhead spending variance	Variable overhead efficiency variance

Fixed overhead is excluded from the unit standard costs because, within the relevant range of normal activity, it does not vary with the volume of production. To facilitate product costing, however, many organizations develop a standard fixed overhead cost per unit.

In the following sections, we analyze the flexible budget cost variances for materials, labor and variable overhead. Our illustration of variance analysis is based on the July activity and costs of McMillan Company's Production Department. There were 11 batches and 4,100 machine hours during the month.

McMILLAN COMPANY—PRODUCTION DEPARTMENT
Actual Manufacturing Costs
For Month of July

Actual units completed.	11,000
Manufacturing costs	
Unit level costs	
Direct materials (24,000 pounds × $4.50) . .	$108,000
Direct labor (2,800 hours × $25.00)	70,000
Waterproofing and inspection.	81,000
Batch level costs (setup and testing)	5,600
Fixed overhead costs	53,000
Total	$317,600

Materials Standards and Variances

The two basic elements contained in the standards for direct materials are the *standard price* and the *standard quantity*. Materials standards indicate how much an organization should pay for each input unit of direct materials and the quantity of direct materials it allows to produce one unit of output. The standard price per unit of direct materials should include all reasonable costs necessary to acquire the materials. These costs include the invoice price of materials, less planned discounts plus freight, insurance, special handling, and any other costs related to the acquisition of the materials. The standard quantity represents the number of units of raw materials allowed for the production of one unit of finished product. This amount should include the amount dictated by the physical characteristics of the process and the product, plus a reasonable allowance for normal spoilage, waste, and other inefficiencies. The quantity standard can be determined by engineering analysis, professional judgment, or by averaging the actual amount used for several periods. An average of actual past materials usage may not be a good standard because it could include excessive wastes and inefficiencies in the standard quantity.

McMillan Company has a direct materials quantity standard of 2.0 pounds per finished unit produced and a materials price standard of $5 per pound. In fact, each unit can physically contain only 1.8 pounds of raw materials, with the additional 0.2 pound representing the amount allowed by the standards for normal spoilage, waste, and other inefficiencies. This is an area for which the company could consider implementing quality cost analysis to see whether the situation can be improved.

The **materials price variance** is the difference between the actual materials cost and the standard cost of actual materials inputs. The **materials quantity variance** is the difference between the standard cost of actual materials inputs and the flexible budget cost for materials. The direct materials variances for McMillan Company follow.

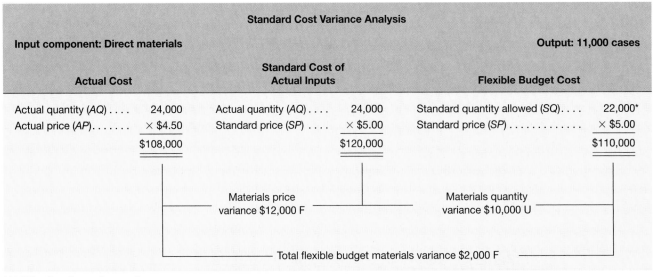

*11,000 units × 2 pounds per unit

McMillan Company had a favorable materials price variance of $12,000 because the actual cost of materials used ($108,000) was less than the standard cost of actual materials used ($120,000). Stated another way, for the materials actually used, the total price paid was $12,000 less than the price allowed by the standards. The price variance can also be viewed as the actual quantity (AQ) used times the difference between the actual price (AP) and the standard price (SP). McMillan Company paid $0.50 per pound below the standard price for 24,000 pounds for a total savings of $12,000. This is readily shown using the formula approach:

$$\textbf{Materials price variance} = \textbf{AQ(AP} - \textbf{SP)}$$
$$= \textbf{24,000(\$4.50} - \textbf{\$5.00)}$$
$$= \textbf{24,000} \times \textbf{\$0.50}$$
$$= \textbf{\$12,000 F}$$

The unfavorable quantity variance of $10,000 occurred because the standard cost of actual materials used, $120,000 (24,000 × $5), was higher than the cost of materials allowed by the flexible budget, $110,000 (22,000 × $5). A total of 22,000 pounds of materials is allowed to produce 11,000 units of finished outputs. This is computed as 11,000 finished units times 2.0 pounds of direct materials per unit. The materials quantity variance can also be computed as the standard price (SP) per pound times the difference between the number of pounds actually used (AQ) and the number of pounds allowed (SQ). This is also readily shown using the formula approach:

$$\textbf{Materials quantity variance} = \textbf{SP(AQ} - \textbf{SQ)}$$
$$= \textbf{\$5(24,000} - \textbf{22,000)}$$
$$= \textbf{\$5} \times \textbf{2,000}$$
$$= \textbf{\$10,000 U}$$

Interpreting Materials Variances

After computing variances, managers must understand how to use them in making decisions relevant to the items being evaluated. A *favorable materials price variance* indicates that the employee responsible for materials purchases paid less per unit than the price allowed by the standards. This could result from receiving discounts for purchasing more than the normal quantities, effective bargaining by the employee, purchasing substandard-quality materials, purchasing from a distress seller, or other factors. Ordinarily, when a favorable price variance is reported, the employee's performance is interpreted as favorable. However, if the favorable price variance results from the purchase of materials of lower than standard quality or from a purchase in more than desirable quantities, the employee's performance would be questionable. Consistent and highly favorable variances could indicate situations that are undermining the responsibility accounting system by building slack into the standards or using incorrect data. These situations should be thoroughly investigated for causes and corrections.

An *unfavorable materials price variance* means that the purchasing employee paid more per unit for materials than the price allowed by the standards. This could be caused by failure to buy in sufficient quantities to receive normal discounts; purchase of higher-quality materials than called for in the product specifications; failure to place materials orders on a timely basis, thereby requiring a more expensive shipping alternative; uncontrollable price changes in the market for the materials; failure to bargain for the best available prices; or other factors. It should be emphasized that an unfavorable variance does not always mean that the employee performed unfavorably. Many noncontrollable factors surround the purchasing function due to timing problems, changing vendors, and changes in materials required by production.

A *favorable materials quantity variance* means that the actual quantity of raw materials used was less than the quantity allowed for the units produced. This could result from factors such as less materials waste than allowed by the standards, better than expected machine efficiency, direct materials of higher quality than required by the standards, and more efficient use of direct materials by employees. An *unfavorable materials quantity variance* occurs when the quantity of raw materials used exceeds the quantity allowed for the units produced. This could result from incurring more waste than provided for in the standards, poorly maintained machinery requiring larger amounts of raw materials, raw materials of lower quality than required by the standards, or poorly trained employees who were unable to use the materials at the level of efficiency required by the standards.

Labor Standards and Variances

To evaluate management performance in controlling labor costs by using a standard cost system, it is necessary to determine the *standard labor rate* for each hour allowed and the *standard time allowed* to produce a unit. Setting labor rate standards can be quite simple or extremely complex. If only one class of employee is used to make each product and if all employees have the same wage rate, determining the standard cost is relatively easy: Simply adopt the normal wage rate as the standard labor rate. If several different classes of employees are used to make each unit of product, separate efficiency and rate standards could be established for each class.

The standard labor time per unit can be determined by an engineering approach or an empirical observation approach. When using an engineering approach, industrial engineers ascertain the amount of time required to produce a unit of finished product by applying time and motion methods or other available techniques. Normal operating conditions are assumed in arriving at the labor standard. Therefore, allowances must be made for normal machine downtime, employee personal breaks, and so forth. Under the empirical approach, the long-run average time required in the past to produce a unit under normal operating conditions is used as a basis for the standard. Use of normal operating conditions automatically factors inefficiencies such as machine downtime and employee breaks into the standard.

Using the general variance model that was used for materials, we can compute the labor rate and efficiency variances. The **labor rate (spending) variance** is the difference between the actual cost and the standard cost of actual labor inputs. The **labor efficiency variance** is the difference between the standard cost of actual inputs and the flexible budget cost for labor.

McMillan Company's labor standards provide for 0.25 hour of labor per unit produced at $24 per hour. During July, 2,800 hours were used at a cost of $25 per hour. Using these data, the labor rate (price) variance and labor efficiency (quantity) variance can be computed as shown in the following illustration.

Standard Cost Variance Analysis

Input component: Direct labor   **Output: 11,000 cases**

Actual Cost		Standard Cost of Actual Inputs		Flexible Budget Cost	
Actual hours (*AH*)	2,800	Actual hours (*AH*)	2,800	Standard hours allowed (*SH*).	2,750*
Actual rate (*AR*)	× $25	Standard rate (*SR*)	× $24	Standard rate (*SR*).	× $24
	$70,000		$67,200		$66,000

Labor rate variance $2,800 U   Labor efficiency variance $1,200 U

Total flexible budget labor variance $4,000 U

*11,000 units × 0.25 hour per unit

The labor rate variance can also be computed in formula form as the actual number of hours used times the difference between the actual rate and the standard rate. The symbols are the same as in the diagram.

$$\textbf{Labor rate variance = AH(AR − SR)}$$
$$= 2,800(\$25 − \$24)$$
$$= 2,800 × \$1$$
$$= \$2,800 \text{ U}$$

This computation of the labor rate variance shows that the company paid $1 more than the standard rate for each of the 2,800 hours worked.

Since 11,000 units of product were finished during the period and 0.25 hour of labor was allowed for each unit, the total number of standard hours allowed was 2,750. The labor efficiency variance can also be computed as the standard rate times the difference between the actual labor hours and the standard hours allowed for the output achieved:

$$\textbf{Labor efficiency variance = SR(AH − SH)}$$
$$= \$24(2,800 − 2,750)$$
$$= \$24 × 50$$
$$= \$1,200 \text{ U}$$

This computation of the labor efficiency variance indicates that the company used 50 more labor hours than the budget permitted for a total of $1,200 more than the standards allowed. Since our illustration avoids the use of more complicated evaluations with multiple drivers, a multiple driver example is provided in the following Business Insight. The approach in this illustration can be used for direct labor or variable overhead.

Interpreting Labor Variances

The possible explanations for labor rate variances are rather limited. An *unfavorable labor rate variance* can be caused by the use of higher paid laborers than the standards provided. Also, a new labor union contract increasing wages could have been implemented after the standards were set. In this case, the standards should have been revised to account for the wage rate change. In a nonunion situation when a negotiated contract does not control wages, a manager could arbitrarily increase employee wages above the standard rate. This also can cause an unfavorable labor rate variance. A *favorable labor rate variance* occurs if lower paid workers were used or if actual wage rates declined.

Unfavorable labor efficiency variances occur when workers or machines require more than the number of hours allowed by the standards to produce a given amount of output. This could be caused

BUSINESS INSIGHT   **Multiple Cost Drivers**

Highly structured activity-based reporting systems usually require the performance reports to indicate all relevant cost drivers associated with the activities being evaluated. This is popular for automated settings such as those of Hewlett-Packard, Advanced Micro Devices, AT&T, and IBM. In these manufacturing environments, labor, as a cost driver, does not dominate. The manufacture and assembly of products are completed in distinct stages, each somewhat independent of others. To illustrate this type of setting, assume that an operating department has three automated processes performing three different tasks. The variances for each activity follow:[6]

Input component: Materials fabrication				Output: 100 units	
Activity	**Actual Cost**	**Standard Cost of Actual Inputs**		**Flexible Budget Cost**	
Cutting . . .	$ 3,400	160 cuts × $20.00 = $ 3,200		150 cuts × $20.00 = $ 3,000	
Shaping . .	7,100	8,000 turns × $ 0.90 = 7,200		8,100 turns × $ 0.90 = 7,290	
Fitting	18,000	80,000 fittings × $ 0.20 = 16,000		63,700 fittings × $ 0.20 = 12,740	
	$28,500	$26,400		$23,030	

Activity spendings   Activity efficiencies

Cutting . . . . . $ 200 U   Cutting . . . . $ 200 U

Shaping . . . . 100 F   Shaping. . . . . 90 F

Fitting . . . . . . 2,000 U   Fitting . . . . 3,260 U

Total spending   Total efficiency . . . .

variance . . . . $2,100 U   variance . . . . $3,370 U

Total flexible budget variance $5,470 U

by a management decision to use poorly trained workers or poorly maintained machinery or by downtime resulting from the use of low-quality materials. Low employee morale and generally poor working conditions could also adversely affect the efficiency of workers, resulting in an unfavorable labor efficiency variance.

A *favorable labor efficiency variance* occurs when fewer hours are used than are allowed by the standards. This above-normal efficiency can be caused by the company's use of higher skilled (and higher paid) workers, better machinery, or raw materials of higher quality than the standards provided. High employee morale, improved job satisfaction, or generally improved working conditions could also account for the above-normal efficiency of the workers.

Overhead Standards and Variances

The traditional unit-level approach usually separates overhead costs into fixed and variable elements for control purposes. This separation is necessary because the variance between actual costs and expected costs is caused by different factors for fixed and variable costs. Unlike direct materials costs, which represent specific cost components, manufacturing overhead represents *groups* of different costs. Consequently, setting standards is often more difficult for overhead costs than it is for materials costs. For mixed manufacturing overhead costs (those that have variable and fixed components), an estimation technique, such as the high-low method, regression analysis (least-squares), or scatter diagram, is often used to separate the fixed and variable overhead components. (These techniques were discussed in Module 15.) If management concludes that the observations used in estimating variable costs reflect normal operating conditions, managers will probably adopt the estimate as the standard variable cost.

Because it includes many heterogeneous costs, manufacturing overhead poses a unique problem in measuring standard quantity and standard price. Direct materials have a natural physical measure of

---

[6] James M. Reeve, "Projects, Models, and Systems—Where Is ABM Headed?" *Journal of Cost Management,* Summer 1996, pp. 5–16.

quantity such as tons, barrels, pounds, and liters. Similarly, labor or assembly is measurable in hours. However, no single quantity measure is common to all overhead items. Overhead is a cost group that can simultaneously include costs measurable in hours, pounds, liters and kilowatts.

To deal with the problem of multiple quantity measures in variable manufacturing overhead, most companies use an artificial (substitute) measure of quantity for all items in a given group. Typical substitute measures are machine hours, units of finished product, direct labor hours, and direct labor dollars. The variable overhead standard is then stated in terms of this single-factor base, and the amount of variable overhead budgeted is based on this artificial activity measure.

Variable Overhead Variances

To illustrate the computation of variable factory overhead variances, assume that McMillan Company's standard unit-level variable overhead costs for waterproofing and inspection consist of the following:

Variable Overhead Cost Item	Quantity Consumed per Pound of Direct Materials	Standard Cost per Pound of Direct Materials*
Indirect materials		
Sealant coating.....................	2 fluid ounces	$1.10
Hinge lubricants	3 milliliters	0.40
Indirect labor		
Inspection workers..................	6 minutes	2.50
Total variable cost per pound of direct materials used		$4.00

*Standard unit-level variable overhead requires 2 pounds of direct materials at $4 per pound for a standard overhead cost per unit of $8. Management assigns 2 pounds of materials as the best base for measuring this part of related costs.

The general model for computing standard cost variances for materials and labor can also be used in computing variable overhead variances. The actual costs of inputs, such as indirect materials, indirect labor, and utilities, are ordinarily obtained, however, directly from the accounting records rather than being computed as quantity times cost.

The **variable overhead spending variance** is the difference between the actual variable overhead cost and the standard variable overhead cost for the actual inputs of the measurement base. The **variable overhead efficiency variance** is the difference between the standard variable overhead cost for the actual inputs of the measurement base and the flexible budget cost allowed for variable overhead based on outputs.

For McMillan Company, the actual variable overhead for waterproofing and inspection is $81,000. This represents the actual cost of overhead items such as indirect materials and indirect labor. Since actual variable overhead is expected to vary with pounds of direct materials used, the standard cost of actual inputs is calculated as actual pounds of direct materials (AP) times the standard variable overhead rate per pound (SRP):

$$\textbf{Standard cost of actual inputs} = \textbf{(AP} \times \textbf{SRP)}$$
$$= \textbf{24,000} \times \textbf{\$4}$$
$$= \textbf{\$96,000}$$

The flexible budget cost for variable overhead allowed for the actual outputs is based on the 22,000 pounds of direct materials allowed (SP) for the units produced during the period (11,000 units $\times$ 2 pounds). The allowed quantities are multiplied by the standard variable overhead rate (SRP). The resulting variable overhead flexible budget cost is $88,000:

$$\textbf{Flexible budget cost} = \textbf{(SP} \times \textbf{SRP)}$$
$$= \textbf{22,000} \times \textbf{\$4}$$
$$= \textbf{\$88,000}$$

Using these data, the variable overhead spending (price) variance and the variable overhead efficiency (quantity) variance follow.

Standard Cost Variance Analysis

Input component: Variable overhead			Output: 11,000 cases	

Actual Costs	Standard Cost of Actual Inputs		Flexible Budget Cost	
$81,000	Actual pounds (AP)	24,000	Pounds allowed (SP)	22,000*
	Standard rate (SRP)	× $4	Standard rate (SRP)	× $4
	Total	$96,000	Total	$88,000

Variable overhead spending variance — $15,000 F

Variable overhead efficiency variance — $8,000 U

Total flexible budget variable overhead variance $7,000 F

*11,000 × 2 lbs.

An alternative to the computation of the variable overhead effectiveness variance follows:

$$\text{Variable overhead efficiency variance} = SRP(AP - SP)$$
$$= \$4(24,000 - 22,000)$$
$$= \$8,000 \text{ U}$$

This approach emphasizes that the 2,000 extra pounds used should have increased variable overhead by $8,000 at the standard rate of $4 per pound.

Interpreting Variable Overhead Variances

A *favorable spending variance* encompasses all factors that cause actual expenditures to be less than the amount expected for the actual inputs of the measurement base, including consumption and payment. Conversely, an *unfavorable spending variance* results when the actual expenditures are more than expected for the inputs of the measurement base. This is caused by consuming more overhead items than expected, or by paying more than the expected amount for overhead items consumed, or by both. Thus, the term *spending variance* is used instead of *price variance*.

The key to understanding the variable overhead spending variance is recognizing that the amount of variable overhead cost allowed is determined by the level of the measurement bases used. Any deviation from this spending budget—due to uncontrolled or mismanaged variable overhead price or quantity variables—causes a spending variance to occur.

The variable overhead efficiency variance measures the difference between the standard variable overhead cost for the actual quantity of the measurement base and the standard variable overhead cost for the allowed quantity of the measurement base. This variance measures the amount of variable overhead that should have been saved (or incurred) because of the efficient (or inefficient) use of the measurement base. It provides no information about the degree of efficiency in using variable overhead items such as indirect materials and indirect labor. This information is reflected in the spending variance.

MANAGERIAL DECISION	You are the Vice President of Manufacturing

Your company has had a practice for many years of budgeting variable overhead costs based on direct labor hours. The managerial accountants have argued that if direct labor hours are controlled, variable overhead costs will take care of themselves since direct labor hours drive variable overhead costs. You (and your plant managers) have become very skeptical of this policy because in recent years variable overhead variances have been very erratic—sometimes being large favorable amounts and other times being large unfavorable amounts. You are beginning to plan for the coming budget year. How do you think you should budget variable overhead and evaluate managers who control of these costs. (Answer p. 21-24)

Fixed Overhead Variances

By definition, the quantity of goods and services purchased by fixed expenditures is not expected to change in proportion to short-run changes in the level of production. For example, in the short run, the production level does not affect the amount of depreciation on buildings, the number of fixed salaried employees, or the amount of real property subject to property taxes. Whether the organization produces 10,000 or 15,000 cases, the same quantity of fixed overhead is expected to be incurred, as long as the production level is within the relevant range of activity provided by the current fixed overhead items. Therefore, an efficiency variance is ordinarily not computed for fixed overhead costs.

Even though the components of fixed overhead are not expected to be affected by the production activity level in the short run, the actual amount spent for fixed overhead items can differ from the amount budgeted by management. For example, higher than budgeted supervisors' salaries could be paid, longer than normal working shifts could cause heating or cooling costs to exceed budget, and price increases could cause the amounts paid for equipment to be higher than expected. Fixed overhead costs in excess of the amount budgeted are reflected in the fixed overhead budget variance. The **fixed overhead budget variance** is, simply, the difference between budgeted and actual fixed overhead. Using the fixed costs of McMillan Company as an example:

$$\textbf{Fixed overhead budget variance} = \textbf{Actual fixed overhead} - \textbf{Budgeted fixed overhead}$$
$$= \$53{,}000 - \$52{,}000$$
$$= \$1{,}000 \ \textbf{U}$$

The fixed overhead budget variance is always the same as the total fixed overhead flexible budget variance. Because budgeted fixed overhead is the same for all outputs within the relevant range, the budget variance explains the total flexible budget variance between actual and allowed fixed overhead. Similar to variable overhead, fixed overhead variances can be caused by a combination of price and quantity factors.

PERFORMANCE REPORTS FOR REVENUE CENTERS

LO4 Calculate Revenue variances and prepare a performance report for a revenue center.

The financial performance reports for revenue centers include a comparison of actual and budgeted revenues, with the difference identified as a variance similar to those of the cost centers. Controllable costs can be deducted from revenues to obtain some bottom-line contribution margin. If the center is then evaluated on the basis of this contribution, it is being treated as a profit center.

If the organization is to meet its budgeted profit goal for a period, with its budgeted fixed and variable costs, the organization's revenue centers must meet their original revenue budgets. Consequently, the original budget (a static budget) rather than a flexible budget is used to evaluate the financial performance of revenue centers.

Assume that McMillan Company's July sales budget called for the sale of 10,000 units at $40 each. If McMillan Company actually sold 11,000 units at $39 each, the total revenue variance is $29,000:

Actual revenues (11,000 × $39)	$429,000
Budgeted revenues (10,000 × $40)	(400,000)
Revenue variance	$ 29,000 F

The **revenue variance** is the difference between the budgeted sales volume at the budgeted selling price and the actual sales volume at the actual selling price. Because actual revenues exceeded budgeted revenues, the revenue variance is favorable. It can be presented as follows:

Revenue variance = (Actual volume × Actual price) − (Budgeted volume × Budgeted price)

After the revenue variance is computed, the impact of changing prices and volume on revenue is then analyzed with the sales price and sales volume variances. The **sales price variance** is computed as the change in selling price times the actual sales volume:

Sales price variance = (Actual selling price − Budgeted selling price) × Actual sales volume

For McMillan, the sales price variance for July follows:

$$\text{Sales price variance} = (\$39 - \$40) \times 11{,}000 \text{ units}$$
$$= \$11{,}000 \text{ U}$$

The **sales volume variance** indicates the impact of the change in sales volume on revenues, assuming there was no change in selling price. The sales volume variance is computed as the difference between the actual and the budgeted sales volumes times the budgeted selling price:

Sales volume variance = (Actual sales volume − Budgeted sales volume) × Budgeted selling price

For McMillan, the sales volume variance for July follows:

$$\text{Sales volume variance} = (11{,}000 \text{ units} - 10{,}000 \text{ units}) \times \$40$$
$$= \$40{,}000 \text{ F}$$

The net of the sales price and the sales volume variances is equal to the revenue variance:

Sales price variance.	$11,000U
Sales volume variance	40,000 F
Revenue variance.	$29,000 F

Interpretation of these variances is subjective. In this case, we could say that if the increase in sales volume had not been accompanied by a decline in selling price, revenues would have increased $40,000 (1,000 units × $40) instead of $29,000. The $1 per unit decline in selling price cost the company $11,000 in revenues. Alternatively, we might note that a $1 reduction in the unit selling price was more than offset by an increase in sales volume. An economic analysis could explain the relationship as volume being sensitive to price (price elasticity).

In any case, variances are merely signals that actual results are not proceeding according to plan. They help managers identify potential problems and opportunities. An investigation into their cause(s) could even indicate that a manager who received a favorable variance was doing a poor job, whereas a manager who received an unfavorable variance was doing an outstanding job. Consider McMillan Company's favorable revenue variance. This occurred because actual sales exceeded budgeted sales by 1,000 units (10 percent), which on the surface indicates good performance. But what if the total market for the company's products exceeded the company's forecast by 15 percent? In this case, McMillan Company's sales volume falls below its expected percentage share of the market; the favorable variance could occur (despite a poor marketing effort) because of strong customer demand that competitors could not fill.

Inclusion of Controllable Costs

Controllable costs should also be considered when evaluating the overall performance of revenue centers. A failure to consider costs could encourage uneconomic selling practices, such as excessive advertising and entertaining, and spending too much time on small accounts. The controllable costs of revenue centers include variable and fixed selling costs. These costs are sometimes further classified into order-getting and order-filling costs. **Order-getting costs** are incurred to obtain customers' orders (for example, advertising, salespersons' salaries and commissions, travel, telephone, and entertainment). **Order-filling costs** are incurred to place finished goods in the hands of purchasers (for example, storing, packaging, and transportation).

The performance of a revenue center in controlling costs can be evaluated with the aid of a flexible budget drawn up for the actual level of activity. Assume that the McMillan Company's July budget for the Sales Department calls for fixed costs of $10,000 and variable costs of $5 per unit sold. If the actual fixed and variable selling expenses for July are $9,500 and $65,000, respectively, the total cost variances assigned to the Sales Department are $9,500 unfavorable. In evaluating the Sales Department's performance as both a cost center and a revenue center, management would consider these cost variances as well as the revenue variances shown in Exhibit 21.2. Although the revenue variances are based on the original budget, the cost variances are based on the flexible budget.

EXHIBIT 21.2	Sales Department Performance Report

McMILLAN COMPANY
Sales Department Performance Report
For Month of July

	Based on Static Budget			Based on Flexible Budget		
	Actual	Original Budget	Static Budget Variance	Actual	Flexible Budget*	Flexible Budget Variance
Revenue						
Units	11,000	10,000	1,000 F			
Dollars.	$429,000	$400,000	$29,000 F			
Selling expenses						
Variable.				$65,000	$55,000	$10,000 U
Fixed.				9,500	10,000	500 F
Total				$74,500	$65,000	$ 9,500 U

*Flexible budget formulas:

Sales ($40 per unit)

Variable selling expenses ($5 per unit)

Fixed selling expenses ($10,000 per month)

Revenue Centers as Profit Centers

Even though we have computed revenue and cost variances for McMillan's Sales Department, we are still left with an incomplete picture of this revenue center's performance. Is the Sales Department's performance best represented by the $29,000 favorable revenue variance, by the $9,500 unfavorable cost variance, or by the net favorable variance of $19,500 ($29,000 F − $9,500 U)? Actually, it is inappropriate to attempt to obtain an overall measure of the Sales Department's performance by combining these separate revenue and cost variances. The combination of revenue and cost variances is appropriate only for a profit center; so far, we have left out one important cost that must be assigned to the Sales Department before it can be treated as a profit center. That cost is the *standard variable cost of goods sold*.

As a profit center, the Sales Department acquires units from the Production Department and sells them outside the firm. Its total responsibilities include revenues, the standard variable cost of goods sold, and actual selling expenses. The Sales Department is assigned the *standard*, rather than the *actual*, *variable cost of goods sold*. Because the Sales Department does not control production activities, it should not be assigned actual production costs. Doing so results in passing the Production Department's variances on to the Sales Department. Fixed manufacturing costs are not assigned to the Sales Department because short-run variations in sales volume do not normally affect the total amount of these costs.

To evaluate the Sales Department as a profit center, the net sales volume variance must be computed. The **net sales volume variance** indicates the impact of a change in sales volume on the contribution margin given the budgeted selling price *and* the standard variable costs. It is computed as the difference between the actual and the budgeted sales volumes times the budgeted unit contribution margin.

Net sales volume variance = (Actual volume − Budgeted volume) × Budgeted contribution margin

Using the $40 budgeted selling price, the standard costs presented for the product (see earlier in the module), and the standard variable selling expenses from Exhibit 21.2, the budgeted contribution margin is $10.50, computed as follows:

Sales.		$40.00
Direct materials	$10.00	
Direct labor.	6.00	
Variable manufacturing overhead		
Unit level	$8.00	
Batch level	0.50*	8.50
Selling.	5.00	29.50
Contribution margin		$10.50

*For simplicity and because production is in complete batches of 1,000 units, we combine unit- and batch-level costs ($0.40 + $0.10).

The net sales volume variance is computed as follows:

$$\text{Net sales volume variance} = (11{,}000 - 10{,}000) \times \$10.50$$
$$= \$10{,}500 \text{ F}$$

As a profit center, the Sales Department has responsibility for the sales price variance, the net sales volume variance, and any cost variances associated with its operations. For July, these cost variances net to $10,000 unfavorable:

Sales price variance	$11,000 U
Net sales volume variance	10,500 F
Selling expense variance	9,500 U
Sales Department variances, net	$10,000 U

In an attempt to improve their overall performance, managers often commit themselves to unfavorable variances in some areas, believing that these variances will be more than offset by favorable variances in other areas. In the case preceding, the favorable sales volume variance appears not to have been sufficient to offset the price reductions and the higher selling expenses. The more complete evaluation of the Sales Department as a profit center (with a $10,000 unfavorable variance) gives a very different impression than the evaluation of the Sales Department as a pure revenue center (with a $29,000 favorable variance) or as a revenue center responsible only for its own direct costs (with a $9,500 unfavorable cost variance).

MODULE-END REVIEW

The flexible budget performance report for Sunset Enterprises Inc. for March follows. The company manufactures only one product, folding chairs.

	Actual Costs	Flexible Budget Cost	Flexible Budget Variances
Output units	5,000	5,000	
Direct materials	$104,125	$100,000	$ 4,125 U
Direct labor.	82,400	75,000	7,400 U
Variable manufacturing overhead			
Category 1	31,000	30,000	1,000 U
Category 2	18,000	20,000	2,000 F
Fixed manufacturing overhead.	42,000	40,000	2,000 U
Total	$277,525	$265,000	$12,525 U

The standard unit cost for folding chairs follows:

Direct materials (4 pounds × $5.00 per pound).	$20
Direct labor (1.25 hours × $12.00 per hour).	15
Variable overhead, Category 1 (1.25 hours × $4.80). . . .	6
Variable overhead, Category 2 ($4 per finished unit)	4
Total standard variable cost per unit	$45

Actual cost of materials is based on 21,250 pounds of direct materials purchased and used at $4.90 per pound; actual cost of assembly is based on 7,000 labor hours. Variable overhead is applied on labor hours for Category 1 and finished units for Category 2.

Required

a. Calculate all standard cost variances for direct materials and direct labor.
b. Calculate all standard cost variances for variable manufacturing overhead.

Solution

a.

Input component: Direct materials		**Output: 5,000 units**
Actual Cost	**Standard Cost of Actual Inputs**	**Flexible Budget Cost**
Actual quantity (AQ). 21,250	Actual quantity (AQ) 21,250	Standard quantity allowed (SQ) 20,000*
Actual price (AP). . . . . × $4.90	Standard price (SP) . . . × $5.00	Standard price (SP) . × $5.00
$104,125	$106,250	$100,000

Materials price variance $2,125 F

Materials quantity variance $6,250 U

Total flexible budget materials variance $4,125 U

*5,000 units × 4 pounds per unit produced

Standard Cost Variance Analysis

Input component: Direct labor		**Output: 5,000 units**
Actual Costs	**Standard Cost of Actual Inputs**	**Flexible Budget Cost**
$82,400	Actual hours (AH) 7,000	Standard hours allowed (SH) 6,250*
	Standard rate (SR). . . . . × $12	Standard rate (SR) . . . . × $12
	Total. $84,000	Total. $75,000

Labor rate variance $1,600 F

Labor efficiency variance $9,000 U

Total flexible budget labor variance $7,400 U

*5,000 units × 1.25 hours per unit

b.

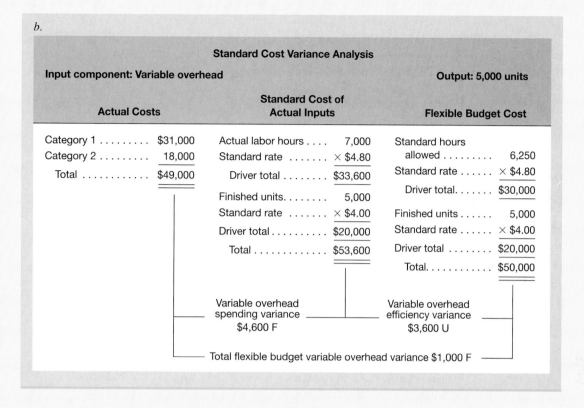

Standard Cost Variance Analysis

Input component: Variable overhead   Output: 5,000 units

	Actual Costs	Standard Cost of Actual Inputs	Flexible Budget Cost

Category 1 . . . . $31,000   Actual labor hours   7,000   Standard hours
Category 2 18,000   Standard rate . . . . × $4.80   allowed   6,250
    Total . . . . $49,000   Driver total . . . . $33,600   Standard rate . . . . . . × $4.80

                                           Finished units.   5,000   Driver total. $30,000
                                           Standard rate . . . . × $4.00   Finished units   5,000
                                           Driver total . . . . $20,000   Standard rate . . . . . . × $4.00
                                               Total . . . . $53,600   Driver total $20,000

                                                                                      Total. $50,000

              Variable overhead   Variable overhead
              spending variance   efficiency variance
                  $4,600 F $3,600 U

              Total flexible budget variable overhead variance $1,000 F

GUIDANCE ANSWER

MANAGERIAL DECISION   **You Are the Vice President of Manufacturing**

It appears that direct labor hours may no longer be a reliable basis for budgeting variable overhead in your company. If actual variable overhead costs do not appear to correlate closely with direct labor hours, this could be an indication that the components of variable overhead have changed since direct labor hours was selected as the cost driver. Your cost accountants should consider other unit-level cost drivers for budgeting variable overhead costs. However, an activity-based costing method using multiple overhead cost pools with separate cost drivers might provide a more reliable basis for budgeting and controlling variable overhead costs.

DISCUSSION QUESTIONS

Q21-1. What is responsibility accounting? Why should noncontrollable costs be excluded from performance reports prepared in accordance with responsibility accounting?

Q21-2. How can responsibility accounting lead to unethical practices?

Q21-3. Responsibility accounting reports must be expanded to include what nonfinancial areas? Give some examples of nonfinancial measures.

Q21-4. What is a cost center? Give some examples.

Q21-5. How is a cost center different from either an investment or a profit center?

Q21-6. What problems can result from the use of tight standards?

Q21-7. What is a standard cost variance, and what is the objective of variance analysis?

Q21-8. Standard cost variances can usually be broken down into two basic types of variances. Identify and describe these two types of variances.

Q21-9. Identify possible causes for (1) a favorable materials price variance; (2) an unfavorable materials price variance; (3) a favorable materials quantity variance; and (4) an unfavorable materials quantity variance.

Q21-10. How is standard labor time determined? Explain the two ways.

Q21-11. In the standard cost system, what is the appropriate treatment of a change in wage rates (per new labor union contract) that dominate the cost of labor?

Q21-12. Explain the difference between the revenue variance and the sales price variance.

Q21-13. Explain the net sales volume variance and list its components.

Q21-14. Explain the difference between how the *actual costs* and the *standard cost of actual inputs* are computed in variable overhead analysis.

Q21-15. Explain what the net sales volume variance measures.

MINI EXERCISES

M21-16. Flexible Budgets and Performance Evaluation (LO2)

Presented is the January performance report for the Production Department of Dover Company.

DOVER COMPANY Production Department Performance Report For Month of January			
	Actual	**Budget**	**Variance**
Volume	30,000	28,000	
Manufacturing costs			
Direct materials	$ 89,600	$ 82,000	$ 7,600 U
Direct labor	165,000	140,000	25,000 U
Variable overhead	62,000	56,000	6,000 U
Fixed overhead	27,500	28,000	500 F
Total	$344,100	$306,000	$38,100 U

Required

a. Evaluate the performance report.

b. Prepare a more appropriate performance report.

M21-17. Materials Variances (LO3)

Lenscrafters

Assume that Lenscrafters uses standard costs to control the materials in its made-to-order sunglasses. The standards call for 2 ounces of material for each pair of lenses. The standard cost per ounce of material is $15. During July, the Palm Beach location produced 4,800 pairs of sunglasses and used 8,800 ounces of materials. The cost of the materials during July was $15.20 per ounce, and there were no beginning or ending inventories.

Required

a. Determine the flexible budget materials cost for the completion of the 4,800 pairs of glasses.

b. Determine the actual materials cost incurred for the completion of the 4,800 pairs of glasses and compute the total materials variance.

c. How much of the total variance was related to the price paid to purchase the materials?

d. How much of the difference between the answers to requirements (a) and (b) was related to the quantity of materials used?

M21-18. Direct Labor Variances (LO3)

Nortel (NT)

Assume that Nortel manufactures specialty electronic circuitry through a unique photoelectronic process. One of the primary products, Model ZX40, has a standard labor time of 0.5 hour and a standard labor rate of $13.50 per hour. During February, the following activities pertaining to direct labor for ZX40 were recorded:

Direct labor hours used	2,180
Direct labor cost	$34,000
Units of ZX40 manufactured . . .	4,600

Required

a. Determine the labor rate variance.

b. Determine the labor efficiency variance.

c. Determine the total flexible budget labor cost variance.

M21-19. Causes for Variances (LO3)

During January, assume that Regal Flags and Poles, Inc. reported the following variances in the production of flagpoles, its only product.

1. Materials price variance
2. Materials quantity variance
3. Labor rate variance
4. Labor efficiency variance
5. Variable overhead spending variance
6. Variable overhead efficiency variance
7. Fixed overhead budget variance

Required

a. Identify the variances that are caused primarily by price factors.

b. Identify the variances that are caused primarily by quantity usage factors.

c. Identify the variances that are caused by both price and quantity factors.

M21-20. Setting Standards (LO3)

Oconee Inc. has just completed one month's testing of a new machine. The manufacturer listed the operating capacity of the machine at 100 feet of material per hour if operated by a skilled employee using top-quality materials. During the month, Oconee used some of its highly skilled employees and medium grade materials (the best price at the time). Test results produced 88 feet per hour on average. Oconee's average work force is 25 percent highly skilled, 65 percent skilled, and 10 percent trainees. Historically, skilled employees work 20 percent faster than trainees and 10 percent slower than the highly skilled employees. All workers will be trained to operate the new equipment.

Required

What should Oconee set as the standard output per hour? Justify with assumptions as necessary.

M21-21. Sales Variances (LO4)

Presented is information pertaining to an item sold by Winding Creek General Store:

	Actual	Budget
Unit sales	150	125
Unit selling price.	$26	$25
Unit standard variable costs.	(20)	(20)
Unit contribution margin	$ 6	$ 5
Revenues	$3,900	$3,125
Standard variable costs	(3,000)	(2,500)
Contribution margin at standard costs	$ 900	$ 625

Required

Compute the revenue, sales price, and the sales volume variances.

EXERCISES

E21-22. Materials Price Variance Based on Purchases and Usage (LO3)

Forza manufactures decorative weather vanes. Assume that weather vanes have a standard cost of $1.50 per pound for direct materials used in the manufacturing process. During September, 11,500 pounds of materials were purchased at $1.55 per pound, and 10,000 pounds were actually used in making 4,800 weather vanes. There were no beginning inventories.

Required

a. Determine the materials price variance, assuming that it is determined when materials are purchased.

b. Determine the materials price variance, assuming that it is determined when materials are used.

c. Determine the materials quantity variance if the standard materials for each weather vane is 2 pounds. Does the price variance method influence the computation of the quantity variance? Explain.

d. Discuss the issues involved in determining the price variance at the point of purchase versus the point of consumption.

E21-23. Direct Labor Variances   (LO3)

Springs Industries,
Inc.

Assume that Springs Industries, Inc., operates its Charlotte plant using a combination of hourly and incentive wage programs for production employees. The guaranteed minimum wage is $14 per hour but with incentive outputs, the wage can increase to $22 per hour. For dye processing, the standard output per hour is 1,000 pounds of yarn processed and dyed. During June, the dye process had an average wage rate of $16 with 920,000 pounds of dyed yarn completing production. Production hours totaled 950.

Required

a. Compute rate and efficiency variances using the minimum wage as the standard.

b. Compute rate and efficiency variances using the maximum wage with incentives as the standard.

c. Why does changing the standard used for the hourly rate change the efficiency variance?

d. Explain which set of variances is most useful for management.

E21-24. Sales Variances   (LO4)

Casio

Assume that Casio Computer Company, LTD. sells handheld communication devices for $110 during August as a back-to-school special. The normal selling price is $150. The standard variable cost for each device is $70. Sales for August had been budgeted for 400,000 units nationwide; however, due to the slowdown in the economy, sales were only 350,000.

Required

Compute the revenue, sales price, sales volume variance, and net sales volume variance.

E21-25. Variable Overhead Variances   (LO3)

Sony (SNE)

Assume that the best cost driver that Sony has for variable factory overhead in the assembly department is machine hours. During April, the company budgeted 480,000 machine hours and $5,000,000 for its Texas plant's assembly department. The actual variable overhead incurred was $5,200,000, which was related to 500,000 machine hours.

Required

a. Determine the variable overhead spending variance.

b. Determine the variable overhead efficiency variance.

E21-26. Variable Overhead Variances   (LO3)

India Leaf Company bases standard variable overhead cost on direct labor hours as the cost driver. Standard variable overhead cost has been set at $15 per unit of output based on $5 of variable overhead per direct labor hour for 3 hours allowed to produce 1 finished unit. Last month, 4,300 direct labor hours were used, and 1,400 units of output were manufactured. The following actual variable overhead costs were incurred:

Indirect materials	$ 4,500
Indirect labor	8,400
Utilities	5,800
Miscellaneous.	3,600
Total variable overhead	$22,300

Required

a. Determine the variable overhead spending variance.

b. Determine the variable overhead efficiency variance.

c. How is the variable overhead efficiency variance related to labor efficiency?

d. If the company used smaller quantities of indirect materials than those reflected in the standards, in which variance would the resulting cost savings be reflected? Explain.

E21-27. Fixed Overhead Variances (LO3)

Huntsville Company uses standard costs for cost control and internal reporting. Fixed costs are budgeted at $7,500 per month at a normal operating level of 10,000 units of production output. During October, actual fixed costs were $8,000, and actual production output was 9,500 units.

Required

a. Determine the fixed overhead budget variance.

b. Assume that the company applied fixed overhead to production on a per-unit basis. Determine the fixed overhead volume variance.

c. Was the fixed overhead budget variance from requirement (a) affected because the company operated below the normal activity level of 10,000 units? Explain.

d. Explain the possible causes for the volume variance computed in requirement (b). How is reporting of the volume variance useful to management?

E21-28. Fixed Overhead Variances (LO3)

Assume that Phillips Petroleum uses a standard cost system for each of its refineries. For the Tulsa refinery, the monthly fixed overhead budget is $21,000,000 for a planned output of 10,000,000 barrels. For September, the actual fixed cost was $22,000,000 for 10,800,000 barrels. The Tulsa refinery's capacity is 11,900,000 barrels.

Phillips Petroleum

Required

a. Determine the fixed overhead budget variance.

b. If fixed overhead is applied on a per-barrel basis, determine the volume variance.

c. What is the refinery's capacity variance?

E21-29. Causes of Standard Cost Variances (Comprehensive) (LO3)

Following are ten unrelated situations that would ordinarily be expected to affect one or more standard cost variances:

1. A salaried production supervisor is given a raise, but no adjustment is made in the labor cost standards.

2. The materials purchasing manager gets a special reduced price on raw materials by purchasing a train carload. A warehouse had to be rented to accommodate the unusually large amount of raw materials. The rental fee was charged to Rent Expense, a fixed overhead item.

3. An unusually hot August caused the company to use 25,000 kilowatts more electricity than provided for in the variable overhead standards.

4. The local electric utility company raised the charge per kilowatt-hour. No adjustment was made in the variable overhead standards.

5. The plant manager traded in his leased company car for a new one in July, increasing the monthly lease payment by $150.

6. A machine malfunction on the assembly line (caused by using cheap and inferior raw materials) resulted in decreased output by the machine operator and higher than normal machine repair costs. Repairs are treated as variable overhead costs.

7. The production maintenance supervisor decreased routine maintenance checks, resulting in lower maintenance costs and lower machine production output per hour. Maintenance costs are treated as fixed costs.

8. An announcement that vacation benefits had been increased resulted in improved employee morale. Consequently, raw materials pilferage and waste declined, and production efficiency increased.

9. The plant manager reclassified her secretary to administrative assistant and gave him an increase in salary.

10. A union contract agreement calling for an immediate 5 percent increase in production worker wages was signed. No changes were made in the standards.

Required

For each of these situations, indicate by letter which of the following standard cost variances would be affected. More than one variance will be affected in some cases.

a. Materials price variance.

b. Materials quantity variance.

c. Labor rate variance.

d. Labor efficiency variance.

e. Variable overhead spending variance.

f. Variable overhead efficiency variance.

g. Fixed overhead budget variance.

PROBLEMS

P21-30. Multiple Product Performance Report (LO2)

Storage Products manufactures two models of DVD storage cases: regular and deluxe. Presented is standard cost information for each model:

Cost Components	Regular	Deluxe
Direct materials		
Lumber	2 board feet × $3 = $ 6.00	3 board feet × $3 = $ 9.00
Assembly kit	= 2.00	= 2.00
Direct labor	1 hour × $4 = 4.00	1.25 hours × $4 = 5.00
Variable overhead . .	1 labor hr. × $2 = 2.00	1.25 labor hrs. × $2 = 2.50
Total	$14.00	$18.50

Budgeted fixed manufacturing overhead is $15,000 per month. During July, the company produced 5,000 regular and 3,000 deluxe storage cases while incurring the following manufacturing costs:

Direct materials	$ 80,000
Direct labor	36,000
Variable overhead	14,000
Fixed overhead	17,500
Total	$147,500

Required

Prepare a flexible budget performance report for the July manufacturing activities.

P21-31. Computation of Variable Cost Variances (LO3)

The following information pertains to the standard costs and actual activity for Tyler Company for September:

Standard cost per unit
    Direct materials . . . .   4 units of material A × $2.00 per unit
                             1 unit of material B × $3.00 per unit
    Direct labor . . . .   3 hours × $8.00 per hour

Activity for September
  Materials purchased
      Material A . . . .   4,500 units × $2.05 per unit
      Material B . . . .   1,100 units × $3.10 per unit
  Materials used
      Material A . . . .   4,150 units
      Material B . . . .   1,005 units
  Direct labor used . . . .   2,950 hours × $8.20 per hour
  Production output . . . .   1,000 units

There were no beginning direct materials inventories.

Required

a. Determine the materials price and quantity variances.
b. Determine the labor rate and efficiency variances.

P21-32. Variance Computations and Explanations (LO3)

Outdoor Company manufactures camping tents from a lightweight synthetic fabric. Each tent has a standard materials cost of $20, consisting of 4 yards of fabric at $5 per yard. The standards call for 2 hours of assembly at $12 per hour. The following data were recorded for October, the first month of operations:

Fabric purchased	9,000 yards × $4.90 per yard
Fabric used in production of 1,700 tents	7,000 yards
Direct labor used	3,600 hours × $12.50 per hour

Required

a. Compute all standard cost variances for materials and labor.

b. Give one possible reason for each of the preceding variances.

c. Determine the standard variable cost of the 1,700 tents produced, separated into direct materials and labor.

P21-33. Determining Unit Costs, Variance Analysis, and Interpretation (LO2, 3)

Big Dog Company, a manufacturer of dog food, produces its product in 1,000-bag batches. The standard cost of each batch consists of 8,000 pounds of direct materials at $0.30 per pound, 48 direct labor hours at $8.50 per hour, and variable overhead cost (based on machine hours) at the rate of $10 per hour with 16 machine hours per batch. The following variable costs were incurred for the last 1,000-bag batch produced:

Direct materials	8,300 pounds costing $2,378 were purchased and used
Direct labor	45 hours costing $450
Variable overhead.	$225
Machine hours used.	18 hours

Required

a. Determine the actual and standard variable costs per bag of dog food produced, separated into direct materials, direct labor, and variable overhead.

b. For the last 1,000-bag batch, determine the standard cost variances for direct materials, direct labor, and variable overhead.

c. Explain the possible causes for each of the variances determined in requirement (b).

P21-34. Computation of Variances and Other Missing Data (LO3)

The following data for O'Keefe Company pertain to the production of 300 units of Product X during December. Selected data items are omitted.

Direct materials (all materials purchased were used during period)
    Standard cost per unit: (a) pounds at $3.20 per pound
    Total actual cost: (b) pounds costing $5,673
    Standard cost allowed for units produced: $5,760
    Materials price variance: (c)
    Materials quantity variance: $96 U
Direct labor
    Standard cost: 2 hours at $7.00
    Actual cost per hour: $7.25
    Total actual cost: (d)
    Labor rate variance: (e)
    Labor efficiency variance: $140 U
Variable overhead
    Standard costs: (f) hours at $4.00 per direct labor hour
    Actual cost: $2,250
    Variable overhead spending variance: (g)
    Variable overhead efficiency variance: (h)

Required

Complete the missing amounts lettered (a) through (h).

P21-35. Measuring the Effects of Decisions on Standard Cost Variances (Comprehensive) (LO3)

The following five unrelated situations affect one or more standard cost variances for materials, labor (assembly), and overhead:

1. Lois Jones, a production worker, announced her intent to resign to accept another job paying $1.20 more per hour. To keep Lois, the production manager agreed to raise her salary from $7.00 to $8.50 per hour. Lois works an average of 175 regular hours per month.

2. At the beginning of the month, a supplier of a component used in our product notified us that, because of a minor design improvement, the price will be increased by 15 percent above the current standard price of $100 per unit. As a result of the improved design, we expect the number of defective components to decrease by 80 units per month. On average, 1,200 units of the component are purchased each month. Defective units are identified prior to use and are not returnable.

3. In an effort to meet a deadline on a rush order in Department A, the plant manager reassigned several higher-skilled workers from Department B, for a total of 300 labor hours. The average salary of the Department B workers was $1.85 more than the standard $7.00 per hour rate of the Department A workers. Since they were not accustomed to the work, the average Department B worker was able to produce only 36 units per hour instead of the standard 48 units per hour. (Consider only the effect on Department A labor variances.)

4. Rob Celiba is an inspector who earns a base salary of $700 per month plus a piece rate of 20 cents per bundle inspected. His company accounts for inspection costs as manufacturing overhead. Because of a payroll department error in June, Rob was paid $500 plus a piece rate of 30 cents per bundle. He received gross wages totaling $1,100.

5. The materials purchasing manager purchased 5,000 units of component K2X from a new source at a price $12 below the standard unit price of $200. These components turned out to be of extremely poor quality with defects occurring at three times the standard rate of 5 percent. The higher rate of defects reduced the output of workers (who earn $8 per hour) from 20 units per hour to 15 units per hour on the units containing the discount components. Each finished unit contains one K2X component. To appease the workers (who were irate at having to work with inferior components), the production manager agreed to pay the workers an additional $0.25 for each of the components (good and bad) in the discount batch. Variable manufacturing overhead is applied at the rate of $4 per direct labor hour. The defective units also caused a 20-hour increase in total machine hours. The actual cost of electricity to run the machines is $2 per hour.

Required

For each of the preceding situations, determine which standard cost variance(s) will be affected, and compute the amount of the effect for one month on each variance. Indicate whether the effect is favorable or unfavorable. Assume that the standards are not changed in response to these situations. (Round calculations to two decimal places.)

P21-36. Fixed Overhead Budget and Volume Variance (LO3)

Lucky Seven Company assigns fixed overhead costs to inventory for external reporting purposes by using a predetermined standard overhead rate based on direct labor hours. The standard rate is based on a normal activity level of 10,000 standard allowed direct labor hours per year. There are five standard allowed hours for each unit of output. Budgeted fixed overhead costs are $200,000 per year. During 2007, the company produced 2,200 units of output, and actual fixed costs were $210,000.

Required

a. Determine the standard fixed overhead rate used to assign fixed costs to inventory.

b. Determine the amount of fixed overhead assigned to inventory in 2007.

c. Determine the fixed overhead budget variance.

P21-37. Profit Center Performance Report (LO4)

Record Rack is a store that specializes in the sale of recordings of classical music. Due to a recent upsurge in the popularity of J. S. Bach's works, Record Rack has established a separate room, Bach's Concert Room, dealing only in recordings of Bach music. The CD's are purchased from a wholesaler for $4.25 each. Although the standard retail price is $7.75 per CD, the manager of Bach's Concert Room can undertake price reductions and other sales promotions in an attempt to increase sales volume. With the exception of the cost of CD's, the operating costs of Bach's Concert Room are fixed. Presented are the budgeted and the actual August contribution statements of Bach's Concert Room.

RECORD RACK—BACH'S CONCERT ROOM
Budgeted and Actual Contribution Statements
For Month of August

	Actual	Budget
Unit sales	4,200	4,000
Unit selling price.	$7.25	$7.75
Sales revenue.	$30,450	$31,000
Cost of goods sold.	(17,850)	(17,000)
Gross profit.	12,600	14,000
Operating costs	(5,000)	(6,000)
Contribution to corporate costs and profits.	$ 7,600	$ 8,000

Required

Compute variances to assist in evaluating the performance of Bach's Concert Room as a profit center. Was the performance satisfactory? Explain.

P21-38. Comprehensive Performance Report   (LO2, 3, 4)

Presented are the budgeted and actual contribution income statements of International Books Ltd. for October. The company has three responsibility centers: a Production Department, a Sales Department, and an Administration Department. Both the Production and Administration Departments are cost centers, and the Sales Department is a profit center.

INTERNATIONAL BOOKS, LTD.
Budgeted Contribution Income Statement
For Month of October

Sales (900 × $300).			$270,000
Less variable costs			
Variable cost of goods sold			
Direct materials (900 × $50)	$45,000		
Direct labor (900 × $20)	18,000		
Manufacturing overhead (900 × $30)	27,000	$ 90,000	
Selling (900 × $70)		63,000	(153,000)
Contribution margin			117,000
Less fixed costs			
Manufacturing overhead.		40,000	
Selling.		50,000	
Administrative.		10,500	(100,500)
Net income.			$ 16,500

INTERNATIONAL BOOKS, LTD. Actual Contribution Income Statement For Month of October			
Sales (1,000 × $330)			$330,000
Less variable costs			
Cost of goods sold			
Direct materials	$50,000		
Direct labor	25,000		
Manufacturing overhead	35,000	$110,000	
Selling		100,000	(210,000)
Contribution margin			120,000
Less fixed costs			
Manufacturing overhead		38,000	
Selling		65,000	
Administrative		22,000	(125,000)
Net income (loss)			$ (5,000)

Required

a. Prepare a performance report for the Production Department that compares actual and allowed costs.
b. Prepare a performance report for selling expenses that compares actual and allowed costs.
c. Determine the sales price and the net sales volume variances.
d. Prepare a report that summarizes the performance of the Sales Department.
e. Determine the amount by which the Administration Department was over- or under budget.
f. Prepare a report reconciling budgeted and actual net income. Your report should focus on the performance of each responsibility center.

CASES

C21-39. Discretionary Cost Center Performance Reports (LO1)

TruckMax had been extremely profitable, but the company has been hurt in recent years by competition and a failure to introduce new consumer products. In 2004, Tom Lopez became head of Consumer Products Research (CPR) and began a number of product development projects. Although the group had good ideas that led to the introduction of several promising products at the start of 2006, Lopez was criticized for poor cost control. The financial performance reports for CPR under his leadership were consistently unfavorable. Management was quite concerned about cost control because profits were low, and the company's cash budget indicated that additional borrowing would be required throughout 2006 to cover out-of-pocket costs. Because of his inability to exert proper cost control, Lopez was relieved of his responsibilities in 2006, and Gabriella Garcia became head of Consumer Products Research. Garcia vowed to improve the performance of CPR and scaled back CPR's development activities to obtain favorable financial performance reports.

By the end of 2007, the company had improved its market position, profitability, and cash position. At this time, the board of directors promoted Garcia to president, congratulating her for the contribution CPR made to the revitalization of the company, as well as her success in improving the financial performance of CPR. Garcia assured the board that the company's financial performance would improve even more in the future as she applied the same cost-reducing measures that had worked so well in CPR to the company as a whole.

Required

a. For the purpose of evaluating financial performance, what responsibility center classification should be given to the Consumer Products Research Department? What unique problems are associated with evaluating the financial performance of this type of responsibility center?
b. Compare the performances of Lopez and Garcia in the role as head of Consumer Products Research. Did Garcia do a much better job, thereby making her deserving of the promotion? Why or why not?

C21-40.   Evaluating Alternative Sales Compensation Plans   (LO2)

Pre-Fab Corporation, a relatively large company in the manufactured housing industry, is known for its aggressive sales promotion campaigns. Pre-Fab's innovative advertising and sales strategies have resulted in generally satisfactory performance in the last few years. One of Pre-Fab's objectives is to increase sales revenue by at least 10 percent annually. This objective has been obtained. Return on investment is considered good and had increased annually until last year when net income decreased for the first time in nine years. The latest economic recession could be the cause of the change, but other factors, such as sales growth, discount this reason.

A significant portion of Pre-Fab's administrative expenses are fixed, but the majority of the manufacturing expenses are variable in nature. The increases in selling prices have been consistent with the 12 percent increase in manufacturing expenses. Pre-Fab has consistently been able to maintain a company wide contribution margin of approximately 30 percent. However, the contribution margin on individual product lines varies from 15 to 45 percent. Sales commission expenses increased 30 percent over the past year. The prefabricated housing industry has always been sales-oriented, and Pre-Fab's management has believed in generously rewarding the efforts of its sales personnel. The sales force compensation plan consists of three segments:

- A guaranteed annual salary, which is increased by about 6 percent per year. The salary is below industry average.
- A sales commission of 9 percent of total sales dollars. This is higher than the industry average.
- A year-end bonus of 5 percent of total sales dollars to each salesperson when his or her total sales dollars exceed the prior year by at least 12 percent.

The current compensation plan has resulted in an average annual income of $62,500 per sales employee, compared with an industry annual average of $50,000. The compensation plan has been effective in generating increased sales. Further, the Sales Department employees are satisfied with the plan. Management, however, is concerned about the financial implications of the current plan. They believe the plan has caused higher selling expenses and a lower net income relative to the sales revenue increase.

At the last staff meeting, the controller suggested that the sales compensation plan be modified so that sales employees could earn an annual average income of $57,500. The controller believed that such a plan would still be attractive to its sales personnel and, at the same time, allow the company to earn a more satisfactory profit. The vice president for sales voiced strong objection to altering the current compensation plan because employee morale and incentive would drop significantly if there were any change. Nevertheless, most of the staff believed that the area of sales compensation merited a review. The president stated that all phases of a company operation can benefit from a periodic review, no matter how successful they have been in the past. Several compensation plans known to be used by other companies in the manufactured housing industry are:

- Straight commission as a percentage of sales
- Straight salary
- Salary plus compensation based on sales to new customers
- Salary plus compensation based on contribution margin
- Salary plus compensation based on unit sales volume

Required

a.   Discuss the advantages and disadvantages of Pre-Fab Corporation's current sales compensation plan with respect to (1) the financial aspects of the company and (2) the behavioral aspects of the sales personnel.

b.   For each of the alternative compensation plans known to be used by other companies in the manufactured housing industry, discuss whether the plan would be an improvement over the current plan in terms of (1) the financial performance of the company and (2) the behavioral implications for the sales personnel.

(CMA Adapted)

C21-41.   Developing Cost Standards for Materials and Labor   (LO2)

After several years of operating without a formal system of cost control, DeWalt Company, a tools manufacturer, has decided to implement a standard cost system. The system will first be established for the department that makes lug wrenches for automobile mechanics. The standard production batch size is 100 wrenches. The actual materials and labor required for eight randomly selected batches from last year's production are as follows:

Batch	Materials Used (in pounds)	Labor Used (in hours)
1	504.0	10.00
2	508.0	9.00
3	506.0	9.00
4	521.0	5.00
5	516.0	8.00
6	518.0	7.00
7	520.0	6.00
8	515.0	8.00
Average	513.5	7.75

Management has obtained the following recommendations concerning what the materials and labor quantity standards should be:

- The manufacturer of the equipment used in making the wrenches advertises in the toolmakers' trade journal that the machine the company uses can produce 100 wrenches with 500 pounds of direct materials and 5 labor hours. Company engineers believe the standards should be based on these facts.
- The accounting department believes more realistic standards would be 505 pounds and 5 hours.
- The production supervisor believes the standards should be 512 pounds and 7.75 hours.
- The production workers argue for standards of 522 pounds and 8 hours.

Required

a. State the arguments for and against each of the recommendations, as well as the probable effects of each recommendation on the quantity variance for materials and labor.

b. Which recommendation provides the best combination of cost control and motivation to the production workers? Explain.

C21-42. Behavioral Effect of Standard Costs (LO1, 2, 3)

Delaware Corp. has used a standard cost system for evaluating the performance of its responsibility center managers for three years. Top management believes that standard costing has not produced the cost savings or increases in productivity and profits promised by the accounting department. Large unfavorable variances are consistently reported for most cost categories, and employee morale has fallen since the system was installed. To help pinpoint the problem with the system, top management asked for separate evaluations of the system by the plant department manager, the accounting department manager, and the personnel department manager. Their responses are summarized here.

Plant Manager—The standards are unrealistic. They assume an ideal work environment that does not allow materials defects or errors by the workers or machines. Consequently, morale has gone down and productivity has declined. Standards should be based on expected actual prices and recent past averages for efficiency. Thus, if we improve over the past, we receive a favorable variance.

Accounting Manager—The goal of accounting reports is to measure performance against an absolute standard and the best approximation of that standard is ideal conditions. Cost standards should be comparable to "par" on a golf course. Just as the game of golf uses a handicap system to allow for differences in individual players' skills and scores, it could be necessary for management to interpret variances based on the circumstances that produced the variances. Accordingly, in one case, a given unfavorable variance could represent poor performance; in another case, it could represent good performance. The managers are just going to have to recognize these subtleties in standard cost systems and depend on upper management to be fair.

Personnel Manager—The key to employee productivity is employee satisfaction and a sense of accomplishment. A set of standards that can never be met denies managers of this vital motivator. The current standards would be appropriate in a laboratory with a controlled environment but not in the factory with its many variables. If we are to recapture our old "team spirit," we must give the managers a goal that they can achieve through hard work.

Required

Discuss the behavioral issues involved in Delaware Corp.'s standard cost dilemma. Evaluate each of the three responses (pros and cons) and recommend a course of action.

C21-43.   Evaluating a Companywide Performance Report   (LO1, 2)

Mr. Micawber, the production supervisor, bursts into your office, carrying the company's 2007 performance report and thundering, "There is villainy here, sir! And I shall get to the bottom of it. I will not stop searching until I have found the answer! Why is Mr. Heep so down on my department? I thought we did a good job last year. But Heep claims my production people and I cost the company $31,500! I plead with you, sir, explain this performance report to me." Trying to calm Micawber, you take the report from him and ask to be left alone for 15 minutes. The report is as follows:

CRUPP COMPANY, LIMITED
Performance Report
For Year 2007

	Actual	Budget	Variance
Unit sales	7,500	5,000	
Sales	$262,500	$225,000	$37,500 F
Less manufacturing costs			
Direct materials	55,500	47,500	8,000 U
Direct labor	48,000	32,500	15,500 U
Manufacturing overhead	40,000	32,000*	8,000 U
Total	(143,500)	(112,000)	(31,500) U
Gross profit	119,000	113,000	6,000 F
Less selling and administrative expenses			
Selling (all fixed)	60,000	40,000	20,000 U
Administrative (all fixed)	55,000	50,000	5,000 U
Total	(115,000)	(90,000)	(25,000) U
Net income	$ 4,000	$ 23,000	$19,000 U

Performance summary

Budgeted net income			$23,000
Sales department variances			
Sales revenue	$ 37,500 F		
Selling expenses	20,000 U	$17,500 F	
Administration department variances		5,000 U	
Production department variances		31,500 U	19,000 U
Actual net income			$ 4,000

*Includes fixed manufacturing overhead of $22,000.

Required

a.   Evaluate the performance report. Is Mr. Heep correct, or is there "villainy here"?
b.   Assume that the Sales Department is a profit center and that the Production and Administration Departments are cost centers. Determine the responsibility of each for cost, revenue, and income variances, and prepare a report reconciling budgeted and actual net income. Your report should focus on the performance of each responsibility center.

Segment Reporting, Transfer Pricing, and Balanced Scorecard

LEARNING OBJECTIVES

LO1 Define a strategic business segment. (p. 22-3)

LO2 Describe the development and use of segment reports. (p. 22-4)

LO3 Explain transfer-pricing and assess alternative transfer pricing methods. (p. 22-7)

LO4 Determine and contrast return on investment and residual income. (p. 22-12)

LO5 Describe the balanced scorecard as a comprehensive performance measurement system. (p. 22-17)

MANAGING BUSINESS SEGMENTS

Many companies offer a variety of products or services. Companies usually organize these products and services into units called *divisions* or *strategic business segments.* Managers of strategic business segments make most of the operating decisions for their units, while senior managers focus on strategic issues such as the investment of assets and the evaluation of performance. We look at three firms in different business sectors, Procter & Gamble, Verizon, and C. H. Robinson Worldwide, to illustrate the challenges of managing business segments.

In managing a consumer products company, executives of Procter & Gamble focus on the success of its many familiar brands. P&G's major brands include Tide (38 percent market share in laundry detergent), Bounty (39 percent market share in paper towels), Downy (46 percent market share in fabric softener), and Folgers (33 percent share in packaged coffee). Although these brands are successful, several of P&G's successful brands recently lost market share. Observers comment that P&G's diverse product line has fallen victim to a group of smaller, more nimble niche firms that can focus on their specific products and markets. At the senior management level, P&G executives must make the appropriate resource allocation decisions to rejuvenate and sustain their brands.

In the telecommunications services industry, Verizon Communications is a major provider. Created through a merger of GTE and Bell Atlantic, the firm has sales of more than $65 billion. With several billion dollars

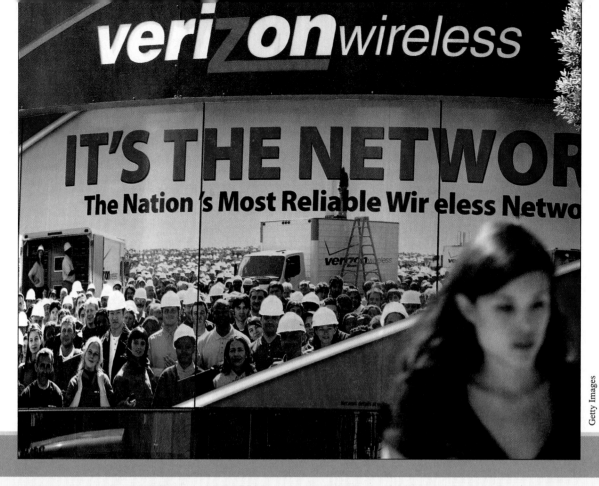

available for capital expenditures, Verizon continues to devote resources to growth markets. Its services include data transmission; wireless communications; local, long distance, and international calling; transmission lines; pay phones; and phone books. Although a telecommunications firm offers many services that share common assets, senior managers must decide where to invest in the next capital projects that will expand the firm's capability in one of several business directions.

Managers at C. H. Robinson Worldwide, a smaller firm than either Verizon or Procter & Gamble, take a decentralized approach to managing the firm's more than 150 branches. This logistics company with annual sales of nearly $4 billion owns no vehicles and ships none of its own freight. It serves as an intermediary between the companies with trucks, ships, and planes and those companies with cargo to move. The firm acts as broker for more than 3 million shipments per year using an operating philosophy that the CEO summarizes as "hire good people and let them attack the marketplace." This decentralized approach allows each of the branch managers to control the branches' own budget, hiring, marketing, and compensation. Essentially, each branch represents a profit center for the firm.

Managers must continually evaluate the performance of their business segments (different brands, different services, or different geographical locations). Managerial accounting provides a variety of tools to analyze the performance of both these units and their managers.

Source: *Business Week*, Forbes, 10-K Reports.[1]

---

[1] Robert Berner. "Can Procter & Gamble Clean Up Its Act?" *Business Week,* March 12, 2001, pp. 80–83; Joanne Gordon, "Green Machine," *Forbes,* October 29, 2001, p. 150; and Scott Woolley, "The New Ma Bell," *Forbes,* April 16, 2001, pp. 68–71.

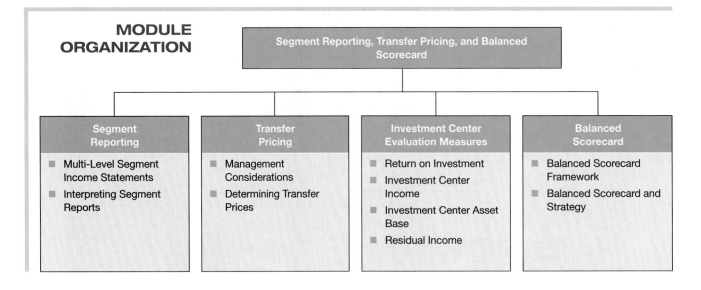

Organizations that maintain multiple product lines or that operate in several industries or in multiple markets often adopt a decentralized organization structure in which managers of major business units or strategic segments enjoy a high degree of autonomy. Examples of strategic business segments include the Chrysler Group of DaimlerChrysler and the Asia Pacific Group of The Coca-Cola Company. Sometimes companies establish segments within segments such as at Coca-Cola, whose Asia Pacific Group has separate business units for individual countries (Japan, Korea, etc.). In organizations such as DaimlerChrysler and Coca-Cola, upper management typically sets specific performance and profitability objectives for each segment and allows the manager of the segment the decision-making freedom to achieve those objectives.

This module explains the ways that an organization evaluates strategic business segments. It also considers transfer pricing and some of the problems that occur when one segment provides goods or services to another segment in the same organization.

STRATEGIC BUSINESS SEGMENTS

LO1 Define a strategic business segment.

A **strategic business segment** has its own mission and set of goals. Its mission influences the decisions that top managers make in both short-run and long-run situations. The organization structure dictates to a large extent the type of financial segment reporting and other measures used to evaluate the segment and its managers. In decentralized organizations, for example, the reporting units (typically called *divisions*) normally are quasi-independent companies, often having their own computer system, cost accounting system, and administrative and marketing staffs. With this type structure, top management monitors the segments to ensure that these independent units are functioning for the benefit of the entire organization.

Although segment reports are normally produced to coincide with managerial lines of responsibility, some companies also produce segment reports for smaller slices of the business that do not represent separate responsibility centers. These parts of the business are not significant enough to be identified as "strategic" business units as defined, but management could want information about them on a continuing basis.

For example, BellSouth Corporation has several strategic business units, including BellSouth Telecommunications Company (BST), which provides traditional regulated telephone services to customers using telephone lines. Within BST are several strategic business units, including units for residential customers, large business customers, and small business customers. Financial reports are prepared for each of these units. Within the residential division, BST can also prepare segment reports on a more detailed basis to determine the profitability of its smaller segments, such as single-line and multi-line customers.

The point is that segment reporting is not constrained by lines of responsibility. A segment report can be prepared for any part of the business for which management believes more detailed information is useful in managing that portion of the business.

SEGMENT REPORTING

Segment reports are income statements for portions or segments of a business. Segment reporting is used primarily for internal purposes, although generally accepted accounting principles also require some disclosure of segment information for public corporations. Even though there are many different types of segment reports, at least three steps are basic to the preparation of all segment reports:

LO2 Describe the development and use of segment reports.

1. Identify the segments.
2. Assign direct costs to segments.
3. Allocate indirect costs to segments.

The format of segment income statements varies depending on the approach adopted by a company for reporting income statements internally. The income statement formats illustrated earlier in this text, including the functional format and the contribution format, can be used for segment reporting. Data availability can, however, dictate the format used. Regardless of the format adopted, it is essential that costs be separable into those directly traceable to the segments and those not directly traceable to segments.

Determining the segment reporting structure is often a more difficult decision than choosing the format for the segment income statements. Companies must decide whether to structure segment reporting along the lines of responsibility reporting, and whether segment reports will be prepared only on one level or on several levels.

For example, consider the hypothetical case of Digital Communications Company (DCC) that has two market divisions, three products, and two geographic territories. DCC's two divisions include the National Division (serving large national accounts) and the Regional Division (serving smaller regional and local accounts). DCC's three product lines are fiber optic cable, twisted pair cable, and coaxial cable. The company is organized into two geographic territories, Atlantic and Pacific. If DCC were using only a single-level segment reporting approach for all three groupings, one report would show the total company income statement broken down into the two divisions, a second report would show the total company income statement broken down into the three products, and a third report would show the total company income statement broken down into the two geographic territories.

Multi-Level Segment Income Statements

If top management of DCC wants to know how much a particular product is contributing to the income of one of the two divisions or how much income a particular product in one of its two geographic territories contributes, it is necessary to prepare multilevel segment income statements. Since DCC sells three products and operates through two divisions in two territories, many combinations of divisions, products, and territories could be used in structuring the company's multilevel segment reporting. The goal is not to slice and dice the revenue and cost data in as many ways as possible but to provide useful and meaningful information to management. Therefore, deciding what type of reporting structure is most useful in managing the company is important.

This decision will be constrained to a great extent by data availability and cost. If there were no data constraints, DCC could look at the company's net income for every possible combination of division, product, and territory. The more data required to support a reporting system, however, the more costly it is to maintain the system, so management must determine the value and the cost of the additional information and make an appropriate cost-benefit judgment.

Panel A of Exhibit 22.1 illustrates multi-level segment reporting for DCC in which the first level shows the total company income statement segmented into the two market divisions, National Accounts and Regional Accounts. Panel B of Exhibit 22.1 shows a second-level report for DCC in which the National Division's segment income statement is broken down into its three product lines, fiber optic cable, twisted pair cable, and coaxial cable. Panel C then provides a third-level income statement for the National Division's fiber optic sales in each of the company's two geographic territories, the Atlantic and Pacific territories. The example in Exhibit 22.1 shows only part of the segment reports for DCC. The complete three-level set of segment reports would also break down the Regional Accounts Division into its product lines and all product lines for both divisions into geographic territories.

In the DCC example in Exhibit 22.1, the first reporting level is the company's divisions, its second reporting level is product lines, and the third is geographic territories. Another approach could be to structure the segment reports with product lines as the first level, geographic territories as the second level, and

EXHIBIT 22.1	Multi-Level Segment Reports

Panel A: First-Level Segment Report of Digital Communications Company—For Divisions (in thousands)

	Segments (Divisions)		
	National Accounts	Regional Accounts	Company Total
Sales....................................	$100,000	$ 200,000	$300,000
Less variable costs........................	(55,000)	(95,000)	(150,000)
Contribution margin........................	45,000	105,000	150,000
Less direct fixed costs.....................	(20,000)	(60,000)	(80,000)
Division margin............................	25,000	45,000	70,000
Less allocated segment costs..............	(10,000)	(25,000)	(35,000)
Division income...........................	$ 15,000	$ 20,000	$ 35,000
Less unallocated common costs...........................			(12,000)
Net income.........................			$ 23,000

Panel B: Second-Level Segment Report of the National Division—For Products (in thousands)

	Segments (Products)			National Division Total
	Fiber Optic	Twisted Pair	Coaxial	
Sales................................	$30,000	$40,000	$30,000	$100,000
Less variable costs......................	(15,000)	(19,000)	(21,000)	(55,000)
Contribution margin.....................	15,000	21,000	9,000	45,000
Less direct fixed costs..................	(9,000)	(4,000)	(2,000)	(15,000)
Product margin.........................	6,000	17,000	7,000	30,000
Less allocated segment costs.............	(5,000)	(4,000)	(1,000)	(10,000)
Product income........................	$ 1,000	$13,000	$ 6,000	$ 20,000
Less unallocated common costs.............				(5,000)
National Division income...................				$ 15,000

Panel C: Third-Level Segment Report of the Fiber Optic Product Line in the National Division—For Geographic Territories (in thousands)

	Segments (Territories)		Fiber Optic Total
	Atlantic	Pacific	
Sales...................................	$20,000	$10,000	$30,000
Less variable costs......................	(11,000)	(4,000)	(15,000)
Contribution margin.....................	9,000	6,000	15,000
Less direct fixed costs...................	(3,000)	(4,000)	(7,000)
Territory margin........................	6,000	2,000	8,000
Less allocated segment costs.............	(2,000)	(3,000)	(5,000)
Territory income........................	$ 4,000	$(1,000)	$ 3,000
Less unallocated common costs................			(2,000)
Fiber optic income..........................			$ 1,000

divisions as the third level. Still another approach would be to make product lines the first level, divisions the second level, and geographic territories the third level.

Regardless of how many different ways the company segments the income statements, at least one set of segment reports follows the company's responsibility reporting system; therefore, one of the segment reports has the operating divisions as the first level. If each division has a product manager for each product, the division segment reports are broken down by products. Finally, if each product within each division has a territory manager, the product segment reports are broken down by territories.

Interpreting Segment Reports

Exhibit 22.1 reports costs in four categories: variable costs, direct fixed costs, allocated common costs, and unallocated common costs. Variable costs vary in proportion to the level of sales and are subtracted from sales in calculating contribution margin. **Direct segment fixed costs** are nonvariable costs directly traceable to the segments incurred for the specific benefit of the respective segments. **Segment margin** equals the contribution margin minus the direct segment fixed costs. For DCC, segment margins are referred to as *division margins, product margins,* and *territory margins.* Segment margins represent the amount that a segment contributes directly to the company's profitability in the short run.

Common segment costs are incurred for the common benefit of all related segments shown on a segment income statement. In some cases, allocating some common costs is reasonable even though they cannot be directly traced to the various segments based on benefits received. For example, if segments share common space, allocating all space-related costs to the segments based on building space occupied could be appropriate. If there is no reasonable basis for allocating common costs, they should not be allocated to the segments. In Panel C of Exhibit 22.1, if advertising costs to promote the company's fiber optic products on national television could not be reasonably allocated to the two geographic territories, they would be charged to the fiber optic product line as an unallocated common cost, not to the individual territories.

If some portion of common costs can be reasonably allocated to the segments, those allocated costs are subtracted from the segment margins to determine segment income. Hence, **segment income** represents all revenues of the segment minus all costs directly or indirectly charged to it.

To properly interpret segment income, we should ask whether segment income represents the amount by which net income of the company will change if that segment is discontinued. For example, if DCC discontinues the coaxial product line in the National Division, does this mean that DCC's net income will decrease by $6 million? Also, does it mean that if the National Division stops selling fiber optic cable in the Pacific territory, DCC's net income will increase by $1 million?

The answer to these questions depends on whether the costs allocated to the segments are avoidable. **Avoidable common costs** are allocated common costs that eventually can be avoided (that is, can be eliminated) if a segment is discontinued. If all allocated common costs are avoidable, the effect of discontinuing the segment on corporate profitability equals the amount of segment income. In most cases, the short-term impact of discontinuing a segment equals the segment margin because allocated costs are capacity costs that cannot be adjusted in the short run. Over time, the company should be able to adjust capacity and eliminate some, or possibly all, of the allocated common costs or find productive uses for that capacity in other segments of the business. The unallocated common costs cannot be changed readily in the short term or the long term without causing major disruptions to the company and its strategy. Therefore, over the long term, the impact of discontinuing a segment should be, approximately, it's segment income.

If DCC discontinues selling fiber optic cable in the Pacific territory (see Exhibit 22.1, Panel C) the short-term effect on the company's profits will probably be a $2 million reduction of profits, which equals the Pacific territory's margin. The revenues and costs that make up the Pacific territory margin would all be lost if fiber optic sales were discontinued in the Pacific territory, but the $3 million of common costs allocated to the Pacific territory would continue, at least in the short term. Over the long term, however, after adjusting the capacity for selling this product in the Pacific territory and eliminating the $3 million of allocated common costs, the effect of discontinuing fiber optics in the Pacific territory on profits should be an increase of about $1 million, which is the amount of the segment loss for fiber optics in the Pacific territory.

To summarize, generally, segment margin is relevant for measuring the short-term effects of decisions to continue or discontinue a segment; however, segment income is relevant for measuring the long-term effects of decisions to continue or discontinue.

MID-MODULE REVIEW

Refer to the Digital Communications (DCC) example in Exhibit 22.1, Panel B. The following additional information is provided for the Coaxial product line in the National Division:

Sales—Atlantic territory	$12,000
Sales—Pacific territory........................	18,000
Direct fixed cost—Atlantic territory	500
Direct fixed cost—Pacific territory	800
Allocated segment costs—Atlantic territory........	200
Allocated segment costs—Pacific territory	600

Required:
a. Prepare a geographic territory segment report of the Coaxial product line in the National division.
b. Explain why the total of the Territory Margins for geographic segments of the Coaxial product line does not equal the product margin of the Coaxial product segment in Panel B of Exhibit 22.1?

Solution
a.

	Segments (Territories)		Coaxial
	Atlantic	**Pacific**	**Total**
Sales....................................	$12,000	$18,000	$30,000
Less variable costs.........................	(8,400)	(12,600)	(21,000)
Contribution margin	3,600	5,400	9,000
Less direct fixed costs	(500)	(800)	(1,300)
Territory margin............................	3,100	4,600	7,700
Less allocated segment costs	(200)	(600)	(800)
Territory income	$ 2,900	$ 4,000	6,900
Less unallocated common costs			(900)
Fiber optic income			$ 6,000

b. The Product Margin for the Coaxial product line in Panel B was $7,000 and reflected $2,000 of direct fixed costs that were attributable to that product line in the National Division. However, when the Coaxial product segment income statement is further segmented into geographic segments, only $1,300 of the $2,000 could be directly traced to the two geographic territories. Therefore, $700 of costs that were direct costs at the product segment level became common costs (either allocated or unallocated) at the territory segment level. This reflects the general notion that as segmentation is extended down to lower and lower levels, the total amount of common costs increase and direct costs decrease. Hence, segmentation rarely is extended to more than three levels.

TRANSFER PRICING

LO3 Explain transfer-pricing and assess alternative transfer pricing methods.

To determine whether each division is achieving its organizational objectives, managers must be accountable for the goods and services they acquire, both externally and internally. When goods or services are exchanged internally between segments of a decentralized organization, the way that the transferor and the transferee will report the transfer must be determined. A **transfer price** is the internal value assigned a product or service that one division provides to another. The transfer price is recognized as revenue by the division providing goods or services and as expense (or cost) by the division receiving them. Transfer-pricing transactions normally occur between profit or investment centers rather than between cost centers of an organization; however, managers often consider cost allocations between cost centers as a type of transfer price. The focus in this module is on transfers between responsibility centers that are evaluated based on profits.

Management Considerations

The desire of the selling and buying divisions of the same company to maximize their individual performance measures often creates transfer-pricing problems. Acting as independent units, divisions could take actions that are not in the best interest(s) of the organization as a whole. The three examples that follow illustrate the need for organizations to maintain a *corporate* profit-maximizing viewpoint while attempting to allow *divisional* autonomy and responsibility.

OmniTech, Inc., has five divisions, some of which transfer products and product components to other OmniTech divisions. The BioTech Division manufactures two products, Alpha and Beta. It sells Alpha externally for $50 per unit and transfers Beta to the GenTech Division for $60 per unit. The costs associated with the two products follow:

	Product	
	Alpha	Beta
Variable costs		
Direct materials.	$15	$14
Direct labor	5	10
Variable manufacturing overhead.	5	16
Selling	4	0
Fixed Costs		
Fixed manufacturing overhead.	6	15
Total	$35	$55

An external company has just proposed to supply a Beta substitute product to the GenTech Division at a price of $52. From the company's viewpoint, this is merely a make or buy decision. The relevant costs are the differential outlay costs of the alternative actions. Assuming that the fixed manufacturing costs of the BioTech Division are unavoidable, the relevant costs of this proposal from the company's perspective are as follows:

Buy		$52
Make		
Direct materials.	$14	
Direct labor	10	
Variable manufacturing overhead.	16	(40)
Difference.		$12

From the corporate viewpoint, the best decision is for the product to be transferred since the relevant cost is $40 rather than to buy it from an external source for $52. The decision for the GenTech Division management is basically one of cost minimization: Buy from the source that charges the lowest price. If BioTech is not willing to transfer Beta at a price of $52 or less, the GenTech management could go to the external supplier to maximize the division's profits. (Although GenTech's managers are concerned about the cost of Beta, they are also concerned about the quality of the goods. If the $52 product does not meet its quality standards, GenTech could decide to buy from BioTech at the higher price. For this discussion, assume that the internal and external products are identical; therefore, acting in its best interest, GenTech purchases Beta for $52 from the external source unless BioTech can match the price.)

Prior to GenTech's receipt of the external offer, BioTech had been transferring Beta to GenTech for $60. BioTech must decide whether to reduce the contribution margin on its transfers of Beta to GenTech and, therefore, lower divisional profits or to try to find an alternative use for its resources. Of course, corporate management could intervene and require the internal transfer even though it would hurt BioTech's profits.

As the second example, assume that the BioTech Division has the option to sell an equivalent amount of Beta externally for $60 per unit if the GenTech Division discontinues its transfers from BioTech. Now the decision for BioTech's management is simple: Sell to the buyer willing to pay the most. From the corporate viewpoint, it is best for BioTech to sell to the external buyer for $60 and for GenTech to purchase from the external provider for $52.

To examine a slightly different transfer-pricing conflict, assume that the BioTech Division can sell all the Alpha that it can produce (it is operating at capacity). Also assume that there is no external market for Beta, but there is a one-to-one trade-off between the production of Alpha and Beta, which use equal amounts of the BioTech Division's limited capacity.

The corporation still regards this as a make or buy decision, but the costs of producing Beta have changed. The cost of Beta now includes an outlay cost and an opportunity cost. The outlay cost of Beta is its variable cost of $40 ($14 + $10 + $16), as previously computed. Beta's opportunity cost is the net benefit forgone if the BioTech Division's limited capacity is used to produce Beta rather than Alpha:

Selling price of Alpha		$50
Outlay costs of Alpha		
Direct materials	$15	
Direct labor	5	
Variable manufacturing overhead	5	
Variable selling	4	(29)
Opportunity cost of making Beta		$21

Accordingly, the relevant costs in the make or buy decision follow.

Make		
Outlay cost of Beta	$40	
Opportunity cost of Beta	21	$61
Buy		$52

From the corporate viewpoint, GenTech should purchase Beta from the outside supplier for $52 because in this case it costs $61 to make the product. If there were no outside suppliers, the corporation's relevant cost of manufacturing Beta would be $61. This is another way of saying that the GenTech Division should not acquire Beta internally unless its revenues cover all outlay costs (including the $40 in the BioTech Division) and provide a contribution of at least $21 ($61 − $40). From the corporate viewpoint, the relevant costs in make or buy decisions are the external price, the outlay costs to manufacture, and the opportunity cost to manufacture. The opportunity cost is zero if there is excess capacity.

Determining Transfer Prices

As illustrated, the transfer price of goods or services can be subject to much controversy. The most widely used and discussed transfer prices are covered in this section. See the following Business Insight for a discussion of transfer-pricing. Although a price must be agreed upon for each item or service transferred between divisions, the selection of the pricing method depends on many factors. The conditions surrounding the transfer determine which of the alternative methods discussed subsequently is selected.

Although no method is likely to be ideal, one must be selected if the profit or investment center concept is used. In considering each method, observe that each transfer results in a revenue entry on the supplier's books and a cost entry on the receiver's books. Transfers can be considered as sales by the supplier and as purchases by the receiver.

Market Price

When there is an existing market with established prices for an intermediate product and the transfer actions of the company will not affect prices, market prices are ideal transfer prices. If divisions are free to buy and sell outside the firm, the use of market prices preserves divisional autonomy and leads divisions to act in a manner that maximizes corporate goal congruence. Unfortunately, not all product transfers have equivalent external markets. Furthermore, the divisions should carefully evaluate whether the market price is competitive or controlled by one or two large companies. When substantial selling expenses are associated with outside sales, many firms specify the transfer price as market price less selling expenses. The internal sale may not require the incurrence of costs to get and fill the order.

BUSINESS INSIGHT **Citigroup's Transfer-Pricing Problems**

Fortune magazine interviewed the CEO of Citigroup in connection with its annual "Fortune 500" article. Citigroup is a diversified financial company that includes such major financial brands as Primerica, Salomon Smith Barney, Citibank, and Travelers. Following is an excerpt from that article discussing some problems of decentralization and transfer pricing at Citigroup.

In a company of Citi's size and complexity, there are dozens of issues—business overlaps, competitive threats, regulations—that cut across divisions. In an institution that promotes cross-selling, for example, there is always the question of how the financial spoils are divided up between the two divisions—a matter that goes under the name "transfer pricing." For example, suppose that a Salomon Smith Barney financial consultant sells a mutual fund "manufactured" by Citi's investment management division. What's the price that the IM division receives? The answer, since it determines profit, is extremely important to executives getting paid (and paying their people) according to what their own bottom line looks like . . . . [The CEO] says testily that he wishes people "would think about doing the business first, and worry about who gets the credit second." But, trying to mediate, he also has his financial people studying plans for internally double counting revenues, so as to make profits (or losses) accrue to both parties involved in a cross-selling event.[2]

To illustrate using the OmniTech example, assume that product Alpha of the BioTech Division can be sold competitively at $50 per unit or transferred to a third division, the Quantum Division, for additional processing. Under most situations, The BioTech Division will never sell Alpha for less than $50, and The Quantum Division will likewise never pay more than $50 for it. However, if any variable expenses related to marketing and shipping can be eliminated by divisional transfers, these costs are generally subtracted from the competitive market price. In our illustration in which variable selling expenses are $4 for Alpha, the transfer price could be reduced to $46 ($50 − $4). A price between $46 and $50 would probably be better than either extreme price. To the extent that these transfer prices represent a nearly competitive situation, the profitability of each division can then be fairly evaluated.

Variable Costs

If excess capacity exists in the supplying division, establishing a transfer price equal to variable costs leads the purchasing division to act in a manner that is optimal from the corporation's viewpoint. The buying division has the corporation's variable cost as its own variable cost as it enters the external market. Unfortunately, establishing the transfer price at variable cost causes the supplying division to report zero profits or a loss equal to any fixed costs. If excess capacity does not exist, establishing a transfer price at variable cost would not lead to optimal action because the supplying division would have to forgo external sales that include a markup for fixed costs and profits. If Beta could be sold externally for $60, the BioTech Division would not want to transfer Beta to the GenTech Division for a $40 transfer price based on the following variable costs:

Direct materials	$14
Direct labor	10
Variable manufacturing overhead	16
Total variable costs	$40

The BioTech Division would much rather sell outside the company for $60, which covers variable costs and provides a profit contribution margin of $20:

Selling price of Beta	$60
Variable costs	(40)
Contribution margin	$20

---

[2] Carol J. Loomis, "The Fortune 500, No. 6 Sandy Weill's Monster," *Fortune,* April 16, 2001

Variable Costs Plus Opportunity Costs

From the organization's viewpoint, this is the optimal transfer price. Because all relevant costs are included in the transfer price, the purchasing division is led to act in a manner optimal for the overall company, whether or not excess capacity exists.

With excess capacity in the supplying division, the transfer price is the variable cost per unit. Without excess capacity, the transfer price is the sum of the variable and opportunity costs. Following this rule in the previous example, if the BioTech Division had excess capacity, the transfer price of Beta would be set at Beta's variable costs of $40 per unit. At this transfer price, the GenTech Division would buy Beta internally, rather than externally at $52 per unit. If the BioTech Division cannot sell Beta externally but can sell all the Alpha it can produce and is operating at capacity, the transfer price per unit would be set at $61, the sum of Beta's variable and opportunity costs ($40 + $21). (Refer back two pages.) At this transfer price, the GenTech Division would buy Beta externally for $52. In both situations, the management of the GenTech Division has acted in accordance with the organization's profit-maximizing goal.

There are two problems with this method. First, when the supplying division has excess capacity, establishing the transfer price at variable cost causes the supplying division to report zero profits or a loss equal to any fixed costs. Second, determining opportunity costs when the supplying division produces several products is difficult. If the problems with the previously mentioned transfer-pricing methods are too great, three other methods can be used: absorption cost plus markup, negotiated prices, and dual prices.

Absorption Cost Plus Markup

According to absorption costing, all variable and fixed manufacturing costs are product costs. Pricing internal transfers at absorption cost eliminates the supplying division's reported loss on each product that can occur using a variable cost transfer price. Absorption cost plus markup provides the supplying division a contribution toward unallocated costs. In "cost-plus" transfer pricing, "cost" should be defined as standard cost rather than as actual cost. This prevents the supplying division from passing on the cost of inefficient operations to other divisions, and it allows the buying division to know its cost in advance of purchase. Even though cost-plus transfer prices may not maximize company profits, they are widely used. Their popularity stems from several factors, including ease of implementation, justifiability, and perceived fairness. Once everyone agrees on absorption cost plus markup pricing rules, internal disputes are minimized.

Negotiated Prices

Negotiated transfer prices are used when the supplying and buying divisions independently agree on a price. As with market-based transfer prices, negotiated transfer prices are believed to preserve divisional autonomy. Negotiated transfer prices can lead to some suboptimal decisions, but this is regarded as a small price to pay for other benefits of decentralization. When they use negotiated transfer prices, some corporations establish arbitration procedures to help settle disputes between divisions. However, the existence of an arbitrator with any real or perceived authority reduces divisional autonomy.

Negotiated prices should have market prices as their ceiling and variable costs as their floor. Although frequently used when an external market for the product or component exists, the most common use of negotiated prices occurs when no identical-product external market exists. Negotiations could start with a floor price plus add-ons such as overhead and profit markups or with a ceiling price less adjustments for selling and administrative expenses and allowances for quantity discounts. When no identical-product external market exists, the market price for a similar completed product can be used, less the estimated cost of completing the product from the transfer stage to the completed stage.

Dual Prices

Dual prices exist when a company allows a difference in the supplier's and receiver's transfer prices for the same product. This method allegedly minimizes internal squabbles of division managers and problems of conflicting divisional and corporate goals. The supplier's transfer price normally approximates market price, which allows the selling division to show a "normal" profit on items that it transfers internally. The receiver's price is usually the internal cost of the product or service, calculated as variable cost plus opportunity cost. This ensures that the buying division will make an internal transfer when it is in the best interest of the company to do so.

In most cases, a market-based transfer price achieves the optimal outcome for both the divisions and the company as a whole. As discussed earlier, an exception occurs when a division is operating below full capacity and has no alternative use for its excess capacity. In this case, it is best for the company to have an internal transfer; therefore, to ensure that the receiving division makes an internal transfer, the company must require the internal transfer as long as its price does not exceed the established market rate. The only time an external price is more attractive when excess capacity exists is when the external price is below the variable cost of the providing internal division, and that scenario is highly unlikely.

A potential transfer pricing problem exists when divisions exchange goods or services for which no established market exists. For example, suppose that a company is operating its information technology (IT) service department as a profit center that transfers services to other profit center departments using a cost-plus transfer price. If the departments using IT services can choose to use those services or to replicate them inside their departments, users might not make a decision that is best for the company. It could be best for the company to have all IT services come from the IT department, but other profit centers could believe that they can provide those services for themselves at lower cost. In this case, the company must decide how important it is to maintain the independence of its profit center. In the interest of maintaining a strong profit center philosophy, top management can decide that it is acceptable to suboptimize by allowing profit centers to provide IT services for themselves.

The ideal transfer pricing arrangement is seldom the same for both the providing and receiving divisions for every situation. In these cases, what is good for one division is likely not to be good for the other division resulting in no transfer, even though a transfer could achieve corporate goals. These conflicts are sometimes overcome by having a higher ranking manager impose a transfer price and insist that a transfer be made. Managers in organizations that have a policy of decentralization, however, often regard these orders as undermining their autonomy. Therefore, the imposition of a price could solve the corporate profit optimization problem but create other problems regarding the company's organization strategy. Transfer pricing thus becomes a problem with no ideal solutions.

INVESTMENT CENTER EVALUATION MEASURES

Two of the most common measures of investment center performance, return on investment and residual income, are discussed in the following sections. Several supporting components of these measures that help clarify the applications are also presented.

LO4 Determine and contrast return on investment and residual income.

Return on Investment

Return on investment (ROI) is a measure of the earnings per dollar of investment. (This assumes that financing decisions are made at the corporate level rather than the division level. Hence, the corporation's investment in the division equals the division's asset base. The computation of ROI, as presented here, is similar to that for return on assets that was discussed in Module 1.) The return on investment of an investment center is computed by dividing the income of the center by its asset base (usually total assets):

$$\text{ROI} = \frac{\text{Investment center income}}{\text{Investment center asset base}}$$

Similar to the disaggregation of return on assets discussed in Module 1, ROI can be disaggregated into investment turnover times the return-on-sales ratio:

$$\text{ROI} = \text{Investment turnover} \times \text{Return-on-sales}$$

where

$$\text{Investment turnover} = \frac{\text{Sales}}{\text{Investment center asset base}}$$

and

$$\text{Return-on-sales} = \frac{\text{Investment center income}}{\text{Sales}}$$

When investment turnover is multiplied by return-on-sales, the product is the same as investment center income divided by investment center asset base:

$$\text{ROI} = \frac{\text{Sales}}{\text{Investment center base}} \times \frac{\text{Investment center income}}{\text{Sales}} = \frac{\text{Investment center income}}{\text{Investment center asset base}}$$

Once ROI has been computed, it is compared to some previously identified performance criteria. These include the investment center's previous ROI, overall company ROI, the ROI of similar divisions, or the ROI of nonaffiliated companies that operate in similar markets. The breakdown of ROI into investment turnover and return-on-sales is useful in determining the source of variance in overall performance.

To illustrate the computation and use of ROI, the following information is available concerning the 2007 operations of North American Steel:

Division	Net Assets	Sales	Divisional Income
Maine	$8,000,000	$12,000,000	$1,440,000
Alberta	4,000,000	8,000,000	960,000
Missouri	7,500,000	5,000,000	1,650,000
Tijuana	3,800,000	5,700,000	1,026,000

Using this information and the preceding equations, a set of Dupont performance measures can be presented as shown in Exhibit 22.2. To illustrate, Maine Division earned a return on its investment base of 18 percent ($1,440,000 ÷ $8,000,000), consisting of an investment turnover of 1.50 ($12,000,000 ÷ $8,000,000) and a return-on-sales of 0.12 ($1,440,000 ÷ $12,000,000). Using such an analysis, the company has three measurement criteria with which to evaluate the performance of Maine Division: (1) ROI, (2) investment turnover, and (3) return-on-sales.

For 2007, North American chose to evaluate its divisions based on company ROI and its interrelated components of investment turnover and return-on-sales. Because each division is different in size, the company evaluation standard is not a simple average of the divisions but is based on desired relationships between assets, sales, and income.

Based on ROI, the Tijuana Division had the best performance, the Alberta Division excelled in investment turnover, and the Missouri Division had the highest return-on-sales. From Exhibit 22.2, the Tijuana Division clearly had the best year because it was the only division that exceeded each of the company's performance criteria. For 2007, each division equaled or exceeded the minimum ROI established by the company even though the component criteria of ROI were not always achieved.

EXHIBIT 22.2	Performance Evaluation Data

NORTH AMERICAN STEEL
Performance Measures
For Year Ending June 30, 2007

	Performance Measures		
	Investment Turnover	× Return-on-Sales	= ROI
Operating unit			
Maine	1.50	0.12	0.18
Alberta	2.00	0.12	0.24
Missouri	0.67	0.33	0.22
Tijuana	1.50	0.18	0.27
Company performance criteria			
Projected minimums	1.20	0.15	0.18

To properly evaluate each division, the company should study the underlying components of ROI. For the Maine Division, management would want to know why the minimum investment turnover was exceeded while the return-on-sales minimum was not. The Maine Division could have incurred unfavorable cost variances by producing inefficiently. As a result of inefficient production, the return-on-sales declined to a point below the minimum desired level. Evaluating a large operating division based on one financial indicator is difficult. Management should select several key indicators of performance when conducting periodic reviews of its operating segments.

A similar analysis of ROI and its components is useful for planning. In developing plans for 2008, management wants to know the possible effect of changes in the major elements of ROI for the Maine Division. Sensitivity analysis can be used to predict the impact of changes in sales, the investment center asset base, or the investment center income.

Assuming the investment base is unchanged, a projected ROI can be determined for the Maine Division for a sales goal of $16,000,000 and an income goal of $1,600,000:

$$
\begin{aligned}
\text{ROI} &= \frac{\text{Sales}}{\text{Investment center asset base}} \times \frac{\text{Investment center income}}{\text{Sales}} \\
&= \frac{\$16,000,000}{\$8,000,000} \times \frac{\$1,600,000}{\$16,000,000} \\
&= 2.0 \times 0.10 \\
&= 0.20, \text{ or } 20 \text{ percent.}
\end{aligned}
$$

ROI increased from 18 to 20 percent, even though the return-on-sales decreased from 12 to 10 percent. The change in turnover from 1.5 to 2.0 more than offset the reduced return-on-sales.

Sensitivity analysis can involve changing only one factor or a combination of factors in the ROI model. When more than one factor is changed, it is important to analyze exactly how much change is caused by each factor.

Statistics such as ROI, investment turnover, and return-on-sales mean little by themselves. They take on meaning only when compared with an objective, a trend, another division, a competitor, or an industry average. Many businesses establish minimum ROIs for each of their divisions, expecting them to attain or exceed this minimum return. The salaries, bonuses, and promotions of division managers can be tied directly to their division's ROI. Without other evaluation techniques, managers often strive for ROI maximization, sometimes to the long-run detriment of the entire organization.

Investment Center Income

Despite the relevance and conceptual simplicity of ROI, a division's ROI cannot be determined until management decides how to measure divisional income and investment. Divisional income equals divisional revenues less divisional operating expenses. Determining divisional revenues is usually a relatively easy task since revenues are typically generated and recorded at the division level, but determining total operating expenses for divisions is more complicated. Because many expenses are incurred at the corporate level for the common benefit of the various operating divisions and to support corporate headquarters operations, the cost assignment issues discussed early in this module affect investment center income.

Direct division expenses are always included in division operating expenses, but there are conflicting viewpoints about how to deal with common corporate expenses. In corporate annual reports, many companies are required to provide segment revenues and expenses segmented by product lines, geographic territories, customer markets, and so on. Companies also show operating income for their various segments in their annual reports, but they include a category called *corporate* or *unallocated* for company expenses that cannot be reasonably allocated to the various segments. For example, the Ericsson, Inc. annual report for a recent year includes the following breakdown of its operating income by segments (stated in millions of Swedish kronas):

Network operators and service providers	33,072 SEK
Consumer products	(16,195)
Enterprises solutions	22
Other operations	1,708
Unallocated	(1,858)
Total operating income	16,749 SEK

A footnote in the Ericsson report indicates that "unallocated consists mainly of costs for corporate staffs, certain goodwill amortization and non-operational gains and losses."

For internal segment reporting, some companies do not allocate corporate costs that cannot be associated closely with individual segments. Other companies insist on allocating all common corporate costs to the operating divisions to emphasize that the company does not earn a profit until revenues have covered all costs. Some top managers believe that since only operating divisions produce revenues, they should also bear all costs, including corporate costs. These managers want to ensure that the sum of the division income for the various segments equals the total income for the company.

Division managers do not control corporate costs; therefore, these costs are seldom relevant in evaluating a division manager's performance. To deal with this conflict, some companies allocate some, or possibly all, common corporate costs in reporting segment operating income, but for ROI calculation purposes exclude allocated corporate costs that are not closely associated with the divisions. These companies include in the ROI calculation costs that represent an identifiable benefit to the divisions but not general corporate costs that provide no identifiable benefits to the divisions. In practice, the treatment of corporate costs for division performance evaluation varies widely.

Investment Center Asset Base

Because the primary purpose for computing ROI is to evaluate the effectiveness of a division's operating management in using the assets entrusted to them, most organizations define *investment* as the average total assets of a division during the evaluation period. For most companies, the *investment base* is defined as each division's operating assets. These normally include those assets held for productive use, such as accounts receivable, inventory, and plant and equipment. Nonproductive assets, such as land for a future plant site, are not included in the investment base of a division but in the investment base for the company.

General corporate assets allocated to divisions should not be included in their bases. Although the divisions might need additional administrative facilities if they were truly independent, they have no control over the headquarters' facilities. The joint nature and use of corporate facility-level expenses make any allocation arbitrary.

Other Valuation Issues

Once divisional investment and income have been operationally defined and ROI computations have been made, the significance of the resulting ratios can still be questioned. Return on investment can be overstated in terms of constant dollars because inflation as well as arbitrary inventory and depreciation procedures cause an undervaluation of the inventory and fixed assets included in the investment center asset base. Asset measurement is particularly troublesome if inventories are valued at last-in, first-out (LIFO) cost and fixed assets were acquired many years ago. A division manager could hesitate to replace an old, inefficient asset with a new, efficient one because the replacement could lower income and ROI through an increased investment base and increased depreciation.

To improve the comparability between divisions with old and new assets when computing ROI, some firms value assets at original cost rather than at net book value (cost less accumulated depreciation). This procedure does not reflect inflation, however. An old asset that cost $120,000 ten years ago is still being compared with an asset that costs $200,000 today. A better solution could be to value old assets at their replacement cost, although obtaining replacement cost data can be a problem.

MANAGERIAL DECISION   **You are the Division Vice President**

Division managers in your company are evaluated primarily based on division return on investment, and you recently received financial reports for your division for the most recent period and discovered that the ROI for your division was 14.5%; whereas, the target ROI for your division set by the CFO and the CEO was 15%. What action can you take to try to avoid missing your performance target for the next period? [Answer p. 22-21]

Residual Income

Residual income is an often-mentioned alternative to ROI for measuring investment center performance. **Residual income** is the excess of investment center income over the minimum rate of return set by top management. The minimum rate of return represents the rate that can be earned on alternative investments of similar risks, which is the opportunity cost of the investment.

The minimum dollar return is computed as a percentage of the investment center's asset base. When residual income is the primary basis of evaluation, the management of each investment center is encouraged to maximize residual income rather than ROI. To illustrate the computation, assume that a company requires a minimum return of 12 percent on each division's investment base. The residual income of a division with an annual net operating income of $2,000,000 and an investment base of $15,000,000 is $200,000 as computed here:

Division income	$2,000,000
Minimum return ($15,000,000 × 0.12)	(1,800,000)
Residual income.	$ 200,000

In recent years, a variation of residual income, referred to as **economic value added** or **EVA®,** has gained in popularity with many corporations. (The term *EVA* is a registered trademark of the financial consulting firm of Stern Stewart and Company.) EVA is a special case of the residual income model applied under specific assumptions. Accordingly, if one can apply the residual income model, then application of EVA is a simple step.

Which Measure Is Best?

Many executives view residual income as a better measure of managers' performance than ROI. They believe that residual income encourages managers to make profitable investments that managers might reject if being measured exclusively by ROI.

To illustrate, assume that two divisions of Color Company have an opportunity to make an investment of $100,000 that requires $10,000 of additional current liabilities and that will generate a return of 20 percent. The manager of the Paint Division is evaluated using ROI and the manager of the Ink Division is evaluated using residual income. The current ROI of each division is 24 percent. Each division has a current income of $120,000, a minimum return of 18 percent on invested capital, and a cost of capital of 14 percent. If each division has a current investment base of $500,000, current liabilities of $40,000, and a tax rate of 30 percent, the effect of the proposed investment on each division's performance is as follows:

	Current	+	Proposed	=	Total
Paint Division					
Investment center income	$120,000		$ 20,000		$140,000
Asset base	$500,000		$100,000		$600,000
ROI	24%		20%		23.3%
Ink Division					
Asset base	$500,000		$100,000		$600,000
Investment center income	$120,000		$ 20,000		$140,000
Minimum return (0.18 × base)	(90,000)		(18,000)		(108,000)
Residual income	$ 30,000		$ 2,000		$ 32,000

The Paint Division manager will not want to make the new investment because it reduces the current ROI from 24 percent to 23.3 percent. This is true, even though the company's minimum return is only 18 percent. Not wanting to explain a decline in the division's ROI, the manager will probably reject the opportunity even though it could have benefited the company as a whole.

The Ink Division manager will probably be happy to accept the new project because it increases residual income by $2,000. Any investment that provides a return more than the required minimum of 18 percent will be acceptable to the Ink Division manager. Given a profit maximization goal for the organization, the residual income method is preferred over ROI evaluations because it encourages division managers to accept all projects with returns above the 18 percent cutoff.

The primary disadvantage of the residual income method as a comparative evaluation tool is that it measures performance in absolute terms. Although it can be used to compare period-to-period results of the same division or with similar-size divisions, it cannot be used to compare the performance of divisions of substantially different sizes. For example, the residual income of a multimillion dollar sales division is expected to be higher than that of a half-million dollar sales division. Because most performance evaluations and comparisons are made between units or alternative investments of different sizes, ROI continues to be extensively used.

BALANCED SCORECARD

LO5 Describe the balanced scorecard as a comprehensive performance measurement system.

Although financial measures have been emphasized throughout this text, several sections stress that other measures, specifically qualitative measures, are important in evaluating managerial performance. This section examines one popular method of performance evaluation using *both* financial and nonfinancial information.

We might ask: why not use just financial measures? First, no single financial measure captures all performance aspects of an organization. More than one measure must be used. Second, financial measures have reporting time lags that could hinder timely decision making. Third, financial measures might not accurately capture the information needed for current decision making because of the delay that sometimes occurs between making financial investments and receiving their results. For example, building a new nuclear power plant can take several years with total assets increasing the entire time without generating revenues.

Balanced Scorecard Framework

Comprehensive performance measurement systems are one suggested solution. The basic premise is to establish a set of diverse key performance indicators to monitor performance. The **balanced scorecard** is a performance measurement system that includes financial and operational measures related to a firm's goals and strategies. The balanced scorecard comprises several categories of measurements, the most common of which include the following:

- Financial
- Customer satisfaction
- Internal processes
- Innovation and learning

A balanced scorecard is usually a set of reports required of all common operating units in an organization. To facilitate the periodic evaluation of performance, a cover sheet (or sheets for a large operation) can be used to summarize the performance of each area using the established criteria for each category.

For example, a chain of bagel shops might have a balanced scorecard that looks something like the one in Exhibit 22.3. This balanced scorecard uses four categories for evaluation and includes financial and nonfinancial information. Each category being monitored has information from the previous period and the standard related to the category. The report should always include the current period, at least one previous period, and some standard. Each store manager should attach documentation and an appropriate explanation as to the change in the measurements during the reporting period.

In making assessments with the evaluation categories, it is important to consider both trailing and leading performance measures. *Trailing measures* look backward at historical data while *leading measures* provide some idea of what to expect currently or in the near future. For example, in the financial category, ROI is a trailing indicator while a budget of production units and costs for the next period is a leading indicator. In the customer category, a chart of sales units per store might tell us whether each store is maintaining its customer base (a trailing indicator) while a weekly chart of product complaints per 100 units sold might be a leading indicator of customer satisfaction, quality control problems, and future sales.

The use of balanced scorecard systems to monitor and assess managerial and organizational performance is increasing worldwide. The following Business Insight provides insights into the key performance indicators used by a group of firms.

A balanced scorecard gives management a perspective of the organization's performance on a recurring set of criteria. Since each reporting unit knows what reports are expected, no one is surprised by changing monthly requests for data. Because the multiple perspectives provide management a broad

EXHIBIT 22.3	Balanced Scorecard Illustration			
		Standard	**Prior Period**	**Current Period**
Key financial indicators				
Cash flow		$ 25,000	$ (4,000)	$ 21,000
Return on investment (ROI).		0.18	0.22	0.19
Sales		$4,400,000	$4,494,000	$4,342,000
Key customer indicators				
Average customers per hour		75	80	71
Number of customer complaints per period.		22	21	17
Number of sales returns per period		10	8	5
Key operating indicators				
Bagels sold/produced per day ratio		0.96	0.93	0.91
Daily units lost (burned, dropped, etc.).		25	32	34
Employee turnover per period		0.10	0.07	0.00
Key growth and innovation indicators				
New products introduced during period.		1	1	0
Products discontinued during period		1	1	1
Number of sales promotions		3	3	2
Special offers, discounts, etc.		4	5	3

analysis of the organization's performance, it allows them to determine how and where the goals and objectives are either being achieved or not achieved.

For most management teams, the balanced scorecard highlights trade-offs between measures. For example, a substantial increase in customer satisfaction can result in a short-run decrease in ROI because the extra effort to please customers is expensive, thereby reducing ROI. A balanced scorecard can be

---

BUSINESS INSIGHT | **Balanced Scorecard Yields Results**

A survey of firms found that a balanced scorecard is more widely used by larger firms. Also, firms having a higher proportion of new products are more likely to include in their scorecard measures related to new products. However, no relation was found between market share of companies and whether or not they used the balanced scorecard. Yet, results indicated that usage of the balanced scorecard is associated with improved performance of companies regardless of company size, stage of product life cycle, or market position. The following were the most commonly used key performance indicators of the surveyed firms:[3]

Financial perspective:
  Operating income
  Sales growth
  Return on investment
Customer perspective:
  Customer satisfaction
  Number of customer complaints
  Market share
  Percentage of shipments returned
    due to poor quality
  On-time delivery
  Warranty repair cost
  Customer response time
  Cycle time from order to delivery

Internal perspective:
  Labor efficiency variance
  Rate of material scrap loss
  Material efficiency variance
  Manufacturing lead time
  Ratio of good output to total output
  Percentage of defective products shipped

Innovation and learning perspective:
  Number of new product launches
  Number of new patents
  Time to market new products

---

[3] Zahirul Hoque and Wendy James, "Linking Balanced Scorecard Measures to Size and Market Factors: Impact on Organizational Performance," *Journal of Management Accounting Research,* Vol. 12, 2000.

filtered down the organization with successively lower level operating units having their own scorecards that mimic those of the higher level units. This provides all levels of management an opportunity to evaluate operations from more than just a financial perspective.

As with all management tools and techniques, the use of the balanced scorecard must be incorporated with the other information sources within the organization. Just as the accounting information system cannot stand alone in managing a business, neither can the balanced scorecard. Some areas could need extensive accounting information in great detail to make the best possible decision while other areas need great detail in production or service integration to be at the right place at the right time. By using a multi-faceted approach to managing, however, the organization should be able to better establish an operating strategy that coincides with its overall goals and objectives.

Balanced Scorecard and Strategy

When a balanced scorecard system is fully utilized to monitor and evaluate an organization's progress, it becomes a system for operationalizing the organization's strategy. Having a goal to maximize shareholder value or generate a certain income does not constitute a strategy. Maximizing shareholder value can be an overarching corporate goal, but it will not likely be realized without a well-developed strategy that identifies and establishes a balanced set of goals on various dimensions of performance.

A balanced scorecard can be the primary vehicle for translating strategy into action and establishing accountability for performance. The balanced scorecard identifies the areas of managerial action that are believed to be the drivers of corporate achievement. If the corporate goal is to increase ROI, the balanced scorecard should include key performance indicators that drive ROI.

An interesting parallel to the successful management of a company can be drawn by considering the key performance indicators the manager of a professional baseball team uses in setting goals and evaluating progress. The manager of the New York Yankees does not just tell his players and managers at the beginning of the baseball season that the team's goal is to win the World Series or even a certain number of ball games. The win-loss record is only one metric used to set goals and evaluate performance for a baseball team. The manager looks at many different drivers of success related to hitting, pitching, and fielding, including the earned run averages of the pitchers, the batting and on-base averages of hitters, the number of errors per game by fielders, and the number of bases stolen by base runners. At the end of the season, the manager measures success not just by whether the Yankees won the World Series, but also by the batting average, number of home runs, and number of bases stolen by individual players, and whether or not a team member won a Golden Glove award or the Cy Young award. These are all measures by which to evaluate achievement and strategic accomplishment. By achieving the goals for each of these areas of the game, the win-loss ratio will take care of itself. If the win-loss results are not acceptable, then the manager adjusts his strategic goals with respect to the key performance indicators (or the manager is dismissed).

Like a baseball team, a company can use a balanced scorecard to develop performance metrics for managers from the top of the company to the lowest-level department. The scorecard becomes a vehicle for communicating the factors that are key to the success of managers, factors that upper management will monitor in evaluating the success of lower managers in carrying out the corporate strategy.

MODULE-END REVIEW

Pareto International, a decentralized organization that manufactures specialty construction products, has three divisions, Commercial, Industrial, and Residential. Corporate management desires a minimum return of 15 percent on its investments and has a 20 percent tax rate with an average cost of capital of 12 percent. The divisions' 2007 results follow (in thousands):

Division	Income	Investment	Current Liabilities
Commercial	$30,000	$200,000	$10,000
Industrial.	50,000	250,000	30,000
Residential	22,000	100,000	5,000

The company is planning an expansion project in 2008 that will cost $50,000,000 and return $9,000,000 per year. It will result in a $10,000 increase in current liabilities.

Required

a. Compute the ROI for each division for 2007.
b. Compute the residual income for each division for 2007.
c. Rank the divisions according to their ROI and residual income.
d. Assume that other income and investments will remain unchanged. Determine the effect of the project by itself. What is the effect on ROI and residual income if the new project is added to each division?

Solution

a.

$$\text{Return on investment} = \frac{\text{Investment center income}}{\text{Investment center asset base}}$$

$$\text{Commercial Division} = \$30,000 \div \$200,000$$
$$= 0.15, \text{ or } 15 \text{ percent}$$
$$\text{Industrial Division} = \$50,000 \div \$250,000$$
$$= 0.20, \text{ or } 20 \text{ percent}$$
$$\text{Residential Division} = \$22,000 \div \$100,000$$
$$= 0.22, \text{ or } 22 \text{ percent}$$

b. Residual income = Investment center income − (Investment center asset base × Minimum return)

$$\text{Commercial Division} = \$30,000 - (0.15 \times \$200,000)$$
$$= \$0.00$$
$$\text{Industrial Division} = \$50,000 - (0.15 \times \$250,000)$$
$$= \$12,500$$
$$\text{Residential Division} = \$22,000 - (0.15 \times \$100,000)$$
$$= \$7,000$$

c. ROI ranks the Residential Division first, the Industrial Division second, and the Commercial Division third. Residual income ranks the Industrial Division first, the Residential Division second, and the Commercial Division third. Because the investments for each division are different, it is somewhat misleading to rank the divisions according to residual income. The Industrial Division had the highest residual income, but it also had the largest investment. The Residential Division's residual income was 56 percent of the Industrial Division's income but only 40 percent of the investment of the Industrial Division. This fact, along with the best ROI ranking, probably justifies the Residential Division being evaluated as the best division of Pareto Company.

d. Return on investment:

$$\text{Investment} = \$9,000 \div \$50,000$$
$$= 0.18, \text{ or } 18 \text{ percent}$$
$$\text{Commercial Division} = (\$30,000 + \$9,000) \div (\$200,000 + \$50,000)$$
$$= 0.156, \text{ or } 15.6 \text{ percent}$$
$$\text{Industrial Division} = (\$50,000 + \$9,000) \div (\$250,000 + \$50,000)$$
$$= 0.1967, \text{ or } 19.67 \text{ percent}$$
$$\text{Residential Division} = (\$22,000 + \$9,000) \div (\$100,000 + \$50,000)$$
$$= 0.2067, \text{ or } 20.67 \text{ percent}$$

ROI will increase for the Commercial Division but decrease for the Industrial and Residential Divisions, even though the project's ROI of 18 percent exceeds the company's minimum return of 15 percent. Residual income:

$$\text{Commercial Division} = (\$30,000 + \$9,000) - [0.15 \times (\$200,000 + \$50,000)]$$
$$= \$1,500$$
$$\text{Industrial Division} = (\$50,000 + \$9,000) - [0.15 \times (\$250,000 + \$50,000)]$$
$$= \$14,000$$
$$\text{Residential Division} = (\$22,000 + \$9,000) - [0.15 \times (\$100,000 + \$50,000)]$$
$$= \$8,500$$

Because the project's ROI exceeds the company's minimum return, the residual income of all divisions will increase.

GUIDANCE ANSWER

ROI is primarily a measure of the profitability of a division's assets, which is in turn a measure of how effectively the investment in assets was used to generate sales, and how profitable those sales were. ROI is driven by investment (or asset) turnover (which is division sales divided by assets) and return on sales (which is division net income divided division sales). Therefore, increasing ROI is similar to a simultaneous balancing act involving controlling sales, expenses, and asset investment. You can increase ROI by increasing sales more than expenses, while holding asset investment constant, or by other combinations of these three variables that ultimately increase ROI. If you adjust one of these variables, at the same time you must keep your eye on the other two variables or you may not achieve your goal of increasing ROI.

DISCUSSION QUESTIONS

Q22-1. What is the relationship between segment reports and product reports?

Q22-2. What is a reporting objective? How is it determined?

Q22-3. Can a company have more than one type of first-level statement in segment reporting?

Q22-4. Explain the relationships between any two levels of statements in segment reporting.

Q22-5. Distinguish between direct and indirect segment costs?

Q22-6. What types of information are needed before management should decide to drop a segment?

Q22-7. In what types of organizations and for what purpose are transfer prices used?

Q22-8. What problems arise when transfer pricing is used?

Q22-9. When do transfer prices lead to suboptimization? How can suboptimization be minimized? Can it be eliminated? Why or why not?

Q22-10. For what purpose do organizations use return on investment? Why is this measure preferred to net income?

Q22-11. What advantages does residual income have over ROI for segment evaluations?

Q22-12. Contrast the difference between residual income and ROI.

Q22-13. Explain how a balanced scorecard helps with the evaluation process of internal operations.

Q22-14. How can a balanced scorecard be used as a strategy implementation tool?

MINI EXERCISES

M22-15. Multiple Levels of Segment Reporting   (LO2)

Gormet Appliances manufactures four different lines of household appliances: cooking, cleaning, convenience, and safety. Each of the product lines is produced in all of the company's three plants: Abbeyville, Bakersville, and Charlottesville. Marketing efforts of the company are divided into five regions: East, West, South, North, and Central.

Required

a. Develop a reporting schematic that illustrates how the company might prepare single-level reports segmented on three different bases.

b. Develop a segment reporting schematic that has three different levels. Be sure to identify each segment's level. Briefly explain why you chose the primary-level segment.

M22-16. Income Statements Segmented by Territory   (LO2)

Script, Inc., has two product lines. The September income statements of each product line and the company are as follows:

SCRIPT, INC.
Product Line and Company Income Statements
For Month of September

	Pens	Pencils	Total
Sales.	$25,000	$30,000	$55,000
Less variable expenses	(10,000)	(12,000)	(22,000)
Contribution margin	15,000	18,000	33,000
Less direct fixed expenses.	(9,000)	(7,000)	(16,000)
Product margin.	$ 6,000	$11,000	17,000
Less common fixed expenses			(6,000)
Net income.			$11,000

Pens and pencils are sold in two territories, Florida and Alabama, as follows:

	Florida	Alabama
Pen sales	$15,000	$10,000
Pencil sales	9,000	21,000
Total sales.	$24,000	$31,000

The preceding common fixed expenses are traceable to each territory as follows:

Florida fixed expenses	$2,000
Alabama fixed expenses	3,000
Home office administration fixed expenses.	1,000
Total common fixed expenses	$6,000

The direct fixed expenses of pens, $9,000, and of pencils, $7,000, cannot be identified with either territory. The company's accountants were unable to allocate any of the common fixed expenses to the various segments.

Required

a. Prepare income statements segmented by territory for September, including a column for the entire firm.

b. Why are the direct expenses of one type of segment report not necessarily the direct expenses of another type of segment report?

M22-17. Income Statements Segmented by Products   (LO2)

Clay Consulting Firm provides three types of client services in three health care-related industries. The income statement for July is as follows:

CLAY CONSULTING FIRM
Income Statement
For Month of July

Sales.		$900,000
Less variable costs.		(605,000)
Contribution margin		295,000
Less fixed expenses		
Service	$70,000	
Selling and administrative.	65,000	(135,000)
Net income.		$160,000

The sales, contribution margin ratios, and direct fixed expenses for the three types of services are as follows:

	Hospitals	Physicians	Nursing Care
Sales.	$350,000	$250,000	$300,000
Contribution margin ratio	30%	40%	30%
Direct fixed expenses of services.	$ 20,000	$ 18,000	$ 16,000
Allocated common fixed services expense	$ 1,000	$ 1,000	$ 1,500

Required
Prepare income statements segmented by client categories. Include a column for the entire firm in the statement.

M22-18. Internal or External Acquisitions: No Opportunity Costs (LO3)
The Van Division of MotoCar Corporation has offered to purchase 180,000 wheels from the Wheel Division for $42 per wheel. At a normal volume of 500,000 wheels per year, production costs per wheel for the Wheel Division are as follows:

Direct materials	$15
Direct labor.	10
Variable overhead.	6
Fixed overhead.	18
Total	$49

The Wheel Division has been selling 500,000 wheels per year to outside buyers at $58 each. Capacity is 700,000 wheels per year. The Van Division has been buying wheels from outside suppliers at $55 per wheel.

Required
a. Should the Wheel Division manager accept the offer? Show computations.
b. From the standpoint of the company, will the internal sale be beneficial?

M22-19. Transfer Prices at Full Cost with Excess Capacity: Divisional Viewpoint (LO3)
Wholesome Dairy's Cheese Division produces cheese that sells for $10 per unit in the open market. The cost of the product is $8 (variable manufacturing of $5, plus fixed manufacturing of $3). Total fixed manufacturing costs are $210,000 at the normal annual production volume of 70,000 units. The Overseas Division has offered to buy 15,000 units at the full cost of $8. The Producing Division has excess capacity, and the 15,000 units can be produced without interfering with the current outside sales of 70,000 units. The total fixed cost of the Cheese Division will not change.

Required
Explain whether the Cheese Division should accept or reject the offer. Show calculations.

M22-20. Transfer Pricing with Excess Capacity: Divisional and Corporate Viewpoints (LO3)
Boyett Art Company has a Print Division that is currently producing 100,000 prints per year but has a capacity of 150,000 prints. The variable costs of each print are $30, and the annual fixed costs are $900,000. The prints sell for $40 in the open market. The company's Retail Division wants to buy 50,000 prints at $28 each. The Print Division manager refuses the order because the price is below variable cost. The Retail Division manager argues that the order should be accepted because it will lower the fixed cost per print from $9 to $6.

Required
a. Should the Retail Division order be accepted? Why or why not?
b. From the viewpoints of the Print Division and the company, should the order be accepted if the manager of the Retail Division intends to sell each print in the outside market for $42 after incurring additional costs of $10 per print?
c. What action should the company take, assuming it believes in divisional autonomy?

M22-21. ROI and Residual Income: Impact of a New Investment (LO4)
The Mustang Division of Detroit Motors had an operating income of $900,000 and net assets of $4,000,000. Detroit Motors has a target rate of return of 16 percent.

Required

a. Compute the return on investment.

b. Compute the residual income.

c. The Mustang Division has an opportunity to increase operating income by $200,000 with an $850,000 investment in assets.

   1. Compute the Mustang Division's return on investment if the project is undertaken. (Round your answer to three decimal places.)

   2. Compute the Mustang Division's residual income if the project is undertaken.

M22-22. ROI: Fill in the Unknowns (LO4)

Provide the missing data in the following situations:

	North American Division	Asian Division	European Division
Sales.	?	$5,000,000	?
Net operating income.	$100,000	$ 200,000	$144,000
Operating assets	?	?	$800,000
Return on investment.	16%	10%	?
Return on sales	0.04	?	0.12
Investment turnover	?	?	1.5

M22-23. Selection of Balanced Scorecard Items (LO5)

The International Accountants' Association is a professional association. Its current membership totals 110,000 worldwide. The association operates from a central headquarters in New Zealand but has local membership chapters throughout the world. The local chapters hold monthly meetings to discuss recent developments in accounting and to hear professional speakers on topics of interests. The association's journal, *International Accountant,* is published monthly with feature articles and topical interest areas. The association publishes books and reports and sponsors continuing education courses. A statement of revenues and expenses follows:

INTERNATIONAL ACCOUNTANTS' ASSOCIATION		
Statement of Revenues and Expenses		
For Year Ending November 30, 2007		
Revenues		$30,275,000
Expenses		
Salaries	$14,000,000	
Other personnel costs	3,400,000	
Occupancy costs	2,000,000	
Reimbursement to local chapters.	800,000	
Other membership services	500,000	
Printing and paper	320,000	
Postage and shipping.	114,000	
General and administrative.	538,000	(21,672,000)
Excess of revenues over expenses		$ 8,603,000

Additional information follows:

- Membership dues are $200 per year, of which $50 is considered to cover a one-year subscription to the association's journal. Other benefits include membership in the association and chapter affiliation.
- One-year subscriptions to *International Accountant* are sold to nonmembers for $80 each. A total of 2,500 of these subscriptions were sold. In addition to subscriptions, the journal generated $200,000 in advertising revenue. The cost per magazine was $20.
- A total of 30,000 technical reports were sold by the Books and Reports Department at an average unit selling price of $45. Average costs per publication were $12.

- The association offers a variety of continuing education courses to both members and nonmembers. During 2007, the one-day course, which cost participants an average of $75 each, was attended by 34,400 people. A total of 2,630 people took two-day courses at a cost of $125 per person.
- General and administrative expenses include all other costs incurred by the corporate staff to operate the association.
- The organization has net capital assets of $44,000,000 and prefers to maintain a cost of capital of 10 percent.

Required

a. Give some examples of key financial performance indicators (no computations needed) that could be part of a balanced scorecard for the IAA.

b. Give some examples of key customer and operating performance indicators (no computations needed) that could be part of a balanced scorecard for IAA.

EXERCISES

E22-24. Appropriate Transfer Prices: Opportunity Costs (LO3)

Plains Peanut Butter Company recently acquired a peanut-processing company that has a normal annual capacity of 4,000,000 pounds and that sold 2,800,000 pounds last year at a price of $2.00 per pound. The purpose of the acquisition is to furnish peanuts for the peanut butter plant, which needs 1,600,000 pounds of peanuts per year. It has been purchasing peanuts from suppliers at the market price. Production costs per pound of the peanut-processing company are as follows:

Direct materials	$0.50
Direct labor	0.25
Variable overhead	0.12
Fixed overhead at normal capacity	0.20
Total	$1.07

Management is trying to decide what transfer price to use for sales from the newly acquired Peanut Division to the Peanut Butter Division. The manager of the Peanut Division argues that $2.00, the market price, is appropriate. The manager of the Peanut Butter Division argues that the cost price of $1.07 (or perhaps even less) should be used since fixed overhead costs should be recomputed. Any output of the Peanut Division up to 2,800,000 pounds that is not sold to the Peanut Butter Division could be sold to regular customers at $2.00 per pound.

Required

a. Compute the annual gross profit for the Peanut Division using a transfer price of $2.00.

b. Compute the annual gross profit for the Peanut Division using a transfer price of $1.07.

c. What transfer price(s) will lead the manager of the Peanut Butter Division to act in a manner that will maximize company profits?

E22-25. Negotiating a Transfer Price with Excess Capacity (LO3)

The Weaving Division of Carolina Textiles Inc. produces cloth that is sold to the company's Dyeing Division and to outside customers. Operating data for the Weaving Division for 2007 are as follows:

	To the Dyeing Division	To Outside Customers
Sales		
450,000 yards × $5.00	$2,250,000	
300,000 yards × $6.00		$1,800,000
Variable expenses at $2.00	(900,000)	(600,000)
Contribution margin	1,350,000	1,200,000
Fixed expenses*	(750,000)	(500,000)
Net income	$ 600,000	$ 700,000

*Allocated on the basis of unit sales.

The Dyeing Division has just received an offer from an outside supplier to supply cloth at $3.50 per yard. The Weaving Division manager is not willing to meet the $3.50 price. She argues that it costs her $3.67 per yard to produce and sell to the Dyeing Division, so she would show no profit on the Dyeing Division sales. Sales to outside customers are at a maximum, 300,000 yards.

Required

a. Verify the Weaving Division's $3.67 unit cost figure.

b. Should the Weaving Division meet the outside price of $3.50 for Dyeing Division sales? Explain.

c. Could the Weaving Division meet the $3.50 price and still show a profit for sales to the Dyeing Division? Show computations.

E22-26. Dual Transfer Pricing (LO3)

The Greek Company has two divisions, Beta and Gamma. Gamma Division produces a product at a variable cost of $6 per unit, and sells 150,000 units to outside customers at $10 per unit and 40,000 units to Beta Division at variable cost plus 40 percent. Under the dual transfer price system, Beta Division pays only the variable cost per unit. Gamma Division's fixed costs are $250,000 per year. Beta Division sells its finished product to outside customers at $23 per unit. Beta has variable costs of $5 per unit, in addition to the costs from Gamma Division. Beta Division's annual fixed costs are $170,000. There are no beginning or ending inventories.

Required

a. Prepare the income statements for the two divisions and the company as a whole.

b. Why is the income for the company less than the sum of the profit figures shown on the income statements for the two divisions? Explain.

E22-27. ROI and Residual Income: Basic Computations (LO4)

Watkins Associated Industries is a highly diversified company with three divisions: Trucking, Seafood, and Construction. Assume that the company uses return on investment and residual income as two of the evaluation tools for division managers. The company has a minimum desired rate of return on investment of 10 percent and a weighted average cost of capital of 7 percent with a 30 percent tax rate. Selected operating data for three divisions of the company follow.

Watkins Associated Industries

	Trucking Division	Seafood Division	Construction Division
Sales.	$1,200,000	$750,000	$900,000
Operating assets	600,000	250,000	350,000
Net operating income.	102,000	56,000	59,000
Current liabilities.	40,000	10,000	30,000

Required

a. Compute the return on investment for each division. (Round answers to three decimal places.)

b. Compute the residual income for each division.

c. Which divisional manager is doing the best job based on ROI? Based on residual income? Why?

E22-28. ROI and Residual Income with Different Bases (LO4)

BMI Company has a target return on capital of 15 percent. The following financial information is available for October ($ thousands):

	Software Division (Value Base)		Consulting Division (Value Base)		Venture Capital Division (Value Base)	
	Book	Current	Book	Current	Book	Current
Sales.	$100,000	$100,000	$200,000	$200,000	$800,000	$800,000
Income	12,000	10,000	16,000	17,000	50,000	52,000
Assets.	60,000	80,000	90,000	100,000	600,000	580,000
Current liabilities.	10,000	10,000	14,000	14,000	40,000	40,000

Required

a. Compute the return on investment using both book and current values for each division. (Round answers to three decimal places.)

b. Compute the residual income for both book and current values for each division.

c. Does book value or current value provide a better basis for performance evaluation? Which division do you consider the most successful?

E22-29. Balanced Scorecard Preparation (LO5)

The following information is in addition to that presented in Mini Exercise 22-23 for the International Accountants' Association. For the year ended November 30, 2007, the organization had set a membership goal of 100,000 members with the following anticipated results:

INTERNATIONAL ACCOUNTANTS' ASSOCIATION Planned Revenues and Expenses For Year Ending November 30, 2007		
Revenues		$28,000,000
Expenses		
Salaries	$13,950,000	
Other personnel costs	3,450,000	
Occupancy costs	1,900,000	
Reimbursement to local chapters.	780,000	
Other membership services	525,000	
Printing and paper	300,000	
Postage and shipping.	103,000	
General and administrative.	550,000	(21,558,000)
Excess of revenues over expenses		$ 6,442,000

Additional information follows:

- Membership dues were increased from $180 to $200 at the beginning of the year.
- One-year subscriptions to *International Accountant* were anticipated to be 2,400 units.
- Advertising revenue was budgeted at $225,000. Each magazine was budgeted at $18.
- A total of 28,000 technical reports were anticipated at an average price of $40 with average costs of $11.
- The budgeted one-day courses had an anticipated attendance of 32,000 with an average fee of $80. The two-day courses had an anticipated attendance of 3,000 with an average fee of $125 per person.
- The organization began the year with net capital assets of $40,000,000 with a planned cost of capital of 10 percent.

Required

a. Prepare a balanced scorecard for IAA for November 2007 with calculated key performance indicators presented in two columns for planned performance and actual performance—include key financial, customer, and operating performance indicators.

b. Which of the evaluation areas you selected indicated success and which indicated failure?

c. Give some explanations of the successes and failures.

PROBLEMS

P22-30. Multiple Segment Reports (LO2)

World Products Incorporated sells throughout the world in three sales territories: Europe, Asia, and the Americas. For July, all $50,000 of administrative expense is traceable to the territories, except $10,000, which is common to all units and cannot be traced or allocated to the sales territories. The percentage of product line sales made in each of the sales territories and the assignment of traceable fixed expenses follow:

	Sales Territory			
	Europe	Asia	The Americas	Total
Cookware sales	40%	50%	10%	100%
China sales.	40	40	20	100
Vases sales.	20	20	60	100
Fixed administrative expense.	$15,000	$15,000	$10,000	$ 40,000
Fixed selling expense.	$30,000	$60,000	$60,000	$150,000

The manufacturing takes place in one large facility with three distinct manufacturing operations. Selected product-line cost data follow.

	Cookware	China	Vases	Total
Variable costs.	$ 9	$ 9	$ 5	
Depreciation and supervision.	15,000	15,000	12,000	$ 45,000*
Other mfg. overhead (common)				10,000
Fixed administrative expense (common)				50,000
Fixed selling expense (common)				150,000

*Includes common costs of $3,000

The unit sales and selling prices for each product follow.

	Unit Sales	Selling Price
Cookware	10,000	$10
China	20,000	15
Vases	15,000	20

Required

a. Prepare an income statement for July segmented by product line. Include a column for the entire firm.

b. Prepare an income statement for July segmented by sales territory. Include a column for the entire firm.

c. Prepare an income statement for July by product line for The Americas sales territory. Include a column for the territory as a whole.

P22-31. Segment Reporting and Analysis (LO2)

Milwaukee Bakery Incorporated bakes three products: donuts, pies, and cakes. It sells them in the cities of Chicago and Milwaukee. For March, the following income statement was prepared:

MILWAUKEE BAKERY, INCORPORATED Territory and Company Income Statements For Month of March			
	Chicago	Milwaukee	Total
Sales.	$2,100	$500	$2,600
Cost of goods sold.	(1,500)	(300)	(1,800)
Gross profit.	600	200	800
Selling and administrative expenses	(400)	(100)	(500)
Net income.	$ 200	$100	$ 300

Sales and selected variable expense data are as follows:

	Products		
	Donuts	Pies	Cakes
Fixed baking expenses.	$200	$140	$100
Variable baking expenses as a percentage of sales	50%	50%	60%
Variable selling expenses as a percentage of sales.	4%	4%	5%
City of Chicago, sales	$800	$900	$400
City of Milwaukee, sales.	$200	$100	$200

The fixed selling expenses were $260 for March, of which $160 was a direct expense of the Chicago market and $100 was a direct expense of the Milwaukee market. Fixed administrative expenses were $130, which management has decided not to allocate when using the contribution approach.

Required

a. Prepare a segment income statement for each sales territory for March. Include a column for the entire firm.
b. Prepare segment income statements for each product. Include a column for the entire firm.
c. If the cake line is dropped and fixed baking expenses do not change, what is the product margin for donuts and pies?

P22-32. Segment Reporting and Analysis (LO2)

Accounting Publishers, Inc. has prepared income statements segmented by divisions, but management is still uncertain about actual performance. Financial information for May is given as follows:

	Textbook Division	Professional Division	Company Total
Sales.	$180,000	$410,000	$590,000
Less variable expenses			
Manufacturing.	32,000	205,000	237,000
Selling and administrative.	4,000	20,500	24,500
Total	(36,000)	(225,500)	(261,500)
Contribution margin	144,000	184,500	328,500
Less direct fixed expenses.	(15,000)	(220,000)	(235,000)
Net income.	$129,000	$(35,500)	$ 93,500

Management is concerned about the Professional Division and requests additional analysis. Additional information regarding May operations of the Professional Division is as follows:

	Accounting	Executive	Management
Sales.	$140,000	$140,000	$130,000
Variable manufacturing expenses			
as a percentage of sales.	60%	40%	50%
Other variable expenses			
as a percentage of sales.	5%	5%	5%
Direct fixed expenses.	$50,000	$75,000	$50,000
Allocated common fixed expenses	$5,000	$2,000	$7,000

The professional accounting books are sold to auditors and controllers. The current information on these markets is as follows:

	Sales Market	
	Auditors	**Controllers**
Sales.	$30,000	$110,000
Variable manufacturing expenses as a percentage of sales.	60%	60%
Other variable expenses as a percentage of sales.	16%	2%
Direct fixed expenses.	$ 5,000	$ 25,000
Allocated common fixed expenses	$ 7,000	$ 8,000

Required

a. Prepare an income statement segmented by product for the Professional Division. Include a column for the division as a whole.

b. Prepare an income statement segmented by market for the accounting books of the Professional Division.

c. Evaluate which accounting books the Professional Division should keep or discontinue in the short run.

d. What is the correct long-run decision?

P22-33. Segment Reports (LO2)

The Entertainment Corporation produces and sells three products. The three products, CDs, DVDs, and videotapes, are sold in a local market and in a regional market. At the end of the first quarter of 2007, the following income statement was prepared:

ENTERTAINMENT CORPORATION **Territory and Company Income Statements** **First Quarter of 2007**			
	Local	**Regional**	**Company**
Sales.	$1,000,000	$300,000	$1,300,000
Cost of goods sold.	(775,000)	(235,000)	(1,010,000)
Gross profit.	225,000	65,000	290,000
Selling expenses	60,000	45,000	105,000
Administrative expenses	40,000	12,000	52,000
Total	(100,000)	(57,000)	(157,000)
Net income.	$ 125,000	$ 8,000	$ 133,000

Management has expressed special concern with the Regional Market because of the extremely poor return on sales. This market was entered a year ago because of excess capacity. Management originally believed that the return on sales would improve with time, but after a year, no noticeable improvement could be seen from the results as reported in the preceding quarterly statement. In attempting to decide whether to eliminate the Regional Market, the following information has been gathered:

	Products		
	CD	**DVD**	**Videotape**
Sales.	$600,000	$500,000	$200,000
Variable manufacturing expenses as a percentage of sales.	60%	70%	60%
Variable selling expenses as a percentage of sales.	3%	2%	2%

Sales by Markets		
Product	Local	Regional
CD	$450,000	$150,000
DVD	350,000	150,000
Videotape	150,000	50,000

All administrative expenses and fixed manufacturing expenses are common to the three products and the two markets; these expenses are fixed for the period. The remaining selling expenses are fixed for the period and separable by market. All fixed expenses are based on a prorated yearly amount.

Required

a.   Prepare the quarterly income statement showing contribution margins by market (territories). Include a column for the company as a whole.

b.   Assuming there are no alternative uses for Entertainment Corporation's present capacity, would you recommend dropping the regional market? Why or why not?

c.   Prepare the quarterly income statement showing contribution margins by product. Include a column for the company as a whole.

d.   It is believed that a new product can be ready for sale next year if Entertainment Corporation decides to go ahead with continued research. The new product can be produced by simply converting equipment now used to produce videotapes. This conversion will increase fixed costs by $10,000 per quarter. What must be the minimum contribution margin per quarter for the new product to make the changeover financially feasible?

(CMA Adapted)

P22-34.   Segment Reports and Cost Allocations   (LO2)

Pacific Products, Inc. has three sales divisions. One of the key evaluation inputs for each division manager is the performance of his or her division based on division income. The division statements for August are as follows:

	Kiwi	Queensland	Hawaii	Total
Sales......................	$400,000	$500,000	$450,000	$1,350,000
Cost of sales................	200,000	240,000	230,000	670,000
Division overhead............	100,000	110,000	110,000	320,000
Division expenses............	(300,000)	(350,000)	(340,000)	(990,000)
Division contribution..........	100,000	150,000	110,000	360,000
Corporate overhead...........	(70,000)	(90,000)	(80,000)	(240,000)
Division income	$ 30,000	$ 60,000	$ 30,000	$ 120,000

The Hawaii manager is unhappy that his profitability is the same as that of the Kiwi Division and one-half that of the Queensland Division when his sales are halfway between these two divisions. The manager knows that his division must carry more product lines because of customer demands, and many of these additional product lines are not very profitable. He has not dropped these marginal product lines because of idle capacity; all of the products cover their own variable costs. After analyzing the product lines with the lowest profit margins, the divisional controller for Hawaii provided the following to the manager:

Sales of marginal products.		$90,000
Cost of sales.	$50,000	
Avoidable fixed costs.................	20,000	(70,000)
Product margin.		20,000
Proportion of corporate overhead		(16,000)
Product income		$ 4,000

Although these products were 20 percent of Hawaii's total sales, they contributed only about 13 percent of the division's profits. The controller also noted that the corporate overhead allocation was based on a formula of sales and divisional contribution margin.

Required

a. Prepare a set of segment statements for August assuming that all facts remain the same except that Hawaii's weak product lines are dropped and corporate overhead is allocated as follows: Kiwi, $80,000; Queensland, $95,000; and Hawaii, $65,000. Does the Hawaii Division appear better after this action? What will be the responses of the other two division managers?

b. Suggest improvements for Pacific Products' reporting process that will better reflect the actual operations of the divisions. Keep in mind the utilization of the reporting process to assist in the evaluation of the managers. What other changes could be made to improve the manager evaluation process?

P22-35. ROI and Residual Income: Impact of a New Investment (LO4)

Business Equipment Inc. is a decentralized organization with four autonomous divisions. The divisions are evaluated on the basis of the change in their return on invested assets. Operating results in the Retail Division for 2007 follow:

BUSINESS EQUIPMENT INC.—RETAIL DIVISION
Income Statement
For Year Ending December 31, 2007

Sales.	$3,125,000
Less variable expenses	(1,562,500)
Contribution margin	1,562,500
Less fixed expenses.	(1,000,000)
Net operating income.	$ 562,500

Operating assets for the Retail Division currently average $2,500,000. The Retail Division can add a new product line for an investment of $300,000. Relevant data for the new product line are as follows:

Sales.	$800,000
Variable expenses (% of sales).	0.60
Fixed expenses	$275,000
Increase in current liabilities.	$ 20,000

Required

a. Determine the effect on ROI of accepting the new product line. (Round calculations to three decimal places.)

b. If a return of 6 percent is the minimum that any division should earn and residual income is used to evaluate managers, would this encourage the division to accept the new product line? Explain and show computations.

P22-36. Valuing Investment Center Assets (LO4)

Six Flags Theme Parks, Inc., operates theme parks in the United States, Mexico, and Europe. One of its first theme parks, Six Flags over Georgia, was built in the 1960s in Atlanta on a large tract of land that has appreciated enormously over the years. Although most of the rides and other attractions have a fairly short life, some of the major buildings that are still in use on the property have been fully depreciated since they were built. Assume that Six Flags over Georgia operates as an investment center with total assets that have a book value of $150 million and current liabilities of $20 million. Assume also that in 2007, this particular theme park had sales of $60 million and pretax division income of $20 million. The replacement cost of all the assets in this park is estimated to be $250 million. The company's cost of capital is 16 percent, and it has a 35 percent tax rate.

Six Flags Theme Parks, Inc. (SIX)

Required

a. Calculate the ROI and residual income for Six Flags over Georgia using book value as the valuation basis for the investment center asset base.

b. Repeat requirement (a) using replacement cost as the investment center asset value.

c. Which valuation, accounting book value or replacement cost do you think the company uses to evaluate the managers of its various theme parks? Discuss.

CASES

IBM Corporation (IBM)

C22-37. Transfer Price Decisions (LO3)

The Consulting Division of IBM Corporation is often involved in assignments for which IBM computer equipment is sold as part of a systems installation. The Computer Equipment Division is frequently a vendor of the Consulting Division in cases for which the Consulting Division purchases the equipment from the Computer Equipment Division. The Consulting Division does not view itself as a sales arm of the Computer Equipment Division but as a strong competitor to the major consulting firms of information systems. The Consulting Division's goal is to maximize its profit contribution to the company, not necessarily to see how much IBM equipment it can sell. If the Consulting Division is truly an autonomous investment center, it has the freedom to purchase equipment from competing vendors if the consultants believe that a competitor's products serve the needs of a client better than the comparable IBM product in a particular situation.

Required

a. In this situation, should corporate management be concerned about whether the Consulting Division sells IBM products or those of other computer companies? Should the Consulting Division be required to sell only IBM products?

b. Discuss the transfer pricing issues that both the Equipment Division manager and the Consulting Division manager should consider. If top management does not have a policy on pricing transfers between these two divisions, what alternative transfer prices should the division managers consider?

c. What is your recommendation regarding how the managers of the Consulting and Equipment Divisions can work together in a way that will benefit each of them individually and the company as a whole?

C22-38. Transfer Pricing at Absorption Cost (LO3)

The Fabrication Division of Metro Sign Company produces large metal numbers that are sold to the Sign Division. This division uses the numbers in constructing signs that are sold to highway departments of local governments. The Fabrication Division contains two operations, stamping and finishing. The unit variable cost of materials and labor used in the stamping operation is $100. The fixed stamping overhead is $800,000 per year. Current production (20,000 units) is at full capacity. The variable cost of labor used in the finishing operation is $12 per number. The fixed overhead in this operation is $340,000 per year. The company uses an absorption-cost transfer price. The price data for each operation presented to the Sign Division by the Fabrication Division follow.

Stamping		
Variable cost per unit	$100	
Fixed overhead cost per unit ($800,000 ÷ 20,000 units)	40	$140
Finishing		
Labor cost per unit	12	
Fixed overhead cost per unit ($340,000 ÷ 20,000 units)	17	29
Total cost per unit.		$169

An outside company has offered to lease machinery to the Sign Division that would perform the finishing part of the number manufacturing for $200,000 per year. With the new machinery, the labor cost per number would remain at $12. If the Fabrication Division transfers the units for $140, the following analysis can be made:

Current process		
Finishing process costs (20,000 × $29).		$580,000
New process		
Machine rental cost per year	$200,000	
Labor cost ($12 × 20,000 units).	240,000	(440,000)
Savings.		$140,000

The manager of the Sign Division wants approval to acquire the new machinery.

Required
a. How would you advise the company concerning the proposed lease?
b. How could the transfer-pricing system be modified or the transfer-pricing problem eliminated?

C22-39. **Transfer Pricing with and without Capacity Constraints** (LO3)
National Carpet Company has just acquired a new backing division that produces a rubber backing, which it sells for $2.10 per square yard. Sales are about 1,200,000 square yards per year. Since the Backing Division has a capacity of 2,000,000 square yards per year, top management is thinking that it might be wise for the company's Tufting Division to start purchasing from the newly acquired Backing Division. The Tufting Division now purchases 600,000 square yards per year from an outside supplier at a price of $1.90 per square yard. The current price is lower than the competitive $2.10 price as a result of the large quantity discounts. The Backing Division's cost per square yard follows.

Direct materials	$1.00
Direct labor.	0.20
Variable overhead.	0.25
Fixed overhead (1,200,000 level)	0.10
Total cost	$1.55

Required
a. If both divisions are to be treated as investment centers and their performance evaluated by the ROI formula, what transfer price would you recommend? Why?
b. Determine the effect on corporate profits of making the backing.
c. Based on your transfer price, would you expect the ROI in the Backing Division to increase, decrease, or remain unchanged? Explain.
d. What would be the effect on the ROI of the Tufting Division using your transfer price? Explain.
e. Assume that the Backing Division is now selling 2,000,000 square yards per year to retail outlets. What transfer price would you recommend? What will be the effect on corporate profits?
f. If the Backing Division is at capacity and decides to sell to the Tufting Division for $1.90 per square yard, what will be the effect on the company's profits?

C22-40. **Transfer Pricing and Special Orders** (LO3)
New England Electronics has several manufacturing divisions. The Pacific Division produces a component part that is used in the manufacture of electronic equipment. The cost per part for July is as follows:

Variable cost.	$ 90
Fixed cost (at 2,000 units per month capacity)	60
Total cost per part	$150

Some of Pacific Division's output is sold to outside manufacturers, and some is sold internally to the Atlantic Division. The price per part is $180. The Atlantic Division's cost and revenue structure follow.

Selling price per unit.		$1,000
Less variable costs per unit		
Cost of parts from the Pacific Division	$180	
Other variable costs	400	(580)
Contribution margin per unit		420
Less fixed costs per unit (at 200 units per month)		(100)
Net income per unit		$ 320

The Atlantic Division received an order for 10 units. The buyer wants to pay only $500 per unit.

Required

a. From the perspective of the Atlantic Division, should the $500 price be accepted? Explain.

b. If both divisions have excess capacity, would the Atlantic Division's action benefit the company as a whole? Explain.

c. If the Atlantic Division has excess capacity but the Pacific Division does not and can sell all of its parts to outside manufacturers, what would be the advantage or disadvantage of accepting the ten-unit order at the $500 price to the Atlantic Division?

d. To make a decision that is in the best interest of the company, what transfer-pricing information does the Atlantic Division need?

C22-41. Transfer Pricing Dispute (LO3)

MBR Inc. consists of three divisions that were formerly three independent manufacturing companies. Bader Corporation and Roper Company merged in 2004, and the merged corporation acquired Mitchell Company in 2005. The name of the corporation was subsequently changed to MBR Inc., and each company became a separate division retaining the name of its former company.

The three divisions have oeprated as if they were still independent companies. Each division has its own sales force and production facilities. Each division management is responsible for sales, cost of operations, acquisition and financing of divisional assets, and working capital management. The corporate management of MBR evaluates the performance of the divisions and division management on the basis of return on investment.

Mitchell Division has just been awarded a contract for a product that uses a component manufactured by the Roper Division and also by outside suppliers. Mitchell used a cost figure of $3.80 for the component manufactured by Roper in preparing its bid for the new product. Roper supplied this cost figure in response to Mitchell's request for the average variable cost of the component; it represents the standard variable manufacturing cost and variable selling and distribution expenses.

Roper has an active sales force that is continually soliciting new prospects. Roper's regular selling price for the component Mitchell needs for the new product is $6.50. Sales of this component are expected to increase. The Roper management has indicated, however, that it could supply Mitchell the required quantities of the component at the regular selling price less variable selling and distribution expenses. Mitchell's management has responded by offering to pay standard variable manufacturing cost plus 20 percent.

The two divisions have been unable to agree on a transfer price. Corporate management has never established a transfer-pricing policy because interdivisional transactions have never occurred. As a compromise, the corporate vice president of finance suggested a price equal to the standard full manufacturing cost (i.e., no selling and distribution expenses) plus a 15 percent markup. The two division managers have also rejected this price because each considered it grossly unfair.

The unit cost structure for the Roper component and the three suggested prices follow.

Standard variable manufacturing cost	$3.20
Standard fixed manufacturing cost	1.20
Variable selling and distribution expenses	0.60
	$5.00
Regular selling price less variable selling and distribution expenses ($6.50 − $0.60)	$5.90
Standard full manufacturing cost plus 15% ($4.40 × 1.15).	$5.06
Variable manufacturing plus 20% ($3.20 × 1.20).	$3.84

Required

a. What should be the attitude of the Roper Division's management toward the three proposed prices?

b. Is the negotiation of a price between the Mitchell and Roper Divisions a satisfactory method of solving the transfer-pricing problem? Explain your answer.

c. Should the corporate management of MBR Inc. become involved in this transfer-price controversy? Explain your answer.

(CMA Adapted)

Pricing and Other Product Management Decisions

LEARNING OBJECTIVES

LO1 Explain the importance of the value chain in managing products and identify the key components of an organization's internal and external value chain. (p. 23-3)

LO2 Distinguish between economic and cost-based approaches to pricing. (p. 23-7)

LO3 Explain target costing and its acceptance in highly competitive industries. (p. 23-12)

LO4 Describe the relation between target costing and continuous improvement costing. (p. 23-17)

LO5 Explain how benchmarking enhances quality management, continuous improvement, and process reengineering. (p.23-18)

GREEN CARS AND STRATEGIC MANAGEMENT

Strong competition exists among Japanese, U.S., and European automakers to develop the next generation of cars—the "green cars" that cut pollution and boost fuel economy. The technological, production, and marketing challenges, however, are substantial. Competing technologies include hydrogen fuel cells and hybrid-powered formats.

Honda and Toyota favor hybrid car technology that combines gasoline and electric power. Ford, General Motors, and DaimlerChrysler favor hydrogen fuel cells that combine hydrogen and oxygen to make electricity and water. Despite competing technological approaches, all of these firms share an important strategic management goal—convincing customers to buy a green car. To achieve this goal, firms must price these cars competitively and create reasonable alternatives for potential customers who are satisfied with a regular car.

To succeed in this emerging market, automakers rely on important management accounting tools, such as target costing and continuous improvement (Kaizen) costing, to achieve a competitive price that is also profitable. With these tools, managers determine the price that yields the desired sales level and then set the product cost to make the product profitable at the target selling price. By constantly improving the design, specifications, and production processes, managers expect to lower product cost until it reaches its target cost.

Two hybrid cars, the Honda *Insight* and Toyota *Prius*, both had initial price tags of around $20,000 and initial yearly target sales between 4,000 and 12,000 units. During development, Toyota relied on continuous

improvement to achieve the cost savings necessary to make the *Prius* profitable. The firm established this price to be competitive with its popular *Corolla* model.

For manufacturers using hydrogen fuel cell technology, the goal is a $20,000 hydrogen fuel cell vehicle before 2010. Managers on these projects count on increased fuel cell performance, reductions in size, and changes in materials to lower the cost of this power source.

Ford and DaimlerChrysler transferred their hydrogen fuel cell research and development to Ballard Power Systems of Canada—a world leader in hydrogen fuel cell technology. In return, both Ford and DaimlerChrysler hold substantial ownership stakes in Ballard. Ballard's mandate from the automakers is clear: Develop a fuel cell automobile propulsion system that has the right size, weight, range, and cost attributes to be commercially successful.

Within this emerging market for green cars as well as other emerging and existing markets, strategic cost management tools such as target costing and continuous improvement costing are important for managers involved in the development, manufacture, and marketing of products and services. Companies that are successful in introducing new products, as well as managing existing products, invariably have a focus on the value chain for all of their products.

Source: *The Wall Street Journal, Forbes,* and *Business Week.*[1]

[1] Jeffrey Ball, "Ballard Power Expands Fuel-Cell Drive as Ford, DaimlerChrysler Boost Stakes, *The Wall Street Journal (Interactive Edition),* October 3, 2001; Terril Ye Jones, "Whose Car Is Greener?" *Forbes,* October 18, 1999, p. 60; Keith Naughton, "Can You Have Green Cars Without Red Ink?" *Business Week,* December 29, 1997, p. 50; Keith Naughton, "Detroit's Impossible Dream," *Business Week,* March 2, 1998, pp. 66 & 68; Emily Thornton, Keith Naughton, and David Woodruff, "Toyota's Green Machine," *Business Week,* December 15, 1997, pp. 108–110; David Woodruff and William C. Symonds, "The Hottest Thing in 'Green' Wheels," *Business Week,* April 28, 1997, p. 42.

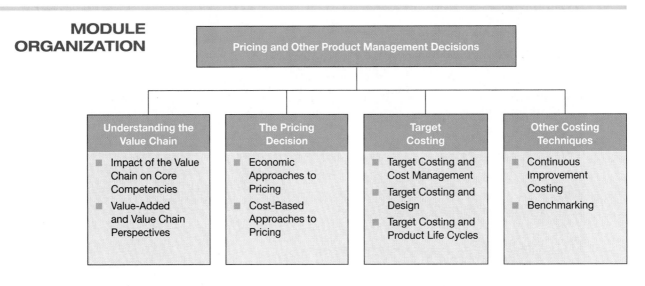

Strategic cost management techniques, such as *target costing* and *continuous improvement costing*, represent important concepts for product management professionals involved in the development, manufacture, and marketing of products and services. Virtually all such techniques are grounded in the notion of managing the value chain. This module examines pricing, the interrelation between price and cost, and the role of quality costs and benchmarking in meeting customer needs at the lowest possible price.

We begin with a discussion of the value chain, followed by an overview of the pricing model economists use to explain price equilibrium. Given the limitations of this long-run equilibrium model for determining price of a product or service, we consider the widely used cost-plus approach to identifying initial prices. We then examine how intense competition (such as that for the green car market) has inverted the cost-plus pricing model into one that starts with an acceptable market price and subtracts a desired profit to determine a target cost. We also consider *life cycle costs* from the perspectives of both the seller, who increasingly plans for all costs before production begins, and the buyer, who regards subsequent operating, maintenance, repair, and disposal costs as important as price. Finally, we consider how *benchmarking* can assist in improving competitiveness and profitability.

UNDERSTANDING THE VALUE CHAIN

LO1 Explain the importance of the value chain in managing products and identify the key components of an organization's internal and external value chain.

The **value chain** for a product or service is the set of value-producing activities that stretches from basic raw materials to the final consumer. Each product or service has a distinct value chain, and all entities along the value chain depend on the final customer's perception of the value and cost of a product or service. It is the final customer who ultimately pays all costs and provides all profits to all organizations along the entire value chain. Consequently, *the goal of every organization is to maximize the value, while minimizing the cost, of a product or service to final customers.*

The value chain provides a viewpoint that encompasses all activities performed to deliver products and services to final customers. Depending on the needs of management, value chains are developed at varying levels of detail. Analyzing a value chain from the perspective of the final consumer requires working backward from the end product or service to the basic raw materials entering into the product or service. Analyzing a value chain from the viewpoint of an organization that is in the middle of a value chain requires working forward (downstream) to the final consumer and backward (upstream) to the source of raw materials. The paper industry provides a convenient context for illustrating the value chain concept.

Exhibit 23.1 presents the value chain for the paperboard cartons used to package beverages, such as Coca-Cola, Pepsi, or Evían products. The value chain is presented at three levels, with each successive level containing additional details. The first level depicts the various business entities in the value chain:

■ Timber producers grow the pulp wood (usually pine) used as the basic input into paper products. Some large paper companies, such as Boise Cascade and Georgia Pacific, harvest much of their pulp wood from timber lands that they manage. Other companies, including Riverwood

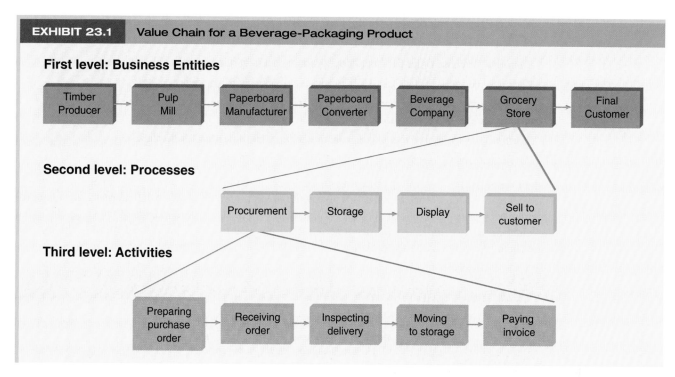

EXHIBIT 23.1   **Value Chain for a Beverage-Packaging Product**

First level: Business Entities

Timber Producer → Pulp Mill → Paperboard Manufacturer → Paperboard Converter → Beverage Company → Grocery Store → Final Customer

Second level: Processes

Procurement → Storage → Display → Sell to customer

Third level: Activities

Preparing purchase order → Receiving order → Inspecting delivery → Moving to storage → Paying invoice

International, which is a leading producer of paperboard for the beverage industry, do not manage their own timber lands, but purchase pulp for their mills on the open market through pulp intermediaries.

- Pulp mills produce the kraft (unbleached) paper used to produce the paperboard. Some of the smaller paperboard manufacturers purchase the kraft paper product from pulp mills; Riverwood International, however, owns its own paper mills that produce paper for its paperboard production facilities.

- Paperboard manufacturers perform a laminating process of coating paperboard material used to produce beverage packages. The paperboard consists of two layers of paper product plus three layers of coating that gives the top surface a high gloss finish that is water resistent and suitable for multi-color printing. Riverwood International is a manufacturer of paperboard for the beverage industry that is marketed under the name of Aqua-Kote.

- The paperboard converter uses manufactured paperboard to print and produce the completed beverage packaging product, such as the cartons used to package the Diet Coca-Cola 12-pack.

- Beverage distributors, such as Coca-Cola Enterprises and Anheuser-Busch, purchase the completed paperboard packages from Riverwood International to package their many different brands in various package sizes and shapes.

- Grocery and convenience stores, such as Safeway and 7-Eleven, display and sell beverages packaged in the paperboard containers.

- The final customer purchases beverages packaged in paperboard packages and uses the packages to carry the beverages and to store them until consumed. The packages not only perform a transport and storage function but also serve as an advertising medium for the beverage company. The beverage company's advertising on the paperboard packages is intended to entice customers to purchase the beverage company's product and to help create a sense of satisfaction for the customer.

To better understand how business entities within the chain add value and incur costs, management might further refine the value chain into **processes,** collections of related activities intended to achieve a common purpose. The second level in Exhibit 23.1 represents major processes concerning the procurement and sale of Coca-Cola products by a grocery store. To simplify our illustration, we show only the processes for the grocery store related to the purchase and sale of Coca-Cola products packaged in paperboard packages. These processes include procuring Coca-Cola products from the bottling company, storing and displaying the product, and selling the product to the final consumer.

An **activity** is a unit of work. In the third level of Exhibit 23.1, the grocery store process to procure Coca-Cola products is further broken up into the following activities:

- *Placing* a purchase order for Coca-Cola products packaged in paper board packages.
- *Receiving* delivery of the Coca-Cola products in paperboard packages.
- *Inspecting* the delivery to make sure it corresponds with the purchase order and to verify that the products are in good condition.
- *Storing* Coca-Cola products in paperboard packages until needed for display.
- *Paying* for Coca-Cola products acquired after the invoice arrives.

Each of the activities involved in procuring product from a vendor is described by a word ending with *ing*. This suggests that most work activities involve action. One way to think about the internal value chain for a particular company is provided in Exhibit 23.2 in terms of the basic components of the value chain that are found in most organizations. This generic model is a good starting point in identifying the internal value chain links for a particular organization.

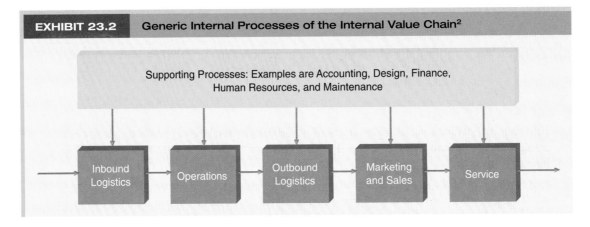

EXHIBIT 23.2 **Generic Internal Processes of the Internal Value Chain[2]**

Supporting Processes: Examples are Accounting, Design, Finance, Human Resources, and Maintenance

Inbound Logistics → Operations → Outbound Logistics → Marketing and Sales → Service

Usefulness of a Value Chain Perspective

The goal of maximizing final customer value while minimizing final customer cost leads organizations to examine *internal* and *external links* in the value chain rather than the departments, processes, or activities independently. From a value chain perspective, it is total cost across the entire value chain, not the cost of individual businesses, departments, processes, or activities that is most important.

Value Chain Perspective Fosters Supplier-Buyer Partnerships

In the past, relationships between suppliers and buyers were often adversarial. Contact between suppliers and buyers was solely through the selling and purchasing departments. Suppliers attempted merely to meet purchasing contract specifications at the lowest possible cost. Buyers encouraged competition among suppliers with the primary—and often single—goal of obtaining the lowest purchase price.

Exploiting cost reduction and value-enhancing opportunities in the value chain has led many buyers and suppliers to view each other as partners rather than as adversaries. Buyers have reduced the number of suppliers they deal with, often developing long-term partnerships with a single supplier. Once they establish mutual trust, both proceed to share detailed information on internal operations and help each other solve problems. Partners work closely to examine mutual opportunities by studying their common value chain. Supplier engineers might determine that a minor relaxation in buyer specifications would significantly reduce supplier manufacturing costs with only minor increases in subsequent buyer processing costs. Working together, they determine how best to modify processes to reduce overall costs and share increased profits.

Companies such as **Hewlett-Packard** and **Ford Motor Company** involve suppliers in design, development, and manufacturing decisions. **Motorola** has even developed a survey asking suppliers to assess

---

[2] The basic idea for this exhibit is based on concepts contained in Michael E. Porter, *Competitive Advantage* (New York: The Free Press, 1985), p. 37. However, we have significantly modified Porter's concepts to fit the purpose and level of this text.

BUSINESS INSIGHT	Value Chain Leads to Virtual Integration of Dell

Dell uses technology and information to integrate the processes of suppliers, manufacturers, and users along the PC value chain. Founder Michael Dell believes this achieves higher levels of efficiency, productivity, and profitability. He also believes the resulting value chain responds to the market like a "virtually integrated" corporation. Working with suppliers, Dell coordinates deliveries to its factories so that components arrive as needed on the shop floor, rather than being delivered to a warehouse for unloading, inspection, storage, removal from storage, and so forth. This requires the continuous sharing of information and schedules. Consider the following examples. Sony Corporation supplies monitors for Dell. The monitors are not delivered to Dell, but instead, Airborne Express or UPS pairs packages containing computers with those containing monitors and delivers them together to customers. Dell also works to enhance the value of its product and to reduce the costs of customers such as Eastman Chemical and Boeing. Eastman requires software on its PCs. Loading this software after delivery was costing Eastman more than $200 per PC. Dell loaded the software on all Eastman PCs during assembly for an extra charge of $15 to $20. Boeing has more than 100,000 Dell PCs. Dell responded with 30 employees permanently stationed at Boeing.[3]

Motorola as a buyer. Among other questions, the survey asks sellers to evaluate Motorola's performance in helping suppliers to identify major cost drivers and to increase their profitability. These questions represent the concerns of a partner rather than those of an adversary. The Business Insight above describes how Dell has molded partnerships with upstream suppliers and downstream customers into what company founder Michael Dell identifies as "virtual integration."

On a smaller scale, the grocery store in Exhibit 23.1 should examine its external links. It may be willing to pay more for Coca-Cola products if the distributors cooperate to help reduce costs such as the following:

- Making more frequent deliveries in small lots would reduce storage costs.

- Being responsible for maintaining and changing the product displays would relieve store workers of these tasks.

- Streamlining ordering and payment procedures would reduce bookkeeping costs.

If partnership arrangements with upstream suppliers enable the grocery store to reduce its total costs, the store can enhance or maintain its competitive position by reducing prices charged to its consumers. Remember that competitors are also striving to reduce costs and enhance their competitive position. Hence, failing to strive for improvements will likely result in reduced sales and profits.

Value Chain Perspective Fosters Focus on Core Competencies

Using value chain concepts, relationships with suppliers often begin to represent an extended family, allowing companies to focus on core competencies; this capability provides a distinct competitive advantage. This has led to the type of super-outsourcing discussed in the opening scenario to Module 17, where Cunningham Motor Company contemplates outsourcing *all* manufacturing functions.

Although Cunningham remains an extreme case, a new breed of contract manufacturers, such as Solectron Corporation and Sanmina-SCI have emerged in recent years. These organizations manufacture products for other companies, ranging from Hewlett-Packard printers to Xerox photocopy machines, with such close partnership arrangements that they behave like a single company. This allows Hewlett-Packard and Xerox to focus on marketing and product development while Solectron and SCI Systems focus on efficient, low-cost manufacturing.

Interestingly, because their facilities are available to all innovators with the necessary financing, the emergence of contract manufacturers may speed innovation. Michael Dell attributes much of Dell's rapid growth and profitability to virtual integration with suppliers (see Business Insight above). **Virtual integration** is the use of information technology and partnership concepts to allow two or more entities along a value chain to act as if they were a single economic entity. According to Michael Dell, "If we had to build our own factories for every single component of the system, growing at 57 percent per year would

---

[3] Joan Magretta, "The Power of Virtual Integration: An Interview with Dell Computers' Michael Dell," *Harvard Business Review*, April–May 1998, pp. 73–83.

not be possible. I would spend 57 percent of my time interviewing prospective vice presidents because the company would not have 15,000 employees but 80,000."

Value-Added and Value Chain Perspectives

The value chain perspective is often contrasted with a value-added perspective. Under a value-added perspective, decision makers consider only the cost of resources to their organization and the selling price of products or services to their immediate customers. Using a value-added perspective, the goal is to maximize the value added (the difference between the selling price and costs) by the organization. To do this, the value-added perspective focuses primarily on internal activities and costs. Under a value chain perspective, the goal is to maximize value and minimize cost to final customers, often by developing linkages or partnerships with suppliers and customers.

Although initial efforts to enhance competitiveness might start with a value-added perspective, it is important to expand to a value chain perspective. World-class competitors utilize both a value-added and a value chain perspective. These firms always keep the final customer in mind and recognize that the profitability of each entity in the value chain depends on the overall value and cost of the products and services delivered to final customers.

The value-added perspective is the foundation of the make or buy (outsourcing) decision considered in Module 17. The key differences between the partnering decisions considered here and the make or buy decision in Module 17 concern time frame, perspective, and attitude. The make or buy decision is a stand-alone decision, often in the short run, that does not view vendors and customers as partners. In contrast, characteristics of the value chain perspective are as follows:

- Comprehensive.
- Focused on the final customers.
- Strategic.
- Basis for partnerships between vendors and customers.

Enhancing or maintaining a competitive position requires an understanding of the entire system used to develop and deliver value to final customers, including interactions among organizations along the value chain. All organizations in the value chain are in business together and should work together as partners rather than as adversaries.

THE PRICING DECISION

LO2 Distinguish between economic and cost-based approaches to pricing.

Pricing products and services is one of the most important and complex decisions facing management. Pricing decisions directly affect the salability of individual products or services, as well as the profitability, and even the survival, of the organization. Many economists have spent their entire careers examining the foundations of pricing. To respond to the needs of pricing hundreds or thousands of individual items, managers have developed pricing guidelines that are typically based on costs. More recently, global competition has turned cost-based approaches upside down. Managers of world-class organizations increasingly start with a price that customers are willing to pay and then determine allowable costs.

Economic Approaches to Pricing

In economic models, the firm has a profit-maximizing goal and known cost and revenue functions. Typically, increases in sales quantity require reductions in selling prices, causing **marginal revenue** (the varying increment in total revenue derived from the sale of an additional unit) to decline as sales increase. Increases in production cause an increase in **marginal cost** (the varying increment in total cost required to produce and sell an additional unit of product). In economic models, profits are maximized at the sales volume at which marginal revenues equal marginal costs. Firms continue to produce as long as the marginal revenue derived from the sale of each additional unit exceeds the marginal cost of producing that unit.

Economic models provide a useful framework for considering pricing decisions. The ideal price is the one that will lead customers to purchase all units a firm can provide up to the point at which the last unit has a marginal cost exactly equal to its marginal revenue.

Despite their conceptual merit, economic models are seldom used for day-to-day pricing decisions. Perfect information and an indefinite time period are required to achieve equilibrium prices at which marginal revenues equal marginal costs. In the short run, most for-profit organizations attempt to achieve a target profit rather than a maximum profit. One reason for this is an inability to determine the single set of actions that will lead to profit maximization. Furthermore, managers are more apt to strive to satisfy a number of goals (such as profits for investors, job security for themselves and their employees, and being a "good" corporate citizen) than to strive for the maximization of a single profit goal. In any case, to maximize profits, a company's management would have to know the cost and revenue functions of every product the firm sells. For most firms, this information cannot be developed at a reasonable cost.

Cost-Based Approaches to Pricing

Although cost is not the only consideration in pricing, it has traditionally been the most important for several reasons.

▪ *Cost data are available.* When hundreds or thousands of different prices must be set in a short time, cost could be the only feasible basis for product pricing.

▪ *Cost-based prices are defensible.* Managers threatened by legal action or public scrutiny feel secure using cost-based prices. They can argue that prices are set in a manner that provides a "fair" profit.

▪ *Revenues must exceed costs if the firm is to remain in business.* In the long run, the selling price must exceed the full cost of each unit.

Cost-based pricing is illustrated in Exhibit 23.3. The process begins with market research to determine customer wants. If the product requires components to be designed and produced by vendors, the process of obtaining prices can be time consuming. When some costs, such as those fixed costs at the facility level, are not assigned to specific products, a markup is added to cover these costs. An additional markup is added to achieve a desired profit. The selling price is then set as the sum of the assigned costs, the markup to cover unassigned costs, and the markup to achieve the desired profit.

The proposed selling price should be evaluated with regard to competitive information and what customers are willing to pay. If the price is acceptable, the product or service is produced. If the price is too high, the product might be redesigned, manufacturing procedures might be changed, and different types of materials might be considered until either an acceptable price is achieved or it is determined that the product cannot be produced at an acceptable price. As shown in the following Business Insight, managers who ignore customer and competitor reactions to proposed prices do so at their peril.

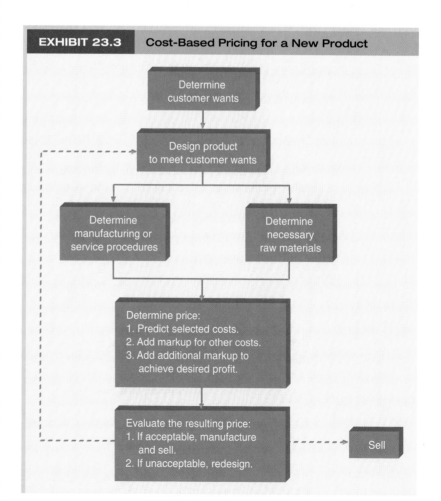

EXHIBIT 23.3   Cost-Based Pricing for a New Product

Determine customer wants

Design product to meet customer wants

Determine manufacturing or service procedures

Determine necessary raw materials

Determine price:
1. Predict selected costs.
2. Add markup for other costs.
3. Add additional markup to achieve desired profit.

Evaluate the resulting price:
1. If acceptable, manufacture and sell.
2. If unacceptable, redesign.

Sell

Cost-Based Pricing in Single-Product Companies

Implementing cost-based pricing in a single-product company is straightforward if everything is known but the selling price. In this case, all known data are entered into the profit formula, which is then solved for the variable price. Assume that Bright Rug Cleaners' annual fixed facility-level costs are $200,000 and the unit cost of cleaning a rug is $10. Management desires to achieve an annual profit of $30,000 at an annual volume of

---

BUSINESS INSIGHT   **Customers Balk at High Prices and Competitors Pounce**

When first introduced, the Ford Taurus, with innovative styling and a competitive price, became the top-selling car in the United States. Within 8 years, the Taurus was generating more than 10 percent of Ford's U.S. auto revenue. Ford then spent several billion on the reinvention of the Taurus. As soon as the redesigned Taurus arrived in the showroom, sales plummeted as customers balked at the price, up to nearly $25,000 for a fully loaded model. "When I think of $20,000, I think of the next level of cars," said a marketing executive. "I didn't want to pay the higher price," commented a retired teacher who opted for a discounted older Taurus. "They priced this car too high and people are resisting it," observed a former Ford dealer.

While Ford was contemplating what to do, Honda and Chrysler started offering special incentives on the Accord and Voyager. "Every manufacturer is attacking our car," said the general manager of Ford Motor's Ford Division. While he placed the cause of soft Taurus sales on a number of factors other than price, he commented, "We're trying to figure out how to keep our dealers competitive." Ford then undertook a major effort to reduce the cost of the Taurus in ways that would be invisible to customers. Hundreds of ideas were considered, including redesigning the door-hinge pins (a savings of $2). The total savings amounted to just $180 per vehicle, demonstrating that cost reductions after the design stage are extraordinarily difficult.[4]

10,000 rugs. To simplify the example, assume that management charges the same price regardless of the type, size, or shape of the rug. Using the profit formula, the cost-based price is determined to be $33:

$$\textbf{Profit} = \textbf{Total revenues} - \textbf{Total costs}$$
$$\$30{,}000 = (\textbf{Price} \times \textbf{10,000 rugs}) - (\$200{,}000 + [\$10 \times \textbf{10,000 rugs}])$$

Solving for the price:

$$(\textbf{Price} \times \textbf{10,000}) = \$300{,}000 + \$30{,}000$$
$$\textbf{Price} = \$330{,}000 \div \textbf{10,000}$$
$$= \$33$$

A price of $33 to clean a rug will allow Bright to achieve its desired profit. However, before setting the price at $33, management should also evaluate the competitive situation and consider what customers are willing to pay for this service.

Cost-Based Pricing in Multiple-Product Companies

In multiple-product companies, desired profits are determined for the entire company, and standard procedures are established for determining the initial selling price of each product. These procedures typically specify the initial selling price as the costs assigned to products or services plus a markup to cover unassigned costs and provide for the desired profit. Depending on the sophistication of the organization's accounting system, possible cost bases in a manufacturing organization include markups based on a *combination of cost behavior and function*. The possible cost bases include:

- Direct materials costs.
- Variable manufacturing costs.
- Total variable costs (manufacturing, selling, and administrative).
- Full manufacturing costs.

Regardless of the cost base, the general approach to developing a markup is to recognize that the markup must be large enough to provide for costs not included in the base plus the desired profit.

$$\textbf{Markup on cost base} = \frac{\textbf{Costs not included in the base} + \textbf{Desired profit}}{\textbf{Costs included in the base}}$$

First we illustrate a pricing decision with variable costs as the cost base; full manufacturing costs is the cost base in the second illustration.

---

[4] "Prices Like These Can't Last," *Business Week,* November 20, 1995, pp. 46–47; Bill Nixon and John Innes, "Management Accounting for Design," *Management Accounting: Magazine for Chartered Management Accountants,* September 1997, p. 40.

1. When the markup is based on variable costs, it must be large enough to cover all fixed costs and the desired profit. Assume that the predicted annual variable and fixed costs for Magnum Enterprises are as follows:

Variable		Fixed	
Manufacturing	$600,000	Manufacturing	$300,000
Selling and administrative	200,000	Selling and administrative	100,000
Total	$800,000	Total	$400,000

Furthermore, assume that Magnum Enterprises has total assets of $1,250,000; management believes that an annual return of 16 percent on total assets is appropriate in Magnum's industry. A 16 percent return translates into a desired annual profit of $200,000 ($1,250,000 × 0.16). Assuming all cost predictions are correct, obtaining a profit of $200,000 requires a 75 percent markup on variable costs:

$$\textbf{Markup on variable costs} = \frac{\$400,000 + \$200,000}{\$800,000}$$
$$= 0.75$$

If the predicted variable costs for Product A1 are $12 per unit, the initial selling price for Product A1 is $21:

$$\textbf{Initial selling price} = \$12 + (\$12 \times 0.75)$$
$$= \$21$$

2. When the markup is based on full manufacturing costs, it must be large enough to cover selling and administrative expenses and to provide for the desired profit. Again, it is necessary to determine the desired profit and predict all costs for the pricing period. The initial prices of individual products are then determined as their unit manufacturing costs plus the markup. For Magnum, the markup on manufacturing costs would be 55.6 percent:

$$\textbf{Markup on manufacturing costs} = \frac{\$300,000 + \$200,000}{\$900,000}$$
$$= 0.556$$

If the predicted manufacturing costs for Product B1 are $10, the initial selling price for Product B1 is $15.56:

$$\textbf{Initial selling price} = \$10 + (\$10 \times 0.556)$$
$$= \$15.56$$

Cost-Based Pricing for Special Orders

Many organizations use cost-based pricing to bid on unique projects. If the project requires dedicated assets, the acquisition of new fixed assets, or an investment in employee training, the desired profit on the special order or project should allow for an adequate return on the dedicated assets or additional investment.

Critique of Cost-Based Pricing

Cost-based pricing has four major drawbacks:

1. Cost-based pricing requires accurate cost assignments. If costs are not accurately assigned, some products could be priced too high, losing market share to competitors; other products could be priced too low, gaining market share but being less profitable than anticipated.

2. The higher the portion of unassigned costs, the greater is the likelihood of over- or under-pricing individual products.

3. Cost-based pricing assumes that goods or services are relatively scarce and, generally, customers who want a product or service are willing to pay the price.

4. In a competitive environment, cost-based approaches increase the time and cost of bringing new products to market.

Cost-based pricing became the dominant approach to pricing during an era when products were relatively long-lived and there was relatively little competition. Also, these systems tend to focus on organizational units such as departments, plants, or divisions and not on activities or cost drivers. While easy to implement, reflecting the need to recover costs and earn a return on investment, and easily justified, cost-based prices might not be competitive. Competition puts intense downward pressure on prices and removes slack from pricing formulas. There is little margin for error in pricing. In a highly competitive market, small variations in pricing make significant differences in success.

MID-MODULE REVIEW

Presented is the 2007 contribution income statement of Knox Company.

KNOX COMPANY Contribution Income Statement For Year Ended December 31, 2007		
Sales (100,000 units at $12 per unit)		$1,200,000
Less variable costs		
Manufacturing.	$300,000	
Selling and administrative.	150,000	(450,000)
Contribution margin		750,000
Less fixed costs		
Manufacturing.	400,000	
Selling and administrative.	200,000	(600,000)
Net income.		$ 150,000

Knox has total assets of $2,000,000, and management desires an annual return of 10 percent on total assets.

Required

a. Determine the dollar amount by which Knox Company exceeded or fell short of the desired annual rate of return in 2007.

b. Given the current sales volume and cost structure, determine the unit selling price required to achieve an annual profit of $250,000.

c. Assume that management wants to state the selling price as a percentage of variable manufacturing costs. Given your answer to requirement (b) and the current sales volume and cost structure, determine the selling price as a percentage of variable manufacturing costs.

d. Restate your answer to requirement (c), dividing into two separate markup percentages:
1. The markup on variable manufacturing costs required to cover unassigned costs.
2. The additional markup on variable manufacturing costs required to achieve an annual profit of $250,000.

Solution

a.

Desired annual profit ($2,000,000 × 0.10)	$200,000
Actual profit	(150,000)
Amount actual profit fell short of achieving the desired return.	$ 50,000

b.

Predicted costs		
Variable..........................	$450,000	
Fixed...........................	600,000	$1,050,000
Desired profit......................		250,000
Required revenue...................		$1,300,000
Unit sales........................		÷ 100,000
Required unit selling price..........		$ 13

c.

Variable manufacturing costs per unit ($300,000/100,000 unit)	= $3
Selling price as a percent of variable manufacturing costs	= $13/3
	= 433⅓%
Markup as a percent of variable manufacturing costs ($10/$3)	= 333⅓.

d.   Detail of markup on variable manufacturing costs:

1. Unassigned costs

Variable selling and administrative......................	$150,000	
Fixed costs.......................................	600,000	$750,000
Variable manufacturing costs...........................		÷300,000
Markup on variable manufacturing costs to cover		
unassigned costs.................................		250%

2. Desired profit.......................................

Desired profit.......................................	$250,000
Variable manufacturing costs...........................	÷300,000
Additional markup on variable manufacturing costs	
to achieve desired profit ($250,000)..................	83⅓%

TARGET COSTING

Peter Drucker has identified cost-based (he calls it "cost-driven") pricing as a "deadly business sin." According to Drucker,

> Most American and practically all European companies arrive at their prices by adding up costs and then putting a profit margin on top. And then, as soon as they have introduced the product, they have to start cutting the price, have to redesign the product at enormous expense, have to take losses—and often have to drop a perfectly good product because it is priced incorrectly."[5]

Drucker believes that cost-based pricing is the reason that, despite its technological success, the United States no longer has a consumer-electronics industry. He believes that the only sound way to price is to start with what the market is willing to pay and then to design a product or service to meet that price. This approach to the pricing and design of new products, referred to as *target costing*, was formalized at Toyota[6] and quickly utilized by other successful Japanese companies such as Nissan, Canon, and Ricoh. On the other hand, the use of target costing is also one of the reasons for the success of U.S.-based personal computer manufacturers such as Dell. These companies set stretch pricing targets, such as breaking the $1,000 barrier, and worked to design a machine that could be profitable with a retail price of $999 or less.

Target Costing Is Proactive for Cost Management

Target costing starts with determining what customers are willing to pay for a product or service and then subtracts a desired profit on sales to determine the allowable, or target, cost of the product or service.

LO3 Explain target costing and its acceptance in highly competitive industries.

---

[5] Peter F. Drucker, "The Five Deadly Business Sins," *The Wall Street Journal,* October 21, 1993, p. A18.

[6] Takao Tanaka, "Target Costing at Toyota," *Journal of Cost Management,* Spring 1993, p. 4.

This target cost is then communicated to a cross-functional team of employees representing such diverse areas as marketing, product design, manufacturing, and management accounting. Reflecting value chain concepts and the notion of partnerships up and down the value chain, suppliers of raw materials and components are often included in the teams. The target costing team is assigned the task of designing a product that meets customer price, function, and quality requirements while providing a desired profit. Its job is not completed until the target cost is met, or a determination is made that the product or service cannot be profitably introduced under the current circumstances. See Exhibit 23.4 for an overview of target costing, and the following Research Insight for some cautions about understanding the market.

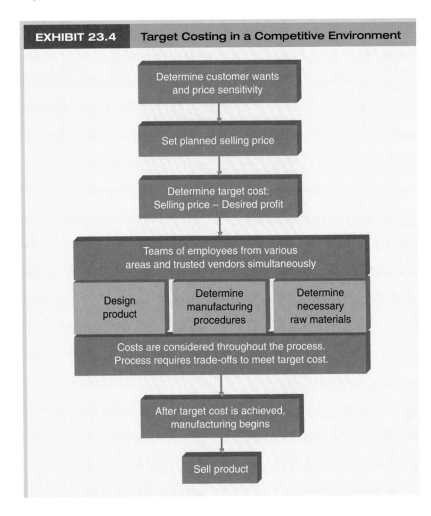

EXHIBIT 23.4 **Target Costing in a Competitive Environment**

Although a formula can be used to determine a markup on cost, it is not possible to develop a formula indicating how to achieve a target cost. Hence, target costing is not a technique. It is more a philosophy or an approach to pricing and cost management. It takes a proactive approach to cost management, reflecting the belief that costs are best managed by decisions made during product development. This contrasts with the more passive cost-plus belief that costs result from design, procurement, and manufacture. Like the value chain, target costing helps orient employees toward the final customer and reinforces the notion that all departments within the organization and all organizations along the value chain must work together. Target costing also empowers employees who will be assigned the responsibility for carrying out activities necessary to deliver a product or service with the authority to determine what activities will be selected. Like process mapping, it helps employees to better understand their role in serving the customer.

Target Costing Encourages Design for Production

In the absence of a target costing approach, design engineers are apt to focus on incorporating leading-edge technology and the maximum number of features in a product. Target costing keeps the customer's function, quality, and price requirements in the forefront at all times. If customers do not want leading-edge

RESEARCH INSIGHT	Target Costing Requires Market Knowledge

Managers must understand that target costing is not just about setting cost targets. It is a value chain approach to managing an organization. Target costing requires an understanding of the market: what the customer or prospective customer wants and is willing to pay. It is important to keep customer expectations at the forefront throughout the entire product development cycle. Otherwise, product features could be added in the development stage that don't reflect what customers want. This is one reason many new products do not sell. The decisions made regarding product development must make business sense to the producer. If a product feature does not add value to a customer, in the long run it probably will not add value to the producer.

Target costing requires management to translate customer value expectations into an acceptable product price. Next, management determines the profit that shareholders expect to make. Netting these two items results in the target cost. Once an organization has determined a product target cost, management must then determine the proper mix of costs that result in a quality product the customer desires. Customers care that the cost of the various product features and functions is in line with the value they receive for what they must pay.[7]

technology (which could be expensive and untested) and several product features, they will resist paying for them. Focusing on achieving a target cost keeps design engineers tuned in to the final customer.

Left on their own, design engineers might believe that their job ends when they design a product that meets the customer's functional requirements. The tendency is to simply pass on the design to manufacturing and let manufacturing determine how best to produce the product. Further down the line, if the product needs servicing, it becomes the service department's responsibility to determine how best to service the product. A target costing approach forces design engineers to explicitly consider the costs of manufacturing and servicing a product while it is being designed. This is known as **design for manufacture**.

Minor changes in design that do not affect the product's functioning can often produce dramatic savings in manufacturing and servicing costs. Examples of design for manufacture include the following:

- Using molded plastic parts to avoid assembling several small parts.
- Designing two parts that must be fit together so that joining them in the correct manner is obvious to assembly workers.
- Placing an access panel in the side of an appliance so service personnel can make repairs quickly.
- Using standard-size parts to reduce inventory requirements, to reduce the possibility of assembly personnel inserting the incorrect part, and to simplify the job of service personnel.
- Ensuring that tolerance requirements for parts that must fit together can be met with available equipment.
- Using manufacturing procedures that are common to other products.

The successful implementation of target costing requires employees from all involved disciplines to be familiar with costing concepts and the notions of value-added and non-value-added activities. When considering the manufacturing process, team members should minimize non-value-added activities such as movement, storage, inspection, and setup. They should also select the lowest-cost value-added activities that do the job properly.

Target Costing Reduces Time to Introduce Products

By designing a product to meet a target cost (rather than evaluating the marketability of a product at a cost-plus price and having to recycle the design through several departments), target costing reduces the time required to introduce new products. Involving vendors in target costing design teams makes the vendors aware of the necessity of meeting a target cost. This facilitates the concurrent engineering of components to be produced outside the organization and reduces the time required to obtain components.

---

[7] David Schwendeman and Al Hartgraves, "Some Myths about Target Costing," *The CPA Letter* (New York: American Institute of CPAs, September 2000), http://www.aicpa.org/pubs.

Target Costing Can Apply to Components

Although it is most frequently associated with the development of new products, target costing can apply to components. A cost management expert at Isuzu Motors once illustrated target costing for components by taking apart a pen. "This is what we do with our competitors' products . . . . analyze the material it is made of, the way it is molded, the process used to assemble it. From this we would determine the product's probable cost." Isuzu would then use the component's probable cost as a target cost to meet or beat.[8]

Target Costing Requires Cost Information

Implementing target costing requires detailed information on the cost of alternative activities. This information allows decision makers to select design and manufacturing alternatives that best meet function and price requirements. Tables that contain detailed databases of cost information for various manufacturing variables are occasionally used in designing products and selecting processes to meet target costs.

Target Costing Requires Coordination

Limitations of target costing are employee and supplier attitudes and the many meetings required to coordinate product design and to select manufacturing processes. All people involved must have a basic understanding of the overall processes required to bring a product to market and an appreciation of the cost consequences of alternative actions. They must also respect, cooperate, and communicate with other team members and be willing to engage in a negotiation process involving trade-offs. Finally, they must understand that although the total time required to bring a new product to market can be reduced, the countless coordinating meetings could be quite intrusive on the individuals' otherwise orderly schedule. See Exhibit 23.5 for an evaluation of target costing.

EXHIBIT 23.5	Pros and Cons of Target Costing

Pros
- Takes proactive approach to cost management.
- Orients organization toward customer.
- Breaks down barriers between departments.
- Enhances employee awareness and empowerment.
- Fosters partnerships with suppliers.
- Minimizes non-value-added activities.
- Encourages selection of lowest-cost value-added activities.
- Reduces time to market.

Cons
- To be effective, requires the development of detailed cost data.
- Requires willingness to cooperate.
- Requires many meetings for coordination.

This aspect of the process is even more difficult when suppliers must be brought in as part of the coordination process. This concept is frequently referred to as **chained target costing** because the supply chain's support is critical for the product to be both competitively priced and delivered to the final customer in a timely manner. When multiple suppliers are required, the organization must obtain everyone's support or the process will probably not be successful due to gaps in the reliability of delivery, quality, and cost control. Each organization and unit must understand that if the product is not brought to market within the defined constraints, all will lose. They must make firm commitments for the project undertaken and to have faith that each participant will carry out whatever part of the supply chain it has promised to fulfill. An example of this process with suppliers of parts and components to Whirlpool Corporation is presented in the following Business Insight. Coordination across the supply chain is vital in the overall process of continuous improvement as discussed later in this module.

---

[8] Ford S. Worthy, "Japan's Smart Secret Weapon," *Fortune*, August 12, 1992, p. 74.

| **BUSINESS INSIGHT** | **Quality Parts Yield Product Success** |

Industry leaders in electric motor manufacturing are attempting to provide their customers, equipment manufacturers, with high efficiency and quieter motors at consistently lower costs as part of the supply chain. An example is Emerson Appliance Solutions, which has teamed with Whirlpool Corporation to develop a customized capacitor motor for the Sears' Kenmore, Kitchen Aid, and Whirlpool brand names. Says Emerson's Whirlpool account manager, "An approximate 20 percent motor energy savings was the result of efforts by engineering teams at both Whirlpool and Emerson that resulted in a smaller, more efficient motor-pump assembly."

Illustrating Emerson's commitment to Whirlpool, the company had three managers who coordinated components for washers, motors, and controls. These managers worked with Whirlpool to achieve its new product objective of emphasizing reduced sound and water consumption while delivering good wash performance. To further enhance the product, Emerson then worked with its supplier, AMP (going up the supply chain), for an improved connection method for the motors' magnet wires and lead wires. Each member of the supply chain was well aware of Whirlpool's concern about cost of the new product and made every effort to contain costs from development to production. As a result, the new product was within the target set by Whirlpool.[9]

Target Costing is Key for Products with Short Life Cycles

From a traditional marketing perspective, products with a relatively long life go through four distinct stages during their life cycle:

1. *Startup*. Sales are low when a product is first introduced. Traditionally, initial selling prices are set high, and customers tend to be relatively affluent trendsetters.

2. *Growth*. Sales increase as the product gains acceptance. Traditionally, prices have remained high during this stage because of customer loyalty and the absence of competitive products.

3. *Maturity*. Sales level off as the product matures. Because of increased competition, pressure on prices is increasing; some price reductions could be necessary.

4. *Decline*. Sales decline as the product becomes obsolete. Significant price cuts could be required to sell remaining inventories.

Target costing is more important for products with a relatively short market life cycle. Products with a long life cycle present many opportunities to continuously improve design and manufacturing procedures that are not available when a product has a short life cycle. Hence, extra care must go into the initial planning for short-lived products. This is especially true when short product life cycles are combined with increased worldwide competition. It is important to introduce a product first and at a price that ensures rapid market penetration.

Target Costing Helps Manage Life Cycle Costs

An awareness of the impact of today's actions on tomorrow's costs underlies the notion of **life cycle costs,** which include all costs associated with a product or service ranging from those incurred with the initial conception through design, pre-production, production, and after-production support.

The lower line in Exhibit 23.6 illustrates the cumulative expenditure of funds over the life of a product. For low-technology products with relatively long product lives, decisions committing the organization to spend money are made at approximately the same time the money is spent. However, for high-technology products with relatively short product lives, most of the critical decisions affecting cost, such as product design and the selection of manufacturing procedures, are made before production begins. The top line in Exhibit 23.6 represents decisions committing the organization to expenditures for a product.

---

[9] Joe Jancsurak, "Value-Added Power," *Appliance Manufacturer Magazine*, February 26, 2001, http://www.ammagazine.com.

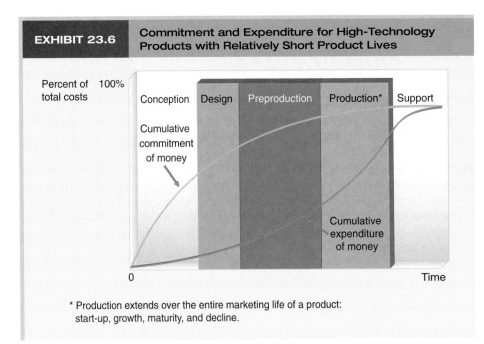

EXHIBIT 23.6 Commitment and Expenditure for High-Technology Products with Relatively Short Product Lives

* Production extends over the entire marketing life of a product: start-up, growth, maturity, and decline.

Reflecting significant changes in vehicle production since the time of Henry Ford and the Model T, General Motors estimates that 70 percent of the cost of manufacturing truck transmissions is determined during design.[10] Others estimate that up to 95 percent of the total costs associated with high-technology products are committed before the first unit is produced.[11]

Life cycle cost concepts have also been usefully applied to low-technology issues, such as repair versus replace decisions. The New York State Throughway Authority uses life cycle concepts to determine the point at which it is more expensive to repair than to replace bridges.

MANAGERIAL DECISION   **You are the Vice President of Product Development**

As head of new product development for your electronics company, you are concerned that so many of the ideas for new products coming from your research and development group are not succeeding in the market. Many recent attempts to take new products to market have failed, not because of technological deficiencies in the products, but because the market would not support the high prices for new products that were necessary to produce a satisfactory profit. What should you do to try to reverse this trend of new product failures? [Answer p. 23-20]

CONTINUOUS IMPROVEMENT COSTING

LO4 Describe the relation between target costing and continuous improvement costing.

Continuous improvement (Kaizen) costing calls for establishing cost reduction targets for products or services that an organization is currently providing to customers. Developed in Japan, this approach to cost management is often referred to as *Kaizen costing. Kaizen* means "continuous improvement" in Japanese. Continuous improvement costing begins where target costing ends. Target costing takes a proactive approach to cost management during the conception, design, and preproduction stages of a product's life; continuous improvement costing takes a proactive approach to cost management during the production stage of a product's life:

---

[10] D.E. Whitney, "Manufacturing by Design," *Harvard Business Review,* July–August 1988, pp. 83–91.

[11] Benjamin S. Blanchard, *Design and Manage to Life Cycle Costs* (Portland, OR: M/A Press, 1978), p. 15.

	Time			
Conception	Design	Preproduction		Production
	Target costing			Continuous improvement costing

Continuous improvement costing adds a specific target to be achieved during a time period to the target costing concept previously discussed. Basically, the mathematics of the concept is quite simple, but its implementation is difficult. Assume that Home Depot wanted to reduce the cost of materials handling in each of its stores, and management set a target reduction of 2 percent a year. If a given store had current annual materials handling costs of $100,000 and expected an increase the next year due to 10 percent growth, the budget for the next year would be $107,800 [($100,000 × 1.10) × 0.98]. The budget for next year based on growth is $110,000 less the continuous improvement factor of 0.02.

Successful companies use continuous improvement costing to avoid complacency. Competitors are constantly striving to win market share through better quality or lower prices. Hewlett-Packard studied Epson to determine its strengths and weaknesses. Isuzu Motors takes competitors' products apart to determine a target cost it must beat. To fend off competition, prices and costs must be continuously reduced. To maintain its competitive position, Hewlett-Packard has reduced the list price of the basic inkjet printer from nearly $400 a decade ago to less than $100 today. This could not have been done without continuous reductions in costs.

The Daihatsu Motor Company sets Kaizen cost reduction targets for each cost element, including purchased parts per car, direct materials per car, labor hours per car, and office utilities.[12] Performance reports developed at the end of each month compare targeted and actual cost reductions. If actual cost reductions are more than the targeted cost reductions, the results are favorable; if the actual cost reductions are less than the targeted cost reductions, the results are unfavorable.

Because cost reduction targets are set before it is known how they will be achieved, continuous improvement costing can be stressful to employees. To help reduce this stress at Daihatsu, a period of about three months following the introduction of a new product is allowed before organizational units are expected to meet target costs and Kaizen costing targets. A critical element in motivating employee cooperation and teamwork in aggressive cost management techniques, such as target and continuous improvement costing, is to avoid using performance reports to place blame for failure. The proper response to an unfavorable performance report must be an offer of assistance to correct the failure.

BENCHMARKING

When Isuzu Motors takes a competitor's product apart to determine the competitor's manufacturing costs, or when Hewlett-Packard studies Epson to identify Epson's strengths and weaknesses, each company is engaging in *benchmarking*, a practice that has been around for centuries. In recent years, however, as globalization and increased competitiveness have forced businesses to more aggressively compete on the bases of cost, quality, and service, benchmarking has become more formalized and open. No longer regarded as spying, **benchmarking** is now a systematic approach to identifying the best practices to help an organization take action to improve performance.

The formalization of benchmarking is largely attributed to a book written in the 1980s by Robert Camp of Xerox. Since then, many managers have come to believe that benchmarking is a requirement for success. Although benchmarking can focus on anything of interest, it typically deals with target costs for a product, service, or operation, customer satisfaction, quality, inventory levels, inventory turnover, cycle time, and productivity. Benchmarking initially focused on studying competitors, but benchmarking efforts have changed dramatically in recent years. According to Camp,

> Although you must focus strongly on the competition, if that is the sole objective, playing catch-up is the best you can do. Watching the competition does not tell you how to outdistance them. The mix

LO5 Explain how benchmarking enhances quality management, continuous improvement, and process reengineering.

---

[12] Yasuhiro Monden and John Lee, "How a Japanese Auto Maker Reduces Costs," *Management Accounting*, August 1993, pp. 22–26.

of our benchmark activities has changed 180 degrees. In the early days, we spent 80 percent of our benchmark time looking at the competition. Today we spend 80 percent of that time outside our industry, because we have found innovative ideas from businesses in other industries.[13]

In considering how to go about benchmarking, an organization must be careful because it must consider nonfinancial limitations. No single numerical measurement can completely describe the performance of a complex device such as a microprocessor or a television camera, but benchmarks can be useful tools for comparing different products, components, and systems. The only totally accurate way to measure the performance of a given product is to test it against other products while performing the exact same activity. The following Business Insight describes how Intel Corporation makes benchmarks available with some information on how to use them.

BUSINESS INSIGHT   **Intel Benchmarks Performance**

Intel Corporation divides its benchmarks into two types, component and system. *Component benchmarks* measure the performance of specific parts of a computer system, such as a microprocessor or hard disk drive. *System benchmarks* typically measure the performance of the entire computer system. The performance obtained will almost certainly vary from benchmark performance for a number of reasons. First, individual components must usually be tested in a complete computer system, and it is not always possible to eliminate the considerable effects that differences in system design and configuration have on benchmark results. For instance, vendors sell systems with a wide variety of disk capabilities and speeds, system memory, and video and graphics capabilities, all of which influence how the system components perform in actual use. Differences in software, including operating systems and compilers, also affect component and system performance. Finally, benchmark tests are typically written to be exemplary for only a certain type of computer application, which might or might not be similar to what is being compared.

A benchmark is, at most, only one type of information that an organization might use during the purchasing or manufacturing process. To get a true picture of the performance of a component or system being considered, the organization should consult industry sources, publicly available research reports, and even government publications of related information.

Benchmarking provides measurements that are useful in setting goals. It can lead to dramatic innovations, and it can help overcome resistance to change. When presented with a major cost reduction target, employees often believe they are being asked to do the impossible. Benchmarking can be a psychological tool that helps overcome resistance to change by showing how others have already met the target.

Although each organization has its own approach to benchmarking, the following six steps used by Alcoa are typical:

1. Decide what to benchmark.
2. Plan the benchmark project.
3. Understand your own performance.
4. Study others.
5. Learn from the data.
6. Take action.[14]

In recent years, professional organizations, such as the Institute of Management Accountants, have set up clearinghouses for benchmark information or have performed benchmarking studies of interest to members as have certain corporations such as Intel.

---

[13] Robert Camp, "A Bible for Benchmarking, by Xerox," *Financial Executive*, July/August 1993, p. 24.

[14] Karen Bemowski, "The Benchmark Bandwagon," *Quality Progress*, January 1991, pp. 22–23.

MODULE-END REVIEW

MBW, Inc. has been conducting early stage research on hydrogen powered automobiles and is nearing the point where product development will soon begin. In order to determine the feasibility of the product, MBW has conducted marketing research that indicates that the price target for the product must be no more than $35,000 if it is to appeal to a large enough market segment to sell a minimum of 150,000 automobiles in the first year of production. The CFO has indicated that the new product must meet a 15% minimum profit margin requirement.

Required

a. Calculate the target cost per unit to produce the hydrogen powered automobile.
b. How would MBW go about determining whether the target cost can be achieved.
c. What should MBW do if the estimated cost to produce the product exceeds the target cost?

Solution

a.

Total revenue (150,000 × $35,000)	$5,250,000,000
Required profit margin (15%)	−787,500,000
Total cost	$4,462,500,000
Number of units	÷ 150,000
Target cost per unit.	$ 29,750

b. A new product such as an automobile is an extremely complex product with hundreds, if not thousands, of different components, involving many different vendors. Once MBW has determined what product features potential customers want, its engineers must determine how best to provide those features, working with vendors and potential vendors. The idea is to determine how best to provide the final product that the customers want at a cost that will provide a reasonable profit to MBW and its vendors.

c. Teams of engineers, accountants, designers, etc. from MBW and its vendors should work together to try to achieve the target cost. If initial cost estimates are too high, they should explore every possibility, including redesign of the product, using components from existing products, developing new production systems, etc. to meet the target cost. If it is finally determined that the target cannot be reached, then management has to decide if it is willing to go forward with the product with a lower than desired initial profit margin. In some cases, managers will proceed with the idea that additional cost savings will be found (using Kaizen Costing methods) after the product is in production.

GUIDANCE ANSWER

MANAGERIAL DECISION	You are the Vice President of Product Development

You should consider adopting target costing methods for new product development. Great product research ideas are successful only when they translate into products that can be produced and sold for an acceptable profit. Creating and producing new products before determining what the customer wants and is willing to pay often leads to failure. Target costing methods reverse this process by applying value chain concepts to bring customers and suppliers along the value chain together to produce a product only if it has features and a selling price that are acceptable to potential customers, and if its production costs allow the seller to make an acceptable profit.

DISCUSION QUESTIONS

Q23-1. What are the relationships among an organization's value chain, processes, and activities?

Q23-2. What should be the goal of every organization along the value chain?

Q23-3. Distinguish between the value added perspective and the value chain perspective.

Q23-4. Why are economic models seldom used for day-to-day pricing decisions?

Q23-5. Identify three reasons that cost-based approaches to pricing have traditionally been important.

Q23-6. Identify four drawbacks to cost-based pricing.

Q23-7. How does target costing differ from cost-based pricing?

Q23-8. Why is cost-based pricing more a technique, and target costing is more a philosophy? Which approach takes a more proactive approach to cost management?

Q23-9. Distinguish between the marketing life cycles of products incorporating advanced technology (such as household electronic equipment) and those using more traditional technology (such as household paper products). Why would life cycle costing be more important to a manufacturer of household electronic equipment than to a manufacturer of household paper products?

Q23-10. What is the relationship between target costing and continuous improvement (Kaizen) costing?

Q23-11. Distinguish between the seller's and the buyer's perspective of life cycle costs.

Q23-12. What advantage is derived from benchmarking against firms other than competitors?

MINI EXERCISES

M23-13. Developing a Value Chain from the Perspective of the Final Customer (LO1)
Prepare a value chain for bottled orange juice that was purchased for personal consumption at an on-campus cafeteria.

M23-14. Developing a Value Chain: Upstream and Downstream Entities (LO1)
Prepare a value chain for a firm that produces gasoline fuel. Clearly identify upstream and downstream entities in the value chain.

M23-15. Classifying Activities Using the Generic Internal Value Chain: Aluminum Cable Manufacturer (LO1)
Using the generic internal value chain shown in Exhibit 23.2, classify each of the following activities of an aluminum cable manufacturer as inbound logistics, operations, outbound logistics, marketing and sales, service, or support.
  a. Advertising in a construction magazine
  b. Inspecting incoming aluminum ingots
  c. Placing bar codes on coils of finished products
  d. Borrowing money to finance a build up of inventory
  e. Hiring new employees
  f. Heating aluminum ingots
  g. Drawing wire from aluminum ingots
  h. Coiling wire
  i. Visiting a customer to determine the cause of cable breakage
  j. Filing tax returns

M23-16. Classifying Activities Using the Generic Internal Value Chain: Cable TV Company (LO1)
Using the generic internal value chain shown in Exhibit 23.2, classify each of the following activities of a cable television company as inbound logistics, operations, outbound logistics, marketing and sales, service, or support.
  a. Installing cable in the apartment of a new customer
  b. Repairing cable after a windstorm
  c. Mailing brochures to prospective customers
  d. Discussing a rate increase with members of a regulatory agency
  e. Selling shares of stock in the company
  f. Monitoring the quality of reception at the company's satellite downlink
  g. Preparing financial statements
  h. Visiting a customer to determine the cause of poor-quality television reception
  i. Traveling to a conference to learn about technological changes affecting the industry
  j. Inspecting television cables for wear

M23-17. Product Pricing: Single Product (LO2)

Sue Bee Honey

Sue Bee Honey is one of the largest processors of its product for the retail market. Assume that it processes honey at one large facility. Its annual fixed costs total $8,000,000, of which $3,000,000 is for administrative and selling efforts. Sales are anticipated to be 800,000 cases a year. Variable costs for processing are $4 per case, and variable selling expenses are 24 percent of selling price. There are no variable administrative expenses.

Required

If the company desires a profit of $4,000,000, what is the selling price per case?

M23-18. Product Pricing: Single Product (LO2)

Assume that you plan to open a soft ice cream franchise in a resort community during the summer months. Fixed operating costs for the three-month period are projected to be $5,250. Variable costs per serving include the cost of the ice cream and cone, $0.25, and a franchise fee payable to Snowdrift Cooler, $0.10. A market analysis prepared by Snowdrift Cooler indicates that summer sales in the resort community should total 24,000 units.

Required

Determine the price you should charge for each ice cream cone to achieve a $7,000 profit for the three-month period.

EXERCISES

E23-19. Product Pricing: Single Product (LO2)

Presented is the 2006 contribution income statement of Colgate Products.

COLGATE PRODUCTS Contribution Income Statement For Year Ended December 31, 2006		
Sales (12,000 units)		$1,440,000
Less variable costs		
Cost of goods sold	$480,000	
Selling and administrative.	132,000	(612,000)
Contribution margin		828,000
Less fixed costs		
Manufacturing overhead.	520,000	
Selling and administrative.	210,000	(730,000)
Net income		$ 98,000

During the coming year, Colgate expects an increase in variable manufacturing costs of $8 per unit and in fixed manufacturing costs of $48,000.

Required

a. If sales for 2007 remain at 12,000 units, what price should Colgate charge to obtain the same profit as last year?

b. Management believes that sales can be increased to 16,000 units if the selling price is lowered to $107. Is this action desirable?

c. After considering the expected increases in costs, what sales volume is needed to earn a profit of $98,000 with a unit selling price of $107?

E23-20. Cost-Based Pricing and Markups with Variable Costs (LO2)

Compu Services provides computerized inventory consulting. The office and computer expenses are $600,000 annually. The consulting hours available for the year total 20,000, and the average consulting hour has $30 of variable costs.

Required

a. If the company desires a profit of $80,000, what should it charge per hour?

b. What is the markup on variable costs if the desired profit is $120,000?

c. If the desired profit is $60,000, what is the markup on variable costs to cover (1) unassigned costs and (2) desired profit?

E23-21. Computing Markups (LO2)

The predicted 2007 costs for Osaka Motors are as follows:

Manufacturing Costs		Selling and Administrative Costs	
Variable................	$100,000	Variable................	$300,000
Fixed..................	220,000	Fixed..................	200,000

Average total assets for 2007 are predicted to be $6,000,000.

Required

a. If management desires a 12 percent rate of return on total assets, what are the markup percentages for total variable costs and for total manufacturing costs?

b. If the company desires a 10 percent rate of return on total assets, what is the markup percentage on total manufacturing costs for (1) unassigned costs and (2) desired profit?

E23-22. Product Pricing: Two Products (LO2)

Quality Data manufactures two products, CD-ROMs and zip disks, both on the same assembly lines and packaged 10 disks per pack. The predicted sales are 400,000 packs of CD-ROMs and 500,000 packs of zip disks. The predicted costs for the year 2007 are as follows:

	Variable Costs	Fixed Costs
Materials..............	$200,000	$500,000
Other.................	250,000	800,000

Each product uses 50 percent of the materials costs. Based on manufacturing time, 40 percent of the other costs are assigned to the CD-ROMs, and 60 percent of the other costs are assigned to the zip disks. The management of Quality Data desires an annual profit of $150,000.

Required

a. What price should Quality Data charge for each disk pack if management believes the zip disks sell for 20 percent more than the CD-ROMs?

b. What is the total profit per product?

c. Based on your answer to requirement (b), how should the company evaluate the status of the two products?

E23-23. Benchmarking (LO5)

Your company is developing a new product for the computer printer industry. You have talked to several material vendors about being able to supply quality components for the new product. The product designers are satisfied with the company's ability to make the product in the current facilities. Numerous potential customers also have been surveyed, and most have indicated a willingness to buy the product if the price is competitive.

Required

What are some means of benchmarking the development and production of your new product?

E23-24. Target Costing (LO3)

Oregon Equipment Company wants to develop a new log-splitting machine for rural homeowners. Market research has determined that the company could sell 5,000 log-splitting machines per year at a retail price of $600 each. An independent catalog company would handle sales for an annual fee of $2,000 plus $50 per unit sold. The cost of the raw materials required to produce the log-splitting machines amounts to $80 per unit.

Required

If company management desires a return equal to 10 percent of the final selling price, what is the target unit cost?

PROBLEMS

P23-25. Product Pricing: Two Products (LO2)

Earthlink, Inc., provides a variety of computer-related services to its clients. Two of the many services offered by each office are Web page design (WPD), and electronic interchange development (EID) services. Assume that each office is expected to earn a 20 percent return on the assets invested. Earthlink has invested $5 million in the Atlanta office since its opening. The annual costs for the coming year are expected to be as follows:

	Variable Costs	Fixed Costs
Consulting support.........	$600,000	$850,000
Sales and administration	100,000	950,000

The two services expend about equal costs per hour, and the predicted hours for the coming year are 50,000 for WPD and 30,000 for EID.

Required

a. If markup is based on variable costs, how much revenue must each service generate by the Atlanta office to provide the profit expected by corporate headquarters? What is the anticipated revenue per hour for each service?

b. If the markup is based on total costs, how much revenue must each service generate to provide the expected profit?

c. Explain why answers in requirements (a) and (b) are either the same or different.

P23-26. Target Costing   (LO3)

Redback Networks, Inc., provides networking services and related systems hardware to its customers. Assume that it is developing a new networking system that small businesses can use. To attract small business owners, Redback must keep the price low without giving up too many of the features of larger networking systems. A marketing research study conducted on the company's behalf found that the price range must be $25,000 to $30,000. Management has determined a target price to be $26,000. The company's minimum profit percentage of sales is normally 20 percent, but the company is willing to reduce it to 15 percent to get the new product on the market. The fixed costs for the first year are anticipated to be $14,000,000. If sales reach 1,200 installed networks, the company needs to know how much it can spend on variable costs, which are primarily related to installation.

Redback Networks, Inc. (RBAK)

Required

a. What is the amount of total cost allowed if the 15 percent profit target is allowed and the sales target is met? Show the amount for fixed and for variable costs.

b. What is the amount of total costs allowed if the 20 percent normal profit target is desired at the 1,200 sales target? Show the amount for fixed and for variable costs.

P23-27. Continuous Improvement (Kaizen) Costing   (LO4)

Matzumi manufactures cameras. At its Pacific plant, cost control has become a concern of management. The actual costs per unit for the years 2006 and 2007 were as follows:

	2006	2007
Direct materials		
Plastic case....................	$ 4.00	$ 3.90
Lens set	17.00	17.20
Electrical component set	6.00	5.40
Film track	11.00	10.00
Direct labor.....................	32.00 (1.6 hours)	30.00 (1.5 hours)
Indirect manufacturing costs		
Variable......................	7.50	7.10
Fixed........................	2.00 (100,000 unit base)	1.90 (120,000 unit base)

The company manufactures all of the camera components except the lens sets, which it purchased from several vendors. The company has used target costing in the past but has not been able to meet the very competitive global pricing. Beginning in 2007, the company implemented a continuous improvement program that requires cost reduction targets.

Required

If continuous improvement (Kaizen) costing sets a first-year target of a 10 percent reduction of the 2006 base, how successful was the company in meeting 2007 per unit cost reduction targets? Support your answer with appropriate computations.

P23-28. Continuous Improvement (Kaizen) Costing (LO4)

GE Capital, a division of General Electric, has been displeased with the costs of servicing its consumer loans. Assume that it has decided to implement a Kaizen-based cost improvement program. For 2007, GE Capital incurred the following costs:

Loan processing.	$14,500,000
Customer relations	3,500,000
Printing, mailing, and postage	800,000

For the next two years, GE Capital expects an increase in consumer loans of 4 percent annually with related increases in costs.

Required

If the company has a continuous improvement of 1 percent each year, develop a budget for the next two years for the consumer loan department.

P23-29. Price Setting: Multiple Products (LO2)

Snap Tools Company's predicted 2008 variable and fixed costs are as follows:

	Variable Costs	Fixed Costs
Manufacturing	$400,000	$260,000
Selling and administrative	100,000	50,000
Total	$500,000	$310,000

Snap Tools produces a wide variety of small tools. Per-unit manufacturing cost information about one of these products, the Type-A Clamp, is as follows:

Direct materials	$ 8
Direct labor	7
Manufacturing overhead	
Variable	6
Fixed	6
Total manufacturing costs	$27

Variable selling and administrative costs for the Type-A Clamp is $3 per unit. Management has set a 2008 target profit of $150,000 on the sale of Type-A Clamps.

Required

a. Determine the markup percentage on variable costs required to earn the desired profit.
b. Use variable cost markup to determine a suggested selling price for the Type-A Clamp.
c. For the Type-A Clamp, break the markup on variable costs into separate parts for fixed costs and profit. Explain the significance of each part.
d. Determine the markup percentage on manufacturing costs required to earn the desired profit.
e. Use the manufacturing costs markup to determine a suggested selling price for the Type-A Clamp.
f. Evaluate the variable and the manufacturing cost approaches to determine the markup percentage.

P23-30. Price Setting: Multiple Products (LO2)

Chesapeake Tackle Company produces a wide variety of commercial fishing equipment. In the past, product managers set prices using their professional judgment. John Marlin, the new controller, believes this practice has led to the significant underpricing of some products (with lost profits) and the significant overpricing of other products (with lost sales volume). You have been asked to assist Marlin in developing a corporate approach to pricing. The output of your work should be a cost-based formula that can be used to develop initial selling prices for each product. Although product managers are allowed to adjust these prices to meet competition and to take advantage of market opportunities, they must explain such deviations in writing. The following 2006 cost information from the accounting records is available:

	Manufacturing Costs	Selling and Administrative Costs
Variable.	$350,000	$ 50,000
Fixed.	150,000	200,000

In 2006, Chesapeake reported earnings of $80,000. However, the controller believes that proper pricing should produce earnings of at least $120,000 on the same sales mix and unit volume. Accordingly, you are to use the preceding cost information and a target profit of $120,000 in developing a cost-based pricing formula. Selling and administrative expenses are not currently associated with individual products. However, you have obtained the following unit production cost information for the Tigershark Reel:

Variable manufacturing costs. . . .	$120
Fixed manufacturing costs.	60
Total	$180

Required

a. Determine the standard markup percentage for each of the following cost bases. Round answers to three decimal places.
   1. Full costs, including fixed and variable manufacturing costs, and fixed and variable selling and administrative costs.
   2. Manufacturing costs plus variable selling and administrative costs.
   3. Manufacturing costs.
   4. Variable costs.
   5. Variable manufacturing costs.

b. Explain why the markup percentages become progressively larger from requirement (a), parts (1) through (5).

c. Determine the initial price of a Tigershark Reel using the manufacturing cost markup and the variable manufacturing cost markup.

d. Do you believe the controller's approach to product pricing is reasonable? Why or why not?

CASES

C23-31. Telephone Pole Rental Rates (LO2, LO3)

Most utility poles carry electric and telephone lines. In areas served by cable television, they also carry television cables. However, cable television companies rarely own any utility poles. Instead, they pay utility companies a rental fee for the use of each pole on a yearly basis. The determination of the rental fee is a source of frequent disagreement between the pole owners and the cable television companies. In one situation, pole owners were arguing for a $7 annual rental fee per pole; this was the standard rate the electric and telephone companies charged each other for the use of poles.

"We object to that," stated the representative of the cable television company. "With two users, the $7 fee represents a rental fee for one-half the pole. This fee is too high because we only use about six inches of each 40-foot pole."

"You are forgetting federal safety regulations," responded a representative of the electric company. "They specify certain distances between different types of lines on a utility pole. Television cables must be a minimum of 40 inches below power lines and 12 inches above telephone lines. If your cable is added to the pole, the total capacity is reduced because this space cannot be used for anything else. Besides, we have an investment in the poles; you don't. We should be entitled to a fair return on this investment. Furthermore, speaking of fair, your company should pay the same rental fee that the telephone company pays us and we pay them. We do not intend to change this fee."

In response, the cable television company representative made two points. First, any fee represents incremental income to the pole owners because the cable company would pay all costs of moving existing lines. Second, because the electric and telephone companies both strive to own the same number of poles in a service area, their pole rental fees cancel themselves. Hence, the fee they charge each other is not relevant.

Required

Evaluate the arguments presented by the cable television and electric company representatives. What factors should be considered in determining a pole rental fee?

C23-32. Target Costing (LO3)

The president of Himatzi Electronics was pleased with the company's newest product, the HE Versatile CD. The product is portable and can be attached to a computer to play or record computer programs or sound, attached to an amplifier to play or record music, or attached to a television to play or record TV programs. It can even be attached to a camcorder to record videos directly on compact disks rather than on tape. It also can be used with a headset to play or record sound. The proud president announced that this unique and innovative product would be an important factor in reestablishing the North American consumer electronics industry.

Based on development costs and predictions of sales volume, manufacturing costs, and distribution costs, the cost-based price of the HE Versatile CD was determined to be $380. Following a market-skimming strategy, management set the initial selling price at $450. The marketing plan was to reduce the selling price by $50 during each of the first two years of the product's life to obtain the highest contribution possible from each market segment.

The initial sales of the HE Versatile CD were strong, and Himatzi Electronics found itself adding second and third production shifts. Although these shifts were expensive, at a selling price of $450, the product had ample contribution margin to remain highly profitable. The president was talking with the company's major investors about the desirability of obtaining financing for a major plant expansion when the bad news arrived. A foreign company had announced that it would shortly introduce a similar product that would incorporate new design features and sell for only $250. The president was shocked. "Why," she remarked, "it costs us $300 to put a complete unit in the hands of customers."

Required

How could the foreign competitor profitably sell a similar product for less than the manufacturing costs to Himatzi Electronics? What advice do you have for the president concerning the HE Versatile CD? What advice would you have to help the company avoid similar problems in the future?

C23-33. Target Pricing (LO3)

A few years ago, Marriott International, the large hotel chain, announced that because occupancy rates had declined during the previous quarter, it was raising room rates to cover the cost of its increase in vacant rooms. Although not referring to accounting or economics, several business journalists during the week following the announcement questioned the basis for the rate increases. One stated that "Marriott increases rates of vacant rooms."[16]

Required

a. Did the journalist mean that vacant rooms would be more expensive? Explain.
b. Do you think Marriott's action to raise room rates was based on economics, accounting, or both?

C23-34. Benchmarking (LO5)

"Rampant downsizing has been sweeping across most parts of Corporate America . . . producing huge layoffs and shutdowns of operations. Commercial banks, though, have been virtually immune. Despite numerous mergers and consolidations, bank employment has remained remarkably steady. And, even though electronic banking is expanding, bank branches, often regarded as relics of the past, have actually increased."[17] Presented is benchmark information on the number of bank employees per 1,000 people in various countries:

Germany	3.2
France	3.5
Japan	3.7
Canada	4.9
United States	5.8

Required

Based on this information, what conclusions can you draw concerning the relative efficiency and operating costs of U.S. commercial banks? Are you aware of any unique circumstances that might lead to these results? What do you predict will happen to employment at U.S. commercial banks during the next several years?

---

[16] "Marriott Increases Rates" *USA Today*, April 16, 2001, p. C1.

[17] Kelly Holland, "Blood on the Marble Floors," *Business Week*, February 27, 1995, p. 98.

Compound Interest Tables

| TABLE 1 | Present Value of Single Amount | | | | | | | | | | $p = 1/(1 + i)^t$ |

	Interest Rate											
Period	0.01	0.02	0.03	0.04	0.05	0.06	0.07	0.08	0.09	0.10	0.11	0.12
1	0.99010	0.98039	0.97087	0.96154	0.95238	0.94340	0.93458	0.92593	0.91743	0.90909	0.90090	0.89286
2	0.98030	0.96117	0.94260	0.92456	0.90703	0.89000	0.87344	0.85734	0.84168	0.82645	0.81162	0.79719
3	0.97059	0.94232	0.91514	0.88900	0.86384	0.83962	0.81630	0.79383	0.77218	0.75131	0.73119	0.71178
4	0.96098	0.92385	0.88849	0.85480	0.82270	0.79209	0.76290	0.73503	0.70843	0.68301	0.65873	0.63552
5	0.95147	0.90573	0.86261	0.82193	0.78353	0.74726	0.71299	0.68058	0.64993	0.62092	0.59345	0.56743
6	0.94205	0.88797	0.83748	0.79031	0.74622	0.70496	0.66634	0.63017	0.59627	0.56447	0.53464	0.50663
7	0.93272	0.87056	0.81309	0.75992	0.71068	0.66506	0.62275	0.58349	0.54703	0.51316	0.48166	0.45235
8	0.92348	0.85349	0.78941	0.73069	0.67684	0.62741	0.58201	0.54027	0.50187	0.46651	0.43393	0.40388
9	0.91434	0.83676	0.76642	0.70259	0.64461	0.59190	0.54393	0.50025	0.46043	0.42410	0.39092	0.36061
10	0.90529	0.82035	0.74409	0.67556	0.61391	0.55839	0.50835	0.46319	0.42241	0.38554	0.35218	0.32197
11	0.89632	0.80426	0.72242	0.64958	0.58468	0.52679	0.47509	0.42888	0.38753	0.35049	0.31728	0.28748
12	0.88745	0.78849	0.70138	0.62460	0.55684	0.49697	0.44401	0.39711	0.35553	0.31863	0.28584	0.25668
13	0.87866	0.77303	0.68095	0.60057	0.53032	0.46884	0.41496	0.36770	0.32618	0.28966	0.25751	0.22917
14	0.86996	0.75788	0.66112	0.57748	0.50507	0.44230	0.38782	0.34046	0.29925	0.26333	0.23199	0.20462
15	0.86135	0.74301	0.64186	0.55526	0.48102	0.41727	0.36245	0.31524	0.27454	0.23939	0.20900	0.18270
16	0.85282	0.72845	0.62317	0.53391	0.45811	0.39365	0.33873	0.29189	0.25187	0.21763	0.18829	0.16312
17	0.84438	0.71416	0.60502	0.51337	0.43630	0.37136	0.31657	0.27027	0.23107	0.19784	0.16963	0.14564
18	0.83602	0.70016	0.58739	0.49363	0.41552	0.35034	0.29586	0.25025	0.21199	0.17986	0.15282	0.13004
19	0.82774	0.68643	0.57029	0.47464	0.39573	0.33051	0.27651	0.23171	0.19449	0.16351	0.13768	0.11611
20	0.81954	0.67297	0.55368	0.45639	0.37689	0.31180	0.25842	0.21455	0.17843	0.14864	0.12403	0.10367
21	0.81143	0.65978	0.53755	0.43883	0.35894	0.29416	0.24151	0.19866	0.16370	0.13513	0.11174	0.09256
22	0.80340	0.64684	0.52189	0.42196	0.34185	0.27751	0.22571	0.18394	0.15018	0.12285	0.10067	0.08264
23	0.79544	0.63416	0.50669	0.40573	0.32557	0.26180	0.21095	0.17032	0.13778	0.11168	0.09069	0.07379
24	0.78757	0.62172	0.49193	0.39012	0.31007	0.24698	0.19715	0.15770	0.12640	0.10153	0.08170	0.06588
25	0.77977	0.60953	0.47761	0.37512	0.29530	0.23300	0.18425	0.14602	0.11597	0.09230	0.07361	0.05882
30	0.74192	0.55207	0.41199	0.30832	0.23138	0.17411	0.13137	0.09938	0.07537	0.05731	0.04368	0.03338
35	0.70591	0.50003	0.35538	0.25342	0.18129	0.13011	0.09366	0.06763	0.04899	0.03558	0.02592	0.01894
40	0.67165	0.45289	0.30656	0.20829	0.14205	0.09722	0.06678	0.04603	0.03184	0.02209	0.01538	0.01075

| TABLE 2 | Present Value of Ordinary Annuity | | | | | | | | | | $p = \{1 - [1/(1 + i)^t]\}/i$ |

	Interest Rate											
Period	0.01	0.02	0.03	0.04	0.05	0.06	0.07	0.08	0.09	0.10	0.11	0.12
1	0.99010	0.98039	0.97087	0.96154	0.95238	0.94340	0.93458	0.92593	0.91743	0.90909	0.90090	0.89286
2	1.97040	1.94156	1.91347	1.88609	1.85941	1.83339	1.80802	1.78326	1.75911	1.73554	1.71252	1.69005
3	2.94099	2.88388	2.82861	2.77509	2.72325	2.67301	2.62432	2.57710	2.53129	2.48685	2.44371	2.40183
4	3.90197	3.80773	3.71710	3.62990	3.54595	3.46511	3.38721	3.31213	3.23972	3.16987	3.10245	3.03735
5	4.85343	4.71346	4.57971	4.45182	4.32948	4.21236	4.10020	3.99271	3.88965	3.79079	3.69590	3.60478
6	5.79548	5.60143	5.41719	5.24214	5.07569	4.91732	4.76654	4.62288	4.48592	4.35526	4.23054	4.11141
7	6.72819	6.47199	6.23028	6.00205	5.78637	5.58238	5.38929	5.20637	5.03295	4.86842	4.71220	4.56376
8	7.65168	7.32548	7.01969	6.73274	6.46321	6.20979	5.97130	5.74664	5.53482	5.33493	5.14612	4.96764
9	8.56602	8.16224	7.78611	7.43533	7.10782	6.80169	6.51523	6.24689	5.99525	5.75902	5.53705	5.32825
10	9.47130	8.98259	8.53020	8.11090	7.72173	7.36009	7.02358	6.71008	6.41766	6.14457	5.88923	5.65022
11	10.36763	9.78685	9.25262	8.76048	8.30641	7.88687	7.49867	7.13896	6.80519	6.49506	6.20652	5.93770
12	11.25508	10.57534	9.95400	9.38507	8.86325	8.38384	7.94269	7.53608	7.16073	6.81369	6.49236	6.19437
13	12.13374	11.34837	10.63496	9.98565	9.39357	8.85268	8.35765	7.90378	7.48690	7.10336	6.74987	6.42355
14	13.00370	12.10625	11.29607	10.56312	9.89864	9.29498	8.74547	8.24424	7.78615	7.36669	6.98187	6.62817
15	13.86505	12.84926	11.93794	11.11839	10.37966	9.71225	9.10791	8.55948	8.06069	7.60608	7.19087	6.81086
16	14.71787	13.57771	12.56110	11.65230	10.83777	10.10590	9.44665	8.85137	8.31256	7.82371	7.37916	6.97399
17	15.56225	14.29187	13.16612	12.16567	11.27407	10.47726	9.76322	9.12164	8.54363	8.02155	7.54879	7.11963
18	16.39827	14.99203	13.75351	12.65930	11.68959	10.82760	10.05909	9.37189	8.75563	8.20141	7.70162	7.24967
19	17.22601	15.67846	14.32380	13.13394	12.08532	11.15812	10.33560	9.60360	8.95011	8.36492	7.83929	7.36578
20	18.04555	16.35143	14.87747	13.59033	12.46221	11.46992	10.59401	9.81815	9.12855	8.51356	7.96333	7.46944
21	18.85698	17.01121	15.41502	14.02916	12.82115	11.76408	10.83553	10.01680	9.29224	8.64869	8.07507	7.56200
22	19.66038	17.65805	15.93692	14.45112	13.16300	12.04158	11.06124	10.20074	9.44243	8.77154	8.17574	7.64465
23	20.45582	18.29220	16.44361	14.85684	13.48857	12.30338	11.27219	10.37106	9.58021	8.88322	8.26643	7.71843
24	21.24339	18.91393	16.93554	15.24696	13.79864	12.55036	11.46933	10.52876	9.70661	8.98474	8.34814	7.78432
25	22.02316	19.52346	17.41315	15.62208	14.09394	12.78336	11.65358	10.67478	9.82258	9.07704	8.42174	7.84314
30	25.80771	22.39646	19.60044	17.29203	15.37245	13.76483	12.40904	11.25778	10.27365	9.42691	8.69379	8.05518
35	29.40858	24.99862	21.48722	18.66461	16.37419	14.49825	12.94767	11.65457	10.56682	9.64416	8.85524	8.17550
40	32.83469	27.35548	23.11477	19.79277	17.15909	15.04630	13.33171	11.92461	10.75736	9.77905	8.95105	8.24378

TABLE 3	Future Value of Single Amount											$f = (1 + i)^t$

						Interest Rate						
Period	0.01	0.02	0.03	0.04	0.05	0.06	0.07	0.08	0.09	0.10	0.11	0.12
1	1.01000	1.02000	1.03000	1.04000	1.05000	1.06000	1.07000	1.08000	1.09000	1.10000	1.11000	1.12000
2	1.02010	1.04040	1.06090	1.08160	1.10250	1.12360	1.14490	1.16640	1.18810	1.21000	1.23210	1.25440
3	1.03030	1.06121	1.09273	1.12486	1.15763	1.19102	1.22504	1.25971	1.29503	1.33100	1.36763	1.40493
4	1.04060	1.08243	1.12551	1.16986	1.21551	1.26248	1.31080	1.36049	1.41158	1.46410	1.51807	1.57352
5	1.05101	1.10408	1.15927	1.21665	1.27628	1.33823	1.40255	1.46933	1.53862	1.61051	1.68506	1.76234
6	1.06152	1.12616	1.19405	1.26532	1.34010	1.41852	1.50073	1.58687	1.67710	1.77156	1.87041	1.97382
7	1.07214	1.14869	1.22987	1.31593	1.40710	1.50363	1.60578	1.71382	1.82804	1.94872	2.07616	2.21068
8	1.08286	1.17166	1.26677	1.36857	1.47746	1.59385	1.71819	1.85093	1.99256	2.14359	2.30454	2.47596
9	1.09369	1.19509	1.30477	1.42331	1.55133	1.68948	1.83846	1.99900	2.17189	2.35795	2.55804	2.77308
10	1.10462	1.21899	1.34392	1.48024	1.62889	1.79085	1.96715	2.15892	2.36736	2.59374	2.83942	3.10585
11	1.11567	1.24337	1.38423	1.53945	1.71034	1.89830	2.10485	2.33164	2.58043	2.85312	3.15176	3.47855
12	1.12683	1.26824	1.42576	1.60103	1.79586	2.01220	2.25219	2.51817	2.81266	3.13843	3.49845	3.89598
13	1.13809	1.29361	1.46853	1.66507	1.88565	2.13293	2.40985	2.71962	3.06580	3.45227	3.88328	4.36349
14	1.14947	1.31948	1.51259	1.73168	1.97993	2.26090	2.57853	2.93719	3.34173	3.79750	4.31044	4.88711
15	1.16097	1.34587	1.55797	1.80094	2.07893	2.39656	2.75903	3.17217	3.64248	4.17725	4.78459	5.47357
16	1.17258	1.37279	1.60471	1.87298	2.18287	2.54035	2.95216	3.42594	3.97031	4.59497	5.31089	6.13039
17	1.18430	1.40024	1.65285	1.94790	2.29202	2.69277	3.15882	3.70002	4.32763	5.05447	5.89509	6.86604
18	1.19615	1.42825	1.70243	2.02582	2.40662	2.85434	3.37993	3.99602	4.71712	5.55992	6.54355	7.68997
19	1.20811	1.45681	1.75351	2.10685	2.52695	3.02560	3.61653	4.31570	5.14166	6.11591	7.26334	8.61276
20	1.22019	1.48595	1.80611	2.19112	2.65330	3.20714	3.86968	4.66096	5.60441	6.72750	8.06231	9.64629
21	1.23239	1.51567	1.86029	2.27877	2.78596	3.39956	4.14056	5.03383	6.10881	7.40025	8.94917	10.80385
22	1.24472	1.54598	1.91610	2.36992	2.92526	3.60354	4.43040	5.43654	6.65860	8.14027	9.93357	12.10031
23	1.25716	1.57690	1.97359	2.46472	3.07152	3.81975	4.74053	5.87146	7.25787	8.95430	11.02627	13.55235
24	1.26973	1.60844	2.03279	2.56330	3.22510	4.04893	5.07237	6.34118	7.91108	9.84973	12.23916	15.17863
25	1.28243	1.64061	2.09378	2.66584	3.38635	4.29187	5.42743	6.84848	8.62308	10.83471	13.58546	17.00006
30	1.34785	1.81136	2.42726	3.24340	4.32194	5.74349	7.61226	10.06266	13.26768	17.44940	22.89230	29.95992
35	1.41660	1.99989	2.81386	3.94609	5.51602	7.68609	10.67658	14.78534	20.41397	28.10244	38.57485	52.79962
40	1.48886	2.20804	3.26204	4.80102	7.03999	10.28572	14.97446	21.72452	31.40942	45.25926	65.00087	93.05097

TABLE 4	Future Value of an Ordinary Annuity											$f = [(1 + i)^t - 1]/i$

						Interest Rate						
Period	0.01	0.02	0.03	0.04	0.05	0.06	0.07	0.08	0.09	0.10	0.11	0.12
1	1.00000	1.00000	1.00000	1.00000	1.00000	1.00000	1.00000	1.00000	1.00000	1.00000	1.00000	1.00000
2	2.01000	2.02000	2.03000	2.04000	2.05000	2.06000	2.07000	2.08000	2.09000	2.10000	2.11000	2.12000
3	3.03010	3.06040	3.09090	3.12160	3.15250	3.18360	3.21490	3.24640	3.27810	3.31000	3.34210	3.37440
4	4.06040	4.12161	4.18363	4.24646	4.31013	4.37462	4.43994	4.50611	4.57313	4.64100	4.70973	4.77933
5	5.10101	5.20404	5.30914	5.41632	5.52563	5.63709	5.75074	5.86660	5.98471	6.10510	6.22780	6.35285
6	6.15202	6.30812	6.46841	6.63298	6.80191	6.97532	7.15329	7.33593	7.52333	7.71561	7.91286	8.11519
7	7.21354	7.43428	7.66246	7.89829	8.14201	8.39384	8.65402	8.92280	9.20043	9.48717	9.78327	10.08901
8	8.28567	8.58297	8.89234	9.21423	9.54911	9.89747	10.25980	10.63663	11.02847	11.43589	11.85943	12.29969
9	9.36853	9.75463	10.15911	10.58280	11.02656	11.49132	11.97799	12.48756	13.02104	13.57948	14.16397	14.77566
10	10.46221	10.94972	11.46388	12.00611	12.57789	13.18079	13.81645	14.48656	15.19293	15.93742	16.72201	17.54874
11	11.56683	12.16872	12.80780	13.48635	14.20679	14.97164	15.78360	16.64549	17.56029	18.53117	19.56143	20.65458
12	12.68250	13.41209	14.19203	15.02581	15.91713	16.86994	17.88845	18.97713	20.14072	21.38428	22.71319	24.13313
13	13.80933	14.68033	15.61779	16.62684	17.71298	18.88214	20.14064	21.49530	22.95338	24.52271	26.21164	28.02911
14	14.94742	15.97394	17.08632	18.29191	19.59863	21.01507	22.55049	24.21492	26.01919	27.97498	30.09492	32.39260
15	16.09690	17.29342	18.59891	20.02359	21.57856	23.27597	25.12902	27.15211	29.36092	31.77248	34.40536	37.27971
16	17.25786	18.63929	20.15688	21.82453	23.65749	25.67253	27.88805	30.32428	33.00340	35.94973	39.18995	42.75328
17	18.43044	20.01207	21.76159	23.69751	25.84037	28.21288	30.84022	33.75023	36.97370	40.54470	44.50084	48.88367
18	19.61475	21.41231	23.41444	25.64541	28.13238	30.90565	33.99903	37.45024	41.30134	45.59917	50.39594	55.74971
19	20.81090	22.84056	25.11687	27.67123	30.53900	33.75999	37.37896	41.44626	46.01846	51.15909	56.93949	63.43968
20	22.01900	24.29737	26.87037	29.77808	33.06595	36.78559	40.99549	45.76196	51.16012	57.27500	64.20283	72.05244
21	23.23919	25.78332	28.67649	31.96920	35.71925	39.99273	44.86518	50.42292	56.76453	64.00250	72.26514	81.69874
22	24.47159	27.29898	30.53678	34.24797	38.50521	43.39229	49.00574	55.45676	62.87334	71.40275	81.21431	92.50258
23	25.71630	28.84496	32.45288	36.61789	41.43048	46.99583	53.43614	60.89330	69.53194	79.54302	91.14788	104.60289
24	26.97346	30.42186	34.42647	39.08260	44.50200	50.81558	58.17667	66.76476	76.78981	88.49733	102.17415	118.15524
25	28.24320	32.03030	36.45926	41.64591	47.72710	54.86451	63.24904	73.10594	84.70090	98.34706	114.41331	133.33387
30	34.78489	40.56808	47.57542	56.08494	66.43885	79.05819	94.46079	113.28321	136.30754	164.49402	199.02088	241.33268
35	41.66028	49.99448	60.46208	73.65222	90.32031	111.43478	138.23688	172.31680	215.71075	271.02437	341.58955	431.66350
40	48.88637	60.40198	75.40126	95.02552	120.79977	154.76197	199.63511	259.05652	337.88245	442.59256	581.82607	767.09142

Constructing the Statement of Cash Flows

LEARNING OBJECTIVES

LO1 Define and describe the framework for the statement of cash flows. (p. B-3)

LO2 Define and explain net cash flows from operating activities. (p. B-7)

LO3 Define and explain net cash flows from investing activities. (p. B-13)

LO4 Define and explain net cash flows from financing activities. (p. B-14)

LO5 Describe and apply ratios based on operating cash flows. (p. B-17)

STARBUCKS

Starbucks Corporation is the leading retailer, roaster, and brander of specialty coffee in the world. It has more than 7,100 company-owned retail locations in North America, Latin America, Europe, the Middle East, and the Pacific Rim. Starbucks sells high quality coffee and the "Starbucks Experience." It also produces and sells bottled Frappuccino® coffee drinks, Starbucks DoubleShot™ coffee drink, and a line of superpremium ice creams through its joint venture partnerships. Its Tazo Tea line of premium teas and Hear Music compact discs further add to its product offerings. Seattle's Best Coffee® and Torrefazione Italia® Coffee brands also help Starbucks appeal to a broader consumer base.

Starbucks' fiscal year 2006 resulted in $7.8 billion in total net revenues, a 22% year-over-year growth, and $564 million in net income, a 14% year-over-year growth. It also reported a 7% comparable store sales growth, which represents the 15th consecutive year of 5% or greater growth. This past year, Starbucks was recognized by *Fortune* magazine as number 5 on its list of America's Most Admired Companies and number 16 in its ranking of 100 Best Companies to Work For. Starbucks was also listed among *Business Ethics* magazine's 100 Best Corporate Citizens.

Product lines of the major U.S. brewed coffee sellers are well defined. On the high end there is Starbucks, with 7,728 U.S. locations. It has made its expensive cappuccinos, frappuccinos, espressos, and lattes part of the common lexicon. On the other end, there is Dunkin' Donuts, which has 4,400 stores. Dunkin' Donuts is the largest seller of regular, nonflavored brewed coffee in the U.S. fast-food outlets. It has an 18% market share, compared with 15% for McDonald's Corporation and 6% for Starbucks.

The Wall Street Journal recently reported that "there's a new brew-haha in Latte-land . . . Starbucks increasingly is looking for growth by opening stores in blue-collar communities where Dunkin' Donuts would typically dominate . . . At the same time, Dunkin' Donuts, a unit of United

Kingdom spirits group **Allied Domecq PLC**, wants to lure Starbucks' well-heeled customers with a new line of Italian brews that it claims it can deliver faster, cheaper and simpler."

Although competition exists, Starbucks' recent performance is difficult to top. In the last 13 years, Starbucks' sales have increased from $285 million to over nearly $8 billion and its income has increased from $29 million to $564 million. An investor purchasing its stock 10 years ago at a split-adjusted price of $3.76 would have seen its value grow to nearly $35 today.

During this same decade, Starbucks' net income and operating cash flows have increased by 10 times and 11 times, respectively. This is graphically portrayed as follows:

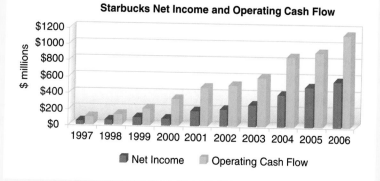

Both net income and operating cash flows are important in assessing the financial health of a company and its value. Starbucks is generating much more cash than it is reporting in income. Why is this? What does it mean? In this module, we describe the process of constructing the statement of cash flows. We also describe how we can use and interpret the statement of cash flows to aid both internal and external decisions.

Sources: Ball and Leung, "Latte Versus Latte—Starbucks, Dunkin' Donuts Seek Growth by Capturing Each Other's Customers," *The Wall Street Journal,* 10 February 2004; Starbucks 2003 through 2006 *Annual Reports* and *10-K Reports.*

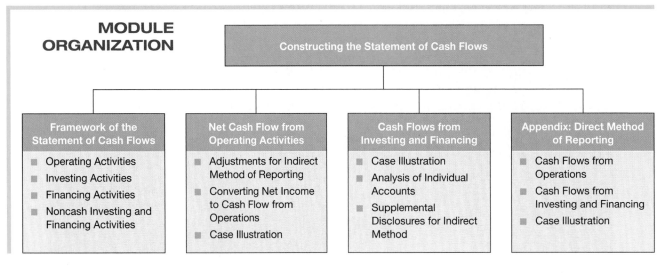

INTRODUCTION

The **statement of cash flows** is a financial statement that summarizes information about the flow of cash into and out of a company. In this appendix, we discuss the preparation, analysis, and interpretation of the statement of cash flows.

The statement of cash flows complements the balance sheet and the income statement. The balance sheet reports the company's financial position at a point in time (the end of each period) whereas the statement of cash flows explains the change in one of its components—cash—from one balance sheet date to the next. The income statement reveals the results of the company's operating activities for the period, and these operating activities are a major contributor to the change in cash as reported in the statement of cash flows.

The statement of cash flows explains the change in a firm's cash *and* cash equivalents. **Cash equivalents** are short-term, highly liquid investments that are (1) easily convertible into a known cash amount and (2) close enough to maturity so that their market value is not sensitive to interest rate changes (generally, investments with initial maturities of three months or less). Treasury bills, commercial paper (short-term notes issued by corporations), and money market funds are typical examples of cash equivalents.

When preparing a statement of cash flows, the cash and cash equivalents are added together and treated as a single sum. This is done because the purchase and sale of investments in cash equivalents are considered to be part of a firm's overall management of cash rather than a source or use of cash. As statement users evaluate and project cash flows, for example, it should not matter whether the cash is readily available, deposited in a bank account, or invested in cash equivalents. Transfers back and forth between a firm's cash account and its investments in cash equivalents, therefore, are not treated as cash inflows and cash outflows in its statement of cash flows.

When discussing the statement of cash flows, managers generally use the word *cash* rather than the term *cash and cash equivalents*. We will follow the same practice in this appendix.

FRAMEWORK FOR THE STATEMENT OF CASH FLOWS

LO1 Define and describe the framework for the statement of cash flows.

In analyzing the statement of cash flows, we must not necessarily conclude that the company is better off if cash increases and worse off if cash decreases. It is not the cash change that is most important, but the sources for that change. For example, what are the sources of cash inflows? Are these sources transitory? Are these sources mainly from operating activities?

We must also review the uses of cash. Has the company invested its cash in operating areas to strengthen its competitive position? Is it able to comfortably meet its debt obligations? Has it diverted cash to creditors or investors at the expense of the other? Such questions and answers are key to properly interpreting the statement of cash flows for business decisions.

The statement of cash flows classifies cash receipts and payments into one of three categories: operating activities, investing activities, or financing activities. Classifying cash flows into these categories identifies the effects on cash of each of the major activities of a firm. The combined effects on cash of all three categories explain the net change in cash for the period. The period's net change in cash is then reconciled with the beginning and ending amounts of cash.

Exhibit B.1 reproduces Starbucks' statement of cash flows ($ thousands). During 2006, Starbucks reported net income of $564.259 million and generated $1,131.633 million of cash from operating activities. The company used $841.040 million of cash for investing activities and $155.326 million of cash for financing activities. In sum, Starbucks increased its cash reserves by $138.797 million (including foreign exchange effects), from $173.809 million at the beginning of fiscal 2006 to $312.606 million at the end of fiscal 2006.

EXHIBIT B.1   Statement of Cash Flows for Starbucks

Consolidated Statements of Cash Flows
Fiscal Year Ended ($ thousands)

	Oct 1, 2006	Oct 2, 2005	Oct 3, 2004
Operating activities			
Net earnings	$ 564,259	$ 494,370	$ 388,880
Adjustments to reconcile net earnings to net cash provided by operating activities			
Cumulative effect accounting change for FIN 47, net of taxes	17,214	—	—
Depreciation and amortization	412,625	367,207	314,047
Provision for impairments and asset disposals	19,622	19,464	17,948
Deferred income taxes, net	(84,324)	(31,253)	(3,770)
Equity in income of investees	(60,570)	(49,537)	(31,707)
Distributions of income from equity investees	49,238	30,919	38,328
Stock-based compensation	105,664	—	—
Tax benefit from exercise of stock options	1,318	109,978	63,405
Excess tax benefit from exercise of stock options	(117,368)	—	—
Net amortization of premium on securities	2,013	10,097	11,603
Cash provided (used) by changes in operating assets and liabilities			
Inventories	(85,527)	(121,618)	(77,662)
Accounts payable	104,966	9,717	27,948
Accrued compensation and related costs	54,424	22,711	54,929
Accrued taxes	132,725	14,435	7,677
Deferred revenue	56,547	53,276	47,590
Other operating assets and liabilities	(41,193)	(6,851)	3,702
Net cash provided by operating activities	1,131,633	922,915	862,918
Investing activities			
Purchase of available-for-sale securities	(639,192)	(643,488)	(887,969)
Maturity of available-for-sale securities	269,134	469,554	170,789
Sale of available-for-sale securities	431,181	626,113	452,467
Acquisitions, net of cash acquired	(91,734)	(21,583)	(7,515)
Net purchases of equity, other investments and other assets	(39,199)	(7,915)	(64,747)
Net additions to property, plant, and equipment	(771,230)	(643,296)	(416,917)
Net cash used by investing activities	(841,040)	(220,615)	(753,892)
Financing activities			
Proceeds from issuance of common stock	159,249	163,555	137,590
Excess tax benefit from exercise of stock options	117,368	—	—
Net borrowing under revolving credit facility	423,000	277,000	—
Principal payments on long-term debt	(898)	(735)	(722)
Repurchase of common stock	(854,045)	(1,113,647)	(203,413)
Net cash used by financing activities	(155,326)	(673,827)	(66,545)
Effect of exchange rate changes on cash and cash equivalents	3,530	283	3,110
Net increase in cash and cash equivalents	138,797	28,756	45,591
Cash and cash equivalents			
Beginning of period	173,809	145,053	99,462
End of period	$ 312,606	$ 173,809	$ 145,053

Operating Activities

A company's income statement reflects primarily the transactions and events that constitute its operating activities. Generally, the cash effects of these operating transactions and events determine the net cash flow from operating activities. The usual focus of a firm's **operating activities** is on selling goods or rendering services, but the activities are defined broadly enough to include any cash receipts or payments that are not classified as investing or financing activities. For example, cash received from collection of receivables and cash payments to purchase inventories are treated as cash flows from operating activities. The following are examples of cash inflows and outflows relating to operating activities.

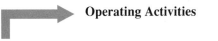

Operating Activities

Cash Inflows	**Cash Outflows**
1. Receipts from customers for sales made or services rendered.	1. Payments to employees or suppliers.
2. Receipts of interest and dividends.	2. Payments to purchase inventories.
3. Other receipts that are not related to investing or financing activities, such as lawsuit settlements and refunds received from suppliers.	3. Payments of interest to creditors.
	4. Payments of taxes to government.
	5. Other payments that are not related to investing or financing activities, such as contributions to charity.

Investing Activities

A firm's transactions involving (1) the acquisition and disposal of property, plant, and equipment (PPE) assets and intangible assets, (2) the purchase and sale of stocks, bonds, and other securities (that are not cash equivalents), and (3) the lending and subsequent collection of money constitute the basic components of its **investing activities**. The related cash receipts and payments appear in the investing activities section of the statement of cash flows. Examples of these cash flows follow.

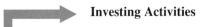

Investing Activities

Cash Inflows	**Cash Outflows**
1. Receipts from sales of property, plant, and equipment (PPE) assets and intangible assets.	1. Payments to purchase property, plant, and equipment (PPE) assets and intangible assets.
2. Receipts from sales of investments in stocks, bonds, and other securities (other than cash equivalents).	2. Payments to purchase stocks, bonds, and-other securities (other than cash equivalents).
3. Receipts from repayments of loans by borrowers.	3. Payments made to lend money to borrowers.

Financing Activities

A firm engages in **financing activities** when it obtains resources from owners, returns resources to owners, borrows resources from creditors, and repays amounts borrowed. Cash flows related to these transactions are reported in the financing activities section of the statement of cash flows. Examples of these cash flows follow.

Financing Activities

Cash Inflows	**Cash Outflows**
1. Receipts from issuances of common stock and preferred stock and from sales of treasury stock.	1. Payments to acquire treasury stock.
2. Receipts from issuances of bonds payable, mortgage notes payable, and other notes payable.	2. Payments of dividends.
	3. Payments to settle outstanding bonds payable, mortgage notes payable, and other notes payable.

Paying cash to settle such obligations as accounts payable, wages payable, interest payable, and income tax payable are operating activities, not financing activities. Also, cash received as interest and dividends and cash paid as interest (but not as dividends) are classified as cash flows from operating activities.

Usefulness of Classifications

The classification of cash flows into three categories of activities helps financial statement users interpret cash flow data. To illustrate, assume that companies D, E, and F are similar companies operating in the same industry. Each company reports a $100,000 cash increase during the current year. Information from their statements of cash flows is summarized below.

	Company D	Company E	Company F
Net cash provided by operating activities	$100,000	$ 0	$ 0
Cash flows from investing activities			
Sale of property, plant, and equipment (PPE).	0	100,000	0
Cash flows from financing activities			
Issuance of notes payable	0	0	100,000
Net increase in cash.	$100,000	$100,000	$100,000

Although each company's net cash increase was the same, the source of the increase varied by company. This variation affects the analysis of the cash flow data, particularly for potential short-term creditors who must evaluate the likelihood of obtaining repayment in the future for any funds loaned to the company. Based only on these cash flow data, a potential creditor would feel more comfortable lending money to D than to either E or F. This is because D's cash increase came from its operating activities, whereas both E and F could only break even on their cash flows from operations. Also, E's cash increase came from the sale of property, plant, and equipment (PPE) assets, a source that is not likely to recur regularly. F's cash increase came entirely from borrowed funds. This means F faces additional cash burdens in the future when the interest and principal payments on the note payable become due.

Noncash Investing and Financing Activities

Another objective of cash flow reporting is to present summary information about a firm's investing and financing activities. Of course, many of these activities affect cash and are therefore already included in the investing and financing sections of the statement of cash flows. Some significant investing and financing events, however, do not affect current cash flows. Examples of **noncash investing and financing activities** are the issuance of stocks, bonds, or leases in exchange for property, plant, and equipment (PPE) assets or intangible assets; the exchange of long-term assets for other long-term assets; and the conversion of long-term debt into common stock. Information about these events must be reported as a supplement to the statement of cash flows.

Noncash investing and financing transactions generally do affect *future* cash flows. Issuing bonds payable to acquire equipment, for example, requires future cash payments for interest and principal on the bonds. On the other hand, converting bonds payable into common stock eliminates future cash payments related to the bonds. Knowledge of these types of events, therefore, is helpful to users of cash flow data who wish to assess a firm's future cash flows.

Information on noncash investing and financing transactions is disclosed in a schedule that is separate from the statement of cash flows. The separate schedule either is reported immediately below the statement of cash flows, or is reported among the notes to the financial statements.

BUSINESS INSIGHT   **Objectivity of Cash**

Usefulness of financial statements is enhanced when the underlying data are objective and verifiable. Measuring cash and the changes in cash are among the most objective measurements that accountants make. Thus, the statement of cash flows is arguably the most objective financial statement. This characteristic of the statement of cash flows is welcomed by those investors and creditors interested in evaluating the quality of a firm's income.

Usefulness of the Statement of Cash Flows

A statement of cash flows shows the periodic cash effects of a firm's operating, investing, and financing activities. Distinguishing among these different categories of cash flows helps users compare, evaluate, and predict cash flows. With cash flow information, creditors and investors are better able to assess a firm's ability to settle its liabilities and pay its dividends. A firm's need for outside financing is also better evaluated when using cash flow data. Over time, the statement of cash flows permits users to observe and access management's investing and financing policies.

A statement of cash flows also provides information useful in evaluating a firm's financial flexibility. *Financial flexibility* is a firm's ability to generate sufficient amounts of cash to respond to unanticipated needs and opportunities. Information about past cash flows, particularly cash flows from operations, helps in assessing financial flexibility. An evaluation of a firm's ability to survive an unexpected drop in demand, for example, should include a review of its past cash flows from operations. The larger these cash flows, the greater is the firm's ability to withstand adverse changes in economic conditions. Other financial statements, particularly the balance sheet and its notes, also contain information useful for judging financial flexibility.

Some investors and creditors find the statement of cash flows useful in evaluating the quality of a firm's income. As we know, determining income under accrual accounting procedures requires many accruals, deferrals, allocations, and valuations. These adjustment and measurement procedures introduce more subjectivity into income determination than some financial statement users prefer. These users relate a more objective performance measure—cash flow from operations—to net income. To these users, the higher this ratio is, the higher is the quality of income.

NET CASH FLOW FROM OPERATING ACTIVITIES

LO2 Define and explain net cash flows from operating activities.

The first section of a statement of cash flows presents a firm's net cash flow from operating activities. Two alternative formats are used to report the net cash flow from operating activities: the *indirect method* and the *direct method. Both methods report the same amount of net cash flow from operating activities.* (Net cash flows from investing and financing activities are prepared in the same manner under both the indirect and direct methods; only the format for cash flows from operating activities differs.)

Indirect Method of Reporting

The *indirect method* starts with net income and applies a series of adjustments to net income to convert it to a cash-basis income number, which is the net cash flow from operating activities. The adjustments to net income do not represent specific cash flows, however, so the indirect method does not report any detail concerning individual operating cash inflows and outflows. In contrast, the *direct method* shows individual amounts of cash inflows and cash outflows for the major operating activities. The net difference between these inflows and outflows is the net cash flow from operating activities.

BUSINESS INSIGHT	Comparison of Accrual and Cash-Basis Amounts

Accountants compute net income, shown on the income statement, using accrual accounting procedures. The net cash flow from operating activities may be larger, smaller, or about the same amount. Financial data from recent annual reports of three companies bear this out.

	Net Income or (Loss)	Net Cash Provided (Used) by Operating Activities
Ford Motor Company....	$(7,091) million	$21,728 million
Lucent	527 million	(478) million
Home Depot	6,169 million	6,494 million

Accountants estimate that *more than 98% of companies preparing the statement of cash flows use the indirect method.* The indirect method is popular because (1) it is easier and less expensive to prepare than the direct method and (2) the direct method requires a supplemental disclosure showing the indirect method (thus, essentially reporting both methods).

The remainder of this appendix discusses the preparation of the statement of cash flows. The indirect method is presented in this section, and the direct method is presented in Appendix B1. (These discussions are independent of each other; both provide complete coverage of the preparation of the statement of cash flows.)

To prepare a statement of cash flows, we need a firm's income statement, comparative balance sheets, and some additional data taken from the accounting records. Exhibit B.2 presents this information for **Java House**. We use these data to prepare Java's 2007 statement of cash flows using the indirect method. Java's statement of cash flows explains the $25,000 increase in cash that occurred during 2007 (from $10,000 to $35,000) by classifying the firm's cash flows into operating, investing, and financing categories. To get the information to construct the statement we do the following:

1. **Use the indirect method to determine the net cash flow from operating activities.** We apply a series of adjustments to the firm's net income. The adjustments include changes in various current asset and current liability accounts.

2. **Determine cash flows from investing activities.** We do this by analyzing changes in noncurrent asset accounts.

3. **Determine cash flows from financing activities.** We do this by analyzing changes in liability and equity accounts.

EXHIBIT B.2	Financial Data of Java House

JAVA HOUSE Income Statement For Year Ended December 31, 2007		
Sales..............		$250,000
Cost of goods sold....	$148,000	
Wages expense	52,000	
Insurance expense....	5,000	
Depreciation expense..	10,000	
Income tax expense...	11,000	
Gain on sale of land ...	(8,000)	218,000
Net income..........		$ 32,000

Additional Data for 2007

1. Purchased all long-term stock investments for cash at year-end.
2. Sold land costing $20,000 for $28,000 cash.
3. Acquired $60,000 patent at year-end by issuing common stock at par.
4. All accounts payable relate to merchandise purchases.
5. Issued common stock at par for $10,000 cash.
6. Declared and paid cash dividends of $13,000.

JAVA HOUSE Balance Sheet	Dec. 31, 2007	Dec. 31, 2006
Assets		
Cash..................	$ 35,000	$ 10,000
Accounts receivable........	39,000	34,000
Inventory................	54,000	60,000
Prepaid insurance.........	17,000	4,000
Long-term investments	15,000	—
PPE assets..............	180,000	200,000
Accumulated depreciation ...	(50,000)	(40,000)
Patent..................	60,000	—
Total assets..............	$350,000	$268,000
Liabilities and Equity		
Accounts payable.........	$ 10,000	$ 19,000
Income tax payable	5,000	3,000
Common stock............	260,000	190,000
Retained earnings	75,000	56,000
Total liabilities and equity....	$350,000	$268,000

The **indirect method** presents the net cash flow from operating activities by applying a series of adjustments to net income to convert it to a cash-basis amount. The adjustment amounts represent differences between revenues, expenses, gains, and losses recorded under accrual accounting and the related operating cash inflows and outflows. The adjustments are added to or subtracted from net income, depending on whether the related cash flow is more or less than the accrual amount. Exhibit B.3 portrays this process.

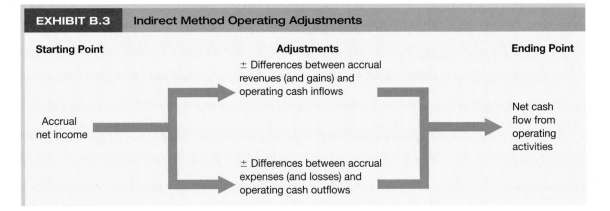

EXHIBIT B.3   Indirect Method Operating Adjustments

Starting Point	Adjustments	Ending Point
Accrual net income	± Differences between accrual revenues (and gains) and operating cash inflows ± Differences between accrual expenses (and losses) and operating cash outflows	Net cash flow from operating activities

Converting Net Income to Net Cash Flow from Operating Activities

Exhibit B.4 summarizes the adjustments to net income in determining operating cash flows. These are the adjustments applied under the indirect method of computing cash flow from operations.

EXHIBIT B.4	**Converting Net Income to Net Cash Flow from Operating Activities**
	Add (+) or Subtract (−) from Net Income
Net income	$ #
Add depreciation	+
Add (subtract): Losses (gains) on asset and liability dispositions	±
Adjust for changes in current assets	
Subtract increases in current assets	−
Add decreases in current assets..	+
Adjust for changes in current liabilities	
Add increases in current liabilities..	+
Subtract decreases in current liabilities	−
Net cash flow from operating activities	$ #

Net income is first adjusted for noncash expenses such as depreciation, amortization, and gains (losses) from asset and liability dispositions and is then adjusted for changes in current assets and current liabilities to yield net cash flow from operating activities, or cash profit. The depreciation adjustment merely zeros out depreciation expense, a noncash expense, which is deducted in computing net income. The following table provides brief explanations of adjustments for receivables, inventories, payables and accruals:

	Change in account balance . . .	Means that . . .	Which requires this adjustment to net income to yield cash profit . . .
Receivables	Increase	Sales and net income increase, but cash is not yet received	Deduct increase in receivables from net income
	Decrease	More cash is received than is reported in sales and net income	Add decrease in receivables to net income
Inventories	Increase	Cash is paid for inventories that are not yet reflected in cost of goods sold	Deduct increase in inventories from net income
	Decrease	Cost of goods sold includes inventory costs that were paid for in a prior period	Add decrease in inventories to net income

Continued

continued

	Change in account balance . . .	Means that . . .	Which requires this adjustment to net income to yield cash profit . . .
Payables and accruals	Increase	More goods and services are acquired on credit, delaying cash payment	Add increase in payables and accruals to net income
	Decrease	More cash is paid than that reflected in cost of goods sold or operating expenses	Deduct decrease in payables and accruals from net income

It is also helpful to use the following decision guide, involving changes in assets, liabilities, and equity, to understand increases and decreases in cash flows.

	Cash flow increases from	Cash flow decreases from
Assets.	Account decreases	Account increases
Liabilities and equity.	Account increases	Account decreases

Using this decision guide we can determine the cash flow effects of the income statement and balance sheet information and categorize them into operating, investing or financing.

Java House Case Illustration

We next explain these adjustments and illustrate them with Java House's data from Exhibit B.2.

Depreciation, Amortization, and Depletion Expenses

Depreciation, amortization, and depletion expenses represent write-offs of previously recorded assets; so-called noncash expenses. Because depreciation, amortization, and depletion expenses are subtracted in computing net income, we add these expenses to net income as we convert it to a related net operating cash flow. Adding these expenses to net income eliminates them from the income statement and is a necessary adjustment to obtain cash income. Java House had $10,000 of 2007 depreciation expense, so this amount is added to Java's net income of $32,000.

Net income.	$32,000
Add: Depreciation.	**10,000**

Gains and Losses Related to Investing or Financing Activities

The income statement may contain gains and losses that relate to investing or financing activities. Gains and losses from the sale of investments, PPE assets, or intangible assets illustrate gains and losses from investing (not operating) activities. A gain or loss from the retirement of bonds payable is an example of a financing gain or loss. The full cash flow effect from these types of events is reported in the investing or financing sections of the statement of cash flows. Therefore, the related gains or losses must be eliminated as we convert net income to net cash flow from operating activities. To eliminate their impact on net income, gains are subtracted and losses are added to net income. Java House had an $8,000 gain from the sale of land in 2007. This gain relates to an investing activity, so it is subtracted from Java's net income.

Net income.	$32,000
Add: Depreciation.	10,000
Deduct: Gain on sale of land	**(8,000)**

Accounts Receivable Change

Credit sales increase accounts receivable; cash collections on account decrease accounts receivable. If, overall, accounts receivable decrease during a year, then cash collections from customers exceed credit sales revenue by the amount of the decrease. Because sales are added in computing net income, the decrease in accounts receivable is added to net income. In essence, this adjustment replaces the sales amount with the larger amount of cash collections from customers. If accounts receivable increase during a year, then sales revenue exceeds the cash collections from customers by the amount of the increase. Because sales are added in computing net income, the increase in accounts receivable is subtracted from net income as we convert it to a net cash flow from operating activities. In essence, this adjustment replaces the sales amount with the smaller amount of cash collections from customers. Java's accounts receivable increased $5,000 during 2007, so this increase is subtracted from net income under the indirect method.

Net income.	$32,000
Add: Depreciation.	10,000
Deduct: Gain on sale of land	(8,000)
Deduct: Accounts receivable increase.	**(5,000)**

Inventory Change

The adjustment for an inventory change is one of two adjustments to net income that together cause the cost of goods sold expense to be replaced by an amount representing the cash paid during the period for merchandise purchased. The second adjustment, which we examine shortly, is for the change in accounts payable. The effect of the inventory adjustment alone is to adjust net income for the difference between the cost of goods sold and the cost of merchandise purchased during the period. The cost of merchandise purchased increases inventory; the cost of goods sold decreases inventory. An overall decrease in inventory during a period must mean, therefore, that the cost of merchandise purchased was less than the cost of goods sold by the amount of the decrease. Because cost of goods sold was subtracted in computing net income, the inventory decrease is added to net income. After this adjustment, the effect of the cost of goods sold on net income has been replaced by the smaller cost of merchandise purchased. Similarly, if inventory increased during a period, the cost of merchandise purchased is larger than the cost of goods sold by the amount of the increase. To replace the cost of goods sold with the cost of merchandise purchased, the inventory increase is subtracted from net income. Java's inventory decreased $6,000 during 2007, so this decrease is added to net income.

Net income.	$32,000
Add: Depreciation.	10,000
Deduct: Gain on sale of land	(8,000)
Deduct: Accounts receivable increase.	(5,000)
Add: Inventory decrease	**6,000**

Prepaid Expenses Change

Cash prepayments of various expenses increase a firm's prepaid expenses. When the related expenses for the period are subsequently recorded, the prepaid expenses decrease. An overall decrease in prepaid expenses for a period means that the cash prepayments were less than the related expenses. Because the expenses were subtracted in determining net income, the indirect method adds the decrease in prepaid expenses to net income as it is converted to a cash flow amount. The effect of the addition is to replace the expense amount with the smaller cash payment amount. Similarly, an increase in prepaid expenses is subtracted from net income because an increase means that the cash prepayments during the year were more than the related expenses. Java's prepaid insurance increased $13,000 during 2007, so this increase is deducted from net income.

Net income.	$32,000
Add: Depreciation.	10,000
Deduct: Gain on sale of land	(8,000)
Deduct: Accounts receivable increase.	(5,000)
Add: Inventory decrease	6,000
Deduct: Prepaid insurance increase.	**(13,000)**

Accounts Payable Change

When merchandise is purchased on account, accounts payable increase by the amount of the goods' cost. Accounts payable decrease when cash payments are made to settle the accounts. An overall decrease in accounts payable during a year means that cash payments for purchases were more than the cost of the purchases. An accounts payable decrease, therefore, is subtracted from net income under the indirect method. The deduction, in effect, replaces the cost of merchandise purchased with the larger cash payments for merchandise purchased. (Recall that the earlier inventory adjustment replaced the cost of goods sold with the cost of merchandise purchased.) In contrast, an increase in accounts payable means that cash payments for purchases were less than the cost of purchases for the period. Thus, an accounts payable increase is added to net income as it is converted to a cash flow amount. Java House shows a $9,000 decrease in accounts payable during 2007. This decrease is subtracted from net income.

Net income	$32,000
Add: Depreciation	10,000
Deduct: Gain on sale of land	(8,000)
Deduct: Accounts receivable increase	(5,000)
Add: Inventory decrease	6,000
Deduct: Prepaid insurance increase	(13,000)
Deduct: Accounts payable decrease	**(9,000)**

Accrued Liabilities Change

Changes in accrued liabilities are interpreted the same way as changes in accounts payable. A decrease means that cash payments exceeded the related expense amounts; an increase means that cash payments were less than the related expenses. Decreases are subtracted from net income; increases are added to net income. Java has one accrued liability, income tax payable, and it increased by $2,000 during 2007. The $2,000 increase is added to net income.

Net income	$32,000
Add: Depreciation	10,000
Deduct: Gain on sale of land	(8,000)
Deduct: Accounts receivable increase	(5,000)
Add: Inventory decrease	6,000
Deduct: Prepaid insurance increase	(13,000)
Deduct: Accounts payable decrease	(9,000)
Add: Income tax payable increase	**2,000**

We have now identified the adjustments to convert Java's net income to its net cash flow from operating activities. The operating activities section of the statement of cash flows appears as follows under the indirect method:

Net income	$32,000
Add (deduct) items to convert net income to cash basis:	
Depreciation	10,000
Gain on sale of land	(8,000)
Accounts receivable increase	(5,000)
Inventory decrease	6,000
Prepaid insurance increase	(13,000)
Accounts payable decrease	(9,000)
Income tax payable increase	2,000
Net cash provided by operating activities	$15,000

To summarize, net cash flows from operating activities begins with net income (loss) and eliminates non-cash expenses (such as depreciation) and any gains and losses that are properly reported in the investing and financing sections. Next, cash inflows (outflows) relating to changes in the level of current operating assets and liabilities are added (subtracted) to yield net cash flows from operating activities. During the period, Java earned cash operating profits of \$34,000 (\$32,000 + \$10,000 − \$8,000), but used \$19,000 of cash (−\$5,000 + \$6,000 − \$13,000 − \$9,000 + \$2,000) to increase net working capital. Cash outflows relating to the increase in net working capital are a common occurrence for growing companies, and this net asset increase must be financed just like the increase in PPE assets.

BUSINESS INSIGHT   **Starbucks' Add-Backs for Operating Cash Flow**

Starbucks reports \$564.259 million of net income for 2006 and \$1,131.633 million of operating cash inflows. The difference between these numbers is mainly due to \$412.625 million of depreciation expense that is included in net income. Depreciation is a noncash charge; an expense not requiring cash payment. It is added back to income in computing operating cash flows. Starbucks also reports a \$19.622 million asset impairment (write-down). This, too, is a noncash charge and is an addback in computing operating cash flows. Starbucks subtracts \$84.324 million for deferred taxes, indicating that cash payments of taxes are greater than tax expense reported in income (this is due to increased deferred tax assets). It also subtracts \$60.570 million for equity in income of investees, meaning that it reported equity income that it did not receive in cash in the form of dividends (see Module 7). Starbucks also adds back its \$105.664 million of stock option expense since that compensation is paid in stock, not in cash, and reclassifies the \$117.368 million of tax benefits it receives for the exercise of these options from operating activities to financing activities as required under current GAAP.

MANAGERIAL DECISION   **You Are the Securities Analyst**

You are analyzing a company's statement of cash flows. The company has two items relating to its accounts receivable. First, the company finances the sale of its products to some customers; the increase to notes receivable is classified as an investing activity. Second, the company sells its accounts receivable to a separate entity, such as a trust. As a result, sale of receivables is reported as an asset sale; this reduces receivables and yields a gain or loss on sale (in this case, the company is not required to consolidate the trust as a Primary Beneficiary of a Variable Interest Entity—see Module 9). This action increases its operating cash flows. How should you interpret this cash flow increase?
[Answer, p. B-26]

CASH FLOWS FROM INVESTING ACTIVITIES

Analyze Remaining Noncash Assets

LO3 Define and explain net cash flows from investing activities.

Investing activities cause changes in asset accounts. Usually the accounts affected (other than cash) are noncurrent asset accounts such as property, plant and equipment assets and long-term investments, although short-term investment accounts can also be affected. To determine the cash flows from investing activities, *we analyze changes in all noncash asset accounts not used in computing net cash flow from operating activities.* Our objective is to identify any investing cash flows related to these changes.

Java House Case Illustration

Analyze Change in Long-Term Investments

Java's comparative balance sheets show that long-term investments increased \$15,000 during 2007. The increase means that investments must have been purchased, and the additional data reported indicates that cash was spent to purchase long-term stock investments. Purchasing stock is an investing activity. Thus, a \$15,000 purchase of stock investments is reported as a cash outflow from investing activities in the statement of cash flows.

Analyze Change in Property, Plant and Equipment Assets

Java's PPE assets decreased \$20,000 during 2007. PPE assets decrease as the result of disposals, and the additional data for Java House indicate that land was sold for cash in 2007. Selling land is an investing activity. Thus, the sale of land for $28,000 is reported as a cash inflow from investing activities in the statement of cash flows. (Recall that the $8,000 gain on sale of land was deducted as a reconciling item in the operating section; see above)

Analyze Change in Accumulated Depreciation

Java's accumulated depreciation increased $10,000 during 2007. Accumulated depreciation increases when depreciation expense is recorded. Java's 2007 depreciation expense was $10,000, so the total change in accumulated depreciation is the result of the recording of depreciation expense. As previously discussed, there is no cash flow related to the recording of depreciation expense, and we have previously adjusted for this expense in our computation of net cash flows from operating activities.

Analyze Change in Patent

We see from the comparative balance sheets that Java had an increase of $60,000 in a patent. The increase means that a patent was acquired, and the additional data indicate that common stock was issued to obtain a patent. This event is a noncash investing (acquiring a patent) and financing (issuing common stock) transaction that must be disclosed as supplementary information to the statement of cash flows.

BUSINESS INSIGHT   **Starbucks' Investing Activities**

Starbucks used $841.040 million cash for investing activities in 2006. Of this, $61.123 million ($431.181 million + $269.134 million − $639.192 million) is related to the purchase of securities. Investing activities are not necessarily related to operating activities (such as purchases of PPE assets). Starbucks also spent $91.734 million on acquisitions of other companies; which is the cash portion of the acquisition cost. It might also have issued debt and stock to finance this acquisition, which would be excluded from this statement and would be identified as noncash financing and investing activities in a footnote. Starbucks invested $771.230 million in property, plant, and equipment (PPE). These expenditures might have been for owned property or for leasehold improvements on leased property. It also spent $39.199 million on other investments.

CASH FLOWS FROM FINANCING ACTIVITIES

Analyze Remaining Liabilities and Equity

Financing activities cause changes in liability and stockholders' equity accounts. Usually the accounts affected are noncurrent accounts such as bonds payable and common stock, although a current liability such as short-term notes payable can also be affected. To determine the cash flows from financing activities, *we analyze changes in all liability and stockholders' equity accounts that were not used in computing net cash flow from operating activities.* Our objective is to identify any financing cash flows related to these changes.

LO4 Define and explain net cash flows from financing activities.

Java House Case Illustration

Analyze Change in Common Stock

Java's common stock increased $70,000 during 2007. Common stock increases when shares of stock are issued. As noted in discussing the patent increase, common stock with a $60,000 par value was issued in exchange for a patent. This event is disclosed as a noncash investing and financing transaction. The other $10,000 increase in common stock, as noted in the additional data, resulted from an issuance of stock for cash. Issuing common stock is a financing activity, so a $10,000 cash inflow from a stock issuance appears as a financing activity in the statement of cash flows.

Analyze Change in Retained Earnings

Retained earnings grew from $56,000 to $75,000 during 2007—a $19,000 increase. This increase is the net result of Java's $32,000 of net income (which increased retained earnings) and a $13,000 cash dividend (which decreased retained earnings). Because every item in Java's income statement was considered in computing the net cash provided by operating activities, only the cash dividend remains to be considered. Paying a cash dividend is a financing activity. Thus, a $13,000 cash dividend appears as a cash outflow from financing activities in the statement of cash flows. We have now completed the analysis of all of Java's noncash balance sheet accounts and can prepare the 2007 statement of cash flows. Exhibit B.5 shows this statement.

If there are cash inflows and outflows from similar types of investing and financing activities, the inflows and outflows are reported separately (rather than reporting only the net difference). For example, proceeds from the sale of plant assets are reported separately from outlays made to acquire plant assets. Similarly, funds borrowed are reported separately from debt repayments, and proceeds from issuing stock are reported separately from outlays to acquire treasury stock.

BUSINESS INSIGHT **Starbucks' Financing Activities**

Starbucks realized cash *outflows* of $694.796 million ($159.249 million − $854.045 million) from issuance of common stock, net of repurchases. Only stock issued for cash is reflected in the statement of cash flows. Stock issued in connection with acquisitions is not reflected because it does not involve cash. Issuance of stock is often related to the exercise of employee stock options, and companies frequently repurchase stock to offset the dilution. Starbucks also reports a cash inflow of $423 million from borrowings during the year and a cash outflow of approximately $0.9 million relating to the repayment of long-term debt. The net effect is a decrease in cash of $155.326 million from financing activities.

SUMMARY OF NET CASH FLOW REPORTING

Preparation of the statement of cash flows draws mainly on information from the income statement and the balance sheet. Each of its three sections uses different portions of these two statements as highlighted in bold font as follows:

	Information from income statement	Information from balance sheet	
Net cash flows from operating activities. . . .	Revenues − Expenses = Net income	**Current assets** Long-term assets	**Current liabilities** Long-term liabilities Equity
Net cash flows from investing activities	Revenues − Expenses = Net income	Current assets **Long-term assets**	Current liabilities Long-term liabilities Equity
Net cash flows from financing activities. . . .	Revenues − Expenses = Net income	Current assets Long-term assets	Current liabilities **Long-term liabilities** **Equity**

Specifically, the three sections draw generally on the following information:

- **Net cash flows from operating activities** draws on the income statement and the current asset and current liabilities sections of the balance sheet
- **Net cash flows from investing activities** draws on the long-term assets section of the balance sheet
- **Net cash flows from financing activities** draws on the long-term liabilities and stockholders' equity sections of the balance sheet.

These relations do not hold exactly, but they provide us a useful way to visualize the construction of the statement of cash flows.

We now summarize the cash flow effects of the income statement and balance sheet information we developed on previous pages, and categorize them into the operating, investing and financing classifications in the following table:

Account	Change	Source or Use	Cash flow effect	Classification on SCF
Current assets				
Accounts receivable	+5,000	Use	−5,000	Operating
Inventories	−6,000	Source	+6,000	Operating
Prepaid insurance.	+13,000	Use	−13,000	Operating
Noncurrent assets				
PPE related.				Investing
Accumulated depreciation . . .	+10,000	Neither	+10,000	Operating
Sale of land				
Proceeds	+28,000	Source	+28,000	Investing
Gain	−8,000	Neither	−8,000	Operating
Investments	+15,000	Use	−15,000	Investing
Current liabilities				
Accounts payable.	−9,000	Use	−9,000	Operating
Income tax payable	+2,000	Source	+2,000	Operating
Long-term liabilities				Financing
Stockholders' equity				
Common stock	+10,000	Source	+10,000	Financing
Retained earnings.				
Net income	+32,000	Source	+32,000	Operating
Dividends	+13,000	Use	−13,000	Financing
Total (net cash flow)			+25,000	

The current year's cash balance increases by $25,000, from $10,000 to $35,000. Formal preparation of the statement of cash flows can proceed once we have addressed one final issue: required supplemental disclosures. We discuss that topic in the next section.

Supplemental Disclosures for Indirect Method

When the indirect method is used in the statement of cash flows, three separate disclosures are required: (1) two specific operating cash outflows—cash paid for interest and cash paid for income taxes, (2) a schedule or description of all noncash investing and financing transactions, and (3) the firm's policy for determining which highly liquid, short-term investments are treated as cash equivalents. A firm's policy regarding cash equivalents is placed in the financial statement notes. The other two separate disclosures are reported either in the notes or at the bottom of the statement of cash flows.

Java House Case Illustration

Java House incurred no interest cost during 2007. It did pay income taxes. Our discussion of the $2,000 change in income tax payable during 2007 revealed that the increase meant that cash tax payments were less than income tax expense by the amount of the increase. Income tax expense was $11,000, so the cash paid for income taxes was $2,000 less than $11,000, or $9,000.

Java House did have one noncash investing and financing event during 2007: the issuance of common stock to acquire a patent. This event, as well as the cash paid for income taxes, is disclosed as supplemental information to the statement of cash flows in Exhibit B.5.

EXHIBIT B.5	Statement of Cash Flows for Indirect Method with Supplemental Disclosures

JAVA HOUSE
Statement of Cash Flows
For Year Ended December 31, 2007

Net cash flow from operating activities		
Net income	$32,000	
Add (deduct) items to convert net income to cash basis		
Depreciation.	10,000	
Gain on sale of land	(8,000)	
Accounts receivable increase	(5,000)	
Inventory decrease.	6,000	
Prepaid insurance increase	(13,000)	
Accounts payable decrease.	(9,000)	
Income tax payable increase	2,000	
Net cash provided by operating activities		$15,000
Cash flows from investing activities		
Purchase of stock investments	(15,000)	
Sale of land	28,000	
Net cash provided by investing activities		13,000
Cash flows from financing activities		
Issuance of common stock	10,000	
Payment of dividends	(13,000)	
Net cash used by financing activities		(3,000)
Net increase in cash		25,000
Cash at beginning of year		10,000
Cash at end of year		$35,000
Supplemental cash flow disclosures		
Cash paid for income taxes.		$ 9,000
Schedule of noncash investing and financing activities		
Issuance of common stock to acquire patent		$60,000

Ratio Analyses of Cash Flows

LO5 Describe and apply ratios based on operating cash flows.

Data from the statement of cash flows enter into various financial ratios. Two such ratios are the operating cash flow to current liabilities ratio and the operating cash flow to capital expenditures ratio.

Operating Cash Flow to Current Liabilities Ratio

Two measures previously introduced—the current ratio and the quick ratio—emphasize the relation of current assets to current liabilities in an attempt to measure the ability of the firm to liquidate current liabilities when they become due. The **operating cash flow to current liabilities ratio** is another measure of the ability to liquidate current liabilities and is calculated as follows:

Operating Cash Flow to Current Liabilities = Net Cash Flow from Operating Activities/Average Current Liabilities

Net cash flow from operating activities is obtained from the statement of cash flows; it represents the excess amount of cash derived from operations during the year after deducting working capital needs and payments required on current liabilities. The denominator is the average of the beginning and ending current liabilities for the year.

To illustrate, the following amounts are taken from the 2006 financial statements for Cisco Systems, Inc.

Net cash flow from operating activities	$ 7,899 million
Current liabilities at beginning of the year	9,511 million
Current liabilities at end of the year	11,313 million

Its operating cash flow to current liabilities ratio of 0.76 is computed as follows:

$$\text{\$7,899 million ([\$9,511 million} + \text{\$11,313 million]/2)} = 0.76$$

Cisco's operating cash flow to current liabilities ratio for the preceding year was 0.83. The higher this ratio, the stronger is a firm's ability to settle current liabilities as they come due. The decrease in Cisco's ratio from 0.83 to 0.76 is unfavorable, although relatively minor. A ratio of 0.5 is considered a good ratio, so, Cisco's ratio of 0.76 is above average.

Operating Cash Flow to Capital Expenditures Ratio

To remain competitive, an entity must be able to replace, and expand when appropriate, its property, plant, and equipment. A ratio that helps assess a firm's ability to do this from internally generated cash flow is the **operating cash flow to capital expenditures ratio**, which is computed as follows:

Operating Cash Flow to Capital Expenditures = Net Cash Flow from Operating Activities/Annual Capital Expenditures

The numerator in this ratio comes from the first section of the statement of cash flows—the section reporting the net cash flow from operating activities. Information for the denominator can be found in one or more places in the financial statements and related disclosures. Data on capital expenditures are part of the required industry segment disclosures in notes to the financial statements. Capital expenditures are often also shown in the investing activities section of the statement of cash flows. Also, capital expenditures often appear in the comparative selected financial data presented as supplementary information to the financial statements. Finally, management's discussion and analysis of the statements commonly identify the annual capital expenditures.

A ratio in excess of 1.0 means that the firm's current operating activities are providing cash in excess of the amount needed to provide the desired level of plant capacity and would normally be considered a sign of financial strength. This ratio is also viewed as an indicator of long-term solvency—a ratio exceeding 1.0 means that there is operating cash flow in excess of capital needs that can then be used to repay outstanding long-term debt.

The interpretation of this ratio for a firm is influenced by its trend in recent years, the ratio size being achieved by other firms in the same industry, and the stage of the firm's life cycle. A firm in the early stages of its life cycle, when periods of rapid expansion occur, is expected to experience a lower ratio than a firm in the mature stage of its life cycle, when maintenance of plant capacity is more likely than expansion of capacity.

To illustrate the ratio's computation, Cicso Systems reported capital expenditures in 2006 of $772 million. Cisco's operating cash flow to capital expenditures ratio for that same year is 10.23, computed as $7,899 million/$772 million. Following are recent operating cash flow to capital expenditures ratios for several companies:

Colgate-Palmolive (consumer grocery products).	4.59
Lockheed Martin (aerospace).	3.69
Verizon Communications (telecommunications)	1.44
Harley-Davidson (motorcycle manufacturer)	4.84
Home Depot (home products).	1.67

APPENDIX-END REVIEW

Part A

1. Which of the following is not disclosed in a statement of cash flows?
   a. A transfer of cash to a cash equivalent investment
   b. The amount of cash at year-end
   c. Cash outflows from investing activities during the period
   d. Cash inflows from financing activities during the period
2. Which of the following events appears in the cash flows from investing activities section of the statement of cash flows?
   a. Cash received as interest
   b. Cash received from issuance of common stock
   c. Cash purchase of equipment
   d. Cash payment of dividends

3. Which of the following events appears in the cash flows from financing activities section of the statement of cash flows?
   a. Cash purchase of equipment
   b. Cash purchase of bonds issued by another company
   c. Cash received as repayment for funds loaned
   d. Cash purchase of treasury stock

4. Tyler Company has a net income of $49,000 and the following related items:

Depreciation expense.	$ 5,000
Accounts receivable increase.	2,000
Inventory decrease.	10,000
Accounts payable decrease.	4,000

   Using the indirect method, what is Tyler's net cash flow from operations?

   a. $42,000   b. $46,000   c. $58,000   d. $38,000

Solution
1. a   2. c   3. d   4. c

Part B

Expresso Royale's income statement and comparative balance sheets follow:

EXPRESSO ROYALE
Income Statement
For Year Ended December 31, 2007

Sales.		$385,000
Dividend income.		5,000
		390,000
Cost of goods sold.	$233,000	
Wages expense	82,000	
Advertising expense.	10,000	
Depreciation expense.	11,000	
Income tax expense.	17,000	
Loss on sale of investments.	2,000	355,000
Net income.		$ 35,000

EXPRESSO ROYALE
Balance Sheets

	Dec. 31, 2007	Dec. 31, 2006
Assets		
Cash.	$ 8,000	$ 12,000
Accounts receivable.	22,000	28,000
Inventory.	94,000	66,000
Prepaid advertising.	12,000	9,000
Long-term investments—Available-for-sale.	30,000	41,000
Fair value adjustment to investments.	—	(1,000)
Plant assets	178,000	130,000
Accumulated depreciation	(72,000)	(61,000)
Total assets.	$272,000	$224,000

Continued

EXPRESSO ROYALE
Balance Sheets

	Dec. 31, 2007	Dec. 31, 2006
Liabilities and Equity		
Accounts payable...........................	$ 27,000	$ 14,000
Wages payable............................	6,000	2,500
Income tax payable	3,000	4,500
Common stock............................	139,000	125,000
Retained earnings	97,000	79,000
Unrealized loss on investments	—	(1,000)
Total liabilities and equity	$272,000	$224,000

Cash dividends of $17,000 were declared and paid during 2007. Plant assets were purchased for cash in 2007, and, later in the year, additional common stock was issued for cash. Investments costing $11,000 were sold for cash at a $2,000 loss in 2007; an unrealized loss of $1,000 on these investments had been recorded in 2006 (at December 31, 2007, the cost and fair value of unsold investments are equal).

Required

a. Compute the change in cash that occurred during 2007.

b. Prepare a 2007 statement of cash flows using the indirect method.

Solution

a. $8,000 ending balance − $12,000 beginning balance = $4,000 decrease in cash

b. (1) Use the indirect method to determine the net cash flow from operating activities.

  • Adjustments to convert Expresso Royale's net income of $35,000 to a net cash provided by operating activities of $38,000 are shown in the following statement of cash flows.

  (2) Analyze changes in remaining noncash asset (and contra asset) accounts to determine cash flows from investing activities.

  • Long-Term Investments: $11,000 decrease resulted from sale of investments for cash at a $2,000 loss. Cash received from sale of investments = $9,000 ($11,000 cost − $2,000 loss).

  • Fair Value Adjustment to Investments: $1,000 decrease resulted from the elimination of this account balance (and the Unrealized Loss of Investments) at the end of 2007. No cash flow effect.

  • Plant Assets: $48,000 increase resulted from purchase of plant assets for cash. Cash paid to purchase plant assets = $48,000.

  • Accumulated Depreciation: $11,000 increase resulted from the recording of 2007 depreciation. No cash flow effect.

  (3) Analyze changes in remaining liability and stockholders' equity accounts to determine cash flows from financing activities.

  • Common Stock: $14,000 increase resulted from the issuance of stock for cash. Cash received from issuance of common stock = $14,000.

  • Retained Earnings: $18,000 increase resulted from net income of $35,000 and dividend declaration of $17,000. Cash dividends paid = $17,000.

  • Unrealized Loss on Investments: $1,000 decrease resulted from the elimination of this account balance (and the Fair Value Adjustment to Investments) at the end of 2007. No cash flow effect.

The statement of cash flows follows:

EXPRESSO ROYALE
Statement of Cash Flows
For Year Ended December 31, 2007

Net cash flow from operating activities

Net income..............................	$35,000	
Add (deduct) items to convert net income to cash basis		
Depreciation	11,000	
Loss on sale of investments.................	2,000	
Accounts receivable decrease	6,000	
Inventory increase........................	(28,000)	
Prepaid advertising increase................	(3,000)	
Accounts payable increase.................	13,000	
Wages payable increase...................	3,500	
Income tax payable decrease...............	(1,500)	
Net cash provided by operating activities		$38,000
Cash flows from investing activities		
Sale of investments	9,000	
Purchase of plant assets	(48,000)	
Net cash used by investing activities............		(39,000)
Cash flows from financing activities		
Issuance of common stock..................	14,000	
Payment of dividends......................	(17,000)	
Net cash used by financing activities............		(3,000)
Net decrease in cash		(4,000)
Cash at beginning of year		12,000
Cash at end of year		$ 8,000

APPENDIX B1: Direct Method Reporting for the Statement of Cash Flows

To prepare a statement of cash flows, we need a firm's income statement, comparative balance sheets, and some additional data taken from the accounting records. Exhibit B.2 presents this information for Java House. We use these data to prepare Java's 2007 statement of cash flows using the direct method. Java's statement of cash flows explains the $25,000 increase in cash that occurred during 2007 (from $10,000 to $35,000) by classifying the firm's cash flows into operating, investing, and financing categories. To get the information to construct the statement, we do the following:

1. **Use the direct method to determine individual cash flows from operating activities.** We use changes that occurred during 2007 in various current asset and current liability accounts.
2. **Determine cash flows from investing activities.** We do this by analyzing changes in noncurrent asset accounts.
3. **Determine cash flows from financing activities.** We do this by analyzing changes in liability and stockholders' equity accounts.

The net cash flows from investing and financing are identical to those prepared using the indirect method. Only the format of the net cash flows from operating activities differs between the two methods, not the total amount of cash generated from operating activities.

Cash Flows from Operating Activities

The **direct method** presents net cash flow from operating activities by showing the major categories of operating cash receipts and payments. The operating cash receipts and payments are usually determined by converting the accrual revenues and expenses to corresponding cash amounts. It is efficient to do it this way because the accrual revenues and expenses are readily available in the income statement.

Converting Revenues and Expenses to Cash Flows

Exhibit B.6 summarizes the procedures for converting individual income statement items to corresponding cash flows from operating activities.

EXHIBIT B.6	Adjustments to Convert Income Statement Items to Operating Activity Cash Flows

Income Statement Item	Adjustment	Operating Activity Cash Flow
Sales	+ Decrease in accounts receivable *or* − Increase in accounts receivable	= Receipts from customers
Cost of goods sold	+ Increase in inventory *or* − Decrease in inventory **and** + Decrease in accounts payable *or* − Increase in accounts payable	= Payments for merchandise
Operating expenses Interest expense Income tax expense (excluding items listed below)	+ Increase in related prepaid expense *or* − Decrease in related prepaid expense **and** + Decrease in related accrued liability *or* − Increase in related accrued liability	= Payments for expenses
Depreciation expense Depletion expense Amortization expense	+ Depreciation expense + Depletion expense + Amortization expense	= 0
Gains (investing and financing) Losses (investing and financing)	Exclude: Not related to cash from operating activities	= 0

Java House Case Illustration

We next explain and illustrate the process of converting Java House's 2007 revenues and expenses to corresponding cash flows from operating activities under the direct method.

Convert Sales to Cash Received from Customers

During 2007, accounts receivable increased $5,000. This increase means that during 2007, cash collections on account (which decrease accounts receivable) were less than credit sales (which increase accounts receivable). We compute cash received from customers as follows (this computation assumes that no accounts were written off as uncollectible during the period):

	Sales	$250,000
−	Increase in accounts receivable	(5,000)
=	Cash received from customers	$245,000

Convert Cost of Goods Sold to Cash Paid for Merchandise Purchased

The conversion of cost of goods sold to cash paid for merchandise purchased is a two-step process. First, cost of goods sold is adjusted for the change in inventory to determine the amount of purchases during the year. Then the purchases amount is adjusted for the change in accounts payable to derive the cash paid for merchandise purchased. Inventory decreased from \$60,000 to \$54,000 during 2007. This \$6,000 decrease indicates that the cost of goods sold exceeded the cost of goods purchased during the year. The year's purchases amount is computed as follows:

	Cost of goods sold	\$148,000
−	Decrease in inventory	(6,000)
=	Purchases	\$142,000

During 2007, accounts payable decreased \$9,000. This decrease reflects the fact that cash payments for merchandise purchased on account (which decrease accounts payable) exceeded purchases on account (which increase accounts payable). The cash paid for merchandise purchased, therefore, is computed as follows:

	Purchases	\$142,000
+	Decrease in accounts payable	9,000
=	Cash paid for merchandise purchased	\$151,000

Convert Wages Expense to Cash Paid to Employees

No adjustment to wages expense is needed. The absence of any beginning or ending accrued liability for wages payable means that wages expense and cash paid to employees as wages are the same amount: \$52,000.

Convert Insurance Expense to Cash Paid for Insurance

Prepaid insurance increased \$13,000 during 2007. The \$13,000 increase reflects the excess of cash paid for insurance during 2007 (which increases prepaid insurance) over the year's insurance expense (which decreases prepaid insurance). Starting with insurance expense the cash paid for insurance is computed as follows:

	Insurance expense	\$ 5,000
+	Increase in prepaid insurance	13,000
=	Cash paid for insurance	\$18,000

Eliminate Depreciation Expense and Other Noncash Operating Expenses

Depreciation expense is a noncash expense. Because it does not represent a cash payment, depreciation expense is eliminated (by adding it back) as we convert accrual expense amounts to the corresponding amounts of cash payments. If Java House had any amortization expense or depletion expense, it would eliminate them for the same reason. The amortization of an intangible asset and the depletion of a natural resource are noncash expenses.

Convert Income Tax Expense to Cash Paid for Income Taxes

The increase in income tax payable from \$3,000 at December 31, 2006, to \$5,000 at December 31, 2007, means that 2007's income tax expense (which increases income tax payable) was \$2,000 more than 2007's tax payments (which decrease income tax payable). If we start with income tax expense, then we calculate cash paid for income taxes as follows:

	Income tax expense	\$11,000
−	Increase in income tax payable	(2,000)
=	Cash paid for income taxes	\$ 9,000

Omit Gains and Losses Related to Investing and Financing Activities

The income statement may contain gains and losses related to investing or financing activities. Examples include gains and losses from the sale of plant assets and gains and losses from the retirement of bonds payable. Because these gains and losses are not related to operating activities, we omit them as we convert income statement items to various cash flows from operating activities. The cash flows relating to these gains and losses are reported in the investing activities or financing activities sections of the statement of cash flows. Java House had an $8,000 gain from the sale of land in 2007. This gain is excluded; no related cash flow appears within the operating activities category.

We have now applied the adjustments to convert each accrual revenue and expense to the corresponding operating cash flow. We use these individual cash flows to prepare the operating activities section of the statement of cash flows; see Exhibit B.7

EXHIBIT B.7	Direct Method Operating Section of Statement of Cash Flows		
Cash received from customers			$245,000
Cash paid for merchandise purchased		$151,000	
Cash paid to employees.		52,000	
Cash paid for insurance		18,000	
Cash paid for income taxes		9,000	230,000
Net cash provided by operating activities			$ 15,000

Cash Flows from Investing and Financing

The reporting of investing and financing activities in the statement of cash flows is identical under the indirect and direct methods. Thus, we simply refer to the previous sections in Appendix B for explanations.

Supplemental Disclosures

When the direct method is used for the statement of cash flows, three separate disclosures are required: (1) a reconciliation of net income to the net cash flow from operating activities, (2) a schedule or description of all noncash investing and financing transactions, and (3) the firm's policy for determining which highly liquid, short-term investments are treated as cash equivalents. The firm's policy regarding cash equivalents is placed in the financial statement notes. The other two separate disclosures are reported either in the notes or at the bottom of the statement of cash flows.

The required reconciliation is essentially the indirect method of computing cash flow from operating activities. *Thus, when the direct method is used in the statement of cash flows, the indirect method is a required separate disclosure.* We discussed the indirect method earlier in this appendix.

Java House did have one noncash investing and financing event during 2007: the issuance of common stock to acquire a patent. This event is disclosed as supplemental information to the statement of cash flows in Exhibit B.5.

APPENDIX-END REVIEW

Expresso Royale's income statement and comparative balance sheets follow:

EXPRESSO ROYALE Income Statement For Year Ended December 31, 2007		
Sales.		$385,000
Dividend income.		5,000
		390,000
Cost of goods sold.	$233,000	
Wages expense	82,000	
Advertising expense.	10,000	
Depreciation expense.	11,000	
Income tax expense.	17,000	
Loss on sale of investments.	2,000	355,000
Net income.		$ 35,000

EXPRESSO ROYALE
Balance Sheets

	Dec. 31, 2007	Dec. 31, 2006
Assets		
Cash	$ 8,000	$ 12,000
Accounts receivable	22,000	28,000
Inventory	94,000	66,000
Prepaid advertising	12,000	9,000
Long-term investments—Available-for-sale	30,000	41,000
Fair value adjustment to investments	—	(1,000)
Plant assets	178,000	130,000
Accumulated depreciation	(72,000)	(61,000)
Total assets	$272,000	$224,000
Liabilities and Equity		
Accounts payable	$ 27,000	$ 14,000
Wages payable	6,000	2,500
Income tax payable	3,000	4,500
Common stock	139,000	125,000
Retained earnings	97,000	79,000
Unrealized loss on investments	—	(1,000)
Total liabilities and equity	$272,000	$224,000

Cash dividends of $17,000 were declared and paid during 2007. Plant assets were purchased for cash in 2007, and later in the year, additional common stock was issued for cash. Investments costing $11,000 were sold for cash at a $2,000 loss in 2007; an unrealized loss of $1,000 on these investments had been recorded in 2006 (at December 31, 2007, the cost and fair value of unsold investments are equal).

Required

a. Compute the change in cash that occurred during 2007.
b. Prepare a 2007 statement of cash flows using the direct method.

Solution

a. $8,000 ending balance − $12,000 beginning balance = $4,000 decrease in cash
b. (1) Use the direct method to determine the individual cash flows from operating activities.
   - $385,000 sales + $6,000 accounts receivable decrease = $391,000 cash received from customers
   - $5,000 dividend income = $5,000 cash received as dividends
   - $233,000 cost of goods sold + $28,000 inventory increase − $13,000 accounts payable increase = $248,000 cash paid for merchandise purchased
   - $82,000 wages expense − $3,500 wages payable increase = $78,500 cash paid to employees
   - $10,000 advertising expense + $3,000 prepaid advertising increase = $13,000 cash paid for advertising
   - $17,000 income tax expense + $1,500 income tax payable decrease = $18,500 cash paid for income taxes
   (2) Analyze changes in remaining noncash asset (and contra asset) accounts to determine cash flows from investing activities.
   - Long-term investments: $11,000 decrease resulted from sale of investments for cash at a $2,000 loss. Cash received from sale of investments = $9,000 ($11,000 cost − $2,000 loss).
   - Fair value adjustment to investments: $1,000 decrease resulted from the elimination of this account balance (and the unrealized loss on investments) at the end of 2007. No cash flow effect.
   - Plant assets: $48,000 increase resulted from purchase of plant assets for cash. Cash paid to purchase plant assets = $48,000.
   - Accumulated depreciation: $11,000 increase resulted from the recording of 2007 depreciation. No cash flow effect.

(3) Analyze changes in remaining liability and stockholders' equity accounts to determine cash flows from financing activities.

- Common stock: $14,000 increase resulted from the issuance of stock for cash. Cash received from issuance of common stock = $14,000.
- Retained earnings: $18,000 increase resulted from net income of $35,000 and dividend declaration of $17,000. Cash dividends paid = $17,000.
- Unrealized loss on investments: $1,000 decrease resulted from the elimination of this account balance (and the fair value adjustment to investments) at the end of 2007. No cash flow effect.

The statement of cash flows under the direct method follows:

EXPRESSO ROYALE
Statement of Cash Flows
For Year Ended December 31, 2007

Cash flows from operating activities		
Cash received from customers...............	$391,000	
Cash received as dividends	5,000	
Cash paid for merchandise purchased.........	(248,000)	
Cash paid to employees.....................	(78,500)	
Cash paid for advertising	(13,000)	
Cash paid for income taxes	(18,500)	
Net cash provided by operating activities		$ 38,000
Cash flows from investing activities		
Sale of investments	9,000	
Purchase of plant assets	(48,000)	
Net cash used by investing activities		(39,000)
Cash flows from financing activities		
Issuance of common stock...................	14,000	
Payment of dividends.......................	(17,000)	
Net cash used by financing activities...........		(3,000)
Net decrease in cash		(4,000)
Cash at beginning of year		12,000
Cash at end of year		$ 8,000

GUIDANCE ANSWERS

MANAGERIAL DECISION   **You Are the Securities Analyst**

Many companies, but not all, treat customers' notes receivable as an investing activity. In 2005, the SEC became concerned with this practice and issued letters to a number of companies objecting to this accounting classification. "Presenting cash receipts from receivables generated by the sale of inventory as investing activities in the company's consolidated statements of cash flows is not in accordance with GAAP," wrote the chief accountant for the SEC's division of corporation finance, in her letter to the companies ("Little Campus Lab Shakes Big Firms—Georgia Tech Crew's Report Spurs Change in Accounting for Operating Cash Flow," March 1, 2005, *The Wall Street Journal*). The SEC's position is that these notes receivable are an operating activity and analysts are certainly justified in treating them likewise. Concerning the sale of receivables, so long as the separate entity (a Trust in this case) is properly structured, the transaction can be treated as a sale (rather than require consolidation) with a consequent reduction in receivables and a gain or loss on the sale recorded in the income statement. Many analysts treat this as a financing activity and argue that the cash inflow should not be regarded as an increase in operating cash flows. Bottom line: many argue that operating cash flows do not increase as a result of these two transactions and analysts should adjust the statement of cash flows to properly classify the financing of receivables as an operating activity and the sale of receivables as a financing activity.

Superscript ^{B1} denotes assignments based on Appendix B1.

DISCUSSION QUESTIONS

Q B-1. What is the definition of *cash equivalents?* Give three examples of cash equivalents.

Q B-2. Why are cash equivalents included with cash in a statement of cash flows?

Q B-3. What are the three major types of activities classified on a statement of cash flows? Give an example of a cash inflow and a cash outflow in each classification.

Q B-4. In which of the three activity categories of a statement of cash flows would each of the following items appear? Indicate for each item whether it represents a cash inflow or a cash outflow:

   a. Cash purchase of equipment.

   b. Cash collection on loans.

   c. Cash dividends paid.

   d. Cash dividends received.

   e. Cash proceeds from issuing stock.

   f. Cash receipts from customers.

   g. Cash interest paid.

   h. Cash interest received.

Q B-5. Traverse Company acquired a $3,000,000 building by issuing $3,000,000 worth of bonds payable. In terms of cash flow reporting, what type of transaction is this? What special disclosure requirements apply to a transaction of this type?

Q B-6. Why are noncash investing and financing transactions disclosed as supplemental information to a statement of cash flows?

Q B-7. Why is a statement of cash flows a useful financial statement?

Q B-8. What is the difference between the direct method and the indirect method of presenting net cash flow from operating activities?

Q B-9. In determining net cash flow from operating activities using the indirect method, why must we add depreciation back to net income? Give an example of another item that is added back to net income under the indirect method.

Q B-10. Vista Company sold for $98,000 cash land originally costing $70,000. The company recorded a gain on the sale of $28,000. How is this event reported in a statement of cash flows using the indirect method?

Q B-11. A firm uses the indirect method. Using the following information, what is its net cash flow from operating activities?

Net income.	$88,000
Accounts receivable decrease	13,000
Inventory increase	9,000
Accounts payable decrease.	3,500
Income tax payable increase	1,500
Depreciation expense.	6,000

Q B-12. What separate disclosures are required for a company that reports a statement of cash flows using the indirect method?

Q B-13. If a business had a net loss for the year, under what circumstances would the statement of cash flows show a positive net cash flow from operating activities?

Q B-14.^{B1} A firm is converting its accrual revenues to corresponding cash amounts using the direct method. Sales on the income statement are $925,000. Beginning and ending accounts receivable on the balance sheet are $58,000 and $44,000, respectively. What is the amount of cash received from customers?

Q B-15.^{B1} A firm reports $86,000 wages expense in its income statement. If beginning and ending wages payable are $3,900 and $2,800, respectively, what is the amount of cash paid to employees?

Q B-16.^{B1} A firm reports $43,000 advertising expense in its income statement. If beginning and ending prepaid advertising are $6,000 and $7,600, respectively, what is the amount of cash paid for advertising?

Q B-17.^{B1} Rusk Company sold equipment for $5,100 cash that had cost $35,000 and had $29,000 of accumulated depreciation. How is this event reported in a statement of cash flows using the direct method?

Q B-18.[B1] What separate disclosures are required for a company that reports a statement of cash flows using the direct method?

Q B-19. How is the operating cash flow to current liabilities ratio calculated? Explain its use.

Q B-20. How is the operating cash flow to capital expenditures ratio calculated? Explain its use.

Q B-21. The statement of cash flows provides information that may be useful in predicting future cash flows, evaluating financial flexibility, assessing liquidity, and identifying financing needs. It is not, however, the best financial statement for learning about a firm's financial performance during a period; information about periodic financial performance is provided by the income statement. Two basic principles—the revenue recognition principle and the matching concept—work to distinguish the income statement from the statement of cash flows. (a) Define the revenue recognition principle and the matching concept. (b) Briefly explain how these two principles work to make the income statement a better report on periodic financial performance than the statement of cash flows.

MINI EXERCISES

M B-22. Classification of Cash Flows **(LO1)**

For each of the items below, indicate whether the cash flow relates to an operating activity, an investing activity, or a financing activity.
a. Cash receipts from customers for services rendered.
b. Sale of long-term investments for cash.
c. Acquisition of plant assets for cash.
d. Payment of income taxes.
e. Bonds payable issued for cash.
f. Payment of cash dividends declared in previous year.
g. Purchase of short-term investments (not cash equivalents) for cash.

M B-23. Classification of Cash Flows **(LO1)**

For each of the items below, indicate whether it is (1) a cash flow from an operating activity, (2) a cash flow from an investing activity, (3) a cash flow from a financing activity, (4) a noncash investing and financing activity, or (5) none of the above.
a. Paid cash to retire bonds payable at a loss.
b. Received cash as settlement of a lawsuit.
c. Acquired a patent in exchange for common stock.
d. Received advance payments from customers on orders for custom-made goods.
e. Gave large cash contribution to local university.
f. Invested cash in 60-day commercial paper (a cash equivalent).

M B-24. Net Cash Flow from Operating Activities (Indirect Method) **(LO2)**

The following information was obtained from Galena Company's comparative balance sheets. Assume that Galena Company's 2007 income statement showed depreciation expense of $8,000, a gain on sale of investments of $9,000, and a net income of $45,000. Calculate the net cash flow from operating activities using the indirect method.

	Dec. 31, 2007	Dec. 31, 2006
Cash	$ 19,000	$ 9,000
Accounts receivable	44,000	35,000
Inventory	55,000	49,000
Prepaid rent	6,000	8,000
Long-term investments	21,000	34,000
Plant assets	150,000	106,000
Accumulated depreciation	40,000	32,000
Accounts payable	24,000	20,000
Income tax payable	4,000	6,000
Common stock	121,000	92,000
Retained earnings	106,000	91,000

M B-25. Net Cash Flow from Operating Activities (Indirect Method)   **(LO2)**

Cairo Company had a $21,000 net loss from operations for 2007. Depreciation expense for 2007 was $8,600 and a 2007 cash dividend of $6,000 was declared and paid. Balances of the current asset and current liability accounts at the beginning and end-of 2007 follow. Did Cairo Company's 2007 operating activities provide or use cash? Use the indirect method to determine your answer.

	Ending	Beginning
Cash.	$ 3,500	$ 7,000
Accounts receivable.	16,000	25,000
Inventory.	50,000	53,000
Prepaid expenses.	6,000	9,000
Accounts payable.	12,000	8,000
Accrued liabilities	5,000	7,600

M B-26.[B1] **Operating Cash Flows (Direct Method)**   **(LO2)**

Calculate the cash flow for each of the following cases.

a.   Cash paid for rent:

Rent expense	$60,000
Prepaid rent, beginning year	10,000
Prepaid rent, end of year	8,000

b.   Cash received as interest:

Interest income.	$16,000
Interest receivable, beginning year. . . .	3,000
Interest receivable, end of year	3,700

c.   Cash paid for merchandise purchased:

Cost of goods sold.	$98,000
Inventory, beginning year	19,000
Inventory, end of year.	22,000
Accounts payable, beginning year. . . .	11,000
Accounts payable, end of year.	7,000

M B-27.[B1] **Operating Cash Flows (Direct Method)**   **(LO2)**

Howell Company's current year income statement reports the following:

Sales.	$825,000
Cost of goods sold.	550,000
Gross profit.	$275,000

Howell's comparative balance sheets show the following (accounts payable relate to merchandise purchases):

	End of Year	Beginning of Year
Accounts receivable.........	$ 71,000	$60,000
Inventory..................	109,000	96,000
Prepaid expenses...........	3,000	8,000
Accounts payable...........	31,000	37,000

Compute Howell's current-year cash received from customers and cash paid for merchandise purchased.

EXERCISES

E B-28. Net Cash Flow from Operating Activities (Indirect Method) (LO2)

Lincoln Company owns no plant assets and reported the following income statement for the current year:

Sales..........................		$750,000
Cost of goods sold..............	$470,000	
Wages expense	110,000	
Rent expense...................	42,000	
Insurance expense..............	15,000	637,000
Net income.....................		$113,000

Additional balance sheet information about the company follows:

	End of Year	Beginning of Year
Accounts receivable.........	$54,000	$49,000
Inventory..................	60,000	66,000
Prepaid insurance...........	8,000	7,000
Accounts payable...........	22,000	18,000
Wages payable.............	9,000	11,000

Use the information to calculate the net cash flow from operating activities under the indirect method.

E B-29. Statement of Cash Flows (Indirect Method) (LO2, 3, 4)

Use the following information about Lund Corporation for 2007 to prepare a statement of cash flows under the indirect method.

Accounts payable increase	$ 9,000
Accounts receivable increase......................	4,000
Accrued liabilities decrease	3,000
Amortization expense............................	6,000
Cash balance, beginning of 2007...................	22,000
Cash balance, end of 2007	15,000
Cash paid as dividends	29,000
Cash paid to purchase land	90,000
Cash paid to retire bonds payable at par..............	60,000
Cash received from issuance of common stock	35,000
Cash received from sale of equipment................	17,000
Depreciation expense............................	29,000
Gain on sale of equipment........................	4,000
Inventory decrease..............................	13,000
Net income....................................	76,000
Prepaid expenses increase	2,000

E B-30.[B1] **Operating Cash Flows (Direct Method)**   **(LO2)**

Calculate the cash flow for each of the following cases.

a.   Cash paid for advertising:

Advertising expense.....................	$62,000
Prepaid advertising, beginning of year......	11,000
Prepaid advertising, end of year...........	15,000

b.   Cash paid for income taxes:

Income tax expense....................	$29,000
Income tax payable, beginning of year	7,100
Income tax payable, end of year	4,900

c.   Cash paid for merchandise purchased:

Cost of goods sold....................	$180,000
Inventory, beginning of year..............	30,000
Inventory, end of year..................	25,000
Accounts payable, beginning of year.......	10,000
Accounts payable, end of year...........	12,000

E B-31.[B1] **Statement of Cash Flows (Direct Method)**   **(LO2, 3, 4)**

Use the following information about the 2007 cash flows of Mason Corporation to prepare a statement of cash flows under the direct method.

Cash balance, end of 2007	$ 12,000
Cash paid to employees and suppliers	148,000
Cash received from sale of land...........	40,000
Cash paid to acquire treasury stock	10,000
Cash balance, beginning of 2007..........	16,000
Cash received as interest................	6,000
Cash paid as income taxes	11,000
Cash paid to purchase equipment.........	89,000
Cash received from customers	194,000
Cash received from issuing bonds payable..	30,000
Cash paid as dividends	16,000

E B-32.[B1] **Operating Cash Flows (Direct Method)**

Refer to the information in Exercise B-28. Calculate the net cash flow from operating activities using the direct method. Show a related cash flow for each revenue and expense.

E B-33. **Investing and Financing Cash Flows**   **(LO3, 4)**

During 2007, Paxon Corporation's long-term investments account (at cost) increased $15,000, which was the net result of purchasing stocks costing $80,000 and selling stocks costing $65,000 at a $6,000 loss. Also, its bonds payable account decreased $40,000, the net result of issuing $100,000 of bonds at $103,000 and retiring bonds with a face value (and book value) of $140,000 at a $9,000 gain. What items and amounts appear in the (a) cash flows from investing activities and (b) cash flows from financing activities sections of its 2007 statement of cash flows?

PROBLEMS

P B-34. **Statement of Cash Flows (Indirect Method)** (LO2, 3, 4)

Wolff Company's income statement and comparative balance sheets follow.

WOLFF COMPANY Income Statement For Year Ended December 31, 2007		
Sales.		$635,000
Cost of goods sold.	$430,000	
Wages expense	86,000	
Insurance expense.	8,000	
Depreciation expense.	17,000	
Interest expense.	9,000	
Income tax expense.	29,000	579,000
Net income.		$ 56,000

WOLFF COMPANY Balance Sheets		
	Dec. 31, 2007	**Dec. 31, 2006**
Assets		
Cash.	$ 11,000	$ 5,000
Accounts receivable.	41,000	32,000
Inventory.	90,000	60,000
Prepaid insurance.	5,000	7,000
Plant assets	250,000	195,000
Accumulated depreciation	(68,000)	(51,000)
Total assets.	$329,000	$248,000
Liabilities and Stockholders' Equity		
Accounts payable.	$ 7,000	$ 10,000
Wages payable.	9,000	6,000
Income tax payable	7,000	8,000
Bonds payable	130,000	75,000
Common stock.	90,000	90,000
Retained earnings	86,000	59,000
Total liabilities and equity	$329,000	$248,000

Cash dividends of $29,000 were declared and paid during 2007. Also in 2007, plant assets were purchased for cash, and bonds payable were issued for cash. Bond interest is paid semiannually on June 30 and December 31. Accounts payable relate to merchandise purchases.

Required

a. Compute the change in cash that occurred during 2007.

b. Prepare a 2007 statement of cash flows using the indirect method.

P B-35.   Statement of Cash Flows (Indirect Method)   (LO2, 3, 4)

Arctic Company's income statement and comparative balance sheets follow.

ARCTIC COMPANY Income Statement For Year Ended December 31, 2007		
Sales.		$ 728,000
Cost of goods sold.	$534,000	
Wages expense	190,000	
Advertising expense.	31,000	
Depreciation expense.	22,000	
Interest expense.	18,000	
Gain on sale of land	(25,000)	770,000
Net loss		$(42,000)

ARCTIC COMPANY Balance Sheets		
	Dec. 31, 2007	**Dec. 31, 2006**
Assets		
Cash.	$ 49,000	$ 28,000
Accounts receivable.	42,000	50,000
Inventory.	107,000	113,000
Prepaid advertising.	10,000	13,000
Plant assets	360,000	222,000
Accumulated depreciation	(78,000)	(56,000)
Total assets.	$490,000	$370,000
Liabilities and Stockholders' Equity		
Accounts payable.	$ 17,000	$ 31,000
Interest payable	6,000	—
Bonds payable	200,000	—
Common stock.	245,000	245,000
Retained earnings	52,000	94,000
Treasury stock	(30,000)	—
Total liabilities and equity	$490,000	$370,000

During 2007, Arctic sold land for $70,000 cash that had originally cost $45,000. Arctic also purchased equipment for cash, acquired treasury stock for cash, and issued bonds payable for cash in 2007. Accounts payable relate to merchandise purchases.

Required

a.   Compute the change in cash that occurred during 2007.

b.   Prepare a 2007 statement of cash flows using the indirect method.

P B-36. **Statement of Cash Flows (Indirect Method)** (LO2, 3, 4)

Dair Company's income statement and comparative balance sheets follow.

DAIR COMPANY Income Statement For Year Ended December 31, 2007		
Sales.		$700,000
Cost of goods sold.	$440,000	
Wages and other operating expenses	95,000	
Depreciation expense.	22,000	
Amortization expense.	7,000	
Interest expense.	10,000	
Income tax expense.	36,000	
Loss on bond retirement	5,000	615,000
Net income.		$ 85,000

DAIR COMPANY Balance Sheets		
	Dec. 31, 2007	**Dec. 31, 2006**
Assets		
Cash.	$ 27,000	$ 18,000
Accounts receivable.	53,000	48,000
Inventory.	103,000	109,000
Prepaid expenses.	12,000	10,000
Plant assets	360,000	336,000
Accumulated depreciation	(87,000)	(84,000)
Intangible assets	43,000	50,000
Total assets.	$511,000	$487,000
Liabilities and Stockholders' Equity		
Accounts payable.	$ 32,000	$ 26,000
Interest payable	4,000	7,000
Income tax payable	6,000	8,000
Bonds payable	60,000	120,000
Common stock.	252,000	228,000
Retained earnings	157,000	98,000
Total liabilities and equity	$511,000	$487,000

During 2007, the company sold for $17,000 cash old equipment that had cost $36,000 and had $19,000 accumulated depreciation. Also in 2007, new equipment worth $60,000 was acquired in exchange for $60,000 of bonds payable, and bonds payable of $120,000 were retired for cash at a loss. A $26,000 cash dividend was declared and paid in 2007. Any stock issuances were for cash.

Required

a. Compute the change in cash that occurred in 2007.

b. Prepare a 2007 statement of cash flows using the indirect method.

c. Prepare separate schedules showing (1) cash paid for interest and for income taxes and (2) noncash investing and financing transactions.

P B-37. **Statement of Cash Flows (Indirect Method)** (LO2, 3, 4)
Rainbow Company's income statement and comparative balance sheets follow.

RAINBOW COMPANY Income Statement For Year Ended December 31, 2007		
Sales.		$750,000
Dividend income.		15,000
		765,000
Cost of goods sold.	$440,000	
Wages and other operating expenses	130,000	
Depreciation expense.	39,000	
Patent amortization expense	7,000	
Interest expense.	13,000	
Income tax expense.	44,000	
Loss on sale of equipment.	5,000	
Gain on sale of investments.	(10,000)	668,000
Net income.		$ 97,000

RAINBOW COMPANY Balance Sheets		
	Dec. 31, 2007	Dec. 31, 2006
Assets		
Cash and cash equivalents	$ 19,000	$ 25,000
Accounts receivable.	40,000	30,000
Inventory.	103,000	77,000
Prepaid expenses.	10,000	6,000
Long-term investments—Available-for-sale.	—	50,000
Fair value adjustment to investments.	—	7,000
Land	190,000	100,000
Buildings.	445,000	350,000
Accumulated depreciation—Buildings.	(91,000)	(75,000)
Equipment	179,000	225,000
Accumulated depreciation—Equipment	(42,000)	(46,000)
Patents	50,000	32,000
Total assets.	$903,000	$781,000
Liabilities and Stockholders' Equity		
Accounts payable.	$ 20,000	$ 16,000
Interest payable	6,000	5,000
Income tax payable	8,000	10,000
Bonds payable	155,000	125,000
Preferred stock ($100 par value)	100,000	75,000
Common stock ($5 par value)	379,000	364,000
Paid-in capital in excess of par value—Common	133,000	124,000
Retained earnings	102,000	55,000
Unrealized gain on investments.	—	7,000
Total liabilities and equity	$903,000	$781,000

During 2007, the following transactions and events occurred:

1. Sold long-term investments costing $50,000 for $60,000 cash. Unrealized gains totaling $7,000 related to these investments had been recorded in earlier years. At year-end, the fair value adjustment and unrealized gain account balances were eliminated.
2. Purchased land for cash.
3. Capitalized an expenditure made to improve the building.
4. Sold equipment for $14,000 cash that originally cost $46,000 and had $27,000 accumulated depreciation.
5. Issued bonds payable at face value for cash.
6. Acquired a patent with a fair value of $25,000 by issuing 250 shares of preferred stock at par value.
7. Declared and paid a $50,000 cash dividend.
8. Issued 3,000 shares of common stock for cash at $8 per share.
9. Recorded depreciation of $16,000 on buildings and $23,000 on equipment.

Required

a. Compute the change in cash and cash equivalents that occurred during 2007.
b. Prepare a 2007 statement of cash flows using the indirect method.
c. Prepare separate schedules showing (1) cash paid for interest and for income taxes and (2) noncash investing and financing transactions.

P B-38.[B1] **Statement of Cash Flows (Direct Method)** (LO2, 3, 4)
Refer to the data for Wolff Company in Problem B-34.

Required

a. Compute the change in cash that occurred during 2007.
b. Prepare a 2007 statement of cash flows using the direct method.

P B-39.[B1] **Statement of Cash Flows (Direct Method)** (LO2, 3, 4)
Refer to the data for Arctic Company in Problem B-35.

Required

a. Compute the change in cash that occurred during 2007.
b. Prepare a 2007 statement of cash flows using the direct method.

P B-40.[B1] **Statement of Cash Flows (Direct Method)** (LO2, 3, 4)
Refer to the data for Dair Company in Problem B-36.

Required

a. Compute the change in cash that occurred in 2007.
b. Prepare a 2007 statement of cash flows using the direct method. Use one cash outflow for "cash paid for wages and other operating expenses." Accounts payable relate to inventory purchases only.
c. Prepare separate schedules showing (1) a reconciliation of net income to net cash flow from operating activities (see Exhibit B.4) and (2) noncash investing and financing transactions.

P B-41.[B1] **Statement of Cash Flows (Direct Method)** (LO2, 3, 4)
Refer to the data for Rainbow Company in Problem B-37.

Required

a. Compute the change in cash that occurred in 2007.
b. Prepare a 2007 statement of cash flows using the direct method. Use one cash outflow for "cash paid for wages and other operating expenses." Accounts payable relate to inventory purchases only.
c. Prepare separate schedules showing (1) a reconciliation of net income to net cash flow from operating activities (see Exhibit B.4) and (2) noncash investing and financing transactions.

P B-42. **Interpreting the Statement of Cash Flows** (LO1, 5)
Following is the statement of cash flows of Amgen, Inc.   Amgen, Inc. (AMGN)

Year Ended December 31 (In millions)	2003	2002
Cash flows from operating activities		
Net income (loss)-	$ 2,259.5	$(1,391.9)
Write-off of acquired in-process R&D....................	—	2,991.8
Depreciation and amortization	686.5	447.3
Tax benefits related to employee stock options............	268.6	251.6
Deferred income taxes	(189.6)	174.7
Other noncash expenses	99.0	24.9
Cash provided by (used in) changes in operating assets and liabilities, net of acquisitions		
Trade receivables, net	(255.5)	(121.9)
Inventories......................................	(167.7)	(101.7)
Other current assets	(32.8)	(5.2)
Accounts payable	74.0	11.0
Accrued liabilities	824.6	(31.8)
Net cash provided by operating activities	3,566.6	2,248.8
Cash flows from investing activities		
Purchases of property, plant, and equipment..............	(1,356.8)	(658.5)
Purchases of marketable securities	(5,320.3)	(2,952.8)
Proceeds from sales of marketable securities	3,338.6	1,621.5
Proceeds from maturities of marketable securities	370.8	778.2
Cash paid for Immunex, net of cash acquired	—	(1,899.0)
Proceeds from sale of Leukine® business................	—	389.9
Purchase of certain rights from Roche...................	—	(137.5)
Other...	(242.5)	(5.6)
Net cash used in investing activities	(3,210.2)	(2,863.8)
Cash flows from financing activities		
Issuance of zero-coupon convertible notes, net of issuance costs	—	2,764.7
Repayment of debt...................................	(123.0)	—
Net proceeds from issuance of common stock upon exercise of employee stock options and in connection with employee stock purchase plan	529.0	427.8
Repurchases of common stock	(1,801.0)	(1,420.4)
Other...	23.5	5.5
Net cash (used in) provided by financing activities	(1,371.5)	1,777.6
(Decrease) increase in cash and cash equivalents...........	(1,015.1)	1,162.6
Cash and cash equivalents at beginning of period	1,851.7	689.1
Cash and cash equivalents at end of period	$ 836.6	$ 1,851.7

Required

a. Amgen reports that it generated $3,566.6 million in net cash from operating activities in 2003. Yet, its net income for the year amounted to only $2,259.5 million. Much of this difference is the result of depreciation. Why is Amgen adding depreciation to net income in the computation of operating cash flows?

b. Amgen reports net cash inflows of $268.6 million in tax benefits arising from employee stock options. These relate to tax benefits the company realizes when employees exercise stock options. Since employees will only exercise stock options when the market price of the stock is above the exercise price, do you feel that this is a reliable source of cash for the company? Explain.

c. Amgen is reporting $(255.5) million relating to trade receivables. What does the sign on this amount signify about the change in receivables during the year?

d. Amgen reports $824.6 million relating to accrued liabilities. Describe what this relates to and its implications for Amgen's future cash flows.

e. Does the composition of Amgen's cash flow present a "healthy" picture for 2003? Explain.

P B-43. **Interpreting the Statement of Cash Flows** (LO1, 5)

Following is the statement of cash flows of Staples, Inc.

Staples, Inc. (SPLS)

In thousands	Year Ended January 31, 2004
Operating activities	
Net income.	$ 490,211
Adjustments to reconcile net income to net cash provided by operating activities:	
Depreciation and amortization	282,811
Asset impairment and other charges	—
Store closure charge.	—
Deferred income taxes (benefit) expense.	(13,725)
Other.	36,434
Change in assets and liabilities, net of companies acquired	
(Increase) decrease in receivables	(4,218)
Decrease (increase) in merchandise inventories.	147,130
Increase in prepaid expenses and other assets	(34)
(Decrease) increase in accounts payable	(27,266)
Increase in accrued expenses and other current liabilities.	95,549
Increase in other long-term obligations	12,840
Net cash provided by operating activities	1,019,732
Investing activities	
Acquisition of property and equipment	(277,793)
Acquisition of businesses, net of cash acquired	(2,910)
Proceeds from sales and maturities of short-term investments.	—
Purchase of short-term investments	(834,100)
Proceeds from sales and maturities of long-term investments	—
Purchase of long-term investments	—
Acquisition of lease rights.	—
Net cash used in investing activities	(1,114,803)
Financing activities	
Proceeds from sale of capital stock.	389,793
Proceeds from borrowings	—
Payments on borrowings	(325,235)
Repayments under receivables securitization agreement	(25,000)
Termination of interest rate swap agreement	—
Purchase of treasury stock.	(4,287)
Net cash provided by (used in) financing activities.	35,271
Effect of exchange rate changes on cash	21,376
Net (decrease) increase in cash and cash equivalents.	(38,424)
Cash and cash equivalents at beginning of period	495,889
Cash and cash equivalents at end of period	$ 457,465

Required

a. Staples reports net income of $490.211 million and net cash inflows from operating activities of $1,019.732 million. Part of the difference relates to depreciation of $282.811 million. Why does Staples add this amount in the computation of operating cash flows?

b. Staples reports a positive amount of $147.130 million relating to merchandise inventories. What does this signify about the change in the dollar amount of inventories during the year? Might this positive cash inflow be of some concern? Explain.

c. Staples reports a cash outflow of $1,114.803 million relating to investing activities. Is this cash outflow a cause for concern? Explain.

d. Staples net cash flows from financing activities is $35.271 million. Does this relatively small amount imply that there is no informational value in this category for the year? Explain.

e. Staples cash balance decreased by $38.424 million during the year. Is this a cause for concern? Explain. Does Staples present a "healthy" cash flow picture for the year? Explain.

Appendix C

Chart of Accounts with Acronyms

Assets

Cash	Cash
MS	Marketable securities
EMI	Equity method investments
AR	Accounts receivable
AU	Allowance for uncollectible accounts
INV	Inventory (or Inventories)
SUP	Supplies
PPD	Prepaid expenses
PPDA	Prepaid advertising
PPRNT	Prepaid rent
PPI	Prepaid insurance
PPE	Property, plant and equipment (PPE)
AD	Accumulated depreciation
INT	Intangible assets
DTA	Deferred tax assets
OA	Other assets

Liabilities

NP	Notes payable
AP	Accounts payable
ACC	Accrued expenses
WP	Wages payable
RNTP	Rent payable
RSL	Restructuring liability
WRP	Warranty payable
IP	Interest payable
CMLTD	Current maturities of long-term debt
UR	Unearned (or deferred) revenues
LTD	Long-term debt
CLO	Capital lease obligations
DTL	Deferred tax liabilities

Equity

CC	Contributed capital
CS	Common stock
APIC	Additional paid-in capital
RE	Retained earnings
DIV	Dividends
TS	Treasury stock
(A)OCI	(Accumulated) other comprehensive income
DC	Deferred compensation expense

Revenues and Expenses

Sales	Sales
REV	Revenues
COGS	Cost of goods sold (or Cost of sales)
OE	Operating expenses
WE	Wages expense
AE	Advertising expense
BDE	Bad debts expense
UTE	Utilities expense
DE	Depreciation expense
RDE	Research and development expense
RNTE	Rent expense
RSE	Restructuring expense
WRE	Warranty expense
AIE	Asset impairment expense
INSE	Insurance expense
SUPE	Supplies expense
GN (LS)	Gain (loss)–operating
TE	Tax expense
OI (OE)	Other nonoperating income (expense)
IE	Interest expense
UG (UL)	Unrealized gain (loss)
DI	Dividend income (or revenue)
EI	Equity income (or revenue)
GN (LS)	Gain (loss)–nonoperating

Closing Account

IS	Income summary

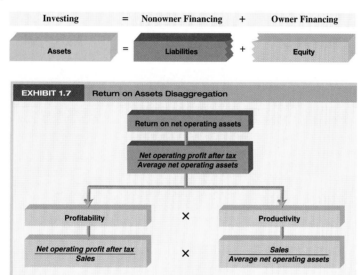

Quick Review

Module 1

Investing	=	Nonowner Financing	+	Owner Financing
Assets	=	Liabilities	+	Equity

EXHIBIT 1.7   Return on Assets Disaggregation

Return on net operating assets

$$\frac{\text{Net operating profit after tax}}{\text{Average net operating assets}}$$

Profitability × Productivity

$$\frac{\text{Net operating profit after tax}}{\text{Sales}} \times \frac{\text{Sales}}{\text{Average net operating assets}}$$

Module 2

Net Working Capital = Current Assets − Current Liabilities

Reconciliation of Retained Earnings

	Beginning retained earnings
±	Net income (loss)
−	Dividends
=	Ending retained earnings

Module 3

EXHIBIT 3.1   Accounting Cycle

1 Analyze Transactions and Prepare (and Post) Entries

2 Prepare (and Post) Accounting Adjustments

4 Complete the Closing Process

3 Prepare Financial Statements from Trial Balance

T-Account Framework

	Assets		=		Liabilities		+		Equity	
	+	−			−	+			−	+
	Increases	Decreases			Decreases	Increases			Decreases	Increases

Account Title	
Debit	Credit
(Left side)	(Right side)

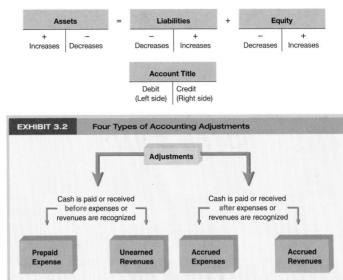

EXHIBIT 3.2   Four Types of Accounting Adjustments

Adjustments

Cash is paid or received *before* expenses or revenues are recognized

Cash is paid or received *after* expenses or revenues are recognized

Prepaid Expense   Unearned Revenues   Accrued Expenses   Accrued Revenues

Adjustments to Net Income to Yield Operating Cash Flows

	Change in account balance . . .	Means that . . .	Which requires this adjustment to net income to yield cash profit . . .
Receivables	Increase	Sales and net income increase, but cash is not yet received	Deduct increase in receivables from net income
	Decrease	More cash is received than is reported in sales and net income	Add decrease in receivables to net income
Inventories	Increase	Cash is paid for inventories that are not yet reflected in cost of goods sold	Deduct increase in inventories from net income
	Decrease	Cost of goods sold includes inventory costs that were paid for in a prior period	Add decrease in inventories to net income
Payables and accruals	Increase	More goods and services are acquired on credit, delaying cash payment	Add increase in payables and accruals to net income
	Decrease	More cash is paid than that reflected in cost of goods sold or operating expenses	Deduct decrease in payables and accruals from net income

	Cash flow increases from	Cash flow decreases from
Assets.	Account decreases	Account increases
Liabilities and equity.	Account increases	Account decreases

Module 4

$$ROE = \frac{\text{Net income}}{\text{Average stockholders' equity}}$$

$$ROE = \text{Operating return} + \text{Nonoperating return}$$

$$\text{Tax on operating profit} = \text{Tax expense} + (\text{Net nonoperating expense} \times \text{Statutory tax rate})$$

Tax Shield

$$\text{Tax rate on operating profit} = \frac{\text{Tax expense} + (\text{Net nonoperating expense} \times \text{Statutory tax rate})}{\text{Net operating profit before taxes}}$$

$$\text{NOPAT} = \text{Net operating profit before tax} \times (1 - \text{Tax rate on operating profit})$$

$$\text{Net operating assets} = \text{Operating assets} - \text{Operating liabilities}$$

$$RNOA = \frac{NOPAT}{Average\ NOA}$$

$$RNOA = \frac{NOPAT}{Average\ NOA} = \frac{NOPAT}{Sales} \times \frac{Sales}{Average\ NOA}$$

Net operating profit margin (NOPM)	Net operating asset turnover (NOAT)

EXHIBIT 4.1	Operating and Nonoperating Items in the Income Statement

Typical Income Statement
Operating Items Highlighted

Revenues
Cost of sales
Gross profit
Operating expenses
   Selling, general and administrative
   Asset impairment expense
   Gains and losses on asset disposal
Total operating expenses
Operating income
Interest expense
Interest and dividend revenue
Investment gains and losses
Total nonoperating expenses
Income before tax, minority interest and discontinued operations
Tax expense
Income before minority interest and discontinued operations
Minority interest (see Appendix 4B)
Discontinued operations (see Appendix 4B)
Net income

EXHIBIT 4.2	Operating and Nonoperating Items in the Balance Sheet

Typical Balance Sheet
Operating Items Highlighted

Current assets
Cash and cash equivalents
Short-term investments
Accounts receivable
Inventories
Prepaid expenses
Deferred income tax assets
Other current assets

Long-term assets
Long-term investments in securities
Property, plant and equipment, net
Capitalized lease assets
Natural resources
Equity method investments
Goodwill and Intangible assets
Deferred income tax assets
Other long-term assets

Current liabilities
Short-term notes and interest payable
Accounts payable
Accrued liabilities
Deferred income tax liabilities
Current maturities of long-term debt

Long-term liabilities
Bonds and notes payable
Capitalized lease obligations
Pension and other post-employment liabilities
Deferred income tax liabilities
Minority Interest

Stockholders' equity
All equity accounts

EXHIBIT 4.3	Key Ratio Definitions

Ratio	Definition
ROE: Return on equity	Net income/Average stockholders' equity
NOPAT: Net operating profit after tax	Operating revenues less operating expenses such as cost of sales, selling, general and administrative expense, and taxes; it excludes nonoperating revenues and expenses such as interest revenue, dividend revenue, interest expense, gains and losses on investments, and minority interest.
NOA: Net operating assets	Operating assets less operating liabilities; it excludes investments in marketable securities and interest-bearing debt.
RNOA: Return on net operating assets. . .	NOPAT/Average NOA
NNE: Net nonoperating expense	NOPAT − Net income; NNE consists of nonoperating expenses and revenues, net of tax

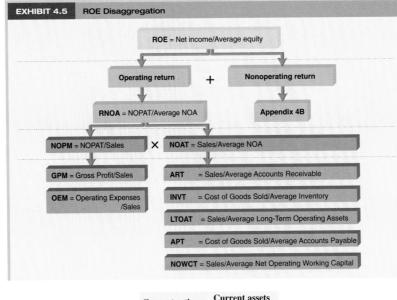

EXHIBIT 4.5 ROE Disaggregation

ROE = Net income/Average equity

Operating return + Nonoperating return

RNOA = NOPAT/Average NOA   Appendix 4B

NOPM = NOPAT/Sales × NOAT = Sales/Average NOA

GPM = Gross Profit/Sales   ART = Sales/Average Accounts Receivable

OEM = Operating Expenses /Sales   INVT = Cost of Goods Sold/Average Inventory

LTOAT = Sales/Average Long-Term Operating Assets

APT = Cost of Goods Sold/Average Accounts Payable

NOWCT = Sales/Average Net Operating Working Capital

$$\text{Current ratio} = \frac{\text{Current assets}}{\text{Current liabilities}}$$

$$\text{Quick ratio} = \frac{\text{Cash + Marketable securities + Accounts receivables}}{\text{Current liabilities}}$$

$$\text{Liabilities-to-equity ratio} = \frac{\text{Total liabilities}}{\text{Stockholders' equity}}$$

Module 5

EXHIBIT 5.1 Distinguishing Operating and Nonoperating Income Components

Operating Activities	Nonoperating Activities
• Sales	• Interest revenues and expenses
• Cost of goods sold	• Dividend revenues
• Selling, general and administrative expenses	• Gains and losses on sales of investments
• Depreciation expense	• Gains and losses on debt retirement
• Research and development expenses	• Gains and losses on discontinued operations
• Restructuring expenses	• Minority interest expense
• Income tax expenses	• Investment write-downs
• Extraordinary gains and losses	
• Gains and losses on sales of operating assets	
• Foreign currency translation effects	
• Operating asset write-downs	
• Other income or expenses	

Tax Expense = Taxes Paid − Increase (or + Decrease) in Deferred Tax Assets + Increase (or − Decrease) in Deferred Tax Liabilities

EXHIBIT 5.4 Sources of Deferred Tax Assets and Liabilities

Net Book Value of Assets		
Financial reporting net book value	> Tax reporting net book value	⟶ Deferred tax liability on balance sheet
Financial reporting net book value	< Tax reporting net book value	⟶ Deferred tax asset on balance sheet

Net Book Value of Liabilities		
Financial reporting net book value	< Tax reporting net book value	⟶ Deferred tax liability on balance sheet
Financial reporting net book value	> Tax reporting net book value	⟶ Deferred tax asset on balance sheet

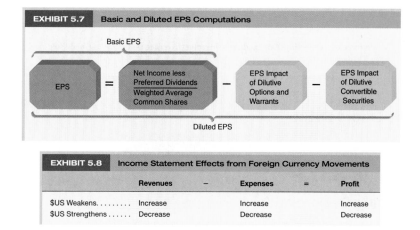

EXHIBIT 5.7 Basic and Diluted EPS Computations

Basic EPS

EPS = Net Income less Preferred Dividends / Weighted Average Common Shares − EPS Impact of Dilutive Options and Warrants − EPS Impact of Dilutive Convertible Securities

Diluted EPS

EXHIBIT 5.8 Income Statement Effects from Foreign Currency Movements

	Revenues	−	Expenses	=	Profit
$US Weakens.........	Increase		Increase		Increase
$US Strengthens......	Decrease		Decrease		Decrease

Module 6

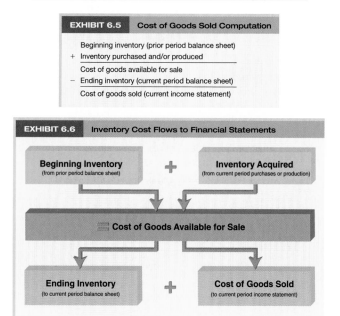

Allowance for Uncollectible Accounts Determination

Beginning allowance for uncollectible accounts..........	$ 2,200
Add: Provision for uncollectible accounts...............	700
Less: Write-offs of accounts receivable.................	0
Ending allowance for uncollectible accounts.............	$ 2,900

EXHIBIT 6.2 Effects of an Accounts Receivable Write-Off

Account	Before Write-Off	Effects of Write-Off	After Write-Off
Accounts receivable...........................	$100,000	$(500)	$99,500
Less: Allowance for uncollectible accounts.........	2,900	(500)	2,400
Accounts receivable, net of allowance.............	$ 97,100		$97,100

Accounts Receivable Turnover = Sales/Average Accounts Receivable

Average Collection Period = Accounts Receivable/Average Daily Sales

EXHIBIT 6.5 Cost of Goods Sold Computation

	Beginning inventory (prior period balance sheet)
+	Inventory purchased and/or produced
	Cost of goods available for sale
−	Ending inventory (current period balance sheet)
	Cost of goods sold (current income statement)

EXHIBIT 6.6 Inventory Cost Flows to Financial Statements

Beginning Inventory (from prior period balance sheet) + **Inventory Acquired** (from current period purchases or production)

Cost of Goods Available for Sale

Ending Inventory (to current period balance sheet) + **Cost of Goods Sold** (to current period income statement)

FIFO Inventory = LIFO Inventory + LIFO Reserve

FIFO COGS = LIFO COGS − Increase in LIFO Reserve (or + Decrease)

$$\text{Inventory Turnover} = \text{Cost of Goods Sold/Average Inventory}$$

$$\text{Average Inventory Days Outstanding} = \text{Inventory/Average Daily Cost of Goods Sold}$$

$$\text{Depreciation Expense} = \text{Depreciation Base} \times \text{Depreciation Rate}$$

Straight-Line Depreciation

Depreciation Base	Depreciation Rate
Cost − Salvage value	1/Estimated useful life

Double-Declining Depreciation

Depreciation Base	Depreciation Rate
Net Book Value = Cost − Accumulated Depreciation	2 × SL rate

EXHIBIT 6.11	Comparison of Straight-Line and Double-Declining-Balance Depreciation			
	Straight-Line		Double-Declining-Balance	
Year	Depreciation Expense	Book Value at End of Year	Depreciation Expense	Book Value at End of Year
1	$18,000	$82,000	$40,000	$60,000
2	18,000	64,000	24,000	36,000
3	18,000	46,000	14,400	21,600
4	18,000	28,000	8,640	12,960
5	18,000	10,000	2,960	10,000
	$90,000		$90,000	

All depreciation methods yield the same salvage value

Total depreciation over asset life is identical for all methods

$$\text{Gain or Loss on Asset Sale} = \text{Proceeds from Sale} - \text{Net Book Value of Asset Sold}$$

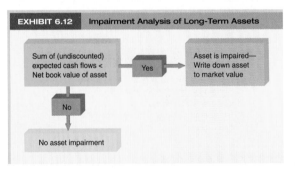

EXHIBIT 6.12 Impairment Analysis of Long-Term Assets

$$\text{PPE Turnover (PPET)} = \text{Sales/Average PPE Assets}$$

$$\text{Estimated Average Useful Life} = \text{Depreciable Asset Cost/Depreciation Expense}$$

$$\text{Percent Used Up} = \text{Accumulated Depreciation/Depreciable Asset Cost}$$

Module 7

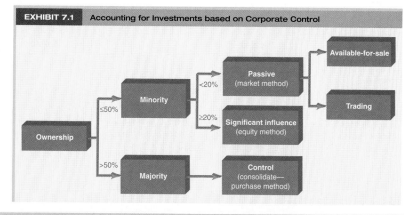

EXHIBIT 7.1   Accounting for Investments based on Corporate Control

EXHIBIT 7.2   Investment Type, Accounting Treatment, and Financial Statement Effects

	Accounting	Balance Sheet Effects	Income Statement Effects	Cash Flow Effects
Passive	Market method	Investment account is reported at current market value	Dividends and capital gains included in income Interim changes in market value may or may not affect income depending on whether the investor actively trades the securities Sale of investment yields capital gain or loss	Dividends and sale proceeds are cash inflows Purchases are cash outflows
Significant influence	Equity method	Investment account equals percent owned of investee company's equity*	Dividends reduce investment account Investor reports income equal to percent owned of investee income Sale of investment yields capital gain or loss	Dividends and sale proceeds are cash inflows Purchases are cash outflows
Control	Consolidation	Balance sheets of investor and investee are combined	Income statements of investor and investee are combined (and sale of investee yields capital gain or loss)	Cash flows of investor and investee are combined (and sale/purchase of investee yields cash inflow/outflow)

*Investments are often acquired at purchase prices in excess of book value (on average, market prices are 1.5 times book value for public companies). In this case the investment account exceeds the proportionate ownership of the investee's equity.

EXHIBIT 7.3   Accounting Treatment for Available-for-Sale and for Trading Investments

Investment Classification	Reporting of Market Value Changes	Reporting of Dividends Received and Gains and Losses on Sale
Available-for-Sale (AFS)	Market value changes bypass the income statement and are reported in accumulated *other comprehensive income* (OCI) as part of equity	Reported as *other income* in income statement
Trading (T)	Market value changes are reported in the income statement as unrealized gains or losses; impacting equity via retained earnings	Reported as *other income* in income statement

Summary of Equity Method Accounting

- Investments are recorded at their purchase cost.
- Dividends received are treated as a recovery of the investment and, thus, reduce the investment balance (dividends are not reported as income as with passive investments).
- The investor reports income equal to its percentage share of the investee's reported income; the investment account is increased by the percentage share of the investee's income or decreased by the percentage share of any loss.
- Changes in market value do not affect the investment's carrying value.

Effects of Equity Method Investments on ROE Components

- **Net operating profit margin (NOPM = NOPAT/Sales).** Most analysts include equity income (sales less expenses) in NOPAT since it relates to operating investments. However, investee's sales are not included in the NOPM denominator. The reported NOPM is, thus, *overstated*.
- **Net operating asset turnover (NOAT = Sales/Average NOA).** Investee's sales are excluded from the NOAT denominator. This means that NOAT is *understated*. (When investee assets exceed the investment balance, the impact on NOAT is *indeterminate*.)
- **Financial leverage (FLEV = Net nonoperating obligations/Average equity).** Financial leverage is understated due to the absence of investee liabilities in the numerator.

EXHIBIT 7.6	Mechanics of Consolidation Accounting (Purchase Price above Book Value)			
	Penman Company	Nissim Company	Consolidating Adjustments	Consolidated
Current assets	$ 5,000	$1,000		$ 6,000
Investment in Nissim	4,000	0	(4,000)	0
PPE, net	10,000	4,000	300	14,300
Goodwill			700	700
Total assets....................	$19,000	$5,000		$21,000
Liabilities......................	$ 5,000	$2,000		$ 7,000
Contributed capital...............	11,000	2,000	(2,000)	11,000
Retained earnings	3,000	1,000	(1,000)	3,000
Total liabilities and equity	$19,000	$5,000		$21,000

Module 8

$$\text{Accounts Payable Turnover (APT)} = \text{Cost of Goods Sold/Average Accounts Payable}$$

$$\text{Accounts Payable Days Outstanding (APDO)} = \text{Accounts Payable/Average Daily Cost of Goods Sold}$$

EXHIBIT 8.1	Coupon Rate, Market Rate, and Bond Pricing
Coupon rate > market rate →	Bond sells at a **premium** (above face amount)
Coupon rate = market rate →	Bond sells at **par** (at face amount)
Coupon rate < market rate →	Bond sells at a **discount** (below face amount)

Interest Expense Computation for Bonds		
Cash interest paid		Cash interest paid
+ Amortization of discount	or	− Amortization of premium
Interest expense		Interest expense

$$\text{Gain or Loss on Bond Repurchase} = \text{Net Bonds Payable} - \text{Repurchase Payment}$$

Module 9

Components of Stockholders' Equity:
- Contributed capital: common stock, preferred stock, additional paid-in capital, treasury stock, minority interest
- Earned capital: retained earnings, accumulated other comprehensive income (AOCI)

Stock Issuance:
- Common stock is increased by number of shares issued $\times$ par value
- Additional paid-in capital is increased for the balance of the issue price

Treasury Stock:
- Record at purchase cost
- When reissued, treasury stock is reduced by the cost of the shares reissued and the balance is reflected as an increase in additional paid-in capital

Dividends and Splits:
- Cash: reduce retained earnings by the cash dividends paid
- Stock (small): reduce retained earnings by the market value of the shared distributed and increase common stock and additional paid-in capital by the market value of the shares issued
- Stock (large): reduce retained earnings by the par value of the shares issued and increase common stock by the same amount (no increase in additional paid-in capital)
- Split: no accounting entry (adjust number of shares outstanding and their par value, if any)

Components of Comprehensive Income:
- Currency translation adjustment
- Unrealized gains and losses on available-for-sale securities
- Minimum pension liability adjustment
- Unrealized gains and losses on certain derivatives

EXHIBIT 9.3	Balance Sheet Effects of Euro Strengthening versus the Dollar					
Currency	**Assets**	=	**Liabilities**	+	**Equity**	
$US weakens	Increase	=	Increase	+	Increase	
$US strengthens.	Decrease	=	Decrease	+	Decrease	

Module 10

EXHIBIT 10.1	Financial Statement Effects of Lease Type for the Lessee			
Lease Type	**Assets**	**Liabilities**	**Expenses**	**Cash Flows**
Capital	Lease asset reported	Lease liability reported	Depreciation and interest expense	Payments per lease contract
Operating	Lease asset **not** reported	Lease liability **not** reported	Rent expense	Payments per lease contract

Pension Plan Assets
Pension plan assets, beginning balance
+ Actual returns on investments (interest, dividends, gains and losses)
+ Company contributions to pension plan
− Benefits paid to retirees
= Pension plan assets, ending balance

Pension Obligation
Projected benefit obligation, beginning balance
+ Service cost
+ Interest cost
+/− Actuarial losses (gains)
− Benefits paid to retirees
= Projected benefit obligation, ending balance

Net Pension Liability (or Asset)
Pension plan assets (at market value)
− Projected benefit obligation (PBO)
Funded status

Net Pension Expense
Service cost
+ Interest cost
− *Expected* return on pension plan assets
± Amortization of deferred amounts
Net pension expense

Effects from Changes in Pension Assumptions		
Estimate change	**Probable effect on pension expense**	**Reason for effect**
Discount rate increase	Increase	While the higher discount rate reduces the PBO, the lower PBO is multiplied by a higher rate. The rate effect is larger than the discount effect, resulting in increased pension expense.*
Investment return increase	Decreases	The dollar amount of expected return on plan assets is the product of the plan assets balance and the expected long-term rate of return. Increasing the return increases the expected return on plan assets, thus reducing pension expense.
Wage inflation increase	Increases	The expected rate of wage inflation affects future wage levels that determine expected pension payments. An increase, thus, increases PBO, which increases both the service and interest cost components of pension expense.

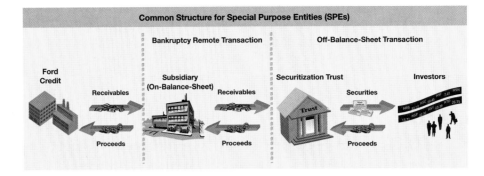

Module 11

EXHIBIT 11.1	Common Income Statement Adjustments

1. Separate persistent and transitory items; examples of items to exclude:
   a. Gains and losses relating to
      - Asset sales of long-term assets and investments
      - Asset write-downs of long-term assets and inventories
      - Stock issuances by subsidiaries
      - Debt retirements
   b. Transitory items reported after income from continued operations
      - Discontinued operations
      - Extraordinary items
   c. Restructuring expenses
   d. Merger costs
   e. LIFO liquidation gains
   f. Liability accruals deemed excessive
   g. Lawsuit gains and losses
   h. Revenue or expense from short-term fluctuations in tax rates and from changes in deferred tax valuation allowance
2. Separate operating and nonoperating items; examples:
   a. Treating interest revenue and expense, and investment gains and losses, as nonoperating
   b. Treating pension service cost as operating, and pension interest costs and expected returns as nonoperating
   c. Treating debt retirement gains and losses as nonoperating
   d. Treating income and losses from discontinued operations as nonoperating
3. Include expenses not reflected in net income; examples:
   a. Inadequate (or excessive) reserves for bad debts or asset impairment
   b. Reductions in R&D, advertising, and other discretionary expenses that were made to achieve short-term income targets; conversely, exclude excessive expenses related to product or market development
   c. Employee stock option expense (for financial statements issued before 2006)

EXHIBIT 11.2	Common Balance Sheet Adjustments

1. Exclude nonoperating assets and liabilities
   a. Eliminate assets and liabilities from discontinued operations
   b. Write-down of assets, including goodwill, that is judged to be impaired
2. Include operating assets and liabilities not reflected in balance sheet; examples:
   a. Capitalize operating assets from operating leases; nonoperating capitalized lease liabilities are also increased
   b. Consolidate off-balance-sheet investments:
      - Equity method investments
      - Special purpose entities (SPEs)
   c. Accrue understated liabilities and assets

EXHIBIT 11.3	Common Statement of Cash Flow Adjustments

1. Adjust operating cash flows for transitory items; examples of adjustments that potentially impact operating cash flows:
   a. Adjust discretionary costs (advertising, R&D, maintenance) to normal, expected levels
   b. Adjust current operating assets (receivables, inventory) to normal, expected levels
   c. Adjust current operating liabilities (payables, accruals) to normal, expected levels
2. Adjust investing cash flows for transitory items, such as cash proceeds from asset disposals (including disposals of discontinued operations) and from tax benefits due to exercise of stock options
3. Review cash flows and reassign them, if necessary, to operating, investing, or financing sections; examples:
   a. Reclassify operating cash inflows from asset securitization to the financing section
   b. Reclassify interest payments from the operating to the financing section

$$\text{Forecasted Year-End Account Balance} = \frac{\text{Forecasted Sales (or Cost of Goods Sold)}}{\text{Estimated Turnover Rate}}$$

Forecasted Cash	Possible Adjustments to Forecasted Balance Sheet and Income Statement
Too low	• Liquidate marketable securities (then adjust forecasted investment income) • Raise cash by increasing long-term debt and/or equity (then adjust forecasted interest expense and/or expected dividends)
Too high	• Invest excess cash in marketable securities (then adjust investment income) • Repay debt or pay out to shareholders as repurchased (treasury) stock or dividends (then adjust forecasted interest expense and/or expected dividends)

Module 12

DCF Valuation Model

$$\text{Firm Value} = \text{Present Value of Expected Free Cash Flows to Firm (FCFF)}$$

$$\text{FCFF} = \text{NOPAT} - \text{Increase in NOA}$$

where

NOPAT = Net operating profit after tax
NOA = Net operating assets

ROPI Valuation Model

$$\text{Firm Value} = \text{NOA} + \text{Present Value of Expected ROPI}$$

$$\text{ROPI} = \underbrace{\text{NOPAT} - (\text{NOA}_{\text{Beg}} \times r_w)}_{\text{Expected NOPAT}}$$

where

NOA_{Beg} = Net operating assets at beginning (*Beg*) of period
r_w = Weighted average cost of capital (WACC)

Module 14

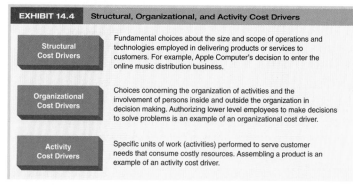

EXHIBIT 14.4	Structural, Organizational, and Activity Cost Drivers
Structural Cost Drivers	Fundamental choices about the size and scope of operations and technologies employed in delivering products or services to customers. For example, Apple Computer's decision to enter the online music distribution business.
Organizational Cost Drivers	Choices concerning the organization of activities and the involvement of persons inside and outside the organization in decision making. Authorizing lower level employees to make decisions to solve problems is an example of an organizational cost driver.
Activity Cost Drivers	Specific units of work (activities) performed to serve customer needs that consume costly resources. Assembling a product is an example of an activity cost driver.

Module 15

$$\frac{\text{Variable costs}}{\text{per unit}} = \frac{\text{Difference in total costs}}{\text{Difference in activity}}$$

$$\text{Fixed costs} = \text{Total costs} - \text{Variable costs}$$

EXHIBIT 15.8	Hierarchy of Activity Costs	
Activity Level	**Reason for Activity**	**Examples of Activity Cost**
1. Unit level	Performed for each unit of product produced or sold	• Cost of raw materials • Cost of inserting a component • Utilities cost of operating equipment • Some costs of packaging • Sales commissions
2. Batch level	Performed for each batch of product produced or sold	• Cost of processing sales order • Cost of issuing and tracking work order • Cost of equipment setup • Cost of moving batch between workstations • Cost of inspection (assuming same number of units inspected in each batch)
3. Product level	Performed to support each different product that can be produced	• Cost of product development • Cost of product marketing such as advertising • Cost of specialized equipment • Cost of maintaining specialized equipment
4. Facility level	Performed to maintain general manufacturing capabilities	• Cost of maintaining general facilities such as buildings and grounds • Cost of nonspecialized equipment • Cost of maintaining nonspecialized equipment • Cost of real property taxes • Cost of general advertising • Cost of general administration such as the plant manager's salary

Module 16

$$\text{Break-even unit sales volume} = \frac{\text{Fixed costs}}{\text{Selling price per unit} - \text{Variable costs per unit}}$$

$$\text{Break-even unit sales volume} = \frac{\text{Fixed costs}}{\text{Unit contribution margin}}$$

$$\text{Target unit sales volume} = \frac{\text{Fixed costs} + \text{Desired Profit}}{\text{Unit contribution margin}}$$

$$\text{Dollar break-even point} = \frac{\text{Fixed costs}}{\text{Contribution margin ratio}}$$

$$\text{Target dollar sales volume} = \frac{\text{Fixed costs} + \text{Desired profit}}{\text{Contribution margin ratio}}$$

Module 17

Relevant Costs		Irrelevant Costs	
Future costs that differ among competing alternatives		Future costs that do not differ among competing alternatives	
Opportunity Costs	**Outlay Costs**		**Sunk Costs**
Net benefits foregone of rejected alternatives	Future costs requiring future expenditures that differ	Future costs requiring future expenditures that do not differ	Historical costs resulting from past decisions

Module 18

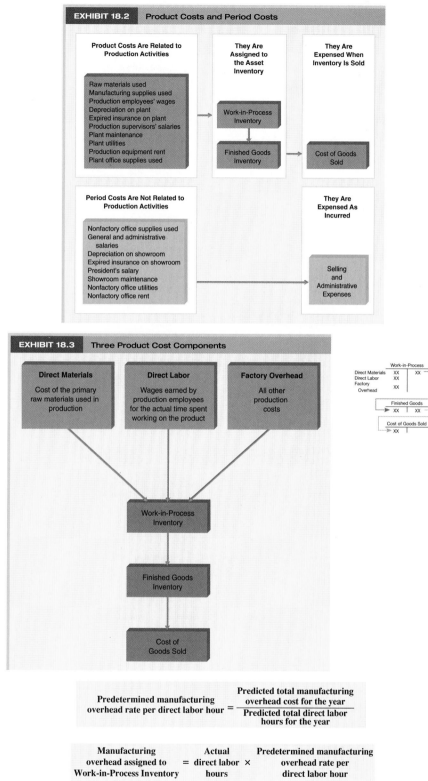

EXHIBIT 18.2 Product Costs and Period Costs

Product Costs Are Related to Production Activities

Raw materials used
Manufacturing supplies used
Production employees' wages
Depreciation on plant
Expired insurance on plant
Production supervisors' salaries
Plant maintenance
Plant utilities
Production equipment rent
Plant office supplies used

They Are Assigned to the Asset Inventory

Work-in-Process Inventory

Finished Goods Inventory

They Are Expensed When Inventory Is Sold

Cost of Goods Sold

Period Costs Are Not Related to Production Activities

Nonfactory office supplies used
General and administrative salaries
Depreciation on showroom
Expired insurance on showroom
President's salary
Showroom maintenance
Nonfactory office utilities
Nonfactory office rent

They Are Expensed As Incurred

Selling and Administrative Expenses

EXHIBIT 18.3 Three Product Cost Components

Direct Materials
Cost of the primary raw materials used in production

Direct Labor
Wages earned by production employees for the actual time spent working on the product

Factory Overhead
All other production costs

Work-in-Process Inventory

Finished Goods Inventory

Cost of Goods Sold

Work-in-Process

Direct Materials	XX	XX
Direct Labor	XX	
Factory Overhead	XX	

Finished Goods

XX	XX

Cost of Goods Sold

XX

$$\text{Predetermined manufacturing overhead rate per direct labor hour} = \frac{\text{Predicted total manufacturing overhead cost for the year}}{\text{Predicted total direct labor hours for the year}}$$

$$\begin{array}{c}\text{Manufacturing} \\ \text{overhead assigned to} \\ \text{Work-in-Process Inventory}\end{array} = \begin{array}{c}\text{Actual} \\ \text{direct labor} \\ \text{hours}\end{array} \times \begin{array}{c}\text{Predetermined manufacturing} \\ \text{overhead rate per} \\ \text{direct labor hour}\end{array}$$

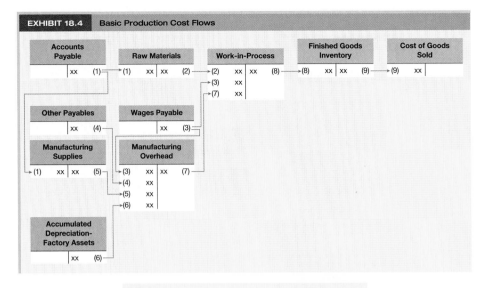

EXHIBIT 18.4   Basic Production Cost Flows

Sales..................................	$X,XXX
Less cost of goods sold	
Beginning inventory	$X,XXX
Plus purchases	X,XXX
Goods available for sale	X,XXX
Less ending inventory...................	(X,XXX)
Cost of goods sold......................	(X,XXX)
Gross profit...........................	X,XXX
Less selling and administrative expenses	(X,XXX)
Net income............................	$X,XXX

Module 19

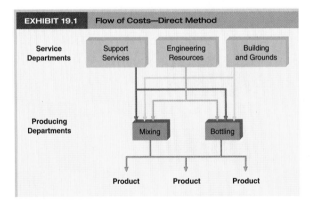

EXHIBIT 19.1   Flow of Costs—Direct Method

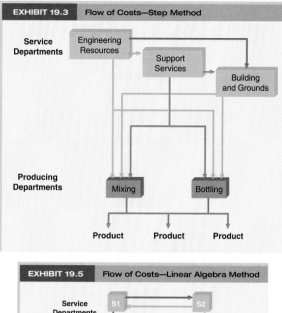

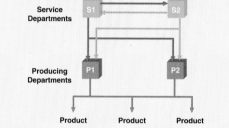

1. Activities performed to fill customer needs consume resources that cost money.

2. The cost of resources consumed by activities should be assigned to cost objectives on the basis of the units of activity consumed by the cost objective.

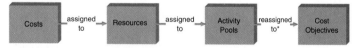

*Based on units of activity utilized by the cost objective.

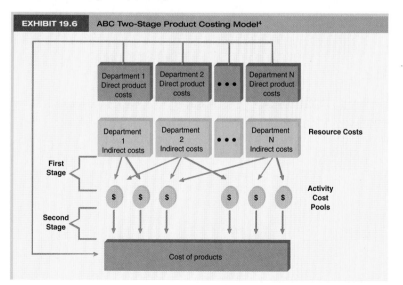

Module 20

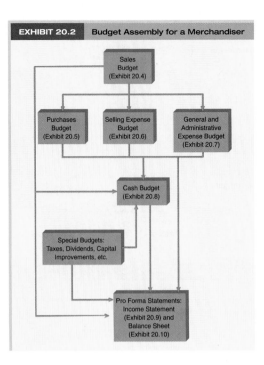

EXHIBIT 20.2 Budget Assembly for a Merchandiser

Module 21

$$\text{Materials price variance} = AQ(AP - SP)$$

$$\text{Materials quantity variance} = SP(AQ - SQ)$$

$$\text{Labor rate variance} = AH(AR - SR)$$

$$\text{Labor efficiency variance} = SR(AH - SH)$$

$$\text{Variable overhead efficiency variance} = SRP(AP - SP)$$

$$\text{Revenue variance} = (\text{Actual volume} \times \text{Actual price}) - (\text{Budgeted volume} \times \text{Budgeted price})$$

$$\text{Sales price variance} = (\text{Actual selling price} - \text{Budgeted selling price}) \times \text{Actual sales volume}$$

$$\text{Sales volume variance} = (\text{Actual sales volume} - \text{Budgeted sales volume}) \times \text{Budgeted selling price}$$

Module 22

$$\text{ROI} = \frac{\text{Sales}}{\text{Investment center base}} \times \frac{\text{Investment center income}}{\text{Sales}} = \frac{\text{Investment center income}}{\text{Investment center asset base}}$$

EXHIBIT 22.3	Balanced Scorecard Illustration		
	Standard	Prior Period	Current Period
Key financial indicators			
Cash flow	$ 25,000	$ (4,000)	$ 21,000
Return on investment (ROI).	0.18	0.22	0.19
Economic value added	$ 130,000	$ 133,000	$ 123,000
Sales.	$4,400,000	$4,494,000	$4,342,000
Key customer indicators			
Average customers per hour	75	80	71
Number of customer complaints per period.	22	21	17
Number of sales returns per period	10	8	5
Key operating indicators			
Bagels sold/produced per day ratio	0.96	0.93	0.91
Daily units lost (burned, dropped, etc.).	25	32	34
Employee turnover per period	0.10	0.07	0.00
Key growth and innovation indicators			
New products introduced during period.	1	1	0
Products discontinued during period	1	1	1
Number of sales promotions	3	3	2
Special offers, discounts, etc.	4	5	3

Module 23

$$\text{Markup on cost base} = \frac{\text{Costs not included in the base} + \text{Desired profit}}{\text{Costs included in the base}}$$

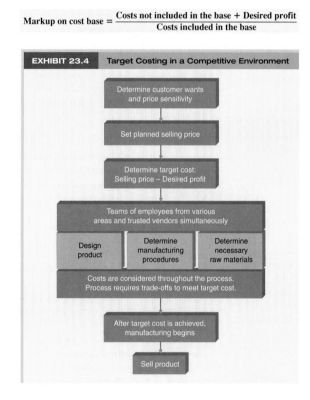

EXHIBIT 23.4	Target Costing in a Competitive Environment

Determine customer wants and price sensitivity

Set planned selling price

Determine target cost: Selling price – Desired profit

Teams of employees from various areas and trusted vendors simultaneously

| Design product | Determine manufacturing procedures | Determine necessary raw materials |

Costs are considered throughout the process. Process requires trade-offs to meet target cost.

After target cost is achieved, manufacturing begins

Sell product

Glossary

A

absorption costing an approach to product costing that treats both variable and fixed manufacturing costs as product costs.

accelerated cost recovery system (ACRS, MACRS) A system of accelerated depreciation for tax purposes introduced in 1981 (ACRS) and modified starting in 1987 (MACRS); it prescribes depreciation rates by asset classification for assets acquired after 1980

accelerated depreciation method Any depreciation method under which the amounts of depreciation expense taken in the early years of an asset's life are larger than the amounts expensed in the later years; includes the double-declining balance method

access control matrix A computerized file that lists the type of access that each computer user is entitled to have to each file and program in the computer system

account A record of the additions, deductions, and balances of individual assets, liabilities, permanent stockholders' equity, revenues, and expenses

accounting cycle A series of basic steps followed to process accounting information during a fiscal year

accounting entity An economic unit that has identifiable boundaries and that is the focus for the accumulation and reporting of financial information

accounting equation An expression of the equivalency of the economic resources and the claims upon those resources of a specific entity; often stated as Assets = Liabilities + Stockholders' Equity

accounting period The time period, typically one year (or quarter), to which periodic accounting reports are related

accounting rate of return the average annual increase in net income that results from acceptance of a capital expenditure proposal divided by either the initial investment or the average investment in the project.

accounting system The structured collection of people, policies, procedures, equipment, files, and records that a company uses to collect, record, classify, process, store, report, and interpret financial data

accounting The process of measuring the economic activity of an entity in money terms and communicating the results to interested parties; the purpose is to provide financial information that is useful in making economic decisions

accounts payable turnover The ratio obtained by dividing annual cost of goods sold by average accounts payable

accounts receivable aging method A procedure that uses an aging schedule to determine the year-end balance needed in the allowance for uncollectible accounts account

accounts receivable turnover Annual net sales divided by average accounts receivable (net)

accounts receivable A current asset that is created by a sale on a credit basis; it represents the amount owed the company by the customer

accrual accounting Accounting procedures whereby revenues are recorded when they are earned and realized and expenses are recorded in the period in which they help to generate revenues

accruals Adjustments that reflect revenues earned but not received or recorded and expenses incurred but not paid or recorded

accrued expense An expense incurred but not yet paid; recognized with an adjusting entry

accrued revenue Revenue earned but not yet billed or received; recognized with an adjusting entry

accumulated depreciation The sum of all depreciation expense recorded to date; it is subtracted from the cost of the asset in order to derive the asset's net book value

acid test ratio more specific than the current ratio as a test of short-term solvency, the acid test ratio (also known as the quick ratio) measures the availability of cash and other current monetary assets that can be quickly generated into cash to pay current liabilities. The general equation for the acid test ratio is: (Cash + Marketable securities + Current receivables)/ Current liabilities.

activities list see operations list.

activity cost drivers specific units of work (activities) performed to serve customer needs that consume costly resources.

activity costing the determination of the cost of specific activities performed to fill customer needs.

activity dictionary a standardized list of processes and related activities.

activity a unit of work.

activity-based budgeting an approach to budgeting that uses an activity cost hierarchy to budget physical inputs and costs as a function of planned activity. It is mechanically similar to the output/input approach to budgeting where physical inputs and costs are budgeted as a function of planned activity.

activity-based costing (ABC) used to develop cost information by determining the cost of activities and tracing their costs to cost objectives on the basis of the cost objective's utilization of units of activity.

activity-based management (ABM) the identification and selection of activities to maximize the value of the activities while minimizing their cost from the perspective of the final consumer.

adjusted trial balance A list of general ledger accounts and their balances taken after adjustments have been made

adjusting entries Entries made at the end of an accounting period under accrual accounting to ensure the proper matching of expenses incurred with revenues earned for the period

adjusting The process of adjusting the historical financial statements prior to the projection of future results; also called recasting and reformulating

aging schedule An analysis that shows how long customers' accounts receivable balances have remained unpaid

allowance for uncollectible accounts A contra asset account with a normal credit balance shown on the balance sheet as a deduction from accounts receivable to reflect the expected realizable amount of accounts receivable

allowance method An accounting procedure whereby the amount of uncollectible accounts expense is estimated and recorded in the period in which the related credit sales occur

Altman's Z-score A predictor of potential bankruptcy based on multiple ratios

amortization The periodic writing off of an account balance to expense; similar to depreciation and usually refers to the periodic writing off of an intangible asset

annuity a series of equal cash flows received or paid over equal intervals of time.

appraisal costs quality costs incurred to identify nonconforming products or services before they are delivered to customers.

articles of incorporation A document prepared by persons organizing a corporation in the United States that sets forth the structure and purpose of the corporation and specifics regarding the stock to be issued

articulation The linkage of financial statements within and across time

assembly efficiency variance the difference between the standard cost of actual assembly inputs and the flexible budget cost for assembly.

assembly rate variance the difference between the actual cost and the standard cost of actual assembly inputs.

asset turnover a measure of performance, the asset turnover ratio measures the firm's ability to use its assets to generate sales. The general equation for asset turnover is: Sales/Average total assets.

asset turnover Net income divided by average total assets

asset write-downs Adjustment of carrying value of assets down to their current salable value

assets The economic resources of an entity that are owned, will provide future benefits and can be reliably measured

audit report A report issued by independent auditors that includes the final version of the financial statements, accompanying notes, and the auditor's opinion on the financial statements

audit An examination of a company's financial statements by a firm of independent certified public accountants

authorized stock The maximum number of shares in a class of stock that a corporation may issue

automatic identification systems (AIS) the use of bar coding of products and production processes that allows inventory and production information to be entered into a computer without writing or keying.

available-for-sale securities Investments in securities that management intends to hold for capital gains and dividend income; although it may sell them if the price is right

average cash cycle Average collection period + modified average inventory days outstanding + modified average payable days outstanding

average collection period Determined by dividing accounts receivable by average daily sales, sometimes referred to as days sales outstanding or DSO

average inventory days outstanding (AIDO) An indication of how long, on average, inventories are on the shelves, computed as inventory divided by average daily cost of goods sold

B

backflush costing an inventory accounting system used in conjunction with JIT in which costs are assigned initially to cost of goods sold. At the end of the period, costs are backed out of cost of goods sold and assigned to appropriate inventory accounts for any inventories that may exist.

balance sheet A financial statement showing an entity's assets, liabilities, and stockholders' equity at a specific date; sometimes called a statement of financial position

balance sheet a picture of the economic health of an organization at a specific time, showing the organization's assets and the claims on those assets.

balanced scorecard a performance measurement system that includes financial and operational measures which are related to the organizational goals. The basic premise is to establish a set of indicators that can be used to monitor performance progress and then compare the goals that are established with the results.

batch level activity an activity performed for each batch of product produced.

bearer One of the terms that may be used to designate the payee on a promissory note; means the note is payable to whoever holds the note

benchmarking a systematic approach to identifying the best practices to help an organization take action to improve performance.

bill of materials a document that specifies the kinds and quantities of raw materials required to produce one unit of product.

bond A long-term debt instrument that promises to pay interest periodically and a principal amount at maturity, usually issued by the borrower to a group of lenders; bonds may incorporate a wide variety of provisions relating to security for the debt involved, methods of paying the periodic interest, retirement provisions, and conversion options

book value per share The dollar amount of net assets represented by one share of stock; computed by dividing the amount of stockholders' equity

associated with a class of stock by the outstanding shares of that class of stock

book value The dollar amount carried in the accounts for a particular item; the book value of a depreciable asset is derived by deducting the contra account accumulated depreciation from the cost of the depreciable asset

borrows at a discount When the face amount of the note is reduced by a calculated cash discount to determine the cash proceeds

bottom-up budget a budget where managers at all levels—and in some cases even non-managers—become involved in the budget preparation.

break-even point the unit or dollar sales volume where total revenues equal total costs.

budget committee a committee responsible for supervising budget preparation. It serves as a review board for evaluating requests for discretionary cost items and new projects.

budget office an organizational unit responsible for the preparation, distribution, and processing of forms used in gathering budget data. It handles most of the work of actually formulating the budget schedules and reports.

budget a formal plan of action expressed in monetary terms.

budgetary slack occurs when managers intentionally understate revenues or overstate expenses in order to produce favorable variances for the department.

budgeted financial statements hypothetical statements that reflect the "as if" effects of the budgeted activities on the actual financial position of the organization. They reflect what the results of operations will be if all the predictions in the budget are correct.

budgeting projecting the operations of an organization and their financial impact on the future.

C

calendar year A fiscal year that ends on December 31

call provision A bond feature that allows the borrower to retire (call in) the bonds after a stated date

capacity costs see committed fixed costs.

capital budgeting a process that involves the identification of potentially desirable projects for capital expenditures, the subsequent evaluation of capital expenditure proposals, and the selection of proposals that meet certain criteria.

capital expenditures Expenditures that increase the book value of long-term assets; sometimes abbreviated as CAPEX

capital expenditures investments of significant financial resources in projects to develop or introduce new products or services, to expand current production or service capacity, or to change current production or service facilities.

capital lease A lease that transfers to the lessee substantially all of the benefits and risks related to ownership of the property; the lessee records the leased property as an asset and establishes a liability for the lease obligation

capital markets Financing sources, which are formalized when companies issue securities that are traded on organized exchanges; they are informal when companies are funded by private sources

capitalization of interest A process that adds interest to an asset's initial cost if a period of time is required to prepare the asset for use

capitalization The recording of a cost as an asset on the balance sheet rather than as an expense on the income statement; these costs are transferred to expense as the asset is used up

cash (operating) cycle The period of time from when cash is invested in inventories until inventory is sold and receivables are collected

cash and cash equivalents The sum of cash plus short-term, highly liquid investments such as treasury bills and money market funds; includes marketable securities maturing within 90 days of the financial statement date

cash budget summarizes all cash receipts and disbursements expected to occur during the budget period.

cash discount An amount that a purchaser of merchandise may deduct from the purchase price for paying within the discount period

cash equivalents short-term, highly liquid investments that are readily convertible into known amounts of cash and so near their maturity date that they present insignificant risk of change in value from interest or money market rate changes; generally, only investments with original maturities of three months or less are considered as possible cash equivalents.

cash An asset category representing the amount of a firm's available cash and funds on deposit at a bank in checking accounts and savings accounts

cash-basis accounting Accounting procedures whereby revenues are recorded when cash is received from operating activities and expenses are recorded when cash payments related to operating activities are made

centralization when top management controls the major functions of an organization (such as manufacturing, sales, accounting, computer operations, marketing, research and development, and management control).

certificate of deposit (CD) An investment security available at financial institutions generally offering a fixed rate of return for a specified period of time

chained target costing bringing in suppliers as part of the coordination process to attain a competitively priced product that is delivered to the customer in a timely manner.

change in accounting estimate Modification to a previous estimate of an uncertain future event, such as the useful life of a depreciable asset, uncollectible accounts receivable, and warranty expenses; applied currently and prospectively only

changes in accounting principles Cumulative income or loss from changes in accounting methods (such as depreciation or inventory costing methods)

chart of accounts A list of all the general ledger account titles and their numerical code

clean surplus accounting Income that explains successive equity balances

closing procedures A step in the accounting cycle in which the balances of all temporary accounts are transferred to the retained earnings account, leaving the temporary accounts with zero balances

coefficient of determination (R2) a measure of the percent of variation in the dependent variable that is explained by variations in the independent variable when the least-squares estimation equation is used.

commitments A contractual arrangement by which both parties to the contract still have acts to perform

committed fixed costs (capacity costs) costs required to maintain the current service or production capacity or to fill a previous legal commitment.

common cost a cost incurred for the benefit of two or more cost objectives—an indirect cost.

common segment costs costs related to more than one segment and not directly traceable to a particular segment. These costs are referred to as common costs because they are incurred at one level for the benefit of two or more segments at a lower level.

common size statement a financial statement that has had all its accounts converted into percentages. As such, a common size statement is very useful for detecting items that are out of line, that deviate from some present amount, or that may be indications of other problems.

common stock The basic ownership class of corporate capital stock, carrying the rights to vote, share in earnings, participate in future stock issues, and share in any liquidation proceeds after prior claims have been settled

common-size financial statement A financial statement in which each item is presented as a percentage of a key figure such as sales or total assets

comparative financial statements A form of horizontal analysis involving comparison of two or more periods' financial statements showing dollar and/ or percentage changes

compensating balance A minimum amount that a financial institution requires a firm to maintain in its account as part of a borrowing arrangement complex capital structure

comprehensive income The total income reported by the company, including net profit and all other changes to stockholders' equity other than those arising from capital (stock) transactions; typical components of other comprehensive income (OCI) are unrealized gains (losses) on available-for-sale securities and derivatives, minimum pension liability adjustment, and foreign currency translation adjustments

computer-aided design (CAD) a method of design that involves the use of computers to design products.

computer-aided manufacturing (CAM) a manufacturing method that involves the use of computers to control the operation of machines.

computer-integrated manufacturing (CIM) the ultimate extension of the CAD, CAM, and FMS concepts to a completely automated and computer-controlled factory where production is self-operating once a product is designed and the decision to produce is made.

conceptual framework A cohesive set of interrelated objectives and fundamentals for external financial reporting developed by the FASB

conservatism An accounting principle stating that judgmental determinations should tend toward understatement rather than overstatement of net assets and income

consistency An accounting principle stating that, unless otherwise disclosed, accounting reports should be prepared on a basis consistent with the preceding period

consolidated financial statements Financial statements reflecting a parent company and one or more subsidiary companies and/or a variable interest entity (VIE) and its primary beneficiary

contingency A possible future event; significant contingent liabilities must be disclosed in the notes to the financial statements

contingent liabilities A potential obligation, the eventual occurrence of which usually depends on some future event beyond the control of the firm; contingent liabilities may originate with such events as lawsuits, credit guarantees, and environmental damages

continuous budgeting budgeting based on a moving time frame that extends over a fixed period. The budget system adds an identical time period to the budget at the end of each period of operations, thereby always maintaining a budget of exactly the same time length.

continuous improvement (Kaizen) budgeting an approach to budgeting that incorporates a targeted improvement (reduction) in costs; management requests that a given process will be improved during the budgeting process. This may be applied to every budget category or to specific areas selected by management. Kaizen budgeting is based upon prior performance and anticipated operating conditions during the upcoming period.

continuous improvement (Kaizen) costing establishing cost reduction targets for products or services that an organization is currently providing to customers.

continuous improvement an approach to activity-based management where the employees constantly evaluate products, services, and processes, seeking ways to do better.

contra account An account related to, and deducted from, another account when financial statements are prepared or when book values are computed

contract rate The rate of interest stated on a bond certificate

contributed capital The net funding that a company receives from issuing and acquiring its equity shares

contribution income statement an income statement format in which variable costs are subtracted from revenues to figure contribution margin, and fixed costs are then subtracted from contribution margin to calculate net income.

contribution margin ratio the portion of each dollar of sales revenue contributed toward covering fixed costs and earning a profit.

contribution margin the difference between total revenues and total variable costs; this amount goes toward covering fixed costs and providing a profit.

controlling the process of ensuring that results agree with plans.

conversion cost the combined costs of direct labor and manufacturing overhead incurred to convert raw materials into finished goods.

convertible bond A bond incorporating the holder's right to convert the bond to capital stock under prescribed terms

convertible securities Debt and equity securities that provide the holder with an option to convert those securities into other securities

copyright An exclusive right that protects an owner against the unauthorized reproduction of a specific written work or artwork

core income A company's income from its usual business activities that is expected to continue (persist) into the future

corporation A legal entity created by the granting of a charter from an appropriate governmental authority and owned by stockholders who have limited liability for corporate debt

cost allocation base a measure of volume of activity, such as direct labor hours or machine hours, that determines how much of a cost pool is assigned to each cost objective.

cost behavior how costs respond to changes in an activity cost driver.

cost center a responsibility center whose manager is responsible only for managing costs.

cost driver analysis the study of factors that influence costs.

cost driver a factor that causes or influences costs.

cost estimation the determination of the relationship between activity and cost.

cost method An investment is reported at its historical cost, and any cash dividends and interest received are recognized in current income

cost objective an object to which costs are assigned. Examples include departments, products, and services.

cost of capital the average cost of obtaining the resources necessary to make investments.

cost of goods sold percentage The ratio of cost of goods sold divided by net sales

cost of goods sold The total cost of merchandise sold to customers during the accounting period

cost of production report used in a process costing system; summarizes unit and cost data for each department or process for each period.

cost pool a collection of related costs, such as departmental manufacturing overhead, that is assigned to one or more cost objectives, such as products.

cost prediction error the difference between a predicted future cost and the actual amount of the cost when, or if, it is incurred.

cost prediction the forecasting of future costs.

cost principle An accounting principle stating that asset measures are based on the prices paid to acquire the assets

cost reduction proposal a proposed action or investment intended to reduce the cost of an activity that the organization is committed to keeping.

cost-volume-profit (CVP) analysis a technique used to examine the relationships among total volume of some independent variable, total costs, total revenues, and profits during a time period (typically a month or a year).

cost-volume-profit graph an illustration of the relationships among activity volume, total revenues, total costs, and profits.

coupon (contract or stated) rate The coupon rate of interest is stated in the bond contract; it is used to compute the dollar amount of (semiannual) interest payments that are paid to bondholder during the life of the bond issue

coupon bond A bond with coupons for interest payable to bearer attached to the bond for each interest period; whenever interest is due, the bondholder detaches a coupon and deposits it with his or her bank for collection

covenants Contractual requirements put into loan or bond agreements by lenders

credit (entry) An entry on the right side (or in the credit column) of any account

credit card fee A fee charged retailers for credit card services provided by financial institutions; the fee is usually stated as a percentage of credit card sales

credit guarantee A guarantee of another company's debt by cosigning a note payable; a guarantor's contingent liability that is usually disclosed in a balance sheet footnote

credit memo A document prepared by a seller to inform the purchaser that the seller has reduced the amount owed by the purchaser due to a return or an allowance

credit period The maximum amount of time, usually stated in days, that the purchaser of merchandise has to pay the seller

credit terms The prescribed payment period for purchases on credit with discount specified for early payment

cumulative (preferred stock) A feature associated with preferred stock whereby any dividends in arrears must be paid before dividends may be paid on common stock

cumulative effect of a change in principle The cumulative effect on net income to the date of a change in accounting principle

cumulative translation adjustment The amount recorded in the equity section as necessary to balance the accounting equation when assets and liabilities of foreign subsidiaries are translated into $US at the rate of exchange prevailing at the statement date

current assets Cash and other assets that will be converted to cash or used up during the normal operating cycle of the business or one year, whichever is longer

current liabilities Obligations that will require within the coming year or operating cycle, whichever is longer, (1) the use of existing current assets or (2) the creation of other current liabilities

current rate method Method of translating foreign currency transactions under which balance sheet amounts are translated using exchange rates in effect at the period-end consolidation date and income statement amounts using the average exchange rate for the period

current ratio A firm's current assets divided by its current liabilities

current ratio a measure of solvency, the current ratio measures the relationship between current assets and current liabilities. The general equation for the current ratio is: Current assets/Current liabilities.

customer level activity an activity performed to obtain or maintain each customer.

cycle efficiency the ratio of value-added to nonvalue-added manufacturing activities.

cycle time the total time required to complete a process. It is composed of the times needed for setup, processing, movement, waiting, and inspection.

D

days' sales in receivables a measure of both solvency and performance, the days receivable outstanding tells how long it takes to convert accounts receivable into cash or how well the firm is managing the credit extended to customers. The general equation for days receivable outstanding is: Ending receivables/Average daily sales.

days' sales in inventory Inventories divided by average cost of goods sold

debenture bond A bond that has no specific property pledged as security for the repayment of funds borrowed

debit (entry) An entry on the left side (or in the debit column) of any account

debt-to-equity ratio a measure of long-term solvency, the debt-to-equity ratio indicates the balance between the amounts of capital that creditors and owners provide. The general equation for the debt-to-equity ratio is: Total liabilities/Total stockholders' equity.

decentralization the delegation of decision-making authority to successively lower management levels in an organization. The lower in the organization the authority is delegated, the greater the decentralization.

declining-balance method An accelerated depreciation method that allocates depreciation expense to each year by applying a constant percentage to the declining book value of the asset

default The nonpayment of interest and principal and/or the failure to adhere to the various terms and conditions of the bond indenture

deferrals Adjustments that allocate various assets and revenues received in advance to the proper accounting periods as expenses and revenues

deferred revenue A liability representing revenues received in advance; also called unearned revenue

deferred tax liability A liability representing the estimated future income taxes payable resulting from an existing temporary difference between an asset's book value and its tax basis

deferred tax valuation allowance Reduction in a reported deferred tax asset to adjust for the amount that is not likely to be realized

defined benefit plan A type of retirement plan under which the company promises to make periodic payments to the employee after retirement

defined contribution plan A retirement plan under which the company makes cash contribution into an employee's account (usually with a third-party trustee like a bank) either solely or as a matching contribution

degree of operating leverage a measure of operating leverage, often computed as the contribution margin divided by income before taxes.

denominator variance see fixed overhead volume variance.

depletion The allocation of the cost of natural resources to the units extracted and sold or, in the case of timberland, the board feet of timber cut

depreciation accounting The process of allocating the cost of equipment, vehicles, and buildings (not land) to expense over the time period benefiting from their use

depreciation base The acquisition cost of an asset less estimated salvage value

depreciation rate An estimate of how the asset will be used up over its useful life—evenly over its useful life, more heavily in the early years, or in proportion to its actual usage

depreciation tax shield the reduction in taxes due to the deductibility of depreciation from taxable revenues.

depreciation The decline in economic potential (using up) of plant assets originating from wear, deterioration, and obsolescence

derivatives Financial instruments such as futures, options, and swaps that are commonly used to hedge (mitigate) some external risk, such as commodity price risk, interest rate risk, or risks relating to foreign currency fluctuations

descriptive model a model that merely specifies the relationships between a series of independent and dependent variables.

design for manufacture explicitly considering the costs of manufacturing and servicing a product while it is being designed.

differential cost analysis an approach to the analysis of relevant costs that focuses on the costs that differ under alternative actions.

diluted earnings per share The earnings per share computation taking into consideration the effects of dilutive securities

dilutive securities Securities that can be exchanged for shares of common stock and, thereby, increase the number of common shares outstanding

direct costing see variable costing.

direct department cost a cost directly traceable to a department upon its incurrence.

direct labor wages earned by production employees for the time they spend working on the conversion of raw materials into finished goods.

direct materials the costs of primary raw materials that are converted into finished goods.

direct method (for cost allocation) a method of allocating service department costs to producing departments based only on the amount of services provided to the producing departments; it does not recognize any interdepartmental services.

direct method (for statement of cash flow) a reporting format for the operating section of the statement of cash flows; where basically, the income statement is reconstructed on a cash basis so that the primary categories of cash inflows and outflows from operating activities are reported.

direct segment fixed costs costs that would not be incurred if the segment being evaluated were discontinued. They are specifically identifiable with a particular segment.

discontinued operations Net income or loss from business segments that are up for sale or have been sold in the current period

discount bond A bond that is sold for less than its par (face) value

discount on notes payable A contra account that is subtracted from the Notes Payable amount on the balance sheet; as the life of the note elapses, the discount is reduced and charged to interest expense

discount period The maximum amount of time, usually stated in days, that the purchaser of merchandise has to pay the seller if the purchaser wants to claim the cash discount

discount rate the minimum rate of return required for the project to be acceptable.

discounted cash flow (DCF) model The value of a security is equal to the present value of the expected free cash flows to the firm, discounted at the weighted average cost of capital (WACC)

discounting The exchanging of notes receivable for cash at a financial institution at an amount that is less than the face value of the notes

discretionary cost center a cost center that does not have clearly defined relationships between effort and accomplishment.

discretionary fixed costs costs set at a fixed amount each period at the discretion of management.

dividend discount model The value of a security today is equal to the present value of that security's expected dividends, discounted at the weighted average cost of capital

dividend payout ratio Annual dividends per share divided by the earnings per share

dividend yield Annual dividends per share divided by the market price per share

dividends account A temporary equity account used to accumulate owner dividends from the business

division margin the amount each division contributes toward covering common corporate expenses and generating corporate profits. It is computed by subtracting all direct fixed expenses identifiable with each division from the contribution margin.

double-entry accounting system A method of accounting that recognizes the duality of a transaction such that the analysis results in a recording of equal amounts of debits and credits

E

earned capital The cumulative net income (losses) retained by the company (not paid out to shareholders as dividends)

earned When referring to revenue, the seller's execution of its duties under the terms of the agreement, with the resultant passing of title to the buyer with no right of return or other contingencies

earnings per share a measure of performance, earnings per share are disclosed on the income statement. The general equation for basic earnings per share is: Net income less preferred stock dividends/ Weighted average number of common shares outstanding for the period.

earnings quality The degree to which reported earnings represent how well the firm has performed from an economic standpoint

earnings smoothing Earnings management with a goal to provide an earnings stream with less variability

economic profit The number of inventory units sold multiplied by the difference between the sales price and the replacement cost of the inventories (approximated by the cost of the most recently purchased inventories)

economic value-added (EVA) a variation of residual income calculated as income after taxes less the cost of capital employed; specifically, net operating profits after tax less a charge for the use of capital equal to beginning capital utilized in the business multiplied by the weighted average cost of capital.

effective interest method A method of amortizing bond premium or discount that results in a constant rate of interest each period and varying amounts of premium or discount amortized each period

effective interest rate The rate determined by dividing the total discount amount by the cash proceeds on a note payable when the borrower borrowed at a discount

effective rate The current rate of interest in the market for a bond or other debt instrument; when issued, a bond is priced to yield the market (effective) rate of interest at the date of issuance

efficient markets hypothesis Capital markets are said to be efficient if at any given time, current equity (stock) prices reflect all relevant information that determines those equity prices

electronic data interchange (EDI) the electronic communication of data between organizations.

employee severance costs Accrued (estimated) costs for termination of employees as part of a restructuring program

employee stock options A form of compensation that grants a select group of employees the right to purchase a fixed number of company shares at a fixed price for a predetermined time period

enterprise resource planning (ERP) enterprise management information systems that provide organizations an integrated set of operating, financial, and management systems.

equity carve out A corporate divestiture of operating units

equity method The prescribed method of accounting for investments in which the investor company has a significant influence over the investee company (usually taken to be ownership between 20-50% of the outstanding common stock of the investee company)

equivalent completed units the number of completed units that is equal, in terms of production effort, to a given number of partially completed units.

ethics the moral quality, fitness, or propriety of a course of action that can injure or benefit people; also, the values, rules, and justifications that governs one's way of life.

expenses Decreases in stockholders' equity incurred by a firm in the process of earning revenues

external failure costs quality costs incurred when nonconforming products or services are delivered to customers.

extraordinary items Revenues and expenses that are both unusual and infrequent and are, therefore, excluded from income from continuing operations

F

face amount The principal amount of a bond or note to be repaid at maturity

facility level activity an activity performed to maintain general manufacturing or marketing capabilities.

factoring Selling an account receivable to another company, typically a finance company or a financial institution, for less than its face value

file a collection of related records.

Financial Accounting Standards Board (FASB) The organization currently responsible for setting accounting standards for reporting financial information

financial accounting an information processing system that generates general-purpose reports of financial operations (income statement and cash flows statement) and financial position (balance sheet) for an organization.

financial assets Normally consist of excess resources held for future expansion or unexpected needs; they are usually invested in the form of other companies' stock, corporate or government bonds, and real estate

financial leverage The proportionate use of borrowed funds in the capital structure, computed as net financial obligations (NFO) divided by average equity; financial leverage is considered favorable if the return on assets is higher than the fixed rate on borrowed funds and unfavorable if the fixed rate is greater than the return it generates.

financial reporting objectives A component of the conceptual framework that specifies that financial statements should provide information (1) useful for investment and credit decisions, (2) helpful in assessing an entity's ability to generate future cash flows, and (3) about an entity's resources, claims to those resources, and the effects of events causing changes in these items

financial reporting the process of preparing financial statements (income statement, balance sheet, and statement of cash flows) for a firm in accordance with generally accepted accounting principles.

financial statement analysis the process of interpreting and evaluating financial statements by using the data contained in them to produce additional financial measures. Financial statement analysis involves comparing financial statements for the current period with those of the previous periods, studying the internal composition of the financial statements, and studying relationships within and among the financial statements.

financial statement elements A part of the conceptual framework that identifies the significant components—such as assets, liabilities, stockholders' equity, revenues, and expenses—used to put financial statements together

financing activities business activities that involve (1) resource transfers between the entity and its owners and (2) the securement of loans from and the repayment of them to nonowners (creditors).

finished goods inventory The dollar amount of inventory that has completed the production process and is awaiting sale to customers

first-in, first-out (FIFO) method in process costing   A costing method that accounts for unit costs of beginning inventory units separately from those started during the current period. The first costs incurred each period are assumed to have been used to complete the unfinished units left over from the previous period.

first-in, first-out (FIFO) method One of the prescribed methods of inventory costing; FIFO assumes that the first costs incurred for the purchase or production of inventory are the first costs relieved from inventory when goods are sold

fiscal year The annual accounting period used by a business firm

five forces of competitive intensity Industry competition, bargaining power of buyers, bargaining power of suppliers, threat of substitution, threat of entry

fixed assets An alternate label for long-term assets; may also be called property, plant, and equipment (PPE)

fixed costs Costs that do not change with changes in sales volume (over a reasonable range); with a unit level cost driver as the independent variable, fixed costs are a constant amount per period of time

fixed manufacturing overhead all fixed costs associated with converting raw materials into finished goods.

fixed overhead budget variance the difference between budgeted and actual fixed overhead.

fixed overhead volume variance the difference between total budgeted fixed overhead and total standard fixed overhead assigned to production.

fixed selling and administrative costs all fixed costs other than those directly associated with converting raw materials into finished goods.

flexible budget variance computed for each cost as the difference between the actual cost and the flexible budget cost of producing a given quantity of product or service.

flexible budgets budgets that are drawn up for a series of possible production and sales volumes or adjusted to a particular level of production after the fact. These budgets, based on cost-volume or cost-activity relationships, are used to determine what costs should have been for an attained level of activity.

flexible manufacturing systems (FMS) an extension of computer-aided manufacturing techniques through a series of manufacturing operations. These operations include the automatic movement of units between operations and the automatic and rapid setup of machines to produce each product.

forecast The projection of financial results over the forecast horizon and terminal periods

foreign currency transaction The $US equivalent of an asset or liability denominated in a foreign currency

foreign exchange gain or loss The gain (loss) recognized in the income statement relating to the change in the $US equivalent of an asset or liability denominated in a foreign currency

for-profit organization an organization that has profit as a primary mission.

franchise Generally, an exclusive right to operate or sell a specific brand of products in a given geographic area

free cash flow This excess cash flow (above that required to manage its growth and development) from which dividends can be paid; computed as NOPAT 2 Increase in NOA

full absorption cost see absorption costing.

full costing see absorption costing.

full costs include all costs, regardless of their behavior patterns (variable or fixed) or activity level.

full disclosure principle An accounting principle stipulating the disclosure of all facts necessary to make financial statements useful to readers

fully diluted earnings per share See diluted earnings per share

functional currency The currency representing the primary currency in which a business unit conducts its operations

functional income statement a type of income statement where costs are classified according to function, rather than behavior. It is typically included in external financial reports.

fundamental analysis Uses financial information to predict future valuation and, hence, buy-sell stock strategies

funded status The difference between the pension obligation and the fair market value of the pension investments

future value the amount a current sum of money (or series of monies) earning a stated rate of interest will accumulate to at the end of a future period.

G

general and administrative expense budget presents the expenses the organization plans to incur in connection with the general administration of the organization. Included are expenses for such things as the accounting department, the computer center, and the president's office.

general journal A journal with enough flexibility so that any type of business transaction can be recorded in it

general ledger A grouping of all of an entity's accounts that are used to prepare the basic financial statements

generally accepted accounting principles (GAAP) A set of standards and procedures that guide the preparation of financial statements

goal a definable, measurable objective.

going concern concept An accounting principle that assumes that, in the absence of evidence to the contrary, a business entity will have an indefinite life

goodwill The value that derives from a firm's ability to earn more than a normal rate of return on the fair market value of its specific, identifiable net assets; computed as the residual of the purchase price less the fair market value of the net tangible and intangible assets acquired

gross margin The difference between net sales and cost of goods sold: also called gross profit

gross profit margin (GPM) (percentage) The ratio of gross profit on sales divided by net sales

gross profit on sales The difference between net sales and cost of goods sold; also called gross margin

H

held-to-maturity securities The designation given to a portfolio of bond investments that are expected to be held until they mature

high-low method of cost estimation utilizes data from two time periods, a representative high activity period and a representative low activity period, to estimate fixed and variable costs.

historical cost Original acquisition or issuance costs

holding company The parent company of a subsidiary

holding gain The increase in replacement cost since the inventories were acquired, which equals the number of units sold multiplied by the difference between the current replacement cost and the original acquisition cost

horizon period The forecast period for which detailed estimates are made, typically 5–10 years

horizontal analysis an evaluative standard, horizontal analysis is the comparison of a firm's current financial measures to those of previous periods. Horizontal analysis is used to evaluate trends in the firm's financial condition covering two or more years.

I

impairment loss A loss recognized on an impaired asset equal to the difference between its book value and current fair value

impairment A reduction in value from that presently recorded

imposed budget see top-down budget.

income statement A financial statement reporting an entity's revenues and expenses for a period of time

income statement a summary of economic events during a period of time, showing the revenues generated by operating activities, the expenses incurred in generating those revenues, and any gains or losses attributed to the period.

incremental budgeting an approach to budgeting where costs for a coming period are budgeted as a dollar or percentage change from the amount budgeted for (or spent during) some previous period.

indirect department cost a cost reassigned, or allocated, to a department from another cost objective.

indirect method (for statement of cash flow) a reporting format for the operating section of the statement of cash flows; wherein net cash flow from operations is computed by entering adjustments to net income from the income statement.

indirect method A presentation format for the statement of cash flows that refers to the operating section only; that section begins with net income and converts it to cash flows from operations

indirect segment costs see common segment costs.

inspection time the amount of time it takes units to be inspected.

intangible assets A term applied to a group of long-term assets, including patents, copyrights, franchises, trademarks, and goodwill, that benefit an entity but do not have physical substance

integer programming a variation of linear programming that determines the solution in whole numbers.

interdepartmental services services provided by one service department to other service departments.

interest cost (pensions) The increase in the pension obligation due to the accrual of an additional year of interest

internal auditing A company function that provides independent appraisals of the company's financial statements, its internal controls, and its operations

internal controls The measures undertaken by a company to ensure the reliability of its accounting data, protect its assets from theft or unauthorized use, make sure that employees are following the company's policies and procedures, and evaluate the performance of employees, departments, divisions, and the company as a whole

internal failure costs quality costs incurred when materials, components, products, or services are identified as defective before delivery to customers.

internal rate of return (IRR) (often called the time-adjusted rate of return) the discount rate that equates the present value of a project's cash inflows with the present value of the project's cash outflows.

inventory carrying costs Costs of holding inventories, including warehousing, logistics, insurance, financing, and the risk of loss due to theft, damage, or technological or fashion change

inventory shrinkage The cost associated with an inventory shortage; the amount by which the perpetual inventory exceeds the physical inventory

inventory turnover (in dollars) often regarded as a measure of both solvency and performance, inventory turnover tells how long it takes to convert inventory into current monetary assets and how well the firm is managing investments in inventory. The general equation for inventory turnover is: Cost of goods sold/Average inventory cost.

inventory turnover (in units) the annual demand in units divided by the average inventory in units.

investing activities business activities that involve transactions related to acquiring and disposing of marketable securities, other long-term investments, and property, plant, and equipment, as well as making and collecting loans unrelated to the sale of goods or services; the acquiring and disposing of resources (assets) that a company uses to acquire and sell its products and services.

investing creditors Those who primarily finance investing activities

investment center a responsibility center whose manager is responsible for the relationship between its profits and the total assets invested in the center. In general, the management of an investment center is expected to earn a target profit per dollar invested.

investment returns The increase in pension investments resulting from interest, dividends, and capital gains on the investment portfolio

investment tax credit a reduction in income taxes of a percent of the cost of a new asset in the year the new asset is placed in service.

invoice price The price that a seller charges the purchaser for merchandise

invoice A document that the seller sends to the purchaser to request payment for items that the seller shipped to the purchaser

IOU A slang term for a receivable

irrelevant costs costs that do not differ among competing decision alternatives.

issued stock Shares of stock that have been sold and issued to stockholders; issued stock may be either outstanding or in the treasury

J

job cost sheet a document used to track the status of and accumulate the costs for a specific job in a job cost system.

job order production the manufacturing of products in single units or in batches of identical units.

job production see job order production.

joint costs all materials and conversion costs of joint products incurred prior to the split-off point.

joint products two or more products simultaneously produced by a single process from a common set of inputs.

journal A tabular record in which business transactions are analyzed in debit and credit terms and recorded in chronological order

just-in-time (JIT) inventory management a comprehensive inventory management philosophy that stresses policies, procedures, and attitudes by managers and other workers that result in the efficient production of high-quality goods while maintaining the minimum level of inventories.

just-in-time (JIT) inventory philosophy Receive inventory from suppliers into the production process just at the point it is needed

K

Kaizen costing see continuous improvement costing.

kanban system see materials pull system.

L

labor efficiency variance the difference between the standard cost of actual labor inputs and the flexible budget cost for labor.

labor rate (spending) variance the difference between the actual cost and the standard cost of actual labor inputs.

land improvements Improvements with limited lives made to land sites, such as paved parking lots and driveways

last-in, first-out (LIFO) method One of the prescribed methods of inventory costing; LIFO assumes that the last costs incurred for the purchase or production of inventory are the first costs relieved form inventory when goods are sold

lease A contract between a lessor (owner) and lessee (tenant) for the rental of property

leasehold improvements Expenditures made by a lessee to alter or improve leased property

leasehold The rights transferred from the lessor to the lessee by a lease

least-squares regression analysis uses a mathematical technique to fit a cost estimating equation to the observed data in a manner that minimizes the sum of the vertical squared estimating errors between the estimated and actual costs at each observation.

lessee The party acquiring the right to the use of property by a lease

lessor The owner of property who transfers the right to use the property to another party by a lease

leveraging The use of borrowed funds in the capital structure of a firm; the expectation is that the funds will earn a return higher than the rate of interest on the borrowed funds

liabilities The obligations, or debts, that an entity must pay in money or services at some time in the future because of past transactions or events

life-cycle budgeting an approach to budgeting when the entire life of the project represents a more useful planning horizon than an artificial period of one year.

life-cycle costs from the seller's perspective, all costs associated with a product or service ranging from those incurred with initial conception through design, pre-production, production, and after-production support. From the buyer's perspective, all costs associated with a purchased product or service, including initial acquisition costs and subsequent costs of operation, maintenance, repair, and disposal.

LIFO conformity rule IRS requirement to cost inventories using LIFO for tax purposes if they are costed using LIFO for financial reporting purposes

LIFO liquidation The reduction in inventory quantities when LIFO costing is used; LIFO liquidation yields an increase in gross profit and income when prices are rising

LIFO reserve The difference between the cost of inventories using FIFO and the cost using LIFO

linear algebra method (reciprocal) method a method of allocating service department costs using a series of linear algebraic equations, which are solved simultaneously, to allocate service department costs both interdepartmentally among service departments and to the producing departments.

linear programming an optimizing model used to assist managers in making decisions under constrained conditions when linear relationships exist between all variables.

liquidation value per share The amount that would be received by a holder of a share of stock if the corporation liquidated

liquidity How much cash the company has, how much is expected, and how much can be raised on short notice

list price The suggested price or reference price of merchandise in a catalog or price list

long-term liabilities Debt obligations not due to be settled within the normal operating cycle or one year, whichever is longer

lower of cost or market (LCM) GAAP requirement to write down the carrying amount of inventories on the balance sheet if the reported cost (using FIFO, for example) exceeds market value (determined by current replacement cost)

M

maker The signer of a promissory note

managed fixed costs see discretionary fixed costs.

management accounting a discipline concerned with financial and related information used by managers and other persons inside specific organizations to make strategic, organizational, and operational decisions.

management by exception an approach to performance assessment whereby management directs attention only to those activities not proceeding according to plan.

management discussion and analysis (MD&A) The section of the 10-K report in which a company provides a detailed discussion of its business activities

managerial accounting The accounting activities carried out by a firm's accounting staff primarily to furnish management with accounting data for decisions related to the firm's operations

manufacturers Companies that convert raw materials and components into finished products through the application of skilled labor and machine operations

manufacturing cost budget a budget detailing the direct materials, direct labor, and manufacturing overhead costs that should be incurred by manufacturing operations to produce the number of units called for in the production budget.

manufacturing costs The costs of direct materials, direct labor, and manufacturing overhead incurred in the manufacture of a product

manufacturing margin the result when direct manufacturing costs (variable costs) are deducted from product sales.

manufacturing organizations organizations that process raw materials into finished products for sale to others.

manufacturing overhead all manufacturing costs other than direct materials and direct labor.

margin of safety the amount by which actual or planned sales exceed the break-even point.

marginal cost the varying increment in total cost required to produce and sell an additional unit of product.

marginal revenue the varying increment in total revenue derived from the sale of an additional unit.

market (yield) rate This is the interest rate that investors expect to earn on the investment in this debt security; this rate is used to price the bond issue

market method accounting Securities are reported at current market values (marked-to-market) on the statement date

market segment level activity performed to obtain or maintain operations in a market segment.

market value per share The current price at which shares of stock may be bought or sold

market value The published price (as listed on a stock exchange) multiplied by the number of shares owned

master budget the grouping together of all budgets and supporting schedules. This budget coordinates all the financial and operational activities and places them into an organization wide set of budgets for a given time period.

matching principle An accounting guideline that states that income is determined by relating expenses, to the extent feasible, with revenues that have been recorded

materiality An accounting guideline that states that transactions so insignificant that they would not affect a user's actions or perception of the company may be recorded in the most expedient manner

materials inventory The physical component of inventory; the other components of manufactured inventory are labor costs and overhead costs

materials price variance the difference between the actual materials cost and the standard cost of actual materials inputs.

materials pull system an inventory production flow system in which employees at each station work to replenish the inventory used by employees at subsequent stations. The building of excess inventories is strictly prohibited. When the number of units in inventory reaches a specified limit, work at the station stops until workers at a subsequent station pull a unit from the in-process storage area.

materials push system an inventory production flow system in which employees work to reduce the pile of inventory building up at their work stations. Workers at each station remove materials from an in-process storage area, complete their operation, and place the output in another in-process storage area. Hence, they push the work to the next work station.

materials quantity variance the difference between the standard cost of actual materials inputs and the flexible budget cost for materials.

materials requisition form a document used to record the type and quantity of each raw material issued to the factory.

maturity date The date on which a note or bond matures

measuring unit concept An accounting guideline noting that the accounting unit of measure is the basic unit of money

merchandise inventory A stock of products that a company buys from another company and makes available for sale to its customers

merchandising firm A company that buys finished products, stores the products for varying periods of time, and then resells the products

merchandising organizations organizations that buy and sell goods without performing manufacturing operations.

method of comparables model Equity valuation or stock values are predicted using price multiples, which are defined as stock price divided by some key financial statement number such as net income, net sales, book value of equity, total assets, or cash flow; companies are then compared with their competitors

minimum level budgeting an approach to budgeting that establishes a base amount for all budget items and requires explanation or justification for any budgeted amount above the minimum (base).

minority interest The equity claim of a shareholder owning less than a majority or controlling interest in the company

mission the basic purpose toward which an organization's activities are directed.

mixed costs costs that contain a fixed and a variable cost element.

model a simplified representation of some real-world phenomenon.

modified accelerated cost recovery system (MACRS) See accelerated cost recovery system

movement time the time units spend moving between work or inspection stations.

mutually exclusive investments two or more capital expenditure proposals where the acceptance of one investment automatically causes the rejection of the other(s).

N

natural resources Assets occurring in a natural state, such as timber, petroleum, natural gas, coal, and other mineral deposits

net asset based valuation model Equity is valued as reported assets less reported liabilities

net assets The difference between an entity's assets and liabilities; net assets are equal to stockholders' equity

net book value (NBV) The cost of the asset less accumulated depreciation; also called carrying value

net financial obligations (NFO) net total of all financial (nonoperating) obligations less financial (nonoperating) assets

net income The excess of a firm's revenues over its expenses

net loss The excess of a firm's expenses over its revenues

net operating assets (NOA) Current and long-term operating assets less current and long-term operating liabilities; or net operating working capital plus long-term net operating assets

net operating profit after tax (NOPAT) Sales less operating expenses (including taxes)

net present value the present value of a project's net cash inflows from operations and disinvestment less the amount of the initial investment.

net realizable value The value at which an asset can be sold, net of any costs of disposition

net sales volume variance indicates the impact of a change in sales volume on the contribution margin, given the budgeted selling price and the standard variable costs. It is computed as the difference between the actual and the budgeted sales volumes times the budgeted unit contribution margin.

net sales The total revenue generated by a company through merchandise sales less the revenue given up through sales returns and allowances and sales discounts

net working capital Current assets less current liabilities

nominal rate The rate of interest stated on a bond certificate or other debt instrument

noncash investing and financing activities Significant business activities during the period that do not impact cash inflows or cash outflows

noncurrent liabilities Obligations not due to be paid within one year or the operating cycle, whichever is longer

nonoperating expenses Expenses that relate to the company's financing activities and include interest income and interest expense, gains and losses on sales of securities, and income or loss on discontinued operations

non-value-added activity an activity that does not add value to a product or service from the viewpoint of the customer.

no-par stock Stock that does not have a par value

NOPAT Net operating profit after tax

normal operating cycle For a particular business, the average period of time between the use of cash in its typical operating activity and the subsequent collection of cash from customers

note receivable A promissory note held by the note's payee

notes to financial statements Footnotes in which companies discuss their accounting policies and estimates used in preparing the statements

not-for-profit organization an organization that does not have profit as a primary goal.

not-sufficient-funds check A check from an individual or company that had an insufficient cash balance in the bank when the holder of the check presented it to the bank for payment

O

objective function in linear programming models, the goal to be minimized or maximized.

objectivity principle An accounting principle requiring that, whenever possible, accounting entries are based on objectively determined evidence

off-balance-sheet financing The structuring of a financing arrangement so that no liability shows on the borrower's balance sheet

operating activities business activities that involve transactions that are related to a company's normal income-earning activity (research, develop, produce, purchase, market, and distribute company products and services) and that enter into the calculation of net income on the income statement.

operating asset turnover The ratio obtained by dividing sales by average net operating assets

operating budget detailed plans to guide operations throughout the budget period.

operating cash flow to capital expenditures ratio A firm's net cash flow from operating activities divided by its annual capital expenditures

operating cash flow to current liabilities ratio A firm's net cash flow from operating activities divided by its average current liabilities

operating creditors Those who primarily finance operating activities

operating cycle The time between paying cash for goods or employee services and receiving cash from customers

operating expense margin (OEM) The ratio obtained by dividing any operating expense item or category by sales

operating expenses The usual and customary costs that a company incurs to support its main business activities; these include cost of goods sold, selling expenses, depreciation expense, amortization expense, research and development expense, and taxes on operating profits

operating lease A lease by which the lessor retains the usual risks and rewards of owning the property

operating leverage a measure of the extent that an organization's costs are fixed.

operating profit margin The ratio obtained by dividing NOPAT by sales

operational audit An evaluation of activities, systems, and internal controls within a company to determine their efficiency, effectiveness, and economy

operations list a document that specifies the manufacturing operations and related times required to produce one unit or batch of product.

opportunity cost the net cash inflow that could be obtained if the resources committed to one action were used in the most desirable other alternative.

optimal solution in linear programming models, the feasible solution than maximizes or minimizes the value of the objective function, depending on the decision maker's goal.

optimizing model a model that suggests a specific choice between decision alternatives.

order level activity an activity performed for each sales order.

order-filling costs costs incurred to place finished goods in the hands of purchasers (for example, storing, packaging, and transportation).

order-getting costs costs incurred to obtain customers' orders (for example, advertising, salespersons' salaries and commissions, travel, telephone, and entertainment).

organization chart an illustration of the formal relationships existing between the elements of an organization.

organization costs Expenditures incurred in launching a business (usually a corporation), including attorney's fees and various fees paid to the state

organization structure the arrangement of lines of responsibility within the organization.

organizational cost drivers choices concerning the organization of activities and the involvement of persons inside and outside the organization in decision making.

organizational-based cost systems used for financial reporting, these systems focus on organizational units such as a company, plant, or department rather than on processes and activities.

organizing the process of making the organization into a well-ordered whole.

outcomes assessment see performance measurement.

outlay costs costs that require future expenditures of cash or other resources.

output/input budgeting an approach to budgeting where physical inputs and costs are budgeted as a function of planned unit level activities. The budgeted inputs are a function of the planned outputs.

outsourcing the external acquisition of services or components.

outstanding checks Checks issued by a firm that have not yet been presented to its bank for payment

outstanding stock Shares of stock that are currently owned by stockholders (excludes treasury stock)

owners' equity The interest of owners in the assets of an entity; equal to the difference between the entity's assets and liabilities; also called stockholders' equity

packing list A document that lists the items of merchandise contained in a carton and the quantity of each item; the packing list is usually attached to the outside of the carton

paid-in capital The amount of capital contributed to a corporation by various transactions; the primary source of paid-in capital is from the issuance of shares of stock

par (bonds) Face value of the bond

par value (stock) An amount specified in the corporate charter for each share of stock and imprinted on the face of each stock certificate, often determines the legal capital of the corporation

parent company A company owning one or more subsidiary companies

parsimonious method to multiyear forecasting Forecasting multiple years using only sales growth, net operating profit margin (NOPM), and the turnover of net operating assets (NOAT)

participation budget see bottom-up budget.

partnership A voluntary association of two or more persons for the purpose of conducting a business

password A string of characters that a computer user enters into a computer terminal to prove to the computer that the person using the computer is truly the person named in the user identification code

patent An exclusive privilege granted for 20 years to an inventor that gives the patent holder the right to exclude others from making, using, or selling the invention

payback period the time required to recover the initial investment in a project from operations.

payee The company or individual to whom a promissory note is made payable

payment approval form A document that authorizes the payment of an invoice

pension plan A plan to pay benefits to employees after they retire from the company; the plan may be a defined contribution plan or a defined benefit plan

percentage of net sales method A procedure that determines the uncollectible accounts expense for the year by multiplying net credit sales by the estimated uncollectible percentage

percentage-of-completion method Recognition of revenue by determining the costs incurred per the contract as compared to its total expected costs

performance measurement the determination of the extent to which actual outcomes correspond to planned outcomes.

period costs expired costs not related to manufacturing inventory; they are recognized as expenses when incurred.

period statement A financial statement accumulating information for a specific period of time; examples are the income statement, the statement of stockholders' equity, and the statement of cash flows

permanent account An account used to prepare the balance sheet; that is, asset, liability, and equity capital (capital stock and retained earnings) accounts; any balance in a permanent account at the end of an accounting period is carried forward to the next period

physical inventory A year-end procedure that involves counting the quantity of each inventory item, determining the unit cost of each item, multiplying the unit cost times quantity, and summing the costs of all the items to determine the total inventory at cost

physical model a scaled-down version or replica of physical reality.

planning the process of selecting goals and strategies to achieve those goals.

plant assets Land, buildings, equipment, vehicles, furniture, and fixtures that a firm uses in its operations; sometimes referred to by the acronym PPE

pooling of interests method A method of accounting for business combinations under which the acquired company is recorded on the acquirer's balance sheet at its book value, rather than market value; this method is no longer acceptable under GAAP for acquisitions occurring after 2001

position statement A financial statement, such as the balance sheet, that presents information as of a particular date

post-closing trial balance A list of general ledger accounts and their balances after closing entries have been recorded and posted

postdated check A check from another person or company with a date that is later than the current date; a postdated check does not become cash until the date of the check

practical capacity the maximum possible activity, allowing for normal repairs and maintenance.

predetermined manufacturing overhead rate an overhead rate established at the start of each year by dividing the predicted overhead costs for the year by the predicted volume of activity in the overhead base for the year.

preemptive right The right of a stockholder to maintain his or her proportionate interest in a corporation by having the right to purchase an appropriate share of any new stock issue

preferred stock A class of corporate capital stock typically receiving priority over common stock in dividend payments and distribution of assets should the corporation be liquidated

premium bond A bond that is sold for more than its par (face) value

present value index the present value of the project's subsequent cash flows divided by the initial investment.

present value the current worth of a specified amount of money to be received at some future date at some specified interest rate.

prevention costs quality costs incurred to prevent nonconforming products from being produced or nonconforming services from being performed.

price discrimination illegally charging different purchasers different prices.

price earnings ratio a measure of performance, price earnings ratio compares the current market price with earnings per share of stock and arrives at a multiple of earnings represented by the selling price.

price fixing the organized setting of prices by competitors.

price-earnings ratio Current market price per common share divided by earnings per share

pro forma income A computation of income that begins with the GAAP income from continuing operations (that excludes discontinued operations, extraordinary items and changes in accounting principle), but then excludes other transitory items (most notably, restructuring charges), and some additional items such as expenses arising from acquisitions (goodwill amortization and other acquisition costs), compensation expense in the form of stock options, and research and development expenditures; pro forma income is not GAAP

process manufacturing a manufacturing environment where production is on a continuous basis.

process map (or process flowchart) a schematic overview of all the activities required to complete a process. Each major activity is represented by a rectangle on the map.

process reengineering the fundamental redesign of a process to serve internal or external customers.

process a collection of related activities intended to achieve a common purpose.

processing time the time spent working on units.

product costs all costs incurred in the manufacturing of products; they are carried in the accounts as an asset (inventory) until the product is sold, at which time they are recognized as an expense (cost of goods sold).

product level activity an activity performed to support the production of each different type of product.

product margin computed as product sales less direct product costs.

production order a document that contains a job's unique identification number and specifies details for the job such as the quantity to be produced, the total raw materials requirements, the manufacturing operations and other activities to be performed, and perhaps even the time when each manufacturing operation should be performed.

productivity the relationship between outputs and inputs.

profit center a responsibility center whose manager is responsible for revenues, costs, and resulting profits. It may be an entire organization, but it is more frequently a segment of an organization such as a product line, marketing territory, or store.

profitability analysis an examination of the relationships between revenues, costs, and profits.

profit-volume graph illustrates the relationship between volume and profits; it does not show revenues and costs.

project-level activity an activity performed to support the completion of each project.

promissory note A written promise to pay a certain sum of money on demand or at a determinable future time

purchase method The prescribed method of accounting for business combinations; under the purchase method, assets and liabilities of the acquired company are recorded at fair market value, together with identifiable intangible assets; the balance is ascribed to goodwill

purchase order A document that formally requests a supplier to sell and deliver specific quantities of particular items of merchandise at specified prices

purchase requisition An internal document that requests that the purchasing department order particular items of merchandise

purchases budget indicates the merchandise or materials that must be acquired to meet current needs and ending inventory requirements.

Q

qualitative characteristics of accounting information The characteristics of accounting information that contribute to decision usefulness; the primary qualities are relevance and reliability

quality circles groups of employees involved in the production of products who have the authority, within certain parameters, to address and resolve quality problems as they occur, without seeking management approval.

quality costs costs incurred because poor quality of conformance does (or may) exist.

quality of conformance the degree of conformance between a product and its design specifications.

quality of design the degree of conformance between customer expectations for a product or service and the design specifications of the product or service.

quality conformance to customer expectations.

quantitative model a set of mathematical relationships.

quarterly data Selected quarterly financial information that is reported in annual reports to stockholders

quick ratio see acid test ratio; defined as quick assets (cash and cash equivalents, short-term investments, and current receivables) divided by current liabilities.

R

raw materials inventories the physical ingredients and components that will be converted by machines and/or human labor into a finished product.

realized (or realizable) When referring to revenue, the receipt of an asset or satisfaction of a liability as a result of a transaction or event

recognition criteria The criteria that must be met before a financial statement element may be recorded in the accounts; essentially, the item must meet the definition of an element and must be measurable

record a related set of alphabetic and/or numeric data items.

registered bond A bond for which the issuer (or the trustee) maintains a record of owners and, at the appropriate times, mails out interest payments

relational (cause-and-effect) cost center a cost center that has clearly defined relationships between effort and accomplishment (cause and effect).

relevance A qualitative characteristic of accounting information; relevant information contributes to the predictive and evaluative decisions made by financial statement users

relevant costs future costs that differ between competing decision alternatives.

relevant range the range of activity within which a linear cost function is valid.

reliability A qualitative characteristic of accounting information; reliable information contains no bias or error and faithfully portrays what it intends to represent

remeasurement The computation of gain or loss in the translation of subsidiaries denominated in a foreign currency into $US when the temporal method is used

residual income for investment center excess of investment center income over the minimum rate of return set by top management. The minimum dollar return is computed as a percentage of the investment center's asset base.

residual net operating income (ROPI) model An equity valuation approach that equates the firm's value to the sum of its net operating assets (NOA) and the present value of its residual operating income (ROPI)

residual operating income Net operating profits after tax (NOPAT) less the product of net operating assets (NOA) at the beginning of the period multiplied by the weighted average cost of capital (WACC)

responsibility accounting the structuring of performance reports addressed to individual (or group) members of an organization in a manner that emphasizes the factors they are able to control. The focus is on specific units within the organization that are responsible for the accomplishment of specific activities or objectives.

retailers Companies that buy products from wholesale distributors and sell the products to individual customers, the general public

retained earnings reconciliation The reconciliation of retained earnings from the beginning to the end of the year; the change in retained earnings includes, at a minimum, the net income (loss) for the period and dividends paid, if any, but may include other components as well; also called statement of retained earnings

retained earnings Earned capital, the cumulative net income and loss, of the company (from its inception) that has not been paid to shareholders as dividends

return on assets A financial ratio computed as net income divided by average total assets; sometimes referred to by the acronym ROA; as a measure of performance, return on assets combines the asset turnover and return on sales ratios to measure directly the firm's ability to use its assets to generate profits

return on common stockholders' equity A financial ratio computed as net income less preferred stock dividends divided by average common stockholders' equity; sometimes referred to by the acronym ROCE

return on equity a measure of performance, the return on equity measures the profits attributable to the shareholders as a percentage of their equity in the firm. The general equation for return on equity is: Net income/Average shareholders' equity; sometimes referred to by the acronym ROE.

return on investment for investment center a measure of the earnings per dollar of investment. The return on investment of an investment center is computed by dividing the income of the center by its asset base (usually average total assets). It can also be computed as investment turnover times the return-on-sales ratio.

return on investment The ratio obtained by dividing income by average investment; sometimes referred to by the acronym ROI

return on net operating assets (RNOA) The ratio obtained by dividing NOPAT by average net operating assets

return on sales a measure of performance, the return on sales measures the firm's ability to generate profits from sales produced by the firm's assets. The general equation for return on sales is: net income divided by net sales; sometimes referred to by the acronym ROS

return The amount earned on an investment; also called yield

revenue center a responsibility center whose manager is responsible for the generation of sales revenues.

revenue recognition principle An accounting principle requiring that revenue be recognized when earned and realized (or realizable)

revenue variance the difference between the budgeted sales volume at the budgeted selling price and the actual sales volume at the actual selling price.

revenues inflows of earned resources from providing goods and services to customers; reflected as increases in stockholders' equity

Robinson-Patman Act prohibits price discrimination when purchasers compete with one another in the sale of their products or services to third parties.

rolling budget see continuous budgeting.

S

sale on account A sale of merchandise made on a credit basis

sales budget a plan of unit sales volume and sales revenue for a future period. It may also contain a forecast of sales collections.

sales mix the relative portion of unit or dollar sales derived from each product or service.

sales price variance the impact on revenues of a change in selling price, given the actual sales volume. It is computed as the change in selling price times the actual sales volume.

sales volume variance indicates the impact on revenues of change in sales volume, assuming there was no change in selling price. It is computed as the difference between the actual and the budgeted sales volumes times the budgeted selling price.

salvage value The expected net recovery when a plant asset is sold or removed from service; also called residual value

scatter diagram a graph of past activity and cost data, with individual observations represented by dots.

secured bond A bond that pledges specific property as security for meeting the terms of the bond agreement

Securities and Exchange Commission (SEC) The commission, created by the 1934 Securities Act, that has broad powers to regulate the issuance and trading of securities, and the financial reporting of companies issuing securities to the public

segment income all revenues of a segment minus all costs directly or indirectly charged to it.

segment margin the amount that a segment contributes toward the common (indirect) costs of the organization and toward profits. It is computed as segment sales less direct segment costs.

segment reports income statements that show operating results for portions or segments of a business. Segment reporting is used primarily for internal purposes, although generally accepted accounting principles also require disclosure of segment information for some public corporations.

segments Subdivisions of a firm for which supplemental financial information is disclosed

selling expense budget presents the expenses the organization plans to incur in connection with sales and distribution.

semi-variable costs see mixed costs.

sensitivity analysis the study of the responsiveness of a model to changes in one or more of its independent variables.

serial bond A bond issue that staggers the bond maturity dates over a series of years

service cost (pensions) The increase in the pension obligation due to employees working another year for the employer

service costing the process of assigning costs to services performed.

service department a department that provides support services to production and/or other support departments.

service organizations nonmanufacturing organizations that perform work for others, including banks, hospitals, and real estate agencies.

setup time the time required to prepare equipment to produce a specific product.

Sherman Antitrust Act prohibits price fixing.

significant influence The ability of the investor to affect the financing or operating policies of the investee

simplex method a mathematical approach to solving linear programming models containing three or more variables.

sinking fund provision A bond feature that requires the borrower to retire a portion of the bonds each year or, in some cases, to make payments each year to a trustee who is responsible for managing the resources needed to retire the bonds at maturity

solvency refers to the firm's ability to pay its debts as they become due.

source document Any written document or computer record evidencing an accounting transaction, such as a bank check or deposit slip, sales invoice, or cash register tape

special purpose entity (See variable interest entity)

spin-off A form of equity carve out in which divestiture is accomplished by distribution of a company's shares in a subsidiary to the company's shareholders who then own the shares in the subsidiary directly rather than through the parent company

split-off point the point in the process where joint products become separately identifiable.

split-off A form of equity carve out in which divestiture is accomplished by the parent company's exchange of stock in the subsidiary in return for shares in the parent owned by its shareholders

spread The difference between the net financial return (NFR) and the return on net operating activities (RNOA)

standard cost variance analysis a system for examining the flexible budget variance, which is the difference between the actual cost and flexible budget cost of producing a given quantity of product or service.

standard cost a budget that indicates what it should cost to provide an activity or produce one batch or unit of product under efficient operating conditions.

stated value A nominal amount that may be assigned to each share of no-par stock and accounted for much as if it were a par value

statement of cash flows a financial statement that reports the major sources and uses of cash classified into operating, investing, and financing activities and that indicates the net increase or decrease in cash; the statement also includes a schedule of any significant noncash investing and financing activities that occur during the period.

statement of cost of goods manufactured a report that summarizes the cost of goods completed and transferred into finished goods inventory during the period.

statement of equity See statement of stockholders' equity

statement of financial position A financial statement showing a firm's assets, liabilities, and stockholders' equity at a specific date; also called a balance sheet

statement of retained earnings See retained earnings reconciliation

statement of stockholders' equity A financial statement presenting information on the events causing a change in stockholders' equity during a period; the statement presents the beginning balance, additions to, deductions from, and the ending balance of stockholders' equity for the period

static budget a budget based on a prior prediction of expected sales and production.

step costs costs that are constant within a narrow range of activity but shift to a higher level with an increased range of activity. Total step costs increase in a step-like fashion as activity increases.

step method A method of allocating service department costs that gives partial recognition to interdepartmental services by using a methodology that allocates service department costs sequentially to both the remaining service departments and the producing departments.

stock dividends The payment of dividends in shares of stock

stock split Additional shares of its own stock issued by a corporation to its current stockholders in proportion to their current ownership interests without changing the balances in the related stockholders' equity accounts; a formal stock split increases the number of shares outstanding and reduces proportionately the stock's per share par value

storyboard a process map developed by employees who perform the component activities within a process.

straight-line depreciation A depreciation procedure that allocates uniform amounts of depreciation expense to each full period of a depreciable asset's useful life

strategic business segment a segment that has its own mission and set of goals to be achieved. The mission of the segment influences the decisions that its top managers make in both short-run and long-run situations.

strategic cost management making decisions concerning specific cost drivers within the context of an organization's business strategy, its internal value chain, and its place in a larger value chain stretching from the development and use of resources to the final consumers.

strategic plan a guideline or framework for making specific medium-range or short-run decisions.

strategic position analysis an organization's basic way of competing to sell products or services.

strategic position how an organization wants to place itself in comparison to the competition.

strategy a course of action that will assist in achieving one or more goals.

structural cost drivers fundamental choices about the size and scope of operations and technologies employed in delivering products or services to customers. These choices affect the types of activities and the costs of activities performed to satisfy customer needs.

suboptimization when managers or operating units, acting in their own best interests, make decisions that are not in the best interest of the organization as a whole.

subsequent events Events occurring shortly after a fiscal year-end that will be reported as supplemental information to the financial statements of the year just ended

subsidiaries Companies that are owned by the parent company

subsidiary ledger A set of accounts or records that contains detailed information about the items included in the balance of one general ledger account

summary of significant accounting policies A financial statement disclosure, usually the initial note to the statements, which identifies the major accounting policies and procedures used by the firm

sum-of-the-years'-digits method An accelerated depreciation method that allocates depreciation expense to each year in a fractional proportion, the denominator of which is the sum of the years' digits in the useful life of the asset and the numerator of which is the remaining useful life of the asset at the beginning of the current depreciation period

sunk costs costs resulting from past decisions that cannot be changed.

T

T-account An abbreviated form of the formal account in the shape of a T; use is usually limited to illustrations of accounting techniques and analysis

target costing establishes the allowable cost of a product or service by starting with determining what customers are willing to pay for the product or service and then subtracting a desired profit on sales.

temporary account An account used to gather information for an accounting period; at the end of the period, the balance is transferred to a permanent stockholders' equity account; revenue, expense, and dividends accounts are temporary accounts

term loan A long-term borrowing, evidenced by a note payable, which is contracted with a single lender

terminal period The forecast period following the horizon period

theory of constraints every process has a bottleneck (constraining resource), and production cannot take place faster than it is processed through the bottleneck. The theory's goal is to maximize throughput in a constrained environment.

throughput sales revenue minus direct materials costs. See also theory of constraints.

time-adjusted rate of return see internal rate of return.

times interest earned ratio a measure of long-term solvency and interest-paying ability; measured as income before interest expense and income taxes divided by interest expense

top-down budget a budget where top management decides on the primary goals and objectives for the organization and communicates them to lower management levels.

total compensation cost The sum of gross pay, payroll taxes, and fringe benefits paid by the employer

trade credit Inventories purchased on credit from other companies

trade discount An amount, usually based on quantity of merchandise purchased, that the seller subtracts from the list price of merchandise to determine the invoice price

trade name An exclusive and continuing right to use a certain term or name to identify a brand or family of products

trademark An exclusive and continuing right to use a certain symbol to identify a brand or family of products

trading on the equity The use of borrowed funds in the capital structure of a firm; the expectation is that the funds will earn a return higher than the rate of interest on the borrowed funds

trading securities Investments in securities that management intends to actively trade (buy and sell) for trading profits as market prices fluctuate

transfer price the internal value assigned a product or service that one division provides to another.

transitory items Transactions or events that are not likely to recur

translation adjustment The change in the value of the net assets of a subsidiary whose assets and liabilities are denominated in a foreign currency

treasury stock Shares of outstanding stock that have been acquired (and not retired) by the issuing corporation; treasury stock is recorded at cost and deducted from stockholders' equity in the balance sheet

trend percentages A comparison of the same financial item over two or more years stated as a percentage of a base-year amount

trial balance A list of the account titles in the general ledger, their respective debit or credit balances, and the totals of the debit and credit amounts

U

unadjusted trial balance A list of general ledger accounts and their balances taken before adjustments have been made

uncollectible accounts expense The expense stemming from the inability of a business to collect an amount previously recorded as a receivable; sometimes called bad debts expense; normally classified as a selling or administrative expense

unearned revenue A liability representing revenues received in advance; also called deferred revenue

unit contribution margin the difference between the unit selling price and the unit variable costs.

unit level activity an activity performed for each unit of product produced or sold.

unit level approach an approach to analyzing cost behavior that assumes changes in costs are best explained by changes in the number of units or sales dollars of products or services provided for customers.

units-of-production method A depreciation method that allocates depreciation expense to each operating period in proportion to the amount of the asset's expected total production capacity used each period

useful life The period of time an asset is used by an entity in its operating activities, running from date of acquisition to date of disposal (or removal from service)

V

value chain analysis the study of value-producing activities, stretching from basic raw materials to the final consumer of a product or service.

value chain the set of value-producing activities stretching from basic raw materials to the final consumer.

value the worth in usefulness or importance of a product or service to the customer.

value-added activity an activity that adds value to a product or service from the viewpoint of the customer.

variable cost ratio variable costs as a portion of sales revenue.

variable costing an approach to product costing that treats variable manufacturing costs as product costs and fixed manufacturing costs as period costs.

variable costs costs that are an identical amount for each incremental unit of activity. Their total amount increases as activity increases, equaling zero dollars when activity is zero and increasing at a constant amount per unit of activity.

variable costs Those costs that change in proportion to changes in sales volume

variable interest entity (VIE) Any form of business organization (such as corporation, partnership, trust) that is established by a sponsoring company and provides benefits to that company in the form of asset securitization or project financing; VIEs were formerly known as special purpose entities (SPEs)

variable manufacturing overhead all variable costs, except direct labor and direct materials, associated with converting raw materials into finished goods.

variable overhead effectiveness variance the difference between the standard variable overhead cost for the actual inputs and the flexible budget cost for variable overhead based on outputs.

variable overhead spending variance the difference between the actual variable overhead cost and the standard variable overhead cost for the actual inputs.

variable selling and administrative costs all variable costs other than those directly associated with converting raw materials into finished goods.

variance a comparison of actual and budgeted (or allowed) costs or revenues which are usually identified in financial performance reports.

vertical analysis an evaluative standard that restates amounts in the current financial statements as a percentage of some base measure such as sales; focused on one period's statements.

virtual integration the use of information technology and partnership concepts to allow two or more entities along a value chain to act as if they were a single economic entity.

voucher Another name for the payment approval form

waiting time the time units spend in temporary storage waiting to be processed, moved, or inspected.

W

warranties Guarantees against product defects for a designated period of time after sale

wasting assets Another name for natural resources; see natural resources

weighted average cost of capital (WACC) The discount rate where the weights are the relative percentages of debt and equity in the capital structure and are applied to the expected returns on debt and equity respectively; an average of the after-tax cost of all long-term borrowings and the cost of equity

weighted average method in process costing, a costing method that spreads the combined beginning inventory cost and current manufacturing costs (for materials, labor, and overhead) over the units completed and those in ending inventory on an average basis.

work in process inventory The cost of inventories that are in the manufacturing process and have not yet reached completion

work ticket a document used to record the time a job spends in a specific manufacturing operation.

working capital a measure of solvency, working capital is the difference between current assets and current liabilities and is the net amount of working funds available in the short run. The general equation for working capital is: Current assets minus Current liabilities.

work-in-process inventories partially completed goods consisting of raw materials that are in the process of being converted into a finished product.

Z

zero coupon bond A bond that offers no periodic interest payments but that is issued at a substantial discount from its face value

zero-based budgeting a variation of the minimum level approach to budgeting where every dollar of expenditure must be justified.

z-score The outcome of the Altman Z-score bankruptcy prediction model

Index

A

Abbott Laboratories, 5:29, 6:48, 11:37, 12:24–26
Abercrombie & Fitch, 1:34, 4:35, 6:39, 10:24, 31, 38, 11:23–24, 31–33, 12:17
Absorption costing, 22:11
    See also under Costing, product: job and process operations
Accenture. *See* Owner financing, reporting/analyzing
Accounting cycle, 3:3
Accounting for MBAs, introducing financial
    Berkshire Hathaway, 1:1–3
    information demand/supply, 1:5–8
    managerial and financial accounting, constrasting, 14:3–5
    principles and governance structures
        environment, financial accounting, 1:23–25
        regulatory and legal environment, 1:25–28
        SEC enforcement actions, 1:28–30
    profitability analysis
        analysis/interpretation of financial statements, 1:18–20
        return on equity, 1:18
        return on net operating assets, 1:16–17
    reporting on business activities, 1:3–5, 21–22
    review, chapter
        cases, 1:38
        discussion questions, 1:30–31
        end-module, 1:21
        exercises/mini-exercises, 1:31–33
        guidance answers, 1:30
        problems, 1:33–38
    statements, financial
        balance sheet, 1:8–10
        beyond, information, 1:15–16
        cash flows, 1:13–14
        income, 1:10–12
        linkages between, 1:14
        overview, 1:8
        stockholders equity, 1:12–13
    See also Managerial accounting for MBAs, introducing
Accounts payable, 8:4–5, B:13
Accounts payable turnover (APT), 8:5–6
Accounts receivable, 13:12–13, B:11–12
    See also under Operating assets, reporting/analyzing
Accrual accounting, 2:13–14, 24–25
    See also under Statement construction and analyzing transactions, financial
Accrued expenses, 3:10, 12
Accrued liabilities, 8:7–9, B:13–14
Accrued revenues, 3:10, 12
Accumulated other comprehensive income/loss, 2:10
Accumulated post-employment benefit obligation (APBO), 10:17, 20
Ace Hardware, 18:2
Activities, planning/financing/investing in business, 1:3–4
    See also Financing activities; Intercorporate investments, reporting/analyzing; Investing activities; Operating activities
Activity-based approach to budgeting, 20:5
Activity-based management (ABM), 19:22
Activity cost drivers, 14:13, 14, 15:16–17
    See also activity-based costing *under* Costing, product: assigning indirect costs

Acura, 14:19
Additional paid-in-capital, 2:10
Adelphia Communications, 1:24, 29–30
Adjusting accounts/process, 2:13–14, 24–25
    See also accrual accounting *under* Statement construction and analyzing transactions, financial; Statements, adjusting/forecasting financial
Administrative costs, 16:5
Advanced Micro Devices, 5:35
Aflac, 14:7
Agilent, 7:25–26
Airline success and cost behavior analysis, 15:1–2
Alamo, 15:8
Albertsons, Inc., 2:39–40
Alcoa, 23:19
Allied Domecq, B:3
Allocation base, cost, 19:4–5
Allstate Insurance Company, 3:29
Amazon.com, 5:37, 14:7, 19, 16:1
American, The, 16:9
American Airlines, 10:2, 16, 18–20, 14:4
American Bar Association (ABA), 14:15
American Institute of Certified Public Accountants (AICPA), 1:23, 14:15
American Stock Exchange Pharmaceutical Index, 5:2
Amgen, 7:42
Amortization, 8:17–19, 10:27–28, B:11
Analyst reports, 2:31–32
Annuities, 8:13, 27, 29
AOLTime Warner, 17:2
Apple Computer, 1:4, 36–38, 15:8, 17:32
    See also Statement construction and analyzing transactions, financial; Statements and transactional analysis, introducing financial
Arctic Company, B:34
Articulation of financial statements, 2:21–23
Assets, 1:8, 2:5–7
    See also Balance sheet; Cash *and* Income *listings;* Operating assets, reporting/analyzing; Return *listings;* Stockholders' equity, statement of; *specific type of asset*
AT&T, 7:39–40, 9:22–23, 29, 17:2
AT&T Wireless, 9:22–23
Audit committee, 1:25–26
Audit firms, independent, 1:27–28, 13:26
Automobiles, green, 23:1–2
Available-for-sale (AFS) marketable securities, 7:7–8
Average cost (AC) inventory costing method, 6:16
Avoidable common segment costs, 22:6

B

Balanced scorecard, 22:18–21, 26, 29
Balance sheet
    adjusting the, 2:25, 11:6–7
    assets: reflecting investing activities, 2:5–7
    book-to-market ratios, 2:12
    budgeting, 20:8, 14, 15
    equation, the accounting, 1:8
    Expresso Royale, B:26
    financing activities, 1:10
    forecasting the, 11:12–16
    investing activities, 1:9
    Java House, B:9

Johnson & Johnson, 12:13–14
    liabilities and equity, 2:7–11
    Lowes, 4:14–16
    operating and nonoperating items, 4:9
    overview, 1:8
    research and development, 5:13
    revenue recognition, 5:9, 11
    template, preparation using effects, 2:26, 28
    See also Intercorporate investments, reporting/analyzing; Kimberly-Clark; Nonowner financing, reporting/analyzing; Off-balance-sheet financing, reporting/analyzing; Operating assets, reporting/analyzing; Owner financing, reporting/analyzing; Statement *listings*
Ballard Power Systems, 23:2
Bank of America, 5:29
Banner AD Corporation, 5:29
Barnes & Noble, 5:36, 14:7, 17:12
Batch-level activity in manufacturing cost hierarchy, 15:17
Bausch & Lomb, 21:4
BearingPoint, 9:23
Bear Stearns, 2:32
Bell Atlantic Corporation, 8:1
Bell Communications Research, 19:5
Bellcore, 19:5
BellSouth Corporation, 22:3
Benchmarks and standards, 21:1–2, 23:18–19
Benihana, Inc., 5:40–41
Berkshire Hathaway, 4:1, 7:35–36
    See also Accounting for MBAs, introducing financial
Best Buy, 1:8, 6:45, 10:39, 11:27, 33–35
Bextra, 5:1
BFI, 17:14
Boeing, 14:8, 17:16
Bombardier, 15:2
Bonds. *See* Nonowner financing, reporting/analyzing
Book-to-market ratios, 2:7, 11, 12, 15
Boston Scientific, 8:31
Bottom-up budget, 20:16
Bowater Incorporated, 18:9
Break-even point. *See under* Cost-volume-profit analysis
Bristol-Myers Squibb, 1:24, 5:29–30, 33, 8:31, 9:28
Budgeting/profit planning, operational
    approaches to budgeting
        activity-based, 20:5
        incremental, 20:5
        minimum level, 20:5–6
        output/input, 20:4, 8–9
    data warehousing, 20:4
    employees, effect on behavior of
        ethics, 20:17
        forecasts, 20:16–17
        participation, employee, 20:15–16
        periods, budgeting, 20:16
        successful budgets, developing, 20:17–18
    future of budgeting, 20:1–2
    master budget
        assembly, procedures involved in budget, 20:8
        balance sheet, 20:8
        cash budget, 20:11–13
        finalizing the budget, 20:14–15
        financial statements, budgeted, 20:13–15

general and administrative expense budget, 20:10–11

goal of developing, 20:7

operating cycle of manufacturer/merchandiser, 20:7

purchases budget, 20:9–10

sales budget, 20:9

selling expense budget, 20:10

performance assessment, 21:6–9

reasons for budgeting, 20:3–4

review, chapter

cases, 20:29–30

discussion questions, 20:20

end-of-module, 20:18–20

exercises/mini-exercises, 20:20–25

guidance answers, 20:20

mid-module, 20:6–7

problems, 20:25–28

Budweiser, 14:8

Buffett, Warren, 1:1–3, 14, 28, 4:1

Burger King, 16:3

Business Ethics, B:2

Business Week, 4:2, 11:2, 14:9, 12

C

California Private Transportation Company, 17:14

Cannon, 14:18

Capital, contributed/earned, 2:10, 10:25, 26

See also Owner financing, reporting/analyzing

Capital distributions, 3:7

Capital investment, 3:5–6

Capitalization, 6:13–14, 26–27, 10:7–10

Capital lease method for the reporting of leases, 10:5

Carnegie Steel Company, 14:7, 15:15

Carnival Cruises, 6:45

Carrying value, 6:28–29

Case, comprehensive. *See* cases *under individual subject headings;* Kimberly-Clark

Cash budget, 20:11–13

Cash cycle, 2:9–10

Cash flows, statement of

accounting for MBAs, introducing financial, 1:13–14

adjusting the, 11:7–9

computations, 2:17–19

direct method reporting of, B:22–25

financing activities, B:15–16, 25

forecasting the, 11:16–17

format of, 2:16–17

framework

classifications, usefulness of, B:7

financing activities, B:6–7

investing activities, B:6

noncash investing and financing activities, B:7

operating activities, B:6

overview, B:4–5

usefulness of statement, B:8

income statement compared to, 2:16

indirect method, supplemental disclosures for, B:17–19

intercorporate investments, reporting/analyzing, 7:5

investing activities, B:14–15, 25

Java House

depreciation/amortization/depletion expenses, B:11

direct method reporting of statement of cash flows, B:23–25

financing activities, B:15–16

income statement/balance sheet, B:9

indirect method of reporting net cash flow from operating activities, B:17–18

investing activities, B:14–15

Johnson & Johnson, 12:15

Kimberly-Clark, 13:25–26

net cash flow from operating activities

accounts payable change, B:13

accounts receivable, B:11–12

accrued liabilities, B:13–14

gains/losses related to financing activities, B:11

income to net cash flow, convert, B:10–11

indirect method of reporting, B:8–10

inventory change, B:12

Java House illustration, B:11–14

prepaid expenses, B:12

operating assets, reporting/analyzing, 6:19

overview, 1:13–14, B:4

review, chapter

discussion questions, B:28–29

end-of-module, B:19–22, 25–27

exercises/mini-exercises, B:29–32

guidance answers, B:27

problems, B:33–39

SEC and FASB requirements, 2:15

Starbucks, B:2–3

summary of net cash flows, B:16–17

template, preparation using effects, 2:28

Caterpillar (CAT), 6:19, 45, 7:38, 46–47

CBS Corporation, 11:11, 41–43

Celebrex, 5:1

Ceridian Corporation, 9:16

C.H. Robinson WorldWide, 22:2

Chambers, John, 6:2

Charge-offs, 5:14

Chart, organizational, 14:10–11

Chartists and predicting equity value, 12:12

Chesapeake Energy Corporation, 9:5

Chrysler, 23:9

Circuit City, 14:8

Cisco Systems, 1:34, 2:7, 5:5, 7, 11:44–48, 16:1

See also Operating assets, reporting/analyzing

Citigroup, 2:7, 32, 7:24

Clear Channel Communications, 7:24

Closing process for preparing financial statements, 3:21–22, 24–25

CNA Financial Corporation, 7:36–37

Coca-Cola Company, 14:5–7, 18:21–22

Codes of ethics, 14:15–16

Coefficient of determination, 15:12–13

Colgate-Palmolive Company, 6:38, 11:20–23, 13:1

Collateral, 8:24

Colleges and service department cost allocation, 19:8

Comcast Corporation, 4:37, 8:32, 40–41

Commentators and demand for financial accounting information, business, 1:6

Committed fixed costs, 15:8

Common segment costs, 22:6

Common-size balance sheet, 13:21, 22

Common-size income statement, 13:8–9

Common stock, 2:10, 9:6

Communication industry and return on net operating assets, 4:13

Compaq Computer, 7:21, 14:1–2

Compensation plans, stock, 9:9–11

Competitive environment, 1:18–20, 13:28, 14:11–12

Compounding, 8:25–28

Comprehensive income, 9:17–18

Consolidation for financial statements and intercorporate investments, 7:18–21, 26–27, 30–31

Constraints and allocation of limited resources, 17:16–19

Construction projects and special purpose entities, 10:24

Continental Airlines, 10:29–30

Continuous budgeting, 20:16

Continuous improvement costing, 23:17–18

Contract rate and pricing debt, 8:12

Contributed capital, 2:10

See also Owner financing, reporting/analyzing

Contribution income statement, 16:6–8, 17:10

Control, investments with. *See under* Intercorporate investments, reporting/analyzing

Controllable costs and performance assessment, 21:20–21

Controlling process and results that agree with plans, 14:11

Conversion costs, 18:6

Convertible securities, 9:23–25

Cook County Hospital, 14:19

Cooper, Robin, 14:4

Coors, 14:8

Core competencies and value chain perspective, 23:6–7

Cornell University, 14:19, 16:3

Corning, 7:23

Corrections Corporation of America, 17:14

Cost-based approaches to pricing, 23:8–11

Cost behavior/activity management/cost estimation, 2:3–5, 5:14–15, 14:1–2, 4–5

airline success, 15:1–2

analysis, cost behavior

additional patterns, 15:6–8

committed and discretionary fixed costs, 15:8

factors affecting patterns, 15:5

patterns, four basic, 15:3–5

total cost function for organization/segment, 15:5–6

cost driver classifications, alternative

customer cost hierarchy, 15:18

manufacturing cost hierarchy, 15:16–17

overview, 15:15–16

estimation, cost

activity and costs, matching, 15:15

high-low estimation, 15:9–11

identifying cost drivers, 15:15

least-square regression analysis, 15:12–13

scatter diagrams, 15:11

technology/prices, changes in, 15:14–15

leadership, cost, 14:7, 9

managerial accounting for MBAs, introducing, 14:1–2, 4–5

review, chapter

cases, 15:27–30

discussion questions, 15:20–21

end-of-module, 15:19–20

exercises/mini-exercises, 15:21–26

guidance answers, 15:20

mid-module, 15:8

problems, 15:26–27

See also Operating assets, reporting/analyzing; Relevant costs/benefits for decision making; Statement *listings; specific type of cost*

Cost center and responsibility accounting system, 21:5

Costco, 3:31, 13:1

Cost Cutters, 16:21

Cost drivers, 14:5

See also under Managerial accounting for MBAs, introducing *and* Cost behavior/activity management/cost estimation

Costing, product: assigning indirect costs

activity-based costing

implementation issues, 19:21–23

limitations of, 19:21

model, two-stage, 19:15–16

overhead rate, inadequacies of a single, 19:13–14

overhead with, applying, 19:19–21

traditional and, comparing, 19:16–17

allocating indirect costs

bases, allocation, 19:4–5

objectives, cost, 19:3–4

pools, cost, 19:4

questions concerning, 19:3

service department costs, 19:5

firms, circumstances of three diverse, 19:1–2

review, chapter

cases, 19:38–40

discussion questions, 19:26–27

end-of-module, 19:23–26

exercises/mini-exercises, 19:27–35

guidance answers, 19:26
mid-module, 19:11–13
problems, 19:35–38
service department cost allocations
direct department costs, 19:5, 7–8
direct method, 19:7–8
dual rates, 19:11
indirect department costs, 19:5
linear algebra (reciprocal) method, 19:10–11
overview, 19:6
peanut butter approach, 19:5
step method, 19:8–10
traditional costing systems
activity-based and, comparing, 19:16–17
department rates, applying overhead with, 19:18–19
plantwide rates, applying overhead with, 19:17–18
Costing, product: job and process operations
absorption and variable costing
alternatives to inventory valuation, 18:32
concepts, basic, 18:28
income statement formats, 18:28–32
inventory valuation differences between, 18:28
overview, 18:27–28
environment, the production, 18:8–10
files and records, production, 18:9–10
inventory
components of product costs, three, 18:5–6
general ledger accounts and subsidiary records, 18:15
organizational classifications, 18:3–4
overhead, manufacturing, 18:6–8
period and product costs, 18:4–5
job costing for products/services
general ledger accounts and subsidiary records, 18:15
illustrated, job costing, 18:11–15
income statement and cost of goods sold, 18:15–16
overhead, overapplied/underapplied, 18:18–19
overview, 18:10–11
service organizations, 18:18–19
software, 18:9
weaknesses in model, 18:14
process costing
first-in-first-out method, 18:25
overview, 18:21–22
report, cost of production, 18:22–25
service organizations, 18:25–26
weighted average method, 18:25
review, chapter
cases, 18:45–46
discussion questions, 18:33
end-of-module, 18:26–27
exercises/mini-exercises, 18:33–38
guidance answers, 18:32
mid-module, 18:19–21
problems, 18:39–44
success, cost competition and company, 18:1–2
Cost of goods sold (COGS), 6:13–14, 19, 8:5, 13:6, 18:15–16, B:23–24
Cost reduction proposal, 17:4
Cost-volume-profit (CVP) analysis
assumptions, key, 16:4
break-even point
determining, 16:8
graph, cost-volume profit, 16:9–10
graph, profit-volume, 16:10–11
planning, profit, 16:8–9
taxes, income, 16:11–12
contribution and functional income statements, 16:6–8
formula, profit, 16:4–6
multiple-product-cost-volume-profit analysis, 16:14–17

operating leverage, 16:17–19
overview, 16:3
review, chapter
cases, 16:30–32
discussion questions, 16:20–21
end-of-module, 16:19–20
exercises/mini-exercises, 16:21–26
guidance answers, 16:20
mid-module, 16:12–14
problems, 16:26–30
sales mix/dollar analysis, 16:14–17
structure (cost) and firm profitability, 16:1–2
Council of Tree and Landscape Appraisers, 15:14
Coupon rate and pricing debt, 8:12
Courts and material misstatements in financial statements, 1:29–30
Covenants, 1:6, 8:24
Credit analysis, 13:28–29
Creditors and demand for financial accounting information, 1:6
Credit services, 2:32
Cunningham Motor Company, 17:1–2
Current assets, 2:6, 9
Current liabilities, 2:8–9, 4:19–20, 13:16–17, B:18–19
See also Nonowner financing, reporting/analyzing
Current ratio, 4:19–20
Customer cost hierarchy, 15:18
Customers and demand for financial accounting information, 1:6
CVS Corporation, 8:38, 12:17

D

Daihatsu Motor Company, 23:18
DaimlerChrysler, 18:2, 23:1
Dair Company, B:35
Data services, 2:33
Data warehousing and budgeting, 20:4
Daufel Enterprises, 17:19
Debt, long/short-term, 8:10–11, 13:17–18
See also Nonowner financing, reporting/analyzing
Debt is reasonable, how much, 2:7
Debt vs. equity, measuring relative use of, 4:18–19
Deere & Company, 5:34, 6:43–44, 8:35
Default risk, 8:22
Deferred tax valuation, 5:19–22, 13:15–16, 19–20
Deferred (unearned) revenue, 2:10
Defined benefit pension plan, 10:12
Defined contribution pension plan, 10:12
Dell Computer, 1:31, 2:37–38, 5:5, 6:23, 14:1–3, 7, 19
Deloitte & Touche, 1:27, 13:26
Delta Airlines, 15:1
Department rates, applying overhead with, 19:18–19
Depletion expenses, B:11
Depreciation, 6:27–31, 35, 13:13–14, B:11, 15, 24
Depression, The Great, 1:23
Derivatives, 7:31–32, 13:24–25
Diary Queen, 15:6
Differential analysis. See under Relevant costs/benefits for decision making
Direct materials/labor, 15:15–16, 16:5, 18:5–6
Direct materials standards and variance analysis for variable costs, 21:12–14
Direct method reporting of statement of cash flows, B:22–25
Directors and demand for financial accounting information, 1:6
Direct segment fixed costs, 22:6
Disclosure, benefits/costs of, 1:7–8, 21–22, 7:8–10
See also Footnote disclosures; Reporting, financial; Statement listings
Discontinued operations, 2:14, 4:29, 5:23
Discount bonds, 8:14, 16
Discounted cash flow model (DCF), 12:4–6, 12, 13:31
Discretionary fixed costs, 15:8
Disney Company, 5:10
Disposal values, 17:5–6

Distributions, capital, 3:7
Dividend discount model for equity valuation, 12:11
Dividend preference and preferred stock, 9:5
Dividends, cash, 9:12–13
Dividends, stock, 9:14–15
Dividends as distributions of income, 3:7
Double-declining-balance depreciation method, 6:29–31
Doubtful accounts, 6:7–8, 13:12–13
Dow Chemical, 5:35, 6:47–48, 10:31, 42–43
Dual prices, 22:12
Dual rates and service department cost allocations, 19:11
Dunkin' Donuts, B:2–3
DuPont, 1:31, 7:37–38, 10:40–41

E

Earned capital, 2:10
See also Owner financing, reporting/analyzing
Earnings as most important metric to report, 1:12
Earnings per share (EPS), 5:3, 24–26, 13:7–8
Earthlink, 23:23–24
EA Systems, 1:35
Ebbers, Bernie, 6:27
Economic value added (EVA), 22:16–17
EDGAR database, 1:21–23
Electronic Data Systems, 9:14
Eli Lilly, 12:1
Embraer, 15:2
Emerging Issues Task Force (EITF), 1:23
Emory University, 14:19
Employee severance costs, 5:14
Enron, 1:23, 24, 30, 2:4
Environmental expenditures, 13:17
Environment and costing systems, the production, 18:8–10
Enviro-Recovery Corporation, 19:2
Epson, 23:18
Equation, the accounting, 1:8–9, 8:3, B:14–15
Equipment costs, 2:4–5, 13:13–14
See also property/plant/equipment under Operating assets, reporting/analyzing
Equity carve outs. See under Owner financing, reporting/ analyzing
Equity/equity investments, 2:8, 10, 13:14, 22–23, 31–32
See also Return listings; Stockholders' equity, statement of
Equity method and accounting for investments with significant influence, 7:13–16, 18, 28–30
Equity securities, analyzing/valuing
assessment of valuation models, 12:11–12
discounted cash flow model, 12:4–6, 12
Johnson & Johnson, 12:1–3, 13–15
managerial insights from the residual operating income model, 12:10–11
models, equity valuation, 12:3–4
residual operating income model, 12:8–12
review, chapter
cases, 12:12:28
discussion questions, 12:16
end-of-module, 12:12–13
exercises/mini-exercises, 12:16–20
guidance answers, 12:15
mid-module, 12:7
problems, 12:20–27
Equivalent completed units, 18:24
Equivalents, cash, B:4
See also Cash flows, statement of
Ericsson, Inc., 22:15
Ernst & Young, 1:27
Ethics
budgeting, 20:17
managerial accounting, 14:15–16
responsibility accounting system, 21:4
sunk costs, 17:5
European Union (EU), 1:24
Excluded intangible assets, 2:7
Expenses, 2:13, 5:14–15

See also Statement *listings; specific type of expense*
Expresso Royale, B:19–22, 25–27
Extraordinary items, 2:14, 5:23–24
Exxon Mobil, 18:9

F

Face amount of the bond, 8:12
Facility-level activity in manufacturing cost hierarchy, 15:17
Falk, Thomas J., 13:1
Fannie Mae, 1:29
FASB. *See* Financial Accounting Standards Board
Federal National Mortgage Association, 1:29
FedEx, 5:32, 39–40, 10:39–40, 14:4, 12
Files/records, production, 18:9–10
Financial Accounting Standards Board (FASB)
    cash flows, statement of, 2:15
    overview, 1:23
    pensions, 10:17
    restructuring costs, 5:14
    special purpose entities, 10:25
Financial leverage (FLEV), 10:3
Financing activities, 1:10, 20:8, B:6–7, 11, 15–16, 25
Finished goods inventories, 18:3
Fiorina, Carly, 14:1
First-in-first-out (FIFO) inventory costing method, 6:15, 19, 20, 13:14, 18:25
Fiscal year, 1:8
Fitch Ratings, 2:32
Fixed costs, 15:3–4, 8, 16:5, 22:6
Flexible budgets, 21:6–9
Foot Locker, 3:27
Footnote disclosures
    cash flows, statement of, B:25
    doubtful accounts, 6:7–8
    inventory, 6:16–17
    Kimberly-Clark, 13:6
    nonowner financing, reporting/analyzing, 8:20–21
    off-balance-sheet financing
        leases, 10:6–7
        pensions, 10:15–20
    property/plant/equipment, 6:33
Ford Motor Company, 1:31, 8:9, 34, 10:22, 23–24, 26, 35–36, 11:11, 14:7, 23:1, 2, 9
Forecasts and budget preparation, 20:16–17
    See also Statements, adjusting/forecasting financial
Foreign currency translation, 5:26–27, 9:17–18
Forms
    8–K, 2:31
    10–K, 1:7, 28, 2:30–31, 5:20, 27, 6:23, 13:9
    10–Q, 1:7, 28
Fortune, 2:3
Fortune Brands, 9:38, 10:32
Free cash flows to the firm (FCFF), 12:4–6
Functional income statement, 16:6–7
Fundamental analysis and demand for financial accounting information, 1:6
Future costs, 14:3, 15:10
Future value concepts, 8:28–29

G

GAAP. *See* Generally accepted accounting principles
Gap, The, 2:7, 4:36, 5:29, 10:24
Gateway Corporation, 21:1–2
General Agreement on Tariffs and Trade (GATT), 14:11
General and administrative expense budget, 20:10–11
General Electric, 5:31, 6:42, 7:20–21, 8:14, 15, 10:20, 15:15, 16:3, 21:4–5, 23:25
General Electric Commercial Credit, 10:1
Generally accepted accounting principles (GAAP)
    accrual accounting, 3:9
    adjusting financial statements, 11:4–9
    book and market value, differences between, 2:11
    capitalization, 6:26
    cash flows, statement of, 2:17
    consolidation for financial statements, 7:18

cost of products sold/ending inventory, 18:1
costs, transferring, 2:4
deferred tax evaluation, 5:19–21
depreciation, 6:29–31
Federal National Mortgage Association, 1:29
goodwill, 13:15
international account standards, 1:24
inventory, 6:3, 14–15
leases, 10:5, 7
limitations of, 4:21–22
off-balance-sheet financing, 10:4, 13
overview, 1:23
pensions, 10:18–19
pro forma income, 5:25
restructuring activities, 5:2–3
retained earnings, 2:21
revenue recognition, 5:1, 5–6, 13:4
special purpose entities, 10:25
stock repurchase, 9:8
truth reflected in financial statements, 11:4
warranty liability, 8:9
General Mills, 7:44–45, 8:32–33, 11:27–29, 35–37
General Motors, 6:24, 10:18, 20, 14:7, 16, 17:16
Glass, Lewis and Co., 1:5
Glidden, Craig, 15:11
Glidden Partners, 15:11
Global Crossing, 1:24
Goals, organizational, 14:6, 9–10
    See also individual subject headings
Goodwill, 7:22–23, 13:14–15
Google. *See* Intercorporate investments, reporting/ analyzing
Government representatives and demand for financial accounting information, 1:7
Graphs, cost-volume profit/profit-volume, 16:9–11
Gross profit margin, 6:20–21
GTE Corporation, 8:1

H

Hallco Builders, 18:9
Halliburton, 3:9
Harley-Davidson, 6:45, 10:38, 11:28, 12:26–27
Hartmarx, 18:9
Herman Miller, 18:41
Hertz, 15:9
Hewlett-Packard (HP), 1:29–30, 6:41, 7:21, 43, 14:1–3, 5, 7, 17:26, 32, 23:18
High-low method of cost estimation, 15:9–11
Hilton Hotels, 14:19
Historical costs, 2:6–7, 9:3, 14:3
Home Depot, 1:11, 26, 5:5, 18:2, 20:2, 23:18
    See also Statements, analyzing/interpreting financial
Honda, 14:19, 23:1, 9
Horizon period and discounted cash flow model, 12:4
Horizontal analysis, 4:23–25
Hospital costing systems, 18:18
Hybrid cars, 23:1–2

I

IBM, 2:7, 9:25, 15:8, 18, 22:35
Impairments, computation/disclosure of asset, 6:31–33
Imposed budget, 20:15
IMS Health, 9:34
Income, revenues/expenses and net, 2:13
    See also Operating income, reporting/analyzing; Statement *listings;* Taxes
Income shifting, 2:4, 6:9
Income statement
    absorption and variable costing, 18:28–32
    accrual accounting, 2:13–14
    adjusting the, 2:25, 11:4–6
    Apple Computer, 2:12
    budgeted, 20:14
    cash flows compared to, statement of, 2:16
    continuing operations and transitory items, 2:14
    contribution, 16:6–8, 17:10
    cost of goods sold, 18:15–16

Expresso Royale, B:25
    forecasting the, 11:10–12
    foreign currency translation, 5:27
    functional, 16:6–7
    Java House, B:9
    Johnson & Johnson, 12:14
    Lowes, 4:8
    net operating profit after tax, 4:5–16
    off-balance-sheet financing, 10:14–15, 23
    operating activities, 1:11–12
    overview, 1:10–11
    research and development, 5:13
    revenue recognition, 5:9, 11
    segments, managing business, 22:4–6
    structure, general, 2:11
    template, preparation using effects, 2:26, 28
    terminology needed to analyze, 2:13
    See also Intercorporate investments, reporting/ analyzing; Kimberly-Clark; Nonowner financing, reporting/analyzing; Operating assets, reporting/analyzing; Owner financing, reporting/analyzing; Statement *listings*
Incremental approach to budgeting, 20:5
Indiana University, 15:8
Indirect costs. *See* Costing, product: assigning indirect costs
Indirect method of reporting net cash flow from operating activities, B:8–10, 17–19
Information, demand/supply of financial accounting, 1:5–8
Inktomi, 16:1
Innovation and profits, 14:9
In-process research and development (IPR&D), 7:22
Input/output approach to budgeting, 20:4
Institute of Management Accountants (IMA), 14:15–16
Intangible assets, 2:6, 7, 7:21–22, 13:21–22
Intel Corporation, 4:44–45, 5:5, 35, 6:40, 11:37, 12:20–22, 23:19
Intellectual assets, 2:7
Intercorporate investments, reporting/analyzing
    aims, strategic, 7:3–4
    consolidation accounting mechanics, 7:30–31
    control, investments with
        accounting for, 7:18–21
        consolidation reporting, limitations of, 7:26
        goodwill, reporting, 7:22–23
        intangible assets, acquired, 7:21–22
        pooling-of-interests, reporting consolidations under, 7:26–27
        subsidiary companies, reporting sale of, 7:24–26
        subsidiary stock issuances, reporting, 7:24
    derivatives, accounting for, 7:31–32
    Google, 7:1–3
    parent company, determining the, 7:27
    passive investments
        acquisition and sale, 7:5–6
        at cost, investments reported, 7:10–11
        defining terms, 7:4
        disclosures, financial statement, 7:8–10
        marked-to-market, 7:7–8
        mark-to-mark *vs.* cost, 7:6
    review, chapter
        cases, 7:48
        discussion questions, 7:33
        end-of-module, 7:27–28
        exercises/mini-exercises, 7:33–43
        guidance answers, 7:33
        mid-module, 7:11–13, 16–18
        problems, 7:43–47
    significant influence, investments with
        control, investments with, 7:4
        defining terms, 7:4
        equity method of accounting, 7:13–16
        reasons for investing, 7:13
        return on equity effects, 7:15–16

Interdepartment services, 19:6
Intermet Corporation, 18:9
International Accounting Standards Board (IASB), 1:24
International Herald Tribune, 16:9
Intuit, 11:39–41
Inventory
    accounts payable turnover, 8:5
    balance sheet, 2:6
    cash flows, statement of, B:12
    cost, transfer of, 2:4
    Kimberly-Clark, 13:6, 13, 17
    statement construction and analyzing transactions,
        financial, 3:6
    turnover, 6:21–23
    See also Costing *listings,* product; Operating assets,
        reporting/analyzing
Investing activities, 1:9, 3:5–6, 20:8, B:6,
    14–15, 25
    See also Intercorporate investments, reporting/
        analyzing; Return *listings;* Stockholders'
        equity, statement of
Investment analysts and demand for financial accounting
    information, 1:6
Investment center evaluation measures
    asset base, 22:15
    best, which measure is, 22:17–18
    economic value added, 22:16–17
    income, divisional, 22:14–15
    other valuation issues, 22:15–16
    residual income, 22:16
    responsibility accounting system, 21:6
    return on investment, 22:12–14
    review, chapter
        end-of-module, 22:21–22
        exercises/mini-exercises, 22:25–26, 28–29
        guidance answers, 22:23
        problems, 22:34–35
iPods, 2:1, 3:1–2
    See also Statement construction and analyzing
        transactions, financial
Iron City Beer, 14:8
Isuzu Motors, 23:18

J

Java House. *See under* Cash flows, statement of
J.C. Penny, 14:8
Jetblue Airways, 9:29, 15:1
J.M. Smucker Company, 18:43
Job cost sheet, 18:9
    See also job costing *under* Costing, product: job and
        process operations
Job order production, 18:9
Jobs, Steve, 1:38, 2:1
John Deere, 5:29
Johnson Controls, 5:29, 36
Johnson & Johnson, 2:34–35
    See also Equity securities, analyzing/valuing
Joint product decisions, relevant costs/benefits and, 17:15
Journal entries, 3:5

K

Kaizen costing, 23:17–18
Kestin, Hersh, 16:9
KeySpan Corporation, 9:2
Kimberly-Clark
    adjusting/forecasting financial performance, 13:29–30
    balance sheet
        common-size, 13:21, 22
        debt, long-term, 13:17–18
        deferred income taxes, 13:19–20
        equity investments, 13:14
        example, 13:11
        goodwill, 13:14–15
        inventory, 13:6, 13, 17
        liabilities, current, 13:16–17
        minority owner's interests in subsidiaries,
            13:20

pensions, 13:18–19
        preferred securities, 13:20
        property/plant/equipment, 13:13–14
        receivable, accounts, 13:12–13
        stockholders' equity, 13:20–21
        taxes, 13:15–16
    cash flows, statement of, 13:25–26
    equity and stock value, valuing firm, 13:31–32
    income statement
        common-size, 13:8–9
        cost of goods sold and gross profit, 13:6
        earnings per share, 13:7–8
        management discussion/analysis, 13:9–10
        marketing/research/general expenses, 13:6–7
        sales, net, 13:4–6
        segments, business, 13:10
        taxes, income, 13:8
        transitory *vs.* persistent classification, 13:7
    line and staff organization, 14:18
    off-balance-sheet reporting/analysis
        audit, independent, 13:26
        derivatives, 13:24–25
        equity method investments, 13:22–23
        intangible assets, internally developed,
            13:21–22
        leases, operating, 13:23–24
        pensions, 13:24
        variable interest entities, 13:24
    overview, 13:1–2
    profitability/creditworthiness, assessing, 13:27–29
    sales, 13:3–6
    segments, organized into three business, 13:3
Kinko's, 16:3
Knowledge-based assets, 2:7
Kohl's, 14:18
Kozlowski, Dennis, 1:24, 11:9
KPMG, 1:27, 36–37

L

Labor and product costs, direct, 15:16, 16:5, 18:5–6
Labor standards and variance analysis for variable costs,
    21:14–16
Lands' End, 14:7
Last-in-first-out (LIFO) inventory costing method, 6:15,
    18–20, 24, 13:6, 13
Learjet, 14:8
Leases, 13:23–24
    See also under Off-balance-sheet financing,
        reporting/analyzing
Least-square regression analysis, 15:12–13
Legislation
    American Jobs Creation Act, 13:8
    Sarbanes-Oxley Act, 1:25, 26, 28, 32
    Securities Act of 1933, 1:23
    Securities Exchange Act of 1934, 1:23
Lenscrafters, 21:25
Liabilities, 2:7–11, 13:16–17, B:13–14, 18–19
    See also Nonowner financing, reporting/analyzing;
        specific type of liability
Liabilities-to-equity ratio, 4:20–21
Life cycle budgeting, 20:16
Life cycle costs and target costing, 23:16–17
Linear algebra (reciprocal) method and service
    department cost allocations, 19:10–11
Line departments, 14:11
Lipitor, 5:1
Liquidation preference and preferred stock, 9:5
Liquidations, last-in-first-out, 6:24
Liquidity, 2:6, 4:18–20, 10:26
L.L. Bean, 14:19
Loan covenants, 1:6
Lockheed Martin, 4:39–41, 10:32, 17:16
Long-term debt, 8:11, 13:17–18
    See also Nonowner financing, reporting/analyzing
Long-term (non-current) assets, 2:6–7

Long-term nonoperating liabilities. *See under* Nonowner
    financing, reporting/analyzing
LookSmart, 7:16
Lower of cost or market, reporting inventory at the,
    6:17–18
Lowes, 3:28, 4:8, 14–16, 38, 18:2
Lucent Technologies, 5:30, 6:12–13, 9:39
Lump sum payment, 8:13

M

Managed fixed costs, 15:8
Management responsibility, statement of, 1:26
Managerial accounting for MBAs, introducing
    cost drivers
        activity, 14:13, 14
        organizational, 14:13–14
        overview, 14:12–13
        structural, 14:13
    cost management, strategic, 14:1–2, 4–5
    demand for, 14:3–5
    ethics, 14:15–16
    financial and managerial accounting, constrasting,
        14:3–5
    mission/goals/strategies, organizational
        competition, 14:11–12
        goal attainment, 14:9–10
        overview, 14:5–6
        planning/organizing/controlling, 14:10–11
        position analysis, strategic, 14:7–9
    review, chapter
        cases, 14:20–22
        discussion questions, 14:17
        end-of-module, 14:16
        exercises/mini-exercises, 14:17–19
        guidance answers, 14:16
        mid-module, 14:11
    themes, blending of three, 14:5
Manufacturing costs, 6:13, 15:15–17
    See also Cost *listings;* Overhead, manufacturing
Manufacturing organizations, 18:3
Margin, segment, 22:6
Margin, unit contribution, 16:7, 17:9
Marginal revenue/cost and the pricing decision, 23:7–8
Margin and turnover of operating assets, operating profit,
    4:12–16
Marked to market investments, 7:7–8
Marketable securities, 2:6
Market niche, 14:8
Market price, 22:9–10
Market rate and pricing debt, 8:12
Market-to-book ratios, 2:7, 11, 12, 15
Market value added (MVA), 22:17
Mark-to-mark *vs.* cost, 7:6
Marriott, 17:12
Master budget. *See under* Budgeting/profit planning,
    operational
Matching Principle, 2:13
Materials and product costs, direct, 15:15–16, 16:5,
    18:5–6
Materials requisition form, 18:10
Materials standards and variance analysis for variable
    costs, 21:12–14
Mayo Clinic, 15:8
McDonald's, 4:35, 11:11, 15:8, B:2
MCI, 8:19
Medco Health, 9:21–22
Med Resorts International, 17:12
Merchandising organizations, 18:3
Merck & Company, 4:45–47, 5:16, 23, 7:34, 9:21–22
Merrill Lynch, 8:12, 11:8
Mesa Air, 15:2
Metric Constructors, Inc., 18:9
MicroAge, 17:32
Microsoft, 6:45, 16:1
Midas Muffler, 15:8
Miller Brewing, 14:8

Milunovich, Steve, 11:8
Minimum level approach to budgeting, 20:5–6
Minority owner's interests in subsidiaries, 13:20
Mission, the organizational, 14:5–6
Mitsubishi Company, 19:5
Mixed costs, 15:3–4
Moody's Investors Service, 2:32, 8:22
MTV, 3:11
Multiples model for equity valuation, 12:11

N

Navistar International Corporation, 18:1–2
Negotiated transfer prices, 22:11–12
Net asset valuation model for equity valuation, 12:11
Net book value (NBV), 6:28–29
Net operating assets (NOA), 4:2, 9–11, 11:23–24, 12:8–11
Net operating asset turnover (NOAT), 1:16, 17, 19, 4:2–3, 13:28
Net operating profit after tax (NOPAT). *See under* Taxes
Net operating profit margin (NOPM), 1:16, 17, 19, 4:12, 10:3, 7, 10, 13:6, 28
Niche, market, 14:8
Nike, 10:31, 11:28
Nippon Kayaku, 18:22
Nokia, 1:35
Noncash investing and financing activities, B:7
Nonconsolidation and special purpose entities, 10:25
Nonoperating activities, 5:3–4
Nonoperating expenses, 2:13
Nonoperating liabilities, 8:10–11
Nonoperating return, 4:16–18, 25–30
Nonowner financing, reporting/analyzing
    bond transactions, financial statement effects of
        amortization, effects of discount/premium, 8:17–19
        footnote disclosures, 8:20–21
        at par, bonds issued at, 8:16
        premium bonds, 8:17
        repurchase, effects of bond, 8:19–20
        zero-coupon convertible notes, 8:17
    current liabilities
        accounts payable, 8:4–5
        accounts payable turnover, 8:5–6
        accrued liabilities, 8:7–9
        nonoperating liabilities, 8:10–11
        overview, 8:4
    debt ratings and cost of debt, 8:21–24
    defining terms, 1:8
    equation, the accounting, 8:3
    future value concepts, 8:28–29
    gains/losses on bond repurchases, 8:29–30
    long-term nonoperating liabilities
        cost of debt, effective, 8:15–16
        overview, 8:12
        pricing of debt, 8:12–15
    present value concepts, 8:25–28
    review, chapter
        cases, 8:42
        discussion questions, 8:31
        exercises/mini-exercises, 8:31–36
        guidance answers, 8:30
        mid-module, 8:6, 9, 11, 25
        problems, 8:36–41
    Verizon Communications, 8:1–2
Nordstrom, 1:33, 10:34, 14:7
Nortel, 21:25
North American Free Trade Agreement (NAFTA), 14:11
Northwest Airlines, 15:1
Not-for-profit organizations, 14:6, 16:3

O

Off-balance-sheet financing, reporting/analyzing
    leases
        capitalization of operating, 10:7–10
        footnote disclosures, 10:6–7
        overview, 10:4–5
        reporting of, lessee, 10:5–6

overview, 10:3–4
pensions
    amortization, 10:27–28
    balance sheet effects, 10:13–16
    cash flows, footnote disclosures of future, 10:16–18
    footnote disclosures, 10:15–20
    income statement effects, 10:14–15
    other post-employment benefits, 10:20
    profit implications, footnote disclosures and, 10:18–20
    reporting of defined benefit plans, 10:12
    types of, two general, 10:12
    review, chapter
        cases, 10:44
        discussion questions, 10:29
        end-of-module, 10:26–27
        exercises/mini-exercises, 10:29–38
        guidance answers, 10:28
        mid-module, 10:11–12
        problems, 10:38–43
Southwest Airlines, 10:1–2
special purpose entities
    characteristics of, 10:22
    popularity of, two main reasons for, 10:25
    project and real estate financing, 10:24
    reporting of consolidated, 10:25–26
    securitization, asset, 10:23–24
    See also under Kimberly-Clark
Operating activities/items, 1:11–12, 4:9–11, 20:8
    See also Cash flows, statement of
Operating assets, reporting/analyzing
    accounts receivable
        analysis implications, 6:8–11
        footnote disclosures, 6:7–8
        overview, 6:4–5
        turnover, asset, 6:9–11
        uncollectible accounts, allowance for, 6:5–7
    Cisco Systems, 6:1–3
    equity method mechanics, 7:28–30
    introduction, 6:3
    inventory
        balance sheet effects, 6:18
        capitalization, 6:13–14
        cash flow effects, 6:19
        costing methods, 6:14–16
        footnote disclosures, 6:16–17
        income statement effects, 6:18
        last-in-first-out liquidations, 6:24
        lower of cost or market, 6:17–18
        overview, 6:13
        tools of inventory analysis, 6:20–23
        value-relevance of inventory disclosures, 6:20
    property/plant/equipment
        analysis implications, 6:33–35
        capitalization, 6:26–27
        depreciation, 6:27–31
        footnote disclosures, 6:33
        impairments, asset sales and, 6:31–33
        overview, 6:26
    review, chapter
        cases, 6:50
        discussion questions, 6:37
        end-of-module, 6:35–36
        exercises/mini-exercises, 6:37–45
        guidance answers, 6:36–37
        mid-module, 6:12–13, 24–25
        problems, 6:45–49
Operating cash flow to capital expenditures ratio, B:19
Operating cash flow to current liabilities ratio, B:18–19
Operating cycle, 2:9–10, 20:7
Operating expenses, 2:13
Operating income, reporting/analyzing
    below-the-line components
        earnings per share, 5:24–26
        extraordinary items, 5:24

foreign currency translation, 5:26–27
        overview, 5:23
    introduction, 5:3–5
    Pfizer, 5:1–3
    research and development expenses, 5:11–13
    restructuring expenses, 5:14–15
    revenues
        percentage-of-completion revenue recognition, 5:9–11
        recognition criteria, 5:5–7
        unearned revenue, recognition of, 5:10–11
    review, chapter
        cases, 5:44
        discussion questions, 5:28
        end-module, 5:27–28
        exercises/mini-exercises, 5:28–36
        guidance answers, 5:28
        mid-module, 5:16, 23
        problems, 5:37–44
    tax expenses, income, 5:17–21
Operating lease method for the reporting of leases, 10:5
Operating leverage, 16:17–19
Opportunity costs, 17:6, 11, 22:11
Options and debt contracts, 8:24
Oracle Corporation, 6:45, 11:37–39, 12:22–23
Order-getting costs, 21:20
Original Bradford Soap Works, 19:14
Oshkosh Truck Corporation, 19:2
Other post-employment benefits (OPEB), 10:20
Outlay costs, 17:4
Output/input approach to budgeting, 20:4, 8–9
Outsourcing, 17:1–2, 12–14
Overhead, manufacturing
    activity-based costs, 19:13–14, 21
    defining terms, 15:16, 18:5
    department rates, applied at, 19:18–19
    determining the amount of, 18:6–8
    fixed, 16:5
    overapplied/underapplied, 18:18–19
    plantwide rates, applied at, 19:17–18
    single overhead rate, inadequacies of a, 19:13–14
    variance analysis for variable costs, 21:16–18
Owner financing, reporting/analyzing
    Accenture, 9:1–3
    balance sheet overview, 1:8
    contributed capital
        Accenture, 9:4–5
        accounting for stock transactions, 9:7–9
        classes of stock, 9:5–6
        compensation plans, stock, 9:9–11
        defining terms, 9:4
    earned capital
        comprehensive income, 9:17–18
        defining terms, 9:4
        dividends, cash, 9:12–13
        dividends, stock, 9:14–15
        overview, 9:12
        splits, stock, 9:15–16
        summary of stockholders' equity, 9:18–20
    equity carve outs and convertibles
        analysis of, 9:23
        convertible securities, 9:23–25
        overview, 9:20
        problems, 9:35–39
        sell-offs, 9:21
        spin-offs, 9:21–22
        split-offs, 9:22–23
    overview, 9:3–4
    review, chapter
        cases, 9:40
        discussion questions, 9:26
        end-of-module, 9:25
        exercises/mini-exercises, 9:26–35
        guidance answers, 9:25
        mid-module, 9:11, 14, 16, 23

P

Papa John's Pizza, 16:21
Paper Mate, 16:25
Parker Brass, 21:11
Parsimonious method for forecasting financial
    statements, 11:23–24
Participative budget, 20:16
Partners and demand for financial accounting
    information, strategic, 1:6
Patents, 5:1, B:15
Payable, accounts, 8:4–6, B:13
Peanut butter approach and service department
    allocations, 19:5
Pensions, 9:17, 13:6–7, 18–19, 24
    See also under Off-balance-sheet financing,
        reporting/analyzing
Pepsi Bottling Group, 8:36–38
Performance assessment
    balanced scorecard, 22:18–21, 26, 29
    budgets, development of flexible, 21:6–9
    cost systems, reporting for
        budgets, development of flexible, 21:6–9
        standard costs, 21:10–11
    reports for revenue centers, 21:19–22
    responsibility accounting system
        centers, types of responsibility, 21:5–6
        ethics, 21:4
        overview, 21:3
        poorly designed, 21:3–4
        structure, organization, 21:4–5
    review, chapter
        cases, 21:33–36
        discussion questions, 21:24–25
        end-of-module, 21:22–24
        exercises/mini-exercises, 21:25–28
        guidance answers, 21:24
        mid-module, 21:9–10
        problems, 21:29–33
    standards gone wild, 21:1–2
    variance analysis for variable costs
        interpreting overhead variances, 21:18
        labor standards, 21:14–16
        materials standards, 21:12–14
        overhead standards, 21:16–18
        overview, 21:11–12
Period costs, 18:4–5
Persistent *vs.* transitory expenses, 13:7
Pfizer, 7:33–34
    See also Operating income, reporting/analyzing
Phillips Petroleum, 20:17
Piper Aircraft, 14:8
Plan, strategic/business, 1:4–5
Plantwide rates, applying overhead with, 19:17–18
Pools, cost, 19:4
Poneman, David, 6:10
Pooling-of-interests, reporting consolidations under,
    7:26–27
Porter, Michael, 14:7, 8
Position analysis, strategic, 14:7–9
Prediction, cost, 15:10
Preferred securities, 13:20
Preferred stock, 2:10, 4:29, 9:5–6
    See also Owner financing, reporting/analyzing
Premium bonds, 8:14, 17
Prepaid expenses, 2:6, 3:10, 11, B:12
Present value concepts, 8:25–28
Prices/pricing
    automobiles, green, 23:1–2
    benchmarking, 23:18–19
    continuous improvement costing, 23:17–18
    cost-based approaches, 23:8–11
    cost estimation, 15:14–15
    economic approaches to, 23:7–8
    review, chapter
        cases, 23:26–27
        discussion questions, 23:20–21

end-of-module, 23:20
exercises/mini-exercises, 23:21–23
guidance answers, 23:20
mid-module, 23:11–12
problems, 23:23–26
target costing
    components, can apply to, 23:15
    coordination, requires, 23:15
    design for production, 23:13–14
    information, requires cost, 23:15
    life cycle costs, 23:16–17
    proactive for cost management, 23:12–13
    pros and cons of, 23:15
    short life cycles, products with, 23:16
    time reduction for product introduction, 23:14
value chain
    core competencies, focusing on, 23:6–7
    supplier-buyer partnerships, 23:5–6
    understanding the, 23:3–5
    value-added perspective, 23:7
    See also Transfer pricing
PricewaterhouseCoopers, 1:27
Prizer, Inc., 11:29
Process manufacturing, 18:9
    See also process costing *under* Costing, product: job
        and process operations
Procter & Gamble (P&G), 1:10, 2:7, 4:35, 5:5, 6:38,
    9:27, 12:7, 12–13, 13:1, 22:1
    See also Statements, adjusting/forecasting financial
Product costs. *See* Costing *listings,* product
Production environment and costing systems, 18:8–10
Productivity relating to net operating assets, 1:16
Product-level activity in manufacturing cost hierarchy,
    15:17
Profit(s)
    cost of goods sold, 6:13–14
    discounted cash flow model, 12:4–5
    forecasting financial statements, 11:23–24
    gross profit margin, 6:20–21
    innovation, 14:9
    Kimberly-Clark, 13:6, 27–29
    margin and turnover of operating assets, operating
        profit, 4:12–16
    not-for-profit organizations, 14:6, 16:3
    off-balance-sheet financing, 10:3, 7, 9, 10, 18–20
    relevant costs/benefits for decision making, 17:9
    residual operating income model, 12:8–11
    responsibility accounting system, 21:6
    revenue centers as profit centers, 21:21–22
    See also Accounting for MBAs, introducing financial;
        Budgeting/profit planning, operational; Cost-
        volume-profit analysis; Return *listings;* return
        on net operating assets *under* Statements,
        analyzing/interpreting financial
Pro forma income, 5:25, 26
Progressive Corporation, 1:21
Project construction and special purpose entities, 10:24
Projected benefit obligation (PBO), 10:13–16
Property/plant/equipment (PPE), 2:4–6, 13:13–14,
    B:14–15
    See also under Operating assets, reporting/analyzing
Purchases budget, 20:9–10

Q

Qualifying special purpose entities (QSPEs), 10:25
Quick ratio, 4:20
Qwest Communications, 1:24

R

Rainbow Company, B:36
Ratio analyses of cash flows, B:18–19
Ratio analysis, limitations of, 4:21–22
Raw materials inventories, 18:3
Real estate financing and special purpose entities, 10:24
Receivable, accounts, 13:12–13, B:11–12

See also account receivables *under* Operating assets,
    reporting/analyzing
Reciprocal method and service department cost
    allocations, 19:10–11
Recording transactions, 2:24
    See also Reporting, financial; Statement *listings*
Red Lobster, 16:3
Regulators and demand for financial accounting
    information, 1:6
    See also Financial Accounting Standards Board;
        Generally accepted accounting principles;
        Securities and Exchange Commission
Relevant costs/benefits for decision making
    differential analysis
        outsourcing, 17:12–14
        overview, 17:6–8
        profit plans, multiple changes in, 17:9
        sell or process further decisions, 17:14–15
        special orders, 17:10–12
    identifying relevant costs
        disposal and salvage values, 17:5–6
        ethical dilemmas caused by sunk costs, 17:5
        future revenues, 17:4
        opportunity costs, 17:6
        outlay costs, 17:4
        overview, 17:3–4
        sunk costs, 17:5
    limited resources, use of
        constraints, theory of, 17:18–19
        multiple constraints, 17:17–18
        overview, 17:15–16
        single constraint, 17:16–17
    outsourcing, 17:1–2
    review, chapter
        cases, 17:31–32
        discussion questions, 17:22
        end-of-module, 17:19–21
        exercises/mini-exercises, 17:22–27
        guidance answers, 17:21–22
        mid-module, 17:7–8
        problems, 17:28–31
Relocation costs, 5:14
Reporting, financial
    accounting for MBAs, introducing financial, 1:21–22,
        13:15
    disclosure, benefits/costs of, 1:7–8
    earnings as most important metric to report, 1:12
    EDGAR, accessing Securities and Exchange
        Commission filings using, 1:21–22
    information demand/supply, 1:5–8
    See also Balance sheet; Cash flows, statement of;
        Footnote disclosures; Income statement;
        Nonowner financing, reporting/analyzing;
        Owner financing, reporting/analyzing;
        Statement *listings;* Stockholders' equity,
        statement of
Repurchase, bond, 8:19–20, 29–30
Repurchase, stock, 9:8–9
Research and development (R&D), 5:1, 11–13, 7:22,
    13:6, 13
Residual income, 22:16, 17
Residual operating income model (ROPI), 12:8–12,
    13:31
Responsibility accounting. *See under* Performance
    assessment
Restricted stock, 9:10–11
Restructuring activities/expenses, 5:2–3, 14–15
Retained earnings, 2:8, 10, 11, 21
Retrospective analysis, 11:4
Return on common equity (ROCE), 4:29–30
Return on equity (ROE), 1:18
    capitalization, 6:26
    defining terms, 4:4
    Home Depot, 4:5
    intercorporate investments, reporting/analyzing,
        7:15–16

Kimberly-Clark, 13:27
nonoperating return component of, 4:25–30
off-balance-sheet financing, 10:3–4, 6–7, 9–10
ratio behavior over time, 4:18
return on common equity, 4:29–30
See also return on net operating assets *under*
    Statements, analyzing/interpreting
    financial
Return on investment (ROI), 22:12–14
Return on net operating assets (RNOA), 1:16–17, 10:3–4,
    6–7, 10, 13:27
    See also under Statements, analyzing/interpreting
    financial
Revenue centers and performance assessment, 21:6,
    19–22
Revenues, 2:13, 3:6–7
    See also Balance sheet; Cash and Income *listings;*
    Operating income, reporting/analyzing; Return
    listings; Stockholders' equity, statement of;
    specific type of revenue
Rigas family and Adelphia Communications Corporation,
    1:29–30
Riverwood International, 18:9
Robert Bosch Tool Corporation, 18:2
Rohm and Haas Company, 6:49
Rolling budget, 20:16
Roto Zip Corporation, 18:1, 2
Royal & SunAlliance, 9:2
Rural/Metro, 17:14
Russian Antonov 124, 17:16

S

Sales budget, 20:9
Sales mix/dollar analysis, 16:14–17
Salvage values, 17:5–6
Salvation Army, 16:3
Scandals, accounting/corporate, 1:24–25, 30, 2:4, 3:9
Scatter diagrams, 15:11
Schonfeld, Mark K., 1:29
SCP Enterprises, 17:12
Sculley, John, 2:1
Sears, 6:10, 14:8, 18:2
SEC. *See* Securities and Exchange Commission
Securities, two types of marketable, 7:7–8
Securities and Exchange Commission (SEC)
    cash flows, statement of, 2:15
    disclosures, accounting, 1:7–8
    EDGAR, accessing filings using, 1:21–22
    enforcement actions, 1:28–30, 5:7–8
    revenue recognition, 5:7–8
    Securities Exchange Act of 1934, 1:23
Securitization, asset, 10:23–24
Segments, managing business
    any part of the business, report can be prepared for,
        22:3
    firms, a look at three, 22:1–2
    Kimberly-Clark, 13:3, 10
    mission and goals, 22:3
    reports
        interpreting, 22:6
        multi-level income statements, 22:4–6
        overview, 22:4
    review, chapter
        discussion questions, 22:23
        exercises/mini-exercises, 22:21–25
        mid-module, 22:7
        problems, 22:29–34
    See also Transfer pricing
Seidenberg, Ivan, 8:1
Selling expense budget, 20:10
Sell-offs, 9:21
Sell or process further decisions, relevant costs/benefits
    and, 17:14–15
Semivariable costs, 15:3–4
Sensitivity analysis, 16:7
Service organizations, 18:3, 18–19, 25–26

See also service department cost allocations *under*
    Costing, product: assigning indirect costs
Severance costs, employee, 5:14
Shareholders and demand for financial accounting
    information, 1:6
Sharper-Image, 6:45
Shin Caterpillar Mitsubishi, 7:38
Short-term debt, 8:10–11
    See also Nonowner financing, reporting/analyzing
Six Flags Theme Parks, 22:34–35
Six Sigma, 21:5
SkyWest, 15:2
Slack, budgetary, 20:16
Solvency analysis, 4:18, 20–21
Southwest Airlines, 1:11, 7:32, 8:39–40, 14:7, 15:1
    See also Off-balance-sheet financing, reporting/
    analyzing
Special orders and relevant costs/benefits for decision
    making, 17:10–12
Special purpose entities (SPEs), 10:2
    See also under Off-balance-sheet financing,
    reporting/analyzing
Spin-offs (divestiture), 9:21–22
Split-off point for joint products, 17:15
Split-offs (divestiture), 9:22–23
Splits, stock, 9:15–16
Springs Industries, 21:27
Sprint Nextel Corporation, 8:25
SRAM Corporation, 19:1
Staff Accounting Bulletin (SAB) *101,* 5:7
Staff departments, 14:11
Standard costs, 21:10–11
Standard & Poor's, 2:32, 8:22, 23
Standards and benchmarks, 21:1–2, 23:18–19
Staples, 4:37, 10:33, B:39
Starbucks, 1:33
    See also Cash flows, statement of
StarTek, 17:1–2
Stated rate and pricing debt, 8:12
Statement construction and analyzing transactions,
    financial
    accounting for MBAs, introducing financial
        balance sheet, 1:8–10
        beyond, information, 1:15–16
        cash flows, 1:13–14
        income, 1:10–12
        linkages between, 1:14
        overview, 1:8
        stockholders equity, 1:12–13
    accrual accounting
        accrued expenses/revenues, 3:12
        good or bad, is it, 3:10
        overview, 3:6–7
        prepaid expenses, 3:11
        scandals, accounting, 3:9
        summary of adjustments, 3:12–13
        trial balance preparation/use, 3:13–15
        types of adjustments, four, 3:10
        unearned revenues, 3:11
    introduction, 3:3–4
    preparation, statement
        balance sheet, 3:17
        cash flows, 3:18–21
        closing process, 3:21–22, 24–25
        income statement, 3:16–17
        stockholders' equity, 3:18
    review, chapter
        cases, 3:35–38
        discussion questions, 3:25–26
        end-of-module, 3:22–23
        exercises/mini-exercises, 3:26–31
        guidance answers, 3:25
        mid-module, 3:8, 15–16
        problems, 3:32–35
    transactions, accounting for/accessing business
        capital distributions, 3:7

capital investment, 3:5–6
inventory acquisition, 3:6
revenue and expense recognition, 3:6–7
template, financial statement effects, 3:4–5
See also Balance sheet; Cash flows, statement of;
    Income statement; Kimberly-Clark; Nonowner
    financing, reporting/analyzing; Owner
    financing, reporting/analyzing; Stockholders'
    equity, statement of
Statements, adjusting/forecasting financial
    adjusting
        balance sheet, 11:6–7
        cash flows, the statement of, 11:7–9
        income statement, 2:25, 11:4–6
    forecasting
        balance sheet, 11:12–16
        cash flows, statement of, 11:16–17
        income statement, 11:10–12
        multiple years, 11:18–19, 23–24
        parsimonious method to multiyear, 11:23–24
        reassessing the forecasts, 11:17–18
    Kimberly-Clark, 13:29–30
    overview, 11:3–4
    Procter & Gamble, 11:1–2
    review, chapter
        cases, 11:44–48
        discussion questions, 11:26
        end-of-module, 11:24–25
        exercises/mini-exercises, 11:26–37
        guidance answers, 11:26
        mid-module, 11:9–10, 20–23
        problems, 11:37–44
Statements, analyzing/interpreting financial
    discussion questions, 4:31
    Home Depot, 4:1–3
    introduction, 4:3–4
    liquidity, 4:18–20
    ratio analysis, limitations of, 4:21–22
    return on equity, 4:4–5, 25–30
    return on net operating assets
        defining terms, 4:5
        disaggregation into margin/turnover, 4:12–16
        net operating profit after tax, 4:5–16
        nonoperating return, 4:16–18
        ratio behavior over time, 4:18
        return on common equity, 4:30
        return on equity and, differences between, 4:3
        two components, 4:2–3
    review, chapter
        cases, 4:49–50
        end-module, 4:22–23
        exercises/mini-exercises, 4:31–39
        guidance answers, 4:30
        mid-module, 4:14–16
        problems, 4:39–49
    solvency analysis, 4:18, 20–21
    vertical/horizontal analysis, 4:23–25
Statements and transactional analysis, introducing
    financial
    Apple Computer, 2:1–3
    articulation of financial statements
        linkages, statement, 2:22–23
        retained earnings reconciliation, 2:21
    balance sheet, 2:5–12
    cash flows, 2:15–19
    costs flowing through the accounting system, 2:3–5
    discussion questions, 2:33–34
    income statement, 2:11–14
    information sources, additional
        analyst reports, 2:31–32
        credit services, 2:32
        data services, 2:33
        Forms 8/10–K, 2:30–31
    leading up to preparing statements, the process,
        2:23–25
    review, chapter

cases, 2:44
end-module, 2:29–30
exercises/mini-exercises, 2:34–39
guidance answers, 2:33
mid-module, 2:19–21
problems, 2:39–43
stockholders' equity, statement of, 2:14–15
template, preparation using effects, 2:23–29
See also under Accounting for MBAs, introducing financial
Static budgets, 21:6
Statistical print production management (SPPM), 18:14
Steelcase Furniture Company, 18:9
Step costs/method, 15:4–5, 19:8–10
Stockholders' equity, statement of
accounting for MBAs, introducing financial, 1:12–13
Apple Computer, 2:15
examples of items included in equity, 2:10
GAAP determining value of the company, 2:11
Kimberly-Clark, 13:20–21
overview, 1:12–13
reconciliation of beginning/ending balances, 2:14
See also Owner financing, reporting/analyzing
Stock repurchase, 9:8
Straight-line method of depreciation, 6:28–31, 35
Strategies, organizational, 1:4–5, 14:6
See also individual subject headings
Structural cost drivers, 14:13
Subsidiary stock/companies and intercorporate investments, 7:24–26
Subway, 15;19
Sue Bee Honey, 23:21–22
Sukumar, Srinivas, 14:5
Sullivan, Scott, 6:27
Sunbeam, 21:4
Sunk costs, 17:5
Supplier-buyer partnerships and value chain perspective, 23:5–6
Suppliers and demand for financial accounting information, 1:6
Symantec Corporation, 3:15–16, 22–23, 9:23–24

T

T-accounts, 3:4–6
Target, 2:7, 36, 4:31–32, 42–43, 5:5, 31, 11:11, 12:16–17, 20:2
Target costing. See under Prices/pricing
Taxes
cash flows, statement of, B:24
cost-volume-profit analysis, 16:11–12
deferred tax valuation, 5:19–22, 13:15–16, 19–20
information, demand for financial accounting information, 1:6
Kimberly-Clark, 13:8, 15–16, 19–20
net operating profit after tax
discounted cash flow model, 12:4–5
forecasting financial statements, 11:23–24
Kimberly-Clark, 13:6, 20
leases, capitalization of operating, 10:7, 9

residual operating income model, 12:8–11
operating income, reporting/analyzing, 5:17–21
See also return on net operating assets under Statements, analyzing/interpreting financial
Technicians and predicting equity value, 12:12
Technology and cost estimation, 15:14–15
TeleTech Holdings, 17:12
Template, financial statement effects, 2:23–29, 3:4–5
See also Statement listings
Terminal period and discounted cash flow model, 12:4
Texas Instruments, 6:40
Thomas Jefferson University Hospital (TJUH), 18:18
Thomson First Call, 12:6
3M Company, 1:36, 2:39, 4:33–34, 6:45, 12:18–20
Times interest earned, 4:21
Time Warner, 11:9–10
TJ Maxx, 6:39
TJX Companies, 1:35–36, 2:38, 4:39
Top-down budget, 20:15
Toyota, 14:18, 23:1–2
Trade credit, 8:5
Trading investments, 7:7–8
Transactional analysis. See Statements and transactional analysis, introducing financial
Transfer pricing
defining terms, 22:7
determining prices
absorption cost plus markup, 22:11
dual prices, 22:12
market price, 22:9–10
negotiated prices, 22:11–12
opportunity costs, 22:11
variable costs, 22:10–11
management considerations, 22:8–9
review, chapter
cases, 22:35–38
exercises/mini-exercises, 22:25, 27–28
Transitory items/expenses, 2:14, 13:7
Travelers Property Casualty, 7:24
Treasury stock, 2:8, 10, 9:8
Trees, cost-based approach for the valuation of, 15:14
Trial balance preparation/use of financial statements, 3:13–15
Tyco, 1:24, 11:9

U

Uncollectible accounts, 6:5–7
Unearned revenue, 2:10, 3:10, 11, 5:10–11
Unit contribution margin (UCM), 16:7, 17:9
United Airlines, 14:10, 15:1
United Parcel Service (UPS), 4:47–48, 14:12, 19
United Way, 14:6
Unit-level activity in manufacturing cost hierarchy, 15:16
Unrealized gains, 9:17
Unrecognized intangible assets, 2:7
USAir, 15:18
USG Corporation, 18:1

V

Valero Energy, 4:35
Value-added and value chain perspective, contrasting the, 23:7
Value chain. See under Prices/pricing
Vanguard Group, 8:12
Variable costs, 15:3–4, 16:5, 22:10–11
See also absorption and variable costing under Costing, product: job and process operations; variance analysis for variable costs under Performance assessment; specific type of cost
Variable interest entities (VIES), 13:8, 24
Variance and performance reports, 21:6
See also variance analysis for variable costs under Performance assessment
Verizon Communications, 2:38, 42, 4:38, 10:33, 37, 22:1–2
See also Nonowner financing, reporting/analyzing
Vertical analysis, 4:23–25
Viacom, 9:28
Voters and demand for financial accounting information, 1:7

W

Wackenhut, 17:14
Waitt, Ted, 21:1–2
Walgreen, 4:36
Wall Street Journal, 6:10, 9:2, B:2
Wal-Mart, 1:19, 2:41, 4:35–36, 14:8, 16:15, 20:2
Walt Disney Company, 5:10
Warranty liabilities, 8:8–9
Webvan, 16:2
Weighted average method, 18:25
Whole Foods, 11:31
Winn-Dixie Stores, 1:31
Wolff Company, B:33
Working capital, 2:9, 19
Work-in-process inventories, 18:3
Work ticket, 18:10
WorldCom, 1:24, 29, 2:4, 3:9, 6:27, 14:15
Write-offs, 5:14
Writers and demand for financial accounting information, press, 1:6
W.W. Grainger, 6:45–46

X

Xerox, 1:24, 3:9, 5:39, 10:36–37, 11:43–44, 14:18

Y

Yahoo!, 7:12–13, 17–18, 16:1
Year, fiscal, 1:8
Yield rate and pricing debt, 8:12
Yum! Brands, Inc., 10:29–30, 34

Z

Zero-coupon convertible notes, 8:17
Zofran, 18:18

Financial Accounting	Managerial Decision (MD) & Research Insight (RI)	Business Insights
MODULE 1 Financial Accounting for MBAs	**MD:** You are the Product Manager **MD:** You are the Chief Financial Officer **RI:** Are Earnings Important?	Accounting Quality Warren Buffett on MD&A Warren Buffett on Audit Committees
MODULE 2 Introducing Financial Statements and Transaction Analysis	**MD:** You are the Securities Analyst **MD:** You are the Operations Manager **RI:** Market-to-Book Ratio	How Much Debt is Reasonable? Apple's Market-to-Book Values Insights into Apple's Statement of Cash Flows
MODULE 3 Constructing Financial Statements and Analyzing Transactions	**MD:** You are the Chief Financial Officer **RI:** Accruals: Good or Bad?	Accounting Scandals and Improper Adjustments
MODULE 4 Analyzing and Interpreting Financial Statements	**MD:** You are the Entrepreneur **RI:** Ratio Behavior Over Time	Home Depot's ROE and RNOA Tax Shield Tax Rates for Computing NOPAT Home Depot's NOPM Home Depot's NOAT
MODULE 5 Reporting and Analyzing Operating Income	**MD:** You are the Financial Analyst **RI:** Restructuring Costs and Managerial Incentives **RI:** "Pro Forma" Income	Ratios Across Industries Cisco's Revenue Recognition Disney's Revenue Recognition Pfizer's R&D Pfizer's Restructuring Pro Forma Income and Managerial Motives
MODULE 6 Reporting and Analyzing Operating Assets	**MD:** You are the Receivables Manager **MD:** You are the Plant Manager **MD:** You are the Division Manager **RI:** LIFO and Stock Prices	Sears' Cookie Jar WorldCom and Improper Cost Capitalization
MODULE 7 Reporting and Analyzing Intercorporate Investments	**MD:** You are the Chief Financial Officer **RI:** Equity Income and Stock Prices	Pitfalls of Acquired Growth Determining the Parent Company in an Acquisition
MODULE 8 Reporting and Analyzing Nonowner Financing	**MD:** You are the Vice President of Finance **RI:** Accounting Conservatism and Cost of Debt **RI:** Valuation of Debt Options	Verizon's Zero Coupon Debt
MODULE 9 Reporting and Analyzing Owner Financing	**MD:** You are the Chief Financial Officer **RI:** Stock Issuance and Stock Returns	
MODULE 10 Reporting and Analyzing Off-Balance-Sheet Financing	**MD:** You are the Division President **RI:** Valuation of Nonpension Postretirement Benefits **RI:** Why Do Companies Offer Pensions?	Why GM's Bonds Were Rated Junk
MODULE 11 Adjusting and Forecasting Financial Statements	**MD:** You are the Corporate Analyst **RI:** Earnings Quality and Accounting Conservatism	What is eBay's Operating Cash Flow? Tyco Buys Operating Cash Flow
MODULE 12 Analyzing and Valuing Equity Securities	**MD:** You are the Division Manager **MD:** You are the Operations Manager **RI:** Power of NOPAT Forecasts **RI:** Using Models to Identify Mispriced Stocks	Analysts' Earnings Forecasts
MODULE 13 Comprehensive Case		